SOCIAL PSYCHOLOGY

A STORYTELLING APPROACH

Expanded First Edition

Leonard Newman
Syracuse University

Ralph Erber
DePaul University

cognella®
academic publishing

Bassim Hamadeh, CEO and Publisher
Michael Simpson, Vice President of Acquisitions
Jamie Giganti, Managing Editor
Jess Busch, Senior Graphic Designer
John Remington, Acquisitions Editor
Brian Fahey, Licensing Specialist
Mandy Licata, Interior Designer

First published in the United States of America in 2015 by Cognella, Inc.

Printed in the United States of America

ISBN: 978-1-63487-136-5 (pbk) / 978-1-63487-137-2 (br)

cognella
academic publishing

www.cognella.com   800-200-3908

CONTENTS

CHAPTER THREE

Person Perception and Social Inference

CHAPTER FOUR

The Self

CHAPTER EIGHT

Group Processes   329

CHAPTER NINE

Attraction   385

CHAPTER TEN

CHAPTER ELEVEN

CHAPTER TWELVE

CHAPTER THIRTEEN

CHAPTER FOURTEEN

The Social Psychology of Genocide, Terrorism—And Heroism   649

Image Credits   701

Index   705

CHAPTER 1

INTRODUCTION TO SOCIAL PSYCHOLOGY

MAKING SENSE OF SOCIAL (AND ANTISOCIAL) BEHAVIOR: THE STORY OF SALVADOR AGRON

Most readers of this book probably will not have heard of Salvador Agron, "the Capeman" (Jacoby, 2000), but for a brief period 40 to 50 years ago, he became a household name. Born in Puerto Rico, Agron moved with his mother and sister to New York in the early 1950s, at about age ten. He did not adjust well to life in the United States, where he got caught up in just about every kind of trouble in which a person can become involved. As a result, he spent much of his adolescence in reform schools and other detention centers. Even when he wasn't incarcerated, Agron spent as little time as possible at his mother's home, because her second husband was a stern Pentecostal preacher with whom he did not get along. Perhaps because of his alienation from his family, Agron joined a series of street gangs with names like the Mau Mau Chaplains of Brooklyn.

By the summer of 1959, Agron was spending most of his time in Manhattan, where he and a group of young Puerto Ricans formed a new gang, the Vampires. On August 29 of that year, he rendezvoused after dark with other gang members in a park on Manhattan's West Side. Expecting a battle with a rival gang, the Norsemen, they instead encountered four boys and a girl who just happened to be walking by. Three of those boys were stabbed in the encounter; two died. Witnesses reported that the murder victims had been attacked by two teenagers, one carrying an umbrella with a sharpened point and the other wearing a black cape with a red satin lining. The one with the cape—"the Capeman"—was said to be the one who did the stabbing. A few days later, after a widely publicized search of the city, the Capeman was apprehended. He turned out to be Salvador Agron, and he confessed to the killings.

Why begin this book with Agron's story? We did so because the key events of Agron's life involve the kinds of human behaviors and experiences that social psychologists seek to explain, and because many of the questions those events raise are questions social psychologists try to answer. In other words, by telling you about Agron's story, we can tell you about the nature of social psychology. Although many of the events of Agron's life were extreme and unusual, his behavior and his reactions to his social environment can be discussed and explained in the same terms as anyone else's.

In this chapter, we will define and introduce social psychology and explain how it differs from other branches of psychology. We will also go over some of the general issues and themes highlighted throughout the book, especially the idea that people typically are not aware of many causes of their social behavior.

WHAT IS SOCIAL PSYCHOLOGY?

You're rushing through your neighborhood, heading toward campus, trying not to be late for class again. Not many people are out at this early hour, but as you turn a corner to take a shortcut down a side street, you find you have some company. Ahead of you is a couple—or at least, a rather unhappy looking man and woman. They're fighting about something—no, maybe they're just bickering. Or would you have to call this a fight? It's hard to say, and hard to figure out what the conflict is about. The two of them are really shouting now, and the guy—a heavyset, disheveled-looking man—is becoming particularly agitated. Is he going to hit the woman, or is he just gesticulating in a particularly emphatic way? And did you just see a look of fear cross her face, or is she only annoyed and disgusted?

What's going on here? And more to the point, what should you do? If someone is about to get hurt, then clearly, the right thing to do would be to intervene and help in some way. But if this is just a heated argument (for all you know, maybe they *always* talk to each other this way), you should mind your own business. You don't want to embarrass yourself by butting into other people's private lives.

If you did want to intervene, what would you do? You could call the police on your cell phone, but by the time help arrived, it might be too late. Will you need to get a little aggressive with the man to get him to back off? Would that be justified? Maybe you could calm the two of them down just by talking to them, but what would you say to influence their behavior?

It might be worth asking yourself if your interpretation of the situation would vary if different kinds of people were involved. What if the man was thin and well dressed—would you judge him and his behavior differently? How about the couple's ethnicity—would your impression change if they were white, black, Asian, or Latino?

If only some other people besides you were on the scene, and you weren't the only onlooker—that would make it easier to figure out what was going on, and what action you should take … at least, you think it would.

If you actually experienced the situation just described, answering all these questions at once might be difficult. And because you weren't standing on that street, you couldn't answer them, even if you wanted to. Yet these are questions social psychologists would ask, and they all relate to the more general issues that interest them. Social psychologists are interested in how people think about other people and themselves; how people's social identities (their race, ethnicity, gender, and age) affect those social judgments; why interactions with other people sometimes go smoothly and sometimes do not; and why some people attract us and others repel us. Social psychologists want to understand how people influence the thoughts, feelings, and behaviors of other individuals; how people's behaviors affect their self-concepts; and how the presence of others can lead ordinary people to do extraordinary things. You will never really know what might have been going on between the man and woman on that side street, but by the time you finish this book, you will know a great deal more about the issues raised by that hypothetical incident.

Social Psychology Defined

A classic definition of social psychology is "an attempt to understand and explain how the thought, feeling and behavior of individuals is influenced by the actual, imagined or implied presence of others" (Allport, 1924). That definition does an admirable job of summarizing a great deal of the work carried out by social psychologists, especially the research covered in this book in Chapters 6 (Persuasion and Attitude Change), 7 (Social Influence: Compliance, Conformity, and Obedience), and 8 (Group Processes). But it does not really do justice to the breadth of issues now studied by social psychologists. For example, for many years, two of the most heavily researched questions in social psychology have been (1) how people go about forming impressions of others and figuring out what they are like (Chapter 3); and (2) the extent to which people's attitudes predict their behavior (Chapter 5).

Of course, one could argue that you cannot form impressions of people until they actually do something, and in that way "influence" you by giving you something to think about. In addition, your beliefs about other people's attitudes affect whether your own attitudes will or will not predict your behavior ("I'd like to go out with him this weekend, but I know my girlfriends hate him"). That is certainly an example of social influence. But many other factors play a role in the relationship between people's attitudes and their behavior. Overall, the stretching and straining we would need to do to make everything social psychologists study fit the classic definition suggests that a broader one may be needed.

A better definition of **social psychology** is the study of how people think, behave, and feel in social contexts (see Brehm, Kassin, & Fein, 2002, for a similar definition). Let's pick this definition apart, starting with "people." If you once believed that social psychologists focus only on how people behave in groups, it should be clear by now that that is not the case. Group processes, as we will see in Chapter 8, are indeed important topics of study, but not the only ones. Individual social behavior, defined more broadly, is another topic of interest. Moreover, as the definition suggests, social psychologists do not concern themselves only with overt, observable social behavior. They are also interested in how people think and feel about their own and other people's behavior, and in how their thoughts, feelings, and behaviors affect each other.

What about "social contexts?" Clearly, that phrase can refer to the actual physical presence of other people, or to what we ordinarily think of as social situations (for example, parties, classrooms, workplaces, sporting events, or your local café). That is not all that it means, however, for the imagined or implied presence of others can, in a variety of ways, be considered a social context. Certainly, the rise of social media and online communities has stretched the definition of what a social experience is. More generally, we think about people even when they are not around. Not only that; the thoughts we have about people can have important implications for our interactions with them.

It should be obvious, for example, that a fistfight is a social psychological phenomenon, and aggression is, in fact, one of the field's classic topics (Chapter 13). But imagine a man sitting alone in his room, ruminating over an unpleasant exchange he recently had with an acquaintance and concluding that the fellow deserves (at the very least) a slap in the face. Is a private experience like that a matter of interest to social psychologists? Absolutely: the man is thinking about a member of his social world—thinking that was triggered by a social event—and what he is thinking might set into motion an interpersonal event, namely a brawl. More generally, human beings spend a great deal of time thinking about themselves, other people, their relationships, and their past and future behavior. Many of our thoughts arise from the fact that we live among other people, and those thoughts have the potential to affect our interpersonal behavior. Thus, a great deal of research in social psychology focuses on understanding our thought processes.

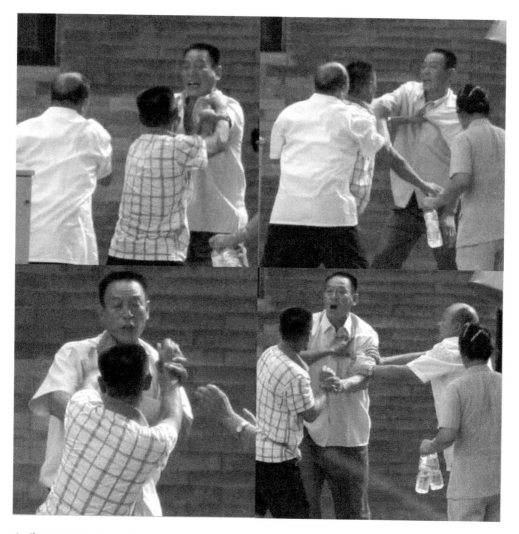

Acting aggressively, thinking about aggressing, observing aggression, encouraging aggression, and intervening to prevent aggression: All are social-psychological phenomena.

Just as we *think* about people when they are not present, we can also be *affected* by them when they are not present. If our enraged friend actually assaults his perceived enemy, he might feel less satisfied afterward than he had anticipated (Carlsmith, Wilson, & Gilbert, 2008). Needless to say, he might fear being punished for his behavior, but he might also be tormented by the knowledge that his father always preached self-control to him—despite the fact that his father died years ago. If his guilt and agitation are too great, the aggressor might try to rationalize his behavior, perhaps by concluding that his victim really deserved the beating (Brock & Buss, 1962; Goldstein, Davis, & Herman, 1975). In fact, he might conclude that a more savage response would have been justified, and this new conviction might cause the conflict to escalate. In sum, the mere fact that we have relationships with other people creates a social context for our actions. How we conduct ourselves from day to day is shaped profoundly—often in ways we are unaware of—by the fact that our lives are intertwined with those of other people.

Overall, we spend a great deal of time thinking about other human beings, and they in turn think about us. We have feelings and attitudes toward other people, just as they do toward us. We behave in ways that affect others, and at the same time are affected by them. All these thoughts, feelings, and behaviors intersect in a variety of ways. Described in this way, everyday life sounds like a hopelessly complex drama, but it is a mess that social psychologists happily plunge into.

Social Psychology Compared to Other Branches of Psychology and Behavioral Science

To appreciate more fully the questions social psychologists ask about people's behavior—and how they differ from the questions other psychologists and social scientists ask—let's revisit the story of Salvador Agron, the "Capeman." Agron's story raises all sorts of issues, but the kinds of issues that psychologists see as most relevant, important, or interesting will differ, depending on their particular area of study (see **Table 1.1**).

Table 1.1: Social psychology compared to other areas of psychology and the social sciences

SOCIAL PSYCHOLOGY	
Focus:	How people think, behave, and feel in social contexts
Sample questions:	What triggered Agron's aggression? What were his beliefs about his victims? What was the immediate context like—how dark, how hot, how crowded? How was he influenced by other people in the immediate context? What was the role of bystanders? How were Agron's attitudes and behaviors changed by the experience?
PERSONALITY PSYCHOLOGY	
Focus:	Individual differences; how people's traits cohere or hang together
Sample questions:	What were Agron's traits? What were his long-term goals, beliefs, and capacities, and how did they combine to turn him into the person he was?
DEVELOPMENTAL PSYCHOLOGY	
Focus:	Age-related differences and the processes that play a role in normal and disturbed development
Sample questions:	What were Agron's early experiences? What were his caretakers like, and who were his biggest social influences?
CLINICAL PSYCHOLOGY	
Focus:	Diagnosis and treatment of psychological problems; factors relating to adjustment and well-being
Sample questions:	How can we best characterize or diagnose Agron's maladaptive behavior? What caused it, and how might we intervene to change it?
SOCIOLOGY	
Focus:	Social institutions and other broad social and cultural forces and their impact on human behavior
Sample questions:	What were conditions like for urban youths in the 1950s, and what were Agron's realistic life choices? What kinds of social support were available to young people? What were the prevailing values in Agron's community?

Other Disciplines

For example, personality psychologists, especially those who fall into the category of "trait psychologists," would be most interested in learning about Agron's traits or dispositions. These researchers believe they can get a fairly complete description of someone's personality by measuring his or her standing on just five major personality dimensions. Known as the Big Five (John & Srivastava, 1999; McCrae & Costa, 2008), those dimensions are Agreeableness, Conscientiousness, Extraversion, Neuroticism, and Openness. The Big Five can be used as a basis for predicting and explaining a person's behavior (McCrae & Costa, 2003), including aggression (Caprara, Barbaranelli, Pastorelli, & Perugini, 1994). Based on past research (John, Caspi, Robins, Moffitt, & Stouthamer-Loeber, 1994), we might expect that an adolescent like Agron, who engages in impulsive violence, would have low levels of Agreeableness (the tendency to be friendly, considerate, and sensitive to others' needs) and Conscientiousness (the tendency to be careful, self-disciplined, and goal oriented).

Developmental psychologists would focus on how Agron became the kind of person who would engage in acts of impulsive violence. For example, they might want to know about his parents' child-rearing practices and disciplinary style. When parents enforce rules harshly or inconsistently, children are less likely to internalize the norms their parents are trying to teach them. In other words, children are less likely to follow those norms (such as rules against harming other people) when no one is around to directly enforce them (Hoffman, 1977). Indeed, throughout most of his childhood, Agron's parents and guardians were not particularly warm and attentive to him. In fact, he lived for years in a poorhouse, cared for (if "cared" is even the right word) by a series of women, who often neglected and physically abused him.

Developmental psychologists might also want to know if important people in Agron's life had modeled aggressive behavior for him. Children imitate high-status models, especially when they see that those models' behavior does not lead to negative consequences (Bandura & Walters, 1963). As we have already pointed out, the behavior of the people who raised Agron was often brutal. Finally, a developmental psychologist would be interested in the level of Agron's cognitive development at the time of the murders. As people mature, their thinking about their own and other people's behavior becomes more sophisticated, although the rate at which they progress and how much they develop varies from person to person (Perry & Bussey, 1983). When he was older, Agron often claimed that at the time he committed his crimes, he had the mind of a five-year-old.

Clinical psychologists might be interested in many of these same aspects of Agron's background, but they would focus more specifically on whether his experiences caused him to develop abnormally. For example, they might conclude that Agron had developed an antisocial personality disorder (Rutter, 2003), defined as "a pervasive pattern of disregard for, and violation of, the rights of others that begins in childhood or early adolescence and continues into adulthood" (American Psychiatric Association, 1994). Clinical psychologists would also be interested in how best to intervene to help people with that diagnosis regain control over their behavior and conform more closely to social norms.

Like social psychologists, sociologists would be interested in a careful examination of the situation in which Agron's act of violence took place. Compared to social psychologists, however, sociologists would concern themselves with broader aspects of the social context. For example, they might be interested in why young men with Agron's background might have been more likely than others to become gang members and involve themselves in criminal activity in New York (and possibly other cities) during the late 1950s. Sociologists might take into consideration the economic and political environment in which Agron's life took shape. In short, compared to social psychologists, sociologists study human behavior at the level of large groups, and their analyses are more likely to focus on social institutions, social classes, ethnic groups, geographic regions, and political entities than on individual people.

Of course, this brief review does not exhaust the many ways in which social scientists other than social psychologists explain what goes on between people and make sense of the way they behave in their everyday lives. We could focus on the genetic material underlying many of the individual differences in personality, like those psychologists who are known as behavior geneticists (Plomin, DeFries, McClearn, & McGuffin, 2009). Likewise, we could focus on people's past learning—how rewards and punishments have shaped their behavior—like psychologists known as behaviorists (Skinner, 1976). Moreover, we should not discount the importance of the point in history at which people are living. As social historians would remind us, the behavior of people in the Middle Ages undoubtedly differed from the behavior of people in the late 1950s. Needless to say, we could learn a lot about people and their behavior by looking at them from all these different perspectives, and social psychologists certainly find these perspectives to be interesting and useful.

Social Psychology

A social psychologist who was analyzing the Capeman murders would tend to focus on the event itself, the immediate context in which it took place, and the individuals who were involved. For instance, how did Agron himself understand what he was doing, and why? How did he explain his actions to himself? What was it about his victims and their behavior that led him to believe that he should assault them? Research on attribution and person perception (Chapter 3) addresses these kinds of issues, as does work on the thought processes underlying aggressive behavior (Chapter 13).

Another set of questions social psychologists would ask focuses on the specific aspects of the situation in which Agron found himself. How dark was it in the park, for example? Research on deindividuation (Chapter 8) shows that any factor that makes people harder to identify as individuals loosens their inhibitions (Zimbardo, 1969). Was it particularly hot that night? High temperatures are associated with a greater propensity for aggressive behavior (Anderson, 2001).

Social psychologists would also emphasize that Agron's violent behavior—though obviously committed by an individual—took place in a situation in which he was acting as part of a group (Chapter 8). Were the murders the culmination of a series of unfortunate group decisions? If so, how were those decisions made? Did the fact that Agron was with other people—and not just any people, but a group of people who were an important part of his personal identity (Chapter 4)—affect his behavior? Did the group encourage him to do what he did (Chapters 6 and 7)?

The behavior of others who witnessed the murders would also interest social psychologists. Were there any bystanders, and if so, did anyone attempt to intervene? How many people called for help, and how many gave information to the police? Research on bystander intervention (Chapter 12) addresses issues such as these.

Finally, social psychologists would want to investigate not just the causes of Agron's behavior, but its effects—especially the effects on his attitudes (Chapter 5) and self-concept (Chapter 4). Although Agron had a history of antisocial and violent behavior, there is no evidence that he had ever killed anyone before. Did his attitudes toward violent behavior change after the stabbings in the park? How would he resolve the psychological discomfort or "cognitive dissonance" (Festinger, 1957; Aronson, 1992) caused by the knowledge that he had committed murder, despite his inhibitions against that socially proscribed act? Would he decide that murder was not as repugnant to him as it had once seemed? What would be the consequences of relabeling himself as a murderer?

Notable in their absence from this list of issues that social psychologists pursue are questions about individual differences in behavior. One might get the impression, then, that social psychologists leave the study of individual differences to personality psychologists, or even downplay their importance. Compared to personality psychologists, social psychologists do put more emphasis on the importance of situational factors than on personality traits. At the same time, they recognize that social behavior is a function of both situational factors and personality variables, as well as the interaction between the two. Just as some situations are more likely than others to elicit aggression, for example, some people are more likely than others to act aggressively.

Not only that; situations do not always have the same effect on everyone. Certain situations will trigger hostile feelings in some people, but not in others. Similarly, some situations—for instance, loud parties—might cause some people (extraverts) to become more outgoing, but others (introverts) to withdraw socially. This insight is the essence of **interactionism** (Endler & Magnusson, 1976; Magnusson, 1990; Murtha, Kanfer, & Ackerman, 1996; Snyder & Ickes, 1985). As we will see, although most of the studies described in this book involve the effects of specific situations on people, a great many also demonstrate how taking personality variables into account allows for a fuller understanding of human social behavior.

Situations do not always have the same effect on everyone.

Social Psychology: Life as It's Lived

In sum, social psychologists take a unique approach, or what might be called a unique level of analysis. The best way to describe that level of analysis might be "life as it's lived," especially life as it is lived among other people. Social psychology basically holds up a magnifying glass to the day-to-day events of our lives. The other approaches to studying people—developmental, clinical, sociological, historical, and so forth—focus on important factors, but those factors typically are not the immediate causes of what people say, think, feel, and do from moment to moment.

For example, being an extraverted 21-year-old upper-middle-class woman in the 21st century with an anxiety disorder and intelligent, supportive parents will have all sorts of implications for how one thinks, feels, and behaves. Social psychologists recognize that, but they focus instead on the thoughts, feelings, and behaviors themselves and the general rules that govern them. Certainly, social psychologists do not dismiss the importance of historical period, temperament, stage of life, social class, mental health, genetic endowment, or even neurochemistry. What they want to know about those characteristics, however, is how they shape the way in which individuals think about and react to different situations, different people, and other aspects of their social world. In other words, the focus of social psychologists is on the implications of all these variables for "life as it's lived."

Social Psychology as a Science

No one needs to read a book about social psychology to speculate about human behavior. Turn on your radio or television, and you will find no shortage of different perspectives on what people are like and why they do what they do. Stroll over to your local coffee shop or park, and you will find even more experts eager to impart their wisdom. Few people will pretend to be authorities on cell biology, nuclear physics, organic chemistry, or computational linguistics, but everybody knows about people. In fact, finding a person who does not consider him- or herself something of an amateur social psychologist would be difficult.

Many people are, of course, very sensitive and perceptive, and social psychologists' intuitions about behavior are not necessarily any more valid than anyone else's. What is true, though, is that social psychologists tend to be more *modest* than most people about their understanding of the complexities of human behavior. For social psychologists, any general statement about people's thoughts, feelings, and behavior is a *hypothesis*—a tentative guess or prediction—that must be tested. Such tests, of course, must be carefully controlled and unbiased, and when the topic of study is human beings, that is no easy task. In fact, producing compelling evidence in support of a hypothesis about the processes underlying human behavior can be extraordinarily difficult.

In sum, social psychologists must test their ideas carefully before taking them seriously and applying them to people's behavior—Salvador Agron's or anyone else's. Chapter 2 will provide a review of the basic research methods social psychologists use to test their hypotheses. And in all of the later chapters, we will explain not only *what* social psychologists have learned about human behavior, but *how* they arrived at their conclusions. In other words, we will present detailed accounts of hundreds of studies.

All the studies you will learn about were conducted using variations of the methods described in Chapter 2, so you should keep the concepts and principles reviewed in that chapter fresh in your mind. To encourage you to do so, every chapter will include questions about research methodology and design, presented under the heading "Think like a social psychologist: Designing research." In addition, each chapter will include a more extended exercise in a separate "Think like a social psychologist" box. A number of those boxes will describe a hypothetical study whose methodology was flawed in some way, and you will be asked to think critically about the study and determine its shortcomings. Solving these puzzles will require you to apply your knowledge of research methodology.

Summary

Social psychology is the study of how people think, behave, and feel in social contexts. It differs from other branches of psychology (personality, developmental, and clinical) in its focus on situational factors and normal psychological processes (that is, psychological processes that are not unique to specific kinds of people). More than other approaches, social psychology focuses on the immediate causes of what people say, think, feel, and do—in other words, on life as it is lived from moment to moment. As we will see, some of those immediate causes are far from obvious, so people are not always aware of them.

The kinds of issues that social psychologists study are also of great interest to other people. In fact, most people speculate frequently about social-psychological phenomena. Social psychologists, on the other hand, do more than speculate. Using the scientific method, they systematically gather data about human social behavior. They formulate testable hypotheses about human behavior, develop procedures to unambiguously test those hypotheses, and analyze the data generated by those procedures using formal statistical tests.

Think Like a Social Psychologist

Confronting social issues

This chapter focuses on a violent incident, though it could also have focused on a more uplifting one. For example, in 2005, a tour boat with many elderly passengers capsized on a lake in upstate New York. A number of people immediately hopped into small boats and put themselves at risk by trying to rescue the passengers. What kinds of questions would social psychologists ask about the rescuers' behavior? What about developmental psychologists and personality psychologists—what kinds of questions would they ask?

SOCIAL PSYCHOLOGY: A PREVIEW OF SOME MAJOR THEMES

Why Did the Capeman Kill?

Each of the chapters that follow this one focuses on a different aspect of people's social behavior. As a result, the chapters' central questions and issues will vary quite a bit. Still, because the research in each one focuses on the same social animals—human beings—we will emphasize the connections between different concepts, ideas, theories, and research studies. In addition, a number of broader themes that run through the book will relate to material in all the chapters. We'll review a few of them here.

Social Psychology and Hidden Influences on Behavior

At any given moment, most of us can provide a reasonable account of our behavior. That is, we usually have something to say about what we are doing, thinking, or feeling and why we are doing, thinking, or feeling it. We can also tell stories that make sense of our past behavior. Though these accounts of our own behavior are not necessarily wrong, we suspect they may often be incomplete. In the course of our daily interactions with others, we may be affected by all sorts of things—that is, "stimuli"—of which we are unaware. In some cases, we may be well aware of the stimuli that affect our behavior, but we may not realize how they affect us. In general, then, the people, places, and things we encounter in our everyday lives can trigger unconscious psychological processes that have profound effects on our behavior. We will refer to these stimuli and the processes they trigger as **hidden influences** on behavior.

In extreme cases, hidden influences can leave us mystified about our own behavior (Wilson & Brekke, 1994). Salvador Agron, for example, could never adequately explain to other people why he stabbed three people. The best he could do was to describe what he had done as "a spontaneous explosion of emotions and feelings" (Jacoby, 2000, p. 335). It is not clear that he could explain his actions even to himself. Although we cannot know for sure, Agron's confusion about his own behavior might explain why, over time, he increasingly denied his part in the violence. Fifteen years after the attacks, he claimed, "I could not see myself committing the killings in the playground. I could not remember the crime." At about the same time, he declared, "I swear, by all that is holy, I do not remember using the knife that was in my hand" (Jacoby, 2000, pp. 123, 176).

A great deal of the research conducted by social psychologists is devoted to revealing hidden influences. These stimuli can be separated into two broad categories. The first consists of *subliminal stimuli*, or visual stimuli that people perceive without being aware of them (Bornstein & Pittman, 1992). As will become clear, people can indeed be influenced subliminally—that is, their thoughts, feelings, and behavior can be affected by stimuli that they do not consciously register. For example, research suggests that if frightening images were flashed on your computer screen for a few milliseconds (a few thousandths of a second), you would subsequently feel more anxious than you would have felt otherwise, as well as more anxious than you would if the images had been pleasant ones (Robles, Smith, Carver, & Wellens, 1987; see **Figure 1.1**). You would, however, be unaware of the *cause* of your anxiety.

Levels of anxiety reported after viewing a film with positive, neutral, or negative subliminal images inserted.

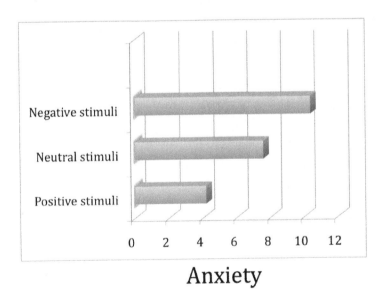

Figure 1.1: Hidden (subliminal) influences on mood.

From Robles, Smith, Carver, and Wellens (1987).

Subliminal effects are fascinating, but in our day-to-day lives, the hidden influences we encounter are more likely to be of another kind. Most hidden influences are not subliminal at all; we are perfectly aware of them, though we are unaware of how they affect us (Nisbett & Wilson, 1977). For example, no one would be surprised to learn that watching a boxing match can have an impact on a person's thoughts and feelings. What is less obvious, however, is that such an experience could have a negative effect on viewers' interactions with other people long after the fight is over (Phillips, 1983). In fact, certain experiences bring particular thoughts to mind—that is, they *prime* them. Those thoughts (in this case, hostile and aggressive ones) can go on to affect a person even after the vivid (and not at all subliminal) experience that primed them is forgotten.

Similarly, there is nothing mysterious about the arousal you experience when you drink heavily caffeinated beverages. Most of the time, we are quite aware of the lift we get from a cup of coffee or a can of cola. How and why that arousal can, depending on the situation, lead you to feel more angry, frightened, or even amorous than you otherwise might is a more complicated story. We will discuss such hidden influences of mood and arousal in Chapter 9. To give one final example, if a person who is a foot taller than everyone else in the room is wearing outlandish clothing, your attention will be drawn to him or her, and you will be quite conscious of that fact. Nevertheless, you are less likely to be aware of the ways in which the tall person's *salience* affects the impressions you form and the judgments you make about him or her (Chapter 3).

We suspect that when you learn about the many hidden influences on your behavior—even when you clearly understand how and why they work—you will be unable to avoid thinking that other people are more affected by them than you. That might be true in some cases, but the odds are that it is not. In fact, research indicates that most people see themselves as being less susceptible than the average person to the biases caused by hidden influences (Pronin, Lin, & Ross, 2002). The reason seems to be that when people introspect about their own behavior, they are unable (not surprisingly) to find any evidence for the nonconscious processes involved (Pronin & Krueger, 2007).

The point of our emphasis on hidden influences is not to make you paranoid about the difficulty of identifying all the immediate influences on your day-to-day behavior. We believe there is a benefit to becoming more conscious of factors that affect how you think about, feel about, and treat other people. Surely, it must be beneficial to understand how your mind works, how your perspective on your experiences might be biased, and how you might treat other people unfairly without being aware of it.

There is nothing subliminal about this wrestling match, but you might not be aware of its effects on your thoughts and behavior—that is, the hidden influences of viewing it.

After all, hidden influences can have unwanted effects on your behavior (Wilson & Brekke, 1994). In sum, we hope that the effect of learning about hidden influences on your behavior will be not to make you paranoid, but to make you just a bit wiser and a lot more humble.

Social Cognition

Just as we can examine human behavior from many different perspectives, we can take several general approaches to studying social psychology in particular. As already noted, social psychologists tend not to be behaviorists. Nevertheless, one could develop a science of social behavior based on the assumption that people are passive beings whose behavior is shaped by reinforcements and other environmental events (Skinner, 1971). Psychoanalytic theorists also have much to say about the issues that interest social psychologists (Hall & Lindzey, 1968; Westen, 1998). Some social psychologists have even proposed Marxist approaches to many of the topics we will cover in this book (Wexler, 1983).

For the last 30 years or so, however, one of the prevailing themes in social psychological research has been **social cognition**. At the broadest level, social cognition research is based on the idea that because people are thinking organisms, social behavior is inextricably related to their cognitive processes (that is, thinking and other mental activity). That definition is admittedly a bit abstract, but that is because social cognition actually has at least two different meanings.

Cognitive Social Psychology

Salvador Agron claimed not to understand why he plunged his knife into the three young men he met in the park. Certainly, to fully explain why the crime took place, we would need to understand why he was carrying a weapon, why he was so ready to engage in violence, why he had joined a gang, and why there was so much tension among gangs on Manhattan's West Side. At the very least, though, we can make an assumption about Agron's state of mind just before he lashed out: he believed his victims posed some sort of threat to him. In other words, the most immediate cause of his behavior was an attribution of hostility (see Chapters 3 and 12). Aggressive behavior is often preceded by an inference that someone is intentionally trying to harm us (Dodge & Crick, 1990). Such inferences can take place without our awareness, and can differ from the conclusions we might reach if we thought more carefully about the other person's behavior (Zelli, Huesmann, & Cervone, 1995; Zelli, Cervone, & Huesmann, 1996).

This way of thinking about an act of aggression, or about any kind of meaningful social behavior, exemplifies a perspective known as **cognitive social psychology**, the first meaning of social cognition. Cognitive social psychology is defined as the study of the thoughts and other mental processes that underlie and lead to social behavior. Research of this kind concerns (1) what people notice and attend to in their social environments; (2) how people interpret or make inferences about what they notice; (3) how they evaluate it, or decide whether they like it; (4) what information people store in memory about different people, groups, relationships, institutions, and other important parts of their social world; (5) how all that information is organized; (6) how and why some of that information later comes to mind; and finally, (7) how all that mental activity ultimately expresses itself in people's behavior (Fiske & Taylor, 1991; Gollwitzer & Bargh, 1996; Isen & Hastorf, 1982; Manis, 1977; Moskowitz, 2005; Schneider, 1991; Sherman, Judd, & Park, 1989).

Described like that, social cognition refers to a general way to think about social psychology, as well as to the research social psychologists carry out based on that orientation. That is, cognitive social psychology is not just

Is she sad, angry, bored, or just sleepy, and why? Was it something you said? How should you react? Cognitive social psychologists study the processes involved in making such judgments, attributions, and decisions.

another topic of study for social psychologists. Instead, it is a way of thinking about and studying just about anything social psychologists are interested in, including aggression, altruism, interpersonal attraction, impression formation, relationships, prejudice, intergroup relations, leadership, social influence, conformity, and attitude

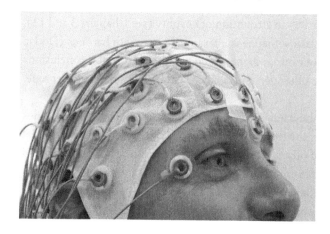

A cap with electrodes connected to an electroencephalograph (EEG). A variety of tools and measurement techniques allow social-cognitive neuroscientists to directly examine the neural activity associated with exposure to different kinds of people, social situations, and social information.

change. Indeed, one could go so far as to say that the cognitive social psychology approach is as central, intrinsic to, and inseparable from the material covered in this book (and more generally, most of the work done by social psychologists over the last few decades) as bubbles are to a glass of club soda.

To summarize, one way of understanding people's social behavior is in terms of how they think about their social worlds. Cognitive social psychologists study those thought processes directly. What that means is that many social psychologists focus less on actual behavior than on what is presumed to come before it, such as people's inferences, judgments, and decisions. This focus on thought processes, especially as they relate to social stimuli, also means that more social psychology experiments than you might guess involve collecting data that might not seem very "social," such as the recall and recognition of information about people, and even reaction times (how quickly people answer questions or identify stimuli). In fact, social cognition researchers—especially those who call themselves **social-cognitive neuroscientists**—are increasingly turning to electrochemical activity in the brain in their search for the underlying causes of social-psychological phenomena (Harmon-Jones & Winkielman, 2007; Lieberman, 2010; Mitchell, 2008; Ochsner & Lieberman, 2001). We will see that such information can tell us a great deal about people's interpersonal behavior.

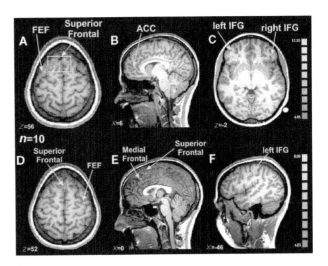

Images of the brain captured via a technique called functional magnetic resonance imaging (fMRI) allow social-cognitive neuroscientists to learn what regions of the brain become active in response to different kinds of social stimuli.

The Social Psychology of Cognition and Socially Shared Cognition

The main idea underlying cognitive social psychology is that we cannot fully understand people's social behavior without taking into account mental processes. The flip side of that statement, on the other hand, is also true. People's thinking does not take place in social isolation. To fully understand people's mental processes, then, we must take into account the social context in which they do their thinking. The way in which people's social environments affect the way they think has been called the **social psychology of cognition** (Higgins, 1992; Levine & Higgins, 1995).

An example of the social psychology of cognition is provided by research on the self-concept (see Chapter 4). People do not always describe themselves in the same way when asked to do so. On different occasions, for example, a reader of this book might think of herself primarily as a student, a psychology major, a sibling, a Canadian, a libertarian, or a fan of techno music. A major factor affecting the perceived importance of these different personal characteristics is the nature of the situation in which she thinks about herself. Different characteristics are distinctive in different settings, and those tend to be the ones that make their way into our descriptions of ourselves (McGuire & Padawer-Singer, 1976). For example, our hypothetical student is more likely to perceive and describe herself as a "woman" in a classroom in which all the other students are males than in a classroom in which the majority of students are female (see **Figure 1.2**). Similarly, an avid swimmer might describe himself in terms of his hobby when talking to a person sitting next to him on an airplane. He would be less likely to describe himself that way to other swimmers in the locker room after a swim.

These different ways of thinking about ourselves have important implications for our behavior. Shortly after Salvador Agron was taken into custody by the police, his sister told a reporter how shocked she was to learn that he was the notorious Capeman. Agron was a "good, quiet kid," she said, "very religious" (Jacoby, 2000, p. 182). That description hardly seems appropriate for the violent hooligan who ran wild through the streets of New York. We should, however, take seriously the possibility that how Agron thought about himself, what he wanted to do and be, and how he evaluated his own behavior was different when he was in the company of his fellow gang members than it was elsewhere. Not only do people behave differently in different settings; to a certain extent, the "self" that directs our behavior in one setting is not the same "self" that does so in a different setting.

How likely are you to mention your sex (male or female) in answering the question "Tell me about yourself" in groups of varying sex compositions?

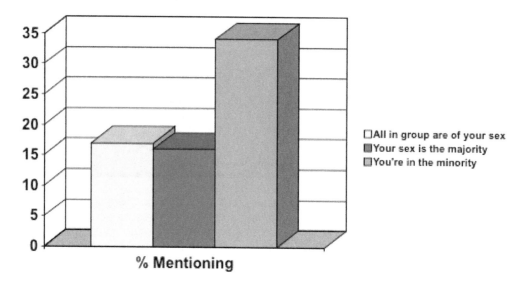

Figure 1.2: *The social psychology of cognition.*

From Cota and Dion (1986). All groups consisted of three people (all male, all female, two females and one male, or two males and one female).

The way you think about what you are doing—and about yourself—changes when others are present.

Because we think about ourselves in very different ways in different situations, the standards by which we judge ourselves also vary. How we think about and evaluate ourselves is affected by our social surroundings, typically without our awareness. Thus, an appreciation of the social psychology of cognition can help us to understand why Salvador Agron might have behaved like the proverbial choirboy in one setting, yet be capable of boasting that "my mother can watch me burn" in another setting.

Cognition is even more social when it takes place in groups of people engaged in some kind of collective or cooperative activity. This kind of social cognition is often referred to as **socially shared cognition** (Resnick, Levine, & Teasley, 1991; Thompson & Fine, 1999). That term refers to the joint cognitive activity that takes place in groups (or even in pairs of people, called *dyads*), especially when that activity is collaborative and goal oriented (Hinsz, Tindale, & Vollrath, 1997; Ickes & Gonzalez, 1994; Larson & Christensen, 1993). If you belong to a group that is trying to reach some conclusion or make a decision, your own knowledge, beliefs, and values will affect that decision, but so will other people's, so will your perception of *their* knowledge and beliefs and values, so will their understanding of what is going on in *your* head, and so will people's perceptions about what other people know about their knowledge and beliefs and values. Clearly, groups are complicated creatures. To understand them, we need to treat them as more than just collections of separate, independent human beings.

Similarly, trying to understand Salvador Agron's behavior on that fateful night in 1959 without taking into account the fact that he was participating in a group activity might be a mistake. Many of the decisions that led up to the murders were group decisions. Understanding how they were made would require more than just an analysis of the thoughts and feelings of individual group members. Agron may have made his own personal judgments and decisions, and the results of his own individual thought processes certainly played a key role in turning him into a notorious killer. But he made the headlines in New York newspapers because he was a Vampire gang member, and on August 29, 1959, the Vampires made some socially shared—but ill-advised—group decisions.

Evolutionary Social Psychology

To some extent, anything we learn about our cognition should help us understand how we think about people, groups, relationships, and all other aspects of our social world. How we reach conclusions about people should be quite similar to how we reach conclusions about anything, and how we remember things about people should be explainable in terms of the basic rules of memory. According to evolutionary social psychologists, though, the mental mechanisms that come into play in social behavior are unique, having been shaped by many millennia of natural selection to guide our social behavior.

For instance, it is safe to say that most social psychologists have long believed that at some basic level, the mental mechanisms people use for categorizing objects—that is, for classifying and making distinctions between things like fruits and vegetables, pieces of furniture, weapons, appliances—are the same mechanisms they use to make distinctions between people and other social entities (for example, personal relationships). Similarly, social psychologists have had little reason to doubt that the thought processes involved in making inferences—that is, reaching conclusions about the underlying properties of one kind of thing (for instance, how dangerous different bodies of water might be)—are the same thought processes involved in making other kinds of inferences, even those about human beings (for example, how dangerous different kinds of people might be). Yet proponents of **evolutionary psychology** (Buss, 1995, 2005; Buss & Kenrick, 1998; Cosmides & Tooby, 1989; Neuberg, Kenrick, & Schaller, 2010; Schaller, Simpson, & Kenrick, 2006; Scher & Rauscher, 2003), an increasingly popular perspective, reject these assumptions.

Evolutionary psychologists stress that natural selection shaped not only our species' physical characteristics, but also our psychological characteristics (Schmitt & Pilcher, 2004; Stevens & Fiske, 1995). Just as certain features of our bodies increased our chances of surviving and reproducing, various **evolved psychological mechanisms** also promoted what biologists refer to as *inclusive fitness*. Those people with the best mental tools for dealing with the challenges our ancestors faced, goes the reasoning, would have been more likely than others to survive and pass down their psychological mechanisms to their descendants. As an illustration, fear of snakes (LoBue & DeLoache, 2008; LoBue, Rakison, & DeLoache, 2010) would probably have motivated a person to engage in behavior that promoted self-preservation (like running away). Similarly, evolution seems to have led human beings to prefer dwellings that provide both a good view of the surrounding area and a place to find shelter and hide (Mealey & Theis, 1995).

Significantly, some of the challenges or "adaptive problems" that our ancestors faced were social ones. In other words, human beings had to develop the capacity to deal with more than predators, scarce resources, harsh climates, and other obvious threats to survival. They had to evolve the capacity to both affiliate with and protect themselves from other people. In other words, they had to evolve a capacity for group living.

An important feature of psychological mechanisms, as described by evolutionary psychologists, is *domain specificity*. That is to say, psychological mechanisms are activated and affect behavior only in certain situations and in response to certain stimuli. The mechanisms that evolved to help people deal with the problem of dangerous animals are not the same as those that evolved to help them cope with threatening people. Similarly, the mechanisms that evolved to help people distinguish between nutritious and poisonous plants, and to categorize them accordingly, are unrelated to the mechanisms that they use to categorize their different kinds of relationships with people.

Evolutionary psychologists suggest that a healthy fear of spiders is innate. Human beings with no inhibitions about handling these creatures were less likely than others to pass on their genes to future generations.

Thus, evolutionary psychologists argue, human beings have developed a set of domain-specific mental mechanisms—evolved social-psychological mechanisms—for dealing with social situations. Specifically, people possess species-general psychological mechanisms that are hypothesized to have evolved to solve adaptive problems in the social domain (Tooby & Cosmides, 1992). Because throughout their evolutionary history, human beings faced countless adaptive problems related to social interaction, evolutionary social psychologists have proposed a great many species-general social-psychological mechanisms (Buss, 1995). Among them are sexual jealousy and gender-specific mate preferences (see Chapter 9 and Buss & Schmidt, 1993; but see Eagly & Wood, 1999, for a counterargument), a tendency to attend to and imitate powerful and high-status models (Abramovitch & Grusec,

1978; Ratcliff, Hugenberg, Shriver, & Bernstein, 2011), fear of strangers (Chapters 11 and 13), and even a procedure for detecting when others are cheating (Cosmides, 1989; Cosmides & Tooby, 1989).

Evolutionary psychology is a broad perspective on human behavior that has inspired new ways of thinking about many of the issues social psychologists study. It should not, however, be confused with the philosophy known as Social Darwinism, or the idea that people (or races of people) who are weak or "unfit" should be dominated by those with superior genes. In fact, evolutionary psychologists assume that the psychological mechanisms they study are species-general—that is, part of the genetic inheritance common to every person. The study of individual differences is only a minor aspect of evolutionary psychology.

Consider, for example, how an evolutionary psychologist would address the issue of violence in impoverished urban areas. Would he or she suggest that inferior or "less fit" people have either gravitated toward or been restricted to these less desirable parts of the community? Nothing could be further from the truth (Wright, 1995). Instead, evolutionary psychologists would focus on the fact that inner cities are often crowded, chaotic, and lacking in critical resources. They would suggest that psychological mechanisms have evolved for coping with such situations, and that those mechanisms might cause people to behave in ways that might seem undesirable today, but which may have enhanced their chances for survival in the past. To put it simply, people in a stressed inner-city area behave in certain ways because that is the way humans are programmed to behave in that kind of social context. Salvador Agron's behavior could be discussed in similar terms. His aggressiveness, his hostility toward authority, his need to find groups (even antisocial ones) with whom to affiliate, and his striving for power within those groups—all could be seen as resulting from the activation of psychological mechanisms designed to help humans cope with low status, alienation from kin, and the need to fend for oneself in a dangerous environment.

In sum, evolutionary psychologists' analysis of inner-city violence would be compatible with a policy of funneling more money and other resources into depressed parts of the city. The point is not, however, that all the predictions of evolutionary psychology are more congenial or consistent with liberal than conservative political ideologies. Instead, it is that evolutionary psychology should not be associated with a particular political agenda at all. It is simply an approach to human behavior that suggests that to a great extent, social behavior is controlled (without our awareness) by inherited psychological mechanisms that evolved specifically to help people manage the complexities of interpersonal behavior in their social worlds.

Boston, Berlin, Bombay, and Beijing: Culture and Social Psychology

Social psychology, you will recall, can be defined as the study of how people think, behave, and feel in social contexts. One important aspect of social contexts is the culture in which they are situated. More and more, social psychologists' theories and hypotheses are taking into account what has been learned about how people of different cultures behave and think about themselves, other people, their relationships, and their social institutions (Bond, 1988; Chiu & Hong, 2006; Fiske, Kitayama, Markus, & Nisbett, 1998; Heine, 2008; Sorrentino, Cohen, Olson, & Zanna, 2005). In short, cross-cultural research has become central to social psychologists' efforts to understand behavior.

As promised, in this book we will describe hundreds of studies of social behavior. But in many (or maybe most) cases, the people involved in those studies are of a certain type: college students. Because research in social psychology is typically conducted in universities, researchers study the people they find in those settings. In addition, much social psychological research has been conducted not only at universities, but at universities with a predominantly white middle-class population. Needless to say, young, white middle-class college students are people like everyone else, so we can learn a great deal from the studies in which they participate. However, there are limits to what we can learn about human beings' thoughts, feelings, and behavior by studying such narrow samples (Henrich, Heine, & Norenzayan, 2010; Henry, 2008; Sears, 1986). This, then, is another consideration that has motivated the recent explosion in cross-cultural research.

Individualistic versus Collectivistic Cultures

Much of the cross-cultural research conducted by social psychologists has been guided by the distinction between **individualistic** and **collectivistic cultures** (Kim, Triandis, Kagitcibasi, Choi, & Yoon, 1994; Markus & Kitayama, 1991; Triandis, 1995; but see Cohen, 2009). Although the boundaries between the two are fuzzy, North American and Western European cultures tend to be dominated more than others by individualism. In those parts of the world, people tend to see themselves as independent individuals who control their own fate. They focus more on their own individual goals than on group goals. Collectivism, on the other hand, is more common in Asia, Africa, much of South America, and Eastern Europe. Collectivists are more likely than individualists to define themselves in terms of their relationships and group memberships, and less likely to assume that their own needs and desires are of primary importance (see **Table 1.2**). As we will see, this distinction has profound implications for a wide range of human behavior (see, for example, Na, Choi, & Sul, 2013).

Understanding how different cultures can affect the way we think and behave is interesting and important, but that is not the only benefit of this research. The study of cross-cultural differences helps us to test the extent to which general statements about human behavior can be considered universal truths. As we will learn in

Table 1.2: Cross-cultural comparisons of the self-concept

People in individualistic cultures like the United States tend to see themselves in terms of personality traits, but people in collectivistic cultures like Japan and India define themselves more in terms of social relationships and roles. Researchers in two studies used the Twenty Statements Test (TST) to measure the relative importance of personality attributes and social role or identities in the different cultures.

COUSINS (1989)

	United States	Japan
Personality attributes	58%	19%
Social roles/identities	9%	27%

DHAWAN et al. (1995)

	United States	India
Personality attributes	49%	3%
Social roles/identities	26%	32%

The TST requires people to complete 20 statements starting with the words "I am." These data were derived from studies by Cousins (1989; "social" and "pure attribute" categories) and Dhawan, Roseman, Naidu, Thapa, and Rettek (1995, "social identity" and "psychological attributes/self-worth" categories).

Chapter 3, a classic finding of social psychology, called the fundamental attribution error, is that we tend to assume human behavior is caused by people's traits, attitudes, beliefs, and abilities, even when other explanations are plausible (Gilbert & Malone, 1995; Ross, 1977). For example, people may conclude that a man who displays fear in the face of a snarling pit bull is a coward, even though that conclusion is not very reasonable. At one time, psychologists explained this phenomenon in terms of basic perceptual processes (Jones, 1979). Because the person stands out from his surroundings, or is salient, went their reasoning, we direct our attention to the person rather than the situation in which his behavior takes place. In general, people tend to attribute more importance to things when they are visually prominent. Thus, it seemed reasonable to conclude that the tendency to overemphasize the role of personality traits in causing behavior was just a specific case of something "people" inevitably do.

Most of the original research on the fundamental attribution error was conducted in the United States. When cross-cultural studies began to indicate that people from Asian countries were not as liable to explain behavior in terms of personal dispositions, the perceptual explanation of

Major league baseball players who go to Japan to play often have trouble adjusting to the more team-oriented, collectivistic style of play there. Top players in Japan are less likely to receive special treatment than top players in the United States. In the words of one team manager in Japan, "if you allow individualism, it will surely spoil your organization" (Whiting, 1990, p. 62).

the phenomenon ran into trouble (Menon, Morris, Chiu, & Hong, 1999; Miller, 1984; Morris & Peng, 1994; Norenzayan, Choi, & Nisbett, 2002; Singelis, 1994). Some of the studies indicated that people from more collectivistic cultures preferred to explain behavior in terms of external, situational influences. Other studies suggested that they focused more on the characteristics of groups than on the characteristics of individuals. Thus, cross-cultural research showed at least one claim about a universal process—a tendency to focus almost exclusively on "person causes" as a result of our visual and perceptual systems—to be incorrect.

Social-psychological research in one culture can also shed light on the behavior of individuals in other cultures, explaining what might otherwise be difficult to analyze. For example, even in an individualistic culture like the United States, situations exist in which people will focus more on group goals than on individual goals, and will be very aware of and concerned about their relationships with others. The same person may behave quite differently when participating in a communal activity with members of his or her church, synagogue, or mosque than when immersed in a competitive work environment. Understanding cultures in which collectivistic values dominate allows us to better understand pockets of collectivism within individualistic cultures.

Cultures of Honor

Another example of how research on a particular culture can help us to understand human nature in general is provided by Nisbett and Cohen's studies of the Southern region of the United States (Cohen & Nisbett, 1994; Nisbett & Cohen, 1996). According to popular stereotypes, Southerners are more prone to violence than Northerners. The truth seems to be more complex, however. In general, Southerners are *not* more violent than people from the North. Instead, they are more likely to feel that aggressive behavior is appropriate in a limited set of situations: those involving direct insults, humiliations, or challenges to their pride. More generally, Nisbett and Cohen characterize the South as a "culture of honor." Indeed, a study of letters written by soldiers during the United States' Civil War revealed that Southerners, but not Northerners, were more likely to justify their participation in the war in terms of "honor" than in terms of "duty" (McPherson, 1997).

Dueling to avenge a perceived insult is more common in cultures of honor than in other cultures.

Research on the Southern "culture of honor" (see also Brown, Osterman, & Barnes, 2009) can shed light on other people's behavior, too—including Salvador Agron's. Recall that he and his fellow Vampires converged on the park in Manhattan hoping to ambush another gang, the Norsemen. What led them to assemble there, however, was not an arbitrary impulse to engage in violence. They had received reports (vague, to be sure) that a Norseman had tried to sell drugs to the mother of a Vampire. They had also heard that Norsemen had beaten up some Puerto Ricans (recall that most of the Vampires were from Puerto Rico). For the Vampires, the proper response to such provocations was clear: immediate retaliation. In this case, even though the provocations were just rumors, the potential consequences of letting the insult go unanswered outweighed the potential costs of lashing out based on faulty information.

One can understand Agron's behavior, then, not just in terms of (1) how he individually perceived his victims' behavior and intentions; (2) how the presence of other people affected his perceptions; (3) how the Vampires collectively perceived the situation; or (4) how his evolutionary heritage predisposed him to respond. Instead, one can focus on the fact that he was immersed in a culture of honor, and that his behavior was a predictable if tragic consequence of embracing that culture's values. We could speculate that in some other context, his reaction to a perceived slight might have been very different from his reaction in the park. Would an insult or snub at his stepfather's Pentecostal church have triggered such a murderous response? That is not likely; we can assume that other values influenced Agron's behavior there. Unfortunately, when Agron encountered people he thought were his enemies, he was surrounded by people who reinforced—even enforced—culture-of-honor values. What followed was his deadly assault, and his arrest, incarceration, murder trial, and death sentence, handed down in October 1960.

Summary

Although social psychologists study a broad range of topics, much of their research involves the study of social cognition and is based on the assumption that to understand social behavior, we must understand the thought processes that lead to that behavior. Research of this kind is also referred to as cognitive social psychology. A great deal of social psychological research also involves the study of how social situations change the way people think (the social psychology of cognition). Social psychologists who study small groups emphasize that the kind of thinking groups do (socially shared cognition) must be distinguished from individual thinking.

A growing movement called evolutionary social psychology involves thinking about social cognition and social behavior as adaptive processes that evolved to increase people's fitness (that is, the likelihood that they will survive to reproduce). From this perspective, social behavior is driven by psychological mechanisms that are common to all human beings' genetic inheritance. At the same time, social psychologists recognize individual and group differences in behavior. In particular, all human beings belong to cultural groups, whose members share important values, basic beliefs, and assumptions about human beings and their behavior. Indeed, cultural differences will be discussed throughout this book.

Although people are profoundly affected by their social contexts, they are not always aware of how those contexts are affecting them. Similarly, although social contexts generally affect our behavior by triggering specific thought processes, those thought processes themselves often take place without our awareness. Overall, people are not always conscious of the factors affecting their thoughts, feelings, and behaviors. Social psychological research sheds a great deal of light on these hidden influences on our behavior.

Think Like a Social Psychologist

Thinking critically

—Most people believe that others are more affected by hidden influences than they themselves are. Why do you think that is so?

—More people die from smoking cigarettes than are killed by spider bites, but more people are afraid of spiders than are afraid of cigarettes. How would an evolutionary psychologist explain these facts?

Understanding everyday behavior

—Can you think of times when you belonged to a group that seemed to have a mind of its own? That is, can you think of cases in which socially shared cognition led your group to make a decision that no individual member would have made?

—Sometimes people who were born and raised in one kind of culture (collectivist, for example) move with their families to another kind of culture (such as an individualist one). Do you think such people adopt blends of the different cultural values, behaving like collectivists in some situations and individualists in others? In general, how do you think they manage their multicultural status?

THE "DARK SIDE" AND THE "BRIGHT SIDE" OF SOCIAL PSYCHOLOGY

As we have noted, despite the fact that we will be focusing on the many ways in which your behavior is affected without your awareness, our intent is not to make you paranoid. Similarly, we would prefer not to depress you. A social psychology book could easily have that effect on a person, because much of social psychological research boils down to a careful analysis of all the nasty things people do and say to each other, and the sometimes unfortunate outcomes of their social interaction. People do aggress against each other (Chapter 13) and fail to help those in distress (Chapter 12). They hate and discriminate against members of other groups (Chapter 11) and try to persuade others to share their prejudices (Chapter 6). Group attempts to solve problems can backfire (Chapter 8); more generally, the presence of others can often bring out the worst in us (Chapters 7 and 14). Out of mental laziness, people may make disastrous decisions. Their relationships fail (Chapter 10). It should not be surprising, though, that social psychologists are drawn to these subjects. In general, people are more interested in trying to explain negative or unexpected events than positive or expected ones (Weiner, 1985).

Our discussion of these phenomena could also leave you confused. The research covered in social psychology textbooks does not typically present a clear picture of human nature. In fact, one could be left with the impression that social psychology is rife with contradictory findings. Are people inherently prejudiced, aggressive, reluctant to help, and prone to shortcuts in their social judgments? Or are they open-minded, congenial, helpful, and thoughtful? One of our goals is to show that depending on the situation, people can be either admirable or reprehensible, and their social interactions can lead either to positive (even wonderful) or negative (even horrifying) outcomes.

For example, we will discuss research showing that people often fail to help others, even when they come face to face with those in need of assistance and could easily offer it (see Chapter 12). Needless to say, when others' suffering is less obvious, people are even less likely to be helpful. Thus, when Salvador Agron was found guilty of murder and sent off to prison, the public forgot him. His mental state deteriorated rapidly, but few people seemed interested in finding out whether he could be rehabilitated, and fewer still acted to prevent him from sinking into madness and despair.

On the other hand, in certain circumstances, some people will respond with empathy to those in distress. When we empathize with others—that is, imagine ourselves in their situation and experience indirectly what they are feeling—we are more likely to help them (Batson, Chang, Orr, & Rowland, 2002), even if we must go to great lengths to do so. Indeed, within a few years of Agron's incarceration, a number of people who were moved by his plight reached out to him, sacrificing a lot of time and energy in the process. These people—strangers at first—contributed greatly to his moral, social, intellectual, and spiritual development. Agron eventually earned a high school diploma and even some college credits behind bars. He became a poet, a leader among his fellow inmates, and an articulate advocate of prison reform.

"We find the defense and prosecution arguments totally confusing without a doubt."

In each chapter, we will highlight the "dark side" and "bright side" of different social psychological issues in separate boxes. By the time you have finished reading this book, you should understand that there are no simple answers to questions about the inherent goodness or badness of human beings, or about the inherent joys or dangers of human interaction.

Think Like a Social Psychologist

Thinking critically

—Are people inherently selfish or generous? Come up with an argument for the "dark side"—that is, make the case that people care basically only about themselves. Now do the same for the "bright side," arguing that people are naturally concerned for others' welfare.

GIVING PSYCHOLOGY AWAY: APPLICATIONS OF SOCIAL PSYCHOLOGY

In a now famous speech before the American Psychological Association, George Miller (then the organization's president) urged members to "give psychology away" (Miller, 1969; see also Fowler, 1999). By that he meant that psychologists should not only share the results of their research with people outside the field, but also communicate their findings in such a way that people can clearly see the relevance of the research to everyday life. We have taken that message to heart. Our goal is not simply to tell you what social psychologists have done

Can basic research in social psychology shed light on why groups of people—like these Darfurian refugees in Africa—might become the victims of ethnic cleansing and genocide?

and learned. We hope too that you will develop a more sophisticated perspective on human behavior, which you can bring with you to your relationships, your workplaces, and all your other everyday interactions.

Another of our goals is to help you apply the principles of social psychology to other fields. Politics, medicine, law, business, education, and sports all involve complex social interactions and relationships. Thus, all the ideas and findings reviewed in this book can be applied to people who work in those (and other) settings. At the same time, some social psychological phenomena are more relevant to some settings and institutions than to others, and some issues and problems are unique to specific domains of human behavior. To illustrate these points, in each chapter we will present brief discussions of how social psychology can shed light on two specific topics.

The first of those topics is the law (Brewer & Williams, 2007; Kovera & Borgida, 2010; Wrightsman, Nietzel, Fortune, & Greene, 2001). According to Salvador Agron, when he was tried in court for his crime, he and his friends were referred to as "Puerto Ricans" and "Spanish boys," while his victims were consistently referred to as "Americans" and "white boys." Can that kind of labeling have an effect on how juries arrive at their verdicts? In Chapter 11 we will consider such issues. The second applied topic we will focus on is health psychology (Friedman & Silver, 2006; Marelich & Erger, 2004; Taylor, 2008). Interest in both topics has been growing in recent years, and social psychologists have made important contributions to both. By the end of the book, you should have a better idea of what social psychology can contribute to these two fields.

The final chapter of this book (Chapter 14) will focus exclusively on what social psychological research can teach us about an even more vital issue: genocide and mass killing. Attempts by one group of people to exterminate another have long plagued human relations (Diamond, 1992; Smith, 2007). In recent history, unfortunately, we have seen some horrendous episodes of human brutality. Perhaps nothing could be more pressing than the need to investigate the causes of such events. Social psychologists, however, have long been modest about applying their research to genocide. That is not too surprising, given the fact that social psychologists so often conduct laboratory research and other forms of direct or controlled observation of human behavior. Needless to say, those research methods are not well suited to the study of genocide.

Nonetheless, at this point, a wealth of social psychological research exists that can shed light on the motives and behavior of perpetrators of genocide, and the group processes that trigger such explosions of violence (Newman & Erber, 2002). Not to examine that research and elaborate on the lessons it teaches us would be a tragedy. In the last chapter, titled "The Social Psychology of Genocide, Terrorism—and Heroism," we will examine such research. As the title suggests, we will also discuss what leads some people to refrain from participating in genocide, and even to actively oppose it.

Think Like a Social Psychologist

Confronting social issues

—More and more, people have not only social lives, but "virtual" social lives on the Internet. Do the interactions people have with each other in cyberspace qualify as social behavior? Can you think of issues that a social psychologist who is interested in such interactions might want to study?

EPILOGUE: WHATEVER HAPPENED TO SALVADOR AGRON?

During his years behind bars, Salvador Agron became a changed person, both through his own efforts and with a helping hand from supporters. The state of New York eventually recognized his growth and development, and in 1979 granted him a parole from prison. Years later, the internationally acclaimed musician Paul Simon produced an album and a Broadway musical based on Agron's story (Simon, 1997). Unfortunately, that story did not end happily. Despite his efforts to educate himself and prepare for life after prison, like many others, Agron found the transition from incarceration to freedom a difficult one. He died in 1986, from an illness that was brought on at least indirectly by heavy drug use.

It is not clear that Agron himself could have explained what caused all the difficulties he experienced after his release. Undoubtedly, many of the factors involved in his decline were hidden influences, of which he would not even have been aware. Social psychologists, though, would have much to say about the difficulties Agron faced after his release. The relevant issues would include (among many others) the stereotyping and prejudice that ex-convicts experience (Harding, 2003), the difficulty of making any kind of major transition in social status (Ruble, 1994), the psychological effects of being deprived of control over one's environment for long periods (Pittman, 1998), and the variables that affect people's ability to resist temptation, such as the short-term stress relief many drugs offer (Baumeister & Heatherton, 1996; Metcalfe & Mischel, 1999). By the end of this book, you should be able to engage in this kind of analysis yourself.

KEY TERMS AND DEFINITIONS

Social psychology: the study of how people think, behave, and feel in social contexts

Interactionism: the idea that a complete understanding of people's social behavior requires us to take into account individual differences, the nature of situations, and how those factors combine and interact

Hidden influences on behavior: stimuli or psychological processes that affect our behavior without our awareness, because we are unaware either of their existence or of the way in which they are affecting us

Social cognition: the study of the cognitive processes involved in people's social behavior

Cognitive social psychology: the study of the thoughts and othher mental processes that underlie and lead to social behavior

Social-cognitive neuroscience: an approach to studying social psychology that employs the methods of cognitive neuroscience (such as the measurement of electrochemical activity in the brain) in order to understand the neural basis of social cognition and social behavior

The social psychology of cognition: the way in which social situations and the presence of other people affect our thinking

Socially shared cognition: the collective thinking engaged in by groups of people; group thinking

Evolutionary psychology: an approach to studying human behavior that assumes that people's thoughts, feelings, and behaviors are directed by psychological mechanisms that evolved because they were adaptive and increased fitness

Evolved social-psychological mechanisms: the psychological mechanisms humans developed as a result of the social challenges they faced throughout their evolutionary history

Individualistic culture: a culture in which people define themselves and others as independent actors with unique attributes, and in which individual goals take precedence over group goals

Collectivistic culture: a culture in which people define themselves and other people in terms of group memberships, and in which group goals take precedence over individual goals

REFERENCES

Abramovitch, R., & Grusec, J. E. (1978). Peer imitation in a natural setting. *Child Development, 49,* 60–65.

Allport, F. (1924). *Social psychology.* New York: Houghton Mifflin.

American Psychiatric Association (1994). *Diagnostic and statistical manual of mental disorders (DSM-IV).* Washington, DC: American Psychiatric Association.

Anderson, C. A. (2001). Heat and violence. *Current Directions in Psychological Science, 10,* 33–38.

Aronson, E. (1992). The return of the repressed: Dissonance theory makes a comeback. *Psychological Inquiry, 3,* 303–311.

Bandura, A., & Walters, R. H. (1963). *Social learning and personality development.* New York: Holt, Rinehart, & Winston.

Batson, C. D., Chang, J., Orr, R., & Rowland, J. (2002). Empathy, attitudes and action: Can feeling for a member of a stigmatized group motivate one to help the group? *Personality and Social Psychology Bulletin, 28,* 1656–1666.

Baumeister, R. F., & Heatherton, T. F. (1996). Self-regulation failure: An overview. *Psychological Inquiry, 7,* 1–15.

Bond, M. H. (1988). *The cross-cultural challenge to social psychology.* Newbury Park, CA: Sage.

Bornstein, R. F., & Pittman, T. S. (1992). *Perception without awareness.* New York: Guilford Press.

Brehm, S. S., Kassin, S. M., & Fein, S. (2002). *Social psychology* (5th ed.). Boston: Houghton Mifflin.

Brewer, N., & Williams, K. D. (Eds.). (2007). *Psychology and law: An empirical perspective.* New York: Guilford Press.

Brock, T., & Buss, A. (1962). Dissonance, aggression, and the evaluation of pain. *Journal of Abnormal and Social Psychology, 65,* 197–202.

Brown, R. P., Osterman, L. L., & Barnes, C. D. (2009). School violence and the culture of honor. *Psychological Science, 20,* 1400–1405.

Goldstein, J. H., Davis, R. W., & Herman, D. (1975). Escalation of aggression: Experimental studies. *Journal of Personality and Social Psychology, 31,* 162–170.

Buss, D. M. (1995). Evolutionary psychology: A new paradigm for psychological science. *Psychological Inquiry, 6,* 1–30.

Buss, D. M. (2005). *The handbook of evolutionary psychology.* New York: Wiley Publications.

Buss, D. M., & Kenrick, D. T. (1998). Evolutionary social psychology. In D. T. Gilbert, S. T. Fiske, & G. Lindzey (Eds.), *The handbook of social psychology* (4th ed., Vol. 2, pp. 982–1026). New York: McGraw Hill.

Buss, D. M., & Schmidt, D. P. (1993). Sexual strategies theory: A contextual evolutionary analysis of human mating. *Psychological Review, 100,* 204–232.

Caprara, G. V., Barbaranelli, C., Pastorelli, C., & Perugini, M. (1994). Individual differences in the study of human aggression. *Aggressive Behavior, 20,* 291–303.

Carlsmith, K. M., Wilson, T. D., & Gilbert, D. T. (2008). The paradoxical consequences of revenge. *Journal of Personality and Social Psychology, 95,* 1316–1324.

Chiu, C.-Y., & Hong, Y.-Y. (2006). *Social psychology of culture.* New York: Psychology Press.

Cohen, A. B. (2009). Many forms of culture. *American Psychologist, 64,* 194–204.

Cohen, D., & Nisbett, R. E. (1994). Self-protection and the culture of honor: Explaining Southern violence. *Personality and Social Psychology Bulletin, 20,* 551–567.

Cosmides, L. (1989). The logic of social exchange: Has natural selection shaped how humans reason? Studies with the Wason selection task. *Cognition, 31,* 187–276.

Cosmides, L., & Tooby, J. (1989). Evolutionary psychology and the generation of culture, Part II. Case study: A computational theory of social exchange. *Ethology and Sociobiology, 10,* 51–97.

Cota, A. A., & Dion, K. L. (1986). Salience of gender and sex composition of ad-hoc groups: An experimental test of distinctiveness theory. *Journal of Personality and Social Psychology, 50,* 770–776.

Cousins, S. D. (1989). Culture and self-perception in Japan and the United States. *Journal of Personality and Social Psychology, 56,* 124–131.

Devine, P. G., Hamilton, D. L., & Ostrom, T. M. (1994). *Social cognition: Impact on social psychology.* San Diego, CA: Academic Press.

Dhawan, N., Roseman, I. J., Naidu, R. K., & Rettek, S. I. (1995). Self-concepts across two cultures: India and the United States. *Journal of Cross-Cultural Psychology, 26,* 606–621.

Diamond, J. (1992). *The third chimpanzee.* New York: Harper Perennial.

Dodge, K. A., & Crick. N. R. (1990). Social information-processing bases of aggressive behavior in children. *Personality and Social Psychology Bulletin, 16,* 8–22.

Eagly, A. H., & Wood, W. (1999). The origins of sex differences in human behavior: Evolved dispositions versus social roles. *American Psychologist, 54,* 408–423.

Endler, N. S., Magnusson, D. (1976). Toward an interactional psychology of personality. *Psychological Bulletin, 83,* 956–974.

Fiske, A. P., Kitayama, S., Markus, H. R., & Nisbett, R. E. (1998). The cultural matrix of social psychology. In D. T. Gilbert, S. T. Fiske, & G. Lindzey (Eds.), *The handbook of social psychology* (4th ed., Vol. 2, pp. 915–981). New York: McGraw Hill.

Festinger, L. (1957). *A theory of cognitive dissonance.* Stanford, CA: Stanford University Press.

Fiske, S. T., & Taylor, S. E. (1991). *Social cognition.* New York: McGraw-Hill.

Fowler, R. D. (May, 1999). Giving psychology away. *Monitor on Psychology, 30* (5).

Friedman, H. S., & Silver, R. C. (Eds.). (2006). *Foundations of health psychology.* New York: Oxford University Press.

Gilbert, D. T., & Malone, P. S. (1995). The correspondence bias. *Psychological Bulletin, 117,* 21–38.

Gollwitzer, P. M., & Bargh, J. A. (Eds.). (1996). *The psychology of action.* New York: Guilford.

Hall, C. S., & Lindzey, G. (1968). The relevance of Freudian psychology and related viewpoints for the social sciences. In G. Lindzey & E. Aronson (Eds.), *The handbook of social psychology* (2nd ed., Vol. 1, pp. 245–319). Reading, MA: Addison-Wesley.

Harding, D. J. (2003). Jean Valjean's dilemma: The management of ex-convict identity in the search for employment. *Deviant Behavior, 24,* 571–595.

Harmon-Jones, E., & Winkielman, P. (Eds.). (2007). *Social neuroscience: Integrating biological and psychological explanations of social behavior.* New York: Guilford Press.

Heine, S. J. (2008). *Cultural psychology.* New York: Norton.

Henrich, J., Heine, S. J., & Norenzayan, A. (2010). The weirdest people in the world? *Behavioral and Brain Sciences, 33,* 61–83.

Henry, P. J. (2008). College sophomores in the laboratory redux: Influences of a narrow data base on social psychology's view of the nature of prejudice. *Psychological Inquiry, 19,* 49–71.

Higgins, E. T. (1992). Social cognition as a social science: How social action creates meaning. In D. N. Ruble, P. R. Costanzo, & M. E. Oliveri (Eds.), *The social psychology of mental health* (pp. 241–278). New York: Guilford.

Hinsz, V. B., Tindale, R. S., & Vollrath, D. A. (1997). The emerging conceptualization of groups as information processors. *Psychological Bulletin, 121,* 43–64.

Hoffman, M. L. (1977). Moral internalization: Current theory and research. In L. Berkowitz (Ed.), *Advances in Experimental Social Psychology* (vol. 10). New York: Academic Press.

Ickes, W., & Gonzalez, R. (1994). "Social" cognition and social cognition: From the subjective to the intersubjective. *Small Group Research, 25,* 294–315.

Isen, A. M., & Hastorf, A. H. (1982). Some perspectives on cognitive social psychology. In A. Hastorf & A. Isen (Eds.), *Cognitive social psychology.* New York: Elsevier/North Holland.

Jacoby, R. (2000). *Conversations with the Capeman: The untold story of Salvador Agron.* New York: Painted Leaf Press.

John, O. P., Caspi, A., Robins, R. W., Moffitt, T. E., & Stouthamer-Loeber, M. (1994). The 'Little Five': Exploring the nomological network of the five-factor model of personality in adolescent boys. *Child Development, 65,* 160–178.

John, O. P., & Srivastava, S. (1999). The big-five factor taxonomy: History, measurement, and theoretical perspectives. In L. A. Pervin & O. P. John (Eds.), *Handbook of personality: Theory and research* (2nd ed., pp. 102–138). New York: Guilford Press.

Jones, E. E. (1979). The rocky road from acts to dispositions. *American Psychologist, 34,* 107–117.

Kim, U., Triandis, H. C., Kagitcibasi, C., Choi, S., & Yoon, G. (1994). *Individualism and collectivism: Theory, method, and applications.* Thousand Oaks, CA: Sage.

Kovera, M. B., Borgida, E. (2010). Social psychology and law. In S. T. Fiske, D. T. Gilbert, & G. Lindzey (Eds.), *The handbook of social psychology* (5th ed., Vol. 2, pp. 1343–1385). Hoboken, NJ: Wiley.

Larson, J. R. Jr., & Christensen, C. (1993). Groups as problem-solving units: Toward a new meaning of social cognition. *British Journal of Social Psychology, 32,* 5–30.

Levine, J. M., & Higgins, E. T. (1995). Social determinants of cognition. *Social Cognition, 13,* 183–187.

Lieberman, M. D. (2010). Social cognitive neuroscience. In S. T. Fiske, D. T. Gilbert, & G. Lindzey (Eds.), *Handbook of social psychology* (5th ed., pp. 143–193). New York: McGraw-Hill.

LoBue, V., & DeLoache, J. S. (2008). Detecting the snake in the grass: Attention to fear-relevant stimuli by adults and young children. *Psychological Science, 19,* 284–289.

LoBue, V., Rakison, D. H., & DeLoache, J. S. (2010). Threat perception across the life span: Evidence for multiple converging pathways. *Current Directions in Psychological Science, 19*(6), 375–379.

Magnusson, D. (1990). Personality development from an interactional perspective. In L. A. Pervin, *Handbook of personality: Theory and research* (pp. 193–22). New York: Guilford Press.

Manis, M. (1977). Cognitive social psychology. *Personality and Social Psychology Bulletin, 3,* 550–566.

Marelich, W. D., & Erger, J. S. (Eds.). (2004). *The social psychology of health: Essays and readings.* Thousand Oaks, CA: Sage Publications.

Markus, H. R., & Kitayama, S. (1991). Culture and the self: Implications for cognition, emotion, and motivation. *Psychological Review, 98,* 224–253.

McCrae, R. R., & Costa, P. T. Jr. (2003). *Personality in adulthood: A five-factor theory perspective* (2nd ed.). New York: Guilford Press.

McCrae, R. R., & Costa, P. T. Jr. (2008). The five-factor theory of personality. In O. P. John, R. W. Robins, & L. A. Pervin (Eds.), *Handbook of personality: Theory and research* (3rd ed., pp. 159–181). New York: Guilford Press.

McGuire, W. J., & Padawer-Singer, A. (1976). Trait salience in the spontaneous self-concept. *Journal of Personality and Social Psychology, 33,* 743–754.

McPherson, J. M. (1997). *For cause and comrades: When men fought in the Civil War.* New York: Oxford University Press.

Mealey, L., & Theis, P. (1995). The relationship between mood and preferences: An evolutionary perspective. *Ethology and Sociobiology, 16,* 247–256.

Menon, T., Morris, M. W., Chiu, C.-Y., & Hong, Y.-Y. (1999). Culture and the construal of agency: Attribution to individual versus group dispositions. *Journal of Personality and Social Psychology, 76,* 701–717.

Metcalfe, J., & Mischel, W. (1999). A hot/cool-system analysis of delay of gratification: Dynamics of willpower. *Psychological Review, 106,* 3–19.

Miller, G. A. (1969). Psychology as a means of promoting human welfare. *American Psychologist, 24,* 1063–1075.

Miller, J. G. (1984). Culture and the development of everyday social explanation. *Journal of Personality and Social Psychology, 46,* 961–978.

Mitchell, J. P. (2008). Contributions of functional neuroimaging to the study of social cognition. *Current Directions in Psychological Science, 17,* 142–146.

Morris, M. W., & Peng, K. (1994). Culture and cause: American and Chinese attributions for social and physical events. *Journal of Personality and Social Psychology, 67,* 949–971.

Moskowitz, G. B. (2005). *Social cognition: Understanding self and others.* New York: Guilford Publications.

Murtha, T. C., Kanfer, R., & Ackerman, P. L. (1996). Toward an interactionist taxonomy of personality and situations: An integrative situational-dispositional representation of personality traits. *Journal of Personality and Social Psychology, 71,* 193–207.

Na, J., Choi, I., & Sul, S. (2013). I like you because you think in the "right" way: Culture and ideal thinking. *Social Cognition, 31,* 390–404.

Neuberg, S. L., Kenrick, D. T., & Schaller, M. (2010). Evolutionary social psychology. In S. T. Fiske, D. T. Gilbert, & G. Lindzey (Eds.), *The handbook of social psychology* (5th ed., Vol. 2, pp. 761–796). Hoboken, NJ: Wiley.

Newman, L. S., & Erber, R. (2002). *Understanding genocide: The social psychology of the Holocaust.* Oxford University Press.

Nisbett, R. E., & Cohen, D. (1996). *Culture of honor: The psychology of violence in the South.* Boulder. CO: Westview Press.

Nisbett, R. E., & Wilson, T. D. (1977). Telling more than we can know: Verbal reports on mental processes. *Psychological Review, 84,* 231–259.

Norenzayan, A., Choi, I., & Nisbett, R. E. (2002). Cultural similarities and differences in social inference: Evidence from behavioral predictions and lay theories of behavior. *Personality and Social Psychology Bulletin, 28,* 109–120.

Ochsner, K. N., & Lieberman, M. D. (2001). The emergence of social cognitive neuroscience. *American Psychologist, 56,* 717–734.

Perry, D. G., & Bussey, K. (1983). *Social development.* Englewood Cliffs, NJ: Prentice Hall.

Phillips, D. P. (1983). The impact of mass media violence on U.S. homicides. *American Sociological Review, 48,* 560–568.

Pittman, T. S. (1998). Motivation. In D. T. Gilbert, S. T. Fiske, & G. Lindzey (Eds.), *The handbook of social psychology* (4th ed., Vol. 1, pp. 549–590). New York: McGraw Hill.

Plomin, R., DeFries, J. C., McClearn, G. E., & McGuffin, P. (2009). *Behavioral genetics* (5th ed.). New York: Worth Publishers.

Pronin, E., Lin, D. Y., & Ross, L. (2002). The bias blind spot: Perceptions of bias in self versus others. *Personality and Social Psychology Bulletin, 28,* 369–381.

Pronin, E., & Kugler, M. B. (2007). Valuing thoughts, ignoring behavior: The introspection illusion as a source of the bias blind spot. *Journal of Experimental Social Psychology, 43,* 565–578.

Ratcliff, N. J., Hugenberg, K., Shriver, E. R., & Bernstein, M. J. (2011). The allure of Status: High-status targets are privileged in face processing and memory. *Personality and Social Psychology Bulletin, 28,* 369–381.

Resnick, L., Levine, J., & Teasley, S. D. (1991). *Perspectives on socially shared cognition.* Washington, DC: American Psychological Association.

Robles, R., Smith, R., Carver, C. S., & Wellens, A. R. (1987). Influence of subliminal visual images on the experience of anxiety. *Personality and Social Psychology Bulletin, 13,* 399–410.

Ross, L. (1977). The intuitive psychologist and his shortcomings. In L. Berkowitz (Ed.), *Advances in experimental social psychology* (Vol. 10, pp. 174–221). New York: Academic Press.

Ruble, D. N. (1994). A phase model of transitions: Cognitive and motivational consequences. In M. Zanna (Ed.), *Advances in Experimental Social Psychology, 26,* 163–214.

Rutter, M. (2003). Commentary: Causal processes leading to antisocial behavior. *Developmental Psychology, 39,* 372–378.

Schaller, M., Simpson, J. A., & Kenrick, D. T. (Eds.). (2006). *Evolution and social psychology.* New York: Psychology Press

Scher, S. J., & Rauscher, F. (Eds.). (2003). *Evolutionary psychology: Alternative approaches.* Dordrecht, Netherlands: Kluwer Academic Publishers.

Schmitt, D. P., & Pilcher, J. J. (2004). Evaluating evidence of psychological adaptation: How do we know one when we see one? *Psychological Science, 15,* 643–649.

Schneider, D. J. (1991). Social cognition. *Annual Review of Psychology, 42,* 527–561.

Sears, D. O. (1986). College sophomores in the laboratory: Influences of a narrow data base on social psychology's view of human nature. *Journal of Personality and Social Psychology, 51,* 515–530.

Sherman, S. J., Judd, C. M., & Park, B. (1989). Social cognition. *Annual Review of Psychology, 40,* 281–326.

Simon, P. (1997). *Songs from the Capeman* [Record]. Warner Brothers.

Singelis, T. M. (1994). The measurement of independent and interdependent self-construals. *Personality and Social Psychology Bulletin, 20,* 580–591.

Skinner, B. F. (1971). *Beyond freedom and dignity.* New York: Alfred A. Knopf.

Skinner, B. F. (1976). *About behaviorism.* New York: Vintage Books.

Smith, D. L. (2007). *The most dangerous animal: Human nature and the origins of war.* New York: St. Martin's Press.

Snyder, M., & Ickes, W. (1985). Personality and social behavior. In G. Lindzey and E. Aronson (Eds.), *Handbook of social psychology* (3rd ed., Vol. 2, pp. 883–947). New York: Random House.

Sorrentino, R. M., Cohen, D., Olson, J. M., & Zanna, M. P. (2005). *Culture and social behavior: The Ontario symposium* (Vol. 10). Mahwah, NJ: Lawrence Erlbaum.

Stevens, L. E., & Fiske, S. T. (1995). Motivation and cognition in social life: A social survival perspective. *Social Cognition, 13,* 189–214.

Taylor, S. E. (2008). *Health Psychology* (7th ed.). New York: McGraw-Hill.

Tooby, J., & Cosmides, L. (1992). Psychological foundations of culture. In J. Barkow, L. Cosmides, & J. Tooby (Eds.), *The adapted mind* (pp. 19–136). New York: Oxford University Press.

Thompson, L., & Fine, G. A. (1999). Social shared cognition, affect, and behavior: A review and integration. *Personality and Social Psychology Review, 3*, 278–302.

Triandis, H. C. (1995). *Individualism and collectivism* (pp. 1–15). Boulder, CO: Westview.

Weiner, B. (1985). "Spontaneous" causal thinking. *Psychological Bulletin, 97*, 74–84.

Westen, D. (1998). The scientific legacy of Sigmund Freud: Toward a psychodynamically informed psychological science. *Psychological Bulletin, 124*, 333–371.

Wexler, P. (1983). *Critical social psychology*. Boston: Routledge & Kegan Paul.

Whiting, R. (1990). *You gotta have Wa*. New York: Vintage.

Wilson, T. D., & Brekke, N. (1994). Mental contamination and mental correction: Unwanted influences on judgments and evaluations. *Psychological Bulletin, 116*, 117–142.

Wright, R. (1995, March 13). The biology of violence. *New Yorker,* pp. 68–77.

Wrightsman, L. S., Nietzel, M. T., Fortune, W. H., & Greene, E. (2001). *Psychology and the legal system*. East Windsor, CT: Wadsworth Publishing.

Zelli, A., Cervone, D., & Huesmann, R. L. (1996). Behavioral experience and social inference: Individual differences in aggressive experience and spontaneous versus deliberate trait inference. *Social Cognition, 14*, 165–190.

Zelli, A., Huesmann, R. L., & Cervone, D. (1995). Social inference and individual differences in aggression: Evidence for spontaneous judgments of hostility. *Aggressive Behavior, 21*, 405–417.

Zimbardo, P. G. (1969). The human choice: Individuation, reason, and order versus deindividuation, impulse, and chaos. *Nebraska symposium on motivation* (vol. 17, pp. 237–307). Lincoln: University of Nebraska Press.

CHAPTER 2

RESEARCH METHODS IN SOCIAL PSYCHOLOGY

SOLOMON ASCH'S STORY: A BEAUTIFUL IDEA

Consider the case of the late Solomon Asch, who became widely known for his work on conformity and how people form impressions of others. By his own admission, Asch became a social psychologist because he was intrigued by the ideas that researchers in the field pursued (Tesser, 1990). Asch's interest in conformity was rooted partly in Muzafer Sherif's (1935, 1936) work on that topic, which made use of the autokinetic effect. In his studies, Sherif had asked participants to look at a bright source of light presented in front of a dark background. The autokinetic effect is the perception that after a time, the bright light appears to move. This illusion, which has to do with our visual-perceptual system, explains why we perceive stars in the night sky to be stationary objects, as long as we don't focus on any single one. Once we do focus on a single star, it appears to wander after a few seconds. The precise reasons for this experience, which happens to everyone, were of little concern to Sherif and Asch.

What mattered to both was that any judgment about the apparent motion of the bright light is entirely subjective and open to interpretation. This particular feature of the autokinetic effect made it a perfect vehicle for studying conformity—that is, people's propensity to go along with a majority. Sherif asked research participants to report on the movements of the bright light. In some instances, they made their judgments in the presence of other apparent research participants, who always gave their answers first. The participants who answered first were really confederates of Sherif, who had been instructed to give a particular answer (for example, "It's moving six inches to the right"). Under these conditions, participants went along with the majority. That is, they adopted the answers given by the confederates.

Asch was both intrigued and troubled by these findings. He felt that participants' reactions, though they clearly indicated conformity, were within reason. After all, the autokinetic effect is a visual illusion; thus, there was no clear right or wrong answer. And when the right answer is less than obvious, agreeing with others makes sense. Yet Asch couldn't help wondering what would happen if the right answer were obvious. Would participants still conform to others' judgments?

Solomon Asch's question would prove to be a fruitful one. What makes a good research idea, and how does it develop into a scientific study? In this chapter, we will begin at the beginning of the research process, with the ideas that eventually develop into research questions. Then we will discuss the research methods social psychologists use, including experiments and surveys. We will see how to analyze experimental data and survey results and interpret their meaning. And we'll see how Asch's question led to some surprising—and disturbing—conclusions.

ASKING THE QUESTION

Whether any field of inquiry can rightfully call itself a science depends on the sophistication and rigor of its methods. Few would disagree with this general idea that good methods translate into good science. Yet great methodology doesn't get us very far if we don't ask the right questions, or ask good questions in the right way. In some ways, researchers are less concerned with establishing facts than they are with exploring the world of ideas. We could even argue that there is an art to every science, one that is exemplified by the beauty of the ideas we pursue.

Intriguing Ideas: The Seemingly Banal, the Surprising, and the Bizarre

Ultimately, what makes for a beautiful idea? Some ideas that seem utterly trivial on the surface may become intriguing because of their surprising implications. Take, for example, the idea that people like to be consistent: it's obvious, boring, and almost embarrassingly trivial. Yet as Leon Festinger (1957; Festinger & Carlsmith, 1959) showed, the consistency principle has some rather unexpected implications for our behavior vis-à-vis our attitudes. Imagine that you think baseball is boring. Imagine further that someone offers you either $5 or $100 to tell a foreign student who knows nothing about the game that baseball is fun. Would your attitude about baseball change as a result of receiving either $5 or $100 for telling this small lie?

According to cognitive dissonance theory (Festinger, 1957), your attitude will not change much if you receive a large reward. The tidy sum of $100 provides enough justification for your lie: You did it for the money. On the other hand, a measly $5 generally won't be enough to justify your false claim about baseball. The only way to resolve this inconsistency is to adjust your attitude to fit your behavior (Festinger & Carlsmith, 1959). Thus, you come to believe that baseball isn't so boring, after all.

Other ideas can be intriguing, not so much because they have wide applications or surprising implications, but because they seem downright bizarre. Do you think you know yourself in a way that others don't? The answer seems obvious—of course you do! However, Daryl Bem (1965) suggested instead that you have no privileged insight into your own attitudes and feelings. According to his self-perception theory (Bem, 1965), when asked whether you like opera, you don't retrieve a stored attitude from memory. Instead, you retrieve memories of opera performances you have attended, count the number of opera CDs you own, and so on. Low totals would suggest that you don't care for opera that much; high totals might suggest you are an opera buff.

That, however, is exactly the way an outside observer would go about assessing your attitude toward opera. In other words, you draw conclusions about your attitude by examining your own behavior, just as others would. Although it seems to violate common sense, self-perception theory explains why doing a small favor for someone makes us more willing to do a large favor later on. Doing a small favor makes us see ourselves as helpful, a self-perception that later comes into play when we are asked to do a large favor (Cialdini, 2008). Similarly, if we are rewarded for doing something we already enjoy, will we like the activity more or less? The answer is less, because we now infer that we're doing it for money rather than pleasure.

Although the research ideas we have introduced up to this point are compelling for different reasons, they share a common feature: None of them is based on the conventional wisdom that good goes with good and bad goes with bad. Applications of this approach, including theorizing about individual differences, often take the form "Do people with high self-esteem have better intimate relationships than people with low self-esteem?" or "Do people who enjoy thinking process a persuasive message more deeply than people who don't?" Research questions of this nature are not particularly compelling, because the answer most often is "yes," although in most cases the reverse is also true. Consequently, there is a limit to how much we can learn by posing such questions.

Translating Intriguing Ideas into Research Questions

No matter how compelling an idea is, it must pass one final test before it can be translated into a research question: we must ask the question at the appropriate level of abstraction. Think about violence, for example. We could ask, "Why are humans as violent as they are?" This kind of question could provoke hours of debate in a coffeehouse, but it cannot easily be translated into a research idea. Now think about the question "Why do people riot after their team wins a championship?" This question, too, concerns violence, but it is raised at a less abstract, more concrete level. It, too, could be debated for hours, but unlike the first question, it can also be translated into a fairly concrete, researchable question.

The process of translating curiosity into a research question requires two important and related steps. First, we need to translate our question into a **hypothesis**. At the most basic level, a hypothesis is a hunch about the relationship between the crucial elements of our question. For example, we could put our question about what makes people violent into the context of exposure to media violence. That would allow us to hypothesize that increased exposure to media violence may lead to increased aggression. Because people *vary* in the extent to which they watch violence on television and in the movies, and because they also *vary* in the extent to which they aggress against each other, these elements of our question are called **variables**. Our hypothesis connects the two variables in a causal fashion by proposing that a change in one will lead to a change in the other.

Restating our question in the form of a hypothesis isn't all we need to do, however. To be viable, our hypothesis must be connected to some existing theory, the second step in converting an idea into a research question. Without theory, our speculations about the relationship between the two variables would be little more than a hunch—not enough to justify the time and effort that goes into research. Employing a theory turns a hypothesis into an educated guess.

Let's return to our hypothesis about the link between aggression and exposure to media violence. We could guess that there is probably *some* relationship between the two variables, such that *more* exposure probably would produce *more* aggression. That hunch would be insufficient grounds for research, however. To strengthen our hypothesis, we might ground it in the social learning theory of aggression (Bandura, 1973), which holds that exposure to aggressive models leads to aggressive behavior. To the extent that media images of violence can serve as vicarious models for aggression, then, we can safely speculate that exposure to media images of violence may have the same effect as exposure to real-life models for aggression.

Without theory it is difficult to generate viable hypotheses.

Asking the Question: A Summary

Social psychologists ask questions about human behavior in a social context. The questions they ask are rooted in ideas about our social world. Ideas can be intriguing if they lead to questions that explain a variety of seemingly unrelated phenomena, or that show surprising implications of seemingly banal truths, or that lead to seemingly bizarre conclusions. Research ideas that are based on individual differences—to the extent that they postulate that good things go with good and bad things go with bad—often are not intriguing. To translate an intriguing idea about human behavior in a social context into a research question, we must first state it as a hypothesis—that is, a statement that specifies the suspected relationship between two or more variables—and then ground the idea in theory.

Think Like a Social Psychologist

Thinking Critically

—On the night before an important test, the obvious thing for a student to do would be to spend as many hours as possible studying. Knowing that people like to feel good about themselves, however, what benefits might you suspect a student could derive from not preparing at all?

Designing Research

—To satisfy your curiosity about self-esteem, you decide to test the hypothesis that people with high self-esteem are happier with their jobs than people with low self-esteem. What possibly important question would your study fail to answer?

ANSWERING QUESTIONS WITH DATA

Solomon Asch's Story, Continued: When the Obvious Right Answer Isn't Obvious

As Solomon Asch continued to think about Sherif's experiment, he wondered what would happen if the right answer were obvious to participants. Would they still conform to others' judgments?

To answer his question, Asch (1955) conducted an experiment very similar to Sherif's. Instead of asking participants to make judgments about an ambiguous stimulus, he presented them with a vertical line drawn on a board, along with a set of comparison lines of obviously varying lengths. He asked participants to pick the one line that matched the target line. The right answer was so obvious that most participants, left to their own devices, could give it immediately.

Yet once again, the results were complicated by the presence of several confederates, who in some cases had been instructed to give the wrong answer. Under these circumstances, a startling number of participants went along with the majority, even though their answers clearly were wrong. What was going on?

Once a question has been translated into a hypothesis and connected to a theory, researchers are in a position to test whether it is, in fact, true. To that end, social psychologists can draw on an extensive array of research tools available to most social scientists. They include naturalistic observations of behavior, surveys, and longitudinal techniques that track people's behavior over long periods. More than any other method, social psychologists like to use experiments to test their hypotheses. As we will see, however, there is a limit to how much we can learn from experiments. Let's look first at the advantages the experimental method has to offer.

The Logic of Experimentation

The most important advantage of the experimental method is that it allows researchers a maximum amount of control in testing hypotheses concerning the causal influence of an **independent variable** (for example, exposure to video game violence) on a **dependent variable** (for example, aggression). Conducting an experiment requires researchers to create a laboratory analog of a real-world phenomenon. That is, they must recreate the real-world conditions surrounding their hypothesis, but in a controlled way that eliminates other variables.

The key elements in this process are *control, random assignment,* and *comparison.* To *control* for extraneous variables, experimenters hold all other variables constant and allow only the variable of interest—the independent variable—to fluctuate. They accomplish this by creating different experimental conditions. Any measurable changes in the behavior of interest—the dependent variable—can then be attributed to differences in the experimental conditions. This type of control minimizes the chances that extraneous variables (those not of interest) might influence the results of the experiment. Extraneous variables—for example, the location of the experiment or the experimenter's demeanor—can subtly and unintentionally influence research participants' responses to the variable of interest. Experimenters can maximize control over these variables by keeping them constant for all participants.

A second form of control, just as important, is **random assignment** of participants to the experimental conditions. The fact that no two people are exactly alike creates a problem for researchers who are trying to determine the relationship between an independent and a dependent variable. One way to control for the myriad individual differences among research participants is to randomly assign them to the different experimental conditions. Random assignment means that every participant has an equal chance of being assigned to any of the

experimental conditions. Assigning participants to conditions in this way distributes individual differences evenly across all the different conditions. It is a way of controlling variables that are otherwise beyond the experimenter's control.

Finally, to allow any kind of *comparison*, an experiment must have more than one condition. How many there are depends in part on the number of independent variables that are of interest you (we'll go into this in more detail in the next section). In its most basic form, an experiment compares the results from an experimental condition with those obtained in a control condition. Even a seemingly simple experiment requires careful consideration of the appropriate control condition, as will become clear in the next section. When researchers

The coin toss at the annual Army-Navy game. In an experiment, flipping a coin is a perfectly appropriate way to randomly assign participants to conditions.

do a good job of controlling the influence of extraneous variables, assigning participants to conditions randomly and providing appropriate comparisons, they can be confident that any difference they observe in the dependent variable is due, in fact, to variations in the independent variable.

The Nuts and Bolts of Experimentation

Let's illustrate how control, random assignment, and comparison work by designing a hypothetical experiment. Suppose you are interested in discovering whether exposure to violent video games causes young children to become more aggressive. There is good reason to suspect that might be the case, based on the results from hundreds of studies of the effects of media violence (Anderson & Bushman, 2002). Still, most of the research done in the past has primarily looked at TV violence, so your hypothesis regarding video game violence is somewhat novel, though it is grounded firmly in theory. Before you can begin your research, you must make a series of decisions, the first of which is how to specify the independent variable.

Will he become more aggressive as a result of playing a violent videogame? Social psychologists have a number of methods at their disposal to answer this question.

Specifying the Independent Variable

First, you need to decide on how many levels your independent variable (exposure to video game violence) should take on. Clearly, you need to expose one group of children to some form of video game violence and then find a way to measure their aggression. But to whom will you compare them? One obvious comparison would be to children *not* exposed to video game violence. However, you need to allow for the possibility that playing any kind of video game may increase aggression to some extent, whether the game in question is *Grand Theft Auto* or *Backyard Baseball*. To take this possibility into account, you could choose three different levels of the independent variable: (1) exposure to a violent video game; (2) exposure to a nonviolent video game; and (3) no exposure, with the last two levels serving as control conditions.

Given the huge selection of commercially available video games, how would you decide which ones to use in your study? This question relates to the way in which you *operationalize* your independent variable. **Operationalization** of an independent variable means identifying a version of the variable that can be made to work in the somewhat sterile and artificial laboratory environment. For your study, you would probably pick a game that is rated as moderately violent. Using a hyper-violent game might limit your ability to draw conclusions about the effects of violence more generally; using a game that is not violent enough might obscure any differences among the conditions. For the nonviolent condition, you probably would pick a game that is rated as nonviolent. What about the group of children who don't get to play a video game, though? Asking them to simply sit around for a while would be both awkward and impractical. Thus, you might want to operationalize "no exposure" by asking these children to draw for a comparable period.

Choosing the Participants

With the levels of the independent variable set and properly operationalized, you can turn to running the experiment. How will you select your participants? Your hypothesis pertains to the effects of video game violence on young children, so you might decide on first, second, or third graders at the local elementary school, making your final decision based on their teachers' enthusiasm for your study. You might even find a room at the school that you could convert into a lab with little more than a chair, a desk, and a video game console. After obtaining consent from the children's parents, you are almost ready to run the experiment. You should, of course, randomly assign the children to your experimental conditions. You could do so in several ways—pulling numbers representing your conditions out of a hat would suffice, or you might decide to use a more high-tech solution, like a random number generator. The point is that the assignment should be random rather than haphazard.

Measuring the Dependent Variable

One decision you must still make is how to measure aggression, your dependent variable. Doing so should not be difficult, since aggression manifests itself in a fairly limited number of observable behaviors. You could observe the children at play after the experiment, and simply count the number of times they push, shove, or kick other children. You could then use the totals you compile over a predetermined period to construct an index of aggression. If you see a higher incidence of pushing, shoving, and kicking among the children who played the violent video game compared to those who played a nonviolent game or played no game at all, your hypothesis will be supported.

This example may suggest that measuring the dependent variable is fairly simple, but that is far from the case. When you decide how to measure a dependent variable, you operationalize it in the sense that you pick one of many possible forms of measurement. Although there is nothing wrong with measuring aggression as the number of pushes and shoves a child engages in, aggression can manifest itself in other ways, including verbal aggression and indirect aggression. Operationalizing aggression as you have tells you little about the effects of violent video games on other forms of aggression.

Furthermore, much of social psychology is devoted to the study of behavior that is not clearly observable, such as thoughts and feelings. As we saw in Chapter 1, social psychologists study attitudes, impressions, and perceptions that frequently do not manifest themselves in overt behavior. Just as frequently, they study hidden influences on behavior, thoughts, and feelings, which by definition tend to occur without a person's conscious awareness.

To ascertain what participants think and how they feel as a result of some variation in their environment, social psychologists often rely on paper-and-pencil measures of everything from their transient moods to their racial attitudes. Scales like these usually include multiple items that measure different aspects of the underlying construct. Mood scales, for example, often contain items that tap into both the positive-negative dimension of moods (for example, happy versus sad) and the arousal dimension (for example, serene versus joyful). Scales designed to measure sexist attitudes include measures of both hostile sexism and benevolent sexism, a seemingly positive but ultimately paternalizing form of prejudice (Glick & Fiske, 1996). Finally, increasing interest in hidden influences has created a cottage industry of methods for measuring implicit prejudice, such as the Implicit Association Test (Greenwald, Banaji, Rudman, Farnham, Nosek, & Mellott, 2002; Greenwald, McGhee, & Schwartz, 1998). For a firsthand experience with the IAT, visit www.yale.edu/implicit

Ensuring Validity and Reliability

Scales like the ones we just described must live up to two relatively independent standards. First, they must have **validity**—that is, they must measure what they claim to measure. Second, they must have **reliability**—that is, they must measure what they claim to measure consistently.

Validity and reliability can be established in a number of ways. To demonstrate the *validity* of a scale, for example, you could compare its results to those obtained with another scale that measures essentially the same concept. You could also compare its results to a scale that measures something entirely different. A high degree of similarity with the first measure, along with a high degree of dissimilarity with the second measure, would suggest that the scale is, in fact, a valid one. Because it measures the underlying construct, it is said to be high in *construct validity*. To establish the *reliability* of the scale, you can simply administer it repeatedly. If it yields consistent results over time, you can consider it reliable.

Validity and reliability do not always go hand in hand. A prime example is the spring-operated bathroom scale you use to weigh yourself. Though it often consistently shows the same weight and thus can be considered a reliable measure, it may give a relatively poor indication of what you actually weigh. The counterweight scale used at your doctor's office provides a measure of your weight that is both valid and reliable. Because social psychologists go to great lengths to ascertain the validity and reliability of the scales they use in their experiments, those measures resemble the doctor's scale far more than your bathroom scale.

Laboratory experiments that present participants with a stripped-down version of reality in an otherwise controlled, somewhat sterile environment are powerful tools for examining potential cause-and-effect relationships. At the same time, however, the **internal validity** that researchers gain by exercising such a high level of control often compromises an experiment's **external validity**—that is, the ability to generalize the results beyond the laboratory. Quite simply, our experimental manipulations may not represent the richness of the underlying concept in the real world. For example, as a matter of convenience, researchers often rely on college students to participate in their experiments. How can we generalize the findings of such experiments beyond their unrepresentative samples?

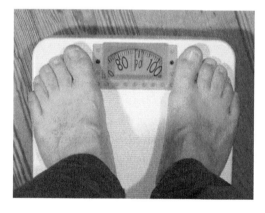

A bathroom scale provides you with a reliable estimate of your weight because it measures it consistently. However, it lacks validity because it does not provide a true estimate of your weight.

One answer is that we cannot generalize them, at least not easily. To some extent, by testing hypotheses in the laboratory, researchers trade away generalizability for control, or external validity for internal validity. To the extent that we manage to replicate these experiments with slightly different operationalizations, however, we can be reasonably sure that we can generalize beyond a given operationalization. Yet we are still left with the artificiality of the laboratory setting, and the inability to generalize the experimental results beyond the chosen samples.

There are two ways of solving the dilemma of internal versus external validity. First, we can decide that our concerns about external validity are misplaced when our primary goal is to test predictions of what will happen in the lab, rather than what will happen in the real world (Mook, 1983). Take your hypothesis about the relationship between video game violence and aggression, for instance. If you test this hypothesis in the laboratory, all you are trying to do is show that the former *can* influence the latter—that is, that there is a cause-and-effect relationship between the two variables. You are fully aware that many real-life conditions may modify this relationship in important ways. For example, parents who condone violence may exacerbate the relationship; parents who condemn violence may attenuate it. Although the real world may often qualify cause-and-effect relationships established in the lab, it rarely invalidates them. Thus, we should evaluate laboratory research primarily in terms of its internal validity.

A second way to solve the dilemma of internal versus external validity is to identify variables and generate hypotheses that highlight concerns specifically with external validity. For example, if you have theoretical reasons to suspect that exposure to violent videogames might affect children differently depending on their age, it would be appropriate to test your hypothesis using children from other age groups. If you have theoretical reasons to suspect that the results of your experiment might not hold up outside the laboratory, you should test your hypothesis in a real-life setting rather than in a lab. Compared to laboratory experiments, field experiments have both advantages and disadvantages.

Field Experiments and Quasi-Experiments

Conducting an experiment in a real-life setting has several advantages. First, it removes the artificiality of the laboratory, allowing us to observe changes in behavior, thoughts, or feelings in their natural context. For this reason, field experiments often give us an opportunity to look at the possible long-term effects of the manipulation of an independent variable. At the same time, the move to the real world means that we must relinquish some control.

Consider your hypothetical experiment concerning the effects of video game violence on aggression. Instead of ferrying groups of second graders back and forth to your lab, allowing them to play various video games and then observing them at play, you could randomly assign them to take either of the two games home. You could then observe their behavior the next day and again in two weeks, which would give you a measure of both the short- and long-term effects. The problem, however, is that even though you assigned participants randomly, you have little or no control over how much time they actually spend playing the video games. You also have little control over the extent to which the children talk with each other about the games. For all you know, a subset of children may be trading the games. Lack of control over these aspects of the experiment threatens its internal validity. That is not to say that field experiments are always a poor way of testing a hypothesis. Quite the contrary; they are often the only way to study relationships such as the predictability of visitors and the well-being of people who live in retirement homes (Schulz, 1976).

Some research questions may force us to relinquish random assignment to conditions. That is often the case when researchers want to study the effects of social interventions—that is, programs designed to reduce drug use, prevent date rape, or increase the likelihood that students will remain in college. In these cases, decisions about who receives a treatment or intervention are often made by others. Given the possible beneficial effects of the treatments, to do otherwise might be unethical. However, the lack of randomly assigned treatment and control groups leaves us unable to control what happens to whom, hampering our ability to draw any kind of comparison.

Do these problems mean that we cannot study the effects of social interventions? The answer is no, because we can still study them through **quasi-experiments**. In fact, we can even study cause-and-effect relationships by gathering data at additional times and places, in order to rule out alternative explanations for the observed results (Cook & Campbell, 1979).

Suppose, for example, that your university has implemented an innovative program to increase the number of freshmen who return for their sophomore year. Suppose further that a wise administrator has given you a grant to study the effectiveness of the new program. One easy way to test whether or not it has made a difference would be to compare the retention rate in the year before the intervention to the retention rate after the intervention. However, such a design would hamper your ability to draw conclusions about cause and effect, for two reasons. First, you are looking at two different groups of people. There may be something unique about either or both freshmen classes that could explain any difference in retention rates that you might observe. Second, you are looking at the two groups a couple of years apart. Much may have happened during that period—for example, the nature of the economy or the availability of financial aid may have changed, either of which could provide an alternative explanation for any difference in retention rates.

A quasi-experiment would provide data on whether these college freshmen may be more likely to return for their sophomore year in response to an intervention aimed at freshmen retention.

To rule out these alternative explanations, you could use one of several quasi-experimental designs. To address the explanation based on the uniqueness of one or both classes, you could compare several freshman classes prior to implementation, with several freshman classes following implementation. To rule out the influence of extraneous events such as changes in the economy, you might want to look at retention rates at a comparable school that does not have such a program. This approach would allow you to identify differences that might result from the intervention, as well as any preexisting differences between the groups. In essence, it would allow you to compare your school's students to students who were subject to the same extraneous influences, but did not experience the intervention.

Quasi-experiments clearly have a place in social psychology, particularly when researchers are interested in studying cause-and-effect relationships in the real world, but cannot make use of random assignment. At the same time, quasi-experiments tend to be costly and time consuming, and are therefore used far less often than they should be.

Survey Methods

Many research questions do not require an experimental procedure; for others, conducting an experiment would be impractical. If we are interested in the relationship between material wealth and life satisfaction (Diener & Biswas-Diener, 2002; Nickerson, Schwarz, Diener, & Kahneman, 2003), do we really want to conduct an experiment? If we want to know whether individuals who idealize their partners are happier with their relationships than those who do not (Murray, Holmes, & Griffin, 1996), can we really devise an experimental procedure to find out? In both cases, we have independent variables (material wealth, partner idealization) and dependent variables (life satisfaction, relationship satisfaction), but we cannot manipulate the independent variables. Nor could we do anything in the lab to affect people's satisfaction with their lives or their life partners.

Questions like these call for the use of nonexperimental methods, chief among them the **survey method**. In doing survey research, we collect data from all or part of a population in order to examine the incidence, distribution, and relationships among naturally occurring phenomena such as life satisfaction. Among the first questions we would ask before conducting such a survey is the extent to which we want to generalize our findings. For example, when we want to know how satisfied people are with a politician's performance in office, we obviously want to generalize our findings to all constituents. The same would be true of the relationship between wealth and life satisfaction.

Selecting the Sample

In both the cases just described, it is important to obtain a representative sample. A sample is representative to the extent that every member of the population has an equal chance to be selected. A **random sample** meets this requirement, because choosing survey respondents from the population in random fashion all but assures that every member of the population has an equal chance of being picked.

When generalizability is not a major concern, a nonrandom sample, also called a **convenience sample**, will often suffice. For example, Murray et al. (1996) wanted to test a hypothesis about the relationship between partner idealization and relationship satisfaction. Consequently, they structured their sample to include couples who had been together for varying amounts of time. Of course, they could have studied a representative sample of American couples, but the additional cost and effort would not have been justified by the additional benefit of increased generalizability. Because the researchers were primarily interested in simply showing a link

To be recruited for a survey is a fact of life in many contexts.

between partner idealization and relationship satisfaction, that benefit would have been small to negligible. If anything, anyone who wished to challenge the findings on the grounds that they lacked generalizability would need to explain why a representative sample might produce different results.

Asking Survey Questions: It's Not as Easy as You Think

Issues of generalizability aside, what we can learn from surveys depends on both the nature of the questions and how we ask them. There is ample research to suggest that the wording of the questions, the order in which we ask them, and the response format can have a surprisingly strong influence on the answers we get (Schwarz, 1999). When respondents read a survey question, for example, they do more than interpret its *literal* meaning; they try to infer its *pragmatic* meaning. A question like "What did you do on Sunday?" is simple enough to allow most respondents to decipher its literal meaning, but which of the respondent's Sunday activities does the researcher want to know about? The question's literal meaning might suggest activities such as tooth brushing and toenail clipping, but its pragmatic meaning—inferred from the questioner's perceived intentions—would suggest more uncommon activities, such as sleeping in or going for a walk.

In settling such questions, respondents tend to invoke conversational rules. In other words, they limit their reports to the kinds of activities they would report to a friend or colleague. Thus, survey questions should be worded so as to take conversational rules into account. For example, if we are interested in obtaining a detailed account of respondents' Sunday activities, rather than just the highlights, we need to ask the question in a way that will elicit the desired response.

Choosing the Response Format

In a number of ways, the response format can also influence the answers researchers obtain. An open response format to the "What did you do on Sunday?" question allows respondents to list everything they did that day, though what they include will ultimately depend on how they interpret the question. The same respondents who omit activities that seem uninteresting from an open response format may include them if asked to check them off on a list. The difference between the two formats can produce profound differences in results. For example, in one study (Schuman & Presser, 1981) researchers asked respondents what they considered to be "the most important thing for children to prepare them for life." Almost two thirds of respondents picked "To think for themselves" from a list of possibilities. However, when presented with an open-response format, less than five percent of respondents listed that activity as most important. Obviously, the results obtained in the two different formats would suggest very different conclusions.

Similar differences surface when survey participants respond to questions using different rating scales. In one study (Schwarz, Knauper, Hippler, Noelle-Neumann, & Clark, 1991), a group of participants responded to the question "How successful are you in life?" using an 11-point rating scale that ranged from 0 (not at all) to 10 (extremely). Another group responded to the same question on an 11-point scale ranging from -5 to +5. The numerical values of the two scales had a profound impact on participants' responses. Only 13 percent of the first group endorsed a value between 0 and 5; 34 percent of the second group endorsed a value between −5 and 0.

The design and wording of a survey question can profoundly impact the answers researchers obtain.

How can we account for this dramatic difference in the responses to the two scales? Presumably, when the scale was anchored with a 0, it prompted participants to interpret "not at all successful" to mean "lacking great achievement." But when the scale was anchored with a −5, it led participants to interpret "not at all successful" to mean "failed." Evidently, the 0 and the −5 led participants to recall different information. Again, the results suggest very different conclusions.

The Ethics of Social Psychological Research

The year was 1961; the place, Yale University. A young social psychologist named Stanley Milgram was about to embark on an experimental study of destructive obedience that would eventually become one of the most celebrated and controversial studies a psychologist ever produced (Milgram, 1963). The experiment he designed focused ostensibly on the effects of punishment on learning. Participants were to teach another person (called the learner) a list of word pairs, punishing him with an electric shock each time he made a mistake.

THINK LIKE A SOCIAL PSYCHOLOGIST: A SURVEY OF VIDEO GAME VIOLENCE AND AGGRESSION

Suppose you have decided to use a survey to test your hypothesis about the relationship between exposure to video game violence and aggression among second graders. How would your choice of method affect the way you state your hypothesis? Should you be concerned about sampling? Whom would you ask to gather your data? What would you need to consider in wording and ordering the questions? Looking at the following response alternatives for video game consumption, would you expect your results to differ, depending on which alternative you use?

Response Alternative 1	Response Alternative 2
(a) Up to ½ hour	(a) Up to 2 ½ hours
(b) ½ hour to 1 hour	(b) 2 ½ hours to 3 hours
(c) 1 hour to 1 ½ hours	(c) 3 hours to 3 ½ hours
(d) 1 ½ hour to 2 hours	(d) 3 ½ hours to 4 hours
(e) More than 2 hours	(e) More than 4 hours

The experimental apparatus, a mock shock generator, contained a set of switches labeled in 15-volt increments, starting with 15 volts and ending with 450 volts. The switches were also labeled descriptively, ranging from "Slight Shock" to "Danger: Severe Shock" and an ominous "XXX" at the highest level. Participants were instructed to begin punishing the learner for incorrect responses at the lowest voltage level, and to increase the voltage each time the learner made a mistake. The learner, a confederate of Milgram, deliberately gave many wrong answers according to a predetermined schedule. Though the mock generator did not actually deliver any shocks, the learner's pretended protests and screams convinced the participants that it did.

Much to Milgram's surprise, most participants showed little reluctance to pull the switch that delivered potentially life-threatening shocks. Even those who balked continued after the experimenter assured them that the shocks were painful but not lethal, or simply demanded that they continue. Though the results of the experiment provided important insights into the nature and consequences of obedience, which we will discuss in detail in Chapter 7, the ethics of the experiment were questionable. Even though many participants willingly applied what they thought was the highest level of shock, most did not do so happily. In fact, participants often expressed discomfort and unease with the procedure.

Did Milgram act ethically in conducting his studies? There is no clear-cut answer to this question. Whether any social psychological experiment can be considered ethical depends on the extent to which the physical and psychological risks to participants are offset by the potential benefits to them or to society. This rule implies that when the risks are severe, the potential benefits must be great. When the risks are minimal, the potential benefits need not be great.

No experiment is ever completely free of risk. Even the most benign study has the potential to threaten participants' privacy and the confidentiality of their responses. Procedures that deceive participants about the true nature of an experiment may also cause them embarrassment. Considerations like these have led some (e.g., Rosenthal, 1994) to suggest that the quality of research should be taken into account in deciding whether it is ethical. This argument suggests that research that has no clear hypothesis, lacks a theoretical foundation, or is poorly conceived from a methodological point of view may not be ethically defensible.

By what process can we decide whether a research project meets a high enough standard of quality to be considered ethically defensible? Decisions of this sort were once left in the hands of researchers. However, all contemporary research in social psychology is conducted in accordance with safeguards that were instituted to minimize the chances of participants being put at unnecessary risk. Guidelines from the American Psychological Association require that at a minimum, researchers must obtain *informed consent* from participants after alerting them to potential risks. Researchers must also *debrief* participants about the nature and purpose of the research at the end of the study, and they must put in place procedures to assure the *anonymity* and *confidentiality* of the data. At most universities, institutional review boards review all research projects to assure their compliance with these safeguards, as well as with federal regulations.

Answering Questions with Data: A Summary

Experimentation is the method social psychologists use most often to test their hypotheses. Its key elements are control of extraneous variables, random assignment of participants, and the comparison of different experimental conditions. At a minimum, an experiment requires least one independent (causal) variable and one dependent (measured) variable. To measure the dependent variable, researchers can take direct measures of the behavior in question, or use paper-and-pencil scales that tap into the construct being measured. Paper-and-pencil measures must be both valid and reliable.

Well-designed experiments have high internal validity—that is, they allow conclusions about cause-and-effect relationships. At the same time, they often lack external validity, which is to say that they limit a researcher's ability to generalize findings to the real world. If the ability to generalize findings is important, social psychologists can use field experiments, quasi-experiments, and survey methods. However, the gains in generalizability that these methods provide come at a cost, for they often require additional research to allow causal inferences. Survey methods also require attention to the sampling of participants and to the wording and ordering of questions.

Regardless of which method a researcher chooses, all research must meet the ethical standards set forth by the American Psychological Association. At a minimum, these standards stipulate that researchers must minimize the potential risk to participants, as well as assure their anonymity and the confidentiality of the data. Researchers must also obtain informed consent from participants and debrief them fully at the end of the study.

Think Like a Social Psychologist

Designing Research
—You decide to conduct an experiment to test the hypothesis that participants who are in a happy mood will find mildly amusing jokes to be funnier than participants who are not in a happy mood.

To create the happy mood condition, you ask one group of participants to spend ten minutes recalling a happy childhood memory. To create the neutral mood condition, you ask another group of participants to wait for ten minutes. Then you randomly assign 40 participants to either of your two conditions. How sound is your experimental procedure? How could you better operationalize the neutral mood condition?

—Suppose your experiment showed that as expected, the happy mood participants rated the jokes as funnier than the neutral mood participants. When you excitedly tell your best friend about these results, she questions them on the grounds that you didn't know what mood participants were in when they came to your experiment. What aspect of your procedure allows you to tell her that her objection does not matter?

Making Connections

—To obtain approval for a new drug, pharmaceutical companies commonly conduct drug trials in which research participants are randomly assigned to receive either the experimental drug or a placebo. Given that the new drug has potentially beneficial effects, how can this procedure be justified? What appears to be the most important consideration in such trials?

Thinking Critically

—A fellow student sends you an e-mail requesting that you complete a "quick survey" for his psychology honors thesis. For your convenience, he supplies you with a link to a website where the data are collected. When you click on the URL, you are taken to a page that asks for your name, along with your response to ten questions about your attitudes regarding safe sex and condom use. List all the ways in which your fellow student has violated the commonly accepted standards for the ethical conduct of research.

MAKING SENSE OF THE DATA

In every study, regardless of whether we use an experiment or a survey to test a hypothesis, we must eventually make sense of the data. To that end, we may first want to look at the distribution of scores for the variable we are interested in. Calculating the means—that is, the averages—can give us a quick overview of the pattern of results we obtained. Yet the means rarely tell the whole story, particularly for experimental results.

Analyzing Experimental Data

To illustrate this point, let's assume that you ran your experiment on the effects of video game violence and aggression with 30 participants, whom you assigned randomly to the three experimental conditions. **Table 2.1** shows the scores from this hypothetical experiment.

You can calculate the mean for the entire experiment by averaging all 30 scores (5.23). Note that this overall mean varies, to a greater or lesser extent, from virtually every individual score. The degree of variation between the individual scores and the overall mean represents the **total variance** in your experiment.

Next, you need to calculate the means for the experimental conditions (8.2, 5.0, and 2.5). They, too, vary to a greater or lesser extent from the overall mean. The degree of variation from one condition to the next—that is, the

Table 2.1: Results from a hypothetical experiment on videogame violence and aggression: Number of pushes, kicks, and shoves observed during a 30-minute play period.

VIOLENT VIDEOGAME CONDITION	NON-VIOLENT VIDEOGAME CONDITION	DRAWING CONDITION
8	6	3
7	5	3
11	9	4
6	4	2
6	4	2
9	5	3
10	5	2
5	2	1
12	6	3
8	4	2
M: 8.2	M: 5.0	M: 2.5

portion of the variance that is accounted for by the researcher's manipulations—represents the **systematic variance**. Finally, if you look at the scores within each condition, you find that few are identical, most likely because of individual differences among the participants. Some children may simply be more aggressive than others. Variation within a condition is called **error variance**, because it is due to variables that are out of your control.

When you compare the means for your experimental conditions, you are interested in more than the relative magnitude of the differences between them. You also need to make sure that they were not caused by chance. To do that, you can use statistical procedures to partition the total variance into the systematic variance and the error variance. If more of the total variance is accounted for by your manipulations than by chance factors like individual differences, then the difference among the means is likely to be significant—that is, not due to chance.

Analyzing Survey Data

We've seen that surveys have some advantages over experiments. Surveys are often better suited than experiments to the study of naturally occurring phenomena. They also allow us to generalize, assuming that the participants were drawn from a random sample. These advantages come at a cost, however. Because in most surveys all variables are measured, drawing conclusions about

Although a survey may measure all relevant variable, the correlational nature of the results makes conclusions about cause and effect difficult.

cause-and-effect relationships is difficult. Instead, we are limited to assessing the degree of association between the variables that interest us.

The Nature of Correlations

Social scientists refer to the degree of association between two variables as a **correlation**. A correlation may be positive or negative, depending on the relationship between the two variables. Variables that are negatively correlated are inversely related; a zero correlation suggests the absence of a relationship. For example, if a survey on the relationship between material wealth and happiness reveals that happiness increases as wealth increases, the two variables would be positively correlated.

If the same survey showed that happiness decreases as wealth increases, the two variables would be negatively correlated. If the survey showed no relationship between wealth and happiness, the correlation would be a zero (see **Figure 2.1** for graphical representations of these outcomes).

The correlation between two variables is expressed mathematically as a correlation coefficient. Its value can range from +1, indicating a perfect positive relationship between the two variables, to −1, indicating a perfect negative relationship. In social psychological research, we rarely find a perfect relationship between two variables. Instead, the correlation coefficients we observe are frequently on the order of .3 (or −.3). Because correlations of .3 are much closer to 0 (no correlation) than to +1 (perfect correlation) (see **Figure 2.2**), critics frequently dismiss them as too low to be meaningful.

Such criticisms are often misplaced, however. A correlation coefficient is much like a batting average in baseball. For the benefit of those who eschew America's favorite pastime, a batting average describes the degree of association between the number of times a player comes up to bat and the number of hits the player gets. As we all know, nobody bats a thousand, but a player with a .300 average is generally considered a slugger, even though his correlation between hits and at-bat appearances is a paltry .300. With the game on the line, any major league manager in need of a pinch hitter would prefer to bring in a player with a .300 average to a player with a .200 average. Similarly, if your life satisfaction survey shows a correlation of .3 between wealth and happiness and a

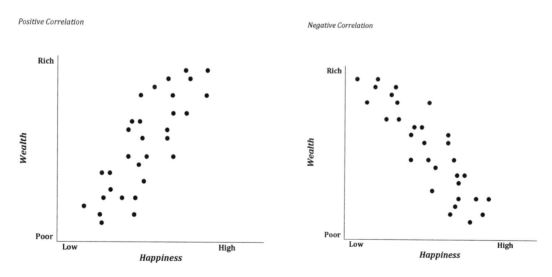

Figure 2.1: Three Possible Correlations in a Hypothetical Study on the Relationship Between Wealth and Happiness.

correlation of .2 between a good sex life and happiness, you would have good reason to suspect that wealth may be more important to life happiness than sex.

Correlation versus Causation

In baseball, although coming up to bat is clearly necessary to get a hit, it does not *cause* the batter to hit the ball. In other words, correlation does not imply causation. Similarly, a positive correlation between two variables like wealth and happiness does not indicate causation. Instead, it can be interpreted in at least three ways: (1) the first variable could affect the second; (2) the second variable could affect the first' or (3) a third variable could affect both. So your .3 correlation could mean that wealth leads to happiness,

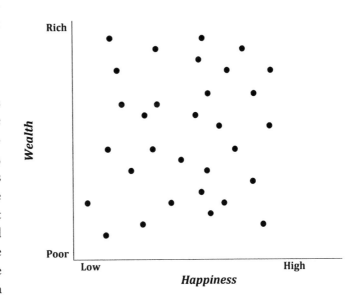

Zero Correlation

but it could also mean that happiness leads to wealth (though that is unlikely). It could also mean that a third variable is responsible for the relationship you observed between wealth and happiness. That is, something

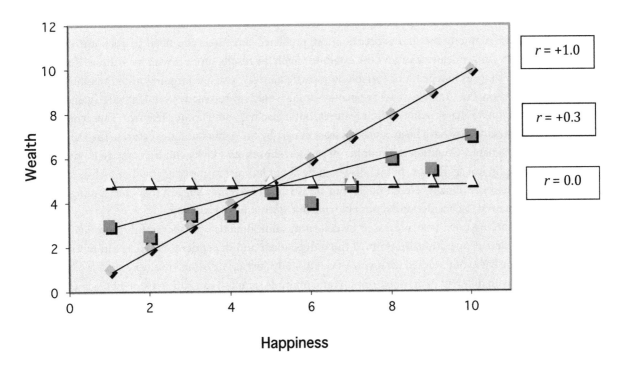

Figure 2.2: Correlations Coefficients (r) of Varying Magnitudes in a Hypothetical Study on the Relationship Between Health and Happiness.

about wealthy, happy people may affect their approach to work and life, creating both financial success and happiness. Similarly, an observed relationship between partner idealization and relationship satisfaction could indicate that continued idealization of one's partner leads to higher relationship satisfaction. Then again, it could mean that people who are happy with their relationships tend to idealize their partners.

In sum, survey data can provide valuable insights into the relationship between two or more variables. Even though a strictly causal interpretation of such data is problematic, the data allow researchers to speculate about the causal nature of a relationship. If one variable occurs before another, they can reasonably infer that the one that came first may have caused a change in the one that came second. Researchers can also measure additional variables and examine their relationship to the variable of interest. Of course, doing so can be fairly onerous, and thinking of every variable that could possibly be related to the variables of interest is often impossible. Ultimately, the choice between the survey method and the experimental method depends on what is more important to researchers. If studying naturally occurring phenomena and generalizing from the findings are of primary concern, the survey method may be more appropriate than an experiment. If drawing causal inferences is the primary goal, an experiment would be more appropriate.

Interpreting the Results

Successful data analysis can be a source of great satisfaction, or at least relief, especially when the data seem to support the hypothesis. Simply finding a significant effect, however, does not by itself imply support for the hypothesis. Rather, the pattern among the means or the correlation between the variables must point in the right direction. In terms of your study of video game violence and aggression, your statistical analysis would yield significant results whether you observed more aggression in the children who played the violent game or in those who played the nonviolent game.

Even if the pattern among the means breaks in the predicted direction, you need to ask some questions before you can draw firm conclusions about the extent to which the results support your hypothesis. Remember that in operationalizing an independent variable in a particular way, you are forgoing other possible ways of looking at the question. For example, there are many—some would say too many—violent video games on the market. *Grand Theft Auto* shares many of their features, but it also has some unique features. Thus, you need to ask whether your results may have been caused at least in part by the game's unique features. The same is true of the dependent variable. Counting the number of pushes, shoves, and kicks children engage in gives you a measure of direct physical aggression, but it tells you little about indirect forms of aggression such as spreading rumors about a classmate. Finally, even though your statistical analysis may suggest that your findings are not due to chance, you need to consider, and if possible rule out, *alternative explanations*.

Issues of this sort are often best addressed by collecting additional data. A successful *replication* of an experiment using different operationalizations of the independent and dependent variables can increase your confidence that you have truly studied what you set out to study. Just as important, multiple studies of the same hypothesis, done with different operationalizations and multiple samples, can add an element of generalizability to your experimental findings. A successful replication that is specifically designed to rule out an alternative explanation would further increase your confidence in your results. Finally, using another research method can compensate for any weaknesses in the original study. Under some circumstances, combining an experiment with a survey can give researchers the advantages of both methods: control and the ability to study naturally occurring phenomena.

Communicating the Results

Eventually, all scientists share the results of their research with others in the field, and sometimes with the public at large. Anthropologists often present their research in the form of a book, especially when it includes detailed observations collected over a long period of a group of people. Mathematicians tend to publish their results in scientific journals that are read by a fairly narrow audience. That makes sense, especially when the work involves the generation of mathematical proofs. Social psychologists fall somewhere between anthropologists and mathematicians in the way they communicate their results. They sometimes publish books on topics like prejudice, persuasion, and relationships, but more often they communicate their findings in one of the many journals devoted to the dissemination of social psychological findings.

Table 2.2 lists some of the most popular and most widely read social psychological journals. All these journals follow a rigorous process of **peer review** before publishing a manuscript. That is, the editors have the paper evaluated by other social psychologists who are familiar with the topic. Though the exact standards vary, all journals take into account the soundness of the methodology used in a study, the appropriateness of the data analysis, and the extent to which the research was conducted in accordance with accepted standards of ethical responsibility. Not surprisingly, most of the journals listed in Table 2.2 accept and publish only a small fraction of the submissions they receive—in some cases, as small as ten percent. As a result, the work published in these journals represents the best in the field.

Papers that are published in these journals share several other features. They generally are written according to the guidelines in the American Psychological Association's (APA) publication manual. APA guidelines stipulate that a research paper should have four distinct parts. The *introduction* presents the research question, along with a theoretical justification for the hypothesis. The *method* section contains information about who participated in the study, along with the details of how it was conducted. The *results* section describes the data

"Let's round it off to 2 and go to lunch."

Although results can be informative, it's how we interpret them that really matters.

Table 2.2: Journals devoted to the publication of social psychological research.

Journal of Personality and Social Psychology

Journal of Experimental Social Psychology

Personality and Social Psychology Bulletin

Social Cognition

Basic and Applied Social Psychology

Journal of Social and Personal Relationships

Journal of Social Issues

that were obtained, along with detailed information on how they were analyzed. Finally, the *discussion* section includes a critical reflection on how the data relate to the hypothesis, along with a consideration of their limitations, implications, and possible applications.

This simple structure provides the backbone for every research article. Alas, because of the technical nature of the material, many students of social psychology—seasoned veterans included—often have difficulty communicating their findings in a compelling way. Articles that are compelling and interesting to readers share some additional features. First, they follow a four-part structure within each of the four parts of the paper. The *introduction* generally begins with a statement of the problem, followed by a review of the relevant literature, identification of the variable(s) of interest, and a theoretical justification for the hypothesis. The *method* section generally begins with a description of the sample of participants, followed by a description of how the variables of interest were operationalized, the design of the experiment, and a detailed account of how the experiment was run (the procedure). The *results* section includes information on what was done to the data, how they were analyzed, and what effects were observed, as well as information about any subsidiary analyses that may have been performed. Finally, the *discussion* section revisits the hypothesis, addresses how the data relate to it, considers possible alternative explanations, and notes the implications of the results beyond the experimental setting.

The way the author discusses the research also has an impact on an article's interest level. There are two ways to talk about science: the language of discovery and the language of debate. According to Wegner (2003), good science writing is all about discovery—about exploring, looking, suspecting, learning. This kind of writing conjures up images of truth seekers searching for something no one has ever seen before. The language of debate is more about battle: claiming, arguing, maintaining, holding. This kind of writing portrays science as a battle between scientists with competing views. Because the language of discovery is far more convincing than the language of debate (which implies that opposition is being mounted even as the findings are described), researchers are generally better off framing their papers in the language of discovery. It greatly increases the chances that an article will reflect the intriguing nature of its ideas, the elegance of its methods, and the sophistication of its data analysis. **Table 2.3** contrasts "discovery words" with "debate words."

Making Sense of the Data: A Summary

The analysis of experimental data involves determining the variance accounted for by manipulations of its independent variables vis-à-vis the variance accounted for by chance factors. The more variance is explained by the manipulated variance, the higher the probability that differences among means are not due to chance. Survey data yield correlations between the variables of interest. Two variables can be positively correlated, negatively correlated, or uncorrelated. Regardless of what methods researchers use, they must consider and rule out alternative explanations for their results.

Social psychologists publish their research in journals. Rigorous peer review prior to publication ensures that researchers used sound methodology and appropriate data analysis, and complied with commonly accepted standards of ethical conduct. Journal articles generally have four parts: (1) an introduction to the research question; (2) a description of the method; (3) a description of the results and procedures for data analysis; and (4) a discussion of the results in light of alternative explanations, together with their theoretical implications. Although many journal articles are written in the language of debate, articles that are written in the language of discovery are particularly likely to reflect the intriguing nature of the ideas researchers pursue.

Table 2.3: Discovery Words versus Debate Words

DISCOVERY WORDS	DEBATE WORDS
Suspect (We suspect that ...)	Argue (We argue that ...)
Find (We found ...)	Show (We showed ...)
Learn (We learned that ...)	Maintain (We maintain ...)
Possibility (It is possible that ...)	Position (Our position is that ...)
Suggest (We suggest ...)	Claim (We claim ...)
Indicate (The findings indicate ...)	Demonstrate (The findings demonstrate ...)
Idea (Our idea is ...)	Point (Our point is ...)
See (We can see that ...)	Hold (We hold that ...)
Expect (We expect to find that ...)	Hope (We hope to find that ...)

Compiled from: Wegner, D.M. (2003). Science Talk: Discover and Debate. Dialogue, 18, 10–11.

EPILOGUE: A BEAUTIFUL IDEA WITH UNLOVELY IMPLICATIONS

What was going on in Asch's experiment, and what was so beautiful about his idea? Apparently, the desire to conform to others' thoughts and behavior is so profound, participants were willing to make patently false statements just to avoid contradicting one another. This conclusion has far-reaching implications. As we will see in Chapters 12 and 14, Asch's findings became the cornerstone for a great deal of theorizing about the roots of atrocities committed during World War II. That is, perpetrators of those atrocities may have been motivated less by sadistic, evil motives than by a desire to conform.

Still, applicability to real life does not by itself render an idea intriguing, for just as we can be intrigued by a poem or painting, we can appreciate a research idea on its own merits. Asch's idea was intriguing because of its ability to explain a variety of seemingly unrelated phenomena as having a common cause. His findings not only helped to explain and predict why people would commit horrific crimes; they proved fundamental to our understanding of why people often fail to do the right thing, such as helping someone in need (Latane & Darley, 1970).

KEY TERMS AND DEFINITIONS

Hypothesis: a statement about the relationship between the crucial elements of a research question

Variables: elements of a research question)

Independent variable: the causal variable of interest in an experiment

Dependent variable: the variable that is measured in an experiment

Random assignment: assignment of research participants in such a way that they have an equal chance to be assigned to any of the conditions of an experiment

Operationalization: the process through which a theoretical variable can be made to work in a laboratory environment

Validity: the extent to which a scale measures what it claims to measure

Reliability: the extent to which a scale yields consistent results

Internal validity: the extent to which an experiment allows conclusions about cause-and-effect relationships

External validity: the extent to which experimental results can be generalized beyond a specific sample or setting

Quasi-experiment: An experiment that is done without random assignment

Survey method: the collection of data from all or part of a population in order to examine the incidence, distribution, and relationships among naturally occurring phenomena

Random sample: a method of selecting survey respondents that assures that every member of a population has an equal chance to be selected

Convenience sample: a nonrandom sample, used when generalizability is not an issue

Total variance: the degree of variation among the scores obtained in an experiment

Systematic variance: the portion of the total variance that is accounted for by the conditions of an experiment

Error variance: the portion of the total variance that is accounted for by variables outside of the experimenter's control

Correlation: the degree to which two variables are associated; ranges from −1 to +1

Peer review: the process by which other scholars in the field evaluate the merits of a research paper submitted for publication in a journal

REFERENCES

Anderson, C. A., & Bushman, B. J. (2002). The effects of media violence on society. *Science, 295*, 2377–2379.

Asch, S. E. (1956). Studies of independence and conformity: A minority of one against a unanimous majority. *Psychological Monographs, 70*, 1–70.

Bem, D. J. (1965). An experimental analysis of self-persuasion. *Journal of Experimental Social Psychology, 1*, 199–218.

Cialdini, R. B. (2008). *Influence: Science and practice* (5th ed.). Needham Heights, MA: Allyn and Bacon.

Cook, T. D., & Campbell, D. T. (1975). The design of quasi-experiments and true experiments in field settings. In M. D. Dunnett (Ed.), *Handbook of industrial and organizational psychology*. New York: Rand McNally.

Diener, E., & Biswas-Diener, R. (2002). Will money increase subjective well-being? *Social Indicators Research, 57*, 119–169.

Festinger, L., & Carlsmith, J. M. (1959). Cognitive consequences of forced compliance. *Journal of Abnormal and Social Psychology, 58*, 202–210.

Fiske, S. T. (2003). *Social beings: A core motives approach to social psychology*. New York: Wiley & Sons.

Greenwald, A. G., Banaji, M. R., Rudman, L. A., Farnham, S. D., Nosek, B. A., & Mellott, D. S. (2002). A unified theory of implicit attitudes, stereotypes, self-esteem, and self-concept. *Psychological Review, 109,* 3–25.

Greenwald, A. G., McGhee, D. E., & Schwartz, J. L. K. (1998). Measuring individual differences in implicit cognition: The implicit association test. *Journal of Personality and Social Psychology, 74,* 1464–1480.

Latane, B., & Darley, J. M. (1970). *The unresponsive bystander: Why doesn't he help?* Englewood Cliffs, NJ: Prentice-Hall.

Milgram, S. (1963). Behavioral study of obedience. *Journal of Abnormal and Social Psychology, 67,* 371–378.

Mook, D. G. (1983). In defense of external invalidity. *American Psychologist, 38,* 379– 387.

Murray, S. L., Holmes, J. G., & Griffin, D. W. (1996). The benefits of positive illusions: Idealization and the construction of satisfaction in close relationships. *Journal of Personality and Social Psychology, 70,* 79–98.

Nickerson, C., Schwarz, N., Diener, E., & Kahneman, D. (2003). Zeroing in on the dark side of the American Dream: A closer look at the negative consequences of the goal for financial success. *Psychological Science, 14,* 531–536.

Rosenthal, R. (1994). Science and ethics in conducting, analyzing, and reporting psychological research. *Psychological Science, 5,* 127–134.

Schulz, R. (1976). Effects of control and predictability on the physical and psychological well-being of the institutionalized aged. *Journal of Personality and Social Psychology, 33,* 563–573.

Schuman, H., & Presser, S. (1981). *Questions and answers in attitude surveys.* New York: Academic Press.

Schwarz, N. (1999). Self-reports: How the questions shape the answers. *American Psychologist, 54,* 93–105.

Schwarz, N., Knauper, B., Hippler, H. J., Noelle-Neumann, E., & Clark, F. (1991). Rating scales: Numeric values may change the meaning of scale labels. *Public Opinion Quarterly, 55,* 570–582.

Sherif, M. (1935). A study of some social factors in perception. *Archives of Psychology, 27,* 1–60.

Sherif, M. (1936). *The psychology of social norms.* Oxford, UK: Harper.

Tesser, A. (1990, August). *Interesting models in social psychology: A personal view.* Paper presented at the annual meeting of the American Psychological Association, Boston, MA.

Wegner, D. M. (2003). Science Talk: Discover and Debate. *Dialogue, 18,* 10–11.

CHAPTER 3

PERSON PERCEPTION AND SOCIAL INFERENCE

CHERYL UNDER THE MICROSCOPE

Filing, photocopying, sorting mail, answering phones—probably not the most exciting part-time work in the world, but Cheryl wanted it. Truth be told, she wanted it badly. Ordinarily, Cheryl would have set her sights on a more challenging job, but this position was in her school's Department of Occupational Therapy (OT), and Cheryl had long ago decided that occupational therapy was the only career for her. Her father had been an occupational therapist, and so had her grandmother. Just spending time around the faculty and graduate students would be an invaluable learning experience; to be paid for it would be a bonus.

As soon as she heard about the opening, Cheryl sat down to write a carefully crafted cover letter for her application. Needless to say, she discussed her long-standing enthusiasm for occupational therapy. But she also wanted to tell whoever would review the application that for her, this was not just a job—it was *the* job. So she pointed out that even though some other jobs might pay better, she was not going to apply for them. She added that although she had a good chance at landing a position at the main library—one of the more popular places to work on campus—she wasn't interested in it.

Cheryl needed letters of recommendation, so she requested them from two faculty members at her school. She asked the first letter-writer, a biology professor who had once employed her as a lab assistant, to talk about her job performance. He wrote in great detail about a complicated experimental procedure that Cheryl had mastered, pointing out that other students usually botched the procedure. He noted, too, that her stellar performance was not restricted to that part of her job. Cheryl had carried out all her duties effectively, despite the fact that she had less research experience than the other assistants in the lab.

Cheryl's second letter-writer was a professor who had been her instructor in two small classes. As a result, she knew Cheryl quite well, and could provide a broader description of her personal qualities: warm, friendly, enthusiastic, intelligent, motivated, conscientious, and quite ambitious. This professor also listed all the projects Cheryl had worked on in her classes, so that whoever read the letter would better understand the context in which she got to know Cheryl.

As soon as Cheryl received the two letters of recommendation, she assembled all her application materials in a folder and rushed off to deliver it to the OT department. Wanting to make the best impression possible, she dressed more formally than usual; it had been a while since she had worn shoes with heels. Her journey across campus hit a snag, though, when she stumbled onto a student demonstration that was blocking her path. Cheryl charged right through it. She was certainly sympathetic to the protesters (the issue was the university's failure to rehire a dean who had been popular with the students), but she did not want to be distracted from her goal.

At last, Cheryl reached her destination. Entering the OT department, she spotted the main office down the hall. Her heart raced, her pace quickened—and unfortunately, her feet flew out from under her. A few unprintable words escaped her mouth as she hit the floor and the pages in her folder scattered all around. Regaining her composure, she realized that her mishap had caught the attention of some department members, who had just emerged from a rather dull meeting. As the bemused professors watched, a janitor ran to her, apologizing profusely. He had just mopped the hallway, and had neglected to put up a "wet floor" sign. In fact, he almost fell himself while rushing to Cheryl's aid.

After delivering the application, Cheryl returned to her dorm room. The department would make its decision about whom to hire in a week or so. Although she was shaken by her fall, Cheryl was confident that she would get the job.

THE ROLE OF PERSON PERCEPTION IN SOCIAL BEHAVIOR

What kind of impression would the members of the OT department form of Cheryl? What kinds of traits and abilities would they infer that she had, and how would they reach those conclusions? More important, how would their conclusions shape their expectations about her future performance and behavior? As we will see, exploring how people make sense of, explain, and predict one another's behavior—that is, understanding the process of **person perception**—has long been a major preoccupation of social psychologists (Gilbert, 1998a; Hastie et al., 1980; Jones, 1990; Macrae & Quadflieg, 2010; Moskowitz, 2005; Schneider, Hastorf, & Ellsworth, 1979; Tagiuri & Petrullo, 1958).

A great deal of our own social behavior depends on how we interpret other people's behavior and the conclusions we reach about them. In fact, social interaction would be inconceivable if people did not have the ability to perceive, explain, and predict one another's behavior. Why do we initiate relationships with some people, but avoid others? Why do we target some for aggression, but heap kindness on others? Why do we eagerly agree with some people, but resist persuasion by others? Often, we have simply decided that the people involved deserve such treatment or consideration. In other words, person perception underlies many—if not most—of the phenomena that are of interest to social psychologists (Newman, 2001). Important real-world outcomes such as hiring and firing, school admission decisions, and jury verdicts arise from the basic processes of person perception.

Thus, research on person perception is central to *cognitive social psychology*, which, as described in Chapter 1, is the study of the thoughts and other mental activities that underlie and lead to social behavior. What makes this kind of research especially challenging is the fact that much of the mental work involved takes place without people being aware of it (Andersen, Moskowitz, Blair, & Nosek, 2007; Bargh, 1997; Bargh & Chartrand, 1999; Greenwald, 1992; Hassin, Uleman, & Bargh, 2005; Kihlstrom, 1987; Uleman & Bargh, 1989; Wegner, 2002; Wilson, 2002).

People are probably not spying on you, but research on person perception assumes that others are constantly observing you, trying to figure out why you're doing what you're doing, and forming impressions of you.

The voluminous research on this topic can be organized into three major approaches, defined by three metaphors: the naive scientist, the cognitive miser, and the motivated tactician (Fiske & Taylor, 1991). Each of these approaches emphasizes different aspects of person perception, and each one tells a very different story about how we make sense of other people's behavior. As we will see, understanding the ups and downs of Cheryl's campaign to win her dream job requires a familiarity with all three of these perspectives on person perception.

THE NAIVE SCIENTIST

Cheryl Gets a Fair Shake

When Cheryl wrote her cover letter, she painstakingly made the case that she was qualified for the job. The two professors who wrote letters of recommendation for her also provided detailed information about her traits and behaviors. All three of them, of course, assumed that the people who would evaluate Cheryl's application would consider everything they had to say in a careful, systematic way. The assumption that people will conscientiously take into account all that they know about another person and then reach a logical conclusion is consistent with the **naive scientist** model of person perception (Fiske & Taylor, 1991).

How do scientists reach conclusions about the objects of their study? Ideally, they do so by means of close observation, careful consideration of all the evidence at their disposal, and logical integration of all that information.

The naive scientist approach to person perception starts with the assumption that people are similarly rational when they reach conclusions about what other people are like. The word naive is not meant to suggest that people are simpleminded or unsophisticated. Rather, the idea is that even though most people are not formally trained in the scientific method, they might nonetheless think like scientists—that is, systematically and logically—in forming their impressions of others. Indeed, such analyses of the way people think about other people and their behavior are often called "rational models." We will now describe a few of those models in detail.

Jones and Davis's Theory of Correspondent Inference

If Keith compliments you, Kim insults you, and Kareem ignores you, you would probably want to know why. Figuring out the causes of their behavior, after all, could help you to decide how to respond. If Keith's compliments were based on sincere admiration, you would probably want to let him know how much you appreciate his comments. If he flatters you in the hope that you would let him peek at your notes for the midterm, however, you would probably want to tell him to get lost. If you are like most people, however, understanding the temporary thoughts, feelings, and goals that cause people to behave in specific ways (for example, Keith's panic over the upcoming test, and his belief that you are a pushover) will not be enough.

In general, we are not satisfied simply with understanding what others do; we want to predict their *future* actions. Thus, we want to know what others are "like," and what traits and attitudes underlie their behavior across time and place (Heider, 1958). Figuring out that Keith's behavior is annoying is one thing; deciding that he is manipulative and lazy is another. When we make a dispositional inference—that is, when we reach a conclusion about another person's enduring traits and/or attitudes—we have information that will be useful to us if we interact with that person again.

When we conclude that another person's behavior reflects a stable, underlying trait—for example, when we conclude that nasty behavior reflects a general nastiness, or that warm behavior reflects warmth—we have made what is called a **correspondent inference** (Jones & Davis, 1965; Jones & McGillis, 1976). Of course, people's behavior does not always correspond directly to their traits. Kim's nasty behavior could have been the result of a really bad day. What determines whether or not we make correspondent inferences?

According to Jones and Davis (also Malle & Holbrook, 2012; Reeder, 2009; Reeder, Vonk, Ronk, Ham, & Lawrence, 2004), before we decide that a person's behavior reflects his or her stable attributes, we must answer a more basic question: What were his or her intentions? In other words, what was he or she trying to accomplish? To address these questions, we need to identify the possible consequences of the behavior—especially those the person could have anticipated. Almost any given behavior produces a variety of different outcomes or effects. Which ones were intended?

Imagine a high school student boarding the school bus one chilly January afternoon during midterms. He finds only two available seats, both of them next to broken windows. One of them is next to the school's most brilliant, but certainly not most popular, student (the nerd). The other one is next to a student who isn't very brainy, but is liked by almost everyone because he knows how to have a good time (the class clown). Wherever the student decides to sit, his choice will produce specific effects. If he chooses to sit next to the nerd, he will get home before dark, but will arrive half frozen from the cold air blasting through the window. Neither of those effects, however, is distinctive to that choice. The same effects would follow if he sat next to the clown.

In Jones and Davis's terms, these "common effects" don't reveal anything about a person's intentions or underlying traits. More useful in making correspondent inferences are noncommon effects—outcomes that are unique to a given choice or behavior. In the student's case, each alternative is associated with a specific noncommon effect. Sitting next to the class clown would probably lead to lots of laughs on the way home; sitting next to the nerd might yield information that would be helpful on an upcoming midterm. In this case, then, the job of an observer who wants to learn something about the student would be relatively simple. If the student sits next to the class clown, we can assume that he is more fun loving and extroverted than he is studious and achievement oriented. If he sits next to the nerd, we can draw the opposite conclusion.

Interpreting other people's behavior is not always so simple, of course. Let's assume that the nerd has an attractive sibling the student wants to meet, and the class clown comes from a wealthy family. Now each choice is associated with multiple noncommon effects. Determining which of those effects is most important to the student (getting exam answers? going on a date? having fun? sailing on a yacht?) would be difficult. The lower the number of noncommon effects, the more easily we can determine a person's intentions and make a correspondent inference.

In making correspondent inferences, moreover, people attend not only to the number and uniqueness of a behavior's effects, but to their social desirability. When people engage in behavior that we could expect from just about anyone (socially desirable behavior), we don't learn much about them. If the student who had to choose between two seats avoided the seat next to a classmate known for carrying a switchblade, we would have little trouble determining what the student's intention was. But while avoiding the possibility of getting stabbed is a perfectly reasonable goal, knowing that a student has that goal doesn't tell us much about his unique personality traits. On the other hand, imagine that the student did choose to sit next to the potentially dangerous young man, and that a propensity toward violence was the only trait that distinguished that young man from the others. This single noncommon effect, because it is so low in social desirability, would be very informative. We could easily make a correspondent inference about the student who made this surprising choice, such as "antisocial."

Pulling all these ideas together leads us to a fairly straightforward prediction. When a person's behavior seems clearly intended to bring about one or two effects in particular, and those effects are not desired by everybody, then we have probably learned something about the person. For example, Jones, Davis, and Gergen (1961) asked

research participants to listen to mock job interviews, in which the applicants were trying to convince interviewers that they were highly qualified for the job of either submariner or astronaut. Submariners, the interviewees had been told, needed to be "outer-directed," or friendly and outgoing; astronauts, on the other had, needed to be "inner-directed," able to tolerate and even enjoy long periods of solitude. When an interviewee who was trying to be hired as a submariner described himself as being "inner-directed," research participants rated him as being truly high on that dimension—more so than when he was trying to be hired as an astronaut. The opposite was true when the interviewee described himself as "outer-directed."

It is difficult to make correspondent inferences from job applicants' self-descriptions when the characteristics they claim to have perfectly match the job description.

These results make perfect sense in terms of Jones and Davis's (1965) theory. There are many socially desirable reasons to describe oneself as having the characteristics appropriate to a particular role or job. One might want to impress the interviewer, increase one's chances of being selected, or simply avoid looking foolish. On the other hand, describing oneself in terms of a trait that is inappropriate would seem to have only one noncommon effect: honesty. Because in this case, revealing one's true nature would also have the undesirable effect of losing an interesting and exciting opportunity (becoming an astronaut or a submariner), most people would make a correspondent inference and conclude that the interviewee was indeed an honest person.

In light of this research, we should be impressed with the way Cheryl crafted the cover letter for her job application. Recall that she took pains to emphasize that the other jobs she might apply for were more lucrative and more widely sought after—in other words, they would increase her spending power and her popularity. But the job in the occupational therapy department, as she described it, was distinguished by just one important (and not universally socially desirable) feature: it was in the occupational therapy department. According to the theory of correspondent inference, a person who read her letter would be likely to conclude that Cheryl was highly motivated to enter the world of occupational therapy.

Kelley's Model of Causal Attribution

In our everyday quest to understand people's behavior, we will sometimes need to take into account causes other than people's attitudes and personality traits. Imagine that while you are waiting for a table at a restaurant, you hear a waitress speak sharply to a customer. How do you interpret her behavior? She could be short-tempered, but she might have been responding to something the customer said or did to her. That, of course, does not exhaust the range of possibilities. Both the waitress and the customer could be perfectly nice people, but the waitress might just have learned that a pay cut was in the works for the restaurant's employees. Regardless, your conclusion could determine whether you continue to wait for a seat or head for the café down the block.

The covariation model. Kelley (1967, 1971a, 1971b, 1973) developed a model for thinking about how people make such **causal attributions**, or judgments about the causes of behaviors and other events. His hypothesis was that people tend to attribute an effect to the possible cause with which it covaries—that is, the one it appears to be associated with over time.

According to this covariation model (Kelley, 1967, 1973), people make judgments about the causes of behavior by seeking out three basic kinds of information: consensus, distinctiveness, and consistency. Getting consensus information involves figuring out whether other people behave in the same way (that is, determining whether or not the behavior you observed is unique to the person who engaged in it). In the case just described, that would mean figuring out whether other members of the restaurant's staff have had unpleasant interactions with the customer. If so, the behavior would be high in consensus; if not, it would be low. Getting distinctiveness information involves figuring out whether the behavior is unique to the person (or other "entity") toward which it was directed. That is, does the waitress treat everyone that way, or just this customer? Finally, consistency is the extent to which a behavior is always triggered by a particular person, situation, or other stimulus (Do these two always clash?).

Obviously, consensus, distinctiveness, and consistency information can combine in several ways, but three patterns are especially meaningful (see **Table 3.1**). When a behavior is high in consistency but low in consensus and distinctiveness, an attribution to the person who engaged in the behavior—the "actor"—is warranted. If the waitress always fights with a particular customer (high consistency), even though no other waitress does (low

Table 3.1: Why did Cheryl make a bad impression on her professor? An analysis based on the covariation model (Kelley (1967, 1971a, 1971b, 1973)

A PERSON ATTRIBUTION	AN ENTITY ATTRIBUTION	A CIRCUMSTANCE ATTRIBUTION
"No one else makes a bad impression on this professor" (**low consensus**)	"Everyone else makes a bad impression on this professor" (**high consensus**)	"No one else makes a bad impression on this professor" (**low consensus**)
"Cheryl makes a bad impression on other professors" (**low distinctiveness**)	"Cheryl does not make a bad impression on other professors" (**high distinctiveness**)	"Cheryl does not make a bad impression on other professors" (**high distinctiveness**)
"In the past, Cheryl has always made a bad impression on this professor" (**high consistency**)	"In the past, Cheryl has always made a bad impression on this professor" (**high consistency**)	"Cheryl has never made a bad impression on this professor before" (**low consistency**)
CONCLUSION: Cheryl is the cause!	CONCLUSION: The professor is the cause!	CONCLUSION: Something just went wrong that day!

consensus) and she also has difficulties with other customers (low distinctiveness), some trait of hers would seem to be the cause. Similarly, if a man constantly trips over his dance partner's feet, even though no one else does, and he also trips over other dance partners' feet, we can infer that he is clumsy.

On the other hand, when a behavior is high in consistency, consensus, and distinctiveness, an "entity" attribution is more logical. In other words, the target of the behavior is probably the cause. The waitress might always argue with a particular patron, but if everyone else does, too, and if her problems are restricted to that customer, the customer would seem to be the culprit. Finally, when a behavior is low in consensus, high in distinctiveness, and low in consistency, a circumstance attribution makes sense. If the waitress usually gets along well with the customer, other people do, too, and the waitress in question gets along well with other customers, then she's just having a bad day—a unique set of circumstances is causing this particular effect.

Research has shown that people can use covariation information to reach the conclusions Kelley's model predicts (but see Foersterling, 1989, and Smith, 1994, for other perspectives on how people use such information). Recall that the biology professor who wrote a letter of recommendation for Cheryl pointed out not only that she had mastered a complicated experimental procedure, but that (1) other students had not; (2) Cheryl always did it perfectly; and (3) she excelled in carrying out other tasks as well. In other words, he made the case that her competent behavior was low in consensus, high in consistency, and low in distinctiveness. Thus, Cheryl could be confident that anyone who read the letter would make a person attribution and conclude that she was a highly competent person.

In research on Kelley's covariation model (e.g., McArthur, 1972; Orvis, Cunningham, & Kelley, 1975), people are typically presented with brief descriptions of behavior, followed by different combinations of consensus, distinctiveness, and consistency information (see **Table 3.1**). Then they are asked to judge the probable cause of the behavior. Curiously, people sometimes seem to ignore the consensus information that is provided to them, preferring to use their own estimates based on their own experience (Nisbett, Borgida, Crandall, & Reed, 1976). Other research shows that covariation information affects not only the attributions people make about others, but also the way they behave toward others (Hazlewood & Olson, 1986; Schuster, Rudolph, & Foersterling, 1998). Yet another body of research looks at the attributions we make about *ourselves*, and shows that they have consequences for our health and well-being: see the Social Psychology and Health box on **pages 68–69**.

SOCIAL PSYCHOLOGY AND HEALTH: CAUSAL ATTRIBUTIONS AND DEPRESSION

Why do people devote so much energy to causal attribution and to social inference in general? A central assumption underlying research on these topics is that people are motivated to *explain* interpersonal events, *predict* future ones, and maintain some *control* over their lives (Heider, 1958; Pittman & Heller, 1987). As a result, when people analyze their own and others' behavior, they might want to do more than just attribute behavior to the person or the situation.

Several researchers have theorized about what kinds of information people seek when they try to make sense of their experiences (e.g., Anderson, 1991; Weiner, 1985; Wimer & Kelley, 1982). One of those theories is particularly important, because it has implications for the most common mental health problem: depression. In any given year, between five and ten percent of the adult population in the United States can be expected to suffer from severe depression. Another three to five percent will suffer from milder forms of the disturbance (Kessler et al., 1994). In fact, depression is so prevalent, it is often referred to as the "common cold" of mental illness.

Depression is multi-determined; that is, no single cause underlies the disorder. There seems to be a genetic component to it, which helps to explain why it tends to run in families (Moldin, Reich, & Rice, 1991). But according to Abramson, Seligman, and Teasdale (1978), another important predictor of depression is the way in which people think about events in their lives, especially negative ones.

According to Abramson et al. (1978), the three most important aspects of a causal explanation are its locus, stability, and globality. *Locus* refers to whether the perceived cause is internal or external. If a date goes badly, you could account for what happened by focusing either on your own characteristics (internal) or on the other person's characteristics (external). *Stability* refers to the endurance of the cause over time. Some causes are transient or temporary; others are longer lasting. A stable cause might be "I'm always awkward on dates"; an unstable one might be "I guess suggesting dinner at a fast food restaurant in a gas station was a bad idea." Finally, *globality* refers to the breadth of the cause, whether very narrow such as a specific area of your life, or at the other extreme, to most or all of your experience. "I'm not a very charming conversationalist when I've had only two hours sleep the night before" applies only to a particular kind of behavior (socializing) in very narrow circumstances (sleeplessness). "I can't meet anyone I like in this town," a more global explanation, has broader applicability **(see Table 3.2)**.

Locus, stability, and globality can combine to produce some very pessimistic or optimistic causal explanations. For example, you could explain a disastrous date by thinking "I can never do anything right"—an internal, stable, global explanation, the most pessimistic type. Or you could conclude that "The person I was set up with was just in a bad mood last night"—an external, unstable, specific explanation. (See **Table 3.2** for another example of different explanatory styles.) Research indicates that a person who comes up with the former explanation would be someone who is more likely to experience depression than a person who comes up with the latter explanation. That is, the tendency to explain your setbacks in terms of internal, stable, and global factors, called a **pessimistic explanatory style**, predicts proneness to depression (Metalsky, Joiner, Hardin, & Abramson, 1993; Peterson & Seligman, 1984).

Table 3.2: Abramson et al.'s (1978) model of explanatory style "I got to the airport late and missed my flight!"

INTERNAL EXPLANATIONS	STABLE	UNSTABLE
GLOBAL	"I can't do anything right."	"I'm not feeling well today, so I'm screwing everything up."
SPECIFIC	"I often have trouble getting places on time."	"I had trouble getting out of the house on time today."

EXTERNAL EXPLANATIONS	STABLE	UNSTABLE
GLOBAL	"The modern world is just becoming too hard to navigate."	"The bad weather and holiday traffic messed everything up today."
SPECIFIC	"This airport is notoriously hard to get to on time."	"Too bad there was traffic today—that's not usually the case on the way to this airport."

The explanation in red (stable, external, global) is the most pessimistic and most likely to be associated with depression. The explanation in green is the least pessimistic.

Some have argued that the logic of the theory is that to trigger depression, a pessimistic explanation must have *all three* characteristics (internality, stability, and globality) (Carver & Scheier, 1991). In practice, however, the three dimensions seem to combine additively to predict negative affect. That means that a highly internal, stable explanation for a negative event can cause depression, even if its globality is not particularly high. Because depression is associated with sleep disturbances, changes in appetite, headaches, and digestive problems, the kinds of causal attributions people tend to fall back on have implications for their physical as well as their mental health.

Discounting and augmentation. What if people don't have all the information they need to make causal attributions according to the covariation model? What if—as is often the case—all they have to go on when trying to figure out why someone did or said something is a single observation, with no background information on consensus, distinctiveness, or consistency? In such cases, people have other tools at their disposal. Kelley (1971a, 1971b, 1973) describes several, two of which have received much more attention than the others.

One of those two tools is the **discounting principle**. When more than one cause of an event seems plausible and one of them is clearly present, people tend to discount the significance of the other causes. In other words, they assume that the other causes are not present. For example, if you learned that a classmate of yours wrote an essay calling for an end to income taxes, you might assume that her essay reflects her conservative political beliefs. If you were to learn that the topic had been assigned to her by a professor, however, you might be less willing to assume she is politically conservative. That is, you would discount conservatism as a cause of her behavior.

Use of the discounting principle plays a role in the **overjustification effect** (Lepper, Greene, & Nisbett, 1973), in which people who have been rewarded for doing things they enjoy report a lessened interest in those activities (Deci & Ryan, 1985; Lepper & Greene, 1978). For example, Lepper et al. (1973) asked preschool children to draw with magic markers—an activity that most found intrinsically enjoyable. The researchers promised some of the children a reward for playing with the markers. Afterward, with great fanfare, they presented those children with a "good player" award. Several days later, in a free play period, the experimenters observed that the rewarded children were less likely than others to choose to play with the magic markers.

What explains this paradoxical effect? Lepper et al. suggested that when rewards are overemphasized, people implicitly assume that the main reason for engaging in the activity is to get a reward. Simultaneously, they discount their own genuine interest, or intrinsic motivation. Thus, rewards can "overjustify" an activity. Interestingly, when people receive *unexpected* rewards, the overjustification effect disappears (Lepper et al. 1973). After all, if they did not expect a reward, then the desire to receive one could not have caused their behavior (see **Figure 3.1**). In that case, they don't discount their own interest. (For another explanation of the overjustification effect, see Pretty & Seligman, 1984; for critical analyses of its importance, see Akin-Little, Eckert, Lovett, & Little, S. G., 2004; Eisenberger & Cameron, 1998; and Eisenberger, Pierce, & Cameron, 1999.)

The flip side of the discounting principle is the **augmentation principle**. According to this principle, when a possible cause for an outcome is *absent*, other potential causes will seem *more* important than they might otherwise. To win election to a high-level political office, for example, one generally needs intelligence, a pleasant personality, and a great deal of money. If one of those causes is not present—and especially if another factor that would make being elected less likely is present—we will assign more importance to (or augment) the other cause or causes. If an unpleasant, not very bright person were to be elected to high office, for example, we might conclude that he must have had ample financial resources to overcome those limitations. Likewise, if we

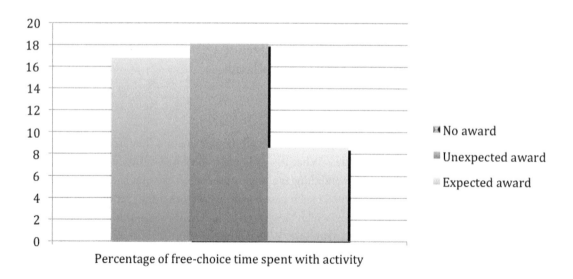

Figure 3.1: The overjustification effect: Expected rewards undermine intrinsic motivation.

From Lepper, Greene, & Nisbett (1973). Participants were three-, four-, and five-year-olds, and the activity was playing with magic markers.

were to learn that a candidate with little money was victorious, we would probably suspect that she had impressive personal qualities.

A study of sharing among preschoolers provides another example. Children who were gently encouraged to give away toys or other attractive objects were later more likely than other children (including children who were essentially forced to share) to continue behaving in a generous way (Chernyak & Kushnir, 2013). In the absence of any other explanation for their sharing (such as lack of choice, or the expectation of some reward for sharing), these children seemed to conclude, consistent with the augmentation principle, that the cause of their sharing was their own personal generosity.

Researchers have found both the discounting and augmentation principles to be useful in understanding the complexities of social judgments (e.g., Morris & Larrick, 1995). Cheryl would have been glad to hear that. Her biology professor had noted that she did great lab work, even though she had less experience in research than his other assistants. Given the presence of a factor that could have inhibited her success (lack of experience), the augmentation principle would lead one to conclude that Cheryl must be exceptionally gifted.

Did this student get candy for doing his homework? If so, research on the overjustification effect suggests that his motivation for completing his assignments could actually be undermined in the long term.

Combining Attributions: The Linear Combination Model

Although the theories we just reviewed are broad and powerful, they have their limitations. For the most part, they explain how people analyze single behaviors by individuals (usually strangers) to reach fairly modest conclusions (generally, specific inferences about personality traits). Such models cannot do justice to the rich, complex impressions we form of the people we deal with in our daily lives. Over long periods, through many interactions with these people, we gather quite a bit of information about them. Clearly, we don't classify the important people in our lives in terms of a single prominent personality trait, like the seven dwarfs in *Snow White*. People are more multifaceted than Dopey, Happy, Sleepy, Sneezy, Bashful, Grumpy, and Doc. Your circle of friends is unlikely to include Generous, Cheerful, Friendly, and Smarty.

Somehow, people have to pull together and integrate the many different inferences they make about others and arrive at overall impressions of them, a process known as **impression formation**. Usually, the most important judgments we make about others are evaluative. In other words, how we interact with others—and whether we choose to do so in the first place—is to a great extent determined by how much we like them (Osgood, Suci,

& Tannenbaum, 1957; Schneider et al., 1979). But how do we arrive at an overall evaluation of someone whom we might believe, for example, to be skillful, determined, cold, and cautious?

According to an extensive series of studies by Anderson (1965a, 1971, 1974), we do it with math—algebra, to be more precise. To each of the person's traits, we assign some value that corresponds to how favorable or unfavorable we consider that trait to be (see **Table 3.3**). We then combine the ratings to create a total favorability score. Combining the ratings could mean either summing them or averaging them. Either way, **linear combination models** assume that we arrive at our impressions of others by assigning some value to each individual piece of information we have and then combining those values in a logical, systematic way.

Of course, not all trait impressions are equal. We can assume that a trait like "homicidal" will carry more weight in an evaluation than a characteristic like "good harmonica player." In some of the earliest research on impression formation (Asch, 1946), certain traits like "warm" and "cold" were found to be better predictors than others of people's overall evaluations. Such traits are called central traits. In linear combination models, these findings can be taken into account by weighting traits differently based on their relative importance. For example, to combine three traits with likeability ratings of 2, 7, and 9 (on a 10-point scale), we might not simply sum them, but increase or decrease the value of each based on its importance. So if the trait with a very positive rating of 9 is "makes good coffee," it might not balance out a trait with a rating of 2 if that trait is more important—"dishonest," for example.

Regardless of the weights we assign to individual traits, we would have to assume that a person described as warm, friendly, enthusiastic, intelligent, motivated, conscientious, and ambitious would be seen positively by others. Those, as you might recall, are the characteristics the second letter-writer attributed to Cheryl. That professor even included a classic central trait—"warm"—in her description of Cheryl. Research on impression formation, then, would predict that her letter of recommendation would be very effective.

Table 3.3: Most and least likable traits

TOP TWELVE MOST LIKABLE	TOP TWELVE LEAST LIKABLE
sincere	liar
honest	phony
understanding	mean
loyal	cruel
truthful	dishonest
trustworthy	untruthful
intelligent	obnoxious
dependable	malicious
open-minded	dishonorable
thoughtful	deceitful
wise	untrustworthy
considerate	unkind

From Anderson (1968). Based on the ratings of 100 college students.

Generous and Vindictive? The Configural Approach to Combining Attributions

Research on linear combination models employs a method developed by Asch (1946): presenting people with a list of traits and asking them to make an overall judgment about the person who has those traits. Asch, however, had a different perspective on how we form impressions. In his view, we do not evaluate people's traits in isolation. Instead, the nature of the other traits a person has subtly alters the perceived meaning of each individual trait. We see people as complex configurations of traits that add up to a coherent whole, rather than as collections of isolated, disconnected characteristics.

Intelligence, for example, is generally seen as a favorable quality. If a person is described as "intelligent" and "warm," we might also describe him or her as "wise." Imagine instead that the two traits were "intelligent" and "cold." Not only would we like the person less, but the term "intelligent" might take on a different meaning. We might see the person more as "calculating" or sinister than as "wise" (Fiske & Taylor, 1991, p. 101).

Diligent, concerned, and intelligent (top); evil, selfish, and intelligent (bottom). A trait can take on different meanings ("wise" vs. "diabolical") in different contexts.

Indeed, when people are presented with multiple traits that supposedly describe a given person, they can and do think about how those traits relate to—and even transform—one another. Asch and Zukier (1984) presented subjects with pairs of seemingly incompatible traits that described particular people. They then asked the subjects to describe each person and explain how the two traits were related. The subjects did so easily. For example, in response to a person described as "generous and vindictive," some subjects suggested that he or she was "generous for ulterior motives; not altruistic but selfish—a scheming, plotting, individual." Others inferred that the person was "generous to those that have treated him benevolently, and vindictive to those who have done him the slightest harm" (Asch & Zukier, 1984, p. 1235).

In terms of overall liking ratings, though, both the linear combination and configural models yield similar predictions. So even though Asch's configural approach seems to do more justice to our subjective experience—that is, the way we really think about other people—the linear combination models still do a good job of accounting for the way we combine bits of knowledge about others into an overall impression.

Thinking Carefully and Systematically: A Summary

When people ask us about our impressions of others and our judgments of their behavior, we usually can justify those impressions and judgments. Most of the time, we can make a case for why our conclusions about other people are logical. When we do so, the reasoning we use probably is not so different from the kind of thinking that goes into the naive scientist models just described. In line with correspondent inference theory, we try to determine people's intentions by taking into account the effects of their actions ("She must have known that her nasty comment would make everyone uncomfortable"). As Kelley's attribution theory suggests, we think about a person's behavior in light of both other people's behavior and the person's own past behavior ("No one else made a comment like that one, and she has made plenty of comments like that in the past"). Finally, as linear combination models suggest, our impressions of people build up over time as a result of our many different judgments of them ("Rude, selfish, conceited—that does it, I've had it with her!"). In fact, to some people, the theories of Jones and Davis, Kelley, and Anderson seem like elaborate descriptions of common sense.

People's thinking is not always so careful and rational, however. As we will see next, person perception can also be based on lazy, irrational thinking—and on hidden influences.

Think Like a Social Psychologist

Making Connections
—Szczurek, Monin, and Gross (2012) found that people whose facial expressions are very unexpected (for example, smiles in response to a revolting image or a tragic scene, or frowns in response to a situation one might expect to be heartwarming) are usually disliked by others. How might you explain this finding in terms of some of the theories of attribution described in this chapter?

Thinking Critically
—People don't lose interest in all the activities they are rewarded for. What might be some of the limitations on the overjustification effect?
—Under what circumstances might people's thinking be as careful and rational as suggested by the naive scientist model? Under what circumstances might it not be?

THE COGNITIVE MISER

Cheryl Gets Derailed

Although Cheryl was sure that she was the best person for the student worker position in the OT department, as the days passed she became less and less certain that her qualifications would make any difference. She did not like what she was hearing from one of her contacts in the department. Apparently, after her pratfall and mildly profane outburst in the hallway, one of the professors had joked about the "drunken sailor" who had applied for the job. Cheryl had also discovered that another applicant was related to a friend of the department chairperson's husband. Finally, Cheryl had just seen the latest edition of the campus newspaper. Prominently featured on the front page (and the paper's website) was a color photo of the recent campus demonstration—and in the center of that photo was Cheryl, the only well-dressed person in a sea of T-shirts and cargo shorts. Cheryl wasn't sure how a reputation as a campus activist—no matter how valid—would strike the OT department's faculty. Meanwhile, all of the other positions for jobs on campus were being filled.

Cheryl was probably right to worry about such things. Another perspective on how people make sense of others' behavior, called the **cognitive miser approach**, suggests that they are not always as fair, rational, and careful as the naive scientist approach assumes. Just as people typically are careful not to spend their money too freely, they also take pains not to expend too much mental energy. In other words, people are miserly with their cognitive resources and can be expected to take mental shortcuts, rather than base every judgment on a systematic analysis of all the information available to them.

The Primacy Effect

Arati and Dipali took a history class together. Over the course of the semester, the students wrote three essays; their final grades were based on their average essay scores. Arati's scores on the three essays were 90, 90, and 75; Dipali was given a score of 75 on the first essay, followed by two 90s. So both students averaged 85—good enough for an A- after the scores were curved. And both students asked the instructor for letters of recommendation. Considering only their test scores, it might seem obvious that the instructor should write equally positive letters for both students. Yet there are reasons to suspect that the letter written for Dipali might be less glowing than the one written for Arati.

Early on in the investigation of impression formation, researchers discovered that the order in which people receive social information has a lot to do with its impact. When Asch (1946) presented research participants with lists of traits and asked them to report how much they liked the people described by the traits, he found a **primacy effect**: the information that was presented first had more of an influence on participants' final impressions than other information. That is, if Person A and Person B were described by the same traits, but the first characteristic listed for Person A was "generous" and the first characteristic for Person B was "careless," participants would be more favorably disposed toward Person A. Because Dipali's first essay score was a less-than-impressive 75, then, her instructor might perceive her to be less intelligent than Arati, who began the semester with two 90s.

Primacy is among the most easily replicated effects in social psychology (Anderson & Barrios, 1961; Anderson & Hubert, 1963; Dreben, Fiske, & Hastie, 1979; Jones & Goethals, 1971). Indeed, the primacy effect was taken into account by linear combination models of impression formation. Trait adjectives (or other kinds of social information) that were presented earlier in a list were assigned larger weights than the others (Anderson, 1965b).

What explains the primacy effect? Several explanations have been proposed. One possibility is that people pay more attention to the information they come across first. Alternatively, they may actively discount or reject information about a person they encounter later if it conflicts with the impressions they formed earlier. Finally, the information people encounter first may change the meaning of later information (Asch, 1946), especially when that information is ambiguous. For instance, if you learn early on that a person is cheerful and

SPEED DATING

i've PREPARED THiS POWERPOINT PRESENTATION ABOUT MYSELF WHICH TAKES PRECiSELY THE ALLOTTED FIVE MiNUTES

First impressions matter.

outgoing, you might see the description "went skydiving" as evidence for the positive trait "adventuresome." However, if you learn early on that a person is "gloomy and depressed," you might evaluate the same fact (skydiving) negatively, as a "self-destructive" characteristic. Similarly, Dipali's initial mediocre essay could have affected how the instructor perceived her comments and questions in class throughout the semester (that is, the instructor might have perceived those comments and questions to be less thoughtful and intelligent than they actually were).

Which explanation is correct? The answer is that all of them are. The thought process that is most important depends on the nature of the information (for example, how ambiguous it is), the nature of the perceiver (for instance, how motivated you are to form an impression, and how much energy you need to devote to the process), the rate at which the information is presented, and a host of other factors. In short, the primacy effect is multi-determined (Jones & Goethals, 1971).

First impressions, then, do matter, unfair as that might seem. Cheryl had been wise to show up well dressed when she delivered her application. She was also lucky that her instructor, in listing Cheryl's most prominent attributes, had begun with "warm and friendly," leaving "quite ambitious" for the end. The term "ambitious" can sometimes have negative connotations—people are more likely to be described as "overambitious" than "over-warm." Had that trait come first in the sequence, it could have put a slightly negative spin on the rest of the traits. Unfortunately, when people in the OT department first caught sight of Cheryl, she was sailing through the air and cursing. No matter how objective and unbiased they were, research on the primacy effect suggests that they could not help but be affected by what they saw.

The Fundamental Attribution Error

In discussing the discounting principle, we noted that if the only information we had about a person was an essay in which she had argued for a position that was *assigned* by a professor, inferring anything about that person's true attitudes would be unreasonable. Similarly, reaching an unflattering conclusion about Cheryl's grace and coordination based on the fall she took in the hallway would be unreasonable. After all, there was no way she could have known that the floor was slippery—and she was wearing heels. Yet decades of research shows that when people form impressions, they do not carefully follow the rules described by early attribution theories. Most prominent among their biases is a tendency to jump to conclusions about people's characteristics based on their behavior, while ignoring situational pressures and other relevant factors. In fact, as one researcher (Jones, 1990, p. 138) puts it, "I have a candidate for the most robust and repeatable finding in social psychology: the tendency to see behavior as caused by the stable personal disposition of the actor when it can be just as easily explained as a natural response to more than adequate situational pressures." This tendency has become known as the **fundamental attribution error** (Ross, 1977), or **correspondence bias** (Gilbert & Malone, 1995).

Some of the earliest evidence for the fundamental attribution error came from a study by Jones and Harris (1967), in which participants were presented with essays or speeches allegedly written by other participants. The topics included school segregation and Fidel Castro's government in Cuba. Half the time, participants were told that the people presenting the arguments were free to take any stand they wished; half the time they were told that the essayists and speakers had no choice in the matter. As predicted by Jones and Davis's theory, participants in the free-choice condition were more likely to believe that people's attitudes were consistent with the arguments they presented than were participants in the no-choice condition. In addition, participants saw the expression of unexpected positions (for example, a pro-Castro speech) as being more informative than expressions of common, socially desirable attitudes.

Another finding, though, was the most memorable one. In the no-choice condition, participants' guesses about people's true attitudes differed significantly between those who argued on opposite sides of an issue. In other words, participants reported believing that the people who wrote essays or speeches in favor of Castro and segregation were truly more pro-segregation and pro-Castro than the people who argued against Castro and segregation. Participants formed these beliefs, even though they knew the speakers were arguing for positions that had been randomly assigned to them. This attitude attribution method, which has been used in many other studies (for example, Miller, 1976; Reeder, Fletcher, & Furman, 1989; Skitka, Mullen, Griffin, Hutchinson, & Chamberlin, 2003), consistently supports the existence of the fundamental attribution error (for reviews of this research, see Gilbert, 1998b; Gilbert & Malone, 1995; Jones, 1979).

There are other ways of demonstrating the fundamental attribution error. Ross, Amabile, and Steinmetz (1979; also Skitka et al., 2003) asked pairs of subjects to participate in a mock quiz show. One member of the pair was randomly assigned to be the questioner; the other, to be the contestant. Questioners were asked to come up with their own difficult (but not impossible) questions for the contestants to answer. Needless to say, thinking up questions about things that you just happen to know, but most other people do not ("What is the second largest city in Bolivia?") is within anyone's capabilities. As you might expect, contestants fared poorly on the quiz. Clearly, this type of exercise is no way to make relative judgments about people's intelligence or knowledge. Yet when neutral observers were asked to rate the subjects, they reported believing that the questioner was more knowledgeable than the contestant. In doing so, they overlooked the role-conferred advantage of the questioner,

Table 3.4: Are arbitrarily assigned "questioners" seen as more knowledgeable than "contestants?" An example of the fundamental attribution error.

RATER	RATINGS OF THE QUESTIONER	RATINGS OF THE CONTESTANT
An observer	82.1	48.9
The contestant	66.8	41.3
The questioner	53.5	50.6

Ratings could range from 1 to 100, with lower numbers meaning "much worse than average" knowledge compared to the average Stanford University student, and higher numbers meaning "much better than average." Based on the results of Ross, Amabile, & Steinmetz (1979), Experiments 1 and 2.

Game show hosts may or may not be very intelligent or knowledgeable—but research on the fundamental attribution error suggests that we will probably perceive them that way (after all, they have all of the answers ...)

a situational variable. Contestants, too, committed the fundamental attribution error, although in this case, the questioners seemed able to avoid it (see **Table 3.4**).

To give just one more example, Snyder and Frankel (1976) asked participants to watch a silent videotape of a woman being interviewed. Some of the participants thought the topic of the interview was "politics"; some thought it was "sex." The woman displayed signs of anxiety during the interview, which would be perfectly understandable if she were talking about her sex life on camera. Nonetheless, participants not only thought she acted more anxiously during the alleged "sex" interview (despite the fact that the videotape was identical in the two conditions), they also rated her as being a more generally anxious person than when she was allegedly discussing politics. In doing so, they did not sufficiently consider the impact of the situation—another example of the fundamental attribution error.

In the studies just described, the situational pressures and constraints on people's behavior were imposed by experimenters. But what if you were imposing the constraints yourself—that is, what if you were essentially pushing people to behave in certain ways? Wouldn't you be aware of the difficulty of reaching conclusions about their attitudes and personalities under those circumstances? Not necessarily, according to research on the phenomenon of **perceiver-induced constraint** (Gilbert & Jones, 1986; Gilbert, Jones, & Pelham, 1987; Ginzel, Jones, & Swann, 1987). Gilbert and Jones (1986) asked participants to "interview" other students about their political opinions. We have placed quotation marks around the word "interview" because participants in one condition signaled (that is, induced) responders to provide a liberal response most of the time, while participants in the other condition signaled for conservative responses. Thus, the interviewers controlled both the situation and the interviewees' behavior. In addition, the experimenter had actually scripted the responses in advance, and all the participants were aware of that. Even under those conditions, the interviewers committed the fundamental attribution error: They reported believing that participants who provided predominantly conservative responses were truly more conservative (and less liberal) than those who provided predominantly liberal responses.

A startling real-world example of the effects (or more precisely, the lack of effects) of perceiver-induced constraint on judgment is described by the historian Pierre Darmon (1986). In 18th-century France, women could terminate their marriages by arguing that their husbands were impotent. Husbands were given the opportunity to refute the charges, but to do so, they were required to demonstrate their virility in front of a group of judges.

Needless to say, such circumstances were not likely to put the accused men "in the mood." However, the judges did not seem to be aware that their presence ensured the outcome they expected.

Just as people often overemphasize the importance of stable dispositions in *explaining* behavior, they often ignore the role of situational factors in *predicting* behavior. Although in general, brave people will be braver than cowardly people, if an escaped lion is loose in the yard, all bets are off. Similarly, Cheryl's stumble on a just-mopped floor should not lead to the expectation that she will be routinely tripping over chairs and walking into walls. Yet people have been shown to predict unreasonably high levels of cross-situational consistency in behavior. For example, participants expect the future behavior of brave or cowardly, introverted or extraverted, and generous or selfish people to be consistent with their traits, regardless of the situations in which they find themselves (Kunda & Nisbett, 1986; Newman, 1996; Nisbett, 1987). The further into the future the predicted behavior is, the hazier and more abstract situational pressures seem to be, and thus the more likely participants are to make simple trait-based predictions (Nussbaum, Trope, & Liberman, 2003).

The implications of this emphasis on personality traits as explanations and predictors of behavior are considerable. For example, the behavior of incarcerated prisoners, women in abusive relationships, and workers stuck in dead-end jobs can, to a great extent, be dictated by their objective circumstances. Yet because of the fundamental attribution error, we run the risk of mislabeling them as fundamentally "violent," "passive," and "lazy and unambitious." Research also suggests that students from universities with lenient grading policies—and who, as a result, tend to have high grades—are often evaluated more favorably than students from other institutions with stricter grading standards (Moore, Swift, Sharek, & Gino, 2010).

When learning about the fundamental attribution error and related biases, students often ask, "How could people be so dumb? How could human beings have survived as long as they have if they are such poor processors of social information?" In response, Ross and Nisbett (1991, p. 143) have argued that throughout evolutionary history, members of "hominid and human troops" interacted mostly with others they had known since birth in familiar situations they had experienced countless times before. There was little call for sophisticated ways of figuring out what people were like and what to expect from them. More complicated analyses of people's behavior based on limited information "probably did not become important until people began to trade and travel, and thus to meet individuals with unfamiliar behavior." From an evolutionary psychology perspective, then, the attributional biases that characterize modern-day humans are residues of an earlier mode of existence, in which relatively complicated psychological mechanisms simply were not necessary.

In sum, our notable lack of attention to situational factors can be a hidden influence on our interactions with others. Unfortunately, making people aware of the fundamental attribution error may not change matters. Even people who are aware of the tendency to overemphasize dispositional factors see themselves as being relatively immune to the bias (Van Boven, Kamada, White, & Gilovich, 2003). Thus, they lack the motivation to reexamine their own judgments. As a result, even if members of the occupational therapy department were to attend a lecture on the fundamental attribution error, and even if their attention were drawn to the fact that most people have trouble maintaining their footing on slippery floors and tend to make unpleasant remarks when they slip and fall on those floors, they might not modify their impressions of Cheryl.

Spontaneous Trait Inference

We have seen that in trying to make sense of what others say and do, people rely too heavily on stable personality traits. In fact, they often make trait inferences without even being aware they are doing so. Research on

spontaneous trait inference (Uleman, Newman, & Moskowitz, 1996)—that is, on the tendency of people to infer others' traits effortlessly, unintentionally, and without awareness—indicates that people infer traits from others' behavior more or less automatically.

Much of our behavior arises from the conscious desire and deliberate effort to accomplish something. In other words, much of our activity occurs because we intend to engage in it, are aware of it, and devote our energy to it. Compared to such **controlled processes**, **automatic processes** take place effortlessly, without intention or awareness. For instance, under normal conditions, experienced drivers can operate a vehicle without much conscious attention to the procedures involved (that is to say, without thinking to themselves "I am now going to press down on the brake with my right foot while reaching for the turn signal with my left hand and glancing at the dashboard to check that my lights are on"). Similarly, experienced typists can produce correctly spelled, coherent documents without thinking about what each finger is doing. As these examples indicate, automatized behaviors tend to be those that have been practiced extensively.

After extensive practice with a keyboard, typing can become automatized.

Just as behaviors can become automatic, so can mental activities (Andersen et al., 2007; Bargh, 1994, 1997; Bargh & Chartrand, 1999). Some of the processes we use to perceive, judge, and evaluate one another may occur automatically. Given how heavily people rely on trait concepts in forming impressions of others, a trait inference would seem to be the kind of well-practiced cognitive process that could eventually become automatic (Smith & Lerner, 1986). Still, how can we determine that people infer others' traits effortlessly, without intention or awareness? Obviously, we can't do so by asking research participants to think about what other people are like, because they would then be aware of what they were doing, and would be devoting effort to it. Nor can we learn about spontaneous trait inference by asking about it after the fact, because people won't be able to report reliably on processes of which they are not aware. Clearly, researchers need indirect methods, and a number of clever techniques have been developed.

If a person thinks about or attends to two different things at once, each of those things will serve as a recall cue for the other (that is, it will make it easier to recall the other thing). This relationship is known as the encoding specificity principle (Tulving & Thomson, 1973). Hence, if a person infers a trait after learning about a behavior—even if the inference takes place without conscious awareness—that trait should help the person to recall the behavior on which the inference was based. A number of researchers (e.g., Moskowitz, 1993; Winter & Uleman, 1984; Winter, Uleman, & Cuniff, 1985) have capitalized on this idea in their studies of spontaneous trait inference. Typically, they present participants with a series of behaviors (for example, "The plumber slips an extra $50 into his wife's purse") without asking them to form impressions of the people described. Rather, they simply ask participants to memorize the behaviors. Later, participants report being unaware of trying to figure out what the people were like. Nonetheless, researchers find that trait words (like "generous") are as effective or more effective than other cues in helping participants to recall the behaviors. These results suggest that participants were unconsciously extracting trait meaning from the behaviors—in other words, making trait judgments.

One limitation of this method is that even though it suggests that people spontaneously infer traits from *behaviors*, it does not provide compelling evidence for an inference that specific *people* have certain traits. One could conceivably decide that some action reflected aggression or generosity without focusing on who performed the action, and without inferring that a specific person is aggressive or generous. Another technique, called the relearning or savings effect method (Carlston & Skowronski, 1994; Carlston, Skowronski, & Sparks, 1995; Skowronski, Carlston, Mae, & Crawford, 1998), provides better evidence that spontaneous trait inferences are really inferences about people. In such studies, researchers present participants with descriptions of behaviors, along with photos of the people who engaged in the behaviors. Later, they ask participants to take part in a memory task in which they must learn to associate specific photos with specific traits. Typically, participants have an easier time memorizing a photo-trait pair (for example, a photo of a person, together with the word "cruel") if the person in the photo has already been shown behaving in a way that would suggest that trait ("I really hate animals ... I saw this puppy, so I kicked it out of the way"; Carlston & Skowronski, 1994, p. 844). In general, relearning material is easier than learning new material (Nelson, 1985), a phenomenon known as the savings effect (Ebbinghaus, 1964). The results of studies like this one suggest that in many cases, participants had already associated particular people with particular traits, even though they had not been asked to do so.

One drawback of the methods just described is that even though participants are not asked to form impressions or infer traits, doing so would be to their advantage. After all, inferring traits might help them remember sentences and learn photo-trait pairings. Could the results of those studies be explained, at least in part, by assuming that some participants intentionally and consciously thought about the trait meanings of behaviors?

The results of studies done using other techniques are harder to explain in this way, however. Newman (1991) and Uleman, Hon, Roman, and Moskowitz (1996) presented participants with sentences that sometimes strongly implied personality traits and then asked them to respond immediately to a "probe word." As quickly and accurately as possible (by pressing one of two buttons), participants had to indicate whether the probe word had appeared in the sentence. Although participants rarely made mistakes, the amount of time they took to respond depended on the type of probe word. Reaction times to trait words that had not been included in the sentences, but which *could have been inferred from them*, were particularly slow. It was as if participants had to overcome the sense that the trait word was familiar, because they had just unconsciously inferred it. A particular strength of this method is that if participants want to perform well on the task, intentionally inferring traits is *not* to their advantage. Doing so would only slow them down (see **Figure 3.2**).

This summary does not exhaust all the methods used to study spontaneous trait inferences (see Fiedler, Schenck, Watling, & Menges, 2005; Todorov & Uleman, 2003, 2004; Uleman et al., 1996; Van Duynslaeger, Sterken, Van Overwalle, & Verstraeten, 2008). Although each method has its limitations, collectively they suggest that people make trait inferences (as well as goal inferences—Hassin, Aarts, & Ferguson, 2005) without intention, awareness, or significant effort. Spontaneous trait inferences can serve as hidden influences on our behavior. Our interactions with others can indeed be affected by conclusions we reached about them without conscious awareness. In Cheryl's case, her potential employers in the OT department might not even be aware of the judgments they made about her when they first caught sight of her in the hallway.

The Dilution Effect

To this point, the biases we have covered have at least one thing in common: they come about because people do not sufficiently take into account the importance of certain pieces of information. In the case of order effects, people may not assign enough weight to the information they encountered later in a sequence of behaviors or

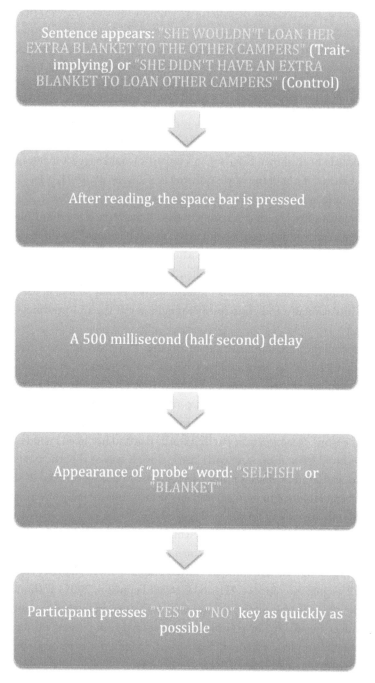

Figure 3.2: A method for studying spontaneous trait inferences: The participant's task was to report whether the "probe" word appeared in the sentence.

From Uleman et al. (1996). If participants spontaneously infer traits, it will take them longer to press "NO" in response to "SELFISH" after the trait-implying sentence.

traits. In the case of the fundamental attribution error and spontaneous trait inferences, they may not note the situation in which behavior took place. As we are about to see, however, people sometimes make suboptimal judgments because they pay *too much* attention to *irrelevant* information.

If you were asked to compare the probable grade point averages (GPAs) of two students, one who studies 31 hours a week and another who studies three hours a week, you would almost certainly predict that the former would have the higher GPA. If you then learned that the first student takes detailed notes in class, but the second does not, your confidence in your prediction would probably increase. Imagine now that you have learned that one of these students plays tennis a couple of times a month, and the other has a pet goldfish. Logically, that kind of information has no bearing on their academic performance; it is *nondiagnostic*. Nonetheless, when Nisbett, Zukier, and Lemley (1981) and Zukier (1982) exposed research participants to scenarios such as this one, the participants became more cautious in making predictions when they were given useless information. In our example, the addition of nondiagnostic information would probably lead you to predict a smaller difference in the two students' GPAs than you would otherwise. The tendency of non-diagnostic information to lead to more conservative judgments is known as the **dilution effect**.

What causes the dilution effect? According to Nisbett et al. (1981), when we try to judge whether a person is likely to have a particular attribute or to experience a particular outcome (such as a high or low GPA), we compare that person to our general beliefs about people with such characteristics. Irrelevant information (for example, "likes oranges") makes a person appear less similar to our abstract mental image of a specific kind of person (for instance, someone with good grades). The dilution effect is hard to eliminate. Encouraging people to be very careful about how they make judgments because they might have to justify them to others has been shown to decrease the kinds of bias that result from insufficient attention to certain pieces of information (such as the fundamental attribution error—see Tetlock, 1985). However, letting people know that they will be held accountable for their judgments actually *magnifies* the dilution effect (Tetlock & Boettger, 1989). When people are trying hard not to be biased, they can unintentionally take useless information too seriously.

Had Cheryl known about the dilution effect, she might have been less thrilled with the second letter of recommendation included with her application. Recall that the letter-writer began by summarizing all the fine qualities she believed Cheryl had. So far, so good. But in the rest of her letter, she listed all the projects Cheryl had worked on in her classes. That kind of information applied to all the students in her classes; it could not be used to predict how successful Cheryl might be as an assistant in the OT department. Thus, the problem is not only that the last paragraphs did not add much to the letter, but rather, they may have detracted from the letter's impact by diluting the effect of the opening paragraphs.

Priming and Concept Accessibility

As we have seen, our perceptions of others may be biased because of the way we do or do not take into account what we know about them and their behavior. Sometimes, though, our impressions may be biased by random events that have nothing to do with the people we are judging and evaluating.

Consider the participants in a classic study by Higgins, Rholes, and Jones (1977) that supposedly focused on color perception. Researchers asked them to identify colors as quickly as possible, while simultaneously holding certain words in memory. Next, researchers asked them to form an impression of a man named Donald (see **Table 3.5**), who was described as someone who (among other things) doggedly stuck to his goals and enjoyed participating in extreme sports. One group of participants tended to see Donald in negative terms—and why not? As they pointed out, he was stubborn and reckless. But participants in a second group formed a more favorable impression of Donald, seeing him as persistent and adventurous.

Table 3.5: Ambiguous descriptions of a person's behavior

Donald spent a great amount of his time in search of what he liked to call excitement. He had already climbed Mt. McKinley, shot the Colorado rapids in a kayak, driven in a demolition derby, and piloted a jet-powered boat—without knowing very much about boats. He had risked injury, and even death, a number of times. Now he was in search of new excitement. He was thinking perhaps he would do some skydiving or maybe cross the Atlantic in a sailboat. (**ADVENTUROUS OR RECKLESS?**)

By the way he acted, one could readily guess that Donald was well aware of his ability to do many things well. (**SELF-CONFIDENT OR CONCEITED?**)

Other than business engagements, Donald's contacts with people were rather limited. He felt he didn't really need to rely on anyone. (**INDEPENDENT OR ALOOF?**)

Once Donald made up his mind to do something, it was as good as done, no matter how long it might take or how difficult the going might be. Only rarely did he change his mind, even when it might well have been better if he had. (**PERSISTENT OR STUBBORN?**)

From Higgins, Rholes, & Jones (1977). Participants' interpretations of the ambiguous descriptions depended on what concepts had been primed and made more accessible.

Why this difference between the two groups' responses? The answer lies in the "memory words" that were presented to participants in the first part of the study. The first group was asked to hold in mind the trait words "stubborn" and "reckless"; the second group, to retain the trait words "persistent" and "adventurous." The different memory words apparently made different concepts cognitively **accessible** to the two groups—that is, they **primed** different concepts. When a concept is cognitively accessible—usually because it has been recently or frequently encountered—it will come to mind easily in the presence of a related person, place, or thing. In this study, when participants were presented with behavior that was ambiguous—in other words, open to more than one interpretation—they fell back on the relevant concepts that were most accessible to them. They did so, even though they did not see any relationship between the first and second parts of the experiment, and had mostly forgotten the words that had been used as trait primes.

Since then, a multitude of studies using these and other priming techniques have produced similar findings (for example, Srull & Wyer, 1979, 1980; for reviews of this research, see DeCoster & Claypool, 2004; Higgins, 1996; Higgins & King, 1981; Schwarz, Bless, Wanke, & Winkielman, 2003; Sedikides & Skowronski, 1991). When people are exposed to a concept that could be used to interpret someone's behavior such as a personality trait just before they encounter a behavior that might be related to that concept, the priming directly influences the way they construe the behavior, even when other interpretations are equally plausible. These effects are not restricted to written descriptions of behavior; they apply to videotaped and live behavior as well (James, 1987; Sinclair, Mark, & Shotland, 1987). (For an example of how *not* to demonstrate how priming affects the interpretation of live behavior, see the Think like a Social Psychologist box **below.**) Priming effects are found even when people are unaware of a potential relationship between the primes and their judgments, and even when they cannot consciously recall the primes. In fact, as we will see later, priming effects of the kind just described are *strongest* in such cases. Indeed, subliminal primes—primes presented so quickly that people cannot consciously

---

THINK LIKE A SOCIAL PSYCHOLOGIST: THE BLIND EXPERIMENTER

After reading about research on priming, a college instructor becomes intrigued by the idea that randomly encountered concepts can affect our impressions of others. She decides to see if she can demonstrate such effects in the classroom. Specifically, she tests the hypothesis that subtly primed traits can significantly affect the way students perceive her.

To do so, she arranges to visit two classes as a guest lecturer. In each class, she gives a brief lecture on human memory, one that she knows from experience is neither a guaranteed crowd pleaser nor exceedingly dull. In addition, she precedes each lecture with a brief "memory test." Most of the words she asks the students to memorize—common, emotionally neutral words like "chair" and "cloud"—are identical. But in the first class she adds unfavorable trait words like "boring" and "hostile," and in the second class she adds favorable trait words such as "interesting" and "warm." The instructor expects that the trait words will serve as primes, affecting how members of the two classes perceive her. At the end of the class, she asks the students to complete a brief questionnaire on her performance, and the results are as she expected. The first class rates her more negatively than the second one.

At first glance, this experiment would seem to be a clever demonstration of how our perceptions of others' behavior (especially when it is ambiguous) can be affected by concepts we have recently encountered, even randomly (Bruner, 1957; Higgins, 1996; Higgins, Rholes, & Jones, 1977). Why should we be cautious about reaching that conclusion, however? What was wrong with the way this study was conducted?

****

Who planned this study? The instructor. Who administered the bogus memory test, which was meant to prime certain concepts? The instructor. Who delivered the lecture that formed the basis for the two classes' impressions? The instructor. Who came up with the hypothesis—and who, we must assume, really wanted to confirm it? Once again, the instructor.

In Chapter 2, we learned about *experimenter expectancy effects*—the danger that experimenters may unintentionally influence research participants in such a way as to confirm a study's hypothesis (Rosenthal, 1966, 1967). Although experimenter expectancy effects can be very subtle, in this case they are easy to see. Because the instructor knew which condition each class was in, she could have subtly and unintentionally adjusted her behavior. She might have delivered the lecture in the first class (the one primed with words like "boring" and "hostile") in more of a monotone, smiling only rarely. In the second class, she might have been a bit more animated and cheerful. Thus, the results could have little or nothing to do with the priming. In general, the people who collect the data should be either ignorant of a study's hypothesis (that is, "blind" to it) or unaware of the condition subjects were assigned to, especially when they have a great deal of contact with the subjects in a study.

identify them—can be especially effective (e.g., Bargh & Pietromonaco, 1982; Bargh, Bond, Lombardi, & Tota, 1986).

Thus, primes are a hidden influence on our interactions with other people. Random events—not just those manipulated by an experimenter—can activate certain thoughts, which then go on to affect how we perceive and react to family, friends, and acquaintances. Priming effects are possible even when we are unaware of the primes. In fact, they can even play a role in spontaneous trait inferences (Newman & Uleman, 1990).

Finally, a wide range of positive or negative concepts can be primed all at once, as a function of changes in one's mood. When Erber (1991) asked participants to make judgments about people with both favorable and unfavorable attributes, participants who were in a bad mood were more likely to attend to and think about those people's negative qualities than participants who were in a good mood. In light of that finding, Cheryl might have worried if she knew that the members of the occupational therapy department who witnessed her pratfall and heard her shouting and cursing had just escaped a boring meeting. Their negative mood undoubtedly increased the chances that they would see her as coarse and graceless, rather than the victim of bad luck.

Salience Effects

In the summer of 1998, one of the authors of this book spent a good deal of time watching the World Cup soccer tournament. As a citizen of the United States, he was especially interested in the U.S. team, which did not perform well. After the team suffered a decisive defeat by Iran, he found himself ruminating over the loss, wondering what had gone wrong. Certain players, he thought, could have been put into the game to turn it around. Where, for example, was Alexi Lalas? He had played a prominent role in the 1994 tournament, when the team had been more successful. If only the coach had allowed him into the game, maybe it would have turned out differently.

The author who had these thoughts actually was not very knowledgeable about soccer. In fact, he had no real reason to believe that Alexi Lalas was any better than the players who had been selected for the game between the United States and Iran. Nor was he even certain that Lalas had been a key player in 1994. Why, then, focus on Lalas?

An individual who would be salient in most contexts.

Alexi Lalas may or may not have been one of the top 11 players in the United States in the 1990s, but he was certainly very tall, with bright red hair and a slightly satanic-looking beard. In short, on the soccer field and probably everywhere else, he stood out—that is, he was **salient**. Salient people are those who are conspicuous, prominent, or otherwise noticeable. As we will see, it would not have been surprising if the author had assigned undue importance to Lalas. That is how we react to salient people and other salient stimuli (Taylor & Fiske, 1978).

There are many reasons why a person might be salient (Fiske & Taylor, 1991). Someone might be especially salient to you because you have a reason to attend to him or her. For example, even on a crowded playground, your own child will be salient to you. In other cases, people may become salient because they behave in unusual ways that violate your expectations. For example, a passenger on a subway car who begins to loudly recite the Ten Commandments will become salient to other passengers. Obviously, such people are salient to you for good reasons. If you are a responsible person, your child should be salient to you, and if you are a wise person, you will be especially vigilant when people behave unpredictably.

In other cases, though, a person's salience is not so obviously related to your goals, needs, and interests. People can be salient simply because they are in some way novel or vivid. The only person in a room who is wearing bright colors can be salient; so can the only person with a nose ring, or the only Asian person in a class of European or European American students. Simply sitting at the head of the table or standing in the part of the room where the light is shining brightest can cause a person to become salient. In other words, people can become salient for reasons that are sometimes quite trivial.

Just as the reasons for being salient can be obvious, so can some of the consequences. Almost by definition, salient people will attract more attention than others. They are also likely to be remembered better than other people. Some other effects of salience are less obvious, however. The first of these hidden influences relates to causal attribution. Salient people, simply by virtue of their salience, seem to others to play a major role in causing the events that occur around them.

Taylor, Fiske, Close, Anderson, and Ruderman (1977) asked participants to listen to a pre-scripted tape of a group conversation. As each member of the group contributed to the discussion, the researchers projected a purported photograph of the person on the wall. To some participants, they showed a set of slides with only one black male. To others, they showed a different set of slides with only one white female. In yet another condition, the person who stood out was a white male. Then the researchers asked the participants to rate each of the members' influence in the group. Regardless of the group members' actual contributions to the discussion, the ones who were salient by virtue of their minority status were rated as more influential than the others in the group's deliberations. In general, visually salient people tend to receive undue credit for setting the tone of discussions, deciding on topics, and leading or guiding the conversation. In a real-world group, the implications of such "solo status"—the first woman to sit on the board of directors, the first Jew to become a partner in a law firm, the only black student in a class—are obvious. A person in such a situation might easily be perceived as having played a bigger role in the group's successes, and unfortunately, in its failures as well.

The tendency to attribute causality to whatever is salient has been used to explain a limitation on the fundamental attribution error. People's eagerness to attribute behavior to dispositional factors is much less pronounced when their *own* behavior is being explained. The attributions they give for their own

In 2007, British police officers ("Bobbies") began strapping video cameras (not shown here) to their hats and helmets so that any incidents in which they were involved could later be reviewed from their perspective. Research on salience suggests that such films would lead to exaggerated perceptions of the suspects' roles in provoking the incidents, and underestimates of the officers' roles.

actions are more likely to be situational. This phenomenon, known as the **actor-observer effect** (Jones & Nisbett, 1971; Nisbett, Caputo, Legant, & Maracek, 1972; but see Goldberg, 1981, and Malle, 2007 for dissenting views), could arise because of differences in what is salient when people explain their own versus others' behavior. For example, when you try to figure out why another person spoke to you in a grouchy tone of voice, you are likely to focus on him or her ("What a jerk"). But in wondering about your own actions, unless you are standing in front of a mirror, your surroundings will be what you see ("This hot, noisy room would put anyone in a bad mood"). The actor-observer effect is less apparent when people are explaining favorable or desirable behaviors. Not surprisingly, we are more likely to want to take credit for the wonderful things we do than for our mistakes. We will discuss such self-serving biases in more detail in Chapter 4.

Salience also affects the way a person is evaluated: it polarizes evaluations. Pleasant salient people are liked more than they would be otherwise, but unpleasant salient people are liked less. In one illustration of this general finding, Eisen and McArthur (1979) asked participants to watch a 20-minute film of a mock trial. The defendant was clearly guilty (he had stabbed someone with a fishing knife). The researcher showed two separate versions of the film. In one, the defendant appeared on camera for five minutes; in the other, he appeared on camera for ten minutes. Aside from the fact that the defendant was more visually salient in the latter condition, all the other information about his crime was identical. Nonetheless, participants who saw the version in which the defendant appeared for ten minutes formed a more negative impression of him than the other participants.

The exact causes of salience effects are not entirely clear. These effects are not simply a function of better memory for salient people. Instead, salience seems to have its effects while people are attending to and thinking about the conspicuous person (Fiske, Kenny, & Taylor, 1982). Either way, the hidden influences of salience on our judgments about other people are considerable. The author's overemphasis on the role of Alexi Lalas in the success or failure of the U.S. soccer team was undoubtedly rooted in Lalas's salience. In light of the research on salience, Cheryl's concern about appearing in the center of a widely distributed photograph of a campus disturbance—while dressed differently from everyone else, no less—was quite sensible. Anyone who was negatively disposed toward the demonstrators would probably be especially aggravated by the woman who appeared to be at the center of it all.

The Costs of Miserliness

One possible reaction to the evidence that people's social judgments are imperfect might be a shrug, along with the observation that "nobody's perfect." Our social judgments, however, are often not only sloppy, they seem deliberately sloppy, allowing us to see others as we want to see them. As a result, others might not see you as you really are, but as they want to see you. In addition, biased judgments can have long-term implications. Once we have reached a conclusion about some aspect of our social world—no matter how accurate or inaccurate it is—it can be difficult to change. Finally, unfair judgments about other people can take on a life of their own. As we will see, even when such judgments are poor reflections of reality, they can go on to *create* reality.

Not just lazy, but biased: Motivated person perception. Our review of biases and shortcuts in person perception does not present a flattering picture of the way people process information about one another. However, there would seem to be at least one saving grace. In our review of the research to this point, we assumed at least implicitly that when people make judgments about others, to the extent that they are motivated at all, they are motivated to be accurate. In other words, even if people sometimes reach incorrect conclusions about one another, they are at least trying to be objective, and not eager to make one inference versus another one.

That, however, is not always the case. Sometimes people have a reason to want to see each other in specific ways. Research shows that when that is the case, people have ways of reaching their desired conclusion without becoming aware that their reasoning is anything but fair and objective (Baumeister & Newman, 1994; Ditto & Lopez, 1992; Kruglanski, 1996; Kunda, 1990).

In a study conducted by Klein and Kunda (1992), for example, student participants were told that they would be paired with other students in a contest involving their knowledge of American history. Before the game started, they were allowed to see a sample of another contestant's answers on a similar quiz. Half the time participants were told that the other contestant would be their partner; half the time they were told that the other contestant would be their opponent. The researchers asked participants to rate the contestant's overall knowledge of American history. When the contestant was supposed to be a partner, participants rated him or her as very knowledgeable, and the questions that were posed were judged to be relatively difficult. When the contestant was supposed to be an opponent, however, participants rated him or her as less knowledgeable, and the questions as relatively easy. Apparently, participants wanted to believe that their partners would be more talented than their opponents, and that is what they concluded, even though they had no rational basis for that conclusion.

Other researchers have also found a tendency for people to reach the conclusions about others that they want to reach (Dunning, 1999, 2003; Murrie, Boccaccini, Guarnera & Rufino, 2013; Spencer, Fein, Zanna, & Olson, 2003). Dunning and Cohen (1992, Study 4) asked participants to evaluate the study habits and general studiousness of other students. Some of those hypothetical students studied quite a lot (for example, 36 hours a week); others spent much less time hitting the books (for instance, nine hours a week). Participants who were themselves very studious distinguished among students with different study habits when evaluating them, but participants who studied very little did not. The less studious participants were motivated to be generous in their evaluations of other students, to avoid feeling bad about themselves. (See **Figure 3.3**.)

People may reach desired conclusions by selectively employing all the mental shortcuts at the cognitive miser's disposal (Chaiken, Liberman, & Eagly, 1989). Nonetheless, when they make motivated inferences about others, they believe they are being evenhanded and unbiased (Newman, 1999). Thus, Cheryl was justly alarmed when she heard that one of the other applicants for the job she sought was related to a person who would play a key role in the hiring decision.

Biased conclusions persevere: Schemas and their functions. In many of the experiments we have reviewed, the targets of participants' judgments were strangers—indeed, they were usually hypothetical people. There is a good reason

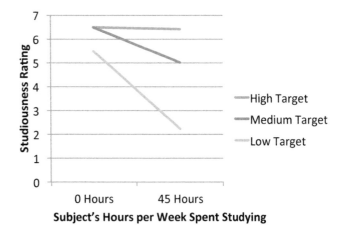

Figure 3.3: *Relationship between participants' own study habits (number of hours per week spent studying) and their judgments of a very studious (high target), moderately studious (medium target), and not very studious (low target) student.*

From Dunning & Cohen (1992). The more studious participants were (see right side of figure), the more they distinguished between the three students. Ratings were made on a seven-point scale, with higher ratings indicating more perceived studiousness.

for that. When experimenters control what research participants know about other people or eliminate prior knowledge entirely, they can see the effects of different experimental manipulations more clearly. Imagine that in the Higgins et al. (1977) study discussed on **page 83**, participants already knew "Donald" and had formed an impression of him. Detecting the effects of the trait primes that were meant to influence participants' interpretations of his behavior would have been more difficult. If you already believed that Donald was reckless, being primed with the word "adventurous" once or twice would not be likely to alter your perspective.

Obviously, we have ongoing relationships with many of the people about whom we make judgments. When we encounter them, we already know a great deal about their personal qualities and past behavior, and have formed expectations for what they are likely to do and say. In short, we have already stored *schemas* for these people in our memories (Augoustinos & Walker, 1995, Chapter 3; Carlston & Smith, 1996; Fiske & Taylor, 1991, Chapter 4; Moskowitz, 2005, Chapter 4; Smith, 1998; Taylor & Crocker, 1981). A **schema** is a mental structure that contains knowledge about a person, group, place, thing, or idea. Although psychologists have studied a wide range of schemas, including schemas for situations and events (Schank & Abelson, 1977), our focus here will be on person schemas. Later in this book we will discuss self-schemas (Chapter 4) and role schemas, especially stereotypes (Chapter 11).

A schema for a person (such as Cheryl) can contain any information about him or her that seems useful or has drawn our attention for some other reason. A person's physical appearance, hobbies, group memberships, relationships with others, and of course, gender and ethnicity (see Chapter 11) can all be contained in the schema we develop for him or her. Much social psychological research on person schemas has focused on the stable characteristics we infer about others, such as their traits and attitudes—which are themselves represented in memory as abstract schemas. Thus, forming an initial impression of a person often involves categorizing his or her behavior in terms of trait schemas. For example, deciding that a person is rude involves matching that person's behavior to the general schema for rude behavior (also known as a trait prototype; Cantor & Mischel, 1979).

Once formed, the schemas corresponding to specific people dominate our thinking about them. Schemas determine what we notice about someone, and in turn, what information we store in memory. If our predominant impression of a woman is that she is rude, we will be more attentive to her interpersonal behavior than we otherwise might be. But if the contents of our schema suggest that she is smart, behavior related to intelligence would be more likely to capture our attention. Schemas also affect what we remember about a person. Although not all the information we have about a person must be consistent with our schema, in most cases the consistent information will be easier to bring to mind (Hastie, 1981). In part, that is because we were probably more attentive to such details in the first place. However, such information can be easier to retrieve after the fact, simply because it is consistent with our expectations (Hirt, McDonald, & Markman, 1998). Thus, once we have convinced ourselves that a person is rude, we are more likely to remember the nasty, impolite remarks she has made than the times when she was considerate and thoughtful.

If by definition, schemas dictate what we expect from people, then it is not surprising that they also affect how we interpret people's behavior. Imagine witnessing an ambiguous behavior that could be interpreted as dishonest. Imagine, too, that you have already formed a schema about the person who is engaging in the behavior, and that your prior knowledge suggests dishonesty. In that case, the sight of him or her essentially primes the trait. In such cases, you are highly likely to interpret the behavior as being consistent with the trait of dishonesty (Reeder, 1993; Trope, 1986; Weisz & Jones, 1993).

The biased and even unfair conclusions we reach about people are incorporated into the schemas we use to remember and think about them. Still, our unfounded beliefs about people's personal qualities can potentially be refuted and corrected in future interactions with them. For example, even if the correspondence bias led you to infer that a classmate who stammered during a presentation was overly anxious (you neglected to take into account the presence of her overbearing parents), her behavior later in the semester may reveal that you were wrong. Unfortunately, once established, schemas resist change, even in the face of seemingly disconfirming evidence, a phenomenon known as the **perseverance effect** (Anderson, Lepper & Ross, 1980; Ross, Lepper, & Hubbard, 1975). Schemas are not completely impervious to change, of course (Weber & Crocker, 1983); beliefs can sometimes be revised. But faced with information that is inconsistent with our expectations, we can choose to ignore it, reinterpret it to fit our expectations, or actively refute it. These efforts can lead to stronger, more confidently held beliefs, even when the new information provides no real support for our expectations (Hill, Lewicki, Czyzewska, & Boss, 1989).

The effort that is involved in maintaining schemas explains a commonly reported finding that might at first seem to contradict this discussion of the effects of schemas on memory. When people are led to believe that a person has a particular personality trait (for example, friendliness) and are then presented with a series of the person's alleged behaviors, they are more likely to remember behaviors that were *inconsistent* with their expectations (unfriendly behaviors) than those that were consistent (Hastie & Kumar, 1979; Srull, 1981; Srull & Wyer, 1989). Why should that be so? Apparently, people attempt to reconcile the inconsistent behaviors with their schema for the person, and because they think more deeply about those behaviors, they find the inconsistent behaviors easier to recall (Bargh & Thein, 1985; Sherman & Hamilton, 1994). However, much of their extra thought involves explaining the unexpected behaviors away (Hastie, 1984). In fact, in these *person memory* studies, even when participants are best able to remember expectancy-violating information, their final impressions are typically consistent with their initial expectations (Hastie & Kumar, 1979).

Recently met this fellow? You were told that he was graceful? Research on person memory suggests that were he to stumble, that's what you would remember best about him—but paradoxically, you might still maintain your belief in his gracefulness.

Support for these findings comes from research using measures other than what participants can recall about people—for example, from research in which participants' brain activation in response to expectancy-violating and expectancy-consistent behaviors is measured. Data from such studies support the hypothesis that people allocate attention to the two types of behavior differently (Bartholow, Pearson, Gratton, & Fabiani, 2003; Van Duynslaeger, Van Overwalle, & Verstraeten, 2007).

What of the more intuitive generalization that we tend to remember those details about people and their behavior that are consistent with our expectations? That is indeed the case for well-established schemas. Once a schema has been well developed and is held with confidence, people seem to devote less mental energy to making all the available data about others' behaviors fit; they focus instead on consistent information (Stangor & McMillan, 1992; Stangor & Ruble, 1989). Only when schemas are "young" and developing (for

SOCIAL PSYCHOLOGY IN THE COURTROOM: EYEWITNESS IDENTIFICATION

Recognizing a person as someone you have encountered before is clearly a very basic aspect of person perception. Although that might seem so obvious that it is not even worth mentioning, it is far from a trivial matter. On an average day, an estimated 200 or more people in the United States become criminal defendants after being identified in a set of photos or a police lineup.

How accurate is this process? Research on identification memory, or the study of eyewitnesses' ability to identify the perpetrators of crimes, is voluminous (Brewer & Wells, 2011; Cutler & Penrod, 1995; Wells et al., 2000). Scholars have reached a consensus on quite a few issues, however (Kassin, Tubb, Hosch, & Memon, 2001). Several variables are reliably associated with the accuracy of eyewitness identifications. People who are stressed (as is often the case when a crime is taking place) are likely to be less accurate than others after the fact (Christianson, 1992). Cross-race identifications also tend to be less trustworthy than those made within one race (Bothwell, Brigham, & Malpass, 1989; Young, Hugenberg, Bernstein, & Sacco, 2012; but see Ackerman et al., 2006), a bias that begins to appear during the first year of life (Anzures, Quinn, Pascalis, Slater, Tanaka, & Lee, 2013; Kelly et al., 2007). And the presence of a deadly weapon seems (understandably) to distract people, drawing their attention away from perpetrators' faces. Later, they are less able than others to accurately identify the perpetrator (Kramer, Buckhout, & Eugenio, 1990; Loftus, Loftus, & Messo, 1987).

"Now take your time. And don't worry, they can't see you. This is a two-way mirror."

Improperly composed police line-ups can lead innocent people to be convicted of crimes.

Other studies have focused on the relationship between confidence and accuracy. When eyewitnesses report being very certain that they can identify a person, one should of course take them more seriously than people who report low levels of confidence. Nonetheless, research indicates that confidence does not always predict accuracy (Bothwell, Deffenbacher, & Brigham, 1987; Sporer, Penrod, Read, & Cutler, 1995). Some have argued that laboratory experiments underestimate the strength of the relationship between confidence and accuracy when people witness actual crimes (Lindsay, Read, & Sharma, 1998), but most students of the topic agree that law enforcement and judicial officials should be more careful in inferring accuracy from a witness's confidence (Wells et al., 2000).

Social psychologists and other researchers who have studied this topic have done more than document the potential pitfalls of eyewitness identification. They have also made some concrete suggestions for improving the way police lineups and other eyewitness identification procedures are conducted (Hasel & Kassin, 2009; Wells et al., 2000). For example, most police lineups include one suspect and a number of other people referred to as distractors, or "fillers." How should the fillers be selected? Luus and Wells (1991) have argued that they should appear similar to the witness's verbal description of the perpetrator (for example, "he was tall and had blue eyes"), but dissimilar to one another in other ways. If the fillers do not have the features and characteristics described by the witness, an eyewitness could easily identify an innocent suspect who just happens to have those features and characteristics. But if the fillers are similar to one another in other ways—for example, if they all wear work boots and have curly hair, even if those details were not part of the description—the witness's ability to correctly identify the perpetrator could be impaired.

In sum, perhaps the most basic person perception process involves determining the identity of the people one encounters. When those people might have been involved in a larceny, assault, or murder, it is a very important process indeed.

example, when you are just getting to know someone) do people focus carefully on inconsistent information and attempt to reconcile it with their expectations. But whether people ignore information that could change their schemas or try to minimize its importance, the end result is often the same. The workings of our minds lead us to resist changes to our schemas, even when their content is based on faulty inferences and questionable conclusions.

Biased inferences become realities: The self-fulfilling prophecy. The night after Cheryl dropped off her application, she had a nightmare. In it, she was called in for a job interview with a member of the occupational therapy department. As soon as Cheryl entered the professor's office, her backpack brushed against a delicate multicolored glass vase, knocking it to the floor and shattering it. To make matters worse, Cheryl tried to minimize the seriousness of the accident by pointing out how ugly the vase was. When she woke up, she laughed at the dream; surely she would not be so clumsy and rude if she were actually invited for an interview. Fortunately, Cheryl was unfamiliar with research on the **self-fulfilling prophecy**, which indicates that our beliefs about others can become a reality when we elicit from them the behavior we expect to see. That research suggests that Cheryl's nightmare was not so far-fetched, even though she was by no means a rude or clumsy person.

In a study that is now well known but still alarming in its implications, Rosenthal and Jacobson (1968) let some elementary school teachers know that certain students in their class had great potential. When those students—who in reality had been randomly selected—were tested eight months later using measures of achievement, they scored higher than their classmates. Even though the teachers' expectations were not grounded in reality, they became reality. Other studies of this phenomenon, also known as the "Pygmalion effect," have replicated Rosenthal and Jacobson's findings. When teachers expect more from students—even if there is no basis for their expectations—they actively nurture those students, calling on them more often, giving them more time to answer, and setting higher goals for them. Eventually, they turn the students into the high achievers they expect them to be (Rosenthal, 1973; Rosenthal & Harris, 1985).

The effects of the self-fulfilling prophecy are not restricted to academic achievement (Darley & Fazio, 1980; Miller & Turnbull, 1986; Snyder, 1984). Snyder, Tanke, and Berscheid (1977) asked male participants to have a get-acquainted telephone conversation with women they did not know. The only information each man had about the woman with whom he spoke was a photograph. Half the participants saw pictures of attractive women; half saw pictures of women who had been judged unattractive by other students. When other participants listened to tapes of the woman's side of the conversation, they formed less favorable impressions of the "unattractive" woman (who was in fact the same person as the "attractive" woman). Apparently, male participants who believed that the woman they were speaking to was unattractive subtly communicated their belief to her. As a result, she became less desirable in the way she presented herself.

In sum, if Cheryl's first appearance in the OT department had left people with the impression that she was awkward and impolite, their erroneous impression could have affected their later interactions with her, without their awareness. Their belief that she was rude could have caused them to be less than pleasant to her; if she were to respond with even mild annoyance, they could easily interpret her understandable reaction as evidence of *her* nasty disposition. Similarly, their expectation that Cheryl was clumsy could have led them to behave with exaggerated care around her. That behavior could make Cheryl self-conscious—a state of mind that can cause one to be less than graceful.

Shortcuts, Biases, and Heuristics: A Summary

Clearly, when people judge and evaluate one another, they do not act like scientists. To put it more precisely, they do not deal with the evidence that is available to them in the objective, impartial manner of a scientist. People put too much emphasis on the first pieces of information they encounter, and on misleading or unimportant details. They often pay little attention to situational information, inferring automatically that behaviors reflect traits. They focus on salient people even when those people are salient for trivial reasons, and they let irrelevant primed thoughts play a role in their judgments. And that is only a partial list of the many hidden influences (or sources of "mental contamination"; Wilson & Brekke, 1994) that affect our social judgments.

Overall, this research is consistent with a view of people as cognitive misers, a perspective on human judgment and decision making that was first clearly articulated by cognitive psychologists (Kahneman, Slovic, & Tevrsky, 1982; Tversky & Kahneman, 1974) who were interested in the "heuristics" (that is, shortcuts) people use to make complex decisions. Their view appealed to social psychologists, who were seeking to portray the way in which people think about one another. As summarized by Fiske and Taylor (1991, p. 13), "The idea is that people are limited in their capacity to process information, so they take shortcuts whenever they can … People adopt strategies that simplify complex problems; the strategies may not be normatively correct or produce normatively correct answers, but they emphasize efficiency" and "rapid adequate solutions, rather than slow accurate solutions." Thus, people behave like cognitive misers not because they want to make biased judgments or because they do not care whether their conclusions about others are unfair. They do so because they really have no choice; there is simply too much social information to process. People need to use mental shortcuts to free up some of their mental energy.

Needless to say, most people would prefer not to be the subject of a suboptimal judgment. They would prefer that people evaluate them accurately—or at least, avoid assigning negative characteristics to them erroneously. To have someone with power over us like a boss, supervisor, or instructor reach such conclusions about us would be even worse. Unfortunately, people with power over others (Guinote & Vescio, 2010) are especially prone to low-effort thinking and self-serving biases (Fiske, 1993; Keltner, Gruenfeld, & Anderson, 2003; Pettit & Sivanathan, 2012). This tendency is a classic example of the "social psychology of cognition" (see Chapter 1), or the potential for our social situations or relationships to affect the way in which we think and process information.

Overall, the social perception process is plagued with inaccuracy and unfairness. (For an opposing perspective, see Funder, 1987.) We should note that the early rational attribution models were, to a certain extent, meant to serve as "straw men." In other words, they were supposed to represent an unattainable ideal of perfection. The ways in which people's judgments departed from that ideal were supposed to serve as clues to the way person perception really worked. But the list of errors and biases that cloud our interpretation of one another's behavior is such a long one that it makes a mockery of the naive scientist metaphor. Most of those errors and biases occur without our awareness (that is, they are hidden influences), which may explain why we see ourselves as relatively immune to them (Pronin, Gilovich, & Ross, 2004).

Think Like a Social Psychologist

Understanding everyday behavior

—In writing their résumés, some people include every personal achievement or unique characteristic they can think of (like coming in second in the class spelling bee in junior high school). In light of the material covered in the cognitive miser section, what might be some of the pluses and minuses of that strategy?

—Imagine not being willing or able to use the shortcuts that cognitive misers use to make judgments. What difficulties would that pose for you?

Confronting social issues

—What are some of the implications of research on the fundamental attribution error, perceiver-induced constraint, and motivated perception for relations between two countries with a history of conflict? How could their relations deteriorate during times of crisis?

Designing research

—How might you adapt some of the methods used to detect spontaneous trait inferences to a study of spontaneous inferences about people's moods or emotional states?

SOCIAL PSYCHOLOGY ENCOUNTERS THE DARK SIDE: BIASED HYPOTHESIS TESTING

Person perception might seem to be a relatively passive process. To learn about other people's character-istics, we simply observe them and then use our observations to reach conclusions—conclusions that often prove faulty. Of course, we could play a more active role in gathering information about others. We could ask direct questions that might help to reveal a person's characteristics. Surely, with that much con-trol over the information-gathering process, we could make more valid trait inferences. Unfortunately, research reveals that during our social interactions, we test our hypotheses about others in a biased way.

In a series of studies described by Snyder (1981), researchers asked participants to test a hypothesis about another person. Usually, the hypothesis was that the person was either extraverted or introverted. To test the hypothesis, participants could choose from a series of questions. Some of those questions related to extraversion ("In what situations are you most talkative?"); some, to introversion ("What things do you dislike about loud parties?"). Other questions were relatively neutral ("What are your career goals?").

Snyder found that participants consistently used a confirmatory strategy in testing their hypotheses. That is, when testing for extraversion, they asked questions predominantly about extraverted behaviors; when testing for introversion, they asked questions predominantly about introverted behaviors. This strategy almost guaranteed that they would gather only hypothesis-confirming evidence. Furthermore, participants used this **confirmatory hypothesis-testing strategy** in a wide range of conditions, some of them despite their belief that the hypothesis was unlikely to be confirmed. Even participants who had a financial incentive to reach the most accurate conclusion possible tested their hypotheses in this way.

The consequences of a confirmatory hypothesis-testing strategy can be far reaching. When people use this strategy, they are likely to find spurious support for their initial hypotheses. That is, they are likely to infer that their first impressions were correct, even when they could easily have reached the opposite con-clusions. Such a line of questioning can also affect the interviewee's behavior. In a study by Fazio, Effrein, and Falender (1981), some research participants were asked a series of extraversion-relevant questions; others were asked a series of introversion-relevant questions. Not surprisingly, when other people listened to tapes of the interviews, they inferred that participants who had been asked extraversion-relevant ques-tions were indeed more extraverted than the other participants. And when confederates of the researcher interacted with participants for a few minutes after the interviews, in a different location, they found similar differences between the two groups of participants. In other words, the effects of the interview carried over to other situations. Finally, when the researchers asked participants to describe themselves just before the end of the experiment, they found that the experimental manipulations had affected the participants' self-concepts. Those who had been asked extraversion-relevant questions rated themselves as being more extraverted than those who had been asked introversion-relevant questions.

In sum, playing an active role in gathering information about people does not guarantee objectiv-ity and accuracy. When we think we know something about someone, the way we go about testing our hypothesis can guarantee that we will confirm it. If someone believes that you are a dull, hostile, or emotionally unstable person, he or she can set in motion a chain of events that predisposes you to behave in those ways.

THE MOTIVATED TACTICIAN

A Ray of Hope for Cheryl

Fortunately, all was not lost for Cheryl. Another perspective on person perception suggests a less careless approach to social judgments. Have you been thinking that even though your own judgments are not as thorough and effortful as the naive scientist's, they also cannot be as thoughtless as those of the cognitive miser? You are not alone. Chaiken et al. (1989) argue that people cannot fairly be labeled as lazy processors of social information; they simply "wish to satisfy their goal-related needs in the most efficient ways possible" (p. 220). To put it more simply, people prefer "satisficing"—making the best decision possible given their circumstances and limitations—to making the best decision that is humanly possible (Simon, 1976). They are not averse to doing some mental work, but would rather do only as much as necessary to achieve their goals.

What are those goals? Sometimes the goal is to reach the most accurate conclusion possible about what others are like. At other times, as we have seen, it is to reach a *particular* conclusion (Kruglanski, 1990). The **motivated tactician model** (Fiske & Taylor, 1991) embraces both these ideas. As motivated tacticians, people take different approaches to social judgments. How extensive and objective their approach will be depends on their goals and needs, as well as on how much time and energy they have for thinking. Sometimes people seek to be thorough and impartial; sometimes they seek to arrive at a particular conclusion. And sometimes they are motivated to make no more than a quick and dirty inference or decision (see **Table 3.6**).

To bring this perspective to life, we will revisit many of the processes the cognitive miser engages in. As we will see, most of them are neither as simple nor as inevitable as they seemed when we first encountered them.

Table 3.6: Three major approaches to person perception (and social thinking in general): A concise summary

THE NAIVE SCIENTIST MODEL

Assumes that people think about others and their behavior carefully, systematically, and objectively. Specifies what people should do if they are rational and take all available information into account in an unbiased way. Describes the way people think in some situations. People's departures from this idealized way of thinking provide clues about how they actually think.

THE COGNITIVE MISER MODEL

Acknowledges that people have limited motivation and ability to make complex social judgments based on a great deal of information. As a result, they take mental shortcuts. Assumes that most of the time, the imperfect and biased processes people actually use to think about each other will be good enough to yield useful information, though they can also lead to major errors and inaccuracies in judgment.

THE MOTIVATED TACTICIAN MODEL

Acknowledges that people can be both scientific and miserly in their thinking. Predicts that people's goals, motives, and abilities, both short-term and long-term, will determine the approach they take to person perception.

Based on Fiske & Taylor (1991).

The Fundamental Attribution Error and Spontaneous Trait Inference Revisited

Research on the fundamental attribution error and spontaneous trait inference may seem to imply that others will inevitably interpret what we say and do in terms of a stable underlying personality trait. In actuality, whether or not people conclude that a mangled sentence indicates a lack of intelligence or that a moment of irritability indicates long-term nastiness depends on a variety of factors. For example, experience with a particular situation and its effects on people can lead us to make less extreme personality inferences about people in those situations (Balcetis & Dunning, 2008). People's goals, immediate circumstances, and basic beliefs about human behavior also have significant effects on the kinds of inferences they make about others.

Motivational factors. Although the mental mechanisms that lead people to commit the fundamental attribution error are powerful, so are other processes. For instance, when people are held *accountable* for their judgments—when they believe they will have to explain or justify their conclusions to others—they are more likely to think carefully about situational factors, and less likely to commit the fundamental attribution error (Tetlock, 1985). In fact, a suspicious state of mind and worries about other people's motives seem to be enough to overcome the fundamental attribution error (Fein, 1996; Hilton, Fein, & Miller, 1993).

Cognitive load. We have described the fundamental attribution error as a mental shortcut. In general, people take shortcuts when they are in a hurry and do not have the luxury of taking the longer, scenic route to a judgment. So it is with the fundamental attribution error; it is most pronounced when, for whatever reason, people do not have the time or energy to mull over all the interesting situational constraints on others' behavior.

Crowded, noisy, distracting—just the kind of environment where we would expect cognitively loaded individuals to be prone to the correspondence bias.

This point was made in studies by Gilbert and his colleagues (Gilbert, 1989). In one study, they adapted the method developed by Snyder and Frankel (1976; see **page 78**): they asked participants to watch a silent videotape of an anxious-looking woman being interviewed. Half the participants thought the interview was about mundane, everyday topics; the other half thought it was about sensitive matters, like the woman's sexual fantasies. In addition, however, the researchers subjected half the participants to a *cognitive load* by asking them to rehearse some words for a memory test as they watched the tape. The researchers found that the cognitively loaded participants did not take notice of the situational information (the topics of the interview). Instead, they rated the woman as anxious, regardless of what she was supposed to be talking about. In contrast, those participants who were able to focus all their attention on the videotape and the interview topics were less likely to ignore the situation and thus less likely to commit the fundamental attribution error (see **Figure 3.4**).

Gilbert and his colleagues based another study on the procedure developed by Jones and Harris (1967; see **page 77**).

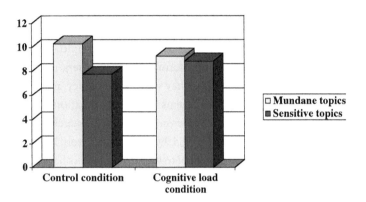

Figure 3.4: Ratings of a woman's anxiety as a function of the topics she discussed and participants' cognitive load.

Based on the results of Gilbert, Pelham, & Krull (1988), Experiment 1. Ratings were made on 13-point scales, where higher numbers mean more dispositional anxiety. Only those participants not dealing with a cognitive load seemed to take the woman's predicament into account.

Participants listened to speeches delivered by other students, some of whom had been forced to argue a particular position. Again, the researchers taxed the mental energy of some of the participants by telling half of them that they themselves would soon have to deliver a speech. Only those participants who were distracted by thoughts of their upcoming performance committed the fundamental attribution error. In guessing the speechmakers' true attitudes, these participants took their words at face value, regardless of the circumstances under which the speeches were written and delivered. (Both studies are described in detail by Gilbert, Pelham, & Krull, 1988.)

These findings and other similar ones led Gilbert (1989, 1998b) to propose a general model of trait inference that could explain the fundamental attribution error (see **Figure 3.5**). According to this model, when we observe others' behavior, we first categorize the behavior in terms of its general meaning ("That was generous")

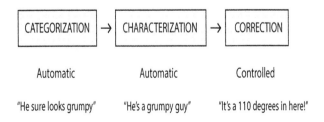

Figure 3.5: A model of the dispositional inference process.

Based on Gilbert (1989, 1998a) and Gilbert, Pelham, & Krull (1988)

and then use that categorization to characterize the person ("He's a generous person"). Both these steps are automatic. The final step, however, takes place only if we have the desire and ability to go further and correct for the situation ("Wait a minute, the person he lent money to was his boss"). Because this last step requires motivation and mental energy (and time—Burger, 1991), we often skip it. If our everyday social interactions are fast-paced and take place in a complicated, stimulus-packed environment, we can predict that the fundamental attribution error will be a common part of our everyday lives.

Gilbert's (1989) model indicates that people seek out certain kinds of information when they first observe someone's behavior; then, they either stick with their initial impression or revise it. In the studies we have reviewed up to now, people have sought information about others' personalities, but were not instructed to think about the meanings of *situations*. What if they were? Would they automatically categorize and characterize the context in which a behavior took place ("Seems like a scary situation"), ignoring information about the person's traits ("But then again, she's always been a nervous wreck")? Research shows that is exactly what happens. Krull and his colleagues (Krull, 1993; Krull & Dill, 1996; Krull & Erikson, 1995) found that in some cases, people can overattribute behavior to the *situation* instead of to traits. Researchers have also found that just as people can make spontaneous trait inferences, they can make spontaneous inferences about situations, without intention, awareness, or the conscious devotion of energy to the process (Ham & Vonk, 2003; Lupfer, Clark, & Hutcherson, 1990).

The idea that perceiving people involves a combination of quick, automatic processes and more effortful and controlled (and optional) cognitive procedures has received compelling support from neuroscientific investigations. Lieberman, Gaunt, Gilbert, and Trope (2002) have described two neurological systems underlying social inference. The first, called the reflexive, or "X," system, involves the lateral temporal cortex, amygdala, and basal ganglia. The neuroanatomy of the second one, called the reflective, or "C," system, is quite different, involving the anterior cingulate, prefrontal cortex, and hippocampus.

The X-system, which humans share with other animals, operates continuously, and corresponds to what we experience as our stream of consciousness. It categorizes people, situations, and objects through a simple pattern-matching procedure. In fact, part of the temporal cortex seems to specialize in identifying behavior in terms of people's intentions. The X-system corresponds more or less to the categorization and characterization phases of Gilbert's (1989) model (see **Figure 3.5**).

The C-system, on the other hand, is the "system that allows us to have the thoughts that dogs cannot" (Lieberman et al., 2002, p. 219). In other words, it controls logical, abstract thinking. The C-system is activated only under special circumstances, such as when the X-system confronts a difficult problem in person perception. For example, the X-system can associate someone's fidgeting, sweating, and darting eyes with anxiety. But if it also detects the presence of a poisonous snake, it will alert the C-system to the need for careful causal analysis of what is going on. The C-system's functioning, unlike that of the X-system, can be disrupted by cognitive load. The "correction" phase of Gilbert's (1989) model matches the C-system quite nicely.

Cultural differences. As we saw in Chapter 1, the fundamental attribution error, like many experimental findings in social psychology, has been documented primarily in North America and western Europe. Does it occur in other parts of the world? Some research suggests that it does. Krull et al. (1999) conducted an attitude attribution study with Chinese participants, and the results replicated other findings (Jones & Harris, 1967). Participants who had been asked to figure out what other people really believed overemphasized dispositional causes for behavior, even in the presence of situational pressures to express specific opinions.

Such studies do not answer the more basic question, however: Do people the world over really focus automatically on others' stable personality traits? When we instruct participants to focus on others' dispositional qualities, as in the Krull et al. (1999) study (and most studies of the fundamental attribution error), we cannot tell what kinds of social inferences they might make spontaneously. To answer this larger question, researchers have conducted several cross-cultural investigations of the causal attributions people make when they are free to make social inferences more naturally. Most of the studies have focused on the differences between individualist and collectivist cultures (Markus & Kitayama, 1991; Triandis, 1995). As we saw in Chapter 1, people in individualist cultures (such as North America and western and northern Europe) see others as independent social beings who are responsible for and control their own behavior. Individualists also emphasize the extent to which people are driven by their own goals, rather than those of their family, community, and nation. Collectivists—people who live in Asia, Africa, Latin America, and eastern Europe—tend to define others in terms of their membership in groups. From a collectivist perspective, behavior does not take place in a social vacuum, but in the context of relationships with other people.

Cross-cultural studies of social inference have yielded fairly consistent findings. People from Asian countries and other collectivist cultures are more likely than people from individualist cultures to explain others' behavior in terms of contextual factors (Lee, Hallahan, & Herzog, 1996; Miller, 1984; Morris & Peng, 1994; Valchev, van de Vijver, Nel, Rothmann, & Meiring, 2013; see **Table 3.7**). In observing prosocial (that is, kind and helpful) and antisocial behavior, for example, Americans, Canadians, and British people offer explanations based on prosocial and

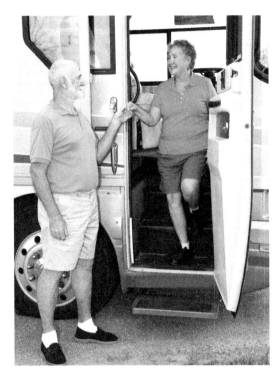

A polite person—or just someone doing what's expected in the situation he is in? People from individualistic and collectivistic cultures might interpret his behavior differently.

Table 3.7: Different causal biases in individualist and collectivist cultures: American and Chinese newspaper reporters explain a murder

AMERICAN EXPLANATIONS	CHINESE EXPLANATIONS
"very bad temper"	"isolation from Chinese community"
"sinister edge to (his) behavior well before the shootings"	"murder can be traced to the availability of guns"
"personal belief that guns were an important means to redress grievances"	"gunman had recently been fired"
"darkly disturbed man who drove himself to success and destruction"	"followed the example of a recent mass slaying in Texas"
"he had a short fuse"	"a victim of the 'Top Students Education Policy'"
"whatever went wrong was internal"	

From Morris & Peng (1994), Study 2. American explanations stressed traits, attitudes, and psychological problems. Chinese explanations stressed social pressures, aspects of society, and situational factors.

antisocial personality traits. Chinese, Koreans, and Indians are more likely to mention situational norms that call for different behaviors. Not surprisingly, people from collectivist cultures are also less likely than people from individualist cultures to overestimate *other* people's tendency to attribute behavior to dispositions (Van Boven, Kamada, & Gilovich, 1999).

Do these findings invalidate Gilbert's (1989) model? Not necessarily. There are at least three ways to adapt his approach to accommodate the cross-cultural data (see also Lieberman, Jarcho, & Obayashi, 2005). Krull (1993), for example, argued that people from individualist and collectivist cultures seek to extract a different kind of meaning from others' behavior. Individualists are interested in diagnosing what is unique about individual people, so they begin the inference process by categorizing the behavior and characterizing the person in terms of traits. Because correcting these initial inferences for situational factors is optional, their explanations of behavior tend to be dominated by personal dispositions. Collectivists, on the other hand, are interested in diagnosing *situations*, so they focus on the nature of the social situation in their automatic categorizations and characterizations. Accordingly, their explanations of behavior tend to be dominated by situational factors, even though they could take people's traits into account if they were motivated to do so.

There is some evidence to support this approach. Duff and Newman (1997) presented participants with ambiguous behaviors that could be understood in terms of either trait or dispositional factors. For example, in "The mailman avoids the big dog at the house on the corner," is the mailman fearful, or is the dog vicious? Using the cued-recall technique (Winter & Uleman, 1984; see **page 81**), they found that participants with individualist views were more likely to spontaneously infer traits. In contrast, people with collectivist views were more likely to infer situational factors. This finding was replicated by Na and Kitayama (2011), whose European American research participants were more likely to spontaneously infer traits than their Asian American participants.

A second approach to cross-cultural differences in person perception (Choi, Nisbett, & Norenzayan, 1999; Knowles, Morris, Chiu, & Hong, 2001; Norenzayan, Choi, & Nisbett, 2002) assumes that at first, people from all cultures categorize behavior and characterize people in terms of traits. People from collectivist cultures, however, might be more motivated to correct their inferences by taking situational factors into account (as in the third and last step in Gilbert's model), especially when those factors are salient. For example, Norenzayan et al. (2001) presented participants with a story about a man who shared money with someone else, but then was asked to share again. Unfortunately, at that point he had only enough money to pay his bus fare to an important meeting. European American participants consistently predicted that the man would still be likely to share. But when the situational constraints on him were made more obvious and salient—when the researchers asked participants to think about the likelihood that the average person would share in such circumstances—Korean participants (and only Korean participants) tempered their predictions by taking the nature of the situation into account. A cross-cultural study of the effects of perceiver-induced constraint—when participants themselves exert situational pressure on others (see **p. 80**)—produced similar findings. Japanese participants were less likely than North Americans to conclude that people they had forced to express particular attitudes really held those attitudes (Masuda & Kitayama, 2004).

Finally, a third way to account for cross-cultural differences in attribution (Menon, Morris, Chiu, & Hong, 1999) suggests that collectivists are just as likely as people from individualist cultures to overattribute behavior to dispositions. The dispositions they infer, however, are characteristics of *groups* rather than individuals. Menon et al. (1999) asked participants to read stories about businesspeople who engaged in unethical and/or incompetent behavior. In the United States, participants made unfavorable attributions about the employee; in Asia, they were more likely to disparage the organization for which the person worked. Again, this cultural difference can be understood in terms of Gilbert's model (see **Figure 3.5**, **page 99**), simply by making different assumptions about the nature of the social actors or entities (individuals or groups) that people in different cultures prefer to categorize in the first step.

Which of these accounts is correct? All of them could be, if people from different cultures use different social inference strategies in different situations. Developing a deep understanding of cross-cultural differences in person perception is a complex endeavor that will occupy researchers for years to come. In part because of the recent explosion in cross-cultural research, the term *correspondence bias* is beginning to replace the term *fundamental attribution error* (Gilbert & Malone, 1995). Regardless of their cultural background, people are biased to draw *some* initial inference about what a person's behavior corresponds to. There may not be anything *fundamental* about the tendency to overemphasize a person's disposition in explaining another's behavior, however.

Priming Revisited: Assimilation and Contrast

At some time or another, most of us have made a clumsy remark that hurt someone's feelings. When that happens, we hope that person will interpret our blunder as nothing more than carelessness. But as we have seen, people's inferences about ambiguous behaviors can be affected by thoughts that just happen to be accessible to them at the time. If the target of our faux pas has recently been exposed to some rude, nasty behavior, our intentions may be misinterpreted. The results of the priming studies we reviewed earlier in the chapter suggest that in cases like these, people will **assimilate** our behavior to the concepts that are accessible to them (in this case, rudeness and nastiness) and evaluate it unfavorably.

Priming, however, does not always produce assimilation effects. For example, thinking about or being reminded of an abstract trait like "cruel" can affect people differently from exposure to an *exemplar* (or typical example) of cruelty, such as Attila the Hun. When people are primed with exemplars of certain traits, they are often *less* likely to infer the trait from others' behavior than they might have been otherwise. That is, exemplars can produce **contrast** effects (Herr, 1986). In cases like these, the primed exemplar serves as a standard of comparison that an ambiguous behavior is not likely to meet. Compared to overrunning Europe and putting tens of thousands of people to death, for instance, an insensitive remark doesn't seem so terrible.

People can prevent even abstract primed trait concepts from having a direct effect on their judgment. One key to experimentally demonstrating the assimilation effects of priming is keeping participants ignorant of the relationship between the priming procedure and the social judgments they are asked to make. For example, in the Higgins et al. (1977) study, researchers presented participants with trait words as part of what they described as a color identification experiment. Then, when they asked participants to interpret an ambiguous behavior, they described the task as a separate experiment. As we noted earlier in the chapter, subtle priming of this kind (especially subliminal priming) tends to produce assimilation effects.

However, when priming is more blatant—when it is clear to people that the priming task brings to mind thoughts that could affect their judgments—participants seem to correct for the effects of primes. For example, a researcher might blatantly prime participants by asking them to carefully attend to and memorize the words and concepts with which they are primed. In such circumstances, people will essentially counter the influence of the primes, which often produces a contrast effect (Lombardi, Higgins, & Bargh, 1987; Martin, Seta, & Crelia, 1990; Newman & Uleman, 1990; Strack, Schwarz, Bless, Kübler, & Wanke, 1993). In other words, when people are primed in an unsubtle way with concepts like "reckless" and "stubborn" and then asked to judge behavior that could be interpreted in those terms, they will bend over backward to avoid bias and to consider the possibility that the behavior could be seen more positively (perhaps as "adventurous" or "persistent").

The effects of accessibility on person perception and social judgment are complex and depend on a combination of many factors (DeCoster & Claypool, 2004; Higgins, 1996; Schwarz, Bless, Wanke, & Winkielman, 2003; Wegener & Petty, 1995). But clearly, both inside and outside the laboratory, motivated tacticians are not at the mercy of whatever thoughts their recent experiences have primed. In general, when people detect influences that could render their judgments less than fair and objective, they will try to control for them or nullify their influence (Wilson & Brekke, 1994). This is a theme we will encounter repeatedly in this book when discussing hidden influences on behavior and the ways in which people deal with them.

Limits on Motivated Person Perception

Though people have ways of drawing the conclusions they want to draw about others, there are limits on their ability to do so. People may want to believe that their friends and loved ones are wonderful and brilliant, and their enemies cruel and stupid. They may also want to believe that those conclusions are reasonable ones with which any objective person would agree (Baumeister & Newman, 1994; Ditto & Lopez, 1992; Newman, 1999). However, concluding that Saddam Hussein was a pacifist, that LeBron James is unathletic, or that Conan O'Brien is introverted is a feat most people cannot manage. Research has shown that biased inferences depend on the presence of at least some partially supportive information (Darley & Gross, 1983; Sanitioso, Kunda, & Fong, 1990). In sum, motivated tacticians may want to believe what they like to believe, but they also know when to give up and reach an alternative conclusion.

Schemas Can Change

Although schemas may stubbornly resist change, eventually many of them will respond to evidence that they are not adequate mirrors of reality. After all, schemas are supposed to be useful, functional indicators of what we can expect from other people. An invalid schema would be of limited value to us.

Consider the perseverance effect (Ross et al., 1975)—the tendency of schemas to persist and even resist disconfirming information (see **page 91**). Anderson (1982; Anderson & Sechler, 1986) altered participants' schemas about firefighters by convincing some of them that a preference for risk was positively associated with success in firefighting, and others that it was negatively associated with success. He then asked them to explain the relationship between the two variables. In addition, he asked half the participants for a hypothetical explanation of the *opposite* relationship (the one presented to the other group of participants). Later, the participants who had been asked to consider the opposite explanation were less prone than the others to perseverance effects (see also Lord, Lepper, & Preston, 1984). Sometimes, then, simply considering alternatives to a schema is enough to raise doubts about its validity.

At other times, people simply respond to the weight of the evidence when it clearly contradicts their expectations. If people have been led to believe that a specific person has a particular trait such as "friendliness," but his or her unfriendly behaviors vastly outnumber the friendly ones, they will eventually revise their impressions (Bargh & Thein, 1986; Helmsley & Marmurek, 1982).

Limits on Self-Fulfilling Prophecies

We should not underestimate the power of the self-fulfilling prophecy to shape people's behavior without their awareness. At the same time, we should not overestimate it. Sometimes our need or desire to form an accurate impression of others allows us to transcend our expectations and give people an opportunity to be themselves. Neuberg (1989) asked participants in his study to conduct mock job interviews with two candidates. One of the candidates, he led them to believe, might be unsuited for the job. Importantly, he urged half the interviewers to form as accurate an impression of each interviewee as they could. The accuracy-motivated interviewers managed not to let their expectations dictate their behavior. They gave the candidates for whom they had negative expectations more encouragement and more time to talk than the other interviewers; they also asked more questions that allowed interviewees to disconfirm their negative expectations (see **Figure 3.6**). Thus, people do not always act to confirm their expectations about other people.

Moreover, the targets of our expectations are not helpless. Just knowing that another person has unfavorable expectations about you can motivate you to disconfirm them (Hilton & Darley, 1985), especially if you believe those expectations are highly unwarranted (Gurwitz & Topol, 1978). That is not to say that targets can always force perceivers to revise their expectancies. Confrontations between people with clear, specific views of their own characteristics (for example, extraversion) and others who expect the opposite (for example, introversion) often result in stalemates (Major, Cozzarelli, Testa, & McFarlin, 1988). But the expectations of others need not always become self-fulfilling prophecies.

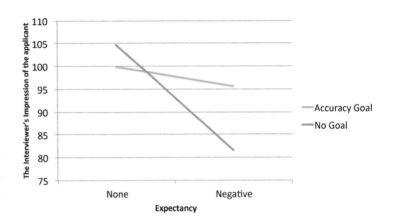

Figure 3.6: *Interviewers' negative expectations about job applicants are not likely to be confirmed when the interviewers are committed to the goal of forming accurate impressions.*

Interviewers had either no expectancies (left side of figure) or negative expectancies (right side), and accuracy goals or no goals. From Neuberg (1989); the scale ranges from 15 to 135. Interviewers with accuracy goals were much less affected by initial expectancies.

Finally, follow-up studies based on Rosenthal and Jacobson's (1968) research on the Pygmalion effect (see **page 94**) have shown that a child's performance in school is predicted more strongly by the child's ability level than by the teacher's expectations (Jussim, 1993; Jussim & Harber, 2005). That is comforting; needless to say, none of us would like to think that we can achieve only at the levels others have set for us based on their expectations. On the other hand, most of us would probably be disturbed to know that our performance at school or work is affected to *any* degree by others' expectations, rather than by our actual aptitude.

The Question of Accuracy Revisited

Given all the biases and errors that characterize person perception, we might conclude that our impressions of one another are completely untrustworthy, perhaps even random. Knowing that we are prone to order effects, the correspondence bias, salience and dilution effects, self-fulfilling prophecies, and other processes that distort our judgments, how could we ever hope to reach accurate conclusions about one another?

In the end, though, our impressions of one another are certainly not random (Human & Biesanz, 2013; Zaki & Ochsner, 2011). People typically show impressive levels of agreement in rating the same individual's personality, and their trait impressions can predict a wide range of behaviors (Funder, 1993, 2012; Kenny & West, 2010; McCrae & Costa, 1987). That is especially true when people are asked to rate how others behave in familiar settings, or when ratings involve traits that are important in the relationship between the person who is doing the rating and the person being rated (Gill & Swann, 2004). People can arrive at surprisingly accurate personality impressions from even very brief exposures to others and their behavior (Ambady, Bernieri, & Richeson, 2000; Hamamura & Li, 2012; Rule, Ambady, Adams, & Macrae, 2008; Borkenau, Brecke, Möttig, & Paelecke, 2009). One study even found that judgments of how powerful future managing partners of law firms appeared to be based on their photographs in their college yearbooks predicted how successful they were years later (as measured by the profits their law firms earned; Rule & Ambady, 2011).

Be warned, however: our judgments of others and our predictions of their behavior are not as accurate as we *believe* them to be (Dunning, Griffin, Milojkovic, & Ross, 1990). For example, judgments of others' trustworthiness based on their appearance tend to be highly inaccurate, even when there is a great deal of agreement about an individual's trustworthiness across judges (Rule, Krendl, Ivcevic, & Ambady, 2013) And while your acquaintances may agree to a certain extent about what you are like, their unique and possibly erroneous impressions of you could have important implications for your interactions with them.

At the very least, though, if you are a brilliant, outgoing person, people are unlikely to see you as dull and mousy. And at least one form of person perception, the interpretation of facial expressions, is associated with particularly high levels of agreement and accuracy, both within and across cultures. Ekman and Friesen (1971) found six emotional expressions to be universal: anger, disgust, fear, happiness, sadness, and surprise. More recent research has added other universal expressions such as pride (Tracy & Robins, 2004), and has also shown that people can reliably distinguish between facial expressions associated with anxiety and fear (Perkins,

Prototypical (and almost universally recognized) pride expressions.

Inchley-Mort, Pickering, Corr, & Burgess, 2012). And although display rules—that is, rules about which emotions should be expressed, to what extent, and in what circumstances—differ cross-culturally (Gudykunst, Ting-Toomey, & Nishida, 1996), throughout the world the basic emotions seem to be expressed and perceived in the same way (Ekman, Friesen, & Ellsworth, 1982).

Overcoming Bias: A Summary

Our review of the cognitive miser perspective may have left you pessimistic about your own and others' social perceptions and judgments. The research we reviewed in that section could be seen as a catalog of biases and hidden influences that consistently and inevitably worm their way into our interactions with one another. Yet several factors reduce the power of those biases. It may not be possible to eliminate all of them, but people can pick their battles and overcome them in certain circumstances. As a result, people are probably best characterized as motivated tacticians.

For example, people are sometimes motivated to be fair and accurate, because they believe the judgments they are making are important and consequential. In such cases, they can often avoid the unwarranted conclusions that mental shortcuts might lead them to. At other times, they are motivated not to let specific biases affect their judgments. Often, simply being aware of the possibility of such a bias is enough to inspire people to attempt to control for its effects. In both cases, being free from distractions and other demands on one's mental resources—that is, being free from cognitive overload—supports their efforts to correct for bias.

In addition, the cognitive miser's distorted perceptions and inaccurate judgments often go down to defeat in the face of reality. Making the dean's list four semesters in a row will probably lead someone to revise his or her unwarranted belief that you are not a very gifted student. People can even take an active role in helping to reshape the inaccurate impressions others have formed of them. Finally, recent cross-cultural research has made social psychologists wary of declaring any bias in social judgment to be inevitable and universal.

Think Like a Social Psychologist

Understanding everyday behavior

—To what extent do you think people are generally under "cognitive load" when they interact with one another in normal, everyday circumstances? What are the implications of that state of affairs for our interpersonal interactions?

—If you are a member of a culture that is considered collectivist (or if you have been exposed to such cultures), is the research on cultural differences in attribution consistent with your personal experiences? Can you think of other cultural differences in attribution that have not yet been studied?

—Can you think of a case in which another person's long-held beliefs about you changed significantly? If so, how did it happen? Does your experience have general implications for the way schemas change?

Designing research

—The ease with which a schema can change could also be related to how long ago a person developed the schema. Think about how you would design an experiment to test the hypothesis that a schema's resistance to change depends on how long ago it was established.

SOCIAL PSYCHOLOGY ENCOUNTERS THE BRIGHT SIDE: BIASED—BUT DIAGNOSTIC—HYPOTHESIS TESTING

Although people may not be perfect hypothesis testers, they aren't *that* bad at the task (Higgins & Bargh, 1987; Jussim, 1993). First of all, their interaction goals—their reasons for testing a hypothesis about another person—affect the way they solicit and interpret information. If they will be interacting with and depending on the other person in the future, they are more likely than usual to probe deeply, to see whether their initial expectations are correct (Darley, Fleming, Hilton, & Swann, 1985).

Second, you may also have noticed a curious aspect of much of the research on hypothesis testing. In most studies, participants must choose from a set of preconstructed questions that would be asked of people already known to have a specific trait. For example, to ask about introversion, participants would select a question such as "What factors make it hard for you to really open up to people?" When left to their own devices, however, people rarely ask such questions to test a hypothesis. Research by Trope and his colleagues reveals that instead, they are much more likely to ask "bi-directional" questions, such as "Do you prefer loud parties or quiet libraries?" and "open-ended" questions, such as "How do you like to spend your time on weekends?" Such questions give people more freedom to reveal who they really are (Trope, Bassok, & Alon, 1984). In general, people prefer diagnostic questions—that is to say, questions that allow them to differentiate between people who do and do not have a specific trait—to confirmatory questions (Sanbonmatsu, Posavac, Vanous, & Ho, 2005; Trope & Bassok, 1982).

We should not conclude, however, that there are no deficiencies in the way people test their hypotheses about one another. People tend not to ask questions to which a "yes" answer could definitively disconfirm a hypothesis (Trope & Thompson, 1997). For instance, if you suspect that a person is very liberal, you are unlikely to ask him if he contributes to a conservative political party; if you suspect that someone is introverted, you are unlikely to ask if she is always the life of the party. A reluctance to ask such questions is somewhat reasonable, of course. You have reason to believe that the answer will be "no," so you will not have learned anything useful if it is. After all, not every conservative person contributes to political parties, and even an extravert might not be the center of attention at every social gathering. Yet these are precisely the kinds of questions, if they elicit a "yes," that could convince you to abandon your hypothesis. Thus, people's hypothesis-testing strategies *are* slightly biased toward confirmation, though not as much as social psychologists once thought.

Finally, people who are on the receiving end of a set of hypothesis-confirming questions are not helpless to dispel others' incorrect beliefs. When they are certain about the trait that is the subject of the interrogation, they are capable of convincing others to abandon their incorrect hypotheses (Swann & Ely, 1984).

EPILOGUE: *JUSTICE FOR CHERYL*

On Cheryl's campus, the continuing controversy over the university's decision to let go of one of its most popular administrators had at least one beneficial effect. For a while, at least, all personnel decisions were made with extra care, and people involved in hiring decisions spent even more time and effort than usual reviewing applications. Because no one wanted to be the next person whose decision would be put under a microscope, no one could afford to be a cognitive miser.

The motivated tacticians on the hiring committee in the OT department were no exception. Of course, the fundamental attribution error and the salience, dilution, and order effects, together with other biases, may have played some role in their deliberations. But in the end, the committee members were able to function as intuitive scientists and correct at least partially for those and other hidden influences on their judgment. As a result, they were able to see that Cheryl was clearly more qualified than the competition. They offered her the job, and she accepted immediately.

Cheryl was as happy in her new job as she expected to be, and her employers were glad they had hired her. In fact, after a couple of months, she was promoted, and found herself supervising other student workers. She was less happy, though, with some of the students who were working under her. Although she had no evidence to back up her suspicions, she couldn't help but think that the tall guy with the green hair, one of many people who worked in the duplicating room, had something to do with the fact that the copy machine was always breaking down. Then there was that other employee who had slipped up and accidentally called her "Sharon" when they first met; Cheryl's negative impression of her had never really changed. Finally, there was the young woman who more often than not was in a grumpy mood. Why was that? And did she behave the same way at the other three jobs she was holding to pay for her tuition?

Clearly, in Cheryl's case and in our own, mere awareness of biases in person perception (in this case, salience effects, primacy effects, and the correspondence bias) is not enough to prevent us from falling victim to them. But with a bit of vigilance, we can keep these hidden influences on our social interactions more or less in check.

HIDDEN INFLUENCES IN PERSON PERCEPTION: A SUMMARY

Primacy effects: The first information we receive about people plays a larger role in our impressions of them than most people realize. First impressions count.

The fundamental attribution error (also called correspondence bias): Although people's behavior often tells us more about the situations they are in than the kind of people they are, we often fail to adequately take into account situational constraints when forming impressions of them.

Spontaneous trait inference: We can draw conclusions about people's personalities without effort, intention, or even awareness. Thus, our behavior toward them can be affected by inferences we do not know we have made.

Dilution effects: Not all the information we have about people is important for forming impressions of them. However, irrelevant information can cloud our judgments about people, making us less certain and more hesitant in our conclusions than we need to be.

Priming and accessibility: When we are simply exposed to (that is, primed with) specific concepts or ideas, they come to mind more easily than other thoughts, and can therefore play an exaggerated role in our judgments of people.

Salience: Our judgments about people who stand out from their surroundings tend to be more extreme than our judgments of others, even when people stand out for trivial reasons. We see salient people as having more of an impact on their surroundings than they actually do.

Actor-observer effects: We are more aware of the effects of situational pressure on our own behavior than on other people's behavior.

Self-fulfilling prophecies: Our beliefs and expectations about others can lead us—without our awareness—to treat them in ways that elicit the behavior we expect.

KEY TERMS AND DEFINITIONS

Person perception: the processes involved in figuring out the meaning of people's behavior and deciding what traits they have

Naive scientist model of person perception: an approach to person perception that assumes people make judgments by using all the information available to them in a logical way

Correspondent inference: the conclusion that someone's behavior directly reflects an underlying personality trait

Causal attribution: a judgment about the cause of a behavior or some other event

Pessimistic explanatory style: the tendency to infer that unpleasant experiences can be attributed to stable, internal, global causes

Discounting principle: a principle of causal attribution that predicts that in the presence of a plausible cause for an outcome, other potential causes will be assigned less importance

Overjustification effect: the finding that when people are rewarded for (or compelled to engage in) activities they already enjoy, their intrinsic motivation to engage in the activities declines

Augmentation principle: a principle of causal attribution that predicts that in the absence of a possible cause for an outcome, other potential causes will be assigned more importance

Impression formation: the processes involved in integrating information about a person to evaluate of that person—that is, deciding how likable he or she is

Linear combination model: an approach to understanding impression formation that assumes we assign a value to each piece of information about a person and then combine the values in a logical, consistent way

Cognitive miser model: an approach to person perception that assumes that people will devote as little mental energy as possible to making judgments about others

Primacy effect: the finding that information that appears earlier in a sequence is more influential than information that appears later

Fundamental attribution error (also called the correspondence bias): the tendency to make judgments about people without taking into account the situations in which they find themselves

Perceiver-induced constraint: constraints or pressure imposed on people by the very individuals who make judgments about them

Spontaneous trait inference: inferring traits effortlessly, unintentionally, and without awareness

Controlled process: a thought process that requires explicit effort and awareness

Automatic process: thinking or behavior that takes place without effort or conscious involvement

Dilution effect: the tendency of information that is of little value to lessen the impact of more useful information

Accessibility: the ease with which a thought or concept comes to mind or can be retrieved from memory; often boosted by priming

Priming: making a concept more accessible by exposing people to some representation of it (typically a word or picture)

Salience: the extent to which a person stands out from his or her surroundings

Actor-observer effect: the tendency of people to see others' behavior as being caused more by traits (and less by situational factors) than their own behavior

Schema: a mental structure that contains knowledge about a person, group, place, thing, or idea

Perseverance effect: the tendency for beliefs and schemas to persist despite disconfirming information

Self-fulfilling prophecy effect: the tendency for people's beliefs to become reality as they elicit from others the behavior they expect from them, without being aware of it

Confirmatory hypothesis-testing strategy: seeking to assess the validity of one's beliefs by looking only for evidence that supports those expectations

Motivated tactician model: a model of person perception that assumes that people adjust their approach to making social judgments depending on their goals, needs, preconceptions, and available mental resources

Assimilation effect: the tendency in some circumstances for people to interpret ambiguous behavior in a way that is consistent with the meaning of primed concepts

Contrast effect: the tendency of people in some circumstances to seemingly bend over backward *not* to allow primed concepts to affect their interpretation of ambiguous behavior

REFERENCES

Abramson, L. Y., Seligman, M. E. P., & Teasdale, J. D. (1978). Learned helplessness in humans: Critique and reformulation. *Journal of Abnormal Psychology, 87*, 49–74.

Ackerman, J. M., Shapiro, J. R., Neuberg, S. L., Kenrick, D. T., Becker, D. V., Griskevicius, V., Maner, J. K., & Schaller, M. (2006). They All Look the Same to Me (Unless They're Angry): From Out-Group Homogeneity to Out-Group Heterogeneity. *Psychological Science, 17*, 836–840.

Akin-Little, K., Eckert, T. L., Lovett, B. J., & Little, S. G. (2004). Extrinsic Reinforcement in the Classroom: Bribery or Best Practice. *School Psychology Review*, 33, 344–362.

Ambady, N., Bernieri, F. J., & Richeson, J. A. (2000). Toward a histology of social behavior: Judgmental accuracy from thin slices of the behavioral stream. In M. P. Zanna (Ed.), *Advances in Experimental Social Psychology* (Vol. 32, pp. 201–271). San Diego, CA: Academic Press.

Andersen, S. M., Moskowitz, G. B., Blair, I. V., & Nosek, B. (2007). Automatic thought. In E. T. Higgins & A. Kruglanski (Eds.), *Social Psychology: Handbook of Basic Principles* (pp. 138–175). New York: Guilford Press.

Anderson, C. A. (1982). Inoculation and counterexplanation: Debiasing techniques in the perseverance of social theories. *Social Cognition, 1*, 126–129.

Anderson, C. A. (1991). How people think about causes: Examination of the typical phenomenal organization of attributions for success and failure. *Social Cognition, 9*, 295–329.

Anderson, C. A., Lepper, M. R., & Ross, L. (1980). Perseverance of social theories: The role of explanation in the persistence of discredited information. *Journal of Personality and Social Psychology, 39*, 1037–1049.

Anderson, C. A., & Sechler, E. S. (1982). Effects of explanation and counterexplanation on the development and use of social theories. *Journal of Personality and Social Psychology, 50*, 24–34.

Anderson, N. H. (1965). Adding versus averaging as a stimulus combination rule in impression formation. *Journal of Experimental Psychology, 70,* 394–400.

Anderson, N. H. (1965). Primacy effects in personality impression formation using a generalized order effect paradigm. *Journal of Personality and Social Psychology, 2,* 1–9.

Anderson, N. H. (1968). Likableness ratings of 555 personality-trait words. *Journal of Personality and Social Psychology, 9,* 272–279.

Anderson, N. H. (1971). Two more test against change of meaning in adjective combinations. *Journal of Verbal Learning and Verbal Behavior, 10,* 75–85.

Anderson, N. H. (1974). Information integration: A brief survey. In D. H. Krantz, R. C. Atkinson, R. D. Luce, & P. Suppes (Eds.), *Contemporary Developments in Mathematical Psychology.* San Francisco: Freeman.

Anderson, N. H., & Barrios, A. A. (1961). Primacy effects in personality impression formation. *Journal of Abnormal and Social Psychology, 63,* 346–350.

Anderson, N. H., & Hubert, S. (1963). Effects of concomitant verbal recall on order effects in personality impression formation. *Journal of Verbal Learning and Verbal Behavior, 2,* 379–391.

Anzures, G., Quinn, P. C., Pascalis, O., Slater, A. M., Tanaka, J. W., & Lee, K. (2013). Developmental origins of the other-race effect. *Current Directions in Psychological Science, 22,* 173–178.

Asch, S. E. (1946). Forming impressions of personality. *Journal of Abnormal and Social Psychology, 41,* 1230–1240.

Asch, S. E., & Zukier, H. (1984). Thinking about persons. *Journal of Personality and Social Psychology, 46,* 1230–1240.

Augoustinos, M., & Walker, I. (1995). *Social cognition: An integrated introduction.* London, UK: Sage Publications.

Balcetis, E., & Dunning, D. A. (2008). A mile in moccasins: How situational experience diminishes dispositionism in social inference. *Personality and Social Psychology Bulletin, 34,* 102–114.

Bargh, J. A. (1994).The four horsemen of automaticity: Awareness, intention, efficiency, and control in social cognition. In R. S. Wyer Jr. & T. K. Srull (Eds.), *Handbook of Social Cognition* (vol. 1, 2nd ed., pp. 1–40). Hillsdale, NJ: Erlbaum.

Bargh, J. A. (1997). The automaticity of everyday life. In R. S. Wyer Jr. (Ed), *Advances in Social Cognition* (vol. 10, pp. 1–61). Mahwah, NJ: Erlbaum.

Bargh, J. A., Bond, R. N., Lombardi, W. J, & Tota, M. E. (1986). The additive nature of chronic and temporary sources of construct accessibility. *Journal of Personality and Social Psychology, 50,* 869–879.

Bargh, J. A., & Chartrand, T. L. (1999). The unbearable automaticity of being. *American Psychologist, 54,* 462–479.

Bargh, J. A., & Pietromonaco, P. (1982). Automatic information processing and social perception: The influence of trait information presented outside of conscious awareness on impression formation. *Journal of Personality and Social Psychology, 43,* 437–449.

Bargh, J. A., & Thein, R. D. (1985). Individual construct accessibility, person memory, and the recall-judgment link: The case of information overload. *Journal of Personality and Social Psychology, 49,* 1129–1146.

Bartholow, B. D., Pearson, M. A., Gratton, G., & Fabiani, M. (2003). Effects of alcohol on person perception: A social cognitive neuroscience approach. *Journal of Personality and Social Psychology, 85,* 627–638.

Baumeister, R. F., & Newman, L. S. (1994). Self-regulation of cognitive inference and decision processes. *Personality and Social Psychology Bulletin, 20,* 3–19.

Borkenau, P., Brecke, S., Möttig, C., & Paelecke, M. (2009). Extraversion is accurately perceived after a 50-ms exposure to a face. *Journal of Research in Personality, 43,* 703–706.

Bothwell, R. K., Brigham, J. C., & Malpass, R. S. (1989). Cross-racial identification. *Personality and Social Psychology Bulletin, 15,* 19–25.

Bothwell, R. K., Deffenbacher, K. A., & Brigham, J. C. (1987). Correlation of eyewitness accuracy and confidence: Optimality hypothesis revisited. *Journal of Applied Psychology, 72,* 691–695.

Brewer, N., & Wells, G. L. (2011). Eyewitness identification. *Current Directions in Psychological Science, 20,* 24–27.

Bruner, J. S. (1957). On perceptual readiness. *Psychological Review, 64,* 123–152.

Burger, J. M. (1991). Changes in attributions over time: The ephemeral attribution error. *Social Cognition, 9,* 182–193.

Cantor, N., & Mischel, W. (1979). Prototypes in person perception. In L. Berkowitz (Ed.), *Advances in Experimental Social Psychology* (Vol. 12, pp. 3–52). New York: Academic Press.

Carlston, D. E., & Skowronski, J. J. (1994). Savings in the relearning of trait information as evidence for spontaneous inference generation. *Journal of Personality and Social Psychology, 66,* 840–856.

Carlston, D. E., Skowronski, J. J., & Sparks, C. (1995). Savings in relearning: II. On the formation of behavior-based trait associations and inferences. *Journal of Personality and Social Psychology, 69,* 429–436.

Carlston, D. E., & Smith, E. R. (1996). Principles of mental representation. In E. T. Higgins and A. W. Kruglanski (Eds.), *Social Psychology: Handbook of Basic Principles* (pp. 184–210). New York: Guilford Publications.

Carver, C. S., & Scheier, M. F. (1991). Unresolved issues regarding the meaning and measurement of explanatory style. *Psychological Inquiry, 2,* 21–24.

Chaiken, S., Liberman, A., & Eagly, A. H. (1989). Heuristic and systematic information processing within and beyond the persuasion context. In J. S. Uleman & J. A. Bargh (Eds.), *Unintended Thought* (pp. 212–252). New York: Guilford Press.

Chernyak, N., & Kushnir, T. (2013). Giving preschoolers choice increases sharing behavior. *Psychological Science, 24,* 1971–1979.

Choi, I., Nisbett, R. E., & Norenzayan, A. (1999). Causal attribution across cultures: Variation and universality. *Psychological Bulletin, 125,* 47–63.

Christianson, S. A. (1992). Emotional stress and eyewitness memory: A critical review. *Psychological Bulletin, 112,* 284–309.

Cutler, B. L., & Penrod, S. D. (1995). *Mistaken identification: The eyewitness, psychology, and the law.* New York: Cambridge University Press.

Darley, J. M., & Fazio, R. H. (1980). Expectancy confirmation processes arising in the social interaction sequence. *American Psychologist, 35,* 867–881.

Darley, J. M., Fleming, J. H., Hilton, J. L., & Swann, W. B. Jr. (1988). Dispelling negative expectancies: The impact of inter-action goals and target characteristics on the expectancy confirmation process. *Journal of Experimental Social Psychology, 24,* 19–36.

Darley, J. M., & Gross, P. H. (1983). A hypothesis-confirming bias in labeling effects. *Journal of Personality and Social Psychology, 44,* 20–33.

Darmon, P. (1986). *Damning the innocent: A history of the persecution of the impotent in pre-revolutionary France.* New York: Viking Press.

Deci, E. L., & Ryan, R. M. (1985). *Intrinsic motivation and self-determination in human behavior.* New York: Plenum.

DeCoster, J., & Claypool, H. M. (2004). A meta-analysis of priming effects on impression formation supporting a general model of informational biases. *Personality and Social Psychology Review, 8,* 2–27.

Ditto, P. H., & Lopez, D. F. (1992). Motivated skepticism: Use of different decision criteria for preferred and nonpreferred conclusions. *Journal of Personality and Social Psychology, 63,* 568–584.

Dreben, E. K., Fiske, S. T., & Hastie, R. (1979). The independence of evaluative and item information: Impression and recall order effects in behavior-based impression formation. *Journal of Personality and Social Psychology, 37,* 1758–1768.

Duff, K. J., & Newman, L. S. (1997). Individual differences in the spontaneous construal of behavior: Idiocentrism and the automatization of the trait inference process. *Social Cognition, 15,* 217–241.

Dunning, D. (1999). A newer look: Motivated social cognition and the schematic representation of social concepts. *Psychological Inquiry, 10,* 1–11.

Dunning, D. (2003). The zealous self-affirmer: How and why the self lurks so pervasively behind social judgment. In S. J. Spencer, S. Fein, M. P. Zanna, & J. M. Olson (Eds.), *Motivated Social Perception: The Ontario Symposium* (vol. 9, pp. 45–72). Mahwah, NJ: Erlbaum.

Dunning, D., & Cohen, G. L. (1992). Egocentric definitions of traits and abilities in social judgment. *Journal of Personality and Social Psychology, 63,* 341–355.

Dunning, D., Griffin, D. W., Milojkovic, J. D., & Ross, L. (1990). The overconfidence effect in social prediction. *Journal of Personality and Social Psychology, 58,* 568–581.

Ebbinghaus, H. (1964). *Memory: A contribution to experimental psychology.* New York: Dover Publications. (Original work published 1885).

Eisen, S. V., & McArthur, L. Z. (1979). Evaluating and sentencing a defendant as a function of his salience and the observer's set. *Personality and Social Psychology Bulletin, 5,* 48–52.

Eisenberger, R., & Cameron, J. (1998). Rewards, intrinsic interest, and creativity. *American Psychologist, 53,* 676–679.

Eisenberger, R., Pierce, W. D., & Cameron, J. (1999). Effects of rewards on intrinsic motivation: Negative, neutral, and positive. *Psychological Bulletin, 125,* 677–691.

Ekman, P., & Friesen, W. V. (1971). Constants across culture in the face and emotion. *Journal of Personality and Social Psychology, 17,* 124–129.

Ekman, P., Friesen, W. V., & Ellsworth, P. (1982). What are the similarities and differences in facial behavior across cultures? In P. Ekman (Ed.), *Emotion in the Human Face* (pp. 128–143). Cambridge, UK: Cambridge University Press.

Erber, R. (1991). Affective and semantic priming: Effects of mood on category accessibility and inference. *Journal of Experimental Social Psychology, 27,* 480–498.

Fazio, R. H., Effrein, E. A., & Falender, V. J. (1981). Self-perceptions following social interaction. *Journal of Personality and Social Psychology, 41,* 232–242.

Fein, S. (1996). Effects of suspicion on attributional thinking and the correspondence bias. *Journal of Personality and Social Psychology, 70,* 1164–1182.

Fiedler, K., Schenck, W., Watling, M., & Menges, J. I. (2005). Priming trait inferences through pictures and moving pictures: The impact of open and closed mindsets. *Journal of Personality and Social Psychology, 88,* 229–244.

Fiske, S. T. (1993). Controlling other people: The impact of power on stereotyping. *American Psychologist, 48,* 621–628.

Fiske, S. T., Kenny, D. A., & Taylor, S. E. (1982). Structural models for the mediation of salience effects on attribution. *Journal of Experimental Social Psychology, 18,* 105–127.

Fiske, S. T., & Taylor, S. E. (1991). *Social cognition.* New York: McGraw Hill.

Försterling, F. (1989). Models of covariation and attribution: How do they relate to the analogy of analysis of variance? *Journal of Personality and Social Psychology, 57,* 615–625.

Funder, D. C. (1987). Errors and mistakes: Evaluating the accuracy of social judgment. *Psychological Bulletin, 101,* 75–90.

Funder, D. C. (1993). Judgments as data for personality and developmental psychology: Error versus accuracy. In D. C. Funder, R. D. Parke, C. Tomlinson-Keasey, & K. Widaman (Eds.), *Studying Lives through Time: Personality and Development* (pp. 121–146). Washington, DC: American Psychological Association.

Funder, D. C. (2012). Accurate personality judgment. *Current Directions in Psychological Science, 21,* 177–182.

Gilbert, D. T. (1989). Thinking lightly about others: Automatic components of the social inference process. In J. S. Uleman & J. A Bargh (Eds.), *Unintended Thought* (pp. 189–211). New York: Guilford Publications.

Gilbert, D. T. (1998a). Ordinary personology. In D. T. Gilbert, S. T. Fiske, & G. Lindzey (Eds.), *The Handbook of Social Psychology* (4th ed., Vol. 2, pp. 89–150). New York: McGraw Hill.

Gilbert, D. T. (1998b). Speeding with Ned: A personal view of the correspondence bias. In J. M. Darley & J. Cooper (Eds.), *Attribution and Social Interaction: The Legacy of Edward E. Jones*. Washington, DC: American Psychological Association.

Gilbert, D. T., & Jones, E. E. (1986). Perceiver-induced constraint: Interpretations of self-generated reality. *Journal of Personality and Social Psychology, 50,* 269–280.

Gilbert, D. T., Jones, E. E., & Pelham, B. W. (1986). Influence and inference: What the active perceiver overlooks. *Journal of Personality and Social Psychology, 52,* 861–870.

Gilbert, D. T., Pelham, B. W., & Krull, D. S. (1988). On cognitive busyness: When person perceivers meet persons perceived. *Journal of Personality and Social Psychology, 54,* 733–740.

Gilbert, D. T., & Malone, P. S. (1995). The correspondence bias. *Psychological Bulletin, 117,* 21–38.

Gill, M. J., & Swann, W. B. Jr. (2004). On what it means to know someone: A matter of pragmatics. *Journal of Personality and Social Psychology, 86,* 405–418.

Ginzel, L. E., Jones, E. E., & Swann, W. B. (1987). How "naïve" is the naïve attributor? Discounting and augmentation in attitude attribution. *Social Cognition, 5,* 108–130.

Goldberg, L. R. (1981). Unconfounding situational attributions from uncertain, neutral, and ambiguous ones: A psychometric analysis of descriptions of oneself and various types of others. *Journal of Personality and Social Psychology, 41,* 517–552.

Greenwald, A. G. (1992). New Look 3: Unconscious cognition reclaimed. *American Psychologist, 47,* 766–779.

Gudykunst, W. B., Ting-Toomey, S., & Nishida, T. (1996). *Communication in personal relationships across cultures.* Thousand Oaks, CA: Sage.

Guinote, A., & Vescio, T. (Eds.). (2010). *The social psychology of power.* New York: Guilford Press.

Gurwitz, S. B., & Topol, B. (1978). Determinants of confirming and disconfirming responses to negative social labels. *Journal of Experimental Social Psychology, 14,* 31–42.

Ham, J., & Vonk, R. (2003). Smart and easy: Co-occurring activation of spontaneous trait inferences and spontaneous situational inferences. *Journal of Experimental Social Psychology, 39,* 434–447.

Hamamura T., & Li, L. M. W. (2012). Discerning cultural identification from a thinly sliced behavioral sample. *Personality and Social Psychology Bulletin, 38,* 1697–1706.

Harris, M. J., & Rosenthal, R. (1985). Mediation of interpersonal expectancy effects: 31 meta-analyses. *Psychological Bulletin, 97,* 363–386.

Hasel, L. E., & Kassin, S. M. (2009). On the presumption of evidentiary independence: Can confessions corrupt eyewitness identifications? *Psychological Science, 20,* 122–126.

Hassin, R. R., Aarts, H., & Ferguson, M. J. (2005). Automatic goal inferences. *Journal of Experimental Social Psychology, 41,* 129–140.

Hassin, R. R., Uleman, J. S., & Bargh, J. A. (2005). *The new unconscious.* New York: Oxford University Press.

Hastie, R. (1981). Schematic principles in human memory. In E. T. Higgins, C. P. Herman, & M. P. Zanna (Eds.), *Social Cognition: The Ontario Symposium* (vol. 1, pp. 19–88). Hillsdale, NJ: Erlbaum.

Hastie, R. (1984). Causes and effects of causal attribution. *Journal of Personality and Social Psychology, 46,* 44–56.

Hastie, R., & Kumar, P. A. (1979). Person memory: Personality traits as organizing principles in memory for behavior. *Journal of Personality and Social Psychology, 37,* 25–38.

Hastie, R., Ostrom, T. M, Ebbesen, E. B., Wyer, R. S. Jr., Hamilton, D. L., & Carlston, D. E. (Eds.) (1980). *Person memory: The cognitive basis of social perception.* Hillsdale, NJ: Erlbaum.

Hazlewood, J. D., & Olson, J. M. (1986). Covariation information, causal reasoning, and interpersonal behavior. *Journal of Experimental Social Psychology, 22,* 276–291.

Heider, F. (1958). *The psychology of interpersonal relations.* New York: John Wiley & Sons.

Helmsley, G. D., & Marmurek, H. H. (1982). Person memory: The processing of consistent and inconsistent person information. *Personality and Social Psychology Bulletin, 8,* 433–438.

Herr, P. M. (1986). Consequence of priming: Judgment and behavior. *Journal of Personality and Social Psychology, 51,* 1106–1115.

Higgins, E. T. (1996). Knowledge activation: Accessibility, applicability, and salience. In E. T. Higgins & A. W. Kruglanski (Eds.), *Social Psychology: Handbook of Basic Principles* (pp. 133–168). New York: Guilford Press.

Higgins, E. T., & Bargh, J. A. (1987). Social cognition and social perception. In M. R. Rosenzweig & L. W. Porter (Eds.), *Annual Review of Psychology* (vol. 38). Palo Alto, CA: Annual Reviews, Inc.

Higgins, E. T., & King, G. (1981). Accessibility of social constructs: Information processing consequences of individual and contextual variability. In N. Cantor & J. Kihlstrom (Eds.), *Personality, Cognition, and Social Interaction* (pp. 69–121). Hillsdale, NJ: Erlbaum.

Higgins, E. T., Rholes, W. S., & Jones, C. R. (1977). Category accessibility and impression formation. *Journal of Experimental Social Psychology, 13,* 141–154.

Hill, T. Lewicki, P., Czyzewska, M., & Boss, A. (1989). Self-perpetuating development of encoding biases in person perception. *Journal of Personality and Social Psychology, 57,* 373–387.

Hilton, J. L., & Darley, J. M. (1985). Constructing other persons: A limit on the effect. *Journal of Experimental Social Psychology, 21,* 1–18.

Hilton, J. L., Fein, S., & Miller, D. T. (1993). Suspicion and dispositional inference. *Personality and Social Psychology Bulletin, 19,* 501–512.

Hirt, E., McDonald, H. E., & Markman, K. D. (1998). Expectancy effects in reconstructive memory: When the past is just what we expected. In S. Lynn & K. M. McConkey (Eds.), *Truth and Memory* (pp. 62–89). New York: Guilford Publications.

Human, L. J., & Biesanz, J. C. (2013). Targeting the good target: An integrative review of the characteristics and consequences of being accurately perceived. *Personality and Social Psychology Review, 17,* 248–272.

James, K. (1987). Priming and social categorizational factors: Impact on awareness of emergency situations. *Personality and Social Psychology Bulletin, 12,* 462–467.

Jones, E. E. (1979). The rocky road from acts to dispositions. *American Psychologist, 34,* 107–117.

Jones, E. E. (1990). *Interpersonal perception.* New York: Macmillan.

Jones, E. E., & Davis, K. E. (1965). From acts to dispositions: The attribution process in person perception. In L. Berkowitz (Ed.), *Advances in Experimental Social Psychology* (Vol. 2, pp. 219–266). New York: Academic Press.

Jones, E. E., Davis, K. E., & Gergen, K. J. (1961). Role playing variations and their informational value for person perception. *Journal of Abnormal and Social Psychology, 63,* 302–310.

Jones, E. E., & Goethals, G. R. (1971). Order effects in impression formation: Attribution context and the nature of the entity. In E. E. Jones, D. E. Kanouse, H. H. Kelley, R. E. Nisbett, S. Valins, & B. Weiner (Eds.), *Attribution: Perceiving the causes of behavior* (pp. 27–46). Morristown, NJ: General Learning Press.

Jones, E. E., & Harris, V. A. (1967). The attribution of attitudes. *Journal of Experimental Social Psychology, 3*, 1–24.

Jones, E. E., & McGillis, D. (1976). Correspondent inferences and the attribution cube: A comparative reappraisal. In J. H. Harvey, W. J. Ickes, & R. F. Kidd (Eds.), *New Directions in Attribution Research* (Vol. 1, pp. 389–420). Hillsdale, NJ: Erlbaum.

Jones, E. E., & Nisbett, R. E. (1971). The actor and the observer: Divergent perceptions of the causes of behavior. In E. E. Jones, D. E. Kanouse, H. H. Kelley, R. E. Nisbett, S. Valins, & B. Weiner (Eds.), *Attribution: Perceiving the causes of behavior* (pp. 79–94). Morristown, NJ: General Learning Press.

Jussim, L. (1993). Accuracy in interpersonal expectations: A reflection-construction analysis of current and classic research. *Journal of Personality, 61*, 637–668.

Jussim, L., & Harber, K. D. (2005). Teacher expectations and self-fulfilling prophecies: Knowns and unknowns, resolved and unresolved controversies. *Personality and Social Psychology Review, 9*, 131–155.

Kahneman, D., Slovic, P., & Tversky, A. (Eds.). (1982). *Judgment under uncertainty: Heuristics and biases.* New York: Cambridge University Press.

Kassin, S. M., Tubb, V. A., Hosch, H. M., & Memon, A. (2001). On the "general acceptance" of eyewitness testimony research: A new survey of the experts. *American Psychologist, 56*, 405–416.

Kelley, H. H. (1967). Attribution theory in social psychology. In D. Levine (Ed.), *Nebraska symposium on motivation* (Vol. 15). Lincoln: University of Nebraska Press.

Kelley, H. H. (1971a). Attribution in social interaction. In E. E. Jones, D. E. Kanouse, H. H. Kelley, R. E. Nisbett, S. Valins, & B. Weiner (Eds.), *Attribution: Perceiving the causes of behavior* (pp. 1–26). Morristown, NJ: General Learning Press.

Kelley, H. H. (1971b). Causal schemata and the attribution process. In E. E. Jones, D. E. Kanouse, H. H. Kelley, R. E. Nisbett, S. Valins, & B. Weiner (Eds.), *Attribution: Perceiving the causes of behavior* (pp. 151–174). Morristown, NJ: General Learning Press.

Kelley, H. H. (1973). The processes of causal attribution. *American Psychologist, 28*, 107–128.

Kelly, D. J., Quinn, P. C., Slater, A. M., Lee, K., Ge, L., & Pascalis, O. (2007). The other-race effect develops during infancy: Evidence of perceptual narrowing. *Psychological Science, 18*, 1084–1089.

Keltner, D., Gruenfeld, D. H., & Anderson, C. (2003). Power, approach, and inhibition. *Psychological Review, 110*, 265–284.

Kenny, D. A., & West, T. V. (2010). Similarity and agreement in self- and other perception: A meta-analysis. *Personality and Social Psychology Review, 14*, 196–213.

Kessler, R. C., McGonagle, K. A., Zhao, S., Nelson, C. B., Hughes, M., Eshleman, S., Wittchen, H. U., & Kendler, K. S. (1994). Lifetime and 12-month prevalence of DSM-III-R psychiatric disorders in the United States. *Archives of General Psychiatry, 51*, 8–19.

Kihlstrom, J. F. (September, 1987) The cognitive unconscious. *Science, 237*, 1445–1452.

Klein, W. M., & Kunda, Z. (1992). Motivated person perception: Constructing justifications for desired beliefs. *Journal of Experimental Social Psychology, 28*, 145–168.

Knowles, E. D., Morris, M. W., Chiu, C., & Hong, Y. (2001). Culture and the process of person perception: Evidence for automaticity among East Asians in correcting for situational influences on behavior. *Personality and Social Psychology Bulletin, 27*, 1344–1356.

Kramer, T. H., Buckhout, R., & Eugenio, P. (1990). Weapon focus, arousal, and eyewitness testimony. *Law and Human Behavior, 14*, 167–184.

Kruglanski, A. W. (1990). Motivations for judging and knowing: Implications for causal attribution. In E. T. Higgins & R. M. Sorrentino (Eds.), *Handbook of motivation and cognition: Foundations of social behavior* (Vol. 2, pp. 333–368). New York: Guilford Press.

Kruglanski, A. W. (1996). Motivated social cognition: Principles of the interface. In E. T. Higgins & A. W. Kruglanski (Eds.), *Social psychology: Handbook of basic principles* (pp. 493–520). New York: Guilford Press.

Krull, D. S. (1993). Does the grist change the mill? The effect of the perceiver's inferential goal on the process of social inference. *Personality and Social Psychology Bulletin, 19,* 340–348.

Krull, D. S., & Dill, J. C. (1996). On thinking first and responding fast: Flexibility in social inference processes. *Personality and Social Psychology Bulletin, 22,* 949–959.

Krull, D. S., & Erikson, D. J. (1995). On judging situations: The effortful process of taking dispositional information into account. *Social Cognition, 13,* 417–438.

Krull, D. S., Loy, M. H., Lin, J., Wang, C. F., Chen, S., & Zhao, X. (1999). The fundamental fundamental attribution error: Correspondence bias in individualist and collectivist cultures. *Personality and Social Psychology Bulletin, 25,* 1208–1219.

Kunda, Z. (1990). The case for motivated reasoning. *Psychological Bulletin, 108,* 480–498.

Kunda, Z., & Nisbett, R. E. (1986). The psychometrics of everyday life. *Cognitive Psychology, 18,* 195–224.

Lee, F., Hallahan, M., & Herzog, T. (1996). Explaining real-life events: How culture and domain shape attributions. *Personality and Social Psychology Bulletin, 22,* 732–741.

Lepper, M. R., & Greene, D. (Eds.) (1978). *The hidden costs of rewards.* Hillsdale, NJ: Erlbaum.

Lepper, M. R., Greene, D., & Nisbett, R. E. (1973). Undermining children's intrinsic interest with extrinsic rewards: A test of the "overjustification" hypothesis. *Journal of Personality and Social Psychology, 28,* 129–137.

Lieberman, M. D., Gaunt, R., Gilbert, D. T., & Trope, Y. (2002). Reflexion and reflection: A social-cognitive neuroscience approach to attributional inference. In M. P. Zanna (Ed.), *Advances in experimental social psychology* (Vol. 34, pp. 199–249). Elsevier Science.

Lieberman, M. D., Jarcho, J. M., & Obayashi, J. (2005). Attributional Inference Across Cultures: Similar Automatic Attributions and Different Controlled Corrections. *Personality and Social Psychology Bulletin, 31,* 889–901.

Lindsay, D. S., Read, J. D., & Sharma, K. (1998). Accuracy and confidence in person identification: The relationship is strong when the conditions vary widely. *Psychological Science, 9,* 215–218.

Lombardi, W. J., Higgins, E. T., & Bargh, J. A. (1987). The role of consciousness in priming effects on categorization: Assimilation versus contrast as a function of awareness of the priming task. *Personality and Social Psychology Bulletin, 13,* 411–429.

Lord, C. G., Lepper, M. R., & Preston, E. (1984). Considering the opposite: A corrective strategy for social judgment. *Journal of Personality and Social Psychology, 47,* 1231–1243.

Loftus, E. F., Loftus, G. R., & Messo, J. (1987). Some facts about "weapons focus." *Law and Human Behavior, 11,* 55–62.

Lupfer, M. B., Clark, L. F., & Hutcherson, H. W. (1990). Impact of context on spontaneous trait and situational inferences. *Journal of Personality and Social Psychology, 58,* 239–249.

Luus, C. A. E., & Wells, G. L. (1991). Eyewitness identification and the selection of distractors for lineups. *Law and Human Behavior, 15,* 43–57.

Macrae, C. N., & Quadflieg, S. (2010). Perceiving people. In S. T. Fiske, D. T. Gilbert, & G. Lindzey (Eds.), *The handbook of social psychology* (5th ed., Vol. 1, pp. 428–463). Hoboken, NJ: Wiley.

Major, B., Cozzarelli, C., Testa, M., & McFarlin, D. B. (1988). Self-verification versus expectancy confirmation in social interaction: The impact of self-focus. *Personality and Social Psychology Bulletin, 14,* 346–359.

Malle, B. F., & Holbrook, J. (2012). Is there a hierarchy of social inferences? The likelihood and speed of inferring intentionality, mind, and personality. *Journal of Personality and Social Psychology, 102*, 661–684.

Malle, B. F., Knobe, J. M., & Nelson, S. E. (2007). Actor-observer asymmetries in explanations of behavior: New answers to an old question. *Journal of Personality and Social Psychology, 93*, 491–514.

Markus, H. R., & Kitayama, S. (1991). Culture and the self: Implications for cognition, emotion, and motivation. *Psychological Review, 98*, 224–253.

Martin, L. L., Seta, J. J., & Crelia, R. (1990). Assimilation and contrast as a function of people's willingness and ability to expend effort in forming an impression. *Journal of Personality and Social Psychology, 59*, 27–37.

Masuda, T., & Kitayama, S. (2004). Perceiver-induced constraint and attitude attribution in Japan and the US: A case for the cultural dependence of the correspondence bias. *Journal of Experimental Social Psychology, 40*, 409–416.

McArthur, L. Z. (1972). The how and what of why: Some determinants and consequences of causal attribution. *Journal of Personality and Social Psychology, 22*, 171–193.

McCrae, R. R., & Costa, P. T. (1987). Validation of the five-factor model of personality across instruments and observers. *Journal of Personality and Social Psychology, 52*, 81–90.

Menon, T., Morris, M. W., Chiu, C.-Y., & Hong, Y.-Y. (1999). Culture and the construal of agency: Attribution to individual versus group dispositions. *Journal of Personality and Social Psychology, 76*, 701–717.

Metalsky, G. I., Joiner, T. E. Jr., Hardin, T. S., & Abramson, L. Y. (1993). Depressive reactions to failure in a naturalistic setting: A test of the hopelessness and self-esteem theories of depression. *Journal of Abnormal Psychology, 102*, 101–109.

Miller, A. G. (1976). Constraint and target effects in the attribution of attitudes. *Journal of Experimental Social Psychology, 12*, 325–229.

Miller, D. T., & Turnbull, W. (1986). Expectancies and interpersonal processes. In M. R. Rozenzweig & L. W. Porter (Eds.), *Annual Review of Psychology*, vol. 37. Palo Alto, CA: Annual Reviews.

Miller, J. G. (1984). Culture and the development of everyday social explanation. *Journal of Personality and Social Psychology, 46*, 961–978.

Moldin, S. O., Reich, T., & Rice, J. P. (1991). Current perspectives on the genetics of unipolar depression. *Behavioral Genetics, 21*, 211–242.

Moore, D. A., Swift, S. A., Sharek, Z. S., & Gino, F. (2010). Correspondence bias in performance evaluation: Why grade inflation works. *Personality and Social Psychology Bulletin, 36*, 843–852.

Morris, M. W., & Larrick, R. (1995). When one cause casts doubt on another: A normative analysis of discounting in causal attribution. *Psychological Review, 102*, 331–355.

Morris, M. W., & Peng, K. (1994). Culture and cause: American and Chinese attributions for social and physical events. *Journal of Personality and Social Psychology, 67*, 949–971.

Moskowitz, G. B. (1993). Individual differences in social categorization: The effects of personal need for structure on spontaneous trait inferences. *Journal of Personality and Social Psychology, 65*, 132–142.

Moskowitz, G. B. (2005). *Social cognition: Understanding self and others.* New York: Guilford Publications.

Murrie, D. C., Boccaccini, M. T., Guarnera, L. A., & Rufino, K. A. (2013). Are forensic experts biased by the side that retained them? *Psychological Science, 24*, 1889–1897.

Na, J., & Kitayama, S. (2011). Spontaneous trait inference is culture-specific: Behavioral and neural evidence. *Psychological Science, 22*, 1025–1032.

Neuberg, S. L. (1989). The goal of forming accurate impressions during social interaction: Attenuating the impact of negative expectancies. *Journal of Personality and Social Psychology, 56*, 374–386.

Newman, L. S. (1991). Why are traits inferred spontaneously? A developmental approach. *Social Cognition, 9*, 221–253.

Newman, L. S. (1996). Trait impressions as heuristics for predicting future behavior. *Personality and Social Psychology Bulletin, 22,* 395–411.

Newman, L. S. (1999). Motivated cognition and self-deception. *Psychological Inquiry, 10,* 59–63.

Newman, L. S. (2001). A cornerstone for the science of interpersonal behavior? Person perception and person memory, past, present, and future. In G. B. Moskowitz (Ed.), *Cognitive social psychology: The Princeton symposium on the legacy and future of social cognition.* Mahwah, NJ: Lawrence Erlbaum Associates.

Newman, L. S., & Uleman, J. S. (1990). Assimilation and contrast effects in spontaneous trait inference. *Personality and Social Psychology Bulletin, 16,* 224–240.

Nisbett, R. E. (1987). Lay personality theory: Its nature, origin, and utility. In N. E. Grunberg, R. E. Nisbett, J. Rodin, & J. E. Singer (Eds.), *A distinctive approach to psychological research: The influence of Stanley Schachter* (pp. 87–117). Hillsdale, NJ: Erlbaum.

Nisbett, R. E., Borgida, E., Crandall, R., & Reed, H. (1976). Popular induction: Information is not necessarily informative. In J. S. Carroll & J. W. Payne (Eds.), *Cognition and Social behavior* (pp. 113–134). Hillsdale, NJ: Erlbaum.

Nisbett, R. E., Caputo, C., Legant, P., & Maracek, J. (1972). Behavior as seen by the actor and as seen by the observer. *Journal of Personality and Social Psychology, 27,* 154–164.

Nisbett, R. E., Zukier, H., & Lemley, R. (1981). The dilution effect: Nondiagnostic information. *Cognitive Psychology, 13,* 248–277.

Norenzayan, A., Choi, I., & Nisbett, R. E. (2002). Cultural similarities and differences in social inference: Evidence from behavioral predictions and lay theories of behavior. *Personality and Social Psychology Bulletin, 28,* 109–120.

Nussbaum, S., Trope, Y., & Liberman, N. (2003). Creeping dispositionism: The temporal dynamics of behavior prediction. *Journal of Personality and Social Psychology, 84,* 485–497.

Orvis, B. R., Cunningham, J. D., & Kelley, H. H. (1975). A closer examination of causal inference: The roles of consensus, consistency, and distinctiveness information. *Journal of Personality and Social Psychology, 32,* 605–616.

Osgood, C., Suci, G. J., & Tannenbaum, P. H. (1957). *The measurement of meaning.* Urbana: University of Illinois Press.

Perkins, A. M., Inchley-Mort, S. L., Pickering, A. D., Corr, P. J., & Burgess, A. P. (2012). A facial expression for anxiety. *Journal of Personality and Social Psychology, 102,* 910–924.

Peterson, C., & Seligman, M. E. P. (1984). Causal explanations as a risk factor for depression: Theory and evidence. *Psychological Review, 91,* 347–374.

Pettit, N. C., & Sivanathan, N. (2012). The eyes and ears of status: How status colors perceptual judgment. *Personality and Social Psychology Bulletin, 38,* 570–582.

Pittman, T. S., & Heller, J. F. (1987). Social motivation. In M. R. Rozenzweig and L. W. Porter (Eds.), *Annual review of psychology* (Vol. 38, pp. 461–489). Palo Alto, CA: Annual Reviews, Inc.

Pretty, G. H., & Seligman, C. (1984). Affect and the overjustification effect. *Journal of Personality and Social Psychology, 46,* 1241–1253.

Pronin, E., Gilovich, T., & Ross, L. (2004). Objectivity in the eye of the beholder: Divergent perceptions of bias in self and others. *Psychological Review, 11,* 781–799.

Reeder, G. D. (1993). Trait-behavior relations and dispositional inference. *Personality and Social Psychology Bulletin, 19,* 586–593.

Reeder, G. D. (2009). Mindreading: Judgments about intentionality and motives in dispositional inference. *Psychological Inquiry, 20,* 1–18.

Reeder, G. D., Fletcher, G. J. O., & Furman, K. (1989). The role of observers' expectations in attitude attribution. *Journal of Experimental Social Psychology, 25,* 168–188.

Reeder, G. D., Vonk, R., Ronk, M. J., Ham, J., & Lawrence, M. (2004). Dispositional attribution: Multiple inferences about motive-related traits. *Journal of Personality and Social Psychology, 86,* 530–544.

Rosenthal, R. (1966). *Experimenter effects in behavior research.* New York: Appleton-Century-Crofts.

Rosenthal, R. (1967). Covert communication in the psychology experiment. *Psychological Bulletin, 67,* 356–367.

Rosenthal, R. (1973, September). The Pygmalion effect lives. *Psychology Today,* 17–23.

Rosenthal, R., & Jacobson, L. (1968). *Pygmalion in the classroom.* New York: Holt, Rhinehart, & Winston.

Ross, L. (1977). The intuitive psychologist and his shortcomings. In L. Berkowitz (Ed.), *Advances in experimental social psychology* (Vol. 10, pp. 173–220). San Diego, CA: Academic Press.

Ross, L., Amabile, T. M., & Steinmetz, J. L. (1979). Social roles, social control, and biases in social-perception processes. *Journal of Personality and Social Psychology, 35,* 485–494.

Ross, L., Lepper, M. R., & Hubbard, M. (1975). Perseverance in self-perception and social perception: Biased attributional processes in the debriefing paradigm. *Journal of Personality and Social Psychology, 32,* 880–892.

Ross, L., & Nisbett, R. E. (1991). *The person and the situation: Perspectives of social psychology.* New York: McGraw-Hill.

Rule, N. O., & Ambady, N. (2011). Judgments of power from college yearbook photos and later career success. *Social Psychological and Personality Science, 2,* 154–158.

Rule, N. O., Ambady, N., Adams, R. B. Jr., & Macrae, C. N. (2008). Accuracy and awareness in the perception and categorization of male sexual orientation. *Journal of Personality and Social Psychology, 95,* 1019–1028.

Rule, N. O., Krendl, A. C., Ivcevic, Z., & Ambady, N. (2013). Accuracy and consensus in judgments of trustworthiness from faces: Behavioral and neural correlates. *Journal of Personality and Social Psychology, 104,* 409–426.

Sanbonmatsu, D. M., Posavac, S. S., Vanous, S., & Ho, E. A. (2005). Information search in the testing of quantified hypotheses: How "All," "Most," "Some," "Few," and "None" hypotheses are tested. *Personality and Social Psychology Bulletin, 31,* 254–266.

Sanitioso, R., Kunda, Z., & Fong, G. T (1990). Motivated recruitment of autobiographical memory. *Journal of Personality and Social Psychology, 59,* 229–241.

Schank, R. C., & Abelson, R. P. (1977). *Scripts, plans, goals, and understanding: An inquiry into human knowledge structures.* Hillsdale, NJ: Erlbaum.

Schneider, D. J., Hastorf, A. H., & Ellsworth, P. C. (1979). *Person perception* (2nd ed.). Reading, MA: Addison-Wesley.

Schuster, B., Rudolph, U., & Försterling, F. (1998). What determines behavioral decisions? Comparing the role covariation information and attributions. *Personality and Social Psychology Bulletin, 24,* 838–854.

Schwarz, N., Bless, H., Wanke, M., & Winkielman, P. (2003). Accessibility revisited. In G.V. Bodenhausen & A. J. Lambert (Eds.), *Foundations of social cognition.* Mahwah, NJ: Erlbaum.

Sedikides, C., & Skowronski, J. J. (1991). The law of cognitive structure activation. *Psychological Inquiry, 2,* 169–184.

Sherman, J. W., & Hamilton, D. L. (1994). On the formation of interitem associative links in person memory. *Journal of Experimental Social Psychology, 30,* 203–217.

Simon, H. (1976). *Administrative behavior* (3rd ed.). New York: Free Press.

Sinclair, R. C., Mark, M. M., & Shotland, R. L. (1987). Construct accessibility and generalizability across response categories. *Personality and Social Psychology Bulletin, 12,* 239–252.

Skitka, L. J., Mullen, E., Griffin, T., Hutchinson, S., & Chamberlin, B. (2003). Dispositions, scripts, or motivated correction? Understanding ideological differences in explanations for social problems. *Journal of Personality and Social Psychology, 83,* 470–487.

Skowronski, J. J., Carlston, D. E., Mae, L., & Crawford, M. T. (1994). Spontaneous trait transference: Communicators take on the qualities they describe in others. *Journal of Personality and Social Psychology, 74,* 837–848.

Smith, E. R. (1994). Social cognition contributions to attribution theory and research. In P. G. Devine, D. L. Hamilton, & T. M. Ostrom (Eds.), *Social cognition: Impact on social psychology* (pp. 77–108). San Diego, CA: Academic Press.

Smith, E. R. (1998). Mental representation and memory. In D. T. Gilbert, S. T. Fiske, & G. Lindzey (Eds.), *The handbook of social psychology* (4th ed., Vol. 1, pp. 109–124). New York: McGraw Hill.

Smith, E. R., & Lerner, M. (1986). Development of automatism of social judgments. *Journal of Personality and Social Psychology, 50,* 246–259.

Snyder, M. (1981). Seek and ye shall find: Testing hypotheses about other people. In E. T. Higgins, C. P. Herman, & M. P. Zanna (Eds.), *Social cognition: The Ontario symposium* (Vol. 1, pp. 277–303). Hillsdale, NJ: Erlbaum.

Snyder, M. (1984). When beliefs create reality. In L. Berkowitz (Ed.), *Advances in experimental social psychology* (Vol. 18). New York: Academic Press.

Snyder, M., & Swann, W. B. Jr. (1978). Behavioral confirmation in social interaction: From social perception to social reality. *Journal of Experimental Social Psychology, 14,* 148–162.

Snyder, M., Tanke, E. D., & Berscheid, E. (1977). Social perception and interpersonal behavior: On the self-fulfilling nature of social stereotypes. *Journal of Personality and Social Psychology, 35,* 656–666.

Snyder, M. L., & Frankel, A. (1976). Observer bias: A stringent test of behavior engulfing the field. *Journal of Personality and Social Psychology, 34,* 857–864.

Spencer, S. J., Fein, S., Zanna, M. P., & Olson, J. M. (Eds). (2003). *Motivated social perception: The Ontario symposium* (Vol. 9). Mahwah, NJ: Erlbaum.

Sporer, S., Penrod, S., Read, D., & Cutler, B. L. (1995). Choosing, confidence, and accuracy: A meta-analysis of the confidence-accuracy relationship in eyewitness identification studies. *Psychological Bulletin, 118,* 315–327.

Srull, T. K. (1981). Person memory: Some tests of associative storage and retrieval models. *Journal of Experimental Psychology: Human Learning and Memory, 7,* 440–463.

Srull, T. K., & Wyer, R. S. Jr. (1979). The role of category accessibility in the interpretation of information about persons: Some determinants and implications. *Journal of Personality and Social Psychology, 37,* 1660–1672.

Srull, T. K., & Wyer, R. S. Jr. (1980). Category accessibility and social perception: Some implications for the study of person memory and interpersonal judgments. *Journal of Personality and Social Psychology, 38,* 841–856.

Srull, T. K., & Wyer, R. S. Jr. (1989). Person memory and judgment. *Psychological Review, 96,* 58–83.

Stangor, C., & McMillan, D. (1992). Memory for expectancy-congruent and expectancy-incongruent information: A review of the social and social developmental literatures. *Psychological Bulletin, 111,* 42–61.

Stangor, C., & Ruble, D. N. (1989). Strength of expectancies and memory for social information: What we remember depends on how much we know. *Journal of Experimental Social Psychology, 25,* 18–35.

Strack, F., Schwarz, N., Bless, H., Kübler, A., & Wanke, M. (1993). Awareness of the influence as a determinant of assimilation versus contrast. *European Journal of Social Psychology, 23,* 53–62.

Swann, W. B. Jr., & Ely, R. J. (1984). A battle of wills: Self-verification versus behavioral confirmation. *Journal of Personality and Social Psychology, 46,* 1287–1302.

Szczurek, L., Monin, B., and Gross, J. J. (2012). The *Stranger* Effect: The rejection of affective deviants. *Psychological Science, 23,* 1105–111.

Tagiuri, R., & Petrullo, L. (Eds.) (1958). *Person perception and interpersonal behavior.* Stanford, CA: Stanford University Press.

Taylor, S. E., & Crocker, J. (1981). Schematic bases of social information processing. In E. T. Higgins, C. P. Herman, & M. P. Zanna (Eds.), *Social cognition: The Ontario symposium* (Vol. 1, pp. 89–134). Hillsdale, NJ: Erlbaum.

Taylor, S. E., & Fiske, S. T. (1978). Salience, attention, and attribution: Top of the head phenomena. In L. Berkowitz (Ed.), *Advances in experimental social psychology* (Vol. 11). New York: Academic Press.

Taylor, S. E., Fiske, S. T., Close, M., Anderson, C., & Ruderman, A. (1977). *Solo status as a psychological variable: The power of being distinctive.* Unpublished manuscript, Harvard University. (Cited in Taylor & Fiske, 1978).

Tetlock, P. E. (1985). Accountability: A social check on the fundamental attribution error. *Social Psychology Quarterly, 48,* 227–236.

Tetlock, P. E., & Boettger, R. (1989). Accountability: A social magnifier of the dilution effect. *Journal of Personality and Social Psychology, 57,* 388–398.

Todorov, A., & Uleman, J. S. (2003). The efficiency of binding spontaneous trait inferences to actors' faces. *Journal of Experimental Social Psychology, 39,* 549–562.

Todorov, A., & Uleman, J. S. (2004). The person reference process in spontaneous trait inferences. *Journal of Personality and Social Psychology, 87,* 482–493.

Tracy, J. L., & Robins, R. W. (2004). Show your pride: Evidence for a discrete emotion expression. *Psychological Science, 15,* 194–197.

Triandis, H. C. (1995). *Individualism and collectivism* (pp. 1–15). Boulder, CO: Westview.

Trope, Y. (1986). Identification and inferential processes in dispositional attribution. *Psychological Review, 93,* 239–257.

Trope, Y., & Bassok, M. (1982). Confirmatory and diagnosing strategies in social information gathering. *Journal of Personality and Social Psychology, 43,* 22–34.

Trope, Y., Bassok, M., & Alon, E. (1984). The questions lay interviewers ask. *Journal of Personality, 52,* 90–106.

Trope, Y., & Thompson, E. P. (1997). Looking for truth in all the wrong places? Asymmetric search of individuating information about stereotyped group members. *Journal of Personality and Social Psychology, 73,* 229–241.

Tulving, E., & Thomson, D. M. (1973). Encoding specificity and retrieval processes in episodic memory. *Psychological Review, 80,* 352–373.

Tversky, A., & Kahneman, D. (1974). Judgment under uncertainty: Heuristics and biases. *Science, 211,* 453–458.

Uleman, J. S., & Bargh, J. A. (1989). *Unintended thought.* New York: Guilford Publications.

Uleman, J. S., Hon, A., Roman, R. J., & Moskowitz, B. B. (1996). On-line evidence for spontaneous trait inferences at encoding. *Personality and Social Psychology Bulletin, 22,* 377–394.

Uleman, J. S., Newman, L. S., & Moskowitz, G. B. (1996). People as spontaneous interpreters: Evidence and issues from spontaneous trait inference. In M. Zanna (Ed.), *Advances in experimental social psychology* (Vol. 28, pp. 211–279). San Diego, CA: Academic Press.

Valchev, V. H., van de Vijver, F. R., Nel, J., Rothmann, S., & Meiring, D. (2013). The use of traits and contextual information in free personality descriptions across ethnocultural groups in South Africa. *Journal of Personality and Social Psychology, 104,* 1077–1091.

Van Boven, L., Kamada, A., & Gilovich, T. (1999). The perceiver as perceived: Everyday intuitions about the correspondence bias. *Journal of Personality and Social Psychology, 77,* 1188–1199.

Van Boven, L., White, K., Kamada, A., & Gilovich, T. (2003). Intuitions about situational correction in self and others. *Journal of Personality and Social Psychology, 85,* 249–258.

Van Duynslaeger, M., Sterken, C., Van Overwalle, F., & Verstraeten, E. (2008). EEG components of spontaneous trait inferences. *Social Neuroscience, 3,* 164–177.

Van Duynslaeger, M., Van Overwalle, F., & Verstraeten, E. (2007). Electrophysiological time course and brain areas of spontaneous and intentional trait inferences. *Social Cognitive and Affective Neuroscience, 2,* 174–188.

Weber, R., & Crocker, J. (1983). Cognitive processes in the revision of stereotypic beliefs. *Journal of Personality and Social Psychology, 45*, 961–977.

Wegener, D. T., & Petty, R. E. (1995). Flexible correction processes in social judgment: The role of naïve theories in corrections for perceived bias. *Journal of Experimental Social Psychology, 68*, 36–51.

Wegner, D. M. (2002). *The illusion of conscious will*. Cambridge, MA: MIT Press.

Weiner, B. (1985). An attributional theory of achievement motivation and emotion. *Psychological Review, 92*, 548–573.

Weisz, C., & Jones, E. E. (1993). Expectancy disconfirmation and dispositional inference: Latent strength of target-based and category-based expectancies. *Personality and Social Psychology Bulletin, 19*, 563–573.

Wells, G. L., Malpass, R. S., Lindsay, R. C. L., Fisher, R. P., Turtle, J. W., & Fulero, S. M. (2000). From the lab to the police station: A successful application of eyewitness research. *American Psychologist, 55*, 581–598.

Wilson, T. D. (2002) *Strangers to ourselves: Discovering the adaptive unconscious*. Cambridge, MA: Harvard University Press.

Wilson, T. D., & Brekke, N. (1994). Mental contamination and mental correction: Unwanted influences on judgments and evaluations. *Psychological Review, 116*, 117–142.

Wimer, S., & Kelley, H. H. (1982). An investigation of the dimensions of causal attribution. *Journal of Personality and Social Psychology, 43*, 1142–1162.

Winter, L., & Uleman, J. S. (1984). When are social judgments made? Evidence for the spontaneousness of trait inferences. *Journal of Personality and Social Psychology, 47*, 237–252.

Winter, L., Uleman, J. S., & Cunniff, C. (1985). How automatic are social judgments? *Journal of Personality and Social Psychology, 49*, 904–917.

Young, S. G., Hugenberg, K., Bernstein, M. J., & Sacco, D. F. (2012). Perception and motivation in face recognition: A critical review of theories of the cross-race effect. *Personality and Social Psychology Review, 16*, 116–142.

Zaki, J., & Ochsner, K. (2011) *Reintegrating the Study of Accuracy into Social Cognition Research. Psychological Inquiry, 22*, 159–182.

Zukier, H. (1982). The dilution effect: The role of the correlation and the dispersion of predictor variables in the use of nondiagnostic information. *Journal of Personality and Social Psychology, 43*, 1163–1174.

CHAPTER 4

THE SELF

GETTING IN SHAPE

To say that Pat is an avid runner would be an understatement. He runs almost every day, usually at the crack of dawn. He has found that with his commitments at work, this is the only way to get his runs in. And he needs those runs. Three years ago, during his regular physical checkup, his weight was out of control and his cholesterol was sky high, especially for someone in his 20s. His physician left no doubt in his mind: either exercise regularly or risk the same health problems his father suffered from.

Pat arrived at running in a roundabout way. He had never really understood its allure, believing in his heart that the famous runner's high was brought on by oxygen deprivation rather than endorphins. Following his visit to the doctor, he joined a weekly pickup game in the gym at the local grade school, and he purchased a membership at a health club across town. Neither really worked for him. The pickup games were often canceled, either because the school needed the gym that day or because not enough people had showed up to play. The hours at the health club were inconvenient during the week, and on weekends it was often packed. So, Pat reluctantly turned to running, primarily because it was a way to exercise without relying on other people.

At first, Pat's runs were little more than grim jogs around the block, but gradually he lengthened them to 45 minutes or an hour. Much to his surprise, as his distance increased, he began to enjoy running. Now the urge to go for a run has replaced the urge for a cigarette each morning, so he heads out to the trail along Chicago's lakefront. On weekends, he often participates in 5k runs, to add some variety and an element of competition to his otherwise solitary pursuit. For two years in a row, Pat has run and finished the Chicago Marathon, with respectable times on both occasions. In fact, the second time he finished within the qualifying time for the Boston Marathon.

The prospect of being able to run in a prestigious and competitive marathon was tantalizing, so Pat kicked his training up a notch. He has gradually increased his pace and mileage to the point that he can now run nine miles at the eight-minute pace required for a 3:30 finish. Today, he's going to try for ten miles, even though an early-morning meeting with some tech people at work has forced him to run in the evening. Not his preferred time, but no sweat, he tells himself, as he sets his stopwatch. *I am a runner.* South on the Lakefront Trail, just past Navy Pier and back ...

Pat knows he is a runner. How do you know who you are? How do you respond when your view of yourself is threatened? And how does the self come into play when you interact with others? This chapter answers these three key questions about the self. Before you continue reading, however, please put down this book and pick up a pen and a piece of paper. We want you to write about yourself. First, imagine that you are writing a personal ad to be placed on the Internet. (We know, of course, that you personally would never resort to that strategy to find a date.) Write down what you would tell a potential date about who you are and what you are looking for in a date. Second, imagine that you're applying for a job, say, as an ice-cream taster. Write something about yourself that you feel would maximize your chances of landing the job.

Now, put your pen down and take a look at what you wrote. Your personal ad is likely to include something about your physical features—your height, weight, hair and eye color. You probably described yourself in terms of your personality traits as well—perhaps you are outgoing, caring, independent, and adventurous. Finally, your self-description may include something about your preferences—what you like to do, whether you like pets, and so on.

Next, take a look at how you described yourself as an ice-cream taster. In all likelihood, your description does not include references to your physical characteristics. Although it may include a list of traits, they are probably different from the ones you listed in the personal ad. Instead of mentioning how outgoing, independent, and adventurous you are, you may have said something about your conscientiousness, reliability, and experience. And again, you may have included something about your preferences—that is, you really like ice cream and enjoy working as part of a team, or something similar that speaks to your desire for the job.

The self is a multifaceted entity. Different facets of the self predominate in different situations, such as a date or a job interview.

In each case, you have described what some (for example, Brown, 1998) have called the "ME" part of yourself. Unlike the "I" part of the self, which describes what you are currently doing (for example, "I read"), the "ME" part has a reflexive quality (for example, "I am a reader," or in Pat's case, "I am a runner"). When you wrote your self-descriptions, you looked in the mirror and focused your attention on various parts of your *self*, and you discovered the "ME" part of yourself. What you saw, however, depended on which aspects of your self were relevant to the task (that is, to the personal ad or the job application). This insight is important, because it suggests that the self is not monolithic, but has many different facets.

Years ago, the psychologist William James divided the self into three parts: the *material self*, the *spiritual self*, and the *social self*. The *material self* includes and extends the boundaries of the body. In other words, it includes your physical self and the physical entities associated with you. Whether any of those entities are part of your self depends on the extent to which you claim psychological ownership. When you refer to physical entities as *my* big toe, *my* running shoes, *my* cat, or *my* car, you claim ownership of them, and they become part of your self. Of course, the reverse can also be true: A tonsorially challenged person may refuse to claim ownership of his bald head, so that "bald" will not be part of his self.

The *spiritual self* includes what might best be called the inner self, and is comprised of everything you own psychologically that is not a physical entity. Thus, it includes your attitudes, beliefs, abilities, feelings, and interests. You can figure out the extent to which you own them by looking at how you react when they are under attack. The more you feel compelled to defend them, the more you own them, and the more they are part of your self. Because Pat, the marathon runner, took increasing ownership of his running, we might expect him to react strongly to any threat to his ability to run marathons. Finally, the *social self* refers to your social identity, as defined by your interpersonal relationships, your ethnic background, your vocation and avocations, your political affiliation, and if applicable, your membership in a stigmatized group (Deaux, Reid, Mizrahi, & Ethier, 1995). Take a look at **Figure 4.1** for a graphical representation of the three aspects of the self identified by William James.

It is easy to see why James proposed that the self is a multifaceted entity comprised of many different elements. The self-descriptions we asked you to write suggest as much. But how do we acquire our sense of self in the first place? How are the ways we think about ourselves related to the ways we feel about ourselves? What role does the self play in our attempts to manage the impressions we make on others, and what does the self do when it comes under attack? In this chapter, we will

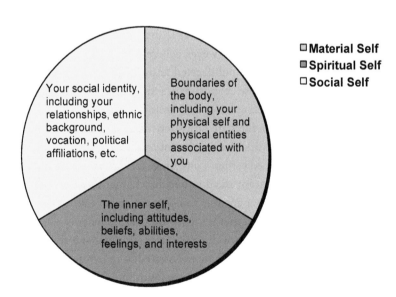

Figure 4.1: The Distinct Parts of the Self According to William James.

answer these questions by looking at three functional, dynamic aspects of the self: the *inquisitive* self, the *managing* self, and the *tactical/strategic* self.

THE INQUISITIVE SELF: GETTING TO KNOW "ME"

Most people have a good idea of who they are, and you are likely no exception. When you wrote your personal ad, you probably took little time to describe yourself in terms of your material, spiritual, and social selves. After all, it doesn't take much to ascertain the color of your eyes and whether you are tall or short, dark-haired or blond (your material self). And it doesn't take much longer to figure out whether you are outgoing, caring, independent, and adventurous, or whether you like cats, hip-hop music, and Democrats or Republicans (your spiritual self). Likewise, it takes little time to ascertain your social identities. You simply know you are a student or a professional, and that you come from a small family or a large one. And you know whether your ethnic background is, for example, African, Asian, Latino, Polish, or some combination of ethnicities (your social self). The reason this process is fast and relatively simple is that your material, spiritual, and social selves are all part of your **self-concept**, a cognitive representation of knowledge about the self that is compiled by your inquisitive self.

Most social psychologists agree that our ideas about ourselves form a complex, highly organized knowledge structure that becomes more differentiated as we go through life. There is less agreement on exactly how we organize this knowledge. Some psychologists (for example, Kihlstrom & Cantor, 1984) have argued for a categorical structure like the ones we use to organize what we know about objects and people. Categorical structures imply a hierarchical organization. For example, your knowledge of animals may include a lower-level category like insects, which may be subdivided into insects that crawl, sting, are beautiful, or give you the creeps. Similarly, your self-knowledge may contain a category for your social identity, subdivided into your identities with family, friends, or coworkers.

Other psychologists (Markus & Wurf, 1987) have argued that our cognitive representations of self-knowledge may be structured like the schemas we have about other people and groups. Schemas aren't all that different from categories. Unlike categories, however, schemas do not necessarily imply a hierarchical organization. Rather, a **self-schema** is a rich and multifaceted knowledge structure that organizes what we know about ourselves, particularly in terms of those characteristics that define us and of which we are highly certain (Markus, 1977).

The concept of the self as a rich and multifaceted knowledge structure has several important implications. Because knowledge structures are ultimately related to memory, it is not surprising that people generally have better recall for information that is relevant to the self than for information that is not self-relevant. Consider again the traits mentioned earlier—outgoing, caring, independent, adventurous—and let's add intelligent, assertive, and silly. If you were asked to decide whether these traits describe you, you would need little time to respond, regardless of your answer. You would also have little trouble recalling this list of traits later on. Now imagine that you must say whether these traits describe your mother. Chances are you would take longer to do so and would recall fewer of the traits later. This **self-reference effect**—superior memory for information that relates to the self—has been demonstrated in numerous studies (Klein, 2012; Klein & Kihlstrom, 1986; Rogers, Kuiper, & Kirker, 1977; Symons & Johnson, 1997). It is a direct outcome of your ability to organize and elaborate on material that relates to the self.

Having a well-developed self-schema has advantages that go beyond memory. In one study (Markus, 1977), participants who were schematic on independence (that is, they thought of themselves as very independent and considered independence an important characteristic) were faster to respond to trait words related to independence (for example, *assertive, self-confident, individualistic*) than participants who were aschematic on independence (that is, independence meant little to them). In addition, participants who were schematic on independence remembered more past behaviors related to independence than other participants, and were more likely to reject the results of a bogus personality test that labeled them as conforming and dependent. Clearly, their self-schemas enabled independent schematics to maintain a coherent and organized sense of themselves. However, this edge in coherence comes at a price. Just like other schemas, self-schemas tend to bias the way we process information. People who are schematic on a trait are selectively attentive to information that fits their schema, and thus have no problem accepting information that confirms their self-views. At the same time, they tend to reject information that is inconsistent with their self-views (Swann, 1990).

People's self-schemas vary, of course, in terms of the specific characteristics they contain. More importantly, like all schemas, they also vary in terms of the number of dimensions they contain. A self-schema with just a few dimensions (for example, female, student) is considerably less complex than a schema with many dimen-

sions related to different aspects of the self (for example, female, student, athletic, activist, independent, interested in the outdoors). In other words, a person who thinks of herself in many different ways has a high degree of self-complexity, whereas a person who thinks of himself in just a few ways has a low degree of self-complexity (Linville, 1985, 1987).

Not surprisingly, the complexity of your self-knowledge increases with age. At around 18 to 24 months you begin to realize that the face in the mirror is yours (Lewis, 1997). In elementary school, your self-representations tend to revolve around features of your material self, like your age, physical characteristics, hobbies, and friends (Montemayor & Eisen, 1977). During adolescence, your self-knowledge expands to include aspects of your spiritual self (for example, your traits, attitudes, and abili-

At age 18-24 months, toddlers begin to recognize the face in the mirror as their own. This realization is necessary for the development of a self-schema.

ties) and your social self (for example, your social identities) (Harter, 2003). When you reach adulthood, your self-knowledge becomes even more differentiated and increases in coherence and stability (Brown, 1998).

In light of this developmental trajectory, it is tempting to assume that high self-complexity may be a good thing, and to some extent it is. During your college career, you may have encountered professors who seem to care only about academic matters like their research and teaching. Because they define themselves primarily on a single dimension, they are low in self-complexity. You may also have encountered professors who care about being good parents and good athletes, as well as about being good scholars. What happens to people in these two groups when they suffer some kind of academic setback? In all likelihood, the setback will devastate the professor who is single-mindedly pursuing her academic career. The professor who defines himself in multiple ways will be less affected by the setback, because he has other identities to fall back on ("Even though I didn't sell a single copy of my book, I'm still a good parent"). Similarly, for someone who thinks of herself as smart *and* athletic rather than just smart, finishing a marathon might help to offset the emotional impact of the breakup of a relationship or a bout with poor grades.

Of course, a complex self-schema can also be detrimental to one's mental health, particularly when it is reflected in multiple identities. When a self-schema incorporates too many identities, role conflicts and identity interference can become burdensome. People who need to juggle career, family, and marriage all at once frequently experience such conflicts. Whether or not more identities are better ultimately depends on the fit among the various identities; see the Social Psychology Encounters the Bright Side box below.

SOCIAL PSYCHOLOGY ENCOUNTERS THE BRIGHT SIDE: THE HIDDEN ADVANTAGES OF MULTIPLE IDENTITIES

Multiple identities can produce interference if they contain incompatible prescriptions for behavior (Van Sell, Brief, & Schuler, 1981). Consider, for example, the female science major who feels she must deemphasize her gender to fit in with her male peers, or the student athlete who feels he must live up to the academic standards of nonathlete peers. The ill effects of such identity interference include stress and lowered self-esteem (Settles, Sellers, & Damas, 2002).

There is some cause for optimism for those who juggle multiple identities, however. One study (Settles, 2004) looksed at the extent of the identity interference experienced by female undergraduates in the sciences. Not surprisingly, given the masculine climate in the sciences, participants who considered their identity as a woman rather than as a scientist to be central to their lives suffered a great deal of identity interference. However, participants who considered their identities as a scientist and as a woman to be equally central suffered relatively little identity interference. Apparently, people can negotiate multiple identities by rendering them equally central to the self.

GETTING TO KNOW YOURSELF

So far we have skirted the question of how the self-concept develops. How do you know who you are? William James' (1890) concept of the self as an empirical entity suggests that your self-concept is based on some kind of cognitive input. Data on your weight, height, gender, and ethnicity are readily available, but how do you know whether you are fat or thin, outgoing or reserved, liberal or conservative? How do you figure out how smart or athletic you are? To answer such questions, you can draw on four sources of information: introspection, reflected appraisals (from others), self-perception, and social comparison.

Introspection

Because your spiritual self is also your "inner self," you might think that all you need to do to figure out who you are is to look inward at your own thoughts and feelings. Introspection can indeed be a good source of information about the self. But although you can easily ascertain your thoughts and feelings, the reasons for your thoughts and feelings will often escape you (Wilson, 2002). For example, if Pat is asked why he enjoys running, he may reply that he likes it because it helps him to keep his weight down. Though he may enjoy it just as much for those triumphant moments when he crosses the finish line at a race, he may not be aware of how much those moments mean to him.

When people introspect, they appear to generate causal theories on the spot to explain their thoughts or feelings (Nisbett & Wilson, 1977). At best, these explanations may simply be misleading. At worst, they may be an illusion (Pronin, 2009). Why do you like chocolate? You may never have thought about the question. Forced to provide an answer, you may fall back on the popular theory that eating chocolate puts people in a good mood. You conclude that you, too, like chocolate because of its mood-altering quality, when in truth you simply like its taste.

At worst, introspection can lead people to change their attitudes altogether. This frequently happens when people try to generate reasons for liking somebody or something. For example, listing all the things you like and dislike about your romantic partner can seriously jeopardize your relationship. You know you like the person, but because the reasons for your liking aren't completely accessible to your consciousness, you may not be able to generate "enough" reasons. Worse, you may come to believe that you like the person for "all the wrong reasons" (Wilson & Kraft, 1993).

The Looking Glass and the Spyglass: Reflected Appraisals

In light of the fallibility of introspection, some have argued that your sense of self derives entirely from your interactions with others, particularly when it is still in the development stage (for example, Cooley, 1902; Mead, 1934). The resulting *looking-glass self* is a representation of the history of your social interactions. It contains not so much what other people think of you, but reflected appraisals of what other people think—that is, what you *think* they think of you.

Consistent with this idea, Kenny and DePaulo (1993) found that people's self-appraisals are not correlated with actual appraisals from others. Instead, they are correlated with they way people perceive others' appraisals. In other words, whether or not I think I'm smart doesn't depend on what you may think and perhaps tell me. Rather, it depends on what I think you think. What's the difference? Others tell us lots of things about ourselves. When we have reason to believe they are guided by ulterior motives, we may not accept what they say. As a result, their comments don't become part of their reflected appraisals, and consequently do not become part of the way we view ourselves.

Reflected appraisals are an important source of data from which to construct the self. They are perhaps most important when the sense of self is still in the making, and there is little in the way of other data. Thus, self-views that are founded on reflected appraisals are most commonly found among children, and to a lesser extent among adults with relatively fixed self-concepts (Demo, 1992). In general, the self-concept does not become static in adulthood—quite the contrary. Others—especially those to whom you feel psychologically close—continue to shape the adult's sense of self in important and unexpected ways.

A great deal of research suggests that psychological closeness can blur the boundaries between the self and the other. Individuals incorporate aspects of the other into their own identities, to the point that the two merge (Aron & Aron, 1986; Aron et al., 1991). This merging of identities creates overlapping mental representations of the self and the other (Mashek et al., 2003), which allows individuals to infer their own attributes based on the attributes of a close other. Because this process may require little more than observing (or spying on) a close other's actions, the result is a spyglass-self (Goldstein & Cialdini, 2007). To the extent that a close other's actions appear to be freely chosen, allowing an internal attribution, any inferences about the other can carry over to the self.

Self-Perception

One way to figure out whether you have a certain trait is to inspect your past behavior. **Self-perception theory** (Bem, 1972) suggests that to decide whether you are outgoing or reserved, you can simply recall how many parties you have gone to, how often you have struck up a conversation with a classmate, and whether or not you prefer to do things with others. Such self-perception of your past behavior allows you to infer whether on balance you are outgoing or reserved. Similarly, you may infer whether you are liberal or conservative by mentally revisiting occasions on which you agreed or disagreed with liberal or conservative views.

Self-perception of this sort involves a form of mental time travel through your *episodic memory* (Tulving, 1972). It suggests a *computational view* of the way you construct aspects of your self. That is, you determine whether or not you have a given trait by retrieving memories of relevant past behaviors and computing their similarity to that trait (Smith & Zarate, 1992). According to this view, Pat would decide whether he is a runner by mentally revisiting past behaviors related to running such as the number of times he went running during the past week, month, or even year. Retrieving a high number of memories like these would give him confidence that he is indeed a runner.

In contrast, the *abstraction view* holds that trait judgments of the self are based on abstractions from relevant behaviors, which are stored in *semantic memory* as abstract representations (Klein & Loftus, 1993). The idea is that you encode behavior as you engage in it, in terms of its implications for a particular trait. As a result, you develop relatively abstract representations of what you are like. The computational and abstraction views yield different predictions regarding the ease (or difficulty) with which people decide whether they possess a certain trait. Because access to episodic memory requires specific retrieval cues that may not always be at hand, deciding how outgoing you are by mentally revisiting all the parties you attended over the past year will be a relatively slow and cumbersome process. Making the same judgment based on a more abstract representation such as "I like to go to parties" would add both ease and speed to the process. To the extent that Pat has a history of running, he is likely to have developed an abstract representation of himself as a runner, which may not require him to consult his episodic memory and compute the number of times he has gone running.

Interestingly, even though the conceptual distinction between the computational and abstraction views is fairly straightforward, distinguishing between the two empirically is far more difficult (Klein, Loftus, & Kihlstrom, 1996). The problem is that at any given moment, people have access to both episodic and semantic memory. Thus, devising an experimental procedure to tease apart the extent to which they rely on computation or abstraction is a challenge (Klein, Rozendal, & Cosmides, 2002).

There is good reason to suspect that your sense of self derives from access to both trait-relevant behaviors (stored in episodic memory) and more abstract information (stored in semantic memory). Evidence to that effect comes from case studies of brain-injured individuals who suffer from a peculiar form of anterograde amnesia that deprives them of episodic memory. This selective memory impairment, which the poet Alexander Pope referred to as "the eternal sunshine of the spotless mind," robs them of personal memories, but leaves their memories of public and impersonal events intact (Klein, Loftus, & Kihlstrom, 1996). Unable to access their episodic memories, these individuals must rely on semantic memory when trying to imagine what their personal experience might be like in the future. In the study by Klein et al. (2002), brain-injured participants had great difficulty imagining their personal futures. To the extent that forecasting of this sort depends on one's sense of self, then, it appears that access to memories of actual past behavior is important. Moreover, these findings suggest that our sense of self is not derived primarily from abstract trait knowledge, stored in semantic memory. If that were the case, anterograde amnesia (which deprives a person of episodic memory) would be less of an impairment than it is in imagining one's personal future.

Abstract representations of the self are nonetheless handy, and are especially characteristic of self-representations in the distant, rather than the near, future, because they necessarily rely on the most essential and invariant attributes of the self (Wakslak, Nussbaum, Liberman, & Trope, 2008). Often, they can be accessed quickly and with relative ease, and provide a way around a problem that is inherent in the scrutiny of behavior. The problem is that you add meaning to your actions at the very moment you observe them. Think about what you are doing right now. Depending on the level of abstraction you choose, there are many possible answers. On a moderate (and probably appropriate) level of abstraction, you could say that you are reading the chapter on the self in your social psychology textbook. You could also think of that behavior in terms of increasing levels of abstraction: you are reading a book, learning about social psychology, gaining important knowledge, furthering your education, and so on. Or you could think of it in terms of decreasing levels of abstraction: reading a page, reading a sentence, moving your eyes from left to right, and so on.

According to action identification theory (Vallacher & Wegner, 1987, 2012; Wegner & Vallacher, 1986), people strive to identify their behavior at an optimal level of abstraction, if for no other reason than to add meaning to their actions. If we asked Pat what he was doing as he shot past us on the running trail, he would probably say that he's running, construing his behavior at a moderate level of abstraction. He most likely would *not* say that he's moving one leg in front of the other (a low level of abstraction). In general, identifying our actions at low levels of abstraction tells us little about the self, including the intentionality of an action (Kozak, Marsh, & Wegner, 2006). However, identifying them at higher levels of abstraction does have implications for the self and may also provide a guide to related behavior. You can learn little about yourself by construing what you are doing as "moving my eyes from left to right," but construing it as "studying for an exam" allows you to conclude that you are a serious student who wants to do well. Of course, you may sometimes want to construe your behavior in a way that is minimally informative: see the Social Psychology and the Law box below.

SOCIAL PSYCHOLOGY AND THE LAW: WHAT DID CRIMINALS THINK THEY WERE DOING?

In an intriguing study, Vallacher and Wegner (1987) asked convicted murderers to retell their crimes. Their study was inspired by the central postulate of action identification theory, that behavior can be construed on different levels of abstraction. On a moderate level of abstraction, for example, the act of murder could be construed as "killing someone." On an excessively high level of abstraction, the same act could be construed in terms of a higher goal (for example, "putting him out of his misery"). And on a very low level of abstraction, the act could be construed in terms of the simple motor actions involved in firing a gun.

How did the convicted murderers recount their crimes? Most chose ways that minimally implicated the self, describing in some detail the motor actions involved in firing the gun. They talked about the sensation of the cold metal on their palms, about squeezing the trigger, and so on. Few spoke of their crimes in terms of moderate or even high levels of abstraction. This approach makes sense. Failure often leads us to lower the level of abstraction with which we construe our actions, because doing so takes the self out of the equation. And for these incarcerated criminals, jail represented failure. Their crimes definitely did not pay.

Similarly, perpetrators of genocide often reconstruct their actions on a concrete rather than an abstract level (Erber, 2002). Claiming only to have followed orders, for example, absolves the self, implying that on a personal level, no crime was committed. When responsibility is assigned to a superior in this way, there is no personal guilt and no need for contrition. To the extent that perpetrators rehearse such descriptions of the crime, they may eventually become part of the automatic self. Our jails may be filled with people who have convinced themselves of their innocence, or at least rectitude, despite their conviction by a jury of their peers.

Social Comparison

Examining our past relevant behaviors can tell us much about our traits, attitudes, and preferences. It helps us to decide whether we are smart or athletic, whether we like foods such as anchovies or tofu. It does not necessarily tell us *how* smart or athletic we are, or *how much* we like tofu, though. To figure out what some have called the "relative self" (Mussweiler, 2003), we need to compare ourselves to others (Festinger, 1954).

At a minimum, **social comparison** involves acquiring, thinking about, and reacting to information about one or more other people relative to the self (Wood, 1996). How athletic are you? The answer may well depend on whether you answer through *downward comparison* to a less athletic other or *upward comparison* to a more athletic other (Wills, 1981). You may conclude that you are very athletic if you compare yourself to an avowed couch potato, but you will arrive at an altogether different conclusion if you compare yourself to a world-class athlete. Similar outcomes can be expected regarding your preference for tofu.

Social comparisons are particularly handy in determining your performance on a task. When Pat ran his first marathon, he finished right in the middle of the pack. How well did he do? To answer this question, he could look at his performance in relation to some objective standard, such as finishing within his desired time. He could also compare his performance to that of others. Comparing himself to someone who is similar in age and gender, but who crossed the finish line after he did, might make him see his performance favorably, because of the downward nature of the comparison. But finding out that a similar other finished well ahead of him would invite an upward comparison that would portray his performance less favorably. Of course, people often use such assessments of their performance to make more general inferences about their ability. Social comparison information appears to be particularly important in that regard (Buckingham & Alicke, 2002).

Both types of social comparison have their benefits. Upward social comparison can help in raising the stakes for yourself and improving your performance. Downward social comparison often produces positive self-evaluations. In fact, an inability to make downward social comparisons can have profoundly detrimental effects. Consider academic environments that are highly selective and competitive, for example. By their very nature, they invite mostly upward social comparisons. Those upward comparisons may in turn have a negative effect on a person's self-concept, even if they were designed with the goal of self-improvement. Because the level of academic achievement in highly selective schools is very high, individual students often find it difficult to escape upward comparisons. As a result, their academic self-concepts are often fairly low, even though by objective standards their achievement level is fairly high (Marsh & Hau, 2003).

When targets for downward social comparison are hard to find, engaging in some form of temporal comparison is often advantageous. Rather than comparing yourself to someone else, you could compare your present level of achievement to your past level of achievement. For example, if you have run a marathon more than once, you can evaluate your most recent performance by comparing it to your time last year. Because such temporal comparisons suggest improvement over time, they may help to offset the negative effects of an upward social comparison (Wilson & Ross, 2000). Discovering that you improved your time from last year, in other words, can soften the realization that you finished near the bottom for your age group. Because temporal comparisons require a look back in time, it is not surprising that adults employ them more often as they grow older (Rickabaugh & Tomlinson-Keasey, 1997).

Everything we have learned to this point emphasizes the importance of your choice of comparison target in assessing your performance and ability. But that isn't the whole story, because upward and downward social comparisons can invite two very different questions. In evaluating your imaginary marathon finish, you can focus on the extent to which your performance was *similar* to that of someone who exemplifies a particular performance standard. Alternatively, you can focus on how *dissimilar* your performance was to the same standard. Regardless of whether the comparison is upward or downward, a similarity focus will bring standard-consistent self-knowledge to mind, leading you to assimilate your performance to the standard. A dissimilarity focus will bring standard-inconsistent knowledge

Photos 4.5: *Comparing our performance against that of others helps us to judge how good we are and how well we did.*

to mind, leading you to move away from the standard (Mussweiler, 2001, 2003). As a result, *downward* comparisons will have more favorable consequences for your self-evaluation if they focus on your *dissimilarity* to the comparison target. Under the same circumstances, *upward* comparisons will have *less* favorable consequences.

How accurate are self-views that are based on social comparisons? For their self-views to be accurate, people would have to make their comparisons in an unbiased fashion, which they often do not do. In general, people tend to believe that they are better than others on easy tasks, but worse than others on difficult tasks. Because people generally have better information about themselves than they do about others, when their performance is exceptionally good (or exceptionally bad), they assume that the performance of others is worse (or better) than their own. Having fairly accurate information about one's own performance exacerbates this effect; having accurate information about the performance of others attenuates it (Moore & Small, 2007).

CULTURAL INFLUENCES ON THE SELF

Some aspects of the self are shaped through the hidden influence of culture (Cross, Hardin, & Gercek-Swing, 2011; Markus & Kitayama, 1991). Cultures vary in many ways, of course. One that has received a fair amount of attention is the level of individualism versus collectivism in a given culture (Triandis, 1989). We discussed this

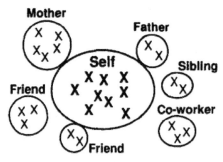

A. Independent View of Self

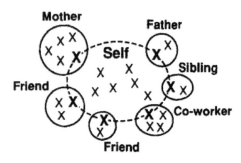

B. Interdependent View of Self

Figure 4.2: Independent and Interdependent Self-Construals

Source: Markus, H.R., & Kitayama, S. (1991). Culture and the Self: Implications for Cognition, Emotion, and Motivation. Journal of Personality and Social Psychology, 98, 224–253.

topic at length in Chapter 3 (see **pages 100–103**), but here is a brief recap.

In general, individualistic cultures emphasize the importance of individual autonomy and personal uniqueness. In collectivistic cultures, on the other hand, individual autonomy and personal uniqueness are considered secondary to the social group and to interpersonal connectedness. Though all cultures incorporate elements of both individualism and collectivism, many differ dramatically in terms of which predominates. Most Western cultures are predominantly individualistic; many Asian and African cultures are predominantly collectivistic. Within the United States, Asians, Asian Americans, Latinos, and Latino Americans are more collectivistic than European Americans. African Americans are more individualistic than European Americans; Asians and Asian Americans are less individualistic than European Americans (Oyserman, Coon, & Kemmelmeier, 2002). In the United States, "the squeaky wheel gets the grease"; in Japan, "the nail that sticks out gets pounded down."

What do these cultural differences in individualism and collectivism imply for the concept of the self? On the most basic level, people in individualistic cultures have an **independent self** that revolves around personal autonomy. Those in collectivistic cultures have an **interdependent self** that revolves around their relationships with others, including the groups to which they belong. **Figure 4.2** contrasts the differences between these two self-construals. They have some important consequences, as shown by comparative studies of American and Japanese students (Kitayama & Markus, 1999, Markus & Kitayama, 1991). When asked to describe themselves, (independent) Americans tend to use abstract traits. *In their self-descriptions*, (interdependent) Japanese students are more likely to refer to their social roles.

Not surprisingly, the American reliance on traits emphasizes the unity and stability of the independent self. Those with an interdependent self adjust themselves more to the demands of a setting or a relationship. For example, someone with an interdependent self can be a respectful son in one context and a competitive tennis player in another. He will likely adjust the competitiveness of his tennis game, depending on whether he is playing against his father or his regular Saturday morning partner. Adjustments of this sort should not be taken to indicate a lack of *self-structure*, however. Rather, it suggests that compared to the independent self, the interdependent self places a higher premium on relationships than on personal preferences (for example, the preference to win every game).

The independent and interdependent selves differ markedly in terms of the *importance* they attach to internal states versus social roles. The independent self is marked by a high degree of personal authenticity—a sense of the "true self"—that renders personal traits, preferences, and feelings important to our behavior. The interdependent self is less consistent internally (Choi & Choi, 2002; Spencer-Rodgers et al., 2009) and more concerned with maintaining social harmony, because to a large degree it is determined by relationships with others. Consequently, maintaining social harmony is more important than indulging personal preferences or feelings. That is not to say that the interdependent self is subordinate to social relationships and social harmony, but that the "true" interdependent self is comprised in large part by one's relationships.

One of the major *life tasks* for those with an independent self is to find a unique identity that sets the self apart from others. Because collectivistic cultures value belonging, fitting in, behaving appropriately, maintaining harmony, and being subtle rather than blunt, finding a unique identity is generally not an

Photos 4.6: The independent self (red) places a strong emphasis on internal states. In comparison, the interdependent self (surrounding individuals) is determined largely by relationships with others.

issue for those with an interdependent self. Instead, the norm of harmony creates an altogether different life task: anger management. Japanese children, for example, are socialized not to express anger. As a result, Japanese adults experience anger far less frequently than their Western counterparts (Kitayama & Markus, 1999). Their suppression of emotions that could upset the social order has some clear benefits for the self: they are happier and better adjusted than individualists, who are less prone to suppress undesirable emotions (Matsumoto et al., 2008).

Interdependent self-construals also provide an advantage when it comes to social comparison. Remember that upward comparisons to another who is doing better generally lead to a lowered self-evaluation. This statement seems particularly true for individuals with independent self-construals that emphasize their personal uniqueness. It is less true for those with interdependent self-construals. Because interdependent self-construals focus on one's relational ties to others, interdependent individuals can bask in the reflected success of a personally relevant other. Thus, for the interdependent self, upward social comparisons can lead to an *improved* self-evaluation (Kemmelmeier & Oyserman, 2001).

Finally, interdependent self-construals are associated with accurate predictions of future behavior, especially in situations with moral or altruistic overtones. Although individualists tend to overestimate their generosity in terms of donating money or avoiding rude behavior, collectivists generally do what they predict they will do (Balcetis, Dunning, & Miller, 2008).

THE AUTOMATIC SELF

The example of the dutiful son and competitive tennis player raises a question about just how willful and difficult it may be to pull out a different self, depending on the characteristics of one's opponent. To the extent that the interdependent self is familiar with his or her social roles and has lots of practice fulfilling them, they may become part of what some scholars (Paulhus, 1993) have called the **automatic self**. Although the automatic self's self-knowledge results from processes that may be hidden from consciousness, it is highly accessible. When you wrote your self-descriptions for the imaginary personal ad, how much conscious self-perception and social comparison did you have to engage in to generate your traits, preferences, and social roles? Probably very little—at least for the ones that came to mind first. Because those traits, preferences, and social roles represent the core of your self, chances are you have activated them repeatedly, so that they come to mind with amazing ease (Bargh & Chartrand, 1999).

The Inquisitive Self: A Summary

You know who you are because the material, spiritual, and social aspects of your identity are part of your self-concept—a cognitive representation of your self-knowledge that is compiled by the inquisitive self. The schematic organization of the self-concept makes self-knowledge highly accessible, as shown by the self-reference effect—that is, superior memory for information related to the self. The self-concept develops and changes through several processes, including self-perception and social comparison. Self-perception involves consulting both episodic and semantic memory for self-relevant information. Through social comparison, you arrive at a sense of self in comparison both to others and to specific standards. Downward social comparison generally has beneficial effects on the way you feel about yourself; upward social comparison helps to improve your performance.

Your self-concept is also strongly shaped by your culture. Individualistic cultures that emphasize individual autonomy and personal uniqueness promote an independent self. Collectivistic cultures that emphasize ties to a social group and interpersonal connectedness promote an interdependent self. Just as you are often unaware of the ways in which your culture shapes your self, your self-esteem is influenced by processes that operate outside your conscious awareness.

Think Like a Social Psychologist

Understanding everyday behavior
—Connor has good reason to think of himself as average in terms of intelligence. Throughout his college career, he consistently pulled a B average; nothing in his coursework suggested either brilliance or incompetence. However, since Connor has been dating Rachel, a pre-med major who regularly makes the dean's list, he feels he has become noticeably smarter. How can you account for this seeming boost in his intelligence?

Confronting social issues
—You are designing social interventions aimed at the prevention of drug use among adolescents. How could you apply action identification theory to this task?

Making connections
—Individualistic cultures promote individual violence, whereas collectivistic cultures promote collective violence. Assuming that this statement is true, what aspects of the independent and interdependent selves would seem to support it?

THE MANAGING SELF: GETTING TO LIKE "ME"

A Disastrous Encounter

Ruth was frazzled. She had agreed to meet Brian at the flower show at Navy Pier after work. Brian was one of the more promising men she had met—good-looking, thoughtful, smart, and very interested in her. He even shared her passion for gardening. She simply had to accept his invitation, even though she knew that getting to Navy Pier from the suburbs would be a challenge, particularly during rush hour. Once on the road, Ruth realized that traffic was even worse than expected. A crash on the Eisenhower Expressway had caused a huge backup, and traffic in downtown Chicago wasn't much better. By the time she reached the intersection of Illinois Street and Lake Shore Drive, she knew she was going to be late. Nothing I can do about that now, she thought, but at least I can let him know I'm almost there. Seeing that the light was green, Ruth reached for the cell phone in her bag. As she was grappling with the zipper, she failed to notice that the light had changed.

Pat, who was approaching Navy Pier, was happy to see the light turn green. He could sprint across the street and loop around the hotdog stand for the second leg of his run. He never saw Ruth's car as it sped through the red light. In fact, he had no memory of what happened, aside from what he learned from the EMTs and the police officer who investigated the accident. His sister had clipped a short newspaper story from the *Tribune*: "Tragic accident leaves runner paralyzed." There was only one thing he was certain about as he left the hospital: He would never walk again.

Adjusting to life in a wheelchair was challenging, at least at first. But to Pat's surprise, he gradually realized that he could function reasonably well. Both his office and apartment building were handicapped accessible—a feature he had never noticed before. His insurance paid for his car to be retrofitted so that he could operate the accelerator by hand. And the weekly meetings with his support group were a big help. Being around people who were in a similar predicament made him feel good; he liked sharing stories about the challenges of getting around on wheels in a world designed for walkers.

Yet there was one adjustment he found difficult to make: He wouldn't be able to run anymore. No more 5k runs, no more marathons, not even a jog around the block. He avoided looking at the medals and T-shirts he had received over the years, which depressed him. One Sunday evening, as he was going through a stack of papers that had piled up next to his desk, he came across the book that listed all the finishers in the last Chicago Marathon. Mournfully, he turned to the page that listed his name and time. "I could have been a contender," he joked to himself.

Before putting the book away, Pat turned almost by accident to the list of finishers in the wheelchair division. He was surprised by how fast they were. Most of them had finished in less time than he took the last time he ran the race.

How does the way you think about yourself relate to the way you feel about yourself? How does the self deal with threats to your feelings? Clearly, the processes of introspection, self-perception, and social comparison produce more than just cognitive representations. They also produce self-evaluations that influence how you feel about yourself. To the extent that being athletic is important to you, finding reason to doubt your athletic ability is likely to make you feel bad about yourself. Similarly, to the extent that being attractive and popular is important to you, confirmation of your good looks and popularity is likely to make you feel good about yourself.

If you think that this relationship between your thoughts and feelings about yourself isn't exactly rocket science, we agree. The relationship between the ways you think and feel about yourself becomes a little more interesting—and far more complex—if we look at the relationship between self-evaluations on specific dimensions and more global measures of self-liking, also known as **self-esteem**. Simply put, both the athletically challenged and the socially advantaged may have similar levels of self-esteem. That is, they may have the same level of affection for the self, despite obvious differences in their self-evaluations.

Thus, even though self-evaluation and self-esteem seem to be related, it is not entirely clear in what way. Because self-esteem has been defined as "feelings of affection for the self" (Brown, 1998), people who think of themselves as possessing many positive qualities probably have higher self-esteem than people who think they possess only a few. However, the nature of the causal link between the two is unclear. Positive self-evaluations could promote self-esteem in a bottom-up fashion, as some cognitive models have suggested (for example, Pelham & Swann, 1989). The process could be as simple as adding up all your positive qualities. Or you could use a more sophisticated way to "compute" your self-esteem, by giving more weight to characteristics that are more important to you than to others. Either way, in the cognitive (bottom-up) model, the causal arrow goes from relatively concrete self-evaluations on specific dimensions (the input) to self-esteem (the output).

Alternatively, high self-esteem may promote positive self-evaluations in a top-down fashion, as affective models would predict (for example, Brown, Dutton, & Cook, 1997). That is, the good (or bad) feelings you have about yourself may influence your self-evaluations on more concrete dimensions. This model suggests that the causal arrow goes from self-esteem as the input to self-evaluation as the output. Even though both models have at least some empirical support, there is reason to give the edge to the affective model. As Brown (1998) has pointed out, although the self-evaluations of people with low self-esteem are generally lower than those of people with high self-esteem, they are by no means negative. Moreover, people with low self-esteem tend to think of themselves as having more positive and fewer negative qualities than most other people.

There is some evidence that self-esteem operates on an implicit level, serving as a hidden influence on your behavior (Buhrmester, Blanton, & Swann, 2011; Greenwald & Banaji, 1995). You may like yourself, but do you really know why (Dijksterhuis, 2004)? Applying the definition of implicit self-esteem (Greenwald & Banaji, 1995) helps provide an answer. The fact is, people are often unaware of their level of self-esteem. Research shows that self-esteem goes hand in hand with your feelings toward and evaluations of the objects and people you associate with. Consequently, your self-esteem is reflected in your evaluations of the things you own (Beggan, 1992) and the people who are part of your group (Tajfel, 1982). Even seemingly innocuous preferences for the letters in your name (Nuttin, 1987) or the numbers in your birth date (Kitayama & Karasawa, 1997) can indicate high implicit self-esteem (see **Figure 4.3**). In other words, to find the level of your implicit self-esteem, you need only look at how much you like the things you own. If you like your car, your clothes, and your pets, you probably have high implicit self-esteem.

The terms "self-esteem" and "self-evaluation" are often used interchangeably, which makes some sense, since both influence the way you feel about yourself. However, the relative independence of these two constructs suggests that there may be some important differences between them. Among them are the ways in which you manage your self-evaluations and your self-esteem. Let's look at how you manage your specific self-evaluations.

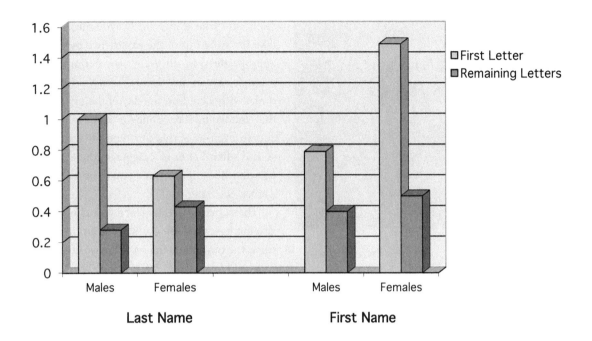

Figure 4.3: Implicit Self-Esteem in Japan: Men's and Women's Preferences for Letters in their Last and First Names.

Source: Kitayama, S., & Karasawa, M. (1997). Implicit self-esteem in Japan: Name letters and birthday numbers. *Personality and Social Psychology Bulletin, 23*, 736–742.

MANAGING SELF-EVALUATIONS

Imagine again that you have finished a marathon (or received a very good grade on an exam). Imagine further that you finished ahead of many runners in your age group (or that your grade is higher than most others in your class). This downward social comparison is likely to leave you feeling good about your performance, and about yourself in general. Now imagine that you prepared for the race (or the exam) with a close friend who ran the race with you and finished well ahead of you. Chances are that his achievement will temper your jubilation. People don't like to be outperformed by others, particularly when the task or performance domain is important to them and the other is psychologically close to them (for example, a friend or romantic partner). Being outperformed in this fashion invites a comparison that can produce negative feelings about the self, and perhaps even the other (Tesser, Millar, & Moore, 1988).

Fortunately, the **self-evaluation maintenance** model (Erber & Tesser, 1994; Tesser, 1988) offers several ways to cope with the consequences of being outperformed by a close other. First, you could reduce your psychological closeness to your friend. Because removing someone from your list of friends would be costly, however, you are likely to take more benign measures, such as cutting down on your interactions with the person (Pleban & Tesser, 1981). Another way to deal with the sting of being outperformed by a close other is to reduce the relevance or importance you place on the performance domain (Tesser & Paulhus, 1983). For example,

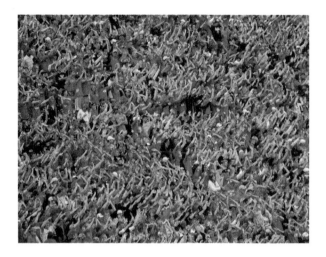

Basking in the reflected glory of your favorite athletic team often leads to a shifting of the boundaries around "me" to include "we."

you could decide that running more than 26 miles really isn't your thing. Finally, you might be able to take the sting out of the experience by putting the appropriate spin on your own performance. For example, you could "decide" that you were coming down with a cold on the day of the marathon, and that you would have done far better without it. Of course, excuses of this sort tend to lack credibility, so it is often better to exaggerate the ability of the person who outperformed you (Alicke, LoSchiavo, Zerbst, & Zhang, 1997).

The superior performance of a close other can also increase your self-evaluations. In close relationships, the other is often part of an expanded sense of your self (Aron, Aron, & Smollan, 1992). That is, the tight boundaries around "me" are redrawn around the "we" that includes your romantic partner or close friend. As a result, your close other's superior performance can be a cause for celebration (Gardner, Gabriel, & Hochschild, 2002). Not surprisingly, a similar effect occurs when the other succeeds on a performance domain that does not matter to you. If you are an avowed couch potato, having a friend who finished the marathon can invite a kind of reflection that will lead to good feelings about yourself. In this case, your friend's accomplishment will allow you to bask in her reflected glory (Cialdini & Richardson, 1980).

As it turns out, your predilection to bask in reflected glory is not limited to cases in which close others succeed. It extends to the success of the athletic teams with which you associate (Cialdini, Borden, Thorne, Walker, Freeman, & Sloan, 1976; Hirt, Zillmann, Erickson, & Kennedy, 1992). Of course, the reverse is also true. When your friends or favorite athletic teams do poorly, you may be quick to cut off their reflected failure by dissociating your self from them (Schimel, Pyszcinski, Greenberg, O'Mahen, & Arndt, 2000).

UNDERSTANDING SELF-ESTEEM

If you examine your self-evaluations across different domains, you are likely to find some variation. For example, you may think of yourself as smart and competent, but perhaps not too athletic. These self-evaluations may be subject to temporal variation as well. Your sense of how smart you are may fluctuate with your academic performance. As we saw earlier, however, such specific self-evaluations may have only a minimal effect on the way you feel about yourself. A poor grade on an exam may have a temporary influence on how smart you think you are, but it may not detract from your self-esteem—that is, the way you feel about yourself overall.

You can get a more precise reading of your self-esteem by completing the Rosenberg (1965) self-esteem scale (see **Table 4.1**), one of the oldest and most common measures of self-esteem used in psychological research.

As you contemplate your score on this measure, keep several things in mind. If you are like everyone else, your score will likely fall into the moderate-to-high range (Banaji & Prentice, 1994; Baumeister, 1998). That

Table 4.1: Rosenberg's (1965) Self-Esteem Scale

1. I feel that I am a person of worth, at least on an equal basis with others.			
1. Strongly agree	2. Agree	3. Disagree	4. Strongly disagree
2. I feel that I have a number of good qualities.			
1. Strongly agree	2. Agree	3. Disagree	4. Strongly disagree
3. All in all, I am inclined to think that I am a failure.			
1. Strongly agree	2. Agree	3. Disagree	4. Strongly disagree
4. I am able to do things as well as most other people.			
1. Strongly agree	2. Agree	3. Disagree	4. Strongly disagree
5. I feel I do not have much to be proud of.			
1. Strongly agree	2. Agree	3. Disagree	4. Strongly disagree
6. I take a positive attitude toward myself.			
1. Strongly agree	2. Agree	3. Disagree	4. Strongly disagree
7. On the whole, I am satisfied with myself.			
1. Strongly agree	2. Agree	3. Disagree	4. Strongly disagree
8. I wish I could have more respect for myself.			
1. Strongly agree	2. Agree	3. Disagree	4. Strongly disagree
9. I certainly feel useless at times.			
1. Strongly agree	2. Agree	3. Disagree	4. Strongly disagree
10. At times I think I am no good at all.			
1. Strongly agree	2. Agree	3. Disagree	4. Strongly disagree

Because some of the scale items are worded in a negative direction to avoid response bias, in order to obtain your overall score you have to reverse-score items 1, 2, 4, 6, and 7 (1 = 4, 2 = 3, 3 = 2, 4 = 1) before adding them to your total score. By this method, higher numbers indicate higher self-esteem.

Source: Rosenberg, M. (1965), *Society and the Adolescent Self-image*. Princeton, NJ: Princeton University Press.

is good news, because high self-esteem has been positively related to everything from resisting persuasion (Rhodes & Wood, 1992) to health, financial success, and personal fulfillment (Branden, 1994). High self-esteem can serve as an effective buffer against stress and failure (Steele, 1988), and has been related more generally to happiness, mental health, and other important life outcomes such as job and relationship satisfaction (Orth, Robins, & Widaman, 2012). At the same time, low self-esteem is often considered a causal antecedent of underachievement, drug use, crime, and various forms of violence, including gang violence and domestic violence (Anderson, 1994; Gondolf, 1985; Mecca, Smelser, & Vasconcellos, 1989; Renzetti, 1992). Based on these and other findings, the California Task Force (1990) suggestsed that programs that are designed to bolster individuals' self-esteem might also be helpful in reducing violence, and possibly in curing a broad range of other social ills.

At the time of its release, the California Task Force's report was met with widespread bemusement. Late-night comedians were quick to ridicule programs for self-esteem enhancement. As it turns out, their reaction was not entirely baseless. To be sure, since high self-esteem is associated with a variety of positive outcomes, it might be desirable to eliminate low self-esteem altogether. Then again, most people already have moderate-to-high self-esteem. Even if it were possible to further raise their self-esteem, how would that benefit them? If we managed to eradicate low self-esteem as successfully as we have managed to eradicate smallpox, would that achievement mark the end of drug use, crime, and violence? Probably not. Part of the problem is that those social ills are at best weakly linked to low self-esteem (Baumeister, Smart, & Boden, 1996).

If anything, high self-esteem—and not low self-esteem—is the root cause of much violence. Think about evildoers like Osama bin Laden, Saddam Hussein, and former Ugandan dictator Idi Amin—to say nothing of Adolf Hitler and Joseph Stalin. Although these tyrants probably suffer(ed) from several mental health problems, none of them appears to have suffered from low self-esteem. To the contrary, they may have harbored a peculiar form of high self-esteem, in which their positive self-views were highly contingent on feedback from others. People with such precarious, highly externalized self-esteem require constant feedback that affirms their positive self-views. Discrepant feedback that challenges their positive self-views is extremely threatening and often elicits aggression and violence (Baumeister, 1998; Baumeister, Smart, & Boden, 1996). Needless to say, people with such an inflated sense of self (that is, an extremely high level of self-esteem) are particularly vulnerable to negative feedback. Take a look at **Figure 4.4** for how threatened egotism can lead to aggression and violence.

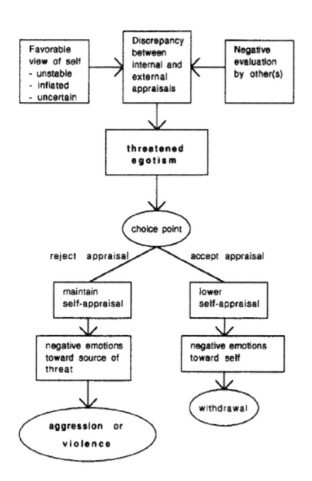

Figure 4.4: The Threatened Egotism Model of Self-Esteem and Aggression.

Source: Baumeister, R. F., Smart, L., & Boden, J. M. (1996). Relation of threatened egotism to violence and aggression: The dark side of high self-esteem. *Psychological Review, 103*, 5–33.

Much of what is true for externalized high self-esteem is also true for unstable high self-esteem. To say that there is such a thing as unstable self-esteem may sound odd, given that self-esteem is defined as a global affection for the self, which is presumed to be rooted in corresponding self-views. However, Kernis (1993) and his colleagues have argued that in some people, self-esteem fluctuates over time, partly as a result of their

unique experience. For example, we can reasonably expect that Pat's self-esteem will suffer as a result of the accident that left him in a wheelchair. To offset such temporary fluctuations, those with unstable high self-esteem embrace positive feedback, but reject negative feedback. On an emotional level, the positive feedback leads to positive feelings, but the negative feedback leads to defensiveness (Kernis, Cornell, Chien-Ru, Berry, & Harlow, 1993). Although these findings do not suggest a direct relationship between unstable high self-esteem and violence, those with unstable high self-esteem often do respond to negative feedback with anger and hostility (Kernis, Grannemann, & Barclay, 1989). As we will see in Chapter 10, defensiveness, anger, and hostility can become the seeds of violence.

Does all this mean that self-esteem is a concept with little or no utility? Not quite. To some extent, self-esteem is tied to a person's self-views: Positive self-views promote high self-esteem, and negative self-views promote low self-esteem. Moreover, positive self-views on a specific dimension help to predict motivation and performance on that dimension. For example, a person who thinks of herself as an athlete is likely to pursue athletic endeavors and do well in them. Because self-esteem is by definition more global than self-evaluation, it tends to predict *bundles of behavior* (Swann, Chang-Schneider, & McClarty, 2007) such as those involved in depression, anxiety disorders, criminal convictions, school refusal, and money or work problems (Donellan et al., 2005; Trzesniewski et al., 2006).

MANAGING SELF-ESTEEM

Kernis and his colleagues have shown that we maintain our self-esteem through more or less active management. They also hint that the way we manage it may depend on our specific goals, such as enhancement or consistency. Because most people have moderate-to-high self-esteem, much of our self-esteem management may be aimed at enhancement. As we will see shortly, however, much as we like to feel good about ourselves, we are frequently just as invested in maintaining an accurate, consistent view of the self.

Self-Enhancement

Because high self-esteem has so many benefits, it is not surprising that a number of processes seem designed to protect or enhance self-esteem. Consider how we make attributions for our successes and failures. First-time marathoners who finish the race often cite their determination and persistence, along with the amount of preparation, for their success (and the first time around, succeeding means finishing). Those who fail to finish are often quick to point to the weather (too hot, too cold, too windy), a lack of sleep, health issues (a cold coming on), or just plain bad luck. Attributions of this sort reveal a **self-serving bias**, a pervasive tendency to attribute our success to internal causes like effort or ability and our failure to external causes beyond our control (Miller & Ross, 1975; Zuckerman, 1979).

Interestingly, the tendency to make self-serving attributions for our successes and failures extends even to the groups we are associated with, like our favorite sports teams (Lau & Russell, 1980). For example, many Chicagoans blamed the collapse of the Cubs in the 2003 National League Championship series on a fan whose attempt to catch a foul ball prevented Moises Alou from getting the second out of the inning. Few blamed the Cubs' short-stop, who later failed to turn a routine double play, and even fewer blamed the manager for not yanking his rapidly tiring pitcher. This self-serving strategy took the blame for the loss away from the team and placed it squarely on the shoulders of a hapless fan.

"There isn't enough blame to go around, there's only enough for you."

The self-serving bias compels us to take credit for our success but blame others for our failures.

It is tempting to suspect that people may be *motivated* to self-enhance by taking credit for their successes and deflecting blame for their failures. That may not be the case, however. Recall from Chapter 3 that we are generally better at processing information that is consistent with our expectations. To the extent that our self-views are positive, we will expect to succeed, and thus will have a relatively easy time integrating our success with relevant aspects of the self, like our effort and ability. On the other hand, failure is not as easy to reconcile with our positive self-views, so we tend attribute it to external causes. At any rate, the self-serving bias enhances our self-images, making us feel good about ourselves (Miller, 1976; Sicoly & Ross, 1979). This statement applies primarily to the independent self. Although self-enhancement is common in all cultures (Kitayama & Uchida, 2003; Sedikides, Gaertner, & Toguchi, 2003), the self-serving bias is rarely found in cultures that promote an interdependent self, perhaps due to cultural norms that preclude blaming others (Sedikides et al., 2003).

Because the self-serving bias is rooted in the way we process information, it may lead indirectly to self-enhancement, without our conscious intention. Several other processes bring about self-enhancement in a more motivated fashion. In general, we value what we are good at and believe that we are good at the things we value (Dunning, Perie, & Story, 1991; Schmader & Major, 1999). If you are smart, there is a good chance you will consider smartness an important characteristic in yourself and others. And if you believe that being smart is important, you are likely to seek feedback that you do indeed have that quality. Similarly, we tend to devalue the characteristics we don't have. If you don't excel at athletic pursuits, there is a good chance that you won't place a premium on athleticism (Gibbons, Benbow, & Gerrard, 1994). Exaggerating your strengths and downplaying your weaknesses is an effective way to feel good about yourself and allow yourself to think you are superior to others. If all else fails and failure has you down, you can improve your sense of self-worth by exaggerating the virtues of your romantic partner (Brown & Han, 2012; For more on the psychological benefits of self-enhancement, see the Social Psychology and Health box below).

SOCIAL PSYCHOLOGY AND HEALTH: THE BENEFITS OF POSITIVE ILLUSIONS AND SELF-ENHANCEMENT

As we have seen, some people with high self-esteem run the risk of becoming defensive—even violent—when their positive self-views are threatened. However, positive self-views also have psychological advantages. Taylor and Brown (1988) have argued that people who believe they have many positive qualities also believe they can effectively use those qualities to create desired outcomes. Consequently, they are more optimistic than others about the future.

The term **positive illusions** describes a combination of positive self-views, a sense of personal control, and optimism that is beneficial in a wide array of psychological functioning. Although positive illusions may seem exaggerated and perhaps unwarranted, they are beneficial in a wide array of psychological functioning. Compared to people with more realistic and accurate self-views, people who hold positive illusions are generally happier. When their positive illusions extend to their partners, they are often happier than others with their personal relationships (Murray, Holmes, & Griffin, 1996). Furthermore, people with an exaggerated sense of control and optimism cope better with stressful life events, including life-threatening illnesses like cancer (Taylor, 1983). The beneficial effects of their positive illusions may extend beyond coping with the psychological distress of the illness to adopting beneficial behaviors such as exercise and a healthy diet (Taylor, Kemeny, Aspinwall, Schneider, Rodriguez, & Herbert, 1992).

Positive self-views are to some extent the outcome of self-enhancement. Could it be that by itself, self-enhancement has beneficial effects on mental health? The answer appears to be yes. Taylor, Lerner, Sherman, Sage, and McDowell (2003) found that research participants who saw themselves in a more favorable light than their friends did fared better on a number of indicators of mental health. Interestingly, this edge in mental health did not have a social cost, because the more self-enhancing participants were also seen more positively by their friends. Thus, positive illusions and self-enhancement appear to be beneficial, as long as the self-views they produce are sturdy and stable.

Although self-enhancement is usually beneficial, at times it can be self-defeating. Self-handicapping (Jones & Berglas, 1978) is the seemingly bizarre tendency to erect obstacles to our own success in order to support self-serving attributions for failure. Suppose you study day and night for an important exam, only to receive a D. By itself, the poor grade could deflate your academic self-esteem, but the effect is compounded by all the effort you poured into studying. If you had handicapped your performance by not studying (Ferrari & Tice, 2000), by taking drugs (Berglas & Jones, 1978) or drinking the night before (Higgins & Harris, 1988), or by subjecting yourself to unusually high levels of stress (Hendrix & Hirt, 2009), the outcome (a poor grade) might not have been all that different. Under those circumstances, however, you would have felt compelled to attribute your poor performance to a lack of effort rather than ability. Because effort, unlike ability, is a variable that is under your control, this kind of self-handicapping allows you to convince yourself that you would have done well if only you had tried harder. Attributing your failure to a lack of effort protects your self-esteem, at least for the short term. In the long run, however, it decreases your chances for future success (Zuckerman, Kieffer, & Knee, 1998), because it may well prevent you from trying harder the next time (McCrea, 2008).

Consistency

Though dramatic, self-handicapping isn't common; it tends to plague people who believe their past achievements do not accurately reflect their abilities (Berglas & Jones, 1978). (The rock band caught in a downward spiral following the smashing success of their first album is a far better, yet less studied, case of self-handicapping than the boozing college student.) Similarly, self-enhancement is only one way to manage your self-esteem. As much as you like to feel good about yourself, you also like to be *consistent*. So, your sense of self—and with it your self-esteem—is determined not only by comparisons with others, but by comparison to the standards you hold for yourself.

According to **self-discrepancy theory** (Higgins, 1987; 1999), you compare your *actual self*—who you are at a given time—to two standards. Your *ought self* exemplifies who you should be or how well you should do on a task. Your *ideal self* exemplifies who you would like to be or how well you would like to do on a task. One way to think about the difference between these two standards is to look at your ought self as reflecting your conscience. Your ideal self is just that—a set of idealized expectations regarding yourself or your performance.

To illustrate this distinction, imagine you have decided to enter a marathon with the realistic expectation of finishing before the course closes. Yet at the same time, you may harbor fantasies of finishing in the top ten percent of your age group. Thus, your ought self and your ideal self suggest different goals and different standards for your performance. Failing to live up to either standard will be reflected in different forms of emotional distress. A discrepancy between your actual and your ought selves (for example, you failed to finish) is likely to lead to feelings of anxiety, tension, and agitation. A discrepancy between your actual and your ideal selves (for example, you finished in 29,000th place) is likely to lead to feelings of depression, dejection, and sadness. Of course, for Pat, feelings of depression, dejection, and sadness will likely be very high because of the magnitude of the discrepancy between his ideal self (wanting to qualify for the Boston Marathon) and his actual self (not having the use of his legs).

Evidence for these differences in the emotional impact of actual-ought and actual-ideal discrepancies comes from a study in which participants first listed attributes characteristic of their actual, ought, and ideal selves (Higgins, Bond, Klein, & Strauman, 1986). In a subsequent experimental session, some participants wrote about the impact that a positive or negative event might have on them. Those with a high actual-ought discrepancy wrote faster than others and reported more agitation. Those with a high actual-ideal discrepancy wrote more slowly than others and reported feeling more dejected. In other words, actual-ought and actual-ideal discrepancies seem to produce specific emotional vulnerabilities: anxiety in the former case and depression in the latter.

Of course, as self-discrepancies decrease or cease to exist, negative emotions will give way to positive emotions. As you reduce an actual-ought discrepancy, agitation will give way to serenity. As you reduce an actual-ideal discrepancy, depression will give way to cheerfulness. With regard to Pat's actual-ideal discrepancy, it may help him to replace his ideal self pre-accident (a Boston qualifier) with an ideal self that is more attainable (racing in a wheelchair and finishing in a respectable time).

The extent to which you can reduce self-discrepancies depends in part on whether you approach a task with a focus on promotion or prevention (Higgins, Shah, & Freedman, 1997). A promotion focus is directed primarily toward obtaining positive consequences, so it is particularly suited to reducing actual-ideal discrepancies like the one Pat is experiencing. A prevention focus is directed toward avoiding negative consequences, so it would be a better bet for reducing or minimizing actual-ought discrepancies. Consistent with this idea, Shah and Higgins (2001) found that participants with a promotion focus were faster than others at appraising how cheerful or dejected a number of positively and negatively valued objects (for example, guns, kitten, garbage, and flowers) would make them feel. Participants with a prevention focus were faster than others at appraising how serene or agitated those same objects would make them feel.

Let's return to the case in which people fail to achieve their goals. Even though these two discrepancies are qualitatively different, the anxiety that arises from actual-ought discrepancies and the dejection that arises from actual-ideal discrepancies have two things in common: Both are aversive, and both arise from inconsistencies among different aspects of the self. We know from **cognitive dissonance theory** (Festinger, 1957) that people like to think of themselves as consistent and will take steps to reduce the negative emotions and physiological arousal caused by the perception of inconsistency. How do they accomplish that goal?

In one of the most famous studies of *dissonance reduction*, Festinger and Carlsmith (1959) asked participants to complete an utterly boring task, like turning a bunch of cubes on a table a quarter turn each. Once participants had completed the task, the experimenter asked them to tell the next participants that the task had been fun and exciting. On the pretense that he had to leave the lab because of an emergency, he offered the participants either a small reward ($1) or a large reward ($20, a large amount in 1959) for telling this lie. Once the participants had completed that part of the experiment, the experimenter returned and asked them to indicate how much they had enjoyed the dull cube-turning task. Those participants who had received the small reward said they had liked the task a great deal more than those who received the large reward.

These results may seem counterintuitive, but they make a great deal of sense when you consider the following. First, participants probably thought of themselves as honest, and thus may have hesitated to comply with the experimenter's request to lie. Those who received the large reward may have been able to justify their behavior on the grounds that they had received a tidy sum of money. Thus, they experienced little cognitive dissonance. For those who received the relatively puny reward, however, the situation was very different. Getting $1 doesn't provide enough justification to lie, especially for people who think of themselves as honest. By convincing themselves that the cube-turning task was, in fact, interesting, participants reduced the dissonance that arose from the inconsistency between their self-views (honest) and their behavior (lying).

To the extent that self-discrepancies involve the realization of an inconsistency (for instance, between your standards and your performance), along with an aversively arousing emotional experience (anxiety or depression), you may reduce this particular form of dissonance by reevaluating the performance-related activity. For example, you could respond to a worse-than-expected finish in a marathon by devaluing marathon running, or by reducing its importance to yourself or its significance as an indication of athleticism. That is not to say that self-discrepancy theory is a special case of dissonance theory, or vice versa. The theoretical power of self-discrepancy theory lies in its ability to make specific predictions about the emotional fallout from coming up short on your goals and standards.

There is some evidence that the experience of cognitive dissonance may depend on a person's self-esteem (Stone, 2003). People with high self-esteem are more likely than others to experience dissonance, because they hold high standards for themselves (Stone, 2003). Conversely, people with low self-esteem are less likely than others to experience dissonance. As Aronson (1968) puts it, "If a person conceives of himself as a 'schnook,' he will expect to behave like a schnook" (p. 24). Low self-esteem, in other words, carries low expectations for the self, so it should produce little pressure to be consistent. Because high self-esteem is tied to high expectations for the self (as reflected in the ought and ideal selves), actual-ought and actual-ideal conflicts are likely to produce relatively large inconsistencies, along with aversive dissonance arousal. People with high self-esteem can reduce this dissonance through **self-affirmation**, the process of affirming one's self-worth in response to threats to the self. Remember that high self-esteem is tied to a variety of positive cognitions about the self. Thus, when people with high self-esteem violate a personal norm, they can reduce the dissonance they experience by affirming their worth in other ways (Steele, 1988), rather than by changing their attitudes (Galinsky, Stone, & Cooper, 2000.)

Accuracy

The motive to be consistent may help to explain why we often seek information that confirms rather than enhances our self-views. In general, we like others to see us as we see ourselves; thus, **self-verification**—the tendency to seek information that confirms our self-views—is often more important than self-enhancement. Because self-verification is ultimately motivated by accuracy, under some circumstances, people may seek feedback that is negative from others. People with high self-esteem generally do not seek negative feedback, because their self-views are confirmed by positive feedback. However, people with negative self-esteem must seek negative feedback to confirm their self-views (Swann, 1984; 2012). This striving for self-verification appears to be culturally universal. In other words, it is prevalent in both individualistic and collectivistic cultures (Seih et al., 2013).

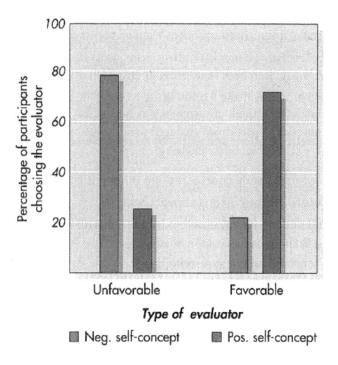

Figure 4.5: Participants' Preferences for Unfavorable and Favorable Evaluators in the Service of Self-verification.

Source: Swann, W.B. Jr., Stein-Seroussi, A., & Giesler, R.B. (1992). Why people self-verify. Journal of Personality and Social Psychology, 62, 392–401.

In support of this idea, researchers have found that people with positive self-views tend to choose romantic partners who evaluate them favorably, while people with negative self-views prefer partners who evaluate them unfavorably (see **Figure 4.5**), thus confirming their own views of themselves (Swann, 1990; Swann, Stein-Seroussi, & Giesler, 1992). Moreover, married couples report a higher level of commitment to their relationship when they feel that their spouses really know them, including their flaws and shortcomings (Swann, Hixon, & De La Ronde, 1992).

Self-verification also plays an important role in the functioning of groups. When people work with others, it is particularly important that they perceive one another's abilities accurately rather than favorably. Research indicates that self-verification improves members' connectedness to the group, which is particularly important for tasks involving creativity (Swann, Milton, & Polzer, 2000). Finally, self-verification promotes both harmony and productivity in diverse work groups (Swann, Kwan, & Polzer, 2003). Of course, in some cases, self-verification can lead to adverse consequences: see the Dark Side of Social Psychology box below.

SOCIAL PSYCHOLOGY ENCOUNTERS THE DARK SIDE: THE LOW SELF-ESTEEM TRAP

Self-verification may be an important mechanism for managing and maintaining a person's self-esteem. Specifically, the preference for accurate rather than favorable feedback from others may help to "fix" a person's self-esteem at a steady level. That is good news for people with positive self-views and high self-esteem. For them, seeking accurate feedback is likely to yield information that enhances the self. However, it may be bad news for people with low self-esteem.

In fact, people with low self-esteem may be caught in what might be called the *low self-esteem trap*. Because their self-views are unfavorable to begin with, accurate feedback is likely to confirm their views. The fact that these people tend to make interpersonal choices that confirm their negative views doesn't help. Because their choices can be counted on to deliver a steady stream of accurate yet negative feedback, their low self-esteem may stabilize over time.

Self-Regulation

Self-enhancement, the need to be consistent, and the desire to be accurate have very different effects on self-esteem. How can we make sense of these seemingly conflicting strategies? One way would be to recognize that they are all part of the more general process of self-regulation, "by which the human psyche exercises control over its functions, states, and inner processes" (Baumeister & Vohs, 2004, p. 1). In general, we may prefer to enhance the self, although at times we may be compelled to manage our self-esteem more for the sake of consistency or accuracy. Consistency may be more important to us when we are interested in self-improvement. One way to reduce a discrepancy between the actual and ought self so as to obtain a more favorable outcome the next time around is to adjust our behavior. Accuracy may be particularly important to group functioning. One way to optimize a group's functioning is to ask others to confirm our strengths and weaknesses through self-verification.

Unlike much of the biological self-regulation that helps to regulate our sleep and calorie intake, the self-regulation of personal goals and social motives is largely volitional—that is, under our conscious control. Volition requires cognitive resources, and self-regulation is certainly no exception. It generally is not a good idea to pursue too many self-regulatory goals at the same time. Thus, New Year's resolutions to lose weight, quit smoking, and get better grades all at once are usually doomed, because pursuing all those goals at the same time exceeds the resources most people have at their disposal. In fact, pursuing even one such goal can lead to a level of **ego-depletion** that makes pursuing another goal at the same time difficult (Baumeister, Bratslavsky, Muraven, & Tice, 1998; Baumeister, Muraven, & Tice, 2000; Baumeister, Vohs, & Tice, 2007) and impairs self-regulation on subsequent tasks (Vohs et al., 2008).

Evidence for the notion that it is perhaps not a good idea to go on a diet and quit smoking at the same time comes from a study that required participants to resist the temptation to eat either chocolate or radishes, while at the same time trying to trace a geometric figure without retracing any lines or lifting the pen from the paper (Baumeister et al., 1998). Unbeknownst to the participants, the task was impossible to complete, so it required persistent repetition. Not surprisingly, participants who had been asked to eat radishes while resisting eating chocolate chip cookies that were left in plain sight spent less time and made fewer attempts to solve the difficult task than participants who had been asked to eat chocolate chip cookies while resisting eating radishes (see **Figure 4.6**). Presumably, resisting chocolate requires a great deal more self-control than resisting radishes. Apparently, resisting the desirable food depleted participants' cognitive resources to the point that they had little willpower left to complete the impossible

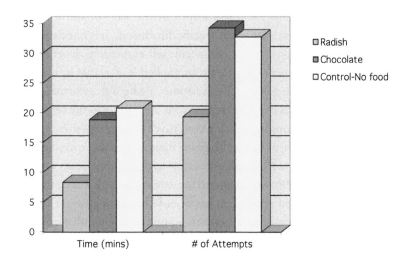

Figure 4.6: Persistence on Unsolvable Puzzles in Baumeister et al., 1998.

Source: Baumeister, R. F., Bratslavsky, E., Muraven, M., & Tice, D. M. (1998). Ego depletion: Is the active self a limited resource? *Journal of Personality and Social Psychology,* 74(5),1252–1265.

Self-regulation and self-control require cognitive resources. Because engaging in one form of self-control depletes the self of resources, attempting other forms of self-control at the same time is bound to fail.

task. Resisting the radishes—a far easier task—left participants with more resources to attempt the task. Similar effects were obtained in studies of the extent to which participants managed to resist fantasizing about or engaging in inappropriate sexual behavior (Gailliot & Baumeister, 2007).

Although feeling good or monitoring one's performance can attenuate the consequences of an ego-depleting activity (Tice, Baumeister, Shmueli, & Muraven, 2007; Wan & Sternthal, 2008), research on the ego-depletion model suggests that volitional self-regulation is not only difficult, but prone to failure (Vohs & Heatherton, 2000). That conclusion may well include the kind of self-regulation that is involved in reducing self-discrepancies. There is also reason to believe that self-enhancement may not be as important as is generally thought. For example, in managing their moods, people often consider the social constraints placed on them by the situation, in addition to their feelings of happiness or sadness. When the situation calls for a more attenuated mood, they often forgo happiness (Erber & Erber, 2000).

THE MANAGING SELF: A SUMMARY

The way you feel about yourself is shaped by the way you think about yourself. Although your self-esteem is related to your self-evaluations on specific dimensions, it is not clear whether your self-esteem is determined by specific self-evaluations, or whether specific self-evaluations depend on your level of self esteem. Some evidence suggests that self-esteem operates on an implicit level—that is, outside your conscious awareness. In general, people tend to protect their self-evaluations. Being outperformed by a close other on a self-relevant performance domain invites negative comparisons. According to the self-evaluation maintenance model, people deal with these comparisons by reducing their psychological closeness to the other, by reducing the relevance of the performance domain, or by handicapping their performance in some way.

Self-esteem differs from self-evaluation in that it represents a more global liking for the self. Self-esteem does vary in its stability over time and the extent to which it is contingent on feedback from the external world. Unstable, externalized self-esteem has been linked to aggression and hostility when threatened. The management of stable, internalized self-esteem is subject to self-enhancement, as well as to pressure for consistency and accuracy. Self-discrepancy theory explains the dynamic tensions between the actual, ought, and ideal selves and predicts the affective consequences of actual-ought and actual-ideal self discrepancies. Pressure for consistency also figures prominently in the theory of cognitive dissonance. At times, people are less interested in self-enhancement and self-consistency than in information that verifies their self-views. All these processes can be conceptualized as instances of self-regulation.

Think Like a Social Psychologist

Designing research
—According to the self-evaluation maintenance model, under what conditions might an individual be inclined to undermine or even sabotage the performance of a close other? How could you design an experiment to test this hypothesis?

Thinking critically
—A news story about an attempted school shooting concludes with the observation that the would-be shooter was suffering from low self-esteem and had been teased by his classmates. On what grounds would you doubt this assessment? What would be the alternative explanation in terms of self-esteem?

Making connections
—The ego depletion model emphasizes the limited ability of the self to execute self-regulatory tasks. In that regard, what are the implications of thinking of the self as a reservoir? The implications of the self as a muscle?

THE TACTICAL AND STRATEGIC SELF: PRESENTING "ME"

On the Road Again

Practicing to race the Chicago Marathon in a wheelchair had been hard. Before Pat could get any kind of distance at a decent speed, he had to spend countless hours lifting weights to build his upper body strength. But that wasn't the worst of it. He had come to hate the pitiful glances he sometimes received from the runners and walkers he encountered as he raced along the Lakefront Trail. It would have been all too easy to accept the labels people use to describe a person like him—terms like "disabled" and "handicapped." But at some point, Pat decided that he would accept none of that. He was going to show the world that though he wasn't a runner anymore, he was still an athlete.

As he was nearing the marathon's finish line, Pat felt that his mission was accomplished. Like all other wheelchair participants, he had started a few minutes ahead of the runners, even the elite ones from Kenya. Those who eventually passed him gave him a big smile and a wave that seemed to indicate he was one of them. And the thousands of spectators who lined the streets had been unbelievable, cheering him on as though he were competing in the Olympics. "I know I'm an athlete, and now the world knows, too," he thought as he crossed the finish line 2 hours and 45 minutes after starting.

The self plays an important role in how we interact with others and the world. As we have seen, the self seeks and processes feedback from others. Self-verification theory suggests that at times we solicit others' candid opinions of us. At other times, we are just as interested in controlling their impressions of us. The self helps us to manage the impressions others form of us, providing strategies for presenting ourselves to them (Goffman, 1959).

Before we discuss the goals, tactics, and strategies that go into managing our impressions, we should note that much **self-presentation** occurs without a great deal of conscious thought or deliberate effort (Tyler, 2012). Under many circumstances, our self-presentations are guided by the hidden influence of the automatic self (Paulhus, 1993). Go back to the self-descriptions you wrote at the beginning of this chapter. Much of what you jotted down probably did not take much effort, and we would guess that your self-descriptions were by and large positive. If that was, in fact, the case, your self-description shows the automatic self in action.

People generally have a lifetime of practice describing themselves, mostly in positive terms. As a result, their self-descriptions tend to be positive, and the constant repetition yields an automatic self that is positive as well (Paulhus, 1993). Because the automatic self requires little in the way of cognitive resources, it should guide self-presentation, particularly when our attention is focused on other tasks. In support of this idea, Paulhus and his colleagues found that the automatic self kicks in whenever we are emotionally aroused (Paulhus & Suedfeld, 1988), pressed for time, or otherwise distracted (Paulhus, Graf, & Van Selst, 1989).

THE TACTICAL SELF: GETTING OTHERS TO LIKE US

Although many self-presentations occur automatically, at times they are guided by specific goals such as wanting to be liked. In those cases, they become more purposeful and deliberate, more like the creation of a desired impression than a revelation of one's true self. This does not mean that self-presentation is necessarily deceitful. As Goffman (1959) emphasized, it frequently involves the "over-communication of some facts and the under-communication of others." In this process, people employ several different tactics, either singly or in combination (Leary, 1995): see **Table 4.2**.

Perhaps the simplest way to create a desired impression is to use verbal *self-descriptions* of our likes and dislikes, accomplishments, family background, and personality characteristics. Often, this type of information is conveyed in face-to-face interactions like a first date. Because of their decidedly verbal nature, self-descriptions are also a great tool for managing written impressions, as in personal ads.

In addition to using verbal descriptions, we often volunteer information about specific attitudes in order to create a desired impression. Sometimes these *attitude expressions* may sound like little more than self-descriptions (for example, "I love running"). However, they allow others to make inferences about us (he's determined, he's conscious of his health, and so on). Similarly, if we hear a person say that she supports legislation designed to reduce air pollution, we can safely infer that she is an environmentally conscious person with generally liberal attitudes.

Sometimes people try to put their past behavior into an appropriate context by complementing their self-descriptions with *attributional statements*. By and large, the attributions they volunteer are self-serving. Frequently,

Table 4.2: Tactics of Self-presentation

Self-descriptions	Describing oneself in ways that communicate a desired impression
Attitude Expressions	Expressing attitudes to convey the presence or absence of certain characteristics
Attributional Statements	Explaining past and present behavior in ways that elicit a desired image
Compliance with Social Norms	Acting in ways that are consistent with the prevailing norms of the situation
Social Associations	Expressing associations with desirable others and dissociations from undesirable others
Changes in Physical Environment	Using and modifying aspects of one's physical environment to elicit a desired impression

Adapted from Leary (1995), Self-presentation: Impression Management and Interpersonal Behavior. Madison, WI: Brown & Benchmark.

people try to convince others that a given behavior sprang from positive motives such as wanting to help someone, rather than from ulterior motives like wanting to look good in the eyes of others (Doherty, Weingold, & Schlenker, 1990). And as we saw earlier, people tend to take credit for their successes ("I got an A in psychology because I worked really hard") while avoiding blame for their failures ("I flunked physics because the instructor hated my guts") (Miller & Ross, 1975). When such attributions are volunteered in an interpersonal context, they can promote a positive impression and deflect a negative impression. Of course, people aren't likely to take statements like these at face value. Thus, under some circumstances, a less self-serving approach may be more effective. By refusing credit for success, one can come across as modest, and by accepting blame for failure, one can create an impression of magnanimity (Miller & Schlenker, 1985).

To some extent, people use *compliance with social norms* to control the impressions they generate. Showing up for a dinner party well groomed and well dressed attests to a person's good judgment, indicating that he is serious about the occasion. Doing so may also allow inferences about the person's good taste and socioeconomic status. Of course, the more general rule is to match one's appearance to the situation. A suit and tie may elicit a good impression when worn to dinner at an expensive restaurant, but at a college football game, the wearer is likely to be seen as nerdy. Similarly, we often try to match our emotional expressions to the situation. We express anger when someone tells us an upsetting story and delight when we hear of someone's good fortune, primarily because we know these reactions are expected from us.

Sometimes people manage the impressions they create by pointing to their *social associations*. In general, people like to be associated with others who are popular, successful, and attractive, if for no other reason than to bask in their reflected glory. How desirable we are in the eyes of others depends to some extent on the desirability of those with whom we associate. People frequently tell about their personal associations, real or imagined, by dropping names ("I ran in the same marathon as Paula Radcliffe"). Sometimes these associations are symbolic in nature. As we saw earlier, when people bask in the reflected glory of their favorite athletic teams, they like to evidence their associations by wearing team-identifying apparel (Cialdini, Borden, Thorne, Freeman, & Sloane, 1976). Regardless of whether the associations we brag about are real, symbolic, or imagined, we tend to mention them in order to create a favorable impression.

Finally, people vary aspects of their *physical environment* in the service of self-presentation. To some extent, such seemingly rational choices as where and how to live may be influenced partly by self-presentational concerns. Some people go to extraordinary lengths to avoid living in the suburbs or driving a minivan. Similar self-presentational concerns may influence their choice of furnishings or coffee table books. After all, our impressions of people who have Plato's *Republic* lying around the living room are likely to be quite different from those of people who keep stacks of *Organic Gardening*. The way people decorate their offices may also be influenced by self-presentational concerns. The professor whose office door is plastered with cartoons probably is not very interested in making his students and colleagues laugh. More likely, he wants to create the impression of a good-natured, likable person.

Self-Presentational Norms

The extent to which any of these self-presentational tactics leads to the desired outcome of creating a favorable impression depends on how well they fit the norms that guide self-presentation. First among those norms is *decorum* (Leary, 1995), which refers to conformity with established standards of behavior. If nothing else, decorum may modify our emotional expressions. If someone tells us a sad story over dinner in a public place, we are likely to respond with an expression of controlled sadness. The public setting prevents us from responding more strongly, perhaps by weeping uncontrollably. In fact, a complete emotional breakdown under such circumstances would likely have the opposite of the intended effect because of the norm it would violate (Baumeister & Tice, 1990).

Similarly, the general norm of *modesty* constrains our choice of self-presentational tactics. It suggests that name-dropping should not be overdone, so as to avoid giving the impression of bragging or showing off. Similarly, modesty prescribes that self-descriptions should not be overly self-aggrandizing. A successful business person is generally better off saying that he makes a good living rather than revealing that he makes an obscenely large amount of money. On the other hand, too much modesty has the potential to backfire. In general, slight modesty is more effective than extreme modesty. Doing well but downplaying the importance of one's performance does not always lead to more favorable impressions, however. If you avoided that approach in the self-description you wrote to get the ice-cream taster job, you made a good choice. Modesty is effective only when the other person is aware of your accomplishments (Schlenker & Leary, 1982).

The norm of *behavioral matching* prescribes that two people's self-presentations should somehow match. If one person is boastful, the other should be boastful in return. If one person is modest, the other should be modest in return. Finally, the norm of self-presentational *consistency* dictates that people should behave in ways that are consistent with their expressed attitudes, and that their consistency should manifest itself in a variety of situations over time. People who say one thing one day and the opposite the next day tend to be perceived as weak, unreliable, and unpredictable.

Self-Presentation in the Heat of the Interaction

In many cases, self-presentations occur as two people are interacting. This situation poses some unique challenges, both for the sender and for the recipient of self-presentational messages. To the extent that self-presentation entails the under-communication of certain facts, the sender can find herself forced to keep a tight lid on whatever she wants to conceal. Self-presentation by way of under-communication can be a daunting task, because suppressing any kind of thought is notoriously difficult (Wegner, 1994). Often, people can succeed at keeping an unwanted thought out of mind for a time by devoting considerable effort to the task. However, any success they may have usually comes at the expense of a massive rebound of the suppressed thought later on (Wegner, Schneider, Carter, & White, 1987).

More importantly, when our attention is divided between suppressing a thought and another task such as conversing with someone, attempting to suppress a thought can make that thought hyper-accessible (Wegner, 1994; Wegner & Erber, 1992). As a result, we often cannot help but blurt out the very thing we are trying to suppress. In the context of self-presentation, suppression may compel us to communicate exactly what we are trying to hide. Even if we should succeed at presenting ourselves in the desired way, our success does not come without a cost. Because careful self-presentation requires considerable cognitive resources, it can deplete our ability to deal with subsequent tasks requiring self-regulation (Vohs, Baumeister, & Ciarocco, 2005).

Although the attentional demands of interacting with another person can be detrimental to the self-presenter, those same demands on the recipient's attention can work to the sender's advantage. In listening to a self-presentation, the recipient must focus her attention on the sender. As we know from Chapter 3, focusing on the person rather than on the situation can lead to dispositional, or personality, attributions (for example, Storms, 1973; Taylor & Fiske, 1975), which are usually easier to generate than situational attributions. The reason is that in forming dispositional attributions, we often rely on implicit personality theories that indicate which traits and behaviors go together. Thus, if someone tells us that she went out of her way to save a neighbor's cat from drowning, we can instantly infer that she is helpful as well as kind. Situational information is generally harder to come by. Even when it is available, recipients may be preoccupied with self-presentational concerns of their own, which deprive them of the attentional resources they need to properly evaluate the information (Gilbert, Pelham, & Krull, 1988).

Detecting Deceit in Self-Presentation

Two people who meet for the purpose of creating a favorable impression in each other find themselves in a paradoxical situation. While they are trying to generate favorable impressions of themselves, they are aware that the other person may have the same goal. Thus, each may be motivated to find out just how truthful the other is in presenting himself. Assessing the truth of a self-presentational communication is often hard to do based only on verbal descriptions, unless they are particularly outrageous ("I used to date Orlando Bloom, but I got bored with him very quickly"). Instead, we must often rely on nonverbal cues to detect whether someone is telling the truth.

If you knew this famous actor personally, would you be tempted to mention the friendship to others? How might such a disclosure affec the impression that others form of you?

Because nonverbal cues like facial expressions are difficult to control, people's thoughts and feelings may show despite their best efforts to conceal them (DePaulo, 1992). If anything, the higher the stakes, the more likely that a nonverbal contradiction will occur (DePaulo, Lanier, & Davis, 1983). One way it manifests itself is through inconsistencies among different channels of nonverbal communication (DePaulo, Stone, & Lassiter, 1985). For example, a person may look us straight in the eye while telling us about his occupational accomplishments, conveying openness and honesty in his face. If at the same time, however, he shifts around nervously in his chair, we can infer from the discrepancy between his facial expressions and his postural movements that he may be lying. Deceit is also reflected in people's speech: Their voices tend to rise in pitch (Zuckerman, Spiegel, DePaulo, & Rosenthal, 1982), and they engage in more sentence repair than usual (Stiff, Miller, Sleight, Mongeau, Garlick, & Rogan, 1989). Interestingly, the more motivated people are to lie, the more likely they are to betray their true thoughts and feelings through their nonverbal behavior (DePaulo, 1992).

THE STRATEGIC SELF: GETTING WHAT WE WANT

Clearly, being liked is an important goal for most people. At times, however, we employ self-presentation strategically, to elicit specific impressions directed at getting what we want. Dale Carnegie (1936) bluntly advised his clients to heap praise on others in order to "make friends and influence people." *Ingratiation* of this sort can indeed work to one's benefit, but only if it succeeds in eliciting the trait attribution the self-presenter desires (Jones & Pittman, 1982). If heaping praise on someone elicits the attribution that you are a nice person, it will work, but it is doomed if it creates the impression that you have an ulterior motive. Complimenting your instructor on a wonderful course after the grades have been turned in will likely elicit the attribution that you are a nice person and a good student who really liked the class. However, the same compliment, made around the time of the mid-term exam, may backfire, because it will elicit the suspicion that it was made with the goal of getting a better grade. And, of course, these two very different outcomes of your attempt at ingratiation will lead your instructor to form very different feelings toward you. In short, flattery is a crude way of eliciting the attribution of being nice and likable. More subtle forms of flattery—nodding, agreeing, smiling, laughing at someone's jokes—are more likely to be successful, because they are more difficult to attribute to ulterior motives. They may not always work, but when they fail, they generally don't backfire.

As much as we want to be liked, we often want to be thought of as competent. Take a look at the self-description you wrote for the job as an ice-cream taster. You probably didn't write it to come across as likable, but focused instead on characteristics that would elicit the attribution of competence at the job. Just like ingratiation, *self-promotion* of this sort should be done with care. When done with moderation, emphasizing your skills, qualifications, and experience can positively influence others' perceptions of your competence without detracting from your likability (Godfrey, Jones, & Lord, 1986). On the other hand, exaggerating your skills, qualifications, and experience can detract from both your competence and your likability, making you look like a shameless and perhaps even fraudulent self-promoter (Jones & Pittman, 1982).

At times, being liked will be the least of your worries. In some situations, you may want to create the impression that you are not to be messed with. If you're embroiled in a dispute over a car repair, for example, you may resort to *intimidation* when other avenues have been exhausted. Some of your instructors may try to come across as scary on the first day of class to get students to attend class religiously and turn in their papers on time. Obviously, the emotion these intimidators are trying to instill is fear—enough of it to control others' behavior (Jones & Pittman, 1982).

People with a lot of power (for example, your instructors) may seem to have an edge in using intimidation effectively. On closer inspection, however, intimidation can also be a great tool for the seemingly powerless. Think, for example, of the young child who responds to a parent's refusal to buy a toy by launching into a temper tantrum. Parents often have little choice but to give in, especially if they want to avoid the glares of everyone in the store. In such cases, the child (seemingly a person of little power) has successfully intimidated the parents (seemingly people of great power), gaining power in the process. On a more adult level, many people who threaten others with a lawsuit probably aren't looking to get their day in court. Rather, the threat is designed to intimidate others into compliance.

For intimidation to succeed, it is important that the threat be perceived as real. Threatening to sue over a small amount of money is often ineffective, especially when the costs of retaining an attorney exceed the amount in dispute. And tough policies on late papers can lose their bite when students realize they aren't enforced. Similarly, intimidation by parents with a history of making empty threats often fails to make the desired impression.

At times, you may be able to get what you want not by intimidating others, but by suggesting that you deserve what you are asking for. Using the strategy of *exemplification*, you can get your way by instilling a sense of guilt in the other for not complying. Rather than threatening a lawsuit against the car repair shop, for example, you could point to your loyalty as a customer, in hopes that the mechanic will give you a break. Rather than throwing a tantrum over a parent's refusal to buy a toy, a child could point out just how good and deserving he has been. Because exemplification works by instilling guilt in others, it is often very effective in gaining compliance. The risk, however, is that the exemplifier will be seen as manipulative or even exploitative. When exemplification is perceived in this way, it is likely to fail, because it does not produce guilt (Jones & Pittman, 1982).

Finally, *supplication* is a self-presentational strategy that is used to convey the idea that one is helpless or needy. The owner's manual of a 1964 Studebaker contained a special insert for women faced with a flat tire: "Put on some fresh lipstick, fluff up your hairdo, stand in a safe spot off the road, wave and look helpless and feminine." More macho drivers were well served not to take this dubious piece of advice. Done by the wrong person and in the wrong situation, displays of strategic incompetence can convey laziness rather than helplessness (Jones & Pittman, 1982). When that is the case, they are not likely to trigger the nurturance that might compel bystanders to help.

INDIVIDUAL DIFFERENCES IN SELF-PRESENTATION

The nature and direction of our self-presentations hinge importantly on our specific goals, as well as on the real or imagined presence of an appropriate target. There is little reason to be self-presentational when we are alone in our rooms. In addition, the extent to which we engage in self-presentation is shaped by at least two dispositional qualities: self-awareness and self-monitoring.

Have you ever found yourself adjusting your gait after glimpsing your reflection in a window? If you have, the change in your behavior resulted from a self-awareness brought on by the sight of your reflection. Such an experience not only conveys an aspect of your actual self (for example, that you walk like a duck); it also brings to mind some aspects of your ideal self (for example, walking like Ben Affleck if you are a man, or like Tyra Banks if you are a woman). As we saw earlier, because negative outcomes of actual-ideal self comparisons are generally aversive, they can compel you to adjust your behavior (Carver, 2003). Of course, the adjustment to your behavior may also be fueled by your concerns about how others view you ("If I think I walk like a duck, other people surely will").

People differ in the extent to which they believe others pay attention to them. Those who are high in *public self-consciousness* (Carver & Scheier, 1981) are highly attuned to how others view them, and are therefore more likely to engage in self-presentation than those who are low in public self-consciousness. Pat''s sentiment, as he crossed the finish line of the Chicago Marathon in his wheelchair, suggests that he was highly self-conscious and that he had succeeded in meeting not only his goal of finishing, but his self-presentational goal.

Our tendency to self-present is also shaped by the extent to which we monitor our own behavior in response to situational demands. People vary in the extent to which they engage in such **self-monitoring**. To find out whether you are a high or low self-monitor, complete the scale in **Table 4.3** by indicating True of False for each item.

What does it mean to be a high or low self-monitor, and what are the implications for self-presentation? High self-monitors are highly sensitive to situational cues and adjust their behavior to fit the situation. Low self-monitors are guided primarily by more internal standards for behavior; thus, they are far less willing to make situational adjustments in their behavior. As a result, high self-monitors are generally better at tailoring their self-presentations to the situation (Danheiser & Graziano, 1982).

Think about self-presentation in the context of a job interview. High and low self-monitors may be equally likely to dress and groom themselves to create a favorable impression. During the interview, however, high self-monitors may try particularly hard to discern what the interviewer might want to hear and adjust their answers accordingly. Low self-monitors, because they are guided primarily by internal standards, may be less likely to make such adjustments. Does that mean that high self-monitors have an edge in such situations? Not necessarily.

Table 4.3: Snyder's (1974) Self-monitoring Scale

1. I find it hard to imitate the behavior of other people.

2. I guess I put on a show to impress or entertain people.

3. I would probably make a good actor.

4. I sometimes appear to others to be experiencing deeper emotions than I actually am.

5. In a group of people I am rarely the center of attention

6. In different situations and with different people I often act like very different persons.

7. I can only argue for ideas I really believe.

8. In order to get along and be liked, I tend to be what people expect me to be.

9. I may deceive people by being friendly when I really dislike them.

10. I am not always the person I appear to be.

To obtain your score, first look at your answers to questions 1, 5, and 7. Give yourself a point for each time you answered False. Next give yourself a point for each time you answered to True to any of the remaining questions. Then total your points. If your total is 7 or higher, you are a high self-monitor; if your total is 3 or lower, you are a low self-monitor.

Adapted from Snyder (1974), Self-monitoring of expressive behavior. *Journal of Personality and Social Psychology*, 30, 526–537.

An interviewer who is interested in hiring someone who seems authentic may well give the nod to the low self-monitor, despite the high self-monitor's attempt to say and do all the right things. (For more on the tradeoff between high and low self-monitoring, see the Think like a Social Psychologist box on **page 161**.)

**THINK LIKE A SOCIAL PSYCHOLOGIST: IS IT BETTER TO BE A
HIGH OR LOW SELF-MONITOR?**

Getting a high score on an IQ test is generally considered good news. But what about getting a high score on Snyder's self-monitoring scale? It seems clear that being a high self-monitor may give you an edge in interacting with others or being part of a group. After all, high self-monitors are, by definition, sensitive to the situation; they are more likely than others to do what is appropriate, what others want (Gangestad & Snyder, 2000). Not surprisingly, then, high self-monitors are more likely than others to emerge as leaders (Dobbins, Long, Dedrick, & Clemons, 1990).

However, there is a downside to being a high self-monitor. Because of their preoccupation with situational cues, these people often behave in ways that contradict their attitudes. They tend to pick their friends on the basis of their looks, and because their self-presentations change with the situation, they may sometimes come across as social chameleons.

On the face of it, being a low self-monitor may seem a liability. Because low self-monitors may be preoccupied with internal rather than social standards for behavior, their social interactions may be quite awkward and lead to largely negative impression. When actor Tom Cruise jumped up and down on the couch on the *Oprah Winfrey Show* while professing his love for Katie Holmes to his host and the nation, many viewers concluded that he must have lost his mind. That the couple subsequently divorced probably didn't help matters. Examples like this suggest that being a low self-monitor has mostly drawbacks, and few, if any, advantages.

Can you think of some situations in which being a low self-monitor could be advantageous? What kind of impression will you form of a person who acts primarily according to internal standards? Are your friends high or low self-monitors? In what ways might you benefit from surrounding yourself with friends who are low self-monitors? How could groups benefit from having both high and low self-monitors?

THE TACTICAL AND STRATEGIC SELF: A SUMMARY

The self has numerous ways to create a desired impression. In general, self-presentation entails the over-communication or under-communication of information about the self, with the goal of eliciting liking from others. We can deploy self-presentation both tactically and strategically to control the impressions we make on others. To elicit liking, the tactical self can use self-descriptions, attitude expressions, attributional statements, compliance with social norms, social association, and changes in the physical environment. To elicit a specific impression, the strategic self can rely on ingratiation, self-promotion, intimidation, exemplification, and supplication. The extent to which people engage in self-presentation is influenced by individual differences in public self-consciousness and self-monitoring. Although much of self-presentation operates on a conscious level, it is also subject to a variety of hidden influences.

Think Like a Social Psychologist

<u>Making connections</u>

—You are feeling undecided about a presidential candidate who is going to give a speech on your campus. He seems to have some good ideas, but until now has been silent on the issues that are important to you. During the speech, he devotes a great deal of time to one of the issues that concern you. What about his self-presentation may make you like him less?

HIDDEN INFLUENCES ON THE SELF: A SUMMARY

<u>Culture:</u> A set of forces that shape aspects of the self such as the independent and interdependent self, without our conscious awareness

<u>The automatic self:</u> Knowledge of the self that is highly accessible, but which results from processes that are hidden from our conscious awareness

<u>Implicit self-esteem:</u> Self-esteem that is not experienced consciously, but is manifested in one's liking for people and objects that are relevant to the self

<u>Automatic self-presentation:</u> Aspects of self-presentation that are generated by the automatic self without our conscious awareness or deliberate thought

KEY TERMS AND DEFINITIONS

Self-concept: the cognitive representation of knowledge about the self

Self-schema: a rich and multifaceted knowledge structure that organizes what we know about ourselves

Self-reference effect: superior memory for information that relates to the self

Self-perception theory: a theory that proposes that people inspect their past relevant behaviors to ascertain whether they have a particular trait

Social comparison: a process that involves acquiring, thinking about, and reacting to information about one or more other people relative to the self

Independent self: a conception of the self that revolves around personal autonomy; common in individualistic cultures

Interdependent self: a conception of the self that revolves around one's relationships with others; common in collectivistic cultures

Automatic self: a highly accessible aspect of the self that contains self-knowledge resulting from processes that may be hidden from consciousness

Self-esteem: a global measure of self-liking

Self-evaluation maintenance: the processes through which individuals cope with the consequences of being outperformed by a close other

Self-serving bias: a pervasive tendency to attribute our success to internal causes and our failure to external causes

Self-discrepancy theory: a theory that describes the consequences of comparing the actual self to the ought self and the ideal self

Cognitive dissonance theory: a theory that proposes that people like to think of themselves as consistent, and will take steps to reduce the negative emotions and physiological arousal caused by the perception of inconsistency

Self-affirmation: the process of affirming one's self-worth in response to threats to the self

Self-verification: the tendency to seek information that confirms our self-views

Ego-depletion: a reduction in mental resources that results from volitional efforts at self-regulation

Self-presentation: the processes—including goals, tactics, and strategies—by which we manage the impressions we make on others

Self-monitoring: the extent to which people monitor their behavior in response to situational demands

Positive illusions: a combination of positive self views, a sense of personal control, and optimism that is beneficial in a wide array of psychological functioning

REFERENCES

Alicke, M. D., LoSchiavo, F. M., Zerbst, J., & Zhang, S. (1997). The person who outperforms me is a genius: Maintaining perceived competence in upward social comparison. *Journal of Personality and Social Psychology, 73*, 781–789.

Aron, A., & Aron, E. N. (1986). *Love and the expansion of the self: Understanding attraction and satisfaction.* Washington, DC: Hemisphere.

Aron, A., Aron, E. N., & Smollan, D. (1992). Inclusion of Other in the Self Scale and the structure of interpersonal closeness. *Journal of Personality and Social Psychology, 63*, 596–612.

Aron, A., Aron, E. N., Tudor, M., & Nelson, G. (1991). Close relationships as including other in the self. *Journal of Personality and Social Psychology, 60*, 241–253.

Aronson, E. (1968). Dissonance theory: Progress and problems. In R. P. Abelson, E. Aronson, W. J. McGuire, T. M. Newcomb, M. J. Rosenberg, & P. H. Tannenbaum (Eds.), *Theories of cognitive consistency: A sourcebook* (pp. 5–27). Skokie, IL: Rand McNally.

Balcetis, E., Dunning, D., & Miller, R. L. (2008). Do collectivists know themselves better than individualists? Cross-cultural studies of the holier than thou phenomenon. *Journal of Personality and Social Psychology, 95*, 1252–1267.

Banaji, M. R., & Prentice, D. A. (1994). The self in social contexts. *Annual Review of Psychology, 45*, 297–332.

Bargh, J. A., & Chartrand, T. L. (1999). The unbearable automaticity of being. *American Psychologist, 54*, 462–479.

Baumeister, R. F. (1998). The self. In D. T. Gilbert, S. T. Fiske, & G. Lindzey, (Eds.), *The handbook of social psychology* (4th ed., Vol. 1, pp. 680–710). New York: Basic Books.

Baumeister, R. F., Muraven, M., & Tice, D. M. (2000). Ego depletion: A resource model of volition, self-regulation, and controlled processing. *Social Cognition, 18*, 130–150.

Baumeister, R. F., Bratslavsky, E., Muraven, M., & Tice, D. M. (1998). Ego depletion: Is the active self a limited resource? *Journal of Personality and Social Psychology, 74*(5), 1252–1265.

Baumeister, R. F., Smart, L., & Boden, J. M. (1996). Relation of threatened egotism to violence and aggression: The dark side of high self-esteem. *Psychological Review, 103*, 5–33.

Baumeister, R. F., & Tice, D. M. (1990). Anxiety and social exclusion. *Journal of Social and Clinical Psychology, 9*, 165–195.

Baumeister, R. F., & Vohs, K. D. (2004). *Handbook of self-regulation: Research, theory, and applications.* New York: Guilford.

Baumeister, R. F., Vohs, K. D., & Tice, D. M. (2007). The strength model of self-control. *Current Directions in Psychological Science, 16*, 351–355.

Beggan, J. K. (1992). On the social nature of nonsocial perception: The mere ownership effect. *Journal of Personality and Social Psychology, 62*, 229–237.

Bem, D. J. (1972). Self-perception theory. In L. Berkowitz (Ed.), *Advances in experimental social psychology* (Vol. 6, pp. 1–63). New York: Academic Press.

Berglas, S., & Jones, E. E. (1978). Drug choice as a self-handicapping strategy in response to noncontingent success. *Journal of Personality and Social Psychology, 36,* 405–417.

Branden, N. (1994). *The six pillars of self-esteem.* New York: Bantam Books.

Brown, J. D. (1998). *The self.* New York: McGraw-Hill.

Brown, J. D., Dutton, K. A., & Cook, K. E. (2001). From the top down: Self-esteem and self- evaluation. *Cognition and Emotion, 15,* 615–631.

Brown, J. D., & Han, A. (2012). My better half: Partner enhancement as self-enhancement. *Social Psychology and Personality Science, 3,* 479–486.

Buckingham, J. T., & Alicke, M. D. (2002). The influence of individual versus aggregate social comparison and the presence of others on self-evaluations. *Journal of Personality and Social Psychology, 83,* 1117–1130.

Buhrmester, M. D., Blanton, H., & Swann, W. B. Jr. (2011). Implicit self-esteem: Nature, measurement, and a new way forward. *Journal of Personality and Social Psychology, 100,* 365–385.

California State Dept. of Education (1990). *Toward a state of esteem. The final report of the California task force to promote self-esteem and personal and social responsibility.* Sacramento, CA.

Carnegie, D. (1936). *How to win friends and influence people.* New York: Simon and Schuster.

Carver, C. S. (2003). Self-awareness. In M. R. Leary & L. P. Tangney (Eds.), *Handbook of self and identity* (pp. 179–196). New York: Guilford Press.

Carver, C. S., & Scheier, M. F. (1981). *Attention and self-regulation: A control-theory approach to human behavior.* New York: Springer-Verlag.

Choi, I., & Choi, Y. (2002). Culture and self-concept flexibility. *Personality and Social Psychology Bulletin, 28,* 1508–1517.

Cialdini, R. B., Borden, R. J., Thorne, A., Walker, M. R., Freeman, S., & Sloan, L. R. (1976). Basking in reflected glory: Three (football) field studies. *Journal of Personality and Social Psychology, 34,* 366–375.

Cialdini, R. B., & Richardson, K. D. (1980). Two indirect tactics of image management: Basking and blasting. *Journal of Personality and Social Psychology, 39,* 406–415.

Cooley, C. H. (1902). *Human nature and the social order.* New York: Charles Scribner's Sons.

Cross, S. E., Hardin, E. E., & Gercek-Swing, B. (2011). The what, how, why, and where of self- construal. *Personality and Social Psychology Review, 15,* 142–179.

Danheiser, P. R., & Graziano, W. G. (1982). Self-monitoring and cooperation as a self- presentational strategy. *Journal of Personality and Social Psychology, 42,* 497–505.

Deaux, K., Reid, A., Mizrahi, K., & Ethier, K. A. (1995). Parameters of social identity. *Journal of Personality and Social Psychology, 68,* 280–291.

Demo, D. H. (1992). The self-concept over time: Research issues and directions. *Annual Review of Sociology, 18,* 303–326.

DePaulo, B. M. (1992). Nonverbal behavior and self-presentation. *Psychological Bulletin, 111,* 203–243.

DePaulo, B. M., Lanier, K., & Davis, T. (1983). Detecting the deceit of the motivated liar. *Journal of Personality and Social Psychology, 45,* 1096–1103.

DePaulo, B. M., Stone, J. I., & Lassiter, G. D. (1985). Telling ingratiating lies: Effects of target sex and target attractiveness on verbal and nonverbal deceptive success. *Journal of Personality and Social Psychology, 48,* 1191–1203.

Dijksterhuis, A. (2004). I like myself but I don't know why: Enhancing implicit self-esteem by subliminal evaluative conditioning. *Journal of Personality and Social Psychology, 86,* 345–355.

Dobbins, G. H., Long, W. S., Dedrick, E. J., & Clemons, T. C. (1990). The role of self- monitoring and gender on leader emergence: A laboratory and field study. *Journal of Management, 16,* 609–618.

Doherty, K., Weingold, M. F., & Schlenker, B. R. (1990). Self-serving interpretations of motives. *Personality and Social Psychology Bulletin, 16,* 485–495.

Donellan, B., Trzesniewski, K., Robins, R., Moffitt, T., & Caspi, A. (2005). Low self-esteem is related to aggression, antisocial behavior, and delinquency. *Psychological Science, 16,* 328–335.

Dunning, D., Perie, M., & Story, A. L. (1991). Self-serving prototypes of social categories. *Journal of Personality and Social Psychology, 61,* 957–968.

Erber, R. (2002). Perpetrators with a clear conscience: Lying self-deception and belief change. In L. S. Newman & R. Erber (Eds.), *Understanding genocide: The social psychology of the Holocaust* (pp. 285–300). New York: Oxford University Press.

Erber, R., & Erber, M. W. (2000). The self-regulation of moods: Second thoughts on the importance of happiness in everyday life. *Psychological Inquiry, 11,* 142–148.

Erber, R., & Tesser, A. (1994). Self-evaluation maintenance: A social psychological approach to interpersonal relationships. In R. Erber, & R. Gilmour (Eds.), *Theoretical frameworks for personal relationships* (pp. 211–233). Hillsdale, NJ: Lawrence Erlbaum Associates.

Ferrari, J. R., & Tice, D. M. (2000). Procrastination as a self-handicap for men and women: A task-avoidance strategy in a laboratory setting. *Journal of Research in Personality, 34,* 73–83.

Festinger, L. (1954). A theory of social comparison processes. *Human Relations, 7,* 117–140.

Festinger, L., & Carlsmith, J. M. (1959).Cognitive consequences of forced compliance. *Journal of Abnormal & Social Psychology, 58,* 203–210.

Gailliot, M. T., & Baumeister, R. F. (2007). Self-regulation and sexual restraint: Dispositionally and temporarily poor self-regulatory abilities contribute to failures at restraining sexual behavior. *Personality and Social Psychology Bulletin, 33,* 173–186.

Galinsky, A. D., Stone, J., & Cooper, J. The reinstatement of dissonance and psychological discomfort following failed affirmation. *European Journal of Social Psychology, 30,* 123–147.

Gangestad, S. W., & Snyder, M. (2000). Self-monitoring: Appraisal and reappraisal. *Psychological Bulletin, 126,* 530–555.

Gardner, W. L., Gabriel, S., & Hochschild, L. (2002). When you and I are "we," you are not threatening: The role of self-expansion in social comparison. *Journal of Personality and Social Psychology, 82,* 239–251.

Gibbons, F. X., Benbow, C. P., & Gerrard, M. (1994). From top dog to bottom half: Social comparison strategies in response to poor performance. *Journal of Personality and Social Psychology, 67,* 638–652.

Gilbert, D. T., Pelham, B. W., & Krull, D. S. (1988). On cognitive busyness: When person perceivers meet persons perceived. *Journal of Personality and Social Psychology, 54,* 733–740.

Godfrey, D. K., Jones, E. E., & Lord, C. G. (1986). Self-promotion is not ingratiating. *Journal of Personality and Social Psychology, 50,* 106–115.

Goffman, E. (1959). *The presentation of self in everyday life.* New York: Doubleday.

Goldstein, N. J., & Cialdini, R. B. (2007). The spyglass self: A model of vicarious self-perception. *Journal of Personality and Social Psychology, 92,* 402–417.

Gondolf, E. W. (1985). Fighting for control: A clinical assessment of men who batter. *Social Casework, 66,* 48–54.

Greenwald, A. G., & Banaji, M. R. (1995). Implicit social cognition: Attitudes, self-esteem, and stereotypes. *Psychological Review, 102,* 4–27.

Harter, S. (2003). The development of self-representations during childhood and adolescence. In M. R. Leary & J. P. Tangney, (Eds.). *Handbook of self and identity* (pp. 610–642). New York: Guilford Press.

Hendrix, K. S., & Hirt, E. R. (2009). Stressed out over possible failure: The role of regulatory fit on claimed self-handicapping. *Journal of Experimental Social Psychology, 45,* 51–59.

Higgins, E. T. (1987). Self-discrepancy: A theory relating self and affect. *Psychological Review, 94,* 319–340.

Higgins, E. T. (1999). Self-discrepancy: A theory relating self and affect. In R. F. Baumeister (Ed.), *The self in social psychology* (pp. 150–181). Philadelphia: Psychology Press.

Higgins, E. T., Bond, R. N., Klein, R., & Strauman, T. (1986). Self-discrepancies and emotional vulnerability: How magnitude, accessibility, and type of discrepancy influence affect. *Journal of Personality and Social Psychology, 51,* 5–15.

Higgins, E. T., Shah, J., & Friedman, R. (1997). Emotional responses to goal attainment: Strength of regulatory focus as moderator. *Journal of Personality and Social Psychology, 72,* 515–525.

Higgins, R. L., & Harris, R. N. (1988). Strategic "alcohol" use: Drinking to self-handicap. *Journal of Social and Clinical Psychology, 6,* 191–202.

Hirt, E. R., Zillmann, D., Erickson, G. A., & Kennedy, C. (1992). Cost and benefits of allegiance: Changes in fans' self-ascribed competencies after team victory versus defeat. *Journal of Personality and Social Psychology, 63,* 724–738.

James, W. (1890). *The principles of psychology* (Vol. 1). New York: Holt.

Jones, E. E., & Berglas, S. (1978). Control of attributions about the self through self- handicapping strategies: The appeal of alcohol and the role of under-achievement. *Personality and Social Psychology Bulletin, 4,* 200–206.

Jones, E. E., & Pittman, T. S. (1982). Toward a general theory of strategic self-presentation. In J. Suls (Ed.), *Psychological perspectives on the self* (Vol. 1, pp. 231–262). Hillsdale, NJ: Lawrence Erlbaum Associates.

Kemmelmeier, M., & Oyserman, D. (2001). The ups and downs of thinking about a successful other: Self-construals and the consequences of social comparisons. *European Journal of Social Psychology, 31,* 311–320.

Kenny, D. A., & DePaulo, B. M. (1993). Do people know how others view them? An empirical and theoretical account. *Psychological Bulletin, 114,* 145–161.

Kernis, M. H. (1993). The role of stability and level of self-esteem in psychological functioning. In R. F. Baumeister (Ed.), *Self-esteem: The puzzle of low self-regard* (pp. 167–182). New York: Plenum Press.

Kernis, M. H., Cornell, D. P., Sun, C., Berry, A., & Harlow, T. (1993). There's more to self- esteem than whether it is high or low: The importance of stability of self-esteem. *Journal of Personality and Social Psychology, 65,* 1190–1204.

Kernis, M. H., Grannemann B. D., & Barclay, L. C. (1989) Stability and level of self-esteem as predictors of anger arousal and hostility. *Journal of Personality and Social Psychology, 56,* 1013–1022.

Kihlstrom, J. F., & Cantor, N. (1984). Mental representations of the self. In L. Berkowitz (Ed.), *Advances in experimental social psychology* (Vol. 17, pp. 1–47). New York: Academic Press.

Kitayama, S., & Karasawa, M. (1997). Implicit self-esteem in Japan: Name letters and birthday numbers. *Personality and Social Psychology Bulletin, 23,* 736–742.

Kitayama, S., & Markus, H. R. (1999). Yin and Yang of the Japanese self: The cultural psychology of personality coherence. In D. Cervone & Y. Shoda, (Eds.). *The coherence of personality: Social-cognitive bases of consistency, variability, and organization* (pp. 242–302). New York: Guilford Press.

Kitayama, S., & Uchida, Y. (2003). Explicit self-criticism and implicit self-regard: Evaluating self and friend in two cultures. *Journal of Experimental Social Psychology, 39,* 476– 482.

Klein, S. B. (2012). Self, memory, and the self-reference effect: An examination of conceptual and methodological issues. *Personality and Social Psychology Review, 16,* 283–300.

Klein, S. B., & Kihlstrom, J. F. (1986). Elaboration, organizations, and the self-reference effect in memory. *Journal of Experimental Psychology: General, 115,* 26–38.

Klein, S. B., & Loftus, J. (1993). Behavioral experience and trait judgments about the self. *Personality and Social Psychology Bulletin, 19,* 740745.

Klein, S. B., Loftus, J., & Kihlstrom, J. F. (1996). Self-knowledge of an amnesic patient: Toward a neuropsychology of personality and social psychology. *Journal of Experimental Psychology: General, 125,* 250–260.

Klein, S. B., Rozendal, K., & Cosmides, L. (2002). A social-cognitive neuroscience analysis of the self. *Social Cognition, 20,* 105–135.

Kozak, M. N., Marsh, A. A., & Wegner, D. M. (2006). What do I think you're doing? Action identification and mind attribution. *Journal of Personality and Social Psychology, 90,* 543–555.

Lau, R. R., & Russell, D. (1980). Attribution in the sports pages: A field test about some current hypotheses about attribution research. *Journal of Personality and Social Psychology, 39,* 29–38.

Leary, M. R. (1995). *Self-presentation: Impression management and interpersonal behavior.* Madison, WI: Brown & Benchmark.

Lewis, M. (1997). The self in self-conscious emotions. In J. G. Snodgrass & R. L. Thompson (Eds.), *The self across psychology: Self-recognition, self-awareness, and the self-concept.* New York: New York Academy of Sciences.

Linville, P. W. (1985). Self-complexity and affective extremity: Don't put all of your eggs in one cognitive basket. *Social Cognition, 3,* 94–120.

Linville, P. W. (1987). Self-complexity as a cognitive buffer against stress-related illness and depression. *Journal of Personality and Social Psychology, 52,* 663–676.

Markus, H. (1977). Self-schemata and processing information about the self. *Journal of Personality and Social Psychology, 35,* 63–78.

Markus, H., & Kitayama, S. (1991). Culture and the self: Implications for cognition, emotion, and motivation. *Psychological Review, 98,* 224–253.

Markus, H., & Wurf, E. (1987). The dynamic self-concept: A social psychological perspective. *Annual Review of Psychology, 38,* 299–337.

Marsh, H. W., & Hau, K. (2003). Big-Fish—Little-Pond effect on academic self-concept: A cross-cultural (26-country) test of the negative effects of academically selective schools. *American Psychologist, 58,* 364–376.

Mashek, D. J., Aron, A., & Boncimino, M. (2003). Confusion of self with close others. *Personality and Social Psychology Bulletin, 29,* 382–392.

Matsumoto, D., Yoo, S. H., Nakagawa, S., and 37 Members of the Multinational Study of Cultural Display Rules (2008). Culture, Emotion Regulation, and Adjustment. *Journal of Personality and Social Psychology, 94,* 925–937.

McCrea, S. M. (2008). Self-handicapping, excuse making, and counterfactual thinking: Consequences for self-esteem and future motivation. *Journal of Personality and Social Psychology, 95,* 274–292.

Mead, G. H. (1934). *Mind, self, and society.* Chicago: University of Chicago Press.

Mecca, A. M., Smelser, N. J., & Vasconcellos, J. (1989). (Eds.). *The social importance of self- esteem.* Berkeley: University of California Press.

Miller, D. T. (1976). Ego involvement and attributions for success and failure. *Journal of Personality and Social Psychology, 34,* 901–906.

Miller, D. T., & Ross, M. (1975). Self-serving biases in the attribution of causality: Fact or fiction? *Psychological Bulletin, 82,* 213–235.

Miller, R. S., & Schlenker, B. R. (1985). Egotism in group members: Public and private attributions of responsibility for group performance. *Social Psychology Quarterly, 48,* 85–89.

Murray, S. L., Holmes, J. G., & Griffin, D. W. (1996). The self-fulfilling nature of positive illusions in romantic relationships: Love is not blind, but prescient. *Journal of Personality and Social Psychology, 71,* 1155–1180.

Montemayor, R., & Eisen, M. (1977). The development of self-conceptions from childhood to adolescence. *Developmental Psychology, 13,* 314–319.

Moore, D. A., & Small, D. A. (2007). Error and bias in comparative judgment: On being both better and worse than we think we are. *Journal of Personality and Social Psychology, 92,* 972–989.

Mussweiler, T. (2001). Focus of comparison as a determinant of assimilation versus contrast in social comparison. *Personality and Social Psychology Bulletin, 27,* 38–47.

Mussweiler, T. (2003). Comparison processes in social judgment: Mechanisms and consequences. *Psychological Review, 110,* 472–489.

Nisbett, R. E., & Wilson, T. D. (1977). Telling more than we can know: Verbal reports on mental processes. *Psychological Review, 84,* 231–259.

Nuttin, J. M. (1987). Affective consequences of mere ownership: The name letter effect in twelve European languages. *European Journal of Social Psychology, 17,* 381–402.

Orth, U., Robins, R. W., & Widaman, K. F. (2012). Life-span development of self-esteem and its effect on important life outcomes. *Journal of Personality and Social Psychology, 102,* 1271–1288.

Oyserman, D., Coon, H. M., & Kemmelmeier, M. (2002). Rethinking individualism and collectivism: Evaluation of theoretical assumptions and meta-analyses. *Psychological Bulletin, 128,* 3–72.

Paulhus, D. L. (1993). Bypassing the will: The automatization of affirmations. In D. M. Wegner & J. W. Pennebaker (Eds.), *Handbook of mental control* (pp. 573–587). Upper Saddle River, NJ: Prentice-Hall.

Paulhus, D. L., & Suedfeld, P. (1988). *Self-deception: An adaptive mechanism.* New York: Prentice-Hall.

Paulhus, D. L., Graf, P., & Van Selst, M. (1989). Attentional load increases the positivity of self-presentation. *Social Cognition, 7,* 389–400.

Pelham, B. W., & Swann, W. B. Jr. (1989). From self-conceptions to self-worth: On the sources and structure of global self-esteem. *Journal of Personality and Social Psychology, 57,* 672–680.

Pleban, R., & Tesser, A. (1981). The effects of relevance and quality of another's performance on interpersonal closeness. *Social Psychology Quarterly, 44,* 278–285.

Pronin, E. (2009). The introspection illusion. In M. P. Zanna (Ed.), *Advances in experimental social psychology* (Vol. 41, pp. 1–67). New York: Elsevier.

Renzetti, C. M. (1992). *Violent betrayal: Partner abuse in lesbian relationships.* Thousand Oaks, CA: Sage Publications.

Rhodes, N., & Wood, W. (1992). Self-esteem and intelligence affect influenceability: The mediating role of message reception. *Psychological Bulletin, 111,* 156–171.

Rickabaugh, C. A., & Tomlinson-Keasey, C. (1997). Social and temporal comparisons in adjustment to aging. *Basic and Applied Social Psychology, 19,* 307–328.

Rogers, T. B., Kuiper, N. A., & Kirker, W. S. (1977). Self-reference and the encoding of personal information. *Journal of Personality and Social Psychology, 35,* 677–688.

Rosenberg, M. (1965). *Society and the adolescent self-image.* Princeton, NJ: Princeton University Press.

Schimel, J., Pyszczynski, T., Greenberg, J., O'Mahen, H., & Arndt, J. (2000). Running from the shadow: Psychological distancing from others to deny characteristics people fear in themselves. *Journal of Personality and Social Psychology, 78,* 446–462.

Schlenker, B. R., & Leary M. R. (1982). Audiences' reactions to self-enhancing, self-denigrating, and accurate self-presentations. *Journal of Experimental Social Psychology, 18,* 89–104.

Schmader, T., & Major, B. (1999). The impact of ingroup vs. outgroup performance on personal values. *Journal of Experimental Social Psychology, 35*, 47–67.

Sedikides, C., Gaertner, L., & Toguchi, Y. (2003). Pancultural self-enhancement. *Journal of Personality and Social Psychology, 84*, 60–79.

Seih, Y., Buhrmester, M. D., Lin, Y., Huang, C., & Swann, W. B. Jr. (2013). Do people want to be flattered or understood? The cross-cultural universality of self-verification. *Journal of Experimental Social Psychology, 49*, 169–172.

Settles, I. H. (2004). When multiple identities interfere: The role of identity centrality. *Personality and Social Psychology Bulletin, 30*, 487–500.

Settles, I. H., Sellers, R. M., & Damas, A. Jr. (2002). One role or two?: The function of psychological separation in role conflict. *Journal of Applied Psychology, 87*, 574–582.

Shah, J., & Higgins, E. T. (2001). Regulatory concerns and appraisal efficiency: The general impact of promotion and prevention. *Journal of Personality and Social Psychology, 80*, 693–705.

Sicoly, F., & Ross, M. (1977). Facilitation of ego-based attributions by means of self-serving observer feedback. *Journal of Personality and Social Psychology, 35*, 734–741.

Smith, E. R., & Zarate, M. A. (1992). Exemplar-based model of judgment. *Psychological Review, 99*, 3–21.

Snyder, M. (1974). Self-monitoring of expressive behavior. *Journal of Personality and Social Psychology, 30*, 526–537.

Spencer-Rodgers, J., Boucher, H. C., Mori, S. C., Wang, L., & Peng, K. (2009). The dialectical self-concept: Contradiction, change, and holism in East Asian cultures. *Personality and Social Psychology Bulletin, 35*, 29–44.

Stiff, J. B., Miller, G. R., Sleight, C., Mongeau, P., Gardelick, R., & Rogan, R. (1989). Explanations for visual cue primacy in judgments of honesty and deceit. *Journal of Personality and Social Psychology, 56*, 555–564.

Steele, C. M. (1988). The psychology of self-affirmation: Sustaining the integrity of the self. In L. Berkowitz (Ed.), *Advances in experimental social psychology* (Vol. 21, pp. 261–302). New York: Academic Press.

Stone, J. (2003). Self-consistency for low self-esteem in dissonance processes: The role of self-standards. *Personality and Social Psychology Bulletin, 29*, 846–858.

Storms, M. D. (1973). Videotape and the attribution process: Reversing actors' and observers' points of view. *Journal of Personality and Social Psychology, 27*, 165–175.

Swann, W. B. Jr. (1984). Quest for accuracy in person perception: A matter of pragmatics. *Psychological Review, 91*, 457–477.

Swann, W. B. Jr. (1990). To be adored or to be known? The interplay of self-enhancement and self-verification. In R. M. Sorrentino & E. T. Higgins (Eds.), *Motivation and cognition* (Vol. 2, pp. 408–448). New York: Guilford Press.

Swann, W. B. Jr. (2012). Self-verification theory. In P. A. M. van Lange, A. W. Kruglanski, & E. T. Higgins (Eds.), *Handbook of theories of social psychology* (Vol. 2, pp. 23–42). Thousand Oaks, CA: Sage.

Swann, W. B. Jr., Chang-Schneider, C., & McClarty, K. L. (2007). Do people's self-views matter? Self-concept and self-esteem in everyday life. *American Psychologist, 62*, 84–94.

Swann, W. B., Hixon, J. G., & De la Ronde, C. (1992). Embracing the bitter "truth": Negative self-concepts and marital commitment. *Psychological Science, 3*, 118–121.

Swann, W. B. Jr., Kwan, V. S. Y., Polzer, J. T., & Milton, L. P. (2003). Fostering group identification and creativity in diverse groups: The role of individuation and self-verification. *Personality and Social Psychology Bulletin, 29*, 1396–1406.

Swann, W. B. Jr., Milton, L. P., & Polzer, J. T. (2000). Should we create a niche or fall in line? Identity negotiation and small group effectiveness. *Journal of Personality and Social Psychology, 79*, 238–250.

Swann, W. B. Jr., Stein-Seroussi, A., & Giesler, R. B. (1992). Why people self-verify. *Journal of Personality and Social Psychology, 62*, 392–401.

Symons, C. S., & Johnson, B. T. (1997). The self-reference effect in memory: A meta-analysis. *Psychological Bulletin, 121,* 371–394.

Tajfel, H. (1982) Social psychology if intergroup relations. *Annual review of psychology, 33,* 1–39.

Taylor, S. E. (1983). Adjustment to threatening events: A theory of cognitive adaptation. *American Psychologist, 38,* 1161–1173.

Taylor, S. E., & Brown, J. D. (1988). Illusion and well-being: A social psychological perspective on mental health. *Psychological Bulletin, 116,* 21–27.

Taylor, S. E., & Fiske, S. T. (1975). Point of view and perceptions of causality. *Journal of Personality and Social Psychology, 32,* 439–445.

Taylor, S. E., Kemeny, M. E., Aspinwall, L. G., Schneider, S. G., Rodriguez, R., & Herbert, M. (1992). Optimism, coping, psychological distress and high-risk sexual behavior among men at risk for AIDS. *Journal of Personality and Social Psychology, 63,* 460–473.

Taylor, S. E., Lerner, J. S., Sherman, D. K., Sage, R. M., & McDowell, N. K. (2003). Portrait of the self-enhancer: Well adjusted and well liked or maladjusted and friendless? *Journal of Personality and Social Psychology, 84,* 165–176.

Tesser, A. (1988). Toward a self-evaluation maintenance model of social behavior. In L. Berkowitz (Ed.), *Advances in experimental social psychology* (Vol. 21, pp. 181–227). New York: Academic Press.

Tesser, A., Millar, M., & Moore, J. (1988). Some affective consequences of social comparison and reflection processes: The pain and pleasure of being close. *Journal of Personality and Social Psychology, 54,* 49–61.

Tesser, A., & Paulhus, D. (1983). The definition of self: Private and public self-evaluation management strategies. *Journal of Personality and Social Psychology, 44,* 672–682.

Tice, D. M., Baumeister, R. F., Shmueli, D., & Muraven, M. (2007). Restoring the self: Positive affect helps improve self-regulation following ego depletion. *Journal of Experimental Social Psychology, 43,* 379–384.

Triandis, H. C. (1989). The self and social behavior in differing cultural contexts. *Psychological Review, 96,* 506–520.

Trzesniewski, K., Donnellan, B., Moffitt, T., Robins, R., Poulton, R., & Caspi, A. (2006). Low self-esteem during adolescence predicts poor health, criminal behavior, and limited economic prospects during adulthood. *Developmental Psychology, 42,* 381–390.

Tulving, E. (1972). Episodic and semantic memory. In E. Tulving & W. Donaldson (Eds.), *Organization of memory.* Oxford, England: Academic Press.

Tyler, J. M. (2012). Triggering self-presentation efforts outside of people's conscious awareness. *Personality and Social Psychology Bulletin, 38,* 619–627.

Vallacher, R. R., & Wegner, D. M. (1987). What do people think they're doing? Action identification and human behavior. *Psychological Review, 94,* 3–15.

Vallacher, R. R., & Wegner, D. M. (2012). Action identification theory. In P. A. M. van Lange, W. Kruglanski, & E. T. Higgins (Eds.), *Handbook of theories of social psychology* (Vol. 2, pp. 327–348). Thousand Oaks, CA: Sage.

Van Sell, M., Brief, A. P., & Schuler, R. S. (1981). Role conflict and role ambiguity: Integration of the literature and directions for future research. *Human Relations, 34,* 43–71.

Vohs, K. D., Baumeister, R. F., & Ciarocco, N. J. (2005). Self-regulation and self-presentation: Regulatory resource depletion impairs impression management and effortful self-presentation depletes resources. *Journal of Personality and Social Psychology, 88,* 632–657.

Vohs, K. D., Baumeister, R. F., Schmeichel, B. J., Twenge, J. M., Nelson, N. M., & Tice, D. M. (2008). Making choices impairs subsequent self-control: A limited-resource account of decision making, self-regulation, and active initiative. *Journal of Personality and Social Psychology, 94,* 883–889.

Vohs, K. D., & Heatherton, T. F. (2000). Self-regulatory failure: A resource-depletion approach. *Psychological Science, 11*(3), 249–254.

Wakslak, C. J., Nussbaum, S., Liberman, N., & Trope, Y. (2008). Representations of the self in the near and distant future. *Journal of Personality and Social Psychology, 95,* 757–773.

Wan, E. W., & Sternthal, B. (2008). Regulating the effects of depletion through monitoring. *Personality and Social Psychology Bulletin, 34,* 32–46.

Wegner, D. M. (1994). Ironic processes of mental control. *Psychological Review, 101,* 34–52.

Wegner, D. M., & Erber, R. (1992). The hyperaccessibility of suppressed thoughts. *Journal of Personality and Social Psychology, 63,* 903–912.

Wegner, D. M., Schneider, D. J., Carter, S. R., & White, T. L. (1987). Paradoxical effects of thought suppression. *Journal of Personality and Social Psychology, 53,* 5–13.

Wegner, D. M., & Vallacher, R. R. (1986) Action identification. In R. M. Sorrentino & E. T. Higgins (Eds.), *Handbook of mMotivation and cCognition: Foundations of sSocial bBehavior.* (pp. 550–582). New York: Guilford Press.

Wills, T. A. (1981). Downward comparison principles in social psychology. *Psychological Bulletin, 90,* 245–271.

Wilson, A. E., & Ross, M. (2000). The frequency of temporal-self and social comparisons in people's personal appraisals. *Journal of Personality and Social Psychology, 78,* 928–942.

Wilson, T. D. (2002). *Strangers to ourselves: Discovering the adaptive unconscious.* Cambridge, MA: Belknap Press/Harvard University Press.

Wilson, T. D., & Kraft, D. (1993). Why do I love thee?: Effects of repeated introspections about a dating relationship on attitudes toward the relationship. *Personality and Social Psychology Bulletin, 19,* 409–418.

Wood, J. V. (1996). What is social comparison and how should we study it? *Personality and Social Psychology Bulletin, 22,* 520–537.

Zuckerman, M. (1979). Attribution of success and failure revisited, or: The motivational bias is alive and well in attribution theory. *Journal of Personality, 47,* 245–287.

Zuckerman, M., Kieffer, S. C., & Knee, C. R. (1998). Consequences of self-handicapping: Effects on coping, academic performance, and adjustment. *Journal of Personality and Social Psychology, 74,* 1619–1628.

Zuckerman, M., Spiegel, N. H., DePaulo, B. M., & Rosenthal, R. (1982). Nonverbal strategies for decoding deception. *Journal of Nonverbal Behavior, 6,* 171–187.

CHAPTER 5

EVALUATION AND ATTITUDES

"WHY AM I BUYING TICKETS TO THIS MOVIE?" THE SELLING OF NO VACANCY

Between the years 1930 and 1932, Richard LaPiere, a sociologist from Stanford University, took frequent breaks from his academic duties to travel extensively through the United States by automobile. Undoubtedly, he stopped to admire all sorts of natural wonders and beautiful landscapes, and we can assume that he also visited important historical sites and cultural institutions. History, however, does not record those details. We know far more about the hotels at which LaPiere stayed and the restaurants at which he dined; those aspects of his journey he documented in great detail. Was LaPiere, despite his scholarly credentials, concerned primarily with filling his belly and finding a warm, comfortable place to sleep for the night? Was he moonlighting as a food critic, or writing a travel guide?

Actually, the information LaPiere left to posterity was simply what was most relevant to the reason for his journey. LaPiere was conducting a field study of people's attitudes. Traveling with him were a "student and his wife," both of whom were "personable, charming, and quick to win the admiration and respect" of everyone they met. They were, however, "foreign-born Chinese, a fact that could not be disguised" (all quotes from LaPiere, 1934, p. 231). Of interest to LaPiere was how his traveling party would be treated at the various establishments they visited. At the time, ethnic Chinese in the United States were concentrated in New York, Chicago, and along the West Coast. They would be perceived as quite alien elsewhere, so LaPiere had reason to believe his traveling companions would elicit decidedly negative reactions. Restaurant personnel, he imagined, would refuse to serve them. Hotel clerks would not rent them rooms, or would pretend that none were available.

The LaPiere study was ambitious; as a social-psychological investigation it was unique. We will learn more about it and the lessons we can draw from it later in this chapter. But LaPiere's adventure also makes for a fascinating *story*. Not many social-psychological investigations feature just a few identifiable people with vividly sketched personalities, or use such rich and unique personal experiences as data. In fact, we (the authors of this book) concluded that just as LaPiere's project became the basis for an interesting and important scientific report, it could also serve as the basis for a compelling motion picture. So excited were we by the idea that we found ourselves meeting with executives at a major movie studio, pitching our proposal for a screenplay tentatively titled *No Vacancy*. (At this point, we should make clear that this story of our foray into show business is a fantasy—or maybe a nightmare.)

Our idea was a hit, and the studio's representatives immediately tried to persuade us not to take our proposal elsewhere. Already they had ideas for how to finance and market the film. Although they were certain that investors could be found to fund the project, they also assured us that some of the production costs could be recovered through "product placement." In other words, the characters in the story could be shown drinking specific commercially available beverages, driving well-known automobile models, and using various other recognizable products. The manufacturers of those products would pay to have them prominently displayed in a widely distributed motion picture. To advertise the film, the studio would print cryptic movie posters showing nothing but a "No Vacancy" sign sitting on a hotel registration desk. One overexcited executive even spoke about splicing subliminal images into the film, to enhance the positive and negative feelings we would want the audience to associate with different characters in the movie.

We were flattered by the enthusiasm our proposal triggered, although a little disturbed that no one seemed very interested in the details of LaPiere's study. The large cash advance that might be coming our way, however, encouraged us to be cooperative and to remain silent about the executives' promotional ideas, all of which were related to social psychological research that was quite familiar to us. After all, we did not want to appear to be condescending toward our new business partners.

The different schemes hatched by our fictional movie executives all had one characteristic in common: they were meant to manipulate people's attitudes. If successful, they would have shaped how the audience evaluated the sponsors' products, the movie itself, and the characters in the movie. Social psychologists use the term *attitude* in much the same way as movie executives, or indeed everyone else—that is, they use it to refer to how we feel about and evaluate things. More precisely, Eagly and Chaiken (1993, p. 1) define an **attitude** as "a psychological tendency that is expressed by evaluating a particular entity with some degree of favor or disfavor."

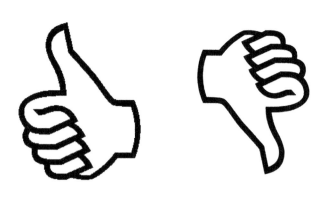

Although attitudes can be complex, any given attitude ranges from extremely positive/favorable (thumbs up) to extremely negative/unfavorable (thumbs down).

Evaluation is one of the most basic psychological processes. It is important for human beings (and other forms of animal life, too, of course) to keep track of what they like and dislike, what they might want to approach, and what they would rather avoid. Clearly, attitudes have important implications for our social behavior. How we interact with other people and groups, our readiness to enter into social situations, and our willingness to take on social roles all depend to a great extent on our attitudes toward those aspects of our social world. As discussed by the Social Psychology in the Courtroom box on **page 175**, attitudes can even determine who goes to prison and for how long. Thus, social psychologists have been at the forefront of research on attitudes.

SOCIAL PSYCHOLOGY IN THE COURTROOM: JUROR ATTITUDES
IN CHILD SEXUAL ASSAULT TRIALS

In the courtroom, attitudes play a role in determining who is imprisoned, who is set free, even who will live or die. In fact, jurors' attitudes on a wide variety of issues can affect the verdicts they reach. For this reason, when juries are selected, lawyers may devote huge amounts of money and effort to determining potential jurors' attitudes (see Toobin, 1996, and Wishner, 1986, for vivid examples).

The importance of jurors' attitudes in child sexual assault trials has been the subject of a great deal of study (Bottoms, Golding, Stevenson, Wiley, & Yozwiak, 2007). Several researchers have reported gender differences in people's reactions to the testimony in such trials. Specifically, women tend to find in favor of victims more often than men (Bottoms, Davis, & Epstein, 2004; Bottoms, Nysse-Carris, Harris, & Tyda, 2003; Duggan et al., 1989; Quas, Bottoms, Haegerich, & Nysse-Carris, 2002). Bottoms (1993) suggested that this gender difference in behavior could be a function of gender differences in attitudes. She identified sexual conservatism, attitudes toward women, and attitudes toward adult/child sexual contact as potential key variables. Indeed, other evidence suggests that independent of gender, such attitudes play a role in people's reactions to child abuse (Hetherton & Beardsall, 1998). Women tend to be more sexually conservative than men, to have (not surprisingly) less negative attitudes toward women, and to have more negative attitudes toward adult/child sexual contact. Perhaps these attitudes can explain the gender differences in the verdicts men and women favor in child sexual assault trials.

A study by Bottoms (1993), in which participants were presented with scenarios based on child sexual assault cases, revealed the expected gender differences in both attitudes and verdicts. More important, statistical analysis of the data revealed that when attitudes were held constant, the gender differences disappeared. In other words, the gender differences in verdicts could be attributed to the gender differences in attitudes.

In a later study, based on different child sexual assault case materials, researchers replicated the finding that women are more pro-victim. However, they failed to find any relationship between either social conservatism or sexism and case judgments (Quas et al., 2002). As discussed in this chapter, though, the relationship between attitudes and behavior can vary, depending on the context. In part, that is because any given behavior is subject to a variety of influences—hidden and otherwise—many of which can operate independently of attitudes. For example, jurors' decisions are also significantly affected by empathy for childhood sexual assault (and other) victims (Haegerich & Bottoms, 2000). At times, the influence of individual differences in empathy for a specific trial participant (which could also be associated with gender differences) could outweigh the influence of more general attitudes.

In this chapter, we will learn how attitudes are formed, how they are measured, and how they affect behavior. In the next chapter, we will cover persuasion and attitude change. The boundaries between these topics are admittedly fuzzy. For example, some of the processes that lead to attitude development can be exploited by people who want to change attitudes. And some of the models of persuasion we will learn about in Chapter 6 tell us not just how to change preexisting attitudes, but how we might encourage people to adopt new attitudes.

Nevertheless, each chapter emphasizes different issues, and both are necessary for a fuller understanding of the social psychology of attitudes.

In the first section of this chapter, we will review many of the ways in which attitudes can develop in "thoughtless" ways. By calling these processes thoughtless, we do not mean to imply that no mental processes are involved. We are simply referring to routes to attitude formation that are based on something other than direct thought about the positive and negative qualities of attitude objects.

"THOUGHTLESS" ATTITUDE FORMATION

In the days leading up to Election Day, most people have settled on their attitudes toward the candidates. And even though people vary widely both in their political sophistication and in their ability to clearly define their political beliefs, most are willing to discuss the objective basis for their attitudes. We would expect such explanations to focus on the candidates' positions on important issues, their past accomplishments, and their promises for the future. Of course, sometimes people fall back on their gut feelings, but even then, most would prefer to believe that their feelings have something to do with the candidates' fitness for office—even if they were triggered by observations that are difficult to recall or describe.

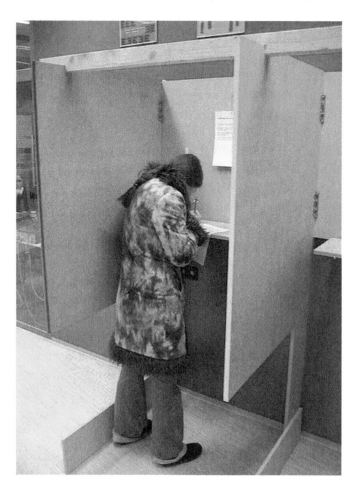

Voters can usually justify their choices, but they are not always aware of the sources of their attitudes toward different candidates and issues.

Other explanations for people's attitudes would be more surprising to us: "I like her because I saw so many of her advertisements on television"; "I'm voting Republican because my parents are Republicans"; "A campaign worker for that candidate gave me a red, white, and blue balloon"; or "I happened to be in a good mood when I heard one of his speeches." We would probably dismiss such attitudes as shallow or mindless. Nonetheless, a great deal of research indicates that our evaluations of people, places, issues, consumer products, and other **attitude objects** (see **Table 5.1**) are often based on factors other than rational thought. A variety of such hidden influences affects our attitudes—typically without our awareness, and independent of any systematic thinking about the merits of those objects.

Table 5.1: What Is an "Attitude Object?" Anything You Can Like or Dislike.

Acquaintances	Ethnic groups
Animals	Foods
Behaviors	Ideas
Books	Movies
Climates	Musicians
Colors	Places
Consumer goods	Relationships
Electoral candidates	Smells

Classical Conditioning

In 2004, Estée Lauder, the billionaire founder of the cosmetics company that bears her name, died at the age of 97. Considered by many to have been a marketing genius, Lauder was the originator of several important business innovations. In the 1940s, she pioneered the "gift with purchase" promotional scheme—the practice of giving customers a free sample of one product with the purchase of another. At the time, her competitors thought she was crazy to give away valuable merchandise, and predicted she would drive herself out of business. But the "gift with purchase" soon became a standard marketing tool. That should not be surprising, because it is essentially a method of classically conditioning positive attitudes toward consumer items.

Classical (or Pavlovian) conditioning is a basic form of learning that can be observed in animals as well as humans. It occurs when some stimulus (called the unconditioned stimulus, or UCS) that already evokes a strong response (called the unconditioned response, or UCR) is paired with a neutral stimulus (the conditioned stimulus, or CS) that is not associated with any particular response. The more consistent the pairing, the more likely that the CS will eventually trigger the same response as the UCS. This response is known as the conditioned response (CR). In the best-known example of this sort of learning, the pioneering physiologist Ivan Pavlov rang a bell whenever he gave food (the UCS) to a hungry dog. Eventually, the ringing of the bell (the CS) was enough to cause the dog to salivate (the CR). Another example, of course, might be the pairing of a purchase with a free gift.

Can a human being's evaluation of a previously neutral attitude object be rendered positive or negative simply by pairing it with an unconditioned stimulus?

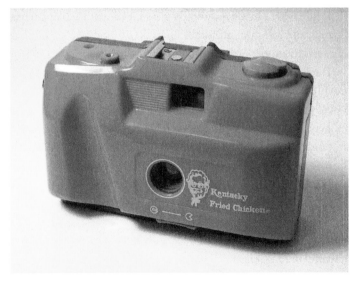

Classical conditioning in the market place; you might not think that a cheap free gift could change your attitude toward a company and its products, but Colonel Sanders knows better.

Long ago, Razran (1938, 1940) showed that people's evaluations of political slogans could be manipulated by pairing them with either foul odors or a free lunch. Similarly, Staats and Staats (1958) manipulated participants' attitudes toward two countries, Sweden and Holland, by mentioning them (along with other countries, to avoid giving away the purpose of the experiment) as participants were reading either favorable or unfavorable words. Some researchers questioned the results of these studies and other similar ones, arguing that participants must have been aware of the associations the experimenters created, and simply played along with what they thought was expected of them (Page, 1969). In other words, what seemed like **classically conditioned attitudes** could simply have been demand effects (see Chapter 2).

More recently, however, Olson and Fazio (2001, 2002) demonstrated that classically conditioned attitudes can develop even when participants are unaware that their attitudes are being manipulated and cannot recall the UCS-CS pairings. In their research, they paired pictures of Pokémon characters with either favorable words and images (*excellent*, puppies) or unfavorable words and images (*terrible*, cockroaches). They presented these pictures so rapidly that participants were unable to remember the pairings. Nonetheless, the procedure did affect participants' attitudes toward the different Pokémon characters.

The ultimate solution to the problem of possible demand effects during attempts to classically condition attitudes would be to devise a way of keeping participants completely unaware of the procedure. In fact, a number of investigators (De Houwer, Baeyens, & Eelen, 1994; De Houwer, Hendrickx, & Baeyens, 1997; Krosnick, Betz, Jussim, Lynn, & Stephens, 1992) have demonstrated that attitudes can be subliminally conditioned with very brief presentations of visual stimuli. When a visual stimulus (that is, a picture or word) can be shown to have affected people's thoughts, feelings, or behavior—even though they could not detect its presence—that stimulus is said to have been **subliminally perceived**, or perceived without awareness.

For example, Krosnick et al. (1992) asked participants to view a series of slides showing a woman engaged in everyday activities such as grocery shopping and dish washing. Unbeknownst to participants, they preceded each slide with a briefly presented image. Half the participants saw favorable images (such as people laughing, kittens), and half saw unfavorable images (a bloody shark, a face on fire). Participants in the first group reported significantly more positive attitudes toward the woman than those in the second group.

The fact that people's attitudes can be shaped by subliminally presented images means that our fictitious movie executive's plan to insert subliminal images into the film *No Vacancy* was not so far-fetched. Some such procedure could indeed affect or reinforce an audience's attitudes toward different characters. Most of us are unlikely, however, to encounter such hidden influences frequently, or even at all, in our everyday lives. In fact, at least one famous story about the effect of subliminal images on a movie audience's attitudes and behavior—that a movie theater in New Jersey once boosted sales of refreshments by subliminally presenting the messages "Eat popcorn" and "Drink Coke"—turns out to have no factual basis (Pratkanis, 1992). And because it is more difficult to present subliminal visual stimuli effectively to large groups of people through the mass media than it is to present them to individuals in a laboratory, such attempts are not likely to be cost-effective (Bornstein, 1989b; Moore, 1982, 1988). Finally, researchers have yet to demonstrate that subliminal attitude change is more powerful or longer lasting than the kind of attitude change produced by more blatant supraliminal stimuli—that is, stimuli that are staring us in the face.

However, classical conditioning certainly can be used effectively to shape people's attitudes (Olson & Fazio, 2006; Walther, Weil, & Düsing, 2011). That would explain the increasingly common practice of product placement in movies and on television (Miller, 1990; Nussbaum, 2008). Thus, soft drink producers are right to believe that the money they spend arranging for Johnny Depp or Jennifer Lawrence to sip a certain beverage on-screen is well worth it. And the producers of *No Vacancy* were probably correct to assume that they could easily find advertisers who were eager to use classical conditioning to create a fondness for their products.

The Mere Exposure Effect

Although it is quite common for judges to hand down criminal penalties less harsh than the ones requested by prosecutors, double-murderers do not usually have their sentences reduced significantly. In 1988, Judge Jack Hampton explained why he took pity on convicted murderer Richard Lee Bednarski, deciding not to send him to prison for life. Bednarski's victims were gay men, and Hampton didn't "care much for queers cruising the streets." He went on to note that he "put prostitutes and gays at about the same level," and would "be hard put to give somebody life for killing a prostitute." Needless to say, his blatantly bigoted comments created a furor, but Hampton did not mind. He seemed pleased that he was becoming well known for his injudicious behavior. "Just spell my name right," he told one reporter. "If it makes anyone mad, they'll forget it" by the next election (Belkin, 1988). Indeed, Hampton was reelected three times before he retired.

The more you see it, the more you like it: Companies saturating the environment with their logos capitalize on the mere exposure effect.

Although many readers will find Judge Hampton's attitudes objectionable, his comments reveal that he had at least an implicit understanding of a remarkable psychological phenomenon. Research on the **mere exposure effect** has shown that repeated exposure to a stimulus—a person, object, image, piece of music, or even the name "Jack Hampton"—leads to more favorable evaluations of that stimulus (Bornstein, 1989a; Harrison, 1977; Zajonc, 1968). Moreover, the increase in positive affect that results from repeated exposure to an attitude object does not depend on pairing it with some other positive stimulus or experience. The mere exposure effect, in other words, is quite different from classical conditioning. All other things held equal, the more often a stimulus is presented to you, the more you will like it.

Consider, for example, the relationship between the frequency with which a word appears in written English (or some other language) and the extent to which people like it or rate its meaning as favorable. Words that appear more frequently elicit much more positive reactions (Zajonc, 1968), a finding that has been replicated with many different kinds of words, including adjectives, personality traits, country and city names, and the names of fruits, flowers, vegetables, and trees. Of course, such findings do not conclusively demonstrate that exposure produces liking; words may be used more frequently *because* people feel more favorable toward them, rather than the other way around. To get around this alternative interpretation, researchers have used novel stimuli—in other words, material that is unfamiliar to most people—and have carefully controlled the frequency with which participants are exposed to them. For example, Zajonc (1968) presented Chinese ideographs, nonsense words, or faces to participants 0, 1, 2, 5, 10, or 25 times and found significant mere exposure effects. The more often participants saw any given stimulus, the more they liked it (see Brickman, Redfield, Harrison, & Crandall, 1972, Rajecki & Wolfson, 1973, and Zajonc & Rajecki, 1969, for similar results).

Hence, research on the mere exposure effect suggests that the fictitious movie executive's plan to bombard the public with *No Vacancy* posters in the months leading up to the movie's release could indeed have favorably predisposed people toward the film. Without really knowing why, many moviegoers would experience positive affect when thinking about the upcoming film.

What if the participants in mere exposure experiments were aware that an attempt had been made to manipulate their attitudes? Indeed, in the experimental investigations described up to now, participants might have been at least partially conscious of the fact that different stimuli had been presented to them at different frequencies. If so, ruling out an alternative explanation for the results of those studies would be difficult. Participants may have assumed that some stimuli were presented more than others because they were in some way better or more important.

Research by Wilson (1979), however, indicates that awareness of a stimulus is not necessary for the mere exposure effect. In Wilson's studies, participants wearing headphones were presented with tone sequences in one ear as they listened to a speaker read a story in the other ear. (This kind of experimental procedure is known as a dichotic listening task.) Afterward, even though participants were generally unable to recognize the melodies they had heard at greater than chance levels, they nonetheless preferred them to others they had not heard. In fact, mere exposure effects are typically much stronger when people are unaware of the number of times they have been exposed to stimuli, and stronger still when people cannot recognize the stimuli at all (Bornstein, 1989a; Bornstein & D'Agostino, 1994). These findings illustrate a principle we have encountered repeatedly in this book: Hidden influences lose much of their power when we become aware of them.

Studies that demonstrate *subliminal* mere exposure effects show even more definitively that the effect does not depend on awareness and is not a demand effect. In these experiments, participants watch a computer screen on which they see what appear to be flashes of light, which are actually fleeting images of faces, shapes, and so on.

Typically, these images (such as polygons) are presented for less than ten milliseconds—that is, less than one hundredth of a second. Remarkably, participants often show a significant preference for images that were subliminally presented, even though they do not recognize the images (Bornstein, 1992; Bornstein & D'Agostino, 1994; Bornstein, Leone, & Galley, 1987; Kunst-Wilson & Zajonc, 1980; Mandler, Nakamura, & Van Zandt, 1987; Monahan, Murphy, & Zajonc, 2000; Seamon, Brody, & Kauff, 1983; see **Figure 5.1**). Subliminal mere exposure effects can even affect people's interpersonal behavior. When participants in a study by Bornstein et al. (1987) took part in an activity with a confederate of the experimenter, they behaved more warmly if they had first been subliminally exposed to the confederate's face several times.

Of course, there are limits to the mere exposure effect (see, for example, de Zilva, Mitchell, & Newell, 2013). You may have been thinking something like

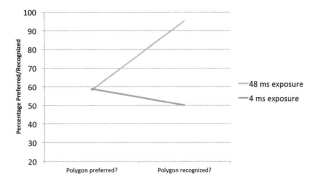

Figure 5.1: The effects of exposure time on recognition on preference.

Recognition of and preferences for polygons after exposures of 4 and 48 milliseconds. At very brief (4 ms) subliminal exposures, the recognition rate falls to chance (50%), but previously viewed (target) polygons are still preferred more often (> 50% of the time) than new polygons—just like those presented long enough (48 ms) to be easily recognizable.

Source: Bornstein, Leone, and Galley (1987).

"I've been exposed to the name *Adolf Hitler* quite a bit along with pictures of him, but I haven't exactly taken a liking to him." In such cases, though, the exposure is typically accompanied by extremely negative information. The name of the phenomenon, after all, is the *mere* exposure effect, not the exposure effect. When increased exposure is associated with a stimulus's unfavorable attributes, our liking for the stimulus will decrease. Thus, Judge Hampton's glee over the number of newspaper stories about him could easily have been misplaced if the gist of all those stories had been that he was an ogre. Without any accompanying negative information, however, exposure to even initially disliked stimuli can eventually produce positive evaluations (Zajonc, Markus, & Wilson, 1974).

In addition, you may have had the experience of hearing an awful song played over and over on the radio, until it is the last thing in the world you want to hear. Indeed, boredom is another factor that limits the mere exposure effect. Bornstein, Kale, and Cornell (1990) found that repeated exposure to very simple drawings produced a weaker mere exposure effect than repeated exposure to more complex drawings, presumably because people lost interest in the simple stimuli more quickly. In another study by Bornstein et al. (1990), the mere exposure effect was less pronounced in people who were known to be very prone to boredom. Similarly, when the presentation of a stimulus is "massed" (for instance, when the same picture is presented ten times in a row) rather than "spaced" (for example, when ten presentations are spread out over time and interspersed with other stimuli), the mere exposure effect is weaker—again, because a massed presentation is likely to trigger boredom. Ultimately, even the most complex stimuli will become familiar and predictable; after a certain point, continued exposure will reduce liking (Bornstein, 1989a).

Although many explanations have been proposed for the mere exposure effect, few have survived scrutiny (Bornstein, 1989a; Harrison, 1977). Researchers do agree, however, that after repeated exposures, a stimulus becomes easier to perceive and recognize. Winkielman and Cacioppo (2001) found that easy-to-process stimuli are inherently preferable to harder-to-process stimuli (such as objects or images that are out of focus or in some way visually obscured). As a result, the easy-to-process stimuli automatically trigger positive feelings. Thus, the mere exposure effect may be a specific example of a more general phenomenon.

Another question is *why* people prefer frequently encountered and easily perceived stimuli. From an evolutionary perspective, that kind of bias would make perfect sense. Bornstein (1989a, p. 282) concisely explains why a preference for the familiar would be adaptive:

The evolutionary roots of the mere exposure effect? Human beings eager to approach novel entities in the environment might not have survived long enough to become our ancestors.

Although there are sometimes advantages to exploring the new and familiar ... some risk is inherent in any venture into the unknown ... Who was more likely to survive longer, reproduce, and pass on genetic material (and inherited traits) to subsequent generations, the cave dweller who had a healthy fear of the strange and unfamiliar beasts lurking outside, or the more risk-taking (albeit short-lived) fellow, who, on spying an unfamiliar animal in the distance, decided that he wanted a closer look?

Mood as Information Effects

As we have seen, research on the classical conditioning of attitudes shows that positive and negative feelings can affect the attitudes we form toward people, places, things, and ideas simply by being paired or associated with them. In such cases, we are not even aware that our attitudes are being shaped. What if we were actively and consciously trying to determine how to evaluate something, though? In that case, incidental and superficial associations would not have a significant effect on our attitudes, would they? Evidence, however, suggests otherwise. Even when we are thinking systematically about how we feel toward an attitude object, we can be influenced by feelings that are irrelevant to our judgments. These hidden influences on our attitudes are known as **mood as information** effects (Clore, Gaspar, & Garvin, 2001; Schwarz, 1990, 2001; Schwarz & Clore, 2003).

In a study in which people reported on how satisfied they were with their lives, Schwarz and Clore (1983) demonstrated how mood could be used as information in making evaluative judgments. The researchers telephoned some participants when the weather was sunny and others on gloomy days. We can assume that participants in the latter group were feeling more depressed than those in the former group, which seems to have led to the study's main finding. That is, the people who were called when the weather was gloomy reported less life satisfaction than those who were called when the weather was sunny.

Other researchers have reported similar effects. For example, Cervone, Kopp, Schaumann, and Scott (1994) manipulated participants' moods by asking them to vividly imagine either happy or sad events. Later, the researchers asked them to reflect on different hypothetical levels of achievement, academic and otherwise. The results were consistent with mood as information effects. Sad participants' attitudes toward reaching any given level of performance (for example, getting a grade of B on a quiz) were more negative than the happy participants' attitudes. In other words, in attempting to estimate how they would feel about a specific outcome, participants used their temporary mood as a relevant piece of information.

We have seen that many hidden influences on behavior tend to lose their power when people become aware of them and their possible effects. The same is true of mood. When Schwarz and Clore (1983) made participants aware of the possibility that their attitude reports could be biased by the weather, either by asking them to describe what kind of day it was (indirect priming) or by telling them that the researchers were interested in the relationship between weather and mood (direct priming), the differences between the two groups disappeared (see **Table 5.2**).

A clever study by Strack, Martin, and Stepper (1988; see also Davis, Senghas, & Ochsner, 2009; Martin, Harlow, & Strack, 1992) eliminated the lingering possibility that (1) participants in these studies were aware that their moods were being manipulated and were affecting their judgments; or that (2) mood was, in fact, a relevant factor for participants to consider in making their judgments. The researchers asked two groups of participants to evaluate the humorousness of a series of cartoons and then gave all participants a pen, but not to use for writing.

Table 5.2: Eliminating Mood as Information Effects

	MENTION OF THE WEATHER		
	NONE	INDIRECT	DIRECT
General Happiness			
Sunny day	7.43	7.29	7.79
Rainy day	5.00	7.00	6.93
Life Satisfaction			
Sunny day	6.57	6.79	7.21
Rainy day	4.86	6.71	7.07

Note: Ratings could range from 1 to 10, with higher ratings indicating more happiness and satisfaction. Calling people's attention either directly or indirectly to the source of their moods (the weather) eliminated mood as information effects. The significant difference between people's happiness and satisfaction on sunny and rainy days disappears in those conditions of the experiment.

Source: Based on the results of Schwarz and Clore (1983), Experiment 2.

Anyone can fake a smile—but not everyone knows that even a posed smile can lead you to more favorably evaluate what or who you are smiling at.

Instead, the researchers asked members of the first group to hold the pen with their front teeth, without letting it touch their lips. Members of the second group were to hold the pen tightly in their puckered lips, without letting it touch their teeth. Participants in the first group were unaware that these odd instructions forced them to smile as they were judging the cartoons. Those in the second group, without being aware of it, were forced to adopt a facial expression that was incompatible with smiling. The results of the study showed that simply engaging in the facial activity associated with a certain mood can affect one's attitudes. Participants who grasped the pen in their teeth thought the cartoons were funnier than participants in the other group.

Inherited Attitudes

The "thoughtless" attitudes we have reviewed so far develop more or less automatically during certain kinds of experiences. There is another reason, though, why a person's attitudes might not develop as the result of a careful, systematic review of all the available evidence. On average, people's attitudes are highly correlated with those of their parents. In the case of political party preference, for example, the political orientation of a person's parents is a strong predictor of that person's own preference (Achen, 2002; Boshier & Thom, 1973).

That finding may not surprise you; after all, parents have years in which to shape their children's perspectives on everything from pizza to poodles to pacifism. Some researchers look at this phenomenon in another way, however. They have suggested that people are born with the potential to hold some attitudes and not others. That is, our attitudes are, to a certain extent, heritable, and are rooted in the genetic material passed on to us by our parents (Tesser, 1993).

Several research strategies can be used to determine the extent to which a personal characteristic is rooted in a genetic component (Loehlin, 1992; Plomin, 1994; Plomin, Chipuer, & Loehlin, 1990). One of those strategies is to compare monozygotic (identical) and dizygotic (fraternal) twins. Members of any given twin pair, of course, are the same age and are usually raised by the same people in the same household, and thus are exposed to the same environmental influences. Identical twins, however, are genetically identical, while fraternal twins are no more similar genetically than other sibling pairs. Thus, if identical twins are more similar than fraternal twins in terms of a particular trait or attitude, we can infer a genetic influence (but see Hoffman, 1991, and Scarr & Carter-Saltzman, 1979, for critical analyses of this assumption).

A twin study by Martin et al. (1986) indicated that many attitudes have a significant genetic component. These highly heritable attitudes include views on the death penalty, racial differences, divorce, and even jazz.

Heritable attitudes have been shown to be important to people, in that they come to mind easily and are resistant to change (Tesser, 1993; Tesser, Whitaker, Martin, & Ward, 1997). And though people tend to be more attracted to those who share the same attitudes (see Chapter 9), the effect is even stronger when the attitudes in question are heritable ones (Tesser, 1993; see also Crelia & Tesser, 1996).

As one researcher (Tesser, 1993, p. 139) notes, it is unlikely that there is a "gene for attitudes toward jazz in the same way as there is a gene for eye color." Heritable attitudes are probably a function of other, more basic characteristics that shape specific attitudes. For example, genetic differences in the preference for complex stimuli, in sensitivity to specific sounds, in preferred levels of activity, and even in intelligence could produce differences in attitudes toward specific kinds of music. Similarly, heritable differences in the ability to tolerate novel stimuli, in proneness to hostility, and in other basic dispositions could combine to predispose certain people to feel prejudice toward out-groups. The point, though, is that if attitudes are heritable, then some of our preferences may have developed relatively passively. Once again, our ability to think about and objectively evaluate the features of attitude objects may be less significant than we realize.

Evolved, Species-General Attitudes

Just as some psychologists suggest that some of our attitudes derive from having *particular* parents, others argue that some of our attitudes can be attributed to having *human* parents. In other words, some of our basic likes and dislikes seem to be species-general—programmed into our genes, if you will, rather than based on personal knowledge or experience. These evolved attitudes include being repelled by spiders and snakes (Marks, 1987; Ohman & Mineka, 2003; see **Figure 5.2**), liking fatty and sugary foods (Rozin, 1976), and preferring

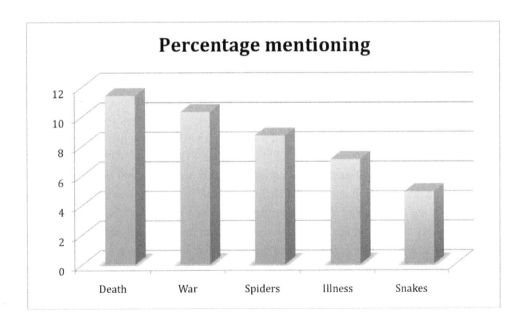

Figure 5.2: Most commonly listed fears among 7–12-year-old boys in the Netherlands.

Children responded to the question "What do you fear most?" Although snakes made the top five, there is only one kind of poisonous snake in the Netherlands, and it is found primarily in just a few nature preserves.

Source: Muris, Merckelbach, Meesters, and Van Lier (1997).

Fear of snakes might be partially learned—but its stubbornness and cross-cultural prevalence suggests that it might also be a function of an evolved psychological mechanism.

certain kinds of landscapes to others, such as those that provide both clear views of the surrounding area and places to hide or find safe refuge (Kaplan, 1992; Mealey & Theis, 1995; Orians & Heerwagen, 1992).

These attitudes may have evolved because they solved the survival problems humans faced. That is to say, holding such attitudes increased the chances that a person would live to pass on his or her genes to the next generation. Fearing snakes, for example, would have led a person to keep away from them, thus avoiding venomous snakebites. Similarly, an attraction to environments that are rich in water, food sources, and shelter would have increased a person's reproductive fitness. People's preferences for leaders of relatively large physical stature (Murray & Schmitz, 2011) have also been interpreted in this way; individuals drawn to physically powerful leaders would have been more likely to survive in dangerous and violent environments.

Thoughtless Attitudes and Hidden Influences on Evaluation: A Summary

Most of us would like to believe that when we prefer one consumer product to another, one person to another, or one stand on an issue to another, our attitudes reflect an ability to discern the important qualities of different attitude objects. Because most of us like to see ourselves as rational and reasonable, we are not flattered to learn that our evaluations can be affected significantly by the random pairing of events, mere exposure to a stimulus, fleeting moods, the genetic material we inherited from our parents, and the life conditions of prehistoric ancestors.

However, the hidden influences of such factors on our likes and dislikes cannot be dismissed. Thus, in the summer of 2005, the owners of a major restaurant chain in Canada may have been horrified by an unwanted endorsement they received from Karla Homolka, a notorious killer who had just been released from prison. Homolka announced that the first thing she wanted to do was get "an iced cappuccino from Tim Horton's" (Brent, 2005). An association—however random and simple it might be—between a restaurant and a series of brutal murders would probably not be great for sales.

Still, the extent to which such "thoughtless" processes dominate our evaluations should not be exaggerated. Typically, our attitudes result from a blend of influences, not just from hidden influences. And we certainly can give thoughtful consideration to what's good and what's bad about an attitude object. In the next section, we will consider some models of "thoughtful" attitude formation.

Think Like a Social Psychologist

Thinking critically

—More and more sports stadiums and arenas are being named (or renamed) for major corporations (such as "Crunchy Crackers Field" or "Lunar Communications Park"). Based on the research just discussed, what are some of the advantages of this marketing strategy? In what ways could it backfire?
—Can you think of some other possible examples of evolved, species-general attitudes?

Confronting social issues

—Young children are less likely than adults to be aware of subtle efforts to manipulate their attitudes. Thus, classical conditioning and mere exposure may be more powerful influences on children's developing preferences than on adults' preferences. What implications does (or should) this possibility have for debates over the regulation of advertising on children's television programs?

"THOUGHTFUL" ATTITUDE FORMATION

What Do Audiences Expect, and What Do They Value?
No Vacancy Gets a Face-Lift

Though we had written only a short synopsis of *No Vacancy*—what is known as a "treatment"—we had all kinds of ideas for the full screenplay. After signing the contract, however, we had trouble getting those ideas heard (or even getting anyone to return our phone calls). In our naïveté, we had overlooked the low status of screenwriters in the movie industry.

When finally another meeting was called, we armed ourselves with extensive notes. Unfortunately, the notes remained in their binders. We learned that after a series of meetings, the studio's "creative people" had concluded that the story needed extensive revisions. The changes they were proposing included (but were not restricted to) replacing the Chinese couple that was traveling with LaPiere with an African American couple; setting the story in the 1960s rather than the 1930s; adding a scene featuring a high-speed automobile chase; and making the character of LaPiere a woman instead of a man. The story would end with the daughter of a racist hotel owner falling in love with the African American man. The movie, we were told, would be a comedy.

We were so stunned by these proposals that we had difficulty hearing the justifications for them, all of which boiled down to the idea that moviegoers respond more positively to certain kinds of plots and scenes than to others. If a film contained those crucial elements, we were told, moviegoers would be more likely to see it. In sum, the recommended revisions were not arbitrary, we were told, but were based on a dispassionate analysis of the available data on moviegoers' preferences.

Attitudes are evaluations—judgments of how good or bad something is or how favorably or unfavorably we react to it. However, some attitude researchers divide the *sources* of these evaluations into two broad categories. **Affectively based attitudes** are based on the simple positive or negative feelings that are associated with an attitude object and triggered by its presence. In contrast, **cognitively based attitudes** are based on beliefs about an attitude object's properties and the desirability of those properties (Breckler, 1984; Eagly & Chaiken, 1998; Edwards, 1990; Millar & Tesser, 1986; Zanna & Rempel, 1988). Consequently, I may react negatively to a

Cognitively based attitudes are based on a dispassionate analysis of an attitude object's features.

certain relative because I encounter her only at funerals or when I am feeling awful (an affectively based attitude). Or my attitude toward her may be based on stories my relatives have told me about her unpleasant personality and the nasty things she has done (a cognitively based attitude).

This distinction between affectively and cognitively based attitudes is hardly crystal clear. Cognitions about an attitude object ("That animal could eat me alive") can, of course, generate affect ("I feel scared whenever I see one approaching"). That affect can go on—independently—to strengthen one's attitudes. Similarly, strong feelings about an attitude object ("That animal makes me anxious"), whatever their source, can lead people to infer that its attributes are consistent with those feelings ("I bet it could eat me alive"). Nonetheless, the distinction between the two sources of attitudes can be useful—indeed, it corresponds roughly to the distinction between "thoughtless" and "thoughtful" attitudes. Put simply, some attitudes are derived primarily from an analysis of an attitude object's characteristics and systematic thought about why one should like or dislike it; other attitudes are not. We have already discussed "thoughtless attitudes"; here, we will focus on "thoughtful" ones.

Expectancy Value Theories

The original version of the television show *Star Trek* featured a half human, half "Vulcan" character named Mr. Spock, who was notable for his devotion to cold, dispassionate logic. If Spock were asked to explain why he evaluated something unfavorably, such as a planet in some far-off galaxy, he would not refer to his gut feelings or to the negative affect he experienced when thinking about the attitude object. Indeed, he distrusted emotions. Instead, he would report that the planet's negative characteristics outweighed its positive ones, and would be careful to note the confidence with which he held his beliefs.

Human beings are not Vulcans, but Spock's approach to attitude formation is quite sensible. In fact, it is not so different from the path to attitude formation described by **expectancy value theories**, which are among the oldest, most influential frameworks for understanding how attitudes develop (Fishbein, 1963, 1967; Peak, 1955). According to expectancy value theories, our attitudes are derived from all the beliefs we hold about an attitude object's attributes.

For example, we may believe that the movie showing at the local cinema has a great deal of action and some steamy romance and that it does not force the viewer to tackle complex ethical or intellectual issues. Each of those attributes will be associated with some positive or negative value. In this case, a potential viewer might value all three of the movie's attributes positively. Each attribute also possesses a subjective probability, or "expectancy," corresponding to the level of confidence we have that the attitude object really has that attribute. For example, moviegoers may hear that *No Vacancy* is an action-packed adventure, rated "R" for nudity, but may also read in a review that the film is based on "the classic study by the social scientist Richard LaPiere." If so, they may worry that the film is too challenging or pretentious for relaxing on a Saturday night. Thus, their confidence that the movie possesses the third salient attribute (easy on the brain) may be shaken.

Pulling all these considerations together, the classic expectancy value formula for determining an attitude is $A = \Sigma (E * V)$, where A = attitude, E = expectancy, and V = value (which can range from very positive to very negative). The Σ symbol indicates that attitudes are calculated by adding up the $E*V$ products for each individual attribute (see **Table 5.3**). In some variants of this method, expectancy is replaced by importance (Rosenberg, 1956)—that is, not the probability that a certain attribute characterizes the attitude object, but the extent to which the attribute matters to someone. If a moviegoer enjoys only movies about love and romance, she would weigh that attribute more heavily than others in evaluating the film.

Quite a bit of research supports this method of accounting for people's attitudes. Carlson (1956), for example, used it to predict white people's attitudes toward minority group members moving into their neighborhood. He found that people with positive attitudes toward that happening tended to favorably evaluate the idea that all individuals should have the "chance to realize their potentialities"; they also believed that integrated neighborhoods would serve that purpose. On the other hand, those who were quite sure that integration would

Table 5.3: Hypothetical Comparison of Two Individuals' Attitudes toward Smoking

PERSON A

	Value?	Expectancy?	Product
Smoking cigarettes can lead to lung cancer	−4	4	−16
Smoking cigarettes is relaxing	+2	3	+6
Smoking cigarettes makes me smell bad	−2	2	−4
Smoking cigarettes is expensive	−3	5	−15
Smoking cigarettes helps me socialize	+4	4	+16
			Sum = −13

PERSON B

	Value?	Expectancy?	Product
Smoking cigarettes can lead to lung cancer	−4	2	−8
Smoking cigarettes is relaxing	+5	4	+20
Smoking cigarettes makes me smell bad	−2	1	−2
Smoking cigarettes is expensive	−2	4	−8
Smoking cigarettes helps me socialize	+4	5	+20
			Sum = +22

Expectancy value theory can be used to calculate the direction (positive or negative) and strength of two people's attitudes toward smoking cigarettes. Attributes were valued on a scale from –5 (very negative) to +5 (very positive), and expectancies were valued from 1 (not very probable) to 5 (very probable). In this example, person B has a more positive attitude toward smoking cigarettes than person A.

have a negative effect on the "value of one's real estate" (another possible attribute of integration) held quite different attitudes.

As we have seen, people's attitudes can be formed through a variety of hidden influences and processes that have little to do with their explicit beliefs about an attitude object's attributes. We are not always aware of or capable of articulating the sources of our attitudes. Clearly, then, the expectancy value approach cannot tell us everything we want to know about attitude formation. It is quite useful, though, for identifying the explicit beliefs that feed into people's attitudes. Even if expectancy value formulas leave out some important variables, they can certainly help to distinguish between people who have strong negative feelings toward some aspect of their social world and those who have strong positive feelings.

The Cognitive Consistency Motive

Expectancy value approaches provide a model for thinking about attitude formation that seems quite rational and reasonable. However, they do not necessarily imply that attitude formation is an unbiased process. What, for instance, is the source of the beliefs and evaluations that combine to create attitudes—for example, the belief that people value "sticking to their own groups," which would contribute to a negative evaluation of integrated neighborhoods (Carlson, 1956)? Does that belief (or any other one) necessarily come from a disinterested, coldly logical and objective analysis?

Several related social psychological theories start from the idea that people are motivated to attain and maintain cognitive consistency (Abelson et al., 1968; Simon, Snow, & Read, 2004). That is, inconsistency among cognitions (beliefs and evaluations) causes psychological discomfort, which people are motivated to eliminate. According to Heider's (1946) balance theory, for example, when a person's attitude differs from the attitude held by someone with whom the person has a "unit relation"—that is, a close associate—he will experience psychological discomfort. For example, if your best friend cannot stand the person you have just started dating, a state of imbalance would exist. You could restore balance by severing the unit relation (perhaps by simply drifting away from your best friend, so that her opinion no longer mattered) or by changing your attitude toward the person you are dating. If you adopt your friend's attitude toward your romantic interest, the inconsistency would disappear. Alternatively, you and the person you are dating could unite in rejecting your best friend.

Pressures for consistency could have played a role in the movie executives' revisions of *No Vacancy*. As an example, some of their beliefs about the moviegoing public's preferences could have been based not on careful inspection of real data, but on a desire to adopt one another's beliefs about what makes for a hit movie. When your colleagues are people whose opinions really matter—your superiors in the company, for instance—the pressure to bring your attitudes into alignment with theirs can be especially powerful.

Certainly the best-known consistency theory is cognitive dissonance theory (Festinger, 1957), which has much in common with balance and congruity theories, but is broader in some ways. Cognitive dissonance theory focuses not just on inconsistencies between attitudes, but on *any* kind of cognitive inconsistency—between beliefs, behaviors, or, most famously, attitudes and behaviors. Elsewhere in this book, we discuss balance theory (Chapter 9) and cognitive dissonance theory (Chapters 4 and 6) in greater detail. For our purposes here, the important point is that consistency theories provide another example of how relatively complex cognitive processes can play a role in attitude formation. And because the thought process that is involved in achieving cognitive consistency is hardly objective or unbiased, we can see how the desire for cognitive consistency (which varies from person to person—see Cialdini, Trost, & Newsom, 1995) could produce an inappropriate or unfortunate evaluative judgment. A person with the desire and aptitude to become, say, an English teacher might begin to denigrate that career choice simply because someone he dislikes also has that same ambition.

Sometimes, then, to avoid psychological discomfort, we reassess and modify attitudes that simply do not fit well with the others we hold. We should not assume, though, that the mental work involved in resolving such inconsistencies is all conscious (Greenwald, Banaji, Rudman, Farnham, Nosek, & Mellott, 2002)—a point we will return to later.

Ambivalence

Though imbalance and dissonance can be unpleasant and people may be motivated to eliminate them, inconsistencies are not always easily resolved. For example, participants in a study by Priester and Petty (2001) reported numerous cases in which their attitudes did not match those of important people in their lives—specifically, their parents. In addition, they did not seem able to persuade themselves that either their own attitudes or their relationships with their parents were unimportant. As a result, their perception of an imbalance in beliefs persisted and was correlated with psychological discomfort.

More generally, people can sometimes evaluate an attitude object both favorably and unfavorably. When people have strong positive *and* negative feelings toward a given person, place, thing, or issue, they are said to be **ambivalent** toward it (Cacioppo, Gardner, & Berntson, 1997; van Harreveld, van der Pligt, & de Liver, 2009; Jonas, Broemer, & Diehl, 2000; Schneider, Eerland, van Harreveld, Rotteveel, van der Pligt, van der Stoep, & Zwaan, 2013; Thompson, Zanna, & Griffin, 1995). For example, a woman may have both positive feelings about cigarettes (because they help her to relax) and negative feelings (because of their health risks). Similarly, many people who love babies because they are so cute also recoil from them because of the time and effort they demand. And Grande Caramel Frappuccinos may be delicious, but a steady diet of them could lead to unhappiness about the shape of your body. In our own case, our feelings about the planned changes to the script of *No Vacancy* were more than a little ambivalent. Certainly, we wanted the movie to be successful, but we also wanted a final product we could be proud of.

Attitudes toward fattening but delicious foods are often characterized by ambivalence.

Ambivalence is another consequence of being a thoughtful creature. After all, there are many ways to categorize, think about, and evaluate a given attitude object, and we cannot always resolve all the conflicting thoughts and feelings they produce. Almost any given attitude object can relate to more than one goal (Newman & Chamberlin, 2002). For example, cigarettes could relate both to the goal of avoiding a bad mood and to the goal of leading a long life. And delicious food has implications both for pleasure and for controlling your weight. Sometimes these goals will conflict.

Ambivalence can be measured and assessed in two ways (Breckler, 1994; Cacioppo et al., 1997; Kaplan, 1972; Locke & Braun, 2009; Priester & Petty, 1996; Thompson et al., 1994). Measures of *potential* ambivalence assess the extent to which people can think of conflicting ways to evaluate an attitude object. Typically, they require people to report the strength of their positive and negative feelings on separate scales. If a person reports high levels of both positive and negative affect toward cigarettes, he or she will score high on such a measure. Measures of *felt* ambivalence, on the other hand, assess the actual state of experiencing ambivalence. Such measures employ a series of adjectives such as "mixed," "muddled," "conflicted," and "confused." People rate the extent to which those terms correspond to their own feelings toward some attitude object.

Thus, a person can have the potential for ambivalence toward something, but feel that way only occasionally. When does potential ambivalence trigger actual ambivalence? According to Newby-Clark, McGregor, and Zanna (2003), actual ambivalence is experienced when both positive and negative feelings (and presumably, the thoughts and goals that led to those feelings) become cognitively accessible—that is, when both come easily to mind (see Chapter 3). Newby-Clark et al. studied people's attitudes toward capital punishment and abortion and assessed the simultaneous accessibility of their conflicting feelings about each issue. In one study, the researchers measured simultaneous accessibility by recording how long participants took to report their positive and negative feelings (quicker responses would indicate greater accessibility). In another study, they manipulated accessibility by asking participants to report their feelings repeatedly. In both studies, the only participants who reported ambivalence (for example, "I have strong mixed emotions both for and against capital punishment, all at the same time") were those whose positive and negative feelings on the issues were accessible simultaneously.

Everyone, we can assume, has experienced ambivalence. Indeed, the vast majority of attitude objects may be associated with some degree of ambivalence. Nonetheless, ambivalence has not received as much attention from social psychologists as one might expect. Thompson et al. (1994) suggested that one reason for the relative lack of interest has been the historical popularity of consistency theories. Because those theories emphasize "the drive to seek consistency across all aspects of experience," they argue, they are "certainly at odds with the notion of ambivalence" (p. 363).

Besides being an interesting phenomenon, ambivalence has important implications for social behavior. For example, several studies have found that when people are ambivalent about some group (such as racial and ethnic minorities, people with disabilities, or people with mental illness), their reactions to members of the group are often polarized, a phenomenon known as **response amplification**. That is, when members of those groups engage in favorable behaviors such as performing brilliantly on some task or behaving generously, people like them more than members of their own group who behave in the same way. However, when members of the same groups engage in unfavorable behaviors such as performing poorly or behaving rudely, people react extremely negatively (Bell & Esses, 1997, 2002; Gibbons, Stephan, Stephenson, & Petty, 1980; Hass, Katz, Rizzo, Bailey, & Eisenstadt, 1991; Katz, Hass, & Bailey, 1988; see **Table 5.4**).

Table 5.4: Ambivalence and Response Amplification When Evaluating One's Partner in a Competition

	RACE OF PARTNER	
OUTCOME	BLACK	WHITE
Success	310	281
Failure	155	196

The higher the score, the more favorable the evaluation of the partner. White participants' evaluations of black teammates differed from their evaluations of white teammates who had performed well (success) or poorly (failure) in a trivia game; responses to the black partner were more extreme. A second study found that this pattern was more pronounced among white participants who held especially ambivalent attitudes toward black people.

Source: Hass, Katz, Rizzo, Bailey, and Eisenstadt (1991), Study 1.

Thoughtful Attitudes: A Summary

Our review of research on "thoughtless" attitude formation may have led you to conclude that attitudes do not really pertain to the attitude object and its qualities. Rather, they derive from the affective experiences with which they are paired, the sheer frequency with which we encounter them, or even the genetic material we are born with. Clearly, however, the way we evaluate attitude objects is also affected by what we know about them, even though that knowledge is sometimes complex and contradictory. Some of our knowledge is direct, involving an attitude object's actual attributes. Indirect knowledge—such as whether our evaluation of an attitude object is consistent with related attitudes—is also important. Determining the origins of any given attitude, then, is a daunting task, but as we will see, determining what a person's attitude is can be even more of a challenge.

Think Like a Social Psychologist

Understanding everyday behavior
—Think of an important political or other public issue about which you have ambivalent feelings. What are the sources of your positive and negative feelings? Can you think of situations in which your positive feelings might temporarily outweigh your negative feelings (and vice versa)?

Thinking critically
—We can easily defend and explain some of our attitudes; others, though they may seem equally strong, are harder to defend and explain. Which attitudes (the ones that are easy to defend or the ones that are difficult to defend) do you think may result from thoughtless attitude formation, and which from thoughtful attitude formation?

Making connections
—Studies of thoughtless versus thoughtful attitude formation paint very different pictures of how people develop their likes and dislikes. Compare the tension between the two processes to the tension between the "naive scientist" and "cognitive miser" models of person perception, discussed in Chapter 3.

ATTITUDE ASSESSMENT

Who Likes the Movie and How Do We Know?
No Vacancy Is Put to the Test

No Vacancy was filmed and edited, and eventually a rough cut was ready for viewing. The people at the movie studio were aware of how upset we were over the changes they had made, but they were confident they could alleviate our distress. They had arranged for some test screenings; once we saw how much audiences loved their version of the movie, they assumed, all would be forgiven. In other words, they set out to measure audience attitudes toward a version of the film that was close to the final product, certain those attitudes would be positive. Measuring attitudes, however, is no simple matter (Krosnick, Judd, & Wittenbrink, 2005), as we will see from our survey of the many different ways to assess them.

Direct Assessment (Self-Reports)

Once a person has formed an attitude, how can we measure and assess it? Perhaps the answer seems obvious: just ask the person. Indeed, in much of the research discussed up to now, including investigations of ambivalence, researchers used self-report measures.

A variety of direct self-report measures can be used to measure attitudes (see Himmelfarb, 1993; Krosnick, Judd, & Wittenbrink, 2005; Petty & Cacioppo, 1981). One of the most popular is the Likert scale (Likert, 1932). When attitudes are assessed in this way, people are presented with a series of statements and must indicate the extent to which they agree with each (typically, using five-point or seven-point scales: see **Table 5.5**). All the statements express positive or negative feelings about an attitude object or issue. For example, an assessment of people's attitudes toward their school might include statements such as "I have received a high-quality education at my university" and "I would advise against seeking admission to my university." The responses to the items are combined (using reverse scoring for items that indicate dislike) to compute an attitude score. Such scores are meaningful only in a relative sense (Blanton & Jaccard, 2006). That is, we can use them to compare a person's attitude to those of other people ("She likes ice cream more than anyone else") or to compare it to the same person's attitude toward other things ("Her least favorite

Door to door surveys typically rely on simple, straightforward self-report measures of attitudes.

Table 5.5: Likert and Semantic Differential Scales (Attitudes toward Technology)

(a) Likert Scale

PLEASE RESPOND TO EACH STATEMENT WITH ONE AND ONLY ONE NUMBER AFTER EACH STATEMENT, USING THE FOLLOWING SCALE:

+2	=	STRONGLY AGREE
+1	=	MODERATELY AGREE
0	=	NEUTRAL
−1	=	MODERATELY DISAGREE
−2	=	STRONGLY DISAGREE

1. I feel that technology complicates my life.

2. I eagerly await the newest models of tablet computers.

3. I dislike having to learn how to use new appliances.

4. I enjoy reading computer magazines.

(b) Semantic Differential Scales

ON EACH OF THE SCALES BELOW, RATE HOW YOU FEEL ABOUT (1) COMPUTERS, (2) SMART PHONES, (3) DIGITAL CAMERAS, AND (4) PORTABLE MUSIC PLAYERS.

Good	+2	+1	0	−1	−2	Bad
Negative	+2	+1	0	−1	−2	Positive
Pleasant	+2	+1	0	−1	−2	Unpleasant
Unfavorable	+2	+1	0	−1	−2	Favorable

---

dessert is rice pudding"). However, the score itself—for example, "5 on a seven-point scale"—does not have independent meaning in the way that a measure of one's height would ("She's five feet tall").

Using an alternative approach known as the **semantic differential technique** (Osgood, Suci, & Tannenbaum, 1957), some researchers present an attitude object of some kind (for example, "coffee," "the New York Yankees," "gay marriage," the movie *No Vacancy*) and then ask respondents to rate the object on several scales whose endpoints are opposite in meaning, such as good–bad, pleasant–unpleasant, and positive–negative. To determine a respondent's attitudes, the researchers combine the responses to all the items (see **Table 5.5**). The advantage of the semantic differential technique is that unlike the Likert method, it employs a standard set of scales that can be applied to any attitude object.

Finally, attitudes can even be assessed using a single-item measure, typically a seven-point scale ranging from positive to negative, favorable to unfavorable, or "like very much" to "dislike very much." A variant of this method—one that has sometimes been found to provide a more valid and useful estimate of people's attitudes—is to ask people how much they like or dislike attitude objects *compared to other people* (Olson, Goffin, & Haynes, 2007). And if researchers are concerned about the possibility that people may be ambivalent about an attitude object, they can use separate scales for positive and negative feelings, ranging from "not at all" to "extremely" (Kaplan, 1972). Clearly, single-item measures are the simplest approach to measuring attitudes. Their drawback is that they tend to have lower reliability than the others (see Chapter 2). That is to say, the attitudes that individuals report on single-item measures are more likely to fluctuate over time.

The advantages of self-report measures are their simplicity and ease of use, and the fact that they have what is known as "face validity." In other words, no great leap of the imagination is required to see how such scales could measure exactly what they are supposed to measure. For these reasons, the movie studio executives decided to use self-report measures at the test screenings for *No Vacancy*. The results of those tests were similarly straightforward: audiences seemed to love the film. As the executives crowed exultantly, "It tested through the roof!"

One disadvantage of self-report measures is that people's responses can be manipulated without too much difficulty by presenting the items in different orders or contexts. For example, a politician who is challenging an incumbent officeholder might want to make the case that voters are pessimistic about their general life situations. The candidate could increase the likelihood of obtaining that finding by asking people to rate their life satisfaction after first rating their satisfaction with some aspect of their lives that most would evaluate negatively ("Rate how happy you are with how much money you make"). The incumbent, on the other hand, could generate much different results by preceding the life satisfaction measure with a question about a more positive aspect of people's lives ("How happy do your children make you?"). By priming happy or unhappy thoughts (see Chapter 3), one can influence the attitudes people report (see Schwarz, 1999, for other examples and a general discussion of this problem).

A more fundamental limitation of self-report measures is that they are based on the assumption that people are willing and able to report their attitudes. Needless to say, people sometimes hesitate to reveal their true feelings. They may be afraid that the attitudes they report will reveal them to be less-than-wonderful people. As we will see in Chapter 11, this problem presents a particular challenge to researchers who are studying prejudice and discrimination. At other times and for other reasons, people are motivated to tell researchers what they think those researchers want to hear. For example, members of the test audiences for *No Vacancy* may have felt that in exchange for the privilege of receiving a sneak preview of a major motion picture, they should reciprocate with flattering feedback. Or they may have wanted to be invited to other free screenings, and so hesitated to alienate the filmmakers with dismissive comments.

Measuring people's perceptions of their past attitudes is particularly challenging. The Social Psychology: The Dark Side and Bright Side boxes on **pages 212 and 213** describe the *congeniality effect*, which occurs when—without being aware of it—we develop a selective memory for facts and arguments that support our attitudes.

Finally, people may sincerely want to report their attitudes, but may not have conscious access to their true feelings. As we will see, a disconnect often exists between the attitudes people believe they have and the feelings an attitude object triggers in them automatically, which guide spontaneous behavior. The indirect attitude measures discussed next are all designed to circumvent one or more of these limitations of self-reports.

INDIRECT ASSESSMENT

What if, for whatever reason, you can't measure or assess attitudes just by directly asking people about them? Social psychologists have devised some ingenious ways to get around this problem, ranging from trickery to the use of physiological measures.

The "bogus pipeline." As we just noted, the attitudes people report are not always trustworthy, because they may not be willing to report attitudes that could prove embarrassing or unacceptable. A simple solution to this problem suggests itself: just hook respondents up to a machine that will indicate whether they are telling the truth. Unfortunately, no such device exists. Even polygraphs (often referred to as "lie detectors") are not as reliable as they are thought to be, despite their extensive use in legal, industrial, and other settings (Fiedler, Schmid, & Stahl, 2002; Lykken, 1998; Ruscio, 2005). (And even if polygraphs can detect lies with slightly greater than chance accuracy, they certainly should not be used to make important decisions about individual people's lives.)

However, Jones and Sigall (1971; Sigall & Page, 1971) introduced a clever variant of this strategy: Why not present people with a machine they *thought* could gauge their true feelings? Jones and Sigall called this strategy the **bogus pipeline**, because it is based on the false belief that researchers have a pipeline to people's thoughts and feelings. As it was originally developed, the procedure involved showing research participants a fancy-looking machine that was supposed to be able to assess their attitudes. The researchers would then connect participants to the machine and present them with a rigged demonstration of its accuracy. (The machine would respond correctly to questions about the participants for which the researchers already knew the answers.) Finally, the participants, impressed by the machine's powers, would report their true attitudes on a variety of issues—or just guess the attitudes they thought the machine would detect. In later studies (Arkin & Lake, 1983, for example) researchers sometimes altered this procedure by simply leading participants to *expect* that the machine would assess their attitudes (that is, they omitted the rigged demonstration of the machine's accuracy).

In one of the earliest of these investigations (Sigall & Page, 1971), researchers found that white participants tested with the bogus pipeline procedure were more likely than others to admit to being prejudiced toward black people. Overall, studies using the bogus pipeline technique reveal that it significantly changes the attitudes people report. Specifically, it leads people to admit to more socially undesirable attitudes than they would otherwise (Grover & Miller, 2012; Roese & Jamieson, 1993).

Despite its effectiveness, the bogus pipeline technique is not widely used today for several reasons (Ostrom, 1973). First, because the technique is difficult to pull off, it is not a practical way to assess the attitudes of large numbers of people. Second, some researchers hesitate to use a method that involves not only lying to participants, but possibly coercing them to reveal aspects of themselves that they would rather conceal. Finally, Roese and Jamieson (1993) suggest that when the attitudes in question are uncertain and weakly held, the bogus pipeline could distort or change rather than reveal them. That is, under the pressures of the situation, people might express—and then actually adopt—offensive or self-denigrating attitudes that they did not hold before.

Physiological measures. The "truth detector" machines used by bogus pipeline researchers are just that—bogus. However, other researchers have attempted to develop authentic techniques for assessing positive and negative evaluations, by examining participants' physical responses to attitude objects. As long ago as the 1930s, researchers were testing the usefulness of the **galvanic skin response (GSR)** as a measure of attitudes. The GSR method is based on the fact that when people have a strong emotional response, their sweat glands become active. If two electrodes are placed on your hand, an electric current will take less time than usual to pass between them if your hands are sweaty (that is, the GSR will be greater). A device called a galvanometer can be used to measure the relative conductance of a participant's skin—and thus, perhaps, to detect the strength of an evaluative response. Indeed, early research revealed that white research participants exhibited higher GSRs when they made physical contact with black (as opposed to white) experimenters (Rankin & Campbell, 1955). Later researchers found that such reactions to black people—even those who were observed simply interacting with whites—were more pronounced among those who were high in prejudice (Westie & DeFleur, 1959).

Unfortunately, the GSR has some major limitations as a measure of attitudes (Cacioppo & Sandman, 1981; Petty & Cacioppo, 1983). First, although it is correlated with the intensity of an attitude, it cannot reveal anything about an attitude's direction. A strong positive reaction will produce the same GSR reading as a strong negative reaction. In addition, the GSR is affected by a variety of factors, such as how novel or unexpected an attitude object is. The same problems bedevil another physiological measure that once seemed to hold great promise: pupillary response (Atwood & Howell, 1971; Hess, 1965). Early research suggested that positive evaluations caused people's pupils to dilate, and negative reactions caused them to constrict. But later research shows that dilation is associated with any strong affective response, either positive or negative. Pupillary responses can also be triggered by any aspect of a stimulus that causes it to attract attention (Petty & Cacioppo, 1983; Woodmansee, 1970).

A much more effective approach is based on **facial electromyographic activity (EMG)**, which associates favorable and unfavorable responses with the contraction of different facial muscles (as measured by an electromyogram; for a recent example, see Stewart et al., 2013). For example, when people think about positive events, they show more electrical activity in the zygomatic and depressor muscles (found on the side of the chin and on the cheek, respectively). When they have negative thoughts, they show more activity in the corrugator and frontalis muscles (found above the eyes and on the forehead) (Schwartz, Fair, Salt, Mandel, & Klerman, 1976). EMG procedures will pick up electrical activity in the muscles even when observers cannot detect facial movements. Cacioppo and Petty (1979) used EMG measures to assess attitudes and found these patterns of activity when they presented participants with arguments they were known to agree with (and evaluate positively) or disagree with (and evaluate negatively).

Neuroscience methods. More recently, researchers have conducted social-cognitive neuroscience studies in an effort to examine patterns of brain activity associated with positive and negative evaluations (Cacioppo, Crites, Berntson, & Coles, 1993; Crites & Cacioppo, 1996; Cunningham, Johnson, Gatenby, Gore, & Banaji, 2003; Cunningham, Espinet, DeYoung, & Zelazo, 2005; Dhont, Van Hiel, Pattyn, Onraet, & Severens, 2012; Lieberman, 2010; McCall, Tipper, Blascovich, & Grafton, 2012). These studies typically use a procedure known as **functional magnetic resonance imaging (fMRI)**, which allows researchers to identify within a few millimeters the regions of the brain that become active in response to specific tasks or stimuli. In the case of attitudes, a key region seems to be the amygdala, where frightening and disliked stimuli have been found to trigger activity (Adolphs & Tranel, 1999; Morris et al., 1996; Whalen et al., 1998). A study by Cunningham et al. (2003), however, suggests that the amygdala is involved primarily in fast, automatic evaluations of stimuli. When people engage in more explicit, intentional thinking about how much they like something, researchers observe greater activity in the prefrontal cortex—especially when people's feelings about the attitude object are complex and ambivalent.

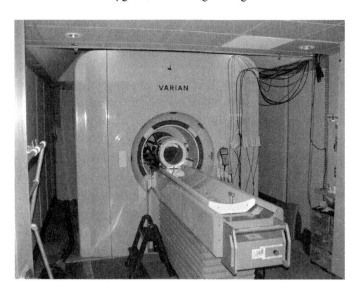

Machinery used for fMRI (Functional Magnetic Resonance Imaging).

Neuroscience research on attitudes is still in an early stage of development. And there are practical limitations on the use of fMRI techniques to measure attitudes: they are expensive, time-consuming, and require specialized equipment. However, new findings in this field promise to deepen our knowledge of the structure and function of attitudes, including the distinction between explicit and automatic (or implicit) attitudes, our next topic.

Automatic and implicit attitude measurement. When something pleasant happens, are you more likely to smile, clap, or yell "hooray" than to frown, make a fist, or shout "boo?" Most people would smile, clap, or shout "hooray"; the opposite is true when something unpleasant happens. This very simple idea is more or less the basis for an innovative and sophisticated technique for detecting **automatically activated attitudes**—attitudes that are triggered quickly and unintentionally, often without our awareness. In a groundbreaking experiment, Fazio, Sanbonmatsu, Powell, and Kardes (1986) asked participants to press one button on a computer keyboard if a clearly favorable word (such as *terrific*) was presented on the computer screen, and another button if a clearly unfavorable word (*awful*) was presented. (In later studies, researchers sometimes used pictures instead of words; see Giner-Sorolla, Garcia, and Bargh, 1999). Furthermore, they asked participants to respond as quickly as possible. Obviously, the task was not difficult, and participants were able to respond to each word in less than a second, with very few errors.

Every adjective, however, was preceded by a very brief presentation of another word—a "prime" word. Sometimes the prime was a word representing a favorable attitude object (such as *gift*); at other times, it represented an unfavorable object (such as *death*). When the prime was a favorable attitude object, participants were then quicker to respond to a favorable word than to an unfavorable word. When the prime was an unfavorable attitude object, the opposite was true (see **Figure 5.4**). Thus, liked attitude objects facilitated positive responses, and disliked objects facilitated negative responses.

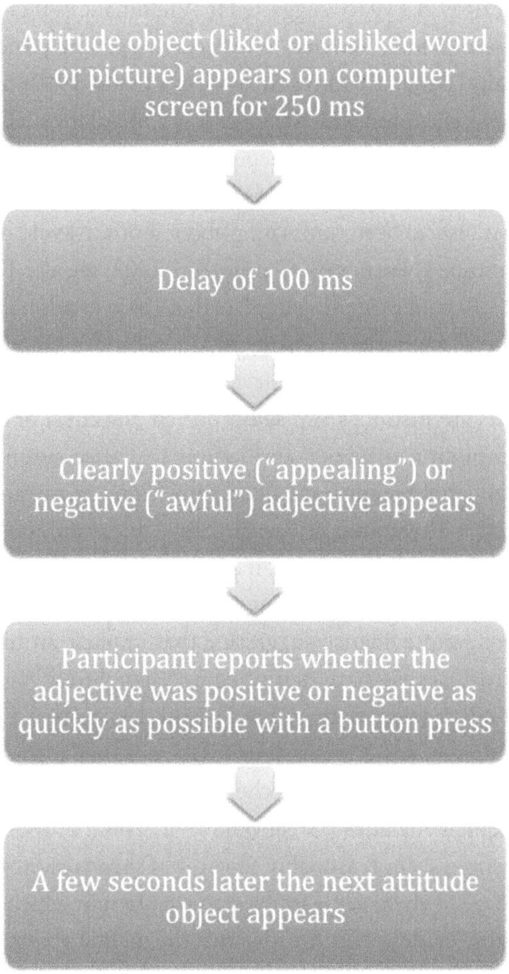

Figure 5.4: Procedure for assessing automatic attitude activation.

People respond more quickly when identifying positive words after liked attitude objects and when identifying negative words after disliked attitude objects.

Source: Experiment 1 of Fazio, Sanbonmatsu, Powell, and Kardes (1986).

These findings make sense if we assume that participants immediately retrieved their attitudes toward the objects from their memories when the objects appeared. Given how quickly participants had to respond, Fazio et al. (1986) concluded that the procedure could be used to assess attitudes that come to mind automatically, without any conscious or strategic thought. Therefore, this method could reveal attitudes that were uncontaminated by people's concern with presenting themselves to others in a socially desirable way.

Later research replicated Fazio et al.'s (1986) findings, extending them in many ways (Hermans, De Houwer, & Eelen, 2001; Herring et al., 2013; Klauer & Musch, 2003; Spruyt, Hermans, De Houwer, & Eelen, 2002). Although

Fazio et al. (1986) suggested that automatic evaluation would occur only for attitudes that are relatively strong, later findings indicated that the effect is surprisingly widespread: weakly held attitudes can also be triggered automatically (Bargh, Chaiken, Govender, & Pratto, 1992; Bargh, Chaiken, Raymond, & Hymes, 1996). Even those attitude objects toward which people feel ambivalent such as ice cream can trigger automatic evaluation. How favorable that evaluation will be depends on the context or the person's current goals. For example, if a person has recently been thinking about foods that taste good, ice cream will automatically activate a positive attitude. If that person has instead been ruminating about foods to avoid on a diet, the word *ice cream* will automatically trigger a negative attitude (Newman & Chamberlin, 2002; see also Ferguson & Bargh, 2004; Mitchell, Nosek, & Banaji, 2003).

Recent evidence suggests that Fazio et al.'s method, along with similar ones that have been developed since then (see Fazio & Olson, 2003), are more than just clever techniques for assessing attitudes that come easily to mind, but that people may hesitate to report. The evaluative tendencies revealed by these indirect methods are distinct from self-reported attitudes, or **explicit attitudes**, in several ways. As such, they may reveal **implicit attitudes**—evaluations that arise automatically when we encounter an attitude object, affecting our thoughts, feelings, and behavior without our awareness (Banaji, 2001; Banaji & Heiphetz, 2010; Fazio & Olson, 2003; Greenwald & Banaji, 1995; Rudman, 2004; Wilson, Lindsey, & Schooler, 2000). Implicit attitudes are often weakly correlated, if at all, with explicit attitudes (Greenwald & Farnham, 2000; Greenwald, McGhee, & Schwartz, 1998; Huntsinger, 2011). The two attitude types also seem to have different sources. Rudman (2004) reviewed evidence suggesting that implicit attitudes are affected more than explicit attitudes by the kinds of processes we have described as "thoughtless" (including affective experiences and other hidden influences). Explicit (that is, thoughtful) attitudes are based more on beliefs that people can recall and describe, and on judgments and evaluations that people make consciously.

Finally, some researchers have found that cognitive consistency principles apply more to implicit than to explicit attitudes (Greenwald et al., 2002; but see Gawronski & Strack, 2004, for an opposing view). Although people seem reasonably tolerant of inconsistency in explicit, conscious cognitions, their implicit attitudes are more likely to settle into a stable pattern in which inconsistencies are kept to a minimum. This finding provides more evidence for the idea that the mental activities that support balance, congruity, and dissonance resolution are not necessarily conscious ones.

The most widely used method for studying implicit attitudes is the Implicit Association Test, or IAT (Greenwald et al., 1998; Greenwald, Nosek, & Banaji, 2003; Nosek, Banaji, & Greenwald, 2002; Nosek, Greenwald, & Banaji, 2005). Because much of the research using that method has been devoted to the study of attitudes toward groups of people, we will postpone discussion of the IAT until our review of research on stereotyping and prejudice in Chapter 11.

Behavioral measures. Imagine that a museum devoted to American history featured two major exhibits, one on the signers of the Declaration of Independence and the other one on reality TV shows. A survey of museum-goers, we might assume, would reveal more favorable opinions about the former exhibit. But an inspection of the two exhibits after the museum closed for the day might well reveal more wear and tear on the floor tiles and more smudges on the display case in the latter area.

One way to assess people's attitudes is to pay attention not to what they say, but to what they do (Webb, Campbell, Schwartz, & Sechrest, 1966). Some researchers (Hazlewood & Olson, 1986; Macrae, Bodenhausen, Milne, & Jetten, 1994), for example, have assessed research participants' attitudes toward others by secretly recording how closely to them they sit. Others such as Wells and Petty (1980) have used the extent to which people nod (as opposed to shaking their heads) while listening to a message as a measure of how much they agree with the message. In the case of *No Vacancy*, the people who were running the screenings could not help but notice that members of the audience were stepping out of the theater for snacks, cigarettes, phone calls, and bathroom breaks more frequently than usual, despite their enthusiastically positive written reactions.

We saw earlier that social psychologists often distinguish between the affective and cognitive sources of attitudes. The **tripartite model of attitudes** (Breckler, 1984; McGuire, 1985; Ostrom, 1969; Rosenberg & Hovland, 1960; Zanna & Rempel, 1988) goes a step further, to include behavior along with cognition (thoughts) and affect (feelings). According to this analysis, attitudes are based on and express themselves in terms of (1) what people think and say about an attitude object; (2) how they feel about it in its presence; and (3) how they behave toward it. This approach implies that people's behavior toward an attitude object will correspond to what they think about it and feel toward it, and that the attitudes they report will predict their behavior. From that perspective, assessing attitudes via behavior makes perfect sense. As we shall see, though, the correlation between how people *say* they evaluate people, places, and things and the way they *behave* toward those attitude objects is often surprisingly weak.

How much do members of this family like cigarettes, coffee, and sugary soft drinks? Can a glance at their trash provide a more reliable estimate of their attitudes than a self-report measure?

We have considered only some of the difficulties of measuring people's attitudes. The Think like a Social Psychologist box on **page 201-202** presents some other biases and pitfalls that can complicate our attempts to gauge attitudes correctly.

THINK LIKE A SOCIAL PSYCHOLOGIST: AVOIDING BIASED ESTIMATES OF OTHERS' ATTITUDES

How good are you at estimating the relative prevalence of different attitudes? Probably not as good as you think you are. A number of biases can cloud our thinking when we try to guess what other people are feeling. For example, people overestimate the extent to which others share their attitudes, a phenomenon known as the **false consensus effect** (Marks & Miller, 1987; Ross, Greene, & House, 1977). Thus, people who oppose the death penalty and prefer Burger King to McDonald's tend to believe their preferences are more common than they actually are. The same is true of people who approve of capital punishment and prefer Big Macs.

A very different bias can manifest itself in group settings, in which people are concerned with how others will judge and evaluate them. In such cases, people may *under*estimate the extent to which others share their attitudes. Imagine, for example, a situation in which a group of young men is presented with the opportunity to steal a car. None of them may be enthusiastic about engaging in such antisocial behavior, but no one may want to admit it for fear of being seen as cowardly. As a result, even though the young men may be in complete agreement on the utter stupidity of the idea, each one will believe that the others favor it. This state of affairs is known as pluralistic ignorance (see Chapter 12 and Miller & Prentice, 1994).

Given the potential for bias in estimating public attitudes, nothing can take the place of hard data. The editors of a campus newspaper suspected that despite their university's reputation as a hotbed of liberalism, student opinion on gun control was actually more negative than most people suspected. They decided to carry out a careful, systematic survey of student attitudes, but realized they did not have the funds to do it. An enterprising staff member came up with a solution to the problem. She turned to a group that had considerable financial resources and was interested in the project: The National Rifle Association (NRA). A grant from the NRA allowed the editors to develop, print, and mail a detailed questionnaire to a large random sample of students. It also allowed them to offer a $10 check to people who completed the questionnaire. In exchange, the editors promised to prominently acknowledge the NRA's support in the cover letter that accompanied the questionnaire.

Why might the results of such a survey be suspect? Why would you doubt that its findings truly reflect students' attitudes?

****

When participants in a study are inadvertently presented with cues that might suggest how they are *supposed* to respond, what they say or do can no longer be considered a reflection of their true attitudes and beliefs. Such cues are known as demand characteristics (see Chapter 2). In 1990, for example, researchers conducted face-to-face interviews to predict the winner of Nicaragua's presidential elections. Some of the interviewers used red and black pens; others used pens that were blue and white. Interviewers who used red and black pens found that 63 percent of the respondents supported the incumbent president, Daniel Ortega. But those who used blue and white pens found that only 44 percent of those surveyed supported Ortega. How can we make sense of these results? The explanation is simple. Red and black were the colors of Ortega's Sandinista party; blue and white were the colors of the opposition party (Schuman, 1990).

Similarly, knowing that a survey on gun control is sponsored by a group with a strong position on the issue—the NRA, or perhaps the Brady Campaign to Prevent Gun Violence —could influence how people respond to the survey. Respondents might want to be cooperative research participants, so they might say what they think the sponsor wants to hear. Alternatively, they might resent what they perceive as pressure to answer the questions in a particular way and bend over backward not to do so. Either way, interpreting the results will be difficult.

ASSESSING ATTITUDES, DIRECTLY AND INDIRECTLY: A SUMMARY

Measuring people's attitudes is clearly less straightforward than measuring their height or weight. Stature and body mass are directly observable; they can be assessed whether or not a person is consciously aware of their magnitude. Nor are these qualities altered by the attempt to measure them. Height and weight cannot be suppressed: When placed on a scale, people cannot withhold information about their weight by refusing to obey the law of gravity. A physical quality like weight can also be boiled down to a single, unambiguous measurement; people's bodies are not associated with separate "heaviness" and "lightness" scores. And finally, if a person weighs 190 pounds on the scale, he cannot "implicitly" weigh 120 pounds.

Attitudes, on the other hand, cannot be viewed directly. They may be difficult to report, can be distorted even as they are being measured, and can be intentionally hidden from others. Attitudes can be complicated by ambivalence, and positive and negative feelings toward an attitude object can exist independently. Finally, attitudes can have separate explicit and implicit aspects. As a result, social psychologists have had to develop a wide variety of direct and indirect methods to uncover and record attitudes accurately.

Regardless of how attitudes are measured, psychologists are interested in them because they provide clues about what people are likely to do, say, and feel. In the next section, we review research on the relationship between attitudes and behavior.

Think Like a Social Psychologist

Designing research

—Come up with your own Likert scale items to assess attitudes toward either (1) fraternity/sorority membership; or (2) multiple-choice examinations.

—Think of some other indirect behavioral measures of people's attitudes. For example, what could you learn about people's attitudes by examining the books on their shelves?

Understanding everyday behavior

—At various points in your life, you may be approached by survey researchers (in person, over the phone, or online) who want you to report your attitudes toward important issues. If a researcher provided you with nothing more than a 7-point Likert scale, how would you differentiate between (a) feeling neutral; (b) feeling ambivalent; and (c) having no opinion? How might survey researchers get around this problem?

ATTITUDES AS PREDICTORS OF BEHAVIOR

What's with All the Empty Seats? Opening Weekend for a "Sure Thing" Movie

Once the people at the movie company accepted the basic premise of *No Vacancy*, they quickly lost interest in the details of LaPiere's study, on which the movie was based. None of them remembered (if they had ever even noticed) how LaPiere followed up his visits to the restaurants, cafés, hotels, and motels on his itinerary. Approximately six months after those visits, LaPiere sent a letter to each place of business. The letter included a questionnaire that asked, "Will you accept members of the Chinese race as guests in your establishment?" Not all the recipients returned the questionnaire, but LaPiere received replies from 81 dining establishments and 47 places of lodging. Their responses did not vary much: "92% of the former and 91% of the latter replied 'no'" (LaPiere, 1934, p. 234).

The racial prejudice LaPiere's questionnaire uncovered seemed to indicate that it would be "foolhardy for a Chinese to attempt to travel in the United States" (LaPiere, 1934, p. 234). But LaPiere had more than just the questionnaires to work with; he had his actual experiences with the people who replied to them. In fact, he and the Chinese couple had met "definite rejection" only once (LaPiere, 1934, p. 232). In other words, the attitudes people reported on the questionnaire were dramatically at odds with their actions. In this case, attitudes did not correlate with behavior, and therefore could not be used to *predict* behavior.

As we will see, the movie executives who produced *No Vacancy* should have paid more attention to this aspect of LaPiere's study. If they had known that attitudes can be poor predictors of behavior, they might have been less carried away by test audiences' reactions to the movie.

LaPiere was not the only social scientist to uncover a disconnect between people's attitudes and their actions. Kutner, Wilkins, and Yarrow (1952) also found little relationship between participants' evaluations of people and their behavior toward those people. And Corey (1937) reported that students' attitudes toward cheating did not predict their actual behavior when taking a test; in fact, their attitudes and their behavior were totally uncorrelated. Finally, in 1969, Allan Wicker (see also Wicker, 1971) came right to the point in his review of the relevant research, writing that "it is considerably more likely that attitudes will be unrelated or only slightly related to overt behaviors than that attitudes will be closely related to actions" (p. 65). That is to say, although people's actions may be predictable and many variables may play a role in eliciting their behavior, a person's subjectively held attitudes are not among those variables. The implication of Wicker's conclusion was that all the work social psychologists had devoted to measuring attitudes amounted to little more than an investigation of an interesting—but irrelevant—mental state.

Effects of Introspection on Attitude-Behavior Consistency

The disappointing performance of attitude measures as predictors of people's behavior might be explained in terms of how much thought people put into completing them. If respondents do not devote much effort to figuring out and reporting their attitudes, we should not be surprised that such data are not very useful in predicting what they are going to do. Maybe if people were encouraged to think about and analyze the reasons for their attitudes before reporting them, the correlation between their attitudes and their behavior would be stronger.

Wilson and his colleagues tested this hypothesis in a series of studies (Wilson & Dunn, 1986; Wilson, Dunn, Bybee, Hyman, & Rotondo, 1984; Wilson, Dunn, Kraft, & Lisle, 1989), with surprising results. As it turns out, introspection about the reasons for your attitudes actually *decreases* attitude-behavior consistency. For example, Wilson and Dunn (1986) asked people who were waiting in line at a university dining hall to report their attitudes toward different beverages (cola, milk, fruit juice, iced tea, and so on). Before doing so, though, they asked some participants to think carefully about and analyze their preferences. Afterward, the experimenters recorded which beverages participants actually selected. Compared to participants in a control group, the attitudes of people in the "analyze reasons" condition were less predictive of their beverage choices. A second study, done in the laboratory using puzzles as attitude objects, revealed the same effect. In this case, the experimenters recorded how much time participants spent playing with different puzzles (see **Figure 5.5**).

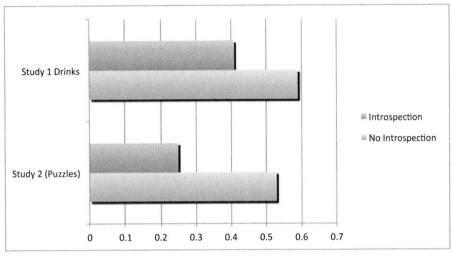

Figure 5.5: The effect of introspection on attitude-behavior consistency

The higher the correlation, the more consistency between attitudes and behavior. Introspecting about the reasons for one's attitudes before reporting those attitudes reduces the correlation.

Source: Wilson and Dunn (1986).

Why does introspection reduce attitude-behavior consistency? Apparently, prolonged introspection causes people to focus on aspects of an attitude object they ordinarily would not consider important, and that typically would not come to mind in dealing with that attitude object. For example, participants in the Wilson and Dunn study might have ended up thinking about the nutritional value of the drinks, or about how popular the drinks were with their fellow students. Those features might then have influenced the attitudes the students reported, even though they were irrelevant to the choices students made when loading up their trays in the cafeteria. Indeed, Wilson and Schooler (1991) found that when people engage in excessive introspection about their attitudes, they tend to focus on unimportant details. When participants in Wilson and Schooler's research analyzed their reasons for preferring some strawberry jams over others, their evaluations were less consistent with experts' ratings of the jams (taken from the magazine *Consumer Reports*) than those of participants who did not introspect.

Attitudes and Behavior: Variables Affecting the Relationship

More recent reviews of the literature have found that attitudes are indeed related to behavior, despite the studies just discussed (Ajzen, 2012; Eagly & Chaiken, 1998; Glasman & Albarracín, 2006; Kraus, 1995). Our intuitions about our behavior may not be perfect, but they aren't *that* far off the mark. Still, Wicker's (1969) critique made important contributions to attitude research. First, he forced psychologists to face the fact that the relationship between the attitudes people report and their behavior was not as strong as they had thought. In addition, he spurred research designed to reveal *when* attitudes do and do not predict behavior. As we will see next, several variables affect the strength of the attitude-behavior relationship.

How specific is the attitude? In the United States, people's attitudes toward affirmative action programs tend to correlate with their political orientations. Self-identified liberals usually favor such programs; conservatives tend to be more skeptical about them. Thus, if we wanted to predict how board members at a particular university would vote on an affirmative action policy proposed for the coming year, assessing their political attitudes might be helpful. Alternatively, we could try to get a measure of the board members' attitudes toward affirmative action in general. At the other extreme, we might want to get a measure of their attitudes toward adopting this specific affirmative action policy next year at this specific school.

Research shows that the narrower the focus of an attitude measure, the more likely it is to predict behavior (Davidson & Jaccard, 1979; Weinstein, 1972). If we want to predict a specific behavior directed at a specific target in a specific context and at a specific time, the best predictor would be an attitude measure that incorporates all that information (Ajzen & Fishbein, 1977). On the other hand, if we want to predict a general trend in behavior over time, the best predictor would be a more general, abstract attitude measure (Weigel & Newman, 1976). For example, if we wanted to predict the board members' votes (especially those involving politically charged issues) over a period of years, then a measure of their conservatism would be more helpful.

What kind of attitude? Many people have a definite and pronounced preference for red or white wine. Very few people are equally committed to red or white shoelaces. Such differences in attitude strength have important implications for attitude-behavior consistency. Attitude strength has been defined and measured in many different ways, including certainty, personal importance, and sheer amount of attitude-related knowledge (Eagly & Chaiken, 1998; Krosnick, Boninger, Chuang, Berent, & Carnot, 1993; Petty & Krosnick, 1995; Pomerantz, Chaiken, & Tordesillas, 1995; Raden, 1985). These different features of attitude strength, while they are often highly correlated, are not totally interchangeable (Krosnick et al., 1993; Raden, 1985; Skitka, Bauman, & Sargis, 2005). Nonetheless, they all have the same effect on attitude-behavior consistency: the stronger the attitude, the greater the consistency between attitude and behavior.

This woman reported a negative attitude toward cotton candy—but not this piece of cotton candy, not today, and not when she's this hungry...

Personal experience with attitude objects also increases attitude-behavior consistency (Fazio & Zanna, 1981). In one study, some participants evaluated different puzzles after working on each of them; others evaluated the puzzles after receiving second-hand information about them from the experimenters. Later, the researchers observed participants during a free-play period. The attitudes reported by participants in the direct-experience condition were more closely correlated with the participants' choice of puzzles than the attitudes of participants in the no-experience condition (Regan & Fazio, 1977).

Another way of assessing an attitude's strength is in terms of its accessibility, or the ease with which it comes to mind (see Chapter 3). Attitude accessibility is positively correlated with attitude-behavior consistency (Fazio

& Williams, 1986; Glasman & Albarracín, 2006). Indeed, the way direct experience may boost attitude-behavior consistency is by increasing an attitude's accessibility (Fazio, Chen, McDonel, & Sherman, 1982). The effects of other aspects of attitude strength on attitude-behavior consistency might also be due to their implications for accessibility. For example, if an attitude is personally important, you will think about it often, which will enhance its accessibility to you. That in and of itself could account for an increase in attitude-behavior consistency.

What kind of person? Some people's actions are more consistent with their attitudes than other people's (Kraus, 1995). In Chapter 4, we introduced the personality variable of self-monitoring. High self-monitors are attentive to the demands and requirements of different situations, adjusting their behavior accordingly. Low self-monitors are more attentive to their own internal states and standards. Based on that distinction, you might predict that attitude-behavior consistency would be more apparent among low self-monitors than among high self-monitors—and you would be right (Snyder & Tanke, 1976; Zanna, Olson, & Fazio, 1980). Interestingly, when researchers ask people to focus attention on themselves rather than on the situation—in other words, when they encourage participants to essentially become low self-monitors, if only temporarily— the correlation between attitudes and behavior increases (Gibbons, 1978; Pryor, Gibbons, Wicklund, Fazio, & Hood, 1977; see **Table 5.6**).

What kind of context? The effects of subjective social norms. Congratulations—you and a friend were among the lucky people invited to one of the test screenings of *No Vacancy*. You loved it, and said as much on the questionnaire you were asked to fill out. Afterward, you and your friend stopped at a local café, where you ran into some acquaintances. When they heard where you had been, they wanted to know about the movie—did you like it? Your attitude, of course, was very favorable, based on direct experience, and highly accessible. So what did you tell your acquaintances about the movie? You scowled and said you did not care for it.

What's going on here? We neglected to remind you of one important detail: your friend loathed the film. Please do not be offended; we have no reason to assume that you are a spineless person (or that your friend would make things miserable for you if you dared to express an independent opinion). The point is simply that sometimes our behavior is inconsistent with our attitudes because the social situation inhibits us from expressing our true feelings.

Ajzen and Fishbein's (1980; Fishbein & Ajzen, 1975) **theory of reasoned action** takes such social influences into account. The theory's first prediction is fairly straightforward: the best predictor of a behavior is a person's intention to engage in that behavior. But what determines our intentions? According to the theory, two

Table 5.6: Self-Focus Leads to Stronger Relationships between Attitudes and Behaviors

ATTITUDE	CONDITION	
	SELF-FOCUS	NO SELF-FOCUS
Playboy/Penthouse	.29	−.22
X-rated movies	.54	.12
Pornography	.71	−.31

Male participants reported their levels of excitement in response to viewing pictures of nude women; those in the self-focus condition did so while sitting in front of a mirror. Self-focus increased the extent to which participants' attitudes toward *Playboy/Penthouse* magazines, X-rated movies, and pornography in general were correlated with the level of excitement experienced.

Correlation coefficients can range from +1.00 (a perfect direct relationship) to −1.00 (a perfect inverse relationship).

Source: Gibbons (1977), Experiment 1.

important variables affect our intentions. The first is our attitude toward the behavior, which is a function of how we evaluate the outcomes we expect to follow from it ("Playing this heavy metal music will make me feel exhilarated"). Our evaluations are weighted by the perceived likelihood of each outcome ("That's what usually happens, but some heavy metal just annoys me"). In other words, embedded in the theory of reasoned action is the expectancy value model, $A = \Sigma\ (E * V)$: see **pages 188–190**.

The second variable that determines our behavioral intentions is subjective social norms. Subjective social norms are our beliefs about what other people prefer—that is, how they would evaluate the outcomes of our behavior ("I'm not sure my grandparents, here on a visit from Florida, would appreciate this music"). Those beliefs are themselves weighted in terms of how important the other people are, or how motivated we are to comply with their wishes ("I love my grandparents even more than Metallica"). Thus, in some circumstances, our expectations about how others will react could constrain the behavior that would follow naturally from our attitudes (Ybarra & Trafimow, 1998). As just one more example, the hotel and restaurant owners who treated the Chinese couple politely might have been concerned about offending LaPiere, their traveling partner.

Some people may habitually place more importance than others on what they perceive to be the social norms in a given situation. For example, we might expect that people from collectivistic cultures would be guided more by subjective social norms than people from individualist cultures, and indeed, some research supports that hypothesis (Abrams, Ando, & Hinkle, 1998).

Thus, the theory of reasoned action explains how attitudes combine with other cognitions to determine your intention to engage in a behavior, and how the relationship between attitudes and behavior varies depending on the context. It has been used successfully to predict behaviors ranging from eating at fast-food restaurants (Brinberg & Durand, 1983) to having an abortion (Smetana & Adler, 1980). Nonetheless, the theory has some limitations (see Eagly & Chaiken, 1993). For example, some behaviors are so habitual and automatic that they proceed independently of any underlying beliefs or evaluations—indeed, they may not even be intentional. Predicting when and where impulsive behaviors will occur is difficult using this model. And at times, strong intentions—derived from both clear and unambiguous attitudes and subjective social norms—will not be enough to produce a given behavior. You may feel positively about answering all the questions on the chemistry midterm correctly, know that your beloved parents feel the same way, and really intend to get that A+, but simply be unable to. To address this problem, Ajzen (1985; Ajzen & Madden, 1986) developed a more elaborate version of the theory of reasoned action, called the theory of planned behavior (see the "Social Psychology and Health" box on **page 209–210** for a description of this theory).

The behavior of people in collectivistic (as oppose to individualistic) cultures is often guided more by subjective social norms than by personal attitudes and preferences.

SOCIAL PSYCHOLOGY AND HEALTH: THE THEORY OF REASONED ACTION AND PUBLIC HEALTH

In the media, schools, and elsewhere, people are exposed to a wide variety of messages intended to change their attitudes toward unsafe or unhealthy habits and activities. What will be the impact of these public health campaigns? Health psychologists are acutely aware that predicting the likelihood that people will smoke, overeat, drive drunk, or engage in unsafe sex requires much more than simply asking them to report their attitudes toward such behaviors (Salovey, Rothman, & Rodin, 1998). Understanding the relationship between attitudes and behavior is critical to changing behavior for the better.

The theory of reasoned action (Ajzen & Fishbein, 1980) has proven useful to psychologists for understanding when and why people's attitudes will predict their health behavior. According to the theory, behavior is best predicted by people's intentions. Intentions, in turn, emerge from (1) people's attitudes toward a behavior (or more precisely, their attitudes toward the expected outcomes of a behavior); and (2) people's beliefs about important subjective norms—that is, their beliefs about what the people they care about think of the behavior. Consequently, according to this theory, if you want to predict whether high school students will experiment with a dangerous drug, you need to know more than their attitudes toward the drug's expected effects.

This woman appears to frequently floss, but the theory of reasoned action (and theory of planned behavior) have been used to shed light on why many people do not.

Knowing how their peers feel about using the drug is also crucial.

Ajzen and Fishbein (1977) also note that to predict behavior, attitudes must be specific. In other words, to predict whether people will use condoms with casual sex partners, researchers should assess their beliefs and attitudes toward using condoms with casual sex partners—not their attitudes toward "safe sex."

The theory of reasoned action has been used successfully to predict dental hygiene behavior (McCaul, O'Neal, & Glasgow, 1988; Toneatto & Binik, 1987), safe sex among gay men (Fishbein et al., 1992, 1993), and several other health-related behaviors. (But see Eagly & Chaiken, 1993, Chapter 4, for complications in applying the theory, and Gibbons & Gerard, 1995, for a different approach to predicting health-related behaviors.) A major limitation of this approach, however, is that some behaviors are difficult for people to bring under control. To address this problem, Ajzen and his colleagues developed the theory of planned behavior (Ajzen, 1985; Ajzen & Madden, 1986). An extension of the theory of reasoned action, the theory of planned behavior takes into account people's actual control of their behavior, as well as their *perceived* control.

Perceived control of a behavior should have an independent effect on behavioral intentions. In general, the things people say they intend to do are more likely to be things they feel they can do rather than things they feel helpless about ("I'll never be able to stop overeating, even though I want to and my spouse wants me to lose weight"). At the same time, if perceived control over a behavior is very different from actual control (such as mistakenly believing that you will really be able to get up at 4:30 A.M. every day to run ten miles), then intentions will be a less powerful predictor of actual behavior. Even with the best possible intentions, people will find some behaviors difficult to enact.

Although measuring these added variables (especially actual control) is difficult, taking them into account seems to improve behavioral predictions (Madden, Ellen, & Ajzen, 1992). The theory of planned behavior has proven useful in predicting health-related behaviors such as exercising (Norman & Smith, 1992) and losing weight (Schifter & Ajzen, 1985). In sum, attitudes do indeed influence behaviors that affect our health, but they do so in concert with other related beliefs (about norms) and expectations (about control).

Explicit versus Implicit Attitudes

Recent interest in the distinction between explicit and implicit attitudes has suggested another approach to the question of attitude-behavior consistency. That is, these two kinds of attitude may be useful for predicting different kinds of behavior (see Fazio, Jackson, Dunton, & Williams, 1995; McClelland, Koestner, & Weinberger, 1989; McConnell & Liebold, 2001; Rydell & McConnell, 2006). Explicit attitudes may be useful for predicting behavior that is conscious and under your control (for example, whether you deliberately purchase food that is low in fat, sodium, and cholesterol). Implicit attitudes, on the other hand, may be more predictive of spontaneous, less deliberate, and less consciously directed actions (such as the look on your face when you eat the zero fat, sodium-free food); thus, they can serve as hidden influences on our behavior.

This generalization is not absolute: Implicit attitudes are related to actions that are under our control, and explicit attitudes can also be related to spontaneous behavior (Cameron, Brown-Iannuzzi, & Payne, 2012; Fazio & Olson, 2003; Rudman, 2004). In addition, there is some disagreement about just how strongly implicit attitudes can predict behavior of any kind (Greenwald, Poehlman, Uhlmann, & Banaji, 2009; Oswald, Mitchell, Blanton, Jaccard, & Tetlock, 2013). Nonetheless, research on the implicit-explicit distinction suggests that the question "Do attitudes predict behavior?" might better be phrased "What kinds of attitudes predict what kinds of behavior in what kinds of situations?"

Attitudes and Behavior: A Summary

The list of factors that play a role in whether or not attitudes predict behavior may seem like just that—a list of unrelated variables. To a great extent, though, we can integrate them by thinking about them in relation to people's goals. Introspection undermines attitude-behavior consistency because it causes people to consider goals that might be associated with an attitude object ("Chocolate milk is not the most sophisticated drink to serve at a party"), but are not the most relevant or important ones ("It sure tastes yummy"). Attitude questions that are specific to a situation ("How do you feel about drinking coffee late at night?") are more likely to bring to mind the goals most relevant to the situation (getting to sleep) than general questions ("Do you like coffee?"). Thus, specific questions are more useful for predicting what people will do in specific situations. Similarly, attitudes that are strong and held with certainty (like attitudes toward death) may be strong because the attitude object in question typically relates to a specific goal (in this case, *avoiding* death). Attitude objects that are associated with multiple goals, on the other hand, are more likely to be associated with ambivalence, so that behavior toward them is more difficult to predict.

The behavior of high self-monitors may be difficult to predict from their attitudes because it is more likely to be influenced by the goal of fitting into a particular situation. High and low self-monitors might both evaluate schoolwork positively because they enjoy the intellectual challenges involved, but if their peers look down on them for caring too much about their grades, the high self-monitor will be less likely than the low self-monitor to hit the books. Finally, regardless of one's level of self-monitoring, salient social norms can make the goal of pleasing others more important than the goals normally associated with an attitude object.

The results of LaPiere's study can be explained in similar terms. People may seek to avoid contact with members of other ethnic or racial groups, a goal that could certainly cause them to report a negative attitude toward those groups privately, in writing ("I will never serve a Chinese person in my restaurant"). A face-to-face encounter with a member of that group is another matter, however. In that context, the goals of avoiding conflict, avoiding a scene, and, of course, not being cruel toward a living, breathing human being (as opposed to an abstract, hypothetical "Chinese person") may produce a more favorable response.

Think Like a Social Psychologist

Understanding everyday behavior
—Why might some attitudes be more important to a given person than other ones? Can the set of attitudes that are most important to a specific person tell us something meaningful about that person?

Confronting social issues
—The theory of reasoned action certainly does not predict that people will always make reasonable or desirable decisions. Using **Table 5.3 (page 189)** as a model, show how a military leader or chief of state could arrive at the intention to use a nuclear weapon against an enemy.

Thinking critically
—Think about why you might be critical of a person who rarely behaves consistently with her attitudes. Then, consider the disadvantages of always behaving consistently with your attitudes, regardless of the situation.

Designing research

—As we saw earlier, high self-monitors' attitudes predict behavior less well than low self-monitors' attitudes. Research that supports that hypothesis, however, examined primarily explicit attitudes. Given what we know about the kind of behavior that is best predicted by *implicit* attitudes, do you think that the same differences in attitude-behavior consistency would be found for high and low self-monitors' implicit attitudes? How would you test that hypothesis?

EPILOGUE: ROTTEN TOMATOES

In light of all the complications involved in measuring attitudes and the variety of influences (many of them hidden) on what people say when asked about their attitudes, you will not be surprised to hear that the attitudes reported by test audiences for *No Vacancy* did not predict most moviegoers' behavior. The film, a total failure at the box office, was pulled from theaters immediately after its opening weekend. The reviews were savage; one reviewer suggested that "though the hapless characters are forced to travel thousands of miles, even a walk down the block would be too far to go to watch this incoherent mess of a movie." Others described the film as "charmless," "unfunny," "formulaic," and (of course) "vacant." Our sense of personal humiliation was tempered somewhat by the fact that our names were buried deep in the closing credits—as Leonard Newmark and Ralph Gerber.

SOCIAL PSYCHOLOGY ENCOUNTERS THE DARK SIDE: REWRITING HISTORY BY MISREMEMBERING YOUR ATTITUDES

Totalitarian governments' efforts to dominate citizens' thinking often include attempts to control the past as well as the present. In other words, the government rewrites history to support its ideology and goals. Current leaders receive more credit for past triumphs than they deserve, and prominent people who have fallen out of favor are either recast as villains or ignored. Sometimes they are literally airbrushed out of photographs.

Most people view this kind of historical tampering with scorn. Needless to say, they would be shocked to discover that *individuals* have a tendency to revise their own memories of the past to support their current attitudes. Some researchers have even characterized the human mind as "totalitarian" (Greenwald, 1980). For example, studies of attitude change—both naturally occurring (Markus, 1986) and experimentally manipulated (Bem & McConnell, 1970; Goethals & Reckman, 1973; Ross, 1989)—reveal that people tend to recall their past attitudes as being more similar to their current attitudes than was actually the case. In other words, you might think that you can easily remember how you felt about capital punishment, Japanese food, or hip hop music five or ten years ago, but it is possible that what you "recall" reflects your current attitudes more than your past ones.

Attitudes have also been shown to bias your memory for related information and events. In a classic demonstration of what has come to be known as the **congeniality effect**, Levine and Murphy (1943) presented Communists and anti-Communists with messages that were either favorable or unfavorable to the Soviet Union (the leading Communist state in the world at the time). Communists could better remember the favorable messages, while anti-Communists could more easily remember the unfavorable messages. Thus, if you have strong attitudes, you are likely to remember facts and arguments that support those attitudes, but forget facts and arguments that undermine them.

The functions of such memory biases seem fairly straightforward. People undoubtedly would prefer not to remember that their attitudes once differed from those they hold now; doing so might cast doubt on the correctness and wisdom of their current beliefs and feelings. For the same reason, people would prefer not to focus on information that flies in the face of their current attitudes and beliefs. However, these distortions of memory come at a cost to the individual, including a tendency to cling too long to dysfunctional attitudes.

SOCIAL PSYCHOLOGY ENCOUNTERS THE BRIGHT SIDE: LIMITS ON THE "CONGENIALITY EFFECT"

Not all researchers have observed the congeniality effect, the finding that people selectively remember information that is consistent with their attitudes. In fact, some research has failed to replicate the finding. For example, people with a great deal of knowledge about a topic have an easier time remembering arguments with which they disagree than other people do (Wiley, 2005; see **Figure 5.3**). Some researchers have even reported the *opposite* result—that is, people remember "uncongenial" facts, ideas, or events better than other facts, ideas, or events.

What explains these findings? As Eagly, Kulesa, Chen, and Chaiken (2001; see also Eagly, Chen, Chaiken, & Shaw-Barnes, 1999) point out, the congeniality hypothesis is based on the idea that people will ignore or try not to think about information that does not fit comfortably with their attitudes. However, people do not always react to attitude-inconsistent information in that way. Instead, they may actively attempt to refute

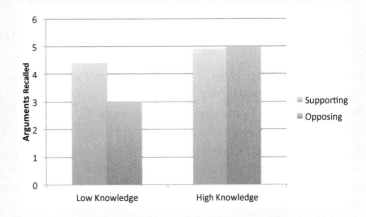

Figure 5.3: *Bias for recalling arguments that support one's attitudes as a function of prior knowledge*

The recall of less knowledgeable people is more biased—they have a harder time recalling arguments opposing their attitudes.

Source: Wiley (2005, Experiment 2).

and discredit it. If so, they should remember the information very well, because thinking long and hard about something makes it easier to recall.

Of course, the fact that people can remember uncongenial information does not mean that they are open to revising strongly held and cherished attitudes. After all, often the only reason that attitude-inconsistent information is so memorable is that people have devoted lots of energy to dismissing it. At the very least, though, this research indicates that people do not always react to unwanted knowledge in the way that a totalitarian political system would (that is, by trying to erase it). Instead, their minds more closely resemble free and open societies, in which dissenting views are heard and discussed (albeit in a biased way).

There is one attitude object toward which almost all people feel positively, and strongly so: the self. But research on autobiographical recall provides more evidence that our memories are not completely distorted by our preferences. Newby-Clark and Ross (2003) found that when people are asked to recall significant life events, they are just as likely to recall negative as positive ones. Certainly some people—especially those whose "repressive" coping style involves avoiding negative affect at all costs (Davis, 1990; Newman & Hedberg, 1999)—try to avoid recalling unpleasant past experiences. And people tend to expect to have favorable experiences in the *future*. But most people do not use their high regard for themselves as a basis for radically editing the past. Given that those who do not remember the past are probably doomed to repeat it, this is good news for us all.

HIDDEN INFLUENCES ON ATTITUDES: A SUMMARY

Classical conditioning (including subliminal classical conditioning): Your evaluation of an attitude object could be a function of the pleasing and/or repellant things with which the attitude object was paired.

The mere exposure effect: Your evaluation of an attitude object could be a function simply of how many times you encountered it.

Mood as information effects: Your evaluation of an attitude object could be a function of the mood you were in when you encountered it.

Inherited attitudes: Your evaluation of an attitude object could be a function of traits and preferences you inherited from your parents.

Evolved, species-general attitudes: Your evaluation of an attitude object could be a function of psychological mechanisms you inherited from your ancestors, common to all human beings.

Automatically activated attitudes and implicit attitudes: Your attitudes themselves could be hidden influences on your behavior if they are activated from memory and guide your behavior without your intention or awareness.

KEY TERMS AND DEFINITIONS

Attitude: a tendency to positively or negatively evaluate some person, object, issue, or other entity

Attitude object: anything toward which a person can have an attitude

Classical conditioning of attitudes: creating attitudes by pairing a conditioned stimulus with an unconditioned stimulus

Subliminal perception: Perceiving stimuli without awareness

Mere exposure effect: the tendency to evaluate stimuli more positively the more you encounter them, all other things held equal

Mood as information effect: the use of mood, no matter what its source, as a simple cue to assess your attitude toward something

Affectively based attitude: An attitude that is based on the simple positive or negative feelings associated with an attitude object

Cognitively based attitude: An attitude that is based on beliefs about an attitude object's properties and the desirability of those properties

Expectancy value theories: Theories stating that attitudes are based on your evaluations of an attitude object's attributes, taking into account your confidence that the object really has those attributes

Ambivalence: a state in which you simultaneously evaluate an object both positively and negatively

Response amplification: the finding that ambivalent feelings about some group (such as a stigmatized group) can lead to extremely positive and negative evaluations of the group's members

Semantic differential technique: a technique for measuring attitudes that involves asking people to rate attitude objects using several scales whose endpoints are opposite in meaning

Bogus pipeline: a technique for encouraging people to report socially unacceptable attitudes by convincing them that a machine can tell whether or not they are lying

Galvanic skin response (GSR): a physiological measure of attitude that is based on the idea that strong evaluative responses will activate people's sweat glands

Facial electromyographic activity (EMG): electrical activity that is caused by subtle movements of the facial muscles associated with positive or negative evaluative responses

Functional magnetic resonance imaging (fMRI): a technique for directly measuring the electrical activity in the brain that is associated with evaluative (and other) responses

Automatically activated attitudes: attitudes that are quickly and unintentionally activated

Explicit attitudes: conscious, self-reported attitudes

Implicit attitudes: attitudes that are based on simple associations activated automatically when you encounter an attitude object, and that may differ from explicit attitudes

Tripartite model of attitudes: the idea that attitudes have cognitive, affective, and behavioral components

False consensus effect: the tendency for people to exaggerate the extent to which others share their attitudes

Theory of reasoned action: a model that predicts people's intentions to behave in certain ways by taking into account their attitudes toward the behaviors; their beliefs about the likelihood of different outcomes of the behaviors; and their beliefs about what other people think of the behaviors

Congeniality effect: the tendency to remember facts and arguments that support your attitudes better than facts and arguments that are inconsistent with your attitudes

REFERENCES

Abelson, R. P., Aronson, E., McGuire, W. J., Newcombe, T. M., Rosenberg, M. J., & Tannenbaum, P. H. (Eds.). (1968). *Theories of cognitive consistency: A sourcebook.* Chicago: Rand McNally.

Abrams, D., Ando, K., & Hinkle, S. (1998). Psychological attachment to the group: Cross-cultural differences in organizational identification and subjective norms as predictors of workers' turnover intentions. *Personality and Social Psychology Bulletin, 24,* 1027–1039.

Achen, C. H. (2002). Parental socialization and rational party identification. *Political Behavior, 24,* 151–170.

Adolphs, R., & Tranel, D. (1999). Preference for visual stimuli following amygdala change. *Journal of Cognitive Neuroscience, 11,* 610–616.

Ajzen, I. (1985). From intentions to actions: A theory of planned behavior. In J. Kuhl & J. Beckman (Eds.), *Action control: From cognition to behavior* (pp. 11–39). Berlin: Springer.

Ajzen, I. (2012). Attitudes and persuasion. In K. Deaux & M. Snyder (Eds.), *The Oxford handbook of personality and social psychology* (pp. 367–393). New York: Oxford University Press.

Ajzen, I., & Fishbein, M. (1977). Attitude-behavior relations: A theoretical analysis and review of empirical research. *Psychological Bulletin, 84,* 888–918.

Ajzen, I., & Fishbein, M. (1980). *Understanding attitudes and predicting social behavior.* Englewood Cliffs, NJ: Prentice Hall.

Ajzen, I., & Madden, T. J. (1986). Prediction of goal-directed behavior: Attitudes, intentions and perceived behavioral control. *Journal of Experimental Social Psychology, 22,* 453–474.

Arkin, R. M., & Lake, E. A. (1983). Plumbing the depths of the bogus pipeline: A reprise. *Journal of Research in Personality, 17,* 81–88.

Atwood, R. W., & Howell, R. J. (1971). Pupilometric and personality test score differences of female aggressing pedophiliacs and normals. *Psychonomic Science, 22,* 115–116.

Banaji, M. R. (2001). Implicit attitudes can be measured. In H. L. Roediger & J. S. Nairne (Eds.), *The nature of remembering: Essays in honor of Robert G. Crowder* (pp. 117–150). Washington, DC: American Psychological Association.

Banaji, M. R., & Heiphetz, L. (2010). Attitudes. In S. T. Fiske, D. T. Gilbert, & G. Lindzey (Eds.), *The handbook of social psychology* (5th ed., Vol. 1, pp. 353–393). Hoboken, NJ: Wiley.

Bargh, J. A., Chaiken, S., Govender, R., & Pratto, F. (1992). The generality of the automatic attitude activation effect. *Journal of Personality and Social Psychology, 62,* 893–912.

Bargh, J. A., Chaiken, S., Raymond, P., & Hymes, C. (1996). The automatic evaluation effect: Unconditional automatic attitude activation with a pronunciation task. *Journal of Experimental Social Psychology, 32,* 104–128.

Belkin, L. (1988, December 17). Texas judge eases sentence for killer of two homosexuals. *New York Times.*

Bell, D. W., & Esses, V. M. (1997). Ambivalence and response amplification toward native peoples. *Journal of Applied Social Psychology, 27,* 1063–1084.

Bell, D. W., & Esses, V. M. (2002). Ambivalence and response amplification: A motivational perspective. *Personality and Social Psychology Bulletin, 28,* 1143–1152.

Bem, D. J., & McConnell, H. K. (1970). Testing the self-perception explanation of dissonance phenomena: On the salience of premanipulation attitudes. *Journal of Personality and Social Psychology, 14,* 23–31.

Billard, M. (1990, July 12–16). Heavy metal goes on trial. *Rolling Stone,* pp. 83–88, 132.

Blanton, H., & Jaccard, J. (2006). Arbitrary metrics in psychology. *American Psychologist, 61,* 27–41.

Bornstein, R. F. (1989a). Exposure and affect: Overview and meta-analysis of research, 1968–1987. *Psychological Bulletin, 106,* 265–289.

Bornstein, R. F. (1989b). Subliminal techniques as propaganda tools: Review and critique. *Journal of Mind and Behavior, 10,* 231–262.

Bornstein, R. F. (1992). Subliminal mere exposure effects. In R. F. Bornstein & T. S. Pittman (Eds.), *Perception without awareness: Cognitive, clinical, and social perspectives* (pp. 191–210). New York: Guilford.

Bornstein, R. F., & D'Agostino, P. R. (1994). The attribution and discounting of perceptual fluency: Preliminary tests of a perceptual fluency/attributional model of the mere exposure effect. *Social Cognition, 12,* 103–128.

Bornstein, R. F., Kale, A. R., & Cornell, K. R. (1990). Boredom as a limiting condition on the mere exposure effect. *Journal of Personality and Social Psychology, 58,* 791–800.

Bornstein, R. F., Leone, D. R., & Galley, D. J. (1987). The generalizability of subliminal mere exposure effects: Influence of stimuli perceived without awareness on social behavior. *Journal of Personality and Social Psychology, 53,* 1070–1079.

Boshier, R., & Thom, E. (1973). Do conservative parents nurture conservative children? *Social Behavior and Personality, 1,* 108–110.

Bottoms, B. L. (1993). Individual differences in perceptions of child sexual assault victims. In G. S. Goodman & B. L. Bottoms (Eds.), *Child victims, child witnesses: Understanding and improving testimony* (pp. 229261). New York: Guilford Press.

Bottoms, B. L., Davis, S. L., & Epstein, M. A. (2004). Effects of victim and defendant race on jurors' decisions in child sexual abuse. *Journal of Applied Social Psychology, 34,* 1–33.

Bottoms, B. L., Golding, J. M., Stevenson, M. C., Wiley, T. R. A., & Yozwiak, J. A. (2007). A review of factors affecting jurors' decisions in cases involving child sexual abuse allegations. In M. Toglia, J. D. Read, D. F. Ross, & C. L. Lindsay (Eds.), *Handbook of eyewitness psychology: Volume 1: Memory for events* (pp. 509–543). Mahwah, NJ: Lawrence Erlbaum.

Bottoms, B. L., Nysse-Carris, K. L., Harris, T., & Tyda, K. (2003). Jurors' perceptions of adolescent sexual assault victims who have intellectual disabilities. *Law and Human Behavior, 27,* 205–227.

Breckler, S. J. (1984). Empirical validation of affect, behavior, and cognitions as distinct components of attitude. *Journal of Personality and Social Psychology, 47,* 1191–1205.

Breckler, S. J. (1994). A comparison of numerical indexes for measuring attitude ambivalence. *Educational and Psychological Measurement, 54,* 350–365.

Brent, P. (2005, July 6). Horton's cool to killer's endorsement. *National Post* (Canada), pp. A1, A4.

Brickman, P., Redfield, J., Harrison, A. A., & Crandall, R. (1972). Drive and predisposition as factors in the attitudinal effects of mere exposure. *Journal of Experimental Social Psychology, 8,* 31–44.

Brinberg, D., & Durand, J. (1983). Eating at fast food restaurants: An analysis using two behavioral intention models. *Journal of Applied Social Psychology, 13,* 459–472.

Cacioppo, J. T., Crites, S. L., Berntson, G. G., & Coles, M. G. (1993). If attitudes affect how stimuli are processed, should they not affect the event-related brain potential? *Psychological Science, 4,* 108–112.

Cacioppo, J. T., Gardner, W. L., & Berntson, G. G. (1997). Beyond bipolar conceptualizations and measures: The case of attitudes and evaluative space. *Personality and Social Psychology Review, 1,* 3–25.

Cacioppo, J. T., & Petty, R. E. (1979). Attitudes and cognitive response: An electrophysiological approach. *Journal of Personality and Social Psychology, 37,* 2181–2199.

Cacioppo, J. T., & Sandman, C. A. (1981). Psychophysiological functioning, cognitive responding, and attitudes. In R. E. Petty, T. M. Ostrom, & T. C. Brock (Eds.), *Cognitive responses in persuasion* (pp. 81–103). Hillsdale, NJ: Erlbaum.

Cameron, C., Brown-Iannuzzi, J. L., & Payne, B. (2012). Sequential priming measures of implicit social cognition: A meta-analysis of associations with behavior and explicit attitudes. *Personality and Social Psychology Review, 16,* 330–350.

Carlson, E. R. (1956). Attitude change through modification of attitude structure. *Journal of Abnormal and Social Psychology, 52,* 256–261.

Cervone, D., Kopp, D. A., Schaumann, L., Scott, W. D. (1994). Mood, self-efficacy, and performance standards: Lower moods induce higher standards for performance. *Journal of Personality and Social Psychology, 67,* 499–512.

Cialdini, R. B., Trost, M. R., & Newsom, T. J. (1995). Preference for consistency: The development of a valid measure and the discovery of surprising behavioral implications. *Journal of Personality and Social Psychology, 69,* 318–328.

Clore, G. L, Gasper, K., & Garvin, E. (2001). Affect as information. In J. P Forgas (Ed.), *Handbook of affect and social cognition* (pp. 121–144). Mahwah, NJ: Lawrence Erlbaum.

Corey, S. M. (1937). Professed attitudes and actual behavior. *Journal of Educational Psychology, 28,* 271–280.

Crelia, R. A., & Tesser, A. (1996). Attitude heritability and attitude reinforcement: A replication. *Personality and Individual Differences, 21,* 803–808.

Crites, S. L. Jr., & Cacioppo, J. T. (1996). Electrocortical differentiation of evaluative and nonevaluative categorizations. *Psychological Science, 7,* 318–321.

Cunningham, W. A., Espinet, S. D., DeYoung, C. G., & Zelazo, P. D. (2005). Attitudes to the right and left: Frontal ERP asymmetries associated with stimulus valence and processing goals. *NeuroImage, 28,* 827–834.

Cunningham, W. A., Johnson, M. K., Gatenby, J. C., Gore, J. C., & Banaji, M. R. (2003). Neural components of social evaluation. *Journal of Personality and Social Psychology, 85,* 639–649.

Davidson, A. R., & Jaccard, J. J. (1979). Variables that moderate the attitude-behavior relationship: Results of a longitudinal survey. *Journal of Personality and Social Psychology, 37,* 1364–1376.

Davis, J., Senghas, A., & Ochsner, K. N. (2009). How does facial feedback modulate emotional experience? *Journal of Research in Personality, 43,* 822–829.

Davis, P. (1990). Repression and the inaccessibility of emotional memories. In J. L. Singer (Ed.), *Repression and dissociation: Implications for personality, psychopathology, and health* (pp. 387–403). Chicago: University of Chicago Press.

De Houwer, J., Baeyens, F., & Eelen, P. (1994). Verbal evaluative conditioning with undetected US presentations. *Behaviour Research and Therapy, 32,* 629–633.

De Houwer, J., Hendrickx, H., & Baeyens, F. (1997). Evaluative learning with "subliminally" presented stimuli. *Cognition and Emotion, 6,* 87–107.

de Zilva, D., Mitchell, C. J., & Newell, B. R. (2013). Eliminating the mere exposure effect through changes in context between exposure and test. *Cognition and Emotion, 27,* 1345–1358.

Dhont, K., Van Hiel, A., Pattyn, S., Onraet, E., & Severens, E. (2012). A step into the anarchist's mind: Examining political attitudes and ideology through event-related brain potentials. *Social Cognitive and Affective Neuroscience, 7,* 296–303.

Duggan, L. M. III, Aubrey, M., Doherty, E., Isquith, P., Levine, M., & Scheiner, J. (1989). The credibility of children as witnesses in a simulated child sex abuse trial. In S. J. Ceci, D. F. Ross, & M. P. Toglia (Eds.), *Perspectives on children's testimony* (pp. 71–99). New York: Springer-Verlag.

Eagly, A. H., & Chaiken, S. (1993). *The psychology of attitudes.* Fort Worth, TX: Harcourt Brace College Publishers.

Eagly, A. H., & Chaiken, S. (1998). Attitude structure and function. In D. T. Gilbert, S. T. Fiske, & G. Lindzey (Eds.), *The handbook of social psychology* (4th ed., Vol. 1, pp. 269–322). New York: McGraw Hill.

Eagly, A. H., Chen, S., Chaiken, S., & Shaw-Barnes, K. (1999). The impact of attitudes on memory: An affair to remember. *Psychological Bulletin, 125,* 64–89.

Eagly, A. H., Kulesa, P., Chen, S., & Chaiken, S. (2001). Do attitudes affect memory? Tests of the congeniality hypothesis. *Current Directions in Psychological Science, 10,* 5–9.

Edwards, K. (1990). The interplay of affect and cognition in attitude formation and change. *Journal of Personality and Social Psychology, 59,* 202–216.

Fazio R. H., Chen J., McDonel, E. C., & Sherman S. J. (1982). Attitude accessibility, attitude-behavior consistency and the strength of the object-evaluation association. *Journal of Experimental Social Psychology, 18,* 339–357.

Fazio, R. H., Jackson, J. R., Dunton, B. C., & Williams, C. J. (1995). Variability in automatic activation as an unobtrusive measure of racial attitudes: A bona fide pipeline? *Journal of Personality and Social Psychology, 69,* 1013–1027.

Fazio, R. H., & Olson, M. A. (2003). Implicit measures in social cognition research: Their meaning and use. *Annual Review of Psychology, 54,* 297–327.

Fazio, R. H., Sanbonmatsu, D. M., Powell, M. C., & Kardes, F. R. (1986). On the automatic activation of attitudes. *Journal of Personality and Social Psychology, 50,* 229–238.

Fazio, R. H., & Williams, C. J. (1986). Attitude accessibility as a moderator of the attitude-perception and attitude-behavior relations: An investigation of the 1984 presidential election. *Journal of Personality and Social Psychology, 51,* 505–514.

Fazio, R. H., & Zanna, M. P. (1981). Direct experience and attitude-behavior consistency. In L. Berkowitz (Ed.), *Advances in experimental social psychology* (Vol. 14, pp. 161–202). San Diego, CA: Academic Press.

Ferguson, M. J., & Bargh, J. A. (2004). Liking is for doing: The effects of goal pursuit on automatic evaluation. *Journal of Personality and Social Psychology, 87,* 557–572.

Festinger, L. (1957). *A theory of cognitive dissonance.* Stanford, CA: Stanford University Press.

Fiedler, K., Schmid, J., & Stahl, T. (2002). What is the current truth about polygraph lie detection? *Basic and Applied Social Psychology, 24,* 313–324.

Fishbein, M. (1963). An investigation of the relationships between beliefs about an object and the attitude toward the object. *Human Relations, 16,* 233–240.

Fishbein, M. (1967). A behavior theory approach to the relations between beliefs about an object and the attitude toward the object. In M. Fishbein (Ed.), *Readings in attitude theory and measurement* (pp. 477–492). New York: Wiley.

Fishbein, M., & Ajzen, I. (1975). *Belief, attitude, intention, and behavior: An introduction to theory and research.* Reading, MA: Addison-Wesley.

Fishbein, M., Chan, D. K.-S., O'Reilly, K., Schnell, D., Wood, R., Beeker, C., & Cohn, D. (1993). Attitudinal and normative factors as determinants of gay men's intentions to perform AIDS-related sexual behaviors: A multi-site analysis. *Journal of Applied Social Psychology, 22,* 999–1011.

Fishbein, M., Chan, D. K.-S., O'Reilly, K., Schnell, D., Wood, R., Beeker, C., & Cohn, D. (1993). Factors influencing gay men's attitudes, subjective norms, and intentions with respect to performing sexual behaviors. *Journal of Applied Social Psychology, 23,* 417–438.

Gawronski B., & Strack, F. (2004). On the propositional nature of cognitive consistency: Dissonance changes explicit, but not implicit attitudes. *Journal of Experimental Social Psychology, 40,* 535–542.

Gibbons, F. X. (1978). Sexual standards and reactions to pornography: Enhancing behavioral consistency through self-focused attention. *Journal of Personality and Social Psychology, 36,* 976–987.

Gibbons, F. X., & Gerard, M. (1995). Predicting young adults' health risk behavior. *Journal of Personality and Social Psychology, 69,* 505–517.

Gibbons, F. X., Stephan, W. G., Stephenson, B., & Petty, C. R. (1980). Reactions to stigmatized others: Response amplification vs. sympathy. *Journal of Experimental Social Psychology, 16,* 591–605.

Giner-Sorolla, R., Garcia, M. T., & Bargh, J. A. (1999). The automatic evaluation of pictures. *Social Cognition, 17,* 76–96.

Glasman, L. R., & Albarracín, D. (2006). Forming attitudes that predict future behavior: A meta-analysis of the attitude-behavior relation. *Psychological Bulletin, 132,* 778–822.

Goethals, G. R., & Reckman, R. F. (1973). The perception of consistency in attitudes. *Journal of Experimental Social Psychology, 9,* 491–501.

Greenwald, A. G. (1980). The totalitarian ego: Fabrication and revision of personal history. *American Psychologist, 35,* 603–618.

Greenwald, A. G., & Banaji, M. R. (1995). Implicit social cognition: Attitudes, self-esteem, and stereotypes. *Psychological Review, 102,* 4–27.

Greenwald, A. G., Banaji, M. R., Rudman, L. A., Farnham, S. D., Nosek, B. A., & Mellott, D. S. (2002). A unified theory of implicit attitudes, stereotypes, self-esteem, and self-concept. *Psychological Review, 109,* 3–25.

Greenwald, A. G., & Farnham, S. D. (2000). Using the Implicit Association test to measure self-esteem and self-concept. *Journal of Personality and Social Psychology, 79,* 1022–1038.

Greenwald, A. G., McGhee, D. E., & Schwartz, J. L. K. (1998). Measuring individual differences in implicit cognition. *Journal of Personality and Social Psychology, 74,* 1464–1480.

Greenwald, A. G., Nosek, B. A., & Banaji, M. R. (2003) Understanding and using the Implicit Association Test: I. An improved scoring algorithm. *Journal of Personality and Social Psychology, 85,* 197–216.

Greenwald, A. G., Poehlman, T., Uhlmann, E., & Banaji, M. R. (2009). Understanding and using the Implicit Association Test: III. Meta-analysis of predictive validity. *Journal of Personality and Social Psychology, 97,* 17–41.

Grover, K. W., & Miller, C. T. (2012). Does expressed acceptance reflect genuine attitudes? A bogus pipeline study of the effects of mortality salience on acceptance of a person with AIDS. *Journal of Social Psychology, 152,* 131–135.

Haegerich, T., & Bottoms, B. L. (2000). Empathy and jurors' decisions in patricide trials involving child sexual assault. *Law and Human Behavior, 24,* 421–448.

van Harreveld, F., van der Pligt, J., & de Liver, Y. N. (2009). The agony of ambivalence and ways to resolve it: Introducing the MAID model. *Personality and Social Psychology Review, 13,* 45–61.

Harrison, A. A. (1977). Mere exposure. In L. Berkowitz (Ed.), *Advances in experimental social psychology* (Vol. 10, pp. 39–83). New York: Academic Press.

Hass, G. R., Katz, I., Rizzo, N., Bailey, J., & Eisenstadt, D. (1991). Cross-racial appraisal as related to attitude ambivalence and cognitive complexity. *Personality and Social Psychology Bulletin, 18,* 786–797.

Hazlewood, J. D., & Olson, J. M. (1986). Covariation information, causal reasoning, and interpersonal behavior. *Journal of Experimental Social Psychology, 22,* 276–291.

Heider, F. (1946). Attitudes and cognitive organization. *Journal of Psychology, 21,* 107–112.

Hermans, D., De Houwer, J., & Eelen, P. (2001). A time course analysis of the affective priming effect. *Cognition and Emotion, 15,* 143–165.

Herring, D. R., White, K. R., Jabeen, L. N., Hinojos, M., Terrazas, G., Reyes, S. M., Taylor, J. H., & Crites, S. L. Jr. (2013). On the automatic activation of attitudes: A quarter century of evaluative priming research. *Psychological Bulletin, 139,* 1062–1089.

Hess, E. H. (1965). Attitude and pupil size. *Scientific American, 212,* 46–54.

Hetherton, J., & Beardsall, L. (1998). Decisions and attitudes concerning child sexual abuse: Does the gender of the perpetrator make a difference to child protection professionals? *Child Abuse and Neglect, 22,* 1265–1283.

Himmelfarb, S. (1993). The measurement of attitudes. In A. H. Eagly & S. Chaiken, *The psychology of attitudes* (Chapter 2, pp. 23–85). Fort Worth, TX: Harcourt Brace College Publishers.

Hoffman, L. W. (1991). The influence of the family environment on personality: Accounting for sibling differences. *Psychological Bulletin, 110,* 187–203.

Huntsinger, J. R. (2011). Mood and trust in intuition interactively orchestrate correspondence between implicit and explicit attitudes. *Personality and Social Psychology Bulletin, 37,* 1245–1258.

Jonas, K., Broemer, P., & Diehl, M. (2000). Attitudinal ambivalence. In W. Stroebe & M. Hewstone (Eds.), *European Review of Psychology* (Vol. 11, pp. 35–74). Chichester, UK: John Wiley & Sons Ltd.

Jones, E. E., & Sigall, H. (1971). The bogus pipeline: A new paradigm for measuring affect and attitude. *Psychological Bulletin, 76,* 349–364.

Kaplan, K. J. (1972). On the ambivalence-indifference problem in attitude theory and measurement: A suggested modification of the semantic differential technique. *Psychological Bulletin, 77,* 361–372.

Kaplan, S. (1992). Environmental preference in a knowledge-seeking knowledge-using organism. In J. Barkow, L. Cosmides, & J. Tooby (Eds.), *The adapted mind* (pp. 581–600). New York: Oxford University Press.

Katz, I., Hass, R. G., & Bailey, J. (1988). Attitudinal ambivalence and behavior towards people with disabilities. In H. Yuker (Ed.), *Attitudes toward persons with disabilities* (pp. 47–57). New York: Springer.

Klauer, K. C., & Musch, J. (2003). Affective priming: Facts and theories. In J. Musch & K. C. Klauer (Eds.), *The psychology of evaluation: Affective processes in cognition and emotion* (pp. 7–49). Mahwah, NJ: Erlbaum.

Kraus, S. J. (1995). Attitudes and the prediction of behavior: A meta-analysis of the empirical literature. *Personality and Social Psychology Bulletin, 21,* 58–75

Krosnick, J. A., Betz, A. L., Jussim, L. J., Lynn, A. R., & Stephens, L. (1992). Subliminal conditioning of attitudes. *Personality and Social Psychology Bulletin, 18,* 152–162.

Krosnick, J. A., Boninger, D. S., Chuang, Y. C., Berent, M. K., & Carnot, C. G. (1993). Attitude strength: One construct or many related constructs? *Journal of Personality and Social Psychology, 65,* 1132–1151.

Krosnick, J. A., Judd, C. M., & Wittenbrink, B. (2005). The measurement of attitudes. In D. Albarracín, B. T. Johnson, & M. P. Zanna (Eds.), *The handbook of attitudes* (pp. 21–76). Mahwah, NJ: Erlbaum.

Kunst-Wilson, W. R., & Zajonc, R. B. (1980). Affective discrimination of stimuli that cannot be recognized. *Science, 207,* 557–558.

Kutner, B., Wilkins, C., & Yarrow, P. R. (1952). Verbal attitudes and overt behavior involving racial prejudice. *Journal of Abnormal and Social Psychology, 47,* 649–652.

LaPiere, R. T. (1934). Attitudes vs. actions. *Social Forces, 13,* 230–237.

Levine, J. M., & Murphy, G. (1943). The learning and forgetting of controversial material. *Journal of Abnormal and Social Psychology, 38,* 507–517.

Lieberman, M. D. (2010). Social cognitive neuroscience. In S. T. Fiske, D. T. Gilbert, & G. Lindzey (Eds.), *The handbook of social psychology* (5th ed., Vol. 1, pp. 143–193). Hoboken, NJ: Wiley.

Likert, R. A. (1932). A technique for the measurement of attitudes. *Archives of Psychology, 140,* 5–53.

Locke, K. D., & Braun, C. C. (2009) Ambivalence versus valence: Analyzing the effects of opposing attitudes. *Social Cognition, 27,* 89–104.

Loehlin, J. C. (1992). *Genes and the environment in personality development.* Newbury Park, NJ: Sage.

Lykken, D. T. (1998). *A tremor in the blood: Uses and abuses of the lie detector.* New York: Plenum Trade.

Macrae, C. N., Bodenhausen, G. V., Milne, A. B., & Jetten, J. (1994). Out of mind but back in sight: Stereotypes on the rebound. *Journal of Personality and Social Psychology, 67,* 808–817.

Madden, T. J., Ellen, P. S., & Ajzen, I. (1992). A comparison of the theory of planned behavior and the theory of reasoned action. *Personality and Social Psychology Bulletin, 18,* 3–9.

Mandler, G., Nakamura, Y., & Van Zandt, B. J. (1987). Nonspecific effects of exposure on stimuli that cannot be recognized. *Journal of Experimental Psychology: Learning, Memory, and Cognition, 13*, 646–648.

Marks, G., & Miller, N. (1987). Ten years of research on the false-consensus effect: An empirical and theoretical overview. *Psychological Bulletin, 102*, 72–90.

Marks, I. M. (1987). *Fears, phobias, and rituals.* New York: Oxford University Press.

Markus, G. B. (1986). Stability and change in political attitudes: Observed, recalled, and explained. *Political Behavior, 8*, 21–44.

Martin, L. L., Harlow, T. F., & Strack, F. (1992). The role of bodily sensations in the evaluation of social events. *Personality and Social Psychology Bulletin, 18*, 412–419.

Martin, N. G., Eaves, L. J., Heath, A. R., Jardine, R., Feingold, L. M., & Eysenck, H. J. (1986). Transmission of social attitudes. *Proceedings of the National Academy of Science, 83*, 4364–4368.

McCall, C., Tipper, C. M., Blascovich, J., & Grafton, S. T. (2012). Attitudes trigger motor behavior through conditioned associations: Neural and behavioral evidence. *Social Cognitive and Affective Neuroscience, 7*, 841–849.

McClelland, D. C., Koestner, R., & Weinberger, J. (1989). How do self-attributed and implicit motives differ? *Psychological Review, 96*, 690–702.

McConnell, A. R., & Leibold, J. M. (2001). Relations among the Implicit Association Test, discriminatory behavior, and explicit measures of racial attitudes. *Journal of Experimental Social Psychology, 37*, 435–442.

McGuire, W. J. (1985). Attitudes and attitude change. In G. Lindzey & E. Aronson (Eds.), *Handbook of social psychology* (3rd ed., Vol. 2, pp. 233–346). New York: Random House.

Mealey, L., & Theis, P. (1995). The relationship between mood and preferences: An evolutionary perspective. *Ethology and Sociobiology, 16*, 247–256.

McCaul, K. D., O'Neill, H. K., & Glasgow, R. E. (1988). Predicting the performance of dental hygiene behaviors: An examination of the Fishbein and Ajzen model and self-efficacy expectations. *Journal of Applied Social Psychology, 18*, 114–128.

Millar, M. G., & Tesser, A. (1986). Effects of affective and cognitive focus on the attitude-behavior relation. *Journal of Personality and Social Psychology, 51*, 270–276.

Miller, D. T., & Prentice, D. A. (1994). Collective errors and errors about the collective. *Personality and Social Psychology Bulletin, 20*, 541–550.

Miller, M. C. (1990). Advertising: End of story. In M. C. Miller (Ed.), *Seeing through movies* (pp. 186–246). New York: Pantheon Books.

Mitchell, J. P., Nosek, B. A., & Banaji, M. R. (2003). Contextual variations in implicit evaluation. *Journal of Experimental Psychology: General, 132*, 455–469.

Monahan, J. L., Murphy, S. T., & Zajonc, R. B. (2000). Subliminal mere exposure: Specific, general, and diffuse effects. *Psychological Science, 11*, 462–466.

Moore, T. E. (1982). Subliminal advertising: What you see is what you get. *Journal of Marketing, 46*, 38–47.

Moore, T. E. (1988). The case against subliminal manipulation. *Psychology and Marketing, 5*, 297–316.

Moore, T. E. (1995). Subliminal self-help auditory tapes: An empirical test of perceptual consequences. *Canadian Journal of Behavioural Science, 27*, 9–20.

Morris, J. S., Frith, C. D., Perrett, D. I., Rowland, D., Young, A. W., Calder, A. J., & Dolan, R. J. (1996, October 31). A differential neural response in the human amygdala to fearful and happy facial expressions. *Nature, 393*, 467–470.

Muris, P., Merckelbach, H., Meesters, C., & Van Lier, P. (1997). What do children fear most often? *Journal of Behavior Therapy and Experimental Psychiatry, 28*, 263–267.

Murray, G. R., & Schmitz, J. (2011). Caveman politics: Evolutionary leadership preferences and physical stature. *Social Science Quarterly, 92,* 1215–1235.

Newby-Clark, I. R., & Ross, M. (2003). Conceiving the past and future. *Personality and Social Psychology Bulletin, 29,* 807–818.

Newby-Clark, I. R., McGregor, I., & Zanna, M. P. (2003). Thinking and caring about cognitive inconsistency: When and for whom does attitudinal ambivalence feel uncomfortable? *Journal of Personality and Social Psychology, 82,* 157–166.

Newman, L. S., & Chamberlin, B. W. (2002, February). *On cigarettes, ice cream, and dentists: The role of ambivalence and context in automatic evaluation.* Paper presented at the annual meeting of the Society for Personality and Social Psychology, Savannah, GA.

Newman, L. S., & Hedberg, D. A. (1999). Repressive coping and the inaccessibility of negative autobiographical memories: Converging evidence. *Personality and Individual Differences, 27,* 45–53.

Norman, P., & Smith, L. (1992). The Theory of Planned Behavior and exercise: An investigation into the role of prior behaviour, behavioural intent, and attitude variability. *European Journal of Social Psychology, 25,* 403–416.

Nosek, B. A., Banaji, M., & Greenwald, A. G. (2002). Harvesting implicit group attitudes and beliefs from a demonstration web site. *Group Dynamics: Theory, Research, & Practice, 6,* 101–115.

Nosek, B. A., Greenwald, A. G., & Banaji, M. (2005). Understanding and using the Implicit Association Test: II. Method variables and construct validity. *Personality and Social Psychology Bulletin, 31,* 166–180.

Nussbaum, E. (2008, October 13). What Tina Fey would do for a Soy Joy. *New York,* pp. 32–37, 90.

Ohman, A., & Mineka, S. (2003). The malicious serpent: Snakes as a prototypical stimulus for an evolved module of fear. *Current Directions in Psychological Science, 12,* 5–9.

Olson, J. M., Goffin, R. D., & Haynes, G. A. (2007). Relative versus absolute measures of explicit attitudes: Implications for predicting diverse attitude-relevant criteria. *Journal of Personality and Social Psychology, 93,* 907–926.

Olson, M. A., & Fazio, R. H. (2001). Implicit attitude formation through classical conditioning. *Psychological Science, 12,* 413–417.

Olson, M. A., & Fazio, R. H. (2002). Implicit acquisition and manifestation of classically conditioned attitudes. *Social Cognition, 20,* 89–104.

Olson, M. A., & Fazio, R. H. (2006). Reducing automatically activated racial prejudice through implicit evaluative conditioning. *Personality and Social Psychology Bulletin, 32,* 421–433.

Orians, G. H., & Heerwagen, J. H. (1992). Evolved responses to landscapes. In J. Barkow, L. Cosmides, & J. Tooby (Eds.), *The adapted mind* (pp. 555–580). New York: Oxford University Press.

Osgood, C., Suci, G. J., & Tannenbaum, P. H. (1957). *The measurement of meaning.* Urbana: University of Illinois Press.

Ostrom, T. M. (1969). The relationship between the affective, behavioral and cognitive components of attitude. *Journal of Experimental Social Psychology, 5,* 12–30.

Ostrom, T. M. (1973). The bogus pipeline: A new ignis fatuus? *Psychological Bulletin, 79,* 252–259.

Oswald, F. L., Mitchell, G., Blanton, H., Jaccard, J., & Tetlock, P. E. (2013). Predicting ethnic and racial discrimination: A meta-analysis of IAT criterion studies. *Journal of Personality and Social Psychology, 105,* 171–192.

Page, M. M. (1969). Social psychology of a classical conditioning of attitudes experiment. *Journal of Personality and Social Psychology, 11,* 177–186.

Peak, H. (1955). Attitude and motivation. In M. R. Jones (Ed.), *Nebraska symposium on motivation* (Vol. 3, pp. 149–188). Lincoln: University of Nebraska Press.

Petty, R. E., & Cacioppo, J. T. (1981). *Attitudes and persuasion: Classic and contemporary approaches.* Dubuque, IA: William C. Brown Company Publishers.

Petty, R. E., & Cacioppo, J. T. (1983). The role of bodily responses in attitude measurement and change. In J. T. Cacioppo and R. E. Petty (Eds.), *Social Psychophysiology: A Sourcebook* (pp. 51–101). New York: Guilford Press.

Petty, R. E., & Krosnick, J. A. (1995). *Attitude strength: Antecedents and consequences*. Hillsdale, NJ: Erlbaum.

Plomin, R. (1994). *Genetics and experience: The interplay between nature and nurture*. Thousand Oaks, CA: Sage Publications.

Plomin, R., Chipuer, H. M., & Loehlin, J. C. (1990). Behavioral genetics and personality. In L. A. Pervin (Ed.), *Handbook of personality: Theory and research* (pp. 225–243). New York: Guilford.

Pomerantz, E. M., Chaiken, S., & Tordesillas, R. S. (1995). Attitude strength and resistance processes. *Journal of Personality and Social Psychology, 69*, 408–419.

Pratkanis, A. R. (1992, spring). The cargo cult science of subliminal persuasion. *Skeptical Inquirer*, pp. 260–272.

Priester, J. R, & Petty, R. E. (1996). The gradual threshold model of ambivalence: Relating the positive and negative bases of attitudes to subjective ambivalence. *Journal of Personality and Social Psychology, 71*, 431–449.

Priester, J. R, & Petty, R. E. (2001). Extending the bases of subjective attitudinal ambivalence: Interpersonal and intrapersonal antecedents of evaluative tension. *Journal of Personality and Social Psychology, 80*, 19–34.

Pryor, J. B., Gibbons, F. X., Wicklund, R. A., Fazio, R. H., & Hood, R. (1977). Self-focused attention and self-report validity. *Journal of Personality, 45*, 513–527.

Quas, J. A., Bottoms, B. L., Haegerich, T. M., & Nysse-Carris, K. L. (2002). Effects of victim, defendant and juror gender on decisions in child sexual assault cases. *Journal of Applied Social Psychology, 32*, 1993–2021.

Raden, D. (1985). Strength-related attitude dimensions. *Social Psychology Quarterly, 48*, 312–330.

Rajecki, D. W, & Wolfson, C. (1973). The rating of materials found in the mailbox: Effects of frequency of receipt. *Public Opinion Quarterly, 37*, 110–114.

Rankin, R. E., & Campbell, D. T. (1955). Galvanic skin response to Negro and white experimenters. *Journal of Abnormal and Social Psychology, 51*, 30–33.

Razran, G. H. S. (1938). Conditioning away social bias by the luncheon technique. *Psychological Bulletin, 35*, 693.

Razran, G. H. S. (1940). Conditioned response changes in rating and appraising sociopolitical slogans. *Psychological Bulletin, 37*, 481.

Regan, D. T., & Fazio, R. H. (1977). On the consistency between attitude and behavior: Look to the method of attitude formation. *Journal of Experimental Social Psychology, 13*, 28–45.

Roese, N. J., & Jamieson, D. W. (1993). Twenty years of bogus pipeline research: A critical review and meta-analysis. *Psychological Bulletin, 114*, 363–375.

Rosenberg, M. J. (1956). Cognitive structure and attitudinal affect. *Journal of Abnormal and Social Psychology, 52*, 367–372.

Rosenberg, M. J., Hovland, C. I. (1960). Cognitive, affective, and behavioral components of attitudes. In C. I. Hovland & M. J. Rosenberg (Eds.), *Attitude organization and change: An analysis of consistency among attitude components* (pp. 1–14). New Haven, CT: Yale University Press.

Ross, L., Greene, D., & House, P. (1977). The "false consensus effect": an egocentric bias in social perception and attribution processes. *Journal of Experimental Social Psychology, 13*, 279–301.

Ross, M. (1989). Relation of implicit theories to the construction of personal histories. *Psychological Review, 96*, 341–357.

Rozin, P. (1976). Psychological and cultural determinants of food choice. In T. Silverstone (Ed.), *Appetite and food intake* (pp. 286–312). Berlin: Dahlem Konferenzen.

Rudman, L. A. (2004). Sources of implicit attitudes. *Current Directions in Psychological Science, 13*, 79–82.

Ruscio, J. (2005, January/February). Exploring controversies on the art and science of polygraph testing. *Skeptical Inquirer, 29*, 34–39.

Rydell, R. J., & McConnell, A. R. (2006). Understanding implicit and explicit attitude change: A systems of reasoning analysis. *Journal of Personality and Social Psychology, 91*, 995–1008.

Salovey, P., Rothman, A. J., & Rodin, J. (1998). Health behavior. In D. T. Gilbert, S. T. Fiske, & G. Lindzey (Eds.), *The handbook of social psychology* (4th ed., Vol. 2, pp. 633–683). New York: McGraw Hill.

Scarr, S., & Carter-Saltzman, L. (1979). Twin method: Defense of a critical assumption, *Behavior Genetics, 9*, 527–542.

Schifter, D. B., & Ajzen, I. (1985). Intention, perceived control, and weight loss: An application of the theory of planned behavior. *Journal of Personality and Social Psychology, 49*, 843851.

Schneider, I. K., Eerland, A., van Harreveld, F., Rotteveel, M., van der Pligt, J., van der Stoep, N., & Zwaan, R. A. (2013). One way and the other: The bidirectional relationship between ambivalence and body movement. *Psychological Science, 24*, 319–325.

Schuman, H. (1990, March 7). Three different pens help tell the story. *New York Times*, A25.

Schwartz, G. E., Fair, P. L., Salt, P., Mandel, M. R., & Klerman, G. L. (1976). Facial muscle patterning to affective imagery in depressed and nondepressed subjects. *Science*, 489–491.

Schwarz, N. (1990). Feelings as information: Informational and motivational functions of affective states. In E. T. Higgins & R. M. Sorrentino (Eds.), *Handbook of motivation and cognition: Foundations of social behavior* (Vol. 2, pp. 527–561). New York: Guilford.

Schwarz, N. (1999). Self-reports: How the questions shape the answers. *American Psychologist, 54*, 93–105

Schwarz, N. (2001). Feelings as information: Implications for affective influences on information processing. In L. L. Martin & G. L. Clore (Eds.), *Theories of mood and cognition: A user's guidebook* (pp. 159–176). Mahwah, NJ: Lawrence Erlbaum.

Schwarz, N., & Clore, G. L. (1983). Mood, misattribution, and judgments of well-being: Informative and directive functions of affective states. *Journal of Personality and Social Psychology, 45*, 513–523.

Schwarz, N., & Clore, G. L. (2003). Mood as Information: 20 Years Later. *Psychological Inquiry, 14*, 296–303.

Seamon, J. G., Brody, N., & Kauff, D. M. (1983). Affective discrimination of stimuli that are not recognized: Effects of shadowing, masking, and cerebral laterality. *Journal of Experimental Psychology: Learning, Memory, and Cognition, 9*, 544–555.

Sigall, H., & Page, R. A. (1971). Current stereotypes: A little fading, a little faking. *Journal of Personality and Social Psychology, 16*, 252–258.

Simon, D., Snow, C. J., & Read, S. J. (2004). The redux of cognitive consistency theories: Evidence judgments by constraint satisfaction. *Journal of Personality and Social Psychology, 86*, 814–837.

Skitka, L. J., Bauman, C. W., & Sargis, E. G. (2005). Moral conviction: Another contributor to attitude strength or something more? *Journal of Personality and Social Psychology, 88*, 895–917.

Smetana, J. G., & Adler, N. E. (1980). Fishbein's Value X Expectancy model: An examination of some assumptions. *Personality and Social Psychology Bulletin, 6*, 89–96.

Snyder, M., & Tanke, E. D. (1976). Behavior and attitude: Some people are more consistent than others. *Journal of Personality, 44*, 501–517.

Spruyt, A., Hermans, D., De Houwer, J., & Eelen, P. (2002). On the nature of the affective priming effect: Affective priming of naming responses. *Social Cognition, 20*, 227–256.

Staats, A. W., & Staats, C. K. (1958). Attitudes established by classical conditioning. *Journal of Abnormal and Social Psychology, 57*, 37–40.

Stewart, T. L., Amoss, R. T., Weiner, B. A., Elliott, L. A., Parrott, D. J., Peacock, C. M., & Vanman, E. J. (2013). The psychophysiology of social action: Facial electromyographic responses to stigmatized groups predict antidiscrimination action. *Basic and Applied Social Psychology, 35*, 418–425.

Strack, F., Martin, L. L., & Stepper, S. (1988). Inhibiting and facilitating conditions of the human smile: A nonobtrusive test of the facial feedback hypothesis. *Journal of Personality and Social Psychology, 54*, 768–777.

Tesser, A. (1993). The importance of heritability in psychological research: The case of attitudes. *Psychological Review, 100*, 129–142.

Tesser, A., Whitaker, D., Martin, L., & Ward, D. (1997). Attitude heritability, attitude change and physiological responsivity. *Personality and Individual Differences, 24*, 89–96.

Thompson, M. M., Zanna, M. P., & Griffin, D. W. (1995). Let's not be indifferent about (attitudinal) ambivalence. In R. E. Petty & J. A. Krosnick (Eds.), *Attitude strength: Antecedents and consequences. Ohio State University series on attitudes and persuasion* (Vol. 4, pp. 361–386). Hillsdale, NJ: Lawrence Erlbaum Associates.

Toneatto, T., & Binik, Y. (1987). The role of intentions, social norms, and attitudes in the performance of dental flossing: A test of the theory of reasoned action. *Journal of Applied Social Psychology, 17*, 593–603.

Toobin, J. (1996). *The run of his life: The people v. O. J. Simpson.* New York: Random House.

Webb, E. J., Campbell, D. T., Schwartz, R. D., & Sechrest, L. (1966). *Unobtrusive measures: Nonreactive research in the social sciences.* Chicago: Rand McNally.

Weigel, R. H., & Newman, L. S. (1976). Increasing attitude-behavior correspondence by broadening the scope of the behavioral measure. *Journal of Personality and Social Psychology, 30*, 724–728.

Weinstein, A. G. (1972). Predicting behavior from attitudes. *Public Opinion Quarterly, 36*, 355–360.

Wells, G. L., & Petty, R. E. (1980). The effects of overt head movements on persuasion: Compatibility and incompatibility of responses. *Basic and Applied Social Psychology, 1*, 219–230.

Westie F. R., & DeFleur, M. L. (1959). Automatic response and their relation to race attitudes. *Journal of Abnormal and Social Psychology, 58*, 340–347.

Whalen, P. J., Rauch, S. L., Etcoff, N. L., McInerney, S. C., Lee, M. B., & Jenike, M. A. (1998). Masked presentations of emotional facial expressions modulate amygdala activity without explicit knowledge. *Journal of Neuroscience, 18*, 411–418.

Wicker, A. W. (1969). Attitudes versus actions: The relationship of verbal and overt behavioral responses to attitude objects. *Journal of Social Issues, 25*, 41–78.

Wicker, A. W. (1971). An examination of the "other variables" explanation of attitude-behavior inconsistency. *Journal of Personality and Social Psychology, 19*, 18–30.

Wiley, J. (2005). A fair and balanced look at the news: What affects memory for controversial arguments? *Journal of Memory and Language, 53*, 95–109.

Wilson, T. D., & Dunn, D. S. (1986). Effects of introspection on attitude-behavior consistency: Analyzing reasons versus focusing on feelings. *Journal of Experimental Social Psychology, 22*, 249–263.

Wilson, T. D., Dunn, D. S., Bybee, J. A., Hyman, D. B., & Rotondo, J. A. (1984). Effects of analyzing reasons on attitude-behavior consistency. *Journal of Personality and Social Psychology, 47*, 5–16.

Wilson, T. D., Dunn, D. S., Kraft, D., & Lisle, D. J. (1989). Introspection, attitude change, and attitude-behavior consistency: The disruptive effects of explaining why we feel the way we do. In L. Berkowitz (Ed.), *Advances in experimental social psychology* (Vol. 19, pp. 123–205). Orlando, FL: Academic Press.

Wilson, T. D., Lindsey, S., & Schooler, T. Y. (2000). A model of dual attitudes. *Psychological Review, 107*, 101–126.

Wilson, T. D., & Schooler, J. W. (1991). Thinking too much: Introspection can reduce the quality of preferences and decisions. *Journal of Personality and Social Psychology, 60*, 181–192.

Wilson, W. R. (1979). Feeling more than we can know: Exposure effects without learning. *Journal of Personality and Social Psychology, 37*, 811–821.

Winkielman, P., & Cacioppo, J. T. (2001). Mind at ease puts a smile on the face: Psychophysiological evidence that processing facilitation elicits positive affect. *Journal of Personality and Social Psychology, 81*, 989–1000.

Wishman, S. (1986). *Anatomy of a jury: The system on trial*. New York: Times Books.

Woodmansee, J. J. (1970). The pupil response as a measure of social attitudes. In G. F. Summers (Ed.), *Attitude measurement* (pp. 514–533). Chicago: Rand McNally.

Ybarra, O., & Trafimow, D. (1998). How priming the private self or collective self affects the relative weights of attitudes and subjective norms. *Personality and Social Psychology Bulletin, 24*, 362–370.

Zajonc, R. B. (1968). Attitudinal effects of mere exposure. *Journal of Personality and Social Psychology Monographs, 9* (2, Pt. 2), 1–27.

Zajonc, R. B, Markus, H., & Wilson, W. R. (1974). Exposure effects and associative learning. *Journal of Experimental Social Psychology, 10*, 248–263.

Zajonc, R. B., & Rajecki, D. W. (1969). Exposure and affect: A field experiment. *Psychonomic Science, 17*, 216–217.

Zanna, M. P., Olson, J. M., & Fazio, R. H. (1980). Attitude-behavior consistency: An individual difference perspective. *Journal of Personality and Social Psychology, 38*, 432–440.

Zanna, M. P., & Rempel, J. K. (1988). Attitudes: A new look at an old concept. In D. Bar-Tal & A. W. Kruglanski (Eds.), *The social psychology of knowledge* (pp. 315–334). Cambridge, England: Cambridge University Press.

CHAPTER 6

PERSUASION AND ATTITUDE CHANGE

VOTE FOR BOB

There is probably no elegant way to eat a corn dog, but Robert (Bob) Marks was determined not to make a spectacle of himself. Marks, a candidate for governor of the state of Ohio, was appearing at the state fair, surrounded by news photographers. For most people, a grease-stained white shirt would be a minor inconvenience. For Bob, it could mean public ridicule.

An embarrassing photo in the next day's papers—or a YouTube clip that went viral—probably would not be a total disaster, however. After all, Bob, a long-time state senator, was well known and well regarded, especially for his support for public education. Legislation he had drafted was widely considered to have increased the quality of the state's schools. Still, would he be able to persuade voters that he had the stature and ability to become the state's chief executive?

Today, Marks would not be doing any persuading. He and his opponent, who was also attending the fair, had agreed not to dominate the day's festivities by delivering speeches. They would, however, be presented to the crowd, and the dignitaries who introduced them would take a few minutes to extol their virtues. Bob's opponent would be introduced (and praised) by the mayor of a nearby town. The local state representative would do the same for Bob. In fact, the mayor had just mounted the stage and was beginning to address the fairgoers. But where was the state representative?

Bob's discomfort increased as the mayor concluded his remarks and the opposing candidate showed his face to the crowd, pumping his fist in the air. Bob's campaign workers were scrambling around, looking for someone who could be pressed into duty as a replacement for the representative. Unfortunately, the problem could not be resolved in just a few minutes, and the crowd was getting restless.

Suddenly, an amplified voice rang out, turning the crowd's attention to "Robert Marks, the next governor of the great state of Ohio!" Bob breathed a sigh of relief and went looking for his aides to congratulate them on turning the situation around. When he found them, however, they didn't look very triumphant—in fact, they seemed frantic. As Bob caught a glimpse of the stage, he saw why: He was being introduced by a carnival worker dressed as a clown. In fact, Bob recognized the man as the guy who ran the dunking booth. Apparently,

During presidential elections, candidates (and their parties) spend huge sums of money trying to persuade people to vote for them (in 2012, for example, approximately 2 billion dollars).

the clown had taken it upon himself to grab the microphone and make a speech. Horrified, Bob noticed for the first time that the sound coming from the crowd resembled laughter more than cheering.

In Chapter 5, we learned how attitudes are formed, how they are measured, and how they affect people's behavior. This chapter focuses on the malleability of attitudes—that is, how they change. We will begin by describing in detail the processes that come into play when others actively attempt to change or shape our attitudes. Next, we'll examine the effects of specific variables on this process. Although **persuasion** (Albarracín & Vargas, 2010; Maio & Haddock, 2007) can be a powerful source of change, it is not the only source. In the third part of this chapter, we'll see that attitudes can also change as a result of our behavior—or, more precisely, our efforts to make sense of and justify our behavior. In the last section, we will examine the ways in which people resist efforts to change their attitudes and the ways in which their resistance can be overcome.

THE PROCESS OF PERSUASION

Social psychologists have sometimes been accused of ignoring activities that play a central role in people's social lives—eating, for example (but see Rozin, 1999; Rozin, Kabnick, Pete, Fischler, & Shields, 2003). Maybe a later edition of this textbook could include a model for predicting when and why people enjoy food. We could categorize the variables associated with enjoyment—the chef's expertise; the ingredients and how they are prepared; the preferences, sophistication, even the ethnicity of the diner; and the context in which food is eaten (time of day, lighting level, the company of others). Next, we could explain how each variable affects our enjoyment. Perhaps meals that are prepared by famous chefs are more enjoyable than others because they are more competently prepared. Diners may prefer sweet food because sugar stimulates certain taste buds. We might consider whether people in France (the birthplace of haute cuisine) enjoy food more than people from other countries. And do we enjoy our meals more when we dine with others than when we dine alone?

By now, the futility of this approach should be obvious. Although all these aspects of dining are important, they do not always affect our enjoyment in the same way. For example, you probably enjoy sweet food more as a dessert than as a main course. And although French people enjoy eating, they may not enjoy Scandinavian food as much as Norwegians do. Similarly, these variables may not always affect diners' enjoyment for the same reason; different processes may be involved at different times. For example, we may not enjoy food prepared by celebrity chefs solely because of how delicious it is, but because we *expect* to enjoy it, and convince ourselves that we do. And good company could enhance a meal because it makes us feel good (which biases our evaluation of the food) or because it distracts us from a poorly prepared meal.

The idea that anyone would adopt this approach to the study of food preferences may seem silly. However, the variable-by-variable approach is not so different from the way psychologists once studied persuasion. Some reviews of research on the topic suggest at least implicitly that certain variables have specific effects, and that they influence people through one particular process. Yet further research has shown that this approach simply does not work (Petty, 1997); a different one is needed. Almost any aspect of a persuasive message—even something as apparently simple as the attractiveness of the communicator—can have several different effects on recipients, via several different underlying processes. Only by focusing on those underlying processes can we make sense of the roles different variables play in persuading people to change their attitudes. In this section, we will review several approaches to thinking about and studying the process of persuasion.

Early Frameworks for Studying Persuasion

New social psychological theories (or scientific theories of any kind, for that matter) do not always follow from their predecessors in a straightforward, logical way. In the case of persuasion, however, we can tell a surprisingly coherent story about how we got from there to here (see also Petty & Wegener, 1998).

Persuasion and attitude change became a major focus of study for social psychologists, largely because of a research project carried out by Carl Hovland and his colleagues in the 1940s and 1950s (Hovland, Janis, & Kelley, 1953). The timing of that development was not a coincidence. During World War II, the U.S. government sponsored research on techniques that might prove useful for rallying the public behind the war effort. Ultimately, Hovland and his colleagues developed a general framework for studying persuasion. For people to accept a message, they hypothesized, they had to (1) attend to it; (2) comprehend it; (3) accept or yield to it; and (4) retain it—that is, remember it. The extent to which people completed those steps—especially the third one—would depend on incentives. In other words, people would be motivated by the rewards they might receive for changing their attitudes.

This approach, which was very fruitful, was later simplified by McGuire (1968), who proposed that all factors playing a role in persuasion (in other words, persuasion variables) could be assigned to one of two categories: those that affect "reception" of the message (for example, variables affecting attention, comprehension, and memory) and those that affect "yielding" (or giving in) to it. Highlighting this distinction allowed McGuire to address an issue researchers had been struggling with: Why were some personality differences positively associated with persuasion at some times and negatively associated with it at other times? According to McGuire, the answer was that the same personality variable could have opposite effects on reception and yielding. For example, highly intelligent people are better able than others to understand complex arguments (more receptive), and so might be persuaded by them. At the same time, they are also better able to refute those arguments (less yielding), and so might not be persuaded by them (Eagly & Warren, 1976).

McGuire's approach inspired psychologists to devote a great deal of effort to studying the relationship between persuasion and how well people can recall a message (a reception variable). Unfortunately, the results of those studies, which were meant to show that people who remember persuasive messages are more likely than others to be affected by them, were quite disappointing (Eagly & Chaiken, 1993; McGuire, 1969). In retrospect, the reason is clear: merely remembering an argument will not change a person's attitude if the argument seems weak and unconvincing. What is important is not verbatim recall of a persuasive message, but a person's *reactions* to the message. The *cognitive response approach* to persuasion (Love & Greenwald, 1978; Petty, Ostrom, & Brock, 1981), the next major development, was based on this insight. Research in this tradition supported the hypothesis that attitude change is related less directly to the persuasive message itself than to a person's interpretation of and reaction to the message.

The cognitive response approach encouraged researchers to look directly at the thoughts triggered by persuasive attempts, and it made a major contribution to the study of attitude change. Are people always motivated to think carefully about persuasive messages, however? And when they are, are they always motivated to take the implications of their thoughts seriously? Furthermore, do the thoughts people have when someone is trying to change their attitudes always concern the content of that person's arguments ("Hey, good point!"), or do they sometimes relate to other aspects of the situation ("Hey, ugly tie")?

Dual-Process Models of Persuasion

Researchers tackled the questions just raised using two new frameworks—the elaboration likelihood model and the heuristic-systematic model—which were developed in the early 1980s and remain dominant to this day. Although there are differences between the two models, both are based on the idea that there are two different ways to be persuaded: (1) through careful consideration of logical arguments; and (2) through reactions that have little to do with a message's content. For this reason, they are called "dual process" models.

The Elaboration Likelihood Model (ELM)

When you are presented with a persuasive message (one that is aimed at getting you to "buy this car," "stop smoking," "support gun control," or "vote for Bob!"), you may carefully attend to its content and critically evaluate it. At other times, you may not. Put another way, the likelihood that you will mentally elaborate on a persuasive message varies from time to time and from situation to situation. This basic idea lies at the heart of the **elaboration likelihood model** (ELM) of the processes that underlie attitude change (Petty & Cacioppo, 1981, 1986a, 1986b; Petty & Wegener, 1999; see **Figure 6.1** for an overview).

What determines the extent to which a person will carefully attend to and think about a message—that is, where that person falls along the **elaboration likelihood continuum**? The key factors are the person's ability and motivation to think about the message. If the person is distracted or is trying to do some other mental work (Petty, Wells, & Brock, 1976), or if many points are made in rapid succession (Smith & Shaffer, 1995), thinking about the arguments will be hard. The same will be true if the person simply is not much of a thinker. Sometimes, however, even people who are perfectly capable of carefully evaluating a message will not do so for another reason: because the subject of the message may not seem terribly important or personally relevant. In such cases, a person's motivation to elaborate on the message will be low (Johnson & Eagly, 1989; Petty & Cacioppo, 1979).

A person's position along the elaboration likelihood continuum—that is, the likelihood that the person will elaborate on a message—can determine which factors affect his or her attitudes. Put another way, it affects the route the person will take in processing persuasive messages. The higher a person is along the continuum, the more likely that person is to take the central route to persuasion. **Central route persuasion** involves paying attention to the merits and flaws of persuasive messages and carefully evaluating the arguments they contain. **Peripheral route persuasion**, on the other hand, involves persuasion by factors extraneous to a message's content, such as the sheer number of points made by the communicator (regardless of how logical or compelling

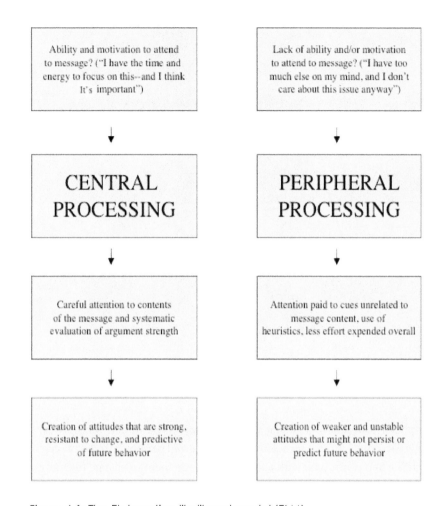

Figure 6.1: The Elaboration likelihood model (ELM).

they are), the attractiveness of the communicator, his or her credentials, other people's reactions, or even your mood. Peripheral processing requires a lot less mental effort and motivation than central processing. In fact, some researchers have argued that peripheral variables can affect people without their awareness (Chaiken, Liberman, & Eagly, 1989), serving as hidden influences on their behavior.

In light of this theory, Bob Marks's distress at being introduced and endorsed by a clown is perfectly understandable. We can assume that people who are enjoying a day at the state fair are not in the mood for deep introspection about their political positions. If so, the difference between being associated with a well-dressed, respectable politician (a highly credible speaker) and one with bright green hair, a big red nose, and a floppy hat might indeed be significant. In such a context, people could well be swayed by peripheral variables.

Finally, the ELM predicts an important consequence of the way people process persuasive messages. Compared to the peripheral route, central route processing should lead to attitudes that are more persistent, resistant to change, and predictive of future behavior. Research supports this hypothesis (Chaiken, 1980; Mackie, 1987). In essence, central route processing produces stronger attitudes, and as we saw in Chapter 5, strength is an important determinant of whether attitudes predict behavior.

In a noisy, distracting environment, people are more likely to process persuasive messages via the peripheral route than the central route.

The central-peripheral distinction is similar in many ways to the distinction between "thoughtful" and "thoughtless" attitudes described in Chapter 5. However, central and peripheral route processing refer to people's actual mental activities when confronted with efforts to persuade them to change their attitudes or adopt new ones. The thoughtful-thoughtless distinction is broader, applying to attitudes developed in any context—not just persuasive situations—for any reason. The thoughtful-thoughtless distinction also encompasses attitude sources that generally are not addressed by the ELM, such as the attitudes we inherit from our parents and attitudes that are shaped by evolution and shared by most humans. Still, an attitude that is arrived at in response to peripheral variables could be classified as a "thoughtless" one, whereas an attitude that results from systematic processing would fit the definition of a "thoughtful" attitude.

Our description of the central processing route—careful, systematic, based on the evidence—may also suggest to you that people who engage in central processing are always neutral, objective, and coldly logical. That is not the case, however, as is recognized by the ELM. How intensely a person thinks about an issue is one thing; the conclusion that person might wish to reach is a different matter (Petty & Cacioppo, 1990). For example, if people learn that their state legislature is debating an extension of the death penalty, they will feel more personal involvement with the issue than if they learn the debate is taking place in some other state. As a result, they will centrally process arguments about the legislation. The nature of central processing will not be the same for death penalty opponents as for death penalty proponents, however. Opponents will be critical of the need for increased executions, while proponents will scoff at attempts to convince them that capital punishment should be eliminated (Lord, Ross, & Lepper, 1979). In short, central processing can be put in the service of a particular bias; people will often work very hard to maintain their attitudes and beliefs.

A related finding is that a person's knowledge of a topic can also change the way he or she responds to a persuasive message. Specifically, greater knowledge and experience can cause a person to be more critical than others of the arguments presented (Wood, Kallgren, & Preisler, 1985). Even one's mood can bias central processing, as we will see shortly.

Research on the ELM

To illustrate the distinction between central and peripheral processing, Cacioppo, Petty, and Morris (1983) presented undergraduate students with one of two "policy statements" justifying tuition increases at their university. Though the statements were of equal length, one contained strong arguments (for example, faculty members had been getting very small raises, and many were starting to leave). The other contained weak arguments (for example, increased tuition could help to beautify the campus). Obviously, we would expect the strong arguments to be more persuasive than the weak ones, and the results of the study confirmed that expectation. The researchers, however, were more interested in *how* participants thought about these arguments. Using a separate questionnaire, they had determined that half the students had high levels of the **need for cognition** (Cacioppo, Petty, Feinstein, & Jarvis, 1996); that is, they enjoyed effortful thinking. The other students had scored low on the need for cognition.

When the researchers analyzed their data, they found that the effects of argument quality were significantly more pronounced among the high-need-for-cognition participants. Those participants were more persuaded by the strong message than the low-need-for-cognition participants and less persuaded by the weak message (see **Figure 6.2**). The researchers concluded that students who were high in the need for cognition were more likely than others to engage in central processing. In other words, they were relatively high on the elaboration likelihood continuum, and thus paid more attention than other students to the quality of the arguments (see also Cacioppo, Petty, Kao, & Rodriguez, 1986). People who are low in the need for cognition are not so strongly affected by argument quality—but other research indicates that they are persuaded more by *peripheral cues* than people who are high in the need for cognition (Haugtvedt, Petty, & Cacioppo, 1992).

The relevance of a message can also affect the likelihood of a person taking the central or the peripheral route to persuasion. Petty, Cacioppo, and Goldman (1981) led participants to believe that their university was considering requiring students to pass a comprehensive exam before graduation. As in the Cacioppo et al. (1983) study, they presented participants with either strong or weak arguments for the new policy. In addition, they told some participants that the

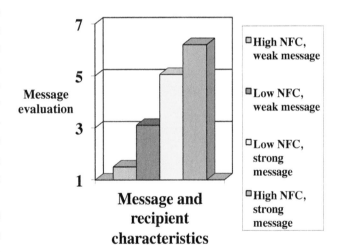

Figure 6.2: *Effectiveness of a persuasive message as a function of argument strength and need for cognition.*

Messages were rated on a scale ranging from 1 to 9, with higher numbers signifying more favorable evaluations. Participants high in the need for cognition (NFC) were more likely than others to distinguish between weak and strong arguments.

Source: Cacioppo, Petty, and Morris (1983).

message had been prepared by a high school class, and others that it had been prepared by a special commission on higher education. This additional information functioned as a peripheral cue (expertise), which participants could use as a shortcut in evaluating the message. Finally, the researchers told half the students that the new policy might go into effect the following year, and the other half that it would take ten years to implement. This last manipulation created two levels of personal involvement, high and low.

Petty et al. (1981) predicted that the attitudes of high-involvement participants would be affected more by argument quality than the attitudes of low-involvement participants. They expected expertise to have a greater impact on low-involvement participants than on high-involvement participants. The results supported these predictions. As **Figure 6.3** shows, the response of high-involvement participants depended more on argument quality than that of low-involvement participants. **Figure 6.4**, on the other hand, indicates that the response of low-involvement participants depended more on their beliefs about who had prepared the message. High personal involvement led to central processing; low personal involvement led to a reliance on low-effort peripheral cues.

What do these results suggest for Bob Marks's predicament, described at the beginning of the chapter? If the clown who spoke on Marks's behalf actually made a speech that was *better* than the one delivered by the politician who preceded him, what would have been the effect on the audience? As we have seen, if the audience was not at all disposed to attend carefully to political messages, the relative quality of the two arguments would have been irrelevant. But if there were any truly interested and involved voters in the crowd, they could well have seen beyond the clown's greasepaint and silly clothes, and discovered through central processing that he was actually making more sense than the first speaker.

When is a Pretty Face a Central Cue? The Multiple-Roles Hypothesis

We might be tempted to assume that any persuasion variable can easily be classified as a central, or peripheral, cue. Indeed, many variables typically *do* fall into one category or the other. For example, personal characteristics of

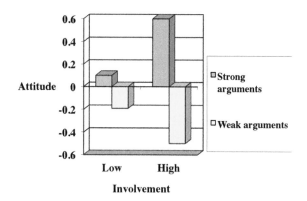

Figure 6.3: Post-message attitudes toward a policy to institute comprehensive exams as a function of involvement and argument quality.

Positive numbers indicate agreement with the policy and negative numbers indicate disagreement. Highly involved participants responded more to argument quality.

Source: Petty, Cacioppo, and Goldman (1981).

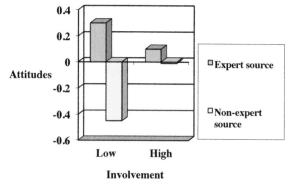

Figure 6.4: Post-message attitudes toward a policy to institute comprehensive exams as a function of involvement and source expertise.

Positive numbers indicate agreement with the policy and negative numbers indicate disagreement. Uninvolved participants, more than highly involved participants, responded to the expertise of the source of the message.

Source: Petty, Cacioppo, and Goldman (1981).

communicators such as their grooming are usually unrelated to a message's validity, but they are often easy to detect. As a result, those characteristics usually will function as peripheral cues. What if a communicator's characteristics are not trivial, however—for instance, she has special expertise that is relevant to the issue at hand—but take some work to discover? In that case, they will affect primarily people with high levels of motivation or ability—those who are high on the elaboration continuum (Kruglanski & Thompson, 1999). Thus, in some cases, a communicator's characteristics can be associated more with the *central* route than the peripheral one.

More generally, according to the **multiple-roles hypothesis**, all persuasion variables can play any of four different roles (Petty & Wegener, 1998). They can serve as (1) actual arguments; (2) peripheral cues; (3) biasers of information processing; or (4) determinants of a person's place along the elaboration likelihood continuum (that is, of their motivation to process messages carefully). Consider, for example, a communicator's attractiveness, a much-studied variable (Chaiken, 1986; Dion & Stein, 1978; Pallak, 1983; Shavitt, Swan, Lowery, & Wänke, 1994). Obviously, attractiveness can serve as a peripheral cue; a mentally lazy audience can simply surrender to a dazzling person. But what if the persuasive message relates to a beauty or grooming product? If the communicator's appearance could be considered a valid testament to the product's value, then attractiveness could serve as an argument for buying the product.

Attractiveness could also serve as a source of bias. Imagine that the topic of a communicator's message is "why you should ask me out on a date." You will likely be biased toward accepting the communicator's arguments if he is attractive ("He likes to enter marathons? He must be in great shape"), but skeptical if he is unattractive ("Does he actually *finish* any of those marathons?"). Finally, the communicator's physical attractiveness could affect a person's willingness to engage in effortful central processing. A beautiful person triggers all sorts

of positive feelings in others (Ashmore & Longo, 1995; Dion, Berscheid, & Walster, 1972; Hatfield & Sprecher, 1986; van Leeuwen & Macrae, 2004). If a beautiful woman were to urge an audience to pay careful attention to what she says, she would probably be more likely to succeed than an unattractive communicator.

Related to the idea that a variable can play multiple *roles* in persuasion is the hypothesis that the final *effect* of any given variable depends on the situation. For instance, we have noted that attractiveness can serve as an "argument," affecting people's attitudes via the central route. In the example we gave—an attempt to persuade people that a beauty or grooming product is worth the money—the effect of the communicator's attractiveness was positive (that is, it increased persuasion).

Why might this well-sculpted bodybuilder be more likely than someone else to persuade you to buy exercise equipment? Could it be simply because you find him to be an impressive individual? Because his appearance argues for the product's effectiveness? Because he grabs your attention, so that you pay close attention to his pitch? Or because you're motivated to believe what he has to say? According to the multiple roles hypothesis, any or all of these explanations are possible.

Imagine instead that an attractive communicator were to argue that a beauty pageant should dispense with talent demonstrations and question-and-answer sessions, and be based instead solely on appearance. In that case, a careful processor might suspect that the communicator's motivation is self-serving and react more *negatively* to the argument than if it had come from someone less stunning. Whether attractiveness enhances persuasion depends on the situation, then.

We began this chapter by showing the pointlessness of attempting to explain why people enjoy their food by focusing on individual variables (such as sweetness) and trying to predict how they affect people's enjoyment. It should now be clear why taking a similar approach to studying persuasion (for example, "Attractive people elicit more agreement because they trigger positive feelings in others") would also be doomed to failure. Although we can identify the general mental processes that are involved in persuasion, the way in which those processes play themselves out will depend on the issue, the communicator, the target audience, the situation, and most importantly, the subtle interactions between these factors. Perhaps because of the complexity of the interactions, most people are unaware of them, and see themselves as relatively invulnerable to efforts to influence or persuade them (Levine, 2003).

The Heuristic-Systematic Model (HSM)

The elaboration likelihood model (ELM) belongs to a family of social psychological theories known as **dual-process models** (Chaiken & Trope, 1999). Such models assume that a wide variety of inferences, judgments, and decisions can be arrived at by means of two very different processes. One of those processes involves deliberate, careful, effortful thinking. The other is a quickly triggered, low-effort process that often takes place without conscious guidance. Gilbert's (1989) account of how we infer people's personality traits (see Chapter 3, **page 99**) is a dual-process model in which an automatic characterization stage was sometimes followed by a more effortful process, allowing people to adjust their initial trait inferences for extenuating factors.

Another dual-process model of persuasion, called the **heuristic-systematic model** (HSM; Chaiken, 1980, 1987; Chaiken, Liberman, & Eagly, 1989; Chen & Chaiken, 1999; Eagly & Chaiken, 1993), is, in many ways, quite similar to the ELM. We will briefly review some of the differences between the two models, because the issues they raise will help to deepen our understanding of persuasion.

Like the ELM, the HSM specifies two basic orientations toward persuasive communications. The first is **systematic processing**, which is essentially identical to the central route in the ELM. The other is **heuristic processing**, a more precise (but narrower) definition of the low-effort process. Heuristic processing involves looking for simple decision rules (that is, heuristics) that can suggest how valid a message is. Some of the heuristics people might use when they are unable or unmotivated to engage in systematic processing are "Experts are to be trusted," "I usually agree with people I like," and "Consensus implies correctness."

Because heuristics are rules that people store in memory, they can be primed to become more cognitively accessible, just like other thoughts. Thus, we can think about how individuals evaluate persuasive messages using some of the ideas introduced in Chapter 3, in connection with how individuals judge and evaluate others. Just as making a trait like "hostile" more accessible can lead a person to apply that trait to someone else, making a heuristic like "Longer messages tend to be stronger" more accessible can lead people to apply that rule to a persuasive appeal.

The HSM also does not share what might be called the ELM's "hydraulic" assumption. According to the ELM, central and peripheral processing fall along a continuum. As a result, the ELM predicts that (1) peripheral and central processing are inversely related; and (2) as the influence of central cues rises, the influence of peripheral cues falls (and vice versa). According to the HSM's *concurrent processing assumption*, in contrast, systematic and heuristic processing can take place at the same time. That means that they can sometimes have independent, additive effects on people's attitudes.

In a test of this hypothesis, Maheswaran and Chaiken (1991) presented people with a bogus description of the "XT-100," said to be a newly developed answering machine. One version of the message asserted that the answering machine was a great product; the other said it was inferior. Some of the participants learned that a majority of consumers who used the product agreed with the assessment they had read. In other words, they were offered an opportunity to use the consensus heuristic to evaluate the XT-100. Not surprisingly, participants' attitudes toward the answering machine were more positive when the description they had read was positive. However, the consensus information strengthened the difference between the two groups, even among a subgroup of participants who engaged in particularly careful thinking, because they believed their evaluations would determine the product's fate. In sum, systematic processing did not switch off heuristic processing; rather, heuristics had an additional effect on motivated thinkers, over and above the content of the message (see also Chaiken & Maheswaran, 1994).

Given the power and pervasiveness of hidden influences on our behavior—including, but not restricted to, heuristic and peripheral cues—it should not be surprising that a simple commitment to think carefully about a persuasive message should not make a person immune to the effects of heuristics. After all, these subtle effects on our thinking often operate without our awareness.

The Distinction between Explicit and Implicit Attitudes

Thus far, we have been discussing attitude change without reference to an important distinction introduced in Chapter 5: explicit versus implicit attitudes. To review, explicit attitudes are evaluations that people are aware of and can report to others. Implicit attitudes are evaluations that people are less able to verbalize, even though those evaluations affect their automatic thoughts and feelings. Indeed, people might not even be aware of their implicit attitudes (Banaji & Heiphetz, 2010; Greenwald, Banaji, Rudman, Farnham, Nosek, & Mellott, 2002; Rudman, 2004). A person's explicit and implicit attitudes are not always consistent. A voter may express admiration for a political candidate but cringe in response to the candidate's photo (and fail to vote for the candidate).

Much remains to be learned about differences in the way explicit and implicit attitudes change (Gawronski & Bodenhausen, 2006; Gawronski & Lebel, 2008). Some evidence suggests that direct, effortful thinking about issues affects primarily explicit attitudes (Rudman, Ashmore, & Gary, 2001; Wilson, Lindsey, & Schooler, 2000). Implicit attitudes are more likely to change in response to indirect influences, such as the feelings people associate with an issue (Rudman, 2004; Rudman et al., 2001). One implication of these findings is that when people take the central route to persuasion, they may end their mental journey with new explicit attitudes. When they take the peripheral route, they may be more likely to experience changes in their implicit attitudes.

The Process of Persuasion: A Summary

No set of general rules or "cookbook" explains *how* people are persuaded to change their attitudes. Nor could one do so. Current models of persuasion recognize how complex the process is. In analyzing or predicting the results of an attempt to persuade, we need to know (1) the kind of thinking the targets of the message can or will do; (2) whether they hold preexisting attitudes or biases about the message's topic; (3) how strong or weak the message is; and (4) what kinds of peripheral cues or heuristics are available to the audience. The ELM and HSM are both powerful frameworks for carrying out this kind of analysis.

Think Like a Social Psychologist

Understanding everyday behavior

—Imagine that a friend of yours, a salesperson, always makes sure that potential clients get to see a photograph of him shaking hands with a famous athlete. What would you tell him about the different roles the photo could play in the persuasive process, and how it could either enhance persuasion or reduce it?

Confronting social issues

—Televised preelection debates can provide people with information about political candidates' beliefs, values, and, plans, but they could also affect people's evaluation of the candidates in other ways. For example, some people believe that Richard Nixon lost votes in the 1960 U.S. presidential election because he looked as if he needed a shave during his debate with John Kennedy. In general, what kinds of peripheral cues might significantly affect the outcome of such debates?

THE EFFECTS OF SPECIFIC VARIABLES ON PERSUASION

The Selling of Bob, Part 1: Take It from Us, He's the Man

Eventually, the clown who had introduced Bob Marks at the Ohio state fair was chased from the stage (by a man dressed as an ear of corn). To Bob's dismay, the red-nosed buffoon delivered a brief lecture about his candidacy before disappearing. Bob had no choice at that point but to make his scheduled appearance onstage and wave to the crowd. There was no time left to try to reverse the disastrous situation; he had a flight to catch at the local airport.

The drive to the airport was the longest 20 minutes of Bob's life. Was there any possible way that the day's events had persuaded even one person to vote for him? If anyone's attitude toward his candidacy or his qualifications had changed, Bob didn't want to hear the details.

The two general theories of persuasion just reviewed help us to think more clearly about persuasion and the different paths to attitude change. The two models can also be used to predict the effects of the many different features of situations where people attempt to change the attitudes of others. What are the implications of hearing a speech in a rich and distracting context like a crowded park or a fair, as opposed to a quiet lecture hall? If your argument can be made simply, should you bother to enlist an expert to deliver the message? Will you be persuaded to wear your seat belt by viewing photos of deadly car crashes? Should you care whether your audience is made up of senior citizens or junior high school students?

As you can probably guess from your reading of the first section of this chapter—especially the discussion of the multiple-roles hypothesis—figuring out the effects of any given persuasion variable requires us to take into account other features of the situation. And though theories of persuasion give us a systematic way to think about the roles of different variables, they do not lend themselves to pat conclusions such as "Always distract your audience," "Smarter people are harder to persuade," or "Never present both sides of an issue." Any such rules would inevitably be overgeneralizations.

Source, Message, Context, and Recipient Variables

Many years ago, Lasswell (1948) suggested that the study of persuasion boils down to the study of "Who says what in which channel to whom with what effect?" (p. 37). Indeed, the variables that affect persuasion can be organized into four categories: **Source variables** ("who"), **message variables** ("what"), **context variables** ("what channel"), and **recipient variables** ("to whom"). In the following sections, we will review research on selected variables in each of those categories. **Table 6.1** provides examples of each type of variable (including some examples not discussed in the text).

Source Variables

Many source variables, or characteristics of communicators, affect their persuasiveness (Levine, 2003), including their attractiveness, how powerful they are (Raven & French, 1958), and their similarity to the message recipients (Brock, 1965; Mills & Jellison, 1968). We have already discussed the effects of attractiveness. Other research shows that similar and powerful communicators also both have an advantage in persuading others. In this section, we will focus on another variable that has received a great deal of attention from researchers: a communicator's **credibility**, defined in terms of his or her expertise and trustworthiness (Kelman, 1958).

People sometimes go to great lengths to provide evidence of their credibility.

Table 6.1: Four types of persuasion variables

TYPE OF VARIABLE	EXAMPLES
SOURCE	Attractiveness, power, similarity to audience, credibility (expertise and trustworthiness), speed of speech, gender, ethnicity, number of sources
MESSAGE	Relevance, strength, number of arguments, argument repetition, one-sided versus two-sided, order of arguments, threat or fear arousal, number of rhetorical questions, discrepancy from audience's preexisting attitudes
RECIPIENT	Attitude strength, need for cognition, intelligence, self-esteem, age, knowledge, gender
CONTEXT	Distraction, anticipation of discussion, audience enthusiasm (consensus), prior warning that persuasion will be attempted

The positive correlation between a communicator's credibility and persuasiveness is one of the oldest, most reliable findings in experimental social psychology (Chaiken & Maheswaran, 1994; Kelman & Hovland, 1953; Lorge, 1936; Petty et al., 1981; Wu & Shaffer, 1987). If the surgeon general of the United States asks people to rethink their attitudes toward suntanning, they are more likely to take the message to heart than if an actor who "plays a doctor on TV" makes the same request. For this reason, Bob Marks certainly would have preferred to be introduced to the crowd at the state fair by a prominent politician or businessperson, rather than a person with more experience balancing beach balls on his nose than balancing budgets.

Consistent with both the ELM and HSM, source credibility matters more to people who are less able or motivated than others to think about the content of a message. Those who engage in central or systematic processing are more likely than others to be concerned with the quality of the argument. Priester and Petty (1995) found that people who are low in the need for cognition (and thus not motivated to think deeply) are more likely than others to abandon the effort to carefully process a message if it comes from a source that is perceived as honest and trustworthy.

Of course, source credibility can serve as more than a simple acceptance versus rejection cue. Sometimes people may be motivated to accurately assess the quality of an argument because the issue at stake is highly relevant to them, yet the validity of the argument may be hard to ascertain. In such cases, we might predict that people would devote so much energy to systematic processing that the communicator's identity would become irrelevant. Instead, source credibility can still affect people in these situations by biasing information processing. In other words, when the communicator is high in expertise and trustworthiness, people tend to conclude that an ambiguous message is stronger than the same message delivered by a less credible source (Chaiken & Maheswaran, 1994).

The fact that a communicator's power, prestige, and attractiveness are such important variables is consistent with the evolutionary approach to social psychology. Buss (1995) suggests that an orientation toward high-status models probably increases fitness, and that such a tendency may have developed into a species-general psychological mechanism. Throughout our evolutionary history, people who attended to and complied with those group members who had the greatest access to knowledge, power, and resources were probably more likely to survive than others. Recall, too, that according to evolutionary psychologists, psychological mechanisms are triggered by specific social contexts. Fiske, Morling, and Stevens (1996) have hypothesized that individuals who find themselves in situations that render them powerless will be especially motivated to attend to high-status people (particularly those with power over them).

Once again, however, the process of persuasion is more complicated than we might imagine. The Social Psychology Encounters the Bright Side and Dark Side boxes on **pages 273** and **274** describe the sleeper effect, which tends to undercut the effects of a source's credibility.

Message Variables

Although communicators' identities—whether similar to you or not, beautiful or plain, expert or uninformed— are important, a person's response to a persuasive message is determined to a great extent by the message itself. Indeed, both the ELM and the HSM highlight the significance of a message's personal relevance. Some issues people care deeply about; others do not affect them much. And, as we have seen, a message's relevance determines a person's approach to thinking about it. People will engage in systematic or central processing if the issue at stake is important and personally meaningful to them. They will fall back on peripheral or heuristic processing if the issue seems trivial.

Clearly, the quality or strength of the arguments in a message is an important variable, one that will affect the extent to which people are persuaded. That is especially true when people are motivated to attend carefully to a message's content—in other words, when they are taking the central rather than the peripheral route. Unfortunately, "relatively little is known about what makes an argument persuasive" (Petty & Wegener, 1998, p. 352). The most that can be said is that a persuasive message should convince people that adopting the advocated position will make bad outcomes less likely and good outcomes more likely.

We do know that what makes a message strong and convincing varies across cultures. Recall from Chapters 1, 3, and 4 that in North America and western Europe, where individualistic values dominate, people tend to focus on their own individual goals and needs. In the more collectivistic cultures of Asia, people define themselves in terms of their relationships to others and think more in terms of group goals. Given those differences, we might hypothesize that what makes for a successful persuasive message in the United States would not have the same effect in South Korea.

That hypothesis has been supported. Han and Shavitt (1994; Zhang & Shavitt, 2003) analyzed advertisements in popular magazines published in the two countries and found systematic differences between them. Ads that appeal to people's desire for self-improvement, independence, and personal pleasure were more common in the United States; those that focus on group benefits, or on how a product can enhance a person's relationship to others, were more common in Korea (see **Figure 6.5**). In a second study, the researchers designed two sets of advertisements, one with individualistic themes ("Treat yourself to a breath-freshening experience") and the other with collectivistic themes ("Share the breath-freshening experience"). Then they presented the ads to participants in the United States and South Korea. Participants in the United States thought that the individualistic ads were more convincing than participants in South Korea did; they also found the collectivistic ads to be significantly less convincing than the South Koreans did.

Even within a given culture, attitude objects may be important to people for different reasons. Persuasive messages pertaining to those objects will be most effective if they target those reasons. In short, attitudes can serve different *functions* (Herek, 1987; Katz, 1960; Smith, Bruner, & White, 1956).

For example, you may feel the way you do about something ("I hate cigarettes") because of your general values ("You should treat your body like a temple"). Such attitudes serve what is called the value-expressive function. Or you may hold an attitude simply because it helps you to behave effectively and avoid negative outcomes ("I dislike cigarettes because research shows they cause cancer"). Such attitudes serve the knowledge function. Attitudes that help people to fit into groups and get along with others ("My friends think smoking is cool, so I do too") serve the social-adjustment function. And attitudes

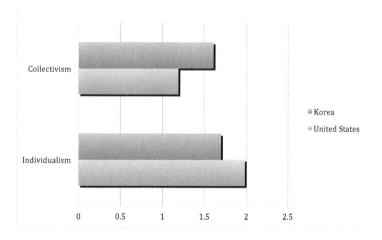

Figure 6.5: *Ratings of individualism and collectivism in advertisements used in the United States and South Korea.*

Ratings could vary from 1 ("not at all individualistic/collectivistic") to 3 ("very individualistic/collectivistic").

Source: Based on data presented by Han & Shavitt (1994).

This advertisement is a classic example of an individualistic appeal.

Although repetition of a message can make it seem more compelling, too much repetition can backfire, reducing its effectiveness.

that prevent you from facing conflicts and contradictions that could prove upsetting or threatening ("What could be wrong with cigarettes? My dear old dad smokes two packs a day") serve the ego-defensive function. Persuasive communications are more likely to lead to attitude change if they are directed specifically at the functions an attitude serves (Snyder & DeBono, 1987).

Messages also vary in ways other than strength or quality. What, for example, are the effects of "piling it on" when trying to persuade someone? Increasing the sheer number of your arguments might seem like a good way to encourage people to adopt a position. That assumption would be correct if the people you are trying to persuade are not able or motivated to carefully process the messages—that is, if the likelihood of elaboration is low. On the other hand, if the targets of persuasion are processing the message carefully, this strategy could backfire, especially if your arguments are weak and unconvincing. In that case, people would notice the flaws in your message (Petty & Cacioppo, 1984).

What about simply repeating the same message several times (Gorn & Goldberg, 1980; McCullough & Ostrom, 1974; Moons, Mackie, & Garcia-Marques, 2009)? As long as the message is reasonably complex (Cox & Cox, 1988) and strong and people are motivated to attend to and think about it, repeating it does indeed seem to be to the communicator's advantage. However, overdoing the repetition—hitting people over the head with an argument—can have the opposite effect (Cacioppo & Petty, 1979). Boring or annoying your listeners is not an effective way to win them over to your side.

In crafting a persuasive message, should you focus only on the position you want to advocate, or would a *two-sided message* (Allen, 1991; Hovland, Lumsdaine, & Sheffield, 1949)—one that acknowledges opposing viewpoints—be more effective? A key consideration in selecting a two-sided message is whether or not the audience is familiar with both sides of an issue (Petty & Wegener, 1988). If people are not even aware of arguments opposing the one you want to make, it might not be a good idea to even bring them up! Either way, if you are trying to persuade people to change their beliefs or behavior, it is better *not* to present both sides of the issue unless you are going to refute the opposing viewpoint (Allen et al., 1990; Hale, Mongeau, & Thomas, 1991).

If the audience is definitely going to hear opposing arguments—from a political opponent, for example—a related issue would be in what *order* they should hear the two sides. In light of the discussion of primacy effects in

In an appeal to obey the speed limit, an image like this one might not necessarily increase the message's effectiveness. Instead, it could overwhelm readers with fear or anxiety, causing them to tune out the message.

Chapter 3, you will not be surprised to hear that you will be more likely to persuade people if you present your own arguments first. Much as with information about people's traits and behaviors, the information about an issue that people encounter first colors their reaction to later information. First-encountered arguments create beliefs and expectations that are hard to shake, placing those who attempt to rebut them at a disadvantage. And the longer the delay between people's exposure to an opposing argument and their report of their attitudes, the greater the advantages of going first (Miller & Campbell, 1959). (Bob Marks, fortunately, was unaware of this research, so he did not have to suffer with the knowledge that being represented by a clown is even worse when the clown is the second act, and the whole fiasco takes place well before Election Day.) When people are asked about their opinion *immediately* after a message, on the other hand, what are called "recency effects" are more likely to occur. At that point, the second message is so much better remembered than the first that it is harder to resist (see also Haugtvedt & Wegener, 1994; Insko, 1964; Wilson & Miller, 1968).

Finally, some messages stand out from others because they are designed to scare people. How effective are **fear** or **threat appeals** (Ruiter, Abraham, & Kok, 2001)? Putting aside the ethical issues, should parents attempt to persuade children to brush their teeth by telling them that their teeth will fall out if they don't? Some of the earliest experimental studies (Janis & Feshbach, 1953) revealed that fear-arousing messages are not always the most effective ones (see also de Hoog, Stroebe, & de Wit, 2004); indeed, they can sometimes be less effective than low-fear messages. Fear or threat appeals that raise the possibility of a fate that is *too* ghastly ("Stay out of the sun, unless you enjoy painful skin grafts") may cause so much arousal and distraction that people will not be able to pay attention to them (Baron, Inman, Kao, & Logan, 1992). When central or systematic processing is disrupted, the subtleties of an argument are lost on a message's recipients. To have their intended effect, threatening messages must do more than highlight a possible negative outcome and convince people that they themselves are vulnerable to the threat. Such messages must also (1) let people know they can take steps to avoid the threat; and (2) leave people feeling that they are capable of taking those steps (Leventhal, 1970; Rogers, 1983).

Considering the examples just presented, you will not be surprised to hear that researchers who want to increase healthy behaviors and decrease unhealthy ones are especially interested in understanding the effects of fear-arousing messages (and messages that are more generally "vivid;" Guadagno, Rhoads, & Sagarin, 2011). They have found that messages about potentially terrible outcomes are more effective for changing some behaviors than others: see the Social Psychology of Health box **below**.

SOCIAL PSYCHOLOGY OF HEALTH: FRAMING PERSUASIVE HEALTH MESSAGES

According to some estimates, smoking costs the United States close to $100 billion a year in health care costs, as well as an equal amount in lost productivity. Thus, persuasive messages that reduce smoking rates even slightly have great social value.

In our day-to-day lives, many of the agents of persuasion we encounter are far from heroic. They include advertisers eager to sell us their clients' products; politicians begging for our votes; and salespeople urging us to purchase the special three-year warranty on the appliance we just bought. The more noble face of persuasion is represented by those who attempt to encourage us to engage in health-promoting behaviors. The persuasive messages they construct are aimed at getting people to stop smoking, lose weight, brush their teeth, and refrain from binge drinking and risky sex.

Two broad approaches are available to communicators seeking to promote healthy behaviors. They can focus on the costs of unhealthy behavior such as a proneness to cancer, obesity, tooth decay, liver damage, and sexually transmitted diseases. Alternatively, they can emphasize the benefits of healthy behaviors (such as physical fitness and strong, white teeth). Which approach is more effective? It depends on the type of behavior you are trying to change (Latimer, Salovey, & Rothman, 2007; Rothman & Salovey, 1997; van 't Riet, J., Ruiter, R. C., Smerecnik, C., & de Vries, H., 2010). To get people to take steps that are associated with some kind of risk (such as being screened for AIDS), you should focus on the negative. To encourage people to engage in risk-free preventive behavior (behavior such as brushing one's teeth to avoid tooth decay that is aimed at reducing the risk of some health-related problem), you should accentuate the positive.

Why is that the case? Messages can focus on, or be framed in terms of, either undesirable outcomes (losses) or desirable outcomes (gains). Research on decision making by Tversky and Kahneman (1981) reveals that people making decisions involving uncertain outcomes are more willing to make risky decisions when they are thinking about the possible losses or costs associated with failure to act. Thus, loss-framed persuasive messages should be more effective when people are asked to take some action that involves risk.

For instance, Meyerowitz and Chaiken (1987) tried to persuade women to engage in breast self-examination (BSE). Such exams, of course, involve some risk: they could cause emotional distress by revealing the presence of a tumor. The researchers had more success with loss-framed messages ("Research shows that women who do not do BSE have an increased chance" of later finding a deadly tumor) than with gain-framed messages ("You can gain several potential health benefits by spending only 5 minutes each month doing BSE"). Research participants who read the loss-framed messages were more likely than others to report an intention to perform BSE. Over the next four months, they also examined themselves more frequently. Such results are consistent with Tversky and Kahneman's predictions.

Rothman, Salovey, Antone, Keough, and Martin (1993) report similar findings in a study of people's willingness to be screened for skin cancer (which involves the risk of a person discovering that he or she suffers from the condition). Participants in this study were more likely to agree to be examined in response to loss-framed messages ("Unless they are detected and treated early, most of these cancers are not curable") than in response to gain-framed messages ("If they are detected early, most of these cancers are curable"). When the goal was to encourage people to engage in preventive behavior (such as using effective sunscreens), which in and of itself poses no risk, gain-framed messages were more effective.

Context Variables

Just as messages have a particular content and come from specific people, they are delivered in places and situations that differ in important ways. Researchers have studied the effects of many context variables. Consistent with the multiple-roles hypothesis, they have found that most context variables have not one effect, but as many as three. First, context variables determine the type of processing that people can or will use. Second, they serve as peripheral cues or heuristics. And third, they bias systematic processing. More often than not, context variables achieve their effects without people's awareness, qualifying as hidden influences on behavior.

We have seen, for example, that distraction prevents people from devoting much energy to thinking about the content of persuasive messages. A distracting environment can therefore lead to peripheral route processing (and lack of attention to an argument's quality). In contrast, anticipating having to discuss or justify one's attitudes causes people to think more carefully about a persuasive message—in other words, it leads to central route processing (Chaiken, 1980; Cialdini et al., 1976). Thus, these and other context variables determine what kind of processing people will adopt.

People often receive persuasive messages when they are in the company of others. In such cases, they may become acutely aware of how those other people are responding. Axsom, Yates, and Chaiken (1987) hypothesized that audience enthusiasm—as long as one has no reason to think that the audience is made up of people very different from oneself (Clarkson, Tormala, Rucker, & Dugan, 2013)—could serve as a heuristic cue. In other words, the laughing and clapping inspired by the clown who introduced Bob Marks at the state fair could

Other people's enthusiastic response to a persuasive message can serve as a powerful heuristic.

have played a significant role in how people responded to his remarks. Consistent with the HSM and ELM, Axsom et al. found that audience enthusiasm affected people's opinions when the issue was not very important to them. More involved participants were affected only by the arguments themselves, which were either high or low in quality.

As we have already noted, sometimes the quality of a message can be ambiguous. In such cases, context variables like audience response could affect how people respond to a message, even when they are highly involved and motivated to focus on its content. Context cues can do so by biasing people's evaluation of the quality of a message's arguments. As discussed by Petty and Wegener (1998), there is some evidence that audience reactions—cheering, applauding, heckling, or booing—can affect persuasion in this way (Petty & Brock, 1976).

Recent research, however, has revealed one interesting circumstance where the perceived popularity of an attitude is *not* an effective way to persuade an individual: when he or she is experiencing romantic desires (Griskevicius, Goldstein, Mortensen, Sundie, Cialdini, & Kenrick, 2009). From an evolutionary perspective, this makes sense. People seeking to attract a mate want to stand out, not conform to what everyone else is saying and doing.

Framing Persuasive Health Messages

Recipient Variables

It will be harder to persuade some people to change specific attitudes than others. Why might that be? Research shows that when people spend an extended period thinking about an attitude, that attitude becomes more extremely positive or negative—and more generally, stronger (Chaiken & Yates, 1985; Liberman & Chaiken, 1991; Tesser, 1978; Tesser, Martin, & Mendolia, 1995). These findings have important implications for the study of persuasion, because when people's attitudes are strong, they are more resistant to change (Bassili, 1996; Petty & Krosnick, 1995). (Although as the Think like a Social Psychologist box **below** discusses, extremely positive or negative attitudes can become more moderate over time.)

THINK LIKE A SOCIAL PSYCHOLOGIST: EXTREME SCORES AND REGRESSION

Bob Marks's opponent was aware that many if not most of the voters were not all that motivated to listen to speeches or read campaign literature. For those voters who were paying attention, however, he and his campaign managers wanted to make the most compelling case possible. After carefully composing a set of arguments that they hoped would provide a knockout blow in the last days before the election, they decided to put it to the toughest test they could imagine. They contacted a group of voters who had been identified in earlier surveys as committed Marks supporters and asked them to read and respond to the message. These people had reported extremely positive attitudes toward Bob Marks. If the message could change their attitudes, the campaign strategists assumed, it would be even more effective with other voters.

Unfortunately, there was a flaw in the campaign workers' thinking. Can you identify it?

****

Though several problems are associated with this test, including the lack of a comparison group, we will focus on the most glaring one. The campaign strategists were clearly unfamiliar with the phenomenon of **regression to the mean** (Kruger, Savitsky, & Gilovich, 1999; Nesselroade, Stigler, & Baltes, 1980). That is, extreme scores or outcomes—extremely positive or negative attitudes, extremely great or dismal athletic performances, extremely good or bad moods—tend to become more moderate over time. The reason for this phenomenon is relatively simple. Any extreme score could reflect either (1) a person's true score (for example, one's stable underlying attitude or actual ability); or (2) chance factors (such as recent experiences or a lucky break). While the factors that produce true scores will tend to remain the same over time, chance factors are wildly unstable. Those random influences are not likely to continue to push a person's score to the extreme end of the distribution.

The famous "sophomore slump" in sports is a classic example. Many sportswriters have noticed that players who excelled during their first year in a league—the "rookies of the year"—tend to be less impressive the following year. People usually assume that the players are choking because of the high expectations everyone has for them. That explanation is unnecessary, however. Outstanding freshman seasons do, of course, result from a player's abilities, at least to a certain extent. However, they tend also to reflect the fact that everything just happened to be going the player's way that season. In baseball, for example, batters have limited control over whether the balls they hit will end up in a part of the field where they can or cannot be easily caught. The laws of probability suggest that some players will experience periods in which they just happen to hit the ball toward the gaps between fielders. Those players will be more likely than others to have award-winning seasons. When the odds catch up with them, though, people will wonder why their play seems to have deteriorated.

Recall that the voters the campaign managers planned to survey had reported extremely positive attitudes toward Bob Marks. There can be little doubt that they truly favored his candidacy, but their high attitude scores probably reflected some random factors, too (such as having recently seen one of his better television ads). One would expect their attitudes toward Marks to regress to the mean over time. Put another way, if people's attitudes are not perfectly stable, then when a person holds an extreme attitude, there is only one direction in which it can move—toward the center. In sum, the campaign managers would probably find that after reading their persuasive communication, extreme pro-Marks voters would have moved ever so slightly in the direction of his opponent. However, they probably could have obtained the same results by asking those voters to read the list of ingredients on a can of soup.

Attitude strength, of course, is a characteristic of the specific attitudes people hold. What about more general recipient variables? Extensive research has not revealed any personality traits that strongly predict a general tendency to be persuaded (Briñol, Rucker, Tormala, & Petty, 2004; Eagly, 1981). Even personality measures designed specifically to differentiate between people who are open or closed to attitude change—such as the dogmatism scale (Rokeach, 1954)—are not very reliable in predicting whether people will resist or yield to persuasive messages.

Of course, one theme of this chapter is that very few, if any, variables will have a simple, straightforward effect on persuasion. So, even though general susceptibility to persuasion remains an elusive concept, personality variables clearly play an important role in persuasion. For example, we have seen that the need for cognition predicts how motivated people will be to carefully attend to arguments, and as a result, how sensitive they will be to the strength of an argument (Cacioppo et al., 1983). We have also seen that intelligence can make people resistant to persuasion, because intelligent people are better able to devise counterarguments. However, when the message is complex, intelligent people may be *more* affected than others, since only they will be able to comprehend and recall it (Eagly & Warren, 1976; McGuire, 1968).

Self-esteem may play a similar role in persuasion (McGuire, 1968). People who are high in self-esteem are more confident in their attitudes and beliefs than people who are low in self-esteem. Hence, they may be less likely to yield to attempts to persuade them. On the other hand, people who are low in self-esteem are generally more passive than others, and less confident in their ability to analyze arguments. If they do not attend to or think about arguments, people with low self-esteem may not be affected by them. One implication of these hypotheses is that the relationship between self-esteem and persuasion will not be straightforward or linear. That is, the people who are the least persuadable (for whatever reason) should be both those with very high *and* those with very low self-esteem (Rhodes & Wood, 1992).

At least one variable, age, has been thought to have a straightforward relationship to susceptibility to persuasion (Glenn, 1980; Mannheim, 1952; Sears, 1983). Young adults are more open to attitude change than people in middle adulthood (people in their 30s, 40s, and 50s; Sears, 1986). With age, people's attitudes become stronger because they are based on greater knowledge and experience. In addition, people make important life decisions based on their attitudes and in the process become increasingly committed to them. And as people age, they "become increasingly entrenched in social networks of others with similar life experiences and worldviews" (Visser & Krosnick, 1998, p. 1389).

Research by Visser and Krosnick (1998), however, suggests a more complicated picture. These researchers found that the people who are most susceptible to persuasion are those in young adulthood and *late* adulthood. Why people in late adulthood should be more prone than others to changing their attitudes is not yet clear. The

Research suggests that the younger and older woman in this photograph will be more open to persuasion and attitude change than the one in middle adulthood (Visser and Krosnick, 1998).

possibilities include (1) a decline in their cognitive abilities that makes it harder for them to counterargue; (2) a decline in the size of their social networks and thus in the number of people who reinforce their attitudes; and (3) the possibility that experience has taught them that life is full of uncertainty and change—in other words, increasing wisdom. As for adults in midlife, a study by Eaton, Visser, Krosnick, and Anand (2009) suggests that their heightened resistance to persuasion can be explained by the fact that this is the stage of life when people are most likely to occupy high-power jobs and positions. High-power social roles call for resoluteness.

Mood

Although mood plays an important role in persuasion, it is difficult to classify in terms of the four types of variables just discussed (Petty & Wegener, 1998). On the one hand, mood can refer to the state of mind of the recipient of a persuasive message. On the other hand, different situations induce specific emotional states, so mood can also be thought of as a context variable. And because persuasive messages are often crafted to trigger certain feelings in people, mood might even be considered a message variable.

No matter how mood is classified, its effects on persuasion can serve as a potent hidden influence on the targets of persuasive appeals. Even when people are conscious of their moods, they are unlikely to be aware of the way mood shapes their reaction to a persuasive message. That is not surprising, because its effects are quite complex.

Does mood play a role in how easily a person can be persuaded? Indeed it does, especially when the message is ambiguous—that is, neither obviously weak nor obviously strong (Bohner, Chaiken, & Hunyadi, 1994). The nature of the effect, however, depends on where a person is on the elaboration likelihood continuum (Forgas, 1995; Petty, Schumann, Richman, & Strathman, 1993).

First, let's consider the case in which people are unable or unwilling to think much about a message. In Chapter 5, we saw how attitudes can be formed through classical conditioning—that is, through the formation of a simple association between an attitude object and good or bad feelings (Olson & Fazio, 2001, 2002). We also saw that people can form attitudes simply by relying on mood as an indication of how they feel about an attitude object, a phenomenon known as the "mood-as-information" effect (Clore, Gasper, & Garvin, 2001; Schwarz, 1990; Schwarz & Clore, 1983). These processes also play a role in the way people respond to persuasive messages, especially through the peripheral route (Gorn,

"I've hired this musician to play a sad melody while I give you a sob story why I didn't do my homework. It's actually quite effective."

The effects of mood on persuasion are more complex than this student realizes.

1982; Petty et al., 1993). Thus, when a person's motivation and interest are not particularly high, a good mood will lead directly to a positive response to a message, and a bad mood will lead directly to a negative response—or even to rejection.

What happens when a message is personally relevant, so that you are motivated to think carefully about it? Mood has an effect in this case as well, but for different reasons. Mood affects the thoughts that come to mind when people are thinking about persuasive communications (or anything else; Blaney, 1986). When people are in a good mood, positive thoughts will be more accessible to them, but when they are in a bad mood, negative thoughts are more likely to spring to mind (Mathur & Chattopadhyay, 1991). Those thoughts, in turn, affect the way people interpret and evaluate persuasive arguments (Petty et al., 1993). People who take the central route to processing a message may try to think deeply about persuasive messages, no matter what their mood. However, they are unaware of the extent to which their moods can bias them toward either dismissing or embracing persuasive arguments.

You may have noticed that mood has the same ultimate effect on persuasion at both levels of motivation and ability. Positive affect makes you more receptive to persuasion; negative affect makes you more resistant. Mood achieves these effects for different reasons, though, depending on whether the target of persuasion is taking the central or peripheral route. These findings would probably give Bob Marks a different perspective on the fiasco at the state fair. The politician who introduced Bob's opponent may have been respectable, but he was more than a little boring. The clown, on the other hand, made people laugh, and when people laugh, they feel good. Whether audience members were interested in gathering information about the upcoming election or just out to relax in the sunshine, the smiles the clown brought to their faces may have made them evaluate Bob's candidacy more favorably.

Other research indicates that mood helps to determine not only how people evaluate a message, but how they process it. One hypothesis that has received some support is that bad moods encourage people to carefully attend to and think about messages (in other words, to do more central processing); good moods cause them to process messages superficially (in other words, to take the peripheral route). To test this hypothesis, Bless, Bohner, Schwarz, and Strack (1990; see also Bless, Mackie, & Schwarz, 1992) led student participants to believe that college administrators were planning to increase fees for the next academic year. Participants heard one of two tape-recorded messages justifying the increase. In one version, the arguments were compelling; in the other, the arguments were weak. The researchers induced a sad mood in some of the participants and a happy mood in others by asking them to write vivid, detailed descriptions of either sad or happy personal experiences. Not surprisingly, participants overall reacted more positively to the strong arguments than to the weak arguments. However, the quality of the argument had a significant effect only on the sad participants; happy participants did not respond very differently to the two messages (see **Figure 6.6**).

Bless et al. (1990) explained these findings by suggesting that sad participants were more motivated than happy ones to think carefully about the content of the messages. Consequently, they were better able to distinguish between impressive and unimpressive arguments. A second study supported this interpretation by showing that when participants were distracted as they listened to the messages, the results were identical for sad and happy participants. That is, neither group reacted differently to the two messages. When sad people are deprived of the mental energy they need to elaborate on persuasive messages, the effect of an argument's quality disappears.

Why does mood have these effects? One possibility is that a bad mood serves as a signal that something is wrong with your current situation. People respond to that signal by paying more attention to what is going on around them, so that they can address the problem (Schwarz, Bless, & Bohner, 1991). From an evolutionary perspective, that response makes a lot of sense. Thus, people who are experiencing negative affect may devote more attention than others to a persuasive communication. Alternatively, there is some evidence that a good mood prevents people from attending carefully to persuasive messages, because a good mood is distracting (Mackie & Worth, 1991; Worth & Mackie, 1987). Not all research replicates the finding that a happy mood leads to lazy thinking, however (Isbell, 2004; Wegener, Petty, & Smith, 1995; Ziegler, Schlett, & Aydinli, 2013).

Less research been conducted on the effects of specific emotions such as sadness or anger, as opposed to bad moods in general (DeSteno, Petty, Rucker, Wegener, & Braverman, 2004). As we have seen elsewhere in this book, though, most hidden influences lose their power when we become aware that they may be affecting our behavior. Thus, the effects of mood on persuasion are likely to be less pronounced when our moods are made salient to us.

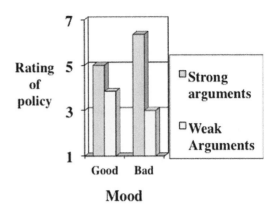

Figure 6.6: Attitude toward a proposed policy as a function of mood and quality of the persuasive arguments.

Ratings were made on a scale from 1 to 9. Higher numbers indicate more favorable attitudes. Participants in a negative mood were more likely than others to distinguish between weak and strong arguments.

Source: Bless, Bohner, Schwarz, and Strack (1990, Study 1).

Head Movements

Could mood play a role in persuasion even at very low levels of affect that are triggered without our awareness? Wells and Petty (1980) played a tape of an editorial to three groups of research participants. They instructed participants in two of the groups to nod or shake their heads while listening. Those participants who nodded their heads while listening to the editorial agreed with it more than other participants; those who shook their heads were less likely to agree with it. These hidden influences on persuasion were independent of participants' initial attitudes.

Why should head movements affect persuasion? Tom, Petterson, Lau, Burton, and Cook (1991) found that nodding induces positive affect, and head shaking induces negative affect. Hence, head movements may affect people's responses to a persuasive message through the process of classical conditioning (see Chapter 5). That is to say, nodding may lead a person to associate the message with good feelings, while head shaking may create an association with bad feelings.

Head movements, however, may influence persuasion in other ways as well (Förster and Strack, 1996). For example, Briñol and Petty (2003) suggest that nodding may increase people's confidence in their response to a message (whatever that response is), while head shaking may signal a lack of confidence. Briñol and Petty supported this "self-validation" hypothesis by showing that when people are presented with weak, unconvincing arguments, nodding actually *reduces* persuasion. That is, nodding can also validate one's conclusion that arguments are feeble.

Subliminal Messages

We have seen that hidden influences can play an important role in persuasion. But can stimuli change people's attitudes, even when people cannot even detect their presence? In other words, to what extent are people prone to subliminal persuasion?

Subliminal perception is a widely known and discussed phenomenon, for understandable reasons. Contemplating the possibility that our attitudes, beliefs, and behaviors could be influenced by other people—some with agendas that we might despise—using invisible stimuli and messages is disturbing, even frightening. After all, without being aware of a plot to implant attitudes or beliefs in us, we would have no way of resisting the attempt.

As we saw in Chapters 3 and 5, words and images that are presented very briefly (for just a few milliseconds) can indeed be perceived unconsciously, and thus can affect our thoughts, feelings, and behavior. Because subliminal visual stimuli generally do not have very powerful effects, however, and because of the technical challenges they pose to those who might wish to make use of them, they are unlikely to play much of a role in attitude change in our everyday lives. In addition, when people have been warned about the possible presence of such subliminal visual stimuli, they can try to adjust their behaviors to compensate for any possible effects the stimuli might have on them (Verwijmeren, Karremans, Bernritter, Stroebe, & Wigboldus, 2013). For these reasons (among others), none of Bob's advisers suggested spending any of his campaign funds on advertisements that included subliminal messages. They may have recalled that in the 2000 U.S. presidential campaign, an apparent attempt to subliminally associate the candidate Al Gore with the word "RATS" (superimposed on his face for one 30th of a second in a television advertisement) was met with ridicule.

Still, other forms of subliminal manipulation are alleged to exist. They include backward messages and subliminal auditory stimuli, even images hidden in print advertisements. What is the evidence for their influence on how we evaluate people, places, things, and even ourselves?

"I think I'm getting subliminal messages from my Rice Krispies!"

Despite the alarming claims in some popular books, the secretive use and effectiveness of subliminal stimuli are greatly exaggerated.

Backward Messages

In late 1985, after spending the day listening to music and getting drunk, Jay Vance and Ray Belknap, both high school dropouts in Reno, Nevada, picked up a shotgun and walked to a nearby schoolyard to blow their heads off. Belknap succeeded; Vance just blew his *face* off and lived to explain his behavior.

An investigation revealed that the two young men had serious long-term problems. Both had a history of drug abuse, petty crime, school failure, and violence. Belknap had attempted suicide before, as had his sister. At a drug treatment center, Vance had reported on a questionnaire that his favorite leisure-time activity was "doing drugs," and that one of his ideal jobs would be "paid assassin." He had also reported that he could think of nothing in his life that was "good." He cited none of those factors, however, in accounting for his attempt to kill himself. Instead, he claimed his actions had been triggered by subliminal messages hidden in a heavy-metal music album (Judas Priest's *Stained Class*). Supposedly, some of those messages were recorded backward; others were simply recorded at low volume and disguised by the accompanying music. Vance was so sure he was the victim of an unscrupulous attempt to affect his attitudes and coerce him into destroying himself that he and his family sued the musicians. *Vance v. Judas Priest* went to trial in 1990.

Backward messages have indeed been placed in commercially produced recorded music, and during the trial, band members admitted they had included reverse speech in some of their recordings. Not all the backward messages that can be found in recorded music were created intentionally, though. Almost any lengthy recording of human speech, when played backward, will yield what sound like meaningful phrases (Vokey & Read, 1985).

Whether or not backward messages are present in a recording, of course, is a separate issue from whether those messages can change people's attitudes and beliefs. Research conducted on the topic shows clearly that they cannot (Begg, Needham, & Bookbinder, 1993; Byrne & Normand, 2000; Swart & Morgan, 1992; Vokey & Read, 1985). More generally, there is no evidence that people are at all capable—either consciously or unconsciously—of decoding or making sense of reverse speech. For that reason, in part, the *Vance v. Judas Priest* trial ended with members of the band being found not guilty on all charges.

Subliminal Self-Help Recordings

Other auditory messages are said to evade our awareness, not because they have been reversed or otherwise scrambled, but because they are presented at very low volume. Consider, for example, subliminal self-help tapes and CDs. Typically, these recordings feature relaxing music or sounds such as ocean waves, light breezes, chirping crickets, and birds flying overhead. The manufacturers, however, claim to have embedded subliminal messages in the soundtrack, at a volume below the threshold of awareness. These messages are supposed to be "inaudible to your conscious hearing, but loud and clear to your subconscious" (Merikle, 1988, p. 356).

A wide variety of such tapes and CDs are marketed. Some are supposed to contain messages that motivate people to lose weight; others supposedly boost academic achievement, improve memory, or even increase sexual confidence. Undoubtedly, we could find a great deal of anecdotal evidence for the effectiveness of many of these products. The real test, of course, is whether the people who listen to them experience more real (or even imagined) changes than people in a control condition—that is, people who listen to recordings with the same surface content, but without the alleged subliminal messages. Numerous studies have failed to find any differences between the two groups (Greenwald, Spangenberg, Pratkanis, & Eskanazi, 1991; Merikle & Skanes, 1992; Phelps & Exum, 1992; Russell, Rowe, & Smouse, 1991). People cannot even guess correctly, at greater-than-chance levels, whether recordings contain any low-volume messages (Merikle, 1988; Moore, 1995), and they certainly cannot determine the content of the messages (Harris, Salus, Rerecich, & Larsen, 1996). That is not surprising, because careful laboratory analyses of subliminal tapes and CDs reveal no evidence that they contain any messages, subliminal or otherwise (Merikle, 1988).

Subliminal Stimuli in Print Advertisements

One of the authors of this book recalls a high school health class in which he was warned to be on the lookout for words and pictures—typically of a sexual nature—hidden cleverly in print advertisements. The instructor even passed around examples of such ads, with the secret images (such as naked people, and the word "sex") circled or otherwise highlighted. Students in the class were asked to be suspicious of a sudden unexplained urge to buy a product; such mysterious urges, we were told, could be an indication of a hidden subliminal influence.

The subliminal advertisements presented during that class were probably from *Subliminal Seduction* (1973) or *Media Sexploitation* (1976), by Wilson Bryan Key. These books, more than anything else, gave rise to the popular belief that people are bombarded with subliminal words and images in magazine advertisements and that those subliminal influences are very effective. But the evidence presented in support of these assertions—especially the latter one—is so weak as to be laughable to anyone who has mastered the concepts reviewed in Chapter 2 of this book.

For example, Key (1973, pp. 3–4) described a study in which over a thousand people stared at an advertisement for a particular brand of gin and reported whatever thoughts or feelings came to mind. Sixty-two percent described feelings of "satisfaction," "sensuousness," "sexuality," "romance," "stimulation," "arousal," and "excitement"; several even reported feeling "horny." Why? According to Key, the source of their feelings was a glass of gin and ice that appeared in the ad. The glass was photographed so that the shadows on the ice cubes and the spaces between them combined in such a way that (with a little squinting) one can make out the word "SEX." Unfortunately, the study did not include a control group. People who are asked to free-associate while staring at *any* picture of an alcoholic beverage might eventually say something related to sex or romance. For all we know, the same could be true of people staring at a blank wall.

More careful studies of this kind of subliminal influence have been conducted (Gable, Wilkens, Harris, & Feinberg, 1987; Kilbourne, Painton, & Ridley, 1985). Overall, the evidence for its effectiveness is no more compelling than Key's. Nor is there any evidence that hidden words and images—whether they can affect people's attitudes or not—are common in printed advertisements.

The Effects of Specific Variables on Persuasion: A Summary

When seeking to persuade others, we must take into account a great deal, including the identity of the communicator; what she is telling people (the content and style of the message); the people in the audience and their moods; and the place and time of the communication. All these variables have an effect on our attitudes. However, our attitudes are not affected by backward messages supposedly embedded in music or by low-volume (and inaudible) messages. Nor can our preferences be traced back to images that are hidden in print advertisements.

Think Like a Social Psychologist

Understanding everyday behavior

—Imagine that a friend (using special software on his computer) played a popular song backward and reported hearing the mysterious phrases "Goodbye, classroom" and "Smoke the fun." What might you tell him to ease his concern that he was being programmed with suggestions to drop out of school and experiment with drugs?

Making connections

—Chapter 4 introduced the personality variable of self-monitoring, a trait that relates to people's tendency to adjust their behavior to their surroundings. How might your strategy for changing the attitudes of low self-monitors differ from your strategy for changing the attitudes of high self-monitors?

—If you were asked to design advertisements for a new line of smartphones, how would your appeal to consumers in individualistic cultures differ from your appeal to consumers in collectivistic cultures? What might be the content of the ads?

CHANGING ATTITUDES THROUGH BEHAVIOR

The Selling of Bob, Part 2: Don't Take It from Us—Convince Yourself

The fiasco at the state fair did not do any irreparable damage to Bob Marks's campaign. All the major newspapers were reporting that he was heading for victory on Election Day. That was great news, of course. Still, Bob was disturbed to learn that his lead in Cleveland, one of the state's biggest cities, was a bit shaky—disturbed, but not surprised. During a recent visit to the city, he had noticed that the number of cars sporting bumper stickers with his opponent's name far outnumbered the cars displaying his own. What was going on? Hadn't thousands of bumper stickers been distributed to his campaign workers? Where were they?

The answer to these questions came not from Bob's top aides, but from a volunteer who had just recently quit his summer job to start work for the campaign. Howard Loranger had asked to meet with Bob personally because he had a story to tell. Apparently, some of his friends were working for the other side, and from them he had learned how the bumper stickers had been distributed. The campaign had used a multistage strategy. First, campaign workers waited for a hot day and spread out among the city's rapid transit stations to distribute inexpensive cardboard fans featuring their candidate's name and face. A few days later, the same workers went to the same stations to hand out free ballpoint pens, also bearing the candidate's name and face. They followed up a few days later with the bumper stickers.

Bob wasn't entirely sure why this sequence of events made sense, but he appreciated the information. He proposed putting a similar plan into action—one that began with the distribution of computer mouse pads. The location of the campaign's website was featured on the mouse pad, along with Bob's name and face. On the website, voters would find a "So you think you know Ohio?' trivia game, which would change every day. Later, the bumper stickers would be distributed. Bob also elevated Howard Loranger to a position of greater responsibility in the campaign.

Howard's promotion was well deserved because his discovery had highlighted an important social-psychological principle. In Chapter 5, we studied the ways in which attitudes can affect behavior, but that causal relationship can be reversed: often, behavior can affect attitudes. That is, our words and actions (such as choosing to use a pen with a candidate's name on it) can lead us to reexamine or even change well-established attitudes. One factor that encourages this kind of attitude change is cognitive dissonance.

Table 6.2: The Preference for Consistency Scale (brief form)

It is important to me that those who know me can predict what I will do.

I want to be described by others as a stable, predictable person.

The appearance of consistency is an important part of the image I present to the world.

An important requirement for any friend of mine is personal consistency.

I typically prefer to do things the same way.

I want my close friends to be predictable.

It is important to me that others view me as a stable person.

I make an effort to appear consistent to others.

It doesn't bother me much if my actions are inconsistent.

All items are paired with a scale ranging from 1 ("Strongly disagree") to 9 ("Strongly agree"). People high in the preference for consistency are more motivated than other people to reduce cognitive dissonance.

Source: Cialdini, Trost, & Newsom (1995).

Cognitive Dissonance and Attitude Change

Persuading people can take a lot of work. But what if we could change people's attitudes simply by creating predicaments that forced them to do all the work? That is, what if we could get them to engage in self-persuasion (Wilson, 1990)?

Persuasion can, in fact, take place in the absence of persuasive communications, through more indirect processes. For example, the behaviors people engage in and the actions they take sometimes cause them to rethink their attitudes, implicitly persuading them to change those attitudes. The theory of cognitive dissonance (Cooper, 2007; Festinger, 1957), introduced in Chapter 4, explains this phenomenon. The theory states that holding two inconsistent beliefs can cause psychological discomfort, leading to a desire to resolve the inconsistency.

As we saw in Chapter 4, self-relevant thoughts are a major source of dissonance (Stone & Cooper, 2001). In general, people like to see themselves as being consistent, although that is true more for some people than for others (Cialdini, Trost, & Newsom, 1995; see **Table 6.2**). Thus, making statements or taking actions that conflict with our own attitudes often arouses dissonance ("I really like Bob Marks" versus "I just refused to donate a dollar to the Bob Marks campaign").

Induced Compliance

This point is illustrated most dramatically by studies of **induced compliance**, in which people are subtly pressured to violate their usual standards of behavior. You may recall one such study, described in Chapter 4, in which Festinger and Carlsmith (1959) aroused dissonance in research participants by coaxing them into lying about how much they enjoyed a boring experimental task (see **page 148**). Other common methods involve asking people to write essays that conflict with their attitudes (Cooper, Zanna, & Taves, 1978) or to deliver a speech favoring a policy or proposal they are against (Goethals, Cooper, & Naficy, 1979). For years, experiments of this kind were among the most common studies conducted by social psychologists (Aronson, 1992; Cooper, 2007; Harmon-Jones & Mills, 1999; Stone, 2001). They revealed that when people comply with such requests (as they usually do), despite feeling that they are not really justified in doing so, they experience dissonance. To eliminate (or at least reduce) the dissonance, they change their attitudes to conform more closely to their behavior.

For instance, in Festinger and Carlsmith's (1959) study, the participants who were paid $1 for lying reported liking the boring task more than those who were paid $20. Because the participants who received $20 could reason that anyone would tell a relatively harmless lie for that sum of money, they did not experience dissonance. Similarly, in the Cooper at al. (1978) study, some participants were instructed to write a disagreeable essay (in favor of pardoning President Richard Nixon, who had recently resigned in disgrace); others were led to believe they had a choice. Members of the latter group were more likely to report dissonance-induced attitude change, because they could not justify their behavior by telling themselves they had written the essay against their will.

There are other ways to deal with dissonance. For example, you could trivialize or minimize the importance of dissonant cognitions (Simon, Greenberg, & Brehm, 1995): "In the grand scheme of things, lying about the experiment is no big deal; the guy I lied to was required to participate in the research, and most of these experiments are boring, anyway." Alternatively, you could change one of the dissonant cognitions, so as to construe your inconsistent behavior differently: "I'll bet the person I lied to didn't believe me anyway and refused to participate in the experiment." These other methods of dissonance reduction are not always feasible, though.

Resolving cognitive dissonance.

If someone you liked asked you to taste a fried grasshopper, you might just chalk it up to something you do for a friend. But how would you deal with the dissonance you would feel if you complied with the same request from a person you loathe? According to Zimbardo, Weisenberg, Firestone, and Levy (1965), you would decide that you like eating grasshoppers.

Preconditions for Cognitive Dissonance

You may be able to recall some occasion on which, without overwhelming pressure, you said or did something that did not reflect your true attitudes, but did not change your attitudes as a result. Indeed, Cooper and Fazio (1984) concluded that several conditions are necessary for arousing dissonance (see **Figure 6.7**). First, the behavior must lead to some sort of negative consequence (Scher & Cooper, 1989). If you were asked to write an essay arguing that

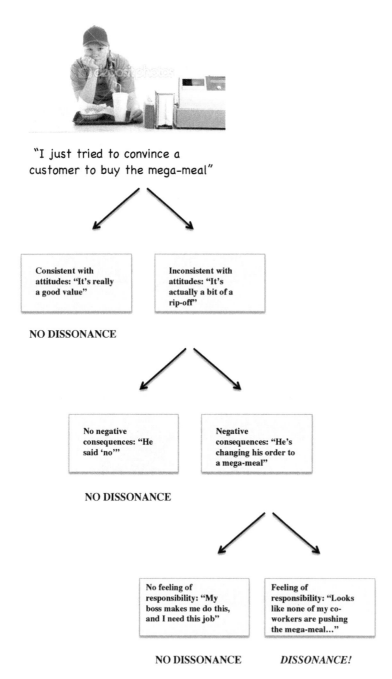

"I just tried to convince a customer to buy the mega-meal"

| Consistent with attitudes: "It's really a good value" | Inconsistent with attitudes: "It's actually a bit of a rip-off" |

NO DISSONANCE

| No negative consequences: "He said 'no'" | Negative consequences: "He's changing his order to a mega-meal" |

NO DISSONANCE

| No feeling of responsibility: "My boss makes me do this, and I need this job" | Feeling of responsibility: "Looks like none of my co-workers are pushing the mega-meal…" |

NO DISSONANCE   *DISSONANCE!*

Figure 6.7: Conditions necessary for dissonance.

young children should be allowed to play with the most violent computer games, but were told that the essay would just be read by an experimenter and then discarded, the only negative outcome would likely be embarrassment. But what if the essay would be used to overturn a law preventing six-year-olds from purchasing computer games with graphic depictions of shootings, stabbings, and beatings? That negative outcome could create a great deal of dissonance for some people.

Cooper and Fazio (1984) suggested that dissonance also depends on a feeling of personal responsibility for your behavior. In other words, people must feel that they had a choice, even if they did not, and must believe that the negative results of their behavior were foreseeable (Goethals et al., 1979). Thus, if you were forced at gunpoint to write an essay extolling the positive benefits of ultraviolent video games, you might not be happy about it, but you would not experience dissonance. Similarly, if you learned only after writing the essay that it would be used to promote the sale of such games to children, you would be less likely to experience dissonance.

Induced Hypocrisy

Stone, Aronson, Crain, Winslow, and Fried (1994; see also Stone, Wiegand, Cooper, & Aronson, 1997) challenged the idea that to induce dissonance, researchers must manipulate people into doing something that they expect will cause a negative outcome. In a variant of the induced compliance procedure that they call "induced hypocrisy," Stone et al. asked college students to compose and deliver speeches that were *consistent* with their attitudes. Half the participants composed a message about safe sex, which they thought would be presented to high school students, and then were videotaped delivering the speech. The other participants simply wrote speeches and were led to believe that only the experimenters would read them. Stone et al. then asked half the participants—whether they had delivered a speech or not—to think about and list the occasions in which they had personally failed to use condoms. The researchers expected that a perceived discrepancy between participants' speeches and their past behavior would produce dissonance, even though participants had been asked to "make a speech that clearly has positive consequences for the audience" (Stone et al., 1994, p. 126).

How could participants in this study reduce their dissonance? The solution was simple: practice safer sex in the future! In fact, when participants were contacted 90 days later, those who had made the safe sex speech and then been made aware of their hypocrisy

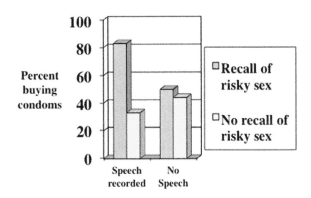

Figure 6.8: *Percentage of students who bought condoms as a function of making a speech advocating safe sex and recalling risky sex.*

Participants who publicly advocated safe sex and also recalled their own risky behavior experienced dissonance, which they resolved by changing their behavior.

Source: Stone, Aronson, Crain, Winslow, and Fried (1994).

were more likely than others to have purchased condoms. Just making a speech or thinking about their past behavior was not enough to trigger dissonance; only a combination of the two was aversive enough to change their attitudes and behaviors (see **Figure 6.8**).

Beyond Induced Compliance

Just as cognitive dissonance theory involves more than attitude change, dissonance-induced attitude change involves more than induced compliance. There are other sources of dissonance. For instance, we would expect that if a group were associated with verbal and physical humiliation, people would not be very fond of that group. What prediction could be simpler? Yet a person's positive attitude toward and devotion to a group like a fraternity or sorority can actually be *enhanced* by the severity of the group's initiation rite (Aronson & Mills, 1959). Apparently, the only way to justify putting oneself through hell to be accepted into a club or organization is to persuade oneself that membership in the group is extraordinarily desirable. Otherwise, the contrast between the cognition "I haven't decided whether I want to join this crowd" and "I just let them throw eggs at my naked body" would produce intolerable dissonance.

Cognitive dissonance theory can also explain why people will try to justify or rationalize a decision after making a difficult choice between two approximately equivalent alternatives—for example, two attractive, reasonably priced high-performance automobiles. In such circumstances, consumers emphasize the favorable features of their chosen alternative and the unfavorable features of the other alternative. Otherwise, the possibility that they have made a bad decision could trigger uncomfortable levels of dissonance (Brehm, 1956). Often—especially when the decision seems irreversible—this kind of post-decisional dissonance reduction includes an active search for information that will justify the choice (Frey, 1986; Frey & Rosch, 1984).

At least one study of post-decisional dissonance indicates that what might seem to us a necessary condition for dissonance—conscious awareness of the dissonance-arousing cognitions—actually is not crucial. Lieberman, Ochsner, Gilbert, and Schachter (2001) found that after choosing between similarly liked stimuli (art prints, in this case), participants liked the ones they chose more than they did before and the ones they rejected less than before. What is notable about this study is the identity of some of their participants: they were people with anterograde amnesia who were unable to form new memories. In other words, they could not even remember being asked to choose between the stimuli. Despite not being able to remember or think about their dissonance-arousing choices, however, their attitudes changed just as much as non-amnesic participants' attitudes. Evidently, the processes that are triggered by cognitive dissonance can take place without our awareness.

Attitude Change Via Self-Perception

The claim that we can change people's attitudes by inducing them to do things they might not otherwise do is universally accepted by social psychologists. Explaining that finding, however, has at times been a matter of dispute. One account is provided by self-perception theory (Bem, 1972). The theory states that people come to know who they are, what they believe, and how they feel, simply by observing and recalling their own behavior (see Chapter 4). People then use the evidence they uncover to reach the same conclusion that any other reasonable person would reach. When asked how you evaluate "television," for example, instead of looking within yourself for some general summary of your feelings—that is, an "attitude"—you might answer based on an estimate of how much time you spend watching TV.

Bem (1967, 1972; Bem & McConnell, 1970) suggested that self-perception theory could explain the results of induced compliance experiments. In the Festinger and Carlsmith (1959) study, for example, participants who were paid one dollar to say that a dull experimental task was interesting might not have claimed to have relatively positive feelings about it in order to reduce dissonance. Instead, they might have done so after noting that they had praised the task without receiving much of an inducement. If they had learned that someone else had done the same thing, they would probably have concluded that he or she also had a positive attitude toward the task, and so reached the same conclusion about themselves.

This explanation may not seem very intuitive. Surely people have more access to their own thoughts and feelings than to other people's, and that knowledge must be useful to them. On the other hand, the self-perception explanation is arguably more parsimonious (see Chapter 2) than the cognitive dissonance explanation, because it does not assume the existence of an internal mental state known as dissonance.

The challenge presented by self-perception theory motivated researchers to seek independent evidence for the existence of cognitive dissonance. They discovered that situations that could be expected to give rise to dissonance really do trigger physiological arousal in people (Croyle & Cooper, 1983; Elkin & Leippe, 1986), and that people perceive that arousal to be unpleasant (Zanna, Higgins, & Taves, 1976). Furthermore, arousal is necessary for attitude change to take place. If a person is given a tranquilizing drug after being put in a dissonance-arousing situation, the degree of resultant attitude change is significantly reduced (Cooper et al., 1978). Although arousal is necessary for attitude change to take place, it is not sufficient (that is, not enough in and of itself). The arousal must be associated with counter-attitudinal behavior, so that it seems to have been caused by an action that a person might regret. If people are encouraged to attribute their arousal to something else like their external surroundings (for example, a cramped, unpleasant research room) or an upcoming event (say, a study that involves electric shocks), attitude change can be made to disappear (Fazio & Cooper, 1983; Pittman, 1975; Zanna & Cooper, 1974).

Do these findings invalidate self-perception theory? Not at all. As Fazio, Zanna, and Cooper (1977) propose, both cognitive dissonance theory and self-perception theory can account for attitude change following behavior, but in different situations (see also Beauvois, Bungert, & Mariette, 1995). When people are led to engage in behavior that violates their usual standards—when they do something they would rather not have done—the attitude change that results can be better explained in terms of dissonance reduction. When their behavior does not conflict with their preexisting attitudes, self-perception theory probably provides a better explanation for changes in attitude. For example, if someone subtly coerces you to sign a petition demanding more lenient sentences for athletes who engage in illegal steroid use, any reduction of the anger and disgust you feel toward those athletes would probably result from dissonance reduction. If, on the other hand, you were manipulated into signing a petition demanding fairer treatment for the people of Zorgonia (a fictional country), any favorable feelings you might develop toward Zorgonians would probably result from self-perception processes.

Similarly, if voters found themselves waving a cardboard fan, writing with a pen, or using a mouse pad bearing a politician's name and face (or constantly visiting a website associated with that politician), they might find themselves feeling more supportive toward his or her campaign. Depending on their initial attitudes, this increase in support would come about via different processes. For those who were initially indifferent, self-perception would explain the change; for those who were initially opposed, cognitive dissonance reduction would more likely explain it. Either way, these people would probably be more willing than in the past to place bumper stickers on their cars extolling the candidate's virtues.

In sum, attitude change that results from actions that make us uncomfortable arises from the need to reduce dissonance; attitude change that results from more trivial behaviors arises from self-perception processes. In either case, we are unlikely to be aware of the hidden influences that led us to change our attitudes. In fact, as we saw in Chapter 5, when our attitudes change, we are often unaware of it (Bem & McConnell, 1970; Goethals & Reckman, 1973; Ross, 1989).

How We Behave Affects How We Feel and What We Believe: A Summary

When we do something shameful or hypocritical, we not only feel bad (that is, experience dissonance), we are motivated to make our bad feelings go away. One way to feel better is to change our attitudes ("I guess I shouldn't feel so bad about insulting that person; she deserved it"). In the absence of such conflicts, even mundane behaviors can shape our attitudes ("I keep lending paper and pens to that person in my class; I must like her"). Knowing about these tendencies is important, because real-life agents of persuasion use them to influence our behavior, and more often than not, to encourage us to part with our hard-earned money. In fact, some prominent researchers have studied these issues not just through experimental work, but by spending time with the real "experts"—that is, by taking time off from academia to work as salespeople (Cialdini, 2000; Levine, 2003).

How can we arm ourselves to resist unwanted attempts at persuasion? And if we find ourselves on the other side of the struggle, what can we do to counteract efforts to resist *our* attempts at persuasion? The final section of this chapter will be devoted to these issues.

Think Like a Social Psychologist

Designing research

—How might you use social-cognitive neuroscience methods to explain when attitudes change as a result of dissonance reduction and when they change as a result of self-perception processes?

Confronting social issues

—Cults often encourage new recruits to master their leader's writings, which can be voluminous, hard to follow, and full of obscure terminology and self-contradictory arguments. From the perspective of cognitive dissonance theory, why might the effort that people put into this task cause them to become more deeply committed to the cult?

Making connections

—In induced compliance studies of cognitive dissonance, half the participants are usually placed in a "no-choice" condition and are told that they must engage in counter-attitudinal behavior. The other half are placed in a "free-choice" condition and are subject to less pressure from the experimenters. Nonetheless, the vast majority of "free-choice" participants go along with the experimenters' request to say or do something that violates their usual standards. Relate this observation to the discussion of the fundamental attribution error in Chapter 3 and to the general finding that people underestimate the effects of situational constraints on their behavior.

RESISTING PERSUASION

The Selling of Bob, Part 3: Bob's Battle with Boos, Barbs, and Bad Press

Bob was breathing easy when he was leading his opponent in the polls by 15 percent. He still slept quite soundly when the papers reported the gap had shrunk to 12 percent (after all, survey results always have some margin of error). But he had to admit to being a little worried when his lead shrank to 10 percent. When yet another survey, taken just a month before the election suggested a gap of just 7 percent, he could not deny the pattern. If he didn't do something to reverse the trend, Bob realized, he might as well start working on his concession speech.

Ordinarily, Bob's way of dealing with his rapidly weakening position would have been to fall back on his strengths, by reminding people why he was an attractive candidate to begin with. Nobody in state government had fought harder for public schools over the last decade, but maybe voters needed to hear again how Bob had increased funding for elementary education, helping to attract and retain high-quality teachers and school administrators. Unfortunately, whenever he touched on the theme in his speeches, he was immediately disrupted by hecklers. They were obviously planted by his opponent—a fact that was probably clear even to many in the audience. Still, their taunts were quite effective at distracting people from what he was saying. "Hey, Bob," shouted one, "what good will it do our kids to learn algebra if they're going to get shot and killed in gang crossfire before they graduate?" Another got laughs when he cut Bob off with "And where are all these brilliant kids going to go? Out of state, of course—it's not like there are any jobs here." By raising questions about Bob's positions on law enforcement and the economy, the hecklers were devaluing his contributions to education.

Bob called a staff meeting and asked for ways to address the problem. Howard Loranger, now part of the campaign's inner circle, did more than generate ideas; he had drafted the text of a pamphlet to be handed out at campaign rallies and posted online. The pamphlet was designed with one strategy in mind: rather than trying to distract people from efforts to undermine Bob's status as the "education candidate," why not confront the attacks directly and show voters how baseless they were? For example, it pointed out that higher school attendance and graduation rates were inversely related to crime levels. And it argued that with a better-educated, more achievement-oriented workforce, the state would be better able to attract new employers.

The pamphlets were produced and widely distributed. Though the hecklers didn't disappear immediately, their comments soon lost their power. Instead of being rewarded with laughs, the hecklers found themselves being told to be quiet by other audience members. In effect, Howard had come up with a way to help people resist the hecklers' attempts to change their attitudes toward Bob. The method he developed has been shown by experimental research to be effective. As we will see, research has found support for other methods, too, and it also sheds light on how to overcome people's resistance.

To a certain extent, of course, resistance to an argument is simply the flip side of persuasion. Any discussion of the variables associated with yielding to a persuasive message is also a discussion of the variables that help make people immune to persuasion. For example, if low intelligence increases the likelihood that one will be persuaded by weak arguments, high intelligence increases resistance to such arguments (Eagly & Warren,

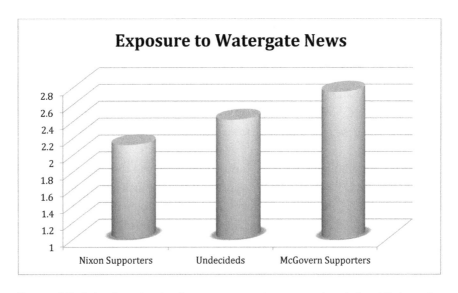

Figure 6.9: Intentional selective exposure to news about the Watergate scandal as it unfolded.

The scandal led to President Richard Nixon's resignation. The question asked participants was, "In keeping up with the news these days, do you find you are paying a great deal of attention to what is going on in the Watergate affair; some attention; or no attention at all?" (1 = none, 2 = some, 3 = a great deal).

Based on data reported by Sweeney & Gruber (1984).

1976). Likewise, if a warning about an imminent attempt to change one's attitudes increases resistance to persuasion (Hass & Grady, 1975), a counter-attitudinal message that is *not* expected increases the likelihood of persuasion.

Nonetheless, a distinction can be made between simply not being persuaded and active resistance to persuasion. As Knowles and Linn (2004b) note, most research on persuasion seems to implicitly adopt the perspective of the persuader, focusing on when different kinds of messages will persuade different kinds of people in different contexts. Much can be learned, however, by taking the perspective of the *targets* of persuasion, especially those who may actively resist assaults on their attitudes and beliefs. How do they resist? Why do they do so? And what can the answers to these questions tell us about how someone with a message to spread might break down their resistance?

General Resistance Processes

A variety of basic strategies can be used to resist persuasion (Levine, 2003). Briñol, Rucker, Tormala, and Petty (2004, p. 95) note that some of those strategies "do not necessitate a great deal of thought." For instance, you can justify dismissing a message simply by derogating (putting down) the person who delivers the message (Jacks & Cameron, 2003; Lapinski & Boster, 2001; Tannenbaum, Macauley, & Norris, 1966). If the person who is trying to change your attitude cannot be taken seriously, then neither can his or her arguments. You can also selectively attend to arguments and information that support your own attitudes and ignore counter-attitudinal information (Frey, 1986; Baumeister & Newman, 1994). For example, in the early 1970s, then president of the United States Richard Nixon was linked to a scandal that led ultimately to his resignation. Most Americans followed the story, known as the Watergate scandal, very closely. But one group of people paid significantly less attention to Watergate news: strong supporters of President Nixon (Sweeney & Gruber, 1984; see **Figure 6.9**).

You can also ignore or discount the content of a message because of doubts about its truth. For example, you could conclude that spokespersons for politicians and other public figures have presented certain arguments simply because they have been told to do so. Or you might suspect that a speaker is just saying what he believes the audience wants to hear. Note, however, that sometimes a certain amount of cognitive work must be done to reach the conclusion that a message should be discounted (Eagly, Chaiken, & Wood, 1981; Eagly, Wood, & Chaiken, 1978).

Other strategies necessitate a bit more mental effort. For instance, you could repulse an assault on your attitudes by reviewing the reasons for holding them, an approach known as **attitude bolstering** (Lydon, Zanna, & Ross, 1988; Wood & Quinn, 2003). Finally, you can actively refute a persuasive appeal through **counterarguing** (Brock, 1967; Petty & Cacioppo, 1977). Although counterarguing may be the most taxing strategy of all, it may also be the most effective (Jacks & Cameron, 2003).

Motivating Resistance through Reactance

We should not be surprised that people often resist attempts to persuade them, especially when they would need to change their cherished attitudes. After all, people value their attitudes as much as or more than their most treasured possessions (Abelson & Prentice, 1989; Prentice, 1987). Still, for most, resistance is not absolute. Needless to say, it would hardly make sense to totally close off the possibility that your attitudes are based on incorrect assumptions.

Certain circumstances, however, have a tendency to arouse so much resistance that attempts at attitude change can produce a boomerang effect—that is, a change in the *opposite* direction from the one encouraged by the message. According to Brehm's (1966; Brehm & Brehm, 1981) theory of psychological **reactance**, when people feel their freedom is being restricted illegitimately, they try to reassert and restore their freedom to think, feel, and behave as they choose (Brehm & Sensenig, 1966). That is especially the case when the perceived assault on a person's freedoms concerns a highly cherished value (Fuegen & Brehm, 2004). For example, Worchel and Brehm (1970) presented participants with persuasive messages about whether or not they should support the Communist Party. Some participants heard freedom-threatening messages containing statements such as, "You cannot believe otherwise." Because of the reactance such statements caused, participants who should have agreed with the message based on their previously stated opinions instead moved *away* from the position it advocated.

Bolstering Resistance through "Inoculation"

One thing Bob Marks had going for him was his reputation for honesty and integrity. His opponent had been involved in some questionable political deals, and everyone knows that an ethical politician is better than a corrupt one. Or is that really true? Running a state government is an incredibly difficult, complicated job that requires endless negotiation, compromise, and of course, deal making. Can a "boy scout" (or "girl scout") really handle the job, or would it be better entrusted to someone with more savvy and experience—someone who is familiar with the kind of backroom deals a governor must inevitably make?

Rest assured, it is probably better to vote for saints than for sinners. However, the idea that a politician with a history of corruption is undesirable is an example of a "cultural truism," a widely accepted belief that seems obviously valid. Although all our attitudes and beliefs are probably vulnerable to attack, cultural truisms can be particularly hard to defend because we have so little practice justifying them. After all, they probably have never been challenged before.

McGuire (1964) developed an **inoculation procedure** for use in helping people to resist attacks on cultural truisms (though a similar technique could be used to protect any attitude or belief). Inoculation is a way of stimulating people's resistance to disease by exposing them to small doses of a germ, so that the body can build up defensive antibodies. People's resistance to persuasive messages can be built up through an analogous method. The procedure involves exposing them to relatively weak attacks against their beliefs (such as challenging the belief that "People should brush their teeth regularly" with "Too frequent brushing can damage the gums and expose the vulnerable parts of the teeth to decay") and either offering them counterarguments ("That would only happen with excessive and improper brushing") or letting them generate counterarguments themselves. Those who have been inoculated in this way are better able to fend off stronger efforts to change their minds than people who have not been inoculated. In fact, inoculation is more effective than simply arming people with arguments in support of a cultural truism; fending off a mock assault seems to be the key (McGuire & Papageorgis, 1961; Papageorgis & McGuire, 1961).

Inoculation helps people to defend themselves not just against familiar attacks, but against novel arguments. Moreover, it strengthens people's attitudes and beliefs in two ways. First, it motivates people to engage in bolstering and defense. The second way has to do with the practice people get in fending off mild attacks, which increases their ability to resist later attacks (Sagarin & Cialdini, 2004). When people are able to ward off attempts to change their attitudes—especially strong attempts—the certainty with which they hold those

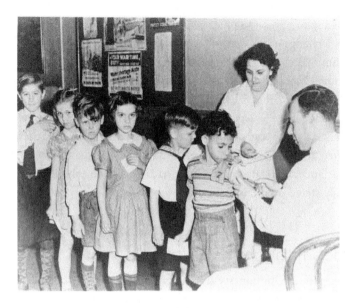

According to inoculation theory, just as exposure to small doses of a disease agent can bolster your physical defenses against a disease, exposure to weak attacks against your attitudes can bolster your psychological defenses against attempts to change your attitudes.

Money back guarantees weaken people's resistance to sales pitches by lowering the stakes involved in deciding to purchase a product or service.

attitudes increases (Tormala & Petty, 2002, 2004).

Howard Loranger's approach to fending off attempts to ridicule Bob Marks's record in support of the schools should now make sense. What could be less controversial than the idea that support for education is good? Such a belief is essentially a cultural truism, much like "Corrupt politicians are bad." As a result, it was highly vulnerable to the hecklers' attacks. Once voters were shown how easily the attacks could be refuted, however, they were able to dismiss them, along with further attacks. They had been inoculated. That was good news for Bob, because when people *cannot* fend off such attacks, or feel that they have done a poor job of doing so, their certainty about their attitudes can actually *decrease* (Tormala & Petty, 2002, 2004; Tormala, Clarkson, & Petty, 2006).

Breaking Down Resistance: A General Framework

The ways in which people resist persuasion can suggest ways to *overcome* resistance. To deal with counterarguing, for example, you could create an even stronger argument. To prevent derogation of the source of a message, you could choose a source so credible that such a strategy would be next to impossible. Bolstering might be prevented by denying people the time to introspect about their attitudes and beliefs. And the tendency to selectively attend to attitude-congruent information might be overcome by motivating (or somehow forcing) people to carefully consider all your arguments. All these strategies could be derived fairly easily from the ELM and HSM, since they are aimed at providing compelling evidence for central/systematic processors, valid persuasion cues for peripheral/heuristic processors, or reasons

Table 6.3: Omega strategies for overcoming resistance to persuasion

SIDESTEPPING RESISTANCE

Discourage people from working up the effort to resist by framing the interaction as if it concerns something else ("I just want to help you reach the right decision") or by pushing the consequence of a decision far into the future.

ADDRESS RESISTANCE DIRECTLY

Make people believe that their reasons for resisting are irrelevant.

ADDRESS RESISTANCE INDIRECTLY

Encourage people to focus their worry and mental effort on something other than the persuasion attempt.

DISTRACT FROM RESISTANCE

Prevent people from marshaling the mental energy needed to argue against a persuasion attempt.

DISRUPT RESISTANCE

Confuse people by making a persuasion attempt in an unusual way, so that their well-practiced methods of resisting persuasion will be less accessible to them.

USING RESISTANCE TO PROMOTE CHANGE

Using "reverse psychology" to challenge people *not* to resist by pretending that you want them to resist.

Source: Knowles and Linn (2004a).

for engaging in careful, unbiased information processing. Knowles and Linn (2004a) label these kinds of efforts to prevent resistance **Alpha strategies**. Alpha strategies focus on direct attempts to make a persuasive message more compelling and attractive.

But another, less direct approach to conquering resistance involves strategies for "removing or disengaging someone's reluctance to change," which Knowles and Linn (2004a, p. 118) call **Omega strategies**. Such strategies are more indirect than alpha strategies; they focus less on strengthening a message than on undermining people's motivation to resist it. Brief descriptions of a few such strategies follow; **Table 6.3** summarizes them and provides some examples.

Sidestepping Resistance

There are a number of ways to sidestep resistance—that is, to prevent the impulse to resist from arising. One way to do so is to cleverly redefine the relationship between the people involved. For example, a person whose goal is to convince you to switch to a new telephone or Internet service provider may claim to want to help you save money. In framing the interaction that way, she might suggest that the two of you have a cooperative relationship and are working toward the same goal. Of course, the persuader's goal might really be to do or say anything within legal limits to make the sale. Compliments and flattery can decrease resistance via similar processes (Grant, Fabrigar, & Lim, 2010).

Another way to sidestep resistance is to push the consequences of a decision far into the future. When the potentially negative consequences of a decision are not immediate, people are likely to be more compliant (Sherman, Crawford, & McConnell, 2004). Common examples of this technique are deals that allow you to take home some major consumer item (a car, a washing machine) without paying anything for a year. If you

SOCIAL PSYCHOLOGY IN THE COURTROOM: INTERROGATION TECHNIQUES

When law enforcement officials have in their custody someone they believe has committed a crime, they would like that person to confess. Of course, sometimes the suspect must be persuaded to make a statement. Researchers who study the persuasive techniques used in police interrogation rooms have noted two broad approaches, similar to Knowles and Linn's (2004a) distinction between Alpha and Omega strategies.

As Kassin (1997, p. 221) notes, "Gone are the days when the police would shine [a] bright light on suspects, grill them for 24 hours at a time, or beat them with a rubber hose." But interrogators still have several tools at their disposal, which Kassin and McNall (1991; Kassin & Gudjonsson, 2004) divide into two broad categories: maximization techniques and minimization techniques. **Maximization techniques** place direct pressure on suspects in an attempt to convince them that they have no choice but to admit their guilt, or would be fools not to. For example, suspects could be told that the evidence pointing to their guilt is overwhelming, even if that is not really the case (in other words, the police could make false or exaggerated claims about the strength of the evidence). Alternatively, suspects could be told that failure to confess will result in a serious sentence, such as death or life imprisonment, while confession (regardless of their actual guilt) will lead to a much more lenient sentence. Such maximization techniques, commonly known as "scare tactics," resemble the Alpha approach to crushing resistance.

Minimization techniques—commonly known as "the soft sell"—involve more indirect attempts to undermine a suspect's reluctance to confess. For instance, the interrogators might express sympathy for the suspect or provide excuses for the crime. A suspected murderer might be told "We all know he got what was coming to him"; someone charged with rape might hear "You really loved her—you just lost control, right?" Instead of exaggerating the seriousness of the charges (a maximization technique), the interrogators might subtly suggest that the alleged crime was not that serious. Such minimization techniques resemble the Omega approach to dealing with resistance.

These strategies may seem benign, even commendable, assuming that only guilty people are pressured to confess to crimes. Tragically, that is not the case (Gudjonsson, 1992; Kassin, 2005; Radelet, Bedau, & Putnam, 1992; Russano, Meissner, Narchet, & Kassin, 2005). Furthermore, not only can innocent people be led to confess by means of such tactics; they can, in some circumstances, actually come to *believe* their own false confessions (Wright, 1994). This phenomenon, known as a false internalized confession, is especially likely to occur when people feel that they cannot trust their own memories (because they were severely intoxicated when the crime allegedly occurred, for example) and are confronted with convincing false evidence (Kassin, 1997).

In a laboratory study, Kassin and Kiechel (1996) induced false internalized confessions in participants whom they had urged not to touch a particular button on a computer keyboard, purportedly because it would cause the computer to crash and ruin an experiment. Shortly after the study began, the computer appeared to malfunction, and the experimenter accused the participant of having pressed the forbidden button. (No one actually did so.) When circumstances caused participants to question their memory of what had happened (because the procedure was fast-paced and confusing) and a confederate of the experimenters claimed to have seen them press the button, all agreed to sign a confession stating that their error had ruined the experiment. In fact, over two-thirds eventually came to believe that they had really pressed the forbidden key. In other conditions that were run at a more leisurely pace, and/or did not include false eyewitness testimony, participants were significantly less likely to confess, much less accept their own guilt.

have ever asked yourself something like, "What was I thinking last month when I agreed to water my friend's houseplants every day during her three-week vacation?" you should recognize this strategy.

Addressing Resistance Directly or Indirectly

Resistance cannot always be dissolved so easily. Even so, there are ways of addressing it. One strategy is to identify the source of the resistance and render it irrelevant. For instance, people might resist pressure to purchase a product or service because they are afraid they will discover it was not worth the money. Providing a money-back guarantee counteracts that reason for resisting. Indeed, such guarantees really do reduce consumer risk. From a retailer's perspective, however, what is more important is that they may mean the difference between a consumer leaving the store with a new toaster or not leaving the store with a new toaster.

Sometimes, resistance may be redirected rather than neutralized. Sagarin and Cialdini (2004) found that when people are encouraged to resist messages from illegitimate sources ("I'm not a doctor, but I play one on TV"), they become more prone than otherwise to persuasion by sources that *do* seem legitimate. One variant of this method is the "good cop, bad cop" approach to police interrogation. When one interrogator plays the role of the vicious, vindictive brute, suspects will focus on protecting themselves from him. As a result, they will become vulnerable to the subtle pressure to confess exerted by the "nice" interviewer (see the Social Psychology in the Courtroom box on **page 270**).

Distracting from Resistance

Resistance often arises from unfavorable thoughts about a persuasive message and/or the person delivering the message. Generating those thoughts can take some work, however (Wheeler, Briñol, & Hermann, 2007). When people are distracted, they may have less time and energy to engage in that kind of thinking (Petty et al., 1976). A classic persuasive technique used by vacuum cleaner salespeople is to pour dirt and ashes on a customer's rug and then clean it up. In part, doing so allows the salesperson to demonstrate the vacuum cleaner's effectiveness. But salespeople may have learned at least implicitly over the years that when customers are worrying about whether their rugs have been ruined, they are less able to mentally compute what all those monthly payments will add up to—and less ready to resist the inevitable sales pitch.

Disrupting Resistance

A few years ago, one of the authors of this book was roused from sleep very early in the morning by a ringing doorbell. The young man at the door said that his car needed a jump-start. He also wanted to know exactly how jump-starting worked. Were some cables better than others for it? Where did the wires from the car battery lead?

How many of them were there? Fortunately, the author knows next to nothing about the workings of automobiles, or he might have been drawn into a conversation about those technical issues and found himself putting on his coat to go outside and demonstrate his expertise. Instead, he became aware of the bizarre nature of the interaction and called the police. Indeed, what he experienced turned out to be the prelude to a complicated scam, for the poor stranded motorist was in reality a con man.

Rather than distracting people, sometimes simply confusing them can lower their resistance. Framing a persuasion attempt in an odd or unexpected way can create confusion about the message's meaning, which can make the target of the attempt vulnerable. Santos, Leve, and Pratkanis (1994) found that panhandlers who requested the odd amount of 37 cents were more likely to receive donations than those who asked for a quarter—even though 37 cents is obviously more than 25 cents. And Davis and Knowles (1999) discovered that by stating a price as "three hundred pennies" instead of "three dollars," they could persuade more people to buy note cards—especially when they took advantage of the confusion people were feeling by encouraging them to believe that the price was a "bargain " (see **Table 6.4**). Another study described by Knowles and Linn (2004a) suggested that calling toothpaste "mouthpaste" could have the same effect.

Using Resistance to Promote Change

Sometimes, resistance can be turned against itself. In other words, if you cannot think of a way to stop people from resisting, actually encouraging them to resist may cause them to drop their guard. This strategy is popularly known as "reverse psychology"; the idea is to pretend that you do *not* want people to do exactly what you *want* them to do. Knowles and Linn (2004a) presented college students with several persuasive messages on topics like the inadequacy of on-campus parking and the possibility of an increase in tuition. The messages were all counter-attitudinal (for example, "Higher tuition leads to a better education"), but half of them were preceded with the phrase "You won't believe this, but … " Students who heard that simple phrase were more likely to accept the arguments.

Resistance and Its Breakdown: A Summary

Resisting persuasion typically involves being aware that your attitudes are being targeted and taking steps to fend off the attack (for instance, via counterarguing, attitude bolstering, and selective attention). Some of the most effective strategies for neutralizing resistance involve creating a situation in which people are unaware that persuasion is being attempted or do not have the time or energy to resist the attempt. In other words,

Table 6.4: Percentage of people who purchased cards from a door-to-door salesman, by type of request

CONDITION	PERCENTAGE OF PEOPLE WHO BOUGHT CARDS
"They're $3"	25
"They're $3. It's a bargain"	30
"They're 300 pennies … That's $3"	35
"They're 300 pennies … That's $3. That's a bargain"	70

Neither the confusing, disruptive comment ("300 pennies") nor the comment defining the transaction as a "bargain" was enough to break down resistance to persuasion. Both were necessary, a strategy known as "disrupt-then-reframe."

Source: Based on the results of Davis & Knowles (1999), Study 2.

overcoming resistance often involves unleashing hidden influences on people's behavior. As always, the best defense against hidden influences is an awareness that they exist, as well as sensitivity to their presence.

Think Like a Social Psychologist

Understanding everyday behavior

—During adolescence, many people see themselves and present themselves to others as being as different as possible from their parents. What might be the role of reactance in that phenomenon?

—You may already have purchased an automobile from a car dealer; if not, you may someday do so. Generate a list of the many different ways that a salesman could use Omega strategies to persuade you to buy a car.

Designing research

—Imagine that you want to convince other students to contribute to a relief effort on behalf of people who are starving in a far-off country. Based on all the material in this chapter, what factors would you need to take into account in developing your appeal? How exactly would you take those factors into account?

Thinking critically

—A great deal (but by no means all) of the research on persuasion and attitude change has been conducted with college students (most commonly, first-year students and sophomores) as research participants. What might be the implications of using that particular population as targets of persuasion for generalizing about the malleability of attitudes?

SOCIAL PSYCHOLOGY ENCOUNTERS THE DARK SIDE: THE SLEEPER EFFECT

Research shows that people take the nature of the source into account when they are presented with a persuasive communication. For example, their reactions to a drug endorsement from a Nobel Prize–winning biochemist will not be the same as their reactions to the same endorsement from the manufacturer's paid representative. If we ask the message recipients about their attitudes toward the drug immediately after they heard the arguments, we would expect those who heard them presented by the trustworthy source to hold more favorable attitudes than those who heard them from the untrustworthy source. What would happen, though, if we measured people's attitudes a month later? (And what would happen if we could get in touch with all those people at the state fair who laughed as a clown endorsed Bob Marks for governor?) Would the message they heard have actually changed their attitudes in a lasting way?

Research on the **sleeper effect** (Gruder, Cook, Hennigan, Flay, Alessis, & Halamaj, 1978; Hovland, Lumsdaine, & Sheffield, 1949; Kumkale & Albarracin, 2004) shows that responses to a persuasive message can change significantly over time. Specifically, the impact of some messages increases after a delay. Over 50 years ago, Hovland and Weiss (1951) presented U.S. college students with arguments about what were then considered controversial issues. Half the time the messages came from a credible, trustworthy source; half the time they came from a source that was suspect. For example, a message in favor of building atomic submarines was said to have come either from a respected U.S. atomic scientist or from the Soviet newspaper *Pravda*. Similarly, an argument about the causes of a steel shortage was associated with either an official-sounding national organization or a journalist who was known to be biased. When asked for their own opinions immediately after being exposed to the arguments, participants reported being significantly persuaded by messages from highly credible sources, but not very persuaded by messages from less credible sources. Four weeks later, however, that difference had disappeared. On average, all participants reported attitude changes that were consistent with the arguments, and they did so to the same degree, regardless of the source.

The most famous demonstrations of the sleeper effect involve messages that gained power over time, despite coming from untrustworthy sources. However, the sleeper effect has also been observed even in the face of other kinds of cues that usually cause people to discount a message's validity. For example, Gruder et al. (1978) presented participants with persuasive appeals that supposedly came from a magazine. Half the time the messages were accompanied with a note from the editor, claiming that the arguments were based on faulty assumptions. Nonetheless, the messages that were paired with this "discounting cue" seemed more compelling to people six weeks later than they did when they were first presented.

Lest you conclude that the sleeper effect arises from lazy thinking, we should note that it is actually *more* pronounced when people pay careful attention to the original message (Kumkale & Albarracin, 2004). Apparently, people are prone to this effect even when they should clearly recognize that an argument may not be valid. Hence, research on the sleeper effect suggests that communications from people who are clearly trying to deceive or manipulate us can affect our attitudes, despite our recognition that they should not be trusted.

SOCIAL PSYCHOLOGY ENCOUNTERS THE BRIGHT SIDE: THE SLEEPER EFFECT REVISITED

Though the sleeper effect is real, it does have limitations. In many cases, people are quite capable of resisting a message that comes from a source they consider suspicious (Gillig & Greenwald, 1974). One of the most important variables to consider is exactly when people learn the communicator's identity. When people become aware of the nature of the source before or while they are processing a persuasive message, they not only are capable of rejecting the message, they also do not fall prey to the sleeper effect. Sleeper effects occur primarily when people learn that a communicator may not be credible *after* they have heard and thought about the message (Pratkanis, Greenwald, Leippe, & Baumgardner, 1988; Kumkale & Albarracin, 2004).

What explains this finding? When people have advance knowledge of a source's identity or some other discounting cue, they will be critical of the message and argue against it. Therefore, the arguments do not have much of an effect on them. When people do not have advance knowledge, they find themselves having just heard (1) some arguments that sounded fairly convincing; and (2) some reasons why they might want to ignore those arguments. According to Pratkanis et al. (1988), though the reasons for discounting an argument may at first have more of an impact on people, over time the effects of the discounting cue (for example, the knowledge that a communicator should not be trusted) tend to weaken more rapidly than the effects of the arguments. That may happen in part because people were exposed to the arguments first (see the discussion of primacy effects in Chapter 3). People may also spend more time processing the message than thinking about the communicator's identity.

The people and groups who pay for the political advertisements presented on television and radio typically identify themselves at the end of a message ("Hi, I'm Bob Marks, and I approve this ad"). Thus, it pays to be on guard against the possibility of a sleeper effect. Nonetheless, recent research shows that people are not always helpless to resist transparently biased attempts at persuasion.

EPILOGUE: *ELECTION DAY*

Even before all the votes were tallied, it was clear that Bob had won the election. Whether the decisive factor was how voters responded to him personally or how they responded to the content of his speeches and political ads, he could not say. Maybe he was simply the right person in the right place at the right time, appealing to the right set of voters. More likely, the interaction of all those factors had the desired persuasive effects—all without anyone's awareness of exactly how their attitudes had been altered.

Needless to say, Bob celebrated with his family, friends, and colleagues. After a couple of days, though, it was time to get back to work; he had to assemble the team that would help him run the state government. Bob was hoping that Howard Loranger could play some sort of role. Besides everything else Howard had done, he had helped to rally the campaign volunteers with a rousing speech during a dark period when every editorial writer in the state had seemed to turn against Bob. What Howard had to say wasn't particularly original—in fact, something about the speech seemed oddly familiar—but it had indeed been effective. Perhaps even more decisive was the way Howard had identified the most demoralized volunteers and subtly coaxed them to resolve their dissonance by publicly affirming their continuing devotion to Bob's candidacy. All those people ended up staying the course.

Unfortunately, Howard could not be persuaded to talk with Bob about the future. Finally, Bob broke down his resistance by waking him up with a phone call at 5:30 in the morning, when he was too groggy to come up with reasons for avoiding a meeting. After some prodding, Howard tried to explain why he was embarrassed by the job offer. His background, he pointed out, was a little different from that of the other higher-ups in the campaign. He was not a lawyer, a businessman, or a white-collar professional of any sort. In fact, Bob might be embarrassed if Howard's work history leaked out. He had enjoyed his last job, which he had taken to earn money for his college education. But "carnival worker" wasn't exactly the most prestigious of occupations—even though running a dunking booth involved some technical skill, and walking around all day in a heavy clown suit required a lot of stamina. Surely Bob remembered how hot it had been the day of the state fair? And by the way, Howard asked, what *did* Bob think about the speech he had given on his behalf that day?

HIDDEN INFLUENCES ON PERSUASION AND ATTITUDE CHANGE: A SUMMARY

Peripheral cues: the extent to which you are persuaded by a message can be affected by aspects of the message (for example, its length), the communicator (for example, her attractiveness), or the context (for example, others' reactions) that may have little do with the message's validity.

Heuristic processing: without being aware of it, you may use simple, well-learned decision rules (for example, "Experts are to be trusted") to decide how to respond to a persuasive message.

Context variables: aspects of the situation (for example, other people's reactions) can affect how you respond to a persuasive message.

Mood effects on persuasion: although the mood you are in when you are exposed to a persuasive message has nothing to do with its validity, your mood could affect how you think about and respond to the message.

Head movements: whether or not you nod or shake your head when you are exposed to a persuasive message could, of course, be determined by your evaluation of the message, but head movements can also have an independent influence on the degree to which you are persuaded.

Omega strategies for breaking down resistance to persuasion: although people may try to overcome your resistance to persuasion by arguing directly with you, more effective strategies involve subtly undermining your reluctance to change your attitudes—ideally, without your awareness that anyone is trying to influence you.

KEY TERMS AND DEFINITIONS

Persuasion: the use of arguments and other messages to try to change people's attitudes, and the process by which that change occurs

Elaboration likelihood model (ELM): a general theory of the causes and effects of persuasion; focuses on the care with which people process persuasive messages

Elaboration likelihood continuum: a hypothetical scale that represents the extent to which people carefully think about or elaborate on persuasive messages

Central route persuasion: attitude development or change that takes place when the motivation and ability to process is high; results from careful, effortful thinking about the arguments presented in persuasive messages

Peripheral route persuasion: attitude development or change that takes place when the motivation and/or ability to process is low; results from the influence of readily available cues that are unrelated to the arguments in persuasive messages

Need for cognition: a personality trait that reflects the extent to which people enjoy engaging in frequent, deep thinking

Multiple roles hypothesis: the idea that any given persuasion variable can play more than one role in persuasion, and therefore will not always have the same effect on attitudes

Dual-process model: any account of how people make inferences, judgments, or decisions that assumes that they do so either quickly and effortlessly and/or carefully and deliberately

Heuristic-systematic model (HSM): a general model of the processes underlying persuasion; focuses on the extent to which people engage in complex thinking or rely on simple mental shortcuts to process persuasive messages

Systematic processing: careful, effortful thought about the content of a persuasive message; similar to the process involved in central route persuasion

Heuristic processing: the use of simple, well-learned decision rules in deciding how to respond to a persuasive message

Source variable: a characteristic of the person (or institution) who is presenting a persuasive message that may affect how people respond to the message

Message variable: an aspect of the persuasive message (topic, content, style) that plays a role in determining the message's impact

Context variable: an aspect of the situation in which a persuasive message is presented that affects the message's impact

Recipient variable: a characteristic of the people to whom a persuasive message is presented that may affect how they respond to the message

Credibility: a potential characteristic of the person who presents a persuasive message; combines trustworthiness and expertise

Sleeper effect: generally, the finding that the impact of some persuasive messages can change after a delay; specifically, the finding that the persuasiveness of messages from sources that are low in credibility can increase over time

Fear or threat appeal: a persuasive message that is meant to affect people by suggesting that they are vulnerable to a negative outcome

Regression to the mean: the statistical principle that extreme scores of any kind will tend to become less extreme over time

Induced compliance procedure: a method for triggering cognitive dissonance in people by subtly inducing them to engage in behaviors that conflict with their attitudes and usual standards for behavior

Attitude bolstering: a method of resisting persuasion that involves actively reviewing the justification for your current attitudes and the reasons you should not change them

Counterarguing: a method of resisting persuasion that involves an active effort to refute the arguments presented in a persuasive message

Reactance: the way people react to constraints on their freedom that are perceived to be illegitimate, including efforts to reclaim that freedom

Inoculation procedure: a technique for preparing people to defend their attitudes against strong attacks by first giving them practice in fending off weaker attacks

Alpha strategy: any method of undermining a person's motivation to resist a persuasive attempt that involves making a message seem more compelling

Omega strategy: any method of undermining a person's motivation to resist a persuasive attempt that involves undermining the person's reluctance to change an attitude or behavior

Maximization technique: a method of interrogation that involves direct pressure on a suspect to confess

Minimization technique: a method of interrogation that involves an indirect attempt to encourage a suspect to confess

REFERENCES

Abelson, R. P., & Prentice, D. A. (1989). Beliefs as possessions: A functional perspective. In A. R. Pratkanis & S. J. Breckler (Eds.), *Attitude structure and function* (pp. 361–381). Hillsdale, NJ: Lawrence Erlbaum Associates.

Albarracin, D., & Vargas, P. (2010). Attitudes and persuasion: From biology to social responses. In S. T. Fiske, D. T. Gilbert, & G. Lindzey (Eds.), *The handbook of social psychology* (5th ed., Vol. 1, pp. 394–427). Hoboken, NJ: Wiley.

Allen, M. (1991). Meta-analysis comparing the persuasiveness of one-sided versus two-sided messages. *Western Journal of Speech Communication, 55*, 390–404.

Allen, M., Hale, J., Mongeau, P., Berkowits-Stafford, S., Stafford, S., Shanahan, W., Agee, P., Dillon, K., Jackson, R., & Ray, C. (1990). Testing a model of message sidedness: Three replications. *Communication Monographs, 57,* 274–291.

Aronson, E. (1992). The return of the repressed: Dissonance theory makes a comeback. *Psychological Inquiry, 3,* 303–311.

Aronson, E., & Mills, J. (1959). The effect of severity of initiation on liking for a group. *Journal of Abnormal and Social Psychology, 59,* 177–181.

Ashmore, R. D., & Longo, L. C. (1995). Accuracy of stereotypes: What research on physical attractiveness can teach us. In Y.-T. Lee, L. J. Jussim, & C. R. McCauley (Eds.), *Stereotype accuracy: Toward appreciating group difference* (pp. 63–86). Washington, DC: American Psychological Association.

Axsom, D., Yates, S. M., & Chaiken, S. (1987). Audience response as a heuristic cue in persuasion. *Journal of Personality and Social Psychology, 53,* 30–40.

Banaji, M. R., & Heiphetz, L. (2010). Attitudes. In S. T. Fiske, D. T. Gilbert, & G. Lindzey (Eds.), *The handbook of social psychology* (5th ed., Vol. 1, pp. 353–393). Hoboken, NJ: Wiley.

Baron, R. S., Inman, M. L., Kao, C. F., & Logan, H. (1992). Negative emotion and superficial social processing. *Motivation and Emotion, 16,* 323–346.

Bassili, J. N. (1996). Meta-judgmental versus operative indexes of psychological attributes: The case of measures of attitude strength. *Journal of Personality and Social Psychology, 71,* 637–653.

Baumeister, R. F., & Newman, L. S. (1994). Self-regulation of cognitive inference and decision processes. *Personality and Social Psychology Bulletin, 20,* 3–19.

Beauvois, J. L., Bungert, M., & Mariette, P. (1995). Forced compliance: Commitment to compliance and commitment to activity. *European Journal of Social Psychology, 25,* 17–26.

Begg, I. M., Needham, D. R., & Bookbinder, M. (1993). Do backwards messages unconsciously affect listeners? No. *Canadian Journal of Experimental Psychology, 47,* 1–14.

Bem, D. J. (1967). Self-perception: An alternative interpretation of cognitive dissonance phenomena. *Psychological Review, 74,* 183–200.

Bem, D. J. (1972). Self-perception theory. In L. Berkowitz (Ed.), *Advances in experimental social psychology* (Vol. 6, pp. 1–62). New York: Academic Press.

Bem, D. J., & McConnell, H. K. (1970). Testing the self-perception explanation of dissonance phenomena: On the salience of premanipulation attitudes. *Journal of Personality and Social Psychology, 14,* 23–31.

Blaney, P. H. (1986). Affect and memory: A review. *Psychological Bulletin, 99,* 229–246.

Bless, H., Bohner, G., Schwarz, N., & Strack, F. (1990). Mood and persuasion: A cognitive response analysis. *Personality and Social Psychology Bulletin, 16,* 331–345.

Bless, H., Mackie, D. M., & Schwarz, N. (1992). Mood effects on attitude judgments: Independent effects of mood before and after message elaboration. *Journal of Personality and Social Psychology, 63,* 585–595.

Bohner, G., Chaiken, S., & Hunyadi, P. (1994). The role of mood and message ambiguity in the interplay of heuristic and systematic processing. *European Journal of Social Psychology, 24,* 207–221.

Brehm, J. W. (1956). Postdecision changes in the desirability of alternatives. *Journal of Abnormal and Social Psychology, 52,* 384–389.

Brehm, J. W. (1966). *A theory of psychological reactance.* New York: Academic Press.

Brehm, S., & Brehm, J. W (1966). *Psychological reactance: A theory of freedom and control.* New York: Academic Press.

Brehm, J. W., & Sensenig, J. (1966). Social influence as a function of attempted and implied usurpation of choice. *Journal of Personality and Social Psychology, 4,* 703–707.

Briñol, P., & Petty, R. E. (2003). Overt head movements and persuasion: A self-validation analysis. *Journal of Personality and Social Psychology, 84,* 1123–1139.

Briñol, P., Rucker, D. D., Tormala, Z. L., & Petty, R. E. (2004). Individual differences in resistance to persuasion: The role of beliefs and meta-beliefs. In E. S. Knowles & J. A. Linn (Eds.), *Resistance and persuasion* (pp. 83–104). Mahwah, NJ: Lawrence Erlbaum Associates.

Brock, T. C. (1965). Communicator-recipient similarity and decision change. *Journal of Personality and Social Psychology, 1,* 650–654.

Brock, T. C. (1967). Communication discrepancy and intent to persuade as determinants of counterargument production. *Journal of Experimental Social Psychology, 3,* 296–309.

Byrne, T., & Normand, M. (2000, April/March). The demon-haunted sentence: A skeptical analysis of reverse speech. *Skeptical Inquirer,* pp. 46–49.

Cacioppo, J. T., & Petty, R. E. (1979). Effects of message repetition and position on cognitive response, recall, and persuasion. *Journal of Personality and Social Psychology, 37,* 97–109.

Cacioppo, J. T., Petty, R. E., Feinstein, J., & Jarvis, B. (1996). Individual differences in cognitive motivation: The life and times of people varying in need for cognition. *Psychological Bulletin, 119,* 197–253.

Cacioppo, J. T., Petty, R. E., Kao, C. F., & Rodriguez, R. (1986). Central and peripheral routes to persuasion: An individual difference perspective. *Journal of Personality and Social Psychology, 51,* 1032–1043.

Cacioppo, J. T., Petty, R. E., & Morris, K. J. (1983). Effects of need for cognition on message evaluation, recall, and persuasion. *Journal of Personality and Social Psychology, 45,* 805–818.

Chaiken, S. (1980). Heuristic versus systematic information processing and the use of source versus message cues in persuasion. *Journal of Personality and Social Psychology, 39,* 752–766.

Chaiken, S. (1986). Physical appearance and social influence. In C. P. Herman, M. P. Zanna, & E. T. Higgins (Eds.), *Physical appearance, stigma, and social behavior: The Ontario symposium* (Vol. 3). Hillsdale, NJ: Erlbaum.

Chaiken, S. (1987). The heuristic model of persuasion. In M. P. Zanna, J. M. Olson, & C. P. Herman (Eds.), *Social influence: The Ontario symposium* (Vol. 5, pp. 3–39). Hillsdale, NJ: Lawrence Erlbaum.

Chaiken, S., Liberman, A., & Eagly, A. H. (1987). Heuristic and systematic processing within and beyond the persuasion context. In J. S. Uleman & J. A. Bargh (Eds.), *Unintended thought* (pp. 212–252). New York: Guilford.

Chaiken, S., & Maheswaran, D. (1994). Heuristic processing can bias systematic processing: Effects of source credibility, argument ambiguity, and task importance on attitude judgment. *Journal of Personality and Social Psychology, 66,* 460–473.

Chaiken, S., & Trope, Y. (Eds.), (1999). *Dual process theories in social psychology.* New York: Guilford.

Chaiken, S., & Yates, S. (1985) Affective-cognitive consistency and thought-induced attitude polarization. *Journal of Personality and Social Psychology, 49,* 1470–1481.

Chen, S., & Chaiken, S. (1999). The heuristic systematic model in its broader context. In S. Chaiken & Y. Trope (Eds.), *Dual process theories in social psychology* (pp. 73–96). New York: Guilford.

Cialdini, R. B. (2000). *Influence: Science and practice* (4th ed.). Boston: Allyn & Bacon.

Cialdini, R. B., Levy, A., Herman, C. P., Koslowski, L., & Petty, R. E. (1976). Elastic shifts of opinion: Determinants of direction and durability. *Journal of Personality and Social Psychology, 34,* 663–672.

Cialdini, R. B., Trost, M. R., & Newsom, T. J. (1975). Preference for consistency: The development of a valid measure and the discovery of surprising behavioral implications. *Journal of Personality and Social Psychology, 69,* 318–328.

Clarkson, J. J., Tormala, Z. L., Rucker, D. D., & Dugan, R. G. (2013). The malleable influence of social consensus on attitude certainty. *Journal of Experimental Social Psychology, 49,* 1019–1022.

Clore, G. L, Gasper, K., & Garvin, E. (2001). Affect as information. In J. P. Forgas (Ed.), *Handbook of affect and social cognition* (pp. 121–144). Mahwah, NJ: Lawrence Erlbaum.

Cooper, J. (2007). *Cognitive dissonance: 50 years of a classic theory.* London, UK: Sage Publications.

Cooper, J., & Fazio, R. H. (1984). A new look at dissonance theory. In L. Berkowitz (Ed.), *Advances in experimental social psychology* (Vol. 17, pp. 229–266). New York: Academic Press.

Cooper, J., Zanna, M. P., & Taves, P. A. (1978). Arousal as a necessary condition for attitude change following induced compliance. *Journal of Personality and Social Psychology, 36,* 1101–1106.

Croyle, R. T., & Cooper, J. (1983). Dissonance arousal: Physiological evidence. *Journal of Personality and Social Psychology, 45,* 782–791.

Cox, D. S., & Cox, A. D. (1988). What does familiarity breed: Complexity as a moderator of repetition effects in advertisement evaluation. *Journal of Consumer Research, 15,* 111–116.

Davis, B. P., & Knowles, E. S. (1999). A disrupt-then-reframe technique of social influence. *Journal of Personality and Social Psychology, 76,* 192–199.

DeSteno, D., Petty, R. E., Rucker, D. D., Wegener, D. T., & Braverman, J. (2004). Discrete emotions and persuasion: The role of emotion-induced expectancies. *Journal of Personality and Social Psychology, 86,* 43–56.

Dion, K., Berscheid, E., & Walster, E. (1972). What is beautiful is good. *Journal of Personality and Social Psychology, 24,* 285–290.

Dion, K. K., Stein, S. (1978). Physical attractiveness and interpersonal influence. *Journal of Experimental Social Psychology, 14,* 97–108.

Eagly, A. H. (1981). Recipient characteristics as determinants of responses to persuasion. In R. E. Petty, T. M. Ostrom, & T. C. Brock (Eds.), *Cognitive responses in persuasion* (pp. 173–195). Hillsdale, NJ: Erlbaum.

Eagly, A. H., & Chaiken, S. (1993). *The psychology of attitudes.* Fort Worth, TX: Harcourt Brace College Publishers.

Eagly, A. H., Chaiken, S., & Wood, W. (1981). An attribution analysis of persuasion. In J. H. Harvey, W. J. Ickes, & R. F. Kidd (Eds.), *New directions in attribution research* (Vol. 3, pp. 37–62). Hillsdale, NJ: Lawrence Erlbaum Associates.

Eagly, A. H., & Warren, R. (1976). Intelligence, comprehension, and opinion change. *Journal of Personality, 44,* 226–242.

Eagly, A. H., Wood, W., & Chaiken, S. (1978). Causal inference about communicators and their effect on opinion change. *Journal of Personality and Social Psychology, 36,* 424–435.

Eaton, A. A., Visser, P. S., Krosnick, J. A., & Anand, S. (2009). Social power and attitude strength over the life course. *Personality and Social Psychology Bulletin, 35,* 1646–1660.

Elkin, R. A., & Leippe, M. R. (1986). Physiological arousal, dissonance, and attitude change: Evidence for a dissonance-arousal link and a "don't remind me" effect. *Journal of Personality and Social Psychology, 51,* 55–65.

Fazio, R. H., & Cooper, J. (1983). Arousal in the dissonance process. In J. T. Cacioppo & R. E. Petty (Eds.), *Social psychophysiology* (pp. 122–152). New York: Guilford Press.

Fazio, R. H., Zanna, M. P., & Cooper, J. (1977). Dissonance and self-perception: An integrative view of each theory's domain of application. *Journal of Experimental Social Psychology, 13,* 464–479.

Festinger, L. (1957). *A theory of cognitive dissonance.* Stanford, CA: Stanford University Press.

Festinger, L., & Carlsmith, J. M. (1959). Cognitive consequences of forced compliance. *Journal of Abnormal and Social Psychology, 58,* 203–211.

Fiske, S. T., Morling, B., & Stevens, L. E. (1996). Controlling self and others: A theory of anxiety, mental control, and social control. *Personality and Social Psychology Bulletin, 22,* 115–123.

Forgas, J. P. (1995). Mood and judgment: The affect infusion model (AIM). *Psychological Bulletin, 117,* 39–66.

Förster, J., & Strack, F. (1996). Influence of overt head movements on memory for valenced words: A case of conceptual-motor compatibility. *Journal of Personality and Social Psychology, 71*, 421–430.

Frey, D. (1986). Recent research on selective exposure to information. In L. Berkowitz (Ed.), *Advances in experimental social psychology* (Vol. 19, pp. 41–80). San Diego, CA: Academic Press.

Frey, D., & Rosch, M. (1984) Information seeking after decisions: The roles of novelty of information and decision reversibility. *Personality and Social Psychology Bulletin, 10*, 91–98.

Fuegen, K., & Brehm, J. W. (2004). The intensity of affect and resistance to social influence. In E. S. Knowles & J. A. Linn (Eds.), *Resistance and persuasion* (pp. 39–63). Mahwah, NJ: Lawrence Erlbaum Associates.

Gable, M., Wilkens, H. T., Harris, L., & Feinberg, R. (1987). An evaluation of subliminally embedded sexual stimuli in graphics. *Journal of Advertising, 16*, 26–31.

Gawronski, B., & Bodenhausen, G. V. (2006). Associative and propositional processes in evaluation: An integrative review of implicit and explicit attitude change. *Psychological Bulletin, 132*, 692–731.

Gawronski, B., & LeBel, E. P. (2008). Understanding patterns of attitude change: When implicit measures show change, but explicit measures do not. *Journal of Experimental Social Psychology, 44*, 1355–1361.

Gilbert, D. T. (1989). Thinking lightly about others: Automatic components of the social inference process. In J. S. Uleman & J. A Bargh (Eds.), *Unintended thought* (pp. 189–211). New York: Guilford Publications.

Gillig, P. M., & Greenwald, A. G. (1974). Is it time to lay the sleeper effect to rest? *Journal of Personality and Social Psychology, 29*, 132–139.

Glenn, N. O. (1980). Values, attitudes, and beliefs. In O. G. Brim, Jr., & J. Kagan (Eds.), *Constancy and change in human development*. Cambridge, MA: Harvard University Press.

Goethals, G. R., Cooper, J., & Naficy, A. (1979). Role of foreseen, foreseeable, and unforeseeable behavioral consequences in the arousal of cognitive dissonance. *Journal of Personality and Social Psychology, 37*, 1179–1185.

Goethals, G. R., & Reckman, R. F. (1973). The perception of consistency in attitudes. *Journal of Experimental Social Psychology, 9*, 491–501.

Gorn, G. J., & Goldberg, M. E. (1980). Children's responses to repetitive TV commercials. *Journal of Consumer Research, 6*, 421–424.

Gorn, G. J. (1982). The effects of music in advertising on choice behavior: A classical conditioning approach. *Journal of Marketing, 46*, 94–101.

Grant, N. K., Fabrigar, L. R., & Lim, H. (2010). Exploring the efficacy of compliments as a tactic for securing compliance. *Basic and Applied Social Psychology, 32*, 226–233.

Greenwald, A. G., Banaji, M. R., Rudman, L. A., Farnham, S. D., Nosek, B. A., & Mellott, D. S. (2002). A unified theory of implicit attitudes, stereotypes, self-esteem, and self-concept. *Psychological Review, 109*, 3–25.

Greenwald, A. G., Spangenberg, E. R., Pratkanis, A. R., & Eskanazi, J. (1991). Double-blind tests of subliminal self-help audiotapes. *Psychological Science, 2*, 119–122.

Griskevicius, V., Goldstein, N. J., Mortensen, C. R., Sundie, J. M., Cialdini, R. B., & Kenrick, D. T. (2009). Fear and loving in Las Vegas: Evolution, emotion, and persuasion. *Journal of Marketing Research, 46*, 384–395.

Gruder, C. L., Cook, T. D., Hennigan, K. M., Flay, B. R., Alessis, C., & Halamaj, J. (1978). Empirical tests of the absolute sleeper effect predicted from the discounting cue hypothesis. *Journal of Personality and Social Psychology, 36*, 1061–1074.

Guadagno, R., Rhoads, K. V. L., & Sagarin, B. (2011). Figural vividness and persuasion: Capturing the "elusive" vividness effect. *Personality and Social Psychology Bulletin, 37*, 626–638.

Gudjonsson, G. H. (1992). *The psychology of interrogations, confessions, and testimony*. London, UK: Wiley.

Hale, J., Mongeau, P. A., & Thomas, R. M. (1991). Cognitive processing of one- and two-sided persuasive messages. *Western Journal of Speech Communication, 55,* 380–389.

Han, S. P., & Shavitt, S. (1994). Persuasion and culture: Advertising appeals in individualistic and collectivistic societies. *Journal of Experimental Social Psychology, 30,* 326–350.

Harmon-Jones, E., & Mills, J. (1999). *Cognitive dissonance: Progress on a pivotal theory in social psychology.* Washington, DC: American Psychological Association.

Harris, J. L., Salus, D., Rerecich, R., & Larsen, D. (1996). Distinguishing detection from identification in subliminal auditory perception: A review and critique of Merikle's study. *Journal of General Psychology, 123,* 41–50.

Hass, R. G., & Grady, K. (1975). Temporal delay, type of forewarning and resistance to influence. *Journal of Experimental Social Psychology, 11,* 459–469.

Hatfield, E., & Sprecher, S. (1986). *Mirror, mirror: The importance of looks in everyday life.* Albany: State University of New York Press.

Haugtvedt, C. P., Petty, R. E., & Cacioppo, J. T. (1992). Need for cognition and advertising: Understanding the role of personality variables in consumer behavior. *Journal of Consumer Psychology, 1,* 239–260.

Haugtvedt, C. P., & Wegener, D. T. (1994). Message order effects in persuasion: An attitude strength perspective. *Journal of Consumer Research, 21,* 205–218.

Herek, G. M. (1987). Can functions be measured? A new perspective on the functional approach to attitudes. *Social Psychology Quarterly, 50,* 285–303.

de Hoog, N., Stroebe, W., & de Wit, J. B. F. (2004). The impact of fear appeals on processing and acceptance of action recommendations. *Personality and Social Psychology Bulletin, 31,* 24–33.

Hovland, C. I., Janis, I. L., & Kelley, H. H. (1953). *Communication and persuasion: Psychological studies of opinion change.* New Haven, CT: Yale University Press.

Hovland, C. I., & Weiss, W. (1951). The influence of source credibility on communication effectiveness. *Public Opinion Quarterly, 15,* 635–650.

Hovland, C. I., Lumsdaine, A. A., & Sheffield, F. D. (1949). *Experiments on mass communications.* Princeton, NJ: Princeton University Press.

Insko, C. A. (1964). Primacy versus recency in persuasion as a function of the timing of arguments and measures. *Journal of Abnormal and Social Psychology, 69,* 381–391.

Isbell, L. M. (2004). Not all happy people are lazy or stupid: Evidence of systematic processing in happy moods. *Journal of Experimental Social Psychology, 40,* 341–349.

Jacks, J. Z., & Cameron, K. A. (2003). Strategies for resisting persuasion. *Basic and Applied Social Psychology, 25,* 145–161.

Johnson, B. T., & Eagly, A. H. (1989). Effects of involvement on persuasion: A meta-analysis. *Psychological Bulletin, 106,* 290–314.

Kassin, S. M. (1997). The psychology of confession evidence. *American Psychologist, 52,* 221–233.

Kassin, S. M. (2005). On the Psychology of Confessions: Does Innocence Put Innocents at Risk? *American Psychologist, 60,* 215–228.

Kassin, S. M., & Gudjonsson, G. H. (2004). The Psychology of Confessions: A Review of the Literature and Issues. *Psychological Science in the Public Interest, 5,* 33–67.

Kassin, S. M., & Kiechel, K. L. (1996). The psychology of false confessions: Compliance, internalization, and confabulation. *Psychological Science, 7,* 125–128.

Kassin, S. M., & McNall, K. (1991). Police interrogations and confessions: Communicating promises and threats by pragmatic implication. *Law and Human Behavior, 15,* 233–251.

Katz, D. (1960). The functional approach to the study of attitudes. *Public Opinion Quarterly, 24*, 163–204.

Kelman. H. C. (1958). Compliance, identification, and internalization: Three processes of attitude change. *Journal of Conflict Resolution, 2*, 51–60.

Kelman, H. C., & Hovland, C. I. (1953). "Reinstatement" of the communicator in delayed measurement of opinion change. *Journal of Abnormal and Social Psychology, 48*, 327–335.

Key, W. B. (1973). *Subliminal seduction*. Englewood Cliffs, NJ: Signet.

Key, W. B. (1976). *Media sexploitation*. Englewood Cliffs, NJ: Signet.

Kilbourne, W. E., Painton, S., & Ridley, D. (1985). The effect of sexual embedding on responses to magazine advertisements. *Journal of Advertising, 14*, 48–56.

Knowles, E. S., & Linn, J. A. (2004a). Approach-avoidance model of persuasion: Alpha and Omega strategies for change. In E. S. Knowles & J. A. Linn (Eds.), *Resistance and persuasion* (pp. 117–148). Mahwah, NJ: Lawrence Erlbaum Associates.

Knowles, E. S., & Linn, J. A. (2004b). The importance of resistance to persuasion. In E. S. Knowles & J. A. Linn (Eds.), *Resistance and persuasion* (pp. 3–9). Mahwah, NJ: Lawrence Erlbaum Associates.

Kruger, J., Savitsky, K., & Gilovich, T. (March/April, 1999). Superstition and the regression effect. *Skeptical Inquirer*, pp. 24–29.

Kruglanski, A. W., & Thompson, E. P (1999). Persuasion by a single route: A view from the unimodel. *Psychological Inquiry, 10*, 83–109.

Kumkale, G. T., & Albarracin, D. (2004). The sleeper effect in persuasion: A meta-analytic review. *Psychological Bulletin, 130*, 143–172.

Lapinski, M. K., & Boster, F. J. (2001). Modeling the ego-defensive function of attitudes. *Communication Monographs, 68*, 14–324.

Lasswell, H. D. (1948). The structure and function of communication in society. In L. Bryson (Ed.), *The communication of ideas: Religion and civilization series* (pp. 37–51). New York: Harper & Row.

Latimer, A. E., Salovey, P., & Rothman, A. J. (2007). The effectiveness of gain-framed messages for encouraging disease prevention behavior: Is all hope lost? *Journal of Health Communication, 12*, 645–649.

Leventhal, H. (1970). Findings and theory in the study of fear communications. In L. Berkowitz (Ed.), *Advances in Experimental Social Psychology* (Vol. 5, pp. 119–186). New York: Academic Press.

Levine, R. (2003). *The power of persuasion: How we're bought and sold*. Hoboken, NJ: John Wiley and Sons.

Liberman, A., & Chaiken, S. (1991). Value conflict and thought-induced attitude change. *Journal of Experimental Social Psychology, 27*, 203–216.

Lieberman, M. D., Ochsner, K. N., Gilbert, D. T., & Schachter, D. L. (2001). Do amnesics exhibit cognitive dissonance reduction? The role of explicit memory and attention in attitude change. *Psychological Science, 12*, 135–140.

Lord, C. G., Ross, L., & Lepper, M. R. (1979). Biased assimilation and attitude polarization: The effects of prior theories on subsequently encountered evidence. *Journal of Personality and Social Psychology, 37*, 2098–2109.

Lorge, I. (1936). Prestige, suggestions, and attitudes. *Journal of Social Psychology, 7*, 386–402.

Love, R. E., & Greenwald, A. G. (1978). Cognitive responses to persuasion as mediators of attitude change. *Journal of Social Psychology, 104*, 231–241.

Lydon, J., Zanna, M. P., & Ross, M. (1988). Bolstering attitudes by autobiographical recall: Attitude persistence and selective memory. *Personality and Social Psychology Bulletin, 14*, 78–86.

Mackie, D. M. (1987). Systematic and nonsystematic processing of majority and minority persuasive communications. *Journal of Personality and Social Psychology, 53*, 41–52.

Mackie, D. M., & Worth, L. T. (1991). Feeling good, but not thinking straight: The impact of positive mood on persuasion. In J. Forgas (Ed.), *Emotion and social judgments* (pp. 210–219). Oxford, England: Pergamon Press.

Maheswaran, D., & Chaiken, S. (1991). Promoting systematic processing in low-motivation settings: Effect of incongruent information on processing and judgment. *Journal of Personality and Social Psychology, 61*, 13–25.

Maio, G. R., & Haddock, G. (2007). Attitude change. In A. W. Kruglanski & E. T. Higgins (Eds.), *Social psychology: Handbook of basic principles* (2nd ed., pp. 565–586). New York: Guilford.

Mannheim, K. (1952). The problem of generations. In P. Kecskemeti (Ed.), *Essays on the sociology of knowledge* (pp. 276–322). London: Routledge & Kegan Paul.

Mathur, M., & Chattopadhyay, A. (1991). The impact of moods generated by television programs on responses to advertising. *Psychology and Marketing, 8*, 59–77.

McCullough, J. L., & Ostrom, T. M. (1974). Repetition of highly similar messages and attitude change. *Journal of Applied Psychology, 59*, 395–397.

McGuire, W. J. (1964). Inducing resistance to persuasion: Some contemporary approaches. In L. Berkowitz (Ed.), *Advances in experimental social psychology* (Vol. 1, pp. 191–229, pp. 136–314). New York: Academic Press.

McGuire, W. J. (1968). Personality and attitude change: An information processing theory. In A. G. Greenwald, T. C. Brock, & T. M. Ostrom (Eds.), *Psychological foundations of attitudes* (pp. 171–196). New York: Academic Press.

McGuire, W. J. (1969). The nature of attitudes and attitude change. In G. Lindzey & E. Aronson (Eds.), *The handbook of social psychology* (2nd ed., Vol. 3). Reading, MA: Addison Wesley.

McGuire, W. J., & Papageorgis, D. (1961). The relative efficacy of various types of prior belief-defense in producing immunity against persuasion. *Journal of Abnormal and Social Psychology, 62*, 327–337.

Merikle, P. M. (1988). Subliminal auditory messages: An evaluation. *Psychology and Marketing, 5*, 355–372.

Merikle, P. M., & Skanes, H. E. (1992). Subliminal self-help audiotapes: A search for placebo effects. *Journal of Applied Psychology, 77*, 772–776.

Meyerowitz, B. E., & Chaiken, S. (1987). The effect of message framing on breast self-examination attitudes, intentions, and behavior. *Journal of Personality and Social Psychology, 52*, 500–510.

Miller, N., & Campbell, D. T. (1959). Recency and primacy in persuasion as a function of timing of speeches and measurement. *Journal of Abnormal Psychology, 59*, 1–9.

Mills, J., & Jellison, J. M. (1968). Effect on opinion change of similarity between the communicator and the audience he addressed. *Journal of Personality and Social Psychology, 9*, 153–156.

Moons, W. G., Mackie, D. M., & Garcia-Marques, T. (2009). The impact of repetition-induced familiarity on agreement with weak and strong arguments. *Journal of Personality and Social Psychology, 96*, 32–44.

Moore, T. E. (1995). Subliminal self-help auditory tapes: An empirical test of perceptual consequences. *Canadian Journal of Behavioural Science, 27*, 9–20.

Nesselroade, J. R., Stigler, S. M., & Baltes, P. B. (1980). Regression towards the mean and the study of change. *Psychological Bulletin, 88*, 622–637.

Olson, M. A., & Fazio, R. H. (2001). Implicit attitude formation through classical conditioning. *Psychological Science, 12*, 413–417.

Olson, M. A., & Fazio, R. H. (2002). Implicit acquisition and manifestation of classically conditioned attitudes. *Social Cognition, 20*, 89–104.

Pallak, S. R. (1983). Salience of a communicator's physical attractiveness and persuasion: A heuristic versus systematic processing interpretation. *Social Cognition, 2*, 158–170.

Papageorgis, D., & McGuire, W. J. (1961). The generality of immunity to persuasion produced by pre-exposure to weakened counterarguments. *Journal of Abnormal and Social Psychology, 62,* 475–481.

Petty, R. E. (1997). The evolution of theory and research in social psychology: From single to multiple effect and process models of persuasion. In C. McGarty & S. A. Haslam (Eds.), *The message of social psychology: Perspectives on mind in society* (pp. 268–290). Oxford, England: Basil Blackwell, Ltd.

Petty, R. E., Brock, T. C. (1976). Effects of responding or not responding to hecklers on audience agreement with a speaker. *Journal of Applied Social Psychology, 6,* 1–17.

Petty, R. E., & Cacioppo, J. T. (1977). Forewarning, cognitive responding, and resistance to persuasion. *Journal of Personality and Social Psychology, 35,* 645–655.

Petty, R. E., & Cacioppo, J. T. (1979). Issue involvement can increase or decrease persuasion by enhancing message-relevant cognitive processes. *Journal of Personality and Social Psychology, 37,* 1915–1926.

Petty, R. E., & Cacioppo, J. T. (1981). *Attitudes and persuasion: Classic and contemporary approaches.* Dubuque, IA: Brown.

Petty, R. E., & Cacioppo, J. T. (1984). The effects of issue involvement on responses to argument quantity and quality: Central and peripheral routes to persuasion. *Journal of Personality and Social Psychology, 46,* 69–81.

Petty, R. E., & Cacioppo, J. T. (1986a). *Communication and persuasion: Central and peripheral routes to attitude change.* New York: Springer-Verlag.

Petty, R. E., & Cacioppo, J. T. (1986b). The elaboration likelihood model of persuasion. In L. Berkowitz (Ed.), *Advances in experimental social psychology* (Vol. 19, pp. 123–205). San Diego, CA: Academic Press.

Petty, R. E., & Cacioppo, J. T. (1990). Involvement and persuasion: Tradition versus integration. *Psychological Bulletin, 107,* 367–374.

Petty, R. E., Cacioppo, J. T., & Goldman, R. (1981). Personal involvement as a predictor of argument-based persuasion. *Journal of Personality and Social Psychology, 41,* 847–855.

Petty, R. E., & Krosnick, J. A. (1995). *Attitude strength: Antecedents and consequences.* Hillsdale, NJ: Erlbaum.

Petty, R. E., Ostrom, T. M., & Brock, T. C. (Eds.) (1981). *Cognitive responses in persuasion.* Hillsdale, NJ: Erlbaum.

Petty, R. E., Schumann, D. W., Richman, S. A., & Strathman, D. J. (1993). Positive mood and persuasion: Different roles for affect under high- and low-elaboration conditions. *Journal of Personality and Social Psychology, 64,* 5–20.

Petty, R. E., & Wegener, D. T. (1998). Attitude change: Multiple roles for persuasion variables. In D. T. Gilbert, S. T. Fiske, & G. Lindzey (Eds.), *The handbook of social psychology* (4th ed., Vol. 1, pp. 323–390). New York: McGraw Hill.

Petty, R. E., & Wegener, D. T. (1999). The elaboration likelihood model: Current status and controversies. In S. Chaiken & Y. Trope (Eds.), *Dual process theories in social psychology* (pp. 41–72). New York: Guilford.

Petty, R. E., Wells, G. L., & Brock, T. C. (1976). Distraction can enhance or reduce yielding to propaganda: Thought disruption versus effort justification. *Journal of Personality and Social Psychology, 34,* 874–884.

Phelps, B. J., & Exum, M. E. (1992, spring). Subliminal tapes: How to get the message across. *Skeptical Inquirer,* pp. 282–286.

Pittman, T. S. (1975). Attribution of arousal as a mediator in dissonance reduction. *Journal of Experimental Social Psychology, 11,* 53–63.

Pratkanis, A. R., Greenwald, A. G., Leippe, M. R., & Baumgardner, M. H. (1988). In search of reliable persuasion effects: III. The sleeper effect is dead. Long live the sleeper effect. *Journal of Personality and Social Psychology, 54,* 203–218.

Prentice, D. A. (1987). Psychological correspondence of possessions, attitudes, and values. *Journal of Personality and Social Psychology, 53,* 993–1003.

Priester, J. R., & Petty, R. E. (1995). Source attributions and persuasion: Perceived honesty as a determinant of message scrutiny. *Personality and Social Psychology Bulletin, 21*, 637–654.

Radelet, M. L., Bedau, H. A., & Putnam, C. E. (1992). *In spite of innocence: Erroneous convictions in capital cases*. Boston: Northeastern University Press.

Raven, B. H., & French, J. R. P. (1958). Legitimate power, coercive power, and observability in social influence. *Sociometry, 21*, 83–97.

Rhodes, N., & Wood, W. (1992). Self-esteem and intelligence affect influenceability: The mediating role of message reception. *Psychological Bulletin, 111*, 156–171.

Rogers, R. W. (1983). Cognitive and physiological processes in fear appeals and attitude change: A revised theory of protection motivation. In J. T. Cacioppo & R. E. Petty (Eds.), *Social psychophysiology: A sourcebook* (pp. 153–176). New York: Guilford.

Rokeach, M. (1954). The nature and meaning of dogmatism. *Psychological Review, 61*, 194–204.

Ross, M. (1989). Relation of implicit theories to the construction of personal histories. *Psychological Review, 96*, 341–357.

Rothman, A. J., & Salovey, P. (1997). Shaping perceptions to motivate healthy behavior: The role of message framing. *Psychological Bulletin, 121*, 3–19.

Rothman, A. J., Salovey, P., Antone, C., Keough, K., & Martin, C. D. (1993). The influence of message framing on intentions to perform health behaviors. *Journal of Experimental Social Psychology, 29*, 408–433.

Rozin, P. (1999). Food is fundamental, fun, frightening, and far-reaching. *Social Research, 66*, 9–30

Rozin, P., Kabnick, K., Pete, E., Fischler, C., & Shields, C. (2003). The ecology of eating: Smaller portion sizes in France than in the United States help explain the French paradox. *Psychological Science, 14*, 450–454.

Rudman, L. A. (2004). Sources of implicit attitudes. *Current Directions in Psychological Science, 13*, 79–82.

Rudman, L. A., Ashmore, R. D., & Gary, M. L. (2001). "Unlearning" automatic biases: The malleability of implicit prejudice and stereotypes. *Journal of Personality and Social Psychology, 81*, 856–868.

Ruiter, R. A. C., Abraham, C., & Kok, G. (2001). Scary warnings and rational precautions: A review of the psychology of fear appeals. *Psychology and Health, 16*, 613–630.

Russano, M. B., Meissner, A. M., Narchet, F. M., & Kassin, S. M. (2005). Investigating true and false confessions within a novel experimental paradigm. *Psychological Science, 16*, 481–486.

Russell, T. G., Rowe, W., & Smouse, A. D. (1991). Subliminal self-help tapes and academic achievement: An evaluation. *Journal of Counseling and Development, 69*, 359–362.

Sagarin, B. J., & Cialdini, R. B. (2004). Creating critical consumers: Motivating receptivity by teaching resistance. In E. S. Knowles & J. A. Linn (Eds.), *Resistance and persuasion* (pp. 259–282). Mahwah, NJ: Lawrence Erlbaum Associates.

Santos, M. D., Leve, C., & Pratkanis, A. R. (1994). Hey buddy, can you spare seventeen cents? Mindful persuasion and the pique technique. *Journal of Applied Social Psychology, 24*, 755–764.

Scher, S. J., & Cooper, J. (1989). Motivational basis of dissonance: The singular role of behavioral consequences. *Journal of Personality and Social Psychology, 56*, 899–906.

Schwarz, N. (1990). Feelings as information: Informational and motivational functions of affective states. In E. T. Higgins & R. M. Sorrentino (Eds.), *Handbook of motivation and cognition: Foundations of social behavior* (Vol. 2, pp. 527–561). New York: Guilford.

Schwarz, N., Bless, H., & Bohner, G. (1991). Mood and persuasion: Affective states influence the processing of persuasive communication. In M. P. Zanna (Ed.), *Advances in experimental social psychology* (Vol. 24, pp. 161–201). San Diego, CA: Academic Press.

Schwarz, N., & Clore, G. L. (1983). Mood, misattribution, and judgments of well-being: Informative and directive functions of affective states. *Journal of Personality and Social Psychology, 45,* 513–523.

Sears, D. O. (1983). The persistence of early political predispositions: The role of attitude object and life stage. In L. Wheeler (Ed.), *Review of personality and social psychology* (Vol. 4, pp. 79–116). Beverly Hills, CA: Sage.

Sears, D. O. (1986). College sophomores in the laboratory: Influences of a narrow data base on social psychology's view of human nature. *Journal of Personality and Social Psychology, 51,* 515–530.

Shavitt, S., Swan, S., Lowery, T. M., & Wänke, M. (1994). The interaction of endorser attractiveness and involvement in persuasion depends on the goal that drives message processing. *Journal of Consumer Psychology, 3,* 137–162.

Sherman, S. J., Crawford, M. T., & McConnell, A. R. (2004). Looking ahead as a technique to reduce resistance to persuasive attempts. In E. S. Knowles & J. A. Linn (Eds.), *Resistance and persuasion* (pp. 149–174). Mahwah, NJ: Lawrence Erlbaum Associates.

Simon, L., Greenberg, J., & Brehm, J. (1995) Trivialization: the forgotten mode of dissonance reduction. *Journal of Personality and Social Psychology, 68,* 247–260.

Smith, M., Bruner, J., & White, R. (1956). *Opinions and personality.* New York: Wiley.

Smith, S. M., & Shaffer, D. R. (1995). Speed of speech and persuasion: Evidence for multiple effects. *Personality and Social Psychology Bulletin, 21,* 1051–1060.

Snyder, M., & DeBono, K. G. (1987). A functional approach to attitudes and persuasion. In M. P. Zanna, J. M. Olson, & C. P. Herman (Eds.), *Social influence: The Ontario symposium* (Vol. 5, pp. 107–128). Hillsdale, NJ: Erlbaum.

Stone, J. (2001). Behavioral discrepancies and the role of construal processes in cognitive dissonance. In G. B. Moskowitz (Ed.), *Cognitive social psychology: The Princeton symposium on the legacy and future of social cognition* (pp. 41–58). Mahwah, NJ: Lawrence Erlbaum Associates.

Stone, J., Aronson, E., Crain, A. L., Winslow, M. P., & Fried, C. B. (1994). Inducing hypocrisy as a means of encouraging young adults to use condoms. *Personality and Social Psychology Bulletin, 20,* 116–128.

Stone, J., & Cooper, J. (2001). A self-standards model of cognitive dissonance. *Journal of Experimental Social Psychology, 37,* 228–243.

Stone, J., Wiegand, A. W., Cooper, J., & Aronson, E. (1997). When exemplification fails: Hypocrisy and the motive for self-integrity. *Journal of Personality and Social Psychology, 72,* 54–65.

Swart, L. C., & Morgan, C. L. (1992). Effects of subliminal backward-recorded messages on attitudes. *Perceptual and Motor Skills, 75,* 1107–1113.

Sweeney, P. D., & Gruber, K. L. (1984). Selective exposure: Voter information preferences and the Watergate affair. *Journal of Personality and Social Psychology, 46,* 1208–1221.

Tannenbaum, P. H., Macauley, J. R., & Norris, E. L. (1966). Principle of congruity and reduction of persuasion. *Journal of Personality and Social Psychology, 3,* 233–238.

Tesser, A. (1978). Self-generated attitude change. In L. Berkowitz (Ed.), *Advances in experimental social psychology* (Vol. 11, pp. 289–338). New York: Academic Press.

Tesser, A., Martin, L., & Mendolia, M. (1995). The impact of thought on attitude extremity and attitude-behavior consistency. In R. E. Petty & J. A Krosnick (Eds.), *Attitude strength: Antecedents and consequences* (pp. 73–92). Hillsdale, NJ: Erlbaum.

Tom, G., Petterson, P., Lau, T., Burton, T., & Cook, J. (1991). The role of overt head movement in the formation of affect. *Basic and Applied Social Psychology, 12,* 281–290.

Tormala, Z. L., Clarkson, J. J., & Petty, R. E. (2006). Resisting persuasion by the skin of one's teeth: The hidden success of resisted persuasive messages. *Journal of Personality and Social Psychology, 91,* 423–435.

Tormala, Z. L., & Petty, R. E. (2002). What doesn't kill me makes me stronger: The effects of resisting persuasion on attitude certainty. *Journal of Personality and Social Psychology, 83*, 1298–1313.

Tormala, Z. L., & Petty, R. E. (2004). Resisting persuasion and attitude certainty: A meta-cognitive analysis. In E. S. Knowles & J. A. Linn (Eds.), *Resistance and persuasion* (pp. 65–82). Mahwah, NJ: Lawrence Erlbaum Associates.

Tversky, A., & Kahneman, D. (1981). The framing of decisions and the psychology of choice. *Science, 211*, 453–458.

van Leeuwen, M. L., & Macrae, C. N. (2004). Is beautiful always good? Implicit benefits of facial attractiveness. *Social Cognition, 22*, 637–649.

van 't Riet, J., Ruiter, R. C., Smerecnik, C., & de Vries, H. (2010). Examining the influence of self-efficacy on message-framing effects: Reducing salt consumption in the general population. *Basic and Applied Social Psychology, 32*, 165–172.

Verwijmeren, T., Karremans, J. C., Bernritter, S. F., Stroebe, W., & Wigboldus, D. J. (2013). Warning: You are being primed! The effect of a warning on the impact of subliminal ads. *Journal of Experimental Social Psychology, 49*, 1124–1129.

Visser, P. S., & Krosnick, J. A. (1998). Development of attitude strength over the life cycle: Surge and decline. *Journal of Personality and Social Psychology, 75*, 1389–1410.

Vokey, J. R., & Read, J. D. (1985). Subliminal messages: Between the devil and the media. *American Psychologist, 40*, 1231–1239.

Wegener, D. T., Petty, R. E., & Smith, S. M. (1995). Positive mood can increase or decrease message scrutiny: The hedonic contingency view of mood and message processing. *Journal of Personality and Social Psychology, 69*, 5–15.

Wells, G. L., & Petty, R. E. (1980). The effects of overt head movements on persuasion: Compatibility and incompatibility of responses. *Basic and Applied Social Psychology, 1*, 219–230.

Wheeler, S. C., Briñol, P., & Hermann, A. D. (2007). Resistance to persuasion as self-regulation: Ego-depletion and its effects on attitude change processes. *Journal of Experimental Social Psychology, 43*, 150–156.

Wilson, T. D. (1990). Self-persuasion via self-reflection. In J. M. Olson & M. P. Zanna (Eds.), *Self-inference processes: The Ontario symposium* (Vol. 6, pp. 43–67). Hillsdale, NJ: Lawrence Erlbaum Associates.

Wilson, W., & Miller, H. (1968). Repetition, order of presentation, and timing of arguments and measures as determinants of opinion change. *Journal of Personality and Social Psychology, 9*, 184–188.

Wood, W., Kallgren, C. A., & Preisler, R. M. (1985). Access to attitude-relevant information in memory as a determinant of persuasion: The role of message attributes. *Journal of Experimental Social Psychology, 21*, 73–85.

Wood, W., & Quinn, J. M. (2003). Forewarned and forearmed? Two meta-analysis syntheses of forewarnings of influence appeals. *Psychological Bulletin, 129*, 119–138.

Worchel, S., Brehm, J. W. (1970). Effect of threats to attitudinal freedom as a function of agreement with the communicator. *Journal of Personality and Social Psychology, 14*, 18–22.

Worth, L. T., & Mackie, D. M. (1987). Cognitive mediation of positive mood in persuasion. *Social Cognition, 5*, 76–94.

Wright, L. (1994). *Remembering Satan*. New York: Knopf.

Wu, C., & Shaffer, D. R. (1987). Susceptibility to persuasive appeals as a function of source credibility and prior experience with the attitude object. *Journal of Personality and Social Psychology, 52*, 677–688.

Zanna, M. P., & Cooper, J. (1974). Dissonance and the pill: An attribution approach to studying the arousal properties of dissonance. *Journal of Personality and Social Psychology, 29*, 703–709.

Zanna, M. P., Higgins, E. T., & Taves, P. A. (1976). Is dissonance phenomenologically aversive? *Journal of Experimental Social Psychology, 12*, 530–538.

Zhang, J., & Shavitt, S. (2003). Cultural values in advertisements to the Chinese X-generation. *Journal of Advertising, 32*, 23–33.

Ziegler, R., Schlett, C., & Aydinli, A. (2013). Mood and threat to attitudinal freedom: Delineating the role of mood congruency and hedonic contingency in counterattitudinal message processing. *Personality and Social Psychology Bulletin, 39,* 1083–1096.

Zimbardo, P. G, Weisenberg, M., Firestone, I., & Levy, B. (1965). Communicator effectiveness in producing public conformity and private attitude change. *Journal of Personality, 33,* 233–255.

CHAPTER 7

SOCIAL INFLUENCE: COMPLIANCE, CONFORMITY, AND OBEDIENCE

THE TROUBLE WITH CASSIDY

Hope was desperate to get some studying done. In her first two years at a high school in suburban Baltimore, she was able to get respectable grades without having to work too terribly hard. But now that she was well into her junior year, the stakes seemed so much higher. College was right around the corner, and every test in every class now seemed to carry much more weight than it had in the past. Hope's newfound concern with grades had a lot to do with her choice of colleges. She had developed a fondness for New England during her family's many vacations in Vermont, Maine, and on Cape Cod, where she had dreamed about going to Brown, Tufts, or Amherst as she rode through the countryside in her parents' van.

Hope was keenly aware that being accepted at any of these colleges would be tough. Getting her GPA as close to 4.0 as possible would be an important step toward making her dream come true—especially in light of the alternative. Hope sensed some pressure from her parents to go to Washington College on Maryland's Eastern Shore as her brother had—that was a choice she would rather not make. Washington College wasn't a bad school, but it was way too close to home. Though she loved her parents dearly, she saw college as a way to gain a measure of independence. Washington College was just an hour from home; if she went there, her parents would likely expect her to come home frequently, just as they had her brother. Going to New England, on the other hand, would mean coming home primarily for the summer and on major holidays. For Hope, that would be often enough; she could see her folks *and* work on her independence.

Though Hope had recognized the importance of studying, she hadn't been very successful finding time for it. Like most juniors, she had a busy life both in and out of school. Judging by the amount of homework she did each day, most of her teachers seemed to think that theirs was the only class students were taking. Playing on the varsity basketball team, volunteering at the local animal shelter, dating a cute but somewhat demanding senior, and just hanging out with her friends added to the load. Juggling these competing demands had become even more complicated when Cassidy arrived halfway through the fall term.

Hope remembered taking an almost immediate dislike to the new girl when they were introduced by their homeroom teacher. Cassidy had transferred from Atlanta when her mother, a high-flying corporate attorney, landed a lucrative job in Baltimore. She did not fit in well at the new school. Although she was quite attractive, she looked, dressed, and spoke like a Southerner. "Just what we need around here—a Georgia Peach!" Hope grumbled to herself.

If Hope's dislike for Cassidy was mild at first, it soon turned to irritation. Over the next couple of months, Cassidy made no attempt to socialize with the other girls, Hope included. She constantly tried to ingratiate herself with her teachers. Worst of all, she managed to turn the heads of all the boys in the class. Hope's increasing dislike for Cassidy was confirmed by her circle of friends, who called themselves the "Benchies" because they spent their lunch breaks on a couple of benches in the park next to the school, weather permitting. On more than one occasion, someone would bring up the idea of "doing something" to put Cassidy in her place, but it never went beyond that. Just talking about it seemed to make them feel better.

The situation changed dramatically when Hope's friend, Danielle, claimed that Cassidy had been trying to steal Brad, fellow Benchie Jennifer's boyfriend. At first the charge was little more than a rumor, but it soon became apparent that nearly half the class believed it. Clearly, Cassidy was a ROTTEN Georgia Peach! The Benchies agreed that something had to be done—all, that is, except Savannah, who felt that Jennifer could do better than Brad. But eventually even she came around, and the focus of their discussions shifted to WHAT should done about it.

When winter drove the Benchies indoors, they continued their discussions by way of text messaging. Whatever they decided to do, it was clear they had to do it outside of school. It was also clear that draping the trees in Cassidy's yard with toilet paper would not do. That had become a way to celebrate the football team's victories. And because parents had complained to the school, the principal had sent home note in which he threatened to suspend any student caught in the act. Hope felt it best to obey the principal in this matter.

Faced with these difficulties, most of the Benchies agreed that an egging might be the best punishment, especially since the cold weather would make the goo stick really well. Hope was on the fence, partly because it seemed that an egging would affect Cassidy's parents more than Cassidy herself. Danielle and Jennifer were strongly in favor. Savannah, as usual, argued against it, favoring continued ostracism instead.

As Hope opened her notebook to study for her algebra test, she tried to put the matter out of her mind. But just as she was ready to begin, the doorbell rang. At first, she ignored it, but whoever was at the door was persistent. After four rings, Hope reluctantly opened the door to find a young man not much older than herself. A citizen's group was collecting signatures for a petition to be sent to the Maryland legislature, he explained. It called for better oversight of rising electricity prices. Hope found it difficult to argue against the petition. Noticing that most of her neighbors had already agreed, she took the young man's clipboard and signed the sheet.

Thinking that she had done a good deed and to end the intrusion that was preventing her from studying, Hope reached for the door. Just then the young man made a new request: he was collecting donations to fund his organization's efforts. Feeling simultaneously put off but obligated by his request, Hope managed to escape by asking him to return when her parents were home. With that she closed the door and went back to her room, where she noticed that a text message had arrived on her cell phone. It was from Danielle: "Egz 4 $ @ Sfway."

This chapter focuses on the social psychological processes that underlie how individuals respond to others' attempts at social influence. Social influence may not seem particularly different from persuasion, but there are some important differences. Persuasion is concerned with *attitude change*, and it does not necessarily require personal interaction. Social influence produces *changes in behavior* such as compliance, conformity, or obedience. Moreover, social influence results from interactions, and it can occur even if the people in question do not intend to change one another's behavior. We begin our discussion of social influence by first looking at specific variables and processes that elicit compliance.

COMPLIANCE

Compliance refers to our tendency to go along with another's direct request. Each day, numerous others ask us for favors—to turn down our stereos, show up for class on time, or part with varying amounts of cash. Those who ask include close others such as our partners, roommates, and friends, as well as distant others—businesses and giant corporations. What determines whether we will comply with such requests?

When it comes to simple requests, at least, the answer seems to be "not much." Compliance often occurs with very little thought on our part, resulting instead from a variety of hidden influences. Imagine you're in the library, making copies of the readings for tomorrow's class, when suddenly you're approached by a fellow student who asks to use the machine to make five copies. Would you comply with her request? Maybe. What if your fellow student were to make the identical request, but add that she is in a rush? Would you be more willing to comply? Probably, because in that form the request seems to contain a justification.

That is exactly what Langer, Blank, and Chanowitz (1978) found when they put unwitting research participants in these situations. Faced with a simple request that did not include a justification, 60 percent of participants stepped aside. When the request seemed to be justified, 94 percent did so. Before you conclude that justified requests elicit more compliance than unjustified requests, however, consider the results Langer et al. (1978) obtained when they added a perfectly nonsensical justification to the original simple request. In this condition, the experimenter added "because I have to make copies." Although the clause added nothing beyond the initial request to make five copies, its inclusion elicited a rate of compliance that was almost identical (93 percent) to the condition in which the request had been justified.

If nothing else, these findings suggest that compliance frequently results from *mindlessness*, operating as a hidden influence on our behavior. Faced with a request, we may implicitly draw on the general conversational rule stipulating that everything that comes after the word "because" justifies or explains everything that goes before. Panhandlers capitalize on our mindlessness when instead of simply asking for a handout, they ask for money to purchase a subway ticket. At other times they may attempt to prevent our frequently mindless refusal to part with any change. In one study (Santos, Leve, & Pratkanis, 1994) people who were approached with the somewhat atypical request for 17 cents expressed more curiosity and responded with more compliance than people who received the more typical request for a quarter. Thus, mindlessness does not always imply compliance; it may simply strengthen the response toward which we were leaning in the first place.

Mindlessness isn't so much gullibility as it is our lack of cognitive processing when we're confronted with relatively small requests. Circumventing cognitive processing can also lead to compliance with larger requests. However, accomplishing that end takes considerably more work on the part of those making the request. The reason is relatively simple: As the size of the request increases, active resistance replaces mindless compliance.

Let's look at three techniques frequently employed to sidestep resistance. Though they differ markedly in terms of their goals, all involve sequential requests (Cialdini, 2008).

The Foot in the Door

Imagine you are a fifth grader who has been asked to choose between two activities. The first option is to play with an assortment of toys; the second is to sort paper into color-coded piles, so that "the sick children in the hospital" can use it for an art project. Will you be able to resist the temptation to play with the latest games, puzzles, dolls, and action figures?

If you were one of the 11-year-olds who participated in Eisenberg, Cialdini, McCreath, and Shell's (1987) study, you probably would have spent at least a *little* of your time on the second activity, but you would not have given it your all. That is what Eisenberg et al. (1987) found—at least, for the control group. A few days earlier, however, the experimenters had persuaded children in the experimental group to engage in a different (and relatively painless) bit of altruistic behavior. After administering a bogus hearing test, the researchers awarded the children special coupons that they could trade in for toys, encouraging them to donate some to "poor children who don't have any toys." All the children but one parted with some of the coupons. When faced later with the choice of activities just described, these children sorted over 50 percent more pieces of paper than those in the control group, who had not previously been induced to share.

The results of this study illustrate the **foot-in-the-door technique**, which involves getting people to comply with a large request by preceding it with a much smaller one that they will find difficult to refuse. Lest you think that only children fall prey to this technique, consider a classic demonstration by Freedman and Fraser (1966). In that study, the researchers found that adults were much more likely to agree to a fairly audacious request—allowing strangers to come to their homes and go through all their personal belongings—if they had previously complied with a small request—answering some questions about consumer goods.

Why does the foot-in-the-door technique work? Complying with the initial request seems to alter one's self-perception (Burger & Caldwell, 2003; Burger & Guadagno, 2003; DeJong, 1979; Snyder & Cunningham, 1975). That is, taking even simple, easy steps to assist others can subtly change people's beliefs about themselves, making them feel more helpful or cooperative. People also infer more specific attitudes from their behavior, attitudes that can drive their future behavior. For example, cults use the foot-in-the-door technique to recruit new members (Zimbardo & Leippe, 1991). By getting people who might be ambivalent about the cult to do some small, seemingly innocuous favors (donate a little money, do some easy work) the cult can often manipulate people's perceptions of their own attitudes toward the cult.

"His foot-in-the-door technique has to be seen to be believed."

Size matters in the successful application of the foot-in-the-door technique

The Door in the Face

The foot-in-the-door technique (Freedman & Fraser, 1966) is a way to sidestep resistance to a *large* request. That is, the strategy of starting with small, painless requests encourages people to lower their guard. For sidestepping resistance to a *small* request, a strategy for eliciting compliance that essentially flips the foot-in-the-door strategy on its head is helpful. The **door-in-the-face technique** (Cialdini et al., 1975; Dillard, 1991) involves first making a large request that people will almost surely refuse, followed by a smaller request that they will then feel obligated to honor.

For example, Cialdini et al. (1975) asked college students if they would be willing to devote two hours a week, for a minimum of two years, to counseling juvenile delinquents. Not one of them agreed, but when the researchers followed with a more modest one—to chaperone a group of the same delinquents on a trip to the zoo—about half the students agreed. The researchers also asked a second group of students to volunteer as chaperones, without first making the more outlandish request. Members of this second group were much less likely to agree to accompany the delinquents to the zoo. The door-in-the-face technique works because once a person has said no to one request, the norm of reciprocity compels them to respond more favorably to the concession of a much smaller request.

Low-Balling

Low-balling is a particularly devious way to sidestep resistance to a large request. Imagine that you've come into enough money to replace the old clunker in front of your house with a brand-new car. After doing some research, you decide on a particular make and model and begin to scour the newspapers for a good deal. You then head for the dealership that offers the most attractive price and ask for a test drive. The car turns out to be everything you expected: It has a great ride, handles well, and even includes a sunroof and a connection for your iPod. You tell the salesperson that you would like to buy the car if he can give you a few hundred dollars off the price advertised in the paper. The salesperson frowns, asks for the ad, and goes to speak with the manager. After about 15 minutes he returns and explains that the car you drove was not the one in the ad. That one was a special value package with few, if any, frills. You drove a model with a special option package that added nearly $2,000 to the car's base.

Will you still buy the car with the higher price? Chances are you will. Consider the results of a study in which students were asked over the phone to participate in an experiment using two different scenarios (Cialdini et al., 1978). In one, the experimenter told participants up front that the experiment was scheduled for 7:00 A.M. In the low-ball scenario, the experimenter mentioned the time of the experiment *after* first securing students' agreement to participate. As expected, a higher percentage of students who had been low-balled agreed to make an appointment to participate and showed up at the appointed time (see **Figure 7.1**).

Low-balling works because once people decide on a course of action, they become committed to it. Commitment involves thinking primarily about all the positive aspects of a decision. As commitment increases, people grow more resistant to changing their minds, even when the reasons for the decision have changed (Kiesler, 1971). In the car-buying example, eliminating possible alternatives to your choice formed the initial basis for your commitment. The test drive cemented your commitment by reaffirming your already positive thoughts and making additional positive aspects of your choice salient. By the time you tell the salesperson that you'll buy the car, you're on the hook!

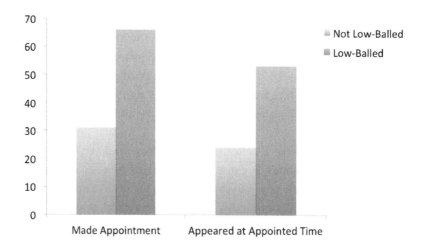

Figure 7.1: The Effects of Low-Balling on Compliance

Source: Cialdini, R.B., Cacioppo, J.T., Bassett, R., & Miller, J.A. (1978). Low-ball procedure for producing compliance: Commitment then cost. *Journal of Personality and Social Psychology, 36*, 463–476

"If you buy the house, I'll throw in the car for free."

A close inspection of low-ball offers usually reveals that they contain little that's free

Low-balling is also known as bait-and-switch. It is effective to the point that in many states, consumers enjoy legal protections against it. Of course, businesses find ways around the law by adding important information in the fine print at the foot of their advertisements. For example, a car dealership may advertise financing at a low interest rate in bold letters at the top of an ad, but bury the important note that "not all buyers will qualify" in fine print at the bottom. The fine print brings the dealership into compliance with the law, but unsuspecting consumers may not realize that they aren't eligible for this particular deal. Once they discover they qualify for financing only at a much higher interest rate, it's often too late. They are committed to their purchase, even if it means paying much more in interest than they had planned.

That's-Not-All and Labeling Techniques

A couple of strategies—ones that disguise their sequential nature somewhat—succeed by subtly changing people's perceptions, including their self-perceptions. The **that's-not-all technique** is based on making a large request that is immediately reduced. In the context of auto sales, for example, a salesperson may ask a relatively high price, but add that the price represents a discount or includes a "free" extended warranty. As transparent as the technique may seem, it is often wildly successful. Imagine yourself rifling through a rack of winter coats in your favorite clothing store. You find one you like, but when you check the tag you realize that it is offered at the regular price of $100. Now imagine the same scenario, but this time the tag shows a "sale price" of $100, allegedly marked down 25% from the regular price. According to Burger (1986), your perception that it is a good deal increases the likelihood that you will buy the coat when it is offered at a supposed discount, even though you will end up paying $100 either way.

Another approach, the **labeling technique**, induces compliance through changes in a person's self-perceptions. Imagine yourself walking into a car dealership and telling the salesperson that you are interested in a certain model. After a brief chat, she announces that you strike her as the kind of person who appreciates value—or, depending on the model, performance, reliability, or some combination of the three. She then proceeds to show you a car that supposedly represents any and all the values you hold dear. Why would this technique make you more likely to purchase the car you planned to buy? The change in your self-perception appears to increase your commitment to your chosen alternative. In support of this explanation, Cialdini et al. (1998) found that elementary school children who had been told that they looked like the kind of boy or girl "who understands how important it is to write correctly" were more likely to choose to work on their penmanship than children who had not received the same compliment.

Although the techniques we have discussed in this section vary in terms of the processes through which they elicit compliance, they share one important feature: All are subtle, covert techniques that may serve as hidden influences on our behavior (Schwarzwald et al., 1979). Consequently, they are often difficult to resist, even for people who know precisely when and how they operate. On several occasions, one of the authors of this book walked away from a car dealership feeling like a complete patsy. The Think like a Social Psychologist box on **below** describes a failed attempt to test the effectiveness of a common strategy for extricating oneself from a high-pressure sales situation.

THINK LIKE A SOCIAL PSYCHOLOGIST

"I Have to Talk to My Wife": An (Almost) True Adventure in Research

You went on a test drive. You offered a price for the car. The salesman talked to his manager, who demanded a much higher price. After lengthy negotiations involving frequent consultations between the salesman and the manager, you finally settle on a price that represents a compromise between their asking price and yours. Do you now accept the deal? Many people do, but some try to gain an edge by claiming that they must first talk to their spouse (or partner) in the hopes that the manager will make additional concessions.

Does this strategy really work? The following account represents a failed attempt to answer that question. Originally reported by Cialdini (2002), we have altered it slightly. To find out whether claiming "I have to talk to my wife" at the end of a price negotiation might compel the seller to reduce the negotiated price further, "Jason," a student at Arizona State University, conducted a field experiment in an open market in Tempe. The vendors there occupy small stalls stocked with goods imported from Mexico. Although there is some variation in what they offer, many sell the same items at roughly the same price, and all conduct their business with the understanding that the final price was to be negotiated.

One item offered by nearly all the vendors was a chess set made out of jade. Prior to conducting his study, Jason made a note of all the vendors who offered the item. He then randomly assigned half the vendors to an experimental condition and the other half to a control condition. In the experimental condition, he would negotiate until the vendor appeared to have made his final offer. At that point, he would indicate that he needed to talk to his wife before he could finalize the purchase. In the control condition, he would negotiate in the same way, but would not claim that he first had to talk to his wife. The final price he was asked to pay in the two conditions would be the dependent variable.

Prices are often negotiable in open markets.

Jason collected the data over two days. On the first day, he ran the experimental condition according to the script and recorded the number of vendors who seemed willing to lower their price further in response to his claim that he needed to talk to his wife. On the second day, he ran the control condition, again according to plan. When the first vendor gave him his "best price," Jason agreed to it. At that point—and with an expression that indicated utter bewilderment—the vendor asked: "Don't you have to talk to your wife?"

The vendor's response made clear to Jason that he would have to abort the experiment, because it seemed obvious that he could not collect the data for the control condition. Where did he go wrong? Jason had randomly assigned his unwitting participants to an experimental and a control condition, but he failed to run the conditions in random fashion. His lapse allowed the participants to communicate with one another about the odd bird who was trying to buy a chess set. Jason could easily have avoided the problem by running both conditions each day.

Randomizing conditions is also important in laboratory experiments. Administering one condition in the morning and the other in the afternoon, for example, confounds the conditions with the time of day. Any differences that result could thus be due either to the experimental manipulations or to the fact that one condition drew primarily morning people, while the other attracted evening people.

COMPLIANCE: A SUMMARY

Compliance refers to our tendency to go along with another's direct request. People often comply with small requests due partly to a lack of cognitive processing. Individuals can often be induced to comply with large requests through the use of sequential techniques. The foot-in-the door technique sidesteps possible resistance to a large request by first securing compliance with a small request. The door-in-the-face technique induces compliance with a small request after the refusal of an unreasonably large request. Low-balling sidesteps resistance by securing a commitment to a low-cost choice and then increasing the cost. The that's-not-all-technique works because it alters the perceived value of an item, and the labeling technique succeeds by changing the self- perceptions of the targets of a request.

Think Like a Social Psychologist

Confronting social issues

—Compliance often has detrimental consequences for the target of a request. The car buyer who is low-balled into spending a great deal more money than he had planned to spend is a case in point. Can you think of ways in which any or all of the techniques for inducing compliance could be used to achieve positive consequences—for example, to induce people to recycle their waste or to vote?

Understanding everyday behavior

—How could you use the door-in-the-face technique to get your parents to pay off a small balance on your credit card? What psychological processes would explain their compliance?

CONFORMITY

Whereas compliance is a behavioral response to social influence attempts from a single other, **conformity** is the tendency to go along with a majority of others. Conformity can result from both *informational* and *normative social influence* (Deutsch & Gerard, 1955). That is, we conform because we like to be right and because we want others to like us. These motives often act as hidden influences on our willingness to go along with a majority's judgment.

Informational Social Influence

Let's face it, we're often asked to make judgments and decisions about truly ambiguous issues. Hope and her friends found themselves in just such a situation. There was no clear-cut answer to *whether* they should do something to teach Cassidy a lesson, and it was equally unclear *what* they should do. In such situations, people often look to others for the answers, a form of **informational social influence**. The power of informational social influence was demonstrated convincingly in a study that took advantage of the **autokinetic effect**, a perceptual illusion created by a stationary point of light surrounded by darkness (Sherif, 1936). After viewers have looked at the point of light for a few seconds, the saccadic motion of their eyes creates the illusion that the light is moving. Some people experience the apparent movement as a circle; others, as a spiral or left-to-right movement. Individual viewers also differ in their estimations of how far the light seems to move, from as little as an inch to as much as two feet. Because the light does not really move, people's perceptions of its movement are truly ambiguous. The central question addressed by Sherif's (1935) now famous experiment was how the presence of others in this situation could help viewers disambiguate the phenomenon.

Sherif (1935) recruited three male participants for a study of visual perception. During the first phase of the experiment, he placed each individual participant in a completely dark room and asked him to provide an estimate of how far a point of light 15 feet in front of him appeared to move. As expected, participants' *individual* estimates varied from one inch to about eight feet. In the second phase of the experiment, participants gave their estimates in one another's presence. Again, participants' estimates varied, but to a much lesser degree (between two and four inches). In additional group sessions, the variation in estimates diminished further, so after the third group session, participants were giving identical estimates (three inches). Evidently, through communication, the group had established norms to which the individuals were now conforming.

Interestingly, participants continued to conform to the group norm, even when they returned to giving their estimates individually (Sherif, 1936). Moreover, they passed the group norm on when they later joined a new group. In one study (Jacobs & Campbell, 1961), the experimenter first replicated Sherif's (1936) conformity effect and then began to gradually substitute new members for the original group members, until only the first participant from the original group remained. Participants in the new group adopted the norm established by the original group, based on the social influence of the one remaining member of the original group.

These findings suggest that participants did not simply go along with a majority judgment. Rather, their conformity reflected their **private acceptance** of the group's norms. That is, they believed they had given the right answer. In fact, the results of a recent study suggest that they adjusted their perceptions to fit the norm (Germar, Schlemmer, Krug, Voss, & Mojzisch, 2014). This conclusion makes a lot of sense, because people want to be right. When there is some ambiguity about what the right answer might be or an answer cannot easily be found, people rely on others' judgments.

Our lives present us with countless examples that attest to the power of informational social influence. Imagine, for example, that you are surfing the web in search of new headphones to replace the cheap ones that keep shorting out on you. Imagine further that your budget is sufficient to treat yourself to either a pair of Beats by Dr. Dre or Soul by Ludacris and that both are similarly priced. One way to decide is to read the consumer reviews available. Once you arrive at a decision, it will likely reflect the judgment of the majority, particularly if the majority is comprised of others who can claim to be experts on the issue (Harkins & Petty, 1987) and if they are unanimous in their endorsement (Nemeth & Chiles, 1988).

Normative Social Influence

Conforming to the opinion of the majority when a judgment is ambiguous makes a great deal of sense. However, majorities can be wrong. This simple observation prompted Solomon Asch to ask whether participants would respond in the same way as Sherif's (1935, 1936) had if they knew the majority's judgment was obviously wrong. To answer his question, Asch (1956) created an experimental scenario that required participants to judge the length of several vertical lines. Between seven and nine participants viewed slides of a target line and three comparison lines (see **Figure 7.2**).

If you were the only participant in this seemingly simple experiment, you would probably take little time and effort to decide that line B is the right answer. But imagine that you are with eight others, who all take their turns before you do and who all seem to agree that line C is the right answer. Would your answer still be line B?

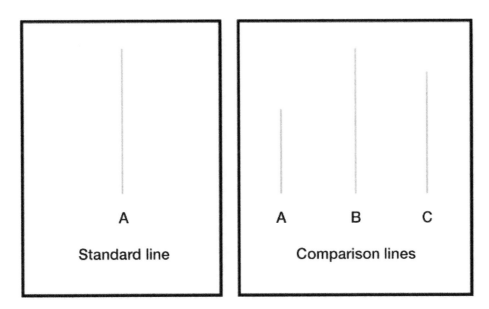

Figure 7.2: Target and Comparisons Lines Used in Asch's (1956) Experiments on Conformity

Source: Asch, S.E. (1956). Studies of independence and conformity: A minority of one against a unanimous majority. *Psychological Monographs, 70*, (whole number 416).

Judging by the results of Asch's (1956) experiment, the odds are that you would change your answer to conform to that of the majority, even though you know it could not be more wrong. Asch's participants made their judgments in the presence of six to eight confederates, all of whom had been instructed to provide the wrong answer on 12 out of 18 trials. The experiment was set up so that the participants always gave their answers last. Faced with this situation, a scant 23.6 percent of participants broke with the majority and gave the correct answers on all trials. A full 76.4 percent went along with the majority on at least one trial. Furthermore, 61.8 percent gave the wrong answer on three or more trials, and 31.9 percent gave the wrong answer on more than nine trials. These results represent a tremendous amount of conformity, given the fact that the majority's answer was obviously wrong.

How can we account for this high level of conformity? Asch's (1956) studies suggest that participants were responding to **normative social influence**. That is, although people like to be right, as Sherif (1936) has shown, they also want to be liked. Going against the majority opinion might upset the group's harmony, earning the scorn of other members of the group. Consistent with this idea, when Asch (1956) allowed participants to give their answers in private, they did not go along with the majority, but instead provided the correct answers. Thus, *normative* social influence leads to **public acceptance** of the majority's point of view, unlike *informational* social influence, which leads to *private acceptance*.

The findings from the studies of the autokinetic effect and of the line judging seem to suggest that informational social influence leads to private acceptance when people are motivated to be right, whereas normative social influence leads to public acceptance when people are concerned with being liked. However, that is not the whole story, because informational and normative social influence can operate at the same time (Turner, 1991). For example, in the autokinetic effect studies, conformity may have resulted primarily from informational social influence (reflecting private acceptance of the group's opinion) and secondarily from the participants' desire not to be too different from everyone else. Similarly, in the line-judging studies, participants' conformity may have resulted primarily from their desire to avoid "rocking the boat." Yet to the extent that they identified with the group, some of their conformity may have reflected private acceptance.

There is some evidence that informational and normative social influence can both influence ambiguous judgments, producing private and public acceptance through different processes. Group size seems to matter in public acceptance, but appears to have little, if any, importance in private acceptance. This conclusion is suggested by a study in which participants were asked to judge whether the color teal was more similar to blue or to green (Insko et al., 1985). Participants made their judgments in the presence of either one or four confederates, who always provided their answers first. Some participants announced their answer publicly; others did so privately, by writing them down on paper. As might be expected, the number of confederates increased participants' conformity only when they gave their answers publicly; it did not influence participants who provided their answers privately. These findings suggest that under some circumstances, normative social influence can produce public acceptance at the same time that informational conformity produces private acceptance.

Hidden Influences on Conformity

It is difficult to argue that in the line-judging studies, participants' willingness to go along with the majority represented mindless conformity. In all likelihood, the pressures of the situation produced an internal conflict between the competing motives to be right and to avoid being ostracized by the group. The fact that not a single participant in Asch's (1956) experiments went along with the majority on *all* the trials suggests that their conformity was indeed not mindless. That is not to say that conformity is always the product of conscious, deliberate processing, however. Instead, growing evidence suggests that conformity frequently results from hidden influences.

Imagine that you are walking down the sidewalk along a busy street in a downtown shopping district. Suddenly, you come upon a group of people who seem to be staring at a window on the top floor of one of the buildings. Will you continue on your way, or will you stop to see what everyone is looking at? Or imagine that you are sitting in a crowded airport, reading a book as you wait for your flight to depart. As you turn the page, you notice that virtually everyone else is using a cell phone. Will you continue to read, or will you feel the sudden urge to make a call?

Chances are your behavior in both situations would be influenced by your observation of what others are doing. When Milgram et al. (1969) created the sidewalk scenario on a busy street in New York City, they found that the percentage of passersby who looked up when others did increased with the number of gapers (see **Figure 7.3**). The presence of a single gaper induced 42 percent of passersby to look up; 15 gapers boosted the rate of this mindless conformity to 86 percent. Because conformity pressures in this type of situation are fairly low, the behavior of participants is perhaps best understood as reflecting the "chameleon effect" (Chartrand & Bargh, 1999)—a form of social imitation executed in the absence of conscious awareness.

Hidden influences on conformity have also been documented in an experiment that used priming to unconsciously alter the accessibility of conforming thoughts (Epley & Gilovich, 1999). Under the guise of a study on psycholinguistics, participants received strings of five scrambled words and were asked to unscramble them to form grammatically correct sentences. Some participants were primed for conformity with strings containing words like *adhere, agree, comply,* and *conform*; others were primed for nonconformity with strings containing words like *challenge, confront, counter,* and *defy*. Once participants finished unscrambling the word strings, they were taken to a separate room, ostensibly to provide feedback about the experiment. They were joined there

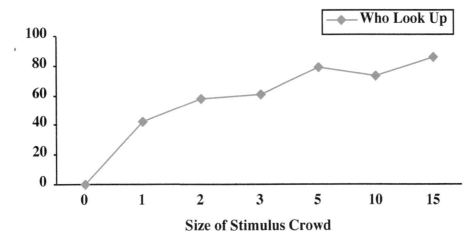

Figure 7.3: Percentage of Passersby Who Looked Up When They Saw Others Look Up

Source: Milgram, S., Bickmann, L., & Berkowitz, L. (1969). Note on the drawing power of crowds of a different size. *Journal of Personality and Social Psychology, 13,* 79–82.

by three confederates, who were identified as having participated in the experiment. Once everyone was seated, the experimenter asked participants to verbally indicate how interesting and enjoyable the experiment was. Two of the three confederates immediately responded by saying that they found it extremely interesting and enjoyable.

The experimenter then asked participants to rate their interest and enjoyment on a brief questionnaire. The responses to the two items on the questionnaire indicated that participants who had been primed with words related to conformity agreed more with the confederates'

The Chameleon Effect

enthusiastic verbal responses than participants who had been primed with words related to nonconformity. In other words, participants who had been primed for conformity responded to the confederates' normative social influence with increased private acceptance. Because participants were unaware of the connection between the sentence construction and the rating tasks, priming appears to have exerted a hidden influence on their tendency to conform to the confederates' judgment.

Priming effects on conformity have even been shown in the absence of confederates. For example, Aarts and Dijksterhuis (2003) led participants to expect that following the experiment, they would either go to the library or a train station. Compared to participants expecting to go to a train station, participants expecting to go to the library were faster at identifying words related to silence in a lexical decision task and spoke in a lower voice, presumably because "going to the library" had primed a mental association with "silence."

The results of a recent survey comparing respondents' stated versus actual reasons for wanting to conserve energy extends the hidden nature of normative social influence in important ways. Nolan et al. (2008) asked respondents to indicate reasons for wanting to conserve energy. Not surprisingly, "to protect the environment" was the most highly endorsed reason, while "other people are doing it" came in dead last. However, when the researchers correlated respondents' stated beliefs with their self-reported behavior directed at energy conservation, the fact that other people were doing it was the single most important predictor. In other words, we may think we're turning down the thermostat or turning off unneeded lights because we want to protect the environment, but we mainly do it because others are doing it.

Predicting the Impact of Normative Social Influence

Recall that in Milgram et al.'s (1969) sidewalk gaping study, the rate of conformity more than doubled when 15 confederates—rather than a single confederate—stared at the window. Looking at the results in that way, however, obscures an equally important finding: that conformity increased most dramatically as the group's size increased from 1 to 5. In fact, doubling the size of the group from 5 to 10 did not further increase conformity, and increasing it to 15 produced only a marginal increase. Thus, while the size of the group is important, it matters only up to a point. Slight increases in the size of a small group appear to have an additive effect. Similar increases in the size of a large group appear to add relatively little to the effect (Seta et al., 1989).

The complex relationship between group size and the impact of social influence is captured by **social impact theory** (Latane, 1981), which we will discuss in Chapter 8. Besides group size, the physical and psychological closeness of the group to the individual also appears to be important. Pressure to conform is highest in a relatively small group (Asch, 1955; Campbell & Fairey, 1989) that is important to the individual (Crandall, 1988; Hogg, 1992) and close to the individual in time and space (Latane et al., 1995).

Cultural and Individual Differences in Conformity

The extent to which research participants respond to normative social influence is affected by a couple of factors that have little to do with the situation, but have everything to do with who they are. One of these factors is culture. Participants from collectivistic cultures show a higher level of conformity in line-judging tasks than participants from individualistic cultures (Bond & Smith, 1996). The difference can be quite dramatic.

For example, Berry (1967) compared conformity rates in a line-judging task (that is, the percentage of participants who went along with the majority on more than half the trials) among the Inuit of Baffin Island and the Temne of Sierra Leone. The Inuit are people who value independence and whose economy is organized around hunting and fishing. The Temne are a farming tribe who value and depend on cooperation. As one might expect, conformity rates were low among the individualistic Inuit (around 18 percent), but fairly high among the more collectivistic Temne (around 60 percent). The Temne's high rate of conformity is not surprising, because collectivistic cultures value conformity to a much greater degree than individualistic cultures, which tend to give the squeaky wheel the proverbial grease. Moreover, in collectivistic cultures, which strive to maintain group harmony, agreeing with others is often seen as a sign of sensitivity, cooperation, and respect rather than conformity (Smith & Bond, 1999).

Are women more susceptible to social influence than men? The prevailing wisdom has been that they are (Crutchfield, 1955). On closer inspection, however, the relationship between gender and conformity becomes more complex. A review of 145 studies on conformity, including well over 20,000 participants (Eagly & Carli,

1981), suggests that, on average, women are more easily influenced than men. But that general finding obscures more specific results that challenge the prevailing wisdom in several ways. First, although male and female participants' responses differed, only a little more than half of the male participants were less susceptible to social influence than the average female participant. Of course, the flip side of that finding was that almost half of all the men were *more* susceptible to social influence than the average woman.

Second, gender differences in conformity are most pronounced in studies that measure public acceptance, as was the case in the line-judgment experiments. Women seem to conform more than men when they provide their answers in public. In private, gender differences disappear. This pattern of results may reflect the different social roles men and women supposedly play. By and large, women are socialized to be supportive and agreeable; men are socialized to be independent and assertive. Such role expectations might easily come into play in public settings (Eagly, 1987).

In collectivistic cultures what appears to be conformity is often considered a sign of agreement and respect

Third—and curiously—gender differences in conformity are reported primarily in studies conducted by male researchers (Eagly & Carli, 1981). Although this finding might be taken to indicate that women are more likely to conform in the presence of male researchers, the truth probably lies elsewhere. One possibility is that male researchers may unconsciously choose experimental materials that are familiar to—and thus less ambiguous to—members of their own sex. If that is the case, much of what appears in the literature on conformity may be more due to hidden influences on the researchers than on the participants.

Normative Social Influence Beyond the Laboratory

Much of what we do in our daily lives represents relatively mindless conformity in response to normative social influence. Although we may think that the way we dress is a form of self-expression, most of us do not stray too far from the norms others have set for us. The speed limit on the highway may be 55 miles per hour, but we often increase our speed to match everyone else's. And although we may never have thought if owning an iPod, we may feel a sudden compulsion to acquire one when we realize that most of our friends already own one. We do these and other things to fit in, to be liked and accepted, to avoid ostracism.

Although the consequences of responding to normative social influence with conformity are often benign, in many instances, our tendency to conform can have negative consequences for the self and others. Take a look in the mirror. Are you happy with what you see? There is a good chance the answer is "no," especially if you are a young woman. We'll discuss changing ideals of beauty in Chapter 9 on attraction. Presently, thinness is in. Perhaps that is why women tend to think of themselves as overweight and perceive themselves as heavier than they actually are (Cohn & Adler, 1992). This distorted perception is especially pronounced after women have been exposed to the ubiquitous media portrayals of slim women. Family and friends are another powerful source of social influence on the desired bodily image. Although influence that suggests the desirable bodily shape is largely informational, it is often complemented by normative social influence that prescribes to achieve it. On a benign level, such prescriptions may include little more than a sensible diet and exercise. More dangerous prescriptions may lead to eating disorders that can result in profound health problems. The Social Psychology and Health box **below** explains how binge eating can arise from the normative social influence exerted by a few members of a group that is both important and physically close to us.

SOCIAL PSYCHOLOGY AND HEALTH: BINGE EATING AS A RESULT OF NORMATIVE SOCIAL INFLUENCE

Binge eating is a symptom of bulimia, a pattern of eating that is characterized by periodic episodes of often uncontrolled eating, followed by periods of fasting or purging through vomiting, diuretics, or laxatives. This eating disorder affects mostly young women who are concerned about their weight (Gandour, 1984).

To determine whether binge eating might result from an individual's desire to conform to group norms, Crandall (1988) studied the relationship between binge eating and popularity in two sororities that differed in their norms for binge eating. In Sorority Alpha, moderate bingeing was associated with popularity; in Sorority Beta, the more the women binged, the more popular they were. Crandall was particularly interested in the extent to which new pledges would adopt the respective norms of the two sororities. To that end, he asked participants to complete measures of binge eating and friendship choices, first at six weeks and then seven months into the academic year.

As expected, just six weeks after participants joined the sorority, there was little evidence that their eating behavior matched that of their closest sorority sisters. After seven months, however, participants' eating had fallen in line with that of their sisters. Those in Sorority Alpha, who had befriended moderate bingers, were more likely to be moderate bingers themselves. Those in Sorority Beta, who had befriended heavy bingers, were more likely to be heavy bingers themselves. Thus, the social influence that unfolded over time was specific to the prevailing norms in the two sororities.

Although Crandall's (1988) findings may be troubling because they demonstrate how normative social influence can promote negative health behaviors, under the right circumstances, the same process can lead to positive outcomes. For example, fraternities and sororities that prohibit alcohol and drugs use their normative social influence to promote positive health behaviors.

MINORITY INFLUENCE: DOES THE MAJORITY ALWAYS WIN?

The Benchies Get Serious

Three hours after she had first sat down at her desk, Hope's study session was a mixed success. On the one hand, she was now sufficiently familiar with the material to take the exam without fear of a panic attack. On the other hand, the text messaging had continued throughout and had become exceedingly distracting. Danielle and Jennifer had sent her three messages each, repeating their call for action. Savannah had sent only one, in which she called again for further deliberations. Realizing that only a meeting of all four Benchies would settle the matter, Hope called them all to suggest they meet at the juice bar across from the movie theater. She was aware that they might be seen in the popular hangout, but it was Monday night when almost everyone was home recovering from the weekend.

Once everyone had arrived (Savannah was habitually late for just about everything), the Benchies began their talk in earnest. Danielle and Jennifer took turns generating reasons for the egging and suggesting ways to minimize the risk of getting caught. Savannah arrived and was quiet until Hope asked for her thoughts. Somewhat timidly, she said that she thought they still had to establish "the facts of the case." (In addition to being habitually late, she was also a *Law & Order* junkie). Her objection was initially met with utter and complete silence.

After what seemed like an eternity, Danielle accused Savannah of not wanting to stand up for her friend. But Jennifer indicated that Savannah's idea might have some merit. It was almost as though she hoped that they might find that there was, in fact, nothing serious between Cassidy and Brad. That would make her feel better than any act of revenge, which would, after all, imply a presumption of guilt on Brad's part. Frustrated by the unexpected turn of events, Danielle rolled her eyes and threw her arms up in the air, asking her friends: "How on earth would we do that?"

The situation that had developed among the Benchies was similar to the jury deliberations in Sidney Lumet's classic movie *Twelve Angry Men*. In the film, 12 jurors gather to render a verdict in a murder trial. The room is extremely hot, so to expedite the proceedings, the foreman polls the jury for a preliminary vote on the defendant's guilt. Without hesitation, six of the jurors raise their hands; a moment later, five more join them, leaving one dissenter.

Instead of raising his hand, the dissenting juror expresses a desire to talk seriously about the case without prejudging the 18-year-old Latino defendant. His request causes a great deal of exasperation, but finally, the foreman relents and asks each juror for an explanation of his vote. At first many of the explanations seem to be aimed at convincing the lone dissenter to change his mind. But eventually, the jury considers some issues surrounding the murder weapon. After the discussion, the foreman asks for another vote, this time in writing instead of by a show of hands. The result of the second round shows ten votes for guilty and two votes for not guilty: one juror has changed his mind. Further discussions of the defendant's alibi and the credibility of the witnesses are followed by additional rounds of voting, in which an increasing number of jurors vote "not guilty." By the end, all jurors are convinced of the defendant's innocence.

Twelve Angry Men presents a somewhat idealized picture of the power of dissenting minorities in the courtroom. In the vast majority of *criminal* trials, the final verdict falls in line with the leanings of the majority at the beginning of the deliberations (Kalven & Zeisel, 1966; Stasser, Kerr, & Bray, 1982). Though the movie doesn't illustrate *when* a dissenting minority can be expected to influence the majority, it does demonstrate *how*. The key is consistency. For each piece of evidence the jury considers, the dissenting juror consistently offers an alternative interpretation.

The importance of the consistency principle for **minority influence** has by now been amply demonstrated (Clark, 2001; Crano, 2000; Moscovici et al., 1969). It was first established experimentally in a study that required participants to decide whether a set of 36 slides were either blue or green (Moscovici et al., 1969). Although differences in brightness and hue suggested that some slides may have been green, they were all, in fact, blue. Not surprisingly, when participants answered by themselves, only one answered "green," and only for two of the 36 slides. A second group of participants answered in groups of six. Each group included four "real" participants and two confederates who had been instructed to answer "green" for all 36 slides. In a third group of participants, also composed of four "real" participants and two confederates, confederates gave the wrong answer inconsistently, for 24 of the 36 slides.

Confederates who provided wrong answers *inconsistently* exerted little influence on the participants' judgments. Virtually all the participants provided the correct answer for most of the slides. However, when the confederates *consistently* gave the wrong answers, 32 percent of the participants gave the wrong answer for four or more slides, and eight percent gave the wrong answer for all 36 slides.

Why was the majority so willing to succumb to the influence of a minority that consistently provided the wrong answers? Participants had little reason to worry that giving the correct answer would jeopardize their standing in the group. They were, after all, in the majority. Consequently, the social influence that minorities exert appears to be informational. A consistently disagreeing minority prompts those in the majority to consider alternative viewpoints and engage in "thinking outside the box" (Nemeth, 1986). In the process, the majority's attention shifts away from their own viewpoints to consider the merits of the minority perspective (Wood et al., 1994).

Of course, espousing a minority opinion is not without risk, because dissent is often met with hostility. In groups that exist over a long period of time, the potential of encountering hostility is reduced to the extent that members have compiled a history of agreement. Previous agreement and conformity endows members with **idiosyncrasy credit** (Hollander, 1958), which enhances their ability to advocate for a minority position (Bray et al., 1987). Not surprisingly, perhaps, a minority group that is merely perceived to have expertise in an area has an improved chance to get its views privately accepted by the majority (Sinaceur et al., 2010).

The informational social influence of minorities appears to serve as a hidden influence on private acceptance, which manifests itself fully over time (Maass & Clark, 1984). Participants in the color judgment experiment by Moscovici et al. completed a second task in which they rated the slides again, but in private and using a continuous scale (from blue to green, rather than blue versus green). Consistent with the idea that minorities exert a hidden influence on majorities, participants who had been exposed to confederates who consistently answered green shaded their answers more toward the green end of the spectrum than participants who had been exposed to the inconsistent minority.

Because minorities can persuade majorities to consider different points of view, they play an important role in situations that require people to generate creative ideas (Nemeth et al., 1990; Peterson & Nemeth, 1996). But their importance goes well beyond creativity. Consider, for example, that slavery was widely accepted in the United States throughout much of the 19th century. Early on, opposition came primarily from small and typically religious groups (the Quakers, for example), who objected to slavery on moral grounds. Because these groups voiced their objections consistently over a fairly long period, their influence on the passing of the Thirteenth Amendment cannot be underestimated.

The war in Iraq provides a more recent example of how a minority may have contributed to a change in public sentiment. At the time of the invasion by the United States in March 2003, a majority of Americans supported the effort. But by the end of 2006, three and a half years into the conflict, only a minority of Americans supported the war. Of course, some of the change in sentiment was probably due to the perception that the war was not going well. But based on the research we have discussed, some of it may also have been the result of the majority gradually adopting the minority's point of view. For an example of how dissenting minorities can influence jury deliberations in *civil* litigation, take a look at the Social Psychology in the Courtroom box below.

SOCIAL PSYCHOLOGY IN THE COURTROOM: MINORITY INFLUENCE IN CIVIL LITIGATION

Although minorities have little social influence on juries in criminal trials, they can exert a powerful influence on civil litigation involving damage awards. Juries in such trials face a situation that differs from those of criminal trial juries in several respects. Rather than rendering guilty or not guilty judgments, they are asked to translate damages into monetary awards, which represent a continuous series of alternatives. Decisions of this nature are notoriously difficult to make. How much money would adequately compensate a victim of a drunk-driving accident? What price tag can you put on the loss of a limb, an eye, or some bodily function that was compromised by medical malpractice? Civil juries can also operate under two different decision rules. Under the unanimity rule, they operate much like criminal juries, but under majority rule, they can render a verdict that not all jurors may agree with.

Civil juries have acquired a reputation for making extreme awards for compensatory and punitive damages. In 1984, Pennzoil sued Texaco for interfering in its attempt to acquire Getty Oil. Twelve presumably angry Texans brought one of the most powerful corporations in the United States to its knees when they awarded Pennzoil a total of $10.5 billion in compensatory and punitive damages.

Could such extreme awards result from the social influence of a minority with extreme opinions? To find out, Kaplan and Miller (1987) recruited students to serve on a mock jury that was to award damages to a plaintiff injured by an improperly constructed furnace. Groups of six participants read the case and were told that a verdict had been reached in favor of the plaintiff. Their task was to first recommend an award by individual ballot and then discuss the case, conducting further balloting as needed. Half the groups operated under a unanimity rule; the other half operated under a majority rule. Some groups were asked to award compensatory damages, others to award punitive damages. Once a group reached a decision, participants were asked to give their personal recommendations privately.

Not unexpectedly, the groups' final decisions represented the mean of the individual recommendations made by their members, regardless of which decision rule they were following. Evidently, the deliberations had led to a compromise, if not a consensus. There was one exception, however: The punitive damage award recommended under the *unanimity rule* was significantly higher than the mean award of the individual members. The problem was that the individual recommendations were positively skewed with one or two group members favoring extremely high awards. Under majority rule, those outliers could be ignored, but under the unanimity rule, they could not. Consequently, the extreme awards resulted from the informational social influence of a minority of the mock jurors.

A follow-up study (Ohtsubo, Miller, Hayashi, & Masuchi, 2003) replicated and expanded Kaplan and Miller's (1987) findings, showing that minority influence on damage awards can cut both ways. Groups in which a minority of members recommend an extremely low award make awards that are lower than the average of individual members' recommendations.

CONFORMITY: A SUMMARY

Conformity refers to our tendency to go along with the majority. Informational social influence generally results in private acceptance of the majority's viewpoint. It works because of people's desire to be accurate. Normative social influence results in public acceptance because of people's desire to be liked and accepted. There is little evidence for gender differences in conformity. However, there is reason to believe that conformity is affected by cultural variables, particularly collectivism versus individualism. Although majorities have a profound effect on conformity both in the social psychological laboratory and in everyday life, minorities can influence a majority if they are consistent in their advocacy.

Think Like a Social Psychologist

Understanding everyday behavior
—Think about a time when you went along with a group's decision, even though you felt it was wrong. What type of social influence did the group exert over you? How did your conformity affect your standing in the group? How did it affect you emotionally?

Making connections
—To what extent might our willingness to conform to numerous unwritten social rules result from social influence? Have you ever violated any of those rules? If so, what happened?

Thinking critically
—What does the experience of "whistleblowers" suggest about the possible limitations of minority influence?

OBEDIENCE TO AUTHORITY

In April 1961, Nazi war criminal Adolf Eichmann was brought to trial in Jerusalem. The summer of that same year, Stanley Milgram began conducting a series of experiments at Yale University, designed to help understand why and how people would respond with **obedience** to orders from an authority. Although the timing of the two events was a coincidence, Milgram had developed an interest in the question because of the atrocities committed in Nazi Germany in the time leading up to and throughout World War II. When those who were responsible for the Holocaust—a genocide unprecedented in both its scope and murderous efficiency—answered for their crimes at the Nuremberg War Trials, many defended themselves by claiming that they had only obeyed orders. Could it be, Milgram wondered, that people would kill for no other reason than having received an order from someone in authority?

The Milgram Experiment

To answer this question, Milgram (1963, 1974) devised an experimental procedure that was both simple and powerful. When participants in the study, who were recruited through newspaper ads in the *New Haven Register* promising financial compensation, arrived at the laboratory, they encountered two men: "Mr. Williams," a stern-looking experimenter holding a clipboard was wearing a white lab coat. "Mr. Wallace," a slightly overweight yet pleasant middle-aged accountant, was ostensibly participating in the experiment as well, but was really a confederate of the experimenter.

Mr. Williams explained that the experiment was concerned with the effects of punishment on learning. One participant would act as a teacher and the other as a learner. The learner was to memorize word pairs read to him by the teacher, who would punish him with an electric shock for giving a wrong answer. The two participants then drew lots to determine who would be the teacher and who would be the learner. The drawing was, of course, rigged so that Mr. Wallace would always be assigned to be the learner.

The experimenter then led both men to an adjacent room, where the learner would give his answers. The teacher watched the learner being strapped to a chair and hooked up to electrodes, through which the shocks would be delivered. The experimenter claimed that the learner had to be strapped in to avoid excessive movement, but it was clear that he would be unable to free himself. To "avoid blisters and burns," the experimenter applied "electrode paste" to the learner's arm. The learner

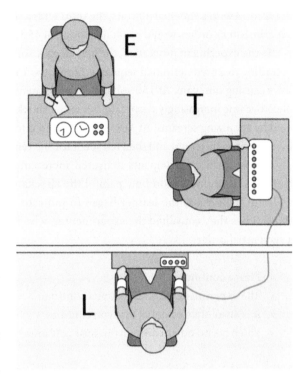

The basic laboratory set-up in Milgram's (1963) study, with the "experimenter" (E), "teacher" (T), and "learner" (L)

mentioned that he had received medical treatment for a heart condition at the local Veteran's Administration Hospital.

Once the learner ("Mr. Wallace") was restrained and ostensibly hooked up to the electrodes, the experimenter escorted the teacher back to the main room and introduced him to an ominous-looking shock generator, complete with 30 lever switches labeled in 15-volt increments from "15 volts" on the far left to "450 volts" on the far right. The switches were also grouped from left to right to indicate Slight Shock, Moderate Shock, Strong Shock, Intense Shock, Extreme Intensity Shock, and Danger: Severe Shock. The remaining two switches were labeled XXX. To demonstrate the shock generator, the experimenter gave the teacher a sample shock of 45 volts. This helped convince participants that the learner would, indeed, receive electric shocks and also provided them with an idea of how painful the shocks might be.

The experimenter then explained that the learner's job was to memorize pairs of words, such as *girl-pretty*, *dress-green*, and *loyalty-secure*. The teacher would first read the list of word pairs to be memorized and then quiz the learner by giving him a target word (for example, *dress*) along with three possible answers (for example, *pretty, green, loud, strong*). The learner would provide his answer by pressing one of four buttons that corresponded to the possible answers, as in a multiple-choice test. Each time he provided a wrong answer, the teacher would deliver a more powerful shock. For example, the first mistake would be punished with a shock of 15 volts, the second with a shock of 30 volts, the third with a shock of 45 volts, and so on. Thus, full compliance with the experimenter's orders would result in a shock of 450 volts after 30 wrong answers.

As the experiment proceeded, the learner gave some correct answers along with a number of wrong answers, according to a predetermined sequence. Starting with the 75-volt shock, the learner began to say that the shocks were causing him pain. At 150 volts, the learner mentioned his heart condition and demanded to be let go. His pleas became increasingly desperate; when the shock levels reached 270 volts and beyond, they were accompanied by agonizing screams. At 315 volts, he refused to answer any more questions, and at 330 volts, he repeated his request to be let out and then fell silent for the remaining eight trials.

Almost all the participants delivered increasingly severe shocks during the first few trials, when they had little or no indication how painful the shocks might be. They became increasingly reluctant to deliver additional shocks as the learner began to indicate his pain, to ask to be let go, and to scream in agony. At those times they consulted the experimenter, who responded with any or all of the following statements, in a sequential order:

- Please continue
- The experiment requires that you continue
- It is absolutely essential that you continue
- You have no other choice; you must continue

When participants expressed concern that the learner might suffer permanent injury, or refused to continue because the learner did not want to go on, the experimenter replied:

- Although the shocks may be painful, they are not harmful
- Whether the learner likes it or not, you must continue until he has learned all the word pairs correctly

Although many participants refused to continue the experiment once they became increasingly aware of the learner's suffering (see **Figure 7.4**), 72.5 percent continued to deliver shocks after the learner had refused to answer any more questions, and 65 percent obeyed fully by going all the way to deliver shocks of 450 volts.

No one was more surprised than Milgram to find such high levels of obedience. He had initially planned to study obedience cross-culturally, perhaps thinking that the Nazi atrocities may have been grounded in cultural variations in obedience (Blass, 2002; Milgram, 1974). Because the rate of obedience he observed among his American participants was so high, however, he shifted the focus of his research to identifying the variables and processes that produce obedience in the first place.

Factors That Increase and Decrease Obedience

When provided with a description of Milgram's experiment and asked to estimate the percentage of participants who would obey the experimenter and go all the way to the switch labeled XXX, most people estimate that only a small percentage of seriously disturbed individuals would do so. Nothing could be further from the truth. Milgram's (1963) participants were, by and large, middle-aged men from all walks of life who gave no hint of pathology. Moreover, when Milgram (1974) replicated his study with female participants, their level of obedience was identical to that of the male participants. His basic findings have since been replicated in many other

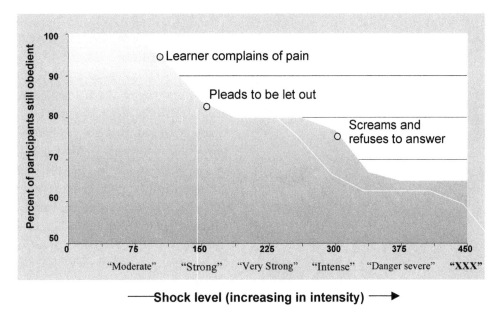

Figure 7.4: Percentage of Participants Who Obeyed at Varying Levels of Shock

Source: Milgram, S. (1974). *Obedience to authority: An experimental view.* New York: Harper & Row.

countries (Kilham & Mann, 1974; Mantell, 1971), using a wide range of samples, including children, college students, and adults (Shanab & Yahya, 1977; 1978).

This is not to say that individual dispositions don't make people vulnerable or resistant to obedience. For an account of how real individuals responded to real orders with obedience, refusals to obey, and even defiance, take a look at the boxes on **pages 314** and **315**.

If individual dispositions do not explain why people would obey orders from an authority, what does? Milgram (1963; 1974) recognized that his participants found themselves caught between two opposing forces. On the one hand, there was the experimenter, who tirelessly reiterated that the experiment must continue. On the other hand, there was the learner, who provided mounting complaints that he was being harmed. To see how these opposing forces could interact to produce increases and decreases in obedience, Milgram (1974) conducted several replications of his original experiment, in which he varied the salience, or psychological immediacy, of both the experimenter and the learner.

Milgram found that if the learner could not be heard complaining of the pain the shocks caused him, the participants' obedience increased even further. It dropped to around 40 percent if both learner and teacher were in the same room. If the teacher had to put the learner's wrist on the shock plate, obedience dropped to about 20 percent. If the experimenter issued his orders over the telephone or through a prerecorded message, obedience dropped below 21 percent for the telephone and even lower for the recording. Clearly, obedience increases with the salience of the authority and decreases with the salience of the victim.

SOCIAL PSYCHOLOGY ENCOUNTERS THE DARK SIDE: THE MY LAI MASSACRE: A CASE OF DESTRUCTIVE OBEDIENCE?

Survivors of the My Lai massacre

On the morning of March 16, 1968, nine helicopters flew the members of the U.S. Army's Charlie Company to a rice paddy outside the tiny Vietnamese village of My Lai 4—known to American soldiers as Pinkville because of its reputation as a Communist stronghold. Their orders were to sweep the village for the Vietcong guerrillas that intelligence reports had placed there. By the time Charlie Company landed, the area had already been peppered with gunfire from assault helicopters. When Lt. William Calley's first platoon reached the main plaza on the southern edge of the village, they encountered mostly families cooking rice in front of their homes.

The killing began soon after the men of Charlie Company began their usual search-and-destroy task: pulling people from their homes, interrogating them, and searching for VC (Vietcong). The first victim was stabbed in the back with a bayonet; a middle-aged man was thrown down a well, and a grenade after him. Then, a group of 15 to 20 mostly older women, who had gathered around a temple, were executed with shots to the back of the head. Meanwhile, about 80 villagers were pulled from their homes and herded into the plaza. As many of them cried, "No VC, No VC," Lt. Calley told one of his men, "You know what I want you to do with them." A few minutes later, when Calley found the villagers still alive, he reissued the order: "Haven't you got rid of them yet? I want them dead! Waste them!" Calley and the soldier then proceeded to fire on the group, killing all but a few who survived because they were covered by dead bodies.

After ordering the killings in the plaza, Calley proceeded to a drainage ditch near the village's eastern boundary, where a group of about 70 to 80 old men, women, and children who had not been killed on the spot had been brought. He ordered a dozen or so his men to push them into the ditch, and three or four of the men did. Calley then ordered his men to shoot into the ditch. Again, some refused as others obeyed. At one point, a two-year-old boy who had miraculously survived the killing began running toward the village. Calley grabbed the boy, threw him back into the ditch and shot him.

By the time Charlie Company broke for lunch around 11 A.M., the killing was pretty much over. My Lai had ceased to exist; its people and buildings were destroyed. Army investigators later found three mass graves containing the bodies of about 500 villagers. Although not all of the men obeyed Lt. Calley's orders, along with his "exemplary" behavior, had proved enough to provoke the atrocious killing of hundreds of defenseless villagers.

SOCIAL PSYCHOLOGY ENCOUNTERS THE BRIGHT SIDE: TWO HEROES OF THE MY LAI MASSACRE

As difficult as it may seem to find heroes in a massacre that killed hundreds of civilians, there were two who emerged during and following My Lai. Chief Warrant Officer Hugh Thompson was flying a recon-naissance helicopter over My Lai that day in support of Charlie Company's operation on the ground. His job was to look for the enemy, draw fire if necessary, and report any enemy activity to two helicopter gunships that were supporting him. At one point, he followed a draft-aged man who was running from the village and reported his position to the pilot of one of the gunships. By Thompson's account, that man was the only enemy he saw that day.

When Thompson returned to My Lai, he found the village covered with bodies, many of them dead, along with some wounded. Unaware that Charlie Company was responsible for the carnage, he landed his helicopter near the drainage ditch. When he noticed that several people in the ditch were still alive, he asked a sergeant to help them. The sergeant responded by shooting them in the head. A little while later, Thompson noticed a group of villagers huddled near a bunker. No longer sure that he could count on Calley's men, he ordered them to stand down, shepherded the villagers to his helicopter, and asked the pilot of the one of the gunships to evacuate them. Thompson saved enough people that day to require two trips by gunship to a place ten miles from My Lai. When he returned to the ditch, he found a small child covered in blood, yet still alive. He took the child into his helicopter and dropped him off at a nearby hospital. Throughout the flight he kept wondering, "How did all these people get into the ditch?"

The answer to his question did not emerge for nearly two years. That we have an answer at all is due in large part to the efforts of Ron Ridenhour, a young man who had been drafted to serve in Vietnam. Ridenhour was not at My Lai on that fateful day, but he heard about it from fellow soldiers who had served with Charlie Company, whom he knew from basic training. He was so appalled by what he learned that he decided to seek an investigation once he was back in the United States. Most of his friends and relatives urged him to leave it alone, except for one who suggested that he write a letter to the Army. Ridenhour followed his friend's advice and in March 1969 sent his letter to the Army and to 30 members of Congress. Mo Udall, a congressional representative from Ridenhour's home state of Arizona, was the only one to act on the letter. He called on the House Armed Services Committee to ask the Pentagon for an investigation into the incident.

A hero of My Lai: Hugh Thompson

In November 1969, the American public learned about what happened at My Lai. The massacre was the cover story in both *Newsweek* and *Time*, and CBS broadcast Mike Wallace's interview with Paul Meadlo, the soldier who had killed the group of villagers in the plaza on orders from Lt. Calley. A year later, Calley stood trial for the massacre in a small courtroom in Fort Benning, Georgia. He was found guilty of premeditated murder and sentenced to hard labor for the remainder of his life. But President Nixon ordered Calley removed from the stockade and placed under house arrest. In 1974, Calley was paroled by the Secretary of the Army and resumed life as a civilian in Columbus, Georgia.

Although justice may not have been served in Lt. Calley's case, My Lai clearly mattered. Two weeks after the verdict was announced, a Harris Poll reported for the first time that a majority of Americans opposed the war in Vietnam. Their change of heart would not have been possible without the determination of Ron Ridenhour. What led him to pursue his cause, despite the opposition and obstacles he encountered? He was likely a man of standing and good character, but he also was a participant in a replication of Milgram's experiment at Princeton University before he served in Vietnam. Ridenhour had been one of the very few participants in the study who refused to deliver even the first shock (Glover, 2001).

Milgram (1974) also found that the legitimacy of authority mattered. When he moved his experiment from prestigious Yale University to a somewhat rundown office in downtown Bridgeport, participants' obedience dropped to 48 percent. When a confederate posing as another participant gave the orders instead of the experimenter, obedience dropped to 20 percent. Finally, the participants' obedience dropped to the lowest level in the presence of two confederates, who rebelled against the experimenter's authority. In that version of the experiment, only 10 percent of the participants obeyed.

Milgram and the Question of *Destructive* Obedience

Milgram's (1963; 1974) research shows just how far people will go in obedience to orders from an authority. Some scholars (for example, Browning, 1992; Sabini & Silver, 1980) have even argued that his experiment provides a framework for genocide and mass killings. Can Milgram's findings really explain the kind of **destructive obedience** found at My Lai? When Paul Meadlo received orders from Lt. William Calley to "waste" villagers who were pleading for their lives, was his situation analogous to that of the teacher in the Milgram experiment?

Milgram (1974) has suggested that though the two situations varied primarily in scope, they were nonetheless guided by a common psychological process. Others (Blass, 1991, 2002; Mixon, 1979) have argued that the situation of the learner in Milgram's experiment bears little resemblance to that of a soldier who has been ordered to kill a group of civilians. Milgram's participants were likely guided by expectations about what can and cannot be done in a scientific experiment (Mixon, 1979). When they expressed concern about the learner's welfare, the experimenter reassured them that the shocks were not harmful. Perpetrators of mass killings may be less certain about what can and cannot be done during a war operation, but they certainly know that their actions will harm their victims. Before we conclude that Milgram (1974) may have overstated his case in arguing that his research could explain *destructive* obedience, let's look at some findings that appear to support his contention.

One study (Meeus & Raaijmakers, 1986) applied a variant of Milgram's procedure to a job interview. Participants were asked to review the credentials of a highly qualified job candidate and then to interview him according to specific instructions. The experimenter, who pretended to be particularly interested in how the applicants would respond to stress, asked participants to make a series of 15 increasingly harassing "stress remarks" (for example, "This job is too hard for you"). The job candidate, who was a confederate of the experimenter, began the interview confident and self-assured and at first shrugged off the demeaning comments. As the remarks became increasingly devastating, however, he became upset, and his performance deteriorated. After repeatedly complaining that the interviewer's remarks were hurting his chances of getting the job, he refused to answer any more questions.

This experimental procedure contained all the elements that were present in Milgram's (1963) original study, with one exception: Participants were aware that their behavior was indeed harmful to the candidate. They knew that by going along with the experimenter's request, they were ruining the candidate's chances. Nonetheless, 92 percent of the participants ignored the applicant's pleas and fully obeyed the experimenter by making all 15 remarks.

In a conceptually similar study (Hofling et al., 1966), nurses working the night shift in a hospital received a phone call from a physician whom they had never met, but who was listed in the hospital's directory as a member of the department of psychiatry. The physician first asked the nurses to check the medicine cabinet for a drug called Astroten. None of the nurses had ever heard of the drug (it does not really exist), but when they checked the cabinet they found a bottle labeled "Astroten," along with specific dosage instructions. When the nurses returned to the phone to confirm that they had found the drug, the physician instructed them to immediately give the drug to a patient on their floor at twice the daily dosage indicated on the bottle's label. He indicated that he would arrive at the hospital shortly to sign the written doctor's order that hospital policy required before any medication could be administered.

Interestingly, 21 nurses who read this scenario indicated unanimously that they would not obey the physician's orders. However, of the 22 nurses who received a call from the physician, 21 obeyed by heading for the patient's room with the medication in hand, even though they (a) knew they were acting in violation of hospital policy; and (b) had reason to believe that the medication could harm the patient at the dosage the physician had prescribed.

Thus, it seems clear that in everyday life, destructive obedience is an all too common response to orders from an authority—just as Milgram had suspected (Meeus & Raaijmakers, 1995). Still, any interpretation of mass killings and genocide from Milgram's perspective is necessarily complicated by the multitude of forces that act upon the perpetrators. For example, many of Charlie Company's men went into the assault on My Lai seeking revenge for the death of one of their comrades two days earlier.

Milgram Revisited: Obedience in the 21st Century

Milgram's dramatic demonstrations of how an authority figure can elicit astonishing levels of obedience in ordinary individuals are among the most well-known social psychological studies. They have been a staple of textbooks for over 30 years, and references to the studies continue to appear in the popular culture (Blass, 2004). And as discussed in Chapter 2, they are also among the most controversial social psychological studies in terms of the ethical issues involved. Thus, it is reasonable to ask whether knowing about the causes and consequences of obedience has made a difference in how we respond to orders from an authority.

If you had the chance (or misfortune) to participate in a 21st-century version of the Milgram experiment, would you refuse to deliver even the first shock, as Ron Ridenhour did? Or would you obey the experimenter's orders more fully, perhaps to a similar extent as Milgram's participants? Before you answer, consider the results of a recent experiment that replicated Milgram's original study in a way that adheres to current ethical standards in research (Burger, 2009). The procedure was identical to the one described on **page 310** (Milgram, 1974)— with one exception. The experimenter did not allow participants to go beyond pressing the 150-volt switch in response to a wrong answer from the learner. **Figure 7.5** shows the results of Burger's (2009) experiment in comparison to those reported by Milgram (1974).

Although the level of obedience observed in 2009 was lower than in 1974, the 12.5 percent decrease in participants who continued the procedure after pressing the 150-volt button is disappointingly small. It is hardly

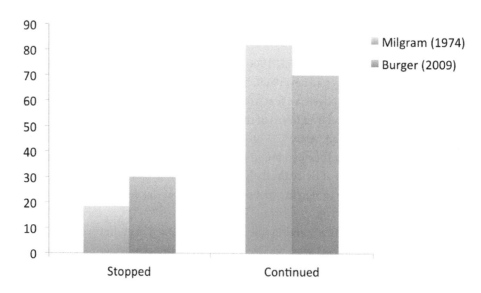

Figure 7.5: Levels of Obedience Then and Now

Source: Burger, J.M. (2009). Replicating Milgram: Would people still obey today? *American Psychologist, 64*, 1–11.

surprising, though, if you consider that the participants' behavior in both studies was shaped by the same powerful situational forces. As Milgram noted, individual dispositions are a poor match for the power of this situation. It appears that knowing how we respond to pressures from an authority is no exception.

Giving Orders: The Stanford Prison Experiment

Research on obedience initiated by Milgram's seminal studies focuses on the behavior of those who receive orders. This line of research has taught us a great deal about what makes people obey. However, we know little about what makes some people give cruel and unjust orders. Why, for example, did Lt. Calley order his men to kill the women and children of My Lai? Of course, he had received orders to conduct a search-and-destroy mission from someone higher up the chain of command. While such missions allowed for civilian casualties under some circumstances, the orders Calley received did not explicitly include the killing of hundreds of defenseless civilians.

It seems that orders give people power, especially when they contain an element of ambiguity. This connection was powerfully demonstrated in the Stanford Prison Experiment (Haney, Banks, & Zimbardo, 1973), in which researchers recruited college- aged men to participate in a "psychological study of prison life." To see a slide show and video clips from the actual experiment, go to www.prisonexp.org. Those who passed a screening for psychological and physical stability were then randomly assigned to be guards or prisoners.

On a Sunday morning, a squad car from the Palo Alto, California, police department pulled up in front of the prisoners' homes. They were arrested and taken to the police station, where they were fingerprinted and charged with burglary. Then they were blindfolded and taken to a mock prison in the basement of the building that housed Stanford University's Psychology Department. To create the prison, the researchers had converted lab rooms into bona fide prison cells, complete with barred doors.

What unfolded once the prisoners arrived bears an uncanny resemblance to the prisoner abuse that took place many years later in Baghdad's Abu Ghraib prison, during the second Gulf War. When the prisoners arrived, the guards decided to force them to strip, sprayed them with a delousing solution, and then required them to stand naked in the cell yard. From that point on, the prisoners spent 24 hours a day in their cells while the guards pulled eight-hour shifts. The humiliation they had experienced when they arrived was only the beginning of their ordeal. The guards began to taunt the prisoners in increasingly hurtful ways and made them wear ankle chains and loose-fitting smocks without underwear. In the middle of the night, the guards roused them from their sleep to have them count off their prisoner numbers. These countdowns, which were at first limited to a few minutes, became longer as the experiment continued. Finally, the abuse escalated from verbal harassment to physical torture. Guards demeaned prisoners by forcing them to beg for bathroom privileges. Prisoners suspected of fomenting a rebellion were denied both food and toilet privileges.

Most of the prisoners responded to the guards' orders with predictable obedience. Unlike the average "teacher" in Milgram's experiments, however, they showed little reluctance to obey. Instead, they willingly followed even the most humiliating orders. Becoming helpless and apathetic, they shuffled back and forth in their cells as though in a trance. Any conversations they had with one another revolved primarily around conditions in the prison. Although their status in the experiment had been determined by the simple flip of a coin, their brief experience had transformed them into real prisoners.

What led the guards to embark on their escalating cycle of abuse and violence, which began almost as soon as the prisoners arrived? The experiment fell short of providing a clear explanation. The prisoners' experience was so stressful to them that after a week, the researchers terminated the experiment out of fear for their welfare. It may be the case, however, that people in power are particularly likely to give cruel and unjust orders when their task is ambiguous. The guards in the Stanford Prison Experiment were charged merely with being guards; they lacked explicit guidelines specifying how they should carry out their duty. Similarly, Lt. Calley was charged with conducting a search-and-destroy mission, and the guards at Abu Ghraib were charged with extracting useable intelligence from their prisoners. In all those cases, how these tasks should be carried out was open to interpretation. The ambiguity of the orders put those in command in a position with a great deal of power, which may have served as a hidden—yet nonetheless corrupting—influence on their behavior.

A Tale of Two Ads: Which One Would You Respond To?

Male college students needed for a psychological study of prison life. $70 per day for 1–2 weeks beginning May 17. For further information and applications, e-mail … .

Male college students needed for a psychological study. $70 per day for 1–2 weeks beginning May 17. For further information and applications, e-mail …

Alternatively, it may be the case that some people are drawn to situations that allow them to be cruel, while others tend to avoid them. In fact, there is reason to believe that the behavior of the guards in the Stanford Prison Experiment may have been partly due to self-selection based on unmeasured individual dispositions. Carnahan and McFarland (2007) recruited participants through the two advertisements shown above. The first is identical to the one that was used to recruit participants for the Stanford Prison Experiment with the amount of financial compensation adjusted for inflation; the second differs only in that it makes no reference to "prison life."

Participants who responded to the ads received an "application package" that asked them to complete measures of five personality traits likely to promote a readiness for abusive behavior (Aggression, Right-Wing Authoritarianism, Machiavellianism, Narcissism, and Social Dominance Orientation). Participants also completed measures of two personality traits (Empathy and Altruism) that should be inversely related with abusive behavior.

As expected, participants who specifically volunteered for the study on prison life differed markedly from the participants who simply volunteered for the unspecified psychological study. As **Figure 7.6** shows, they scored higher on the traits likely to promote abusive behavior and lower on the traits that would prevent it.

Hence, it seems that the results of the Stanford Prison Experiment were to some extent due to participant self-selection. This makes sense in light of some of the behavioral implications of the traits measured in Carnahan & McFarland's (2007) study. Highly aggressive individuals are prone to anger and hostility generally, and right-wing authoritarianism is related to a desire to intentionally harm another. Machiavellianism includes a tendency to injure others without compunction. Narcissism includes fantasies of unlimited power, and individuals high

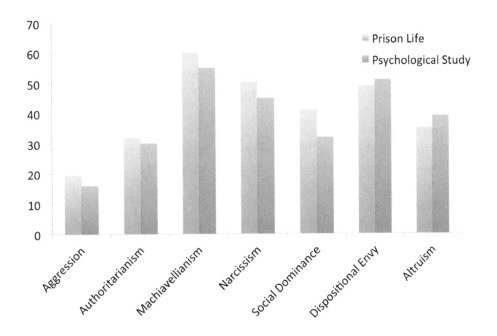

Figure 7.6: Personality Characteristics of Volunteers for Two Different Experiments

Source: Carnahan, T., & McFarland, S. (2007). Revisiting the Stanford Prison Experiment: Could participant self-selection have led to the cruelty? *Personality and Social Psychology Bulletin, 33*, 603–614

in social dominance believe in the domination of inferior groups by superior groups. At the same time, a lack of empathy prevents individuals from taking the perspective of the victim, and a lack of altruism is characteristic of individuals high in aggression.

OBEDIENCE: A SUMMARY

People will obey orders to the extent that they believe those orders were issued by a legitimate authority. In Milgram's (1963) original experiment, a majority of participants delivered what they thought might be potentially lethal electric shocks to a confederate in response to the experimenter's instructions. Additional studies (Milgram, 1974) showed that obedience increased as the experimenter's psychological immediacy increased and decreased as the victim's psychological immediacy increased. Some researchers have cast doubt on whether Milgram's findings can be applied to destructive obedience. However, others have replicated his findings by designing experiments in which participants were unambiguously aware that their actions could harm their victims. The Stanford Prison Experiment further extends Milgram's findings, shedding light on the psychological forces that compel some individuals to give orders that violate basic human rights.

Think Like a Social Psychologist

Making connections

—Milgram (1974) reported that participants' obedience decreased when they had to deliver shocks in the presence of confederates who rebelled against the experimenter's orders. What kind of social influence did those confederates exert over participants?

Designing research

—How could you adapt Milgram's (1963) procedure in designing your own experiment to study the effects of rebellious confederates on participants' obedience?

Understanding everyday behavior

—When the American Psychological Association (APA) celebrated its centennial, the Smithsonian Institution put on a special exhibit that coincided with APA's annual meeting. To enter the exhibit, visitors—most of whom were psychologists attending the APA meeting—had to traverse a corridor with a floor made of black and white tiles. A sign at the entrance instructed them to "walk on black tiles" only, and most did so willingly. When they reached the end of the corridor, they saw the first exhibit on display: the shock generator Milgram had used in his studies. What happened? What might this "finding" suggest about your own willingness or reluctance to obey orders?

Confronting social issues

—Given what we know about the destructive powers of obedience, what measures could the United States military take to prevent future incidents such as occurred at My Lai and Abu Ghraib? What measures might be aimed specifically at (a) those who give orders; and (b) those who obey them?

EPILOGUE: THE BENCHIES MAKE A SURPRISING DISCOVERY

As it happened, discovering the truth about Cassidy and Brad was not as difficult as the Benchies had at first suspected. The evening following their meeting at the juice bar, Hope received a call from Jennifer that began with the words "You're not gonna believe this!" Evidently, she had gone over to Brad's house to confront him about the rumors that he was involved with Cassidy. Much to Jennifer's surprise, Brad was all smiles, and seemed almost elated to see her. Before she could say anything, he led her to his room and pointed to the PS 2 on his desk.

On top of the PS 2 was a football—not just any football, but one that was signed by Hershel Walker, the legendary University of Georgia running back who had won the Heisman Trophy in 1982 before becoming a successful pro football player. Brad was really into college football, and the Georgia Bulldogs were his favorite team. Cassidy had found out about his leaning when Brad showed up for class in gym shorts sporting the letters "UGA." If the two had developed any kind of relationship, it was entirely centered on their shared affinity for Georgia football. Cassidy had been so happy to find a kindred spirit that she offered to let Brad borrow the signed football even though (or perhaps because) it was a valuable collector's item.

Jennifer had reacted to Brad's revelations with mixed emotions. She felt at once relieved that the rumors about Brad and Cassidy were unfounded, and embarrassed that she hadn't given him more credit. More than anything else, she felt the need to immediately break the news to her fellow Benchies. She excused herself to use the bathroom and called her friends.

Hope was greatly relieved to learn about the new developments. She no longer felt torn between obeying the principal and sticking up for her friend. Because there was no longer any need to teach Cassidy a lesson, she didn't have to risk a suspension that could have wreaked havoc on her grades. But mostly she was relieved because suddenly it seemed that she and her friends might be able to get along with the new kid on the block. "I have no use for a Georgia peach," Hope thought, "but a Georgia Bulldog is an altogether different matter."

HIDDEN INFLUENCES ON COMPLIANCE, CONFORMITY, AND OBEDIENCE: A SUMMARY

Mindlessness: going along with a direct request from another without giving deliberate thought to its nature

Sequential requests: Compliance requests, such as the foot-in-the-door and the door-in-the-face techniques, which are effective because they are subtle and hide their true purpose

The chameleon effect: a form of social imitation that is executed in the absence of conscious awareness

Conformity primes: the unconscious influence of situational information that increases the accessibility of conformity-related thoughts

Gender bias in conformity experiments: the tendency of researchers to unconsciously choose experimental materials familiar primarily to members of their own sex

Minority influence on private acceptance: over time, the unconscious private acceptance of the social influence of a minority

Power: the psychological force that unconsciously corrupts those in a position to give orders in an ambiguous situation

KEY TERMS AND DEFINITIONS

Compliance: going along with another's direct request

Foot-in-the-door technique: a way to sidestep resistance to a large request by first getting compliance with a small request

Door-in-the-face technique: a way to sidestep resistance to a small request by first making an unreasonably large request

Low-balling: a way to sidestep resistance to a large request by first creating a commitment to a smaller request

That's-not-all technique: a way to sidestep resistance to a large request by immediately reducing the perceived size of the request

Labeling technique: a way to induce compliance by changing a target's self-perceptions

Conformity: the tendency to go along with the decisions or actions of a majority

Informational social influence: social influence that leads to conformity in situations in which people want to be accurate

Autokinetic effect: the illusion of apparent movement that is created by a stationary light surrounded by darkness

Private acceptance: the type of conformity that results from informational social influence

Normative social influence: social influence that leads to conformity because people want others to like and accept them

Public acceptance: the type of conformity that results from normative social influence

Social impact theory: a theory that predicts conformity based on a group's size, as well as its physical and psychological closeness

Minority influence: the process by which an initially small number of dissenters can change the opinion of a majority

Idiosyncrasy credit: the credibility dissenters gain through a prior history of agreeing with a group

Obedience: Changes in behavior in response to orders or commands from an authority

Destructive obedience: Obedience to an authority that has detrimental consequences for those affected by the orders

REFERENCES

Aarts, H., & Dijksterhuis, A. (2003). The silence of the library: Environment, situational norms, and social behavior. *Journal of Personality and Social Psychology, 84,* 18–28.

Asch, S. E. (1955). Opinions and social pressure. *Scientific American, 193,* 31–35.

Asch, S. E. (1956). Studies of independence and conformity: A minority of one against a unanimous majority. *Psychological Monographs, 70,* (whole number 416).

Beaman, A. L., Cole, C. M., Preston, M., Klenty, B., & Steblay, N. H. (1983). Fifteen years of foot-in-the-door research. *Personality and Social Psychology Bulletin, 9,* 181–196.

Berry, J. W. (1967). Independence and conformity in subsistence-level societies. *Journal of Personality and Social Psychology, 7,* 415–418.

Blass, T. (1991). Understanding the behavior in the Milgram obedience experiment: The role of personality, situations, and their interactions. *Journal of Personality and Social Psychology, 60,* 398–413.

Blass, T. (2002). Perpetrator behavior as destructive obedience. In L.S. Newman & R. Erber (Eds.), *Understanding genocide: The social psychology of the Holocaust* (pp. 91–109). New York: Oxford University Press.

Blass, T. (2004). *The man who shocked the world: The life and legacy of Stanley Milgram.* New York: Basic Books.

Bond, R., & Smith, P. B. (1996). Culture and conformity: A meta-analysis of studies using Asch's (1952b, 1956) line judgment task. *Psychological Bulletin, 119,* 111–137.

Bray, R. M., Johnson, D., & Chilstrom, J. T. Jr. (1982). Social influence by group members with minority opinions: A comparison of Hollander and Moscovici. *Journal of Personality and Social Psychology, 43,* 78–88.

Browning, C. (1992). *Ordinary men: Reserve Police Battalion 101 and the Final Solution in Poland.* New York: HarperCollins.

Burger, J. M. (1986). Increasing compliance by improving the deal: The that's-not-all technique. *Journal of Personality and Social Psychology, 51,* 277–283.

Burger, J. M. (1999). The foot-in-the-door compliance procedure: A multiple-process analysis and review. *Personality and Social Psychology Review, 3,* 303–325.

Burger, J. M. (2009). Replicating Milgram: Would people still obey today? *American Psychologist, 64,* 1–11.

Burger, J. M., & Caldwell, D. F. (2003). The effects of monetary incentives and labeling on the Foot-in-the-Door Effect: Evidence for a self-perception process. *Basic and Applied Social Psychology, 25,* 235–241.

Burger, J. M., & Guadagno, R. E. (2003). Self-concept clarity and the foot-in-the-door procedure. *Basic and Applied Social Psychology, 25,* 79–86.

Campbell, J. D., & Fairey, P. J. (1989). Informational and normative routes to conformity: The effect of faction size as a function of norm extremity and attention to the stimulus. *Journal of Personality and Social Psychology, 57,* 457–468.

Carnahan, T., & McFarland, S. (2007). Revisiting the Stanford Prison Experiment: Could participant self-selection have led to the cruelty? *Personality and Social Psychology Bulletin, 33,* 603–614.

Cialdini, R. B. (2002, May). Personal communication. Chicago, IL.

Cialdini, R. B. (2008). *Influence: Science and practice* (5th ed.). Needham Heights, MA: Allyn and Bacon.

Cialdini, R. B., Cacioppo, J. T., Bassett, R., & Miller, J. A. (1978). Low-ball procedure for producing compliance: Commitment then cost. *Journal of Personality and Social Psychology, 36,* 463–476.

Cialdini, R. B., Eisenberg, N., Green, B. L., Rhoads, K., & Bator, R. (1998). Undermining the undermining effect of reward on sustained interest. *Journal of Applied Social Psychology, 28,* 253–267.

Cialdini, R. B., Vincent, J. E., Lewis, S. K., Catalan, J., Wheeler, D., & Darby, B. L. (1975). Reciprocal concessions procedure for inducing compliance: The door-in-the- face technique. *Journal of Personality and Social Psychology, 31,* 206–215.

Chartrand, T. L., & Bargh, J. A. (1999). The chameleon effect: The perception-behavior link and social interaction. *Journal of Personality and Social Psychology, 76,* 893–910.

Clark, R. D. III. (2001). Effects of majority defection and multiple minority sources on minority influence. *Group Dynamics, 5,* 57–62.

Cohn, L. D., & Adler, N. E. (1992). Female and male perceptions of ideal bodily shapes. *Psychology of Women Quarterly, 16,* 69–79.

Crandall, C. S. (1988). Social contagion of binge eating. *Journal of Personality and Social Psychology, 55,* 588–598.

Crano, W. D. (2000). Milestones in the psychological analysis of social influence. *Group Dynamics: Theory, Research, and Practice, 4,* 68–80.

Crutchfield, R. A. (1955). Conformity and character. *American Psychologist, 10,* 191– 198.

DeJong, W. (1979). An examination of self-perception mediation of the foot-in-the-door effect. *Journal of Personality and Social Psychology, 37,* 2221–2239.

Dillard, J. P. (1991). The current status of research on sequential-request compliance techniques. *Personality and Social Psychology Bulletin, 17,* 283–288.

Eagly, A. H. (1987). *Sex differences in social behavior: A socio-cultural interpretation.* Hillsdale, NJ: Erlbaum.

Eagly, A. H., & Carli, L. L. (1981). Sex of researchers and sex-typed communications as determinants of sex differences in influenceability: A meta-analysis of social influence studies. *Psychological Bulletin, 90,* 1–20.

Eisenberg, N., Cialdini, R. B., McCreath, H., & Shell, R. (1987). Consistency-based compliance: When and why do children become vulnerable? *Journal of Personality and Social Psychology, 52,* 1174–1181.

Elms, A., & Milgram, S. (1966). Personality characteristics associated with obedience and defiance toward authoritative command. *Journal of Experimental Research in Personality, 1,* 282–289.

Epley, N., & Gilovich, T. (1999). Just going along: Nonconscious priming and conformity to social pressure. *Journal of Experimental Social Psychology, 35,* 578–589.

Freedman, J. L., & Fraser, S. C. (1966). Compliance without pressure: The foot-in-the- door technique. *Journal of Personality and Social Psychology, 4,* 195–202.

Germar, M., Schlemmer, A., Krug, K., Voss, A., & Mojzisch, A. (2014). Social influence and perceptual decision making: A diffusion model analysis. *Personality and Social Psychology Bulletin, 40,* 217–231.

Glover, J. (2001). *Humanity: A moral history of the 20th century.* New Haven, CT: Yale University Press.

Haney, C., Banks, C., & Zimbardo, P. (1973). Interpersonal dynamics in a simulated prison. *International Journal of Criminology and Penology, 1,* 69–97.

Harkins, S. G., & Petty, R. E. (1987). Information utility and the multiple source effect. *Journal of Personality and Social Psychology, 52,* 260–268.

Hofling, C. K., Brotzman, E., Dalrymple, S., Graves, N., & Pierce, C. M. (1966). An experimental study in nurse-physician relationships. *Journal of Nervous and Mental Disease, 143,* 171–180.

Hogg, M. A. (1992). *The social psychology of group cohesiveness: From attraction to social identity.* London: Harvester-Wheatsheaf.

Hollander, E. P. (1958). Conformity, status, and idiosyncrasy credit. *Psychological Review, 65,* 117–127.

Insko, C. A., Smith, R. H., Alicke, M. D., Wade, J., & Taylor, S. (1985). Conformity and group size: The concern with being right and the concern with being liked. *Personality and Social Psychology Bulletin, 11,* 41–50.

Jacobs, R., & Campbell, D. T. (1961). The perpetuation of an arbitrary decision through several generations of a laboratory micro-culture. *Journal of Abnormal and Social Psychology, 62,* 649–658.

Kalven, H. Jr., & Zeisel, H. (1966). *The American jury.* Boston: Little, Brown.

Kaplan, M. F., & Miller, C. E. (1987). Group decision making and normative versus informational influence: Effects of type of issue and assigned decision rule. *Journal of Personality and Social Psychology, 53,* 306–313.

Kiesler, C. A. (1971). *The psychology of commitment.* New York: Academic Press. Kilham, W., & Mann, L. (1974). Level of destructive obedience as a function of transmitter and executant roles in the Milgram obedience paradigm. *Journal of Personality and Social Psychology, 29,* 696–702.

Langer, E. J., Blank, A., & Chanowitz, B. (1978). The mindlessness of ostensibly thoughtful action. *Journal of Personality and Social Psychology, 36,* 635–642.

Latane, B. (1981). The psychology of social impact. *American Psychologist, 36,* 343–356.

Latane, B., Liu, J. H., Nowak, A., Bonevento, M., & Zheng, L. (1995). Distance matters: Physical space and social impact. *Personality and Social Psychology Bulletin, 21,* 795–805.

Maass, A., & Clark, R. D. III (1984). Hidden impact of minorities: Fifteen years of minority influence research. *Psychological Bulletin, 95,* 428–450.

Mantell, D. M. (1971). The potential for violence in Germany. *Journal of Social Issues, 27,* 101–112.

Meeus, W. H. J., & Raaijmakers, Q. A. W. (1986). Administrative obedience: Carrying out orders to use psychological-administrative violence. *European Journal of Social Psychology, 16,* 311–324.

Meeus, W. H. J., & Raaijmakers, Q. A. W. (1995). Obedience in modern society: The Utrecht Studies. *Journal of Social Issues, 51,* 155–175.

Milgram, S. (1963). Behavioral study of obedience. *Journal of Abnormal and Social Psychology, 67,* 371–378.

Milgram, S. (1974). *Obedience to authority: An experimental view.* New York: Harper & Row.

Milgram, S., Bickmann, L., & Berkowitz, L. (1969). Note on the drawing power of crowds of a different size. *Journal of Personality and Social Psychology, 13,* 79–82.

Mixon, D. (1979). Understanding shocking and puzzling conduct. In P. Ginsburg (Ed.), *Emerging strategies in social psychological research* (pp. 155–176). New York: Wiley.

Moscovici, S., Lage, E., & Naffrechoux, M. (1969). Influence of a consistent minority on the responses of a majority in a color perception task. *Sociometry, 32,* 365–380.

Nemeth, C. (1986). Differential contributions of majority and minority influence. *Psychological Review, 93,* 23–32.

Nemeth, C., Mayeseless, O., Sherman, J., & Brown, Y. (1990). Exposure to dissent and recall of information. *Journal of Personality and Social Psychology, 58,* 429–437.

Nemeth, C. J., & Chiles, C. (1988). Modeling courage: The role of dissent in fostering independence. *European Journal of Social Psychology, 18,* 275–280.

Nolan, J. M., Schultz, P. W., Cialdini, R. B., Goldstein, N. J., & Griskevicius, V. (2008). Normative social influence is under-detected. *Personality and Social Psychology Bulletin, 34,* 913–923.

Ohtsubo, Y., Miller, C. E., Hayashi, N., & Masuchi, A. (2004). Effects of group decision rules on decisions involving continuous alternatives. *Journal of Experimental Social Psychology, 40,* 320–331.

Peterson, R. S., & Nemeth, C. J. (1996). Focus versus flexibility: Majority and minority influence can both improve performance. *Personality and Social Psychology Bulletin, 22,* 14–23.

Sabini, J. P., & Silver, M. (1980). Destroying the innocent with a clear conscience: A sociopsychology of the Holocaust. In J. E. Dimsdale (Ed.), *Survivors, victims, and perpetrators: Essays on the Nazi Holocaust* (pp. 329–358). New York: Hemisphere.

Santos, M. D., Leve, C., & Pratkanis, A. R. (1994). Hey, buddy, can you spare seventeen cents? Mindful persuasion and the pique technique. *Journal of Applied Social Psychology, 24,* 755–764.

Schwarzwald, J., Raz, M., & Zvibel, M. (1979). The applicability of the door-in-the-face technique when established behavioral customs exist. *Journal of Applied Social Psychology, 9,* 576–586.

Seta, J., Crisson, J. E., Seta, C. E., & Wang, M. A. (1989). Task performance and perceptions of anxiety: Averaging and summation in an evaluative setting. *Journal of Personality and Social Psychology, 56,* 387–396.

Shanab, M. E., & Yahya, K. A. (1977). A behavioral study of obedience in children. *Journal of Personality and Social Psychology, 35,* 530–536.

Shanab, M. E., & Yahya, K. A. (1978). A cross-cultural study of obedience. *Bulletin of the Psychonomic Society, 11,* 267–269)

Sherif, M. (1936). *The psychology of social norms.* New York: Harper.

Sinaceur, M., Thomas-Hunt, M. C., Neale, M. A., O'Neill, O. A., & Haag, C. (2010). Accuracy and perceived expert status in group decisions: When minority members make majority members more accurate privately. *Personality and Social Psychology Bulletin, 36,* 423–437.

Smith, P. B., & Bond, M. H. (1999). *Social psychology across cultures* (2nd ed.). Needham Heights, MA: Allyn & Bacon.

Snyder, M., & Cunningham, M. R. (1975). To comply or not to comply: Testing the self- perception explanation of the "foot-in-the-door" phenomenon. *Journal of Personality and Social Psychology, 31,* 64–67.

Stasser, G., Kerr, N. L., & Bray, R. M. (1982). The social psychology of jury deliberations. In N. L. Kerr & R. M. Bray (Eds.), *The social psychology of the courtroom* (pp. 221–256). New York: Academic Press.

Wood, W., Lundgren, S., Ouellette, J. A., Busceme, S., & Blackstone, T. (1994). Minority influence: A meta-analytic review of social influence processes. *Psychological Bulletin, 115,* 323–345.

Zimbardo, P. G., & Leippe, M. R. (1991). *The psychology of attitude change and social influence.* New York: McGraw-Hill.

CHAPTER 8

GROUP PROCESSES

THE MAKING OF A (COLLABORATIVE) RESEARCH PROJECT

Just about everyone was busy that week, but Eric couldn't help thinking that his own life was even more hectic. His parents, siblings, and cousins were constantly calling, texting, and e-mailing him. They were planning a major family reunion, and it was time to finalize the arrangements. Where should it be held? On what weekend? Eric's extended family was spread out across the country, and it was clear that no matter what they decided, someone was going to be inconvenienced.

Unfortunately, many of those conversations were interrupted by calls from members of Eric's band. They had been looking for a new drummer, and had by now auditioned so many candidates that they were having trouble keeping track of what they had liked and disliked about each one. Too bad they hadn't taken notes; to make the right choice, Eric and his bandmates were going to have to try to reconstruct all that information from memory. Their choice of a drummer had important consequences: firing the last one had been more than a bit unpleasant, and they didn't want to go through that again.

To make matters worse, Eric was also racing from one meeting to another. On Tuesday, he headed straight from a late-afternoon lecture to catch up with some other students from his English class. They were all pretty upset about the way the class was being run. Their papers weren't being returned in a timely manner, and when they were, the instructor's comments weren't particularly extensive or helpful. Rather than complain individually, they had decided to join together to figure out the best way to approach the instructor with their concerns and convince him to make some changes.

Finally, Eric felt obligated to attend some meetings of his neighborhood association. Plans were afoot to tear down a historic building a couple of blocks from where he lived: a fast-food restaurant was going to replace the landmark. People in the community worried that their neighborhood's character would change for the worse.

In sum, Eric was involved in a great deal of social activity. But the nature of that activity differed in an important way from most of the social behaviors we have so far considered. For the most part, the research we reviewed in earlier chapters focused on how individuals react to social situations and behave within them. We have discussed, for example, how individuals form impressions of (and make impressions on) others; how they

329

Group decision-making is complex. When twelve people try to speak as one, they can produce brilliant ideas that no one individual could have generated, or disastrous decisions that no single member of the group would ever have taken seriously.

see themselves, and the implications of different kinds of self-concepts; how they form their attitudes, and the relationship between their attitudes and their behavior; when and why they can be persuaded to change their attitudes; and how they respond to pressure to conform and obey.

People are not just individuals, however; like Eric, they are also members of groups—and like Eric, often of many groups. And as Eric's experiences make clear, groups are distinct social entities. Groups form impressions, set goals (Mackie & Goethals, 1987), devise plans to solve problems, make decisions, take action, and try to perform as well as possible. They have their own attitudes, and they often try to change others' attitudes. Like individuals, they have feelings and self-images, and they experience stress. Groups even try to remember things (Betts & Hinsz, 2013).

These phenomena are the topic of this chapter. Specifically, we will review research on **group processes**—that is, the social and psychological processes that underlie the behavior of groups (Kerr & Tindale, 2004; Hackman & Katz, 2010; Larson, 2009; Levine & Moreland, 1998; Steiner, 1972). Understanding social behavior requires understanding group processes, for as we will discuss, people have an intrinsic need to congregate and form connections with others.

Sometimes groups convene to weigh evidence and make decisions or recommendations. At other times, they come together to get something concrete done—to create some sort of physical or intellectual product, or to solve a problem that has only one correct solution (see Kerr & Tindale, 2004). We will discuss research on both these kinds of activities, referred to as *group decision making* and *group performance*. Then, in the final section of the chapter, we will narrow our focus to the experience of individuals within groups—specifically, how people's thoughts, feelings, and behaviors are affected by being part of a group.

GROUPS AS THINKERS

Groups, of course, are collections of individuals. To understand a group and predict how it will behave, then, can we focus only on the individuals in the group? In other words, does figuring out what to expect of a group that is composed of Eric, Eva, and Enrique boil down to figuring out what Eric, Eva, and Enrique are each thinking and feeling? The answer, as you might suspect, is no. To understand the collaborative thinking, or socially shared cognition, that people do in groups, we need to take a different approach (Ickes & Gonzalez, 1994; Larson & Christensen, 1993; Resnick, Levine, & Teasley, 1991; Thompson & Fine, 1999).

By way of analogy, imagine trying to analyze the behavior of a flock of birds. Would you try to figure out how each bird decides when and where to fly? Or would you think about the flock as a collective unit that behaves in predictable ways and responds as a whole to changes in the environment? Certainly, individual birds are worthy of study, but the rules of behavior that flocks obey would be difficult to discover if you devoted all your effort to examining individual birds in isolation.

Groups think (Hinz & Tindale, 1997; Wilson, Timmel, & Miller, 2004), and understanding how they do so means treating them as distinct entities that are more than just the sum of their members. This is true for three basic reasons. First, group members influence each other, and as a result, groups can reach conclusions or take actions that might have been impossible to predict based on their members' beliefs and attitudes. Second, the kind of thinking that takes place in groups is not identical to the kind of thinking that individuals do. Some of the processes we will discuss here can be studied only in the context of collective thinking.

Finally, group thinking is more complex than individual thinking in many ways. *Individuals* who are making decisions must bring to mind pieces of relevant information, evaluate all that information, and determine its implications for what should be done. That's complicated enough. In *group* settings, though, what one person brings to mind must be reconciled with what other people recall and bring up, and all that information must be combined in some way. In a group, deciding on the implications of everything that is discussed is a negotiated process, one that depends not just on what members are thinking, but on their understanding of what *other* group members are thinking.

Making sense of group processes is among the greatest of the challenges that social psychologists face. As we will see, much has been learned that can shed light on how the groups Eric belonged to function and make decisions.

THE NEED TO BELONG

In E. M. Forster's story, "The Machine Stops" (Forster, 1928/1973), people live alone in isolated underground chambers, communicating with one another by means of "view screens." All their material needs are taken care of by an enormous machine. To satisfy their desire for intellectual or artistic stimulation, they retrieve information with the machine's help or listen to lectures broadcast by people in other chambers. They have no need to band together with others to solve problems, overcome obstacles, or defeat their enemies, because they have no problems, obstacles, or enemies. Even parents and children live separately from one another, assigned randomly to different chambers, often on opposite sides of the globe.

How likely is it that human beings could exist in this way? Not very, according to recent theory. Baumeister and Leary (1995; see also Case & Williams, 2004) have proposed that people have a fundamental **need to belong**—specifically, "a pervasive drive to form and maintain at least a minimum quantity of lasting, positive, and significant interpersonal relationships" (p. 497). This need, Baumeister and Leary suggest, is as strong as any other, even as strong as the need for food.

A great deal of evidence supports this theory. First, groups form very easily. Even those that are created arbitrarily quickly become cohesive, and members begin to treat and perceive one another differently from out-group members (Tajfel, Flament, Billig, & Bundy, 1971). Furthermore, being excluded from or rejected by groups is among the most common and powerful sources of anxiety (Baumeister & Tice, 1990; Kurzban & Leary, 2001; Williams, 2001). In a study by Zadro, Williams, and Richardson (2004), participants who played a game against a computer reacted negatively to being ostracized by the *computer*, even after being told that it was programmed to behave that way (see **Figure 8.1**). Simply imagining a social rejection is enough to cause a person stress (Craighead, Kimball, & Rehak, 1979).

Recent research, in fact, reveals that the brain's response to the pain of social rejection is remarkably similar to its response to physical pain (Eisenberger, Lieberman, & Williams, 2003). Not surprisingly, then, social isolation can result in physical symptoms such as sleep disturbances (Cacioppo et al., 2002). It also has negative effects on the immune system, leaving a lonely person more prone to physical illness than others (Kielcolt-Glaser et al., 1984).

Why would people have such a strong need to belong? It is reasonable to suppose that this need has an evolutionary basis (Baumeister & Leary, 1995). The desire to form and maintain relationships with others would have had a lot of survival value for early human beings. After all, groups can care for one another's children, cooperate in finding food and other resources, and band together to fight off predators. As a result, people today—products of that evolutionary history—may be born with a psychological mechanism that encourages them to seek out others and causes them to feel distress when social contact is disrupted.

It goes without saying that even if the need to belong is basic to human nature, people will differ in the intensity of their need. Cultural differences in the need to belong may also exist: Western cultures in particular tend to view groups with suspicion (Waller, 2002). Many Western thinkers have suggested that groups bring out the worst in people, and that individuals who become part of a "mob" regress to a more primitive state of mind (most famously, Le Bon, 1895/1968). Not surprisingly, ingrained distrust of groups is less apparent in

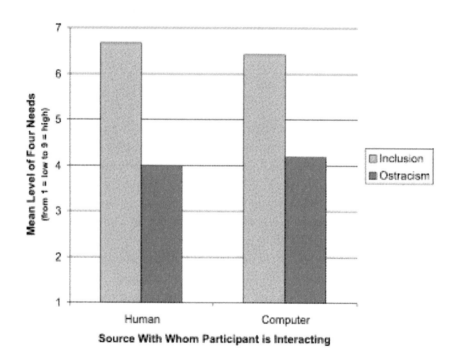

Figure 8.1: The effects of being ostracized by a human or by a computer: No difference.

Ostracized participants reported feeling lower levels of self-esteem, control, belongingness, and meaningfulness (all measured on 9-point scales, and averaged here to create one overall score). Based on the results of Zadro, Williams, and Richardson (2004).

collectivistic cultures. In fact, people in collectivistic societies tend to think about their social worlds more in terms of groups than individuals (Menon, Morris, Chiu, & Hong, 1999).

Might we predict, then, that people in collectivistic cultures belong to more groups than people in individualistic ones? Surprisingly, a study by Curtis, Grabb, and Baer (1992) suggests the opposite. For example, people in Japan report belonging to significantly fewer voluntary organizations (political parties, professional associations, consumer groups, trade unions, arts groups, and so on) than people in the United States and Great Britain. These findings are not difficult to reconcile with the idea that groups are more important sources of identity in collectivistic cultures than in individualistic cultures, however (Levine & Moreland, 1998). People who take group membership and its associated obligations seriously may be less likely to commit to a large number of groups than people who see group membership as a superficial affiliation.

Because human beings are essentially programmed to think, feel, and behave in concert with others, the study of groups is central to social psychology. E. M. Forster, the author of "The Machine Stops," grasped this idea intuitively. In his story, the protagonist rebels against the machine, struggling to escape his isolated existence and establish contact with others like himself.

Think Like a Social Psychologist

Making connections

—Any given person belongs to many different groups—North Americans, women or men, students, Latinas, psychology majors, country music fans, and so on—many of which overlap with each other. Based on what you learned in Chapters 3 and 4, what factors do you think may determine which groups are more important and significant than others to a particular person at a particular time?

GROUP DECISION MAKING

Making a (Hasty?) Decision

Eric soon found himself attending meetings of yet another group. Students in the laboratory section of his Social and Personality Psychology class had been organized into four-person teams to plan and carry out research projects. The instructor asked them to do more than just collect data on a topic; research teams had to use the information they gathered to test a specific hypothesis (see Chapter 2). In other words, they had to come up with a specific, falsifiable proposition.

For the next few weeks, Eric and his fellow team members would spend many hours together engaged in interdependent thinking and behavior. But they were looking forward to it. The need to belong could help to explain why members of Eric's research team responded positively to the opportunity to work collaboratively, and why they took care not to say or do anything that might make anyone want to exclude them from the group.

Brainstorming

The term *brainstorming* has become quite commonplace. In everyday speech, it is used to describe what happens when people get together to come up with new ideas, regardless of how they do it. **Group brainstorming** has

A brainstorming group.

a more specific meaning: It is a method for generating new ideas that involves (1) bringing up as many new ideas as possible, without worrying about how good they are; (2) not criticizing others' ideas; and (3) combining and improving on the ideas that have been generated (Osborn, 1957; Paulus, Dugosh, Dzindolet, Coskun, & Putman, 2002). The technique is very popular; people who participate in group brainstorming sessions believe that it is highly effective (Paulus, Dzindolet, Poletes, & Camacho, 1993).

Research has consistently shown, however, that group brainstorming is not that effective a method for generating ideas (Mullen, Johnson, & Salas, 1991; Stroebe & Diehl, 1994). When researchers compare brainstorming groups to equal-sized groups of individuals who have been asked to come up with their ideas by working alone, the outcome is quite consistent. The brainstorming groups produce fewer ideas than the groups of individuals, which are referred to as *nominal groups*. The ideas they do come up with are also no higher in quality than the ideas generated by nominal groups.

There are at least three explanations for the disappointing performance of brainstorming groups (Diehl & Stroebe, 1987). The first is that people in such groups may experience evaluation apprehension—that is, they may not want to share their ideas for fear that other group members will disparage their intelligence or creativity. Another possibility is that individuals who generate ideas as part of a group may put less effort into it than members of a nominal group because they feel less responsibility for the outcome. This effect is known as free riding (a phenomenon we will return to later, when we discuss *social loafing*). A third explanation depends on what is known as production blocking: because only one person can talk at a time in a brainstorming group, members are prevented from voicing as many ideas as they could come up with if they were working alone. Listening to others may also interfere with their ability to think of their own ideas. The longer members must wait for their turn to speak, the more likely they are to forget some of their ideas.

In support of the idea that evaluation apprehension and production blocking may depress the performance of brainstorming groups, a variant of group brainstorming—electronic group brainstorming—has been found to produce better results than either traditional brainstorming groups or nominal groups (Dennis & Valacich, 1999; Valacich, Dennis, & Connolly, 1994). Although the people in electronic brainstorming groups work together, they are physically isolated from one another (they use a computer network to share their ideas). Because everyone in the group can contribute ideas to an on-screen session at the same time, production blocking is eliminated. And because group members do not know who contributed a specific idea, evaluation apprehension is reduced.

Evaluation apprehension, free riding, and production blocking may all affect brainstorming groups. The relative importance of each effect may depend on the specific group setting. Significantly, research by Paulus and Dzindolet (1993; see also Larey & Paulus, 1995) indicates that once any of these influences has reduced the group's output, members' standards for the quantity and quality of their contributions change. They expect less from themselves, and their lowered expectations begin to depress the group's productivity.

Like most people, Eric and the other members of his research team were unaware of these studies of group brainstorming, so they used a similar procedure to decide on a topic for their research project. Among the ideas they rejected were "interpersonal dynamics in supermarket checkout lines" (or "That looks like more than 15 items to me, buddy"); "personality and pen choice" (or "What's with the green ink?"); and "spying on old boyfriends/girlfriends on Facebook—mental health implications." Ultimately, the group settled on a topic that seemed a little more conventional and that all agreed was interesting: the relationship between birth order and achievement. They decided to review the research literature and conduct an independent, questionnaire-based study to address the issue of whether or not firstborn children in families are more successful than those born later (later-borns).

Shared and Unshared Information

Coming up with a falsifiable hypothesis about birth order turned out to be easy for Eric and his group. One of the reasons the topic seemed promising to them was that they had discovered that all of them were firstborn children, and all had younger siblings who were not, in their estimation, "college material." The implication seemed obvious: firstborn siblings, they predicted, would be more likely than later-borns to possess the psychological qualities that lead to success.

The way in which Eric and his group decided on their hypothesis was typical of group decision making. Making a decision involves reviewing whatever one knows that is relevant to the decision. When a group is making the decision, that knowledge is distributed across the members; as a result, they must all pool their knowledge. Although there are many ways to classify the bits of knowledge that people bring to a group, one important distinction is the one between shared and unshared information (Stasser & Titus, 1985, 1987). **Shared information** refers to knowledge that all or most group members possess; **unshared information** is unique to individual members. When researchers analyze the content of group discussions, they generally find that shared information has been discussed at greater length than unshared information (Gigone & Hastie, 1993, 1997; Larson, Christensen, Abbot, & Franz, 1996; Larson, Foster-Fishman, & Keys, 1994; Stasser & Titus, 1985, 1987; Toma & Butera, 2009) and is perceived by group members as being more valid (Boos, Schauenburg, Strack, & Belz, 2013; Wittenbaum, Hubbell, & Zuckerman, 1999). In addition, shared information tends to be brought up earlier in discussions (Larson et al., 1994; Larson, Christensen, Franz, & Abbott, 1998), so that if a conversation is rushed or ends early, it may be the *only* information that is reviewed. These effects are especially strong when groups make subjective decisions—that is, when there is more than one correct solution to a problem (Stasser, 1999).

What makes these differences important in the way shared and unshared knowledge are treated? Quite simply, sometimes the implications of shared knowledge are very different from the implications of unshared knowledge (Stasser & Titus, 1985; Winquist & Larson, 1998; see **Table 8.1**). Imagine, for example, that the members of a selective club or organization are considering whether to admit a new member. If the candidate made a good impression on occasions when all the decision makers were present, the details of those events (shared information) would be likely to come up during the group's deliberations. In one-on-one interactions, when her guard was down or she felt less pressure to impress, she may have shown a less agreeable side of her personality. However, those unshared experiences would be less likely to be mentioned and discussed at a group meeting. As a result, the group might vote to admit the applicant, even though no individual member would have made the same decision.

Table 8.1: Distribution of shared and unshared information: A hypothetical example

Given what members of this hiring committee knew, should they have offered the position of office manager to this job applicant?

COMMITTEE MEMBER A: RELEVANT KNOWLEDGE	COMMITTEE MEMBER B: RELEVANT KNOWLEDGE	COMMITTEE MEMBER C: RELEVANT KNOWLEDGE
Strong letter of recommendation from previous boss	Strong letter of recommendation from previous boss	Strong letter of recommendation from previous boss
Good knowledge of computers and business software	Good knowledge of computers and business software	Good knowledge of computers and business software
Has business degree from Community College	Has business degree from Community College	Has business degree from Community College
Lives close to the office	Lives close to the office	Lives close to the office
Was an hour late for job interview	Had personal conflicts with fellow employees at last job	Had a C- GPA in college
Plans to move soon to a town 2 hours distant	Rescheduled job interview 3 times	Recent email message received from the candidate was full of misspellings and grammatical errors

Based on the shared (and thoroughly discussed) information in this example, the candidate received an offer, although much of the unshared (and mostly neglected) information suggests that decision was unwise.

Similarly, given some time, every member of Eric's group probably could have thought of families in which the later-born children were the high achievers and the older children the slackers. They kept that unshared information to themselves, however. In general, the more unshared information a group discusses, the higher the quality of its decisions, especially when that information has a different implication from the shared information (Scholten, van Knippenberg, Nijstad, & De Dreu, 2007; Winquist & Larson, 1998). Unfortunately, much of this valuable unshared information never comes up during group discussions. Thus, the distribution of information within a group is a hidden influence on decision making. (For more on the serious consequences of neglecting unshared information, see the Social Psychology of Health box **below.**)

SOCIAL PSYCHOLOGY AND HEALTH: MEDICAL DECISION-MAKING TEAMS

Much of the research on the role of shared and unshared information in decision making, like much of social psychology research in general (Sears, 1986), has been conducted using student volunteers. Participants in these studies also make decisions concerning matters about which they typically have little expertise. In addition, their commitment to making informed, accurate decisions is probably limited. Would the results of these studies be replicated in groups whose members possess more expertise, and who are clearly motivated to be careful and accurate decision-makers?

The answer to this question is yes. Larson, Christensen, Franz, and Abbott (1998; see also Larson et al., 1996) assembled several groups of medical interns and students employed at U.S. hospitals. They then presented information about a patient's symptoms selectively to members of each group. For example, some members learned that a 25-year-old patient had both short-term and long-term symptoms consistent with a diagnosis of Lyme disease; others learned that she had symptoms consistent with a diagnosis of infectious mononucleosis. The researchers controlled the distribution of different pieces of information so that the knowledge of some of the patient's symptoms was shared, but the knowledge of other symptoms was unshared (that is, available to only one group member). The participants in each three-member group then convened to discuss what they had learned and make a diagnosis.

The researchers found that these groups behaved just as the college students had when presented with decision-making tasks. That is, they were more likely to bring up and discuss shared information, and more likely to mention

Education and intelligence do not immunize people from the perils of group decision-making. Even medical professionals over-utilize shared information.

a given piece of shared information early in the discussion than a given piece of unshared information. In addition, the groups' diagnoses tended to be more consistent with the shared information than with the equally valid unshared information. Finally, the less unshared information the groups discussed, the less accurate were their diagnoses.

Medical errors often arise when individual physicians are compelled to make decisions on the spot under stressful conditions (see Gawande, 2002, pp. 47–74). But Larson et al.'s research suggests that even when groups of physicians have the time and energy to make decisions carefully and deliberately, they can make poor diagnoses. Fortunately, medical decision-making teams can take corrective measures to control for the disproportionate influence of shared information. For example, group leaders who are aware of the potential underuse of unshared information can strive to actively elicit it and ensure that it receives sufficient attention (Cicourel, 1999; Larson et al., 1998).

Groupthink

Not only do groups make decisions that are less than ideal; sometimes their decisions are disastrous. Of course, some of those disastrous decisions result from developments that could not have been anticipated. For example, Eric and his family might have thoughtfully and carefully chosen a date for their family reunion and then had to cancel it because of a major hurricane.

Some psychologists suggest, however, that certain characteristics of groups and their decision-making processes make them especially prone to poor decision making. Janis (1982), who analyzed a phenomenon he called **groupthink**, provided perhaps the best description of how group decisions can lead to fiascos. According to Janis, groupthink emerges when a group's members (1) are pressured by stressful circumstances to make decisions; (2) are isolated from outside opinions and influences; (3) are led by someone who promotes his or her own ideas and discourages critical thinking; (4) strongly desire one another's respect, and value group consensus; and (5) have no formal, preestablished rules or procedures for weighing evidence and reaching conclusions. Under these circumstances, groups are likely to develop a belief in their own infallibility, and to actively discourage one another from expressing doubts about the group's decisions. They will also ignore any warning signs that they may be making a mistake. The ultimate result is a terrible, often tragic, decision.

The most famous example of groupthink is the decision to launch the Bay of Pigs invasion of Cuba by President John F. Kennedy and his advisers in 1961. In an operation that, in retrospect, seems the height of absurdity, a small group of poorly armed exiles was transported to Cuba, where they were supposed to overthrow the government with virtually no military support from the United States. The belief was that the country's population would spontaneously rise up to support the invaders. Instead, the scheme was an immediate and total failure. Janis (1982) found that the conditions under which the plan was developed and the way in which the decision to invade was made closely matched his description of groupthink.

Though researchers have identified other prototypical examples of groupthink, studies of both established real-world groups and short-term laboratory groups do not strongly support Janis's theory (Aldag & Fuller, 1993; Longley & Pruitt, 1980; but see Turner, Pratkanis, Probasco, & Leve, 1992). The most consistent support for the model has been the finding that the symptoms of groupthink are correlated with rigid, controlling group leaders who do not tolerate dissent (Flowers, 1977; Tetlock, Peterson, McGuire, Chang, & Feld, 1992). We will return to the topic of leadership style later in this chapter. For now, we will simply suggest (along with others—see Kerr & Tindale, 2004) that even though Janis's ideas about groupthink have not all been well supported, they still proved to be extremely important and valuable to group researchers. The groupthink model highlighted the possibility that some qualities which, at first glance, might seem to be desirable in groups—like self-confidence and camaraderie—could, in extreme cases, turn out to be toxic.

Group Polarization

Early in their review of the relevant research, Eric and his group came across evidence suggesting that the relationship between success, achievement, and birth order was more complicated than they had suspected. When they met to discuss their findings, however, no one seemed inclined to modify their initial hypothesis. In fact, a couple of people even argued in favor of ignoring the studies that contradicted their hypothesis. One of those studies, for example, did not have a very large sample size. Another, when examined closely, included some confusing and contradictory findings. By the time the group concluded its discussion, members were no less committed to their hypothesis than they had been when they started. In fact, they were even more convinced that their own research would support it.

What happened in Eric's group, irrational as it may seem, is not unusual. It illustrates **group polarization**, or the tendency of a group's attitudes, beliefs, and decisions to become more extreme after discussion (Isenberg, 1986; Moscovici & Zavalloni, 1969; Myers & Lamm, 1976). Group polarization has been found in a wide variety of groups and in discussions focusing on topics as diverse as policy recommendations, criminal sentencing decisions, how much money to wager in games of chance,

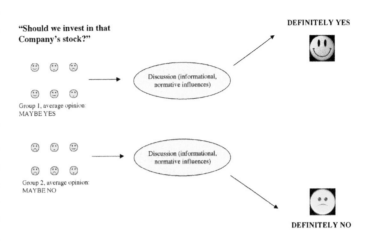

Figure 8.2: Group polarization: Another example.

and intergroup attitudes. For example, Myers and Bishop (1970) grouped white research participants into two groups; one consisted of people known to be prejudiced, and another consisted of unprejudiced people. After the groups discussed issues involving race relations, their attitudes were even more polarized (extremely different from each other) than they had been before (see **Figure 8.2**).

Research supports two explanations for group polarization effects, one based on what are called "informational influences" and the other on "normative influences" (Deutsch & Gerard, 1955). According to the persuasive argument explanation (an example of informational influence), if a group is leaning in a particular direction, discussion will inevitably involve justifications for moving in that direction. In other words, by the end of their discussion, group members will have heard more arguments in favor of a particular decision than for a contrasting decision. If the decision to take a particular course of action is based on the number of arguments for or against the decision that members can bring to mind, then discussion could strengthen members' conviction that their initial stance was correct.

The social comparison explanation (an example of normative influence) is that the members of a group want to present themselves favorably, which often means conforming to other members' thoughts and feelings. Discussion will suggest what the average tendency in the group is with regard to particular attitudes and beliefs. Members might want not just to match what they think is the average tendency, but to exceed it—that is, to strongly endorse the group's norms. If the group member believes that the groups' attitudes and beliefs are even more extreme than they really are—a phenomenon known as pluralistic ignorance (Isenberg, 1980; Miller & Prentice, 1994; see Chapter 12)—then he or she will feel pressure to support especially extreme positions. Either way, polarization will result.

Although several researchers have designed experiments to demonstrate the importance of one of these explanations for the polarization effect while ruling out the other, decades of research suggest that both persuasion and social comparison contribute to the effect (Isenberg, 1986). For example, studies in which people are provided only with information about other group members' preferences, but not their reasons for those preferences (which eliminates the role of persuasion) have revealed polarization effects (Goethals & Zanna, 1979). Similarly, studies in which people are exposed to other group members' reasoning, but not their overall preferences (which eliminates the role of social comparison) have also revealed polarization effects (Burnstein & Vinokur, 1977).

The More the Meaner: The Discontinuity Effect

The extreme decisions that groups sometimes make can lead to extreme behavior. Imagine, for example, that one group is competing with another group. A discussion of how to behave in this situation could intensify feelings of distrust toward the other group, and also reinforce the tentative belief that aggressive behavior may be necessary for one's own group to prevail. In fact, research has repeatedly shown that relationships between groups are more competitive than relationships between individuals, a finding known as the **discontinuity effect** (Insko, Schopler, Hoyle, Dardis, & Graetz, 1990; McCallum et al., 1985; Schopler, Insko, & Wieselquist, 2001).

We have already noted one explanation for this effect: group polarization. Specifically, it is likely that during group deliberations, members will be exposed to arguments about the possible evil intentions of their opponents and/or the benefits of erring on the side of greediness. This explanation (social support for shared self-interest) boils down to saying that something about belonging to a group leads people to become more competitive than they otherwise would be (Wildschut, Insko, & Gaertner, 2002).

Another explanation, group schema–based distrust, focuses instead on the possibility that something about playing against or negotiating with a group makes people more competitive. In support of this idea, Hoyle, Pinkley, and Insko (1989) found that in general, people believe that groups are more competitive than individuals. That, in turn, would lead them to behave more competitively against groups, so as not to be taken advantage of by them.

Winquist and Larson (2004) designed a study to pit these two explanations against each other. They asked participants to play the Prisoner's Dilemma Game (PDG; Dawes, 1980; Messick & Brewer, 1983), in which opponents must choose between cooperative and competitive moves. Competitive moves lead to the highest payoff, provided that your opponent (foolishly, in this case) chooses cooperative moves. At the same time, opponents will receive the highest *joint* payoff if both behave cooperatively (see **Figure 8.7** and the "Social Dilemmas" section, **page 365**). In one condition of this experiment, individuals played against individuals; in another, groups played against groups; and in a third, individuals played against groups.

The results of this study supported both explanations for the discontinuity effect. That is, both group polarization and group schema–based distrust contributed to the discontinuity effect. Groups were more competitive than individuals, regardless of whom they played against. At the same time, individuals and groups were more competitive when playing against groups than when playing against individuals. Both belonging to a group and playing against a group seemed to heighten competitiveness, primarily by increasing feelings of distrust toward opponents. In sum, more than one process contributes to overly aggressive encounters between groups.

THINK LIKE A SOCIAL PSYCHOLOGIST: VARIABLES THAT INTERACT

Sometimes what seems like the tiniest change in the way an experiment is run can have dramatic effects on its outcome. Suppose a researcher set out to test the hypothesis that when groups negotiate, teams of men make more aggressive opening offers than teams of women. In the experiment this researcher conducted, teams of women and men, each with three members, faced off against each other. In all cases, the subject of the negotiation was the sale of a property; the researcher was especially interested in the initial sale prices that the two teams would suggest.

To make sure the results of the study would be general rather than specific to a particular negotiation task, the researcher developed two different versions of the task. In one, teams negotiated the sale of an apartment building; in the other, they negotiated the sale of a factory. Teams were randomly assigned to one task or the other. The instructions they received before they began to negotiate were essentially the same, regardless of the task. As part of those instructions, they were told that successful negotiators are rational, assertive, attend to their own self-interest, and do not allow their emotions to get in the way of what they are doing. However, in the factory condition, without thinking much about it, the researcher added to the instructions a comment that he probably thought went without saying: that the attributes of successful negotiators would be described by most people as "male" characteristics.

When the study was completed, the researcher was surprised to find that there were no overall gender differences in the initial offers. On average, the dollar amounts proposed by the male teams did not differ from the amounts proposed by the female teams. However, one of his research assistants suggested they look more carefully at the data and consider more than just the gender composition of the groups. What else do you think the researcher should have examined, and why?

****

Initially, the researcher combined the data from the two conditions (apartment building and factory). But when he looked at them separately—taking into account the different instructions given to groups in the two conditions—he found the results were considerably more interesting. Teams of women who had simply been told of the attributes that were supposedly associated with successful negotiating (which were stereotypically male attributes) were significantly less aggressive in their opening offers than the men's teams. However, teams of women who had been explicitly and directly told that those attributes were more likely to be found among males (the factory condition) were significantly *more* aggressive than teams of men. Apparently, subtly linking the task to gender stereotypes led women to conform to those stereotypes. Blatantly linking the two, however, led to *reactance* (see Chapter 6): the women rebelled against the stereotype and bent over backward *not* to conform to it.

This hypothetical experiment is based on a study by Kray, Thompson, and Galinsky (2001). If such an experiment were actually conducted, then, we would expect to obtain essentially the same findings (although in Kray et al.'s study—which did *not* include the flawed feature of our hypothetical study—the negotiators were individuals, rather than groups). One problem with our hypothetical study, of course, is that the content of the task (apartment building versus factory) was *confounded* (see Chapter 2) by the difference in the instructions (subtle versus blatant mention of stereotypes). In such cases, it is impossible to know with certainty which of the two variables (content or instructions) made more of a difference. The most important lesson to draw from this experiment, though, is that the effects of some variables—in this case, gender—often depend on other variables—in this case, how blatantly relevant stereotypes are to a task. As we saw in Chapter 2, in cases like these, the two variables *interact*, so that the effects of one (gender) cannot be understood without taking the other (the precise instructions provided to participants) into account. Another way of expressing this idea is to say that one variable *moderates* the effects of the other. As this example demonstrates, not taking such moderators into account can make a variable that played a significant role in participants' behavior (gender) seem to have no relationship at all to their behavior.

So that we do not present too dark a picture of groups, we should note that in some situations, interactions between groups produce a better outcome than interactions between individuals. When negotiations are extended, complex, and involve many overlapping issues, groups are better able than individuals to figure out how to arrive at an agreement that benefits everyone (Thompson, Peterson, & Brodt, 1996). (For an example of the complicated role of gender in negotiations, see the Think like a Social Psychologist box on **page 341-342**.)

The discontinuity effect could shed light on an unpleasant interaction between Eric's group and another research team in his class. Because quite a few of the computers in the classroom had crashed, both groups converged on the same machine at the same time to conduct an online search for material. Unfortunately, the negotiations that followed consisted of little more than repeated (and increasingly shrill) assertions that "we got here first." To restore order, the instructor had to intervene. After a cooling-down period, Eric quietly approached a member of the other group individually, and the two quickly worked out an agreement to share the computer equally—a happy ending, although everyone involved was more than a little embarrassed and puzzled about how the conflict had escalated so quickly. The students should not have been so hard on themselves, however. People generally are not aware of the effects that belonging to a group has on them. Group membership, in other words, can be a hidden influence on our behavior.

Group Decision Making, for Better or Worse: A Summary

Groups can make decisions their members can be proud of, often simply by basing them on what the majority of members prefer (Hastie & Kameda, 2005). At times, many heads can indeed be better than one. But everyone should be alert to the problems that can emerge during group decision making. The processes we have reviewed are subtle and can unfold over time in complex interactions involving many people. As a result, they typically take place without awareness by the group members. At times, the costs of these hidden influences can be immense. In extreme cases, being blind to the downside of group decision making can lead to group polarization, groupthink, and ultimately to political, military, and technological disasters.

Prominent among the problems that plague group decision making is the fact that although group members typically have lots of information at their disposal, they do not always make use of it. In particular, groups are more likely to focus on widely shared information than on important unshared information. In addition, if shared knowledge steers a group toward a particular conclusion, powerful psychological forces may polarize the group, causing members to embrace their conclusion with a fervor that might not be warranted. The outcome, including a commitment to overly aggressive and competitive behavior, could be regrettable. Unfortunately, popular techniques such as brainstorming for maximizing the advantages of group thinking do not necessarily help to overcome these problems; in some cases, they may make them worse.

Think Like a Social Psychologist

Thinking critically
—As we have seen, groups can get into serious trouble by ignoring unshared information. Can you think of some reasons why downplaying unshared information might seem rational to group members?

Understanding everyday behavior
—Imagine that a group of friends got together on Halloween to engage in a little mischief—tossing an egg or two—but ended up seriously vandalizing their neighbors' homes. How might you explain what happened?

Confronting social issues
—Imagine that two governments are preparing to negotiate some sensitive and potentially explosive issues. You have been hired as a consultant to help manage their meeting. In light of research on the discontinuity effect and competitiveness, what might you suggest?

MAKING (FITFUL?) PROGRESS

Eric's research team very quickly came up with a plan of action and figured out who would be responsible for what. For example, one of the group members became the go-to person who knew which relevant published studies they had already reviewed and which they had not. Another was the expert on different theories of birth order. Eric kept track of the group's progress in administering the questionnaire they had designed. By the end of the first week, they were convinced they would complete their project well before the end of the semester.

A week or two later, however, the group was no longer feeling so complacent. Members were becoming more and more confused and frustrated by the seemingly endless studies on the effects of birth order, and were feeling increasingly unsure that they would ever make sense of them all. Tensions developed within the group, and the fact that no one was in charge and empowered to resolve those tensions was becoming a problem. One day, Eric decided to take matters into his own hands and essentially appointed himself the group's leader. No one objected much. Unfortunately, his heavy-handed, no-nonsense attempt to reorganize the way the group was conducting its work was not met with much gratitude. In fact, Eric started to wonder whether he was really cut out for the role of leader.

GROUP PERFORMANCE

The research presented in the last section focused for the most part on situations in which groups had to sift through large collections of facts and observations to make a judgment or decision. Clearly, some judgments are better than others, and some decisions produce better outcomes than others. Still, to a great extent, decisions tend to be subjective. In other words, there is some room for disagreement about how good a decision is.

Groups, however, also engage in other kinds of tasks, some of which lend themselves to more objective evaluation. For example, if two groups work to solve a set of math problems, and the first group comes up with more correct answers than the second group, we can easily evaluate their performance: the first group did better than the second. In this section, we will review research relating to how effectively and efficiently groups perform.

Members' Abilities

One aspect of a group that should obviously affect the quality of its performance is the average ability level of the people in the group. Clearly, the more competent, talented, and knowledgeable a group's members, the better the group should perform. Not surprisingly, research supports that prediction (Terborg, Castore, & DeNinno, 1976). Yet the role of members' abilities in a group's performance can be more complicated. Two groups could have the same mean ability level but differ in terms of the *variability* of individual ability levels. For example, one group could consist of people who all have approximately average ability levels; another could consist of people with a mix of low-, average-, and high-ability levels. The first group would be considered *homogeneous* in terms of ability; the latter would be considered *heterogeneous*.

Which kind of group is better, a homogeneous or a heterogeneous one? The answer depends on the nature of the task. **Disjunctive tasks** can be completed, even if only one member knows the answer or solution. Finding the solution to a crossword puzzle clue is an example of a disjunctive task; only one person needs to know that a 10-letter word meaning "askew" (16 across) is "catawampus." **Conjunctive tasks**, on the other hand, can be completed only if everyone contributes. Many team sports are relatively conjunctive. For example, a volleyball team would be hard pressed to win if one member was an extremely poor player. In general, heterogeneous groups are better at disjunctive tasks than at conjunctive tasks

Conjunctive group tasks require effective performances from everyone

(Levine & Moreland, 1998; Steiner, 1972). The reason is fairly simple: heterogeneous groups are more likely than homogeneous groups to have at least one brilliant member who can ensure the group's success when the outcome depends on the performance of its best member (disjunctive tasks). But heterogeneous groups are also more likely

SOCIAL PSYCHOLOGY ENCOUNTERS THE DARK SIDE: THE COMPLICATED EFFECTS OF DIVERSITY

Groups come in a wide variety of sizes, shapes, and colors. As a result, they have different goals (to make sales, promote friendships, pass laws, win competitions), different norms and traditions, and different sources of pride. In recent years, however, the large majority of organizations, corporations, clubs, and other institutions in the United States and other Western nations have had at least one common characteristic: they claim to value diversity. For example, universities often proudly publicize their programs to support and celebrate a diverse student body.

There are many different kinds of diversity: Groups can be heterogeneous in terms of their gender, age, attitudes, personality traits, and many other characteristics. We will focus here on one aspect of diversity that has been particularly prominent in public discussions of the topic: racial, national, and ethnic diversity (in other words, cultural diversity). Why is this kind of diversity so highly valued? A common misconception is that concern with diversity is based solely on the desire to compensate members of minority groups for past exclusion and injustices. For example, if all the firefighters in a community belong to a particular racial group, members of other groups may have been systematically excluded. As a result, people might lobby for diversity simply as a way to eliminate such discriminatory policies.

Certainly, in many cases (including the hypothetical one just described), concern with diversity can be better described as concern with a *lack* of diversity. In other words, increasing diversity can be a way of addressing a negative situation. But diversity is also valuable because of its *positive* effects. A group that is culturally diverse is also diverse in terms of its members' knowledge, attitudes, skills, and life experiences. As a result, the group is less likely than others to get stuck in a rut, and more likely to take advantage of novel ideas and perspectives (Guerin et al., 2004; Hurtado, 2005; Sommers, 2006). Diversity, then, is a goal of many institutions because it can improve performance (Sommers, Warp, & Mahoney, 2008).

The benefits of diversity are far from automatic, however. In fact, the effects of diversity on groups can be quite complicated (Cummings, Kiesler, Zadeh, & Balakrishnan, 2013; Kaiser, Major, Jurcevic, Dover, Brady, & Shapiro, 2013; Levine & Moreland, 1998; Milliken & Martins, 1996; Plaut, Garnett, Buffardi, & Sanchez-Burks, 2011; Triandis, Kurowski, & Gelfand, 1994). One thing is clear, though: merely assembling a group of people from different cultural backgrounds can be a recipe for disaster. Consider, for example, this description of a multinational team in one business organization:

> Their members mistrusted each other, guarded information jealously, and took every opportunity to attack other members. One European member explained his team's poor performance to us forcefully: "Those Brits on our team are too serious, the Germans are so stuck up about engineering they don't think anyone else has a brain, and the French couldn't care less about production quotas." (DiStefano & Maznevski, 2000, p. 47)

When attempts to promote diversity do not succeed, the individuals involved emerge from the experience with less tolerance for other people's differences and more negative attitudes toward policies aimed at promoting diversity (Hurtado, 2005).

SOCIAL PSYCHOLOGY ENCOUNTERS THE BRIGHT SIDE: THE BENEFITS OF DIVERSITY

Though diverse groups can be among the unhappiest of groups (Mannix & Neale, 2005), the reverse can also be true: they can be effective and rewarding in ways that would be impossible for homogeneous groups. At least two variables seem to determine the outcome. First, groups sometimes need time to learn how to take advantage of their diversity. As we have seen, when group members come from different backgrounds, they can bring different perspectives to the decisions a group makes and the problems it must solve. For those different perspectives to be heard and taken seriously, though, groups need to develop procedures and norms that will allow them to be aired. In a study by Watson, Kumar, and Michaelson (1993), business students in the United States were divided into groups of four or five people. Some groups consisted solely of white students; others contained a mix of students who were white, black, Latino, or foreign nationals (that is, students from Asia, Africa, Latin America, or the Middle East). For 17 weeks, the groups worked together on a variety of tasks and problems. Every four weeks or so, the researchers assessed the quality of both their performance and their interactions.

Initially, the less diverse groups seemed to have higher-quality interactions, but by the end of the study, those differences had disappeared. As for the level of performance, the diverse groups seemed at a disadvantage during the early phases of the study, but by the time of the last measurement, they were scoring *higher* than the others on some measures of performance, and lower on none of them.

The passage of time is no guarantee of success in diverse groups, however. In Watson et al.'s (1993) studies, groups not only received frequent feedback about the quality of their interactions and their work; they were given time to talk about the feedback and consider how they might improve their performance. This second feature of the study was almost certainly essential to its outcome. Indeed, a common feature of those diverse groups that are happy and successful is that members acknowledge their differences and talk about what the effects of those differences might be (DiStefano & Maznevski, 2000; Maznevski, 1994). Thus, if groups try actively to increase their diversity, they need to do so in a careful and deliberate way, not just because it is the "right" thing to do, but because it is in the group's best interest to have a more diverse membership.

Finally, positive experiences with diversity build on themselves. When people have good experiences in diverse groups, they feel more positive about a wide range of efforts that are designed to expand opportunities for others. On a more basic level, they are also better able to take other people's perspectives (Hurtado, 2005).

Diverse groups, when assembled carefully and run effectively, can be especially effective and creative

to have at least one incompetent member who can doom the group to failure on a task that requires everyone to contribute (a conjunctive task; For discussions of the benefits and perils of racially, ethnically, and nationally diverse groups, see the Social Psychology Encounters the Dark Side box on **page 345** and the Social Psychology Encounters the Bright Side box on **page 346**).

In general, though, groups tend not to perform as well as might be expected, given their members' abilities. Pooling everyone's knowledge and skills and coordinating everyone's efforts is a difficult task. Because groups rarely perform these tasks as efficiently as possible, the result can be underperformance, a phenomenon known as **process loss** (Hill, 1982; Steiner, 1972). In other words, groups do not achieve the level of productivity that might be expected from them based on their members' talents.

A different question is whether groups even outperform individuals. On some kinds of tasks, such as physical ones, the answer clearly is yes. For instance, half a dozen people can stack more bales of hay per hour than one person. But when a group is trying to produce a judgment, a solution to a problem, or some other intellectual product, the answer is not so clear. In fact, convincing demonstrations of the ability of groups to perform better than their best individual members are so rare (Kerr & Tindale, 2004; Tindale & Larson, 1992), such a finding has a specific name: the *assembly bonus effect* (Collins & Guetzkow, 1964; Michaelson, Watson, & Black, 1989). This effect is most likely to occur when tasks are complex and involve several different intellectual problems. Because no one person is likely to excel at solving all the problems, a combination of people is more likely than an individual to succeed (Laughlin, Bonner, & Miner, 2002; Laughlin, Hatch, Silver, & Boh, 2006; see **Figure 8.3**).

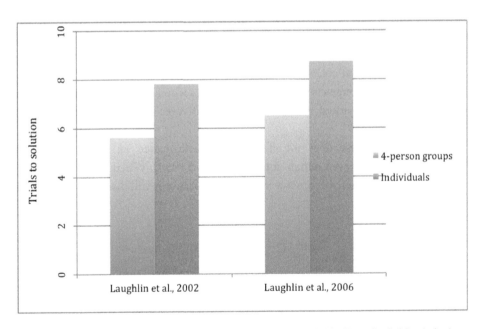

Figure 8.3: Groups solve complex problems more quickly than individuals in two studies.

Participants had to solve "letters to numbers" problems individually or in groups of four people. The task involved determining what numbers various letters symbolized based on a series of equations presented in successive trials.

Based on the results of Laughlin, Bonner, and Miner (2002) and Laughlin, Hatch, Silver, and Boh (2006).

Based even on this brief review, it should be clear that group dynamics are so complex that any rules for assembling a successful group will almost always need to be qualified by other considerations. Even the principle with which we began this section—pick people with the most ability—is far from absolute. Consider, for example, the experience of a major research-and-development company that set out to create a healthy yet delicious cookie (Gladwell, 2005). One of the teams assembled to develop the cookie consisted of the most knowledgeable and successful experts the company could find to work on the project. Called the Dream Team, it was possibly "the most talented group of people ever to work together in the history of the food industry" (p. 127). Unfortunately, the group's members found it hard to work together, and the cookie they produced was not the one that was put into production. The winning cookie was developed by a competing group of less-stellar food industry professionals. Talent, perhaps, is often associated with other characteristics, like high self-regard or "big egos," which can interfere with group processes.

Group Cohesiveness

The Dream Team assembled to develop the perfect cookie might have been bursting with expertise, but it likely was lacking in another quality that could be important for high-level performance: cohesiveness. Groups that are cohesive consist of members who like each other, feel pride in the group, and are committed to the group's task. Cohesiveness, as defined in this way—especially in terms of commitment to the task—is positively correlated with performance (Mullen & Copper, 1994).

This finding should be interpreted with caution, however. As we saw in Chapter 2, when two variables are correlated, it is not always possible to tell which of them is the cause and which the effect. Thus, just as group cohesiveness could lead to better performance, it is also possible that when a group performs well, the experience of success increases its cohesiveness. Indeed, Mullen and Copper (1994) found that the evidence for the effects of successful performance on cohesiveness may outweigh the evidence for the effects of cohesiveness on performance. Note that cohesiveness is *not* defined in terms of whether or not a group's members share the same opinions and beliefs. As we learned, research on groupthink reveals that such a state of affairs can lead to disastrous results.

A group's cohesiveness, of course, does not affect only its performance; on a more basic level, it helps to determine whether the group will even remain intact (Festinger, 1950). When a group's cohesiveness drops below a certain level, its effectiveness becomes a moot issue, because it will disintegrate (Sani, 2005; Sani & Todman, 2002).

Transactive Memory

In groups, people know and remember different things. They also know something about what other group members with different experiences, interests, and expertise might be able to remember. And they are aware of what those other members expect them to remember. For these reasons, people expect different group members to be responsible for attending to and storing in memory different kinds of information. Recall that Eric's group also divvied up the responsibility for who should remember what.

Couples and families do the same thing (Wegner, Erber, & Raymond, 1991). One person might be the one who remembers social plans, another the one who keeps track of which bills have been paid. In sum, just as individual people have memory systems, so do groups. Specifically, groups can develop what is called a **transactive memory system** (Wegner, 1987, 1995). Of course, it takes time to develop such a system. Earlier in this chapter, when we reviewed the use of shared and unshared information, we found that groups of people who do not have a history of working together often fail to take advantage of the fact that different members know different things.

There are a number of advantages to being part of a transactive memory system. For individuals, the upside is obvious: one can benefit from others' knowledge and expertise in a way that one could not if carrying out a task alone. For groups, the benefit is enhanced performance: groups that have developed transactive memory systems perform better than those that have not. Liang, Moreland, and Argote (1995) asked groups of people to work together to assemble transistor radios from kits with dozens of parts. They provided different kinds of training to different groups. Members of some groups received individual training; members of other groups were trained together. The groups that were trained together were better able to recall information about assembling radios than the other groups, and they made fewer errors in completing the task.

These findings suggest that people who were trained together developed a transactive memory system. In other words, members of the groups developed different types of expertise, made note of who knew what, and used that knowledge to their advantage. There are some alternative explanations for these findings, however. For example, people who are introduced to a new group often experience anxiety about the extent to which they will be accepted by other members. Perhaps the group training helped members to feel more relaxed, which in turn helped them to perform better. Or perhaps the groups who were trained together simply learned how to communicate with one another about the task—that is, how to talk clearly about the task of assembling radios. That would be different from developing a transactive memory system, and it might have been the key factor in the study.

Later research helped to rule out these alternative interpretations, however. For example, any way of allowing group members to interact and get to know one another before working together should reduce anxiety and help them to feel more comfortable. Yet allowing group members to participate in team-building exercises that have nothing to do with their task (such as assembling radios) does not provide the same advantage as group training (Moreland, 1999). In another study (Moreland & Myaskovsky, 2000), researchers added an experimental condition, in which group members were not allowed to interact in advance of the task—and thus had no experience communicating with one another—but did receive information about one another's skills. In other words, the experimenters provided them with the information they would need to develop a transactive memory system. Groups in that condition performed as well as those whose members had trained together (see **Table 8.2**).

Overall, the results of these studies indicate that when groups create transactive memory systems, they perform better. (Direct observations of the groups' interactions and discussions also supported that conclusion.)

Table 8.2: Group performance on a radio assembly task as a function of type of training

	INDIVIDUAL TRAINING	GROUP TRAINING	INDIVIDUAL TRAINING WITH INFORMATION ABOUT OTHERS' SKILLS
Recall of procedures	18.80	25.50	25.78
Errors	49.85	35.30	28.70

Higher scores indicate greater recall of procedures and a greater number of errors. The "group training" and "individual with information about other group members' skills" conditions did not differ significantly on either measure.

Source: Based on the results of Moreland & Myaskovsky (2000).

However, spreading knowledge across different members of a group can also have disadvantages (Wegner, 1987). For example, people may make incorrect assumptions about what others know and remember (Baumann & Bonner, 2013), or they may overestimate the knowledge the group has at its disposal ("Hey, I thought one of you knew how to open these parachutes"). In addition, if and when a group dissolves, individuals who once relied on others' storehouses of knowledge may suddenly find they are helpless to complete certain tasks themselves ("My old roommate was the only one who could remember how to deal with the furnace when it acted up"). This shortcoming of a transactive memory system may explain why an elderly person's functioning often deteriorates after the death of a spouse.

The Mere Presence of Others: Social Facilitation

Clearly, understanding how groups shape the experiences of the people in them often requires knowing something about the characteristics of their members—their opinions, abilities, and knowledge. One of social psychology's oldest research topics, however, is how the presence of *any* other people, regardless of who they are, can affect human behavior. Triplett (1898), for example, measured how quickly people performed a straightforward task—winding string onto fishing reels—in two conditions. In one condition, research participants were alone; in the other, they performed the task in the presence of others. Triplett found that the presence of others caused people to wind the string faster. Similarly, Eric found that he entered questionnaire data much more quickly and with fewer errors when he worked in the company of one or more of his research partners.

Although Triplett's study is celebrated as one of social psychology's earliest experiments, some argue that the results were actually quite weak and difficult to interpret (Strube, 2005). Nonetheless, his work inspired many other investigations of **social facilitation** (for reviews, see Bond & Titus, 1982; Guerin, 1986, 1993; Uziel, 2007; Zajonc, 1965, 1980). Although the researchers who conducted those studies generally predicted that the presence of others would boost performance, it became clear after a while that social facilitation effects were more complex than had at first been thought. Sometimes, the presence of others caused people to perform tasks more quickly, efficiently, and accurately; at other times, the opposite occurred.

This confusing state of affairs was clarified by Zajonc (1965, 1980), whose careful review of the research on the topic revealed that the presence of others led to better performance only when the task was simple and well learned. When the task was difficult or novel, the presence of others led to worse performance. Later studies confirmed this

Will she sink more free throws when practicing alone or with an audience watching her? Social facilitation research addresses this issue

general principle (Bond & Titus, 1983), which could explain why Eric's experience when using statistical software to analyze data from the questionnaires was very different from his experience when simply entering the data. When others were around, he became confused, made poor decisions, and even pressed the wrong keys. Though Eric had taken a class in statistics, he was far from comfortable running t-tests, correlations, and analyses of variance. In other words, doing so was essentially a novel task for him, so the presence of others caused his performance to deteriorate in this case.

Why do the effects of the presence of others depend on the situation? The answer is that the proximity of other people leads to arousal (Moore & Baron, 1983; Mullen, Bryant, & Driskell, 1987). According to Zajonc (1965, 1980), arousal energizes dominant responses—actions or thought processes that are extensively practiced and easily executed. When the task is simple and familiar (for example, a right-handed person copying text with her right hand), dominant responses are likely to boost performance. When the task is more difficult and less familiar (for example, a right-handed person copying text with her left hand), dominant responses will be less helpful, and might even interfere with performance.

One way of explaining why the presence of others leads to arousal is in terms of our worries about how onlookers will evaluate our performance and judge us—that is, in terms of evaluation apprehension (Cottrell, Wack, Sekerak, & Rittle, 1968; Geen, 1981). In support of this hypothesis, researchers have found that although the presence of other people can trigger stress and undermine performance, the presence of *pets* can reduce stress and help people to perform well (Allen, Blascovich, Tomaka, & Kelsey, 1991; Allen, Blascovich, & Mendes, 2002). People are unlikely to worry about how Spot the dog or Mr. Whiskers the cat will react to their low score on a test of mental arithmetic. Another way of explaining social facilitation is in terms of the distractions other people can present. The difficulty people experience in focusing their attention on a task when others are present and competing for their attention can lead to arousal (Sanders, 1981).

Zajonc (1965), however, predicted that the *mere* presence of others, regardless of how judgmental or distracting they were, would lead to social facilitation effects. A number of studies have supported that hypothesis. Markus (1978) asked participants to put on socks, shoes, and lab coats, supposedly to make their appearance identical to that of other participants in an experiment. A few minutes later, participants were told to put their own clothes back on because the other participants (who were nonexistent) had not shown up. Some participants were alone; others were in the presence of a confederate of the experimenter, who busied himself with something on the other side of the room, his back to the participant. Markus found that the mere presence of the confederate led participants to put on the experimenter-provided clothing (a novel task) more slowly than those who were alone, but to put on their own clothes (a familiar task) more quickly than the others.

Schmitt, Gilovich, Goore, and Joseph (1986) pointed out that participants in Markus's experiment might have worried that the confederate would turn his head and watch them as they struggled with the clothing. Thus, in their own experiment, they asked participants to complete a familiar or novel task, either alone or with another person present. That person, however, was as "merely" present as possible—he was blindfolded, wore headphones, and had his back turned to the participant. As in Markus's experiment, the presence of the other person led people to perform a well-practiced, easy task (typing their own names) more quickly than usual, but slowed them down when they performed a novel, difficult task (typing their names backward, while inserting ascending digits between the letters). The effects of the merely present person were as strong as the effect of the experimenter peering over the participant's shoulder as he or she typed (see **Figure 8.4**).

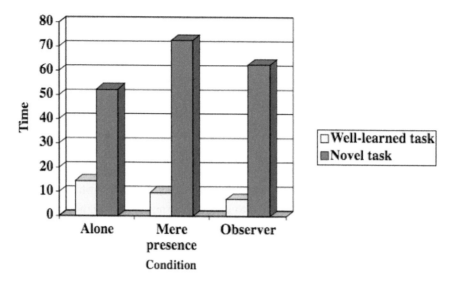

Figure 8.4: The mere presence of others and social facilitation effects.

Mean times are reported in seconds. The well-learned task (speeded up by the presence of others) was typing one's name; the novel task (slowed down by the presence of others) was typing one's name backward with interspersed digits. Mere presence had the same effect as an observer inspecting participants' performance.

Source: Based on the results of Schmitt, Gilovich, Goore, & Joseph (1986).

Social facilitation effects on performance are not restricted to human beings. Even rats' behavior is influenced by the presence of an audience.

An evolutionary psychologist would interpret these findings to mean that people are born with a basic psychological mechanism that triggers arousal in the presence of other human beings. The fact that social facilitation has been shown in other species, including rats and even ants and cockroaches (Benedict, Cofer, & Cole, 1980; Chen, 1937; Zajonc, Heingartner, & Herman, 1969), further supports the idea that its effects depend on simple, primitive responses that have little to do with our ability to reflect on our behavior or worry about others' reactions (see **Figure 8.7**).

The existence of mere presence effects does not mean that the nature and number of people present is always unimportant, however. According to social impact theory (Latané, 1981), the greater the number of people who are present, the closer they are; and the more socially significant they are, the greater the social facilitation effects. In other words, your performance on a difficult task may be affected by the presence of a stranger sitting across the room reading the newspaper, but it will probably be more affected by four of your professors sitting three feet from you, staring at your work. Similarly, the bigger and more densely packed a crowd of people, the greater the arousal (Evans, 1979; Nagar & Pandey, 1987).

Finally, though most people believe their performance on difficult tasks will benefit from a supportive audience such as close friends or family members, the opposite has been found to be true. That is, supportive audiences can cause a person to "choke" and become too hesitant and cautious. Butler and Baumeister (1998) asked college students to perform a mental arithmetic task that most found difficult: counting backward out loud by 13s for two minutes, as quickly as possible, beginning with the number 1,470. Half the participants thought they were being observed by a friend standing behind a one-way mirror; half thought some other student was observing them. (In reality, all were being watched only by one of the experimenters.) Participants reported feeling less stressed and distracted when they thought a friend was watching, although ironically, their performance was actually worse (see **Table 8.3**). Supportive audiences had a hidden influence on participants, causing their performance to deteriorate.

Leadership

One theme we keep returning to in this chapter is that groups are more than just collections of the individuals who make them up. Still, group members *are* individuals, and as such, they are far from interchangeable. Each member brings different qualities and strengths to the group, and each can serve different functions and play different roles. Most obviously, in many groups of people, some members stand out as leaders (Chemers, 1987, 1997; Chemers & Ayman, 1993; Goethals, 2005; Hollander, 1985; Northouse, 2003). A **leader** can be defined as a person who directs and organizes group members and their activities, and who takes responsibility for the attainment of the group's goals.

Who's a Good leader? Leadership Styles

Eric had trouble taking charge of his group's activities. Does this mean he was not a "leader type?" Trying to answer that question would make sense only if there were a clear "leader type" to begin with. Certainly, some people are more suited to leadership than others. But as we will see, it is more accurate to say that *within any given situation*, some people with specific combinations of traits are more suited to leadership than others (Zaccaro, 2007). Psychologists long ago gave up the quest to define specific personality traits that would predispose a person to consistently emerge as a leader in all situations (Stogdill, 1948).

One of the reasons why it is difficult to identify a single set of traits correlated with leadership ability is that leaders have two basic jobs (Bales, 1950; Halpin & Winer, 1957). Some leaders—including some very effective ones—focus more on one of those jobs than the other. **Task specialists** excel at *initiating structure*; that is, their

Table 8.3: Performance on a mental arithmetic task in front of different audiences

	FRIEND (SUPPORTIVE)	STRANGER (NONSUPPORTIVE)
Number of subtractions	18.9	25.8
Percentage of errors	9%	11%

Participants spent two minutes counting backward by 13s from 1,470. Though the percentage of errors did not differ significantly between conditions, the speed of performance (number of subtractions made) did.

Source: Based on the results of Butler & Baumeister (1998).

strength lies in organizing group members, clarifying their roles and hierarchical relationships, pushing them to get the job done, and making sure that work gets done on schedule. **Social-emotional specialists**, on the other hand, excel at *interpersonal consideration*. They let the people they are supervising know how much they care for them, do favors for them, and make sure that everyone feels included and heard. Typically, the best leaders can handle both aspects of the role. Still, the clearest message to emerge from leadership research is that different situations call for different types of leaders with different personal strengths.

Interactional approaches

Chapter 1 introduced the concept of interactionism, the idea that social behavior cannot be explained in terms of either personality traits or situational influences alone. Some people, for example, may be more generally aggressive than others, but they will express their aggressiveness only in certain situations. Similarly, some situations may elicit more aggressiveness than other situations, but certain people will react to those situations with more aggressiveness than others. In other words, aggressiveness emerges from a combination of specific kinds of people and specific kinds of situations.

The same can be said about effective leadership: Different situations demand different leaders with different personal qualities. The people who have those specific qualities will be best suited to leadership in those specific situations (Riggio, Murphy, & Pirozzolo, 2001). A number of different interactional theories of leadership have been proposed (see Hogg, 2001; House, 1971; Hollander, 1993; Vroom & Jago, 2007). Hogg, for example, has suggested that people become leaders when they are seen as prototypical members of their group (see Chapter 3). In other words, groups are led by people whose attitudes, beliefs, and behaviors are representative of the group as a whole (and distinct from the attitudes, beliefs, and behaviors of other groups). Those same people, of course, will not inevitably emerge as leaders in all groups. Someone might become a leader of his soccer team (because he is seen as the prototypical athlete), but not of his student government (because he is not seen as the prototypical politician).

The most influential interactional theory of leadership, however, is probably Fiedler's (1967, 1978) **contingency model**. Consistent with other research on leadership, Fiedler identified two basic leadership styles, one involving a focus on completing tasks successfully and efficiently (task-oriented leadership) and the other involving a concern with interpersonal relations (relationship-oriented leadership). Neither style, he found, was effective in all groups and all situations. The key factor in determining which of the two styles was the better match for a particular group was a variable he called situational control—that is, the extent to which the leader can influence his or her subordinates. Situations that are high in control are those in which (1) the leader's authority is formal and recognized by all; (2) group members feel a sense of loyalty or obligation to the leader; and (3) the group's task or goal is well defined.

The relationship between situational control and the optimal leadership style is complicated. Task-oriented leaders are best suited to both high-control *and* low-control situations. In high-control situations, they can take advantage of the opportunity to maximize the group's performance and output. In low-control situations, their decisive style is necessary to overcome the confusion found in unstructured, chaotic situations. What about moderate-control situations? In those very common cases, a relationship-oriented leader will be more effective. Moderate-control situations consist of a mix of favorable and unfavorable features—for example, clear objectives, but low employee morale, or loyal employees, but ambiguous objectives. Leaders who are sensitive to group dynamics and perceptive about the strengths and weaknesses of different members will be in a better position than others to deal creatively with the situation.

Quite a bit of research supports Fiedler's contingency theory (Peters, Hartke, & Pohlmann, 1985; Schriesheim, Tepper, & Tetrault, 1994; Strube & Garcia, 1981). Other research has shown that when leaders are properly matched to the situation, it is not only the group that benefits. Leaders who are a poor fit for a group (for example, task-oriented leaders in moderate-control situations, or relationship-oriented leaders in high- or low-control situations) experience much more job stress than leaders who are a good fit (Chemers, Hays, Rhodewalt, & Wysocki, 1985). This research could shed light on Eric's predicament. Although the situation in his group was deteriorating, it had by no means fallen to the low end of the control dimension. A strict task-oriented leader is not what his group needed, but that unfortunately was the style Eric adopted.

As we noted earlier, not many personality traits have been found to predict how effective people will be as leaders. One exception to this rule is assertiveness: people who are either extremely assertive or extremely unassertive are perceived negatively in leadership roles (Ames & Flynn, 2007). One of the other few exceptions is arguably consistent with contingency theory. Kenny and Zaccaro (1983; Zaccaro, Foti, & Kenny, 1991) found that people who are high in social perceptiveness (the ability to perceive others' needs and goals) and flexibility (the ability to adjust one's approach based on the nature of the situation) are more likely than others to emerge as leaders. People with these characteristics, we can assume, will be better than others at judging the nature of their groups and the challenges they face, and more capable of adopting a different leadership style as needed. Thus, such people can adjust their leadership style to match the level of situational control they have.

The late Nelson Mandela, President of South Africa from 1994 to 1999, was perceived by many throughout the world to be a transformational leader

Transformational Versus Transactive Leaders

Another distinction that has proven useful in understanding the nature of leadership is the difference between transformational and transactional leaders (Bass & Avolio, 1993; Burns, 1978; Eagly, Johannesen-Schmidt, & van Engen, 2003). **Transformational leaders** do more than control and direct their followers; they change them in fundamental ways. Rather than merely helping people to accomplish their goals, they inspire them to adopt new goals (see **Table 8.4**). **Transactional leaders**, on the other hand, simply do their jobs—that is, they help followers to get the things they want (money, security, prestige) and to avoid negative outcomes. These leaders are essentially managers who do not question or try to change the group's perspective. The distinction between transformational and transactional leadership, we should note, is based not only on research in individualistic cultures; it has been found to be valid cross-culturally (Walumbwa & Lawler, 2003).

Table 8.4: The qualities of transformational leaders

Demonstrate qualities that motivate respect and pride
Communicate values, purpose, and importance of an organization's mission
Exhibit optimism and excitement
Examine new perspectives for solving problems and completing tasks
Focus on development and mentoring of followers and attend to followers' individual needs

Source: Eagly, Johannesen-Schmidt, & van Engen (2003).

Which kind of leadership is more effective, transformational or transactional? Once again, to answer this question, we must take an interactional approach. Research by Waldman, Ramirez, House, and Puranam (2001) shows us once again that any given leader's effectiveness depends on the situation. In uncertain, unstable, or chaotic environments, transformational leaders seem to excel, because they can better rally and refocus group members. But in stable, smoothly functioning situations, transactional leaders do just fine. In such environments, there is no pressing need for a transformational leader to shake things up.

Transformational leaders are typically charismatic individuals (Bass, 1997; House & Shamir, 1993) who can use their powers to radically change people's value systems and beliefs. Abraham Lincoln and Mahatma Gandhi are thought to have been transformational leaders. It is worth noting, though, that Adolph Hitler and Osama bin Laden also fit the profile. Overall, there is nothing inherently good or admirable in any leadership style; what matters are the ends that leaders pursue.

Gender Differences

Whether he or she is task oriented or relationship oriented, transformational or transactional, one thing that can be said about the typical leader of large, prominent groups is that he or she is a he. That is, in most groups, men are more likely to emerge as leaders than women (Eagly & Karau, 1991). Clearly, there is a gender difference in the sheer number of political, business, military, and other leaders. Just as clearly, there are many possible explanations for that difference (Heilman, Block, Martell, & Simon, 1989; Simon & Hoyt, 2013). One is that bias and discrimination keep women out of many leadership roles. Another (not mutually exclusive) explanation is that women are socialized to shy away from such roles. A third hypothesis, of course, is that women simply are not as effective as men in leadership roles.

This last hypothesis was tested by Eagly, Karau, and Makhijani (1995) in a major "meta-analysis" of the research literature. (Meta-analysis is a technique for combining the results of many studies for statistical analysis.) Did they find a gender difference in leader effectiveness? In a word, no. But the story of gender differences in leadership is more interesting than that.

Even before Eagly et al.'s (1995) study, many social scientists were skeptical about the existence of gender differences in leader effectiveness. But what about the *style* with which men and women lead organizations and groups? There was little consensus on that issue, and even less evidence, until the publication of another meta-analysis by Eagly and Johnson (1990), this one of studies of gender differences in leadership style. Eagly and Johnson tested the hypothesis that men would be more task oriented as leaders and women more relationship oriented—a hypothesis that is consistent with gender stereotypes. They did, in fact, find some evidence to support that hypothesis, although the differences they identified were weak and inconsistent. Their analysis revealed stronger, more consistent evidence for another gender difference: overall, women are significantly more democratic than men as leaders. In other words, women are more likely than men to encourage all members of an organization to participate in decision making. Men, in contrast, are generally more autocratic—that is, less open to broad-based participation in decision making.

In light of this finding, we must conclude that the answer to the question "Is there a relationship between gender and leadership effectiveness?" is more complicated than a simple yes or no. You will not be surprised to learn that the answer is "it depends." Again, we need to take an interactional approach to answer the question. Eagly et al. (1995) found that men are more effective in some situations and women in others. Specifically, men are more effective in leadership roles that are defined in masculine terms—that is to say, roles in which the leader can behave autocratically. Women are more effective in roles that are defined in feminine terms—that is, roles requiring the interpersonal skills possessed by a democratic leader. One reason why women are relatively ineffective in leadership roles that call for stereotypically masculine behavior is that women who are perceived to be "acting like men"—behaving autocratically, in other words—tend to be disliked and devalued (Eagly, Makhijani, & Klonsky, 1992).

The Ups and Downs of Group Performance: A Summary

Which kinds of groups perform best? Intuitively, the answer seems straightforward: groups whose members are talented, like each other, and are led by a person with leadership ability. Yet as we have seen, the true answer is much more complicated. Groups do not always perform as well as expected based on the abilities of their members. Because the difficulties members have in coordinating their efforts can lead to inefficiencies—process losses—groups have a surprisingly hard time outperforming even a single talented individual. And although experience may suggest that cohesiveness increases a group's chances for success, cohesiveness is more often the result of success, not the cause. Similarly, figuring out who will be an effective leader in any given situation is far from simple. Different leadership styles—task oriented versus relationship oriented, transformational versus transactional, autocratic versus democratic—are appropriate for different groups. Finally, if group members face novel challenges or unfamiliar tasks, the mere presence of other people can cause their performance to deteriorate.

In sum, there is no simple formula for constructing a high-performing group; the requirements depend on the situation and the group's task (see also Wiley & Bailey, 2006; Wilson et al., 2004). Nevertheless, groups that function smoothly and effectively—for example, groups that have developed a transactive memory system—can perform even better than one would expect based on their members' average ability levels.

Think Like a Social Psychologist

Understanding everyday behavior

—Have you ever belonged to a group with the wrong mix of abilities for the kind of task (conjunctive or disjunctive) it faced? What went wrong in that situation?

Making connections

—Understanding a leader's effectiveness requires us to think in terms of interacting variables. How is an interactional approach also necessary for understanding the effects of others' presence on a person's performance (social facilitation effects)? For understanding the relationship between the distribution of group members' abilities and the group's performance?

Designing research

—How might you design an experiment to show that the same form of leadership could be perceived differently, depending on whether group members thought the leader was male or female? How could you make sure that no other variables were confounded with the leader's gender?

MAKING A (TOKEN?) CONTRIBUTION

Recall that consistent with research on social facilitation, the quality of Eric's data entry improved in the presence of others, but his ability to analyze the data was impaired. Unfortunately, these interesting social psychological effects were less notable than the fact that he was not spending all that much time on *either* of those tasks. As for working in others' presence—well, the group was not meeting as often as it could or should, either. In fact, Eric was spending much more time working on a political science paper that was due at the end of the semester. The other members of his group were also focusing more on their individual work for other classes.

We might suspect that given some of the recent tumult in the group, members were avoiding the project because they were feeling annoyed with one another. Perhaps ill will played a role in the group's behavior, but as we will see, there is no reason to make that assumption.

THE INDIVIDUAL WITHIN THE GROUP

As we have emphasized repeatedly, to understand how groups operate, we must both study them in action and consider them as objects of study in and of themselves. Because groups are more than the sum of their parts, we cannot make sense of them by focusing on their individual members, any more than we can say anything meaningful about a snowstorm by focusing on individual snowflakes.

Nonetheless, group members *are* individuals, and some things that individuals do take place only in a group setting. For a person to "let the group down," for example—that is, behave in ways that are destructive to the group—he or she must belong to a group to begin with. The same goes for feeling cheated or unappreciated by a group. The final section of this chapter focuses on three aspects of individual people's thoughts, feelings, and behavior that can be studied and discussed only with respect to groups of individuals.

Social Loafing

Why did members of Eric's group withdraw effort from their project? Research on **social loafing** (Ingham, Levinger, Graves, & Peckham, 1974; Karau & Williams, 1993; Latané, Williams, & Harkins, 1979; Sheppard, 1993) reveals that people who work on collective tasks often do not exert as much effort as they do when they work on individual tasks. (This phenomenon is sometimes called the "Ringelmann effect," after the German psychologist who first reported it in the early 1920s: see Kravitz & Martin, 1986.) Many people become "free riders" when working in groups.

In a classic study by Latané, Williams, and Harkins (1979; see Hunt, 1985, for a vivid description), participants were assigned a straightforward task: yelling as loud as they could. When they shouted together with other people, the average sound produced per person was less loud than when they shouted individually. A second study replicated that finding in a condition with participants who merely *thought* they were shouting along with others (they were wearing blindfolds and headphones). Although the task in that study might seem artificial, social loafing has since been found among people who participate in a wide variety of activities, including work-related tasks (such as reviewing job applications and typing), jury deliberation (Najdowski, 2010), creative projects, physical challenges (like rope pulling), cognitive challenges (solving problems or finding a path through a maze), and athletic performances.

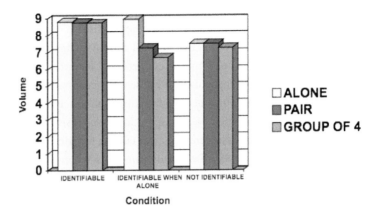

Figure 8.5: Social loafing on a shouting task.

Effort depends on how identifiable your efforts are. Subjects always shouted alone, but did so either while knowing that they were alone or while thinking that they had one or three partners. In the Identifiable condition, they always thought that their individual effort could be directly measured; in the Identifiable When Alone condition, they thought that their own effort could be directly measured only when they shouted alone; and in the Not Identifiable condition, they thought that their individual effort could never be directly measured. The sound volume produced was measured as Dynes/cm^2.

Source: Based on the results of Williams, Harkins, & Latané (1981).

Why do people tend to let the team down by holding back their effort while working and playing in groups? After conducting a thorough review of research on the topic, Karau and Williams (1995, p. 137) concluded that "individuals will be willing to exert effort on a collective task only to the degree that they expect their efforts to be instrumental in obtaining outcomes that they value personally." In other words, if people are to work hard on a group activity, they must care about the outcome and believe they can affect it. Thus, it is not enough that people think that what they are working on matters; they must feel that their efforts will not be wasted.

One thing most people care a great deal about is how others perceive them (see Chapter 4). For that reason, one of the factors that reduces people's tendency to engage in social loafing is how identifiable or open to scrutiny their own work will be (Kerr & Bruun, 1981; Williams, Harkins, & Latané, 1981; see **Figure 8.5**). When a group's members believe that no one will be able to tell just how much work they did or did not do, social loafing is especially pronounced. Conversely, when they believe that someone will be able to evaluate their contributions, the effect has been known to disappear—members work as hard in a group as they do alone. In sum, people are less likely to loaf if they think that doing so will make them look bad.

Just as people in groups may not be motivated to exert themselves when they see no benefit to doing so, they will also be less willing to put in their best effort when they feel that *costs* are involved (Shepperd, 1993, 1995). For instance, people may feel that working on a group task will drain time and energy from other projects, especially individual ones for which they could take all the credit. This principle may explain why fatigue increases a person's social loafing (Hoeksema-van Orden, Gaillard, & Buunk, 1998).

The work we have reviewed so far presents a pessimistic picture of human nature; indeed, Latané et al. (1979, p. 831) referred to social loafing as a "social disease." Are there circumstances in which people care about group outcomes as well as individual ones? It should be heartening to hear that there are. First, although social loafing has been noted in collectivistic cultures, it is less pronounced than in individualistic cultures (Karau & Williams, 1993). This finding makes a lot of sense, given that an essential characteristic of such cultures is strong identification with in-groups. But even in individualistic cultures, people can be motivated to overcome social loafing when the groups they belong to are highly cohesive (Worchel, Rothberger, Day, Hart, & Butemeyer, 1998) or when they are presented with clear criteria for comparing their performances to those of other groups (Harkins & Szymanski, 1989). Finally, in some cases, when a group's success is very important to members who perceive themselves to be more talented or capable than others, those members will significantly increase their efforts to compensate for what they see as others' weak performance. This phenomenon is known as the social compensation effect (Williams & Karau, 1991; see also Kerr & Tindale, 2004).

You may be wondering how to reconcile social loafing with social facilitation. Research on social facilitation reveals that sometimes (specifically, on easy tasks), the presence of others leads people to perform better than otherwise. That research generally involves people who are working individually while in the presence of either observers or others who are not working on the same task. In other words, social facilitation research focuses on what happens when people are or could be the focus of others' attention. Social loafing research, on the other hand, deals with situations in which individuals can become anonymous, or lost in the group.

Deindividuation

Research on social loafing demonstrates that disappearing into a group can lead people *not* to do things they might otherwise have done (like expending effort or acting conscientiously). But the anonymity that results from being an unidentifiable member of a group also increases the probability that people *will* do other things— specifically, things that violate their normal standards of behavior. In other words, people in crowds, or "mobs," often engage in behavior that might seem unthinkable to them as individuals.

Imagine, for example, spotting a man who is clinging to the ledge of a building, threatening to commit suicide by jumping off. Would you mock him and encourage him to jump? We hope the answer is "no," but unfortunately, you would be more likely to do so if you were part of a large crowd (Mann, 1981). Now, imagine that one of your school's athletic teams has just won a major championship. Does overturning cars, smashing windows, setting fires, and looting stores seem like an appropriate way to celebrate? Most *individual* celebrants would say no, but *mobs* of celebrating people often think differently.

We will not even ask you to imagine yourself as a white citizen of Tulsa, Oklahoma, in 1921—the year and place of one of the United States' deadliest race riots (Madigan, 2003). Over the course of two days, 35 city blocks were burned, 10,000 people left homeless, and over 800 treated at hospitals for injuries. The number of black residents who were killed is unclear; though the official number was 39, most scholars agree that the deaths numbered in the hundreds. What triggered this apocalyptic event? A black man stumbling in an elevator and falling on a white woman.

Many of the people in situations like this, we must assume, experienced **deindividuation**, a psychological state in which people become anonymous members of a crowd, lose their sense of individuality, and cease to be constrained by their usual standards of behavior (Diener, 1979; Postmes & Spears, 1998; Zimbardo, 1970). Two factors lead to deindividuation. The first is the anonymity and lack of identifiability that comes from being just one person of many in a large group. In such situations, a person is less likely to be held accountable for contributing to an act of violence or destructiveness than in other situations. Thus, people will be less motivated to attend to their usual personal norms or rules for proper behavior (like, say, not looting stores).

Another factor that leads to deindividuation makes it unlikely that a person will even be *able* to attend to those norms. Large crowds are arousing and distracting; they absorb our attention and make it difficult to think about anything else—and that includes the self and one's typical standards of behavior. The second factor that contributes to deindividuation, then, is a loss of self-awareness. As a result, people let themselves be guided by whatever group norms arise in a given situation. Unfortunately, those norms may dictate destroying as much property as possible, or even killing members of some out-group.

Of course, group norms are not always antisocial. If a positive or admirable group norm becomes salient, deindividuation has been known to lead to positive behavior (Johnson & Downing, 1979; Postmes & Spears, 1998; see **Figure 8.6**). If you were part of a crowd that happened to be on a burning building, for example, you might end up participating in a frenzied effort to rescue those trying to escape from the fire, even if you are not ordinarily a bold risk-taker.

Deindividuation can also arise under other circumstances. Uniforms, for example, can promote anonymity and

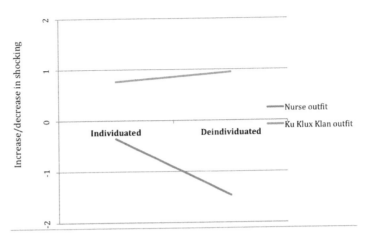

Figure 8.6: Deindividuation can sometimes decrease antisocial behavior.

Participants wore either Ku Klux Klan outfits (antisocial norm cues) or nurse outfits (prosocial norm cues), and were either identifiable (individuated) or not (deindividuated). They decided whether to increase or decrease the number of shocks administered to a person who performed poorly on a learning task.

Source: Johnson and Downing (1979).

Crowds do not always bring out the worst in people. When Flight 1549 made an emergency water landing in New York's Hudson River in 2009, the behavior of many passengers was notable for its generosity and bravery

a loss of awareness of oneself as an individual (Zimbardo, 1970). The brutal behavior of the uniformed guards in the Stanford prison experiment (Zimbardo, Maslach, & Haney, 2000; see Chapter 7), in which they acted in accordance with norms that would have seemed unacceptable in any other environment, was probably due to

There are many forms of deindividuation, but all can potentially lead to extreme behavior

their losing themselves in their roles. Some people have suggested that "flaming"—the tendency to make outrageous and hostile comments via electronic mail that one would never make face to face—is an example of deindividuation (Suler, 2004). Deindividuation might even play a role in software piracy (Hinduja, 2008).

Still, the kind of deindividuation that occurs in crowds often leads to particularly extreme and vivid violence. The American writer and editor, Bill Buford, became fascinated with the English football fans—"soccer hooligans"—who were responsible for outbreaks of violence in Europe in the 1980s (Buford, 1992). He infiltrated one such group, supporters of the Manchester United team, and traveled with them to observe up close the mayhem they created. Over time, Buford found himself gradually drawn into their activities, and eventually began to participate in their brutal brawls with fans of other teams, and even the police. Buford's description of what it felt like to lose himself in a violent mob is consistent with the conclusions reached by social psychologists. Such experiences, he wrote, "exclude the possibility of all other thought except the experience itself, incinerate self-consciousness, transcend (or obliterate?) our sense of the personal, of individuality, of being an individual in any way"

(p. 193). In other words, "being in a crowd in an act of violence" (p. 193) seemed to Buford to involve becoming anonymous and merging with the group, without reflecting on the meaning of his behavior.

Social Dilemmas

Public Goods and Resource Dilemmas

Although research on social loafing typically focuses on small groups, people also belong to larger communities. As a result, sometimes the consequences of failing to cooperate with others or to contribute to the greater good can be more serious than not finishing a project on time or not screaming as loudly as other groups. For example, most cities in the United States have public radio stations, which typically broadcast a few programs that are quite popular. To hear those shows, all you have to do is turn on the radio and tune in the station. However, public broadcasting stations need more than just your rapt attention; they need money. In a situation like this, it is easy to become a free rider. Because appeals for donations are broadcast rather than made face to face, hardly anyone will ever know whether you have contributed. And surely, at least some of the other thousands of listeners (most of whom probably make more money than you, after all) will pay up. Unfortunately, when too many people fail to contribute, their favorite programs may be canceled.

A more famous example of this phenomenon (a hypothetical one, but based closely on real-world events) is the "tragedy of the commons," described by Hardin (1968). A community of herdsmen shares a piece of public land—the commons—for grazing their herds. Each herdsman wants as many animals as possible, because the more animals he has, the more money he will make. Of course, the more animals the herdsmen graze, the more damage will be done to the commons. In the short term, the damage seems minimal, and the costs of the damage are spread across all the herdsmen. Consequently, from a single herdsman's perspective, adding another animal to the herd always seems the smart thing to do. Because everyone is thinking the same way, however, all the herds keep growing. Eventually, the commons becomes overgrazed, and the grass and all the animals die.

The tragedy of the commons is a classic illustration of a **social dilemma**, a situation in which what seems like the smart, desirable decision for individuals has negative consequences for the group as a whole (Dawes, 1980; Komorita & Parks, 1995; Messick & Brewer, 1983; Pruitt, 1998; Van Vugt, 2009). In a social dilemma, people are faced with the choice of maximizing either their own short-term self-interest or the group's long-term collective interest.

There are two basic kinds of social dilemma, the public goods dilemma and the resource dilemma (Brewer & Kramer, 1986; Komorita & Parks, 1995). **Public goods dilemmas** involve situations in which the upkeep of

You might face public goods dilemmas in the office. If you fail to toss a few coins into the payment box, they won't be missed, but if no one pays up, there will be no more coffee

Diamond (2005) on the decline of Easter Island as a result of deforestation—and a maladaptive response to a social dilemma: "... what were Easter islanders saying as they cut down the last tree on their island?... how on earth could a society make such an obviously disastrous decision as to cut down all the trees on which it depended? ... Many of the reasons for such failure fall under the heading of what economists and other social scientists term 'rational behavior' ... That is, some people may reason correctly that they can advance their own interests by behavior harmful to other people. Scientists term such behavior 'rational' precisely because it employs correct reasoning, even though it may be morally reprehensible." (Diamond, 2005, pp. 23, 427)

some service, facility, or other commodity that is available to everyone depends on voluntary contributions of time, money, or effort. Contributing to public broadcasting is just one example; working on a community garden would be another, as would be participating in a neighborhood security watch. **Resource dilemmas** involve a common, shared resource to which everyone has access, but which will disappear if everyone simply takes as much as they want. The tragedy of the commons is an example of a resource dilemma. So is the issue of water conservation—if everyone waters the lawn and washes the car and takes a 30-minute shower every day, eventually there may not be enough water for anyone. Both dilemmas show that sometimes, what seems rational for an individual is not rational for a group of individuals. And because "In most societies, it is to each individual's advantage to use as much energy, to pollute as much, and to have as many children as possible" (Dawes, 1980, p. 171), in extreme cases, social dilemmas can lead to the complete collapse of a society (Diamond, 2005).

Fortunately, people do not always respond selfishly in the face of social dilemmas. Research has identified a number of factors that are associated with cooperation. One is group size (Kerr, 1989): the smaller the group, the more cooperative its behavior. In small groups, people realize that any person's decision will have consequences for the group as a whole. They also realize that they are not anonymous. Indeed, the more clearly identifiable people's behavior is, the more they will try to transcend their narrow self-interest (Sniezek, May, & Sawyer, 1990). As in the case of social loafing, then, people are less likely to free-ride when they feel their behavior will make a difference and when they know that people will notice their contributions to the group.

Encouraging communication among the people who are involved in a social dilemma also enhances their cooperation (Orbell, van de Kragt, & Dawes, 1988). Finally, establishing, encouraging, or even just reminding people of the general social norm of cooperation can make a difference (Weber & Murnighan, 2008). For

		YOUR CHOICE	
		Cooperate	Compete
OPPONENT'S CHOICE	Cooperate	You get 15 points	You get 25 points
		Opponent gets 15 points	Opponent gets 0 points
	Compete	You get 0 points	You get 5 points
		Opponent gets 25 points	Opponent gets 5 points

Figure 8.7: A typical prisoner's dilemma game.

The payoffs for each of your moves are shown in colored text; your opponent's payoffs are shown in plain text. Note that competing while your opponent cooperates pays off handsomely for you (25 points), and vice versa. When both of you opt for a competitive move, you each get less than you would if both of you had opted for a cooperative move (5 points compared to 15 points).

instance, many people litter. After all, if you don't see a garbage can nearby and you don't feel like carrying an empty soda can around, what difference could one little can tossed into the street make? Yet Reno, Cialdini, and Kallgren (1993) reduced people's tendency to drop their junk on the ground by subtly exposing them to evidence that other people are motivated to avoid littering (for example, by arranging for them to see another person—a confederate of the experimenters—picking up some litter).

The Prisoner's Dilemma

The psychological processes that underlie people's behavior in everyday social dilemmas, from participating in recycling programs to making the suggested contribution at museums, are difficult to examine directly. Instead, researchers have used a relatively simple approach called the

SOCIAL PSYCHOLOGY IN THE COURTROOM: JURY DECISION MAKING

Although the research covered in this chapter has been applied to groups of all kinds, some groups have attracted more attention than others. The way in which juries arrive at decisions has been of particular interest to social psychologists. Every year, over 150,000 jury trials take place in the United States (Saks & Marti, 1997). In many of them, juries must make life-or-death decisions. Not surprisingly, then, a great deal of research has been conducted on jury decision making (Davis, 1989; Devine, 2012; Devine, Clayton, Dunford, Seying, & Price, 2001; Diamond, 1997; Ellsworth, 1989).

Some of this research focuses on how individual jurors make sense of the information presented to them at a trial, and how they then use that

In a Japanese courtroom, a defendant faces judges—but no jury. Japan, a collectivistic society, did not adopt a jury system until 2009. Because of the reluctance of many Japanese to "express opinions in public" and "to argue with one another," such a system still does not appeal to many people in that country (Onishi, 2007).

information to judge a defendant's guilt or innocence (Pennington & Hastie, 1986, 1992). Although these studies cannot tell us what goes on in jury rooms once jurors have convened to discuss the evidence, they have important implications for the verdicts that juries reach. Around 90 percent of the time, the verdict that the majority of jurors prefer before their deliberations begin is the verdict that they ultimately reach (Kalven & Zeisel, 1966; Sandys & Dillehay, 1995).

Still, in thousands of trials, the fate of defendants and plaintiffs depends on how jurors collectively arrive at a difficult decision. Understanding how they make those decisions is thus of great importance, especially because juries very often do not follow the detailed instructions judges give to them (Devine et al., 2001). In other words, although the legal system presents an idealized conception of how evidence should be evaluated, once the door to the jury room closes, jurors are prone to all the biases discussed in this chapter, from overuse of shared information to polarization effects and social loafing.

Hence, other research focuses on the collective decision making of juries. Because in some cases, juries can be composed of fewer than the typical 12 people, a number of researchers have examined the effects of jury size. The results of that research are complex. To give just one example, some studies find that in civil trials, larger juries award significantly more money for damages than smaller juries; other studies show the opposite (Davis, Hulbert, Au, Chen, & Zarnoth, 1997). Although more research is needed on this issue, it is clear that with juries, size matters. Another issue that some researchers have addressed is the effects of early polling—that is, the practice of taking an initial poll on the verdict that members favor before any discussion takes place. Not surprisingly, given what we learned about primacy effects in Chapter 3, the results of such a poll can strongly affect the course of the discussion that follows (Davis, Kameda, Parks, & Stasson, 1989). Similarly, the order in which jurors consider criminal charges is important; defendants are more likely to be convicted on a given charge if juries discuss it after considering a more serious one (Davis, Tindale, Nagao, Hinsz, & Robertson, 1984).

Research on jury decision making is very difficult to conduct (Devine et al., 2001). Ideally, researchers would prefer to videotape actual juries and then analyze the processes they observe. However, cameras and other types of recording equipment are almost never allowed in jury rooms. Therefore, researchers have three alternatives: (1) to study "mock" (simulated) juries; (2) to interview jurors after the trial has concluded; or (3) to analyze written (archival) records of jury verdicts. All these methods are useful, but all have limitations. Studies of mock juries are appealing because they allow experimenters to manipulate variables and observe the deliberations, but their external validity (see Chapter 2) can be questioned. Interviews rely on jurors' memories, which can be hazy, biased, or otherwise distorted. And written records do not usually provide much detail about what took place during the group decision-making process.

One thing is clear, however: defendants generally fare better by placing their fate in the hands of a jury rather than a trial judge. Compared to judges, juries have a *leniency bias* (Kalven & Zeisel, 1966). Although judges and juries do agree most of the time, when they differ, the judges' verdicts are usually more severe than those rendered by juries. And although juries, like all groups, are subject to the influence of the majority, smaller majorities are needed to convince other jurors to acquit than to convince them to convict a defendant (MacCoun & Kerr, 1988).

to study the way people think about social dilemmas (Axelrod, 1984; Dawes, 1980; Pruitt, 1998). **Figure 8.7** shows a simple example of such a game. On each trial of the game, the two opponents (either individuals or groups) decide on a response, or "move," which is generally either clearly competitive ("defecting") or cooperative. *Collectively*, the two sides will do better (earn the most points, dollars, or whatever else is being distributed) if both cooperate; they will do worse if both compete (in the figure, 30 points versus 10 points). At the same time—and this is the sinister, paradoxical feature of these games—in response to any single move by an opponent, *individually*, the other player will gain more by competing. For this reason, the majority of moves in most prisoner's dilemma games are competing moves.

This game is called the prisoner's dilemma because it mimics the situation of two criminals in separate cells trying to decide whether or not to confess to a crime they committed together. If both confess, they will probably receive moderate sentences; if neither confesses, they will be released after a relatively short period. But if only one of the prisoners agrees to cooperate with law enforcement and confesses to the crime, then he or she will go free immediately, and the other will go to prison for a long time.

Many other versions of the prisoner's dilemma game are possible. In general, though, they share a common characteristic with social dilemmas: behavior that seems to be in an individual's short-term interest is not in everyone's long-term interest. For that reason, these games have been found to be useful in studying how people think about and react to social dilemmas. Indeed, some of the same variables that affect people's behavior in social dilemmas have been found to be important in prisoner's dilemma games, including group size (Maxwell & Schmidt, 1972), opportunities for communication (Dawes, McTavish, & Shaklee, 1977), and the salience of different norms (Liberman, Samuels, & Ross, 2002). (To learn how group size, among other variables, affects jury deliberations, see the Social Psychology in the Courtroom box on **page 366-367**.)

Perceptions of Fairness and Justice within Groups

To a certain extent, members of groups experience common outcomes. For example, they receive resources (money, equipment, and so on) to do their work; they receive credit, praise, or bonuses when all goes well; and, of course, they are blamed when all does not go well. Yet within groups, individuals sometimes experience different outcomes. Group resources and rewards may not be parceled out equally; credit and blame may be assigned more to some individuals than to others. How are rewards and blame distributed, and what happens when members become unhappy with the way they are faring as individuals?

There are many different rules for the distribution of rewards and punishments, and many different perspectives on which rules are more just (Skitka & Crosby, 2003). Different rules are used in different kinds of groups, and the rules can change over time, even within a specific group (Schroeder, Steel, Woodell, & Bembenek, 2003). The three most common rules are equality, relative need, and equity. As we will see in Chapter 10 (see also Austin, 1980; Clark, Graham, & Grote, 2002), in intimate relationships—families, marriages, civil unions, and other committed partnerships—who gets what is often guided by the principles of equality and relative need. That is, resources are divided equally, with adjustments made for those who need more of a given resource. These rules apply to both concrete resources like food and abstract resources such as attention.

In many of the groups people belong to at school, work, or other public settings, however, **equity** is the more common basis for determining who gets what. Equity (Adams, 1965; Hatfield, Traupmann, Sprecher, Utne, & Hay, 1985; Walster, Walster, & Berscheid, 1978) is based on the idea that the benefits people receive should be proportional to their contributions. According to the equity principle, people who work hard or are in other ways responsible for a group's success should be rewarded more than those who are not instrumental to its success. People such as extreme social loafers who hinder a group's progress should benefit least of all. Competitive situations and those in which people become focused on material concerns are especially likely to raise the issue of equity (Skitka, 2003). If money, property, promotions, or grades are at

off the mark.com   by Mark Parisi

LIFE'S UNFAIR...

© Mark Parisi, Permission required for use.

Issues of fairness, equity and justice are inescapable

stake, people will be keeping track of the relationship between their contributions (time, effort, innovation) and what they receive in return.

Needless to say, someone has to decide what constitutes an equitable distribution of resources. That decision might be made collectively by the whole group, by a committee, or by the group's leader. Because individuals do not control their outcomes directly, it is common for people to feel they have been treated inequitably. In fact, people typically overestimate their contributions to group projects (Ross & Sicoly, 1979), so that perceiving inequity may well be the norm when people work together. When two or more people are asked to estimate their percentage contribution to some joint effort (How much effort do you contribute to keeping your dorm room clean? What percentage of the laundry do you do? What proportion of the data did you enter for the group project?), the percentages almost always add up to significantly more than 100 (which is impossible, of course).

People who are dissatisfied with the way their contributions have been evaluated (or with any of the group's decisions, for that matter) are more likely than others to criticize another aspect of the group's functioning: the *process* by which these and other decisions are made (Skitka, 2002; Skitka & Mullen, 2002). That is, they are more likely to focus on **procedural justice** (Lind & Tyler, 1988; Thibault & Walker, 1975). Obviously, people who are satisfied with their salaries, grades, or bonuses probably will not be motivated to carefully assess the procedure through which they were handsomely rewarded. But people who are less satisfied may well be motivated to understand the precise process that led to what they believe is an injustice. More generally, procedural justice becomes important to people when they are concerned about their status in a group (Skitka, 2003; Tyler, 1994; Tyler & Lind, 1992; van Prooijen, van den Bos, & Wilke, 2002).

Concerns about justice and equity became very salient to Eric and his fellow researchers when the instructor made a surprise announcement just before the due date for their final report. She asked all the groups in the class to prepare a memo summarizing each group member's individual contribution to the project. It was clear to everyone that the memo would affect people's grades. In fact, one member of Eric's group, claiming that he was in danger of getting a C for his final grade, pleaded with the others to give his contribution extra emphasis. However, the other members quickly rejected the idea of using relative need as a guide to preparing their memo.

At the same time, though, the members of Eric's group did not want to just divide up the credit equally. After all the time and effort they had put into the project, they wanted their contributions to be accurately and justly recognized. Fortunately, before the discussion became uncomfortable, Eric took control of the situation. He reminded everyone that once they had recognized each other's strengths, each of them had concentrated on a certain aspect of the project (library research, data entry, analysis and interpretation of the results). Therefore, each of them had played an indispensable role in the project. And because each had filled a niche in the project so effectively, distributing credit equally would in this case be the equitable thing to do.

Everyone was satisfied with this conclusion. In fact, they were so satisfied that no one took the time to notice that Eric's ideas about everyone finding a niche had probably been influenced by a theory of birth order they had recently learned about. As we will see shortly, the theory had clarified for them why their research had not revealed simple differences in success and achievement between firstborn siblings and later-borns.

Individuals in Group Settings: A Summary

When people are immersed in groups, they are not as accountable for their actions as when they are functioning and being perceived as individuals. The result is often social loafing (relaxing and letting others do the work) and the pursuit of self-interest, even when such behavior leads to disaster for the group as a whole. In extreme cases, deindividuation can lead people to become not just lazy and selfish, but violent and destructive. Fortunately, when people feel that their actions will be valued and recognized by others, and when prosocial and cooperative values are made salient, individuals tend to behave more admirably.

Most people are only vaguely aware of the psychological processes—the hidden influences—that lead them to engage in social loafing, to fall prey to deindividuation, and to behave selfishly when confronted with social dilemmas. However, they are certainly aware of another aspect of being a group member: the possibility that their efforts, accomplishments, talents, and virtues may not be recognized by others, and that they may not be treated fairly by the group. Several rules are used to determine whether or not group members have been treated justly. Prominent among them is the equity rule, or the idea that people should be rewarded in proportion to their contributions to the group. Concern with justice and fair treatment is so important that some evolutionary psychologists have argued that people are programmed with psychological mechanisms designed to detect signs of cheating and exploitation (Cosmides, 1989; Cosmides & Tooby, 1989).

Think Like a Social Psychologist

Thinking critically
—To what extent do you think people are aware of the factors that lead to social loafing? To what extent are those factors hidden influences?

Making connections
—Do you think that the criteria used to decide whether the procedures for distributing a group's resources are fair might differ in individualistic and collectivistic cultures? Why or why not?

Understanding everyday behavior
—What social dilemmas do you face in everyday life? Can you come up with a hypothesis about why you sometimes behave cooperatively and sometimes selfishly in such situations?

EPILOGUE: *MAKING SENSE OF GROUP DYNAMICS*

Birth order is not a standard topic in the study of group processes, but as Eric and his friends discovered, perhaps it should be. There are many different approaches to understanding why the talents and personalities of firstborn and later-born children might differ (Adler, 1931; Ernst & Angst, 1983; Newman, Higgins, & Vookles, 1992; Schooler, 1972; Zajonc & Markus, 1975). Some focus on differences in the way parents treat their oldest, youngest, and middle children; others emphasize the importance of sibling relationships; still others speculate about biological factors that might differentiate firstborn children from later-born children.

One theory (Sulloway, 1996), however, is based on the idea that families are small groups with complicated internal dynamics, or patterns of interaction. Although the theory is quite elaborate, it can be boiled down to the thesis that families are groups in which the less powerful members (the children) vie for the attention and resources of the powerful and dominant leaders (the parents). Firstborn children have the advantage of entering the family group before their younger siblings. As a result, they have a head start on the most direct route to status: pursuing conventional goals and excelling at activities their parents value. In addition, because firstborn children are, by definition, older than their siblings, they will generally be seen as the children most likely to survive into adulthood. As a result, parents will tend to focus their efforts on supporting their firstborn's efforts to become prominent in areas they and society value most.

Later-born children must find another niche for themselves. In their quest for other ways to stand out, they are drawn to less obvious paths to success and fulfillment. The differences between firstborn and later-born children are starkly illustrated by Sulloway's (1996) analysis of the positions taken by scientists and politicians during periods of major upheaval, such as the French Revolution and the introduction of Darwin's theory of evolution. Firstborn siblings tended to support the status quo; later-born children tended to be revolutionaries and supporters of new, even radical, approaches. For Eric and his group, the most important implication of this theory was that we should not expect to find overall differences in success or prominence between firstborn and later-born children. Children who are born to different positions in the family simply find different ways to achieve and stand out—just as members of Eric's group had each found different niches and different ways to stand out and make contributions to their research project.

The lessons Eric and his team learned from Sulloway's theory extended beyond birth order. One is that people's behavior cannot be understood without knowing something about the nature and composition of the groups to which they belong (the family, in this case). Another is that groups are complicated systems that cannot be understood by considering each individual separately; they must be understood as separate entities with their own dynamics—dynamics that their members may not even be aware of. Those lessons, we hope, are also the ones you will take from this chapter.

KEY HIDDEN INFLUENCES IN GROUPS: A SUMMARY

The distribution of information in a group: in any given group, some pieces of information are shared by more members than other pieces of information. Although group members are rarely aware of the uneven distribution of knowledge, it plays a major role in decision making: shared information is more likely to be influential than unshared information.

Groupthink: subtle interpersonal processes can lead groups of people—even talented, knowledgeable people—to confidently and enthusiastically make decisions that an outsider would recognize as disastrous.

Group polarization: when a group is already leaning toward a particular decision, even a seemingly objective, dispassionate discussion can move the group toward a more extreme position.

The discontinuity effect: groups, even more than individuals, can become unreasonably competitive and distrustful when negotiating with each other.

Social facilitation effects: although many people suspect that the presence of others can affect their performance on mental and physical tasks, the nature of the effect is not obvious. In general, the presence of others enhances performance on well-learned tasks, but undermines performance on more difficult or novel tasks.

Social loafing: being in a group affects people's decisions about how much effort to contribute to a given task or project. Without being aware of why they are doing so, people often withdraw their efforts in group settings.

Deindividuation: people are unaware of how the anonymity and arousal they experience in large groups can loosen their usual standards of behavior, leading them to engage in antisocial acts that would ordinarily shock them.

KEY TERMS AND DEFINITIONS

Group processes: the social and psychological processes that underlie the behavior of groups

Need to belong: the human need to have close and enduring relationships with other people

Group brainstorming: a method used by groups to generate as many new ideas as possible, in which people are encouraged not to be critical of their own or others' contributions

Shared information: knowledge that all or most members of a group possesses

Unshared information: knowledge possessed by only one group member, or very few of them

Groupthink: a group process that can lead to disastrous decisions, characterized by pressure for unanimity, isolation from outside influences, belief in the group's superiority, and leadership that is intolerant of dissent

Group polarization: the tendency for a group's attitudes, beliefs, and decisions to become more extreme after discussion

Discontinuity effect: the tendency for relationships between groups to be more competitive than relationships between individuals

Disjunctive task: a task that can be completed even if only one member of a group knows the answer or solution

Conjunctive task: a task that can be completed only if all group members can make a meaningful contribution

Process loss: the decrease in performance that occurs when a group fails to combine members' talents as efficiently as possible

Transactive memory system: a group in which the information needed to accomplish some task or tasks is distributed in an organized and predictable way across different group members

Social facilitation: the effects of the presence of other people on one's performance

Leader: a person who directs and organizes group members and their activities and takes responsibility for the attainment of the group's goals

Task specialist: a leader with a task orientation, who focuses on organizing group members and their activities, establishing and enforcing hierarchies, and making sure that work gets done properly and efficiently

Social-emotional specialist: a leader with an interpersonal orientation, who focuses on relationships with subordinates and subordinates' relationships with one another

Contingency model: a model of leadership that specifies which kinds of leadership are appropriate to different kinds of groups, with the key situational variable being how much control the leader has

Transformational leader: a charismatic leader who can inspire followers to adopt new values and goals

Transactional leader: a leader who is concerned primarily with managing a group's efforts to make gains, avoid losses, and fulfill existing goals

Social loafing: the tendency for people who are working on a collective task not to exert as much effort as when they work on individual tasks

Deindividuation: a state of mind brought about by being part of a crowd or by otherwise becoming anonymous, in which people become less aware of themselves as individuals, less attentive to their usual standards of behavior, and more likely to engage in antisocial behavior

Social dilemma: a situation in which behavior that is in a group member's short-term self-interest has negative long-term consequences for the group as a whole

Public goods dilemma: a social dilemma in which people must decide whether to contribute to the upkeep of some service or facility that is available to everyone (for example, a public radio station)

Resource dilemma: a social dilemma in which people must decide whether to use more than their share of some limited resource (for example, gasoline)

Prisoner's dilemma game: an experimental method for studying how people react to social dilemmas, involving a game in which opponents must choose between cooperative and competitive moves

Equity: the idea that people should be rewarded in proportion to their contribution to the group

Procedural justice: the fairness of the process with which groups decide how to allocate resources

REFERENCES

Adams, J. S. (1965). Inequality in social exchange. In L. Berkowitz (Ed.), *Advances in Experimental social psychology* (Vol. 2, pp. 267–299). New York: Academic Press.

Adler, A. (1931). *What life should mean to you.* Boston: Little, Brown.

Aldag, R. J., & Fuller, S. R. (1993). Beyond fiasco: A reappraisal of the groupthink phenomenon and a new model of group decision processes. *Psychological Bulletin, 113,* 533–552.

Allen, K. M., Blascovich, J., & Mendes, W. B. (1991). Cardiovascular reactivity in the presence of pets, friends, and spouses: The truth about cats and dogs. *Psychosomatic Medicine, 64,* 727–739.

Allen, K. M., Blascovich, J., Tomaka, J., & Kelsey, R. M. (1991). Presence of human friends and pet dogs as moderators of autonomic responses to stress in women. *Journal of Personality and Social Psychology, 61,* 582–589.

Ames, D. R., & Flynn, F. J. (2007). What breaks a leader: The curvilinear relation between assertiveness and leadership. *Journal of Personality and Social Psychology, 92,* 307–324.

Austin, W. (1980). Friendship and fairness: Effects of type of relationship and task performance on choice distribution rules. *Personality and Social Psychology Bulletin, 6,* 402–408.

Axelrod, R. (1984). *The evolution of cooperation.* New York: Basic Books.

Bales, R. F. (1950). *Interaction process analysis: A method for the study of small groups.* Reading, MA: Addison-Wesley.

Bass, B. M. (1997). Does the transactional-transformational leadership paradigm transcend organizational and national boundaries? *American Psychologist, 52,* 130–139.

Bass, B. M., & Avolio, B. J. (1993). Transformational leadership: A response to critiques. In M. M. Chemers & R. Ayman (Eds.), *Leadership theory and research: Perspectives and directions* (pp. 49–80). San Diego, CA: Academic Press.

Baumann, M. R., & Bonner, B. L. (2013). Member awareness of expertise, information sharing, information weighting, and group decision making. *Small Group Research, 44,* 532–562.

Baumeister, R. F., & Leary, M. R. (1995). The need to belong: Desire for interpersonal attachments as a fundamental human motivation. *Psychological Bulletin, 117,* 497–529.

Baumeister, R. F., & Tice, D. M. (1990). Anxiety and social exclusion. *Journal of Social and Clinical Psychology, 9,* 165–195.

Benedict, J. O., Cofer, J. L., & Cole, M. W. (1980). A study of Zajonc's theory of social facilitation using a wheel turn Sidman avoidance response in rats. *Bulletin of the Psychonomic Society, 15,* 236–238.

Betts, K. R., & Hinsz, V. B. (2013). Strong shared representations promote schema-consistent memory errors in groups. *Group Processes & Intergroup Relations, 16,* 734–751.

Bond, C. F. Jr., & Titus, L. J. (1983). Social facilitation: A meta-analysis of 241 studies. *Psychological Bulletin, 94,* 265–292.

Boos, M., Schauenburg, B., Strack, M., & Belz, M. (2013). Social validation of shared and nonvalidation of unshared information in group discussions. *Small Group Research, 44,* 257–271.

Brewer, M. B., & Kramer, R. M. (1986). Choice behavior in social dilemmas: Effects of social identity, group size, and decision framing. *Journal of Personality and Social Psychology, 50,* 543–549.

Buford, B. (1992). *Among the thugs: The experience, and the seduction, of crowd violence.* New York: Norton.

Burns, J. M. (1978). *Leadership*. New York: Harper & Row.

Burnstein, E., & Vinokur, A. (1977). Persuasive argumentation and social comparison as determinants of attitude polarization. *Journal of Experimental Social Psychology, 13*, 315–332.

Butler, J. L., & Baumeister, R. F. (1998). The trouble with friendly faces: Skilled performance with a supportive audience. *Journal of Personality and Social Psychology, 75*, 1213–1230.

Cacioppo, J. T., Hawkley, L. C., Bernston, G. C., Ernst, J. M., Gibbs, A. C., Stickgold, R., & Hobson, J. A. (2002). Do lonely days invade the nights? Potential social modulation of sleep efficiency. *Psychological Science, 13*, 384–387.

Case, T. I., & Williams, K. D. (2004). Ostracism: A Metaphor for Death. In J. Greenberg, S. L. Koole, & T. Pyszczynski (Eds.), *Handbook of experimental existential psychology* (pp. 336–351). New York: Guilford Press.

Chemers, M. M. (1987). Leadership processes: Intrapersonal, interpersonal, and societal influences. In C. Hendrick (Ed.), *Review of personality and social psychology* (Vol. 8, pp. 252–277). Newbury Park, CA: Sage.

Chemers, M. M. (1997). *An integrative theory of leadership*. Mahwah, NJ: Erlbaum.

Chemers, M. M., & Ayman, R. (Eds.). (1993). *Leadership theory and research: Perspectives and directions*. San Diego, CA: Academic Press.

Chemers, M. M., Hays, R. B., Rhodewalt, F., & Wysocki, J. (1985). A person-environment analysis of job stress: A contingency model explanation. *Journal of Personality and Social Psychology, 49*, 628–635.

Chen, S. C. (1937). Social modification of the activity of ants in nest-building. *Physiological Zoology, 10*, 420–436.

Cicourel, A. V. (1990). The integration of distributed knowledge in collaborative medical diagnosis. In J. Galegher, R. E. Kraut, & C. Egido (Eds.), *Intellectual teamwork: Social and technological foundations of cooperative work* (pp. 221–242). Hillsdale, NJ: Erlbaum.

Clark, M. S., Graham, S., & Grote, N. (2002). Bases for giving benefits in marriage: What is ideal? What is realistic? What really happens? In P. Noller & J. A. Feeney (Eds.), *Understanding marriage* (pp. 150–176). New York: Cambridge University Press.

Collins, B. E., & Guetzkow, H. (1964). *A social psychology of group processes for decision making*. New York: Wiley.

Cosmides, L. (1989). The logic of social exchange: Has natural selection shaped how humans reason? Studies with the Wason selection task. *Cognition, 31*, 187–276.

Cosmides, L., & Tooby, J. (1989). Evolutionary psychology and the generation of culture, Part II. Case study: A computational theory of social exchange. *Ethology and Sociobiology, 10*, 51–97.

Cottrell, N. B., Wack, D. L., Sekerak, G. J., & Rittle, R. H. (1968). Social facilitation of dominant responses by the presence of an audience and the mere presence of others. *Journal of Personality and Social Psychology, 9*, 245–250.

Craighead, W. E., Kimball, W. H., & Rehak, R. S. (1979). Mood changes, physiological responses, and self-statements during social rejection imagery. *Journal of Consulting and Clinical Psychology, 47*, 385–396.

Cummings, J. N., Kiesler, S., Zadeh, R., & Balakrishnan, A. D. (2013). Group heterogeneity increases the risks of large group size: A longitudinal study of productivity in research groups. *Psychological Science, 24*, 880–890.

Curtis, J. E., Grabb, E. G., & Baer, D. E. (1992). Voluntary association membership in fifteen countries: A comparative analysis. *American Sociological Review, 57*, 139–152.

Davis, J. H. (1989). Psychology and law: The last 15 years. *Journal of Applied Social Psychology, 19*, 199–230.

Davis, J. H., Au, W. T., Hulbert, L., Chen, X., & Zarnoth, P. (1997). Effects of group size and procedural influence on consensual judgments of quality: The example of damage awards and mock civil juries. *Journal of Personality and Social Psychology, 73*, 703–718.

Davis, J. H., Kameda, T., Parks, C., & Stasson, M. (1989). Some social mechanics of group decision making: The distribution of opinion, polling sequence, and implications for consensus. *Journal of Personality and Social Psychology, 57,* 1000–1012.

Davis, J. H., Tindale, R. S., Nagao, D. H., Hinsz, V. B., & Robertson, B. (1984). Order effects in multiple decisions by groups: A demonstration with mock juries and trial procedures. *Journal of Personality and Social Psychology, 49,* 1003–1012.

Dawes, R. M. (1980). Social dilemmas. In M. R. Rosenzweig & L. W. Porter (Eds.), *Annual review of psychology* (Vol. 31, pp. 169–193). Palo Alto, CA: Annual Reviews, Inc.

Dawes, R. M., McTavish, J., & Shaklee, H. (1977). Behavior, communication, and assumptions about other people's behavior in a commons dilemma situation. *Journal of Personality and Social Psychology, 35,* 1–11.

Dennis, A. R., & Valacich, J. S. (1999). Research note. Electronic brainstorming: Illusions and patterns of productivity. *Information Systems Research, 10,* 375–377.

Deutsch, M., & Gerard, H. B. (1955). A study of normative and informational social influences upon individual judgment. *Journal of Abnormal and Social Psychology, 51,* 629–636.

Devine, D. J. (2012). *Jury decision making: The state of the science.* New York: NYU Press.

Devine, D. J., Clayton, L. D., Dunford, D. D., Seying, R., & Pryce, J. (2001). Jury decision making: 45 years of empirical research on deliberating groups. *Psychology, Public Policy, and Law, 7,* 622–727.

Diamond, J. (2005). *Collapse: How societies choose to fail or succeed.* New York: Viking.

Diamond, S. S. (1997). Illuminations and shadows from jury simulations. *Law and Human Behavior, 21,* 561–571.

Diehl, M., & Stroebe, W. (1987). Productivity loss in brainstorming groups: Toward the solution of a riddle. *Journal of Personality and Social Psychology, 53,* 497–509.

Diehl, M., & Stroebe, W. (1991). Productivity loss in idea-generating groups: Tracking down the blocking effect. *Journal of Personality and Social Psychology, 61,* 392–403.

Diener, E. (1979). Deindividuation, self-awareness, and disinhibition. *Journal of Personality and Social Psychology, 37,* 1160–1171.

Diener, E. (1980). Deindividuation: The absence of self-awareness and self-regulation in group members. In P. B. Paulus (Ed.), *Psychology of group influence* (pp. 209–242). Hillsdale, NJ: Erlbaum.

DiStefano, J. J., & Maznevski, M. L. (2000). Creating value with diverse teams in global management. *Organizational Dynamics, 29,* 45–63.

Eagly, A. H., & Johnson, B. T. (1990). Gender and leadership style: A meta-analysis. *Psychological Bulletin, 108,* 233–256.

Eagly, A. H., & Karau, S. J. (1991). Gender and the emergence of leaders: A meta-analysis. *Journal of Personality and Social Psychology, 60,* 685–710.

Eagly, A. H., Johannesen-Schmidt, M. C., & van Engen, M. L. (2003). Transformational, transactional, and laissez-faire leadership styles: A meta-analysis comparing women and men. *Psychological Bulletin, 129,* 569–591.

Eagly, A. H., Karau, S. J., & Makhijani, M. G. (1995). Gender and the effectiveness of leaders: A meta-analysis. *Psychological Bulletin, 117,* 125–145.

Eagly, A. H., Makhijani, M. G., & Klonsky, B. G. (1992). Gender and the evaluation of leaders: A meta-analysis. *Psychological Bulletin, 111,* 3–22.

Eisenberger, N. I., Lieberman, M. D., & Williams, K. D. (2003). Does rejection hurt? An fMRI study of social exclusion. *Science, 302,* 290–292.

Ellsworth, P. C. (1989). Are twelve heads better than one? *Law and Contemporary Problems, 52,* 207–224.

Ernst, C., & Angst, J. (1983). *Birth order: Its influence on personality.* New York: Springer-Verlag.

Evans, G. W. (1979). Behavioral and physiological consequences of crowding in humans. *Journal of Applied Social Psychology, 9*, 27–46.

Festinger, L. (1950). Informal social communication. *Psychological Review, 57*, 271–282.

Fiedler, F. E. (1967). *A theory of leadership effectiveness.* New York: McGraw-Hill.

Fiedler, F. E. (1978). The contingency model and the dynamics of the leadership process. In L. Berkowitz (Ed.), *Advances in Experimental Social Psychology* (Vol. 11, pp. 59–112). New York: Academic Press.

Flowers, M. L. (1977). A laboratory test of some implications of Janis's groupthink hypothesis. *Journal of Personality and Social Psychology, 35*, 888–896

Forster, E. M. (1928/1973). "The machine stops." In B. Bora (Ed.), *The science fiction hall of fame* (Vol. IIB, pp. 248–279). New York: Avon.

Gawande, A. (2002). *Complications: A surgeon's notes on an imperfect science.* New York: Picador.

Geen, R. G. (1981). Evaluation apprehension and social facilitation: A reply to Sanders. *Journal of Experimental Social Psychology, 17*, 252–256.

Gigone, D., & Hastie, R. (1993). The common knowledge effect: Information sharing and group judgment. *Journal of Personality and Social Psychology, 65*, 959–974.

Gigone, D., & Hastie, R. (1997). The impact of information on small group choice. *Journal of Personality and Social Psychology, 72*, 132–140.

Gladwell, M. (2005, September 5). The bakeoff: Competing to create the ultimate cookie. *New Yorker*, pp. 125–133.

Goethals, G. R. (2005). Presidential leadership. Group performance and decision making. *Annual Review of Psychology, 56*, 545–570.

Goethals, G. R., & Zanna, M. P. (1979). The role of social comparison in choice shifts. *Journal of Personality and Social Psychology, 37*, 1469–1476.

Guerin, B. (1986). Mere presence effects in humans: A review. *Journal of Experimental Social Psychology, 22*, 38–77.

Guerin, B. (1993). *Social facilitation.* Paris, France: Cambridge University Press.

Gurin, P., Lehman, J. S., Lewis, E., Dey, E. L., Gurin, G., & Hurtado, S. (2004). *Defending diversity: Affirmative action at the University of Michigan.* Ann Arbor: University of Michigan Press.

Hackman, J. R., & Katz, N. (2010). Group behavior and performance. In S. T. Fiske, D. T. Gilbert, & G. Lindzey (Eds.), *The handbook of social psychology* (5th ed., Vol. 2, pp. 1208–1251). Hoboken, NJ: Wiley.

Halpin, A. W., & Winer, B. J. (1957). A factorial study of leader behavior descriptions. In. R. M. Stogdill & A. E. Coons (Eds.), *Leader behavior: Its description and measurement* (pp. 39–51). Columbus: Bureau of Business Research, Ohio State University.

Hardin, G. R. (1968). The tragedy of the commons. *Science, 162*, 1243–1248.

Harkins, S. G., & Szymanski, K. (1989). Social loafing and group evaluation. *Journal of Personality and Social Psychology, 56*, 934–941.

Hastie, R., & Kameda, T. (2005). The robust beauty of majority rules in group decisions. *Psychological Review, 112*, 494–508.

Hatfield, E., Traupmann, J., Sprecher, S., Utne, M., & Hay, J. (1985). Equity and intimate relations: Recent research. In W. Ickes (Ed.), *Compatible and incompatible relationships* (pp. 91–118). New York: Springer-Verlag.

Heilman, M. E., Block, C. J., Martell, R. F., & Simon, M. C. (1989). Has anything changed? Current characterizations of men, women, and managers. *Journal of Applied Psychology, 74*, 935–942.

Hill, G. W. (1982). Group versus individual performance: Are N+1 heads better than one? *Psychological Bulletin, 91*, 517–539.

Hinduja, S. (2008). Deindividuation and Internet software piracy. *Cyberpsychology & Behavior, 11,* 391–398.

Hinsz, V. B., Tindale, R. S., & Vollrath, D. A. (1997). The emerging conceptualization of groups as information processors. *Psychological Bulletin, 121,* 43–64.

Hoeksema-van Orden, C. Y. D., Gaillard, A. W. K., & Buunk, B. P. (1998). Social loafing under fatigue. *Journal of Personality and Social Psychology, 75,* 1179–1190.

Hogg, M. A. (2001). A social identity theory of leadership. *Personality and Social Psychology Review, 5,* 184–200.

Hollander, E. P. (1985). Leadership and power. In G. Lindzey & E. Aronson (Eds.), *Handbook of social psychology* (3rd ed., Vol. 2, pp. 485–537). New York: Random House.

Hollander, E. P. (1993). Legitimacy, power, and influence: A perspective on relational features of leadership. In M. M. Chemers & R. Ayman (Eds.), *Leadership theory and research: Perspectives and directions* (pp. 29–47). San Diego, CA: Academic Press.

House, R. J. (1971). A path-goal theory of leader effectiveness. *Administrative Science Quarterly, 16,* 321–338.

House, R. J., & Shamir, B. (1993). Toward the integration of transformational, charismatic, and visionary theories. In M. M. Chemers & R. Ayman (Eds.), *Leadership theory and research: Perspectives and directions* (pp. 81–107). San Diego, CA: Academic Press.

Hoyle, R. H., Pinkley, R. L., & Insko, C. A. (1989). Perceptions of social behavior: Evidence of differing expectations for interpersonal and intergroup interaction. *Personality and Social Psychology Bulletin, 15,* 365–376.

Hunt, M. B. (1985). *Social research: The scientific study of human interactions* ("One thing at a time," Chapter 4, pp. 155–199). New York: Russell Sage.

Hurtado, S. (2005). The next generation of diversity and intergroup relations research. *Journal of Social Issues, 61,* 595–610.

Ickes, W., & Gonzalez, R. (1994). "Social" cognition and social cognition: From the subjective to the intersubjective. *Small Group Research, 25,* 294–315.

Ingham, A. G., Levinger, G., Graves, J., & Peckham, V. (1974). The Ringelmann effect: Studies of group size and group performance. *Journal of Experimental Social Psychology, 10,* 371–384.

Insko, C. A., Schopler, J., Hoyle, R. H., Dardis, G. J., & Graetz, K. A. (1990). Individual-group discontinuity as a function of fear and greed. *Journal of Personality and Social Psychology, 58,* 68–79.

Isenberg, D. J. (1980). Levels of analysis of pluralistic ignorance phenomena: The case of receptiveness to interpersonal feedback. *Journal of Applied Social Psychology, 10,* 457–467.

Isenberg, D. J. (1986). Group polarization: A critical review and meta-analysis. *Journal of Personality and Social Psychology, 50,* 1141–1151.

Janis, I. L. (1982). *Groupthink: Psychological studies of policy decisions and fiascoes* (2nd ed.). Boston: Houghton Mifflin.

Johnson, D. J., and Downing, L. L. (1979) Deindividuation and valence of cues: Effects on prosocial and antisocial behavior. *Journal of Personality and Social Psychology, 37,* 1532–1538.

Kaiser, C. R., Major, B., Jurcevic, I., Dover, T. L., Brady, L. M., & Shapiro, J. R. (2013). Presumed fair: Ironic effects of organizational diversity structures. *Journal of Personality and Social Psychology, 104,* 504–519.

Kalven, H., & Zeisel, H. (1966). *The American jury.* Chicago: University of Chicago Press.

Karau, S. J., & Williams, K. D. (1993). Social loafing: A meta-analytic review and theoretical integration. *Journal of Personality and Social Psychology, 65,* 681–706.

Karau, S. J., & Williams, K. D. (1995). Social loafing: Research findings, implications, and future directions. *Current Directions in Psychological Science, 4,* 134–140.

Kenny, D. A., & Zaccaro, S. J. (1983). An estimate of variance due to traits in leadership. *Journal of Applied Psychology, 68*, 678–685.

Kerr, N. L. (1989). Illusions of efficacy: The effects of group size on perceived efficacy in social dilemmas. *Journal of Experimental Social Psychology, 25*, 287–313.

Kerr, N. L. (1994). Norms in social dilemmas. In D. Schroeder (Ed.), *Social dilemmas: Perspectives on individuals and groups* (pp. 31–47). Westport, CT: Praeger.

Kerr, N. L., & Bruun, S. (1981). Ringelmann revisited: Alternative explanations for the social loafing effect. *Personality and Social Psychology Bulletin, 7*, 224–231.

Kerr, N. L., & Tindale, R. S. (2004). Group performance and decision making. *Annual Review of Psychology, 55*, 623–655.

Kielcolt-Glaser, J. K., Garner, W., Speicher, C., Penn, G. M., Holliday, J., & Glaser, R. (1984). Psychosocial modifiers of immunocompetence in medical students. *Psychosomatic Medicine, 46*, 7–14.

Komorita, S. S., & Parks, C. D. (1995). Interpersonal relations: Mixed motive interaction. *Annual Review of Psychology, 46*, 183–207.

Kravitz, D. A., & Martin, B. (1986). Ringelmann rediscovered: The original article. *Journal of Personality and Social Psychology, 50*, 936–941.

Kray, L. J., Thompson, L., & Galinsky, A. (2001). Battle of the sexes: Gender stereotype confirmation and reactance in negotiations. *Journal of Personality and Social Psychology, 80*, 942–958.

Kurzban, R., & Leary, M. R. (2001). Evolutionary origins of stigmatization: The functions of social exclusion. *Psychological Bulletin, 127*, 187–208.

Larey, T. S., & Paulus, P. B. (1995). Social comparison goal setting in brainstorming groups. *Journal of Applied Social Psychology, 26*, 1597–1596.

Larson, J. R. Jr. (2009). *In search of synergy in small group performance.* New York: Psychology Press.

Larson, J. R. Jr., & Christensen, C. (1993). Groups as problem-solving units: Toward a new meaning of social cognition. *British Journal of Social Psychology, 32*, 5–30.

Larson, J. R. Jr., Christensen, C., Abbot, A. S., & Franz, T. M. (1996). Diagnosing groups: Charting the flow of information in medical decision-making teams. *Journal of Personality and Social Psychology, 71*, 315–330.

Larson, J. R. Jr., Christensen, C., Franz, T. M., & Abbot, A. S. (1998). Diagnosing groups: The pooling, management, and impact of shared and unshared case information in team-based medical decision-making. *Journal of Personality and Social Psychology, 75*, 93–108.

Larson, J. R. Jr., Foster-Fishman, P. G., & Keys, C. B. (1994). Discussion of shared and unshared information in decision-making groups. *Journal of Personality and Social Psychology, 67*, 446–461.

Latané, B. (1981). The psychology of social impact. *American Psychologist, 36*, 343–356.

Latané, B., Williams, K., & Harkins, S. (1979). Many hands make light the work: The causes and consequences of social loafing. *Journal of Personality and Social Psychology, 37*, 822–832.

Laughlin, P. R., Bonner, B. L., & Miner, A. G. (2002). Groups perform better than the best individuals on letters-to-numbers problems. *Organizational Behavior and Human Decision Processes, 88*, 605–620.

Laughlin, P. R., Hatch, E. C., Silver, J. S., & Boh, L. (2006). Groups perform better than the best individuals on letters-to-numbers problems: Effects of group size. *Journal of Personality and Social Psychology, 90*, 644–651.

Le Bon, G. (1895/1968). *The crowd: A study of the popular mind.* Dunwoody, GA: Norman S. Berg.

Levine, J. M., & Moreland, R. L. (1998). Small groups. In D. T. Gilbert, S. T. Fiske, & G. Lindzey (Eds.), *The handbook of social psychology* (4th ed., Vol. 2, pp. 415–469). New York: McGraw Hill.

Liang, D. W., Moreland, R. L., & Argote, L. (1995). Group versus individual training and group performance: The mediating role of transactive memory. *Personality and Social Psychology Bulletin, 21,* 384–393.

Liberman, V., Samuels, S. M., & Ross, L. (2004). The name of the game: Predictive power of reputations versus situational labels in determining prisoner's dilemma game moves. *Personality and Social Psychology Bulletin, 30,* 1175–1185.

Lind, E. A., & Tyler, T. R. (1988). *The social psychology of procedural justice.* New York: Plenum.

Longley, J., & Pruitt, D. G. (1980). Groupthink: A critique of Janis' theory. In L. Wheeler (Ed.), *Review of Personality and Social Psychology* (Vol. 1, pp. 74–93). Beverly Hills, CA: Sage.

MacCoun, R. J., & Kerr, N. L. (1988). Asymmetric influence in mock jury deliberation: Jurors' bias for leniency. *Journal of Personality and Social Psychology, 54,* 21–33.

Mackie, D. M., & Goethals, G. R. (1987). Individual and group goals. In C. Hendrick (Ed.), *Review of personality and social psychology* (Vol. 8, pp. 144–166). Newbury Park, CA: Sage.

Madigan, T. (2003). *The burning: Massacre, destruction, and the Tulsa Race Riot of 1921.* New York: St. Martin's Griffin.

Mann, L. (1981). The baiting crowd in episodes of threatened suicide. *Journal of Personality and Social Psychology, 41,* 703–709.

Mannix, E., & Neale, M. A. (2005). What difference makes a difference? The promise and reality of diverse teams in organizations. *Psychological Science in the Public Interest, 6,* 31–55.

Markus, H. (1978). The effect of mere presence on social facilitation: An unobtrusive test. *Journal of Experimental Social Psychology, 14,* 389–397.

Maxwell, G., & Schmidt, D. R. (1972). Cooperation in a three-person prisoner's dilemma. *Journal of Personality and Social Psychology, 31,* 376–383.

Maznevski, M. L. (1994). Understanding our differences: Performance in decision-making groups with diverse members. *Human Relations, 47,* 531–552.

McCallum, D. M., Harring, K., Gilmore, R., Drenan, S., Chase, J. P., Insko, C. A., & Thibaut, J. (1985). Competition and cooperation between groups and between individuals. *Journal of Experimental Social Psychology, 21,* 301–320.

Menon, T., Morris, M. W., Chiu, C.-Y., & Hong, Y.-Y. (1999). Culture and the construal of agency: Attribution to individual versus group dispositions. *Journal of Personality and Social Psychology, 76,* 701–717.

Messick, D. M., & Brewer, M. B. (1983). Solving social dilemmas: A review. In L. Wheeler & P. Shaver (Eds.), *Review of personality and social psychology* (Vol. 4, pp. 11–44). Beverly Hills, CA: Sage.

Michaelson, L. K., Watson, W. E., & Black, R. H. (1989). A realistic test of individual versus group consensus decision making, *Journal of Applied Psychology, 74,* 834–839.

Miller, D. T., & Prentice, D. A. (1994). Collective errors and errors about the collective. *Personality and Social Psychology Bulletin, 20,* 541–550.

Milliken, F. J., & Martins, L. L. (1996). Searching for common threads: Understanding the multiple effects of diversity in organizational groups. *Academy of Management Review, 21,* 402–433.

Moore, D. L., & Baron, R. S. (1983). Social facilitation: A physiological analysis. In J. T. Cacioppo & R. Petty (Eds.), *Social psychophysiology.* New York: Guilford Press.

Moreland, R. L. (1999). Transactive memory: Learning who knows what in work groups and organizations. In L. Thompson, D. Messick, & J. Levine (Eds.), *Shared cognition in organizations: The management of knowledge* (pp. 3–31). Mahwah, NJ: Erlbaum.

Moreland, R. L., & Myaskovsky, L. (2000). Exploring the performance benefits of group training: Transactive memory or improved communication? *Organizational Behavior and Human Decision Processes, 82,* 117–133.

Moscovici, S., & Zavalloni, M. (1969). The group as a polarizer of attitudes. *Journal of Personality and Social Psychology, 12*, 125–135.

Mullen, B., Bryant, B., & Driskell, J. E. (1997). Presence of others and arousal: An integration. *Group Dynamics: Theory, Research, and Practice, 1*, 52–64.

Mullen, B., & Copper, C. (1994). The relation between group cohesiveness and performance: An integration. *Psychological Bulletin, 115*, 210–227.

Mullen, B., Johnson, C., & Salas, E. (1991). Productivity loss in brainstorming groups: A meta-analytic integration. *Basic and Applied Social Psychology, 12*, 3–24.

Myers, D. G., & Bishop, G. D. (1970). Discussion effects on racial attitudes. *Science, 169*, 778–789.

Myers, D. G., & Lamm, H. (1976). The group polarization phenomenon. *Psychological Bulletin, 83*, 602–627.

Nagar, D., & Pandey, J. (1987). Affect and performance on cognitive task as a function of crowding and noise. *Journal of Applied Social Psychology, 17*, 147–157.

Najdowski, C. J. (2010). Jurors and social loafing: Factors that reduce participation during jury deliberations. *American Journal of Forensic Psychology, 28*, 39–64.

Newman, L. S., Higgins, E. T., & Vookles, J. (1992). Self-guide strength and emotional vulnerability: Birth order as a moderator of self-affect relations. *Personality and Social Psychology Bulletin, 18*, 402–411.

Northouse, P. G. (2003). *Leadership: Theory and practice* (3rd ed.). Thousand Oaks, CA: Sage Publications.

Onishi, N. (2007, July 16). Japan Learns Dreaded Task of Jury Duty. *New York Times*, p. A1.

Orbell, J. M., van de Kragt, A. J. C., & Dawes, R. M. (1988). Explaining discussion-induced cooperation. *Journal of Personality and Social Psychology, 54*, 811–819.

Osborn, A. F. (1957). *Applied imagination.* New York: Scribner.

Paulus, P. B., Dugosh, K. L., Dzindolet, M. T., Coskun, H., & Putman, V. L. (2002). Social and cognitive influences in group brainstorming: Predicting production gains and losses. In W. Stroebe & M. Hewstone (Eds.), *European review of social psychology* (Vol. 12, pp. 299–325). Hoboken, NJ: John Wiley & Sons Ltd.

Paulus, P. B., Dzindolet, M. T., Poletes, G., & Camacho, L. M. (1993). Perception of performance in group brainstorming: The illusion of group productivity. *Personality and Social Psychology Bulletin, 19*, 78–89.

Paulus, P. B., & Dzindolet, M. T. (1993). Social influence processes in group brainstorming. *Journal of Personality and Social Psychology, 64*, 575–586.

Pennington, N., & Hastie, R. (1986). Evidence evaluation in complex decision-making. *Journal of Personality and Social Psychology, 51*, 242–258.

Pennington, N., & Hastie, R. (1992). Explaining the evidence: Tests of the story model for juror decision-making. *Journal of Personality and Social Psychology, 62*, 189–206.

Peters, L. H., Hartke, D. D., & Pohlmann, J. T. (1985). Fiedler's contingency theory of leadership: An application of the meta-analytic procedures of Schmidt and Hunter. *Psychological Bulletin, 97*, 274–285.

Plaut, V. C., Garnett, F. G., Buffardi, L. E., & Sanchez-Burks, J. (2011). "What about me?" Perceptions of exclusion and Whites' reactions to multiculturalism. *Journal of Personality and Social Psychology, 101*, 337–353.

Postmes, T., & Spears, R. (1998). Deindividuation and antinormative behavior. *Psychological Bulletin, 123*, 238–259.

Prentice-Dunn, S., & Rogers, R. W. (1989). Deindividuation and the self-regulation of behavior. In P. B. Paulus (Ed.), *Psychology of group influence* (2nd ed., pp. 87–109). Hillsdale, NJ: Erlbaum.

Pruitt, D. G. (1998). Social conflict. In D. T. Gilbert, S. T. Fiske, & G. Lindzey (Eds.), *The handbook of social psychology* (4th ed., Vol. 2, pp. 470–503). New York: McGraw Hill.

Reno, R. R., Cialdini, R. B., & Kallgren, C. A. (1993). The transsituational influence of social norms. *Journal of Personality and Social Psychology, 64*, 104–112.

Resnick, L., Levine, J., & Teasley, S. D. (1991). *Perspectives on socially shared cognition.* Washington, DC: American Psychological Association.

Riggio, R., Murphy, S. E., & Pirozzolo, F. J. (Eds.) (2001). *Multiple intelligences and leadership.* Mahwah, NJ: Erlbaum.

Ross, M., & Sicoly, F. (1979). Egocentric biases in availability and attribution. *Journal of Personality and Social Psychology, 37*, 322–337.

Saks, M. J., & Marti, M. W. (1997). A meta-analysis of the effects of jury size. *Law and Human Behavior, 21*, 451–466.

Sandys, M., & Dillehay, R. C. (1995). First-ballot votes, predeliberation dispositions, and final verdicts in jury trials. *Law and Human Behavior, 19*, 175–195.

Sanders, G. S. (1981). Driven by distraction: An integrative review of social facilitation theory and research. *Journal of Experimental Social Psychology, 17*, 227–251.

Sani, F. (2005). When subgroups secede: Extending and refining the social psychological model of schism in groups. *Personality and Social Psychology Bulletin, 31*, 1074–1086.

Sani, F., & Todman, J. (2002). Should we stay or should we go? A social-psychological model of schism in groups. *Personality and Social Psychology Bulletin, 28*, 1647–1655.

Schmitt, B. H., Gilovich, T., Goore, N., & Joseph, L. (1986). Mere presence and social facilitation: One more time. *Journal of Experimental Social Psychology, 22*, 228–241.

Scholten, L., van Knippenberg, D., Nijstad, B. A., & De Dreu, C. K. W. (2007). Motivated information processing and group decision-making: Effects of process accountability on information processing and decision quality. *Journal of Experimental Social Psychology, 43*, 539–552.

Schooler, C. (1972). Birth order effects: Not here, not now! *Psychological Bulletin, 78*, 161–175.

Schopler, J., Insko, C., & Wieselquist, J. (2001). When groups are more competitive than individuals: The domain of the discontinuity effect. *Journal of Personality and Social Psychology, 80*, 632–644.

Schriesheim, C. A., Tepper, B. J., & Tetrault, L. A. (1994). Least preferred co-worker score, situational control, and leadership effectiveness: A meta-analysis of contingency model performance predictions. *Journal of Applied Psychology, 79*, 561–573.

Schroeder, D. A., Steel, J. E., Woodell, A. J., & Bembenek, A. F. (2003). Justice within social dilemmas. *Personality and Social Psychology Review, 7*, 374–387.

Sears, D. O. (1986). College sophomores in the laboratory: Influences of a narrow data base on psychology's view of human nature. *Journal of Personality and Social Psychology, 51*, 515–530.

Shepperd, J. A. (1993). Productivity loss in performance groups: A motivation analysis. *Psychological Bulletin, 113*, 67–81.

Shepperd, J. A. (1995). Remedying motivation and productivity loss in collective settings. *Current Directions in Psychological Science, 4*, 131–134.

Simon, S., & Hoyt, C. L. (2013). Exploring the effect of media images on women's leadership self-perceptions and aspirations. *Group Processes & Intergroup Relations, 16*, 232–245.

Skitka, L. J. (2002). Do the means justify the ends, or do the ends justify the means? A value protection model of justice reasoning. *Personality and Social Psychology Bulletin, 28*, 452–461.

Skitka, L. J. (2003). On different minds: An accessible identity model of justice reasoning. *Personality and Social Psychology Review, 7*, 286–297.

Skitka, L. J., & Crosby, F. J. (2003). Trends in the social psychological study of justice. *Personality and Social Psychology Review, 7,* 282–285.

Skitka, L. J., & Mullen, E. (2002). Understanding judgments of fairness in a real-world political context: A test of the value protection model of justice reasoning. *Personality and Social Psychology Bulletin, 28,* 1419–1429.

Sniezek, J. A., May, D. R., & Sawyer, J. E. (1990). Social uncertainty and interdependence: A study of resource allocations in groups. *Organizational Behavior and Human Decision Processes, 46,* 155–180.

Sommers, S. R. (2006). On racial diversity and group decision-making: Identifying multiple effects of racial composition on jury deliberations. *Journal of Personality and Social Psychology, 90,* 597–612.

Sommers, S. R., Warp, L. S., & Mahoney, C. C. (2008). Cognitive effects of racial diversity: White individuals' information processing in heterogeneous groups. *Journal of Experimental Social Psychology, 44,* 1129–1136.

Stasser, G. (1999). The uncertain role of unshared information in collective choice. In L. L. Thompson, J. M. Levine, & D. M. Messick (Eds.), *Shared cognition in organizations: The management of knowledge* (pp. 49–70). Mahwah, NJ: Lawrence Erlbaum Associates, Inc.

Stasser, G., & Titus, W. (1985). Pooling of unshared information in group decision making: Biased information sampling during discussion. *Journal of Personality and Social Psychology, 48,* 1467–1478.

Stasser, G., & Titus, W. (1987). Effects of information load and percentage of shared information on the dissemination of unshared information during group discussion. *Journal of Personality and Social Psychology, 53,* 81–93.

Steiner, I. D. (1972). *Group process and productivity.* New York: Academic Press.

Stogdill, R. M. (1948). Personal factors associated with leadership: A survey of the literature. *Journal of Psychology, 25,* 35–71.

Stroebe, W., & Diehl, M. (1994). Why groups are less effective than their members: On productivity losses in idea-generating groups. In W. Stroebe & M. Hewstone (Eds.), *European review of social psychology* (Vol. 5, pp. 271–303). Chichester, England: Wiley.

Strube, M. J. (2005). What did Triplett really find? A contemporary analysis of the first experiment in social psychology. *American Journal of Psychology, 118,* 271–286.

Strube, M. J., & Garcia, J. E. (1981). A meta-analytical investigation of Fiedler's contingency model of leadership effectiveness. *Psychological Bulletin, 90,* 307–321.

Suler, J. R. (2004). The online disinhibition effect. *CyberPsychology and Behavior, 7,* 321–326.

Sulloway, F. J. (1996). *Born to rebel: Birth order, family dynamics, and creative lives.* New York: Vintage Books.

Tajfel, H., Billig, M. G., Bundy, R. P., & Flament, C. (1971). Social categorization and intergroup behavior. *European Journal of Social Psychology, 1,* 149–178.

Terborg, J. R., Castore, C., DeNinno, J. A. (1976). A longitudinal field investigation of the impact of group composition on group performance and cohesion. *Journal of Personality and Social Psychology, 34,* 782–790.

Tetlock, P. E., Peterson, R. S., McGuire, C., Chang, S., & Feld, P. (1992). Assessing political group dynamics: A test of the groupthink model. *Journal of Personality and Social Psychology, 63,* 403–425.

Thibaut, J., & Walker, L. (1975). *Procedural justice: A psychological analysis.* Hillsdale, NJ: Lawrence Erlbaum Associates, Inc.

Thompson, L., Peterson, E., & Brodt, S. E. (1996). Team negotiation: An examination of integrative and distributive bargaining. *Journal of Personality and Social Psychology, 70,* 66–78.

Thompson, L., & Fine, G. A. (1999). Socially shared cognition, affect, and behavior: A review and integration. *Personality and Social Psychology Review, 3,* 278–302.

Tindale, R. S., & Larson, J. R. Jr. (1992). Assembly bonus effect or typical group performance? A comment on Michaelson, Watson, and Black (1989). *Journal of Applied Psychology, 77*, 102–105.

Toma, C., & Butera, F. (2009). Hidden profiles and concealed information: Strategic information sharing and use in group decision making. *Personality and Social Psychology Bulletin, 35*, 793–806.

Triandis, H. C., Kurowski, L. L., & Gelfand, M. J. (1994). Workplace diversity. In H. C.

Triandis, M. D. Dunnette, & L. M. Hough (Eds.), *Handbook of industrial and organizational psychology* (2nd ed., Vol. 4, pp. 769–827). Palo Alto, CA: Consulting Psychologists Press, Inc.

Triplett, N. (1898). The dynamogenic factors in pacemaking and competition. *American Journal of Psychology, 9*, 507–533.

Turner, M. E., Pratkanis, A. R., Probasco, P., & Leve, C. (1992). Threat, cohesion, and group effectiveness: Testing a social identity maintenance perspective on groupthink. *Journal of Personality and Social Psychology, 63*, 781–796.

Tyler, T. R. (1994). Psychological models of the justice motive: Antecedents of distributive and procedural justice. *Journal of Personality and Social Psychology, 67*, 850–863.

Tyler, T. R., & Lynd, E. A. (1992). A relational model of authority in groups. In M. Zanna (Ed.), *Advances in experimental social psychology* (Vol. 25, pp. 115–191). San Diego, CA: Academic Press.

Uziel, L. (2007). Individual differences in the social facilitation effect: A review and meta-analysis. *Journal of Research in Personality, 41*, 579–601.

Valacich, J. S., Dennis, A. R., & Connolly, T. (1994). Idea generation in computer-based groups: A new ending to an old story. *Organizational Behavior and Human Decision Processes, 57*, 448–467.

van Prooijen, J. W., van den Bos., K., & Wilke, H. A. M. (2002). Procedural justice and status: Status salience as antecedent of procedural fairness effects. *Journal of Personality and Social Psychology, 83*, 1353–1361.

Van Vugt, M. (2009). Averting the tragedy of the commons: Using social psychological science to protect the environment. *Current Directions in Psychological Science, 18*, 169–173.

Vroom, V. H., & Jago, A. G. (2007). The role of situation in leadership. *American Psychologist, 62*, 17–24.

Waldman, D. A., Ramirez, G. G., House, R. J., & Puranam, P. (2001). Does leadership matter? CEO leadership attributes and profitability under conditions of perceived environmental uncertainty. *Academy of Management Journal, 44*, 134–143.

Waller, J. (2002). *Becoming evil: How ordinary people commit genocide and mass killing*. New York: Oxford University Press.

Walster, E. G., Walster, W., & Berscheid, E. (1978). *Equity: Theory and research*. Boston: Allyn & Bacon.

Walumbwa, F. O., & Lawler, J. J. (2003). Building effective organizations: Transformational leadership, collectivist orientation, work-related attitudes and withdrawal behaviours in three emerging economies. *International Journal of Human Resource Management, 14*, 1083–1101.

Watson, W. E., Kumar, K., & Michaelson, L. K. (1993). Cultural diversity's impact on interaction process and performance: Comparing homogeneous and diverse task groups. *Academy of Management Journal, 36*, 590–602.

Weber, J. M., & Murnighan, J. K. (2008). Suckers or saviors? Consistent contributors in social dilemmas. *Journal of Personality and Social Psychology, 95*, 1340–1353.

Wegner, D. M. (1987). Transactive memory: A contemporary analysis of the group mind. In B. Mullen & G. R. Goethals (Eds.), *Theories of group behavior* (pp. 185–208). New York: Springer.

Wegner, D. M. (1995). A computer network model of human transactive memory. *Social Cognition, 13*, 319–339.

Wegner, D. M., Erber, R., & Raymond, P. (1991). Transactive memory in close relationships. *Journal of Personality and Social Psychology, 61*, 923–929.

Wildschut, T., Insko, C. A., & Gaertner, L. (2002). Intragroup social influence and intergroup competition. *Journal of Personality and Social Psychology, 82,* 975–992.

Wiley, J., & Bailey, J. (2006). Effects of collaboration and argumentation on learning from web pages. In A. M. O'Donnell, C. E. Hmelo-Silver, & G. Erkins (Eds.), *Collaborative learning, reasoning, and technology* (pp. 297–321). Mahwah, NJ: Lawrence Erlbaum.

Williams, K., Harkins, S., & Latané, B. (1981). Identifiability as a deterrent to social loafing: Two cheering experiments. *Journal of Personality and Social Psychology, 40,* 303–311.

Williams, K. D. (2001). *Ostracism: The power of silence.* New York: Guilford Publications.

Williams, K. D., & Karau, S. J. (1991). Social loafing and social compensation: The effects of expectations of co-worker performance. *Journal of Personality and Social Psychology, 61,* 570–581.

Wilson, D. S., Timmel, J. J., & Miller, R. R. (2004). Cognitive cooperation: When the going gets tough, think as a group. *Human Nature, 15,* 225–250.

Winquist, J. R., & Larson, J. R. Jr. (1998). Information pooling: When it impacts group decision making. *Journal of Personality and Social Psychology, 74,* 371–377.

Winquist, J. R., & Larson, J. R. Jr. (2004). Sources of the discontinuity effect: Playing against a group versus being in a group. *Journal of Experimental Social Psychology, 40,* 675–682.

Wittenbaum, G. M., Hubbell, A. P., & Zuckerman, C. (1999). Mutual enhancement: Toward an understanding of the collective preference for shared information. *Journal of Personality and Social Psychology, 77,* 967–978

Worchel, S., Rothberger, H., Day, E. A., Hart, D., & Butemeyer, J. (1998). Social identity and individual productivity within groups. *British Journal of Social Psychology, 37,* 389–413.

Zaccaro, S. J. (2007). Trait-based perspectives on leadership. *American Psychologist, 62,* 6–16.

Zaccaro, S. J., Foti, R. J., & Kenny, D. A. (1991). Self-monitoring and trait-based variance in leadership: An investigation of leader flexibility across multiple group situations. *Journal of Applied Psychology, 76,* 308–315.

Zadro, L., Williams, K. D., & Richardson, R. (2004). How low can you go? Ostracism by a computer is sufficient to lower self-reported levels of belonging, control, self-esteem, and meaningful existence. *Journal of Experimental Social Psychology, 40,* 560–567.

Zajonc, R. B. (1965). Social facilitation. *Science, 149,* 269–274.

Zajonc, R. B. (1980). Compresence. In P. B. Paulus (Ed.), *Psychology of group influence* (pp. 35–60). Hillsdale, NJ: Erlbaum.

Zajonc, R. B., Heingartner, A., & Herman, E. M. (1969). Social enhancement and impairment of performance in the cockroach. *Journal of Personality and Social Psychology, 13,* 83–92.

Zajonc, R. B., & Markus, G. B. (1975). Birth order and intellectual development. *Psychological Review, 82,* 74–88.

Zimbardo, P. G. (1970). The human choice: Individuation, reason, and order versus deindividuation, impulse, and chaos. In W. J. Arnold & D. Levine (Eds.), *1969 Nebraska symposium on motivation* (Vol. 27, pp. 237–307). Lincoln: University of Nebraska Press.

Zimbardo, P. G., Maslach, C., & Haney, C. (2000). Reflections on the Stanford Prison Experiment: Genesis, transformations, consequences. In T. Blass (Ed.), *Obedience to authority: Current perspectives on the Milgram paradigm* (pp. 193–237). Mahwah, NJ: Erlbaum.

CHAPTER 9

ATTRACTION

AT THE BUS STOP

Kalei's mom had dropped her off near Kalani High School, where she could catch the bus that would take her to the University of Hawaii at Manoa. It was a beautiful morning. After several days of stifling Kona weather, the trade winds had picked up again and were pushing wispy clouds through the sky. Behind her, the undersized Kalani High football team was practicing for their game against mighty Kaiser High.

Realizing just how much time she had before the bus arrived, Kalei reached into her backpack for the study notes she needed to review for her chemistry exam later that morning. As she wrestled the papers from her bag, her phone rang to announce that she had received a text message from Chad, her boyfriend of two years. Kalei was briefly tempted to ignore it, but then realized that he was probably calling to get in touch with her about the tickets for the Cazimero Brothers' show at the Waikiki Shell.

A love for Hawaiian music was one of the many things Kalei shared with Chad. They both loved hanging out at Yami Soft Frozen Yogurt Shoppe on Ala Moana Boulevard and looking for bargains at the flea market in the Aloha Stadium parking lot. They had grown up in the same neighborhood and gone to the same schools. Before Chad decided that Sunday mornings should be reserved for surfing, they had even attended the same church. Their parents knew each other and had generally supported their relationship—except for a brief time when they had had to date secretly, after her dad suggested that she find someone who would put the Bible ahead of the surfboard. But that blew over, perhaps because her dad realized the two were good for each other. They rarely disagreed about anything, and Chad always went out of his way to compliment her on her appearance. As a busy college student, Kalei liked the fact that Chad always took charge of planning their dates; otherwise, she would never get see the Cazimeros live!

The message on the phone was from Chad. He was asking if she wanted to go to the concert with him—just as she expected. Kalei tapped out a quick "Sure thing" just as the bus arrived. She climbed on and found a seat across from a man she had seen there before. A nametag clipped to his shirt pocket identified him as Kekoa Wang, a staff member at Kaiser Hospital on King Street.

What will happen on this bus ride? Will Kalei, the Kalani High School graduate, become attracted to Kekoa, who works at Kaiser Hospital on King Street? What makes some people attractive to us, more so than others? Is it just a matter of physical appearance, or do we like people for all sorts of reasons, many of them not obvious to us? In this chapter, we discuss the social psychological variables and processes that explain why we become attracted to others.

PSYCHOLOGICAL INFLUENCES ON LIKING AND ATTRACTION

In Chapter 5, we saw that people often don't know the reasons why they like some things while they dislike others, or why they feel about something the way they do. Much of what is true for attitudes about objects and issues also holds for interpersonal preferences. Our friendship and dating choices are influenced by psychological influences that often operate outside of conscious awareness.

Implicit Egotism

Research suggests that Kalei may well become attracted to Kekoa on her way to class. Why? The results of an archival study (Pelham, Mirenberg, & Jones (2002) suggest that people often prefer things that are connected to themselves even arbitrarily—through the letters in their names, for example. This **implicit egotism** manifests itself in several ways. For example, people tend to live in cities with names that resemble their own names. There is a disproportionate number of Jacks in Jacksonville, Phils in Philadelphia, Virginias in Virginia Beach, and Mildreds in Milwaukee. In the United States, dentists are more likely than the average American to be named Dennis, Denise, or Dena; hardware store owners, more likely to be named Harold or Harris; and roofers, more likely to be named Rashid, Roy, or Ray (Pelham, Mirenberg, & Jones (2002). Moreover, studies show that participants in experiments are especially likely to be attracted to other participants whose experimental codes resemble their birthday, or whose surnames share letters with their own (Jones, Pelham, Carvallo, & Mirenberg, 2004). Admittedly, these name-letter effects are small, and there is a debate about whether they truly exist (Pelham & Carvallo, 2011; Simonsohn, 2011). Nonetheless, much of the research on attraction has demonstrated the influence of such hidden influences—that is, processes that operate outside of conscious awareness.

Learning to Like Someone

In the days when parents exerted a strong influence on whom their children married, romance novels often featured a young woman dreaming of love and romance, but forced to marry a man she doesn't love. Friends and sympathetic family members suggest that perhaps she can learn to love her partner. The remainder of the story revolves around her struggle with this seemingly impossible task. Whether or not she ultimately escapes the loveless marriage, the conclusion is always the same: you cannot *learn* to love someone. However, you can learn to *like* someone, in the same way that you learn to like things associated with pleasant experiences.

Pavlov's (1927) principle of **classical conditioning** suggests that we will come to like those with whom good things are associated. This principle has been succinctly expressed to mean "that liking for a person will result under those conditions in which an individual experiences reward in the presence of that person, regardless of the relationship between the other person and the rewarding event or state of affairs" (Lott & Lott, 1974,

p. 172). In other words, we should like others if we meet them on a sunny day, at the beach, or in a stimulating class, rather than on a rainy day, in a cramped study hall, or during a boring lecture. Supposedly, the positive feelings induced by pleasant surroundings become conditioned to the people we meet in those surroundings, so that we like them as well as the surroundings. This idea seems almost self-evident, and, not surprisingly, numerous experimental studies have supported the hidden influence of classical conditioning (e.g., Byrne, 1971; Byrne & Rhamey, 1965; Clore & Byrne, 1974; Lott & Lott, 1974).

At the same time, we tend to dislike others whom we meet under adverse conditions (Gouaux, 1971; Griffit, 1969; Griffit & Veitch, 1971; Veitch & Griffit, 1976). In a typical experiment, participants evaluate fictitious others while seated in lab rooms ranging from comfortable to hot or roomy to crowded (Griffit & Veitch, 1971). Consistent with classical conditioning principles, the less favorable the conditions, the worse the evaluations, as **Figure 9.1** shows. Again, the negative affect induced by the adverse situation appears to become conditioned to the person being evaluated, leading to a decrease in liking.

Before we can conclude that we like those we meet under pleasant circumstances and dislike those we meet under adverse circumstances, we need to take a closer look at one noteworthy feature of the research on the classical conditioning of negative affect. In most studies, participants rate a fictitious stranger (that is, a verbal description of a person) rather than a real stranger (for example, another participant in the study). Imagine that you and three fellow students have just finished participating in a study, in which your job was to fill out questionnaires in a comfortable, spacious room. At lunchtime, you spot one of your fellow participants in the cafeteria. How likely are you to sit with him? If you are like most people, you will probably reply, "That depends."

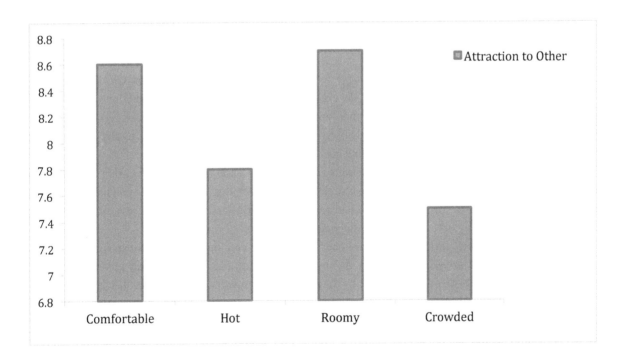

Figure 9.1: Attraction to a Fictitious Other Under Different Environmental Conditions

Source: Griffit, W.B., & Veitch, R. (1971). Hot and crowded: Influence of population density and temperature on interpersonal affective behavior. *Journal of Personality and Social Psychology, 17,* 92–98.

What if you had done the same study in a crowded, overheated room? Surprisingly, doing so could increase the chances that you would seek out your fellow participants. The reason is that your shared negative experience created an affective bond among you. When you find yourself in aversive circumstances, the mere presence of others is rewarding because it provides a sense of comfort. Similar results were found in at least one laboratory study (Rotton, Barry, Frey, & Soler, 1978) that showed increased attraction among participants who met in an environment polluted by ammonium sulfide.

For the same reason, soldiers who have shared combat duty often forge friendships that last a lifetime, despite geographical separation. These results cannot easily be explained in terms of classical conditioning, which would predict that the negative affect induced by being fired on should carry over to others who were present. The key to this puzzle is that aversive conditioning occurs primarily with *fictitious* strangers. When the strangers are *real*, their presence provides a sense of comfort that helps us to cope with the aversive situation, especially if the situation arouses fear. Indeed, our **need for affiliation** (Schachter, 1959) is most pronounced when we experience fear and uncertainty because the presence of others helps to reduce both emotions. By virtue of the hidden influence of **operant conditioning** (Kenrick & Johnson, 1979), then, we find ourselves more attracted to people with whom we share adversity.

Arousal and Attraction

It is possible to explain attraction to a stranger under extremely pleasant or unpleasant circumstances without referring to either classical or operant conditioning. The fact is, either situation increases a person's level of physiological arousal, which is experienced as accelerated heart rate, perspiration, and breathing. Such increases in physiological functioning are equally characteristic of positive and negative emotions. Thus, heightened arousal can be interpreted as either a positive or negative emotional state, depending on the attribution a person makes for it (Schachter & Singer, 1962).

The attributions you make may, in turn, be suggested by the situation. For example, if you notice an increase in arousal at the same time you realize that it has been raining for days, you may blame your arousal on the bad weather and label it irritation. However, if that same increase in arousal is accompanied by the realization that spring has finally arrived, you may label it happiness. By itself, arousal is not specific to any emotion. The emotional experience is determined by situational cues (Schachter & Singer, 1962).

In many cases, situational cues are unambiguous and readily available (such as the fact that it is sunny or rainy outside). Over the course of your life, you also develop a general idea of what makes you happy, irritated, or angry. Thus, the process of attributing heightened arousal to a particular cause is not necessarily a conscious, effortful task. Instead, it can serve as a hidden influence on attraction.

In other situations, labels or explanations are hard to come by; you may need to choose among multiple cues to the source of your arousal. For example, if you are standing alone at a bus stop, any increase in arousal you feel may be caused either by the weather or by the realization that you are running late. If you find yourself in the company of an attractive person, however, you may explain your arousal differently. Instead of feeling irritated, you may decide that you are on the verge of falling in love. In short, attraction can result from the **misattribution of arousal**.

The idea that attraction can result from a misattribution of arousal is well supported by experimental studies. For example, Dutton and Aron (1974) conducted a field experiment involving male (and presumably heterosexual) college students who had just crossed either a shaky bridge or a sturdy bridge. At that point, an attractive female interviewer approached and asked them to fill out a short questionnaire, giving them an opportunity to contact her later if they had any questions. The difference between the two bridges the participants had crossed—and thus between the two experimental conditions—was dramatic. The shaky bridge was a five-foot wide, 450-foot long suspension bridge constructed of wooden boards attached to wire cables. Hung over a 230-foot-deep canyon, it had a tendency to tilt, sway, and wobble. Those characteristics, along with low handrails made of wire cables, gave participants the impression that they were in danger of falling over the side. The sturdy bridge was 10 feet wide, hung only 10 feet above a shallow creek, and was constructed of heavy cedar.

The researchers were interested primarily in the number of participants who would accept the interviewer's phone number and avail themselves of the opportunity to call her. As expected, 9 of the 18 participants who had crossed the shaky bridge ended up calling the attractive *female* interviewer. Of the 16 participants who had crossed the sturdy bridge, only 2 called her. Regardless of which bridge they had crossed, participants who were met by a *male* interviewer rarely called him. Evidently, participants who had crossed the shaky bridge attributed their arousal to the presence of the attractive female interviewer. Much less misattribution occurred among those participants who experienced little arousal and among those who were met by a male interviewer, who provided a relatively poor cue to participants' arousal.

This finding that arousal brought on by external stimuli can be misattributed to a potential object of attraction has been replicated across many situations. For example, male participants who were expecting to receive a painful electric shock were more attracted to a female confederate than participants who were expecting to receive only a mild shock (Dutton & Aron, 1974; Experiment 3). Similar results were obtained in experiments that manipulated participants' level of arousal through exposure to erotic material (Stephan, Berscheid, & Walster, 1971) or unflattering feedback on a personality test (Jacobs, Berscheid, & Walster, 1971). Perhaps the most revealing evidence for the notion that "adrenaline makes the heart grow fonder" comes from a study of young dating couples, who rated (a) the extent of romantic love they felt for their partners; and (b) the amount of parental interference to which their relationship was subjected (Driscoll, Davis, & Lipetz, 1972). Not surprisingly, the researchers found a positive relationship between the degree of love and the amount of parental interference. The more parental interference, the more in love couples felt. Along these same lines, Rubin (1973) discovered that dating couples who came from different religious backgrounds reported more romantic love than dating couples from similar religious backgrounds. Presumably, they attributed the arousal produced by conflicts over their religious orientations to their partner's attractiveness.

Some (Kenrick & Cialdini, 1977) have argued that the increased attraction resulting from heightened arousal could just as easily be explained in terms of operant conditioning. According to this argument, an increase in attraction could be due to the other person's fear-reducing qualities, rather than to a misattribution of the arousal produced by a fearful situation. This point is valid, although the empirical evidence for it does not seem strong (Foster, Witcher, Campbell, & Green, 1998). For arousal to be attributed to a stranger or romantic partner, its source needs to be at least somewhat ambiguous. Under those circumstances, arousal seems to affect attraction by way of misattribution of arousal (Foster et al., 1998; White & Kight, 1984). However, when heightened arousal clearly results from the anticipation of a painful electric shock, to the extent that the person correctly identifies its source, it may not lead to increased attraction. Finally, if operant conditioning were the correct explanation, participants in Dutton and Aron's (1974) experiment should have been just as attracted to the male interviewer as to the female interviewer because his presence should have been just as fear reducing.

The misattribution view of attraction has some clear-cut implications for the early stages of dating. Rubin (1973) points out that in Roman times, courtship experts advised men to take their would-be lovers to watch

Research on misattribution of arousal explains how the thrill of these rides can add to the thrill of a relationship.

the gladiators, on the chance that the arousal created by watching the bloody contests might be misperceived as attraction, or even love. Today's couples might benefit from seeing a scary movie or watching an exciting athletic competition.

Of course, it is possible that neither operant conditioning nor misattribution of arousal provides the best explanation of attraction. Some researchers suggest that arousal may contribute to attraction by facilitating what they call the *dominant response* (Allen, Kenrick, Linder, & McCall, 1989). According to this *response facilitation* perspective, in an aversive environment, liking is the dominant response to a same-sex person for heterosexual individuals, and romantic attraction the dominant response to a potential date. Arousal simply facilitates these responses, producing increased liking for a same-sex other and increased romantic attraction to an opposite-sex other, regardless of whether the source of arousal is ambiguous or obvious.

The Gleam of Praise

So far we have treated others primarily as passive bystanders, whose presence reduces fear and uncertainty or provides convenient labels for our physiological states. But, of course, others do more than just stand around. By responding to what we do and say, they influence how much we like or dislike them. All else equal, we tend to like those who respond to us with praise more than those who respond with disapproval or indifference.

Based on this simple principle, Dale Carnegie (1936) advised that heaping praise on someone was a foolproof means of gaining a person's friendship. This simple idea is so well-established that to this day, you can sign up for workshops (called Dale Carnegie Seminars) on the importance of using praise and other means of ingratiation to "make friends and influence people."

Before you sign up for a Dale Carnegie Seminar—certainly before you pay for it—read what the Dutch philosopher Baruch Spinoza (1981) wrote in proposition 44 of *The Ethics* several hundred years ago:

> *Hatred which is completely vanquished by love passes into love: and love is thereupon greater than if hatred had not preceded it. For he who begins to love a thing, which he has wont to hate or regard with pain, from the very fact of loving feels pleasure. To this pleasure involved in love is added the pleasure arising from aid given to the endeavor to remove the pain involved in hatred. ...*

Although Spinoza was concerned with hatred turned to love, proposition 44 may have similar implications for praise following on the heels of derogation. That is, praise may be particularly effective following derogation because of its propensity to elicit more liking than praise alone.

A study by Aronson and Linder (1965) lends support to this idea. Following several brief interactions, participants overheard a confederate talking about them. In one condition, the confederate consistently conveyed a positive impression of them (intelligent, good conversationalist, outstanding person). In another condition, the confederate consistently conveyed the opposite impression. Needless to say, there were marked differences in how much participants in the two conditions liked the confederate. However, when the confederate began by conveying a negative impression and then became more positive, participants liked her even more than those who heard her make entirely positive comments. Not surprisingly, when the confederate's evaluation went from positive to negative, participants liked her even less than when she had conveyed a consistently negative impression. **Figure 9.2** summarizes the effects of such gains and losses on attraction.

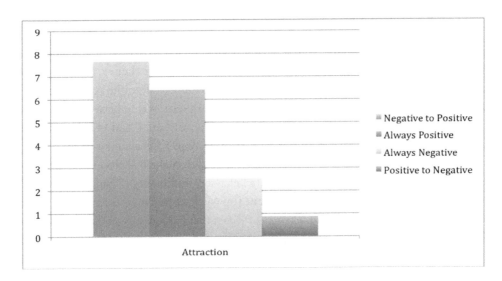

Figure 9.2: The Gain-Loss Effect on Attraction

Source: Aronson, E., & Linder, D.E. (1965). Gain and loss of esteem as determinants of interpersonal attraction. *Journal of Experimental and Social Psychology, 1,* 156–171.

Why would we like someone who begins by thinking poorly of us, but who later becomes positive, more than someone who always liked us? One reason is that we perceive the switch from a negative to a favorable evaluation as a relative gain, just as Spinoza (1981) suggestsed for hatred and love. Similarly, we like someone who switches from a positive to a negative evaluation less than someone who is consistently negative because the change represents a relative loss. Such **gain-loss effects** may be due to an attributional analysis aimed at discerning the other's motives for praising us. Did she praise us for what we did or said, or to cull favors or gain our approval? Praise that is attributed to an ulterior motive reduces rather than increases attraction (Jones & Pittman, 1982; Jones & Wortman, 1973). However, the realization that someone has raised her opinion of us adds credibility to the praise, increasing attraction. Likewise, a switch from praise to derogation may suggest that the initial praise was insincere and thus will likely reduce attraction.

Dispositions on the part of those on the receiving end of praise further complicate the simple picture drawn by Dale Carnegie. As we saw in Chapter 4, the striving for self-verification implies that people with positive self-concepts prefer positive feedback, including praise. On the other hand, people with negative self-concepts prefer negative feedback (Swann, 1992). In terms of interpersonal preferences, people with positive self-views tend to choose partners who evaluate them favorably; people with negative self-views prefer partners who evaluate them unfavorably, confirming their views of themselves (Swann, Hixon, Stein-Seroussi, & Gilbert, 1990; Swann, Stein-Seroussi, & Giesler, 1992). Consequently, married couples report a higher level of commitment when they feel that a spouse really knows them, including their shortcomings and flaws (Swann, Hixon, & De La Ronde, 1992). Not surprisingly, people tend to be most attracted to partners who provide equal opportunities for both self-enhancement *and* self-verification (Katz & Joiner, 2002).

The Importance of Agreement

On some level, we can think of praise as a specific—perhaps exaggerated—form of agreement. People who compliment us on our choice of wardrobe or political opinions are essentially communicating their agreement. Not surprisingly, agreement produces attraction, but the reverse is also true: attraction can produce agreement.

The reciprocal nature of the relationship between agreement and attraction was first recognized by Heider (1958) and elaborated by Newcomb (1961) in their formulations of **balance theory**. According to this theory, to fully understand attraction in interpersonal relationships, we must analyze the relationship between two people in terms of three distinct units or elements. First, there is a relationship between one person (P) and another (O) that is characterized by mutual liking or disliking. In addition, P and O each have a relationship with regard to some issue (X), which could represent an attitude, object, behavior, or personality trait. For example, their relationships with X could involve the identity of the best basketball player of all time (an attitude), an ice cream flavor (an object), nose-picking in public (a behavior), or honesty (a personality trait). These two relationships with X may be marked by overt agreement (on Michael Jordan as the greatest basketball player ever, for example), or by mere association (for example, the fact that P frequently picks his nose in public). The P-O-X triad can be formally represented as a triangle, in which a plus sign (+) denotes liking, agreement, or the presence of some attribute, and a minus sign (–) denotes the opposite (see **Figure 9.3**).

By and large, people gravitate toward balanced triads. A triad is said to be in a state of balance when the elements and their relationships agree with one another—that is, when the multiplication of their signs yields a positive outcome (Heider, 1958). Balance exists in the first triad in **Figure 9.3**, in which the two people like each other, and both evaluate issue X positively. Balance also exists in the second triad, in which the two people like each other, and both evaluate issue X negatively. In both cases, the two people and their sentiments coexist in perfect harmony.

The third triad, however, is marked by a state of *imbalance*, which is created by P and O's disagreement about X. The resulting tension may motivate P to restore balance in one of several ways. They include (a) a change in P's attitude toward X; (b) a change in P's perception of O's attitude toward X; (c) a reduction in the importance P assigns to X; (d) a reduction in P's attraction to O; and (e) a reduction in the relevance both P and O assign to X (Newcomb, 1961). The path P chooses depends to some extent on the nature of the relationship and the situation. If P is not heavily invested in X, a change in P's attitude toward X is a likely solution. If P has a strong, entrenched belief in X, however, a change in P's perception of O's attitude may be the way to restore balance.

People tend to avoid states of *unbalance*, which are marked by mutual dislike between P and O (see the fourth and fifth triads in **Figure 9.3**). In these cases, a reduction in the attraction between P and O is unlikely to restore balance (Tashakkori & Insko, 1981), especially in relationships that were formed without free choice (for example, those formed among coworkers or tenants). In such situations, people are more likely to increase their liking for the people they disliked initially (Tyler & Sears, 1977).

Speaking of people we dislike, balance theory can explain why we sometimes like those who dislike the same people we do. Remember that people gravitate toward balanced triads. With a shared dislike of X, balance can be obtained only by rendering the sign for the relationship between P and O positive (see the second triad in **Figure 9.3**). Thus, our enemy's enemy becomes our friend (Aronson & Cope, 1968).

Balance theory does a good job of explaining the motivational forces at work when the P-O-X triad is out of balance. At the same time, it is a bit simplistic, because it does not take into account the fact that agreement with some people may be more important than agreement with others. For example, you probably put a relatively high premium on agreement with someone who is highly competent in matters that are important to you. Agreeing with a noted film critic's opinion of a movie you have just seen, then, is inherently more rewarding than agreeing with someone who lives down the hall. Consequently, your liking for the critic will increase more as a result of your agreement than your liking for the stranger down the

Balance:

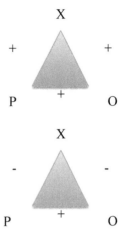

Imbalance:

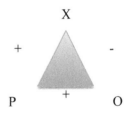

Unbalance

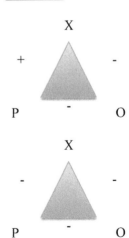

Figure 9.3: Balance, Imbalance, and Unbalance in the P-O-X Triad

Source: Heider, F. (1958). *The psychology of interpersonal relations.* New York: Wiley.

States of balance are marked by agreement and positive feelings; states of imbalance, by disagreement and negative feelings.

hall who agrees with you. Of course, the reverse is also true: disagreeing with the noted film critic will lead to a steeper decrease in your liking for her than disagreeing with the fellow down the hall would affect your liking for him (Mills, Cooper, & Duncan, 2002).

Similarity: Birds of a Feather Flock Together

If we like those who agree with us, might we also be attracted to those who share our attitudes and personal characteristics? If you answered yes to this question, you're right. The evidence is overwhelming that we like those who are similar to us in age (Ellis, Rogoff, & Cramer, 1981), race and religion (Kandel, 1978), emotional experience (Rosenblatt & Greenberg, 1988), sense of humor (Murstein & Brust, 1985; Treger, Sprecher, & Erber, 2013), music preferences (Boer et al., 2011), intelligence (Lewak, Wakefield, & Briggs, 1985), performance or skill level (Tesser, Campbell, & Smith, 1984), and speaking or writing style (Ireland et al., 2011). We even prefer those who share our identity as a morning person or an evening person (Watts, 1982). And people who share similar physical features (for example, hair length and color) tend to flock together spontaneously (Mackinnon, Jordan, & Wilson, 2011). Similarity on such dimensions may promote the ease with which two people communicate and interact. For example, morning people may simply have a hard time coordinating their activities with evening people. What is more, superficial similarities may indicate attitudinal similarity: someone who dresses the way we do or likes the same kind of music may also share some of our attitudes, beliefs, and values.

The importance of **attitude similarity** to attraction was established by Byrne and his colleagues (Byrne, 1971; Byrne & Nelson, 1965; Byrne & Rhamey, 1965; Clore & Byrne, 1974), whose experimental research shows that a stranger with similar attitudes elicits more liking than a stranger with dissimilar attitudes (Byrne, 1971). The degree of attraction between two people is determined by the *proportion* of attitudes on which they agree, rather than the total number of agreements. In other words, we like a stranger who agrees with us on 5 out of 10 attitudes just as much as a stranger who agrees with us 50 out of 100 times (Byrne & Nelson, 1965). The degree of attraction is further determined by the *magnitude* of similarity. In general, we like others more when they are similar to us in terms of both attitudes *and* personality than when they are similar to us on only one of those dimensions (Byrne & Rhamey, 1965).

All else being equal, then, we will be more attracted to people who agree with us than to people who do not. Yet some research casts doubt on the pervasiveness of this phenomenon. Most of the experimental work on attitude similarity relies on paper-and-pencil measures of attraction. When behavioral measures are employed, a different picture emerges. In one study (Gormly, 1979), participants reported on paper that they liked an attitudinally similar other more than an attitudinally dissimilar other (see **Figure 9.4a**). However, when they were asked to choose one of the two people for continued discussion, two-thirds of the participants picked the one whose attitudes were *dissimilar* (see **Figure 9.4b**).

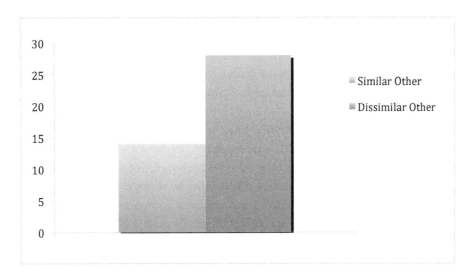

Figure 9.4a: Liking for an Attitudinally Similar and Dissimilar Other

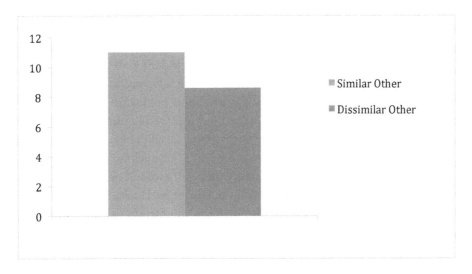

Figure 9.4b: Number of Participants Preferring a Discussion With an Attitudinally Similar and Dissimilar Other

Source: Gormly, A.V. (1979). Behavioral effects of receiving agreement or disagreement from a peer. *Personality and Social Psychology Bulletin, 5,* 405–408.

Several other studies employing paper-and-pencil measures also seem to qualify the similarity-attraction relationship. For example, similarity seems to matter primarily to people who have a favorable self-concept (Leonard, 1975). And in romantically tinged relationships, physical attractiveness is often more important than attitudinal similarity (Kleck & Rubenstein, 1975). As long as two people's level of physical attractiveness is comparable, romantic settings can produce attraction to a *dissimilar*, rather than a similar, other (Gold, Ryckman, & Mosley, 1984). Finally, during the early stages of a friendship, attitude *dissimilarity* produces more attraction than similarity. In well-established friendships, similarity attracts (McCarthy & Duck, 1976). Although some researchers (e.g., Sunnafrank, 1984) have argued that these findings suggest that the relationship between similarity and attraction may be an artifact of the psychological laboratory, most researchers agree that the empirical evidence is solid and reliable. Other researchers have raised questions about how the similarity-attraction relationship should be explained. There are at least five possibilities. Byrne and his colleagues favor a *reinforcement-affect* explanation, meaning that similarity is rewarding. That is, we like those who are similar to us because they are associated with certain rewards. However, a *balance* explanation could account for the importance of similarity just as well.

Alternatively, the similarity-attraction relationship may be due partly to *impression management*—that is, a desire to create a favorable impression through the expression of liking for someone. Similarity may also produce attraction through *uncertainty reduction*. To the extent that we are not sure of our views, that is, agreement with another provides consensual validation. Conversely, dissimilarity increases our uncertainty (Goethals, 1986). Finally, a *rewards of interaction* interpretation suggests that similarity is important, primarily because it has positive implications for interactions with others, especially strangers (Kandel, 1978).

In light of the strong theoretical and empirical support for the link between similarity and attraction, raising the possibility that similarity may be unrelated to attraction may seem silly. However, Rosenbaum (1986) did just that when he introduced the **repulsion hypothesis**, which proposes that at first, people respond to all strangers with liking. Once dissimilarity surfaces, however, this initial liking turns to disliking or repulsion. In other words, people are not attracted to a select few who share their attitudes; they are repelled by those who *don't* share their attitudes. Similarity matters only to the extent that it prevents the repulsion that arises from dissimilarity.

To make this point empirically, Rosenbaum (1986) replicated Byrne's work, with the addition of a control condition that contained no information about similarity. This "no-information" condition produced levels of attraction comparable to those obtained in the similarity condition, but higher than those in the dissimilarity condition. Rosenbaum (1986) concluded that dissimilarity—rather than similarity—determined attraction.

To conclude from such findings that similarity is irrelevant for attraction may be premature, however. Specifically, there is a problem with the no-information condition on which Rosenbaum based his conclusion. By and large, people assume that most other people share their attitudes and opinions, a phenomenon known as the false consensus effect (Marks & Miller, 1987; Ross, Greene, & House, 1977). When participants are confronted with a description of a stranger that is devoid of any information regarding attitudinal similarity or dissimilarity, as in Rosenbaum's (1986) no-information condition, they may very well assume a false consensus. In fact, under those conditions, participants assume that the other person will agree with them 73 percent of the time (Singh & Tan, 1992). Given this high level of assumed similarity, Rosenbaum may not have managed to create a true no-information condition (Byrne, Clore, & Smeaton, 1986). More important, we cannot know whether such a condition ever exists in real life. Thus, the safest conclusion at this point seems to be that both similarity and dissimilarity contribute to attraction and repulsion (Singh & Ho, 2000).

Results from a more recent study (Amodio & Showers, 2005) provide further insights into the role of similarity and dissimilarity in attraction. Over a year's time, dating partners reported their level of commitment to their partner, the degree to which they perceived themselves as similar, and their satisfaction with the relationship. The results showed that whether similarity and dissimilarity increase or decrease attraction depends on individuals' commitment to a relationship. **Table 9.1** summarizes the ways in which commitment interacts with similarity.

Table 9.1: Relationship Styles by Level of Commitment and Perceived Similarity

		Commitment to Relationship	
		Low	**High**
Perceived Similarity	**Low**	*Exploration* • Novelty seeking • Similar to Self-expansion (Aron & Aron, 1997) • Liking: Moderate with no decrease over time	*Fatal Attractions* • Focus on positive "extrinsic" qualities (not on similarity) and reluctant to recognize negative partner attributes, qualities • Liking: Moderate with substantial decreases over time
	High	*Convenience* • Unattractive or little-liked partners bonded via similarity • Liking: low with substantial decreases over time	*Prototypic Committed Relationship* • Realistic appraisal of partner, recognition of both positive and negative traits • Liking: High with decreases over time

Adapted from Amodio & Showers (2005)

Specifically, although similar partners in *committed* relationships reported a high degree of satisfaction with their relationship, similar partners in *uncommitted* relationships did not. Among committed couples, similarity was associated with initially high levels of attraction that decreased over time. Among uncommitted couples, similarity was associated with low levels of initial attraction that decreased further over time. Although these couples may have been drawn together because of their similarity, they clearly did not like each other.

The effects of dissimilarity on attraction were also mediated by commitment. In *committed* relationships, dissimilar partners subscribed to unrealistic, idealized appraisals of their partners' faults, turning a blind eye to their partner's troubling qualities. These relationships faltered over time. Surprisingly, in *uncommitted* relationships, dissimilar partners displayed the most stable level of liking. Amodio and Showers (2005) suggest that these couples should be considered "explorers," who view their dissimilarity as an opportunity for growth and self-expansion (Aron & Aron, 1997).

Complementarity: Opposites Attract

If attitudinal dissimilarity can destroy attraction, can other forms of dissimilarity contribute to it? Can a person who is dominant be attracted to someone who is submissive, for instance? Or can a person who is nurturing find happiness with someone who enjoys being nurtured? The answer may be yes, because of the **complementarity** of these respective needs. Submissiveness complements dominance, and succorance complements nurturance.

Sporadic observations by family therapists have supported this intuitively appealing idea (Kubie, 1956; Mittelman, 1956). In the most systematic, ambitious attempt to study the role of need complementarity to date, Winch (1958) tried to reconcile the seeming importance of similarity with the apparent importance of complementarity. He reasoned that similarity may be most important in meeting new people. For example, a person who spends his weekends playing softball is unlikely to meet someone who enjoys the theater. Likewise, a devout churchgoer is unlikely to meet a Bohemian atheist. Once two people have met on the basis of similar interests, however, their relationship will succeed based less on how similar they are than on how well they complement each other's needs.

From Murray's (1938) list of psychogenic needs, Winch extracted those needs that he considered most relevant to human mate selection: abasement (a tendency to yield dignity and prestige), achievement, approach, autonomy, deference, dominance, hostility, nurturance, succorance, recognition, status aspirations, and status strivings. To these he added the personality dimensions of anxiety, emotionality, and vicariousness. These needs and traits can complement one another in two ways. In Type I complementarity, one partner is high on a need and the other partner is low. For example, one might be high on dominance and the other low. In Type II complementarity, one partner is high on one need and the other partner is high on a different need. For example, one person might be high on hostility and the other high on abasement.

To find out which dimensions might be complementary, Winch (1958) picked 25 married couples who were students at Northwestern University. He administered a battery of objective tests to assess their needs and personalities and then subjected the results to statistical analysis. Winch concluded that the couples did indeed show complementarity, especially on needs such as achievement and passivity, nurturance and receptiveness, dominance and submission. Furthermore, he found that most of the marriages he studied could be classified according to the degree of dominance and nurturance expressed by husband and wife. This combination of dominance/submissiveness and nurturance/receptiveness yielded four categories of marriage, as shown in **Table 9.2**.

According to this categorization, a nurturing and dominant husband paired with a receptive and submissive wife produces *Ibsenian complementarity*, in which the husband plays the role of protector and caretaker, and the wife the role of a passive, incompetent doll-child. The name for this type of marriage derives from Henrik Ibsen's play, *A Doll's House*. In this kind of marriage, the husband seeks to control and mold his wife into the kind of woman he wants her to be. In contrast, a nurturing and submissive husband paired with a receptive and dominant wife produces *Thurberian complementarity*, named after the writer James Thurber. In this rather comical type of marriage, the wife is a dominant, active woman, and the husband a passive man who harbors a latent hostility that he expresses only under great provocation. The relationship between the cartoon characters Charlie Brown and Lucy in "Peanuts" is a case in point, as are the relationships between General Halftrack and his wife in "Beetle Bailey" and between Mr. and Mrs. Dithers in "Blondie."

Table 9.2: Dimensions and types of complementarity

		Nurturance-Receptiveness	
		Husband Nurturant/ Wife Receptive	Wife Nurturant/ Husband Receptive
Dominance-Submissiveness	Husband Dominant/ Wife Submissive	*Ibsenian*	*Master-Servant Girl*
	Husband Submissive/ Wife Dominant	*Thurberian*	*Mother-Son*

Source: Winch (1958).

A receptive and dominant husband paired with a nurturing, submissive wife produces a *master–servant girl complementarity*. In this type of marriage, the wife is more competent than the Ibsenian wife. The husband is the head of the house, and she is the capable and worthy servant. Although on the surface, the husband is dominating and self-assured, on a deeper level he is also dependent on his wife's emotional support. Finally, a receptive and submissive husband paired with a nurturing and dominant wife produces a *mother-son complementarity*. In this type of marriage, the wife is nurturing, and the husband seeks the kind of succorance he once received from his mother.

Winch conceded that his classification scheme did not describe all marriages. Furthermore, he acknowledged that needs can exist on an overt, conscious level, as well as on a covert, unconscious level. A person who is dominant and self-assured on one level (perhaps because of role expectations) might nevertheless be dependent and emotionally needy on another level. In such cases, how should we classify the person and the resulting relationship? Finally, Winch's sample of 25 couples was fairly small and perhaps atypical, given that it included only married college students.

Not surprisingly, subsequent tests of Winch's model have provided a mixed bag of evidence for the role of complementarity in close relationships. Some studies found support for Winch's ideas in the context of friendship choices (Schutz, 1958), relationship development (Kerckhoff & Davis, 1962), and attachment (Luo & Klohnen, 2005). Other studies found no evidence for complementarity in dating couples, newlyweds, and veteran couples (Bowerman & Day, 1956; Murstein, 1961). And one set of studies found that Thurberian complementarity can be downright precarious (Swann, Rentfrow, & Gosling, 2003): verbally inhibited men became alienated by their verbally uninhibited partners. In light of such inconsistent findings, several reviews of the literature (Barry, 1970; Tharp, 1963; White & Hatcher, 1984) have concluded that Winch's hypothesis lacks sufficient empirical support, despite its appeal among laypeople and family therapists.

Given the strong evidence for the importance of similarity and the relatively weaker evidence for the importance of complementarity, should we conclude that birds of a feather flock together, but opposites don't attract? The answer is both yes and no. On the one hand, the similarity hypothesis has withstood the test of time. On the other hand, much of the inconsistencies in the findings regarding complementarity stem from differences in the measurement of needs. Projective tests, such as the Thematic Apperception Test, tend to tap into more covert needs. Objective paper-and-pencil tests, such as the Edwards Personal Preference Scale, tend to tap into more overt needs.

In these studies, then, distinguishing between covert and overt needs may be important. A person with a covert need for dominance may not seek submissiveness from others at all times and under all circumstances. Instead, whether or not a covert tendency toward dominance leads to overt demands for submission may depend on the presence or absence of certain interpersonal goals. For example, Shawna may feel somewhat conflicted about her desire to dominate Tyrone, and may therefore camouflage her wish behaviorally. Alternatively, Tyrone's behavior may indicate that he does not wish to be submissive, which may cause Shawna to refrain from overt demands for submissive behavior.

Based on such reasoning, Dryer & Horowitz (1997) have argued that attraction cannot be predicted from need complementarity without taking into account differences in interpersonal style and goals. From this perspective, interpersonal behaviors *invite* rather than evoke complimentary responses. Because people can refuse such invitations, one would expect to find that in the most satisfactory relationships, the wish of one partner to dominate is met by the desire of the other to be submissive. To test this idea, Dryer & Horowitz (1997) asked research participants who had been classified as endorsing either a dominant or a submissive interpersonal style to interact with a confederate who behaved in either a dominant or submissive fashion. At the conclusion of the experiment, participants rated their satisfaction with the interaction. As expected, participants who had a dominant interpersonal style were happiest when the confederate behaved in a submissive fashion. Participants who endorsed a submissive interpersonal style were happiest when the confederate acted in a dominant fashion (see **Figure 9.5**).

Findings like these indicate that the connection between complementarity and relationship satisfaction is far more complicated than Winch (1958) assumed. At the same time, when we look beyond covert needs for dominance and submissiveness to take into account specific interpersonal and situational variables, we find that the link between complementarity and relationship satisfaction is considerably stronger than was suspected in the past.

Proximity: The Girl (or Boy) Next Door

Friendships, dating relationships, and marriages do not result primarily from fate and random pairings. Instead, people tend to marry those who live close by. One early study (Bossard, 1932) revealed that of the first 5,000 marriages formed in Philadelphia in the year 1931, a third of the brides and grooms lived within five blocks of each other, and slightly more than half lived within 20 blocks. Studies of friendship formation in college dormitories (Lundberg & Beazley, 1948; Lundberg, Hertzler, & Dickson, 1949) and housing projects (Festinger,

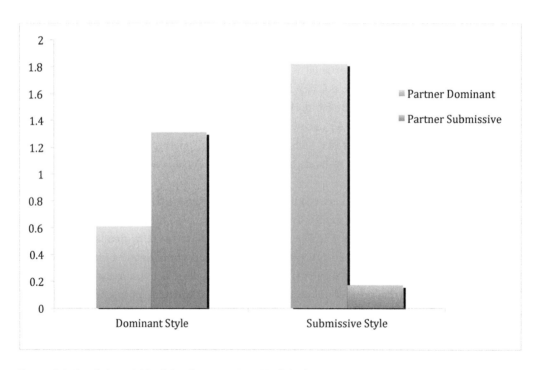

Figure 9.5: Participants' Satisfaction As a Result of Their Interpersonal Styles and Their Partner's Behavior

Based on: Dryer, D.C., & Horowitz, L.M. (1997). When do opposites attract? Interpersonal complementarity versus similarity. *Journal of Personality and Social Psychology, 72,* 592–603.

Schachter, & Back, 1950; Nahemow & Lawton, 1975) also show that physical proximity is the most important predictor of who becomes friends with whom. Similar effects have even been obtained using state police trainees' place in the alphabet as a measure of proximity (Segal, 1974).

How can we explain the importance of a seemingly trivial factor like proximity in the development of attraction? One answer may be that people who live in close proximity are similar on some important dimensions. To the extent that neighborhoods are often defined in terms of ethnicity and socioeconomic status, this type of explanation could account for the high rate of within-neighborhood marriages. On the other hand, dormitory assignments are, for the most part, random, so that the resulting friendships cannot easily be explained in terms of similarity. A more likely explanation is that attraction to those who are close to us may be a hidden influence resulting from mere exposure. This idea has its roots in experimental demonstrations showing that the more people are exposed to anything—from a character in the Chinese alphabet to a political candidate—the more favorably they will evaluate it (Moreland & Zajonc, 1982; Zajonc, 1968).

There is good reason to suspect that the mere exposure effect holds for attraction to people as well. In one study (Brockner & Swap, 1976), participants were exposed one, two, four, or eight times to others who were either attitudinally similar or dissimilar. Consistent with the mere exposure hypothesis, participants rated the most frequently seen others more favorably. The effect was more pronounced when the other was attitudinally similar, suggesting that mere exposure increases attraction primarily when the initial evaluation is positive or neutral (Grush, 1976). Interestingly, similar effects have been observed online, a venue where proximity can be related to a particular chat room. Regular attendance at these sites aids in forming an attraction (Levine, 2000).

Playing Hard to Get

Throughout the ages, one of the cardinal rules of dating has held that a person who appears to be hard to get is a more desirable catch than a person who seems overly eager to forge a union. At least two social psychological theories suggest that there is an advantage in **playing hard to get**. According to both dissonance theory (Festinger, 1956) and personal equity theory (Seta & Seta, 1982; Seta, Seta, & Martin, 1987), expending a great deal of effort to achieve a goal increases the goal's value, in part, perhaps, to justify the effort (Aronson & Mills, 1959). Alternatively, frustrated efforts may increase a suitor's physiological arousal, which becomes a hidden influence on love or desire through misattribution (Dutton & Aron, 1974).

Though the hard-to-get rule is intuitively and theoretically appealing, experiments have shown it to be more elusive than we might expect. In five different studies that varied a woman's availability for dating, Walster, Walster, Pilliavin, & Schmidt (1973) found no evidence for the idea that playing hard to get makes for a more desirable date. The reason for this result became clear when the investigators looked at how participants perceived the women. Perceptions of both easy-to-get and hard-to-get women included interpersonal assets as well as liabilities. The easy-to-get woman was perceived as friendly, warm, and flexible, yet unpopular and unselective. The hard-to-get woman was perceived as unfriendly, cold, and rigid, yet popular and selective. Clearly, one woman's assets were the other woman's liabilities. However, a sixth study showed that a woman who is selectively hard to get (relatively easy for participants, but hard for everyone else) was perceived to have no liabilities. Because she was considered friendly, warm, flexible, popular, and *selective*, she turned out to be the most desirable date. These findings suggest that playing hard to get is fraught with pitfalls; it seems to work only when the game is played selectively. Some (Eastwick, Finkel, Mochon, & Ariely, 2007) have argued that coming across as selective may determine attraction in the increasingly popular practice of speed dating. However, results from a recent study (Gomez & Erber, 2013) suggest that the matching principle provides a better predictor of attraction in such situations.

Secrecy

Initial attraction can be amplified by the need for secrecy, as in the case of institutional prohibitions against dating. When teachers fall in love with their students or supervisors are drawn to their employees, the resulting relationships may need to be concealed from others. Often, the need for secrecy becomes a hidden influence that renders these relationships more exciting than they would be otherwise.

Why would a need for secrecy increase attraction? There are two possible answers. First, striving to keep a relationship secret from others may increase our arousal, which we can easily misattribute to the object of our desire. Second, keeping a relationship secret requires us to banish from consciousness all thoughts about the other, especially in situations in which we might be tempted to talk about the relationship. Suppressing any kind of thought is more difficult than we might think, however. We may succeed for a time, but usually only at the expense of a massive rebound, in which the suppressed thought returns with even stronger force (Wegner, Schneider, Carter, & White, 1987). Moreover, the very attempt to suppress a thought often renders it hyperaccessible to consciousness—especially when we need to attend to other matters (Wegner, 1994; Wegner & Erber, 1992).

Whichever explanation we adopt, suppressing thoughts about someone to whom we are attracted can lead to a preoccupation with that person that increases the initial attraction (Lane & Wegner, 1994). In an experimental demonstration of this phenomenon, Wegner, Lane, and Dimitri (1994) asked mixed-sex pairs of participants to play a card game. Some pairs were asked to make foot contact under the table; others were not. Of those who were asked to make foot contact, some were asked to keep the contact secret from the other pair; others were not required to maintain secrecy. As we might expect, participants who were told to secretly maintain foot contact were more attracted to their partners than other participants. They were more likely to see themselves going out together, to think that their partners would be a good romantic match, and to feel close to their partners. At the conclusion of the experiment, these participants also reported more intrusive thoughts about their partners than other participants. These results suggest that keeping a relationship secret can indeed increase attraction, and that the increase results primarily from the cognitive preoccupation created by the need for secrecy.

This heightened attraction comes at a price, however. Studies that have examined real couples found that the anxiety associated with concealing their relationship resulted in decreased levels of relationship satisfaction (Foster & Campbell, 2005) and decreases in commitment and self-esteem, along with a higher incidence of health-related problems (Lehmiller, 2009).

Fatal Attractions

For many of us, thinking about **fatal attractions** brings to mind the motion picture, *Fatal Attraction*. In that movie, a middle-aged man has a brief and intense sexual encounter with a sexually assertive single woman while his wife and children are away for the weekend. After a few days of steamy sex, all hell breaks loose, and the end result is one dead lover, one seriously boiled pet rabbit, and in the U.S. version of the movie, a reaffirmation of family values. In real life, however, these experiences are rarely lethal to the individuals who become involved in them. In a typical situation, two individuals are drawn to one another because of characteristics that they at first find pleasing, but later come to dislike. Thus, the word *fatal* refers to the death of the relationship (Felmlee, 1995; 1998a). In the movie *Fatal Attraction*, the single woman's sexual assertiveness was at first attractive to the married man. Once his wife returned, however, it became a major inconvenience, causing the death of the relationship.

For most of us, the characteristics that produce fatal attractions are much more innocuous. We may be attracted to someone because he or she is funny, but later become annoyed by the constant silliness. Or we may appreciate another's refreshing innocence, only to become troubled by the accompanying lack of maturity (Felmlee, 1995). People are especially prone to fatal attractions when the characteristics they admire in another differs from their own characteristics, from the average, or from the norm (Felmlee, 1998b). Consequently, a timid person may be attracted to someone who appears adventurous; a middle-aged man may be attracted to a young woman with an unusual sexual appetite.

Attractions of this sort can become fatal for several reasons. Our initial impressions of the other may have been carefully crafted to obscure the drawbacks that lead to eventual repulsion. We also tend to idealize others in the early stages of a relationship. As infatuation fades, we become increasingly aware of the other's liabilities. Finally, behavior that is different or novel may simply grow stale over time, spoiling a partner's initial likability.

Psychological Influences on Liking and Attraction: A Summary

The extent to which we are attracted to others depends on several hidden influences that operate outside of conscious awareness. Implicit egotism compels us to like others with characteristics that are similar to our own, including superficial characteristics like the letters in our name. Classical conditioning principles predict that we will like others whom we meet under favorable circumstances; operant conditioning, that we will like others whose presence helps to alleviate our fear or uncertainty. Praise promotes attraction, especially when it follows on the heels of derogation or indifference. Agreement promotes attraction because it establishes balance.

Similarity in attitudes is of paramount importance to attraction; the proportion of agreed-upon attitudes is more influential than the total number. Although need complementarity can lead to attraction, its effects are complicated and have been difficult to establish in the laboratory. Playing hard to get increases attraction primarily when the game is played selectively—that is, when a person appears to be hard to get for everyone else. Keeping a relationship secret promotes attraction because it creates intrusive thoughts about the secret partner. Fatal attractions come about when we are attracted to someone with unusual or novel characteristics that later become liabilities.

Think Like a Social Psychologist

Designing research
—Why are data about friendships that were formed in dormitories more useful than marriage records as a test of the hypothesis that proximity leads to attraction?

Understanding everyday behavior

—Speed dating, a matchmaking service that allows people to interact briefly with many different dates in the same venue, is enjoying increased popularity in many U.S. cities. Imagine yourself participating in a speed dating session. With just a few minutes to interact with each person, what questions would you to ask?

Making connections

—Many workplaces have strict prohibitions against dating among employees, to limit the potential for harassment. Based on the research on secrecy and attraction, what might be an unintended consequence of such policies?

THE MAN ON THE BUS

Kalei had seen Kekoa on the bus before, usually when she had to be at school early for her chemistry class. However, the two had never spoken, and they rarely exchanged glances. Kekoa's head seemed forever buried in the *Honolulu Advertiser*. On the rare occasions when he looked up, Kalei never knew whether he was looking at her or out the window behind her. His seeming indifference to her presence had not discouraged Kalei's fascination with his handsome appearance, however.

Sneaking a quick glance, Kalei once again marveled at Kekoa's perfectly symmetrical, clean-shaven face, large eyes, and prominent cheekbones and chin. His short, wavy hair, slightly gray around the temples, suggested that he was a bit older than Kalei. Kekoa's tall, athletic body was clad in an expensive Hawaiian shirt, neatly tucked into pleated slacks. A pair of expensive-looking loafers completed the outfit, convincing Kalei that he must be a physician who took the bus because it was convenient.

Compared to Kekoa, Chad seemed just a boy. A surfer, he seemed to care little about his appearance, from his perpetually unkempt hair to what Kalei called his "uniform": T-shirt, shorts, and rubber slippers from Long's Drug Store. Moreover, Chad seemed to lack ambition. Kalei was working toward a college degree, but he seemed perfectly content with his sales job at Town and Country Surf. Except for an occasional class at Leeward Community College, he showed little interest in furthering his education. And his idea of a night on the town was to take her to Zippy's for a plate lunch, then to a friend's house to relive the weekend's best waves.

Most of the time, Kalei wasn't troubled by Chad's lack of ambition, and she found his boyishness charming. But as the bus slowed down in the rush-hour traffic, Kalei couldn't resist fantasizing about what life with Kekoa would be like. "A girl can dream, right?" she thought.

PHYSICAL ATTRACTIVENESS

That good looks matter in dating is something most of us know or at least suspect, even though many of us would like to believe that love is more than skin-deep. In fact, evidence shows that our thoughts, feelings, and behavior toward others are influenced far more by a person's good looks than any of us wants to admit.

Consider the results of a classic field experiment conducted 50 years ago at the University of Minnesota (Walster, Aronson, Abrahams, & Rottman, 1966). In that study, more than 700 freshmen participated in a dance held the week before classes started. Participants who chose to attend were assigned a date by computer. The experiment was set up so that students could obtain tickets only by appearing in person at the Student Union. When they did, they were asked to show their ID cards to one person, to sign for their tickets with a second person, and to pick up the tickets from a third person. The people who handled the ticket distribution had been employed by the experimenters to rate the **physical attractiveness** of participants and then randomly assign them a date of the opposite sex. Halfway through the dance, participants were asked to rate their dates on several dimensions, including physical attractiveness, their comfort level with the date, and whether or not they would like to see the person again.

This procedure may sound straightforward, but both the collection and the analysis of the data turned out to be more complicated than anticipated. First, in terms of providing students with dates, the experiment worked all too well. By intermission, a large number of couples had traded the dance floor for more private venues, and had to be chased down to fill out the questionnaire. Second, because in 1966 computers were bulky machines that were operated primarily by highly trained technicians, the computer was not used either to match the participants or to analyze their responses. Instead, the researchers had to record and analyze the data manually (Hatfield, 2004).

As it turns out, the only predictor of participants' satisfaction with their dates was physical attractiveness. How much participants liked their dates, how comfortable they felt during the dance, and how much they wanted to see the person again was determined solely by the person's physical appearance. The idea that people may base their dating choices solely on physical attractiveness is disheartening. After all, it flies in the face of the admonition not to judge a book by its cover, and the truism that beauty is only skin-deep. However, the phenomenon is fairly robust (e.g., Sprecher, 1989), as well as universal across cultures (Hatfield & Sprecher, 1986) and sexual orientations (Sergios & Cody, 1986). To the extent that physical attractiveness is more important than cultural prescriptions to the contrary, our dating choices may result from hidden influences operating outside of conscious awareness.

Because the influence of physical attractiveness is strong, observers can usually predict the dating choices of others with a high degree of accuracy (Chapdelaine, Levesque, & Cuadro, 1999). At the same time, the power of physical attractiveness does have limits. For example, women seem to place a lower premium on physical attractiveness than men (Feingold, 1990; 1991). When we examine what men and women *do*, however, this gender difference weakens, although it does not disappear entirely (Sprecher, 1986). Similarly, among married couples, the wife's physical attractiveness is more of an issue than the husband's. In one study, husbands reported reduced sexual satisfaction as their wives' physical attractiveness declined with age. The same was not true of wives, however (Margolin & White, 1987).

Those who are uncomfortable with the idea that good looks really matter often point out that "real" couples—that is, couples who have been together for some time—seem well matched in terms of attractiveness. Such observations suggest that *similarity* in attractiveness may be more important than absolute beauty. The idea that couples in ongoing relationships tend to be well matched in attractiveness has received some empirical support (Murstein, 1972; Price & Vandenberg, 1979). Although some studies indicate that matching levels of attractiveness are common mostly among long-term, committed couples (Murstein & Christy, 1976; White, 1980), others suggest that matching may be especially important in the early stages of a relationship (Feingold, 1988). Some studies indicate that matching levels of attractiveness may be important even in same-sex friendships (Cash & Derlega, 1978), especially among women (Feingold, 1988).

One of the earliest and most dramatic confirmations of the **matching hypothesis** in the initiation of romantic relationships came from a study (Berscheid et al., 1971) that used the same method employed by Walster et al. (1966), with one major difference. Rather than being assigned a date, participants could choose from several potential dates of varying levels of attractiveness. In this study, participants chose dates who matched their own self-reported levels of attractiveness, regardless of whether they thought their chosen dates might accept or reject them. At first glance, this finding may seem to contradict Walster et al.'s observations. After all, we can't all seek both the most attractive date and a date who matches our own level of attractiveness. A close inspection of the results of the two studies shows that they may be more complementary than contradictory,

Research strongly suggests that couples are well matched in terms of physical attractiveness. However, evidence that the matching principle applies to pets and their owners is purely anecdotal.

however. The matching hypothesis may accurately describe dating choices from a range of potential partners, as in the Berscheid et al. study. But when fate or a computer arranges a date with a highly attractive person, as in the Walster et al. study, we will try to maintain that contact, especially if the date went well. In other words, matching may be a motive in obtaining a date; attractiveness may be a motive in holding onto a date.

Issues of timing aside, few people appear to think of themselves as unattractive. In a survey of 2,000 men and women, Hatfield & Sprecher (1986) found that most *adults* are quite happy with the way they look. Only four percent of the men and seven percent of the women surveyed indicated they were dissatisfied with their appearance. Similarly, the majority of people rate their partners as *attractive* or *very attractive* (Gagne & Lydon,

THINK LIKE A SOCIAL PSYCHOLOGIST: RESEARCHING ATTRACTIVENESS: WHEN THE RESPONDENTS AND THE QUESTIONS MATTER

Zach has read about the importance of physical attractiveness very carefully, and with great interest. He is a bit puzzled about the way the authors reconciled the findings of Walster et al. (1966) with those of Berscheid et al. (1971). The first study seems to suggest that people seek dates who are highly attractive;

the second, that people seek dates who match their own level of attractiveness. Looking at himself in the mirror, he sees a gangly adolescent with little muscle tone and hardly any facial hair—and an angry red zit near the base of his nose. Not at all happy with the way he looks, he wonders about the truth of the assertion that most people find themselves attractive, or at least moderately so.

To get to the bottom of this question, Zach decides to survey his classmates. He sits down at his computer and whips up a simple questionnaire. "In general, I am satisfied with my appearance," it reads. He decides to measure agreement on a 9-point scale, with 1 meaning "completely disagree" and 9 meaning "completely agree." He also asks respondents to indicate whether they are female or male.

The next day, Zach passes out his survey in class and collects responses from all but 5 of his 59 classmates. He takes the completed questionnaires to his dorm room, checks his zit, and then tabulates the responses. Just as he expected—and contrary to the assertion in his textbook—he finds that the average response is 4.23, slightly below the scale's midpoint. He also finds that there is no difference between the men's and women's ratings. He decides to write to the authors of his textbook, but after finding their e-mail addresses, he pauses. Did he make any mistakes in conducting his study?

Zach has good reason to reevaluate his research. In thinking it over, he finds two flaws. First, even though external validity is rarely an issue in experimental social psychology, in this case, it may actually be important. We know that as a group, adolescents tend to be unhappy with their body images, given the huge changes they experience at their age. Consequently, Zach needs to broaden his sample to include mature adults, and he needs to break down the data by age group.

Second, asking a single question generally is not a good way to study anything. In this case, Zach left it up to participants to interpret the meaning of the word *appearance*. Some of them may have focused on facial features; others, on bodily features or even the clothes they were wearing that day. Some may even have responded based on the bad hair day they were having. To get a reliable measure, Zach needs to operationalize the term *appearance* by creating separate items to capture its different dimensions. He should then use a composite score such as an average of the scores on various items as the basis for further analysis.

2001). From this perspective, the results of the two dating studies are entirely compatible. People look for dating partners who match their own level of attractiveness, but because they tend to think of themselves as attractive, they look for partners who are high in attractiveness. Take a look at the Think like a Social Psychologist Box above for possible pitfalls in gathering evidence to support our speculations.

Matching is perhaps best understood by taking into account people's sense of self-worth (Taylor et al., 2011) along with their objective and subjective physical attractiveness. *Objective* physical attractiveness may provide a *lower limit* for the physical attractiveness of others whom we might approach for a relationship, because it allows us to define potentially unattractive dates as attractive and desirable. Subjective physical attractiveness may provide an upper limit that prevents us from seeking a relationship with others who are more attractive. Thus, the two limits work in tandem to generate a range of dating choices that result in people dating others of similar physical attractiveness (Montoya, 2008). These issues aside, physical attractiveness is of paramount importance in the initiation and maintenance of romantic relationships.

Cultural Standards of Attractiveness

The old adage that beauty lies in the eye of the beholder suggests that standards of beauty vary from one person to the next. But standards of beauty also vary across cultures, in terms of which parts of the body are considered important and which characteristics make them attractive. Consider the results of a classic anthropological study (Ford & Beach, 1951) of the value that 100 "primitive" cultures place on body build in females. The researchers found that a slim body build was considered beautiful in five cultures, a medium body build in another five, and a plump body build in 18 cultures. In the vast majority of cultures, however, body build was *not* considered an important determinant of attractiveness. More recent research that compared 26 countries across 10 world regions suggests that thinness is universally desired, especially among those high in socioeconomic status with access and exposure to Western media (Swami et al., 2010).

There is some evidence for cultural universality regarding *facial features*. In one cross-cultural study of women's facial attractiveness (Cunningham, Roberts, Barbee, Druen, & Wu, 1995), Asians, Latinos, and whites favored neonatal features, including large eyes, a small nose, and a small chin. These preferences held regardless of whether the face in question was Asian, Latino, or white. There was some variation in how participants from the three cultures evaluated facial features indicating sexual maturity and emotional expressiveness, however. Latino and white participants considered such features attractive, but Asian participants were not influenced by them. Significantly, the extent to which participants had been exposed to media portrayals of Western ideals of beauty did *not* influence participants' ratings.

In addition to this variation across cultures, standards of beauty may change over time. The beauty ideal exemplified by the voluptuous women portrayed in baroque paintings has little in common with the busty yet slim-waisted ideal exemplified by Marilyn Monroe and Jane Russell in the 1950s, or by the tall and slender ideal exemplified today by supermodels Heidi Klum, Naomi Campbell, and Gisele Bündchen.

What Men and Women Want

In Western culture today, heterosexual standards of attractiveness appear to vary by gender. For both sexes, bodily and facial features, as well as facial expressions, appear to be important in determining a person's attractiveness. Men tend to value a low waist-to-hip ratio (Singh, 1993), low weight (Franzoi & Herzog, 1987), and physiques with relatively little curvature (Horvath, 1981). These are features men consider to be ideal in women, but in terms of what they find acceptable, men more than women tend to appreciate a wide range of body sizes (Miller, Smith, & Trembath, 2000). Regarding facial features, men prefer women with large eyes, a small nose, a small chin, narrow cheeks, and high eyebrows (Cunningham, 1986). Furthermore, men like smiles (Cunningham, 1986) and other facial expressions indicative of happiness (Mueser, Grau, & Sussman, 1984; Raines, Hechtman, & Rosenthal 1990). Interestingly, the face and body seem to be equally important in determining a woman's physical attractiveness, although an unattractive body can decrease an overall attractiveness rating, even if the face is attractive (Alicke, Smith, & Klotz, 1986).

What do women like? Masculinity seems to be the key to women's perceptions of men's physical attractiveness. By and large, they favor men with a muscular physique over men with low levels of muscularity, although they also prefer moderate muscularity to more exaggerated features (Frederick & Haselton, 2007; Lavrakas, 1975). Facial masculinity, as evidenced by large eyes and prominent cheekbones and chin, also matters (Johnston et al., 2001), as do high-status clothing and good grooming habits (Cunningham, Barbie, & Pike, 1990). Interestingly, like men's judgments of women, women's judgments of men's attractiveness are influenced by the waist-to-hip ratio. Women also like men with a .9 ratio of waist to hip, although their perceptions of attractiveness are equally influenced by cues suggesting a man's income (Singh, 1995).

In addition to these gender-specific features, men and women's perceptions of an attractive face are influenced by averageness and symmetry. In a series of computer-assisted studies, Langlois, Roggman, and Musselman (1994) created "average" faces by blending the images of 32 or more individual faces to create a single composite face. In trial after trial, research participants found the composite or "average" face the most attractive—more attractive than any of the individual faces from which the composite was constructed. One way to interpret this finding is that the averaging process created faces that approximated prototypes of the human face, representing its modal features. Participants may have responded favorably to those prototypes because they exemplify an idealized human facial configuration.

Facial averageness overlaps to some degree with facial symmetry. Average faces are more likely than others to be symmetrical, for the obvious reason that the process of creating them is likely to yield features evenly proportioned about the mean. Thus, it is not surprising to learn that symmetrical faces are perceived as more attractive than nonsymmetrical or somewhat asymmetrical faces (Gangestad & Scheyd, 2005; Gangestad, Haselton, & Buss, 2006; Langlois & Roggman, 1990; Langlois, Roggman, & Musselman, 1994). As we shall see, there is good reason to believe that facial symmetry has unique effects, despite its overlap with facial averageness.

What about those who are attracted to their own sex? Are gay men attracted to men with masculine physical features? Are lesbian women attracted to women with feminine physical features? The answer to both questions appears to be yes, according to a study of the preferences expressed in gay and lesbian personal ads, as well as the direct responses from a community sample (Bailey, Kim, Hills, & Linsenmeyer, 1997). Gay men consistently search for men who look and act masculine. In fact, "masculine" and "straight-acting" were among the most common descriptors in gay men's personal ads. Lesbian women consistently search for feminine-looking partners and reject partners with masculine characteristics, such as short hair, a muscular build, and a high waist-to-hip ratio. A more recent study of all-male personal ads further suggests that gay men place a strong emphasis on physical appearance (Bartholome, Tewksbury, & Bruzzone, 2000).

Other Determinants of Attractiveness

Although perceptions of attractiveness are determined to a large extent by the nature and configuration of facial and bodily features, that is not the whole story. We do not perceive others in a psychological vacuum. Instead, our judgments of attractiveness are often profoundly shaped by the context in which they take place, including our moods and whether or not we are currently in a relationship.

Contrast effects. How attractive we perceive a person to be depends in part on the attractiveness of others we are exposed to. For example, our perceptions of an average-looking person can be affected by prior exposure to an extremely attractive person. Perceptual contrast effects of this nature are most pronounced when we are conscious of the prior stimulus (Martin, 1986), and when the discrepancy between the prior stimulus and the one to be judged is large (Herr, Sherman, & Fazio, 1983).

Several experiments have demonstrated **contrast effects** on judgments of attractiveness. In one study (Kenrick & Gutierres, 1980), male dormitory residents were asked to rate a photograph of an average-looking female. Half the participants made their ratings after watching an episode of *Charlie's Angels*, a popular TV show from the 1970s that featured three strikingly attractive women. The remaining participants made their ratings after watching TV programs that did not include attractive women. As expected, the men who had watched *Charlie's Angels* rated the woman in the photograph as less attractive than the men who had watched the other programs. This contrast has been replicated in more controlled laboratory settings (Kenrick & Gutierres, 1980, Studies 2 and 3).

Prior exposure to relatively unattractive others produced a contrast effect in the opposite direction. Participants who had seen a series of photographs of faces low in attractiveness rated an average-looking female's photograph as more attractive than participants who saw the unattractive faces after her photograph. Note that the sequence of events seems to be essential to this contrast effect: it is obtained primarily when attractive or unattractive stimuli *precede* the stimulus to be judged. When the same moderately attractive picture is *embedded* in a series of pictures of either high or low attractiveness, exactly the opposite effect is observed. Under those circumstances, the perceived attractiveness of the average-looking person is assimilated to the context. That is, it is perceived as *less* attractive when embedded in a series of pictures showing people *low* in attractiveness, and as *more* attractive when it is embedded in a series of pictures showing people *high* in attractiveness (Geiselman, Haight, & Kimata, 1984; Wedell, Parducci, & Geiselman, 1987).

The message from these studies of perceptual contrast and assimilation is straightforward: Attractive people are tough acts to follow. On the other hand, if we can surround ourselves with attractive others, they can serve as beneficial influences on others' perceptions of our attractiveness.

Mood effects. To some extent, our perceptions and evaluations of other people are influenced by how we feel. Generally speaking, we tend to look at others more favorably when we are in a good mood and less favorably when we are in a bad mood (Erber, 1991; Forgas & Bower, 1987). This tendency seems to include our perceptions of others' physical attractiveness. In one study (May & Hamilton, 1980), female participants rated photographs of men who had already been judged physically attractive or unattractive while listening to either pleasant rock music or unpleasant avant-garde music. A control group heard no music at all. As one might expect, participants in whom a positive mood had been induced rated the photographs as more attractive than participants in whom a negative mood had been induced, regardless of how attractive the men in the photographs really were.

Relationship effects. Our perceptions of others' physical attractiveness are also shaped by whether or not we are involved in a romantic relationship. Compared to people who are not romantically involved, people who are dating tend to perceive those of the opposite sex as less attractive (Simpson, Gangestad, & Lerma, 1990). This perceptual shift does not appear to be influenced by extraneous factors such as self-esteem. Instead, it may be a powerful mechanism for the maintenance of ongoing relationships, one that reduces the susceptibility to temptation. Like the contrast effect, however, this phenomenon can sometimes produce the opposite effect. In one study (Kenrick, Neuberg, Zierk, & Krones, 1994), male participants who had been exposed to photographs of *extremely attractive* females evaluated their current relationships less favorably than participants who had been exposed to photographs of average-looking females.

On the other hand, unattached people who desire a dating relationship seem to become less discriminating as they become progressively more desperate. In one study conducted to provide an answer to country-and-western singer Mickey Gilley's (1975) question *"Don't all the girls get prettier at closing time, don't they all start to look like movie stars?"* male bar patrons were approached by an experimenter at 9:00 P.M., 10:30 P.M., and 12:00 A.M. and asked to rate the collective attractiveness of the female patrons. The results provided an affirmative answer to Gilley's question: As closing time approached and the number of possible choices decreased, men rated the female patrons as more attractive. And no, the effect was not caused by increased alcohol consumption. Women's perceptions of men's attractiveness were similarly affected by the decrease in choices, suggesting that boys, too, get prettier at closing time.

Ironically, being in a committed relationship can amplify a person's attractiveness because it marks the person as a good romantic choice (Uller & Johansson, 2003). That is, being in a relationship suggests a person's fitness to be in a relationship, confirming to others the "invisible" positive qualities that make the person commitment worthy.

Physical Attractiveness: A Summary

Physical attractiveness is of paramount importance in dating. Established couples are generally well matched in their level of physical attractiveness, and people gravitate toward the most attractive others within the constraints imposed by their own level of attractiveness. Although standards of beauty vary across cultures, there is also a great deal of cultural universality in perceptions of beauty. Across cultures, men prefer women with neonatal facial features, a low waist-to-hip ratio, and facial expressions that are indicative of happiness. Likewise, women prefer men with dominant facial features and a muscular physique. Both sexes show a strong preference for symmetry in the face and body.

In addition to these physical features, our perceptions of another's physical attractiveness are influenced by contextual factors. Prior exposure to extremely attractive or unattractive individuals produces contrast effects. A good mood increases the perceived level of another person's attractiveness; a bad mood decreases it. Relationship status also influences attractiveness ratings, in two ways. Being in a committed relationship generally decreases the perceived level of others' attractiveness. However, it also amplifies others' perception of the committed person's attractiveness, because it confirms their worthiness of the relationship.

Think Like a Social Psychologist

Making connections

—In Chapter 5, we discussed attitude change as a result of mere exposure. How could mere exposure influence the perception of another's attractiveness? What specific processes might be at work? Give examples of celebrities who illustrate the mere exposure effect on perceptions of attractiveness.

Understanding everyday behavior

—What do TV shows like *The Powerpuff Girls* or *Teen Titans*, both produced in Japan, tell us about the cultural universality of standards of physical attractiveness?

WHY PHYSICAL ATTRACTIVENESS IS IMPORTANT

Just why is physical attractiveness so important? And why do men and women differ on the physical characteristics they value in others? Three theoretical perspectives shed light on these questions. The evolutionary perspective traces the origins of gender differences in such preferences to evolved dispositions. The social-cultural perspective sees these differences in terms of women and men's places in the social structure. And the social-cognitive model suggests that men and women alike favor physically attractive people because of a culturally shared stereotype of beauty.

The Evolutionary Perspective

The evolutionary perspective on human behavior considers all psychological processes in terms of their adaptive value. According to this view, gender differences reflect adaptations to the pressures of the different physical and social environments men and women found themselves in during the Pleistocene Epoch, 1.8 million to 11,000 years ago. Commonly known as the Ice Age, the Pleistocene was marked by periods of glaciation that tied up vast amounts of water, lowering sea levels and permitting species to migrate across previously impassable barriers. In this environment of evolutionary adaptedness (EEA; Barkow, Cosmides, & Tooby, 1992), modern humans evolved and began their global dispersion, enabled by adaptations to their changing environment. Men and women acquired a variety of new learning skills, along with a larger brain that served as the neurological basis for these new abilities.

Of most concern to us, men and women developed different strategies to maximize their reproductive success—and consequently, their survival. Evolution has a way of selecting against maladaptive processes and for processes that aid the survival of the species (Darwin, 1871). Humans are concerned not so much with their collective survival, however, as they are with the survival of their own genes (Wilson, 1975). From an evolutionary perspective, dating is part of the process of sexual selection that ends with reproduction. Unlike nonmammalian species, which tend to feature a wide discrepancy in the parental investment of males and females (Trivers, 1972), human males and females have relatively similar *levels* of parental investment (Trivers, 1972). Nonetheless, the *nature* of men's and women's parental investment differs, so that they play the dating game according to different rules.

To reproduce successfully, males must find females who are likely to produce viable offspring. Thus, they look for cues that are indicative of a woman's fertility (how likely she is to produce offspring) and reproductive value (how long she will be able to produce offspring). These cues can be found in a woman's physical appearance. Because a woman's reproductive capacity is relatively short, men should be attracted to females who have the physical features associated with youth, including neonatal facial features, smooth skin, good muscle tone, lustrous hair, and full lips (Symons, 1979).

Hence, the **evolutionary perspective on attraction** helps to explain why men place a higher premium on physical attractiveness than women. Because men can produce offspring until they reach a fairly old age (Pablo Picasso fathered a child when he was well into his eighties), physical indicators of their youth are of little importance. What is important in a man is his ability to provide the resources such as food, shelter, territory, and protection needed to raise offspring. Among modern-day humans, those resources typically translate into earning potential. As a result, women should be attracted to men who are ambitious, industrious, and otherwise able to acquire resources. Interestingly, recent advances in reproductive technology have enabled postmenopausal women to bear offspring, reducing the importance of youth. However, at present, the promise of this technology is offset by a double standard in which having a child late in life is seen as a sign of virility on the part of the father, but of irresponsibility on the part of the mother (*Newsweek*, May 1, 1997).

These speculations about the differential importance of youth and good looks versus ambition and industriousness were confirmed in a study that assessed the importance of those characteristics for men and women in 37 nations, from Belgium to Zambia (Buss, 1989). In all countries, males preferred spouses who were an average of 2.66 years younger than they were. The preferred age discrepancy was as low as .38 years in the Netherlands and as high as 7.38 years in Zambia. Women, on the other hand, preferred men who were an average of 3.42 years older. In all but three countries (India, Poland, and Sweden), men more than women rated good looks as important. In all countries except Spain, women rated earning potential as significantly more important than men did. The highest ratings on this dimension were obtained in Indonesia, Nigeria, and Zambia; the lowest ratings, in the Netherlands, Great Britain, and among South African Zulus. Analogous results were obtained for ambition and industriousness in men. On this variable, gender differences were obtained in 29 of the 37 cultures (Iran, Finland, the Netherlands, Norway, Spain, Sweden, and Colombia were the exceptions).

Considering the diversity of Buss's (1989) sample and the consistency of the findings, the study would seem to provide overwhelming evidence for the evolutionary perspective on physical attractiveness, including the differential importance of age to males and females. To the extent that human preferences in this regard reflect adaptations, they act as hidden influences on our dating behavior. In fact, gender differences in the importance of physical attractiveness may be part of a more general adaptation to avoid potentially costly errors.

According to **error management theory** (Haselton & Buss, 2000), any judgment made under conditions of uncertainty carries two possible types of error. First, decision makers can assume that something is

This woman's face seems to be almost perfectly symmetrical. According to evolutionary psychology, we perceive this face to be attractive because it suggests both good health and good genes.

true when it is, in fact, false (a false positive). Alternatively, they can assume that something is false when it is, in fact, true (a false negative). For a woman, overestimating a man's earning potential could have very adverse consequences. Thus, we would expect her to look for a man with features that minimize the chances of a false positive—that is to say, the possibility that her mate will not be a capable provider. Similarly, a man would be ill served if he overestimated a woman's fertility and reproductive potential. Consequently, he should look for a broad range of physical features that indicate a woman's ability to reproduce. In support of this theory, women (but not men) tend to under-perceive a man's level of commitment, and men (but not women) tend to over-perceive a woman's sexual intent (Haselton & Buss, 2000; 2009), especially when they are in a position of power and have indications that the woman may be romantically available (Kunstman & Maner, 2011).

Why, then, is facial symmetry so important to both sexes? Symmetrical faces are not just pleasing to the eye. Instead, they convey information about a person's health and fitness (Jones et al., 2001; Simmons, Rhodes,

Peters, & Koehler, 2004), to the extent that environmental stress and poor health during earlier stages of development produced deviations from bilateral symmetry (for example, Fink & Penton-Voak, 2002; Hönekopp, Bartholome, & Jansen, 2004). Moreover, facial symmetry indicates the presence of good genes, including the ability to resist parasitic infections (Gangestad, Haselton, & Buss, 2006; Thornhill & Gangestad, 1999). From an evolutionary perspective, facial symmetry and physical attractiveness serve as "health certificates" that indicate the presence of health in a potential mate (Sugiyama, 2005).

Critics of the evolutionary perspective have pointed out that we know too little about the nature of humans' primeval environment to validate evolutionary hypotheses (Eagly & Wood, 1999). They further suggest that gender differences in the importance of physical attractiveness may have developed far more recently than the Pleistocene Epoch.

The Social-Cultural Perspective

According to the **social-cultural perspective on attraction** (Eagly & Wood, 1999; 2003), gender roles have multiple determinants, including a consideration of men's and women's biological endowments. Men's greater size and strength gives them priority in jobs demanding strenuous activity; women's childbearing and lactation give them priority in the care of young children. This division of labor is a mixed blessing. Men and women could maximize their welfare by joining together in cooperative relationships. But because men typically specialize in activities that bring greater status, wealth, and power than women's activities, the result can be best described as patriarchy.

This lopsided social structure affects the ways in which men and women accommodate themselves to their respective roles. First, men's accommodation to roles of power and status produces relatively more dominant behavior; women's accommodation to roles with little power and status produces relatively more subordinate behavior. Second, women and men seek to fulfill their gender-typical roles by acquiring the specific skills and resources necessary to successful role performance, and by adapting their social behavior to their gender roles. These methods of role differentiation explain the different characteristics men and women find attractive in potential partners. In industrial economies that operate on a gender-based division of labor, women will benefit from seeking a mate who is likely to succeed in a wage-earning role. Thus, they will look for features indicative of dominance and status. Men, on the other hand, will benefit from seeking a mate who is likely to be successful in a domestic role. Consequently, men will favor younger women because of their superior childbearing ability, and they will put a premium on characteristics that are predictive of successful motherhood, including health, kindness, and warmth.

Eagly and Wood (1999) based these conclusions on a reanalysis of the very data Buss (1989) presented in support of the evolutionary view. They found that across cultures, men value being a good cook and housekeeper in a woman just as much as they value physical attractiveness. Because good housekeeping is an important aspect of life in industrialized societies, Eagly and Wood (1999) concluded that gender differences in the importance of attractiveness may have originated around the time of the industrial revolution, rather than during the Pleistocene.

How these gender differences can best be explained is subject to continuing debate (Eagly & Wood, 2006; Gangestad, Haselton, & Buss, 2006). Regardless of which period they originated in, however, good looks are important because they form the basis of a powerful stereotype.

The Social-Cognitive Perspective: The Power of Stereotypes

As we will see in Chapter 11, stereotypes are often organized around the physical features people share, which shape our perceptions of them in important ways. Likewise, our perceptions of physically attractive others may be shaped by a stereotype that suggests that attractive people are better people. Through a similar process, we judge a book by its cover: if it looks good on the outside, we reason, it must be good on the inside.

The **attractiveness stereotype** on judgments of others was discovered in a classic study, in which participants viewed photographs of men and women of varying levels of attractiveness (Dion, Berscheid, & Walster, 1972). Participants of both sexes were asked to evaluate the men and women shown in the photographs in terms of their personalities and the quality of their lives. As we might expect, attractive people were perceived to be warmer, kinder, and more sensitive, interesting, strong, poised, modest, sociable, and outgoing than people of

SOCIAL PSYCHOLOGY ENCOUNTERS THE DARK SIDE: DISCRIMINATION BASED ON ATTRACTIVENESS

On the face of it, discriminating among potential dates on the basis of physical attractiveness may not be particularly disturbing. After all, dating choices are deeply personal. As one participant in the Walster et al. (1966) study put it, somewhat chauvinistically: "Every man should have the right to be with a beautiful woman!"

The problem is, discrimination based on attractiveness is not limited to dating. Rather, good-looking people enjoy several potentially "unfair" advantages. For example, we tend to think of attractive people as being higher in status—especially those aspects of status that are inherited (Kalick, 1988). And we tend to evaluate the work of attractive people more favorably than that of others, especially when it is objectively poor (Landy & Sigall, 1974). Moreover, evidence shows that the ratings of college professors on ratemyprofessor.com are influenced by attractiveness (Riniolo, Johnson, Sherman, & Misso, 2006). "Hot" instructors receive higher ratings on helpfulness, ease, and overall quality than instructors without superior attractiveness (Bonds-Raacke & Raacke, 2007). Perhaps biases like these are among the reasons why attractive people often have an edge in promotion decisions (Morrow, McElroy, Stamper, & Wilson, 1990).

SOCIAL PSYCHOLOGY AND HEALTH: BEING UNATTRACTIVE MAY BE DANGEROUS TO YOUR MENTAL HEALTH

To some extent, the advantages attractive people enjoy stem not so much from an attractiveness stereotype as from a stereotype about those who are unattractive. In other words, if what is beautiful is good, what is ugly is bad.

Several research findings support the existence of an ugliness stereotype. In one study (O'Grady, 1982), participants were asked to indicate the extent to which people of varying levels of attractiveness might be at risk for several mental disorders. Not surprisingly, participants' risk assessments were strongly influenced by the attractiveness of the person they were rating. That is, the likelihood of the perceived risk increased as the person's attractiveness decreased. However, the bias extended beyond those mental disorders that are often accompanied by poor hygiene (such as disorganized schizophrenia), which could detract from a person's appearance. Moreover, it manifested itself regardless of whether participants had been told that a person had a diagnosed mental disorder. Even when participants were explicitly told that attractiveness was irrelevant to their judgments, they continued to attribute more psychological disturbances to unattractive targets than to others (Jones, Hanson, & Philips, 1978).

This last finding is of special importance, because it suggests that the unattractiveness stereotype is so ingrained that conscious, deliberate attempts to control it are likely to fail. Even mental health professionals are influenced by the stereotype. A study of incarcerated mental patients (Farina et al., 1977) showed that unattractive patients receive more severe diagnoses and remain hospitalized longer than attractive patients.

SOCIAL PSYCHOLOGY IN THE COURTROOM: LOOKS, GUILT, AND SENTENCING

Findings about the relationship between attractiveness and the perceived risk for mental illness are mirrored by analogous findings in the legal domain. In general, participants who have been instructed to behave as if they are jurors tend to be more lenient in their convictions and recommended sentences when the offender is highly attractive (Efran, 1974.).

In some cases, this effect can be traced to the stereotype of *attractive* people. In one study (Solomon & Schopler, 1978), male participants were asked to judge the case of a young woman accused of embezzling $10,000. In different conditions, the woman was presented to them as highly attractive, of average attractiveness, or unattractive. Not surprisingly, the attractive woman received the most lenient sentence (12 months in prison); the average-looking woman received a sentence about 50 percent longer (19.5 months). Interestingly, the unattractive woman was not penalized because of her looks: her sentence was slightly shorter (18.5 months) than the sentence for the average-looking woman.

In other cases, differences in punitiveness can be traced to the stereotype of *unattractive* people. Participants in another study (Esses & Webster, 1988) received hypothetical information about an attractive, average-looking, or unattractive sex offender. Asked to decide whether he met the criteria for a dangerous offender (which would mandate stiffer penalties), they perceived the unattractive offender to be significantly more likely to meet the criteria than the average-looking or attractive offender. These effects are not limited to studies in which undergraduate students served as mock jurors. In criminal cases, attractive defendants are acquitted more frequently than unattractive ones. Even if they are found guilty, they receive lighter sentences than unattractive defendants (Sigall & Ostrove, 1975).

Why this leniency toward attractive people and harshness toward unattractive people? One answer may be that our attributions of responsibility are influenced by a person's attractiveness. Simply put, we may hold attractive people less responsible for situations that have negative outcomes. Perhaps we are more apt to consider mitigating information ("She needed the money to care for her dying father") when the offender is attractive. After all, our stereotype holds that attractive people are better people; thus, we may place the blame elsewhere. Because we believe that people who are less attractive are far from superior, we are more likely to blame them for their transgressions.

Even so, the connection between attractiveness and leniency appears to have some clear boundaries. When a defendant's transgressions are particularly heinous, his or her attractiveness matters little. The courts applied the law with equal harshness to serial killers Ted Bundy and John Wayne Gacy, despite the obvious differences in their physical attractiveness. And an Italian court convicted Amanda Knox not once, but twice of murdering her roommate.

Still, an unattractive defendant can level the playing field by smiling. Because people who smile are perceived as more attractive, sincere, sociable, and competent than those who don't (Reis et al., 1990), their transgressions are judged more leniently (LaFrance & Hecht, 1995).

average or low physical attractiveness. Attractive people were also perceived to have happier marriages, better jobs, and more fulfilling lives. The only dimension on which attractive people did not come out ahead was on parenting skills. Perhaps the participants thought that attractive people have such busy social lives, they can't be bothered to change diapers or drive the kids to baseball practice. If you think drawing such sweeping conclusions is based on physical attractiveness alone, think again. Inferences about dispositional characteristics based on another's physical appearance can be surprisingly accurate (Naumann et al., 2009).

Given the positive characteristics with which we imbue physically attractive people, it is not surprising that they receive preferential treatment in dating. In the eyes of others, simply being associated with a physically attractive person makes us better people. This stereotype holds more for men with attractive partners than for women (Sigall & Landy, 1973). Although the attractiveness stereotype is relatively benign in the context of dating, it has a profoundly dark side: see the Social Psychology: The Dark Side box on **page 415**. In addition, attractiveness confers advantages—and a lack of attractiveness confers disadvantages—in health, as well as in legal matters: see the Social Psychology and Health box on **pages 415–416** and the Social Psychology in the Courtroom box on **pages 416–417** The attractiveness stereotype is by no means limited to adults' perceptions of other adults. We also discriminate in favor of attractive children, in several ways. Clifford & Hatfield (1973) asked participants to look at academic records that ostensibly belonged to either attractive or plain-looking fifth graders. Cute boys and girls were perceived to be more intelligent and more likely to pursue and receive an advanced degree than plain-looking children. Furthermore, participants thought the attractive children's parents were more interested in their children's education than the parents of the plain-looking children.

Not surprisingly, teachers share this bias toward good-looking children (Lerner & Lerner, 1977). In one particularly illustrative study (Ross & Salvia, 1975), elementary school teachers looked at the files of either an attractive or an unattractive eight-year-old child with an alleged IQ of 78. They were then asked to recommend whether the child should be placed in a class for mentally retarded children. Despite the children's identical records, the unattractive child was more likely to be recommended for the special program than the attractive child.

Differences in physical attractiveness also play a role in adults' treatment of children who make mistakes. Dion (1972) asked male and female participants to observe an experimenter interacting with a child who was made to appear either attractive or unattractive. Participants then administered penalties (of one to five pennies) to the child for incorrect responses on a picture-matching task. Male participants were not influenced by the child's attractiveness, but female participants penalized the unattractive child more severely than the attractive child.

Children exhibit the attractiveness bias just as adults do, even before they are out of diapers. When presented with pictures of attractive and unattractive children, infants as young as six months of age prefer to look at pictures of the attractive children (Ramsey, Langlois, Hoss, Rubenstein, & Griffin, 2004). Of course,

Cartoons like these exemplify the physical attractiveness stereotype, which applies to men and women alike: beautiful goes with good and ugly goes with bad.

people of all ages probably prefer to look at "nice" pictures, whether they show people, sunsets, or landscapes. Still, there is reason to suspect that these preferences may be due in part to the attractiveness stereotype. In one study (Dion, 1974), researchers asked preschoolers ranging from age four to six to indicate which of their classmates they liked and disliked, and to nominate peers who displayed various types of social behavior.

Not surprisingly, children's liking for their peers was determined primarily by perceived physical attractiveness. Unattractive children were nominated more frequently than others as exemplars of antisocial behavior. Attractive children of both sexes, but particularly boys, were rated as more independent and self-sufficient than unattractive children.

These findings suggest that some aspects of the attractiveness stereotype are acquired at an early age. Experience does not seem to ameliorate reliance on the stereotype. Rather, the stereotype seems to grow stronger and more complex with age, in the sense that the adult version includes more attributes than the childhood version. Compared to young adults, older people seem to hold stronger stereotypes about physical attractiveness (Adams & Huston, 1975).

Origins of the Attractiveness Stereotype

The existence of a pervasive bias in favor of physically attractive people is intriguing. What is the source of this stereotype? Some (Lemay, Clark, & Greenberg, 2010) have argued that it may be a matter of projection. When we desire to bond with beautiful others, we assume that they desire us as well, thus rendering them good. Alternatively, the attractiveness stereotype may be rooted in the widespread belief that people tend to get what they deserve. This belief in a **just world** (Lerner, 1980) allows us to view our environment as a safe, predictable place where we can achieve our goals through ability and effort. The news of someone else's misfortune threatens our belief in a just world, reminding us that we, too, could suffer the same fate. To reduce this threat, we conclude that innocent or not, the victim probably deserved it.

From this vantage point, our bias toward physically attractive people may stem from a complementary bias toward winners. That is, those who are fortunate enough to be attractive must be good, deserving people. Consistent with this idea, Dion (1987) found that participants who were particularly strong believers in a just world held the attractiveness stereotype more strongly than more tentative believers. This finding applied only to the perception of attractive men, however—not to the perception of attractive women.

The idea that attractive people might be better people is both odd and obvious. It seems odd because we are at a loss to explain how their attractiveness could, in fact, make them better. It seems obvious because research suggests that we have vastly different expectations for attractive and unattractive people. Attractive people may become better people by living up to our odd expectations, creating real differences between themselves and those who are unattractive. Yet evidence shows that we react very differently to attractive and unattractive people, providing a qualitatively superior reality for those who are good-looking. When physically attractive people need help, for example, they are more likely than unattractive people to receive it (Benson, Karabenick, & Lerner, 1977), especially if the emergency is perceived to be severe (West & Brown, 1975).

Curiously, attractive people show greater reluctance to seek help from others, especially if they expect to interact with the prospective helper in the future (Nadler, 1980). There may be a couple of reasons for this effect. First, asking for help exposes people's neediness, which may have adverse implications for their self-esteem. Second, coming across as needy may alter the prospective helper's otherwise favorable reaction to the victim's physical attractiveness. Both these possibilities diminish if a person receives help without solicitation. In such cases, victims might even convince themselves that they got help because they deserved it.

The privileged social reality that we create for attractive people manifests itself in more subtle ways, as well. Reis and his colleagues (Reis, Nezlek, & Wheeler, 1980; Reis, Wheeler, Spiegel, Kernis, Nezlek, & Perri, 1982) asked college seniors of varying levels of attractiveness to keep track of their everyday social interactions over a

15-day period, using the Rochester Dyadic Interaction Record (Wheeler & Nezlek, 1977). Among other things, this measure asks participants to indicate the frequency, level of intimacy, and pleasantness of their interactions with members of the same and opposite sex. Participants' physical attractiveness had been independently assessed based on a photograph.

An analysis of the records kept by participants showed that their relative physical attractiveness and gender strongly influenced many aspects of their social lives. For both men and women, physical attractiveness was positively related to the affective quality of their social experiences. In other words, physically attractive

SOCIAL PSYCHOLOGY ENCOUNTERS THE BRIGHT SIDE: ATTRACTIVENESS MAY NOT BE EVERYTHING

Despite the seemingly overwhelming evidence for a pervasive bias toward attractive people, the underlying stereotype may not be as strong as we might expect. Two meta-analyses of virtually all the published studies on the attractiveness stereotype (Eagly, Ashmore, Makhijani, & Longo, 1991; Feingold, 1992) found it to be most pronounced when researchers asked participants to judge attractive versus unattractive people on dimensions related to their social competence (such as social skills). Participants' judgments of intelligence and adjustment were less influenced by physical attractiveness, and their judgments of honesty and concern for others were unbiased. Finally, they judged attractive targets to be less modest and vainer than their less attractive counterparts.

These findings suggest that the results of such experimental studies depend to some extent on the nature of the questions that are asked. Along these lines, Dermer & Thiel (1975) showed participants pictures of people of varying levels of attractiveness, as in Dion et al. (1972). Then, they asked participants to judge how materialistic, vain, and snobbish the people were, as well as how committed they were to their marriages and how sympathetic toward oppressed people. The participants rated attractive targets *less favorably* on all these dimensions.

Even if we interpret these findings as exceptions to the rule, being physically attractive can sometimes be more of a curse than a blessing. Just like everyone else, attractive people are aware of the prevailing stereotype and the reactions it tends to elicit from others. One consequence is that they have more difficulty than others dealing with praise, which creates attributional ambiguity for them. Often, an attractive person cannot tell whether an evaluator's praise is sincere (Sigall & Michela, 1976). Thus, they frequently discount the praise they receive (Major, Carrington, & Carnevale, 1984).

Furthermore, some of the advantages that physically attractive people enjoy can be offset by several disadvantages. Attractive people frequently have a difficult time starting a relationship because their attractiveness can scare people away. And they sometimes have trouble maintaining relationships because their looks may elicit jealousy (Hatfield & Sprecher, 1986). Attractive job seekers are also at a disadvantage when interviewed by a same-sex person because their attractiveness is perceived as threatening (Agthe, Spörrle, & Maner, 2011). Finally, although physically attractive people have an edge in dating, they are often rejected as friends by their same-sex peers (Krebs & Adinolfi, 1975). Of course, difficulties like these are not likely to trigger a massive outbreak of sympathy for the plight of the good-looking. All things considered, the advantages of physical attractiveness outnumber the disadvantages.

participants perceived both same-sex interactions and opposite-sex interactions to be more intimate and pleasant than physically unattractive participants. Attractive males tended to have more interactions with females and fewer interactions with males than unattractive males. No such effect was observed for females. Attractive males were also more assertive in their interactions, and less fearful of rejection by the other sex, than unattractive males. Interestingly, attractive females were less assertive and less trusting of the opposite sex than unattractive females.

These gender differences aside, attractive people's social reality clearly differs from that of less attractive people. Of course, there is a chicken-and-egg problem here. To some extent, these different social realities are created by the attractiveness stereotype, which compels us to treat attractive people better than others. As a consequence, however, attractive people may acquire some of the positive characteristics with which we imbue them, creating real differences in their dispositions. Does that mean there is little hope for those of us with a less-than-perfect appearance? The Social Psychology: The Bright Side box on **page 420** notes some important limitations of the attractiveness stereotype.

Universality of the Attractiveness Stereotype

Until recently, the attractiveness stereotype had been demonstrated almost exclusively in Western cultures. Some (for example, Dion, 1986) have suggested that its prevalence in the West may be related to the individualistic nature of Western cultures. In the United States, identity is based primarily on personal attributes; in collectivistic cultures like Korea and China, identity is based more on family and group ties (Triandis, 1995). Theoretically, in cultures in which identity is based on something other than personal attributes (such as physical attractiveness), the attractiveness stereotype should be less pronounced, or even nonexistent.

The evidence for this speculation is somewhat mixed. In one study that compared Chinese and North American students at a Canadian university, the Chinese were less influenced by physical attractiveness than the North Americans in their inferences about others' personality traits. Yet in speculating about desirable life outcomes, such as getting a good job, Chinese and North American participants were equally influenced by the attractiveness stereotype. Other studies (Wheeler & Kim, 1997; Zebrowitz, Montepare, & Lee, 1993) have found the attractiveness stereotype to be just as prevalent in Asia as in Western cultures, although its content is somewhat different. In most cultures, attractiveness is related to culturally valued characteristics. Western participants perceive attractive people to be stronger, more assertive, and more dominant than others; Korean participants perceive them to be more honest and more concerned for others (Wheeler & Kim, 1997). Thus, the attractiveness stereotype appears to some extent to be culturally universal.

Why Physical Attractiveness Is Important: A Summary

According to the evolutionary perspective, physical attractiveness is important because it signals fitness for reproduction and genetic survival. In women, neonatal features indicate fertility and reproductive potential. In men, physical features related to dominance indicate the potential to be a good provider. Beauty, as evidenced by facial and bodily symmetry, is important to both genders, because it signals good health and good genes. According to the social-cultural perspective, physical attractiveness is important because it signals an ability to meet the demands of the male and female gender roles (good housekeeping included). According to the social-cognitive perspective, physical attractiveness is important because it is part of a stereotype that equates good looks with being a good person.

Think Like a Social Psychologist

Thinking critically

—The evolutionary perspective suggests that to improve their reproductive success, women look for mates whose physical appearance suggests they may be good providers. However, around the time of ovulation, women tend to be attracted to men whose appearance indicates good health, even when they are in a committed relationship (Haselton & Gangestad, 2006). How might such a shift in preferences be related to a woman's desire to improve her inclusive fitness?

Confronting social issues

—In light of the pervasive bias in favor of attractive defendants, what steps might the legal system take to eliminate it? What are the limitations in trying to level the playing field for attractive and unattractive defendants?

Designing research

—The evolutionary perspective traces men's and women's preferences for specific physical characteristics to the Pleistocene Epoch. The social-cultural perspective claims that those preferences developed around the 19th century. How could a look at drawings of men and women inform this debate? What observations would lead you to agree with the evolutionary perspective? What observations would lead you to agree with the social-cultural perspective?

EPILOGUE: IMAGINATION IS GOD'S GIFT TO THE DREAMERS

Kalei had no trouble imagining a life with Kekoa. In her fantasy, his good looks never faded, providing a solid basis for continued attraction and romance. Being a successful physician, he provided her with a spacious home in Kahala, complete with a pool and access to the oceanfront. Kalei imagined intimate evenings watching the sun set behind Diamondhead Crater—that is, when they weren't out enjoying the nightlife in Waikiki. Being a wealthy couple, they often visited the mainland – to go skiing in Colorado, or spend a weekend in San Francisco.

What Kalei couldn't figure out was why the song "The Wind Beneath My Wings" by the late, great Iz kept playing through the latter part of her fantasy. Then she realized it was the ringtone on her cell phone. Before she could retrieve it from her bag, she realized that the unthinkable was happening: Kekoa was looking straight at her. He couldn't have picked a worse time. Having just indulged in a fantasy about him, she felt quite embarrassed, and was sure she must be blushing. Unable to meet his gaze, she rose from her seat and moved toward the door. Fortunately, she could see her stop approaching; soon she would escape from this uncomfortable situation.

On the short walk from the bus stop to the campus, Kalei's relief was tempered by the realization of just how foolish her fantasy had been. She had always thought of herself as a strong, independent woman, and had dreamed about going to law school after graduating from college. She really had no need of a man to take care of her. Nor did she need anyone to provide her with the good life; she was quite able to acquire that herself. Realizing that she needed to stop beating herself up over her fantasy and concentrate on the chemistry exam, she allowed herself one final thought as she entered the classroom: "He is very good looking!"

HIDDEN INFLUENCES ON ATTRACTION: A SUMMARY

Implicit egotism: attraction to another person that results from a superficial similarity to the self, such as the letters in their names

Classical and operant conditioning: learning principles that produce attraction in the absence of conscious awareness

Misattribution of arousal: physiological arousal from one source that is mistakenly attributed to another source, usually a person, producing attraction to that person

Proximity effects: increased attraction to others who live in close proximity, resulting from mere exposure

Playing hard to get: A dating tool through which a person can indicate that he or she is both selective and desirable

Secrecy: A situation in which the need to keep a relationship secret creates a sense of cognitive preoccupation that adds to feelings of attraction

Evolutionary influences on attraction: the unconscious human tendency to be attracted to people whose physical features indicate fitness

Attractiveness stereotype: the basis for unconscious processes through which people infer that physically attractive others have superior dispositions and deserve better outcomes than physically unattractive others

KEY TERMS AND DEFINITIONS

Implicit egotism: a preference for things that are associated with the self

Classical conditioning: a learning principle that predicts a liking for others who are associated with good things

Need for affiliation: The human tendency to seek the company of others, especially in situations marked by fear or uncertainty

Operant conditioning: a learning principle that predicts attraction to others with whom we share adversity

Misattribution of arousal: the process by which the physiological arousal created by one source is attributed to another source

Gain-loss effect: increased liking for an evaluator who shifts from derogation to praise, compared to one who delivers consistent praise; decreased liking for an evaluator who shifts from praise to derogation

Balance theory: A theory that recognizes the reciprocal nature of agreement and attraction

Attitude similarity: The idea that similarity in attitudes produces attraction

Repulsion hypothesis: An alternative account for the relationship between attitude similarity and attraction, which proposes that dissimilarity leads to repulsion rather than similarity leading to attraction

Complementarity: A special form of dissimilarity in two people's needs that produces attraction

Playing hard to get: A strategy through which a person communicates the extent to which he or she is both selective and desirable

Fatal attraction: An attraction based on characteristics that eventually cease to please, leading to the death of the relationship

Physical attractiveness: Perceptions of attractiveness that are conveyed primarily through a person's physical features

Matching hypothesis: The idea that people like to date others who match their own level of attractiveness

Contrast effect: A change in the perception of an average-looking person as a result of prior exposure to an extremely attractive person

Evolutionary perspective on attraction: an approach that explains gender differences in physical attractiveness in terms of their adaptive value

Error management theory: A variant of the evolutionary perspective that explains the adaptive value of gender differences in attractiveness in terms of the reduced fitness of men and women who make erroneous choices

Social-cultural perspective on attraction: An alternative to the evolutionary perspective that traces gender differences in attraction to the gender roles assigned to men and women in modern society

Attractiveness stereotype: The belief that attractive people are better people than unattractive people, and deserve better outcomes

Just world: The belief that people tend to get what they deserve; reduces the threat posed by learning of another's misfortune

REFERENCES

Adams, G. R., & Huston, T. L. (1975). Social perception of middle-aged persons varying in physical attractiveness. *Developmental Psychology, 11,* 657–658.

Agthe, M., Spörrle, M., & Maner, J. K. (2011). Does being attractive always help? Positive and negative effects of attractiveness on social decision making. *Personality and Social Psychology Bulletin, 37,* 1042–1054.

Alicke, M. D., Smith, R. H., & Klotz, M. L. (1986). Judgments of physical attractiveness: The role of faces and bodies. *Personality and Social Psychology Bulletin, 12,* 381–389.

Allen, J. B., Kenrick, D. T., Linder, D. E., & McCall, M. A. (1989). Arousal and attraction: A response-facilitation alternative to misattribution and negative-reinforcement models. *Journal of Personality and Social Psychology, 57,* 261–270.

Amodio, D. M., & Showers, C. J. (2005). "Similarity breeds liking" revisited: The moderating role of commitment. *Journal of Social and Personal Relationships, 22,* 817–836.

Aron, A., & Aron, E. N. (1997). Self-expansion motivation and including other in the self. In S. Duck (Ed.), *Handbook of personal relationships: Theory, research, and interventions* (2nd ed., pp. 251–270). Chichester, England: John Wiley & Sons.

Aronson, E., & Cope, V. (1968). My enemy's enemy is my friend. *Journal of Personality and Social Psychology, 8,* 8–12.

Aronson, E., & Linder, D. E. (1965). Gain and loss of esteem as determinants of interpersonal attraction. *Journal of Experimental and Social Psychology, 1,* 156–171.

Aronson, E., & Mills, J. (1959). The effect of severity of initiation on liking for a group. *Journal of Abnormal and Social Psychology, 59,* 177–181.

Bailey, J. M., Kim, P. Y., Hills, A., & Linsenmeyer, J. A. W. (1997). Butch, femme, or straight-acting? Partner preferences of gay men and lesbians. *Journal of Personality and Social Psychology, 73,* 960–973.

Barkow, J. H., Cosmides, L., & Tooby, J. (1992). *The adapted mind: Evolutionary psychology and the generation of culture.* New York: Oxford University Press.

Barry, W. A. (1970). Marriage research and conflict: An integrative review. *Psychological Bulletin, 73,* 41–54.

Bartholome, A., Tewksbury, R., & Bruzzone, A. (2000). "I want a man": Patterns of attraction in all-male personal ads. *Journal of Men's Studies, 8,* 309–321.

Benson, P. L., Karabenick, S. A., & Lerner, R. M. (1976). Pretty pleases: The effects of physical attractiveness, race, and sex on receiving help. *Journal of Experimental Social Psychology, 12,* 409–415.

Berscheid, E., Dion, K., Walster, E., & Walster, G. W. (1971). Physical attractiveness and dating choice: A test of the matching hypothesis. *Journal of Experimental Social Psychology, 7,* 173–189.

Bossard, J. H. S. (1932). Residential propinquity as a factor in mate selection. *American Journal of Sociology, 38,* 219–224.

Bowerman, C. E., & Day, B. R. (1956). A test of the theory of complementarity needs as applied to couples during courtship. *American Sociological Review, 21,* 602–605.

Brockner, J., & Swap, W. C. (1976). Effects of repeated exposure and attitude similarity on self-disclosure and attraction. *Journal of Personality and Social Psychology, 33,* 531–540.

Boer, D., Fisher, R., Strack, M., Bond, M. H., Lo, E., & Lam, J. (2011). How shared preferences in music create bonds between people: Values as the missing link. *Personality and Social Psychology Bulletin, 37,* 1159–1171.

Bonds-Raacke, J., & Raacke, J. (2007). The relationship between physical attractiveness of professors and students' ratings of professor quality. *Journal of Psychiatry, Psychology, and Mental Health, 1,* 1–5.

Buss, D. M. (1989). Sex differences in human mate preferences: Evolutionary hypotheses tested in 37 cultures. *Behavioral and Brain Sciences, 12,* 1–14.

Byrne, D. (1971). *The attraction paradigm.* New York: Academic Press.

Byrne, D., & Nelson, D. (1965). Attraction as a linear function of proportion of positive reinforcements. *Journal of Personality and Social Psychology, 1,* 659–663.

Byrne, D., & Rhamey, R. (1965). Magnitude of positive and negative reinforcement as a determinant of attraction. *Journal of Personality and Social Psychology, 2,* 884–889.

Carnegie, D. (1936). *How to win friends and influence people.* New York: Simon & Schuster.

Cash, T. L., & Derlega, V. J. (1978). The matching hypothesis: Physical attractiveness among same-sex friends. *Personality and Social Psychology Bulletin, 4,* 240–243.

Chapdelaine, A., Levesque, M. J., & Raymund, M. (1999). Playing the dating game: Do we know whom others would like to date? *Basic and Applied Social Psychology, 21,* 139–147.

Clifford, M. M., & Walster, E. (1973). Research note: The effects of physical attractiveness on teacher expectations. *Sociology of Education, 46,* 248–258.

Clore, G. L., & Byrne, D. (1974). A reinforcement-affect model of attraction. In T. Huston (Ed.), *Foundations of interpersonal attraction* (pp. 143–170). New York: Academic Press.

Cunningham, M. R. (1986). Measuring the physical in physical attractiveness: Quasi-experiments on the sociobiology of female facial beauty. *Journal of Personality and Social Psychology, 50,* 625–635.

Cunningham, M. R., Barbee, A. R., & Pike, C. L. (1990). What do women want? Facialmetric assessment of multiple motives in the perception of male physical attractiveness. *Journal of Personality and Social Psychology, 59,* 61–72.

Cunningham, M. R., Roberts, A. R., Barbee, A. P., Druen, P. B., & Wu, C. F. (1995). "Their ideas of beauty are, on the whole, the same as ours": Consistency and variability in the cross-cultural perception of female physical attractiveness. *Journal of Personality and Social Psychology, 68,* 261–279.

Darwin, C. (1871). *The descent of man, and selection in relation to sex.* London: John Murray.

Dermer, M., & Thiel, D. M. (1975). When beauty may fail. *Journal of Personality and Social Psychology, 31,* 1168–1176.

Dion, K. K. (1972). Physical attractiveness and evaluation of children's transgressions. *Journal of Personality and Social Psychology, 24*, 207–213.

Dion, K. K., (1974). Children's physical attractiveness and sex as determinants of adult punitiveness. *Developmental Psychology, 10*, 772–778.

Dion, K. K. (1977). The incentive value of physical attractiveness for young children. *Personality and Social Psychology Bulletin, 3*, 67–70.

Dion, K. K. (1986). Stereotyping based on physical attractiveness: Issues and conceptual perspectives. In C. P. Herman, M. P. Zanna, & E. T. Higgins (Eds.), *The Ontario symposium: Physical appearance, stigma, and social behavior* (Vol. 3, pp. 7–21). Hillsdale, NJ: Erlbaum.

Dion, K. K., Berscheid, E., & Walster, E. (1972). What is beautiful is good. *Journal of Personality and Social Psychology, 24*, 285–290.

Driscoll, R., Davis, K. W., & Lipetz, M. E. (1972). Parental interference and romantic love. *Journal of Personality and Social Psychology, 24*, 1–10.

Dryer, D. C., & Horowitz, L. M. (1997). When do opposites attract? Interpersonal complementarity versus similarity. *Journal of Personality and Social Psychology, 72*, 592–603.

Dutton, D. G., & Aron, A. P. (1974). Some evidence for heightened sexual attraction under conditions of high anxiety. *Journal of Personality and Social Psychology, 30*, 510–517.

Eagly, A. H., Ashmore, R.D., Makhijani, M. G., & Longo, L. C. (1991). What is beautiful is good, but …: A meta-analytic review of research on the physical attractiveness stereotype. *Psychological Bulletin, 110*, 109–128.

Eagly, A. H., & Wood, W. (1999). The origins of sex differences in human behavior: Evolved dispositions versus social roles. *American Psychologist, 54*, 408–423.

Eagly, A. H., & Wood, W. (2006). Three ways that data can misinform: Inappropriate partialling, small samples, and anyway, they're not playing our song. *Psychological Inquiry, 17*, 131–137.

Eastwick, P. W., Finkel, E. J., Mochon, D., & Ariely, D. (2007). Selective versus unselective romantic desire: Not all reciprocity is created equal. *Psychological Science, 18*, 317–319.

Efran, M. G. (1974). The effect of physical appearance on the judgment of guilt, interpersonal attraction, and severity of recommended punishment in a simulated jury task. *Journal of Research in Personality, 8*, 45–54.

Ellis, S., Rogoff, B., & Cramer, C. C. (1981). Age segregation in children's social interactions. *Developmental Psychology, 17*, 399–407.

Erber, R. (1991). Affective and semantic priming: Effects of mood on category accessibility and inference. *Journal of Experimental Social Psychology, 27*, 480–498.

Esses, V., & Webster, C. D. (1988). Physical attractiveness, dangerousness, and the Canadian Criminal Code. *Journal of Applied Social Psychology, 18*, 1017–1031.

Farina, A., Fischer, E. H., Sehrman, S., Smith, W. T., Groh, T., & Mermin, P. (1977). Physical attractiveness and mental illness. *Journal of Abnormal Psychology, 86*, 510–517.

Feingold, A. (1988). Matching for attractiveness in romantic partners and same-sex friends: A meta-analysis and theoretical critique. *Psychological Bulletin, 104*, 226–235.

Feingold, A. (1990). Gender differences in effects of physical attractiveness on romantic attraction: A comparison across five research paradigms. *Journal of Personality and Social Psychology, 59*, 981–993.

Feingold, A. (1991). Sex differences in the effects of similarity and physical attractiveness on opposite-sex attraction. *Basic and Applied Social Psychology, 12*, 357–367.

Feingold, A. (1992). Good looking people are not what we think. *Psychological Bulletin, 111*, 304–341.

Felmlee, D. H. (1995). Fatal attractions: Affection and disaffection in intimate relationships. *Journal of Personal and Social Relationships, 12,* 295–311.

Felmlee, D. H. (1998a). "Be careful what you wish for … ": A quantitative and qualitative investigation of "fatal attractions." *Personal Relationships, 5,* 235–253.

Felmlee, D. H. (1998b). Fatal attraction. In B. H. Spitzberg & W. R. Cupach (Eds.), *The dark side of close relationships* (pp. 3–31). Mahwah, NJ: Erlbaum.

Festinger, L. (1956). *A theory of cognitive dissonance.* Stanford, CA: Stanford University Press.

Festinger, L., Schachter, S., & Back, K. W. (1950*). Social pressures in informal groups: A study of human factors in housing.* New York: Harper & Row.

Fink, B., & Penton-Voak, I. S. (2002). Evolutionary psychology of facial attractiveness. *Current Directions in Psychological Science, 11,* 54–58.

Ford, C. S., & Beach, F. A. (1951). *Patterns of sexual behavior.* New York: Harper & Row.

Forgas, J. P., & Bower, G. H. (1987). Mood effects on person perception judgments. *Journal of Personality and Social Psychology, 53,* 53–60.

Foster, C. A., & Campbell, W. K. (2005). The adversity of secret relationships. *Personal Relationships, 12,* 125–143.

Foster, C. A., Witcher, B. S., Campbell, W. K., & Green, J. D. (1998). Arousal and attraction: Evidence for automatic and controlled processes. *Journal of Personality and Social Psychology, 74,* 86–101.

Franzoi, S. L., & Herzog, M. E. (1987). Judging physical attractiveness: What body aspects do we use? *Personality and Social Psychology Bulletin, 13,* 19–33.

Frederick, G. A., & Haselton, M. G. (2007). Why is muscularity sexy? Tests of the fitness indicator hypothesis. *Personality and Social Psychology Bulletin, 33,* 1167–1183.

Gagne, F. M., & Lydon, J. E. (2004). Bias and accuracy in close relationships: An integrative review. *Personality and Social Psychology Review, 8,* 322–338.

Gangestad, S. W., Haselton, M. G., & Buss, D. M. (2006). Evolutionary foundations of cultural variation: Evoked cultures and mate preferences. *Psychological Inquiry, 17,* 75–95.

Gangestad, S. W., & Scheyd, G. J. (2005). The evolution of human physical attractiveness. *Annual Review of Anthropology, 34,* 523–548.

Geiselman, R. E., Haight, N. A., & Kimata, L. G. (1984). Context effects in the perceived physical attractiveness of faces. *Journal of Experimental Social Psychology, 20,* 409–424.

Goethals, G. R. (1986). Social comparison theory: Psychology from the lost and found. *Personality and Social Psychology Bulletin, 12,* 1101–1120.

Gold, J. A., Ryckman, R. M., & Mosley, N. R. (1984). Romantic mood induction and attraction to a dissimilar other: Is love blind? *Personality and Social Psychology Bulletin, 12,* 261–278.

Gomez, P., & Erber, R. (2013). Is selectivity an aphrodisiac? *Universitas Psychologica, 12.* DOI:10.11144/Javeriana. UPSY12-5.isaa.

Gormly, A. V. (1979). Behavioral effects of receiving agreement or disagreement from a peer. *Personality and Social Psychology Bulletin, 5,* 405–408.

Gouaux, C. (1971). Induced affective states and interpersonal attraction. *Journal of Personality and Social Psychology, 20,* 37–43.

Griffit, W. B. (1969). Personality similarity and the self-concept as determinants of interpersonal attraction. *Journal of Social Psychology, 78,* 137–146.

Griffit, W. B., & Veitch, R. (1971). Hot and crowded: Influence of population density and temperature on interpersonal affective behavior. *Journal of Personality and Social Psychology, 17,* 92–98.

Grush, J. E. (1976). Attitude formation and mere exposure phenomena: A non-artificial explanation of empirical findings. *Journal of Personality and Social Psychology, 33,* 281–290.

Haselton, M. G., & Buss, D. M. (2000). Error management theory: A new perspective on biases in cross-sex mind reading. *Journal of Personality and Social Psychology, 78,* 81–91.

Haselton, M. G., & Buss, D. M. (2009). Error management theory and the evolution of misbelief. *Behavioral and Brain Sciences, 32,* 522–523.

Haselton, M. G., & Gangestad, S. W. (2006). Conditional expression of women's desires and men's mateguarding across the ovulatory cycle. *Hormones and Behavior, 49,* 509–518.

Hatfield, E. (2004, January). *Personal communication.*

Hatfield, E., & Sprecher, B. (1986). *Mirror, mirror … The importance of looks in everyday life.* Albany, NY: SUNY Press.

Heider, F. (1958). *The psychology of interpersonal relations.* New York: Wiley.

Herr, P. M., Sherman, S. J., & Fazio, R. H. (1983). On the consequences of priming: Assimilation and contrast effects. *Journal of Experimental Social Psychology, 19,* 323–340.

Hönekopp, J., Bartholome, T., & Jansen, G. (2004). Facial attractiveness, symmetry, and physical fitness in young women. *Human Nature, 15,* 147–167.

Horvath, T. (1981). Physical attractiveness: The influence of selected torso parameters. *Archives of Sexual Behavior, 10,* 21–24.

Ireland, M. E., Slatcher, R. B., Eastwick, P. W., Scissors, L. E., Finkel, E. J., & Pennebaker, J. M. (2011). Language style matching predicts relationship initiation and stability. *Psychological Science, 22,* 29–44.

Jacobs, L. E., Berscheid, E., & Walster, E. (1971). Self-esteem and attraction. *Journal of Personality and Social Psychology, 17,* 84–91.

Johnston, V. S., Hagel, R., Franklin, M., Fink, B., & Grammer, K. (2001). Male facial attractiveness: Evidence for hormone-mediated adaptive design. *Evolution and Human Behavior, 22,* 251–267.

Jones, B. C., Little, A. C., Penton-Voak, I. S., Tiddeman, B. P., Burt, D. M., & Perrett, D. I. (2001). Facial symmetry and judgements of apparent health: Support for a "good "genes" explanation of the attractiveness-symmetry relationship. *Evolution and Human Behavior, 22,* 417–429.

Jones, E. E., & Pittman, T. S. (1982). Toward a general theory of strategic self-presentation. In J. Suls (Ed.), *Psychological perspectives on the self* (pp. 231–262). Hillsdale, NJ: Erlbaum.

Jones, E. E., & Wortman, C. (1973). *Ingratiation: An attributional approach.* Morristown, NJ: General Learning Press.

Jones, J. T., Pelham, B. W., Carvallo, M., & Mirenberg, M. C. (2004). How do I love thee? Let me count the J's: Implicit egotism and interpersonal attraction. *Journal of Personality and Social Psychology, 87,* 665–683.

Jones, W. H., Hanson, R. O., & Phillips, A. L. (1978). Physical attractiveness and judgments of psychopathology. *Journal of Social Psychology, 55,* 79–84.

Kalick, S. M. (1988). Physical attractiveness as a status cue. *Journal of Experimental Social Psychology, 24,* 469–489.

Kandel, D. B. (1978). Similarity in real-life adolescent friendship pairs. *Journal of Personality and Social Psychology, 36,* 306–312.

Katz, J., & Joiner, T. E. Jr. (2002). Being known, intimate, and valued: Global self-verification and dyadic adjustment in couples and roommates. *Journal of Personality, 70,* 33–58.

Kenrick, D. T., & Cialdini, R. B. (1977). Romantic attraction: Misattribution versus reinforcement explanations. *Journal of Personality and Social Psychology, 35,* 381–391.

Kenrick, D. T., & Gutierres, S. E. (1980). Contrast effects and judgments of physical attractiveness. When beauty becomes a social problem. *Journal of Personality and Social Psychology, 38*, 131–140.

Kenrick, D. T., & Johnson, G. A. (1979). Interpersonal attraction in aversive environments: A problem for the classical conditioning paradigm? *Journal of Personality and Social Psychology, 37*, 572–579.

Kenrick, D. T., Neuberg, S. L., Zierk, K., & Krones, J. (1994). Evolution and social cognition: Contrast effects as a function of sex, dominance, and physical attractiveness. *Personality and Social Psychology Bulletin, 20*, 210–217.

Kerckhoff, A. C., & Davis, K. E. (1962). Value consensus and need complementarity in mate selection. *American Sociological Review, 27*, 295–303.

Kleck, R. E., & Rubenstein, C. (1975). Physical attractiveness, perceived attitude similarity, and interpersonal attraction in an opposite-sex encounter. *Journal of Personality and Social Psychology, 31*, 107–114.

Krebs, D., & Adinolfi, A. A. (1975). Physical attractiveness, social relations, and personality style. *Journal of Personality and Social Psychology, 31*, 24–253.

Kubie, L. S. (1956). Psychoanalysis and marriage: Practical and theoretical issues. In V. W. Eisenstein (Ed.), *Neurotic interaction in marriage* (pp. 10–43). New York: Basic Books.

Kunstman, J. W., & Maner, J. K. (2011). Sexual overperception: Power, mating motives, and biases in social judgment. *Journal of Personality and Social Psychology, 100*, 282–294.

LaFrance, M., & Hecht, M. A. (1995). Why smiles generate leniency. *Personality and Social Psychology Bulletin, 21*, 207–214.

Landy, D., & Sigall, H. (1974). Beauty is talent: Task evaluation as a function of the performer's physical attractiveness. *Journal of Personality and Social Psychology, 29*, 299–304.

Lane, J. D., & Wegner, D. M. (1994). Secret relationships: The back alley to love. In R. Erber & R. Gilmour (Eds.), *Theoretical frameworks for personal relationships*. Hillsdale, NJ: Erlbaum.

Langlois, J. H., & Roggman, L. A. (1990). Attractive faces are only average. *Psychological Science, 1*, 115–121.

Langlois, J. H., Roggman, L. A., and Musselman, L. (1994). What is average and what is not average about attractive faces. *Psychological Science, 5*, 214–220.

Lavrakas, P. (1975). Female preferences for male physiques. *Journal of Research in Personality, 9*, 324–334.

Lehmiller, J. J. (2009). Secret relationships: Consequences for personal and relational well- being. *Personality and Social Psychology Bulletin, 35*, 1452–1466.

Lemay, E. P., Clark, M. S., & Greenberg, A. (2010). What is beautiful is good because what is beautiful is what is desired: Physical attractiveness stereotyping as projection of interpersonal goals. *Personality and Social Psychology Bulletin, 36*, 339–353.

Leonard, D. W. (1975). Partial reinforcement effects in classical aversive conditioning in rabbits and human beings. *Journal of Comparative and Physiological Psychology, 88*, 539–547.

Lerner, M. J. (1980). *The belief in a just world: A fundamental delusion*. New York: Plenum.

Lerner, R. M., & Lerner, J. V. (1977). Effects of age, sex, and physical attractiveness on child-peer relations, academic performance, and elementary school adjustment. *Developmental Psychology, 1*, 585–590.

Levine, D. (2000). Virtual attraction: What rocks your boat. *CyberPsychology and Behavior, 3*, 565–573.

Lewak, R. W., Wakefield, J. A., & Briggs, P. F. (1985). Intelligence and personality in mate choice and marital satisfaction. *Personality and Individual Differences, 6*, 471–477.

Lott, A. J., & Lott, B. E. (1974). The role of reward in the formation of positive interpersonal attitudes. In T. Huston (Ed.), *Foundations of interpersonal attraction* (pp. 171–189). New York: Academic Press.

Lundberg, G. A., & Beazley, V. (1948). "Consciousness of kind" in a college population. *Sociometry, 11*, 59–74.

Lundberg, G. A., Hertzler, V. B., & Dickson, L. (1949). Attraction patterns in a university. *Sociometry, 12,* 158–169.

Luo, S., & Klohnen, E. C. (2005). Assortative mating and marital quality in newlyweds: A couple-centered approach. *Journal of Personality and Social Psychology, 88,* 304–326.

Mackinnon, S. P., Jordan, C. H., & Wilson, A. E. (2011). Birds of a feather sit together: Physical similarity predicts seating choice. *Personality and Social Psychology Bulletin, 37,* 879–892.

Major, B., Carrington, P. I., & Carnevale, P. J. D. (1984). Physical attractiveness and self-esteem: Attributions for praise from an other-sex evaluator. *Personality and Social Psychology Bulletin, 10,* 43–50.

Margolin, L., & White, L. (1987). The continuing role of physical attractiveness in marriage. *Journal of Marriage and the Family, 49,* 21–28.

Marks, G., & Miller, N. (1987). Ten years of research on the false consensus effect: An empirical and theoretical review. *Psychological Bulletin, 102,* 72–90.

Martin, L. L. (1986). Set/reset: Use and disuse of concepts in impression formation. *Journal of Personality and Social Psychology, 51,* 493–504.

May, J. L., & Hamilton, P. A. (1980). Effects of musically evoked affect on women's interpersonal attraction toward and perceptual judgments of physical attractiveness of men. *Motivation and Emotion, 4,* 217–228.

McCarthy, B., & Duck, S. (1976). Friendship duration and responses to attitudinal agreement- disagreement. *British Journal of Social and Clinical Psychology, 15,* 377–386.

Miller, E. J., Smith, J. E., & Trembath, D. L. (2000). The "skinny" on body size requests in personal ads. *Sex Roles, 43,* 129–141.

Mills, J., Cooper, D., & Duncan, F. (2002). Polarization of interpersonal attraction: The effect of perceived potency. *Basic and Applied Social Psychology, 24,* 156–162.

Mittelman, B. (1956). Analysis of reciprocal neurotic patterns in family relationships. In V. W. Eisenstein (Ed.), *Neurotic interaction in marriage* (pp. 81–100). New York: Basic Books.

Montoya, R. M. (2008). I'm hot, so I'd say you're not: The influence of objective physical attractiveness on mate selection. *Personality and Social Psychology Bulletin, 34,* 1315–1331.

Moreland, R. L., & Zajonc, R. B. (1982). Exposure effects in person perception: Familiarity, similarity, and attraction. *Journal of Experimental Social Psychology, 18,* 395–415.

Morrow, P. C., McElroy, J. C., Stamper, B. G., & Wilson, M. A. (1990). The effects of physical attractiveness and other demographic characteristics on promotion decisions. *Journal of Management, 16,* 723–736.

Mueser, K. T., Grau, B. W., Sussman, S., & Rosen, A. J. (1984). You're only as pretty as you feel: Facial expression as a determinant of physical attractiveness. *Journal of Personality and Social Psychology, 46,* 469–478.

Murray, H. A. (1938). *Explorations in personality.* New York: Oxford University Press.

Murstein, B. I. (1961). A complementarity need hypothesis in newlyweds and middle-aged married couples. *Journal of Abnormal and Social Psychology, 22,* 8–12.

Murstein, B. I. (1972). Physical attractiveness and marital choice. *Journal of Personality and Social Psychology, 22,* 8–12.

Murstein, B. I., & Brust, R. G. (1985). Humor and interpersonal attraction. *Journal of Personality Assessment, 49,* 637–640.

Murstein, B. I., & Christy, P. (1976). Physical attractiveness and marital adjustment in middle- aged couples. *Journal of Personality and Social Psychology, 34,* 537–542.

Nadler, A. (1980). Good looks do not help: Effects of helper's perceived physical attractiveness and expectation for future interaction on help-seeking behavior. *Personality and Social Psychology Bulletin, 6,* 378–383.

Nahemow, L., & Lawton, M. P. (1975). Similarity and propinquity in friendship formation. *Journal of Personality and Social Psychology, 32,* 204–213.

Newcomb, T. M. (1961). *The acquaintance process*. New York: Holt, Rinehart, and Winston.

Naumann, L. P., Vazire, S., Rentfrow, P. J., & Gosling, S. D. (2009). *Personality and Social Psychology Bulletin, 35,* 1661–1671.

O'Grady, K. E. (1982). Sex, physical attractiveness, and perceived risk for mental illness. *Journal of Personality and Social Psychology, 43,* 1064–1071.

Pavlov, I. P. (1927). *Conditioned reflexes*. London: Oxford University Press.

Pelham, B. W., & Carvallo, M. (2011). The surprising potency of implicit egotism: A reply to Simonsohn. *Journal of Personality and Social Psychology, 101,* 25–30.

Pelham, B. W., Mirenberg, M. C., & Jones, J. T. (2002). Why Susie sells seashells by the seashore: Implicit egotism and major life decisions. *Journal of Personality and Social Psychology, 82,* 469–487.

Raines, R. S., Hechtman, S. B., & Rosenthal, R. (1990). Nonverbal behavior and gender as determinants of physical attractiveness. *Journal of Nonverbal Behavior, 14,* 253–267.

Ramsey, J. L., Langlois, J. H., Hoss, R. A., Rubenstein, A. J., & Griffin, A. M. (2004). Origins of a stereotype: Categorization of facial attractiveness by 6-month-old infants. *Developmental Science, 7,* 201–211.

Reis, H. T., Nezlek, J., & Wheeler, L. (1980). Physical attractiveness in social interaction. *Journal of Personality and Social Psychology, 38,* 604–617.

Reis, H. T., Wheeler, L., Spiegel, N., Kernis, M. H., Nezlek, J., & Perri, M. (1982). Physical attractiveness in social interaction II: Why does appearance affect social experience? *Journal of Personality and Social Psychology, 43,* 979–996.

Reis, H. T., Wilson, I., Monestere, C., Bernstein, S., Clark, A., Seidl, E., Franco, M., Gioioso, E., Freeman, L., & Radoane, K. (1990). What is smiling is beautiful and good. *European Journal of Social Psychology, 20,* 259–267.

Riniolo, T. C., Johnson, K. C., Sherman, T. R., & Misso, J. A. (2006). Hot or not: Do professors perceived as physically attractive receive higher student evaluations? *Journal of General Psychology, 133,* 19–35.

Rosenbaum, M. E. (1986). The repulsion hypothesis: On the nondevelopment of relationships. *Journal of Personality and Social Psychology, 51,* 1156–1166.

Rosenblatt, A., & Greenberg, J. (1988). Depression and interpersonal attraction: The role of perceived similarity. *Journal of Personality and Social Psychology, 55,* 112–119.

Ross, L., Greene, D., & House, P. (1977). The "false consensus effect": An egocentric bias in social perception and attribution processes. *Journal of Experimental Social Psychology, 13,* 279–301.

Ross, M. B., & Salvia, J. (1975). Attractiveness as a biasing factor in teaching judgments. *American Journal of Mental Deficiency, 80,* 96–98.

Rotton, J., Barry, T., Frey, J., & Soler, E. (1978). Air pollution and interpersonal attraction. *Journal of Applied Social Psychology, 8,* 57–71.

Rubin, Z. (1973). *Liking and loving*. New York: Holt, Rinehart, and Winston.

Schachter, S. (1959). *The psychology of affiliation: Experimental studies of the source of gregariousness*. Stanford, CA: Stanford University Press.

Schachter, S., & Singer, J. (1962). Cognitive, social, and physiological determinants of the emotional state. *Psychological Review, 69,* 379–399.

Schutz, R. E. (1958). Patterns of personal problems of adolescent girls. *Journal of Educational Psychology, 49,* 1–5.

Segal, M. W. (1974). Alphabet and attraction: An unobtrusive measure of the effect of propinquity in a field setting. *Journal of Personality and Social Psychology, 30,* 654–657.

Sergios, P. A., & Cody, J. (1986). Importance of physical attractiveness and social assertiveness skills in male homosexual dating behavior and partner selection. *Journal of Homosexuality, 12,* 71–84.

Seta, J. J., & Seta, C. E. (1982). Personal equity: An interpersonal comparator system analysis of reward value. *Journal of Personality and Social Psychology, 43,* 222–235.

Seta, J. J., & Martin, L. L. (1987). Payment and value: The generation of an evaluation standard and its effect on value. *Journal of Experimental Social Psychology, 23,* 285–301.

Sigall, H., & Landy, D. (1973). Radiating beauty: The effects of having a physically attractive partner on person perception. *Journal of Personality and Social Psychology, 28,* 218–224.

Sigall, H., & Michela, J. (1976). I'll bet you say that to all the girls: Physical attractiveness and reactions to praise. *Journal of Personality, 44,* 611–626.

Sigall, H., & Ostrove, N. (1975). Beautiful but dangerous: Effects of offender attractiveness and nature of the crime on juridic judgments. *Journal of Personality and Social Psychology, 31,* 410–414.

Simmons, L. W., Rhodes, G., Peters, M., & Koehler, N. (2004). Are human preferences for facial symmetry focused on signals of developmental instability? *Behavioral Ecology, 15,* 864–871.

Simonsohn, U. (2011). Spurious? Similarity effects (implicit egotism) in marriage, job, and moving decisions. *Journal of Personality and Social Psychology, 101,* 1–24.

Simpson, J. A., Gangestad, S. W., & Lerma, M. (1990). Perception of physical attractiveness: Mechanisms involved in the maintenance of romantic relationships. *Journal of Personality and Social Psychology, 59,* 1192–1201.

Singh, D. (1993). Adaptive significance of female physical attractiveness: Role of waist-to-hip ratio. *Journal of Personality and Social Psychology, 65,* 293–307.

Singh, D. (1995). Female judgment of male attractiveness and desirability for relationships: Role of waist-to-hip ratio and financial status. *Journal of Personality and Social Psychology, 69,* 1089–1101.

Singh, R., & Ho, S. Y. (2000). Attitudes and attraction: A new test of the attraction, repulsion and similarity-dissimilarity asymmetry hypotheses. *British Journal of Social Psychology, 39,* 197–211.

Singh, R., & Tan, L. S. (1992). Attitudes and attraction: A test of the similarity-attraction and dissimilarity-repulsion hypotheses. *British Journal of Social Psychology, 31,* 227–238.

Solomon, M. R., & Schopler, J. (1978). The relationship between physical attractiveness and punitiveness: Is the linearity assumption out of line? *Personality and Social Psychology Bulletin, 4,* 483–486.

Spinoza, B. (1981) *The ethics.* Malibu, CA: Simon.

Sprecher, S. (1989). The importance to males and females of physical attractiveness, earning potential, and expressiveness in initial attraction. *Sex Roles, 21,* 318–328.

Stephan, W., Berscheid, E., & Walster, E. (1971). Sexual arousal and heterosexual perception. *Journal of Personality and Social Psychology, 20,* 93–101.

Sugiyama, L. S. (2005). Physical attractiveness in adaptionist perspective. In D. M. Buss (Ed.), *The handbook of evolutionary psychology* (pp. 292–343). New York: Wiley.

Sunnafrank, M. (1984). Attitude similarity and interpersonal attraction in communication processes. *Communication Monographs, 50,* 273–284.

Swami, V., et al. (2010). The attractive female body weight and female body dissatisfaction in 26 countries across 10 world regions: Results of the international body project I. *Personality and Social Psychology Bulletin, 36,* 309–325.

Swann, W. B. Jr. (1992). Seeking "truth," finding despair: Some unhappy consequences of a negative self-concept. *Psychological Science, 1,* 15–17.

Swann, W. B. Jr., Hixon, J. D., & De La Ronde, C. (1992). Embracing the bitter "truth": Negative self-concepts and marital commitment. *Psychological Science, 3,* 118–121.

Swann, W. B. Jr., Hixon, J. G., Stein-Seroussi, A., & Gilbert, D. T. (1990). The fleeting gleam of praise: Cognitive processes underlying behavioral reactions to self-relevant feedback. *Journal of Personality and Social Psychology, 59*, 17–26.

Swann, W. B. Jr., Rentfrow, P. J., & Gosling, S. D. (2003). The precarious couple effect: Verbally inhibited men + critical, disinhibited women = bad chemistry. *Journal of Personality and Social Psychology, 85*, 1095–1106.

Swann, W. B. Jr., Stein-Seroussi, A., & Giesler, R. B. (1992). Why people self-verify. *Journal of Personality and Social Psychology, 62*, 392–401.

Tashakkori, A., & Insko, C. A. (1981). Interpersonal attraction and person perception: Two tests of three balance models. *Journal of Experimental Social Psychology, 17*, 247–255.

Taylor, L. S., Fiore, A. T., Mendelsohn, G. A., & Cheshire, C. (2011). "Out of my league": A real-world test of the matching hypothesis. *Personality and Social Psychology Bulletin, 37*, 942–954.

Tesser, A., Campbell, J., & Smith, M. (1984). Friendship choice and performance: Self-evaluation maintenance in children. *Journal of Personality and Social Psychology, 46*, 561–574.

Tharp, R. G. (1963). Psychological patterning in marriage. *Psychological Bulletin, 60*, 97–117.

Thornhill, R., & Gangestad, S. W. (1999). Facial attractiveness. *Trends in Cognitive Science, 3*, 452–460.

Treger, S., Sprecher, S., & Erber, R. (2013). Laughing and liking: Exploring the interpersonal effects of humor use in initial interactions. *European Journal of Social Psychology, 43*, 532–543.

Triandis, H. C. (1995). *Individualism and collectivism*. Boulder, CO: Westview.

Trivers, R. L. (1972). Parental investment and sexual selection. In B. Campbell (Ed.), *Sexual selection and the descent of man* (pp. 136–179). Chicago: Aldine.

Tyler, T. R., & Sears, D. O. (1977). Coming to like obnoxious people when we have to live with them. *Journal of Personality and Social Psychology, 35*, 200–211.

Veitch, R., & Griffit, W. (1976). Good news-bad news: Affective and interpersonal effects. *Journal of Applied Social Psychology, 6*, 69–75.

Walster, E., Aronson, V., Abrahams, D., & Rottman, L. (1966). Importance of physical attractiveness in dating behavior. *Journal of Personality and Social Psychology, 4*, 508–516.

Walster, E., Walster, G. W., Pilliavin, J., & Schmitt, L. (1973). "Playing hard-to-get": Understanding an elusive phenomenon. *Journal of Personality and Social Psychology, 26*, 113–121.

Watts, B. L. (1982). Individual differences in circadian activity rhythms and their effects on roommate relationships. *Journal of Personality, 50*, 374–384.

Weddell, D. H., Parducci, A., & Geiselman, R. E. (1987). A formal analysis of ratings of physical attractiveness: Successive contrast and simultaneous assimilation. *Journal of Experimental Social Psychology, 23*, 230–249.

Wegner, D. M. (1994). Ironic processes of mental control. *Psychological Review, 101*, 34–52.

Wegner, D. M., & Erber, R. (1992). The hyperaccesibility of suppressed thought. *Journal of Personality and Social Psychology, 63*, 903–912.

Wegner, D. M., Lane, J. D., & Dimitri, S. (1994). The allure of secret relationships. *Journal of Personality and Social Psychology, 66*, 287–300.

Wegner, D. M., Schneider, D. J., Carter, S. III, & White, L. (1987). Paradoxical effects of thought suppression. *Journal of Personality and Social Psychology, 58*, 409–418.

West, S. T., & Brown, T. J. (1975). Physical attractiveness, the severity of the emergency, and helping: A field experiment and interpersonal simulation. *Journal of Experimental Social Psychology, 11*, 531–538.

White, G. L., & Knight, T. D. (1984). Misattribution of arousal and attraction: Effects of salience of explanations of arousal. *Journal of Experimental Social Psychology, 20*, 55–64.

Wilson, E. O. (1975). *Sociobiology*. Cambridge, MA: Belknap Press.

Wheeler, L., & Kim, Y. (1997). What is beautiful is culturally good. The physical attractiveness stereotype has different content in different cultures. *Personality and Social Psychology Bulletin, 23,* 795–800.

Wheeler, L., & Nezlek, J. (1977). Sex differences in social participation. *Journal of Personality and Social Psychology, 35,* 742–754.

White, G. L. (1980). Physical attractiveness and courtship progress. *Journal of Personality and Social Psychology, 39,* 660–668.

White, S. G., & Hatcher, C. (1984). Couple complementarity and similarity: A review of the literature. *American Journal of Family Therapy, 12,* 15–25.

Winch, R. F. (1958). *Mate selection: A theory of complementarity of needs.* New York: Harper & Row.

Zajonc, R. B. (1968). Attitudinal effects of mere exposure. *Journal of Personality and Social Psychology Monograph Supplement, 9,* Part 2, 1–27.

Zebrowitz, L. A., Montepare, J. M., & Lee, H. K. (1993). They don't all look alike: Individuated impressions of other racial groups. *Journal of Personality and Social Psychology, 65,* 85–101.

CHAPTER 10

INTIMATE RELATIONSHIPS

THE GRADUATE II

n the 1968 movie classic, *The Graduate*, Ben returns home to California after graduating from an East Coast college. With no idea what he wants to do with his life, he spends most of his days hanging around the pool, trying to escape his parents' admiring friends. Despite his best efforts, Ben falls prey to the middle-aged Mrs. Robinson, the alcoholic wife of his father's boss, who seduces him into a torrid affair. Ben's unsuspecting parents, worried about 'his lack of direction, try to interest him in Elaine, the Robinsons' attractive daughter. Almost half-heartedly, he asks Elaine out, and after a rough start, the two become interested in each other. But when Elaine finds out about Ben's affair with her mother, she breaks off her relationship with him and goes off to college in Berkeley. There she meets Carl, a clean-cut medical student who is a friend of her family.

In the meantime, Ben has decided he wants to marry Elaine. In a desperate attempt to win her back, he moves to Berkeley and begins following her around. But she is already engaged to Carl and still hurt by Ben's betrayal. Anxious to push Ben out of Elaine's life, her parents set a date for her wedding to Carl. When Ben finds out about it, he drives day and night until he reaches the church, snatching Elaine from Carl just seconds after she says "I do." He and Elaine run out of the church, catch a bus, and ride off. In the final scene, we see them sitting at the back of the bus as Simon and Garfunkel sing "Mrs. Robinson." The two make an odd couple. Elaine is still wearing her wedding dress, while Ben's appearance shows that he's just spent a couple of days behind the wheel, with the top down. Even stranger is the absence of any interaction between the two. Both look straight ahead, their facial expressions suggesting they have no idea where they might be going – literally or figuratively.

How does the mutual attraction they feel translate into a lasting relationship? What are the processes through which they will maintain their relationship? How will they deal with conflict? To some extent, this chapter represents a sequel to *The Graduate* and begins once Ben and Elaine step off the bus. In this chapter, we explore some of the most fundamental processes in intimate relationships: the nature of love, self-disclosure, fairness, commitment, conflict, and forgiving.

Dustin Hoffman and Katherine Ross, stars of "The Graduate"

WHAT IS THIS THING CALLED LOVE?

The world of music may seem like an appropriate place to find an answer to the musical question first raised by Cole Porter. Type www.links2love.com into your web browser, and you get access to the lyrics of over 13,000 love songs. Many of them provide a number of more or less lyrical answers about the nature of that "Crazy Little Thing Called Love." You may, for example, hear that love hurts, that it's a secondhand emotion, and that it's something money can't buy. Still confused? Go to the library and head for the section that houses literature, philosophy, and religious studies. You may find that love is a many-splendored thing and that there are all kinds of love—romantic love, brotherly love, platonic love, and Christian love, to name just a few. Chances are your quest to find the meaning of love will leave you just as confused as the protagonists of the film *Love Story*, who famously (but not correctly) maintained that "love means never having to say you're sorry."

Until recently, psychology has done little to clear up such confusion about the nature of love. To some extent, the failure to address one of the most intriguing of human emotions stems from the discipline's unique intellectual history. Freud's seemingly obsessive preoccupation with sex as a major motivator of human behavior compelled him to define love as a compensatory mechanism that kicked in when the desire for a sexual union was blocked. Presumably, sexual frustration leads to idealization of the other person, along with the subjective feeling of falling in love (Freud, 1922). For behaviorists, with their exclusive focus on stimulus-response connections, sex was equally important to the experience of love, yet for very different reasons. Watson (1924) looked at love as little more than an innate response to the cutaneous stimulation of the erogenous zones. In other words, touch someone in all the right places, and he or she can't help but respond with feelings of love.

Many 20th-century social psychologists considered love as an attitude—a general disposition to think, feel, and act toward another in certain ways (see Chapter 5). Presumably, if Jane thinks John is a neat guy, she will have positive feelings about him and will entertain a request for a dinner date with some degree of seriousness. Note the underlying assumption of consistency here. Favorable or unfavorable beliefs about an object or person usually correspond to positive or negative feelings and behavioral intentions.

From the perspective of the attitude framework, your attitude toward your romantic partner isn't all that different from your attitude toward your favorite brand of running shoes. The love you feel for your partner is merely a more intense form of the liking you have for your iPod (Heider, 1958). To be sure, the idea that love is little more than an intense form of liking seems supported by the way we use language. We often claim to "love" a variety of objects, issues, or things (cars, stereos, or football teams, for example) when we really mean to say that we like them a whole lot. At the same time, however, we often go to great lengths to assure others that we like them, but do not necessarily love them. When we tell someone that we should "just be friends," we generally aren't asking for less love, but are suggesting instead that liking should be the predominant sentiment in the relationship. Recent research suggests that there are important differences between the two kinds of feelings.

Liking and Loving: A Conceptual Distinction

Rubin (1970) was among the first to realize the profound implications of labeling one's feelings for another as "love" versus "liking." He developed separate scales to measure the extent to which a person *likes* or *loves* another. **Table 10.1** presents some items from the two scales.

A look at the items shows several important differences between liking and love. Liking appears to be a matter of favorable evaluation ("I think that ____ is unusually well adjusted"), respect ("I think that ____ is one of those people who quickly wins respect"), and the perception of similarity ("I think that ____ and I are quite similar to each other"). Love, on the other hand, seems to have elements of affiliation and dependency ("If I could never be with ____, I would be miserable."), exclusiveness and absorption ("I feel very possessive toward ____"), and a predisposition to help ("I would do almost anything for ____").

To further explore the differences between liking and love, Rubin administered both scales to 158 dating couples and asked them to respond once with their dating partner in mind, and once with a close same-sex

Table 10.1: Sample Items from Rubin's Love and Liking Scales

<u>Liking Items</u>

1. I think that _____ is unusually well-adjusted.

2. I think that _____ is one of those people who quickly wins respect

3. I think that _____ and I are quite similar to each other.

4. I have great confidence in _____ good judgment.

<u>Love Items</u>

1. If I could never be with _____ I would be miserable.

2. I feel very possessive toward _____.

3. I would do almost anything for _____.

4. I feel I can confide in _____ about virtually everything

Source: Rubin, Z. (1973), Liking and Loving. New York: Holt, Rinehart, and Winston

friend in mind. The findings from his study corroborate many of his theoretical speculations about the difference between liking and love, though there were a few surprises. As expected, the two scales were only moderately correlated, suggesting that while liking and love often go hand in hand, they are not two forms of the same sentiment. As we all know, we can like others without loving them, and we may sometimes love others without really liking them that much. Along these same lines, participants liked their dating partners only slightly more than their same-sex friends, but they loved them much more than they loved their friends.

Somewhat surprisingly, scores on the love and liking scales were more highly correlated for men than for women. Men may be more confused about the true nature of their feelings than women, who are prone to make more subtle distinctions. Consequently, men may have a more difficult time maintaining pure friendships with women—a point illustrated by the movie *When Harry Met Sally*. Finally, women tended to like their partners more than they were liked in return. This difference was due almost entirely to differences in the ratings on task-related dimensions such as good judgment, intelligence, and leadership potential. Bear in mind that this study was conducted almost 30 years ago. In these days of increased equality between men and women, this finding may no longer be relevant.

The Prototype of Love

Though Rubin's work (1970) iwas an important first step in clarifying the nature of love, his main objective was to distinguish love from liking. He was less concerned with establishing what love is in most people's minds. That may well be an empirical question that can be answered by asking a sufficient number of people to list the features of love as they see it and then looking for a consensus about the central features. Doing so would establish a **prototype of love**—that is, a list of features most commonly associated with love. Fehr (1988) took such an approach by asking a large number of undergraduates to list as many features of love as they could in three minutes. This procedure yielded a list of 68 features mentioned by two or more participants. She then asked a second group of undergraduates to rate each item on the list in terms of how central it was to love, using an 8-point scale ranging from 1 (extremely poor feature of love) to 8 (extremely good feature of love). **Table 10.2** lists the ten most central and the ten most peripheral features as the students ranked them.

Table 10.2: The 10 Most Central and the 10 Most Peripheral Features of Love

MOST CENTRAL	MOST PERIPHERAL
1. Trust	1. Scary
2. Caring	2. Dependency
3. Honesty	3. Uncertainty
4. Friendship	4. Butterflies in stomach
5. Respect	5. See only other's good qualities
6. Concern for other's well-being	6. Gazing at the other
7. Loyalty	7. Euphoria
8. Commitment	8. Heart rate increases
9. Acceptance	9. Energy
10. Supportiveness	10. Thinking about the other all the time

Source: Fehr, B. (1988). Prototype analysis of the concepts of love and commitment. *Journal of Personality and Social Psychology, 55,* 557–579.

The picture of love that emerges from Fehr's study is slightly different from Rubin's. On the one hand, Rubin's predisposition to help seems reflected in "Concern for other's well-being" and "Supportiveness." On the other hand, Rubin had classified friendship and respect, two of Fehr's most central features of love, as being part of liking. For more on the differences between the two studies and to explore possible reasons for their divergent findings, see the Think like a Social Psychologist box **below**).

THINK LIKE A SOCIAL PSYCHOLOGIST: DEFINING LOVE

Rubin (1970) and Fehr (1988) took very different paths in search of the defining features of love. In creating the Love and Liking Scales, Rubin was inspired by the writings of anthropologists, psychologists, and sociologists. Consequently, one could argue that he may have relied on a somewhat biased sample of highly educated academics. Fehr, on the other hand, relied on undergraduates to generate the central features of love. At first blush, her approach may appear superior to Rubin's, since it relied on respondents whose thinking was not contaminated by years of advanced academic training.

At the same time, it is not clear that Fehr's sample yielded unbiased responses. Curiously, Fehr's participants considered "Friendship" and "Respect" as central features of love, but not sexual passion. What kinds of biases may have crept into her study because she relied on college students? What aspect of her methodology may have contributed to this result?

The differences in the two studies aside, for most people, love is probably a strange mixture of trusting, caring, helping, wanting, and commitment. With this in mind, let's look at some theories about the origins of this peculiar emotion.

CAUSAL THEORIES OF LOVE

Why do people—fools included—fall in love? Evolutionary theory suggests that it acts as a hidden influence on issues related to reproduction and the survival of the species. Humans face some unique reproductive challenges, which have required unique adaptations. Compared to other primates, human offspring are weak, slow to develop, and dependent on adult caretakers until well into their teens (Martin, 2003; Hill & Kaplan, 1999). At the same time, humans are weaned at a much earlier age than most other primates, which allows for shorter intervals between births. One adaptation to the challenges of raising several highly dependent children at the same time is biparental care (Pillsworth & Haselton, 2005). Two parents are better than one in providing for high-maintenance offspring. Fathers in particular provide nutritional and social resources, protection against predators, and models for learning (e.g., Marlowe, 2003).

Successful biparental care requires a strong parental investment on the father's part, which, in turn, requires a high degree of certainty about a child's paternity (Trivers, 1972). Pair bonding provides the basis for that certainty, maximizing the parental investment on the father's part. Though pair bonding is not unique to humans, it is the primary context for human reproduction. Thus, the institution of marriage can be found in some form among most human cultures (Brown, 1991). Admittedly, there is some variation in terms of specific marriage traditions across cultures, but most encourage relatively long-term reproductive relationships (Buss, 2003).

Love enables relationships of this sort and provides the emotional glue that keeps them together (Pillsworth & Haselton, 2005). As a result, the cultural universality of marriage is paralleled by a similar **cultural universality of romantic love**. One cross-cultural study (Jankowiak & Fisher, 1992) found that romantic love was present in 89 percent of the 166 cultures surveyed. And across cultures, reciprocal liking appears to be the most common precursor to love (Riela et al., 2010). To be sure, the way in which individuals *experience* love may be influenced by their culture. The distinction between individualism and collectivism that was discussed at length in Chapters 3 and 4 provides some clues to the ways love may be experienced in various cultures. In most Western cultures, love is generally experienced in the context of individual self-expression and self-fulfillment. But cultures that emphasize harmony and respect for social relationships are more likely to endorse a friendship-based form of romantic love that minimizes the potential for disruption of existing family relationships (Dion & Dion, 1993). Consequently, marrying for love tends to be more important in individualistic societies than in societies marked by a high degree of collectivism (Levine et al., 1995). And while Westerners see love as a path to happiness, the Chinese conception of love includes a more mixed set of emotional experiences, including sorrow and pity along with happiness (Shaver, Wu, & Schwartz, 1992).

Cross-cultural research suggests that this couple's experience of love included a more mixed set of emotions than is common among Western couples

These differences aside, the universality of love strongly suggests that our capacity and desire for romantic love may have its origins in our evolutionary history. In support of the idea that love is an evolved adaptation, researchers have identified dedicated neurotransmitters in the human brain that render the experience of love rewarding (Aron, Fisher, Mashek, Li, & Brown, 2006). Falling in love isn't something meant for fools at all; rather, it may represent a uniquely human adaptation to our reproductive needs that also has implications for our health and well-being. For a closer look at the real and not-so real benefits of being married, see the **Social Psychology and Health** box **below**.

SOCIAL PSYCHOLOGY AND HEALTH: THE REAL AND NOT-SO REAL BENEFITS OF BEING MARRIED

The benefits of pair bonding may not be limited to a couple's children (Pillsworth & Haselton, 2005), but may extend to the parents as well. Being married, or at least romantically involved, has been linked to happiness to such a degree that their equation has become a fundamental truth (Hetherington & Kelly,

2002; Myers, 1999; Seligman, 2002). Empirical support for the link between marriage and happiness comes from a number of surveys conducted in the United States and Europe. All show that married people are generally happier than single people (Diener, Suh, Lucas, & Smith, 1999; Diener & Seligman, 2002; Inglehart, 1990).

If findings like these should tempt you to close your book and rush out in search of that special someone, we would certainly understand. But in light of the high stakes, we would ask you to first look more closely at the data. The empirical evidence in favor of the relationship between marriage and happiness is correlational. Consequently, we cannot conclude that getting married will necessarily increase your happiness. Furthermore, virtually all the surveys took a snapshot of people's happiness at a single point in time. Thus, the causal arrow between marital status and happiness may operate in reverse. In other words, happy people may be more likely to get married than unhappy people.

Support for this idea comes from a longitudinal study that tracked the reported happiness of thousands of participants over a 15-year period, with special attention paid to those who did and did not marry (Lucas, Clark, Georgellis, & Diener, 2003). The results indicated that those who married during the study were, on average, slightly happier to begin with than those who did not marry. Getting married increased their happiness further, but only to a small degree and for a short period of time. On average, veterans of married life "are no happier in the years after marriage than they were in the years before marriage" (Lucas, et al., 2003, p. 532). In other words, happy people are more likely to marry than unhappy people, but married people aren't necessarily happier than their unmarried counterparts.

Given love's importance for human reproduction and survival, we should not be surprised to learn that people are generally not aware of the cognitive and affective processes that contribute to the experience of love. We return to our story of Ben and Elaine for a closer look at these processes.

Love as Misattribution of Arousal

Mr. and Mrs. Robinson's attempts to keep Ben and Elaine apart were a glorious failure. Admittedly, riding off in the back of a bus isn't the same as riding off into the sunset, but the two lovers may well have ended up spending their lives together. In fact, the Robinsons' parental interference may have amplified any affection Ben and Elaine had for each other. This "Romeo and Juliet effect" is well documented (e.g. Driscoll, Davis, & Lipetz, 1972), and may result from a **misattribution of arousal** (Schachter & Singer, 1961) produced by the obstacles parents throw in a couple's way. We discussed misattribution of arousal at length in Chapter 9. You may recall that within the framework of this theory, emotion results from a change in the level of physiological arousal (for example, an increase in heart rate, perspiration, pupil dilation) that is then labeled according to available cues. While no single study has explored the possible effects of misattribution of arousal for the experience of love, we can speculate that any arousing event or situation might intensify the emotion. In addition to parental interference, then, trouble at work or school, societal or cultural disapproval, or the need to keep a relationship secret (Lane & Wegner, 1994; Wegner, Lane, & Dimitri, 1995) could produce extraneous sources of arousal. Within the dynamics of a relationship, disagreement or sexual frustration may have a similar effect, as long as the source of the arousal is sufficiently ambiguous. To the extent that individuals are of this process, we can consider misattribution of arousal a hidden influence on our experience of love.

Love as Preoccupation with the Other

Misattribution emphasizes the importance of unexplained arousal, limiting the role of cognition to the task of explaining arousal. However, thinking, particularly thinking about the other, can be an important component in the generation and intensification of subjective feelings of love. Think about the last time you fell in love. Chances are you had a hard time concentrating on the most elementary tasks, such as studying, working, and enjoying time with friends. People who are in love often can't stop thinking about the other, to the point where it impairs their cognitive functioning (Steenbergen, Langeslag, Band, & Hommel, 2013).

This cognitive preoccupation may have a causal effect on the experience of love. If nothing else, thinking about the other may intensify feelings of love, just as our thoughts about a variety of things can change our evaluations of them. For example, if we leave a movie theater with a sense of disappointment, further thinking is only likely to increase our letdown. But if we liked the movie we saw, continued thinking about it will further increase our evaluation. Presumably, preoccupation with the movie brings to mind thoughts that are congruent with the initial evaluation, and thus additional thinking tends to further polarize it (Tesser, 1978).

This type of reasoning may explain the intensification of love over time, as suggested by a study in which dating couples recorded how often they thought about their partner over a period of two weeks (Tesser & Paulhus, 1976). Additionally, participants reported how much in love they were at the beginning and end of the study (using the Love part of Rubin's Liking and Love scale), and they recorded the number of dates during that time. To measure any reality constraints that may have entered into their thinking, participants kept track of any unpleasant discoveries they had made about the other that could have decreased their feelings of love (strange and intolerable personal habits, for example). As expected, the frequency with which couples thought about each other was strongly correlated with their subjective experience of love.

The connection between thinking and feeling manifested itself in a couple of ways. First, the frequency of thought at Time 1 (the beginning of the two-week period) was highly predictive of how much in love participants felt at Time 2 (the end of the two-week period). At the same time, the degree of love participants felt at Time 1 predicted the frequency of thinking at Time 2. In other words, the more participants felt in love, the more they thought about each other and the more their love. Not surprisingly, dating frequency was positively correlated with love, but reality constraints were negatively correlated. The latter finding is important because it suggests that love is not completely blind. Although a couple's obsessive preoccupation with each other may border on idealization, unpleasant discoveries may constrain the extent to which they are able to idealize each other. Obsessive thinking may have its most profound impact when couples lack information about each other—perhaps because their relationship is in an early stage (and little self-disclosure has occurred), or because the lovers have been kept apart by circumstances (Beach & Tesser, 1978).

WHAT IS THIS THING CALLED LOVE?: A SUMMARY

Love is not just an extreme form of liking, but instead differs from it in important ways (Rubin, 1970). The prototype of love has distinct central features, including trust, caring, honesty, loyalty, and commitment (Fehr,

1988). Love may have evolved in response to evolutionary pressures that favored bonding for the care of weak and dependent offspring. Not surprisingly, on the individual level, several psychological mechanisms promote the experience of love. They include the misattribution of physiological arousal from other sources as love (Driscoll, Davis, & Lipetz, 1972), and a cognitive preoccupation with the other that results in increased feelings of love (Tesser & Paulhus, 1976).

Think Like a Social Psychologist

Designing research

—Simply asking research participants to list the features of characteristics they associate with love can be problematic because participants may list features they think *ought* to be associated with love, rather than features they personally think are associated with it. How could you design an experiment that might avoid such biased responses? What measurement technique(s) might be particularly suited to uncover participants' "true" feelings?

Understanding everyday behavior

—Frequent and heated arguments are generally not considered beneficial for a relationship. What theory of love would predict that they could contribute to the love two people feel for one another? What mechanisms would produce this increase in the subjective experience of love?

Confronting social issues

—Based on the evolutionary perspective on love, who would be most suited to raise a young child: a single mother? A single father? A loving gay couple?

TYPOLOGIES OF LOVE

Causal theories help us to understand how attraction can turn into love and how arousal, obsessive thinking, and extraneous events can intensify emotion. At the same time, they concentrate mainly on its *quantitative* aspects, devoting little or no attention to *qualitative* differences in the experience of love. Clearly, the kind of love we have for a sibling differs from the kind of love we feel for a romantic partner. Even within intimate relationships, love can manifest itself in different ways. We may think of one relationship as marked by infatuation, another as marked by companionship. The fact that love has many manifestations, even in the context of intimate relationships, is addressed by theories stressing individual differences in love. Common to those approaches is the theme that people vary in the types of love they prefer and experience.

Love Styles

The intellectual grandfather of the individual difference approach to love is John Alan Lee (1973, 1988), who developed a typology of **love styles**. Lee identified three primary love styles and three secondary styles that represent mixtures and compounds of the primary styles. To correspond to descriptions of love he had found in classical literature, he gave them Greek and Latin names.

Primary Love Styles

The first love style Lee identified was *Eros*, the passionate love often caused by a strong attraction to the physical attributes of the other. Eros is love that is certainly not blind. People characterized by this style tend to think that finding the perfect mate is the most important thing in life. Once they have found the partner of their dreams, they manifest a strong desire for abundant physical and verbal acknowledgments of their love. The polar opposite to Eros is *Storge*, a companionate love, which develops out of friendship and interaction. Storge is most common in agrarian societies, in which partner choice is limited because people stay in one place most of their lives. It is less typical of societies with high mobility. Overt expressions of love and passion are rare in this style; the emphasis is on commonly shared interests. Carl, whom Elaine left at the altar, seems to have been characterized by this love style. A third style, *Ludus*, is a playful love, mostly for the short term. Ludus generally lacks a sense of falling in love and usually does not involve commitment, either in time or exclusivity. It can be found among people who prefer to remain single.

Secondary Love Styles

Mixing Eros and Ludus produces *Mania*, the kind of dependent and possessive love characterized by obsessive preoccupation and intense jealousy. Like erotic lovers, manic lovers require constant and tangible assurances of love, but they have no preference for any particular type of person. As the term implies, lovers who are characterized by mania appear to have lost their senses; they vacillate between demonstrating their love and vying for control of the relationship. As such, manic love has an element of pathology, one that is amplified by a tendency to project desired qualities onto their partners.

Mixing Storge and Ludus produces the very different love style called *Pragma*, which is anchored in logic and practicality. For pragmatic lovers, finding the compatible mate is primarily a practical problem that can be solved through effort and persistence. Like Storge, Pragma tends to develop slowly, because pragmatic lovers are wary of warning signs. They typically avoid commitment and talk of the future until they are convinced they have found the right partner. Sexual compatibility is important to these lovers, but they consider it a matter of sharpening skills, rather than finding the right chemistry. Not surprisingly, pragmatic lovers look for mates by joining organizations such as singles clubs. Finally, mixing Eros with Storge yields *Agape*, a form of love that is

"When it comes to men, I'm more into trust <u>fund</u> than trust <u>worthy</u>."

For pragmatic lovers finding a compatible mate is a practical problem that can be solved through effort and persistence

PRIMARY LOVE STYES   **SECONDARY LOVE STYLES**

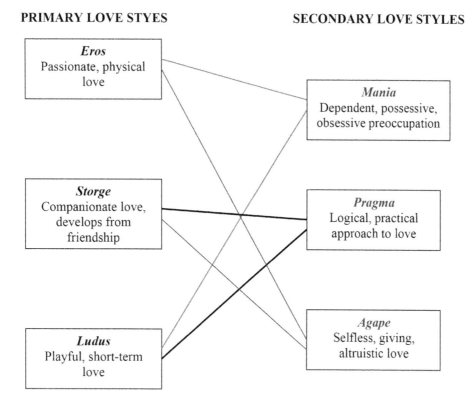

Figure 10.1: Primary and Secondary Love Styles According to Lee (1973)

Source: Lee, J. A. (1973). *The colors of love: An exploration of the ways of loving.* Don Mills, Ontario, Canada: New Press.

selfless, giving, and altruistic. These lovers consider it a duty to respond to the needs of the other, even if their love is not reciprocated. While the New Testament espouses agape as the ultimate form of love, it is perhaps the least common form in adult romantic relationships. Agape may be more typical of the love parents have for their children. **Figure 10.1** provides a graphic representation of the different love styles.

Research on Love Styles

Lee's typology has a great deal of face validity. As you read through the descriptions of the six different love styles, you probably identified the one that characterizes you. You have probably encountered others whose style is different from yours. But the ultimate test of a theory is the extent to which it explains a variety of phenomena. In this case, we need to ask how well Lee's typology predicts the way people choose their partners, their satisfaction with their relationships, and the stability of their relationships. The available evidence is mixed.

Looking at partner choice first, several studies using the Love Attitude Scale (LAS), a 42-item measure that corresponds to distinctions among Lee's love styles (Hendrick & Hendrick, 1986), have reported generally positive correlations between partners' love styles (Davis & Latty-Mann, 1987; Hendrick, Hendrick, & Adler, 1988). Erotic lovers were especially likely to be paired with one another. Of course, this finding can be interpreted in at least two ways. It may indicate an attempt on the part of both partners to find someone who matches their own love style. Alternatively, partners may simply have come to share each other's views of the relationship. In other words, if one partner sees a lot of eros in the relationship, the other partner may eventually come to see it in the same way. Thus, the positive correlation may result from continued interaction, rather than from partner choice per se. Of course, partners are less likely to share the view that their relationship should be marked by intense jealousy or a lack of commitment. Thus, ludus lovers and manic lovers are rarely paired with lovers of the same style (Davis & Latty-Mann, 1987; Hendrick et al., 1988).

Although these findings on the relationship between love styles and partner choice are difficult to interpret, the results of research on the correlation between love styles and relationship satisfaction are relatively straightforward. Eros and agape are generally associated with measures of relationship satisfaction, whereas ludus tends to be negatively correlated with relationship satisfaction (e.g., Bierhoff, 1991; Davis & Latty-Mann, 1987; Hendrick et al., 1988; Levy & Davis, 1988). That is hardly surprising in light of the importance people place on passion and altruism in relationships. Finally, matching levels of eros and agape along with pragma seems to predict the stability of a relationship, as well as the number of children a couple has (Bierhoff, 1991). But as with partner choice, it is unclear how best to explain these findings. Matching love styles may produce outcomes such as commitment and investment that would predict relationship stability more directly. Because such variables were not measured, the question remains an open one.

A Triangular Theory of Love

Despite its shortcomings, Lee's (1973, 1988) typology provided the foundation for other typologies that avoid some of the same problems. Sternberg (1986) proposed that love has three basic ingredients: intimacy, passion, and decision/commitment. Intimacy refers to feelings that promote closeness, bondedness, and connectedness, including concern for the welfare of the other, subjective happiness, positive regard, sharing, support, mutual understanding, and intimate communication. Passion refers to sources of arousal that promote the experience of passion such as sexual needs and the need for self-esteem, affiliation, submission, dominance, and self-actualization. Finally, decision/commitment refers to (a) the decision that one is in love with the other; and (b) the commitment to maintain that love.

Intimacy, passion, and commitment follow a unique pattern as a relationship develops. In successful relationships, intimacy increases steadily; dying relationships are characterized by a decrease in intimacy. Passion develops rapidly at the beginning of a relationship and is eventually replaced by habituation. However, drastic decreases of passion, or even a loss of passion, may produce a cyclical pattern in which a relationship returns to its beginning.

Of course, the larger question is, what generates increases and decreases in passion in the first place? One possibility is that passion is a function of intimacy. In the early stages of a relationship, passion will be high because of rapid increases in intimacy (Baumeister & Bratslavsky, 1999). Simply put, learning about another, sharing experiences, and discovering that the other person cares about you are exciting and thus provide fuel for passion. As two people reach the point where they feel they know everything about one another, have run out of new experiences to share, and feel they understand each other completely, passion should decrease.

The development of decision/commitment depends to some extent on the success of a relationship, which itself is influenced by the development of intimacy and passion. In successful relationships with rapidly increasing passion and gradually increasing intimacy, commitment develops slowly at first. Dramatic events, like having sex

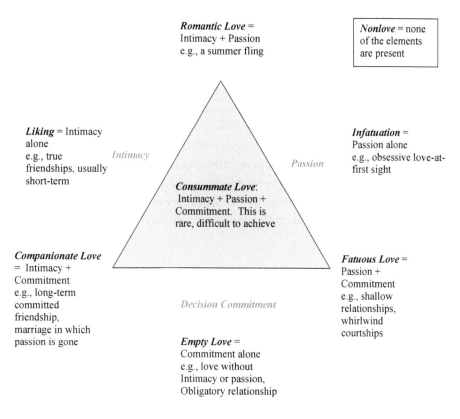

Figure 10.2: Eight Types of Love and Their Characteristics

Based on Sternberg, R.J. (1986). A triangular theory of love. *Psychological Review, 93*, 119–135

for the first time or moving in together, generally bring a drastic increase in commitment. Once couples have married, bought a home, and had children, commitment levels off, primarily because it cannot increase any further.

Sternberg's three components of love can be found in all close relationships to varying degrees. Assuming that in any given relationship, intimacy, passion, and commitment can be either low or high, Sternberg (1986) came up with eight forms of love that produce qualitatively different relationships (see **Figure 10.2**).

As the term implies, consummate love describes the kind of relationship for which many strive and perhaps few achieve. Realistically, most intimate relationships may be lacking in one or more components. Romantic love, with its emphasis on intimacy and passion in the absence of strong commitment, is perhaps characteristic of couples in the early stages of dating. Fatuous love, with its emphasis on passion and commitment, seems to describe sex without intimacy—the kind of relationship Ben had with Mrs. Robinson. Companionate love, with its lack of passion, describes many mature relationships, in which sex has been supplanted by intimacy and commitment. Empty love, with its focus on commitment in the absence of anything else, describes couples who stay together for matters of convenience, child-rearing, or tax purposes. Liking, with its emphasis on intimacy, describes the relationship of two friends. Finally, although non-love may seem to be an artifact of the classification (if everything can be high, it can also be low), it does perhaps describe the sentiment that exists among two people whose relationship has ended.

Sternberg's (1986) **triangular theory of love** is useful in understanding how different forms of love can produce qualitatively different relationships. However, its utility depends to some extent on how well it explains relationship satisfaction and stability. At this point, there is little, if any, research on those issues. Nonetheless, we can speculate that on the most basic level, a couple will be happy with their relationship to the extent that it meets their mutual expectations. For example, two people may be quite satisfied with a relationship that is low in commitment, as long as they both agree that commitment is not important. Mismatches in expectations regarding any of the components of love are likely to lead to conflicted relationships, and help keep advice columnists in business. On the other hand, Sternberg (1986) felt that in close relationships, the three components of love were equally important. From his perspective, we would expect relationships that contain equal parts of intimacy, passion, and commitment to be the most successful. However, when Sumter, Valkenburg, and Peter (2013) looked at relationships across the life span, they found that commitment is equally present from adolescence through older adulthood, while passion and intimacy are especially prevalent in relationships among young adults.

Passionate and Companionate Love

The eight different types of relationships Sternberg (1986) describesd represent a range of theoretical possibilities. By themselves, they give no indication of which ones are more likely to occur empirically. Some (Hatfield, 1988) have argued that most close relationships fall into either one of two categories. **Passionate love** is characterized by an intense longing for complete union with the other and is represented by both the unadulterated passion of infatuation and the intimate passion of romantic love in Sternberg's (1988) typology. According to Hatfield (1988), passionate love comes in two forms. Reciprocated passionate love creates a sense of fulfillment, along with feelings of elation and even ecstasy on the part of both partners. And it affects our brain: the mere mention of a loved one's name instantly activates neural pathways associated with pleasure and reward (Cacioppo, Grafton, & Bianchi-DeMicheli, 2012). Unrequited passionate love, on the other hand, often produces feelings of emptiness, anxiety, and despair in those whose love is rejected (Hatfield & Sprecher, 2010).

As it turns out, **unrequited love** is unrewarding for the would-be lover and the rejecter. Would-be lovers often look back on such relationships with a mixture of positive and intensely negative emotions. They often feel that their love was mutual, that they had been led on, or that the rejection had not been communicated clearly. Rejecters are by no means better off. They look back on the relationship with mostly negative emotions. While they may feel innocent of any wrongdoing, they often feel guilty about their inability to return the other's love. At the same time, they perceive any attempts on the part of the would-be lover to keep the relationship going as intrusive and annoying (Baumeister, Wotman, & Stillwell, 1993).

Companionate love lacks the longing of passionate love. It describes instead the attraction we feel toward others with whom our lives are deeply intertwined. Cognitively, this type of love entails the sharing of information about each other, even if it is of an embarrassing nature. The emotional component of companionate love is characterized by the attainment of intimacy, rather than a longing for it. The couple's shared life creates a sense of comfort, as opposed to arousal.

It is tempting to think of intimate relationships as being either passionate or companionate. Realistically, however, many successful relationships probably have elements of both. For many people, their lover is also their best friend. Moreover, as relationships mature, they may undergo a transformation from being primarily passionate to primarily companionate. As Sternberg (1986) has argued, passion is subject to habituation, and the focus of a relationship may change in response to specific events.

To investigate this idea, Tucker and Aron (1993) measured the amount of passionate love couples experienced at three important transition points in their relationships: before and after they got married, before and after they had their first child, and before and after their children were old enough to leave the home. The two researchers found that passionate love declined steadily over time, as well as with transitions in the relationships. However, the decreases they found were relatively small. Even couples who were anticipating or experiencing an "empty nest" reported at least moderate levels of passionate love. In a similar vein, Sprecher (1999) monitored 101 heterosexual couples over a four-year period and found little change in objective measures of love. However, those couples who were still together at the conclusion of the study (about 40 percent) reported increased *feelings* of love, commitment, and satisfaction.

How well does the distinction between passionate and companionate love explain differences in relationship satisfaction and stability? One could argue that passionate love is perhaps more rewarding, in part because of the overwhelming longing for union with the other. One could also argue that companionate love may be more predictive of success over the long term because it lacks the emotional turmoil often created by the experience of passionate love. Unfortunately, there is little research to address these issues. One study (Aron & Henkemeyer, 1995) reports that women who experience a great deal of passionate love are happier, more satisfied with their relationships, and more excited about them than women who experience little passionate love.

TYPOLOGIES OF LOVE: A SUMMARY

Typologies of love revolve around the many ways in which individuals experience love. The love styles identified by Lee (1973, 1988) have been used to predict individual differences in partner choice, relationship satisfaction, and relationship stability. Sternberg's triangular theory of love (Sternberg, 1986) points to the differences in passion, intimacy, and commitment for the experience of love and charts the developmental course of the three components as a relationship progresses. Hatfield (1988) emphasizes the differences between passionate and companionate love and between reciprocated and unrequited love.

Think Like a Social Psychologist

Explaining everyday behavior
—After a period of blissful singlehood, Erin signs up for a singles cruise to meet Mr. Right. Which of Lee's love styles does her behavior exemplify?

Making connections
—Laura and Luke have been dating for about a year, even though Laura does not completely reciprocate Luke's feelings for her. What specific emotions might motivate the two to carry on with the relationship nonetheless?

LOVE AS ATTACHMENT

One final way to look at individual differences in the experience of love is to conceptualize it as **attachment**. Much in the same way as the emotional bonds between infants and their caregivers are characterized by different styles of attachment, the emotional bonds between intimate partners have different styles that can act as hidden influences on a relationship.

In Ainsworth's Strange Situation children's reactions to the unexpected departure and the subsequent return of a caregiver provide an indication of their attachment style

According to Bowlby (1969, 1973, 1980), all infants form an attachment to their caregivers. Developed from interactions infants have with their caregivers, it becomes the foundation for the infant's expectation about the self and relationships with others. By examining infants' responses to a caregiver's sudden departure, followed by an equally sudden reappearance (an experimental procedure known as the "Strange Situation"), Ainsworth et al. (1978) empirically established three distinct attachment styles that represent adaptations to their environment (Roisman & Fraley, 2008). Securely attached infants have caregivers who are involved with them, respond to their needs, and interact with them in positive ways (Isabella, 1993). As a result, these infants feel good about themselves; they trust their caregivers and do not fear abandonment. Faced with the Strange Situation, they show mild distress when the caregiver leaves, but experience and display positive emotions when she returns. Anxiously attached infants generally have caregivers who are either inconsistent or overbearing in their affection and in their responses to the infant's needs. In the Strange Situation, these infants become inconsolable when the caregiver departs, and their distress persists beyond the reunion. Finally, avoidantly attached infants have caregivers who are distant, emotionally aloof, and feel uncomfortable about physical closeness. In the Strange Situation, these infants may or may not become distressed at the caregiver's departure, and do not seek closeness with her when she returns.

The attachment styles acquired during infancy are fairly stable and persist into adulthood (Bowlby, 1982; Fraley, 2002; Simpson et al., 2007). Of course, in adulthood, the partner in a close, intimate relationship becomes the new attachment figure, taking the place of the parents (Kerns, 1994). In other words, the attachment style that marked the infant's relationship to the mother is transferred to the adult, the romantic partner (Brumbaugh & Fraley, 2006).

There is some evidence that different attachment styles may be localized in different parts of the brain. Emotional positivity and approach behavior seem to be localized in the left hemisphere; emotional negativity and avoidance behavior in the right hemisphere. Cohen and Shaver (2004) hypothesized that the two hemispheres may also be differentially sensitive to positive and negative words related to attachment. Using a divided visual field task that allowed the processing of such words by either the left or right hemisphere, but not both,

Table 10.3: What is Your Attachment Style?

_____ I find it relatively easy to get close to others and am comfortable depending on them and having them depend on me. I don't often worry about being abandoned or about someone getting too close to me. (*Secure Attachment*)

_____ I find that others are reluctant to get as close as I would like. I often worry that my partner doesn't really love me or won't stay with me. I want to merge completely with another person, and this desire sometimes scares people away. (*Anxious Attachment*)

_____ I am somewhat uncomfortable being close to others; I find it difficult to trust them completely, difficult to allow myself to depend on them. I am nervous when anyone gets too close, and often, love partners want me to be more intimate than I feel comfortable being. (*Avoidant Attachment*)

Source: Hazan, C., & Shaver, P. (1987). Romantic love conceptualized as an attachment process. *Journal of Personality and Social Psychology, 52*, 511–524.

they found that avoidant participants had a more difficult time processing positive words related to attachment presented to the right hemisphere—that is, the seat of emotional negativity.

The finding that different attachment styles are localized in different hemispheres of the brain further attests to the idea that they may serve as hidden influences. But just how does adult attachment influence intimate relationships? In one study (Hazan & Shaver, 1987), over 1,200 adults responded to a questionnaire that appeared in the *Rocky Mountain News*. It contained a total of "95 questions about your most important romance." The crucial item on the questionnaire asked respondents to check off which of three statements best described their feelings about relationships. Take a look at **Table 10.3** to see which one describes your attachment style.

The nature and scope of this study revealed a wealth of data about the importance of attachment in romantic relationships. To begin with, the percentages of adults who displayed the three attachment styles were remarkably similar to the percentages of infants who displayed the same style. Fifty-six percent of adults displayed a secure attachment, compared to 65 percent of infants; 19 percent of adults displayed an anxious attachment, compared to 23 percent of infants; and 25 percent of adults displayed an avoidant attachment, as compared to 12 percent of infants. Moreover, the different attachment styles were associated with markedly different experiences of love. Secure lovers characterized their most important relationship as happy, friendly, and trusting. They emphasized their ability to accept and support their partner unconditionally. Anxious lovers reported experiencing love in terms of obsession, a desire for reciprocation and union, and emotional ups and downs, along with extreme sexual attraction and jealousy. Avoidant lovers' relationships were characterized by a fear of intimacy, emotional ups and downs, and jealousy (in the absence of sexual attraction). Given these qualitatively different experiences, it is not surprising that the relationships of secure lovers lasted longer than those of anxious and avoidant lovers (on average, about ten years, compared to six years and five years, respectively). Although Hazan and Shaver (1987) did not report sex differences for the different attachment styles, recent research (Del Giudice, 2011) indicates that men tend to be higher in avoidance, while women tend to be higher in anxiety, just as the steretype suggests.

Bowlby's (1982) speculations about the transfer of attachment from mother to adult romantic partner received some support as well. Most adults would have difficulty recalling the nature of their attachment to their caregivers at the tender age of 18 months. To circumvent this problem, Hazan & Shaver (1987) asked respondents a series of questions about their parents' general behavior toward them during their childhood, as well as their parents' behavior toward each other. Compared to insecure respondents, secure respondents reported warmer relationships with both parents, as well as between parents. Anxious respondents recalled their fathers as having been unfair; avoidant respondents described their mothers as cold and rejecting. A more recent study that tracked more than 700 children from birth through age 18 (Fraley, Rosiman, Booth-LaForce, Owen, & Holland, 2013) paints a similar, yet more detailed, picture. Adult attachment appears to be primarily shaped by the nature of one's caregiving environment in childhood. The quality of one's best friendships matters as well, but temperament plays no role. Across the remainder of the life span, attachment anxiety is highest among young adults and decreases as we move through middle age into older adulthood. At the same time, attachment avoidance is highest among those of middle age, and individuals in relationships generally feel less anxiety and avoidance than young adults (Chopik, Edelstein, & Fraley, 2013). Evidently, the nature and quality of our romantic relationships in adulthood continue to shape our attachment styles.

Most of the research on adult attachment built on Bowlby's classification. It describes mental models of relationships that include the self *and* the other. Some (Bartholomew & Horowitz, 1991) have argued in favor of separating the mental models for the self from the mental models for the other. This separation yields four styles, including two distinct avoidant attachments. *Secure* individuals feel good about themselves and the other. *Preoccupied*, or anxious, individuals think of themselves as unacceptable and unlovable, but feel that others are basically good. Avoidant individuals think of others as untrustworthy. But *dismissive* individuals feel good about themselves, yet see others as undeserving of a relationship. *Fearful* individuals feel bad about themselves and bad about others. In essence, they think of themselves as unlovable and of others as untrustworthy—a combination of mental models that makes them fearful of intimacy.

Consequences of Adult Attachment Styles

Hazan and Shaver's (1987) study of adult attachment styles draws a clear picture of how these styles produce differences in the experience of love. Other research indicates that differences in attachment style have a variety of consequences for individuals and their relationships.

Emotional Control

Couples frequently find themselves in circumstances that resemble the Strange Situation, since separation from one's partner is an unavoidable fact of life. Fortunately, many separations are both short and benign. An hour or two for a dental appointment, a day apart because of school or work do not pose problems for most couples. Attachment styles should not affect how couples deal with such routine separations. But what happens when one partner has to travel out of town, perhaps for an extended period of time?

To find out how attachment styles influence responses to more prolonged or drastic separations, Fraley and Shaver (1998) studied couples waiting at an airport. They asked those couples who were separating to complete a questionnaire designed to assess the length of their relationship, their attachment style, and their degree of distress. Then, unobtrusively, the researchers observed the couples' behavior. Not surprisingly, most couples engaged in some form of proximity maintenance. That is, they held on to, followed, and searched for their partners more than couples traveling together. Couples who had been together for a relatively short period of time stayed especially close together. Anxious women who had reported a great deal of distress on the questionnaire also exhibited a great deal of proximity maintenance behavior. But fearful women pulled away from their partners, even though they had reported a high level of stress on the questionnaire. Both these findings are consistent with

How you say goodbye to your partner says a lot about your attachment style

attachment theory. Oddly enough, anxious and avoidant men failed to exhibit a similar behavior pattern in this situation. Their behavior may have been more constrained by the airport's public setting.

To the extent that securely attached individuals see their partners as a source of comfort, we would expect different attachment styles to be related to a more general ability for emotional self-control. In support of this reasoning, Feeney and Kirkpatrick (1996) found a marked difference in how secure, anxious, and avoidant individuals responded to stress when their partners were either present or absent. Compared to secure participants, anxious and avoidant individuals showed increased anxiety when they had to complete a stressful task (counting backward by 13 as quickly and accurately as possible) in their partner's absence. Their increased level of anxiety persisted when they tried to complete a similar task in their partner's presence. These findings suggest that secure attachment tends to *reduce* generalized anxiety, whereas insecure attachment *produces* anxiety in a stressful situation related to separation. Moreover, the observation that in a stressful situation, the presence of one's partner does little to reduce anxiety levels in insecure individuals suggests an approach-avoidance conflict likely brought on by the generalized expectation that the other cannot be counted on for emotional support (Carpenter & Kirkpatrick, 1996; Collins & Feeney, 2004).

Studies that look at support-seeking and support-giving among individuals with different attachment styles lend further support to the idea that those who are securely attached are more likely to seek *and* receive support from their partners when confronted with an anxiety-provoking situation. Simpson, Rholes, & Nelligan (1992) observed the behavior of heterosexual couples as the female partners were about to enter into an anxiety-provoking situation. As expected, securely attached women used their partners as a source of reassurance and comfort as their anxiety about the upcoming task increased. Avoidant women looked for emotional support from their partner mainly when their anxiety level was low. Anxious women did not seek support from their partners regardless of the level of anxiety they experienced. Their lack of support seeking may have risen from an internal conflict over their proximity needs. Anxious women may need and desire comfort and reassurance, yet they know that their partners are not consistently available to provide it. Thus, the need for proximity becomes associated with anger and resentment, which further increases their level of stress. Not surprisingly, when the researchers looked at male partners' behavior, they found that secure men offered greater reassurance, comfort, and support than anxious and avoidant men.

Of course, findings like these should not be taken as an indication that individuals with insecure attachment styles are unable to control emotions such as fear and anxiety. Instead, such individuals appear to have an edge in emotional self-control because they have learned that they cannot rely on their partner as a source of comfort and reassurance. Consistent with this idea, one study (Feeney, 1995) found that a proclivity for emotional self-control was most pronounced among couples in which both partners endorsed insecure attachment styles.

Partner Choice

Given the importance of similarity in attraction (see Chapter 9), we should not be surprised that individuals would prefer and date others with similar attachment styles (Frazier, Byer, Fisher, Wright, & DeBord, 1996). This is particularly true for individuals with a secure attachment style, who seek others who are equally comfortable getting close (Collins & Read, 1990). The preferences among insecurely attached individuals are a little more complex. Some have produced evidence for a similarity principle (e.g., Frazier et al., 1996); others have found that anxiously and avoidantly attached individuals do not seek others with the same attachment style (e.g., Kirkpatrick & Davis, 1994). Instead, they often prefer partners who meet their expectations about close relationships. That is, anxious women frequently date avoidant men, while anxious men seek out anxious or avoidant women (Collins & Read, 1990; Simpson, 1990). In all likelihood, these choices are not made consciously; instead, they may represent the hidden influences of attachment.

Relationship Satisfaction and Stability

Our speculations about attachment style and partner choice are further supported by research on the quality of ongoing relationships. Compared to individuals with secure attachment styles, those with anxious and avoidant styles tend to have relationships that are marked by less trust, commitment, and satisfaction (Kane et al., 2007), along with more frequent and more severe conflicts (Campbell, Simpson, Boldry, & Kashy, 2005). Interestingly, a lack of commitment and interdependence is particularly descriptive of the avoidant attachment style, whereas a lack of trust was more descriptive of the anxious attachment style (Collins & Read, 1990; Feeney & Noller, 1990; Simpson, 1990). Moreover, individuals with anxious and avoidant attachment styles report their relationships to be more frequently a source of negative emotions and less frequently a source of positive emotions. The reverse is true for those with secure attachment styles (Fuller & Fincham 1995; Simpson, 1990). Not surprisingly, both partners in a relationship tend to become particularly dissatisfied when either suffers high anxiety over abandonment (anxious attachment) or low comfort with closeness (avoidant attachment) (Jones & Cunningham, 1996). Not surprisingly, relationship problems stemming from avoidant attachment are more common in collectivistic societies that place a premium on closeness and harmony than in individualistic societies that value emotional distance and independence (Friedman et al., 2010).

Attachment styles may help to predict why some relationships persist, even though they appear to be doomed in terms of the couple's level of satisfaction. Similarly, they may help explain why relationships that are marked by relatively high degrees of satisfaction nonetheless break apart. For example, an anxious individual's preoccupation with the reciprocation of affection, along with a concern about potential abandonment, may motivate special efforts to maintain the relationship, even if it falls well short of expectations. Avoidant individuals, on the other hand, may be compelled to break up out of fear of becoming overly dependent, even though their satisfaction with the relationship is high.

There is evidence in favor of both sets of speculations. Remember that in Hazan & Shaver's (1987) study, secure respondents reported that their current relationship had lasted for about ten years, while anxious and avoidant respondents reported relationships that had lasted for five or six years, respectively. Secure respondents were less likely to be divorced (six percent) than anxious and avoidant respondents (10 percent and 12 percent, respectively). A study that tracked couples over a four-month period (Keelan, Dion, & Dion, 1994) suggests that these differences may be due to the different qualitative nature of the relationships, based on various attachment styles. In this sample, secure individuals reported consistent levels of relationship satisfaction, relationship costs, commitment, and trust. But anxious and avoidant individuals evidenced decreasing levels of satisfaction, commitment, and trust, along with increasing relationship costs.

However, the results of at least one study (Kirkpatrick & Davis, 1994), which tracked well over 300 couples over three years, suggests that the connection among attachment, relationship satisfaction, and relationship stability may be complicated by sex differences. As might be expected, securely attached individuals displayed high levels of satisfaction and stability. In couples in which the *woman* was *anxiously attached,* both partners tended to be unhappy with their relationship. But in couples in which the *man* was *avoidantly attached,* the men (but not the women) rated the relationship negatively. Still, the relationships of avoidant men and anxious women were remarkably stable over time.

Why would anxious women's and avoidant men's relationships be just as stable as those of secure men and women? The answer to this question may be related to gender stereotypes. Women are generally expected to seek and maintain intimacy and to be the general caretakers of relationships. Anxious women, for whom the possibility of abandonment is a central concern, may be more motivated than others to work at holding the relationship together, which may account for the relatively high stability of their relationships, especially with avoidant men. This process may be aided by the relatively low expectations that avoidant men have for their partners and their relationships.

Of course, the observation that relationships between anxious women and avoidant men can be surprisingly stable should not be taken as an indication that they are marked by happiness and bliss. Instead, they appear to be lacking in trust, which, according to some researchers (Holmes & Rempel, 1989), is one of the most sought-after qualities of close relationships. Indeed, trust in one's partner is one of the cornerstones of intimacy (Sternberg, 1986) and a necessary precondition for the development of commitment and feelings of security (Holmes & Rempel, 1989). Securely attached individuals appear to have an edge in the ability to trust their partners.

In one study using a diary technique (Mikulincer, 1998), securely attached partners remembered more experiences that were marked by trust and reported more constructive coping techniques in response to violations of trust (talking to their partners, for example) than anxious and avoidant partners. Unsurprisingly, anxious and avoidant individuals remembered fewer past relationships marked by trust. Furthermore, anxious individuals tended to respond to violations of trust with rumination and worry; avoidant individuals responded with attempts to distance themselves from their partners. Though everyone, regardless of attachment style, considered achieving intimacy important, anxious individuals struggled to attain a sense of security, while avoidant individuals attempted to gain control over their relationships.

Much of the early research on attachment involved measuring attachment styles and comparing their effects on a number of dependent variables. To the extent that unmeasured variables associated with attachment may be at least partly responsible for any results, that approach is problematic. For example, if we assume that securely attached individuals are happier than anxiously attached individuals, differences in happiness—rather than differences in attachment—may be responsible for any differences in results. However, more recent research that uses priming procedures to elicit a sense of security or anxiety in participants has not supported this alternative explanation.

For example, Mikulincer and Shaver (2001) primed a "secure base schema" by subliminally exposing some participants to words like *closeness, love, hug,* and *support*. They primed other participants with words that had positive connotations unrelated to security (for example, *happiness, honesty, luck,* and *success*). Finally, they primed a third group of participants with neutral words (for example, *office, table, boat,* and *picture*). They then asked all participants to form impressions of two people, one of whom was identified as an in-group member and the other as an out-group member. As expected, participants in whom a secure base schema had been primed provided more favorable evaluations of the out-group member than participants who had been primed with positive or neutral words. How can we explain these effects? Using a similar procedure, Mikulincer et al. (2002) found that priming a secure base schema produces increased empathy—a quality that may have affected participants' evaluation of the out-group member. Other studies found that participants in whom a secure base schema had been primed disclosed more about themselves, were more likely to seek support, and were faster to identify words related to security (Gillath et al., 2006; Mikulincer, Gillath, & Shaver, 2002). Because priming can have its effects outside of conscious awareness, this line of research provides perhaps the clearest evidence to date that attachment serves as a hidden influence on a number of processes in relationships.

LOVE AS ATTACHMENT: A SUMMARY

Individual differences in the experience of love have been traced to differences in adult attachment styles (Hazan & Shaver, 1987; Mikulincer & Shaver, 2001). Attachment style influences partner choice, along with relationship satisfaction and stability (Collins & Read, 1990; Frazier et al., 1996; Kirkpatrick & Davis, 1994). Differences in attachment style also influence individuals' ability to control their emotions (Carpenter & Kirkpatrick, 1996).

Think Like a Social Psychologist

Making connections

—From a developmental perspective, how could one account for the remarkable stability of attachment? What different social realities may securely, anxiously, and avoidantly attached individuals face as they progress through the various stages of childhood and adolescence?

Thinking critically

—Early research treated adult attachment as an individual difference variable. What are the limits of that approach? To what extent does the work by Mikulincer and Shaver (2001) represent an improvement?

THE DEVELOPMENT OF INTIMACY

A Career in Plastics

Love may have brought Ben and Elaine together, but it provides no guarantee for a rewarding, lasting relationship. In *The Graduate II*, we see Ben and Elaine get off the bus and establish their relationship in a physical sense. Ben retrieves his car and other belongings and moves into Elaine's studio apartment in Berkeley. Broke and jobless, he remembers the advice he received from a family friend and decides to pursue a career in plastics at a company in Oakland. The job, which was advertised as a "ground-floor opportunity," lives up to its billing. Ben is the newest member of a growing sales force that pitches brand-new products to largely skeptical customers. The hours are long, and because his salary is based on commissions, his income is never predictable. It doesn't help that the Robinsons no longer support Elaine financially. Nonetheless, Ben's salary, along with Elaine's income from working at Berkeley's law library, is more than enough to make ends meet. Within a few months, they are able to move to a larger apartment in San Francisco's vibrant Haight-Ashbury district. While the move increases Elaine's commute, the hippie culture so prevalent in the "Haight" provides a stimulating context for their fledgling relationship—one that more than makes up for the hours Elaine spends on the subway each day.

Will love prevail? That depends. Ben and Elaine still face numerous obstacles that have very little to do with buying groceries and paying the rent. They both have a fair amount of explaining to do. Elaine is still stung by Ben's relationship with her mother. Ben wants to know about Elaine's aborted marriage to Carl. Getting answers to such "How-could-you?" questions is part of obtaining a general sense of who the other really is. In addition, they need to establish norms to guide their interactions to assure each other that they are getting a fair shake. As we will see, both self-disclosure and norms regarding fairness are related to a couple's satisfaction and the stability of their relationship. In this section, we'll take a closer look at self-disclosure and norms for intimate relationships.

Self-Disclosure

Self-disclosure has been defined as a process that involves the sharing of thoughts, feelings, and experiences (Derlega, Metts, Petronio, & Margulis, 1993). It is obviously important for developing relationships, as mutual self-disclosure helps individuals establish a sense of intimacy. But it is equally important in established relationships because continued self-disclosure helps maintain that sense of intimacy and promotes relationship satisfaction (Campbell, Lackenbauer, & Muise, 2006). Let's first take a look at how self-disclosure develops among individuals who are just getting to know each other. To that end, imagine you have just returned from a first date, during which your partner talked incessantly about

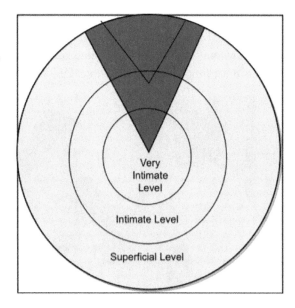

Figure 10.3: The Social Penetration Model of Self-disclosure and Intimacy

Based on: Altman, I., & Taylor, D. A. (1973). *Social Penetration: The development of interpersonal relationships.* New York: Holt, Rinehart and Winston.

a wide range of deeply personal issues and provided you with vivid and detailed accounts of past relationships. You never got a word in yourself and hardly got to ask any questions. When you made a suggestion for the wine to go with dinner, you got an earful about past health problems, including uncomfortably vivid descriptions of skin rashes stemming from allergic reactions. You are probably unhappy and very exhausted. And in your mind, there is absolutely no chance that you would go on a second date with that person. There may be many reasons for your disinclination, but chief among them may be the sense of discomfort that your date created by violating the two major norms of self-presentation.

First, your date failed to understand that self-disclosure is supposed to unfold in a gradual fashion. According to the **social penetration** model (Altman & Taylor, 1973), self-disclosure grows in terms of both the number of topics (breadth) and their personal significance (depth). Early in a relationship, self-disclosure is limited to a small range of topics that are explored on a relatively superficial level. A couple exchanges information about simple preferences that are not overly revealing. As the relationship develops, the breadth and depth of self-disclosure increases to include a wider range of topics that are covered more thoroughly (see **Figure 10.3**).

Self-disclosure and relationships are mutually transformative: self-disclosure increases as a relationship develops, and relationships develop as a result of increased self-disclosure (Derlega et al., 1993). Intimacy, the hallmark of a close relationship, develops as a result of self-disclosure (especially disclosure of an emotional nature) and partner responsiveness (Laurenceau, Feldman Barrett, & Pietromonaco, 1998).

According to the social penetration model, the gradual nature of self-disclosure does not imply that it is necessarily linear. Rather, changes in the breadth and depth of self-disclosure can occur at different rates. In developing relationships, people tend to expand on the number of topics they discuss before they increase the depth of their disclosures. The rate at which self-disclosure increases also depends on the nature of the relationship. In "love at first sight," the level of self-disclosure increases sharply rather than gradually (Berg, 1984, Berg & Clark, 1986). Contrary to popular belief, couples who follow this pattern are more likely to stay together than those for whom self-disclosure is a more gradual process (Berg & McQuinn, 1986). The key here is that both partners must proceed at the same rate. One reason you were so put off by your imaginary date was the premature disclosure of too many facts at an uncomfortable level of intimacy.

In addition to violating the norms of social penetration, your date violated another important norm of self-disclosure. How do two people on a date figure out what and how much to disclose? The answer is simple: They take their cues from each other—a principle known as **self-disclosure reciprocity** (Berg & Archer, 1980, 1982). That is, they match their self-disclosures in the intimacy and emotional tone of each other (Taylor & Belgrave, 1986). One highly intimate self-disclosure is reciprocated with another highly intimate self-disclosure; one unrevealing self-disclosure is reciprocated

Self-disclosure – the sharing of thoughts, feelings, and experiences – is of paramount importance for the development of intimacy

with another unrevealing self-disclosure. Similarly, positive self-disclosures are reciprocated with positive self-disclosures and negative self-disclosures with negative self-disclosures. If someone tells you about a death in the family, then responding with news about your excellent grades or new car would be wildly inappropriate.

Adhering to the principle of reciprocity is patently important because it helps to promote intimacy (Laurenceau, Feldman Barrett, & Pietromonaco, 1998; Reis & Shaver, 1988) and attraction (Gable, Reis, Impett, & Asher, 2004; Sprecher et al., 2013). In addition, the extent to which a person reciprocates another's self-disclosure by itself conveys information. Responsiveness to the level of intimacy and emotional tone of another's disclosure can elicit positive attributions about one's personality (that one is sensitive, for example) and can result in increased liking and attraction (Reis et al., 2011). Failure to reciprocate appropriately is likely to elicit negative attributions (that one is insensitive, for example) and can lead to a corresponding decrease in liking.

Evidence for the suspected relationship between self-disclosure reciprocity and liking comes from a study in which participants listened to taped conversations that had allegedly taken place between two strangers (Berg & Archer, 1980). On the first tape participants heard, one of the strangers disclosed something that was either high or low in intimacy. Some participants then heard another tape where a second stranger responded at the same level of intimacy. Other participants heard a tape in which the second stranger responded to a highly intimate disclosure with a disclosure low in intimacy, and a third group heard a tape where the second stranger responded to a disclosure low in intimacy with a highly intimate self-disclosure. All participants were then asked to indicate their liking for the second stranger. As expected, liking was high for the stranger who responded in kind and low for the stranger who failed to reciprocate on the appropriate level of intimacy.

Although self-disclosure reciprocity is important for the development of intimacy and romantic attraction, it also has its limits. For example, sharing one's vulnerabilities doesn't increase closeness, but can instead lead to insecurities about the relationship (Lemay & Clark, 2008). Similarly, disclosing one's values (for example, "Education is the most powerful tool to end poverty") doesn't increase closeness because others don't find them particularly useful or revealing (Pronin, Fleming, & Steffel, 2008). Finally, the extent to which two people reciprocate each other's self-disclosure seems to depend on their mood. People who are happy tend to disclose more intimate and varied information, whereas people in sad moods tend to be more attentive to the behavior of others and reciprocate their self-disclosures more accurately (Forgas, 2011).

Self-Disclosure in Mature Relationships

Clearly, self-disclosure is important for the development of intimate relationships. But what happens once a couple has gone beyond the stage of getting to know each other? For most couples, the amount of self-disclosure levels off once the relationship has become mature—generally, after about a year (Huston, McHale, & Crouter, 1986). Beyond the first year, self-disclosure begins a slow and steady decline that continues as partners grow older and the relationship matures (Antill & Cotton, 1987).

This decline in self-disclosure is no cause for alarm. In mature relationships, partners know each other fairly well, and so the need for self-disclosure is lower than in relationships that are still getting off the ground. This is not to say that mature relationships are devoid of self-disclosure. Instead, almost by necessity, they are characterized by a decrease in the amount of information disclosed (Antill & Cotton, 1987) and a shift from self-disclosures that are high in *evaluative intimacy* to those that convey *descriptive intimacy*. Evaluative intimacy refers to how we feel about something that happened ("I'm devastated by the D I got on my midterm"); descriptive intimacy refers to the actual event that may have taken place ("I got a D on my midterm"). This shift in content makes a great deal of sense. Once we know a person intimately, we know how certain events will make them feel; they no longer need to tell us.

There is one notable exception, however. Couples who are on the verge of a breakup decrease the number of topics they talk about, but increase the depth of their self-disclosures (Tolstead & Stokes, 1984). That is, they talk about fewer topics with a greater degree of intimacy. A couple's pattern of self-disclosures can also change quickly and dramatically in response to stressful events outside the relationship. Distress is often accompanied by cognitive preoccupation, which triggers a need to confide in others, including intimate partners (McDaniel, Stiles, & McGaughey, 1981). Confessions of this sort can relieve stress, partly because they transfer some aspect of the problem to another (Pennebaker, 1990). Needless to say, this is a zero-sum game where one partner's gain is the other partner's loss. Once the stressor has been removed, however, the couple's communicative pattern returns to one of descriptive self-disclosure.

ALL'S FAIR IN LOVE AND WAR? NORMS FOR INTIMATE RELATIONSHIPS

In time, Ben and Elaine establish a pattern of mutual self-disclosure in which Elaine talks a great deal about her emotions, but Ben confines himself to simply recounting what has happened to him. Will Elaine grow unhappy with their relationship because of the obvious imbalance between intimate and descriptive self-disclosure? Will she reach a point at which she ponders leaving Ben? Applying the reciprocity principle, she may indeed come to resent Ben's stubborn refusal (or inability) to match her affective disclosures (Davidson, Balswick, & Halverson, 1983).

Does this imply that a more general lack of reciprocity produces unhappiness and dissatisfaction? According to one perspective (Levinger & Huesman, 1980), two people in an intimate relationship exchange a variety of things. In addition to affection, companionship, and sympathy, they can provide each other with a range of commodities, including love, status, money, and goods (Turner, Foa, & Foa, 1971). When U.S. Secretary of State John Kerry quipped that he had "married up" when he wed ketchup heiress Teresa Heinz, he referred to an exchange by which the two traded wealth for status. By suggesting that his gains were perhaps larger than hers, he implied that the exchange, while evidently in his favor, wasn't entirely fair. However, before we conclude that his happiness about the interpersonal profit he reaped is accompanied by a similar level of unhappiness on the part of his wife, we need to submit the idea that intimate relationships can be characterized as exchange relationships to further scrutiny.

Clearly, many of our interactions with others are marked by principles of exchange. The most straightforward of these would involve a like-for-like exchange, as is the case in self-disclosure. A classmate may give you her notes from a class you have to miss in exchange for an implicit promise that you will reciprocate later in the semester. You put a reasonable amount of effort into your job, expecting that your employer will compensate you adequately. And when you shell out $50 to hear you favorite band, you expect them to show up on time and entertain you for a couple of hours. For the most part, uneven exchanges that seem to favor us aren't particularly troublesome. When you manage to buy a $100 sweater for $25 at your favorite store's "Blowout Clearance" sale, you likely will not be overcome by guilt. However, exchanges in which you yourself end up being short-changed may well leave you profoundly unhappy.

Communal versus Exchange Norms

The fact that all the foregoing examples involve relationships with relative strangers is no accident. It is primarily in casual relationships that people give things with the expectation of receiving something of comparable value in return, either immediately or in the near future (Clark & Mills, 1979). Other kinds of relationships are not necessarily guided by exchange norms. Think about parents and children, for example. True, raising children has its own rewards, but did your parents send you to college, drive you to sleepovers and soccer games with the expectation that you will perhaps provide for them in their old age? Maybe not. In all likelihood, your parents have some sort of retirement plan that will cover their financial needs in old age. Or think about a time you went out of your way to help a friend in need. Did you lend a hand with the idea that your help would be repaid some day?

Our guess is that the answer to these questions is probably "no." In **communal relationships**—the kinds we have with our family, our romantic partners, and our close friends—the giving and receiving of benefits is guided by different norms. That makes them qualitatively distinct from **exchange relationships**—the types we have with strangers and acquaintances. Specifically, in close relationships, the giving of benefits is guided primarily by need or our desire to please others (Clark & Mills, 1979). How do you decide on a wedding gift for a couple of close friends? Chances are you will carefully examine their gift registry and choose what they need, without considering the value of what they gave you, or might give you at your own wedding. In fact, when close others respond to your attempts at giving in a tit-for-tat fashion, you may experience a sense of discomfort, and perhaps even like them less. The reason is that they have violated the need-based norms of giving in communal relationships.

Research on Relationship Norms

The existence of need-based norms for the giving and receipt of benefits in close relationships has received a fair amount of empirical support. One of the earliest investigations was designed to test the idea that in exchange relationships, benefits are given in exchange for past benefits, or with the expectation of future benefits, while in communal relationships, benefits are given according to the other's needs (Clark & Mills, 1979). In this study, researchers led male research participants to believe that they could expect either an exchange or a communal relationship with a female confederate by informing them that she was either married or new in town and anxious to meet people. Participants then worked on a task that required them to create as many words as they could from a set of letters in return for points from the experimenter. They were led to believe that the female confederate was doing the same task in a separate room, using fewer letters. Because that made the confederate's task harder, the experimenter gave participants the opportunity to send her any extra letters if she requested so through an elaborate message system. This manipulation allowed participants to give benefits to another with whom they expected either an exchange relationship or a communal relationship. The female confederate responded to participants' benefits in one of two ways. To communicate a desire for an exchange relationship, she sent participants a note thanking them for the letter, and included a letter from her set in return. Alternatively, she sent participants a simple thank-you note without returning the favor. At the end of the experiment, all participants indicated their liking for the confederate.

The results were as Clark and Mills (1979) predicted. Participants who had expected an exchange relationship with the allegedly married confederate liked her better when she followed exchange-based norms; that is, when she returned their favors. That result made sense, because they thought she was unavailable, and thus the chances of establishing an intimate relationship with her were nonexistent. Participants who had expected the possibility of a communal relationship with the female confederate liked her better when she followed communal norms; that is to say, when she offered her thanks, but no repayment. When the confederate violated the norms of the expected relationship by following communal norms in the exchange situation or exchange norms in the communal situation, participants' liking of her decreased substantially.

There are several reasons why violating the norms that guide exchange and communal relationships may lead to decreased liking. In an exchange relationship, *giving* a benefit comes with the *expectation* of repayment in the form of a comparable benefit. At the same time, *receiving* a benefit creates an *obligation* to respond with a comparable benefit. When these expectations are violated, people feel shortchanged, and perhaps even exploited. In communal relationships, on the other hand, receiving a benefit does not come with an obligation to respond in kind. In fact, when close others respond in such a fashion, we often feel quite awkward. By focusing on comparability and equity, they seem to be ignoring what we want or need (e.g., Mills & Clark, 1994). Thus, the extent to which people stick to the norms guiding the giving and receiving of benefits has implications for liking. Those who follow the rules should be liked more than those who violate them.

Similarly, we would expect to find differences in how closely people keep track of their inputs to casual and close relationships. Specifically, we would expect people in casual relationships to monitor their inputs more closely than people in communal relationships. These expectations about the monitoring of benefits were borne out in two studies (Clark, 1984) that looked at the communal/exchange distinction in two ways. In the first study, pairs of strangers were led to believe that their partners desired either an exchange or a communal relationship, using a procedure similar to the one used by Clark and Mills (1979). All participants then worked on a joint task for which they expected a reward. The task consisted of circling numbers that were arranged in a matrix; the reward would be given according to how well the pair (rather than the individuals) performed. Participants could choose pens of the same or a different color as the one their partners used, to either obscure or highlight their unique contributions to the task.

As expected, participants who thought they had an exchange relationship with their partner chose the different-color pen significantly more often (87.5 percent of the time) than one would expect by chance. Apparently, their choice was motivated by a desire to keep track of each other's inputs so as to divide the joint reward proportionately. Participants who desired a communal relationship chose the different-color pen significantly less often than one would expect by chance (12.5 percent of the time), presumably because they felt compelled to obscure any differences in their inputs. The researchers obtained similar results when they compared the behavior of friends to the behavior of strangers. Because friendships operate according to communal norms, friends chose the same-color pen more often. And because relationships with strangers operate according to exchange norms, strangers chose the different-color pen more often.

As keeping track of inputs becomes less important in communal relationships, keeping track of the other's *needs* increases in importance. That should be true regardless of whether or not the other can reciprocate. The giving of benefits in communal relationships should be guided exclusively by an orientation to the other's needs. Such should not be the case in exchange relationships in which reciprocation—expected or actual—should determine the willingness to give a benefit. These hypotheses were confirmed in a study (Clark, Mills, & Powell, 1986) that employed a paradigm similar to the one used by Clark (1984). The main difference was that instead of actually returning benefits, participants had a chance to check whether or not their partners needed help under two conditions, reciprocation and no reciprocation. Participants who expected an exchange relationship checked more often when they knew the other might reciprocate. Participants who expected a communal relationship were not influenced by the possibility of reciprocation in checking whether their partners needed help.

Criticisms of the Communal/Exchange Distinction

Despite the impressive amount of research in its favor, the distinction between exchange and communal relationships has not been without critics. One frequent criticism is that the distinction is based on research conducted in an artificial laboratory setting, in which the type of relationship is manipulated experimentally. However, that argument is not particularly compelling because studies of the behavior of friends (e.g., Clark, 1984; Clark, Mills, & Corcoran, 1989) have produced results consistent with those obtained in studies that involve experimental manipulations of the type of relationship.

A second criticism relates to the idea that communal relationships might really be exchange relationships with a fairly long time perspective. In other words, people in communal relationships may not expect reciprocation right away, but may instead expect the giving and receiving of benefits to be even in the long run. However, that idea is not easily reconciled with the findings showing that in communal relationships people do not keep track of their inputs. Without a knowledge or awareness of one's inputs, how could people determine what to expect in the future?

The distinction between exchange and communal relationships appears then to be a meaningful one in terms of both its theoretical and its empirical foundation. However, in some ways, a communal relationship may represent an ideal world in which benefits are given solely on the basis of perceived need. In real life, that may not always be the case. Whether or not we respond to another's need may, to some extent, be determined by how legitimate we perceive the need to be. Most people, for example, are reluctant to accommodate a partner's need for "more space." Furthermore, some (Leventhal, 1976) have argued that the giving of benefits is jointly determined by need, contributions, and various distributive norms. Neither of these issues is likely to shatter the usefulness of the distinction between communal and exchange relationships, however.

INTIMACY AND RELATIONSHIP NORMS: A SUMMARY

Self-disclosure and intimate relationships are mutually transformative. Self-disclosure increases as a relationship develops, and relationships develop as a result of increased self-disclosure (Derlega et al., 1993). Early in a relationship, self-disclosure is limited to a small number of topics covered at a fairly superficial level. As the relationship develops, the breadth and depth of self-disclosure increase to include a wider range of topics covered in more depth (Altman & Taylor, 1973). Adhering to the principle of self-disclosure reciprocity promotes intimacy and allows attributions about an individual's positive characteristics (Berg & Archer, 1980; Reis & Shaver, 1988). Self-disclosure continues to be important in mature relationships, though it declines as partners come to know each other better. Much of the decline is explained by a shift from disclosures that are high in evaluative intimacy to disclosures that are high in descriptive intimacy (Antill & Cotton, 1987). Unlike relationships with strangers, intimate relationships are guided by communal norms (Clark & Mills, 1979). Intimates generally are not concerned with the comparability of benefits given and received (Mills & Clark, 1994). The giving and receiving of benefits is based on the other's need, rather than expectations about the possibility of reciprocation (Clark, 1984). Consequently, partners in a communal relationship do not keep track of their inputs into a joint task (Clark, 1984), but closely monitor their partners' needs (Clark, Mills, & Powell, 1986). Liking depends on the extent to which individuals follow the norms guiding communal and exchange relationships (Clark & Mills, 1979).

Think Like a Social Psychologist

Making connections

—In Chapter 4, we divided the self into the material, spiritual, and the social self. Which part of the self would you disclose about on a first date? Which aspects might you disclose early? Which ones might you disclose later?

Thinking critically

—How would you counter the claim that communal relationships are simply exchange relationships for the long term? What specific evidence would support your position?

EVALUATING RELATIONSHIP OUTCOMES: SHOULD I STAY OR SHOULD I GO?

To say that communal relationships are guided by norms centered on the other's needs provides no guarantee for a happy and lasting relationship. Communal and exchange relationships alike can be unrewarding and may be terminated. The extent to which a relationship produces unhappiness depends importantly on the degree to which it meets relationship expectations. But whether or not two people decide to go their own way depends on expectations about the availability of alternatives.

"He's not 'Mr. Right', but he's definitely 'Mr. Better-than-the-Other-ones!'"

An individual's comparison level for alternatives (CLalt) describes the outcomes she could expect from an alternative relationship

Expectations for the Relationship

Regardless of whether a relationship between two people is based on exchange or communal norms, they will occasionally be compelled to evaluate what they are getting from it. In an exchange relationship, such evaluations are determined primarily by perceptions of fairness. If your mechanic regularly overcharges you for repairs on your car, you will likely become unhappy. Whether you decide to take your business elsewhere depends at least in part on the availability of other mechanics, however. If there is little or no choice, you will probably stay with him, even though you're not a happy customer.

In communal relationships, people's evaluations are primarily determined by the extent to which the relationship meets their needs. Relationship distress can lead individuals to scrutinize what they give and what they receive. To the extent that such scrutiny results in perceptions of unfairness, it may exacerbate the distress (Grote & Clark, 2001). Thus, while perceptions of unfairness are associated with unhappiness in both exchange and communal relationships, the causal sequence is very different. In exchange relationships, perceptions of unfairness cause unhappiness. In communal relationships, unhappiness may lead to perceptions of unfairness. In either case, the decision to look for a new mechanic or a new partner depends to some extent on the availability of suitable alternatives.

Let's return to Ben and Elaine to further illustrate these points about satisfaction and stability in communal relationships. As you may recall, Ben took an entry level job to support Elaine through college and perhaps even through law school. While Elaine is perfectly happy with that sacrifice, she has some issues with Ben's reluctance to discuss his feelings. On the surface, both have at least some reason to be unhappy, but whether or not they are unhappy will depend on the standard against which they compare their outcomes. Thibaut and Kelly (1959) referred to this standard as a **comparison level (CL)**—a summary of expectations for what one should get from a relationship.

For Elaine, Ben, and just about everyone else, the comparison level can be an idealized standard such as perpetual romance, undivided loyalty, or reliable companionship. Alternatively, it can be a set of conscious expectations and hidden influences based on experiences in past relationships, parental modeling, or social comparison. As such, it can vary widely from one person to the next, and can even change over time. For example, Ben's CL may be fairly low, based on his previous relationship with Mrs. Robinson, which was limited to casual sex. Elaine's CL may be low to the extent that it is based on her parents' relationship, but may be high to the extent

SOCIAL PSYCHOLOGY AND THE LAW: LEGAL DISCRIMINATION AGAINST SINGLES?

The national debate over gay marriage has heightened our collective awareness of the many benefits, legal and otherwise, of being married. Does that mean society discriminates against singles? Some (DePaulo, 2006; DePaulo & Morris, 2005; Morris, Sinclair & DePaulo, 2007) have argued that single people suffer a number of disadvantages, including forms of outright legal discrimination. The U.S. Civil Rights Commission and the Equal Employment Opportunity Commission aim to assure equal protection under the law, regardless of race, color, national origin, sex, age, religion, or disability. However, neither covers civil (marital) status.

Why should civil status be included in the list of protected categories? Numerous studies have shown that compared to married men, single men earn lower salaries and are less likely to receive promotions in a broad range of professions (Bellas, 1992; Budig & England, 2001; Keith, 1986). Single and married people contribute to Social Security at the same rate, but their contributions are treated differently when they die. A surviving spouse may be eligible for a portion of the deceased spouse's benefits, but a single person's contributions go back into the system at his or her death. Singles also receive less favorable treatment regarding their estate taxes, capital gains on the sale of their homes, auto insurance, and housing. Finally, compared to married women, single women have more difficulty qualifying for in vitro fertilization and adoption (Millbank, 1997).

Legal discrimination against singles may be rooted in a pervasive ideology of marriage and family (DePaulo, 2006; DePaulo & Morris, 2005). Support for this idea comes from an experimental study, in which undergraduate research participants were asked to act as landlords (Morris, Sinclair, & DePaulo, 2007). In considering rental applications from a married couple, an unmarried heterosexual couple, and a pair of same-sex friends, 80 percent of participants decided to rent their property to the married couple. Only 12 percent chose to rent to the unmarried couple, and 8 percent to the same-sex friends.

that it is based on social comparisons to friends with devoted and perhaps doting husbands. To make a long story short, whether Ben and Elaine are happy depends not on some absolute measure of what they get from their relationship, but on how their outcomes stack up against their expectations.

	I	II	III	IV
High				
	O	CLalt	CL	CLalt
	CL	O	O	CL
	CLalt	CL	CLalt	O
Low				

Figure 10.4: Four Possible Ways in which Relationship Outcomes (O) can be Compared Against Expectations for the Relationship (CL) and Expectations for Alternatives (CLalt)

Source: Thibaut, J. W., & Kelley, H. H. (1959). *The social psychology of groups.* New York: Wiley.

While experiencing outcomes that fall below their expectations may make Ben and Elaine unhappy, whether or not they will contemplate leaving the relationship depends on their **comparison level for alternatives (CLalt)**, a standard that describes the outcomes they could expect from an alternative relationship. To the extent that their current outcomes exceed their CLalt, they are dependent on their relationship, even when their outcomes fall below their CLs. If Elaine's only alternatives are to return to her parents or beg stodgy Carl to take her back, she is likely to stay with Ben, even if she thinks she deserves more from the relationship. In any event, trading a relationship for singlehood has some surprising and adverse consequences, as the Social Psychology and the Law box on **page 465** shows.

Theoretically, the permutations of outcomes (O), comparison levels (CL), and comparison levels for alternatives (CLalt) can produce eight different configurations of varying satisfaction and dependence. The most empirically probable scenarios are depicted in **Figure 10.4**.

In scenario I, Elaine finds herself in a relationship marked by *attractive stability*. Her outcomes exceed both her expectations for the relationship (CL) and her expectations regarding alternatives. She is happy with the relationship, yet at the same time highly dependent, because her outcomes from an alternative relationship would be lower than her outcomes from her relationship with Ben. In scenario II, Elaine finds herself in a relationship marked by *attractive instability*. Although her outcomes exceed her expectations, she could do even better in an alternative relationship. Scenario III shows Elaine in a relationship marked by *unattractive stability* that mimics the situation mentioned at the beginning of this section. She may not be happy with what she's getting, but the alternative (stodgy Carl) is even worse. She is thus highly dependent on the relationship, and is likely to stick with Ben, despite her obvious unhappiness. Finally, in scenario IV, Elaine finds herself in a relationship marked by *unattractive instability*. She is unhappy, yet not dependent.

In scenario IV, whether or not Elaine decides to end her relationship with Ben depends on at least one additional variable—her level of **investment** in the relationship (Rusbult, Martz, & Agnew, 1998). Investments are defined as all the things a person has put into a relationship that would be lost by ending it (Rusbult, 1983). They include temporal investments, such as the time already spent in the relationship, along with the tangible investments of coupled life like homeownership, children, and friends (Goodfriend & Agnew, 2009). The

SOCIAL PSYCHOLOGY ENCOUNTERS THE BRIGHT SIDE: MAKING RELATIONSHIPS LAST THROUGH COMMITMENT AND SACRIFICE

Rusbult's (1983) investment model predicts that a partner's satisfaction, alternatives, and level of investment will determine his or her level of commitment to a relationship. Consequently, they should all contribute to a relationship's stability and longevity. This idea has been supported by studies of heterosexual dating relationships among college students, married couples of various ages, gay and lesbian couples, and close friendships (Rusbult, 1983; Kurdek, 1992; Lin & Rusbult; 1995; Rusbult & Buunk, 1993). These studies also show that in the presence of an attractive alternative, low levels of satisfaction and investment are highly predictive of a decision to leave the relationship. Strong commitment thus appears to be an important mechanism for the maintenance of close relationships. Strongly committed individuals may be more willing than others to make personal sacrifices for their partners and their relationships (Van Lange, Rusbult, Drigotas, Arriaga, Witcher, & Cox, 1997).

chances that a person will leave a relationship decrease as the level of investment in the relationship increases (Rusbult, 1983). Elaine's investment in her relationship with Ben is high—after all, she alienated her parents and left her husband at the altar. Consequently, she may be reluctant to leave Ben, even in the presence of a promising alternative.

Ultimately, a person's level of investment, relationship satisfaction, and alternatives combine to determine her level of **commitment** to a relationship (Rusbult, 1983). At the same time, a person's level of commitment determines her evaluation of alternatives. People who are strongly committed to a relationship tend to devalue the attractiveness of possible alternatives (Johnson & Rusbult, 1989). In other words, they are less likely to find greener grass on the other side of the fence, even though they may not be completely satisfied with their relationships (Arriaga, Reed, Goodfriend, & Agnew, 2006; Le & Agnew, 2003). For more on the importance of commitment to a relationship, see the Social Psychology Encounters the Bright Side box **above.**

Expectations for One's Partner

By now, we hope we have convinced you that people's expectations of what they should get out of a relationship play an important role in how happy or satisfied they are with their real-life relationships. Of course, in addition to such abstract ideas, people also have specific expectations of their partners. Does holding positive expectations about a partner's virtues and faults help a relationship? There are some good reasons to ask this question. On the one hand, and in keeping with poet Alexander Pope's exhortation, we can avoid disappointment by holding low expectations. Conversely, as we saw in Chapter 4, positive illusions can have profound beneficial effects on our well-being. As a result, holding positive illusions about our partners may have similarly beneficial effects for our relationships.

Support for this idea comes from a couple of studies (Murray, Homes, & Griffin, 1996a; 1996b) that looked at the extent to which individuals' relationship satisfaction was influenced by the degree to which they idealized their partners' virtues (for example, patience, understanding), faults (for example, moodiness, childishness), and general social commodities (for example, self-assuredness, intelligence). In general, participants in these studies saw their partners in a more positive light than they saw themselves, suggesting a tendency toward **idealization**. More important, the extent to which the partners in a relationship idealized each other was correlated with how happy and satisfied they were with their relationship. In other words, those who looked at their partners in an idealized fashion were relatively happy, whereas those who looked at their partners more realistically were relatively unhappy. One possible reason for the positive relationship between idealization and happiness may be the propensity of those who idealize their partners to persist in a relationship, even in light of doubts and conflicts (Murray, Holmes, & Griffin, 1996b).

Before we conclude that idealizing one's partner is the key to happiness in a relationship, we need to keep two things in mind. First, the findings from both studies are correlational, to the extent that they are based on variables that were measured at the same time. This makes pinpointing the causal direction between idealization and happiness difficult. Of course, idealization could lead to happiness, but the possibility that happiness may lead to idealization is equally plausible. Second, the results present a snapshot of couples who had been together for an average of only 19 months (Murray, Holmes, & Griffin, 1996a) and 6.5 years (Murray, Holmes, & Griffin, 1996b). Thus, they tell us little about the effects of idealization over time. Finally, as with everything else in life, moderation seems to be key when it comes to idealizing our partners. Too little or too much of it can have detrimental effects on how much they like us (Tomlinson et al., 2014).

Figure 10.5: The Moderating Effects of Behavior on the Association Between Expectations and the Trajectory of Marital Satisfaction

Source: McNulty, J. K., & Karney, B. R. (2004). Positive expectations in the early years of marriage: Should couples expect the best or brace for the worst? *Journal of Personality and Social Psychology, 86*, 729–743.

When examined over a period of time, the rosy picture between positive expectations and relationship satisfaction becomes a bit more blurry. McNulty and Karney (2004) measured partner expectations and relationship satisfaction among 300 married couples over a period of four years. Measures were taken at five points in time, beginning at six months and ending with four years. The findings from this study not only qualify the power of positive expectations; they also shed light on the processes through which partner expectations exert their effects.

Over the four-year period, positive expectations had their most beneficial effects on relationship satisfaction in individuals who made positive attributions for their partners' behavior. Initially positive expectations were related to a decrease in relationship satisfaction among those who made negative attributions for their partners' behavior. In other words, positive expectations appear to be most beneficial for individuals who are able to confirm them through positive attributions for relevant behavior. They have a detrimental effect on those who fail to confirm them through their attributions (see **Figure 10.5**).

Imagine, for example, that Elaine entered her relationship with Ben believing that he was trustworthy (a positive expectation). But imagine that Ben often comes home late from work and often does not call when his job takes him out of town. If Elaine explains Ben's behavior by reasoning that he is busy supporting her financially, she will likely remain happy with the relationship. But if she attributes his behavior to cheating (remember that he once had an affair with her mother), her expectations will be shattered, and her satisfaction with the relationship will decline more profoundly than it would have in the absence of positive expectations about his trustworthiness.

Moreover, specific partner expectations can interact with more general relationship expectations. Consider, for example, a couple's transition to parenthood. The birth of the first child represents a major transition that often decreases relationship satisfaction, particularly for mothers (Belsky, Rovine, & Fish, 1989; Cowan & Cowan, 1988). Part of this decrease in satisfaction may be due to societal norms that place the responsibility for child rearing squarely on the mother's shoulders. Not surprisingly, then, relationship satisfaction among mothers tends to bottom out when children are very young (and very needy) and when the distribution of household chores is uneven (Dew & Wilcox, 2011, Keyzer & Schenk, 2012). At the same time, such a decline in relationship satisfaction is neither universal nor inevitable. For example, Ruble, Fleming, Hackel, and Stangor (1988) found that among many first-time parents, relationship satisfaction remained relatively high and was quite comparable to that of nonparents.

To make sense of these seemingly contradictory findings, Hackel and Ruble (1992) compared married couples' relationship satisfaction during pregnancy with their satisfaction four months after the first baby was born. Men and women alike reported a decline in marital happiness, along with an unequal distribution of child rearing and housekeeping chores. And yes, by and large, mothers did more than their fair share of those chores, and more than they had expected to do. Although this finding suggests a straightforward relationship between disconfirmed positive partner expectations and marital dissatisfaction, one group of mothers provided a curious, yet theoretically important, exception. Mothers with traditional attitudes about the division of labor in marriage actually became happier when their husbands contributed less than they had expected. Even though their husbands' behavior disconfirmed their specific expectations, it confirmed their expectations about the divergent roles of men and women in domestic matters. Of course, marital happiness declined steeply for mothers with egalitarian expectations whose husbands contributed less than they had expected. In fact, the disillusionment caused by such massive disconfirmation of their expectations could become the seed of later conflicts.

EVALUATING RELATIONSHIP OUTCOMES: A SUMMARY

Relationship distress may cause individuals to scrutinize their outcomes more closely (Grote & Clark, 2001). The extent to which such scrutiny leads to unhappiness with the relationship depends on individuals' expectations of what they deserve (Thibaut & Kelly, 1959). Decisions about whether or not to leave an unsatisfying relationship hinge on the availability of attractive alternatives (Thibaut & Kelly, 1959), as well as the level of commitment to the relationship (Rusbult, 1983). Maintaining positive or even idealistic expectations about one's partner can increase relationship satisfaction (Murray, Holmes, & Griffin, 1996). Doing so is most beneficial to individuals who are able to confirm their positive expectations by making positive attributions of their partners' behavior (McNulty & Karney, 2004).

Think Like a Social Psychologist

<u>Understanding everyday behavior</u>

—In terms of comparison level theory, how might you explain the situation of a person who is "trapped" in an abusive relationship?

<u>Thinking critically</u>

—According to Rusbult's model, a person's investment, relationship satisfaction, and alternatives determine his or her commitment to a relationship. Can you think of ways in which the causal arrow might operate in reverse?

CONFLICT

The Long Shadow of Mrs. Robinson

Conflicts in relationships do not necessarily have to lead to a breakup but can be resolved in a number of positive ways

It's been 18 months since Ben snatched Elaine from the altar and "rescued" her from a doomed relationship with Carl, and just about a year since the two got married in a small, quiet ceremony at Berkeley's city hall. Elaine has few regrets. Sure, Carl was a good guy with good prospects, but she always knew he wasn't right for her. Today, as she rides the train back to San Francisco, her relationship with Ben is very much on her mind. The bright sunshine and blue sky provide a stark contrast to the gloom that has settled over their apartment in the Haight. Ben never was much of a talker, especially about his feelings. But ever since she brought up the idea of going to law school, Ben seems to have gone into an impenetrable cocoon. She knew he wouldn't be thrilled at the prospect of remaining the primary breadwinner, especially since he found little enjoyment in his job.

Suddenly, Elaine catches herself thinking that law school probably wouldn't be an issue if she had married Carl. Nor would it be an issue if Ben hadn't gotten involved in that sick relationship with her mother. Both Carl and her parents could have supported her aspirations to become an attorney without much financial sacrifice. For Ben, sending her to law school meant another four years of selling plastics, of putting his own ambitions on hold. Maybe I'm just too selfish, she thinks. Maybe I should be more like my mother and devote myself to supporting my husband. (Then again, Mom cheated on Dad—how supportive is that?)

At this point, Elaine realizes the full extent of her unhappiness. She never fully forgave Ben for his transgression. Perhaps that is the root cause of all their problems, she thinks. As she exits the train, she decides that she needs to resolve all these issues tonight, regardless of whether or not Ben is in the mood for talking.

Ben and Elaine took a circuitous route to becoming a couple. However, what's happening to them now is far from unusual. Marital satisfaction begins to decline almost as soon as the honeymoon is over. The sharpest decline occurs during the first year of marriage (Kurdek, 1992). Conflicts of one sort or another are commonplace. If nothing else, the simultaneous strivings for autonomy and affiliation, intimacy and privacy, openness and closedness can be incompatible, causing inevitable friction and planting the seeds for conflict (Gottman, 1993). The question is not so much whether a couple will experience conflict. Rather, it is *when* a conflict will occur and how the couple will deal with it.

Sources of Conflict

Take a moment to reflect on the conflicts you have experienced in a past or present relationship. Chances are, some of those conflicts may have originated from something you (the self) or your partner (the other) said, thought, or felt. Other conflicts may have been fundamental to your relationship ("I was looking for intimacy, but all he wanted to do was party"). Still other conflicts may have been aroused by the relationship's social context ("I was too overwhelmed by the demands of my senior year to give him what he needed)". In some instances, a conflict may have arisen simply because the relationship was not meant to be (a simple matter of fate). Because the self, the other, the relationship, and the social context all contribute to conflict (Bradbury & Fincham, 1990; 1992), virtually any close relationship will experience conflict at some point.

That is not to say that conflict is always bad for a relationship. Conflict is first and foremost transformational for a relationship, in that it can provide the impetus for change (e.g., Gottman, 1993; Peterson, 1983). The direction of the transformation is primarily a matter of conflict resolution. Conflicts that are resolved constructively can lead to growth and greater unity. In fact, in the long term, satisfaction with a relationship is strongly influenced by the extent to which it makes allowances for the expression of disagreement and even anger (Gottman & Krokoff, 1989). On the other hand, destructive conflicts that are marked by hurtful communication and continued escalation are generally damaging to all involved and frequently lead to the end of a relationship.

Stages of Conflict

The transformational view suggests that whether a conflict becomes constructive or destructive may depend in large part on how people respond to and deal with it. To better understand how people's responses can determine the course and outcome of a conflict, it is helpful to divide a conflict into stages (Peterson, 1983). In this regard, conflict has something in common with the game of chess, in the sense that both can be analyzed in terms of what happens in the beginning, middle, and end stages.

The Beginning Stages

Every conflict begins with a set of predisposing conditions, along with a specific initiating event. Unless a specific event brings predisposing conditions to the forefront, they may never lead to conflict. Elaine's continuing unhappiness with Ben's lack of communication merely predisposes the relationship toward conflict. It may have simmered for some time, but becomes particularly problematic when it gets in the way of her legal aspirations. If it brings her resentment to a boil, it could become the event that initiates the conflict. Similarly, Ben may resent having to take a job he doesn't like to support Elaine. The prospect of having to do it longer than he had expected may provoke him to initiate conflict.

In the presence of these predisposing conditions and a potential initiating event, Ben and Elaine have a choice. They can attempt to avoid the conflict and hope that the passage of time will eventually make the problem go away (Gottman, 1993). Or they can decide to engage in the conflict, in the hope that they can resolve it. At this point, their conflict moves into the middle stages.

The Middle Stages

On the face of it, engaging in conflict may seem superior to avoiding conflict. After all, negative emotions can be kept under wraps only so long and are bound to haunt us down the road (Wegner, Erber, & Zanakos, 1994). Negative emotions stemming from conflict are no exception. Trying to suppress them only exacerbates them, especially among those who are anxiously attached (Ben-Naim, Hirschberger, Ein-Dor, & Mikulincer, 2013). However, expressing negative emotions is no cakewalk, either. The way in which these are communicated determines whether a conflict will be resolved constructively or destructively.

The trouble with communicating negative emotions is that most likely, both partners in a relationship will feel bad. That situation can easily lead to a communication pattern characterized by **negative affect reciprocity**. If Ben responds to Elaine's disclosure of her resentment by disclosing his own resentment, accusing her of being unreasonable, or storming out of the apartment, he may set in motion a vicious cycle of tit-for-tat exchanges of negative feelings, which may well lead to further escalation of the conflict. Negative affect reciprocity is most common among couples who are experiencing general dissatisfaction with their relationship (Fincham, 2003; Levenson & Gottman, 1983). That is not entirely surprising, since dissatisfied couples have more negative emotions to begin with (Levenson & Gottman, 1985) and see their problems as more severe than couples who are generally happy, in spite of the conflict they are experiencing (Gottman & Levenson, 1992).

Relationship conflict is stressful (Powers, Pietromonaco, Gunlicks, & Sayer, 2006; Swann, McClarty, & Rentfrow, 2007), but whether or not a conflict is headed for a constructive solution also depends on the attributions couples make for their problems. Placing the blame on one's partner generally leads to further escalation of the conflict, pushing it toward a destructive resolution. More benevolent attributions have the opposite effect. They can lay the groundwork for constructive resolution by allowing conciliatory responses, like a reframing of the problem and a willingness to negotiate (Bradbury & Fincham, 1992; Peterson, 1983).

Closer inspection of the potential responses to conflict reveals a more detailed picture. Four types of behaviors are possible, since both destructive and constructive behavior can be either active or passive (Rusbult & Zembrodt, 1983; Rusbult, Zembrodt, & Gunn, 1982). Abusing or threatening one's partner actively harms the relationship; ignoring one's partner or refusing to deal with a problem harms the relationship in a more passive way. On the constructive side, discussing the problem or seeking counseling can actively benefit the relationship; hoping for an improvement or being supportive in the face of conflict can benefit the relationship in a more passive way. In general, the harmful effects of destructive behavior are stronger than the beneficial effects of constructive behavior (Rusbult, Johnson, & Morrow, 1986; Rusbult, Yovetich, & Verette, 1996), especially if both partners respond destructively. Research shows that couples who are generally satisfied with their relationship are more likely to choose constructive strategies. Those who are profoundly unhappy often resort to destructive strategies (Rusbult, Zembrodt, & Gunn, 1982). However, those who approach life in general with a sense of optimism are more likely to resolve common conflicts and disagreements in a constructive fashion and thus have happier and more rewarding relationships (Assad, Donnellan, & Conger, 2007; Srivastava et al., 2006).

The Termination Stage

Regardless of whether couples respond constructively or destructively, their conflict will eventually end. That does not mean it has necessarily been resolved, however. Destructive avoidance is likely to result in the termination of the relationship, as is destructive engagement, especially when both partners pursue the strategy (Rusbult, Yovetich, & Verette, 1996). Interestingly, the termination of a relationship is not a single, cataclysmic event. Rather, breakups tend to unfold in four stages (Duck, 1982). In the first intrapersonal stage, an individual thinks a lot about his or her unhappiness with the relationship. In the second dyadic stage, the couple discusses the problem and confronts the prospect of breaking up. In the third, or social, stage, the couple brings the impending breakup to the attention of friends and family. Finally, in the second intrapersonal stage, the now-separated partners attempt to figure out what went wrong and how to get over the breakup. In the process, they need to redefine themselves in the absence of a partner with whom their life was deeply intertwined, requiring adjustments to the structure and clarity of their self-concept (Slotter, Gardner, & Finkel, 2010). Struggling to find the answer to the question of "who am I without you?" contributes greatly to the emotional distress associated with most romantic breakups.

Constructive engagement is likely to result in negotiation communication in the service of a solution (Peterson, 1983). Couples may resolve the conflict by agreeing to structural improvements that create more favorable conditions for the relationship. For example, they may decide to spend more time together or to avoid going to sleep upset. The success of such structural improvements depends on the strength of their initial affection. Open communication, assertions of personal worth, and allowances for personal differences all improve the chances for a positive solution.

When a conflict can be resolved only by satisfying the original goals of both partners, a couple may reach an integrative agreement that permits both partners to achieve their respective goals. If one partner's striving for autonomy clashes with the other partner's desire for intimacy, the couple may find ways to allow for both. For example, they may decide to devote Saturdays to couple activities and Sundays to watching football.

Because integrative agreements allow both partners to meet their respective goals, they may not work when the conflict stems from finite resources such as money. In such situations, a compromise that reduces the aspirations of both partners may be the best bet for a successful resolution. For example, a couple that is experiencing a conflict over pocket money may decide to allocate equal amounts of money to both partners.

Structural improvements, integrative agreements, and compromise all benefit both partners in the couple. Of course, resolution of a conflict may be achieved by one partner dominating the other, so that one partner wins and the other loses. Such a solution has some undesirable side effects. It distributes power unevenly, adding an element of coercion that puts the relationship on shaky ground and may become the predisposing condition for a new conflict.

Ben and Elaine finally had the talk Elaine wanted to have, yet dreaded. Much to her surprise, it went far better than she had expected. After some initial defensiveness, Ben began to open up. As it turned out, Ben had no objection to her going to law school. In fact, he found the idea of being married to a high-flying trial lawyer almost titillating. Elaine learned that Ben's strange quietness did not indicate detachment or even alienation; he had just been preoccupied. Steven, one of his coworkers, had been telling him that the future was not in plastics per se, but in one particular form of plastic: silicon. Computers were getting smaller and smaller, and might someday reach the point at which they could fit on a desk. Such computers might actually become a household item. Ben realized that it was a bit of a pipe dream, but he talked about it with such excitement that Elaine felt she should help him to pursue the idea. She decided to spend a couple of years as a paralegal before applying to law school. That way she could contribute to making ends meet while building up her law school credentials.

Ben and Elaine talked well into the night—not just about what had troubled them, but about everything under the sun. They laughed more than they had in months, and the sex that followed was great. Their newfound bliss was interrupted only briefly by Ben's apology for his affair with Elaine's mother. Even though they didn't talk much about it, Elaine knew then that she would find a way to forgive Ben.

Forgiving

When interpersonal transgressions are the cause of conflict in a relationship, **forgiving** is often called for. Interpersonal transgressions are behaviors that violate the implicit or explicit norms governing relationships (Finkel, Rusbult, Kumashiro, & Hannon, 2002). As such, they can include everything from belittling one's partner in public to violating the norm of sexual exclusivity. These transgressions frequently cause feelings of betrayal, sadness, and anger in the victim (Finkel et al., 2002). Perpetrators may experience sadness, shame, and guilt (Baumeister, Stillwell, & Wotman, 1990; Riek, Root-Luna, & Schnabelrauch, in press). Victims may seek vengeance or retribution; perpetrators may try to explain their transgressions in ways that would justify their behavior (Finkel et al., 2002; Stillwell & Baumeister, 1997).

Clearly, both victims and perpetrators of an interpersonal transgression are in a difficult position. However, the couple's ability to move beyond the pain created by a transgression depends on the victim's willingness to forgive. Forgiving involves a transformation of motivation that replaces the destructive tendencies in the relationship with constructive feelings, thoughts, and behavior (McCullough, Worthington, & Rachal, 1997). This transformation is especially likely to occur among individuals who are otherwise highly satisfied with their relationship (Schumann, 2012), as well as those who place a high value on it and don't feel that forgiving would put them at risk of being exploited by their partner (Burnette, McCullough, Van Tongeren, & Davis, 2012; McCullough, Kurzban, & Tabak, 2012). In forgiving the perpetrator, the victim essentially cancels the interpersonal debt created by the perpetrator's act of betrayal (Finkel et al., 2002).

To be sure, the cancellation of such debts is not a simple process. It is especially difficult

"HOW MANY TIMES DO I HAVE TO SAY I'M SORRY?"

Apologies can lead to forgiving to the extent that they elicit empathy for the transgressor for those with attachment anxiety (Finkel, Burnette, & Scissors, 2007) and those whose anger fuels prolonged rumination (McCullough, Bono, & Root, 2007). Yet forgiving has obvious benefits. For the couple, enacting forgiving responses following a transgression helps initiate efforts at repairing the damage to a relationship and fosters the restoration of interpersonal harmony (Fincham, Beach, & Davila, 2004; Rusbult et al., 2005). For individuals, forgiving has tangible benefits in the form of lessened negative feelings (Worthington & Scherer, 2004), as well as improved physical health (Toussaint et al., 2001) and psychological functioning (Witvliet et al.,

Figure 10.6: The Sequential Process by which an Apology Can Lead to Conflict Resolution

Source: McCullough, M. E., Worthington, E. L., & Rachal, K. C. (1997). Interpersonal forgiving in close relationships. *Journal of Personality and Social Psychology, 73,* 321–336.

2001). To some, these benefits can be offset by some steep costs, as victims who forgive put themselves at risk of being victimized by their partners in the future (McNulty, 2011).

How do victims of betrayal manage to forgive? It appears that the behavior of the perpetrators following the transgression plays a key role. Making amends greatly increases victims' motivation to forgive and can serve as a starting point for a successful resolution of a prior betrayal (Hannon et al., 2010). But even a simple apology can often go a long way toward eliciting forgiveness, especially if it is elaborate and includes an admission of guilt (Darby & Schlenker, 1982; Weiner, Graham, Peter, & Zmuidinas, 1991). But just why is an apology so important? Apologies help transform relationship-destructive motivation because they elicit empathy for the transgressor. As we will see in Chapter 12, empathy—taking another's perspective—lies at the heart of altruistic behavior. Putting one's own bad feelings and destructive inclinations aside for the greater good of the relationship requires altruism. Thus, apologies prompt forgiveness by eliciting empathy for the perpetrator. Forgiveness, in turn, brings opportunities for conciliatory behavior, allowing the relationship to get back on track (McCollough, Worthington, & Rachal, 1997): see **Figure 10.6**.

Though apologies are important, forgiving can occur for other reasons as well. Have you ever forgiven someone even in the absence of an apology, or before the apology was offered? Have you ever failed to forgive, even though you received a sincere apology filled with admissions of guilt? If so, your level of commitment may have influenced your willingness to forgive in the first instance and your refusal to forgive in the second. Commitment is related to forgiveness and positive relationship behaviors in a couple of ways. First, commitment is linked to interdependence. Because highly committed couples depend on one another for many different outcomes, their interdependence may compel them to take a broader view of each other's transgressions. Second, commitment inspires behavior that is directed toward the other's welfare, which is antithetical to holding a grudge. Finkel and his colleagues (2002) have shown that commitment is indeed predictive of participants' willingness to forgive acts of betrayal. Finkel et al.'s study also provides evidence that commitment may influence willingness to forgive outside of their awareness. Rather than measuring how committed participants were to their relationships, these researchers primed different levels of commitment by asking participants to either

SOCIAL PSYCHOLOGY ENCOUNTERS THE DARK SIDE: FORGIVENESS CAN BE HAZARDOUS TO YOUR HEALTH

Complete the following sentence: "The most dangerous place for a woman is the _____." Surveys conducted in the United States and elsewhere suggest that "the home" may provide the most appropriate completion for this sentence. An estimated 21 percent to 34 percent of all women in the United States will be assaulted by a male partner during their lifetimes (Browne, 1993). Each year, well over four million women are *severely* assaulted by their male partners (Strauss & Gelles, 1990). Studies conducted in Japan (Kozu, 1999) and Russia (Horne, 1999) paint an even bleaker picture.

The causes of relationship violence are manifold. Some have to do with the abuser's dispositions. Men with a high need for power and control and a low need for affiliation are particularly likely to strike out against their female partners (Mason & Blankenship, 1987). Another cause is the lack of legal protection afforded to victims of relationship violence. Violence against a stranger usually leads to arrest and full prosecution. Domestic violence will lead to arrest and prosecution only if the victim demands it and presses charges. Such differential treatment may well convince an abuser that he is not really committing a crime.

In describing the "battered woman syndrome," Walker (1984) pointed out that relationship violence is often cyclical. During times of rising tension, the woman may withdraw to avoid doing anything to anger her partner. Rather than producing the desired outcome, however, her withdrawal often contributes to an acute incident of battery, after which the abuser may become contrite and apologize for his actions.

As we have seen, receiving an apology is the first step in a causal sequence that leads to forgiveness (McCullough, Worthington, & Rachal, 1997). Although forgiveness can have many positive outcomes for a relationship, there is evidence that it can also make victims susceptible to future abuse. A longitudinal study that followed 72 newlywed couples over their first four years of marriage (McNulty, 2011) found that spouses who tended to forgive their partners for the verbal and physical abuse they inflicted continued to suffer abuse at a steady and consistent rate. Spouses who were less willing to forgive experienced declines in both forms of aggression over the four-year period. Evidently, forgiveness removes the victim's anger and criticism that would hold the abuser at bay (McNulty & Russell, 2010; Overall et al., 2009).

write about dependence and commitment (for example, "Describe two ways in which your life has become linked to your partner's") or about independence and lack of commitment (for example, "Describe an activity you enjoy engaging in when your partner is not around"). Following the priming task, participants responded to several hypothetical scenarios of betrayal. Participants in whom high commitment had been primed were more likely than others to indicate that they would respond to acts of betrayal by discussing them with their partners. Those in whom low commitment had been primed were more likely than others to indicate that they would terminate the relationship. So, commitment appears to act as a hidden influence on forgiving.

These findings on the relationship between commitment and forgiveness highlight the importance of a relationship's characteristics. A willingness or unwillingness to forgive may not be determined primarily by individual dispositions such as the presence or absence of a tendency for vengeance. Nor does it seem to primarily be determined by specific emotions or events like an apology. Rather, commitment may be the critical ingredient that transforms initially negative motivations into the positive, relationship-enhancing motivation to forgive. For the adverse effects of forgiving, see the Social Psychology Encounters the Dark Side box on **page 476**.

CONFLICT: A SUMMARY

All intimate relationships include conflict, which can arise from the behavior of either partner, from aspects of the relationship itself, or from the couple's social context (Bradbury & Fincham, 1990; 1992). Conflict can transform a relationship either positively or negatively, depending on how the couple manages it (Gottman, 1993). Reciprocal negative affect during the middle stages of a conflict will often have destructive outcomes for the relationship (Levenson & Gottman, 1985. Other destructive conflict resolution strategies include actively threatening or harming the other and passively ignoring the other. Positive attributions for a partner's behavior, on the other hand, can contribute to constructive conflict resolution (Bradbury & Fincham, 1992), as can discussion of the problem, or counseling, and even the hope that the passage of time will lead to improvement (Rusbult & Zembrodt, 1983). Happy couples are more likely than unhappy couples to choose constructive strategies (Rusbult, Zembrodt, & Gunn, 1982). In the termination stage of conflict, they may achieve a positive resolution through structural improvements in the relationship, integrative agreements, or compromise (Peterson, 1983).

When interpersonal transgressions produce conflict, forgiving the perpetrator is often the most appropriate path to conflict resolution. Victims are most likely to forgive a betrayal following an apology, which helps to transform relationship-destructive response into relationship-enhancing responses by producing empathy for the perpetrator (McCullough, Worthington, & Rachal, 1997). The willingness to forgive is further determined by characteristics of the relationship, particularly the couple's level of commitment (Finkel et al., 2002).

Think Like a Social Psychologist

Explaining everyday behavior
—A couple experiences frequent conflicts about the level of affection that is exchanged in their relationship (one wants more while the other is fine with the way things are). Which of the three conflict resolution strategies—integrative agreement, structural improvement, compromise—would be best suited to resolve the conflict? What additional conditions must be met to make the particular strategy work?

Thinking critically
—According to McCullough et al. (1997), forgiving involves a transformation of motivation that replaces destructive tendencies with constructive thoughts, feelings, and behaviors. How might the strength of the initial motivation influence this process?

HIDDEN INFLUENCES ON RELATIONSHIPS: A SUMMARY

Evolutionary perspective on love: considers love the emotional glue that promotes survival of offspring through pair bonding

Misattribution of arousal: the process that promotes the experience of love through arousing events external and internal to intimate relationships

Attachment: the emotional bond that exists between infants and caregivers as well as romantic partners; the basis for partner choices

Secure base schema: feelings of closeness, love, and support that influence relationship processing by producing empathy

Comparison levels: A set of consciously or unconsciously derived expectations regarding what a person deserves from a relationship

Commitment: A quality of a relationship or a relationship prime related to forgiving

KEY TERMS AND DEFINITIONS

Prototype of love: a cognitive representation that contains the features most commonly associated with love

Cultural universality of romantic love: the observation that romantic love is present in the vast majority of cultures; it parallels the universality of marriage

Misattribution of arousal: the process by which arousal generated by one source is erroneously attributed to a different source

Love styles: individual differences in the ways people experience love

Triangular theory of love: a theory that describes different forms of love, based on the level of intimacy, passion, and commitment in a relationship

Passionate love: a form of love characterized by an intense longing for another

Unrequited love: love for another who does not reciprocate

Companionate love: the attraction we feel for others with whom our lives are deeply intertwined

Attachment: the emotional bond that exists between infants and caregivers, as well as among adult romantic partners

Self-disclosure: a process that involves the sharing of thoughts, feelings, and experiences

Social penetration: the growth of self-disclosure in terms of breadth and depth as a relationship develops

Self-disclosure reciprocity: the matching of self-disclosures between two people in terms of intimacy and emotional tone

Communal relationships: relationships between close others, in which the giving and receiving of benefits is based on need and the desire to please the other

Exchange relationships: relationships between strangers and casual acquaintances, where the giving and receiving of benefits is guided by principles of equal exchange

Comparison level (CL): a summary of expectations for what one should get from a relationship

Comparison level for alternatives (CLALT): expectations regarding the outcomes a person would expect from an alternative relationship

Relationship investment: the things a person has put into a relationship that would be lost by ending it

Commitment: an orientation toward a relationship determined by a person's level of investment, relationship satisfaction, and alternatives

Idealization: a tendency to see one's partner in a more positive light than they see themselves that is related to relationship satisfaction

Negative affect reciprocity: a communication pattern, in which two people respond to disclosures of negative affect in kind, resulting in the escalation of a conflict

Forgiving: a response to a relationship transgression that involves the transformation of motivation to replace destructive tendencies with constructive feelings, thoughts, and behaviors

REFERENCES

Ainsworth, M. D. S., Blehar, M. C., Waters, E., & Wall, S. (1978). *Patterns of attachment: A psychological study of the strange situation*. Hillsdale, NJ: Erlbaum.

Altman, I., & Taylor, D. A. (1973). *Social penetration: The development of interpersonal relationships*. New York: Holt, Rinehart and Winston.

Antill, J. K., & Cotton, S. (1987). Self-disclosure between husbands and wives: Its relationship to sex roles and marital happiness. *Australian Journal of Psychology, 39*, 11–24.

Aron, A., Fisher, H., Mashek, D. J., Strong, G., Li, H., & Brown, L. L. (2005). Reward, motivation, and emotion systems associated with early-stage intense romantic love. *Journal of Neurophysiology, 94*, 327–337.

Aron, A., & Henkemeyer, L. (1995). Marital satisfaction and passionate love. *Journal of Social and Personal Relationships, 12*, 139–146.

Arriaga, X. B., Reed, J. T., Goodfriend, W., & Agnew, C. R. (2006). Relationship perceptions and persistence: Do fluctuations in perceived partner commitment undermine dating relationships? *Journal of Personality and Social Psychology, 91*, 1045–1065.

Assad, K. K., Donnellan, M. B., & Conger, R. D. (2007). Optimism: An enduring resource for romantic relationships. *Journal of Personality and Social Psychology, 93*, 285–297.

Bartholomew, K., & Horowitz, L. M. (1991). Attachment styles among young adults: A test of the four category model. *Journal of Personality and Social Psychology, 61*, 226–244.

Baumeister, R. F., & Bratslavsky, E. (1999). Passion, intimacy, and time: Passionate love as a function of change in intimacy. *Personality and Social Psychology Review, 3*, 49–67.

Baumeister, R. F., Stillwell, A., & Wotman, S. R. (1990). Victim and perpetrator accounts of interpersonal conflict: Autobiographical narratives about anger. *Journal of Personality and Social Psychology, 59*, 994–1005.

Baumeister, R. F., Wotman, S. R., & Stillwell, M. A. (1993). Unrequited love: On heartbreak, anger, guilt, scriptlessness, and humiliation. *Journal of Personality and Social Psychology, 64*, 377–394.

Beach, S. R. H., & Tesser, A. (1978). Love in marriage: A cognitive account. In R. J. Sternberg & M. L. Barnes (Eds.), *The psychology of love* (pp. 330–355). New Haven, CT: Yale University Press.

Bellas, M. (1992). The effects of marital status and wives' employment on the salaries of faculty men: The (house) wife bonus. *Gender and Society, 6*, 609–622.

Belsky, J., Rovine, M., & Fish, M. (1989). The developing family system. In M. Gunnar (Ed.), *Systems and development: Minnesota symposium on child psychology* (Vol. 22). Hillsdale, NJ: Erlbaum.

Ben-Naim, S., Hirschberger, G., Ein-Dor, T., & Mikulincer, M. (2013). An experimental study of emotion regulation during conflict interactions: The moderating role of attachment orientation. *Emotion, 13*, 506–519.

Berg, J. H. (1984). Development of friendship between roommates. *Journal of Personality and Social Psychology, 46*, 346–356.

Berg, J. H., & Archer, R. L (1980). Disclosure or concern: A second look at liking for the norm breaker. *Journal of Personality, 48*, 245–257.

Berg, J. H., & Archer, R. L. (1982). Responses to self-disclosure and interaction goals. *Journal of Experimental Social Psychology, 18*, 501–512.

Berg, J. H., & Clark, M. S. (1986). Differences in social exchange between intimate and other relationships: Gradually evolving or quickly apparent? In V. J. Derlega & B. A.

Winstead (Eds.), *Friendship and social interaction* (pp. 101–128). New York: Springer-Verlag.

Berg, J. H., & McQuinn, R. D. (1986). Attraction and exchange in continuing and noncontinuing dating relationships. *Journal of Personality and Social Psychology, 50*, 942–952.

Bierhoff, H. (1991). Twenty years of research on love: Theory, results, and prospects for the future. *German Journal of Psychology, 15*, 95–117.

Bowlby, J. (1969). *Attachment and loss: Vol. 1. Attachment.* New York: Basic Books.

Bowlby, J. (1973). *Attachment and loss: Vol. 2. Separation.* New York: Basic Books.

Bowlby, J. (1980). *Attachment and loss: Vol. 3. Loss, sadness, and depression.* New York: Basic Books.

Bowlby, J. (1982). Attachment and loss: Retrospect and prospect. *American Journal of Orthopsychiatry, 53*, 664–678.

Bradbury, T. N., & Fincham, F. D. (1990). Attributions in marriage: Review and critique. *Psychological Bulletin, 107*, 3–33.

Bradbury, T. N., & Fincham, F. D. (1992). Attributions and behavior in marital interaction. *Journal of Personality and Social Psychology, 63*, 613–628.

Brumbaugh, C. C., & Fraley, R. C. (2006). Transference and attachment: How do attachment patterns get carried forward from one relationship to the next? *Personality and Social Psychology Bulletin, 32*, 552–560.

Brown, D. E. (1991). *Human universals.* New York: McGraw-Hill.

Browne, A. (1993). Violence against women by male partners: Prevalence, outcomes, and policy implications. *American Psychologist, 48*, 1077–1087.

Budig, M. J., & England, P. (2001). The wage penalty for motherhood. *American Sociological Review, 662*, 204–225.

Burnette, J. L., McCullough, M. E., Van Tongeren, D. R., & Davis, D. E. (2012). Forgiveness results from integrating information about relationship value and exploitation risk. *Personality and Social Psychology Bulletin, 38*, 345–356.

Buss, D. M. (2003). *The evolution of desire: Strategies of human mating* (revised ed.). New York: Basic Books.

Cacioppo, S., Grafton, S. T., & Bianchi-DeMicheli, F. (2012). The speed of passionate love as a subliminal prime: A high-density electrical neuroimaging study. *NeuroQuantology, 10*, 715–724.

Campbell, L., Lackenbauer, S. D., & Muise, A. (2006). When is being known or adored by romantic partners most beneficial? Self-perceptions, relationship length, and responses to partner's self-verifying and enhancing appraisals. *Personality and Social Psychology Bulletin, 32*, 1283–1294.

Campbell, L., Simpson, J. A., Boldry, J., & Kashy, D. A. (2005). Perceptions of conflict and support in romantic relationships: The role of attachment anxiety. *Journal of Personality and Social Psychology, 88*, 510–531.

Carpenter, E. M., & Kirkpatrick, L. A. (1996). Attachment style and presence of a romantic partner as moderators of psychophysiological responses to a stressful laboratory situation. *Personal Relationships, 3,* 351–367.

Chopik, W. J., Edelstein, R. S., & Fraley, R. C. (2013). From the cradle to the grave: Age differences in attachment from early adulthood to old age. *Journal of Personality, 81,* 171–183.

Clark, M. S. (1984). Record keeping in two types of relationships. *Journal of Personality and Social Psychology, 47,* 549–577.

Clark, M. S., & Mills, J. (1979). Interpersonal attraction in exchange and communal relationships. *Journal of Personality and Social Psychology, 37,* 12–24.

Clark, M. S., Mills, J., & Corcoran, D. M. (1989). Keeping track of needs and inputs of friends and strangers. *Personality and Social Psychology Bulletin, 15,* 533–542.

Clark, M. S., Mills, J., & Powell, M. C. (1986). Keeping track of needs in communal and exchange relationships. *Journal of Personality and Social Psychology, 51,* 333–338.

Cohen, M. X., & Shaver, P. R. (2004). Avoidant attachment and hemispheric lateralization of the processing of attachment and emotion-related words. *Cognition and Emotion, 18,* 799–813.

Collins, N. L., & Feeney, B. C. (2004). Working models of attachment shape perceptions of social support: Evidence from experimental and observational studies. *Journal of Personality and Social Psychology, 87,* 363–383.

Collins, N. L., & Read, S. J. (1990). Adult attachment, working models, and relationship quality in dating couples. *Journal of Personality and Social Psychology, 58,* 644–663.

Cowan, P. A., & Cowan, C. P. (1988). Changes in marriage during the transition to parenthood: Must we blame the baby? In G. Y. Michaels & W. A. Goldberg (Eds.), *The transition to parenthood: Current theory and research.* Cambridge, UK: Cambridge University Press.

Darby, B. W., & Schlenker, B. R. (1982). Children's reactions to apologies. *Journal of Personality and Social Psychology, 43,* 742–753.

Davidson, B., Balswick, J., & Halverson, C. F. (1983). Affective self-disclosure and marital adjustment: A test of equity theory. *Journal of Marriage and the Family, 45,* 93–102.

Davis, K. E., & Latty-Mann, H. (1987). Lovestyles and relationship quality: A contribution to validation. *Journal of Social and Personal Relationships, 4,* 409–428.

DePaulo, B. M. (2006). *Singled out: How singles are stereotyped, stigmatized, and ignored, and still live happily ever after.* New York: St. Martin's Press.

DePaulo, B. M., & Morris, W. L. (2005). Singles in Society and Science. *Psychological Inquiry, 16,* 57–83.

Del Giudice, M. (2011). Sex differences in romantic attachment: A meta-analysis. *Personality and Social Psychology Bulletin, 37,* 193–214.

Derlega, V. J., Metts, S., Petronio, S., & Margulis, S. T. (1993). *Self-disclosure.* Newbury Park, CA: Sage.

Dew, J., & Wilcox, W. B. (2011). If momma ain't happy: Explaining declines in marital satisfaction among new mothers. *Journal of Marriage and Family, 73,* 1–12.

Diener, E., & Seligman, M. E. P. (2002). Very happy people. *Psychological Science, 13,* 81–84.

Diener, E., Suh, E. M., Lucas, R. E., & Smith, H. L. (1999). Subjective well-being: Three decades of progress. *Psychological Bulletin, 125,* 276–302.

Dion, K. L., & Dion, K. K. (1993). Gender and ethnocultural comparisons in styles of love. *Psychology of Women Quarterly, 17,* 463–473.

Driscoll, R., Davis, K. W., & Lipetz, M. E. (1972). Parental interference and romantic love. *Journal of Personality and Social Psychology, 24,* 1–10.

Duck, S. (1982). A topography of relationship disengagement and dissolution. In S. Duck (Ed.), *Personal relationships 4: Dissolving personal relationships.* New York: Academic Press.

Feeney, J. A. (1995). Adult attachment and emotional control. *Personal Relationships, 2,* 143– 159.

Feeney, B. C., & Kirkpatrick, L. A. (1996). Effects of adult attachment and presence of romantic partners on physiological responses to stress. *Journal of Personality and Social Psychology, 70,* 255–270.

Feeney, B. C., & Noller, P. (1990). Attachment style as a predictor of adult romantic relationships. *Journal of Personality and Social Psychology, 58,* 281–291.

Fehr, B. (1988). Prototype analysis of the concepts of love and commitment. *Journal of Personality and Social Psychology, 55,* 557–579.

Fincham, F. D. (2003). Marital conflict: Correlates, structure, and context. *Current Directions in Psychological Science, 12,* 23–27.

Fincham, F. D., Beach, S. R. H., & Davila, J. (2004). Forgiveness and conflict resolution in marriage. *Journal of Family Psychology, 18,* 72–81.

Finkel, E. J., Rusbult, C. E., Kumashiro, M., & Hannon, P. A. (2002). Dealing with betrayal in close relationships: Does commitment promote forgiveness? *Journal of Personality and Social Psychology, 82,* 956–974.

Finkel, E. J., Burnette, J. L., & Scissors, L. E. (2007). Vengefully ever after: Destiny beliefs, state attachment anxiety, and forgiveness. *Journal of Personality and Social Psychology, 92,* 871–886.

Forgas, J. P. (2011). Affective influences on self-disclosure: Mood effects on the intimacy and reciprocity of disclosing personal information. *Journal of Personality and Social Psychology, 100,* 449–461.

Fraley, R. C. (2002). Attachment stability from infancy to adulthood: Meta-analysis and dynamic modeling of developmental mechanism. *Personality and Social Psychology Review, 6,* 123–151.

Fraley, R. C., & Shaver, P. R. (1998). Airport separations: A naturalistic study of adult attachment dynamics in separating couples. *Journal of Personality and Social Psychology, 75,* 1198–1212.

Fraley, R. C., Roisman, G. I., Booth-LaForce, C., Owen, M. T., & Holland, A. S. (2013). Interpersonal and genetic origins of adult attachment styles: A longitudinal study from infancy into early adulthood. *Journal of Personality and Social Psychology, 104,* 817–838.

Frazier, P. A., Byer, A. L., Fisher, A. R., Wright, D. M., & DeBord, K. A. (1996). Adult attachment style and partner choice: Correlational and experimental findings. *Personal Relationships, 3,* 117–136.

Freud, S. (1922). Certain neurotic mechanisms in jealousy, paranoia, and homosexuality. In *Collected papers* (Vol. 2). London: Hogarth Press.

Friedman, M., Rholes, W. S., Simpson, J., Bond, M., Diaz-Loving, R., & Chan, C. (2010). Attachment avoidance and the cultural fit hypothesis: A cross-cultural investigation. *Personal Relationships, 17,* 107–127.

Fuller, T. L., & Fincham, F. D. (1995). Attachment style in married couples: Relation to current marital functioning, stability over time, and method of assessment. *Personal Relationships, 2,* 17–34.

Gable, S. L., Reis, H. T., Impett, E., & Asher, E. R. (2004). What do you when things go right? The intrapersonal and interpersonal benefits of sharing positive events. *Journal of Personality and Social Psychology, 87,* 228–245.

Gillath, O., Mikulincer, M., Fitzsimons, G. M., Shaver, P. R., Schachner, D. A., & Bargh, J. A. (2006). Automatic activation of attachment-related goals. *Personality and Social Psychology Bulletin, 32,* 1375–1389.

Goodfriend, W., & Agnew, C. R. (2009). Sunken costs and desired plans: Examining different types of investments in close relationships. *Personality and Social Psychology Bulletin.*

Gottman, J. M. (1993). The roles of conflict engagement, escalation, and avoidance in marital interaction: A longitudinal view of five types of couples. *Journal of Consulting and Clinical Psychology, 61,* 6–15.

Gottman, J. M., & Krokoff, L. J. (1989). Marital interaction and satisfaction: A longitudinal view. *Journal of Consulting and Clinical Psychology, 57*, 47–52.

Gottman, J. M., & Levenson, R. W. (1992). Marital processes predictive of later dissolution: Behavior, physiology, and health. *Journal of Personality and Social Psychology, 63*, 221–233.

Grote, N. C., & Clark, M. S. (2001). Perceiving unfairness in the family: Cause or consequence of marital distress? *Journal of Personality and Social Psychology, 80*, 281–293.

Hackel, L. S., & Ruble, D. N. (1992). Changes in the marital relationship after the first baby is born: Predicting the impact of expectancy disconfirmation. *Journal of Personality and Social Psychology, 62*, 944–957.

Hannon, P. A., Rusbult, C. E., Finkel, E. J., & Kamashiro, M. (2010). In the wake of betrayal: Amends, forgiveness, and the resolution of betrayal. *Personal Relationships, 17*, 253–278.

Hatfield, E. (1988). Passionate and companionate love. In R. J. Sternberg and M. L. Barnes (Eds.), *The psychology of love* (pp. 191–217). New Haven, CT: Yale University Press.

Hatfield, E., & Sprecher, S. (2010). The passionate love scale. In T. E. Fisher, C. M. Davis, W. L Yaber, & S. L. Davis (Eds.), *Handbook of sexuality-related measures: A compendium* (3rd ed.). (pp. 466–468). Thousand Oaks, CA: Taylor & Francis.

Hazan, C., & Shaver, P. (1987). Romantic love conceptualized as an attachment process. *Journal of Personality and Social Psychology, 52*, 511–524.

Heider, F. (1958). The psychology of interpersonal relations. *Psychological Review, 51*, 358–374.

Hendrick, C., & Hendrick, S. S. (1986). A theory and method of love. *Journal of Personality and Social Psychology, 50*, 392–402.

Hendrick, S. S., Hendrick, C., & Adler, N. L. (1988). Romantic relationships: Love, satisfaction, and staying together. *Journal of Personality and Social Psychology, 54*, 980–988.

Hetherington, E. M., & Kelly, J. (2002). *For better or for worse: Divorce reconsidered*. New York: W. W. Norton & Co, Inc.

Hill, K. R., & Kaplan, H. S. (1999). Life history traits in humans: Theory and empirical studies. *Annual Review of Anthropology, 28*, 397–430.

Holmes, J. G., & Rempel, J. T. (1989). Trust in close relationships. In C. Hendrick (Ed.), *Close relationships: Review of personality and social psychology* (Vol. 10, pp. 187–220). Newbury Park, CA: Sage.

Horne, S. (1999). Domestic violence in Russia. *American Psychologist, 54*, 55–61.

Huston, T. L., McHale, S. M., & Crouter, A. C. (1986). When the honeymoon's over: Changes in the marriage relationship over the first year. In R. Gilmour & S. Duck (Eds.), *The emerging field of personal relationships* (pp. 109–132). Hillsdale, NJ: Erlbaum.

Inglehart, R. (1990). *Culture shift in advanced industrial society*. Princeton, NJ: Princeton University Press.

Isabella, R. A. (1993). Origins of attachment: Maternal interaction behavior across the first year. *Child Development, 64*, 605–621.

Jankowiak, W. R., & Fisher, E. F. (1992). A cross-cultural perspective on romantic love. *Ethnology, 31*, 149–155.

Johnson, D. L., & Rusbult, C. E. (1989). Resisting temptation: Devaluation of alternative partners as a means of maintaining commitment in close relationships. *Journal of Personality and Social Psychology, 57*, 967–980.

Jones, J. T., & Cunningham, J. D. (1996). Attachment styles and other predictors of relationship satisfaction in dating couples. *Personal Relationships, 3*, 387–399.

Kane, H. S., Jaremka, L. M., Guichard, A. C., Ford, M. B., Collins, N. L., & Feeney, B. C. (2007). Feeling supported and feeling satisfied: How one partner's attachment style predicts the other partner's relationship experience. *Journal of Social and Personal Relationships, 24*, 535–556.

Keelan, J. P., Dion, K. L., & Dion, K. K. (1994). Attachment style and heterosexual relationships among young adults: A short-term panel study. *Journal of Social and Personal Relationships, 11*, 201–214.

Kearns, J. N., & Fincham, F. D. (2004). A prototype analysis of forgiveness. *Personality and Social Psychology Bulletin, 30*, 838–855.

Keith, P. M. (1986). The social context and resources of the unmarried in old age. *International Journal of Aging and Human Development, 23*, 81–96.

Keizer, R., & Schenk, N. (2012). Becoming a parent and relationship satisfaction: A longitudinal dyadic perspective. *Journal of Marriage and Family, 74*, 759–773.

Kerns, K. A. (1994). A development model of the relations between mother-child attachment and friendship. In R. Erber & R. Gilmour (Eds.), *Theoretical frameworks for personal relationships* (pp. 129–156). Hillsdale, NJ: Erlbaum.

Kirkpatrick, L. A., & Davis, K. E. (1994). Attachment style, gender, and relationship stability: A longitudinal analysis. *Journal of Personality and Social Psychology, 66*, 502–512.

Kozu, J. (1999). Domestic violence in Japan. *American Psychologist, 54*, 50–54.

Kurdek, L. A. (1992). Relationship stability and relationship satisfaction in cohabiting gay and lesbian couples: A prospective longitudinal test of the contextual and interdependence model. *Journal of Personality and Social Psychology, 9*, 125–142.

Lane, J. D., & Wegner, D. M. (1994). Secret relationships: The back alley to love. In R. Erber & R. Gilmour (Eds.), *Theoretical frameworks for personal relationships*. Hillsdale, NJ: Erlbaum.

Laurenceau, J. P., Feldman Barrett, L., & Pietromonaco, P. R. (1998). Intimacy as an interpersonal process: The importance of self-disclosure, partner disclosure, and perceived partner responsiveness in interpersonal exchanges. *Journal of Personality and Social Psychology, 74*, 1237–1251.

Le, B. & Agnew, C. R. (2003). Commitment and its theorized determinants: A meta-analysis of the investment model. *Personal Relationships, 10*, 37–57.

Lee, J. A. (1973). *The colors of love: An exploration of the ways of loving.* Don Mills, Ontario, Canada: New Press.

Lee, J. A. (1988). Love-styles. In R. J. Sternberg & M. L. Barnes (Eds.), *The psychology of love* (pp. 38–67). New Haven, CT: Yale University Press.

Lemay, E. P. Jr., & Clark, M. S. (2008). "Walking on Eggshells": How expressing relationship insecurities perpetuates them. *Journal of Personality and Social Psychology, 95*, 420–441.

Levenson, R. W., & Gottman, J. M. (1983). Marital interaction: Physiological linkage and affective exchange. *Journal of Personality and Social Psychology, 45*, 587–597.

Levenson, R. W., & Gottman, J. M. (1985). Physiological and affective predictors of change in relationship satisfaction. *Journal of Personality and Social Psychology, 49*, 85–94.

Leventhal, G. S. (1976). The distribution of rewards and resources in groups and organizations. In L. Berkowitz & E. Hatfield (Eds.), *Advances in experimental social psychology* (Vol. 9, pp. 92–132). New York: Academic Press.

Levine, R., Sato, S., Hashimoto, T., & Verma, J. (1995). Love and marriage in eleven cultures. *Journal of Cross-Cultural Psychology, 26*, 554–571.

Levinger, G., & Huesman, L. R. (1980). An "incremental exchange" perspective on the pair relationship: Interpersonal reward and level of involvement. In K. K. Gergen, M. S. Greenberg, & R. H. Willis (Eds.), *Social exchange: Advances in theory and research* (pp. 165–188). New York: Plenum.

Levy, M. B., & Davis, K. E. (1988). Love styles and attachment styles compared: Their relation to each other and to various relationship characteristics. *Journal of Social and Personal Relationships, 5*, 439–471.

Lin, Y. W., & Rusbult, C. E. (1995). Commitment to dating relationships and cross-sex friendships in America and China. *Journal of Social and Personal Relationships, 12*, 7– 26.

Lucas, R. E., Clark, A. E., Georgellis, Y., & Diener, E. (2003). Reexamining adaptation and the set point model of happiness: Reactions to changes in marital status. *Journal of Personality and Social Psychology, 84*, 527–539.

Marlowe, F. (2003). A critical period for provisioning by Hadza men: Implications for pair bonding. *Evolution and Human Behavior, 24*, 217–229.

Martin, R. D. (2003). Human reproduction: A comparative background for medical hypotheses. *Journal of Reproductive Immunology, 59*, 111–135.

Mason, A., & Blankenship, V. (1987). Power and affiliation motivation, stress and abuse in intimate relationships. *Journal of Personality and Social Psychology, 52*, 203–210.

McCullough, M. E., Bono, G., & Root, L. M. (2007). Rumination, emotion, and forgiveness: Three longitudinal studies. *Journal of Personality and Social Psychology, 92*, 490–505.

McCullough, M. E., Fincham, F. D., & Tsang, J. (2003). Forgiveness, forbearance, and time: The temporal unfolding of transgression-related interpersonal motivation. *Journal of Personality and Social Psychology, 84*, 540–557.

McCullough, M. E., Kurzban, R., & Tabak, B. A. (2012). Cognitive systems for revenge and forgiveness. *Behavioral and Brain Sciences, 36*, 1–58

McCullough, M. E., Worthington, E. L., & Rachal, K. C. (1997). Interpersonal forgiving in close relationships. *Journal of Personality and Social Psychology, 73*, 321–336.

McDaniel, S. H., Stiles, W. B., & McGaughey, K. J. (1981). Correlations of male college students' verbal response mode use in psychotherapy with measures of psychological disturbance and psychotherapy outcome. *Journal of Consulting and Clinical Psychology, 49*, 571–582.

McNulty, J. K. (2011). The dark side of forgiveness: The tendency to forgive predicts continued psychological and physical aggression in marriage. *Personality and Social Psychology Bulletin, 37*, 770–783.

McNulty, J. K., & Karney, B. R. (2004). Positive expectations in the early years of marriage: Should couples expect the best or brace for the worst? *Journal of Personality and Social Psychology, 86*, 729–743.

McNulty, J. K., & Russell, V. M. (2010). When "negative" behaviors are positive: A contextual analysis of the long-term effects of problem-solving behaviors on changes in relationship satisfaction. *Journal of Personality and Social Psychology, 98*, 587–604.

Mikulincer, M. (1998). Attachment working models and the sense of trust: An exploration of interaction goals and affect regulation. *Journal of Personality and Social Psychology, 74*, 1209–1224.

Mikulincer, M., Gillath, O., & Shaver, P. (2002). Activation of the attachment system in adulthood: Threat-related primes increase the accessibility of mental representations of attachment figures. *Journal of Personality and Social Psychology, 83*, 881–895.

Mikulincer, M., & Shaver, P. R. (2001). Attachment theory and intergroup bias: Evidence that priming the secure base schema attenuates negative reactions to others. *Journal of Personality and Social Psychology, 81*, 97–115.

Millbank, J. (1997). Every sperm is sacred? Denying women access to fertility services on the basis of sexuality or marital status. *Alternative Law Journal, 22*, 126–129.

Mills, J., & Clark, M. S. (1994). Communal and exchange relationships: Controversies and research. In R. Erber & R. Gilmour (Eds.), *Theoretical frameworks for personal relationships*. Hillsdale, NJ: Erlbaum.

Morris, W. L., Sinclair, S., & DePaulo, B. M. (2007). No shelter for singles: The perceived legitimacy of marital status discrimination. *Group Processes and Intergroup Relations, 10*, 457–470.

Murray, S. L., Holmes, J. G., & Griffin, D. W. (1996a). The benefits of positive illusions: Idealization and the construction of satisfaction in close relationships. *Journal of Personality and Social Psychology, 70,* 79–98.

Murray, S. L., Holmes, J. G., & Griffin, D. W. (1996b). The self-fulfilling nature of positive illusions in romantic relationships: Love is not blind, but prescient. *Journal of Personality and Social Psychology, 71,* 1155–1180.

Myers, D. G. (1999). Close relationships and quality of life. In D. Kahneman, E. Diener, & N. Schwarz (Eds.), *Well-being: The foundation of hedonic psychology* (pp. 374–391). New York: Russell Sage.

Overall, N. C., Fletcher, G. J. O., Simpson, J. A., & Sibley, C. G. (2009). Regulating partners in intimate relationships: The costs and benefits of different communication strategies. *Journal of Personality and Social Psychology, 96,* 620–639.

Pennebaker, J. W. (1990). *Opening up: The healing power of confiding in others.* New York: Morrow.

Peterson, D. R. (1983). Conflict. In H. H. Kelley, E. Berscheid, A. Christensen, J. H. Harvey, T. L. Huston, G. Levinger, E. McClintock, L. A. Peplau, & D. R. Peterson (Eds.), *Close relationships* (pp. 360–396). New York: Freeman.

Pillsworth, E. G., & Haselton, M. G. (2005). The evolution of coupling. *Psychological Inquiry, 16,* 98–103.

Powers, S. I., Pietromonaco, P. R., Gunlicks, M., & Sayer, A. (2006). Dating couples' attachment styles and patterns of cortisol reactivity and recovery in response to a relationship conflict. *Journal of Personality and Social Psychology, 90,* 613–628.

Pronin, E., Fleming, J. J., & Steffel, M. (2008). Value revelations: Disclosure is in the eye of the beholder. *Journal of Personality and Social Psychology, 95,* 795–809.

Reis, H. T., Maniaci, M. R., Caprariello, P. A., Eastwick, P. W., & Finkel, E. J. (2011). Familiarity does indeed promote attraction in live interaction. *Journal of Personality and Social Psychology, 101,* 557–570.

Reis, H. T., & Shaver, P. (1988). Intimacy as an interpersonal process. In S. Duck and D. F. Hale (Eds.), *Handbook of personal relationships: Theory, research and interventions.* (pp. 367–389). Oxford, England: John Wiley & Sons.

Riek, B. M., Root-Luna, L. M., & Schnabelrauch, C. (in press). Transgressors' guilt and shame: A longitudinal examination of forgiveness seeking. *Journal of Social and Personal Relationships.*

Riela, S., Rodriguez, G., Aron, A., Xu, X., & Acevedo, B. P. (2010). Experiences of falling in love: Investigating culture, ethnicity, gender, and speed. *Journal of Social and Personal Relationships, 27,* 473–493.

Roisman, G. I. & Fraley, R. C. (2008). A behavior-genetic study of parenting quality, infant attachment security, and their covariation in a nationally representative sample. *Developmental Psychology, 44,* 831–839.

Ruble, D. N., Fleming, A. S., Hackel, L., & Stangor, C. (1988). Changes in the marital relationship during the transition to first-time motherhood: Effects of violated expectations concerning division of household labor. *Journal of Personality and Social Psychology, 55,* 78–87.

Rubin, Z. (1970). Measurement of romantic love. *Journal of Personality and Social Psychology, 16,* 265–273.

Rubin, Z. (1973). *Liking and loving.* New York: Holt, Rinehart, and Winston.

Rusbult, C. E. (1983). A longitudinal test of the investment model: The development (and deterioration) of satisfaction and commitment in heterosexual involvement. *Journal of Personality and Social Psychology, 45,* 101–117.

Rusbult, C. E., & Buunk, B. P. (1993). Commitment processes in close relationships: An interdependence analysis. *Journal of Social and Personal Relationships, 10,* 175–204.

Rusbult, C. E., Hannon, P. A., Stocker, S. L., & Finkel, E. J. (2005). Forgiveness and relational repair. In E. L. Worthington Jr. (Ed.), *Handbook of forgiveness* (pp. 185–205). New York: Brunner-Routledge.

Rusbult, C. E., Johnson, D. J., & Morrow, G. D. (1986). Impact of couple patterns of problem solving on distress and nondistress in dating relationships. *Journal of Personality and Social Psychology, 50,* 744–753.

Rusbult, C. E., Martz, J. M., & Agnew, C. R. (1998). The Investment Model Scale: Measuring commitment level, satisfaction level, quality of alternatives, and investment size. *Personal Relationships, 5,* 357–391.

Rusbult, C. E., Yovetich, N. A., & Verette, J. (1996). An interdependence analysis of accommodation processes. In G. Fletcher & J. Fitness (Eds.), *Knowledge structures in close relationships: A social psychological approach* (pp. 63–90). Hillsdale, NJ: Lawrence Erlbaum Associates.

Rusbult, C. E., & Zembrodt, I. M. (1983). Responses to dissatisfaction in romantic involvements: A multidimensional scaling analysis. *Journal of Experimental Social Psychology, 19,* 274–293.

Rusbult, C. E., Zembrodt, I. M., & Gunn, L. K. (1982). Exit, voice, loyalty, and neglect: Responses to dissatisfaction in romantic involvements. *Journal of Personality and Social Psychology, 43,* 1230–1242.

Schachter, S., & Singer, J. (1962). Cognitive, social, and physiological determinants of the emotional state. *Psychological Review, 69,* 379–399.

Schumann, K. (2012). Does love mean never having to say you're sorry? Associations between relationship satisfaction, perceived apology sincerity, and forgiveness. *Journal of Social and Personal Relationships, 29,* 997–1010.

Seligman, M. E. P. (2002). *Authentic happiness: Using the new positive psychology to realize your potential for lasting fulfillment.* New York: Free Press.

Shaver, P. R., Wu, S., & Schwartz, J. C. (1992). Cross-cultural similarities and differences in emotion and its representation. In M. Clark (Ed.), *Emotion: Review of personality and social psychology,* No. 13 (pp. 175–212). Thousand Oaks, CA: Sage Publications, Inc.

Simpson, J. A. (1990). The influence of attachment styles on romantic relationships. *Journal of Personality and Social Psychology, 59,* 971–980.

Simpson, J. A., Rhodes, W. S., & Nelligan, J. S. (1992). Support-seeking and support-giving within couple members in an anxiety-provoking situation: The role of attachment styles. *Journal of Personality and Social Psychology, 62,* 434–446.

Simpson, J. A., Collins, W. A., Tran, S., & Hayden, K. C. (2007). Attachment and the experience and expression of emotions in romantic relationships. *Journal of Personality and Social Psychology, 92,* 355–367.

Slotter, E. B., Gardner, W. L., & Finkel, E. J. (2010). Who am I without you? The influence of romantic breakup on the self-concept. *Personality and Social Psychology Bulletin, 36,* 147–160.

Sprecher, S. (1999). "I love you more today than yesterday": Romantic partners' perceptions of changes in love and related affect over time. *Journal of Personality and Social Psychology, 76,* 46–53.

Sprecher, S., Treger, S., Wondra, J. D., Hilaire, N., & Wallpe, K. (2013). Taking turns: Reciprocal self-disclosure promotes liking in initial interactions. *Journal of Experimental Social Psychology, 49,* 860–866.

Srivastava, S., McGonigal, K. M., Richards, J. M., Butler, E. A., & Gross, J. J. (2006). Optimism in close relationships: How seeing things in a positive light makes them so. *Journal of Personality and Social Psychology, 91,* 143–153.

Sternberg, R. J. (1986). A triangular theory of love. *Psychological Review, 93,* 119–135.

Sternberg, R. J. (1988). Triangulating love. In R. J. Sternberg & M. L. Barnes (Eds.), *The psychology of love* (pp. 119–138). New Haven, CT: Yale University Press.

Stillwell, A. M., & Baumeister, R. F. (1997). The construction of victim and perpetrator memories: Accuracy and distortion in role-based accounts. *Personality and Social Psychology Bulletin, 23,* 1157–1172.

Straus, M. A., & Gelles, R. J. (1986). Societal change and change in family violence from 1975 to 1985 as revealed in two national surveys. *Journal of Marriage and the Family, 48,* 465–479.

Sumter, S. R., Valkenburg, P. M., & Peter, J. (2013). Perceptions of love across the lifespan: Differences in passion, intimacy, and commitment. *International Journal of Behavioral Development, 37,* 41–427.

Swann, W. B. Jr., McClarty, K. L., & Rentfrow, P. J. (2007). Shelter from the storm? Flawed reactions to stress in precarious couples. *Journal of Social and Personal Relationships, 24,* 793–809.

Taylor, D. A., & Belgrave, F. Z. (1986). The effects of perceived intimacy and valence on self- disclosure reciprocity. *Personality and Social Psychology Bulletin, 12,* 247–255.

Tesser, A. (1978). Self-generated attitude change. In L. Berkowitz (Ed.), *Advances in experimental social psychology* (Vol. 11, pp. 289–338). New York: Academic Press.

Tesser, A., & Paulhus, D. L. (1976). Toward a causal model of love. *Journal of Personality and Social Psychology, 34,* 1095–1105.

Thibaut, J. W., & Kelley, H. H. (1959). *The social psychology of groups.* New York: Wiley.

Tolstedt, B. E., & Stokes, J. P. (1984). Self-disclosure, intimacy, and the depenetration process. *Journal of Personality and Social Psychology, 46,* 84–90.

Tomlinson, J. M., Aron, A., Carmichael, C. L., Reis, H. T., & Holmes, J. G. (in press). The costs of being put on a pedestal: Effects of feeling over-idealized. *Journal of Personal and Social Relationships.*

Toussaint, L. L., Williams, D. R., Musick, M. A., & Everson, S. A. (2001). Forgiveness and health: Age differences in a U.S. probability sample. *Journal of Adult Development, 8,* 249–257.

Trivers, R. L. (1972). Parental investment and sexual selection. In B. Campbell (Ed.), *Sexual selection and the descent of man* (pp. 136–179). Chicago: Aldine.

Tucker, P., & Aron, A. (1993). Passionate love and marital satisfaction at key transition points in the family life cycle. *Journal of Social and Clinical Psychology, 12,* 135–147.

Turner, J. L., Foa, E. B., & Foa, U. G. (1971). Interpersonal reinforcers: Classification, interrelationship, and some differential properties. *Journal of Personality and Social Psychology, 19,* 168–180.

Van Lange, P. A. M., Rusbult, C. E., Drigotas, S. M., Arriaga, X. B., Witcher, B. S., & Cox, C. L. (1997). Willingness to sacrifice in close relationships. *Journal of Personality & Social Psychology, 72,* 1373–1395.

van Steenbergen, H., Langeslag, S. J. E., Band, G. P. H., & Hommel, B. (2013). Reduced cognitive control in passionate lovers. Motivation and Emotion, published online November 2.

Walker, L. E. A. (1984). *The battered woman syndrome.* New York: Springer.

Watson, J. B. (1924). *Behaviorism.* New York: Norton.

Wegner, D. M., Erber, R., & Zanakos, S. (1993). Ironic processes in the mental control of mood and mood-related thought. *Journal of Personality and Social Psychology, 65,* 1093–1104.

Wegner, D. M., Lane, J. D., & Dimitri, S. (1994). The allure of secret relationships. *Journal of Personality and Social Psychology, 66,* 287–300.

Weiner, B., Graham, S., Peter, O., & Zmuidinas, M. (1991). Public confession and forgiveness. *Journal of Personality, 59,* 281–312.

Witvliet, C. V. O., Ludwig, T. E., & Vander Laan, K. L. (2001). Granting forgiveness or harboring grudges: Implications for emotion, physiology, and health. *Psychological Science, 121,* 117–123.

Worthington, E. L., & Scherer, M. (2004). Forgiveness as an emotion-focused coping strategy that can reduce health risks and promote health resilience: Theory, review, and hypotheses. *Psychology and Health, 19,* 385–405.

CHAPTER 11

STEREOTYPING, PREJUDICE, AND DISCRIMINATION

BIAS, BIGOTRY, AND BROTHERHOOD: A RESEARCH EPIC

Many of the topics discussed in this book have been major areas of research ever since social psychology became recognized as a field of study. That is not true for all of them, however, as a glance at the first *Handbook of Social Psychology* (Murchison, 1935) will reveal. Then, as now, the Handbook was considered to be the most authoritative review of the social psychology literature. It is over 1000 pages long, but the index indicates that "stereotypes" and "prejudice" are discussed on only two of those pages. These topics' lack of prominence in the book is not surprising, given their lack of prominence as a focus of research at the time. In the decade of the 1930s, no more than 10 papers with the word "stereotype" and no more than 20 with the word "prejudice" in their titles appeared in the psychological literature.

In contrast, the 1998 version of the *Handbook of Social Psychology* (Gilbert, Fiske, & Lindzey, 1998) included a lengthy chapter on stereotyping, prejudice, and discrimination (Fiske, 1998), and two chapters on related areas of research (social stigma and intergroup relations). In 1999, the major American and European experimental social psychology conferences featured a total of 51 symposia, and 19 of them (37 percent) focused on these topics (Fiske, 2000). Today, it is not unheard of for single issues of social psychology journals to contain more papers on stereotyping than the ten that appeared between 1930 and 1939.

What caused this change in emphasis? The answer is simple: the events of World War II. Not only was that conflict one of the most brutal and destructive in human history, it was also fueled to a great extent by racism and intergroup hatred. In order to better understand the malevolent forces that led to the deaths of tens of millions, researchers turned their attention to stereotyping, prejudice, and discrimination with an intensity that has not let up to this day (Dovidio & Gaertner, 2010; Dovidio, Glick, & Rudman, 2005; Nelson, 2009; Yzerbyt & Demoulin, 2010). The civil rights struggles of the 1950s and 1960s also added to the urgency of this work.

Social psychologists have tackled bigotry and hatred with all of the research methods at their disposal. This chapter tells the story of how they confronted and made sense of these destructive aspects of human relations, a story with discrete chapters and even a few plot twists. It is a story that is still ongoing.

STEREOTYPING, PREJUDICE, AND DISCRIMINATION: AN OVERVIEW

Although stereotyping, prejudice, and discrimination are related, they are distinct concepts. **Prejudice** consists of unfavorable *feelings* about a group of people—feelings that can develop very early in childhood (Raabe & Beelmann, 2011). The intense dislike that homophobic people feel toward gay people, as well as overt expressions of that hatred, are examples of prejudice. **Discrimination** is unfair *behavior* toward members of some group, such as depriving them of the opportunities and resources available to others. Banning gay people from jobs that would put them in contact with young people would be an illustration of discriminatory behavior. Finally, *beliefs* about the characteristics of particular categories of people—characteristics that distinguish those people from others—are referred to as **stereotypes**. A person who believes that gay people are especially likely to make sexual advances toward children is stereotyping gay people.

Almost any identifiable group of people can be unfairly stereotyped. Redheads are alleged to be hot-tempered and promiscuous.

Prejudice, discrimination, and stereotyping are often closely related. A person with unfavorable thoughts and beliefs about a particular group can be expected to feel hostility toward that group and will probably treat members of the group with disdain. And if a person aggressively supports laws targeted against the group, it would be reasonable to assume that he or she holds unfavorable beliefs about the group's personality traits and other characteristics. Thus, groups who are on the receiving end of one of these types of bias are typically subject to all of them. When a group is highly devalued in all three ways—when it is the target of extremely negative thoughts, feelings, and behavior—that group is said to be **stigmatized** (Crocker, Major, & Steele, 1998; Heatherton, Kleck, Hebl, & Hull, 2000; Levin & van Laar, 2006; see **Table 11.1**).

Yet because prejudice, discrimination, and stereotyping are not perfectly correlated, treating them as separate phenomena makes sense. First of all, stereotypes are not always negative. Members of some groups are seen as being *more* intelligent, athletic, or even-tempered than members of other groups. Asian Americans, for example, are sometimes stereotyped as being academically gifted. These favorable stereotypes are not entirely harmless; they can burden the people who are saddled with them, and lead other people to resent them. Still, the fact remains that stereotypes do not necessarily trigger hatred or other negative feelings. In addition, some of the more intriguing research in recent years has raised the possibility that even well-meaning, unprejudiced people may harbor stereotypes that affect their interactions without their awareness. In other words, stereotypes can serve as hidden influences on behavior, giving rise to discrimination without prejudice. Finally, some people, regardless of how they perceive and feel about people who differ from them in terms of their race, ethnicity, nationality, gender, age, or sexual orientation (and even accent—Gluszek & Dovidio, 2010; Kinzler, Shutts, DeJesus, & Spelke, 2009) are motivated to avoid treating others in biased ways.

Table 11.1 Stigmatization of people with illnesses and disabilities

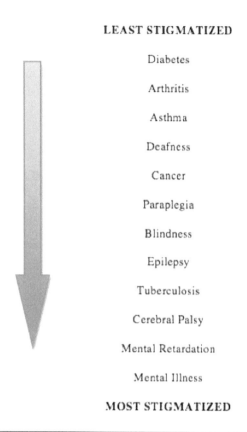

LEAST STIGMATIZED

Diabetes

Arthritis

Asthma

Deafness

Cancer

Paraplegia

Blindness

Epilepsy

Tuberculosis

Cerebral Palsy

Mental Retardation

Mental Illness

MOST STIGMATIZED

People with mental illness are often highly devalued. A review of studies examining willingness to employ people with different disabilities and illnesses, willingness to marry them or have them as neighbors, and many other indications of social rejection found people with mental illness to be the most stigmatized group.

Source: Subset of data presented by Yuker (1988).

In sum, although stereotyping, prejudice, and discrimination can sometimes be difficult to disentangle, they are not identical concepts. Research conducted by social psychologists often focuses more on one of these aspects of intergroup tension than on the others.

Postwar Social Psychologists: Battling Bigotry, Breaking Down Barriers

Much of the early research on stereotyping and prejudice was guided by the **sociocultural perspective**. This perspective is based on the idea that negative intergroup beliefs and attitudes are learned from other people (family, friends, teachers, etc.), the media (books, movies, television, etc.) and other sources in one's environment and culture (Ashmore & Del Boca, 1981; Degner & Dalege, 2013; Hamilton, Stroessner, & Driscoll, 1994; Paluck, 2011). From this perspective, changing people's attitudes and beliefs about other groups requires changing what people are exposed to.

Sociocultural influences do not have to involve direct instruction. If women are portrayed on television as "scantily clad half-wits who need to be rescued" (Atkin, Moorman, & Linn, 1991, p. 679) or in children's books as never being without cooking utensils or brooms (Crabb & Bielawski, 1994), these messages will affect the development of gender stereotypes without anyone having to be explicitly taught that women are more helpless and nurturing than men. And stereotypes can be transmitted in even more indirect ways than that. A child whose parents (or other adults) consistently tense up when in the presence of members of a particular group will implicitly learn to associate that group with hostility and danger (Castelli, De Dea, & Nesdale, 2008).

The messages children receive about stereotypical gender-appropriate behaviors are often far from subtle.

THE CONTACT HYPOTHESIS

Social experiences can also *reduce* stereotyping and prejudice. For example, what better way to learn that your fears and suspicions about another group are baseless than to spend time interacting with members of the group? According to the **contact hypothesis** (Amir, 1969; Hodson, 2011; Pettigrew, 1986; van Laar, Levin, Sinclair, & Sidanius, 2005), direct contact between members of different groups can sometimes reduce stereotyping and prejudice. Much research in the decade following World War II was designed to test this hypothesis.

The Contact Hypothesis: Early Research

The results of a number of early studies of the effects of intergroup contact were quite encouraging. For example, Deutsch and Collins (1951) interviewed white housewives who lived in either integrated or segregated public housing projects. They found that women who lived in close proximity to black people were over ten times more likely than women with no black neighbors to support a policy of integrating city housing projects (53 percent versus 5 percent). Wilner, Walkley, and Cook (1952) reported similar findings.

Another study that supported the contact hypothesis focused on prejudice toward a different group, Japanese Americans. During World War II, Japanese Americans who lived on the West Coast of the United States were regarded with such suspicion that they were confined in internment camps. Hostility toward them persisted for many years afterward. Irish (1952), however, identified a group of Americans whose attitudes toward Japanese Americans were significantly more positive than the norm: those who had counted Japanese Americans among their neighbors during the war.

Early research on the contact hypothesis was not only exciting and inspiring; it was also influential. In the landmark 1954 *Brown v. Board of Education* decision, the U.S. Supreme Court ruled that racially segregated schools were unconstitutional because they were inherently unequal.

Social psychological research on race relations played a role in the landmark 1954 Brown v. Board of Education decision. The U.S. Supreme Court ruled that racially segregated schools were inherently unequal and thus unconstitutional. Thurgood Marshall, memorialized here, argued the case before the court (which he himself later joined).

The justices were influenced in part by research indicating that enforced separation of the races could lower the self-esteem of minority children (see the Dark Side and the Bright Side boxes on **pages 493** and **494–495**). However, they were also swayed by the claim that increased contact between white and black schoolchildren could foster more harmonious race relations. Social psychologists' research on the effects of intergroup contact had inspired optimism that integrated educational institutions could have such an effect.

SOCIAL PSYCHOLOGY: THE DARK SIDE—STIGMA AND LOW SELF-ESTEEM

What are the consequences of belonging to a stigmatized group? Some of the negative effects of the stereotyping and prejudice that stigmatized people experience are fairly straightforward. Those who are seen by the dominant groups in a society as being incompetent and disagreeable will be discriminated against and will be unfairly denied access to all sorts of privileges, opportunities, and resources. For example, they will be less likely than others to live in safe, attractive neighborhoods and less likely to have satisfying, well-paying jobs.

In the 1930s and 1940s, Kenneth and Mamie Phipps Clark developed a simple—but ingenious—method for demonstrating another, more subtle effect of stigmatization (Clark & Clark, 1947). In studies using their doll technique, the Clarks presented black children with two dolls that were identical in every way but one: color. One doll was white, the other was brown. Then the Clarks asked the children a series of questions about the dolls, including "Show me the doll that is the 'nice' doll," and "Show me the doll that looks 'bad.'" They found that a majority of the children identified the white doll as the nice one and the brown doll as the bad one. The children did so, despite the fact that the vast majority of them had identified the brown doll as the one that looked like a "colored" or "Negro" child. Similar findings have been reported for other minority groups (Aboud, 1988).

According to Clark and Clark, these results indicated that being treated as inferior can result in low self-esteem, and even self-hatred. By extension, these negative effects of discrimination can maintain and even increase inequality, because people who think poorly of themselves probably will not be motivated to combat injustice. The results of studies using the doll technique were so compelling that they played an important role in arguments made before the U.S. Supreme Court in *Brown v. Board of Education* (1954). The justices' ruling on the case struck down laws that enforced racial segregation in public schools and discredited the concept of "separate but equal" facilities. As one scholar has noted, the Clarks' research was "used by the highest court to make one of the most far-reaching decisions of the 20th century" (Tomes, 2002, p. 56).

SOCIAL PSYCHOLOGY: THE BRIGHT SIDE—STIGMA AND SELF-PROTECTION

The fact that minority children often prefer dolls (and other images) that look like people from a dominant group in their society is intriguing (and disturbing), but it offers only indirect evidence that members of stigmatized groups may suffer from low self-esteem. In fact, direct tests of that hypothesis generally do *not* support it (Aboud, 1988; Crocker & Major, 1989; Gray-Little & Hafdahl, 2000).

Crocker and Major (1989) provide several explanations for this finding. First, people who belong to oppressed groups can attribute disappointments and other negative experiences (bad grades, failure to be hired for a job) to prejudice and discrimination (Sechrist, Swim, & Stangor, 2004). For example, studies of black soldiers during World War II revealed that they were less worried than white soldiers about accusations of cowardice because those accusations could be attributed to racism (Bourke, 1999). Although that way of explaining negative experiences might not always be valid or well received by others (Schultz & Maddox, 2013), it is not unreasonable for members of a stigmatized group. Attributing a failure or a disappointment to others' prejudice will leave one feeling less depressed than attributing it to one's own shortcomings (Major, Kaiser, & McCoy, 2003).

Another way in which members of stigmatized groups can maintain their self-esteem is by comparing their talents and achievements to those of other members of their group, rather than to members of more advantaged groups. After all, if you want to see how you measure up against others, it seems only fair to choose people who operate under the same social pressures and constraints. Finally, stigmatized people tend to base their sense of self-worth on qualities that correspond to their own—and their group's—strengths. For example, people with serious physical disabilities would not evaluate themselves in terms of their capacity to engage in physical activities that are no longer within their range of capabilities.

As Crocker and Major note, the idea that stigmatized people can buffer themselves from prejudice and discrimination should not be interpreted to mean that prejudice and discrimination do not affect well-being. Each of these self-protective strategies has a drawback. For example, if you repeatedly attribute your failures to prejudice against your group, you may come to believe that discrimination is so pervasive and powerful that nothing you attempt will ever meet with success. Thus, of all the "Bright Sides" discussed in this book, this one is probably the dimmest. At the very least, though, Crocker and Major have explained why people who belong to stigmatized groups can often feel quite good about themselves. They are not doomed to lives of self-doubt and self-loathing.

In sum, early research on the contact hypothesis suggested that integrating neighborhoods, workplaces, and schools would do more than just correct the injustice of discrimination based on race or ethnicity. Social psychologists believed that contact between groups had the potential to undermine the very psychological forces that led to segregation in the first place.

The Contact Hypothesis Revisited

The deadly assaults on the Pentagon and New York's World Trade Center caught most Americans by surprise on September 11, 2001. In the aftermath of the destruction, scholars, journalists, government officials, and others tried to make sense of what had happened. They studied the history and goals of radical Islamic groups like Al Qaeda, Hezbollah, and Islamic Jihad. Several observers concluded that whatever the differences between those groups, all seemed to owe an intellectual debt to the Egyptian scholar Sayyid Qutb, an Islamic fundamentalist and political activist. Although Qutb was executed in 1966 (Berman, 2003), his philosophy outlived him. He argued that Western liberalism and modernity were corrupting Muslims and that Christianity and Judaism were false religions. The only hope for humanity, he believed, was to organize society around Koranic principles. To hasten the arrival of a more perfect world, Qutb urged Muslims to declare war on the West and its values.

You may be thinking that if Qutb had had the opportunity to get to know Westerners, he would have felt differently. If he had enjoyed extended contacts with the Christians and Jews who inspired so much fear and hostility in him, surely he would have moderated his views. As it turns out, however, Qutb did interact quite a bit with Westerners. In his childhood, he received a modern, secular education, and in the late 1940s, he studied in the United States, earning a master's degree from the Colorado State College of Education. Qutb's beliefs actually became *more* radical after his years in the West; his contact with members of another culture only led him to demonize them.

One could argue that Qutb was an unusual individual. Certainly, his extreme views do not reflect those of the majority of Muslims. Unfortunately, his story illustrates a more general point: that contact between people of different races, religions, nationalities, and social classes does not always reduce hostility between them. Many people's everyday experiences confirm this point, as does history.

Consider, for example, one of the more violent spasms of genocidal killing in recent history. In 1994, following a period of political instability in the African nation of Rwanda, one group, the Hutus, rose up and in a matter of weeks slaughtered hundreds of thousands of members of another group, the Tutsis. The underlying causes of this tragic event were many and complex (Gourevitch, 1998; Smith, 1998), but one aspect of the slaughter made it especially hard to comprehend. Hutus and Tutsis had lived as neighbors for centuries, and intermarriage between the two groups was becoming increasingly common. Group contact apparently had done nothing to shield the Tutsis from the most horrible consequence of intergroup hatred imaginable.

Long before then, social psychologists had recognized as far too simplistic the idea that "merely by assembling people without regard to race, color, religion, or national origin, we can thereby destroy stereotypes and develop friendly attitudes" (Allport, 1954, p. 261). For example, Campbell (1958) assessed the attitudes of white high school students on two occasions, just before and six months after the integration of their school. He found that some of the students became less prejudiced toward black people during that period, but just as many became *more* prejudiced. When Mussen (1950) conducted a similar study in a summer camp, his findings were the same: contact between the two groups changed some people's attitudes, but change occurred in *both* directions. Over time, such discouraging results began to pile up (Harding, Kutner, Proshansky, & Chein, 1969). Moreover, broader studies of the effects of school integration have led some researchers to conclude that the desegregation mandated by *Brown v. Board of Education* had few—if any—significant effects on racial attitudes (Stephan, 1986).

Integrated classrooms can help reduce students' negative intergroup attitudes, but they do not always have that effect.

Four Critical Aspects of Intergroup Contact

More than half a century of research on the contact hypothesis has identified at least four aspects of intergroup contact that are critical to the reduction of prejudice (Allport, 1954; Brewer & Brown, 1998; Pettigrew & Tropp, 2000, 2006). The first is that members of the two or more groups involved must have the opportunity for *meaningful social interaction*. In other words, the situation must have high "acquaintance potential" (Cook, 1978, p. 97). When people get to know one another, they often discover shared interests, and may even find that the stereotypes they learned as children are untrue.

The second critical factor is the *pursuit of common objectives*, or cooperation. For example, members of two antagonistic groups may develop warm feelings by attending the same school, but they will be even more likely to do so if they play on the same sports teams. Even extensive interaction on a joint project may not be enough to reduce prejudice, however, unless members of the two groups are of *equal status*—the third critical factor. If minority group members are assigned subordinate roles (for example, if black soldiers are commanded by white officers), both groups will have fewer opportunities to see each other in a new light, and their views of one another will probably not be transformed.

Finally, contact must take place in the context of clear *social and/or institutional support*. In other words, the groups involved must believe that harmonious relationships are expected, desired, or at least tolerated by friends, family, and respected authority figures. This factor explains a scandal that emerged in the United States Air Force Academy in 2003. Male and female cadets worked closely together at the academy, often participating in exercises in which they cooperated to achieve desired outcomes. Although there were no official status differences between men and women, female cadets were not universally respected by their male peers. In fact, they were subject to alarmingly high levels of sexual assault. Investigations of the situation indicated that the institution's leaders bore a great deal of the responsibility, for they looked the other way as the female cadets became a stigmatized group. Despite mounting evidence that the climate at the academy was unacceptably hostile toward women, they made little effort to develop adequate support systems, to provide women with fair hearings for their grievances, or to ensure they would not be retaliated against when they spoke up about the violence that was directed at them.

In contrast, recall that white residents of the housing projects studied by Deutsch and Collins (1951) and Wilner et al. (1952) developed more positive attitudes toward their black neighbors as a result of intergroup contact. In that case, the social climate encouraged tolerance, acceptance, and harmony. People were aware that they were living in experimental housing projects, where authorities hoped and expected that racial barriers would break down. In situations like these, in which intergroup contact is likely to have a positive outcome, the interracial and interethnic friendships that develop can even reduce the physiological stress people have been found to experience while interacting with out-group members (Page-Gould, Mendoza-Denton, & Tropp, 2008). (For a summary of the four critical aspects of intergroup contact, see **Table 11.2**.)

Table 11.2: Four critical aspects of intergroup contact

Meaningful social interaction
Group members must get to know each other; mere physical proximity is not enough.
Pursuit of common objectives
Mutual affection and respect are more likely when members of the other group are seen as allies working toward the same goals as one's own group.
Equal status
When neither group is dominant, it is more difficult to develop a view of the out-group as being inferior or less worthy of respect.
Social and/or institutional support
Group contact is more likely to be successful when it is encouraged and rewarded by those whose opinions we value and respect.

THE ROBBERS CAVE EXPERIMENT

A legendary field study known as the "Robbers Cave experiment" (Sherif, Harvey, White, Hood, & Sherif, 1961) provides what might be the best illustration of these principles. In a state park, Sherif and his colleagues set up a summer camp for 22 boys age 11. They divided them into two groups, who were at first unaware of each other's existence. During that period, which lasted about a week, a certain amount of group solidarity developed. One group of boys named themselves the Eagles; the other became the Rattlers.

When members of the two groups finally came face to face, they did not simply intermingle. Instead, the researchers pitted the Eagles against the Rattlers in contests and athletic tournaments, and prizes were awarded to the victors. As you might imagine, the competitive atmosphere did not lead to friendly relations between the two groups: All-out warfare broke out. At one point, the researchers had to intervene because the Eagles had armed themselves with socks stuffed with rocks.

Needless to say, the researchers' goal was not to see how much hatred and violence they could whip up in a group of happy, well-adjusted boys. In fact, creating intergroup hostility was easy; what was of more interest to the researchers was how to eliminate it. To that end, Sherif and his colleagues arranged a series of joint activities. However, they found that watching movies together and sharing meals did little to promote harmony between the two groups.

Two other events turned out to be more helpful in ending the conflict between the Eagles and the Rattlers. First, the campers' water supply was disrupted. Then, a truck in which they were traveling together broke down. Both these crises were staged, and in both, the solution to the apparent problem required cooperation and coordination between the two groups. For example, all 20 boys had to work together to pull the truck to get it started. These final activities did the trick. Tensions began to subside, and when the time came to return home, the boys asked to travel together on the same bus. Eagles and Rattlers sat together and chatted on the ride home, friends at last.

How did Sherif and his colleagues turn an explosive intergroup situation into a peaceful one? They did so by putting into place all the conditions required for that to happen. The two groups were of equal status, and the researchers made sure that did not change (they arranged competitions very carefully so that neither group would dominate). Through joint activities, they gave the boys a chance to interact and become acquainted. Of course, not just any activity would do; the most important ones involved cooperation and shared goals. Finally, the researchers created a context in which peaceful relations were not just tolerated, but supported.

The Robbers Cave study, with its happy ending, is justifiably a classic. Note, however, the lengths to which the researchers had to go to reduce prejudice and conflict. Most group interactions do not have all of the features that make contact a positive, constructive experience, and some do not have any of them (Gerard, 1988; Slavin, 1985). Even if the situation does allow for more than superficial social interaction, intergroup contact is likely to be complicated by differences in power and status. And there is no reason to assume that people will share goals, or that administrative or social support will be available. From a "glass is half empty" perspective, the Robbers Cave study suggests that the typical outcome of group encounters will *not* necessarily be group hugs and promises to keep in touch.

The Robbers Cave study was a carefully constructed experiment. To see how difficult it is to draw conclusions from nonexperimental studies of interracial and interethnic contact, see the Think like a Social Psychologist box on **pages 498-499.**

THINK LIKE A SOCIAL PYCHOLOGIST: THE LIMITATIONS OF NONEXPERIMENTAL METHODS

Brian and Ken were psychology majors who had become friends after taking several psychology classes together. One day, after a lecture on stereotyping, they found themselves in a particularly intense discussion of the implications of research on stereotyping for their everyday lives. Ken, an Asian American, lived in a racially and ethnically mixed fraternity house. Brian, who was white, lived in a fraternity house that was almost totally white. Could the very different social compositions of their fraternities affect the attitudes and beliefs of the students who lived there?

To answer this question, the two designed and conducted an independent study and recruited white students in the two fraternities to participate. They asked the participants to fill out a survey developed to measure stereotyping of blacks, Latinos, and Asians. Brian administered the questionnaires to participants in his frat house, and Ken did the same for participants in his.

The results turned out as predicted: the white students where Brian lived were more likely to endorse stereotypical beliefs about other groups than the white students in Ken's more diverse fraternity. The findings were consistent with Brian and Ken's belief that living with people from different cultures and backgrounds can undermine the influence of racial and ethnic stereotypes. However, when Brian and Ken wrote up the results of their study, *they did not strongly argue that their data supported that conclusion.* Why not? What might have been some methodological shortcomings of their research?

****

As we have seen, contact between different racial and ethnic groups can help to break down barriers and promote harmony between them, but only in certain circumstances. When members of the different groups enjoy equal status, have a variety of extended interactions, work together to achieve collective goals, and interact in a setting or institution that encourages and supports friendly relations, stereotyping and prejudice become less of a problem. Ken's fraternity seems to have those characteristics, and social psychological research does indeed suggest that diverse living situations of that sort promote tolerance. Nonetheless, for a couple of reasons, Brian and Ken were correct in recognizing that their research could not, in and of itself, strongly support that conclusion.

First, because Brian and Ken's study was not an experiment, *participants were not randomly assigned to conditions*; they themselves had decided where they would live. Hence, the more positive intergroup attitudes at Ken's fraternity might not have been a consequence of living there—they might be the reason some people chose to live there in the first place. In addition, Ken and Brian's role as the experimenters could have led to *demand effects*. When white American participants report their feelings and beliefs about minority groups to a member of one of those groups, they may claim to have more favorable attitudes than they would when speaking with a white interviewer. Indeed, several studies have reported such "race of the experimenter" effects (Fazio, Jackson, Dunton, & Williams, 1995).

INAUSPICIOUS CONTACT: REALISTIC CONFLICT AND RELATIVE DEPRIVATION

One might argue that the conflict and competition between the Eagles and Rattlers was staged and artificial. But the situation created was by no means unusual; in reality, it is more common than not for group interests to conflict and for resources to be distributed unequally. Such inequalities and divergent goals can have serious consequences. According to **realistic group conflict theory** (Levine & Campbell, 1972; Palmer, 1996), prejudice is caused by competition for scarce resources—money, jobs, land, power, and status.

In the American South in the late 19th and early 20th centuries, for example, lynchings of black people were associated with stressful economic conditions. As the price of cotton went down, the number of lynchings increased (Hovland & Sears, 1940; Hepworth & West, 1988). Similarly, the rise of anti-Semitism in Germany between the first and second world wars coincided with the collapse of the German economy. Although the processes through which economic distress and other difficult life conditions lead to such **scapegoating** is quite complicated—and by no means inevitable (Green, Glaser, & Rich, 1998; Glick, 2002)—group conflict is clearly more likely to erupt during conditions of scarcity and insecurity than during times of plenty and security.

Of course, one might argue that although scarcity and insecurity are all too common, they certainly are not universal conditions. Would it not be reasonable to expect that groups would coexist peacefully, as long as there are enough resources to go around? Unfortunately, such an assumption would not necessarily be valid. "Enough" is a fuzzy concept that is very dependent on one's circumstances. According to **relative deprivation theory** (Olson, Herman, & Zanna, 1986; Smith, Pettigrew, Pippin, & Bialosiewicz, 2012), dissatisfaction arises not from objectively unfavorable circumstances (in other words, from specific levels of food, property, status, power, and other resources), but from the perception that one is doing less well than others. Among African Americans, for example, urban unrest peaked in the 1960s, at a time when the group was making significant economic strides. Unfortunately, their perception was that the gap in wealth between blacks and whites was not narrowing, and was perhaps even widening (Sears & McConahy, 1973). Although objectively, circumstances were improving, in relative terms they were not.

Overall, as research on and theorizing about the effects of group contact became increasingly sophisticated, social psychologists developed a deeper understanding of the circumstances in which contact might reduce stereotyping and prejudice. However, they had difficulty escaping the conclusion that in practice, the effect of intergroup contact is not necessarily—or even typically—a reduction in hostility.

The Contact Hypothesis: A Summary

Social psychologists have tried to develop procedures for reducing intergroup tension and conflict. Early tests of the contact hypothesis indicated that arranging for members of different groups to have extended interactions with each other would accomplish that goal. However, further research punctured their hopes, undermining social psychologists' faith in the idea that stereotyping, prejudice, and discrimination could be tackled head-on through straightforward measures. Make no mistake: group contact, when it takes place in the right circumstances, can reduce prejudice. But those circumstances are by no means universal (see also Becker, Wright, Lubensky, & Zhou, 2013; Sengupta & Sibley, 2013). And contact that does *not* take place with the right conditions in place has the potential to *increase* prejudice, even more than contact in favorable conditions can *reduce* prejudice (Barlow et al., 2012).

Think like a Social Psychologist

Making connections

—Chapter 5 reviewed the different ways in which attitudes can develop. Prejudice against a specific group is essentially an unfavorable attitude. What are some of the ways in which prejudices might develop that would qualify them as "thoughtless attitudes," as defined in Chapter 5?

Thinking critically

—In light of relative deprivation theory, would it be possible to specify a situation in which a group's average income level is going down, yet members of the group feel *less* resentment toward other groups than they once did?

THE COGNITIVE APPROACH TO STEREOTYPING AND PREJUDICE

How you perceive and treat members of different groups is an issue of global importance. Animosity and conflict between people who differ in terms of their race, ethnicity, nationality, or religion can have disastrous consequences—all too often including armed conflict.

Yet intergroup relationships are also *local* issues, because they affect your everyday encounters with others. What do people notice about you—what attracts their attention? What impressions are others likely to form of you? What features of your personality and what elements of your behavior are they apt to remember? How much room do they give you to be yourself? The outcome of all these aspects of everyday social interaction (and others) can be affected by how people label you in terms of your group membership. In other words, the processes underlying stereotyping, prejudice, and discrimination unfold in everyday encounters with other people in the course of what might otherwise seem like routine social experiences.

Social Psychologists Meet the "Cognitive Monster": Do Good Intentions Matter?

Researchers in the **cognitive** tradition (see Ashmore & Del Boca, 1981; Fiske, 1998; Hamilton, Stroessner, & Driscoll, 1994; Monteith, Zuwerink, & Devine, 1994), which first became dominant in the late 1970s and early 1980s, focus directly on the kinds of questions posed in the previous paragraph. They investigate how our beliefs and feelings about groups affect our reactions to other people. Does simply identifying someone as "Mexican," "a Buddhist," "a lawyer," or "a senior citizen" make a difference in what goes on between you and that person? According to research in the cognitive tradition, the answer is yes. How you categorize people will affect what you decide is worth attending to about them, what details of your interactions with them are stored in your memory, which of those details you will later recall, what you conclude about their personal characteristics, how you evaluate them, and, of course, how you behave toward them.

The cognitive approach to stereotyping, prejudice, and discrimination involves a fine-grained analysis of the role of stereotypes and bias in our social interactions. Two features of this approach should be emphasized: the idea that stereotyping is related to normal, universal cognitive processes and the fact that many of those processes take place automatically and without our awareness. Research based on this approach helped write a new chapter in the history of research on stereotyping, prejudice, and discrimination—and overall, it led social psychologists to the conclusion that people are essentially wired to stereotype others.

Stereotyping as a Basic Cognitive Process—and a Hidden Influence

As you enter the produce section of your local market, you see more than just "produce." The colorful shapes before you are instantly recognizable as bananas, apples, cucumbers, onions, and dozens of other fruits and vegetables. You make these distinctions without trying (if not, you are unlikely to be sent on the weekly run to the grocery store). Similarly, when you step into a friend's dining room, you can identify some objects as tables and some as chairs—not just as "furniture." If you are unable or unwilling to differentiate between the two, you probably will not be invited back.

The point is, to avoid categorizing all the stimuli you encounter is next to impossible; even if you could, doing so would be inadvisable. Because the world is a complicated place, you need categories in order to make your way through it. By grouping things based on their characteristics and functions, you can make sense of and manage the complexity of your environment. Knowledge about categories also serves as a guide for your behavior in different situations (Cantor & Mischel, 1979; Medin, 1989, 2000). Other people, of course, are a very important part of your social world. Therefore, just as you cannot help but assign labels to household items or fruits and vegetables, you cannot help but categorize people (Bodenhausen & Macrae, 1998; Fiske, 1998; Hamilton & Sherman, 1994).

Stereotyping, then, is a product of normal, universal cognitive processes (Hamilton & Sherman, 1994). It follows that the byproducts of stereotyping—that is, prejudice and discrimination—spring at least indirectly from basic aspects of human thought processes. Viewed from a cognitive perspective, then, stereotypes are not a feature of irrational thinking, and people who stereotype others are not necessarily motivated by hostility. Nor are competition and conflict necessary to the development of stereotypes. In short, stereotypes are not aberrations; people categorize one another and make assumptions based on those categorizations because doing so is helpful in many different ways (Macrae, Stangor, & Milne, 1994).

This way of thinking about stereotyping has some disturbing implications. First, prejudice is more subtle in its effects than we might think. One expert has estimated that only about ten percent of people in Western democracies are "blatantly biased" or "ill-intentioned extremists" (Fiske, 2002, pp. 123, 126). Most readers of this book, for example, probably would not feel much sympathy for George Wallace, the former governor

In a notorious display of blatant bias, Alabama Governor George Wallace blocked the entrance to the University of Alabama, prepared to prevent the registration of the school's first Black students, 1963

of Alabama, who in the 1960s personally stood in the doorway to prevent two black students from enrolling in the University of Alabama (Picture 11.5). More often, beliefs and feelings about groups make themselves felt in subtler, less public ways. Research rooted in the cognitive approach demonstrates how those subtle effects come about and how stereotypes can serve as hidden influences on our interactions with others (Bodenhausen & Macrae, 1998; Dovidio & Gaertner, 2010; Fiske, 1998; Hamilton & Sherman, 1994). One of the more unsettling conclusions from this research is that stereotypes affect the thoughts, feelings, and behaviors of even well-intentioned people who would prefer to be unprejudiced.

Biased Inferences

We dislike mean people and avoid them; admire smart people; and protect vulnerable people. To a great extent, our feelings and behavior toward others follow naturally from what we infer about them and their behavior. What determines our inferences, though? The answer should seem obvious: We decide what people are like based on what they say and do. A person's words and actions should speak for themselves, so that whether a person is male, female, black, or white should be beside the point. But the meaning of what people say and do is often far from straightforward (see Chapter 3). Because it is not always clear what people are thinking, feeling, and intending, we use stereotypes to resolve the ambiguity.

In two different studies, Duncan (1976) and Sagar and Schofield (1980) asked people to interpret behavior that could have been aggressive in intent. On a television monitor, Duncan's subjects, who were college students, watched what they thought was a real, ongoing social interaction between two male students, one that culminated in an ambiguous shove. In Sagar and Schofield's (1980) study, elementary school children viewed

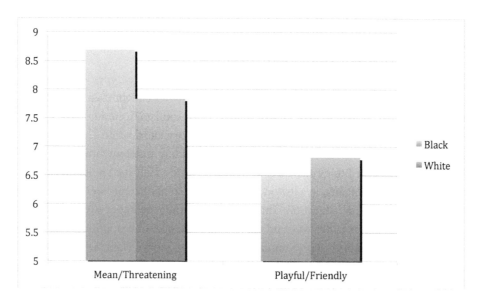

Figure 11.1: *Judgments of how mean/threatening and playful/friendly a child who engaged in ambiguously aggressive behavior seemed to be.*

Black children were judged to be more mean and threatening and less playful and friendly. Data derived from Sagar & Schofield (1980).

pictures of other children and listened to stories about the pictures ("David started poking him in the back with the eraser end of his pencil"). In both studies, the experimenters manipulated the race of the possible aggressor: half the time he was black, half the time, white.

Although these two studies involved different populations and used different methods, the results were quite similar. In both cases, the black protagonist's behavior—which was, of course, identical to the white protagonist's behavior—was seen as being meaner, more threatening, or violent (see **Figure 11.1**). Thus, a white person and a black person can do the same thing, yet elicit very different reactions from others (see also Stone, Perry, & Darley, 1997). When people make judgments about groups of people (as opposed to individuals), these differences in judgment can be even more exaggerated (Gill, 2003).

Such findings, of course, are not restricted to stereotypes associated with race. Condry and Condry (1976) screened a movie about a nine-month-old baby called Dana. To half the people in the study, Dana was said to be a boy; when they saw his strong reaction to a jack-in-the-box toy, they were sorry to see him become "angry." To the other half of the participants, Dana was a girl, and they were sorry to see her so "frightened" by the toy. The gender that researchers assigned to Dana affected how the participants construed the baby's other behaviors as well. Similarly, a person's gender affects how people interpret his or her performance on difficult tasks. When men succeed, their triumphs are attributed to ability; when they fail, their poor performance is blamed on bad luck or insufficient effort. In contrast, women's successes are more likely to be attributed to hard work, while their failures are chalked up to low ability or a task that was too difficult (Swim & Sanna, 1996).

As these examples show, when a stereotype is associated with a group, people are quick to assume that the behavior of a specific member of that group reflects the stereotype. This statement holds true, especially when the group in question is not one's own **in-group**, but an **out-group**. In part, this is because people tend to believe that members of out-groups are more similar to each other than members of their own in-groups, a bias known as the **out-group homogeneity effect** (Linville, Fischer, & Salovey, 1989; Park & Judd, 1990; Quattrone & Jones, 1980; Rubin & Badea, 2012). One implication of the out-group homogeneity effect is that people are more likely to see any given member of an out-group as having the traits that are stereotypical of his or her group than they are to see a member of their own in-group in a stereotypical way.

It is possible, of course, that participants in these studies applied their stereotypes without any qualms. They might have been fully aware that they were making biased judgments, and might even have cheerfully admitted as much to the experimenters. Other research, however, has shown similar effects among people who would be horrified to learn that their judgments were affected by social category information.

In a study by Darley and Gross (1983), students viewed one of four different videotapes of a white female fourth-grader and then were asked to evaluate her academic abilities. Half the videotapes opened with a sequence that presented the child, Hanna, in a low-income urban area; her parents were said to hold blue-collar jobs and to have only a high-school education. The other half of the videotapes showed the same child in a middle-class suburban setting; her father was said to be an attorney and her mother, a freelance writer. The purpose of this manipulation was to bring to mind the participants' social class stereotypes; the researchers assumed that their expectancies for Hanna's performance would be affected by their knowledge of her social class. Half the participants also viewed a second, relatively uninformative tape that showed Hanna working on problems from an achievement test. The remaining participants were not shown this segment. Thus, some participants learned only that Hanna's background was either blue-collar or middle class; others learned that information, but were also exposed to a sample of her performance (which was always identical). After viewing the tape(s), participants rated Hanna's achievement and academic level.

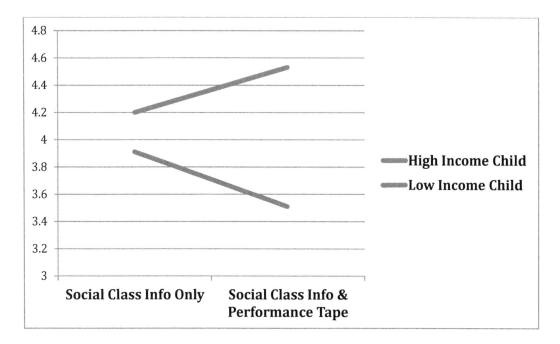

Figure 11.2: Judgments of a child's academic abilities as a function of alleged social class (high or low income) and performance sample (none or an ambiguous 12–minute long tape).

From Darley & Gross (1983), based on mean judgments of Hannah's reading, mathematics, and liberal arts abilities (expressed as grade levels).

Participants who viewed Hanna's performance reached conclusions about her abilities that were consistent with their social class stereotypes. Those who learned that the girl was from a low-income family saw her as being less talented academically than participants who thought she was from a more privileged family. What, though, of participants who had been given only social class information? In that case, there were no differences between the two groups: participants refused to make assumptions about Hanna's ability based only on her social class (see **Figure 11.2**). Thus, the subjects in this study were not bigoted and were not willing to make assumptions

SOCIAL PSYCHOLOGY IN THE COURTROOM: JUROR BIAS

Every few years or so, a high-profile trial involving a minority defendant seems to capture the attention of the media and the public. The cases differ, of course, but behind-the-scenes accounts usually include at least one common element: a serious concern about the composition of the jury. Defendants' lawyers typically devote a great deal of effort to ensuring that their clients will be judged by a true "jury of their peers," not those who might be prejudiced against them because of their race or ethnicity. The issue of race, for example, preoccupied both the prosecution and the defense in O. J. Simpson's 1995 murder trial

(Toobin, 1996). These kinds of concerns seem reasonable, given what is known about the ways in which stereotyping and prejudice affect how people process information.

Indeed, quite a few experimental simulations involving mock trials confirm that a person's race, ethnicity, gender, and sexual orientation do play a role in determining his or her fate. Bodenhausen (1988), for example, asked college students to play the role of jurors in an assault trial. The information presented to them was mixed—in other words, the case was far from open and shut. As a result, there was quite a bit of variability in the way participants made sense of what had happened. Nonetheless, participants were significantly more likely to lean toward a guilty verdict when the defendant was identified as "Carlos Ramirez" (from New Mexico) than when he was given the more nondescript name "Robert Johnson" (from Ohio). Bodenhausen and Lichtenstein (1987), Crawford and Skowronski (1998), and others have reported similar findings.

Other research involving mock trials has demonstrated less straightforward effects of social categories. In a study by Shaffer and Case (1982), mock jurors who were heterosexual gave more lenient sentences to defendants identified as being gay than to heterosexual defendants accused of the same crimes. Presumably, the participants were aware that they might be biased by the defendant's sexual orientation, and so bent over backward to avoid being unfair—so far backward, in fact, that they over-corrected for any possible bias. Other research indicates that mock jurors who are white sometimes make similar adjustments when making judgments about black defendants (Sargent & Bradfield, 2004). And in a broad review of the research literature, although Mazzella and Feingold (1994) found support for the hypothesis that black defendants receive harsher punishments than White defendants for many crimes, an exception to that rule was "white collar" crimes like embezzlement. In connection with those crimes, mock jurors tended to be more punitive toward *White* defendants than toward black defendants.

What do we know, though, about the role of stereotypes and prejudice in "real-world" courtrooms? Quite a bit, it turns out. Some researchers have concluded that in the United States, blacks in particular are subject to discrimination in terms of the severity of their sentences (Haney, 1991). To give just one example, young black people are more likely than whites of the same age to be held in detention while their cases are pending, instead of being released to a parent's custody (Leonard, Pope, & Feyerherm, 1995). On the other hand, a major study of court cases involving capital offenses (Baldus, Woodworth, and Pulaski, 1990) found that on average, black defendants were treated more leniently than white defendants. In part, however, that finding was due to the fact that when the *victim* of a murder was black, murderers were treated more leniently than when the victim was white, and most murder cases involve persons of the same race.

It seems clear that prejudice and stereotyping play an important role in the courtroom. And overall, it seems fair to say that members of stigmatized groups are at a disadvantage when they are judged by members of a society's dominant group. For example, black defendants are especially likely to receive harsh sentences if they have Afrocentric facial features—that is, features that are perceived to be more typical of African Americans than of whites (Blair, Judd, & Chapleau, 2004). Yet it is hard to argue with journalist Jeffrey Toobin, who suggests that lawyers "tread on dangerous ground when they make decisions about jurors based on generalizations about their ethnic backgrounds" (1996, p. 188).

about others based only on social categories. Apparently, they sincerely wanted to be fair and objective. Once they were given some raw behavioral data to work with, however, their stereotypes affected what they saw. From their perspective, their judgments were based on nothing but the facts. So even when people would not think of making judgments about others based on social class, ethnic background, race, gender, or sexual orientation, stereotypes can serve as hidden influences on how they see them.

In sum, avoiding generalizations about groups of people in judging individuals can be difficult, even when we are trying hard to prevent stereotypes from unduly influencing our judgments (Nelson, Biernat, & Manis, 1990). For a discussion of how stereotyping affects jurors' judgments, see the Social Psychology in the Courtroom box **below.**

Automatic Stereotyping and Prejudice

If stereotypes can affect our judgments when we do not want them to and bias our thinking without our awareness, can they do the same when we are not even aware that we are making judgments? In Chapter 3, we reviewed evidence for *spontaneous trait inferences*, in which people automatically form impressions of others' traits unintentionally, effortlessly, and without awareness (Uleman, Newman, & Moskowitz, 1996). Often, the people whose traits we infer can be categorized in a variety of ways. Can the stereotypes associated with those categories affect our spontaneous trait inferences? That is, if sentences like "Fred solves the mystery halfway through the book" can lead people to spontaneously infer the trait "clever," does it matter whether Fred is identified as a short-order cook or an investment banker?

To answer these questions, Wigboldus, Dijksterhuis, and van Knippenberg (2003; Wigboldus, Sherman, Franzese, & van Knippenberg, 2004) used the method developed by Newman (1991) and Uleman, Hon, Roman, and Moskowitz (1996) for studying spontaneous trait inferences. Subjects believed they were participating in a study of memory. Sentences were presented to them, followed by a single word. They were asked to quickly indicate whether or not that word had appeared in the preceding sentence by pressing a "yes" or "no" button on a keyboard. As in the Newman (1991) and Uleman et al. (1996) studies, the sentences of interest to the experimenters described behaviors that were clearly associated with a trait such as "hits the saleswoman" (aggressive) and "wins the science quiz" (smart). In Wigboldus et al.'s research, though, the type of person who was engaging in the behavior varied. In some cases it was a "skinhead" doing the hitting; in others, a "girl," and so forth. Some participants learned that a "professor" was the quiz winner; others, that the winner was a "garbage man."

Recall that people make few mistakes in this kind of experiment; what is of interest is how long they take to respond. When a word that was *not* in a sentence ("aggressive") matches an inference made in response to the sentence ("hits the saleswoman"), people are slower to respond correctly with a "no." The automatic inferences they make confuse them, slowing them down. For example, Wigboldus et al. found that when the actors in a sentence were engaging in stereotypical behavior (such as a professor winning a quiz), participants' reaction times were slower for trait words that were not in the sentence but were *consistent* with the behavior (intelligent) than for trait words that were not in the sentence, but were *inconsistent* with the behavior. In other words, stereotypes affected the participants' spontaneous trait inferences. Some of the results suggested that stereotypes are more likely to *inhibit* spontaneous inferences (for example, to discourage the inference that a garbage man is smart) than to facilitate them (for instance, to encourage the inference that a skinhead is violent). The important point, though, is that this research illustrates the hidden influences of stereotypes on person perception. Stereotypes affect the impressions we form of others, even when we are unaware that we are forming impressions.

The influences of stereotypes on spontaneous trait inferences are perhaps not surprising, given other research indicating that when a group is associated with a stereotype, simply seeing a member of that group can bring the stereotype to mind. Moreover, members of stigmatized groups can elicit instantaneously negative reactions (especially when people are cognitively loaded, and do not have the ability to second-guess their reactions). In a word, stereotyping and prejudice can be automatic (Bargh, 1994).

Consider, for example, the results of a study by Wittenbrink, Judd, and Park (1997; see Dovidio, Evans, & Tyler, 1986, for related findings). Wittenbrink et al. presented a series of favorable and unfavorable traits on a computer screen. Before each trait, the word "black" or "white" flashed very briefly (for a few milliseconds) across the screen; participants were almost never consciously aware of seeing those words. They were not asked to think about groups or group differences, but simply to decide whether the trait words they saw were real words (some were nonsense words). Researchers found that in this type of procedure, known as a lexical decision task, participants will identify words such as "fork" more quickly when they are presented right after related words like "spoon." Thus, lexical decision tasks can shed light on the associations people have made—consciously or unconsciously—between different concepts. Wittenbrink et al. used this method to determine the kinds of traits that white college students automatically associate with black people and white people.

Did participants automatically associate black people with *any* negative trait term? No. Nor did they associate whites with all positive attributes. However, they were quick to respond to (that is, identify as words) unflattering traits that are part of the cultural stereotype of African Americans (such as violent, lazy) when those trait words followed the subliminal appearance of the word "black." In addition, participants were quick to respond to flattering trait words that are stereotypic of whites (such as intelligent, responsible) when those trait words followed the subliminal appearance of the word "white." Consequently, people in this study revealed very specific prejudices, and they did so without awareness.

Given Wittenbrink et al.'s findings, we might expect that our typical affective reactions to people from other groups will tend to be more negative than our reactions to fellow group members. In other words, automatic stereotyping could lead to automatic prejudice. Fazio, Jackson, Dunton, and Williams (1995) tested that hypothesis using another method designed to get people to reveal their thoughts and feelings about different groups without being aware of it. They presented white participants with adjectives such as "wonderful," "disgusting," "attractive," and "annoying" and asked them to indicate as quickly as possible whether the words were "good" or "bad" by pressing one of two buttons. There was a catch, however: each adjective was preceded by a brief presentation of a person's face. Half the time the face belonged to a white person and half the time to a black person.

Fazio et al. wanted to know whether there would be a relationship between the race of the face in the photograph and the time participants took to make their judgments about the adjectives. They reasoned that if people had just been exposed to faces they felt positively about, they would be quick to identify good words. On the other hand, if they had just been exposed to faces they felt negatively about, they would be quick to identify bad words. That is, if participants' attitudes toward the faces were automatically activated, those attitudes would prepare the participants for—and make it easier for them to identify—words that matched those attitudes. (See Chapter 5 for more discussion of this experimental procedure.)

Given the results of the other studies reviewed in this section, Fazio et al.'s findings probably will not surprise you. When white participants were primed with white faces, they were quicker to determine that favorable adjectives were "good." When they were primed with black faces, they were quicker to determine that unfavorable adjectives were "bad." For a few black students who participated in Fazio et al.'s study, the results were essentially the opposite of those for the white participants. In sum, this study revealed that people have a tendency to

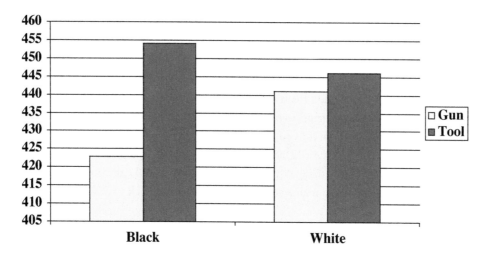

Figure 11.3: Mean times (in milliseconds) to identify guns and tools as a function of prime type (black faces or white faces).

Participants primed with black faces were quicker to identify weapons. From Payne (2001), Experiment 1.

automatically evaluate members of other groups, and that evaluation is negative. Prejudice can make itself felt as soon as people categorize each other.

A study by Payne (2001; Payne, Lambert, & Jacoby, 2002) suggests that in certain circumstances, these automatic reactions could have deadly consequences. As in Fazio et al.'s study, researchers primed nonblack participants with brief presentations of white and black faces and asked them to make a judgment immediately after each face. In this study, though, the judgment involved identifying an object. Half the time, the object was a tool (an electric drill, for example); half the time, it was a weapon (a handgun). Participants made their judgments by pressing one of two buttons. Although the objects were presented for just a fraction of a second, they made few errors. However, they were quicker to identify handguns as weapons when the guns were preceded by the brief appearance of a black person's face (see **Figure 11.3**). In a second study, in which participants were required to respond very quickly, the researchers found that they were more likely to identify the tools *errone-ously* as weapons when the tools were paired with a photograph of a black person's face. (For related findings, see Correll, Park, Judd, & Wittenbrink, 2002; Eberhardt, Goff, Purdie, & Davies, 2004; Greenwald, Oakes, & Hoffman, 2003; and Unkelbach, Forgas, & Denson, 2008).

These findings may simply demonstrate, once again, that dangerousness is an important component of the African American stereotype. But if we can generalize from the college students who participated in this study to other people—police officers, for example (Plant & Peruche, 2005; Sim, Correll, & Sadler, 2013; but see Correll et al., 2006)—then Payne's results assume more importance. Serious consequences could follow from the finding that if you belong to a specific group, other people could be biased to perceive an object in your hands as a weapon. In 1999, a man named Amadou Diallo was killed after being shot at 41 times by four New York City police officers, who thought he was brandishing a weapon. Unfortunately, the object in his hand was not a weapon at all: it was a wallet. Given the results of Payne's studies, it should come as no surprise that Diallo was a black man.

Implicit Attitudes

Imagine that you are working in a supermarket stock room. You have been asked to shelve a small truckload of newly arrived items. Four products are being unloaded, and your job is to quickly shelve them as they come off the truck. Bagels and hot dog buns are to be deposited on the shelf to your left, oranges and lemons on the shelf to your right. Needless to say, this is not a mind-bending task, but it is made even easier if you boil it down to a simple decision rule: bread to the left and citrus fruits to the right. The fact that bagels and hot dog buns "go together," as do oranges and lemons, will make it easier for you to keep up with the rapid flow of items from the truck.

Now imagine a slightly different scenario. This time, the rule is hot dog buns and oranges to the left, bagels and lemons to the right. We will assume that most readers of this book would still be able to handle the job. But in this case, it is a little more likely that a manager who wanders over to check your work would find squashed fruit and sesame bagels rolling off into the dairy aisle. Trying to group things that you would not ordinarily categorize together can be challenging.

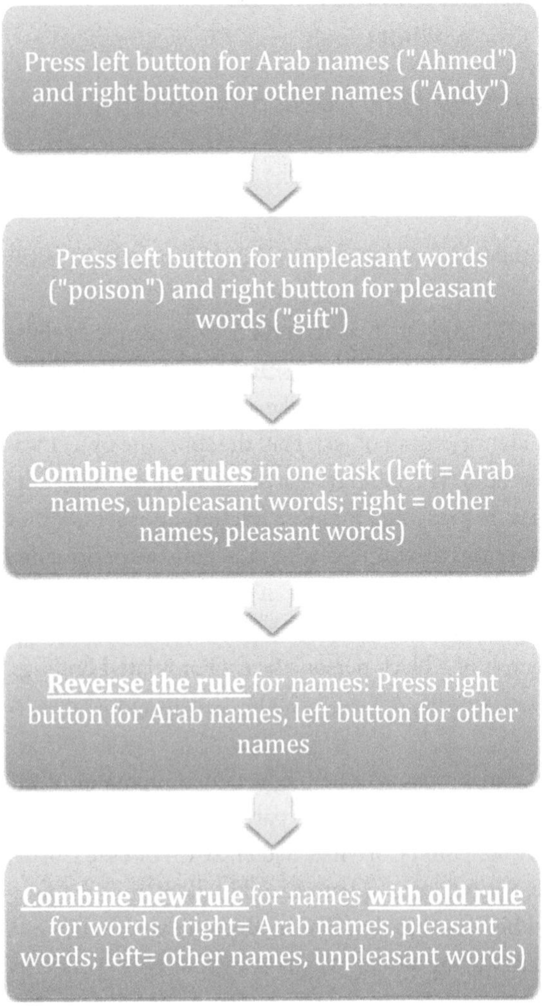

If that logic is clear to you, then the rationale for the **Implicit Association Test** (IAT; Greenwald, McGhee, & Schwartz, 1998; Greenwald, Banaji, Rudman, Farnham, Nosek, & Mellott, 2002; Nosek, Banaji, & Greenwald, 2002; Nosek, Greenwald, & Banaji, 2007) will also be clear. The IAT is a computer-administered measure involving a sequence of tasks. In the first stage, people learn to respond to words or pictures representing two social categories (elderly and young people, in some cases) by quickly pressing buttons with either the left or right hand (for example, elderly = left, and young = right). Then they repeat the task, this time responding with one button press or the other to favorable and unfavorable words, like "rotten" and "pleasant." The next task is a little more challenging: the two tasks are *combined*. This time, both types of stimuli—youths versus the elderly and positive versus negative—are presented, and participants must respond to each one as they did earlier.

At this point, a new rule is established for the social category stimuli (now elderly = right, and young = left), and participants practice making the distinction. In the fifth and last stage, the new rule for the social category words or pictures is combined with the one for the positive and negative words. What is most interesting to researchers is which of the "combined" tasks proves easier for participants—that is, which is performed more quickly, with fewer errors. That piece of information, it is believed, can reveal something

Figure 11.4: An example of the Implicit Association Test (IAT).

Based on Greenwald, McGhee, and Schwartz (1998).

about a person's *implicit attitudes* (see Chapter 5), which are defined as those attitudes that people either will not or cannot admit to others, or even to themselves. For example, if a person has an easier time with the task when young people and favorable words call for the same response, and thus "go together" (and when simultaneously, old people and unfavorable words are paired), she is probably biased to evaluate young people more favorably than old people (Nelson, 2005; North & Fiske, 2012). If the opposite is true, the participant probably has a pro-elderly bias (see **Figure 11.4**).

An interesting feature of implicit attitudes toward different groups, as measured in this way, is that they do not necessarily correlate highly with *explicit attitudes* (see Chapter 5)—that is, attitudes that are consciously and intentionally expressed (Greenwald et al., 1998, 2002; Karpinski & Hilton, 2001; Nosek, 2007). This discrepancy could be due in part to people's reluctance to admit to socially unacceptable thoughts and feelings about racial, ethnic, age, and other groups. However, it could also be due to their lack of awareness of their own attitudes.

Why, though, should we believe that what the IAT measures is an attitude? First of all, the IAT produces the results we would expect when it is used to confirm widely shared, socially acceptable attitudes. For example, when insects are compared to flowers, almost everyone has an easier time responding when insects are paired with negative words and flowers are paired with positive words (Greenwald et al., 1998). The meaning of that result is clear, so why should we not take IAT results seriously when what is compared are attitudes toward white people and black people (Smith-McLallen, Johnson, Dovidio, & Pearson, 2006)? If "black" and "awful," on the one hand, and "white" and "wonderful," on the other, seem to go together as naturally and easily as oranges and lemons, it is hard to imagine that we have not learned something important about a person's attitudes.

Implicit attitudes, as measured by the IAT, have also been shown to be associated with other indicators of stereotyping and prejudice (Greenwald, Poehlman, Uhlmann, & Banaji, 2009). For example, in studies by Gawronski, Ehrenberg, Banse, Zukova, and Klauer (2003), participants completed a version of the IAT that was designed to measure the extent to which they associated men with career-related words (like salary and economy) and women with household-related words (such as children and kitchen). They then watched men and women either being interviewed or having a group discussion. Gawronski et al. found that participants with implicitly sexist attitudes were more likely than others to attribute gender stereotypical traits to the men ("assertive," among others) and women ("domestic")

Posture and body language are the kinds of implicit indicators of prejudice that the IAT can predict. Is this man perhaps interacting with a member of a stigmatized group?

in the group. Similarly, Hugenberg and Bodenhausen (2003) and Hutchings and Haddock (2008) found that white people's implicit prejudice toward black people predicts their readiness to perceive anger in black—but not white—faces. Note, however that the extent to which the IAT reveals negative or ambivalent attitudes toward black people by black people themselves is a more complicated issue, and not all of the variables associated with implicit in-group or out-group preferences have been identified (but see Ashburn-Nardo, Knowles, & Monteith, 2003; Livingston, 2002; Nosek et al., 2002).

Some researchers urge caution in interpreting IAT results (Oswald, Mitchell, Blanton, Jaccard, & Tetlock, 2013). Andreychik and Gill (2012), Arkes and Tetlock (2004), and Uhlmann, Brescoll, and Paluck (2006) all point out that people could associate an out-group with negative thoughts and feelings because they feel bad about the way that group has been treated, not because they dislike that group. If so, then the IAT scores of a white person who feels chronically guilty about the discrimination black Americans face could be identical to those of a white person with deep-seated prejudice against blacks. Both might associate black people with the concept "awful," but for different reasons. Another matter of concern is that with practice, people can "fake" their performance, so that they appear to be less biased than they actually are (Czellar, 2006; De Houwer, Beckers, & Moors, 2007; Fiedler & Bluemke, 2005; Hu, Rosenfeld, & Bodenhausen, 2012; Rohner, Schroder-Abe, & Schutz, 2013). Finally, some researchers (Blanton & Jaccard, 2006; Blanton, Jaccard, Gonzales, & Christie, 2006) emphasize that even if the IAT can be used to assess *relative* levels of bias in a sample of participants (for example, liking young people more than old people), there are no criteria for using it to confidently label someone as clearly "prejudiced" against a given group.

Nonetheless, and as we just saw, the IAT has been shown in a number of studies (including also McConnell & Liebold, 2001, and Neumann, Hülsenbeck, & Seibt, 2004) to be a significant predictor of discriminatory behaviors—especially spontaneous, subtle behaviors that people do not consciously plan or control. Hence, this research provides more evidence that our attitudes toward members of different groups are automatically activated whenever we encounter them. The IAT is one of the more easily administered measures for demonstrating this phenomenon and produces stronger effects than other measures (Devine, 2001).

The Cognitive Approach: A Summary

The cognitive approach suggests that stereotyping is a natural consequence of the way we gather and process information about others. It also suggests that prejudice is deeply embedded in people's everyday social interactions and behaviors, in ways that are often hard for them to detect. That is, stereotypes are another of the many hidden influences on our dealings with others. Our biased beliefs and feelings about groups unintentionally color our interpretations of other people's behavior. That is true both for our immediate, spontaneous social inferences and for our more careful, deliberate judgments. A number of different measures have been developed to show that stereotypes are activated automatically and become cognitively accessible as soon as we have determined a person's gender, race, ethnicity, occupation, or other meaningful social category (for yet another example, see Banaji & Hardin, 1996).

As we will see in the next section, the importance of these effects is magnified by the fact that once stereotypes are in place, they are remarkably hard to eliminate.

Think Like a Social Psychologist

Making connections

—Stereotypes are often well learned and cognitively accessible. In light of that, consider the implications of research on social facilitation (see Chapter 8) for the expression of stereotypes in social situations. In what situations might stereotyping be a "dominant response?"

Designing research

—An implicit measure of stereotyping or prejudice reveals that people have thoughts and feelings about out-group members that they do not consciously control. Besides the measures described in this chapter, can you think of other ways to detect people's implicit biases?

THE STUBBORN AND SELF-PERPETUATING NATURE OF STEREOTYPES

What accounts for the staying power of our beliefs about other groups of people? In part, it could be the fact that biased inferences seem to provide support for the beliefs that led to those inferences. For example, if we expect girls to be more easily frightened than boys, that expectation could lead us to interpret as fear a girl's ambiguous response to a surprising event (Condry & Condry, 1976). We could then treat our interpretation of the girl's response as objective evidence that girls are indeed more fragile than boys. Many of our expectations have this self-perpetuating quality (Hill, Lewicki, Czyzewska, & Boss, 1989).

Other processes contribute to the stubbornness of stereotypes, making them more difficult to change than early researchers ever imagined. One of those processes is memory.

Stereotypes and Memory

In Chapter 3, we learned that when people have an expectation for the way a particular person is likely to behave, they tend to remember expectancy-inconsistent (or "incongruent") information about that person's behavior better than expectancy-consistent information. In other words, if we think that Albert is smart and then see him complete both the *New York Times* crossword puzzle in five minutes and back his car into a tree, we will more easily recall the driving mishap (Hastie & Kumar, 1979; Bargh & Thein, 1985; Srull & Wyer, 1989). Recall why that is so: When people act in ways that are surprising, we usually want to understand why. We think about those behaviors more, which makes them more memorable. Remember, though, that when expectancies are very well established, this incongruency effect can disappear (Stangor & McMillan, 1992).

What happens when an expectation is based on a stereotype? In that case, the expectation that a person will be smart, dumb, kind, or hostile will be based solely on the person's social category—in other words, the racial, ethnic, occupational, or gender group to which we have assigned the person. Stereotypes, of course, are often very well established. In addition, people generally acknowledge that some group members do not perfectly fit the stereotypes for their groups. Therefore, behavior that does not fit a stereotype will not be so surprising that we would feel compelled to explain it (Srull, 1981).

Overall, then, we might expect that people will tend *not* to remember stereotype-inconsistent behaviors more than consistent ones. And we would be right. When we observe others' behavior, and all we know about those people is that they are "women," "Latinos," "business majors," "jocks," or members of some other social category, we are more likely to remember all the ways in which those people confirmed the stereotypes associated with their groups than the ways in which they did not (Rothbart, Evans, & Fulero, 1979; Stangor & McMillan, 1992). For example, Cohen (1981) showed participants a videotape of a woman celebrating her birthday with her husband. Some participants were told that she was a librarian, others that she was a waitress. What did participants remember about her? Those who thought she was a librarian were more likely than others to remember that she wore glasses and had a collection of classical music. Those who thought she was a waitress remembered that she drank beer and watched television.

Stereotypes, then, maintain themselves by affecting what we attend to and what we store in memory. They also confirm themselves *retroactively*. In other words, even categorizing people after the fact can result in our remembering things about them that confirm our stereotypes. Snyder and Uranowitz (1979) asked people to read about the life of one "Betty K." Later, some of the participants in the study were told that Betty had self-identified as gay and was leading a lesbian lifestyle. Others were told that she was heterosexual. This new information affected participants' memories about Betty. Those who were told that she was a lesbian were more likely to report incorrectly that in high school she never went out with men. Those who thought she was heterosexual were more likely to remember that Betty had gone out on several dates, but they *incorrectly* remembered and reported various details that were consistent with her not being gay. Though these findings have been controversial (Belezza & Bower, 1981), other research indicates that people often reconstruct past events in a biased way that conforms to their expectations (Hirt, McDonald, and Markman, 1998).

Normal memory processes not only contribute to the stability and tenacity of preexisting stereotypes; they can also contribute to the development of those stereotypes in the first place. In a classic study, Hamilton and Gifford (1976) presented participants with a series of behaviors performed by members of two groups. They presented twice as many "Group A" behaviors as "Group B" behaviors. Some of the behaviors were desirable ("is rarely late for work") and some undesirable ("always talks about himself"), but within each group, the ratio of desirable to undesirable behaviors was the same: there were more than twice as many desirable behaviors. Afterward, people were asked to recall as many of the behaviors as they could and to report their impressions of the groups.

In a world without bias, in which people's minds function like well-oiled machines, the results of this study would be straightforward and uninteresting. Perfectly rational people would recall similar proportions of desirable and undesirable behaviors for both Group A and Group B and would not differ in how favorably they perceived the two groups. In the real world, however, people have a tendency to recall distinctive events (that is, events that stand out) more than nondistinctive events. Thus, we would expect them to be more likely to recall a given Group B behavior than a given Group A behavior and to recall a given undesirable behavior better than a desirable one. After all, there were fewer Group B behaviors than Group A behaviors, and fewer undesirable behaviors than desirable behaviors. Furthermore, an event that is *doubly* distinctive is especially memorable. Undesirable Group B behaviors fall into that category, and indeed, participants recalled a greater proportion of such behaviors. Their impressions of the two groups followed suit: they evaluated Group B more negatively.

This phenomenon, called the **illusory correlation** effect, has been replicated many times (Hamilton & Sherman, 1994; Stroessner & Plaks, 2001). In everyday life, desirable behaviors are more common than undesirable ones. People usually behave in a normative, socially acceptable manner; nasty or unpleasant behavior is the exception to the rule. Moreover, in everyday life, interactions with members of minority groups are more distinctive than interactions with members of the dominant group, for by definition, members of minority groups are less numerous than members of other groups. Research on illusory correlations indicates that even if there were no basis whatsoever for attributing negative traits to a minority group, stereotypes about the group would develop anyway. To a person in England, for example, a hostile interaction with a Jamaican or an annoying experience with an Arab would stand out in memory more than similar experiences with native British

Table 11.3: Men and women: Examples of subtypes

WOMEN	MEN
Housewife	Blue collar worker
Businesswoman	Businessman
Athletic woman	Athlete
Sexy woman	Ladies' man
Midlife woman	Family man
Menopausal woman	Macho man

Sources: Deaux, Winton, Crowley, & Lewis, (1985); Edwards (1992); Marcus-Newhall, Thompson, & Thomas (2001).

People could maintain a stereotype of a "college student" while at the same time mentally constructing a variety of college student subtypes, such as art students, fraternity brothers, Asian students, nerds, and older students

people. Stereotypes need not be based on even a grain of truth. They can come into being simply because of the way in which well-meaning people remember things.

Subtyping

Surely there must be times when we simply cannot confirm our stereotypes. It is one thing to interpret ambiguous behavior in terms of our preconceptions about different groups of people. It is quite another to encounter strong, self-confident women who can repair the trucks they drive; brilliant, articulate, hardworking black professors; and Jewish mixed martial arts fighters with embarrassingly low SAT scores, and yet pretend that they fit our stereotypes.

But even in the face of disconfirming evidence of this sort (which people often find instinctively disturbing—Flannigan, Miles, Quadflieg, & Macrae, 2013), our stereotypes can remain surprisingly unscathed. When faced with individuals who definitely do not conform to our expectations for them based on their race, ethnicity, age, or gender, we can create category **subtypes** (Deutsch & Fazio, 2008; Kunda & Oleson, 1995; Weber & Crocker, 1983; Rothbart & John, 1985; see **Table 11.3**). In other words, we store these people in memory as special instances of more general types. Subtyping is especially likely to happen if several of the disconfirming examples share similar features. Thus, after interacting with a black computer programmer, a black lawyer, and a black cardiologist, a white person might construct a new subcategory of black people, "black professionals."

Interestingly, subtyping seems to leave the broader, more general stereotype intact. Rothbart, Sriram, and Davis-Stitt (1996) found that even when people had created new subtypes of Asian, black, and gay people, they could more easily retrieve from memory information about people who were more prototypically (from their perspective) Asian, black, and gay. Even if you have categorized a Republican reader of the *Wall Street Journal* as a "politically conservative gay man," for example, he will not be the person who springs to mind when you are asked to name a gay person. Nor will his characteristics be incorporated into the stereotypes you might continue to use to form impressions of others you label as gay.

The Self-Fulfilling Prophecy Revisited

Based on observations of classroom behavior, researchers have concluded that many teachers have different expectations for the boys and girls in their classes. Specifically, they expect boys to be more persistent and academically assertive than girls, and as a result, they treat boys differently from girls. When boys get stuck trying to answer a question, teachers are more likely to give them extra help so they can come up with the answer themselves. When boys speak out of turn, teachers answer them, but when girls speak out of turn, they are told to raise their hands (Long, 1993).

One might argue that if so many teachers have such gender-biased expectations, those expectations must be based on real gender differences. Furthermore, if teachers' beliefs about boys' more energetic classroom behavior were wrong, wouldn't they eventually realize their mistake and stop treating male and female students differently? Expectations, after all, should be based on reality.

As we saw in Chapter 3, however, expectations can *create* reality. Research on the *self-fulfilling prophecy* (Darley & Fazio, 1980) shows that our beliefs about people can lead to behaviors that confirm those beliefs. That is, teachers' stereotypes about girls and boys could actually create the expected gender differences—and in doing so, "confirm" their reality. If girls are treated differently from boys—if less is expected from them and they get the message that asserting themselves is not acceptable—they could well become less confident, less likely to raise their hands, and less likely to persist in trying to answer a question. An observer in the classroom, however, would see only the gender differences in behavior, not the complicated interpersonal processes that led to those differences. In fact, teachers themselves are unlikely to be aware of their role in creating such self-fulfilling prophecies.

A study by Word, Zanna, and Cooper (1974) shows how stereotypes can lead us to induce the kind of

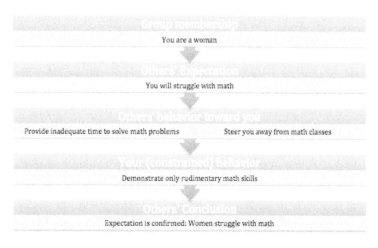

Figure 11.5: Gender stereotypes and the self-fulfilling prophecy: An illustrative example.

behavior we expect to see in others. In the first part of the study, white participants each played the role of an interviewer and met with white and black people, who they thought were playing the role of job applicants. The interviewees were actually confederates of the experimenter, who had been trained to behave alike and give the same answers to questions. The researchers found that the interviewers treated white and black applicants differently: They made less eye contact with black applicants, were less likely to sit facing them, and asked fewer questions of them. Clearly, the participants had different attitudes toward white and black people.

What were the consequences of this differential treatment of job applicants? In a second part of the study, participants—all white—played the role of job applicants, and this time, the confederates served as the *interviewers*. The confederates were trained to treat applicants in one of two ways: warmly, as the white applicants had been treated in the first part of the study, or coolly, as the black applicants had been treated. Later, the researchers showed videotapes of the interviews to a separate group of people—who had not participated in the experiment—and asked them to rate the applicants. Participants who interacted with the chilly interviewer—that is, those who were treated as if they were black—were evaluated more negatively than the other participants. In sum, behaviors that are rooted in generalizations about groups of people can constrain members of those groups in such a way that there is little else they can do but act out the roles we have forced on them. Consequently, we create the evidence that confirms our stereotypes (see **Figure 11.5**).

The Consequences of Suppressing Stereotypes

One psychologist has offered a more optimistic perspective on stereotyping. In line with many of the findings already reviewed in this chapter, Devine (1989a, b) assumed that well-learned, widely shared cultural stereotypes are activated automatically when we encounter members of other groups. This unintentional activation of stereotypes, she thought, was independent of prejudice—that is, independent of a person's conscious acceptance or rejection of stereotypes. Nonetheless, Devine hypothesized that important differences exist between people who are prejudiced or unprejudiced. Prejudiced people, she suggested, allow their automatically activated stereotypes to guide their interactions with others. In contrast, people who are low in prejudice engage in both "intentional inhibition of the automatically activated stereotype" and "intentional activation of nonprejudiced beliefs" (Devine, 1989b, pp. 6, 7). In other words, despite the automatic activation of stereotypes, such people can consciously strive to override them and treat others fairly.

How easy is it, though, for people to correct for the possible effects of stereotypes on their impressions and evaluations of others? Studies by Macrae, Bodenhausen, Milne, and Jetten (1994) show how surprisingly difficult it is to suppress thoughts about stereotypes, simply by trying to do so. In one of these studies, participants were asked to spend five minutes making up a story about a person known to them only from a photograph—a person who happened to be a skinhead. Half the participants were asked not to allow any stereotypes they might have about skinheads to color their stories. They complied with those instructions: the stories they told were freer of stereotypical traits and behaviors than the ones told by other participants. (For example, their stories were less likely to suggest that the person in the photo was hostile and violent.) The participants were then shown a second photograph of a different skinhead and asked to tell a story about a day in his life. This time, however, they received no special instructions regarding stereotypes.

You might not be surprised to learn that the stories told by participants who had previously been asked to suppress their stereotypes were more stereotypical than before. After all, those participants were no longer constrained in what they could think and say. More striking was that their stories were even more packed with stereotypes than the stories told by people who had never been asked to suppress stereotypes (see **Table 11.4**). Trying to suppress their thoughts about stereotypes seemed to cause an avalanche of stereotypical thoughts when they ceased their efforts at suppression. In a second study by Macrae et al. (1994), after participants had made up their initial stories, they were told they would have an opportunity to meet the skinhead in the photograph. Those who had tried to suppress their thoughts about skinhead stereotypes chose to sit further away from the person than the other participants. Thus, the preoccupation with an unfavorable stereotype that is caused by trying to avoid thinking about it can affect people's behavior toward targets of the stereotype.

Many other studies have confirmed that trying not to think about stereotypes can be difficult (Geeraert, 2013; Monteith, Sherman, & Devine, 1998; Wegner, 1994; Zhang & Hunt, 2008). In general, research shows that suppressing thoughts of *any* kind can be quite difficult (Wegner, 1992). Although thinking about things or not thinking about them is easy, trying not to think about one thing in particular is more challenging. Suppressed thoughts tend to return later with a vengeance, a phenomenon known as the rebound effect (Wegner, Schneider, Carter, & White, 1987). In addition, when people are pressured or distracted as they try to suppress a thought (as is often the case in everyday life), they have difficulty not blurting it out or acting on it. In such circumstances, the suppressed thought is said to be hyperaccessible (Wegner & Erber, 1992). Thus, suppressing thoughts about food while on a diet, about alcohol while trying to abstain, or about romance while in the presence of someone

Table 11.4: Suppression of stereotypes and their rebound

STORY	FIRST SUPPRESS, THEN NO INSTRUCTIONS	NO INSTRUCTIONS FOR EITHER STORY
First story	5.54	6.95
Second story	7.83	7.08

Stories (about skinheads) were rated for stereotypicality, with scores that could range from 1 (not at all stereotypic) to 9 (very stereotypic). Participants who told the most stereotypical stories were those who had previously tried to suppress thoughts about the stereotype.

Source: Macrae, Bodenhausen, Milne, & Jetten (1994), Experiment 1.

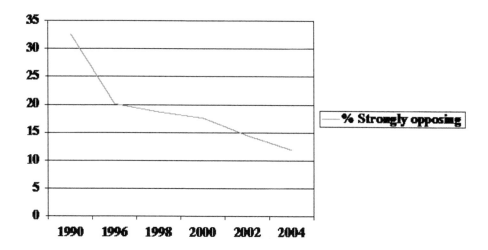

Figure 11.6: Percentage of white Americans strongly opposing "having a close relative or family member marrying a black person," 1990–2004.

From Davis, Smith, & Marsden (2005), data from the General Social Surveys (http://sda.berkeley.edu/).

who is unattainable might have unanticipated effects. The same is true of suppressing stereotypes. Apparently, people cannot easily will themselves to be unbiased.

Modern and Symbolic Racism

By the late 1980s, it was clear to researchers that stereotypes are hard-to-control hidden influences on behavior—in the words of one social psychologist (Bargh, 1999), "cognitive monsters." Ironically, surveys taken at the time indicated that at least in the United States, overt prejudice was becoming less common than in the past. Between the 1950s and 1980s, the number of people who subscribed to overt antiblack biases declined dramatically (Dovidio & Gaertner, 1986), and some data indicate a continuation of that trend today (see **Figure 11.6**).

How can we reconcile these cheery survey results with the growing conviction among social psychologists that intergroup bias is even more pervasive and difficult to eradicate than they had ever suspected? One answer is that the relationship between people's true feelings and what they report on surveys can be less than straightforward (Crandall & Eshelman, 2003). As Crosby, Bromley, and Saxe (1980) argue, people's explicit reports of their attitudes in response to such surveys are as much a reflection of their desire to *appear* unprejudiced as of their internalized beliefs and feelings.

For this reason, psychologists who wish to measure individual differences in explicit racism have relied less and less on straightforward questions about hostile feelings toward different ethnic and racial groups. Subtler measures seem to be called for. Among those are the Modern Racism Scale (MRS; McConahay, Hardee, & Batts, 1981) and the Symbolic Racism Scale (Henry & Sears, 2002), which were designed to allow respondents to express their dislike of black Americans by reporting opposition to social policies and trends they thought favorable or advantageous to black people. Someone who might be embarrassed to report outright hostility toward black people, the reasoning went, might still agree with statements like "Blacks are getting too demanding in their push for equal rights," or "Over the past few years, blacks have gotten more economically than they deserve." Although endorsing those statements might not necessarily be a consequence of unacknowledged racism, doing so would be one way to express such feelings.

Intransigent Stereotypes: A Summary

Once established, stereotypes are hard to change. What we remember about other people's behavior tends to be consistent with how we stereotype the groups they belong to. In some cases, the fact that we can recall people behaving in stereotypical ways is not surprising, because without being aware of it, we actually *elicit* such behavior from people. That is, our stereotypes can lead to self-fulfilling prophecies. Stereotypes can even survive our encounters with people who clearly contradict them. When that happens, we respond by subtyping people—seeing them as exceptions to the general rule.

What if a person tries to purge stereotypes from his or her thinking? Research on thought suppression shows that doing so is no simple matter. In fact, vigorous efforts not to think about stereotypes can paradoxically make them even *more* likely to affect our interactions with others. Overall, then, even people with the best of intentions, who deplore bigotry, seem vulnerable to stereotyping and prejudice in a variety of subtle ways.

Think Like a Social Psychologist

Making connections
—In Chapter 3, we reviewed research on circumstances that might weaken or eliminate self-fulfilling prophecies. In light of that research, outline some of the conditions under which stereotypes might *not* lead to behavioral confirmation via self-fulfilling prophecies.

Understanding everyday behavior
—People who are prejudiced toward another group sometimes claim that "some of my best friends" are members of that group. Could any of the research we just reviewed help to explain how people might be sincere in making such a claim?

IS IT HUMAN NATURE TO BE PREJUDICED? MORE EVIDENCE

The ease with which we adopt stereotypes, how pervasively they affect our impressions and judgments, and how difficult they are to modify may be less surprising to you after we review evidence for how deeply rooted "us versus them" thinking is in human behavior. In addition, you will see how your own responses to being stereotyped can paradoxically reaffirm the stereotype.

In-Group Bias and Minimal Groups

Obviously, people like their own groups more than they like other groups. Not only that; they give preferential treatment to members of their own groups and are more likely to feel empathy for them than for out-group members (Cikara, Bruneau, & Saxe, 2011). This phenomenon, known as *in-group bias* (Brewer & Brown, 1998; Castelli, Tomelleri, & Zogmaister, 2008; Wilder, 1981), might not be so surprising were it not for how pervasive it is. Research done using the **minimal group technique** (Tajfel, 1982; Tajfel & Billig, 1974) reveals that just about any criterion that can be used to divide people into groups, no matter how trivial, can and will be used as a basis for discrimination.

In one of the best-known studies of this kind, Tajfel, Billig, Bundy, and Flament (1971), presented teenage boys with slides consisting of clusters of dots and asked them to estimate how many dots were on each slide. They then informed the boys that each of them belonged to one of two groups, either "dot overestimators" or "dot underestimators." This distinction would not seem to be terribly important. In the next part of the study, researchers asked the boys to allocate "points" to the two groups—points that could supposedly be exchanged for money. Although each boy knew that he himself would not be getting any of the money, on average, participants awarded more points to their own groups. Minimal group effects like this one can be created on just about any basis, from a coin toss to who gets a blue or green badge.

There is a physiological basis for this effect. Van Bavel, Packer, and Cunningham (2008) found that people who are randomly assigned to groups immediately begin to demonstrate different patterns of neural activity in response to in-group and out-group members. Activation of one brain region in particular, the orbitofrontal cortex, was found to be a significant predictor of the extent to which research participants preferred people in their in-group to people in the out-group.

Minimal group effects are most often explained in terms of social identity theory (Kuhl, 1997; Tajfel & Turner, 1979, 1986). According to this theory, people want to feel good about themselves, but the "self" consists not just of one's personal identity, but of one's **social identity**. Our social identities are based on the groups we belong to, and the overall positivity or negativity of our social identities depends on how we feel about those groups. Hence, we are biased to evaluate our in-groups positively, even to favor them over other groups. In sum, according to social identity theory, our tendency to want to like ourselves will lead us almost inevitably to discriminate against members of other groups.

Social identity theory represents another broad approach to thinking about stereotyping, prejudice, and discrimination: the **motivational perspective** (also sometimes referred to as the psychodynamic perspective—Allport, 1954; Ashmore & Del Boca, 1981; Monteith, Zuwerink, & Devine, 1994; Newman & Caldwell, 2005). From this perspective, people's motives and needs underlie their tendency to create negative images of out-groups and discriminate against them. Denigrating another group and its traditions can serve as a strategy—albeit indirect, destructive, and, in the end, not terribly effective—for helping people feel better about themselves.

As we might infer from this discussion, social identity theory predicts that when a person discriminates, his self-esteem will get a boost. In a review of the literature, Rubin and Hewstone (1998) found that the evidence tends to support that hypothesis. However, social identity theory also suggests that low self-esteem *predicts* discrimination: that is, people with low levels of self-esteem are supposed to be more likely to discriminate than people with high self-esteem (Hogg & Abrams, 1990). Research has been less supportive of this prediction. Indeed, a review of the literature by Aberson, Healy, and Romero (2000) revealed that people with *high* self-esteem discriminate more readily than others against out-groups. Apparently, discrimination is more effective for maintaining high self-esteem than it is for raising low self-esteem. Experimental studies, though, show that when people are directly threatened, insulted, or given false negative feedback, they often respond to such assaults on their self-esteem by stereotyping out-group members (Fein & Spencer, 1997; Kunda & Sinclair, 1999).

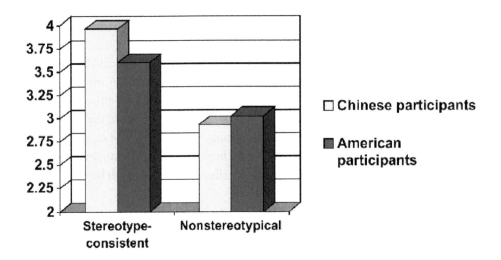

Figure 11.7: Chinese and American participants' ratings of the likelihood of members of hypothetical groups having stereotype-consistent or nonstereotypical personality traits.

Spencer-Rodgers, Williams, Hamilton, Peng, and Wang (2007). Likelihood ratings were made on 7-point scales, with higher numbers meaning greater likelihood.

Social identity theory might form the basis for some predictions about cross-cultural differences in stereotyping, prejudice, and discrimination. In collectivistic cultures (see Chapter 1), people are more likely to define themselves in terms of their group memberships than are people from individualistic cultures. Not just their self-concepts, but the sources of their self worth derive more from their social identities than is the case in individualistic cultures (Markus & Kitayama, 1991). It would seem to follow from social identity theory that the kind of behavior that results from the need to defend important social identities (that is, hostility toward other groups) should be more common among collectivists than among individualists. Indeed, some have suggested that intergroup disparagement and antagonism is more common in societies in which collectivistic values dominate than in individualistic cultures (Oyserman & Lauffer, 2002). In keeping with that idea, when Spencer-Rodgers, Williams, Hamilton, Peng, and Wang (2007) told research participants that one fictional group (the Snoets) had a reputation for being artistic, and another (the Frints) for scientific achievement, Chinese participants were more likely than American participants to infer that specific members of those groups would have personality traits consistent with those stereotypes (see **Figure 11.7**). In other words, participants from a more collectivistic culture (Chinese participants) were quicker than those for an individualistic culture to apply stereotypes to individuals.

Triandis (1995), however, argues that the story is more complicated. Collectivists, he admits, do identify more strongly with their groups than individualists. However, the competitiveness and striving that characterizes individualistic cultures could lead individualists to defend and enhance more intensely *any* aspect of their self-concept, whether personal or social (Heine & Lehman, 1997). On that basis, we might expect individualists to be more aggressive than collectivists toward members of other groups. In the end, Triandis suggests, it might not be possible to make blanket statements about the correlation between culture and prejudice.

Prejudice and hate knows no national or cultural boundaries. Pictured here are a Neo-Nazi in Russia; a member of the Ku Klux Klan in the United States; a refugee camp for victims of ethnic cleansing in Africa (Darfur); and a memorial for victims of Islamic terrorists in Mumbai, India

Interestingly, Oyserman, Sakamoto, and Lauffer (1998) found that people who hold both collectivistic *and* individualistic values might be the ones who feel most connected to and obligated to humankind as a whole, without regard to race, nationality, or other such distinctions. In their study, those people who were encouraged to focus on their individualistic values preferred helping other individuals they knew; those who were encouraged to focus on their collectivistic values preferred helping their in-groups. However, those who were primed with both kinds of values felt more committed to the larger society. Thus, a combination of feeling connected to other people (collectivism) and respecting individual differences (individualism) led to the most altruistic and unprejudiced motives and intentions.

Prejudice as an Inherited Psychological Mechanism

To most people, the results of studies using the minimal group procedure are remarkable. Who could imagine that being arbitrarily assigned to a blue-badge group could lead to prejudice toward people with green badges? To some people, though, the results are not at all surprising. These findings are quite compatible with the perspective of social psychologists who analyze behavior in terms of evolutionary principles (Buss, 1995; Buss & Kenrick, 1998; Neuberg, Kenrick, & Schaller, 2010; see Chapter 1). Evolutionary psychologists begin from the hypothesis that people are genetically disposed to be more helpful and supportive to their relatives (who are genetically similar to them) than to other people (Burnstein, Crandall, and Kitayama, 1994; Buss & Kenrick, 1998). Throughout human evolutionary history (in what is known as the ancestral environment), group membership was correlated with genetic overlap. Being kinder to members of one's in-group than to members of other bands of people increased the probability that one's own genes would be passed on to later generations. Such considerations could account for ethnocentrism, the tendency to idealize one's own group—a tendency found even in rhesus monkeys (Mahajan, Martinez, Gutierrez, Diesendruck, Banaji, & Santos, 2011).

Of course, treating one's own group more favorably than others often entails treating other groups less favorably. Hence, it would have been both natural and adaptive for people to develop a wariness about—even a fear toward—out-groups (Kurzban & Leary, 2001; Suedfeld & Schaller, 2002). After all, people who expected that members of another tribe would treat them with as much kindness and generosity as they would each other might not have survived to pass on this trusting nature to their children. Under these conditions, xenophobia, the tendency to fear strangers, might have made adaptive sense. So a psychological mechanism that caused people to react to out-group members with hostility and aggression might have increased inclusive fitness.

Although the evolutionary account might seem somewhat speculative, some of its implications can and have been tested. Schaller, Park, and Mueller (2003; Schaller, 2003) hypothesized that the tendency to react to members of other groups in a prejudiced way might be enhanced by aspects of the environment historically associated with the possibility that out-group members could do one harm. For example, people often feel more vulnerable in the dark. If you cannot see what is threatening you, you will be less able to avoid the threat or to prepare for it than you would be during the day. As a result, people who were predisposed to be especially wary of out-group members at night might have had a survival advantage over those who were not.

In two studies, Schaller et al. presented participants—none of whom were black—with a slide show featuring several black men. Half the participants watched the show in a well-lighted room, and half in a dark one. In the first study, participants were then asked to complete a survey of their beliefs about the stereotype of blacks. In the second study, researchers assessed participants' attitudes toward black people indirectly, using the Implicit Association Test (IAT). In both studies, the participants' belief that the world is a dangerous place (as measured by a separate questionnaire) predicted their tendency to associate black people with dangerous traits and behaviors, but *only* among those who saw the slide show in darkness. Thus, among those who tend to see the world as a threatening place, danger signals like darkness seem to activate thoughts about the dangerousness of strangers, outsiders, and people who are "different."

As we have seen, some people distrust and despise members of other groups because they have been taught to do so by parents or peers. Others give themselves over to prejudice in a misguided effort to feel better about themselves. Moreover, basic cognitive mechanisms may bias people to associate out-groups with unfavorable characteristics. Evolutionary psychologists would not necessarily dispute these conclusions, but they would see all of them as secondary to a more basic truth. Human beings, they argue, are prejudiced against members of other groups because that is how human beings evolved (Diamond, 1992; Kurzban & Leary. 2001; Navarrete,

McDonald, Molina, & Sidanius, 2010; Neuberg & Cottrell, 2006; Waller, 2002).

The Prejudiced Brain: Social-Cognitive Neuroscience

The inherited psychological mechanisms that evolutionary psychologists have proposed are abstractions. In other words, they cannot be located in a particular area of the brain or associated with a particular pattern of neural activity. However, if psychological mechanisms developed as a function of natural selection and were passed on to offspring through genetic transmission, they must have some physical reality.

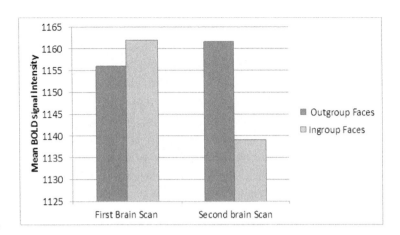

Figure 11.8: Early and late amygdala activation (blood-oxygen-level-dependent, or BOLD signals) in response to racial in-group and out-group faces.

From Hart et al. (2000). Participants habituated to in-group faces between the first and second brain scan (BOLD signals decreased), but did not habituate to out-group faces.

Research in social-cognitive neuroscience (Harmon-Jones & Devine, 2003; Lieberman, 2010; Ochsner, 2007) has revealed that specific regions of the brain are involved in responses to members of out-groups (Amodio, 2009; Brosch, Bar-David, & Phelps, 2013; Eberhardt, 2005; Ochsner & Lieberman, 2001). The amygdala, for example, is a part of the brain that is associated with the experiences of fear and anxiety. Brain imaging studies

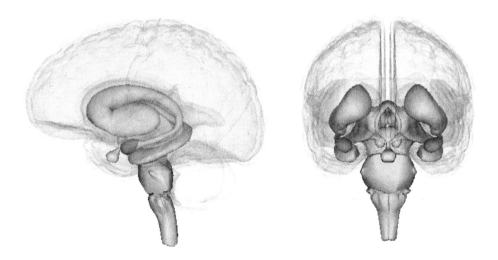

Differences in people's reactions to in-group and out-group members are to a great extent correlated with activity in the amygdala (shown in red here).

show that viewing the faces of members of out-groups activates the amygdala (Cunningham et al., 2004; Fiske, 2002; but see Van Bavel et al. [2008] for a more complex interpretation of amygdala activity). It would be reasonable to suspect that the amygdala might become active in response to *any* unfamiliar face, whether from an in-group or an out-group—and that, in fact, is the case. However, experiments conducted by Hart et al. (2000) and Phelps et al. (2000) show that responses to in-group faces will habituate (that is, decrease or disappear) over time; in contrast, responses to out-group faces do not (see **Figure 11.8**). Brain imaging studies reveal that our responses to those who belong to out-groups are unique.

These findings should not be interpreted to mean that the amygdala is the area of the brain devoted to stereotyping and prejudice. The amygdala plays a role in a wide variety of social-psychological phenomena, especially those associated with high levels of affect (Ochsner & Lieberman, 2001). Nor should these findings be taken as proof that people are predisposed to be prejudiced. Brain activation also reflects learned responses. However, social psychologists' work on the neural level of analysis does suggest that human brains are, at the very least, well prepared to categorize other people (Ito & Urland, 2003; Ito, Thompson, & Cacioppo, 2004) and to efficiently divide the world into "us" and "them." This suggestion, of course, is compatible with the theorizing of evolutionary psychologists. It is further evidence that stereotyping and prejudice are deeply rooted in the way human beings process information about their social worlds.

Doing a Number on Ourselves: Stereotype Threat

When intelligence and achievement tests are administered to large populations, some group differences emerge. For example, black Americans score lower on average than white Americans on IQ tests. This finding is not a stereotype, but a fact about which there is no debate. What *is* hotly debated are the causes of this and similar differences.

Some people have suggested that genetic differences between groups may be responsible for differences in test scores, although the general consensus among psychologists is that there is no compelling evidence for that explanation. Others emphasize social-cultural explanations. For historical reasons, for example, some groups of people occupy less advantageous positions within their societies. As a result, they have less access than others to the resources and experiences that would allow them to develop the skills measured by intelligence and achievement tests. To put it more simply, people with less money and status than others do not attend the best schools, and consequently cannot get the same education as people with more money. A variant of this idea is that in many ways, intelligence and achievement tests are geared toward dominant groups. In other words, they are not "culture fair."

The social-cultural explanation is compelling, and a great deal of evidence supports it. However, Steele and Aronson (1995; Steele, 1997) proposed another possible explanation. When people find themselves in situations in which they might fail, embarrass themselves, or be diminished in some other way, then needless to say, they feel burdened. That situation might be made worse, though, if they thought they might fail in a way that would confirm stereotypes about the groups they belong to. For example, as Steele and Aronson put it:

> whenever African-American students perform an explicitly scholastic or intellectual task, they face the threat of confirming or being judged by a negative societal stereotype—a suspicion—about their group's intellectual ability and competence … And the self-threat it causes—through a variety of

mechanisms—may interfere with the intellectual functioning of these students, particularly during standardized tests. (p. 797)

In this kind of situation, black students—and other people in similar situations—will experience **stereotype threat**, the risk of confirming by their own behavior a stereotype that is associated with their in-group.

To demonstrate this phenomenon, Steele and Aronson (1995) presented black students and white students with a 30-minute test composed of difficult items from the Graduate Record Examination (GRE). In one condition, they told participants that the test was a "genuine test of your verbal abilities and limitations." In the other condition, they described the test as a problem-solving task. When participants' Scholastic Aptitude Test (SAT) scores were taken into account, Steele and Aronson found that in the latter condition—in which the stakes were not terribly high—both black and white students performed just as well as would be expected. But in the former condition, in which the test was described as a test of mental abilities, black students' performance deteriorated. In another study, Steele and Aronson found that simply making people's race salient to them before a test (by asking them to report it to the experimenter) had the same effect, even when the test was not described as a test of ability or intelligence. Just filling out a form that included a question about race was enough to produce the stereotype threat.

The effects of stereotype threat have been replicated many times, using a number of different groups and stereotypes (Steele, Spencer, & Aronson, 2002). For example, women are said to be less competent than men at math, so when their math abilities are tested, they run the risk of being judged by that stereotype. Research by Spencer, Steele, and Quinn (1999) shows that stereotype threat can disrupt women's math performance. When the researchers described a math test as one on which women usually score lower than men, female participants performed worse than equally qualified men (see **Figure 11.9**). The gender difference in scores disappeared

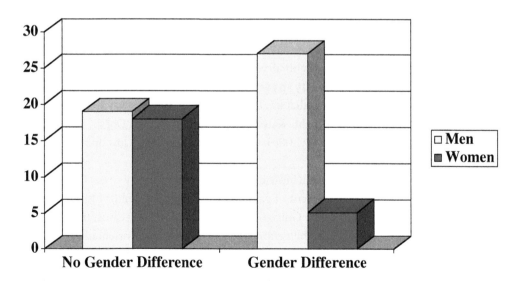

Figure 11.9: Men and women's performance on a difficult math test as a function of how the test was characterized ("shown to produce gender differences" versus "shown not to produce gender differences").

From Spencer, Steele, & Quinn (1999), with scores corrected for guessing.

when they described the test as one that was not usually associated with gender differences. (See also Brown & Josephs, 1999; Rydell, Rydell, & Boucher, 2010; Steinberg, Okun, & Aiken, 2012).

A person does not have to be a member of a minority or stigmatized group to experience stereotype threat. One study of the role of stereotype threat in athletic performance showed that in certain cases, members of majority groups—in this case, white people in the United States—can also succumb to stereotype threat. Stone, Lynch, Sjomeling, and Darley (1999) argued that just as knowing about stereotypes related to intelligence can affect intellectual performance, knowing about stereotypes related to athletic ability can affect athletic performance. In this study, there were no overall differences between the athletic performances of black and white participants. However, there was a difference in performance that depended on how the task—a game of miniature golf—was described. When the task was described as a test of "natural athletic ability," whites did worse than blacks; when it was described as a test of "sports intelligence," blacks performed worse than whites. Apparently, blacks did not want to be judged to be low in sports intelligence, and whites did not want to exemplify a lack of innate athletic ability.

Research on stereotype threat shows that stereotypes can cause people to undermine their own efforts—and in the long term, even abandon their interest in excelling in academic and other domains (Woodcock, Hernandez, Estrada, & Schultz, 2012). Exactly how people's awareness of bias and discrimination might affect their performance is still being investigated (Aronson & Inzlicht, 2004; Beilock, Jellison, Rydell, McConnell, & Carr, 2006; Croizet et al., 2004; Régner, Smeding, Gimmig, Thinus-Blanc, Monteil, & Huguet, 2010; Schmader & Johns, 2003). Being at risk of confirming a stereotype could cause a person to become self-conscious or distracted by

SOCIAL PSYCHOLOGY AND HEALTH: MINORITY STRESS

Being the target of prejudice or discrimination can make a person agitated and miserable (Jamieson, Koslov, Nock, & Mendes, 2013)—but that is not all. In the long run, being stigmatized can make it hard to maintain your mental health and well-being (Major, 2006). For example, being subject to bigotry can increase the risk that you will abuse drugs and alcohol (Gibbons, Gerrard, Cleveland, Wills, & Brody, 2004). More generally, it can lead to **minority stress**—stress that is caused not only by overt discrimination by others, but by constantly expecting that kind of treatment and always watching out for it (Clark, Anderson, Clark, & Williams, 1999; Inzlicht, Kaiser, & Major, 2008; Lick, Durso, & Johnson, 2013; Meyer, 2003; Ong, Fuller-Rowell, & Burrow, 2009). Coming to accept others' low opinion of your group could be another source of stress.

In most parts of the world, gay and lesbian individuals are prone to minority stress. One study showed that 20 percent of gay women and 25 percent of gay men had been assaulted or otherwise victimized because of their sexual orientation (Herek, Gillis, & Cogan, 1999). In many cases, the minority stress that gay people experience is intensified by their efforts to conceal their sexual orientation (Quinn, 2006) and their fear of being discovered. Not surprisingly, then, when Meyer (2003) reviewed studies comparing the mental health of heterosexual and LGB (lesbian, gay, bisexual) people, he found that "whenever significant differences in prevalences of disorders between LGB and heterosexual groups were found, LGB groups had higher prevalences than heterosexual groups" (p. 684).

Until 1973, the American Psychiatric Association classified homosexuality as a mental disorder. The message of recent research, however, is *not* that LGBT (lesbian, gay, bisexual, and transgender) identity is a form of mental illness. Rather, the way LGBT people are *treated* makes them vulnerable to a variety of mental health problems. This conclusion is supported by evidence that within the LGBT population, those who are subject to greater amounts of minority stress also suffer more mental health problems (Meyer, 2003).

Belonging to a minority group does not automatically increase a person's risk of suffering from a mental disorder. Supportive and accepting environments can buffer people from minority stress. If attitudes toward LGB people continue to change in the United States and elsewhere, future studies of the relationship between sexual orientation and mental health may show less evidence of differences between heterosexuals and LGBT people.

anxious thoughts (Brodish & Devine, 2009). In both cases, the result would be to divert the person's attention away from the task at hand. Alternatively, stereotype threat could affect task strategies: a person might become reckless or overcautious, or simply withdraw effort. Finally, stereotype threat could lead to arousal, which could interfere with a person's performance.

Ultimately, a combination of some or all these factors may underlie the effect of stereotype threat. In different situations, different threats may decrease performance for different reasons (Cohen & Garcia, 2008; Schmader, Johns, & Forbes, 2008; Steele et al., 2002; see Josephs, Newman, Brown, & Beer, 2003, for evidence of the role of hormonal factors). As is true of many of the subtle hidden influences on our behavior, however, there are some benefits to being aware of stereotype threat. Johns, Schmader, and Martens (2005) found that educating women about the phenomenon eliminated the effect of stereotype threat on their math performance.

Persistent stereotype threat can lead to a phenomenon called minority stress, which affects people's physical and mental health in addition to their academic and athletic performance: see the Social Psychology of Health box on **pages 528–529**.

Deeply Rooted Biases: A Summary

The message of much recent research seems to be that the hidden influences of stereotypes and prejudice are inevitable. Even more disturbing is the idea that throughout our evolutionary history, the pressure of natural selection has wired us to stereotype members of all kinds of social categories. In support of this idea, research in social-cognitive neuroscience shows that encounters with out-group members activate different areas of the brain than do encounters with in-group members.

Stereotypes even affect the extent to which people can demonstrate their *own* talents and abilities. Simply knowing that you can be stereotyped in a given situation is enough to disrupt your performance. Without your awareness, stereotype threat can lead you to confirm others' low expectations for members of your group. In light of these findings, we might suspect that the best we can hope for is to learn to live with stereotypes and prejudice. But our story does not end there.

Think Like a Social Psychologist

Designing research
—As we have noted, researchers are still investigating just how stereotype threat causes a person's performance on mental and other tasks to deteriorate. In other words, they are still studying the *mediating processes* (distraction, arousal, and so on) involved in the effect. How would you go about designing an experiment to test the importance of one or more of those processes?

Thinking critically
—Even if human beings inherit the psychological mechanisms that predispose them to be suspicious and hostile toward out-group members, not every situation would trigger those mechanisms. Can you come up with an evolutionary hypothesis about situations that might trigger psychological mechanisms promoting *cooperation* with out-group members?

BEYOND BIAS: OVERCOMING STEREOTYPING, PREJUDICE, AND DISCRIMINATION

Is prejudice really inescapable? Are intergroup tension and animosity inevitable? As we have seen, much of the research conducted by social psychologists seems to suggest as much. On the other hand, consider the evolution of Chop-Chop (Ma, 2001; Zimmerman, 2002), a comic book character introduced in 1941. Chop-Chop is a member of the Blackhawks, an international team originally organized to fight the Nazis. In the early years of this series, all the Blackhawks represented crude national or ethnic stereotypes (including Olaf, the "big dumb Swede"). However, the characterization of Chop-Chop, the Chinese member, was particularly grotesque. The other Blackhawks were drawn in realistic style and wore sharp leather uniforms. In contrast, Chop-Chop was short and fat, with big ears and heavily slanted eyes. He wore a clown-like red, yellow, and green costume, and his facial expression was almost always a hideous grin. The writers of the *Blackhawk* stories rarely gave him much dialogue; more often than not, what he did have to say was something like "Yipsie Doodle!" or "Oh wobbly woes!"

In the mid-1950s, as the world was still coming to grips with the implications of the shocking ethnic hatred that bubbled to the surface in World War II, Chop-Chop underwent his first transformation. He was redrawn as a man with more or less Caucasian features, who happened to have a yellowish complexion and a funny name. Apparently, the only acceptable way to deal "sensitively" with Chop-Chop's Chinese heritage was to bend over backward to ignore it. It was as if readers would consider any culturally distinct characteristics shameful and embarrassing.

The 1960s were characterized by a resurgence of ethnic pride in the United States, and a widespread interest in exploring one's roots. Comic book writers and artists became less cautious, and Chop-Chop became a martial arts expert who spoke with a Confucian-like air of wisdom. The new characteristics that were bestowed on him were positive, but they were stereotypes nonetheless. Chop-Chop's final makeover took place in the 1980s. For the first time in years, he was drawn to look Chinese; gone was the fear that his appearance would mark him as inferior. He was made a regular member of the team, with his own airplane and the same leather uniform as the other Blackhawks. Most important, he was called by his "real" name: Wu Cheng.

Today, a character as offensive as Chop-Chop would cause a major public outcry. Yet we should not conclude that the media no longer promote negative and unfair images of whole groups of people. For example, when people with mental illness appear as characters on television and in the movies, they are typically portrayed as being dangerous and prone to violence (Diefenbach, 1997; Wahl, 1995). And studies done in several countries (Germany, New Zealand, Canada, and the United States) find that news stories about people with mental illness tend to focus on criminal behavior (Angermeyer & Schulze, 2001; Nairn, Coverdale, & Claasen, 2001; Whitley & Berry, 2013). In reality, people's beliefs about the association between mental illness—including schizophrenia—and violent behavior are wildly exaggerated (Steadman, 1981). Prejudice against overweight people is also widely accepted (Crandall, 1994; Crandall et al., 2001; Kenrick, Shapiro, & Neuberg, 2013), so that fat people are commonly shown in unflattering ways in the media.

The Monster Can Be Tamed: Good Intentions Matter

Social psychologists acknowledge that overt biases and prejudices of all sorts are still acceptable to a significant segment of the population. And as we have seen, our awareness of all the hidden influences of stereotypes and prejudices is limited. But the fact remains that intergroup relations are not static. Societies have changed in the past, and they continue to change today. Individuals, too, are not powerless to control how they interact with their neighbors. There really are some important differences between bigots and people who want to be fair and unbiased. Furthermore, a person who leans on stereotypes in one situation might not do so in another (Kunda & Spencer, 2003).

More and more, then, research by social psychologists focuses on such differences across people and situations—how they come about and how they express themselves. The latest chapters in the history of research on stereotyping, prejudice, and discrimination tell a more hopeful story than those that preceded them.

A Brainy Cheerleader? Two Ways to Form Impressions

Common sense and intuition might lead us to rebel against the implication that our encounters with others are always characterized by automatic stereotyping and mindless prejudice. Surely we can

The late Jack Kemp exemplifies the importance of personalized, piecemeal, attribute-based processing. Obsessed with sports as a child, a college jock, a quarterback in the National football League—but also a congressman, Housing Secretary, economic policy expert, and candidate for Vice President of the United States

sometimes form objective and accurate impressions of others based on what they say and do. Certainly we can differentiate between the individual members of different groups. If psychologists denied that could ever happen, they would be wrong. On the other hand, if you were to argue that your impressions of others are always unbiased and carefully formed, *you* would be wrong.

Psychologists now recognize that when we form our impressions of others, we can follow one of two major routes. Sometimes the conclusions we reach about others are largely **category-based**, or driven almost exclusively by stereotypes. Yet it is possible to override that relatively effortless procedure. When we carefully attend to the details of others' behavior—in other words, when we focus on individuating information—the process we use to form our impressions is said to be *personalized* (Brewer, 1988), *attribute-based*, or **piecemeal** (Fiske, 1988; Fiske & Neuberg, 1990). Cheerleaders, for example—especially female cheerleaders—are associated with a fairly well-defined stereotype. A category-based impression of a cheerleader probably would not result in her being invited to join the chess club or the debate team. A shopping trip to the mall or a pool party would probably seem more appropriate. Clearly, brainy cheerleaders do exist, but without personalized processing, they will escape detection. Only careful attention to a cheerleader's unique characteristics would allow us to notice the thick philosophy book in her backpack and the A+ she received in calculus and organic chemistry.

Several variables will influence the approach you take in forming an impression. For instance, if you cannot easily fit a person into any of your existing categories, you have no stereotype to fall back on, and your only alternative will be to focus on that person's unique set of traits, abilities, and attitudes (Fiske, Neuberg, Beattie, & Milberg, 1987). Your own needs and goals, however, are also important. When you encounter people in circumstances that motivate you to form accurate impressions of them, you are more likely to engage in piecemeal processing. Outcome-dependent situations are one example of such circumstances. When two people are outcome dependent, that means that they must rely on each other to achieve some goal. People have been shown to pay more attention to important, meaningful information about others under outcome-dependent conditions (Erber & Fiske, 1984). Not surprisingly, outcome dependency causes people to rely less on stereotypes and to pay more attention to individuating information (Neuberg & Fiske, 1987).

Research suggests that the approach you take to forming an impression can have profound effects on your immediate, spontaneous reactions to others. As we saw earlier, seeing out-group members' faces typically activates the amygdala, the part of the brain that is associated with fear and anxiety. But when people are asked to see and treat others as unique individuals—in other words, to avoid category-based processing—they can prevent that neurological response (Fiske, 2002).

These theories (Brewer, 1988; Fiske & Neuberg, 1990), we should note, do not depend on hard-and-fast definitions of categories and individuating information. In fact, depending on the situation, a given characteristic could serve *both* functions. You could categorize someone as a "cheerleader," but take into account individuating information such as intellectual strength. On the other hand, imagine encountering a conservatively dressed professor who later turns out to have been a cheerleader in high school. In that case, "intellectual" would be the automatically applied category, and "cheerleader" would serve as the individuating information. The important point, then, is not whether you can determine if a given piece of information is a "category" or an "attribute." Instead, these theories shed light on when and how people will do more than just settle for the stereotypes associated with a category, whatever that category happens to be.

Personalized, piecemeal, or attribute-based processing will not necessarily eliminate the effects of stereotypes on our impressions of others. "Individuating information" is not always clear in its implications; often, it is ambiguous. For example, if a man asks another person to stop smoking, is his action an indication of concern for his own health, concern for the smoker's health, or just plain rudeness? The answer might not be clear, so stereotypes could affect how an onlooker resolves the ambiguity (Kunda & Sherman-Williams, 1993). If the man who asks the smoker to snuff out the cigarette is a nurse, one might be more likely to infer concern for the smoker's health than if the man is a bouncer at a bar. In general, category-based and attribute-based processing are not mutually exclusive (Nelson, Acker, & Manis, 1996; Sherman, 2001). Even when people think they are engaged in objective, piecemeal processing of others' behavior, stereotypes can exert hidden influences, especially when people are, for whatever reason, low in cognitive capacity and unable to monitor their thought processes (Ma, Correll, Wittenbrink, Bar-Anan, Sriram, & Nosek, 2013).

Nonetheless, it is clear that we have the capacity to note people's unique attributes (see also Posten & Mussweiler, 2013). How we perceive others is not always totally determined by the stereotypes that pop automatically into our minds.

Automatic Bias Revisited: Individual Differences

We are not at the mercy of whatever pops into our minds when we interact with others. Still, some researchers suggest that members of a stigmatized group will automatically trigger negative stereotypes, whether or not one is explicitly prejudiced (Devine, 1989a, b). A study done by Lepore and Brown (1997) indicated otherwise, however. In this study, done in Great Britain, white psychology students were split into two groups, based on how much prejudice they had expressed toward black people on a questionnaire. Then, in the first part of the study, half the participants were subliminally primed with words related to the general category of "black people," such as "Afro," "colored," "dreadlocks," and "blacks." Finally, the participants were asked to form an impression of a person whose behavior was described ambiguously with respect to level of aggressiveness or unreliability. For example, the statement "He can easily get angry at people who disagree with him" suggests only the potential for aggression.

Lepore and Brown found that the effects of the priming depended on participants' preexisting levels of prejudice. As expected, those who were high in prejudice and were primed with words meant to activate the "black people" category saw the target person as being more aggressive and unreliable than the high-prejudice participants, who had not been primed. For the primed high-prejudice participants, it seems, unfavorable stereotypical attributes were linked inextricably to thinking about black people. Participants who were low in prejudice were unaffected by the primes. Reminding them about black people did *not* seem to automatically bring stereotypical traits to mind.

Other data support this conclusion (Brown, Croizet, Bohner, Fournet, & Payne, 2003; Kawakami, Dion, & Dovidio, 1998; but see Stewart, Weeks, & Lupfer, 2003). Recall that Wittenbrink et al. (1997), in a study described earlier in this chapter, used a lexical decision task to demonstrate automatic antiblack stereotyping and prejudice among white research participants. These effects, however, were more pronounced in participants who were high in prejudice.

Evidence also suggests that one's level of prejudice is related to neuropsychological responses to out-group members. Phelps et al. (2000), as you might recall, found that the sight of black faces activates the amygdala in white people. Not everyone reacts in the same way, however; the degree of activation was found to be correlated with people's antiblack bias, as measured by the IAT.

Thus, people vary not only in terms of explicit or overt prejudice, but in the extent to which they automatically stereotype or evaluate negatively members of out-groups. These findings have led to renewed interest in

Table 11.5: A measure of motivation to respond to black people without racial prejudice

---

External motivation items

    Because of today's PC (politically correct) standards, I try to appear nonprejudiced toward black people.

    I try to hide any negative thoughts about black people in order to avoid negative reactions from others.

    If I acted prejudiced toward black people, I would be concerned that others would be angry with me.

    I attempt to appear nonprejudiced toward black people in order to avoid disapproval from others.

    I try to act nonprejudiced toward black people because of pressure from others.

Internal motivation items

    I attempt to act in nonprejudiced ways toward black people because it is personally important to me.

    *According to my personal values, using stereotypes about black people is OK.

    I am personally motivated by my beliefs to be nonprejudiced toward black people.

    Because of my personal values, I believe that using stereotypes about black people is wrong.

    Being nonprejudiced toward black people is important to my self-concept.

From Plant & Devine (1998). Each statement is rated on a scale ranging from 1 (strongly disagree) to 9 (strongly agree). The item marked with a * is reverse scored—that is, *dis*agreement suggests internal motivation to respond without prejudice. The measure can be modified to apply to other groups.

individual differences in the way people think about and react to other groups. For the most part, the goal of this kind of research is not to discover or identify a "prejudiced personality." Instead, researchers have tried to shed light on how various motives, beliefs, and values shape the ways in which stereotypes and prejudice affect people's interactions with others (Son Hing, Chung-Yan, Hamilton, & Zanna, 2008).

For example, Plant and Devine (1998) developed a measure to distinguish between the *external* and *internal* motivation to respond without prejudice (see **Table 11.5**; for a similar measure, see Dunton & Fazio, 1997). In one study, they asked participants, 97 percent of whom were white, to report their stereotypic beliefs about blacks. Some participants thought they were giving their answers anonymously; others had to answer orally (that is, publicly). What people who were primarily high in external motivation were willing to say depended on how anonymous they thought their answers would be; they endorsed more stereotypes in private than in public. People who were primarily high in internal motivation were less affected by context. Plant and Devine concluded that rather than focusing on how generally prejudiced people are, it might be more useful to examine *when and why* they are willing or unwilling to express bias. (See Klonis, Plant, & Devine, 2005, for a measure of the internal and external motivation to respond without sexism.)

Other researchers have studied more general values and orientations that might relate to prejudice. Moskowitz, Gollwitzer, Wasel, and Schaal (1999) found that male students with egalitarian goals—specifically, the goal of judging women in an unbiased manner—were better able than other male students to control the automatic activation of gender stereotypes. On the other hand, Pratto, Sidanius, Stallworth, and Malle, (1994; also Cohrs, Kämpfe-Hargrave, & Riemann, 2012; Levin et al., 2012) found that another set of values, social dominance orientation (SDO), is *positively* correlated with bias. SDO refers to the extent to which one wants one's own group to dominate and be superior to other groups. People who are high in SDO are more likely than others to agree with statements like "Some people are just more worthy than others," and less likely to agree with statements such as "In an ideal world, all nations would be equal." More to the point, SDO is predictive of racism and sexism.

Finally, research by Altemeyer (1981, 1988) has focused on an aspect of personality called authoritarianism. Altemeyer's Right Wing Authoritarian (RWA) measure (an update of an earlier one developed by Adorno, Frenkel-Brunswik, Levinson, & Sanford, 1950) includes items such as "What our country really needs is a strong, determined leader who will crush evil and take us back on our true path," and "Our country will be destroyed someday if we do not smash the perversions eating away at our moral fiber and traditional beliefs." Unsurprisingly, those are statements with which people who are high in RWA agree. RWA correlates significantly with prejudice of all sorts; for example, it is highly predictive of hostility toward gay people (Altemeyer, 1994). Altemeyer suggests that people who are high in RWA have been exposed to only a narrow range of experiences and are therefore suspicious and fearful of unfamiliar people and ideas.

Consequently, although we are all prone to stereotype, to be prejudiced (Chambers, Schlenker, & Collisson, 2013, and to engage in discrimination, our motives, goals, beliefs, and values distinguish between those of us who are more bigoted than tolerant and those of us who treat others more fairly than not. Fazio et al. (1995) concluded that in regard to the automatic and uncontrollable activation of stereotypes, there are at least three basic types of people. One type includes those who experience negative thoughts and feelings when they encounter members of a specific out-group and are relatively unconcerned about them (truly prejudiced people). A second type includes those for whom such thoughts and feelings simply are not activated (truly unprejudiced people). A third type includes those who are prone to automatic stereotyping and prejudice, but are motivated to counter such bias when they become aware of it. Gaertner and Dovidio (1986; Dovidio & Gaertner, 2004) refer to the last group as "aversive racists"; such people, it has been said, experience "prejudice with compunction" (Devine, Monteith, Zuwerink, & Elliot, 1991).

The Malleability of Implicit and Automatic Biases

Aversive racists would appear to be in an uncomfortable predicament: they seem to be stuck with automatic thoughts and feelings they would rather not have. Research indicates, however, that people's automatic and implicit evaluations of out-group members are at least somewhat malleable (Devine, Forscher, Austin, & Cox, 2012). Rudman, Ashmore, and Gary (2001) found that after students completed a seminar on diversity issues, their antiblack biases, as measured by the IAT, were significantly reduced. Pairing white college freshmen with black roommates can have the same effect (Shook & Fazio, 2008). Blair, Ma, and Lenton (2001) found that they could undermine the implicit bias to see men as stronger than women (again, as measured by the IAT) by directing people to engage in counterstereotypic mental imagery (for example, thinking about traits and behaviors that would be characteristic of a strong woman). Similarly, Dasgupta and Asgari (2004) discovered they could reduce the implicit bias among women to see themselves more as followers than as leaders by exposing them to women in leadership positions. And finally, Dasgupta and Greenwald (2001) found that simply presenting college students with pictures of admired elderly people (for example, Albert Einstein) was enough to decrease their implicit bias against the elderly.

Table 11.6: Different kinds of basic prejudices and their associated stereotypes

Out-group status	Interdependence (Type of Relationship)	
	COOPERATIVE	COMPETITIVE
HIGH	**Admiration** (lack of prejudice)	**Envious prejudice**
	Stereotypes: Competent, warm	**Stereotypes:** Competent, not warm
LOW	**Paternalistic prejudice**	**Contemptuous prejudice**
	Stereotypes: Incompetent, warm	**Stereotypes:** Incompetent, not warm

From Fiske, Cuddy, Glick, and Xu (2002); Glick (2002); Glick and Fiske (2002).

A New Model of Stereotype Content

The cognitive approach to stereotyping and prejudice focuses on the complicated interplay of thoughts, feelings, and behaviors that ensues when people from different groups encounter each other. Social psychologists who conduct this kind of research are more interested in the consequences of categorizing people in different ways than in the actual *content* of the stereotypes. For the most part, they have assumed that the insights they gain from their research apply to *any* stereotyped group, be it Latinos, Native Americans, accountants, vegetarians, or ice hockey fans.

Research by Glick and Fiske (2001; Fiske, Cuddy, Glick, & Xu, 2002; Glick, 2002), however, reminds us that there are important differences between different kinds of stereotypes. They proposed a model of stereotypes and prejudice that helps to explain some aspects of the beliefs groups develop about each other in terms of two broad traits: competence and warmth (see **Table 11.6**). Most stereotypes, of course, indicate how likable or smart people are supposed to be. This model relates those stereotypic traits to two aspects of intergroup relations, the relative status of the groups and their interdependence. Here, the term *status* refers to the fact that some groups are more socially and economically successful than others. The term *interdependence* refers to the fact that relations between groups are sometimes cooperative and sometimes competitive.

Glick and Fiske found that when another group is high in status and cooperative with your group (for example, when it is your ally during war), you are likely to perceive members of that group as being warm and competent. When a group is seen as being cooperative, but *low* in status (for example, foreign domestic workers), you are likely to perceive them as warm and *in*competent.

What about groups that are seen as competitors? Naturally, they are seen as being low in warmth. High-status competitors are seen as cold and competent; low-status competitors, as cold and incompetent. Clearly, many factors play a role in the way groups see each other, but Glick and Fiske's model suggests that the overall shape of a group's stereotype can be predicted by focusing on just two basic aspects of the *perceived* relationship between the two groups.

Glick and Fiske's model also speaks to the different types of prejudice and discrimination that are associated with these different kinds of stereotypes. Groups that are seen as warm and competent receive admiration—in other words, they are not the targets of prejudice. Groups that are seen as warm and incompetent, on the other hand, are subject to **paternalistic prejudice**. Members of these groups might be liked and their presence tolerated, but they will also be disrespected, pitied, and treated with condescension. Enslaved people and people who live in colonized nations experience prejudice of this kind.

A group that is seen as cold and competent becomes the target of **envious prejudice**. Although other groups grudgingly admire such a group's success, its members are envied, feared, and resented. Successful minority groups such as Asian Americans in the early 21st century or Jews in early-20th-century Germany often become the targets of this kind of prejudice. Finally, **contemptuous prejudice** is reserved for groups that are both disliked and seen as low in competence. Members of these groups will experience hostility and disrespect. In fact, they might even be seen as barely human; a part of the brain that is necessary for thinking about other people, the medial prefrontal cortex, is less likely than usual to be activated when a person encounters the target of contemptuous prejudice (Harris & Fiske, 2006). In Chapter 14, we will discuss the role of envious and contemptuous prejudice in the most extreme form of intergroup conflict—genocide.

Taking Control of Group Contact: The Jigsaw Classroom

Some social psychologists have tried to apply the lessons they have learned from research on group contact to improve intergroup relations (Johnson & Johnson, 1987). The best-known technique to emerge from their research is the **jigsaw classroom** (Aronson & Patnoe, 1997).

Children working together and learning from each other like those in Jigsaw Classrooms

Just as a jigsaw puzzle cannot be completed unless all its pieces fit together harmoniously, in a jigsaw classroom, children cannot complete their assignments unless they work together cooperatively.

The basic method is to divide children into groups, give each group some problems to solve, and then assign each member of the group to master some bit of knowledge that is essential to the solution. For example, wars are typically triggered by many interrelated events. To see the big picture, one must learn about all those events and then figure out how one followed from the other. In a jigsaw classroom, if a group were asked to learn about and report on the causes of World War I, each student in the group would master part of the information. Group members would then teach each other what they learned, and together they would arrive at a coherent account of how the conflict began.

This method could provide any class with a meaningful educational experience, but it was developed for a specific purpose: to improve the classroom atmosphere in desegregated schools. When African American, Latino, and white children from different communities are simply thrown together in a classroom, too often the result is hostility, mistrust, resentment, and even violence. Social psychologist Elliot Aronson designed the jigsaw classroom to defuse this kind of tension (Aronson & Bridgeman, 1979). In jigsaw classrooms, children from different backgrounds engage in extended, socially sanctioned, goal-oriented activities with peers of equal status.

In short, in such classrooms, everything is arranged for the purpose of fostering positive interactions between students. Experiments have shown that the jigsaw technique lowers the levels of stereotyping and prejudice in the classroom and increases students' self-esteem. In some cases, it even improves academic performance.

Responsibility, Control, and Change: A Summary

Humans are not doomed to be prejudiced or to discriminate against others. Good intentions matter; people who strive to form accurate, objective impressions of others can reduce the role of stereotypes in their thinking. The same is true of people who simply try their best to take other people's perspectives (Galinsky & Moskowitz, 2000; Todd, Bodenhausen, Richeson, & Galinsky, 2011). Unprejudiced people are less likely than prejudiced people (those who are high in authoritarianism or social dominance) to react unfavorably to out-group members, either intentionally or automatically.

Although few, if any, of us should congratulate ourselves for our immunity from bias, neither should we despair. People are capable of exerting a significant amount of control over the way they think, feel, and act toward members of other groups; they can even exert some control over activation of their amygdalas when faced with out-group members (Wheeler & Fiske, 2005). Although people with egalitarian values who strive to treat others impartially must always be on guard against the hidden influences of stereotyping and prejudice (including paternalistic, envious, and contemptuous prejudice), their vigilance can pay off. In fact, extremely unprejudiced people might even be biased to *dis*confirm stereotypes (Wyer, 2004).

Controlling one's own prejudiced responses is important, but more active responses are necessary to fight discrimination. Unfortunately, most people in the United States remained silent in the early 1940s when Japanese-Americans were expelled from their homes, rounded up, and imprisoned in grim and isolated internment camps.

Think Like a Social Psychologist

Confronting social issues

—Imagine that with your new expertise in stereotyping and prejudice, you have been asked to testify in a court case involving workplace discrimination. The defense attorney asks you to confirm that recent research shows that stereotypes can be activated automatically and can affect people's behavior without their awareness. Then she asks you to agree that the implication of that research is that her client cannot be held responsible for his discriminatory actions. How would you respond? (For one perspective on this dilemma, see Fiske, 1989.)

Understanding everyday behavior

—At your school, are subgroups of students stereotyped in specific ways? Based on the material in this chapter, what are some conditions that might lead your fellow students to change or abandon those stereotypes?

Civil rights marchers in the 1960s, speaking out against prejudice and discrimination.

EPILOGUE: *A PERSONAL BATTLE (IT'S UP TO YOU)*

Early research on intergroup relations—research that was meant to find straightforward ways to undermine discrimination—gave way to studies that seemed to indicate that stereotyping, prejudice, and discrimination are inevitable and unalterable. More recent research is more encouraging; it has helped write a new chapter in the history of attempts to understand these important social psychological issues. Although racial, ethnic, and other biases can indeed serve as potent hidden influences on behavior, with vigilance, an unprejudiced person can dampen their effects.

Confronting our own prejudice is not the same as confronting the prejudice of others, however. Ultimately, fighting prejudice requires more than exercising individual control over our own cognitive processes. A study done by Swim and Hyers (1999) vividly illustrates this point. The female college students who participated in the research were led to believe they were taking part in a group discussion with three other people, who were actually confederates of the experimenters. One of the confederates, a male student, had been instructed to make some offensive sexist remarks.

Whether they were the only women in the group or one of three women, most of the participants (55 percent) did not respond at all to the confederate's remarks. A large majority (84 percent) let the comments pass without directly and unambiguously expressing their disapproval, although later questioning revealed that most had indeed been offended by the remarks. Unfortunately, the women believed that others would have found them to be rude and would have thought poorly of them if they had spoken up. Indeed, researchers find that when women behave assertively, they are seen as being less likable and approachable than they were before, and less likable and approachable than men who engage in the same behavior (Rudman, 1998).

Presumably, these participants hoped that others in the group felt the same way they did, so we can assume that they would have admired anyone who did confront the insensitive remarks. In the end, though, most participants let it slide. Of course, lashing out at anyone who dares to utter a remark that does not sit well with one's own values probably will not lead to a comfortable environment in which people trust and support each other.

However, there are costs to letting blatantly biased people live comfortably with their assumptions that others share their attitudes and beliefs (see also Rasinski, Geers, & Czopp, 2013). Fighting stereotyping, prejudice, and discrimination sometimes requires taking the battle outside yourself.

KEY HIDDEN INFLUENCES ON STEREOTYPING, PREJUDICE, AND DISCRIMINATION

Automatic stereotype activation: Simply encountering a member of a group can make stereotypes about that group cognitively accessible, with or without your awareness.

Automatic negative evaluation of out-groups: Merely encountering a member of an out-group group can trigger negative affect, with or without your awareness.

Stereotype-based inferences: Without your awareness, the stereotypes associated with a group can affect your perception of the members' behavior, whether or not you think the stereotypes are valid.

The out-group homogeneity effect: Other groups seem to be less diverse than your own—that is, members of other groups seem to be more similar than members of your own group.

Illusory correlations: Although members of all groups engage in more favorable than unfavorable behaviors, the unfavorable behaviors of minority groups are more memorable than the favorable ones, and play a disproportionate role in others' impressions of those groups.

In-group bias: You tend to favor your own group over others, even when group membership is based on trivial criteria.

Stereotype threat: Simply knowing that a group you belong to is stereotyped in a particular way—whether or not you accept the stereotype's validity—can be threatening and can affect how you perform and behave, ultimately leading you to confirm the stereotype.

KEY TERMS AND DEFINITIONS

Prejudice: unfavorable feelings about a group of people

Discrimination: unfair behavior toward members of a group

Stereotype: a belief (often exaggerated or unjustified) about the characteristics of a particular group of people

Stigmatized group: a group that is devalued and ostracized by others and the subject of extremely negative thoughts, feelings, and behaviors

Sociocultural perspective: an approach to stereotyping, prejudice, and discrimination that emphasizes how intergroup beliefs, attitudes, and behaviors are shaped by cultural and interpersonal influences

Contact hypothesis: the hypothesis that direct contact between members of different groups reduces stereotyping and prejudice

Realistic group conflict theory: the theory that prejudice is caused by competition for scarce resources

Scapegoat: A group or individual who is unfairly blamed for other groups' or individuals' problems

Relative deprivation theory: the theory that resentment toward other groups stems from the perception that one's group is not comparing as favorably as expected with other groups

Cognitive perspective: an approach to stereotyping, prejudice, and discrimination that emphasizes how intergroup beliefs, attitudes, and behaviors are shaped by the cognitive processes people use to perceive, categorize, and think about members of other groups

In-group: a group with which an individual identifies

Out-group: a group with which an individual does not identify

Out-group homogeneity effect: the tendency to believe that members of out-groups are more similar than members of one's own in-group

Implicit Association Test (IAT): a test that can be used to assess people's implicit attitudes toward other groups—that is, their tendency to spontaneously or unconsciously associate other groups with specific stereotypes or evaluations

Illusory correlation: a mistaken belief about associations or correlations, such as seeing a nonexistent relationship between a group of people and some personality characteristic

Subtype: a category of people who are seen as special cases of a broader category, such as "career women" or "student athletes"

Minimal group technique: a method for studying intergroup behavior that involves creating groups based on arbitrary criteria

Social identity: the aspect of one's self-concept that is based on the groups to which one belongs, rather than on one's own unique personal characteristics

The motivational perspective: an approach to stereotyping, prejudice and discrimination that emphasizes how intergroup beliefs, attitudes, and behaviors are shaped by people's needs, motives, and fears

Stereotype threat: the discomfort triggered by situations in which one's behavior or performance could confirm a stereotype associated with a group to which one belongs

Minority stress: psychological stress that results from being stigmatized (which can lead to physical symptoms and self-destructive behavior)

Category-based impression: an impression of a person that is based on the way one labels that person (and the stereotypes associated with that label)

Piecemeal or attribute-based impression: an impression of a person that is based on that person's specific behaviors and personal characteristics

Paternalistic prejudice: negative feelings about another group that are based on the belief that members of the group are agreeable, but low in intelligence and competence

Envious prejudice: negative feelings about another group that are based on the belief that members of the group are intelligent and competent, but hostile and disagreeable

Contemptuous prejudice: negative feelings about another group that are based on the belief that members of the group are both disagreeable/hostile and low in intelligence and competence

Jigsaw classroom: a classroom in which children who may come from different groups and backgrounds can complete assignments and solve problems only by cooperating and pooling their knowledge

REFERENCES

Aberson, C. L., Healy, M., & Romero, V. (2000). Ingroup bias and self-esteem: A meta-analysis. *Personality and Social Psychology Review, 4*, 157–173.

Aboud, F. (1988). *Children and prejudice*. New York: Basil Blackwell.

Adorno, T. W., Frenkel-Brunswik, E., Levinson, D. J., & Sanford, R. (1950). *The authoritarian personality*. New York: Harper.

Allport, G. W. (1954). *The nature of prejudice*. Reading, MA: Addison-Wesley.

Altemeyer, B. (1981). *Right-wing authoritarianism*. Winnipeg: University of Manitoba Press.

Altemeyer, B. (1988). *Enemies of freedom: Understanding right-wing authoritarianism*. San Francisco: Jossey-Bass.

Altemeyer, B. (1994). Reducing prejudice in right-wing authoritarians. In M. P. Zanna & J. M. Olson (Eds.), *The psychology of prejudice: The Ontario symposium* (Vol. 7, pp. 131–148). Hillsdale, NJ: Erlbaum.

Amir, Y. (1969). Contact hypothesis in ethnic relations. *Psychological Bulletin, 71*, 319–342.

Amodio, D. M. (2009). The social neuroscience of intergroup relations. *European Review of Social Psychology, 19*, 1–54.

Andreychik, M. R., & Gill, M. J. (2012). Do negative implicit associations indicate negative attitudes? Social explanations moderate whether ostensible "negative" associations are prejudice-based or empathy-based. *Journal of Experimental Social Psychology, 48*, 1082–1093.

Angermeyer, M. C., & Schulze, B. (2001). Reinforcing stereotypes: How the focus on forensic cases in news reporting may influence public attitudes towards the mentally ill. *International Journal of Law and Psychiatry, 24*, 469–486.

Arkes, H. R., & Tetlock, P. E. (2004). Attributions of implicit prejudice, or "Would Jesse Jackson 'fail" the Implicit Association Test?" *Psychological Inquiry, 15*, 257–278.

Aronson, E., & Bridgeman, D. (1979). Jigsaw groups and the desegregated classroom: In pursuit of common goals. *Personality and Social Psychology Bulletin, 5*, 438–446.

Aronson, E., & Patnoe, S. (1997). *Cooperation in the classroom: The jigsaw method*. New York: Longman.

Aronson, J., & Inzlicht, M. (2004). The ups and downs of atributional ambiguity: Sterotype vulnerability and the academic self-knowledge of African-American college students. *Psychological Science, 15*, 829–836.

Ashburn-Nardo, L., Knowles, M. L., & Monteith, M. J. (2003). Black Americans' implicit racial associations and their implications for intergroup judgment. *Social Cognition, 21*, 61–87.

Ashmore, R. D., & Del Boca, F. K. (1981). Conceptual approaches to stereotypes and stereotyping. In D. L. Hamilton (Ed.), *Cognitive processes in stereotyping and intergroup behavior* (pp. 1–35). Hillsdale, NJ: Lawrence Erlbaum Associates.

Atkin, D. J., Moorman, J., & Linn, C. A. (1991). Ready for prime-time: Network series devoted to working women in the 1980's. *Sex Roles, 25*, 677–685.

Baldus, D. C., Woodworth, G., & Pulaski, C. A. Jr. (1990). *Equal justice and the death penalty*. Boston: Northeastern University Press.

Banaji, M. R., & Hardin, C. (1996). Automatic stereotyping. *Psychological Science, 7*, 136–141.

Bargh, J. A. (1994).The four horsemen of automaticity: Awareness, intention, efficiency, and control in social cognition. In R. S. Wyer Jr. & T. K. Srull (Eds.), *Handbook of social cognition* (Vol. 1, 2nd ed., pp. 1–40). Hillsdale, NJ: Erlbaum.

Bargh, J. A. (1999). The cognitive monster: The case against the controllability of automatic stereotype effects. In S. Chaiken & Y. Trope (Eds.) *Dual-process theories in social psychology* (pp. 361–382). New York: Guilford.

Bargh, J. A., & Thein, R. D. (1985). Individual construct accessibility, person memory, and the recall-judgment link: The case of information overload. *Journal of Personality and Social Psychology, 49*, 1129–1146.

Barlow, F. K., Paolini, S., Pedersen, A., Hornsey, M. J., Radke, H. R. M., Harwood, J., Rubin, M., & Sibley, C. G. (2012). The contact caveat: Negative contact predicts increased prejudice more than positive contact predicts reduced prejudice. *Personality and Social Psychology Bulletin, 38,* 1629–1643.

Becker, J. C., Wright, S. C., Lubensky, M. E., & Zhou, S. (2013). Friend or ally: Whether cross-group contact undermines collective action depends on what advantaged group members say (or don't say). *Personality and Social Psychology Bulletin, 39,* 442–455.

Beilock, S. L., Jellison, W. A., Rydell, R. J., McConnell, A. R., & Carr, T. H. (2006). On the causal mechanisms of stereotype threat: Can skills that don't rely heavily on working memory still be threatened? *Personality and Social Psychology Bulletin, 32,* 1059–1071.

Bellezza, F. S., & Bower, G. H. (1981). Person stereotypes and memory for people. *Journal of Personality and Social Psychology, 41,* 856–865.

Berman, P. (March 23, 2003). The philosopher of Islamic terror. *New York Times Magazine,* pp. 24–29, 56–59, 65–67.

Blair, I. V., Judd, C. M., & Chapleau, K. M. (2004). The influence of Afrocentric facial features in criminal sentencing. *Psychological Science, 15,* 674–679.

Blair, I. V., Ma, J. E., & Lenton, A. P. (2001). Imagining stereotypes away: The moderation of implicit stereotypes through mental imagery. *Journal of Personality and Social Psychology, 81,* 828–841.

Blanton, H., & Jaccard, J. (2006). Arbitrary metrics in psychology. *American Psychologist, 61,* 27–41.

Blanton, H., Jaccard, J., Gonzales, P., & Christie, C. (2006). Decoding the implicit association test: Implications for criterion prediction. *Journal of Experimental Social Psychology, 42,* 192–212.

Bodenhausen, G. V. (1988). Stereotypic biases in social decision making and memory: Testing process models of stereotype use. *Journal of Personality and Social Psychology, 55,* 726–737.

Bodenhausen, G. V., & Lichtenstein, M. (1987). Social stereotypes and information processing strategies: The impact of task complexity. *Journal of Personality and Social Psychology, 52,* 871–880.

Bodenhausen, G. V., & Macrae, C. N. (1998). Stereotype activation and inhibition. In R. S. Wyer Jr. (Ed.), *Advances in social cognition* (Vol. 11, pp. 1–52). Mahwah, NJ: Erlbaum.

Bourke, J. (1999). *An intimate history of killing: Face-to-face killing in twentieth-century warfare.* London, UK: Granta Books.

Brewer, M. B. (1988). A dual process model of impression formation. In T. K. Srull & R. S. Wyer Jr. (Eds.), *Advances in social cognition* (Vol. 1, pp. 1–36). Hillsdale, NJ: Erlbaum.

Brewer, M. B., & Brown, R. J. (1998). Intergroup relations. In D. T. Gilbert, S. T. Fiske, & G. Lindzey (Eds.), *The handbook of social psychology* (4th ed., Vol. 2, pp. 554–594). New York: McGraw Hill.

Brodish, A. B., & Devine, P. G. (2009). The role of performance-avoidance goals and worry in mediating the relationship between stereotype threat and performance. *Journal of Experimental Social Psychology, 45,* 180–185.

Brosch, T., Bar-David, E., & Phelps, E. A. (2013). Implicit race bias decreases the similarity of neural representations of Black and White faces. *Psychological Science, 24,* 160–166.

Brown, R., Croizet, J. C., Bohner, G., Fournet, F., & Payne, A. (2003). Automatic category activation and social behavior: The moderating role of prejudiced beliefs. *Social Cognition, 21,* 167–193.

Brown, R. P., & Josephs, R. A. (1999). A burden of proof: Stereotype relevance and gender differences in math performance. *Journal of Personality and Social Psychology, 76,* 246–257.

Burnstein, E., Crandall, C., & Kitayama, S. (1994). Some neo-Darwinian rules for altruism: Weighing cues for inclusive fitness as a function of the biological importance of the decision. *Journal of Personality and Social Psychology, 67,* 773–789.

Buss, D. M. (1995). Evolutionary psychology: A new paradigm for psychological science. *Psychological Inquiry, 6,* 1–30.

Buss, D. M., & Kenrick, D. T. (1998). Evolutionary social psychology. In D. T. Gilbert, S. T. Fiske, & G. Lindzey (Eds.), *The handbook of social psychology* (4th ed., Vol. 2, pp. 982–1026). New York: McGraw Hill.

Cantor, N., & Mischel, W. (1979). Prototypes in person perception. In L. Berkowitz (Ed.), *Advances in experimental social psychology* (Vol. 12, pp. 3–52). New York: Academic Press.

Castelli, L., De Dea, C., & Nesdale, D. (2008). Learning social attitudes: Children's sensitivity to the nonverbal behaviors of adult models during interracial interactions. *Personality and Social Psychology Bulletin, 34,* 1504–1513.

Castelli, L., Tomelleri, S., & Zogmaister, C. (2008). Implicit ingroup metafavoritism: Subtle preference for ingroup members displaying ingroup bias. *Personality and Social Psychology Bulletin, 34,* 807–818.

Campbell, E. Q. (1958). Some social-psychological correlates of direction in attitude change. *Social Forces, 36,* 335–340.

Chambers, J. R., Schlenker, B. R., & Collisson, B. (2013). Ideology and prejudice: The role of value conflicts. *Psychological Science, 24,* 140–149.

Cikara, M., Bruneau, E. G., & Saxe, R. R. (2011). Us and them: Intergroup failures of empathy. *Current Directions in Psychological Science, 20,* 149–153.

Clark, K. B., & Clark, M. P. (1947). Racial identification and preference in Negro children. In T. M. Newcomb and E. L. Hartley (Eds.), *Readings in social psychology* (pp. 169–178). New York: Holt.

Clark, R., Anderson, N. B., Clark, V. R., & Williams, D. R. (1999). Racism as a stressor for African-Americans: A biopsychosocial model. *American Psychologist, 54,* 805–816.

Cohen, C. E. (1981). Person categories and social perception: Testing some boundaries of the processing effect of prior knowledge. *Journal of Personality and Social Psychology, 40,* 441–452.

Cohen, G. L., & Garcia, J. (2008). Identity, belonging, and achievement: A model, interventions, and implications. *Current Directions in Psychological Science, 17,* 365–369.

Cohrs, J., Kämpfe-Hargrave, N., & Riemann, R. (2012). Individual differences in ideological attitudes and prejudice: Evidence from peer-report data. *Journal of Personality and Social Psychology, 103,* 343–361.

Condry, J., & Condry, S. (1976). Sex differences: A study in the eye of the beholder. *Child Development, 47,* 812–819.

Cook, S. W. (1978). Interpersonal and attitudinal outcomes in cooperating interracial groups. *Journal of Research and Development in Education, 12,* 97–113.

Correll, J., Park, B., Judd, C. M., & Wittenbrink, B. (2002). The police officer's dilemma: Using ethnicity to disambiguate potentially threatening individuals. *Journal of Personality and Social Psychology, 83,* 1314–1329.

Correll, J., Park, B., Judd, C. M., Wittenbrink, B., Sadler, M. S., & Keesee, T. (2006). Across the thin blue line: Police officers and racial bias in the decision to shoot. *Journal of Personality and Social Psychology, 92,* 1006–1023.

Crabb, P. B., & Bielawski, D. (1994). The social representation of material culture and gender in children's books. *Sex Roles, 30,* 69–79.

Crandall, C. S. (1994). Prejudice against fat people: Ideology and self-interest. *Journal of Personality and Social Psychology, 66,* 882–894.

Crandall, C. S., D'Anello, S., Sakalli, N., Lazarus, E., Wieczorkowska, G., & Feather, N. T. (2001). An Attribution-Value model of prejudice: Anti-fat attitudes in six nations. *Personality and Social Psychology Bulletin, 27,* 30–37.

Crandall, C. S., & Eshelman, A. (2003). A justification-suppression model of the expression and experience of prejudice. *Psychological Bulletin, 129,* 414–446.

Crawford, M. T., & Skowronski, J. J. (1998). When motivated thought leads to heightened bias: High need for cognition can enhance the impact of stereotypes on memory. *Personality and Social Psychology Bulletin, 24,* 1075–1088.

Crocker, J., & Major, B. (1989). Social stigma and self-esteem: The self-protective properties of stigma. *Psychological Review, 96*, 608–630.

Crocker, J., Major, B., & Steele, C. (1998). Social stigma. In D. T. Gilbert, S. T. Fiske, & G. Lindzey (Eds.), *The handbook of social psychology* (4th ed., Vol. 2, pp. 504–553). New York: McGraw Hill.

Croizet, J. C., Després, G., Gauzins, M., Huguet, P., Leyens, J.-P., & Méot, A. (2004). Stereotype threat undermines intellectual performance by triggering a disruptive mental load. *Personality and Social Psychology Bulletin, 30*, 721–731.

Crosby, F., Bromley, S., & Saxe, L. (1980). Recent unobtrusive studies of black and white discrimination and prejudice: A literature review. *Psychological Bulletin, 87*, 546–563.

Cunningham, W. A., Johnson, M. K., Raye, C. L., Gatenby, C., Gore, J. C., & Banaji, M. R. (2004). Separable neural components in the processing of Black and White faces. *Psychological Science, 15*, 806–813.

Czellar, S. (2006). Self-presentational effects in the implicit association test. *Journal of Consumer Psychology, 16*, 92–100.

Darley, J. M., & Fazio, R. H. (1980). Expectancy confirmation processes arising in the social interaction sequence. *American Psychologist, 35*, 867–881.

Darley, J. M., & Gross, P. H. (1983). A hypothesis-confirming bias in labeling effects. *Journal of Personality and Social Psychology, 44*, 20–33.

Dasgupta, N., & Asgari, S. (2004). Seeing is believing: Exposure to counterstereotypic women leaders and its effect on the malleability of automatic gender stereotyping. *Journal of Experimental Social Psychology, 40*, 642–658.

Dasgupta, N., & Greenwald, A. G. (2001). On the malleability of automatic attitudes: Combating automatic prejudice with images of admired and disliked individuals. *Journal of Personality and Social Psychology, 81*, 800–814.

Davis, J. A., Smith, T. W., & Marsden, P. V. (2005). GENERAL SOCIAL SURVEYS, 1972–2004: [CUMULATIVE FILE] [Computer file]. 2nd ICPSR version. Chicago, IL: National Opinion Research Center [producer], 2005. Storrs, CT: Roper Center for Public Opinion Research, University of Connecticut/Ann Arbor, MI: Inter-university Consortium for Political and Social Research/Berkeley, CA: Computer-assisted Survey Methods Program (http://sda.berkeley.edu), University of California [distributors].

Deaux, K., Winton, W., Crowley, M., & Lewis, L. L. (1985). Level of categorization and content of gender stereotypes. *Social Cognition, 3*, 145–167.

Degner, J., & Dalege, J. (2013). The apple does not fall far from the tree, or does it? A meta-analysis of parent-child similarity in intergroup attitudes. *Psychological Bulletin, 139*, 1270–1304.

De Houwer, J., Beckers, T., & Moors, A. (2007). Novel attitudes can be faked on the Implicit Association Test. *Journal of Experimental Social Psychology, 43*, 972–978.

Deutsch, M., Collins, M. E. (1951). *Interracial housing: A psychological evaluation of a social experiment.* Minneapolis: University of Minnesota press.

Deutsch, R., & Fazio, R. H. (2008). How subtyping shapes perception: Predictable exceptions to the rule reduce attention to stereotype-associated dimensions. *Journal of Experimental Social Psychology, 44*, 1020–1034.

Devine, P. G. (1989a). Automatic and controlled processes in prejudice: The role of stereotypes and personal beliefs. In A. R. Pratkanis, S. J. Breckler, & A. G. Greenwald (Eds.), *Attitude structure and function* (pp. 181–212). Hillsdale, NJ: Erlbaum.

Devine, P. G. (1989b). Stereotypes and prejudice: Their automatic and controlled components. *Journal of Personality and Social Psychology, 56*, 5–18.

Devine, P. G. (2001). Implicit prejudice and stereotyping: How automatic are they? Introduction to the special section, *Journal of Personality and Social Psychology, 81*, 757–759.

Devine, P. G., Forscher, P. S., Austin, A. J., & Cox, W. L. (2012). Long-term reduction in implicit race bias: A prejudice habit–breaking intervention. *Journal of Experimental Social Psychology, 48,* 1267–1278.

Devine, P. G., Monteith, M. J., Zuwerink, J. R., & Elliot, A. J. (1991). Prejudice with and without compunction. *Journal of Personality and Social Psychology, 60,* 817–830.

Diamond, J. (1992). *The third chimpanzee.* New York: Harper Perennial.

Diefenbach, D. (1997). The portrayal of mental illness on prime-time television. *Journal of Community Psychology, 25,* 289–302.

Dovidio, J. F., Evans, N., & Tyler, R. (1986). Racial stereotypes: The contents of their cognitive representations. *Journal of Experimental Social Psychology, 22,* 22–37.

Dovidio, J. F., & Gaertner, S. L. (1986). Prejudice, discrimination, and racism: Historical trends and contemporary approaches. In J. F. Dovidio & S. L. Gaertner (Eds.), *Prejudice, discrimination, and racism* (pp. 1–34). New York: Academic Press.

Dovidio, J. F., & Gaertner, S. L. (2004). Aversive racism. In M. P. Zanna (Ed.), *Advances in experimental social psychology* (Vol. 37, pp. 1–52). San Diego, CA: Academic Press.

Dovidio, J. F., & Gaertner, S. L. (2010). Intergroup bias. In S. T. Fiske, D. T. Gilbert, & G. Lindzey (Eds.), *The handbook of social psychology* (5th ed., Vol. 2, pp. 1084–1121). Hoboken, NJ: Wiley.

Dovidio, J. F., Glick, P., & Rudman, L. A. (Eds.). (2005). *On the nature of prejudice: Fifty years after Allport.* Malden, MA: Blackwell Publishing.

Duncan, B. L. (1976). Differential social perception and attribution of ingroup violence: Testing the lower limits of stereotyping of blacks. *Journal of Personality and Social Psychology, 34,* 590–598.

Dunton, B. C., & Fazio, R. H. (1997). An individual difference measure of motivation to control prejudiced reactions. *Personality and Social Psychology Bulletin, 23,* 316–326.

Eberhardt, J. L. (2005). Imaging Race. *American Psychologist, 60,* 181–190.

Eberhardt, J. L., Goff, P. A., Purdie, V. J., & Davies, P. G. (2004). Seeing Black: Race, crime, and visual processing. *Journal of Personality and Social Psychology, 87,* 876–893.

Edwards, G. H. (1992). The structure and content of the male gender role stereotype: An exploration of subtypes. *Sex Roles, 27,* 533–551.

Erber, R. & Fiske, S. T. (1984). Outcome dependency and attention to inconsistent information. *Journal of Personality and Social Psychology, 47,* 709–726.

Fazio, R. H., Jackson, J. R., Dunton, B. C., & Williams, C. J. (1995). Variability in automatic activation as an unobtrusive measure of racial attitudes: A bona fide pipeline? *Journal of Personality and Social Psychology, 69,* 1013–1027.

Fein, S., & Spencer, S. J. (1997). Prejudice as self-image maintenance: Affirming the self through derogating others. *Journal of Personality and Social Psychology, 73,* 31–44.

Fiedler, K., & Bluemke, M. (2005). Faking the IAT: Aided and unaided response control on the Implicit Association Tests. *Basic and Applied Social Psychology, 27,* 307–316.

Fiske, S. T. (1988). Compare and contrast: Brewer's dual process model and Fiske et al.'s continuum model. In T. K. Srull & R. S. Wyer Jr. (Eds.), *Advances in social cognition* (Vol. 1, pp. 65–76). Hillsdale, NJ: Erlbaum.

Fiske, S. T. (1989). Examining the role of intent: Toward understanding its role in stereotyping and prejudice. In J. S. Uleman & J. A Bargh (Eds.), *Unintended thought* (pp. 253–286). New York: Guilford Publications.

Fiske, S. T. (1998). Stereotyping, prejudice, and discrimination. In D. T. Gilbert, S. T. Fiske, & G. Lindzey (Eds.), *The handbook of social psychology* (4th ed., Vol. 2, pp. 357–411). New York: McGraw Hill.

Fiske, S. T. (2000). Stereotyping, prejudice, and discrimination at the seam between the centuries: Evolution, culture, mind, and brain. *European Journal of Social Psychology, 30*, 299–322.

Fiske, S. T. (2002). What we know about bias and intergroup conflict, the problem of the century. *Current Directions in Psychological Science, 11*, 123–128.

Fiske, S. T., Cuddy, A. C., Glick, P., & Xu, J. (2002). A model of (often mixed) stereotype content: Competence and warmth respectively follow from perceived status and competition. *Journal of Personality and Social Psychology, 82*, 878–902.

Fiske, S. T., & Neuberg, S. L. (1990). A continuum model of impression formation from category-based to individuating responses: Influences of information and motivation on attention and interpretation. In M. P. Zanna (Ed.), *Advances in experimental social psychology* (Vol. 23, pp. 1–74). New York: Academic Press.

Fiske, S. T., Neuberg, S. L., Beattie, A. E., & Milberg, S. J. (1987). Category-based and attribute-based reactions to others: Some informational conditions and stereotyping and individuating processes. *Journal of Experimental Social Psychology, 23*, 399–427.

Flannigan, N., Miles, L. K., Quadflieg, S., & Macrae, C. (2013). Seeing the unexpected: Counterstereotypes are implicitly bad. *Social Cognition, 31*, 712–720.

Gaertner, S. L., & Dovidio, J. F. (1986). The aversive form of racism. In J. F. Dovidio & S. L. Gaertner (Eds.), *Prejudice, discrimination, and racism* (pp. 61–89). Orlando, FL: Academic Press.

Galinsky, A. D., & Moskowitz, G. B. (2000). Perspective-taking: Decreasing stereotype expression, stereotype accessibility, and in-group favoritism. *Journal of Personality and Social Psychology, 78*, 708–724.

Gawronski, B., Ehrenberg, K., Banse, R., Zukova, J., & Klauer, K. C. (2003). It's in the mind of the beholder: The impact of stereotypic associations on category-based and individuating impression formation. *Journal of Experimental Social Psychology, 39*, 16–30.

Geeraert, N. (2013). When suppressing one stereotype leads to rebound of another: On the procedural nature of stereotype rebound. *Personality and Social Psychology Bulletin, 39*, 1173–1183.

Gerard, H. B. (1988). School desegregation: The social science role. In P. A. Katz & D. A. Taylor (Eds.), *Eliminating racism: Profiles in controversy* (pp. 225–236). New York: Plenum Press.

Gibbons, F. X., Gerrard, M., Cleveland, M. J., Wills, T. A., & Brody, G. (2004). Perceived discrimination and substance use in African American parents and their children: A panel study. *Journal of Personality and Social Psychology, 86*, 517–529.

Gilbert, D. T., Fiske, S. T., & Lindzey G. (Eds.). *The handbook of social psychology* (4th ed.). New York: McGraw Hill.

Gill, M. J. (2003). Biased against "them" more than "him": Stereotype use in group-directed and individual-directed judgments. *Social Cognition, 21*, 321–348.

Glick, P. (2002). Sacrificial lambs dressed in wolves' clothing: Envious prejudice, ideology, and the scapegoating of Jews. In L. S. Newman & R. Erber (Eds.), *Understanding genocide: The social psychology of the Holocaust* (pp. 113–142). New York: Oxford University Press.

Glick, P., & Fiske, S. T. (2001). Ambivalent stereotypes as legitimizing ideologies: Differentiating paternalistic and envious prejudice. In J. T. Jost & B. Major (Eds.), *The psychology of legitimacy: Emerging perspectives on ideology, justice, and intergroup relations* (pp. 278–306). Cambridge, UK: Cambridge University Press.

Gluszek, A., & Dovidio, J. F. (2010). The way they speak: A social psychological perspective on the stigma of nonnative accents in communication. *Personality and Social Psychology Review, 14*, 214–237.

Gourevitch, P. (1998). *We wish to inform you that tomorrow we will be killed with our families.* New York: Farrar, Straus, & Giroux.

Gray-Little, B., & Hafdahl, A. R. (2000). Factors influencing racial comparisons of self-esteem: A quantitative review. *Psychological Bulletin, 126,* 26–54.

Green, D. P., Glaser, J., & Rich, A. (1998). From lynching to gay bashing: The elusive connection between economic conditions and hate crime. *Journal of Personality and Social Psychology, 75,* 82–92.

Greenwald, A. G., Banaji, M. R., Rudman, L. A., Farnham, S. D., Nosek, B. A., & Mellott, D. S. (2002). A unified theory of implicit attitudes, stereotypes, self-esteem, and self-concept. *Psychological Review, 109,* 3–25.

Greenwald, A. G., McGhee, D. E., & Schwartz, J. L. K. (1998). Measuring individual differences in implicit cognition. *Journal of Personality and Social Psychology, 74,* 1464–1480.

Greenwald, A. G., Oakes, M. A., & Hoffman, H. G. (2003). Targets of discrimination: Effects of race on responses to weapons holders. *Journal of Experimental Social Psychology, 39,* 399–405.

Greenwald, A. G., Poehlman, T. A., Uhlmann, E. L., & Banaji, M. R. (2009). Understanding and using the Implicit Association Test: III. Meta-analysis of predictive validity. *Journal of Personality and Social Psychology, 97,* 17–41.

Hamilton, D. L., & Gifford, R. K. (1976). Illusory correlation in interpersonal perception: A cognitive basis of stereotypic judgments. *Journal of Experimental Social Psychology, 12,* 392–407.

Hamilton, D. L., & Sherman, J. W. (1994). Stereotypes. In R. S. Wyer Jr. & T. K. Srull (Eds.), *Handbook of social cognition* (2nd ed., Vol. 2, pp. 1–68). Hillsdale, NJ: Erlbaum.

Hamilton, D. L., Stroessner, S. J., & Driscoll, D. M. (1994). Social cognition and the study of stereotyping. In P. G. Devine, D. L. Hamilton, & T. M. Ostrom (Eds.), *Social cognition: Impact on social psychology* (pp. 291–321). San Diego, CA: Academic Press.

Haney, C. (1991). The fourteenth amendment and symbolic legality: Let them eat due process. *Law and Human Behavior, 15,* 183–204,

Harding, J., Kutner, B., Proshansky, N., & Chein, I. (1969). Prejudice and ethnic relations. In G. Lindzey & E. Aronson (Eds.), *Handbook of social psychology* (2nd ed., Vol. 5, pp. 1–76). Reading, MA: Addison-Wesley.

Harmon-Jones, E., & Devine, P. G. (2003). Introduction to the special issue on social neuroscience: Promises and caveats. *Journal of Personality and Social Psychology, 85,* 589–593.

Harris, L T., & Fiske, S. T. (2006). Dehumanizing the lowest of the low: Neuroimaging responses to extreme out-groups. *Psychological Science, 17,* 847–853.

Hart, A. J., Whalen, P. J., Shin, L. M., McInerney, S. C., Fischer, H., & Rauch, S. L. (2000). Differential response in the human amygdala to racial outgroup vs. ingroup face stimuli. *Neuroreport, 11,* 2351–2355.

Hastie, R., & Kumar, P. A. (1979). Person memory: Personality traits as organizing principles in memory for behaviors. *Journal of Personality and Social Psychology, 37,* 25–38.

Heatherton, T. F., Kleck, R. E., Hebl, M. R., & Hull, J. G. (2000). *The social psychology of stigma.* New York: Guilford Press.

Heine, S. J., & Lehman, D. R. (1997). The cultural construction of self-enhancement: An examination of group-serving biases. *Journal of Personality and Social Psychology, 72,* 1268–1283.

Henry, P. J., & Sears, D. O. (2002). The Symbolic Racism 200 Scale. *Political Psychology, 23,* 253–283.

Hepworth, J. T., & West, S. G. (1988). Lynchings and the economy: A time-series reanalysis of Hovland and Sears (1940). *Journal of Personality and Social Psychology, 55,* 239–247.

Herek, G. M., Gillis, J. R., & Cogan, J. C. (1999). Psychological sequalae of hate-crime victimization among lesbian, gay, and bisexual adults. *Journal of Consulting and Clinical Psychology, 67,* 945–951.

Hill, T., Lewicki, P., Czyzewska, M., & Boss, A. (1989). Self-perpetuating development of encoding biases in person perception. *Journal of Personality and Social Psychology, 57,* 373–387.

Hirt, E., McDonald, H. E., & Markman, K. D. (1998). Expectancy effects in reconstructive memory: When the past is just what we expected. In S. Lynn & K. M. McConkey (Eds.), *Truth and memory* (pp. 62–89). New York: Guilford Publications.

Hodson, G. (2011). Do ideologically intolerant people benefit from intergroup contact? *Current Directions in Psychological Science, 20,* 154–159.

Hogg, M. A., & Abrams, D. (1990). Social motivation, self-esteem, and social identity. In D. Abrams and M. Hogg (Eds.), *Social identity theory: Constructive and critical advances* (pp. 28–47). New York: Harvester Wheatsheaf.

Hovland, C. I., & Sears, R. R. (1940). Minor studies of aggression: VI. Correlation of lynching with economic indices. *Journal of Psychology, 9,* 301–310.

Hu, X., Rosenfeld, J., & Bodenhausen, G. V. (2012). Combating automatic autobiographical associations: The effect of instruction and training in strategically concealing information in the autobiographical Implicit Association Test. *Psychological Science, 23,* 1079–1085.

Hugenberg, K., & Bodenhausen, G. V. (2003). Facing prejudice: Implicit prejudice and the perception of facial threat. *Psychological Science, 14,* 640–643.

Hutchings, P. B., & Haddock, G. (2008). Look black in anger: The role of implicit prejudice in the categorization and perceived emotional intensity of racially ambiguous faces. *Journal of Experimental Social Psychology, 44,* 1418–1420.

Inzlicht, M., Kaiser, C. R., & Major, B. (2008). The face of chauvinism: How prejudice expectations shape perceptions of facial affect. *Journal of Experimental Social Psychology, 44,* 758–766.

Irish, D. P. (1952). Reactions of Caucasian residents to Japanese-American neighbors. *Journal of Social Issues, 8,* 10–17.

Ito, T. A., Thompson, E., & Cacioppo, J. T. (2004). Tracking the timecourse of social perception: The effects of racial cues on event-related brain potentials. *Personality and Social Psychology Bulletin, 30,* 1267–1280.

Ito, T. A., & Urland, G. R. (2003). Race and gender on the brain: Electrocortical measures of attention to the race and gender of multiply categorizable individuals. *Journal of Personality and Social Psychology, 85,* 616–626.

Jamieson, J. P., Koslov, K., Nock, M. K., & Mendes, W. (2013). Experiencing discrimination increases risk taking. *Psychological Science, 24,* 131–139.

Johns, M., Schmader, T., & Martens, A. (2005). Knowing is half the battle: Teaching stereotype threat as a means of improving women's math performance. *Psychological Science, 16,* 175–179.

Johnson, D. W., & Johnson, R. T. (1987). *Learning together and alone: Cooperative, competitive, and individualistic learning* (2nd ed.). Englewood Cliffs, NJ: Prentice Hall.

Josephs, R. A., Newman, M. L., Brown, R. P., & Beer, J. M. (2003). Status, testosterone, and human intellectual performance: Stereotype threat as status concern. *Psychological Science, 14,* 158–163.

Karpinski, A., & Hilton, J. L. (2001). Attitudes and the implicit association test. *Journal of Personality and Social Psychology, 81,* 774–788.

Kawakami, K., Dion, K. L., & Dovidio, J. F. (1998). Racial prejudice and stereotype activation. *Personality and Social Psychology Bulletin, 24,* 407–416.

Kenrick, A. C., Shapiro, J. R., & Neuberg, S. L. (2013). Do parental bonds break anti-fat stereotyping?: Parental work ethic ideology and disease concerns predict bias against heavyweight children. *Social Psychological and Personality Science, 4,* 721–729.

Kinzler, K. D., Shutts, K., DeJesus, J., & Spelke, E. S. (2009). Accent trumps race in guiding children's social preferences. *Social Cognition, 27,* 623–634.

Klonis, S. C., Plant, E. A., & Devine, P. G. (2005). Internal and external motivation to respond without sexism. *Personality and Social Psychology Bulletin, 31,* 1237–1249.

Kuhl, V. (1997). Disparities in judgments of the O. J. Simpson case: A social identity perspective. *Journal of Social Issues, 53*, 531–545.

Kunda, Z., & Oleson, K. C. (1995). Maintaining stereotypes in the face of disconfirmation: Constructing grounds for subtyping deviants. *Journal of Personality and Social Psychology, 68*, 565–580.

Kunda, Z., & Sherman-Williams, B. (1993). Stereotypes and the construal of individuating information. *Personality and Social Psychology Bulletin, 19*, 90–99.

Kunda, Z., & Sinclair, L. (1999). Motivated reasoning with stereotypes: Activation, application, and inhibition. *Psychological Inquiry, 10*, 12–22.

Kunda, Z., & Spencer, S. J. (2003). When do stereotypes come to mind and when do they color judgment? A goal-based theoretical framework for stereotype activation and application. *Psychological Bulletin, 129*, 522–544.

Kurzban, R., & Leary, M. R. (2001). Evolutionary origins of stigmatization: The functions of social exclusion. *Psychological Bulletin, 127*, 187–208.

Leonard, K., Pope, C. E., & Feyerherm, W. H. (1995). *Minorities in juvenile justice.* Thousand Oaks, CA: Sage.

Lepore, L., & Brown, R. (1997). Category and stereotype activation: Is prejudice inevitable? *Journal of Personality and Social Psychology, 72*, 275–287.

Levin, S., Matthews, M., Guimond, S., Sidanius, J., Pratto, F., Kteily, N., Pitpitan, E. V., & Dover, T. (2012). Assimilation, multiculturalism, and colorblindness: Mediated and moderated relationships between social dominance orientation and prejudice. *Journal of Experimental Social Psychology, 48*, 20–212.

Levin, S., & van Laar, C. (2006). *Stigma and group inequality: Social psychological perspectives.* Mahwah, NJ: Erlbaum.

Levine, R. A., & Campbell, D. T. (1972). *Ethnocentrism: Theories of conflict, ethnic attitudes, and group behavior.* New York: Wiley.

Lick, D. J., Durso, L. E., & Johnson, K. L. (2013). Minority stress and physical health among sexual minorities. *Perspectives on Psychological Science, 8*, 521–548.

Lieberman, M. D. (2010). Social cognitive neuroscience. In S. T. Fiske, D. T. Gilbert, & G. Lindzey (Eds.), *The handbook of social psychology* (5th ed., Vol. 1, pp. 143–193). Hoboken, NJ: Wiley.

Linville, P. W., Fischer, G. W., & Salovey, P. (1989). Perceived distributions and characteristics of in-group and out-group members: Empirical evidence and a computer simulation. *Journal of Personality and Social Psychology, 57*, 165–188.

Livingston, R. W. (2002). The role of perceived negativity in the moderation of African Americans' implicit and explicit racial attitudes. *Journal of Experimental Social Psychology, 38*, 405–413.

Long, K. R. (1993). Professors say girls get short shrift in class. *Cleveland Plain Dealer.*

Ma, D. S., Correll, J., Wittenbrink, B., Bar-Anan, Y., Sriram, N., & Nosek, B. A. (2013). When fatigue turns deadly: The association between fatigue and racial bias in the decision to shoot. *Basic and Applied Social Psychology, 35*, 515–524.

Ma, S. (2001). The nine lives of *Blackhawk's* Oriental: Chop Chop, Wa Cheng, and Weng Chan. *International Journal of Comic Art, 3*, 120–148.

Macrae, C. N., Bodenhausen, G. V., Milne, A. B., & Jetten, J. (1994). Out of mind but back in sight: Stereotypes on the rebound. *Journal of Personality and Social Psychology, 67*, 808–817.

Macrae, C. N., Stangor, C., & Milne, A. B. (1994). Activating social stereotypes: A functional analysis. *Journal of Experimental Social Psychology, 30*, 370–389.

Mahajan, N., Martinez, M. A., Gutierrez, N. L., Diesendruck, G., Banaji, M. R., & Santos, L. R. (2011). The evolution of intergroup bias: Perceptions and attitudes in rhesus macaques. *Journal of Personality and Social Psychology, 100*, 387–405.

Major, B. (2006). New perspectives on stigma and psychological well-being. In S. Levin & C. van Laar (Eds.), *Stigma and group inequality: Social psychological perspectives* (pp. 193–210). Mahwah, NJ: Erlbaum.

Major, B., Kaiser, C. R., & McCoy, S. K. (2003). It's not my fault: When and why attributions to prejudice protect self-esteem. *Personality and Social Psychology Bulletin, 29,* 772–781.

Marcus-Newhall, A., Thompson, S., & Thomas, C. (2001). Examining a gender stereotype: Menopausal women. *Journal of Applied Social Psychology, 31,* 698–719.

Markus, H. R., & Kitayama, S. (1991). Culture and the self: Implications for cognition, emotion, and motivation. *Psychological Review, 98,* 224–253.

Mazzella, R., & Feingold, A. (1994). The effects of physical attractiveness, race, socioeconomic status, and gender of defendants and victims on judgments of mock jurors: A meta-analysis. *Journal of Applied Social Psychology, 24,* 1351–1344.

McConahay, J. B., Hardee, B. B., & Batts, V. (1981). Has racism declined? It depends upon who's asking and what is asked. *Journal of Conflict Resolution, 25,* 563–579.

McConnell, A. R., & Leibold, J. M. (2001). Relations among the Implicit Association Test, discriminatory behavior, and explicit measures of racial attitudes. *Journal of Experimental Social Psychology, 37,* 435–442.

McPherson, J. (1988). *Battle cry of freedom: The Civil War era.* New York: Oxford University Press.

Medin, D. L. (1989). Concepts and conceptual structure. *American Psychologist, 44,* 1469–1481.

Medin, D. L. (2000). Are there kinds of concepts? *Annual Review of Psychology, 51,* 121–147.

Meyer, I. H. (2003). Prejudice, social stress, and mental health in lesbian, gay, and bisexual populations: Conceptual issues and research evidence. *Psychological Bulletin, 129,* 674–697.

Monteith, M. J., Sherman, J. W., & Devine, P. G. (1998). Suppression as a stereotype control strategy. *Personality and Social Psychology Review, 2,* 63–82.

Monteith, M. J., Zuwerink, J. R., & Devine, P. G. (1994). Prejudice and prejudice reduction: Classic challenges, contemporary approaches. In P. G. Devine, D. L. Hamilton, & T. M. Ostrom (Eds.), *Social cognition: Impact on social psychology* (pp. 323–346). San Diego, CA: Academic Press.

Moskowitz, G. B., Gollwitzer, P. M., Wasel, W., & Schall, B. (1999). Preconscious control of stereotype activation through chronic egalitarian goals. *Journal of Personality and Social Psychology, 77,* 167–184.

Murchison, C. (1935). *Handbook of social psychology.* Worcester, MA: Clark University Press.

Mussen, P. H. (1950). Some personality and social factors related to changes in children's attitudes towards Negroes. *Journal of Abnormal and Social Psychology, 45,* 423–441.

Nairn, R., Coverdale, J., & Claasen, D. (2001). From source material to news story in New Zealand print media: A prospective study of the stigmatizing processes in depicting mental illness. *Australian and New Zealand Journal of Psychiatry, 35,* 654–659.

Navarrete, C., McDonald, M. M., Molina, L. E., & Sidanius, J. (2010). Prejudice at the nexus of race and gender: An outgroup male target hypothesis. *Journal of Personality and Social Psychology, 98,* 933–945.

Nelson, T. D. (2005). Ageism: Prejudice against our feared future self. *Journal of Social Issues, 61,* 207–222.

Nelson, T. D. (2009). *Handbook of prejudice, stereotyping, and discrimination.* New York: Psychology Press.

Nelson, T. E., Acker, M., & Manis, M. (1996). Irrepressible stereotypes. *Journal of Experimental Social Psychology, 32,* 13–38.

Nelson, T. E., Biernat, M. R., & Manis, M. (1990). Everyday base rates (sex stereotypes): Potent and resilient. *Journal of Personality and Social Psychology, 59,* 664–675.

Neuberg, S. L., & Cottrell, C. A. (2006). Evolutionary bases of prejudice. In M. Schaller, J. A. Simpson, & D. T. Kenrick (Eds.), *Evolution and social psychology* (pp. 163–187). New York: Psychology Press.

Neuberg, S. L., & Fiske, S. T. (1987). Motivational influences on impression formation: Outcome dependency, accuracy-driven attention, and individuating processes. *Journal of Personality and Social Psychology, 53,* 431–444.

Neuberg, S. L., Kenrick, D. T., & Schaller, M. (2010). Evolutionary social psychology. In S. T. Fiske, D. T. Gilbert, & G. Lindzey (Eds.), *The handbook of social psychology* (5th ed., Vol. 2, pp. 761–796). Hoboken, NJ: Wiley.

Neumann, R., Hülsenbeck, K., & Seibt, B. (2004). Attitudes towards people with AIDS and avoidance behavior: Automatic and reflective bases of behavior. *Journal of Experimental Social Psychology, 40,* 543–550.

Newman, L. S. (1991). Why are traits inferred spontaneously? A developmental approach. *Social Cognition, 9,* 221–253.

Newman, L. S., & Caldwell, T. L. (2005). Allport's "Living Inkblots": The role of defensive projection in stereotyping and prejudice. In J. F. Dovidio, P. Glick, and L. A. Rudman (Eds.), *On the nature of prejudice: Fifty years after Allport* (pp. 377–392). Malden, MA: Blackwell Publishing.

North, M. S., & Fiske, S. T. (2012). An inconvenienced youth? Ageism and its potential intergenerational roots. *Psychological Bulletin, 138,* 982–997.

Nosek, B. A. (2007). Implicit-explicit relations. *Current Directions in Psychological Science, 16,* 65–69.

Nosek, B. A., Banaji, M. R., & Greenwald, A. G. (2002). Harvesting implicit group attitudes and beliefs from a demonstration website. *Group Dynamics, 6,* 101–115.

Nosek, B. A., Greenwald, A. G., & Banaji, M. R. (2007). The Implicit Association Test at age 7: A methodological and conceptual review. In J. A. Bargh (Ed.), *Automatic processes in social thinking and behavior* (pp. 265–292). Psychology Press.

Ochsner, K. N. (2007). Social cognitive neuroscience: Historical development, core principles, and future promise. In A. Kruglanksi & E. T. Higgins (Eds.), *Social psychology: A handbook of basic principles* (2nd ed., pp. 39–66). New York: Guilford Press.

Ochsner, K. N., & Lieberman, M. D. (2001). The emergence of social cognitive neuroscience. *American Psychologist, 56,* 717–734.

Olson, J. M., Herman, C. P., & Zanna, M. P. (1986). *Relative deprivation and social comparison: The Ontario symposium* (Vol. 4). Hillsdale, NJ: Erlbaum.

Ong, A. D., Fuller-Rowell, T., & Burrow, A. L. (2009). Racial discrimination and the stress process. *Journal of Personality and Social Psychology, 96,* 1259–1271.

Oswald, F. L., Mitchell, G., Blanton, H., Jaccard, J., & Tetlock, P. E. (2013). Predicting ethnic and racial discrimination: A meta-analysis of IAT criterion studies. *Journal of Personality and Social Psychology, 105,* 171–192.

Oyserman, D., & Lauffer, A. (2002). Examining the implications of cultural frames on social movements and group action. In L. S. Newman & R. Erber (Eds.), *Understanding genocide: The social psychology of the Holocaust* (pp. 162–187). New York: Oxford University Press.

Oyserman, D., Sakamoto, I., Lauffer, A. (1998). Cultural accommodation: Hybridity and the framing of social obligation. *Journal of Personality and Social Psychology, 74,* 1606–1618.

Page-Gould, E., Mendoza-Denton, R., & Tropp, L. R. (2008). With a little help from my cross-group friend: Reducing anxiety in intergroup contexts through cross-group friendship. *Journal of Personality and Social Psychology, 95,* 1080–1094.

Palmer, D. L. (1996). Determinants of Canadian attitudes towards immigration: More than just racism? *Canadian Journal of Behavioural Science, 28,* 180–192.

Paluck, E. (2011). Peer pressure against prejudice: A high school field experiment examining social network change. *Journal of Experimental Social Psychology, 47,* 350–358.

Park, B., & Judd, C. M. (1990). Measures and models of perceived group variability. *Journal of Personality and Social Psychology, 59,* 173–191.

Payne, B. K. (2001). Prejudice and perception: The role of automatic and controlled processes in misperceiving a weapon. *Journal of Personality and Social Psychology, 81,* 181–192.

Payne, B. K., Lambert, A. J., & Jacoby, L. L. (2002). Best laid plans: Effects of goals on accessibility bias and cognitive control in race-based misperceptions of weapons. *Journal of Experimental Social Psychology, 38,* 384–396.

Pettigrew, T. F. (1986). The intergroup contact hypothesis reconsidered. In M. Hewstone & R. Brown (Eds.), *Contact and conflict in intergroup encounters.* Oxford, UK: Basil Blackwell.

Pettigrew, T. F., & Tropp, L. R. (2000). Does intergroup contact reduce prejudice? Recent meta-analytic findings. In S. Oskamp (Ed.), *Reducing prejudice and discrimination: The Claremont symposium on applied psychology* (pp. 93–114). Mahwah, NJ: Erlbaum.

Pettigrew, T. F., & Tropp, L. R. (2006). A meta-analytic test of intergroup contact theory. *Journal of Personality and Social Psychology, 90,* 751–783.

Phelps, E. A., O'Connor, K. J., Cunningham, W. A., Funayama, E. S., Gatenby, J. C., Gore, J. C., & Banaji, M. J. (2000). Performance on indirect measures of race evaluation predicts amygdala activation. *Journal of Cognitive Neuroscience, 12,* 729–738.

Plant, E. A., & Devine, P. G. (1998). Internal and external motivation to respond with prejudice. *Journal of Personality and Social Psychology, 75,* 811–832.

Plant, E. A., & Peruche, B. M. (2005). The consequences of race for police officers' responses to criminal suspects. *Psychological Science, 16,* 180–183.

Posten, A.-C., & Mussweiler, T. (2013). When distrust frees your mind: The stereotype-reducing effects of distrust. *Journal of Personality and Social Psychology, 105,* 567–584.

Pratto, F., Sidanius, J., Stallworth, L. M., & Malle, B. F. (1994). Social dominance orientation: A personality variable predicting social and political attitudes. *Journal of Personality and Social Psychology, 67,* 741–763.

Quattrone, G. A., & Jones, E. E. (1980). The perception of variability within in-groups and out-groups: Implications for the law of small numbers. *Journal of Personality and Social Psychology, 38,* 141–152.

Quinn, D. M. (2006). Concealable versus conspicuous stigmatized identities. In S. Levin & C. van Laar (Eds.), *Stigma and group inequality: Social psychological perspectives* (pp. 83–103). Mahwah, NJ: Erlbaum.

Raabe, T., & Beelmann, A. (2011). Development of ethnic, racial, and national prejudice in childhood and adolescence: A multinational meta-analysis of age differences. *Child Development, 82,* 1715–1737.

Rasinski, H. M., Geers, A. L., & Czopp, A. M. (2013). "I guess what he said wasn't that bad": Dissonance in nonconfronting targets of prejudice. *Personality and Social Psychology Bulletin, 39,* 856–869.

Régner, I., Smeding, A., Gimmig, D., Thinus-Blanc, C., Monteil, J., & Huguet, P. (2010). Individual differences in working memory moderate stereotype-threat effects. *Psychological Science, 21,* 1646–1648.

Röhner, J., Schröder-Abé, M. & Schütz, A. (2013). What do fakers actually do to fake the IAT? An investigation of faking strategies under different faking conditions. *Journal of Research in Personality, 47,* 330–338.

Rothbart, M., Evans, M., & Fulero, S. (1979). Recall for confirming events: memory processes and the maintenance of social stereotypes. *Journal of Experimental Social Psychology, 15,* 343–355.

Rothbart, M., & John, O. P. (1985). Social categorization and behavioral episodes: A cognitive analysis of the effects of intergroup contact. *Journal of Social Issues, 41,* 81–104.

Rothbart, M., Sriram, N., & Davis-Stitt, C. (1996). The retrieval of typical and atypical category members. *Journal of Experimental Social Psychology, 32,* 309–336.

Rubin, M., & Badea, C. (2012). They're All the Same! … but for Several Different Reasons: A Review of the Multicausal Nature of Perceived Group Variability. *Current Directions in Psychological Science, 21,* 367–372.

Rubin, M., & Hewstone, M. (1998). Social identity theory's self-esteem hypothesis: A review and some suggestions for clarification. *Personality and Social Psychology Review, 2,* 40–62.

Rudman, L. A. (1998). Self-promotion as a risk factor for women: The costs and benefits of counterstereotypical impression management. *Journal of Personality and Social Psychology, 74,* 629–645.

Rudman, L. A., Ashmore, R. D., & Gary, M. L. (2001). "Unlearning" automatic biases: The malleability of implicit prejudice and stereotypes. *Journal of Personality and Social Psychology, 81,* 856–868.

Rydell, R. J., Rydell, M. T., & Boucher, K. L. (2010). The effect of negative performance stereotypes on learning. *Journal of Personality and Social Psychology, 99,* 883–886.

Sagar, H. A, & Schofield, J. W. (1980). Racial and behavioral cues in black and white children's perceptions of ambiguously aggressive acts. *Journal of Personality and Social Psychology, 39,* 590–598.

Sargent, M. J., & Bradfield, A. L. (2004). Race and information processing in criminal trials: Does the defendant's race affect how the facts are evaluated? *Personality and Social Psychology Bulletin, 30,* 995–1008.

Schaller, M. (2003). Ancestral environments and motivated social perception: Goal-like blasts from the evolutionary past. In S. J. Spencer, S. Fein, M. P. Zanna, and J. M. Olson (Eds.), *Motivated social perception: The Ontario symposium* (Vol. 9, pp. 215–231). Mahwah, NJ: Erlbaum.

Schaller, M., Park, J. H., & Mueller, A. (2003). Fear of the dark: Interactive effects of beliefs about danger and ambient darkness on ethnic stereotypes. *Personality and Social Psychology Bulletin, 29,* 637–649.

Schmader, T., & Johns, M. (2003). Converging evidence that stereotype threat reduces working memory capacity. *Journal of Personality and Social Psychology, 85,* 440–452.

Schmader, T., Johns, M., & Forbes, C. (2008). An integrated process model of stereotype threat effects on performance. *Psychological Review, 115,* 336–356.

Schultz, J. R., & Maddox, K. B. (2013). Shooting the messenger to spite the message? Exploring reactions to claims of racial bias. *Personality and Social Psychology Bulletin, 39,* 346–358.

Sears, D. O., & McConahy, J. N. (1973). *The politics of violence: The new urban blacks and the Watts riot.* Boston: Houghton Mifflin.

Sechrist, G. B., Swim, J. K., & Stangor, C. (2004). When do the stigmatized make attributions to discrimination occurring to the self and others?: The roles of self-presentation and need for control. *Journal of Personality and Social Psychology, 87,* 111–122.

Sengupta, N. K., & Sibley, C. G. (2013). Perpetuating one's own disadvantage: Intergroup contact enables the ideological legitimation of inequality. *Personality and Social Psychology Bulletin, 39,* 1391–1403.

Seuss, Dr. (1961). *The Sneetches and other stories.* New York: Random House.

Shaffer, D. R., & Case, T. (1982). On the decision to testify in one's own behalf: Effects of withheld evidence, defendant's sexual preferences, and juror dogmatism on juridic decisions. *Journal of Personality and Social Psychology, 42,* 335–346.

Sherif, M., Harvey, L. J., White, B. J., Hood, W. R., & Sherif, C. W. (1961). *The Robbers Cave experiment: Intergroup conflict and cooperation.* Middletown, CT: Wesleyan University Press.

Sherman, J. W. (2001). The dynamic relationship between stereotype efficiency and mental representation. In G. B. Moskowitz (Ed.), *Cognitive social psychology: The Princeton symposium on the legacy and future of social cognition* (pp. 177–190). Mahwah, NJ: Lawrence Erlbaum Associates.

Shook, N. J., & Fazio, R. H. (2008). Interracial roommate relationships: An experimental field test of the contact hypothesis. *Psychological Science, 19,* 717–723.

Sim, J. J., Correll, J., & Sadler, M. S. (2013). Understanding police and expert performance: When training attenuates (vs. exacerbates) stereotypic bias in the decision to shoot. *Personality and Social Psychology Bulletin, 39,* 291–304.

Slavin, R. E. (1985). Cooperative learning: Applying Contact Theory in desegregated schools. *Journal of Social Issues, 41*(2), 45–62.

Smith, D. N. (1998). The psychocultural roots of genocide: Legitimacy and crisis in Rwanda. *American Psychologist, 7,* 743–753.

Smith, H. J., Pettigrew, T. F., Pippin, G. M., & Bialosiewicz, S. (2012). Relative deprivation: A theoretical and meta-analytic review. *Personality and Social Psychology Review, 16,* 203–232.

Smith-McLallen, A., Johnson, B. T., Dovidio, J. F., & Pearson, A. R. (2006). Black and White: The role of color bias in implicit race bias. *Social Cognition, 24,* 46–73.

Snyder, M., & Uranowitz, S. W. (1978). Reconstructing the past: Some cognitive consequences of person perception. *Journal of Personality and Social Psychology, 36,* 941–950.

Son Hing, L. S., Chung-Yan, G. A., Hamilton, L. K., & Zanna, M. P. (2008). A two-dimensional model that employs explicit and implicit attitudes to characterize prejudice. *Journal of Personality and Social Psychology, 94,* 971–987.

Spencer, S. J, Steele, C. M., & Quinn, D. M. (1999). Stereotype threat and women's math performance. *Journal of Experimental Social Psychology, 35,* 4–28.

Spencer-Rodgers, J., Williams, M. J., Hamilton, D. L., Peng, K., & Wang, L. (2007). Culture and group perception: Dispositional and stereotypic inferences about novel and national groups. *Journal of Personality and Social Psychology, 93,* 525–543.

Srull, T. K. (1981). Person memory: Some tests of associative storage and retrieval models. *Journal of Experimental Psychology: Human Learning and Memory, 7,* 440–463.

Srull, T. K., & Wyer, R. S. Jr. (1989). Person memory and judgment. *Psychological Review, 96,* 58–83.

Stangor, C., & McMillan, D. (1992). Memory for expectancy-congruent and expectancy-incongruent information: A review of the social and social developmental literatures. *Psychological Bulletin, 111,* 42–61.

Steadman, H. (1981). Critically reassessing the accuracy of public perceptions of the dangerousness of the mentally ill. *Journal of Health and Social Behavior, 22,* 310–316.

Steele, C. M. (1997). A threat in the air: How stereotypes shape intellectual identity and performance. *American Psychologist, 52,* 613–629.

Steele, C. M., & Aronson, J. (1995). Stereotype threat and the intellectual test performance of African Americans. *Journal of Personality and Social Psychology, 69,* 797–811.

Steele, C. M., Spencer, S. J., & Aronson, J. (2002). Contending with group image: The psychology of stereotype and social identity threat. In M. P. Zanna (Ed.), *Advances in experimental social psychology* (Vol. 34, pp. 379–440). San Diego, CA: Academic Press.

Steinberg, J. R., Okun, M. A., & Aiken, L. S. (2012). Calculus GPA and math identification as moderators of stereotype threat in highly persistent women. *Basic and Applied Social Psychology, 34,* 534–543.

Stephan, W. G. (1986). The effects of school desegregation: An evaluation 30 years after *Brown.* In R. Kidd, L. Saxe, & M. Saks (Eds.), *Advances in applied social psychology.* Hillsdale, NJ: Erlbaum.

Stewart, T. L., Weeks, M., & Lupfer, M. B. (2003). Spontaneous stereotyping: A matter of prejudice? *Social Cognition, 21,* 263–298.

Stone, J., Perry, Z. W., & Darley, J. M. (1997). "White men can't jump": Evidence for the perceptual confirmation of stereotypes following a basketball game. *Basic and Applied Social Psychology, 19*, 291–306.

Stone, J., Lynch, C. I., Sjomeling, M., & Darley, J. M. (1999). Stereotype threat effects on Black and White athletic performance. *Journal of Personality and Social Psychology, 77*, 1213–1227.

Stroessner, S. J., & Plaks, J. E. (2001). Illusory correlation and stereotype formation: Tracing the arc of research over a quarter century. In G.B. Moskowitz (Ed.), *Cognitive social psychology: The Princeton symposium on the legacy and future of social cognition* (pp. 247–259). Mahwah, NJ: Lawrence Erlbaum Associates.

Suedfeld, P., & Schaller, M. (2002). Authoritarianism and the Holocaust: Some Cognitive and Affective Implications. In L. S. Newman & R. Erber (Eds.), *Understanding genocide: The social psychology of the Holocaust* (pp. 68–90). New York: Oxford University Press.

Swim, J. K., & Hyers, L. L. (1999). Excuse me—What did you just say?: Women's public and private responses to sexist remarks. *Journal of Experimental Social Psychology, 35*, 68–88.

Swim, J. K., & Sanna, L. (1996). He's skilled, she's lucky: A meta-analysis of observers' attributions for women's and men's successes and failures. *Personality and Social Psychology Bulletin, 22*, 507–519.

Tajfel, H. (1982). *Social identity and intergroup relations.* Cambridge, UK: Cambridge University Press.

Tajfel, H., & Turner, J. C. (1979). An integrative theory of intergroup conflict. In W. Austin & S. Worchel (Eds.), *The social psychology of intergroup relations* (pp. 33–47). Monterey, CA: Brooks-Cole.

Tajfel, H., & Turner, J. C. (1986). The social identity theory of intergroup behavior. In S. Worchel & W. Austin (Eds.), *Psychology of intergroup relations* (2nd ed., pp. 7–24). Chicago: Nelson-Hall Publishers.

Tajfel, H., & Billig, M. G. (1974). Familiarity and categorization in intergroup behavior. *Journal of Experimental Social Psychology, 10*, 159–170.

Tajfel, H., Billig, M. G., Bundy, R. P., & Flament, C. (1971). Social categorization and intergroup behavior. *European Journal of Social Psychology, 1*, 149–178.

Todd, A. R., Bodenhausen, G. V., Richeson, J. A., & Galinsky, A. D. (2011). Perspective taking combats automatic expressions of racial bias. *Journal of Personality and Social Psychology, 100*, 1027–1042.

Tomes, H. (December, 2002). Recognizing Kenneth B. Clark's legacy. *Monitor on Psychology, 33*(11), p. 56.

Toobin, J. (1996). *The run of his life: The people v. O. J. Simpson.* New York: Random House.

Triandis, H. C. (1995). *Individualism and collectivism.* Boulder, CO: Westview.

Uhlmann, E., Brescoll, V. L., & Paluck, E. L. (2006). Are members of low status groups perceived as bad, or badly off? Egalitarian negative associations and automatic prejudice. *Journal of Experimental Social Psychology, 42*, 491–499.

Uleman, J. S., Hon, A., Roman, R. J., & Moskowitz, G. B. (1996). On-line evidence for spontaneous trait inferences at encoding. *Personality and Social Psychology Bulletin, 22*, 377–394.

Uleman, J. S., Newman, L. S., & Moskowitz, G. B. (1996). People as spontaneous interpreters: Evidence and issues from spontaneous trait inference. In M. Zanna (Ed.), *Advances in experimental social psychology* (Vol. 28, pp. 211–279). San Diego, CA: Academic Press.

Unkelbach, C., Forgas, J. P., & Denson, T. F. (2008). The turban effect: The influence of Muslim headgear and induced affect on aggressive responses in the shooter bias paradigm. *Journal of Experimental Social Psychology, 44*, 1409–1413.

Van Bavel, J. J., Packer, D. J., & Cunningham, W. A. (2008). The neural substrates of in-group bias: A functional magnetic resonance imaging investigation. *Psychological Science, 19*, 1131–1139.

Van Laar, C., Levin, S., Sinclair, S., & Sidanius, J. (2005). The effect of university roommate contact on ethnic attitudes and behavior. *Journal of Experimental Social Psychology, 41*, 329–345.

Wahl, O. F. (1995). *Media madness: Public images of mental illness.* New Brunswick, NJ: Rutgers University Press.

Waller, J. (2002). *Becoming evil: How ordinary people commit genocide and mass killing*. New York: Oxford University Press.

Weber, R., & Crocker, J. (1983). Cognitive processes in the revision of stereotypic beliefs. *Journal of Personality and Social Psychology, 45*, 961–977.

Wegner, D. M. (1992). You can't always think what you want: Problems in the suppression of unwanted thoughts. In M. Zanna (Ed.), *Advances in experimental social psychology* (Vol. 25, pp. 193–225). San Diego, CA: Academic Press.

Wegner, D. M. (1994). Ironic processes of mental control. *Psychological Review, 101*, 34–52.

Wegner, D. M., & Erber, R, (1992). The hyperaccessibility of suppressed thoughts. *Journal of Personality and Social Psychology, 63*, 903–912.

Wegner, D. M., Schneider, D. J., Carter, S. III, & White, L. (1987). Paradoxical effects of thought suppression. *Journal of Personality and Social Psychology, 53*, 409–418.

Wheeler, M. E., & Fiske, S. T (2005). Controlling racial prejudice: Social-cognitive goals affect amygdala and stereotype activation. *Psychological Science, 16*, 56–63.

Whitley, R., & Berry, S. (2013). Trends in Newspaper Coverage of Mental Illness in Canada: 2005–2010. *Canadian Journal of Psychiatry, 58*, 107–112.

Wigboldus, D. H. J., Dijksterhuis, A., & van Knippenberg, A. (2003). When stereotypes get in the way: Stereotypes obstruct stereotype-inconsistent trait inferences. *Journal of Personality and Social Psychology, 84*, 470–484.

Wigboldus, D. H. J., Sherman, J. W., Franzese, H. L., & van Knippenberg, A. (2004). Capacity and comprehension: Spontaneous stereotyping under cognitive load. *Social Cognition, 22*, 292–309.

Wilder, D. A. (1981). Perceiving persons as a group: Categorization in intergroup relations. In D. L. Hamilton (Ed.), *Cognitive processes in stereotyping and intergroup behavior* (pp. 213–257). Hillsdale, NJ: Erlbaum.

Wilner, D. M., Walkley, R. P., & Cook, S. W. (1952). Residential proximity and intergroup relations in public housing projects. *Journal of Social Issues, 8*, 45–69.

Wittenbrink, B., Judd, C. M., & Park, B. (1997). Evidence for racial prejudice at the implicit level and its relationship with questionnaire measures. *Journal of Personality and Social Psychology, 72*, 262–274.

Woodcock, A., Hernandez, P. R., Estrada, M., & Schultz, P. (2012). The consequences of chronic stereotype threat: Domain disidentification and abandonment. *Journal of Personality and Social Psychology, 103*, 635–646.

Word, C. H., Zanna, M. P., & Cooper, J. (1974). The nonverbal mediation of self-fulfilling prophecies in interracial interaction. *Journal of Experimental Social Psychology, 10*, 109–120.

Wyer, N. A. (2004). Not all stereotypic biases are created equal: Evidence for a stereotype-disconfirming bias. *Personality and Social Psychology Bulletin, 30*, 706–720.

Yuker, H. E. (1988). Perceptions of severely and multiply disabled persons. *Journal of the Multihandicapped Person, 1*, 5–16.

Yzerbyt, V., & Demoulin, S. (2010). Intergroup relations. In S. T. Fiske, D. T. Gilbert, & G. Lindzey (Eds.), *The handbook of social psychology* (5th ed., Vol. 2, pp. 1024–1083). Hoboken, NJ: Wiley.

Zhang, S., & Hunt, J. S. (2008). The stereotype rebound effect: Universal or culturally bounded process? *Journal of Experimental Social Psychology, 44*, 489–500.

Zimmerman, C. From Chop-Chop to Wu Cheng: The evolution of the Chinese character in Blackhawk comic books. (http://web.archive.org/web/20030608121315/http://www.balchinstitute.org/museum/comics/chop.html)

CHAPTER 12

PROSOCIAL BEHAVIOR AND ALTRUISM

THE MORNING OF A BUSY DAY

Ana knew she had a busy day ahead of her that morning as she watched the Weather Channel and munched on her Corn Pops. Her recent promotion by the ad agency had given her new responsibilities for a long-standing client known to have deep pockets. That client's ad proposal absolutely had to be done by the end of the week. The deadline made her somewhat anxious, but at the same time it excited her. The boost in her salary would allow her to replace that old Chevy her father had handed down to her when she was a college sophomore. It had served its purpose, dragging the laundry to and from her parents' house, but recently some ominous clanking sounds suggested it was time to look for a new car.

What Ana didn't know was that throughout the day, she would be busy fielding numerous requests for help, and at the end of the day, she would be asking for help from someone else. It all began with a pitch for donations that aired just before the local forecast. The short, commercial-length video showed the devastation a massive tornado had caused to the small town of Joplin, Missouri. Video footage of entire neighborhoods with completely destroyed homes alternated with images of the disaster's human toll. One particularly powerful photo showed a father embracing his son amidst a pile of rubble that used to be their home. And the narrator of the story was none other than Jim Cantore, Ana's favorite Weather Channel broadcaster, who asked viewers to make a donation to help the victims. Just ten dollars could go a long way, he said. Ana wanted make a donation right away, but looking at her watch, she realized she was running late. So she scribbled down the toll-free number and resolved to call it from the office during her lunch break.

For most social animals, humans included, helping others and receiving help are part of daily life. At times, we help others without being asked, such as when we slow down to let a fellow driver change lanes. At other times, we help in response to a specific request, agreeing, for example, to take notes for a fellow student or responding to a charitable appeal with a donation. On rare occasions, circumstances may require heroic effort from us, at considerable risk to our well-being. Although on the surface these responses may appear quite different, all ultimately benefit others. Indeed, that is the essence of prosocial behavior. In this chapter, we will look at

The material and human toll of the Joplin, Mo. tornado

the nature of prosocial behavior, asking two questions that have intrigued social psychologists: Why do people help? and why do people fail to help?

THE NATURE OF PROSOCIAL BEHAVIOR

Prosocial behavior refers to a broad category of actions intended to benefit others in socially defined ways (Piliavin, Dovidio, Gaertner, & Clark, 1981). This seemingly simple definition clarifies the nature of prosocial behavior in several ways. First, prosocial behavior is necessarily *interpersonal*, involving an interaction between a benefactor and one or more beneficiaries. Second, for a behavior to be prosocial, it must be *intentional*. If we slow down intentionally to enable a fellow motorist to change lanes, we are acting in a prosocial manner. If we slow down to change the radio station, we may accomplish the same thing, but the outcome is not the result of intentional, prosocial behavior. Third, to qualify as prosocial behavior, the act must benefit *others* more than ourselves. Interpersonal exchanges from which both parties benefit equally aren't really prosocial.

Finally, what benefits others is *socially defined*. That is, by and large, the social context defines which acts are prosocial and which are not. Years ago, before the dangers of smoking were well known, giving a stranger a cigarette would in all likelihood have been seen as a prosocial act. Today, however, that same act may not be seen as prosocial, because of the obvious drawbacks of smoking. Similarly, we don't generally think of relentless criticism as a form of prosocial behavior. However, to a student who is trying to get a paper published, offering the strongest criticism possible may well be a prosocial act.

The term *prosocial behavior* is sometimes used interchangeably with *helping* and *altruism*. These three terms are quite different, however. *Prosocial behavior* is an umbrella term that includes cooperation, helping, and altruism. This chapter focuses on helping and altruism.

Helping

Helping may be defined as any action that provides some benefit to or improves the well-being of another person (Schroeder, Penner, Dovidio, & Piliavin, 1995). It can be classified in three different ways (Pearce & Amato, 1980). First, helping can be seen as either spontaneous and informal (for example, holding the door for a fellow student), or planned and formal (say, making a sizable charitable donation). Second, helping can be categorized according to the relative seriousness of the situation (for example, giving someone directions versus giving first aid to an accident victim). Third, helping can be seen as having indirect benefits (for example, a donation to a charitable fund) or direct benefits (perhaps the donation of spare change to a homeless person).

A slightly different classification scheme emerged when McGuire (1994) asked college students to list the kinds of help they had given to and received from others. Students' responses suggested four different kinds of helping. *Casual helping* includes small favors, such as lending someone change for the copy machine. *Substantial personal helping* involves considerably more effort—for example, helping a friend to move. *Emotional helping* includes social support given to a friend with personal problems. (See the Social Psychology and Health box on **page 562** for some specific benefits of social support.) Finally, *emergency helping* includes assistance to a stranger with a severe emergency, such as an accident victim.

SOCIAL PSYCHOLOGY AND HEALTH: THE STRESS-BUFFERING EFFECTS OF SOCIAL SUPPORT

Close others form a social network that can provide psychological and material resources to an individual who is coping with stress (Cohen, 2004). Social support provides three specific three types of resources (House & Kahn, 1985). *Instrumental support* is material aid such as financial assistance or help with daily tasks. *Informational support* is advice and guidance on how to cope with one's problems. *Emotional support* includes empathy, caring, reassurance, and trust, along with opportunities for emotional expression. The lack of such social support can impede a person's ability to cope with a stressful event, promoting negative coping mechanisms such as smoking, drinking, and drug use (Cohen, Kessler, & Gordon, 1995).

Does that mean our ability to cope with stress increases with the *amount* of social support we receive? Not necessarily. A review of the extensive literature on social support and stress (Cohen & Wills, 1985) concludes that the mere *perception* that support is available tends to buffer the effects of stress, even if support is available from only a single source. In other words, simply knowing that social support is there when we need it can help us to cope with a stressful event. Unsurprisingly, the type of support that is available also matters. If we're suffering from romantic problems, for example, an offer of money will do little to help. At the same time, if we can't pay our bills, emotional support in the form of a shoulder to cry on will not get us very far.

Regardless of how we classify helping, it is prosocial to the extent that it is intended to benefit another. Getting something in return matters very little. For the benefactor, the benefits of helping can be relatively small—for example, gratitude from the beneficiary, a good feeling about oneself, or the avoidance of guilt for not helping. Or they can be more tangible, such as receiving a picture of the child who benefits from one's donation. As long as the help is offered with the intent of benefiting another, it constitutes a prosocial act, regardless of whether it also benefits the helper.

Altruism

Altruism is characterized by the lack of any expectation that helping will bring external rewards (Macauley & Berkowitz, 1970). Because of the emphasis on expected or anticipated rewards rather than actual benefits, this definition is unrestrictive. That is, helping that has unexpected or incidental benefits would still by definition be considered altruistic. Defining altruism in this way makes sense. For example, the meaning of returning a lost wallet to its rightful owner changes, depending on whether or not we expect a finder's fee.

What about the less tangible rewards of helping? If you find yourself feeling good after helping someone in an emergency, does that make your act less altruistic than it would be if you had no (unexpected) good feelings? Some scholars (e.g., Krebs, 1982) have argued that helping isn't truly altruistic unless it comes at a cost to the helper. The self-sacrifice criterion puts a strong emphasis on the consequences of helping to the benefactor. That is, helping is not truly altruistic unless the cost to the helper outweighs any possible benefits. From this perspective, instances of helping that are truly altruistic are extremely rare.

Altruism implies helping others without expecting benefits for the self

Others (Batson, 1991) have argued that whether or not a prosocial act can be considered altruistic should be defined not by the *consequences* to the helper, but by the helper's *motivation* for the act. From this perspective, help provided to ease a victim's suffering would be considered altruistic. Help provided with the expectation of some type of reward, or to avoid feeling guilty, would be considered prosocial because of its benefits to the victim, but it would not be considered altruistic because it is rooted in ultimately selfish motives.

WHY DO PEOPLE HELP?

Serena Calls

It was only noon, but Ana's day at work had been far busier than she had imagined. To make matters worse, much of what she had to deal with had very little to do with work. Soon after arriving, she called Steve, the systems manager, to ask for a different e-mail account. Ana had always received more than her share of spam, but when she opened her e-mail today, it was out of control. Her feminist sensibilities were outraged by the multiple e-mails offering "male enhancement" and the avalanche of solicitations from adult websites. Steve had promised to get back to her ASAP, but he was living up to his reputation as a snail.

Serena, her older sister, had called to find out if Ana could babysit so she could go to a doctor's appointment that evening. Ana was reluctant at first because it meant leaving work early. Then again, it was her sister asking; how could she decline? And then at 10 A.M., Vicki, Ana's best friend, called to say she wanted to have lunch with her that day. Ana had planned to get a salad from the grocery store across the street, but Vicky was persistent, mentioning "boy problems," so Ana gave in. She checked her watch and realized she might have time to call that 800 number to make a donation toward hurricane relief. Before she could retrieve the piece of paper from her cluttered purse, however, Vicki arrived and motioned toward the door.

Ana put down the paper, grabbed her purse and coat, and accompanied Vicki down what she thought must be the slowest elevator in Chicago. At least it gave her time to convince Vicki they should go to the deli nearby rather than the Mexican restaurant on the river. As the two were about to cross the street, they were approached by a homeless person selling copies of *Streetwise*, a weekly publication meant to provide benefactors of the homeless with something in return for their money. Without breaking stride, Ana extracted a dollar bill from her purse and handed it to him as she grabbed the latest copy of the newspaper.

PROSOCIAL BEHAVIOR AS EGOISM

To ask why people help each other may strike some of us as strange. After all, helping is the right thing to do, as prescribed by the norm of social responsibility or the idea that people are responsible for one another's welfare (Berkowitz, 1972). Yet philosophers from Socrates to Hobbes have espoused a view of human nature in which individuals are motivated first and foremost by self-interest. This view suggests that people comply with the norm of social responsibility primarily when doing so serves their self-interest. Not surprisingly, evolutionary psychology provides ample evidence that a great deal of prosocial behavior is indeed motivated by egoism.

Evolutionary Psychology I: Kin Selection and Helping

In evolutionary psychology, helping is explained through the principle of **inclusive fitness** (Hamilton, 1964). According to this principle, humans have a vested interest in preserving their genetic material, not only in their own offspring, but in the offspring of genetically related relatives. Consequently, they are more likely to help relatives than strangers and more likely to help close relatives than distant ones.

To illustrate this point, imagine that you've just arrived home for a family celebration, only to find your house engulfed in flames. Many of your relatives made it out of the house safely, but four people are trapped: your younger brother, your brother's son, your cousin, and the son of an acquaintance. These four are not beyond rescue, but they are scattered around the house, and the fire is burning with such a vengeance that you will be lucky to save just one, even if you act without hesitating. Who will you attempt to save first?

Burnstein, Crandall, and Kitayama (1994) presented scenarios like this one to a large number of American and Japanese undergraduates. Like them, you would probably opt to save your younger brother first, your brother's son second, your cousin third, and the son of an acquaintance last. The reason is simple and entirely compatible with the principle of inclusive fitness: you share 50 percent of your genetic material with your brother, but only 25 percent with his son, 12.5 percent with your cousin, and none with the son of a mere acquaintance. Consequently, saving your brother provides the best chance of your genes surviving into future generations—especially if you yourself don't survive your heroic actions. Interestingly, the results were similar when participants made decisions about helping that did not involve life-or-death consequences. This finding suggests that the tendency to help closely related kin first may be a generalized response that evolved in reaction to evolutionary pressures. As with most human behaviors that are rooted in evolutionary history, it does not require purposeful thought, but is executed outside of conscious awareness.

According to the evolutionary perspective on helping, we are particularly likely to help those who share our genes

Using a similar methodology, Burnstein et al. (1995) identified some additional variables that support the evolutionary explanation of helping, particularly the imperative to save women and children first. They found that in a life-or-death scenario, participants were generally more willing to help females than males—but only to a point. As predicted by the principle of inclusive fitness, women lost their advantage when they reached the age of diminished reproductive potential. In general, the willingness of participants to help closely related others decreased as a function of the victims' age and declined at a particularly steep rate past the age of diminished reproductive capacity. With more mundane kinds of help, the decrease in helping as a function of age reversed as the other approached old age.

The favorable prejudice toward the young was so pervasive that participants were generally more willing to help their three-day-old brother than their 10- or 18-year-old brother, even though the latter was closer to the reproductive stage. This general tendency prevailed primarily in environments that posed little threat to an infant's life, however. In situations marked by high infant mortality, participants showed a decreased tendency to rescue an infant brother, and an increased tendency to help a brother close to reproductive age.

One could argue that findings like those from Burnstein et al. (1995) are limited in value because they represent responses to hypothetical scenarios, rather than actual situations. However, the results of two studies of real-world helping suggest that the principle of inclusive fitness does figure prominently in people's responses to emergencies. Sime (1983) reported that survivors of a fire at a vacation complex were more likely, once they became aware of the fire, to search for relatives than for friends. And Laube (1985) found that emergency workers who were called on to help during a natural disaster reported to duty only after they had made sure their families were safe. Finally, the proclivity to help kin is not unique to humans; it is commonplace in the animal world as well (see Batson, 1995). Because the tendency to preserve inclusive fitness is innate and requires little in the way of higher-order cognitive processing, it can be considered a hidden influence on helping behavior.

Evolutionary Psychology II: Indirect Reciprocity and the Adaptive Value of Following Social Norms

Returning to our opening story, the principle of inclusive fitness can explain why Ana was willing to help her sister, even at considerable cost to herself. Although the situation was not a life-or-death matter, contributing to the welfare of her sister's offspring would ultimately contribute to her own inclusive fitness. However, inclusive fitness does not explain why Ana helped the homeless man, because helping him would provide no genetic benefit to her.

Why did Ana help the homeless man, then? More generally, why do we help others who are not genetically related to us? Evolutionary psychology offers two perspectives. The first is based on the idea of reciprocity (Axelrod, 1984; Trivers, 1971). If we help others, they become willing and available to reciprocate later. So Ana may not have helped the homeless man primarily to get something tangible in return (that is, the newspaper). Rather, she may have done so because he might be able to assist her in the future in some way. Helping based on the principle of **indirect reciprocity** (Alexander, 1987) is particularly likely when the benefit to the recipient exceeds the cost to the helper and when the helper and recipient recognize each other and are likely to interact in the future.

Of course, neither inclusive fitness nor indirect reciprocity can account for the anonymous help from strangers that is commonplace among humans, and at times can be dramatic. Less than two weeks after Hurricane Katrina devastated New Orleans and much of the Gulf Coast in September 2005, charitable relief organizations received pledges totaling $500 million. Only a fraction of them came from big donors like the Rolling Stones and the National Football League; most came from small donors—high school students who washed cars and grade-school children who sold bracelets to benefit the victims. Nine-year-old Johnny Wilson, who swam from Alcatraz to San Francisco's Aquatic Park, single-handedly raised $30,000.

Why do people help strangers, even when there is little chance of reciprocity and possibly a risk to their own inclusive fitness (when, for example, their heroic actions jeopardize their own well-being)? Evolutionary psychology suggests that the adaptive value of following societal and cultural norms can explain such behaviors. In general, those who follow societal norms are better off than those who ignore or defy them (Simon, 1990). Because humans tend to live together and are highly interdependent, cooperation and mutual responsibility for the welfare of others is paramount for a social group to function optimally and compete for resources with other groups (Tomasello et al., 2012). Consequently, most societies reward those who comply with social norms and punish those who do not (Cosmides, 1989). Because such rewards and punishments often operate outside of conscious awareness, they may serve as a hidden influence on people's willingness to help.

Societal mechanisms that promote help for strangers are complemented by two processes that operate on the individual level. McGuire (2003) identified an important cognitive bias that comes into play when people assess the perceived cost of helping to the benefactor, as well as the value of help to the beneficiary. Specifically, people show a modesty bias in estimating the cost of the help they provide relative to the help they receive. In other words, helpers tend to downplay both the cost of their actions to themselves and the benefits to the recipient. Beneficiaries, on the other hand, tend to overestimate the value of the help they receive. Although the modesty bias may sound counterintuitive, taking an "it was nothing" view of the perceived cost and value of our help ultimately promotes future helping, because it leaves us feeling chronically short in our attempts to be socially responsible.

Although the evolutionary account of helping (e.g., Wood & Eagly, 2002) is not without its critics, it is intriguing for a couple of reasons. First, because humans have acquired their propensity to help through evolutionary history, the processes that lead to their decisions to help generally operate outside of conscious awareness. For example, the decision to save your younger brother before you save your brother's son does not require a conscious calculation of relative fitness gains. Instead, the action occurs more or less automatically because evolution has rendered it the optimally adaptive response. The evolutionary account suggests that ultimately, every prosocial act arises from egoism. Help that is provided to genetically related others raises the odds that one's genes will survive into future generations. Help that is provided to strangers may result in reciprocal aid in the future, but even without reciprocal gains, helpers are rewarded through the many positive consequences of complying with social norms.

For the benefactor, these benefits of helping have two features in common. First, the gains often materialize over the long term. Inclusive fitness gains, for example, generally do not manifest themselves for generations. Other benefits of helping—such as reciprocal aid and rewards for complying with social norms—are likewise postponed. Second, the benefits of helping are far from certain. Saving your younger brother from a burning house at the cost of your own life will provide inclusive fitness gains, only to the extent that he survives future threats to his reproductive ability. Similarly, though doing someone a favor increases the *likelihood* that the person will return it in the future, there is no guarantee. And though society looks more kindly on those who comply with social norms, it also teaches us—at least occasionally—that no good deed goes unpunished. As we will see, however, helping has a number of benefits that are fairly immediate and certain.

Why Do People Help?: A Summary

Prosocial behavior is generally defined as behavior that is intended to benefit another. Helping, however, has been classified in different ways. One classification differentiates help in terms of its spontaneity, the seriousness of the situation, and the benefits, whether direct or indirect. Another scheme differentiates among casual helping, substantial personal helping, emotional helping, and emergency helping. Altruism is a form of prosocial behavior that is offered without expectation of a reward.

The evolutionary perspective on prosocial behavior suggests that all helping is selfishly motivated. According to the principle of inclusive fitness, humans have a vested interest in preserving their genetic material. Consequently, they are more likely to help others to whom they are closely related, particularly in life-or-death situations. Prosocial behavior that is intended to benefit strangers is explained on the basis of indirect reciprocity. When there is little or no chance that the beneficiary of help will reciprocate, people still help in order to comply with prevailing social norms because their compliance has adaptive value.

Think Like a Social Psychologist

Making Connections

—Critics of the evolutionary approach to helping often cite alternative explanations. In that regard, how can the distinction between communal and exchange relationships, discussed in Chapter 10, be used to account for the human tendency to save family members rather than strangers from a fire? What other plausible explanations, not based on the concept of inclusive fitness, can you think of?

PROSOCIAL BEHAVIOR AS MOOD MANAGEMENT

Helping has consequences for the way we feel. Although the modesty bias shown by McGuire (2003) suggests that we downplay the cost, helping nonetheless makes us feel good, and refusing to help often makes us feel bad. At the same time, the way we are feeling has consequences for our willingness to help others.

Protecting Good Moods

Imagine that your psychology instructor has just returned your first test. Much to your surprise, you did far better than you had expected. You leave the class with a sense of accomplishment and a feeling of elation. As you head for the exit, you see a fellow student slip on the stairs. He appears to be unharmed, but the fall has dislodged his backpack and spilled its contents all over the staircase. How likely are you to stop and help him gather his belongings? More specifically, will the good feelings that you experienced from doing so well on your

Good moods promote helping because they make us focus on the benefits of helping and the good in other people. They also promote helping because it preserves good moods.

test increase the odds that you will help? Research on the effect of good moods on helping suggests that the answer is an unqualified "yes" (Isen & Levin, 1972).

What is it about a good mood that makes people more likely to help? A meta-analytic review that compared a large number of studies (Carlson, Charlin, & Miller, 1988) indicates that good moods promote helping through three mechanisms. First, people who are in a good mood tend to see the world through the proverbial rose-colored glasses (Clark & Isen, 1982), which allow them to see the benefits of helping more than the costs (Clark & Waddell, 1983) and the good in other people more than the bad (Isen, Shalker, Clark, & Karp. 1978). Second, helping is a good way to maintain or even enhance a good mood because of its positive consequences for the benefactor (Carlson, Charlin, & Miller, 1988; Isen & Levin, 1972). At a minimum, when we help someone in need, we can feel good for having done the right thing. We may also receive gratitude from the beneficiary. Both those outcomes can prolong a good mood. Not surprisingly, it helps when the appeal for help is positive (Cunningham, Steinberg, & Grev, 1980), and it hurts when the act of helping involves an unpleasant task (Isen & Simmonds, 1978).

Finally, even when helping is unpleasant, refusing to help could have disastrous consequences for a good mood. We may be haunted by thoughts of what we should have done, and we may feel bad for not helping, especially when the cost of doing so was small. Thus, a good mood may vanish with the cognitive and affective consequences of not helping.

Relieving Bad Moods

If good moods promote helping, do bad moods discourage it? Let's return to the example of the unfortunate student who has lost the contents of his backpack after slipping on the stairs. This time, however, imagine that you are in a bad mood because you performed much worse on the test than you had expected. Will you stop to help the student gather his belongings? As it turns out, research on the effects of a bad mood on helping suggests that the answer is again an unqualified "yes" (e.g., Carlson & Miller, 1987; Cialdini, Darby, & Vincent, 1973). How can that be?

Because helping can be a positive, mood-enhancing experience, people who are in a bad mood often engage in prosocial activities to make themselves feel better. According to the **negative state relief model** (Cialdini, Kenrick, & Baumann, 1982; Schaller & Cialdini, 1988), that is especially true for people who are experiencing sadness or guilt (Baumeister, Stillwell, & Heatherton, 1994; Cialdini, Darby, & Vincent, 1973).

In a clever test of the hypothesis that sadness and guilt would promote helping, Cialdini, Darby, and Vincent (1973) made some participants feel guilty by leading them to believe they had accidentally ruined a graduate student's research data. Other participants were made to feel sad by seeing the experimenter ruin the student's data. All participants then completed a task that required them to track a maze. Half the participants in the guilt and sadness conditions received praise for their performance; the other half received no praise. Then all participants were asked if they were willing to help another student, who was not part of the experiment, with a class project. **Figure 12.1** shows the effect of these experimental conditions on the dependent variable (willingness to help another student).

The results indicate that when participants who were feeling guilty or sad and received no praise for their performance on the maze-tracking task, they were quite willing to help the imaginary "other student." However, when participants' moods were alleviated by the praise they received for their performance, their willingness to help the other student dropped dramatically. In other words, participants looked at helping as a means to rid

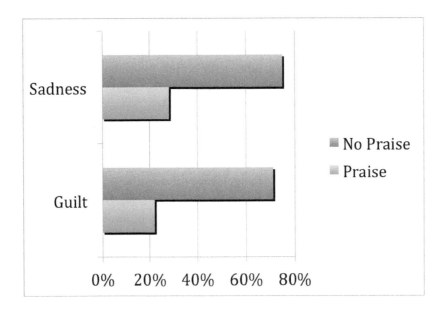

Figure 12.1: Willingness to help as a result of mood and guilt

Source: Cialdini, R.B., Darby, B.L., & Vincent, J.E. (1973). Transgression and altruism: A case for hedonism. *Journal of Experimental Social Psychology*, 9, 502–516.

themselves of their guilt or sadness. The increased willingness to help observed among participants who are in a bad mood hinges on the extent to which other means of relief are available to them. Merely anticipating that one's mood will improve is often enough to reduce the willingness to help to levels more characteristic of those who are not in a bad mood. For example, Schaller and Cialdini (1988) found that sad participants who expected to watch a funny video helped less than sad participants who expected to watch a video described as not funny.

Our heightened willingness to help as a result of being in a bad mood also depends on the extent to which we believe that helping will in fact improve our mood. At times, we may feel so bad that we can think of absolutely nothing we could do to make ourselves feel better. Evidence that such extreme moods do not promote helping comes from a clever experiment in which researchers convinced some participants that their moods could not be changed (Manucia, Baumann, & Cialdini, 1984). In this study, all participants swallowed a pill that they believed was a fast-acting memory drug. It was, of course, a placebo that allowed the experimenters to "inform" participants of its effects. Half the participants were led to believe that the drug would freeze any mood they were experiencing and prolong it for 30 minutes. The rest of the participants were told that the drug would have no effect on their moods. Some participants then recalled and wrote about a sad event in their lives, while others wrote about an event that was not sad. Once they had completed their writing, all participants were given an opportunity to help another student with a project.

The results of this experiment supported the negative state relief model in two ways. First, participants who felt sad and believed that the pill had no side effects were more willing to help than participants who were in a neutral mood. Presumably, they expected helping to improve their mood. Second, sad participants who believed that the pill had frozen their mood—and that helping therefore would not improve their sadness—were less willing to help than sad participants, who believed their mood was malleable.

Although the negative state relief model is well supported empirically, it is not without critics. Citing a paucity of research demonstrating the effects of helping on mood, Carlson and colleagues (Carlson & Miller, 1987; Carlson et al., 1988) suggested that sad people's increased willingness to help may not be motivated by a desire to alleviate a negative mood. Furthermore, happy people's increased willingness to help may not be motivated by a desire to preserve their good mood. Instead, the researchers suggested, both good and bad moods may have an effect on helping, because both promote self-focus. As we saw in Chapter 4, directing attention to the self increases the salience of internal standards of behavior. When we encounter someone who is in need of help, being in a good or bad mood may simply remind us that offering to help is the right thing to do.

Researchers may differ on whether moods affect helping because people want to maintain or improve them, or because they make helping-related standards salient. However, there is little controversy that moods do promote helping. Still, understanding the link between mood and helping is important, because the two competing explanations have vastly different implications. If happy people help in order to maintain their mood and guilty people help in order to improve it, both groups are motivated ultimately by self-interest. If they help because of a heightened self-focus, then their motivation is not an issue.

Managing Emotions Related to an Emergency

The negative state relief model is concerned primarily with the effects of moods that exist independently of an emergency requiring help. However, seeing another who is in need of help can by itself cause a strong emotional reaction among those in a position to help. Ana's distress in response to Jim Cantore's appeal on behalf of victims of the Joplin tornado is a case in point. According to the **arousal/cost-reward model** of helping (Dovidio, Piliavin, Gaertner, Schroeder, & Clark, 1991; Piliavin, Dovidio, Gaertner, & Clark, 1981), her decision to take action may have been motivated partly by a desire to relieve her distress at the plight of the mother and child. More generally, the arousal/cost-reward model proposes that the decision to help is determined by the level of

According to the arousal/cost-reward model of helping, the motivation to help stems from a desire to relieve the distress experienced at the plight of the children

negative emotional arousal experienced by a witness to an emergency, along with a consideration of the cost of helping to the witness and the cost of not helping to the victim.

How much arousal a witness experiences depends to some extent on the severity of the emergency (Dovidio, 1984), but is also influenced by the victim's characteristics and the nature of the relationship between the victim and the witness. For example, the plight of an attractive victim and of victims we feel connected to psychologically elicit especially high levels of arousal, so those victims are most likely to receive our help (Piliavin et al., 1981). At the same time, witnesses are less likely to help when they attribute their arousal to something other than the emergency. Gaertner and Dovidio (1977) led some participants in a study to believe that any arousal they felt might be due to ingesting a pill with arousing side effects. When those participants later encountered what appeared to be an accident involving another student, slightly more than half of them offered to help. Among participants who had not been informed about the arousing side effects of the pill, 85 percent helped. Thus, though the level of arousal is clearly important to helping behavior, the perception that the arousal stems from the emergency is equally important.

How do costs and rewards interact with arousal to predict helping? Not surprisingly, as the cost to the helper increases, helping decreases (Dovidio, 1984). That is particularly true when the act of helping is more unpleasant than the arousal produced by the emergency (Piliavin & Piliavin, 1972). At the same time, helping increases as the personal cost of not helping increases, because the victim might die as a result of our inaction (Dovidio et al., 1991). On the surface, this finding may suggest that helping is the result of a conscious, deliberate cost-benefit analysis by the helper. However, the strong arousal that is commonly felt by witnesses to an emergency often renders the decision to help automatic and spontaneous, thus serving as a hidden influence on helping. That would explain acts of heroic helping, including those displayed by participants in a study by Clark and Word (1974), who rushed to the help of a victim who was apparently being electrocuted. If participants had consciously thought about the consequences of touching the victim (almost certain death), few would have helped.

Of course, one could argue that the participants who risked their lives to save a fellow student from electrocution were motivated by something other than the selfish desire to relieve their distress. In fact, as we will see next, in many instances, people do help primarily out of a concern for the welfare of others.

Prosocial Behavior as Mood Management: A Summary

Models of helping that are based on the emotional antecedents and consequences of helping also suggest that helping is selfishly motivated. Both good moods and bad moods appear to increase helping. According to the mood management hypothesis, people who are happy help in order to maintain their happiness. People who are in a bad mood, such as sadness or guilt, help in order to make themselves feel better. An alternative hypothesis is that the relationship between mood and helping results from a heightened focus on the self brought on by a happy or sad mood. Presumably, a heightened focus on the self renders salient internal standards for behavior. The arousal/cost-reward model of helping explains helping in severe emergencies in terms of the emotional distress a witness experiences, the perceived cost of helping to the self, and the perceived cost of not helping to the victim.

Think Like a Social Psychologist

Thinking critically

—According to the mood management hypothesis, people who are feeling sad help others in order to make themselves feel better. To the extent that they consider the possible consequences of not helping, what related concern may motivate helping among people in a sad mood?

Designing research

—What kind of experiment would allow you to decide whether increased helping as a result of a happy or sad mood results from mood management or self-focus? What conditions would you need to include? What pattern of results would support the different explanations?

PROSOCIAL BEHAVIOR AS ALTRUISM

Trying to Make the Call

By the time Ana arrived at her sister's apartment on Chicago's West Side, the irritation she felt when her sister asked her to babysit had waned. Instead, she felt exasperated by the horrendous rush-hour traffic and the difficulty of finding a parking space that wouldn't require her to walk several blocks. To make matters worse, the ominous clanking sounds from her car seemed to have gotten louder as she crawled from one light to the next. As much as she tried to convince herself that it was a product of her imagination, there was no denying that it sounded a lot worse than it had in the morning.

Fortunately, Serena was in a good mood and visibly grateful that Ana had come to her aid. Ana appreciated the chance to spend some time with her nephew, who was equally happy to see her, even though he was suffering from a cold and soon fell asleep on her shoulder. After putting the baby in his crib, Ana wandered into the kitchen to get something to eat. She and Vicki had talked a lot over lunch, and had not had time to finish their sandwiches. But the kitchen cupboards didn't offer anything that appealed to her; Serena appeared to subsist entirely on diet soda and Tostitos. With nothing else to do, Ana straightened out the kitchen and washed a few dishes left in the sink before settling down on the couch with the day's newspaper.

As had been the case for days, the front page was once again devoted to the Joplin tornado. It featured the story of M. "Dean" Wells, the floor manager of the local Home Depot. As 200 mph tornado winds bore down, he ordered customers and employees to the back of the store. Hearing frantic knocking at the doors, he rushed to the front of the store to let another dozen people in. They all survived, but Dean Wells was killed when a wall collapsed on him. The story brought the Weather Channel's appeal back to Ana's mind. Remembering that she had meant to call that 800 number, she pulled her cell phone and the slip of paper from her purse. Before she could finish dialing the number, however, a noise from the nursery signaled that the baby's nap was over. He was awake, and he wasn't happy.

Was Ana's inclination to aid the victims of the Joplin tornado selfishly motivated? Probably not; none of the victims was genetically related to her. And because she felt neither particularly happy nor sad, helping them likely would not have changed her mood. Most important, the victims' plight didn't cause her emotional distress so much as it moved her. That is, Ana felt *empathy* for the victims.

According to Batson (1991, 2002), **empathy**—or helping that is designed purely to benefit another who is in need—lies at the heart of altruism. Empathy promotes helping for two reasons. First, it involves taking another's perspective (Davis, 1994; Krebs & Russell, 1981). Cognitively, we put ourselves in the shoes of the victim. Second, in doing so, we vicariously experience the victim's distress (Davis, 1994; Eisenberg & Miller, 1987). This combination of perspective taking and vicarious experience of distress produces empathic concern, a state in which we feel compassion for the victim (Batson & Shaw, 1991).

According to this definition, prosocial behavior is altruistic whenever empathic concern is present. This kind of compassion is very different from the aversive empathic arousal in the arousal/cost-reward model, however. Empathic arousal is about the self; empathic concern is for the victim. Whereas helping that is motivated by a desire to relieve one's own distress ultimately benefits the helper (Hoffman, 1981), helping that is motivated by empathic concern always benefits the victim.

To test the idea that helping can result from altruistic empathy, Batson and his colleagues (Batson, 2002; Batson & Powell, 2003) developed an experimental procedure that allowed them to differentiate altruism from egoistic motivations. In one study (Batson, Duncan, Ackerman, Buckley, & Birch, 1981), they asked participants to watch a video in which "Elaine," a fellow participant, reacted badly to a series of uncomfortable electric shocks. Participants could then volunteer to take the remaining shocks in her place, under one of several different conditions. To induce empathic concern, the researchers told a subset of participants that Elaine was similar to them in her interests and values. Batson et al. also told some participants that if they didn't help, they would continue to watch Elaine take the remaining shocks. They told others that they would not have to watch further shocks.

Varying the ease with which participants could escape from the aversive situation in this way was of crucial importance to the experiment. It allowed the experimenters to disentangle the extent to which helping may have been due to aversive arousal reduction from the extent to which it may have been due to empathic concern. If participants helped primarily to reduce their own arousal, as the arousal/cost-reward model suggests, empathy would matter only when escape from the situation was difficult. To the extent that participants could easily reduce their arousal by escaping the situation, helping rates should be relatively low (see the top part of **Figure 12.2**).

AVERSIVE AROUSAL REDUCTION HYPOTHESIS

	Low Empathy	High Empathy
Easy Escape	Low	Low
Difficult Escape	High	High

EMPATHY-ALTRUISM HYPOTHESIS

	Low Empathy	High Empathy
Easy Escape	Low	Low
Difficult Escape	High	High

Figure 12.2: Helping Rates Predicted by Two Different Hypotheses in the Empathy by Escape Design

Adapted from Batson, D. (1995). "Prosocial motivation: Why do we help others?" In A. Tesser (Ed.), *Advanced Social Psychology*. New York: McGraw-Hill.

However, if participants helped in order to alleviate Elaine's suffering, as the empathy-altruism model suggests, then their empathy should lead to helping regardless of whether or not they could escape from the situation (see the bottom part of **Figure 12.2**).

Results from several such experiments (for example, Batson, Duncan, Ackerman, Buckley, & Birch, 1981; Toi & Batson, 1982) consistently favor the empathy-altruism hypothesis. That is, when participants are made to feel empathy for Elaine, they volunteer to take the remaining shocks themselves, even if they could easily escape witnessing her continued suffering. Evidently, for empathically aroused participants, physical escape does not translate into psychological escape (Stocks, Lishner, & Decker, 2009). This finding runs counter to the aversive arousal reduction hypothesis, which does not explain why even participants who could easily avoid arousal still helped Elaine.

Using a similar experimental procedure, Batson and colleagues ruled out another hypothesis for the high rate of helping among those with an easy means of escape. According to this alternative explanation, the high rate of helping may have been due less to feelings of empathy than to egoistic concern about the consequences of *not* helping. The general idea is that failing to help often produces guilt and shame—emotions that may be further amplified by empathy for the victim. So the high rate of helping among participants who felt empathy for Elaine, yet could easily escape, may have been generated by a desire to avoid guilt and shame. If that were the case, participants should help less when they can rationalize not helping, on the basis that no one else is helping. However, when Batson and colleagues (Batson et al. 1988) tested that idea experimentally, they found that empathic participants who had such an excuse still helped as much as participants who didn't. Thus, there is good reason to believe that true altruism—helping others solely for their benefit—does indeed exist: We find it whenever empathy is present.

Proximal Altruism as Ultimate Egoism?

Although the evidence for the empathy-altruism hypothesis seems overwhelming, some (Kenrick, 1991; Krebs, 1991) have argued that even helping that is born of empathy may be selfishly motivated. Kenrick (1991) in particular suggestsed that the factors that cause empathy are rooted in shared heredity. In the laboratory, empathy is frequently induced by similarity or by specific instructions to take another's perspective (Batson, 1995). In real life, however, similarity is something that we share, especially with our kin. Moreover, we can assume that during the course of our evolutionary history, communication based on empathic concern occurred most frequently with those who were genetically similar to us. Consequently, our propensity toward empathy may have been rooted, at least initially, in selfish concerns with inclusive fitness.

Of course, it is difficult to see how the participants in Batson's studies could mistake Elaine for a genetic relative. Nevertheless, helping strangers out of empathic concern may be a generalized, ultimately egoistic response that was once highly adaptive and now serves as a hidden influence on our behavior (Cialdini, Brown, Lewis, Luce, & Neuberg, 1997). Alternatively, empathy may be an evolved mechanism that directs helping toward familiar others and those who previously cooperated with us (de Waal, 2008). The finding that empathy has a stronger effect on helping when the helper and victim belong to the same cultural group, rather than to different cultural groups (Stuermer, Snyder, Kropp, & Siem, 2006), further attests to empathy's adaptive value.

Attempting to interpret what appears to be altruistic helping as a selfish behavior may strike some readers as odd or even misplaced. It flies in the face of countless cases of heroic helping, in which individuals risked—or even lost—their own lives to save someone in need. Was the unknown hero who survived the crash of Air

Florida flight number 90, only to lose his life saving fellow passengers from the icy waters of the Potomac River in January 1982, motivated by some kind of self-benefit (the *Washington Post*, 1982)? Did the firefighters and police officers who rushed into the burning towers of the World Trade Center on 9/11 act out of self-interest? Did the Dutch family that hid Anne Frank from the Nazis act out of selfishness?

All these cases seem to represent altruism in its purest form: Helping not only with no self-benefit, but at considerable risk to the self. Why, then, would social psychologists doubt that altruism exists? The problem is that social psychologists have traditionally subscribed to the doctrine of **psychological hedonism** (Allport, 1954), which originated in the writings of philosopher Jeremy Bentham (1789, 1879). Bentham proposesd that humans act simply to gain pleasure or happiness (positive hedonism) or to avoid pain (negative hedonism). At times, a person can gain happiness by contributing to the welfare of others, but as Mill (1863) argued, the pursuit of one's own happiness is ultimately what motivates the help.

A great deal of research supports this cynical view of prosocial behavior (Batson, 1987). Thus, Batson's assertion that altruism exists is subject to ongoing, and at times heated, debate (Batson et al., 1997; Cialdini et al., 1997). Much of the debate revolves around the question of whether the experience of empathy blurs the usual distinction between self and other. To the extent that the vicarious experience of what another is suffering results in the incorporation of the self in the other, helping that is induced by empathy could indeed benefit the self (Cialdini et al., 1997). Regardless of whether that is the case, there can be little doubt that taking another's perspective increases our willingness to help.

Empathy, Collectivism, and Group Identity

Helping out of self-interest or to benefit another are by no means the only motives for prosocial behavior. At times, we may be less concerned about our individual welfare or the welfare of a specific other because we are motivated by a collective interest in the groups to which we belong. Imagine that you have received a letter from your local public radio station, asking you to make a donation. The request creates a **social dilemma** for you. On the one hand, public radio benefits everyone, including you. On the other hand, the benefit to you is somewhat diminished if you must pay for it. The prosocial thing to do would be to "do your share" and donate a small amount of money. However, self-interest would compel you to keep your hard-earned dollars, in the hopes that others will donate enough to keep public radio on the air. That way, you can reap the benefits without incurring any costs.

How you respond to such social dilemmas depends on the extent to which you approach it with a **collective interest**—that is, concern for the welfare of the group to which you belong, rather than for your own self-interest. Dawes and his colleagues (Dawes, van de Kragt, & Orbell, 1990; Orbell, van de Kragt, & Dawes, 1988) conducted a series of experiments that demonstrated the conditions that arouse collective interest, as well as its effect on the choices people make in social dilemmas.

In one study, participants who had been recruited for a study on group decision making received $5, which they could either keep or give away with the prospect of receiving a $10 bonus in return. The experimenters varied the rules by which each participant did or did not receive the bonus. Some participants were led to believe that they would receive the $10 bonus if four or more participants *other than themselves* donated their $5. (This rule is called a *noncontingent rule*—that is, receiving the reward was not contingent on the participant donating his or her own money.) Other participants were led to believe that everyone in their group would receive the $10 bonus if five or more participants, *one of whom could be themselves*, were to donate their money. (This rule is called a *contingent rule*—that is, receiving the reward is contingent partly on whether participants donate their own money.) In addition to manipulating the conditions under which participants would receive the $10 reward, the experimenters instructed some, but not all, groups of participants to discuss their choices.

Figure 12.3 shows the results of this experiment. In the absence of any discussion, a higher percentage of participants who thought that receiving the reward was contingent on their own donations (45 percent) donated their $5 than participants who thought it was not contingent (30 percent). Interestingly, discussion increased participants' willingness to donate in both conditions (85 percent and 75 percent, respectively). Presumably, the discussions aroused a sense of collective interest that prompted even those who could have gained the most by holding on to their money to donate it to the group.

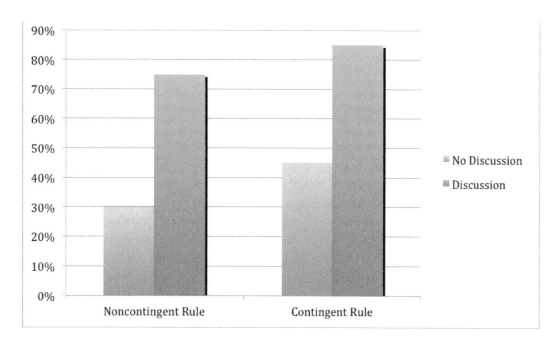

Figure 12.3: Effects of Rules and Discussion on Donation Rates

Source: Dawes, van de Kragt, and Orbell (1990), Cooperation for the benefit of us – not me, or my conscience. In J. Mansbridge (Ed.), *Beyond self-interest* (pp. 97–110). Chicago, IL: The University of Chicago Press.

Additional experiments using a similar methodology indicate that prosocial behavior stemming from a collective interest is limited to the specific groups to which we belong. When asked to donate money to another group (for example, the one doing the experiment across the hall), participants were once again guided primarily by self-interest (Orbell, van de Kragt, & Dawes, 1988). This finding points to the importance of group identity in the development and influence of collective interest. The more we identify with a group, the more we are willing to act to benefit the group, even if doing so may result in a personal loss. At the same time, the more we identify with a group, the less willing we are to sacrifice for groups to which we don't belong.

We have already seen that empathy can supersede self-interest. How does empathy interact with collective interest? What happens when self-interest, collective interest, and empathy conflict? To answer this question,

Batson et al. (1995) presented participants with a social dilemma that forced them to divide raffle tickets among themselves, their group, and another individual (Jenny or Mike), who happened to be the victim of a romantic breakup. Some participants received this news with the instruction to treat Jenny or Mike objectively, without getting caught up in how he or she felt (low empathy). Others were instructed to imagine how Jenny or Mike might feel as a result of the breakup, and how it had affected their lives individually (high empathy).

In the absence of such instructions, most participants (62.5 percent) allocated half their tickets to themselves and half to the group, suggesting that they were motivated by a combination of self-interest and collective interest. A much smaller percentage of participants acted purely in the collective interest (20 percent), donating all the tickets to the group, or in their own self-interest, by keeping all their tickets to themselves (12.5 percent). A mere 5 percent divided their tickets between themselves and Jennifer or Mike. Among participants who did receive instructions, the division of tickets differed dramatically: 37.5 percent of them wanted to split the tickets with Jenny or Mike. Another 32.5 percent based their decision on a combination of self-interest and collective interest. The percentage of participants who based their decision purely on the collective interest dropped to 15 percent, and the percentage who kept all the tickets to themselves remained about the same (15 percent).

The findings from this study reinforce the importance of empathy in predicting prosocial behavior. As we have seen, self-interest and collective interest are important motives for prosocial behavior. Under the right circumstances, collective interest trumps self-interest, but empathy trumps both. Interestingly, though the empathy-altruism link has been demonstrated primarily with individual victims, there is some evidence that it operates on the group level as well (Penner & Finkelstein, 1998). In one study of AIDS volunteers (Stuermer, Snyder, & Omoto, 2005), researchers found that empathy was a stronger predictor of helping when the victim belonged to an in-group. Among gay and lesbian AIDS volunteers for whom the victim was part of the in-group, empathy was the strongest predictor of helping. Among heterosexual volunteers for whom the victim was part of an out-group, helping was determined primarily by the victim's level of attractiveness.

Just how does empathy promote helping? It appears that people high in empathic concern or induced to feel empathy help, not so much because they perceive pressure from others or fear disapproval for not helping. They primarily help because they consider it an important choice that is consistent with their personal values and life goals (Pavey, Greitemeyer, & Sparks, 2012).

Are There Gender and Age Differences in Altruism?

The stereotype of the social role of females holds that women are more empathic than men. Research suggests that this stereotype may hold a kernel of truth. Numerous studies have shown women to respond with more empathy, using a variety of subjective and self-report measures, than men (Eisenberg & Lennon, 1983; Lennon & Eisenberg, 1987; Martin & Clark, 1982). Research further shows that this gender difference reflects differences in motivation rather than ability (Eisenberg & Lennon, 1983; Ickes, Gesn, & Graham, 2005).

To the extent that altruism depends on empathy, one would expect that women should also be the more helpful gender. However, by one measure, men seem to have the edge. Since 1904, the Carnegie Hero Fund Commission has awarded recognition to heroes who voluntarily risked their lives trying to save the life of another. As of 2003, 91 percent of those who received medals for their heroism were men (Becker & Eagly, 2004), even though Andrew Carnegie, the commission's founder, had left explicit instructions to not discriminate against women.

YES, i WANTED A KniGHT iN SHiNiNG
ARMOUR, BUT i DiDN'T KNOW iT'D BE
ME DOiNG ALL THE SHiNiNG!

Heroic helping conjures up the image of The Knight in Shining Armor. As a result, acts of heroism typical of women often go unrecognized

Before you conclude from these statistics that men are more altruistic than women, consider that Carnegie Hero Medals are typically awarded for acts of helping such as saving others from fires, drowning, animal attacks, electrocution, suffocation, and assaults by criminals (Wooster, 2000). Because such emergencies require immediate, physical intervention, they are more typical of men (Becker & Eagly, 2004). When one considers acts of heroism that require more sustained helping, women are the more helpful gender in many cases. Women were overrepresented among those who rescued Jews from the Nazi Holocaust, and women are more likely than men to donate a kidney or volunteer for the Peace Corps (Becker & Eagly, 2004).

How can we explain the gender differences in empathy-based altruistic helping? The finding that men are more likely to provide immediate help while women are more likely to provide sustained help fit well with a social role account (Eagly & Crowley, 1986) that emphasizes the different norms underlying the male and female gender roles.

Men are supposed to be risk takers and adventurous; women are supposed to be nurturant and caring. However, the observation that gender differences in empathy are evident in infancy (Martin & Clark, 1982) suggests that there may also be innate differences in the mechanisms underlying the experience of empathy among men and women.

In support of this speculation, fMRI studies of neural activity in the human brain suggest that empathy at the sight of another's pain can be divided into an early automatic emotional sharing component and a late cognitive evaluation process (Gu & Han, 2007). Although women and men show no differences in the automatic sharing component of empathy, women show more neural activity than men in the late cognitive evaluation process (Han, Fan, & Mao, 2008).

Age also matters when it comes to empathy-based altruism. Both seem to peak late in life. Sze et al. (2011) had groups of young adults (age 20–30), middle-aged adults (age 40–50) and older adults (age 60–80) watch videos of individuals in need. In addition, they were given an opportunity to make a monetary contribution to charities supporting these individuals. They found that the size of the contribution increased with age in a linear fashion: Young adults contributed the least, older adults the most. This finding resonates nicely with developmental models that indicate that generativity is a key component to successful aging (Erikson, 1982).

Prosocial Behavior as Altruism: A Summary

According to Batson and colleagues, altruism—helping with no benefit to the self—is related to empathy. When a victim's plight triggers empathic concern, people will help, even if they can escape from the situation and/or they can justify not helping. Although the empathy-altruism model has garnered considerable empirical support, some researchers claim that what appears to be altruistic helping may ultimately be caused by selfish motives. For example, the variables that trigger empathy may arise from genetic relatedness. Others have argued that empathy blurs the distinction between the self and the other. Thus, any action that benefits the other ultimately benefits the self.

In a social dilemma, collective interest can lead to helping that benefits the group at the expense of self-interest. Under conditions that elicit empathy for a single member of a group, however, helping based on empathy replaces helping for the common good.

Gender differences in the experience of empathy compel men toward altruistic helping that is immediate and compel women toward altruistic behavior that is more sustained. Although these differences can be explained in terms of the norms underlying the male and female gender role, there is also evidence of an innate component. The finding that older adults show increased empathy-based altruism is explained by a developmental focus on generativity.

THINK LIKE A SOCIAL PSYCHOLOGIST: ADVENTURES IN RANDOM ASSIGNMENT

Bill Scholar, professor of psychology at Hats off to Science University, decides to conduct a study of the effects of priming of the positive emotional consequences of helping on rates of helping. He conducts the experiment with the help of the students in the two sections of his social psychology class. Bill delivers identical lectures in his day class, which meets on Tuesdays and Thursdays at 10 and his night class on Wednesday evening, except that he sprinkles his lecture to the day students with anecdotes about people who felt better after helping someone. (Bill flipped a coin to decide which section he would prime for helping.) At the end of both classes, he explains that he needs help with an experiment, and asks students to come to his lab on Friday afternoon. The percentage of students who show up from each section will be the dependent variable.

At the assigned time, almost 60 percent of the students from the day class visit Bill's lab, along with a little more than a third of the night students. Bill concludes that his experiment has failed, because the students in his day class were probably more helpful to begin with. What aspect of his method does not warrant his conclusion?

The answer is that Professor Scholar randomly assigned the two sections to the conditions of his experiment when he should have randomly assigned *individual* participants. The problem is that the two sections, or groups, may differ importantly in ways that could well affect the outcome of the experiment. In all likelihood, many of the evening students may have day jobs, which could prevent them from taking time off, especially on short notice. The lesson to be learned from this example is that in collecting experimental data, true random assignment should always take precedence over convenience.

Think Like a Social Psychologist

Thinking critically

—According to one view, the variables that trigger empathy may also provide cues to genetic related-ness. Can you make an argument for why this relationship may, in fact, be maladaptive?

Making connections

—The doctrine of psychological hedonism holds that all human behavior, prosocial behavior in-cluded, is ultimately motivated by selfishness or egoism. To the extent that it is difficult to identify behavior that is not hedonistically motivated, what does that say about the doctrine's value as a basis for hypotheses about why people help?

WHY DO PEOPLE FAIL TO HELP?

The Long Way Home

It was well past 7 P.M. when Ana drove home that day. Not unexpectedly, Serena had had to wait longer than expected at the doctor's office. When she finally returned, the two had chatted for a while and discussed their plans for Thanksgiving.

SOCIAL PSYCHOLOGY AND THE LAW: CAN PROSOCIAL BEHAVIOR BE LEGISLATED?

Good Samaritan laws exist in many countries, including Japan, France, Germany, and Spain. Most of them require citizens to assist people in distress, unless doing so would cause harm to themselves. In Germany, failure to provide assistance in an emergency is a criminal offense. Citizens are obliged to provide first aid when necessary and are immune from prosecution if the assistance they provide in good faith turns out to be harmful.

In the United States, Good Samaritan laws protect those who help the injured or ill from blame. The intention is to reduce bystanders' hesitation or unwillingness to help, for fear of causing unintentional injury or wrongful death. Laws vary from state to state. Most, like the one in Illinois, exempt helpers from prosecution or liability in the event their actions cause unintended harm. Some, like Minnesota's law, declare a "duty to assist" in an emergency:

> A person at the scene of an emergency who knows that another person is exposed to or has suffered grave physical harm shall, to the extent that the person can do so without danger or peril to self or others, give reasonable assistance to the exposed person. Reasonable assistance may include obtaining or attempting to obtain aid from law enforcement or medical personnel. A person who violates this subdivision is guilty of a petty misdemeanor.

How effective are Good Samaritan laws in promoting help during an emergency? There is no clear answer to this question. The photographers at the scene of Princess Diana's car accident were investigated for violating France's Good Samaritan law, though they were later exonerated. Evidently, the law did not compel them to do the right thing. As we will see, failure to provide assistance often has little to do with the fear of prosecution (Latane & Darley, 1970). Consequently, Good Samaritan laws are probably less effective than legislators might think.

Traffic on the Eisenhower Expressway should have been light, since it was well past rush hour. However, a light but steady rain had settled over the city, just as the Weather Channel had predicted. The rain slowed traffic to a crawl. Ordinarily, Ana wouldn't have minded, because she considered traffic hassles a relatively minor price to pay for living in a great city. Tonight, though, she was tired and hungry, and quite anxious about the noise emanating from her car's engine.

Just as she was about to exhort the old Chevy to get her home one last time, the engine sputtered and refused to turn over. As it took its last gasps, Ana pulled over to the shoulder. On impulse, she reached for her cell phone, only to realize that the battery was dead. Briefly, she entertained the idea of getting out of the car to wave down a fellow motorist, but the rain and the spray from passing cars discouraged her. Ana slumped down in the driver's seat, hoping someone would eventually stop to help her. Gazing out the driver's side window at the steady flow of cars, she figured it wouldn't be long.

Ana may have been unduly optimistic about her chances of getting help. Consider the circumstances that led to the death of Princess Diana on August 30, 1997. Trying to shake a group of rapacious papparazzi, her driver had crashed the car into a concrete pillar at high speed. The impact of the crash killed her fiancé, Dodi Fayed, and left Diana gravely injured. The papparazzi, who had followed closely, immediately pulled over and began snapping photos of the dying princess. Their apparent callousness caused an international uproar, prompting

Figure 12.4: Helping in an Emergency: Five Necessary Decisions

Source: Latane, B., & Darley, J.M. (1970). *The unresponsive bystander: Why doesn't he help?* New York: Apple-Century-Croft.

renewed calls for a Good Samaritan law that would make withholding help from the victim of an emergency a crime punishable by law (see the Social Psychology and the Law box on **page 582**).

Failure to help is not always the result of callousness. Consider an incident that took place more than 30 years before Princess Diana's death. During the early morning hours of March 13, 1964, Catherine (Kitty) Genovese was stabbed to death by an unknown assailant as she returned to her apartment in Queens, New York. A brief report of her murder appeared in the *Long Island Press* that same day. Two weeks later, a more grizzly account of the circumstances under which she died appeared on the front page of the *New York Times*. According to that account, Kitty died slowly. She was stabbed repeatedly over a period of about 30 minutes, while screaming for help and pleading for her life. Her cries were so loud that 38 of her neighbors rose from their beds to watch her die. Not a single one picked up the phone to call the police. Although the veracity of this part of the story has since been questioned (Manning, Levine, & Collins, 2007), it received widespread attention at the time. Some (for example, Rosenthal, 1964) suggested that the bystanders' inaction was brought on by callousness, or complete—and perhaps uniquely urban—disregard for the welfare of others. Rosenthal's (1964 account of the incident provoked a landmark research program (Latane & Darley, 1970) into the reasons why people often fail to help others in emergencies.

Latane and Darley (1970) reasoned that attributing the causes of inaction to bystanders' dispositions does not sufficiently explain **bystander apathy**. Instead, these researchers proposed that we must look at the situation from the bystander's perspective. Their cognitive model of helping suggests that before bystanders can offer assistance, they must make a series of sequential decisions (as shown in **Figure 12.4**). An incorrect decision at any point during this sequence will result in the failure to help (Latane & Darley, 1970).

Noticing the Event

Failure to help often is not the result of apathy, callousness, or disregard for the welfare of others. Instead, potential helpers frequently do not recognize an event as an emergency, particularly when they are in a hurry or otherwise distracted. In our opening story, although Ana hoped that one of the many passing motorists would pull over to offer assistance, the circumstances of her emergency suggested otherwise. It was dark and rainy. The traffic was making everyone late, feeling they were in a rush. Some drivers were undoubtedly talking on their cell phones, conducting business or telling their families they would be late for dinner. As a result, many drivers simply may not have noticed her car parked on the shoulder.

Evidence for this speculation comes from an experiment in which participants were asked to walk to another building across campus and deliver a speech (Darley & Batson, 1973). Some participants expected to speak about the kinds of jobs they preferred; others expected to talk about the parable of the Good Samaritan. In addition, some participants were told they were running late and would have to hurry. Others were led to believe they were on schedule for their appointments. A third group believed they were running ahead of schedule.

On the way to their appointments, all participants came across a confederate of the experimenters, who was slumped in a doorway, acting as though he was in distress. The experimenters were interested in the percentage of participants who would stop to help the confederate under the different experimental conditions. As expected, whether or not participants stopped to help depended primarily on whether they were in a rush.

Most passersby will probably notice this man soliciting money, but whether they will offer assistance depends on whether they interpret his situation as an emergency.

MISTAKEN AS PRANK, BODY LEFT HANGING

Associated Press

FREDERICA, Del.—The presumed suicide of a woman found hanging from a tree went unreported for hours because passersby thought the body was a Halloween decoration, authorities said.

The 42-year-old woman used rope to hang herself across the street from some homes on a moderately busy road late Tuesday or early Wednesday, Delaware state police said.

The body, suspended about 15 feet above the ground, could be seen easily from passing vehicles.

State police spokesman Cpl. Jeff Oldham and neighbors said people noticed the body at breakfast time Wednesday but dismissed it as a holiday prank. Authorities were called to the scene about three hours later.

"They thought it was a Halloween decoration," Fay Glanden, wife of Mayor William Glanden, told the News Journal newspaper in Wilmington.

"It looked like something somebody would have rigged up," she said.

Sixty-three percent of those who believed they were running ahead of schedule and had ample time to make their appointments offered to help. Forty-five percent of those who believed they were on schedule stopped to help. Among those who were in a rush because they were running behind, however, only 10 percent stopped to offer assistance.

Whether participants expected to talk about jobs or the parable of the Good Samaritan made little difference to their rates of helping. When questioned at the end of the experiment, the majority of those who had rushed to their appointments indicated that they hadn't noticed the man slumped in the doorway. Ironically, the participants in this study were seminary students. Surely, if people who are training for a life of helping others—many of them with thoughts of helping on their minds—can fail to notice someone in distress, the power of distraction and time pressure must loom large.

Interpreting the Event as an Emergency

Noticing an event is necessary for helping to be offered, but by no means does it guarantee help. Once an event has been noticed, bystanders must still interpret it as an emergency. This is generally not an issue when the situation is clearly dangerous. In this case, people often rush to another's help as predicted by the arousal/cost-reward model, whether bystanders are present or not (Fisher et al., 2011). However, many situations carry some ambiguity as to whether they are real emergencies. The man slumped over in a doorway, coughing and groaning, may be in real need of assistance. Then again, he may only be sleeping off a drinking binge.

Ana's situation, too, was marked by ambiguity. From the perspective of passersby, the car on the shoulder may have held a motorist in distress. Then again, it may have been abandoned by its owner hours before. Frequently, the context in which an event is noticed contributes to the difficulties of recognizing it as an emergency, as the newspaper story in **Box 12.1** illustrates.

Two powerful contextual cues appear to have caused inaction among those who noticed the body dangling from the tree. First, on most days of the year, such a sight would be unexpected, and thus would alarm most passersby. Because the same sight is commonplace the week before Halloween, however, it takes on an entirely different meaning. Instead of being considered a potential emergency, it is seen as a decoration or a prank. Second, from the perspective of passersby, the apparent inaction of others who may have encountered the situation further complicated the matter. Those who may have been unsure about the dangling body may have concluded that it was a prank because if it had been an emergency, someone else would already have taken action. This phenomenon is known as **pluralistic ignorance**: because there is no evidence that others are concerned, we assume that nothing is wrong.

To demonstrate how pluralistic ignorance can shape the way people interpret an apparent emergency, Latane and Darley (1968) recruited participants for a study that required them to complete several questionnaires about their attitudes on a variety of issues. Some participants worked on the questionnaires by themselves; others, in the presence of two strangers. A third group worked in the presence of two confederates. As participants answered the questionnaires, the experimenters began to pump white smoke through a heating vent in the wall.

You may have guessed that the experimenters had little interest in the participants' responses to the questionnaires. Instead, they wanted to see how participants in the three experimental conditions would respond to the smoke. Would they continue marking their questionnaires, or would they leave the room to alert the experimenters? In most cases, smoke emanating from a heating vent signals a potential fire, but *white* smoke can indicate a more benign problem, such as condensation in the ventilation system. Of course, in light of such ambiguity, the safe thing to do would be to report the problem.

Because *the presence of others diffuses responsibility for helping,* having an automobile accident on a busy street reduces the chances that a motorist will receive assistance

Most participants who worked on the questionnaires by themselves did just that: 50 percent of them went to see the experimenter within two minutes of noticing the smoke, and 75 percent did so within six minutes. However, when participants worked with two others, only 12 percent of them responded within two minutes, and 38 percent within six minutes. Some participants kept working, even when there was so much smoke in the room that they could barely see the questionnaires. Working with two confederates who acted unconcerned (for example, by shrugging their shoulders when participants made eye contact with them) did not reduce response rates much further. Evidently, subtle cues from others are sufficient to induce pluralistic ignorance. Although participants may have been worried about the smoke, realizing that neither of the other participants seemed concerned caused the majority of them to dismiss its importance.

Taking Responsibility for Helping

Pluralistic ignorance prevents helping because it prevents individuals from recognizing an event as an emergency. But what happens in situations that are not ambiguous? Does the presence of others promote or inhibit helping?

Kitty Genovese's murder suggests the latter answer. Remember that, by one account, it was witnessed by 38 neighbors, not a single one of whom did anything to help. Latane and Darley (1970) reasoned that their failure to take action was directly related to the number of bystanders. From their perspective, it was clear that others had noticed her screams as well. That recognition led to a **diffusion of responsibility**: Everyone thought that taking action was someone else's responsibility. This conclusion is unsettling, because it suggests that there is no safety in numbers. The more bystanders, the more responsibility can be diffused. Kitty Genovese's murder might have been prevented had it been witnessed by just two or three bystanders. Similarly, Ana's chances of getting help would be greater if her car had broken down on a street where traffic was light rather than on the busy expressway.

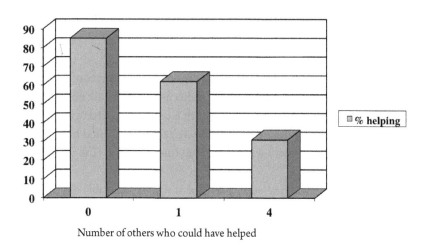

Figure 12.5: The Inhibiting Effects of Bystanders on Rates of Helping

Based on: Darley & Latane (1968). Bystander intervention in emergencies: Diffusion of responsibility. *Journal of Personality and Social Psychology*, 8, 377–383.

That the presence of others diffuses responsibility has been shown in numerous studies. In one particularly powerful demonstration, Latane and Darley (1968) asked participants to discuss personal issues related to their lives at the university. Participants sat in individual cubicles where they could not see one another. Ostensibly to avoid embarrassment to them, the discussion was held via intercom. Some participants were led to believe that

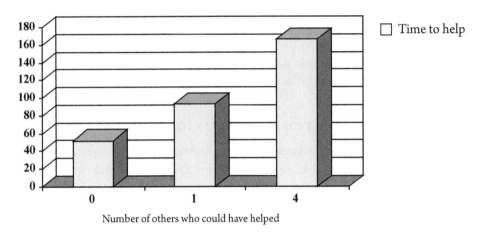

Number of others who could have helped

Figure 12.6: The Inhibiting Effect of Bystanders on Time Taken to Help

Based on: Darley & Latane (1968). Bystander intervention in emergencies: Diffusion of responsibility. *Journal of Personality and Social Psychology*, 8, 377–383.

the discussion took place with just one other student; others thought the discussion involved two others, and some believed it involved five others. In reality, there was only one participant in each discussion. The rest were prerecorded voices, and the "discussion" was rigged so that the participant was always the last to speak.

Early in the discussion, one of the "other participants" hesitantly volunteered that he was prone to seizures, especially during times of stress. As the discussion unfolded, it became clear that he was having a violent seizure, during which he repeatedly stated that he would die if he did not get help. The researchers recorded the percentage of participants who either tried to find him or alerted the experimenter to the problem. They also kept track of how long participants waited to intervene.

Figure 12.5 shows the results for the first measure. As expected, the number of bystanders affected the rate of helping. When participants believed they were having a discussion with just one other person, that person was necessarily the one having the seizure. Consequently, in that condition, participants were the only ones who could help. There was no possibility that their responsibility to take action could be diffused. Not surprisingly, 85 percent of the participants responded within 60 seconds in this condition. The remainder did so within two and a half minutes.

When participants believed there was one other participant who conceivably could intervene, only 62 percent helped within 60 seconds. Although the percentage increased to just over 80 percent within two and a half minutes, it never reached the 100 percent mark. When participants thought there were three others who could help, the decrease in response was even more dramatic. In that condition, a mere 31 percent intervened within the first 60 seconds. Even after six minutes, when the experiment was terminated, well over a third still had not sought help.

SOCIAL PSYCHOLOGY ENCOUNTERS THE DARK SIDE: THE IMPLICIT BYSTANDER EFFECT

The presence of bystanders greatly affects helping because it decreases the chance that people will recognize a situation as an emergency and thus feel responsible for offering aid. There is evidence that bystander effects will manifest themselves, even when others are not present. The *implicit bystander effect* was demonstrated in a series of studies (Garcia, Weaver, Moskowitz, & Darley, 2002) that primed the presence of others in various ways and noted the effect on helping rates in an unrelated situation.

In one study, participants first imagined they had won a free dinner for themselves or for themselves and ten friends. Later, during the experiment, they were asked how much time they would be willing to spend helping the experimenter with another study. As expected, participants who had imagined dinner with ten friends volunteered less time than participants who had imagined dinner by themselves.

A second study looked at the processes that may lead to the implicit bystander effect. Participants imagined that they and a friend were at a movie theater that was either crowded or empty. They then completed a lexical decision task that required them to decide whether words flashed on a computer screen for a brief time were indeed words on nonwords. All the critical words were related to unaccountability (*unaccountable, innocent, exempt*). As expected, participants who had imagined themselves in a crowded movie theater responded to the words faster than participants who had imagined themselves in an empty movie theater.

These findings suggest that bystander effects may not depend on the physical presence of others. Merely imagining their presence can reduce helping. Under such conditions, reduced help may result from a decreased sense of responsibility and accountability.

The identification of the implicit bystander effect complements earlier research in an important way. Though we may be the only bystander to an emergency, whether or not we feel compelled to offer help may depend on whether we have just exited an empty or crowded bus.

The number of bystanders also had an effect on the time participants took before intervening (see **Figure 12.6**). When there was no one else who could help, participants took an average of 53 seconds to intervene. The presence of one additional participant increased response times to 93 seconds among those who intervened. The presence of four additional participants boosted it to 166 seconds.

These inhibiting effects of bystanders, as demonstrated by Darley and Latane (1968), are dramatic, especially considering the fact that the gender of the "other participants" did not matter. It also made no difference when some participants were led to believe that another participant was a premed student, who would appear to be particularly well suited to help.

Would it make a difference if the other bystanders were friends rather than strangers? To find out, Latane and Rodin (1969) recruited participants for a study ostensibly meant to evaluate their game and puzzle preferences for a fictitious Consumer Testing Bureau. Participants completed their surveys by themselves, with two strangers, or with two friends. As they were working, they overheard the experimenter falling and hurting her ankle in the next room. Consistent with earlier findings, when participants were by themselves, 70 percent of them sought to intervene within two minutes of hearing the experimenter's fall. When they were with two strangers,

"Is there a healthcare representative in the house?!"

Helping is often complicated by our inability to decide on the proper course of action

the percentage of participants who tried to intervene dropped to 40 percent. However, when they were with friends, the percentage who intervened returned to 70 percent.

Does this finding mean that the presence of friends, as opposed to the presence of strangers, facilitates helping? Not really. Given that 70 percent of the participants who were alone helped, the odds that *at least* one of three participants would help would actually be higher than 70 percent. In other words, the presence of friends, too, inhibits helping.

Given the pervasiveness of this effect, the presence of bystanders may serve as a hidden influence that inhibits helping through processes operating outside of conscious awareness. The Social Psychology Encounters the Dark Side box on **page 589** describes a series of studies of such implicit bystander effects.

Considering Appropriate Forms of Helping

Taking responsibility is clearly an important step toward helping, but a potential helper must still determine the appropriate response. In some cases, doing so may merely delay a response to the emergency. Consider, for example, the situation in which the participants of the Latane and Rodin (1969) study found themselves. After deciding that it was their responsibility to come to the aid of the injured experimenter, they could have done

Because this nurse is capable of providing assistance, the presence of bystanders is unlikely to reduce her willingness to help in an emergency

so in several ways. Most of them pulled down the room divider; a slightly smaller group simply yelled "Help!" A few participants left the room and entered the experimenter's room through a separate door.

In some emergencies, people may fail to help because they feel they are incapable of responding appropriately (Schwartz & Clausen, 1970). Put yourself in the shoes of participants in Darley and Latane's (1968) seizure study. It may be perfectly clear that the person needs assistance–and equally clear that you should help—but would you know what to do? If you were in the presence of others, would you be tempted to see whether someone else who might be better qualified to help would step up?

Unfortunately, the recognition that we are unable to help can have consequences beyond mere inaction. Instead of helping victims out of their predicament, too often we blame them for it. For example, we often derogate the destitute by (a) holding them responsible for their poverty (Henry, Reyna, & Weiner, 2004); and (b) assuming that any action we might take will make no difference (Lerner, 1980; Lerner & Miller, 1978). Such a response may seem odd, but it is firmly grounded in our belief in a just world (Lerner, 1980). We would like to believe that the world is a fair place in which people get what they deserve and deserve what they get. Learning that something bad happened to someone else has the potential to threaten our just-world belief. We deal with the threat by concluding that the person must have done something to deserve the bad luck.

As we might expect, people who feel incapable of helping have a difficult time choosing the appropriate course of action. Those who feel particularly capable are more likely to help. In one study (Cramer, McMaster, Bartell, & Dragna, 1988), education majors and registered nurses encountered an emergency involving a man who was trapped under a collapsed ladder. They were traveling either by themselves or in the presence of a confederate trained to behave as if nothing had happened. As in past research, the presence of the passive bystander affected the willingness to help among those students who did not feel particularly well-equipped to provide assistance (that is, the education majors). However, the passive bystander's presence did not affect the nurses, who went to help the trapped workman.

Implementing the Chosen Action

Once the appropriate form of assistance has been decided on, we might expect the chance that it will be implemented to be fairly high. That certainly is the case, although there are some notable exceptions. For example, the presence of visibly passive bystanders can reduce helping because their inaction can signal that an offer of help is inappropriate (Schwartz & Gottlieb, 1976). Fears that one's help may not be wanted can also reduce the chance of implementing a solution. Imagine you have witnessed a confrontation between a man and a woman. If you are like most people, you will probably assume that the two are romantically linked. That may lead you to conclude that an offer of assistance might not be welcome. Consistent with this conclusion, participants who witnessed a staged fight between a man and a woman were less likely to help when they thought the combatants were a married couple than when they thought the combatants were strangers (Shotland & Straw, 1976).

Even situations that are relatively unambiguous can sometimes be complicated because of confusion over who is responsible for the victim's plight. Imagine finding a person slumped over on a sidewalk. You rush to find out what is wrong; as you are doing so, other pedestrians join you. What do you think they will think about your relationship to the victim? What will you be thinking about what they are thinking? The results of two studies in which participants took either the helper's perspective or the onlooker's (Cacioppo, Petty, & Losch, 1986) suggest that you will expect the others to hold you responsible for the person's situation. This expectation isn't born out of paranoia, but has an objective basis. Onlookers who observe a victim with another person generally assume that the other person had something to do with the victim's situation.

SOCIAL PSYCHOLOGY ENCOUNTERS THE BRIGHT SIDE: OF STUDENTS AND SUPERHEROES

If simply imagining the presence of others can decrease helping, could imagining someone who is particularly helpful increase helping? The answer appears to be yes, with one qualification. In a series of studies (Nelson & Norton, 2005), researchers asked some participants to list the characteristics of a superhero, and others to list the characteristics of an example of a superhero—Superman. Later, researchers asked both groups to indicate their willingness to volunteer as tutors to children in neighboring communities. Compared to participants in a control group, who had been asked to describe a typical dorm room, participants who had described the characteristics of a superhero volunteered more hours. However, those who had described Superman's characteristics volunteered for fewer hours than even those in the control group.

Why did the superhero prime increase helping, but the Superman prime decrease it? The answer lies in the comparisons participants may have drawn between themselves and the target of the priming. Participants who were primed with the category of superhero may have assessed the extent to which they were similar to a superhero. Because Superman is such an extreme example of that category, however, students who received the Superman prime may have focused on the extent to which they were *dissimilar* to Superman. Because their own powers paled next to Superman's, they may have underestimated their own, including their ability to help.

How Can Helping Be Improved?

Latane and Darley's decision-making model explains in detail why people often fail to help in an emergency. At each step, an incorrect decision leads to a failure to help. Frequently, the presence of mostly passive bystanders lies at the heart of faulty decision making. The behavior of others appears to serve as a source of information as we interpret the situation, decide whether or not to take responsibility, and choose and implement a course of action.

Others do not always have to be a negative influence on helping, however. They can model helpful behavior by being helpful themselves. Imagine the following scenario: The holiday season has arrived, and a Salvation Army volunteer has once again stationed himself at the entrance to the local grocery store. On your way in, you see a customer who is leaving drop some coins in the kettle. Would witnessing this act of kindness increase your willingness to make a donation on your way out?

Research suggests that it would, especially if the customer parts with her money cheerfully (Hornstein, 1970). That is why charities often frame their requests in terms of how many people have already responded. There is also good reason to believe that exposure to helpful models increases helping in emergency situations. In a classic study (Bryan & Test, 1967), motorists were more likely to pull over and offer help to the driver of a disabled vehicle after they had witnessed another motorist doing the same thing.

More subtle contextual cues may also serve as hidden influences that promote helping. For example, in one study, participants who had been primed with words related to helping were more likely to help someone pick up spilled pens than participants who had been primed with words unrelated to helping (Macrae & Johnston, 1998). Evidently, the priming task made helping thoughts more accessible, resulting in more help. Moreover, priming prosocial cues promotes helping, even in the presence of bystanders (Abbate, Ruggieri, & Boca, 2013). The Social Psychology Encounters the Bright Side box on **pages 592-593** describes a study that shows how a subtle priming technique influenced sustained helping (volunteering) in both hypothetical and real-world situations.

Finally, there is evidence from laboratory and field studies to suggest that helping promotes future helping behavior, especially when helpers reflect on their actions. In one study, participants who wrote about their thoughts, feelings, and actions related to a situation in which they helped another were subsequently more likely to help in an unrelated situation than participants who reflected on being the recipients of help. Presumably, reflecting on giving help encourages future helping because it increases the salience and strength of one's identity as a capable and caring human being (Grant & Dutton, 2012).

Why Do People Fail to Help?: A Summary

People often fail to help in emergencies, usually because of an incorrect decision somewhere in a sequence of steps that leads to action. First, people may fail to notice an event. Even if they do, they may fail to interpret it as an emergency, to take responsibility, or to choose and implement the appropriate action. These failures are caused primarily by the presence of bystanders, whose behavior becomes an important source of information. Inaction on their part can lead to pluralistic ignorance, causing the situation to be misinterpreted. Bystanders' inaction can also result in the diffusion of responsibility—a situation in which individuals believe that others will take the responsibility for helping. Even when individuals do take responsibility, they often fail to choose the appropriate action, because they feel incapable of offering aid. Implementing a chosen action may be further complicated if bystanders believe that helping will bring social disapproval.

Think Like a Social Psychologist

Thinking critically

—When seminary students rushed across campus to give a speech on the parable of the Good Samaritan, many failed to help a man they passed, who was slumped in a hallway. This finding is generally interpreted as showing that it is all too easy not to notice an emergency, even for those who should have helping on their minds. Can you think of anything in the parable of the Good Samaritan that may not have been a good prime for helping?

ALL'S WELL THAT ENDS WELL

Ana knew that she only felt as if she had been sitting in her car for hours. She was tired and hungry, and there was little to occupy her mind other than wondering how on earth she was going to get home. A quick look at her wristwatch, however, indicated that she had waited less than half an hour when a car pulled over in front of her. A tall, heavy-set middle-aged man emerged from the car and knocked on her passenger-side window. "Need a tow?" he asked in a deep, booming voice. Grateful that he had stopped for her, Ana explained her situation, including the part about the inoperable cell phone. He handed her his phone and disappeared into his car.

Ana had no trouble reaching the emergency operator at the auto club, who told her that a tow truck would arrive momentarily, and asked her to wait by her car. When Ana went to return the phone to the Good Samaritan, she was prepared to thank him and send him on his way. To her surprise, he practically insisted that they wait together in his car, and even offered to drive her home. Unlike her own car, his had a working heater, so Ana was happy to accept his invitation. She was less sure about the offer of a ride home. As a single woman, she was keenly aware of the many cases in which young women were assaulted by strangers offering aid. She wasn't really afraid that harm might come to her, though; there was something avuncular about this man, which put her at ease. Instead, she worried that in accepting his offer, she might be imposing on someone who, like everyone else, was probably anxious to get home. He assured her, however, that taking her home was no trouble at all.

The tow truck arrived and put Ana's car on the hook, to be towed to the shop that had serviced it in the past. On the way to her apartment, the Good Samaritan did most of the talking. He explained that he had passed another disabled car a couple of miles back. He had thought of stopping then, but continued when he realized that someone else had already pulled over. He went on about how everyone seems to be in rush nowadays, and how people don't seem to look out for each other the way they used to. The only time he stopped talking was when the Beatles' song "Help!" played on the stereo system. Even then, he sang along to the tune: "Help, I need somebody—help, not just anybody …"

Ana didn't mind listening to his monologue, because she felt too exhausted to carry on a conversation. When the car pulled up in front of her apartment building, she realized she had never asked the Good Samaritan for his name. "Name's Al," he said, as he handed her his business card. "Looks like you need some new wheels. Stop by the dealership and we'll see if I can fix you up. I sell new and used, and I'm there every day except Tuesdays."

Ana stuffed Al's card into her purse without looking at it. Later, as her frozen low-carb, low-fat, low-taste dinner entrée warmed in the microwave oven, she retrieved the card to see what kind of cars Al sold. With it came the little slip of paper on which she had scribbled the 800 number earlier that day. Ana dialed it and was greatly relieved when she heard a friendly voice ask, "Joplin Tornado Relief, would you like to make a donation?"

HIDDEN INFLUENCES ON HELPING: A SUMMARY

Inclusive fitness: An evolutionary principle that predicts we will help others to whom we are genetically related in order to preserve our genetic material

Reward-and-punishment mechanisms: Mechanisms that reward those who comply with cooperative norms and punish those who cheat. Compliance with such norms often occurs in the absence of conscious awareness

Arousal from witnessing an emergency: Arousal that directs our attention to the most central aspects of an emergency, making helping often automatic and spontaneous

Ultimate egoism: The idea that empathic concern is a generalized response that in evolutionary terms is highly adaptive and occurs without conscious awareness

Bystander effect: The inhibiting influence—often experienced outside of conscious awareness—that the presence of bystanders to an emergency exerts on those who could help

Contextual cues: The influence, for example, of surreptitious priming on a person's willingness to help

KEY TERMS AND DEFINITIONS

Prosocial behavior: a category of actions intended to benefit others in socially defined ways

Helping: any action that provides some benefit to or improves the well-being of another person

Altruism: helping in the absence of any expectation that doing so will bring external rewards

Inclusive fitness: the human interest in preserving genetic material, not only in one's own offspring, but in the offspring of relatives

Indirect reciprocity: the expectation that helping others will make them available and willing to reciprocate later

Negative state relief model: a theoretical model that predicts that people who are in a bad mood will help others in order to make themselves feel better

Arousal/cost-reward model: a theoretical model that explains helping as being caused by the desire to relieve the emotional distress of witnessing an emergency

Empathy: a state in which we take another's perspective and vicariously experience the other's emotions

Psychological hedonism: a doctrine proposing that humans act primarily in order to seek pleasure and avoid pain

Social dilemma: a situation that pits the greater good of the group against the good of the individual

Collective interest: concern for the group to which we belong, rather than for the self

Bystander apathy: the tendency not to help when in the presence of others

Pluralistic ignorance: assuming that there is nothing wrong because there is no evidence that others are concerned

Diffusion of responsibility: the failure of individuals to take appropriate action in the presence of bystanders; in general, as the number of bystanders increases, the less likely we are to take responsibility for helping

REFERENCES

Abbate, C. S., Ruggieri, S., & Boca, S. (2013). The effect of prosocial priming in the presence of bystanders. *Journal of Social Psychology, 153,* 619–622.

Alexander, R. D. (1987). *The biology of moral systems.* Chicago: Aldine Transaction.

Allport, G. (1954). The historical background of modern social psychology. In G. Lindzey (Ed.), *Handbook of social psychology* (pp. 3–56). Cambridge, MA: Addison-Wesley.

Axelrod, R. (1984). *The evolution of cooperation.* New York: Basic Books.

Batson, C. D. (1987). Prosocial motivation: Is it ever truly altruistic? In L. Berkowitz (Ed.), *Advances in Experimental Social Psychology* (Vol. 20, pp. 65-122).

Batson, C. D. (1991). *The altruism question: Toward a social-psychological answer.* Hillsdale, NJ: Erlbaum

Batson, C. D. (1995). Prosocial motivation: Why do we help others? In A. Tesser (Ed.), *Advanced social psychology* (pp. 333–381). New York: McGraw-Hill.

Batson, C. D. (2002). Addressing the altruism question experimentally. In S. G. Post & L. G. Underwood (Eds.), *Altruism and altruistic love: Science, philosophy, and religion in dialogue* (pp. 89–105). Oxford, UK: Oxford University Press.

Batson, C. D., Batson, J. G., Todd, R. M., Brummett, B. H., Shaw, L. L., & Aldeguer, C. M. R. (1995). Empathy and the collective good: Caring for one of the others in a social dilemma. *Journal of Personality and Social Psychology, 68,* 619–631.

Batson, C. D., Duncan, B., Ackerman, P., Buckley, T., & Birch, K. (1981). Is empathic emotion a source of altruistic motivation? *Journal of Personality and Social Psychology, 40,* 290–302.

Batson, C. D., Dyck, J. L., Brandt, J. R., Batson, J. G., Powell, A. L., McMaster, M. R., & Griffitt, C. (1988). Five studies testing two new egoistic alternatives to the empathy-altruism hypothesis. *Journal of Personality and Social Psychology, 55,* 52–77.

Batson, C. D., & Powell, A. A. (2003). Altruism and prosocial behavior. In T. Milton & M. J. Lerner (Eds.), *Handbook of psychology: Personality and social psychology* (Vol. 5, pp. 463–484). New York: Wiley.

Batson, C. D., Sager, K., Garst, E., Kang, M., Rubchinsky, K., & Dawson, K. (1997). Is empathy-induced helping due to self-other merging? *Journal of Personality and Social Psychology, 73,* 495–509.

Batson, C. D., & Shaw, L. L. (1991). Evidence for altruism: Toward a pluralism of prosocial motives. *Psychological Inquiry, 2,* 107–122.

Baumeister, R. F., Stillwell, A. M., & Heatherton, T. F. (1994). Guilt: an interpersonal approach. *Psychological Bulletin, 115,* 243–267.

Becker, S. W., & Eagly, A. H. (2004). The heroism of women and men. *American Psychologist, 59,* 163–178.

Bentham, J. (1879). *An introduction to the principles of morals and legislation* (First published in 1789). Oxford, UK: Clarendon Press.

Berkowitz, L. (1972). Social norms, feelings, and other factors affecting helping behavior and altruism. In L. Berkowitz (Ed.), *Advances in experimental social psychology* (Vol. 6, pp. 63–108). New York: Academic Press.

Bryan, J. H., & Test, M. A. (1967). Models and helping: Naturalistic studies in aiding behavior. *Journal of Personality and Social Psychology, 6*, 400–407.

Burnstein, E., Crandall, C., & Kitayama, S. (1994). Some neo-Darwinian decision rules for altruism: Weighing cues for inclusive fitness as a function of the biological importance of the decision. *Journal of Personality and Social Psychology, 67*, 773–789.

Cacioppo, J. T., Petty, R. E., & Losch, M. E. (1986). Attributions of responsibility for helping and doing harm: Evidence for confusion of responsibility. *Journal of Personality and Social Psychology, 50*, 100–105.

Carlson, M., Charlin, V., & Miller, N. (1988). Positive mood and helping behavior. *Journal of Personality and Social Psychology, 55*, 211–229.

Carlson, M., & Miller, N. (1987). Explanation of the relationship between negative mood and helping. *Psychological Bulletin, 102*, 91–108.

Cialdini, R. B., Brown, S. L., Lewis, B. P., Luce, C., & Neuberg, S. L. (1997). Reinterpreting the empathy-altruism relationship: When one into one equals one. *Journal of Personality and Social Psychology, 73*, 481–494.

Cialdini, R. B., Darby, B. L., & Vincent, J. E. (1973). Transgression and altruism: A case for hedonism. *Journal of Experimental Social Psychology, 9*, 502–516.

Cialdini, R. B., Kenrick, D. T., & Baumann, D. J. (1982). Effects of mood on prosocial behavior in children and adults. In N. Eisenberg (Ed.), *The development of prosocial behavior* (pp. 339–359). New York: Academic Press.

Cohen, S. (2004). Social relationships and health. *American Psychologist, 59*, 676–684.

Cohen, S., Kessler, R. C., & Gordon, L. U. (1995). Strategies for measuring stress in psychiatric and physical disorders. In S. Cohen, R. C. Kessler, & L. U. Gordon (Eds.), *Measuring stress* (pp. 3–28). New York: Oxford University Press.

Cohen, S., & Wills, T. A. (1985). Stress, social support, and the buffering hypothesis. *Psychological Bulletin, 98*, 310–357.

Clark, M. S., & Isen, A. M. (1982). Toward understanding the relationship between feeling states and social behavior. In A. H. Hastorf & A. M. Isen (Eds.), *Cognitive social psychology* (pp. 73–108). New York: Elsevier.

Clark, M. S., & Waddell, B. A. (1983). Effects of moods on thoughts about helping, attraction, and information acquisition. *Social Psychology Quarterly, 46*, 31–35.

Clark, R. D. III, & Word, L. E. (1974). Where is the apathetic bystander? Situational characteristics of the emergency. *Journal of Personality and Social Psychology, 29*, 279–287.

Cosmides, L. (1989). The logic of social exchange: Has natural selection shaped how humans reason? Studies with the Wason selection task. *Cognition, 31*, 187–276.

Cramer, R. E., McMaster, M. R., Bartell, P. A., & Dragna, M. (1988). Subject competence and minimization of the bystander effect. *Journal of Applied Social Psychology, 18*, 1133–1148.

Cunningham, M. R., Steinberg, J., & Grev, R. (1980). Wanting to and having to help: Separate motivations for positive mood and guilt-induced helping. *Journal of Personality and Social Psychology, 38*, 181–192.

Darley, J. M., & Batson, C. D. (1973). From Jerusalem to Jericho: A study of situational and dispositional variables in helping behavior. *Journal of Personality and Social Psychology, 27*, 100–108.

Darley, J. M., & Latane, B. (1968). Bystander intervention in emergencies: Diffusion of responsibility. *Journal of Personality and Social Psychology, 8*, 377–383.

Davis, M. H. (1994). *Empathy: A social psychological approach.* Madison, WI: Brown Benchmark.

Dawes, R., van de Kragt, A. J. C., & Orbell, J. M. (1990). Cooperation for the benefit of us—not me, or my conscience. In J. J. Mansbridge (Ed.), *Beyond self-interest* (pp. 97–110). Chicago: University of Chicago Press. de Waal, F. B. M. (2008). Putting the altruism back into altruism: The evolution of empathy. *Annual Review of Psychology, 59,* 279–300.

De Waal, F. B. M. (2008). Putting the altruism back into altruism: The evolution of empathy. *Annual Review of Psychology, 59,* 279–300.

Dovidio, J. F. (1984). Helping behavior and altruism: An empirical and conceptual overview. In L. Berkowitz (Ed.), *Advances in experimental social psychology* (Vol. 17, pp. 361–427). New York: Academic Press.

Dovidio, J. F., Piliavin, J. A., Gaertner, S. L., Schroeder, D. A., & Clark, R. D. III (1991). The arousal: Cost-reward model and the process of intervention: A review of the evidence. In M. S. Clark (Ed.), *Review of personality and social psychology: Vol. 12. Prosocial behavior* (pp. 86–118). Newbury Park, CA: Sage.

Eagly, A. H., & Crowley, M. (1986). Gender and helping behavior: A meta-analytic review of the social psychological literature. *American Psychologist, 100,* 283–308.

Eisenberg, N., & Lennon, R. (1983). Sex differences in empathy and related capacities. *Psychological Bulletin, 94,* 100–131.

Eisenberg, N., & Miller, P. (1987). The relation of empathy to prosocial and related behaviors. *Psychological Bulletin, 101,* 91–119.

Erkison, E. H. (1982). *The life cycle completed: A review.* New York: Norton.

Fisher, P., et al. (2011). The bystander-effect: A meta-analytic review on bystander intervention in dangerous and non-dangerous situations. *Psychological Bulletin, 137,* 517–537.

Gaertner, S. L., & Dovidio, J. F. (1977). The subtlety of white racism, arousal, and helping behavior. *Journal of Personality and Social Psychology, 35,* 691–707.

Garcia, S. M., Weaver, K., Moskowitz, G. M., & Darley, J. M. (2002). Crowded minds: The implicit bystander effect. *Journal of Personality and Social Psychology, 83,* 843–853.

Grant, A., & Dutton, J. (2012). Beneficiary or benefactor: Are people more prosocial when they reflect on receiving or giving? *Psychological Science, 23,* 1033–1039.

Gu, X., & Han, S. (2007). Attention and reality constraints on the neural processes of empathy for pain. *Neuroimage, 36,* 256–267.

Hamilton, W. D. (1964). The genetic evolution of social behavior. *Journal of Theoretical Biology, 7,* 1–52.

Han, S., Fan, Y., & Mao, L. (2008). Gender differences in empathy for pain: An electrophysiologial investigation. *Brain Research, 1196,* 85–93.

Henry, P., Reyna, C., & Weiner, B. (2004). Hate welfare but help the poor: How the attributional content of stereotypes explains the paradox of reactions to the destitute in America. *Journal of Applied Social Psychology, 34,* 34–58.

Hoffman, M. L. (1981). Is altruism part of human nature? *Journal of Personality and Social Psychology, 40,* 121–137.

Hornstein, H. A. (1970). The influence of social models on helping behavior. In J. Macauley & L. Berkowitz (Eds.), *Altruism and helping behavior* (pp. 29–42). New York: Academic Press.

House, J. S., & Kahn, R. L. (1985). Measures and concepts of social support. In S. Cohen & S. L. Syme (Eds.), *Social support and health* (pp. 83–108). New York: Academic Press.

Ickes, W., Gesn, P. R., & Graham, T. (2005). Gender differences in empathic accuracy: Differential ability or differential motivation? *Personal Relationships, 7,* 95–109.

Isen, A. M., & Levin, P. A. (1972). Effects of feeling good on helping: Cookies and kindness. *Journal of Personality and Social Psychology, 21,* 384–388.

Isen, A. M., Shalker, T. E., Clark, M. S., & Karp, L. (1978). Affect, accessibility of material in memory, and behavior. *Journal of Personality and Social Psychology, 36,* 1–12.

Isen, A. M., & Simmonds, S. F. (1978). The effect of feeling good on a helping task that is incompatible with good mood. *Social Psychology, 41,* 346–349.

Kenrick, D. T. (1991). Proximate altruism and ultimate selfishness. *Psychological Inquiry, 2,* 135–137.

Krebs, D. L. (1982). Psychological approaches to altruism: An evaluation. *Ethics, 92,* 447–458.

Krebs, D. L. (1991). Altruism and egoism: A false dichotomy? *Psychological Inquiry, 2,* 137–139.

Krebs, D. L., & Russell, C. (1981) Role taking and altruism: When you put yourself in another's shoes, will they take you to their owner's aid? In J. P. Rushton & R. M. Sorrentino (Eds.), *Altruism and helping behavior: Social, personality, and developmental perspectives* (pp. 137–165). Hillsdale, NJ: Erlbaum.

Laube, J. (1985). Health care providers as disaster victims. In J. Laube & S. Murphy (Eds.), *Perspectives on disaster recovery* (pp. 210–228). Norwalk, CT: Appleton-Century-Crofts.

Latane, B., & Darley, J. M. (1968). Group inhibition of bystander intervention. *Journal of Personality and Social Psychology, 10,* 215–221.

Latane, B., & Darley, J. M. (1970). *The unresponsive bystander: Why doesn't he help?* New York: Apple-Century-Croft.

Latane, B., & Rodin, J. (1969). A lady in distress: Inhibiting effects of friends and strangers on bystander intervention. *Journal of Experimental Social Psychology, 5,* 189–202.

Lennon, R., & Eisenberg, N. (1987). Gender and age differences in empathy and sympathy. In N. Eisenberg & J. Strayer (Eds.), *Empathy and its development* (pp. 195–217). New York: Cambridge University Press.

Lerner, M. J. (1980). *The belief in a just world: A fundamental delusion.* New York: Plenum.

Lerner, M. J., & Miller, D. T. (1978). Just world research and the attribution process: Looking back and looking ahead. *Psychological Bulletin, 85,* 1030–1051.

Macauley, J. R., & Berkowitz, L. (Eds.). (1970). *Altruism and helping behavior.* New York: Academic Press

Macrae, C. N., & Johnston, L. (1998). Help, I need somebody: Automatic action and inaction. *Social Cognition, 16,* 400–417.

Manning, R., Levine, M., & Collins, A. (2007). The Kitty Genovese murder and the social psychology of helping: The parable of the 38 witnesses. *American Psychologist, 62,* 555–562.

Manucia, G. K., Baumann, D. J., & Cialdini, R. B. (1984). Mood influences on helping: Direct effects or side effects? *Journal of Personality and Social Psychology, 46,* 357–364.

Martin, G. B., & Clark, R. D. III (1982). Distress crying in neonates: Species and peer specificity. *Developmental Psychology, 18,* 3–9.

McGuire, A. M. (1994). Helping behaviors in the natural environment: Dimensions and correlates of helping. *Personality and Social Psychology Bulletin, 20,* 45–56.

McGuire, A. M. (2003). "It was nothing"—Extending evolutionary models of altruism by two social cognitive biases in judgments of the costs and benefits of helping. *Social Cognition, 21,* 363–394.

Mill, J. S. (1863). *Utilitarianism.* London: Parker, Son, & Bourn.

Nelson, L. D., & Norton, M. I. (2005). From student to superhero: Situational primes shape future helping. *Journal of Experimental Social Psychology, 41,* 423–430.

Orbell, J. M., van de Kragt, A. J., & Dawes, R. M. (1988). Explaining discussion-induced cooperation. *Journal of Personality and Social Psychology, 54,* 811–819.

Pavey, L., Greitemeyer, T., & Sparks, P. (2012). "I help because I want to, not because you tell me to": Empathy increases autonomously motivated helping. *Personality and Social Psychology Bulletin, 38,* 681–689.

Pearce, P. L., & Amato, P. R. (1980). A taxonomy of helping: A multidimensional scaling analysis. *Social Psychology Quarterly, 43,* 363–371.

Penner, L. A., & Finkelstein, M. A. (1998). Dispositional and structural determinants of volunteerism. *Journal of Personality and Social Psychology, 74,* 525–537.

Piliavin, J. A., Dovidio, J. F., Gaertner, S. L., & Clark, R. D. (1981). *Emergency intervention.* New York: Academic Press.

Piliavin, J. A., & Piliavin, I. M. (1972). The effects of blood on reactions to a victim. *Journal of Personality and Social Psychology, 23,* 253–261.

Rosenthal, A. M. (1964). *Thirty-eight witnesses.* New York: McGraw-Hill.

Schaller, M., & Cialdini, R. B. (1988). The economics of empathic helping: Support for a mood management motive. *Journal of Experimental Social Psychology, 24,* 163–181.

Schroeder, D. A., Penner, L. A., Dovidio, J. F., & Piliavin, J. A. (1995). *The psychology of helping and altruism: Problems and puzzles.* New York: McGraw-Hill.

Schwartz, S. H., & Clausen, G. T. (1970). Responsibility, norms, and helping in an emergency. *Journal of Personality and Social Psychology, 16,* 299–310.

Schwartz, S. H., & Gottlieb, A. (1976). Bystander reactions to a violent theft: Crime in Jerusalem. *Journal of Personality and Social Psychology, 34,* 1188–1199.

Shotland, R. L., & Straw, M. (1976). Bystander response to an assault: When a man attacks a woman. *Journal of Personality and Social Psychology, 34,* 990–999.

Sime, J. D. (1983). Affiliative behavior during escape to building exits. *Journal of Environmental Psychology, 3,* 21–41.

Simon, H. A. (1990). A mechanism for social selection and successful altruism. *Science, 250,* 1665–1668.

Stocks, E. L., Lishner, D. A., & Decker, S. K. (2009). Altruism or psychological escape: Why does empathy promote prosocial behavior? *European Journal of Social Psychology, 39,* 649-655.

Stuermer, S., Snyder, M., Kropp, A., & Siem, B. (2006). Empathy-motivated helping: The moderating role of group membership. *Personality and Social Psychology Bulletin, 32,* 943–956.

Stuermer, S., Snyder, M., & Omoto, A. M. (2005). Prosocial emotions and helping: The moderating role of group membership. *Journal of Personality and Social Psychology, 88,* 532–546.

Sze, J. A., Gyurak, A., Goodkind, M. S., & Levenson, R. W. (2011). Greater emotional empathy and prosocial behavior in late life. *Emotion, 12,* 1129–1140.

Washington Post Editorial (1982, January 21). The unknown hero. *Washington Post.*

Toi, M., & Batson, C. D. (1982). More evidence that empathy is a source of altruistic motivation. *Journal of Personality and Social Psychology, 43,* 281–292.

Tomasello, M., Melis, A. P., Tennie, C., Wyman, E., & Herrmann, E. (2012). Two key steps in the evolution of human cooperation. *Current Anthropology, 53,* 673–692.

Trivers, R. L. (1971). The evolution of reciprocal altruism. *Quarterly Review of Biology, 46,* 35–37.

Wood, W., & Eagly, A. H. (2002). A cross-cultural analysis of the behavior of women and men: Implications for the origins of sex differences. *Psychological Bulletin, 129,* 119–138.

Wooster, M. M. (2000). Ordinary people, extraordinary rescues. *American Enterprise, 11,* 18–21.

CHAPTER 13

AGGRESSION AND VIOLENCE

B rian had heard these words before. Maybe not the exact words, but whether the line was "I think we should see other people," or "Let's just be friends," what it really meant was "I don't want to see you anymore," or "I don't want to be your partner anymore." He knew that lines like these were spoken out of consideration to break the fall, but in his experience they never helped: Being dumped always hurt. The feelings of loss, emptiness, and despair were the same, regardless of the language. And this was the worst breakup he had ever experienced—and not just because it was the most recent, either.

Brian wasn't sure what to make of it when Suzie called him to suggest they meet for coffee at the shop where he once worked while he was a student at the University of Kentucky. For days, he had tried to get her to go there with him, because it was the place where they had met three years ago. In his mind, the coffee shop was the perfect setting for him to propose to her. Suzie was the best thing that had ever happened to him, and a week ago—feeling ready to take their relationship to the next level—Brian bought an engagement ring. But Suzie had been unusually aloof for some time now, and had consistently thwarted his attempts to set up the date. Unsettled by her standoffishness, Brian had chalked it up to her hectic schedule at work. Now, he found it just as unsettling that she wanted the meeting on such short notice. However, his trepidation had been quickly dispelled by the realization that this might be the opportunity he needed to pop the question.

The coffee shop was crowded, but Brian found a table near the window from which he could see the door. In his excitement he had arrived ridiculously early, which gave him an opportunity to take another look at the ring he was carrying in his coat pocket. Within minutes, Suzie breezed through the door, her long, dark hair tucked into the collar of her denim jacket. Brian waved, and Suzie spotted him and walked toward his table. Something wasn't right, though. Ordinarily, Suzie would have looked at him the entire time she was crossing the room, and walking with a bounce in her step that suggested she was glad to see him. Today was different: Her gaze was fixed on the floor as she moved slowly toward him. When she sat down next to him, she omitted the customary hug and peck on the cheek. What was wrong?

After a brief exchange about life at the office, Suzie placed her hand on Brian's arm and said, "There's something I need to talk to you about." She began by telling him what a great guy he was, and what a great time they had had together. The more she talked, the less Brian was able to hear what she was saying. He knew from experience where Suzie was heading, and he was stunned. It was almost as though he was watching the whole scene from a vantage point somewhere outside his body. He wasn't even sure whether Suzie had ever said "Let's just be friends," but when she checked her watch and said "I gotta go," Brian knew it was over. Still in shock, he watched her head for the door. He couldn't help noticing that the bounce was back in her step.

When Brian returned to his apartment later that evening, the message light on his answering machine was blinking. He knew in his heart that it was Suzie. Before he pressed the Play button, he thought briefly how nice it would be if she had realized she made a terrible mistake and wanted to get back together with him. But she had merely called to say that she would pick up the things she had left in his apartment and return her key the next morning while he was at work. Brian's rational side knew that she wanted to do it that way to avoid the awkwardness they would feel if he was there when she collected her belongings. But his irrational side resented what he perceived to be cowardice on her part. It was his irrational side that made him call in sick at work the next morning.

Suzie arrived just before 8 A.M., accompanied by Eric, whom she introduced as a friend who owned a pickup truck. Watching the two remove the tangible evidence that he and Suzie were a couple was too much for Brian. To disguise his dismay, he put on his running shoes and went for a jog. "I may be a real mess," he thought, "but I'm not going to advertise it." Running through the crisp early-morning air for nearly an hour made Brian feel almost normal again. For a brief moment, the fateful meeting at the coffee shop seemed like a distant memory to him. But when he rounded the corner to his street, he noticed Suzie and Eric standing on the sidewalk together. He slowed down, not wanting to be seen. What followed next made his blood boil. After taking a last look at the building, Suzie turned toward Eric and the two embraced, then walked hand in hand to Eric's truck. Anger was beginning to replace the sense of sadness and loss Brian had been experiencing. Moreover, thoughts of revenge against the truck-driving interloper were beginning to replace thoughts about winning Suzie back.

In this chapter, we will examine the social psychological literature on human aggression—behavior that is *intended* to harm another who does not want to be harmed (Anderson & Bushman, 2002; Bushman & Huesmann, 2010). We will discuss the personal and situational variables that promote aggression and review social psychological theories of why humans aggress against one another. Before we do that, however, let's take a closer look at how aggression is generally defined.

DEFINING AGGRESSION

There is a reason why social psychological definitions of aggression emphasize the intent of the behavior, rather than its harmful consequences. Otherwise, a whole host of behaviors, including many that are socially acceptable, would be mislabeled as aggression. For example, dentists regularly hurt their patients when they perform root canals; parents often cause their children emotional pain when they punish them for their transgressions. Neither dentists nor parents act with the intention of causing harm, however. Similarly, accidents often have harmful, sometimes lethal, consequences for others. Yet, even a drunk driver who causes an accident that results in multiple fatalities does not intend to cause harm when he gets behind the wheel.

Instrumental versus Hostile Aggression

Just as not all hurtful behaviors are aggressive, not all forms of aggression are the same. Taking into account motives and emotions, social psychologists distinguish between two types of aggression, *instrumental aggression* and *hostile aggression* (Baron & Richardson, 1994). Both types involve doing harm to another. **Instrumental aggression**, however, is only a means to another end, like gaining status or money—or sacking the quarterback on the opposing team. As such, instrumental aggression is proactive, and is often premeditated and controlled. In **hostile aggression**, doing harm to someone is the primary—perhaps the only—goal. Although hostile aggression can be premeditated and controlled, it generally arises out of anger, in which case it is reactive, impulsive, and automatic.

Needless to say, this distinction between instrumental and hostile aggression is not as clear-cut as it may at first seem. Take self-defense, for example. An aggressive act that may appear to be reactive, self-defense serves an instrumental purpose, even if it appears to be impulsive and automatic. Similarly, if instrumental aggression

Instrumental aggression turns to hostile aggression

fails to achieve its goal, it can lead to anger, turning into hostile aggression. The fistfights that often break out at hockey games are a good example of instrumental-turned-into-hostile aggression.

Categorizing Aggression

When we think of the kind of aggression that is born of anger and hostility, the punch thrown at an opponent—the prototypical aggressive act—comes to mind most easily. Yet, aggressing against the source of a provocation is often not feasible. For example, a student who is reprimanded by his teacher for coming late to class may be ill-served by aggressing against him. In such cases, aggression is often displaced toward an innocent target who happens to be in the wrong place at the wrong time (Marcus-Newhall, Pederson, Carlson, & Miller, 2000) or a target who is guilty of a relatively minor provocation (Miller, Pederson, Earlywine, & Pollock, 2003). Whether individuals who are prevented from direct retaliation engage in displaced aggression depends on the extent to which they ruminate about the original provocation (Bushman, Bonacci, Pederson, Vasquez, & Miller, 2005). Angry rumination promotes aggression because it undermines individuals' capacity for self-control (Denson et al., 2011).

Regardless of its target, aggression comes in many different guises. According to Buss (1961), acts of aggression can be classified along three independent dimensions: physical-verbal, direct-indirect, and active-passive. **Table 13.1** lists and classifies eight different ways that Brian, the protagonist of this chapter's opening story, can aggress against Eric.

Table 13.1: Eight Ways Brian Can Aggress against Eric

	ACTIVE		PASSIVE	
	Direct	**Indirect**	**Direct**	**Indirect**
Physical	Punching, stabbing, shooting him	Tampering with the brakes	Blocking his driveway	Refusing to get out of his way
Verbal	Derogating him	Spreading rumors about him	Refusing to help or answer him	Not speaking up in his defense

Admittedly, active aggression is far easier to imagine than passive aggression. That does not mean that passive aggression is less common, however. If you've ever received "the silent treatment" from a friend, partner, or parent, you were victimized by a passive form of verbal aggression aimed directly at causing you harm.

Although there are many different ways Brian can retaliate against Eric, which one he chooses—even whether or not he does choose to aggress against Eric—depends on several personal and situational variables. We'll consider first those that pertain to Brian as a person.

AGGRESSION—THE PERSON

On a personal level, human aggression raises troubling questions. What motivated the terrorists who hijacked four airplanes on September 11, 2001, and crashed them into the Pentagon and World Trade Center? What compelled Dylan Klebold and Eric Harris to kill 12 students and a teacher at Columbine High School before they killed themselves? Why, during the 1990s, did the citizens of Rwanda and the former Yugoslavia turn on their neighbors—and in some cases, even their relatives—and slaughter them by the thousands?

It is possible, of course, to answer these and related questions by citing unique circumstances—political zealotry, a history of ostracism, or ethnic strife. In doing so, however, we would be overlooking the fact that with few exceptions, aggression and violence are universal: they have characterized human existence throughout history (Bonta, 1997). Furthermore, in citing unique circumstances, we would fail to answer a larger question put forth by Rodney King, himself a victim of violent aggression: "Can we all get along?"

The Roman proverb *Homo homini lupus* ("Man is wolf to man") tells us that the answer to Rodney King's question is human nature itself. That is, humans are simply predisposed to aggress against other humans. Twentieth-century psychologists conceptualized this predisposition in the form of animal instincts that function much like hidden influences on aggression. For example, Freud (1920) speculated that much of human behavior results from two unconscious desires: *Eros*, or the life instinct, which motivates humans to reproduce and preserve their own lives; and *Thanatos*, or the death instinct, which motivates people to escape from life's travails. Because these two instincts have vastly different consequences (life versus death), they necessarily conflict. One way to resolve the conflict, Freud theorized, is to direct the death instinct not toward the self, but against others. Aggression occurs, Freud wrote, when the life instinct gains the upper hand over the death instinct.

Konrad Lorenz, who achieved lasting fame for his studies on imprinting in ducklings, also thought of aggression as an instinctual behavior. Unlike Freud, however, Lorenz saw aggression as neither uniquely human nor incompatible with the desire to live, preserve the self, and procreate (Lorenz, 1966). In his view, successful aggression promotes individual and genetic survival over both the short and long term. In the short term, it helps individuals to gain valuable resources such as food and shelter. Over the long term, it aids in genetic survival because it increases the individual's access to desirable mates.

Lorenz's speculations about the adaptive value of aggression foreshadowed more recent theorizing by evolutionary psychologists. However, they do not really explain why aggression occurs, because his theory is circular in nature. That is, Lorenz inferred the instinct from his observations of aggressive behavior. Explaining aggression as the result of an instinct, then, doesn't tell us very much.

Instinct theories also do not explain why some people are more aggressive than others. We can learn a great deal more about aggression by looking at individual differences in aggression, particularly sex differences, and their causes.

Sex Differences in Aggression

In terms of physical aggression, the evidence is overwhelming: men are more aggressive than women. Worldwide, more than 99 percent of same-sex homicides involve a male perpetrator and a male victim (Daly & Wilson, 1988). Across the life span, moreover, males are consistently more physically aggressive than females (Archer, 2004). Young boys play aggressive, rough-and-tumble games three to six times as frequently as girls (DiPietro, 1981; Singer, 1994). Boys are also far more likely than girls to engage in pushing, shoving, and hitting that has little to do with the game they are playing (Deaux & LaFrance, 1998).

Physical aggression manifests itself early in life, perhaps as early as the end of the first year (Tremblay et al., 2005). At that age, most aggression is instrumental—taking things from others or pushing others to get something. About a quarter of the 17-month- olds studied by Tremblay and colleagues (2005), however, bit, kicked, and hit others for seemingly no other reason than to inflict harm. Not surprisingly, boys outbit, outkicked, and outhit girls at a rate of eight to one. Starting around the third year of life, the boys' rate of physical aggression began to decline steadily, presumably because the boys became increasingly able to inhibit their aggressive impulses (Nagin & Tremblay, 1999). Though that may sound like good news, the gap in the rates of physical aggression among boys and girls never closed entirely. By age 11, boys were still three times more likely than girls to physically aggress against others (Tremblay et al., 2002).

Sex differences in aggression: Boys are more likely than girls to engage in pushing, shoving, and hitting as part of their play

Although sex differences in physical aggression are profound, there is little to indicate that the sexes differ in the extent to which they experience anger. In fact, little girls and grown women experience anger at the same rate as little boys and grown men (Kring, 2000). To the extent that anger fuels hostile aggression, why is there such a marked difference in physical aggression between the sexes? The answer is not that females are less aggressive than males. Rather, females tend to aggress against others in more indirect ways, by gossiping, spreading rumors, or ostracizing others (Archer, 2005; Coie et al., 1999; Österman et al., 1998).

Some have argued that girls may be more prone than boys to indirect relational aggression, as opposed to direct physical aggression, because they care more about relationships than boys (e.g., Crick & Rose, 2000). Thus, by gossiping and spreading rumors, they hit others where it hurts most. This explanation has some appeal, yet it does not account for the origin of sex differences in caring about relationships.

One could argue that these differences are related to differences in the socialization of boys and girls. There are two complications to that argument. First, as we have seen, sex differences in aggression have been observed at an age when gender socialization has barely begun. Second, as boys get older, they resort less to physical aggression and rely far more often on indirect aggression—a shift that becomes particularly dramatic between the ages of six and 17 (Archer, 2004). In other words, as boys reach adolescence, their patterns of aggression become more similar to those of girls. If gender-specific socialization accounts for aggression, then the differences between boys and girls should be more pronounced during adolescence than at the tender age of two. Because they are not, we need to consider a different explanation. Sex differences in aggression may instead be gender-specific adaptations to differences in the evolutionary pressures placed on women and men.

The Evolution of Sex Differences in Aggression

Evolutionary theory traces sex differences in the tendency toward physical aggression to differences in **parental investment** (Campbell, 2002; Daly & Wilson, 1988). For males, both animal and human, physical aggression serves as an incentive. That is, males have much to gain by aggressing against other males. Aggression establishes their dominance and gives them an edge in their pursuit of the most desirable mates—just as Lorenz (1966) suspected. Their parental investment ends at the point of mating, however—just where the infinitely greater parental investment of females begins.

In contrast, females are in charge of gestation (in the mammalian species), as well as the upbringing and protection of their offspring. For them, direct physical aggression serves as a disincentive. They have little to gain and everything to lose by aggressing against others, given the risks that physical confrontations carry. For example, the death of a mother has far more serious consequences for her offspring than the death of a father. Thus, lowered physical aggression among females reflects their need to avoid exposing themselves and their offspring to danger (Taylor et al., 2000).

From an evolutionary perspective, then, sex differences in aggression reflect gender-specific adaptations that are rooted in differences in parental investment. There is also reason to believe that the heightened aggression seen in males is supported by hormonal influences.

The Neuroendocrinology of Aggression

Men differ from women in a myriad of ways. On an endocrinologic level, men have higher **testosterone** levels than women. To the extent that they are also more prone to physical aggression than women, we might suspect that testosterone contributes to their heightened aggression. Indeed, numerous studies of diverse samples of people, including prison inmates (Dabbs et al., 1995), college fraternity members (Dabbs, Hargrove, & Heusel, 1996), military veterans (Dabbs, Hooper, & Jukovic, 1990), and young boys (Chance et al., 2000), show a positive correlation between testosterone levels and various measures of aggression. Of course, correlations do not imply causality. In this case, numerous studies suggest that the link between testosterone and aggression is a complicated one.

Positive correlations between testosterone and aggression are obtained most frequently in situations marked by competition or a challenge to a person's social status (Higley, 1996). This observation raises the possibility that aggression itself can produce increases in testosterone, especially when it is associated with winning (Mazur, 1983; Mazur, Booth, & Dabbs, 1992). Testosterone is also correlated with beneficial, socially desirable traits such as toughness, social dominance, competitiveness, physical vigor, and social assertiveness (Higley, 1996). In fact, most individuals with high testosterone levels are restrained in their aggression and express it only in socially acceptable ways. Individuals of low socioeconomic status are the notable exception to this generalization (Dabbs & Morris, 1990).

Animal studies indicate that the neurotransmitter **serotonin** (CSF 5-HIAA) affects the expression and regulation of aggression by providing the biological basis for successful impulse control. (Higley, 1996; Westergaard et al., 2002). In several studies of free-ranging adolescent male rhesus monkeys, animals with low concentrations of serotonin in their central nervous systems were no more or less aggressive than those with high concentrations of serotonin. However, the low-serotonin animals had many more scars and wounds than the others, suggesting they were reckless and unable to stay out of fights they couldn't win (Higley et al., 1996). In the human world, low levels of serotonin have been similarly linked to impaired impulse control, severe aggression, and lack of social competence among both men and women (Linnoila & Virkkunen (1992).

The most straightforward way of interpreting the data on testosterone and serotonin is that they contribute differently to the expression of aggressive behavior. Testosterone contributes to aggressive motivation; serotonin regulates the threshold, intensity, and frequency of aggressive behavior. Individuals with high levels of testosterone but normal levels of serotonin may be aggressive in a variety of contexts, but in general, their aggression is neither violent nor unrestrained, serving primarily to assert their social dominance. Individuals with high testosterone levels but lower-than-average serotonin levels are not just aggressive, but prone to aggress more easily, more frequently, and more violently than others because of their lack of impulse control (Higley et al., 1996).

The Hostile Attribution Bias

Individual differences in gender and hormones are important predictors of aggression. However, they do not provide a complete account of the variables that may predispose an individual toward aggression. A more complete account would include a person's attitudes, beliefs, and values as they pertain to aggression and violence. Personality traits may matter as well. In Chapter 6, we saw that inflated or unstable self- esteem can lead to aggression when a person's self-image is threatened (Bushman & Baumeister, 1998; Kernis et al., 1989).

Chronic differences in the way individuals interpret another's ambiguous intent are also important to the expression of aggression. Most of us have little difficulty correctly interpreting another person's intentions when they are clearly benign or hostile, but what about when the situation is less than perfectly clear? Suppose a fellow student bumps into you as you are riding in an elevator. Was it an accident? Was he trying to pick a fight or clumsily trying to flirt with you? To answer these questions, you may look for additional information. If the

"What's that funny look for? You think my
girlfriend's an airhead, don't you?!"

The hostile attribution bias leads individuals to interpret ambiguous behavior as intentionally hostile

elevator is particularly crowded, you may decide that the bump was indeed an accident. A closer look at the person's facial expression may reveal whether you're dealing with a threat or a flirtation.

Unfortunately, chronically aggressive individuals often eschew this type of analysis. Their interpretation of the situation is guided instead by a **hostile attribution bias** (Nasby, Hayden, & DePaulo, 1979), which is to say that they explain ambiguous behavior as intentionally hostile. The hostile attribution bias is characteristic of children who have been the targets of aggression (Crick & Dodge, 1994; Dodge & Tomlin, 1987).

At least at first, they may correctly attribute others' aggressive behavior to hostility. Over time, however, they may begin to perceive hostile intent everywhere. Of course, their overperception of others' hostility increases their aggression, decreasing the extent to which they are accepted by others (Reijntjes et al., 2011).

Aggression—The Person: A Summary

Faced with the pervasiveness of human aggression, some theorists (Freud, 1920, Lorenz, 1966) proposed that aggression may arise from a basic human instinct. Gender differences in aggression may result from adaptations to evolutionary pressures. Specifically, they may be rooted in differences in parental investment that provide the males of most mammalian species with an incentive to aggress, but the females with a disincentive because of their role in gestation and nurturing. On a neuroendocrinologic level, sex differences in aggression are manifested in different levels of testosterone, a hormone that contributes to aggressive motivation. The neurotransmitter serotonin helps to keep aggressive behavior in check. Besides chemical influences on aggression, a hostile attribution bias, which causes individuals to interpret the behavior of others as intentionally hostile, can also produce chronic differences in aggressiveness.

Think Like a Social Psychologist

Making connections
—Testosterone is related to aggression, and men generally have higher levels of testosterone than women. Does that imply that chemistry is destiny? Can you identify circumstances under which women might be more prone to aggression than men?

Thinking critically
—The finding that men of lower socioeconomic status are less restrained in their aggression and express it in less socially desirable ways than men of higher socioeconomic status is intriguing, because it suggests that the difference in aggression between the two groups may be due to different serotonin levels. However, the nature of the link between the two variables is unclear. Make an argument for why lower socioeconomic status might lead to lowered levels of serotonin. Then make an argument for why low levels of serotonin might lead to lower socioeconomic status. Which argument makes more sense to you?

Understanding everyday behavior
—Suppose you have a friend who is reluctant to go out on dates because of her belief that "men want only one thing." To what extent does her belief reflect a hostile attribution bias? How might she have acquired it? What functions does it serve for her?

AGGRESSION—THE SITUATION

Brian Tries to Cope

As the noon hour approached, Brian wished he had gone to work. He didn't quite know what to do with himself, and his jog earlier that morning had left him more jittery than relaxed. The cool morning breeze had vanished and was gradually being replaced by heat and humidity. To make matters worse, his air conditioner, which had been limping along for some time, had finally quit on him. Oddly enough, it had happened without a bang. If not for the increasing heat and humidity, he would never have noticed that the unit was merely recycling the hot air in his living room.

Opening the windows, Brian decided to visit his parents. He could count on their home to be cool, and his mother had asked him to come over some time ago. His parents were planning to sell the house, which had become an empty nest, and move to a condominium. In preparing for the move, they had found several things that belonged to Brian, and they wanted him to sort through the items. Brian dreaded the task, and had been putting it off. He didn't cherish the thought of his boyhood home being sold, perhaps to a developer who would raze it and replace it with one of those new McMansions. He was also afraid that his mom would ask him how things were going with Suzie. His parents liked Suzie far more than anyone else he had ever dated and were looking forward to their son's wedding and the possibility of grandchildren.

When Brian arrived at his parents' house, his dad offered him a cold beer, which he gladly accepted. They sat around the kitchen table, talking about the weather and other mundane things, until his mom directed him to the hallway closet, which was filled with assorted boxes. Going through them didn't take Brian long at all. They held mostly things he had left behind on purpose—papers he had written in high school, an obsolete video game system, and countless other games he had long since outgrown. The few things that had any sentimental value fit neatly into one medium-sized box that he could store easily in the trunk of his car. Brian was going to leave the other boxes in the closet, but at his mother's urging, he put them out at the curb for garbage pickup the next day.

As he removed the last items from the closet, Brian noticed another box on the top shelf. It was smaller, and it looked quite different from the moving boxes that were piled up on the floor. Piqued by curiosity, he removed the lid and was shocked at what he found. The box contained a small handgun that must have belonged to his father. "Son of a gun," he thought, without realizing the pun, "my own father, that gentle man who never missed church on Sunday, owns a gun!" Briefly, Brian entertained the notion of spinning it on his index finger, like a gun fighter in an old Hollywood movie. But just then his mother called him, so he quickly replaced the lid and closed the closet door.

When Brian returned to the kitchen, his mother apologized for not inviting him to dinner—an invitation Brian had secretly wished for. His parents were headed for a potluck supper in honor of the church's outgoing pastor. After chatting with his mother for a few more minutes, Brian got into his car and headed home.

The heat in Brian's apartment was stifling, even though he had left the windows wide open. The lack of any breeze provided him with absolutely no relief. Brian opened the refrigerator and found several bottles of cold beer. He would have to cool off the old- fashioned way. Opening one of the bottles, he sat down in front of the TV, picked up the remote, and began flipping through the channels. The network stations were all showing the local news, ESPN was broadcasting live a poker tournament, and the Comedy Channel was running some sort of "Best of *Saturday Night Live*" special. Nothing really grabbed him.

Brian was about to turn off the TV when he came across one of those 24/7 movie channels. The movie had already started, but it didn't take him long to recognize one of his all-time favorites. In light of everything that had happened over the past 24 hours, watching *The Texas Chain Saw Massacre* while having a few cold ones seemed a good way to spend the evening, especially if he could top it off with *Grand Theft Auto*, his favorite Xbox game.

Brian was unaware that his many attempts to distract himself from Suzie's rejection and his jealousy of Eric were predisposing him to aggression. As we will see, ample research indicates that the stifling heat, the alcohol he was drinking, his exposure to violent movies and video games, the sight of his father's gun, and even his morning jog were contributing to a propensity for aggression.

Heat and Aggression

Social psychological research on the relationship between ambient temperature and aggression confirms the common suspicion that people become more aggressive as the weather grows hotter (Anderson, Anderson, Dorr, DeNeve, & Flanagan, 2000; Bushman, Wang, & Anderson, 2004). Motorists riding in cars without air conditioning are more prone to respond with rage to traffic-related frustrations than those who are cruising along in comfort (Kenrick & McFarlane, 1986). Major-league pitchers hit opposing batters at nearly twice the usual rate when the temperature is 90 degrees or higher. Yet the number of wild pitches they throw does not increase, suggesting that they hit the batters out of aggression rather than heat-induced fatigue or wildness (Reifman, Larrick, & Fein, 1991).

More serious aggressive acts that increase with the heat include assaults, rapes, homicides, and riots, even politically motivated riots. Studies of the correlation between weather records and crime statistics (Anderson, 1989, for example) show that worldwide, more violent crimes are committed during the summer than in any other season.

Moreover, studies of the violence rates in regions that differ in climate generally show higher crime rates in hotter regions (Anderson & Anderson, 1996). Finally, studies that compare violence rates during hot and more temperate years generally report more violence in the years marked by hotter temperatures (Anderson, Bushman, & Groom, 1997).

There is general agreement that the relationship between heat and aggression is *linear*. That is, the hotter it gets, the more aggressive people become. However, some archival studies have reported data that suggest a *curvilinear* relationship between heat and aggression (Baron & Ransberger, 1978; Cohn & Rotton, 1997): That is, heat promotes aggression up to a point, but at extremely high temperatures, aggression begins to decrease. This finding makes good intuitive sense: when the temperature hovers above 90 degrees, most of us find it difficult to engage in any kind of activity, physical aggression included. It also makes good theoretical sense: To the extent that extreme heat is aversive, it may trigger a motive to escape that is incompatible with the motive to aggress (Baron, 1972). Because the data on which the curvilinear relationship rests are archival rather than experimental, however, they are subject to alternative interpretations: see the Think like a Social Psychologist box on **pages 612-613**.

THINK LIKE A SOCIAL PSYCHOLOGIST: THE PITFALLS OF INTERPRETING ARCHIVAL DATA

Baron and Ransberger (1978) were among the first to advance the idea of a curvilinear relationship between heat and aggression. They based their case on an analysis of ambient temperature records during episodes of collective violence—specifically the riots and civil disturbances that swept the United States during the "long, hot summers" of the late 1960s and early 1970s. Consistent with their predictions, they found that of the 102 riots they analyzed, 38 (37.25 percent) took place on days when the temperature was between 81 and 90 degrees Fahrenheit. Only 9 riots (8.8 percent) occurred when the temperature was above 90 degrees. The pattern became even more dramatic when Baron and Ransberger (1978) restricted their analysis to riots that were unrelated to Dr. Martin Luther King's assassination on April 4, 1968. Of the remaining 86 riots, more than 44 percent took place at temperatures between 81 and 90 degrees; only about 10 percent occurred when the temperature was above 90 degrees.

Can we take these results to indicate that the relationship between heat and collective violence is indeed curvilinear rather than linear (see Figure 13.1 for the difference between the two types of relationships)? What might argue against interpreting the data in this way? To answer these questions, let's think about another experiment. Assume you have found that over the past five summers, more people have fallen in love when the temperature was in the 80s than in the 90s. If so, you probably won't be tempted to conclude that the ambient temperature played a causal role in the relationship you observed. The problem is, during any given summer, days in the 80s far outnumber days in the 90s, providing many more opportunities to fall in love on days in the 80s. The curvilinear relationship between heat and collective violence observed by Baron and Ransberger (1978) may be another artifact of the base temperature rates during summer.

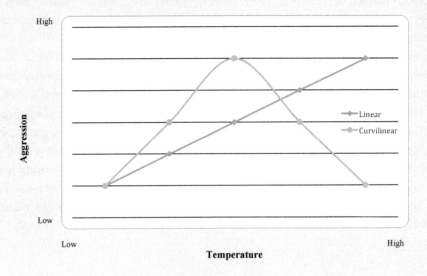

Figure 13.1: Hypothetical Relationships Between Heat and Aggression

Carlsmith and Anderson (1979) made exactly that point when they analyzed the relationship between ambient temperatures and the number of baseball games played by the New York Mets in the 1977 season. Their analysis revealed a curvilinear relationship: Many more games were played when the temperature was in the 80s, many fewer when it was in the 90s. Because Major League Baseball games are scheduled months in advance, however, there is little reason to conclude that game frequency is causally related to the temperature. Not surprisingly, when Carlsmith and Anderson (1979) took into account the difference in base temperature rates in their reanalysis of Baron and Ransberger's (1978) data, the results suggested that the relationship between heat and collective violence was linear, rather than curvilinear.

Surprisingly, Carlsmith and Anderson's (1979 reanalysis did not bury the curvilinearity hypothesis. A year later, Cohn and Rotton (1997) analyzed the relationship between temperature and assaults, first in Minneapolis and later in Dallas (Rotton & Cohn, 2000). Both studies suggest a curvilinear relationship: assaults increased up to a temperature of about 75 degrees, but decreased as the temperature rose further. Could these findings also be misleading?

According to Bushman, Wang, and Anderson (2005), the answer appears to be yes. The problem is that most assaults take place between 9:00 P.M. and 3:00 A.M., when most people engage in discretionary activities. That, of course, is the coldest period in the day. During the day, when temperatures in both Minneapolis and Dallas are highest and most people engage in obligatory activities like school or work, assaults are infrequent. Consequently, the time of day may influence temperature in one direction and assaults in the opposite direction. When Bushman et al. (2005) compared temperatures with assaults during the high-assault period between 9:00 P.M. and 3:00 A.M., they found that the frequency of assaults *increased* as a linear function of the temperature.

The debate over whether the relationship between heat and aggression is linear or curvilinear is likely to continue (see Cohn & Rotton, 2005), as long as theoretical claims are made based solely on archival data. As is the case with all naturally occurring variables, temperature varies for a host of reasons. Thus, any relationship between heat and aggression (or falling in love, for that matter) could be explained in many different ways.

Alcohol and Aggression

According to some estimates (for example, Anderson & Bushman, 1997), about half of all violent crimes reported in the United States are committed by an intoxicated assailant. Alcohol consumption may not cause aggression, but there is ample evidence that it facilitates it (Bushman & Cooper, 1990; Ito, Miller, & Pollock, 1996; Steele & Josephs, 1990), especially when people have been provoked and cannot manage to distract themselves or respond nonaggressively (Bushman & Cooper, 1990). Intoxication causes **alcohol myopia**, a general impairment of all cognitive processes (Steele & Southwick, 1985). This inability to think clearly affects the way people sort out conflicting impulses such as the simultaneous desire to aggress in response to a provocation and withdraw from it. Sober people are perfectly capable of inhibiting an aggressive impulse when they know the other person is likely to retaliate. Intoxicated people, however, focus on the provocation (Giancola & Corman, 2007) and often fail to realize the harm their aggression might cause (Bushman & Cooper, 1990). Alcohol can also exacerbate the effect of rumination on aggression toward the source of a subsequent minor annoyance, especially among individuals already predisposed toward displaced aggression (Denson, White, &

Warburton, 2009). Alcohol can further increase aggression because it magnifies the perceived intentionality of another's behavior, compelling intoxicated people to interpret a harmless bump in a crowded bar as a hostile act (Bègue et al., 2010).

Consuming large amounts of alcohol facilitates aggression

Although alcohol myopia and the magnification of the intentionality bias are psychological phenomena marked by cognitive impairment, their causes are entirely physiological. For one thing, the effects of alcohol depend on how much was consumed. Moderate-to-high amounts of alcohol facilitate aggression; low amounts do not. Moreover, merely thinking that one is drunk does not promote aggression. In several studies, research participants who believed they were drinking alcohol, when in fact they had received a placebo, were no more aggressive than participants in a control group, who were correctly informed about the nonalcoholic beverage they had consumed. Regardless of their expectations, participants who had consumed alcohol were far more aggressive than those who did not (Bègue et al., 2010; Bushman & Cooper, 1990; Hull & Bond, 1986).

Exercise and Aggression

The idea that physical exercise could promote aggression may strike some people as odd. After all, running 3 miles or spending an hour in the gym is supposed to make us feel better. However, exercise also increases physiological arousal, and as we saw in Chapter 9, people often misattribute the causes of their arousal. Recall the participants in Dutton and Aron's (1974) study, who were more attracted to a female experimenter after having crossed a shaky bridge than those who had crossed a sturdy bridge. Evidently, participants who had crossed the shaky bridge mislabeled the arousal produced by their scary experience as sexual attraction. What might have happened had the same participants met an experimenter who insulted them instead of stirring their romantic desire? Chances are they would have misattributed their arousal to the insult and responded more aggressively than those who had crossed the sturdy bridge.

Research on **excitation transfer** (Zillmann, 1988)—the spillover of arousal from one setting to the next—corroborates this speculation. In one study (Ramirez, Bryant, & Zillmann, 1982), male undergraduates viewed (1) a short, sexually explicit film; (2) a set of sexually suggestive pictures; or (3) facial photographs with no erotic content while in the presence of an experimenter who behaved rudely. When they later evaluated the experimenter, participants who had seen the sexually explicit film expressed more hostility toward him than participants who had seen the less arousing pictures and photographs (see **Figure 13.2**). Evidently, the arousal produced by the sexually explicit film carried over into the evaluation period, when participants, having misattributed it to the experimenter's rude behavior, responded with high levels of hostility. In case you're wondering, women, too, become more aggressive when they are provoked after being exposed to sexually explicit material (Zillmann, Bryant, & Carveth, 1981).

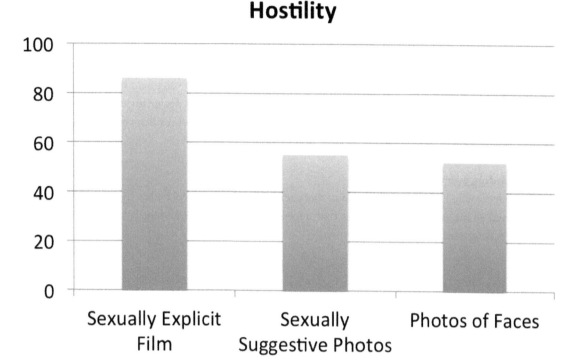

Figure 13.2: Hostility toward a Rude Experimenter Following Exposure to Different Types of Erotic and Non-erotic Stimuli

Source: Ramirez, J., Bryant, J., & Zillmann, D. (1982). Effects of erotica on retaliatory behavior as a function of level of prior provocation. *Journal of Personality and Social Psychology, 43*, 971–978.

Although the link between aggression and excitation has been demonstrated primarily through exposure to sexually explicit material, there is good reason to believe that other sources of arousal would have a similar effect. In other words, anything that is arousing—physical exercise included—has the potential to create excitation, which can then transfer or spill over into another situation. Because the original source of arousal tends to some extent to recede from conscious awareness, excitation transfer can be considered a hidden influence on aggression.

Aggression—The Situation: A Summary

Ambient heat, alcohol consumption, and any activity that produces physiological arousal are all related to aggression. The bulk of the evidence suggests that the effects of heat on aggression are linear and result from the negative feelings associated with discomfort. However, some studies suggest that the relationship between heat and aggression may be curvilinear because extreme heat may compel individuals to escape the situation, rather than aggress against others. Alcohol promotes aggression because it impairs most cognitive processes. Alcohol myopia prevents individuals from effectively dealing with conflicting impulses toward fight (aggression) and flight (escape or withdrawal). Physical arousal can promote aggression through excitation transfer, even when the source of the arousal is irrelevant to the situation.

Think Like a Social Psychologist

Designing research

—Having read about the effects of heat and alcohol on aggression, you can't help but wonder about their combined effects. What would you hypothesize? How would you design an experiment to test the combined effects of heat and alcohol on aggression? What pattern of results would support your hypothesis? What would refute it?

Understanding everyday behavior

—Most people who exercise regularly claim that exercise makes them feel better. In light of what you have learned about excitation transfer, is that necessarily true? Can you identify conditions under which exercising may make people feel worse?

AGGRESSION—THE CULTURE

Although aggression can be explained in terms of personal dispositions and situational variables, unique features of one's culture contribute importantly to variations in aggression. Cultures vary in the extent to which they convey that aggression is acceptable. Easy access to guns, positive portrayals of violence in the media, and a culture of honor all promote aggression and violence.

Weapons Effects on Aggression

Fortunately, Brian had looked at his father's handgun only briefly before putting it back into the box. Taking it might well have increased the chances of his eventually using it. Among Western industrialized nations, the United States has both the highest rate of gun ownership and the highest rate of homicides committed with a gun (Berkowitz, 1994). Every year in the United States, almost 3,000 children are killed by gun-related violence—about one child every three hours (Geen & Donnerstein, 1998). Statistics like these have prompted repeated calls for gun control, yet some (the National Rifle Association, for example) reject those calls, in part on the premise that "people, not guns, kill people." Social psychology is not likely to settle this political debate. What seems clear, however, is that the mere presence of guns can increase aggression in general—not just violence that is committed with a gun.

This **weapons effect** was first demonstrated by Berkowitz and LePage (1967), who recruited undergraduates for an experiment on physiological reactions to the stress of receiving mild electric shocks. The experiment was to be completed with another participant, who was really a confederate of the experimenter. In the first phase of the experiment, the participant spent five minutes listing ideas that might improve a popular singer's record sales and public image, while the confederate pretended to generate a list of ways a used car salesman might improve sales. The participant and confederate were then led to separate rooms to "evaluate" each other. A set of good ideas was to be "rewarded" by a single shock; a bad idea was to be "punished" by ten shocks.

The participant was always evaluated first, and received either a single shock (non-angered condition) or seven shocks (angered condition) from the confederate. The participant then switched rooms with the confederate to evaluate his ideas.

The setup of the room was the crucial manipulation in the experiment. For one group of participants, the room contained nothing but the shock generator. For another group of participants, the room also held a 12-gauge shotgun and a .38 caliber revolver, which were ostensibly part of an unrelated experiment (unassociated weapons condition). Participants in a third group also saw the shotgun and the revolver, but were told they belonged to an experiment the confederate was working on (associated weapons condition). For a fourth group of participants, the room held the shock generator and a couple of badminton racquets.

The researchers expected that angered participants would retaliate against the confederate by delivering more shocks than participants who had not been angered. That was, in fact, the case. However, as **Figure 13.3**

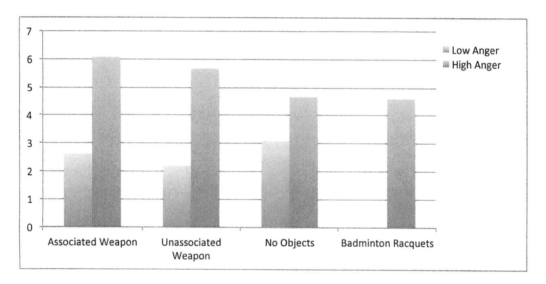

Figure 13.3: Mean Number of Shocks Delivered as a Result of Anger and Aggressive Cues

Adapted from: Berkowitz, L., & LePage, A. (1967). Weapons as aggression-eliciting stimuli. *Journal of Personality and Social Psychology, 7*, 202–207.

shows, when angered participants delivered the shocks in the presence of aggressive cues (that is, the weapons), they retaliated with far greater fury than either angered participants who were not exposed to the weapons or participants who had not been angered.

What do these results say about the question of whether the finger pulls the trigger or the trigger pulls the finger? It seems clear that to those who are already angry and predisposed to aggression, the mere sight of a gun serves as an aggressive cue. At the same time, the presence of weapons increases aggression in general—not just aggression with a gun—as shown by participants' willingness to deliver more electric shocks in the weapons conditions than in the conditions that lacked cues to aggression. Do these findings support the use of gun control? The Social Psychology and the Law box on **page 618** explores the issue.

What social-cognitive processes are responsible for the weapons effect? According to Berkowitz's (1993) cognitive neoassociation theory, negative feelings produced by an insult or a provocation automatically activate cognitions that compel an individual to respond either aggressively or by escaping from the situation. Situational cues like weapons automatically activate aggression-related thoughts, which can promote an aggressive response. In support of this idea, among participants working on a lexical decision task, those who were surreptitiously exposed to pictures of guns identified aggression-related words like *assault*, *punch*, and *torture* faster

SOCIAL PSYCHOLOGY AND THE LAW: WOULD GUN CONTROL REDUCE THE MURDER RATE?

A well-regulated militia being necessary to the security of a free State, the right to keep and bear arms shall not be infringed. Second Amendment to the United States Constitution

The United States is the only country in the world that awards citizens the constitutional right "to keep and bear arms." At the same time, international crime statistics compiled by organizations like the United Nations suggest that the United States is a remarkably violent country. Among industrialized nations, the murder rate in the United States is one of the highest: roughly seven times higher than in Australia and Germany, and about ten times higher than in the United Kingdom and Spain, where gun ownership is closely restricted. Could the ease of owning a gun in the United States contribute to this country's high murder rate?

Proponents of gun control frequently cite comparative murder rates in support of tighter restrictions on gun ownership. Such comparisons are less straightforward than they appear to be, however, because the United States differs from Australia, Great Britain, Germany, and Spain in many other ways that have little to do with restrictions on gun ownership. Unmeasured cultural differences, rather than gun ownership per se, may contribute significantly to the differences in national murder rates.

A comparison of the murder rates in Seattle and Vancouver provides better support for the idea that gun control might reduce at least some forms of violence (Sloan et al., 1988). Seattle and Vancouver are close to each other, share the same climate, and are similar in terms of their size and residents' income and education levels. Just as important, they are similar in their burglary and robbery rates. The main difference between the two cities is that Vancouver is located in Canada, where gun ownership is restricted, and Seattle is located in the United States, where guns are easily available. Yet Sloan and colleagues (Sloan et al., 1988) found that the rate of assault with a gun was seven times higher in Seattle than in Vancouver.

Not surprisingly, the risk of becoming a murder victim was also significantly higher in Seattle than in Vancouver. Moreover, the risk of dying from an assault with a handgun was five times higher in Seattle than in Vancouver. Interestingly, homicide rates involving means other than a gun (for example, stabbing or strangulation) were about the same in the two cities. Although this finding seems to run counter to the idea that guns can serve as cues to general aggression, the authors' conclusion that a community's homicide rate may be reduced by restricting access to firearms—especially handguns—appears to be warranted.

than participants who had not been primed with those cues (Anderson, Benjamin, & Bartholow, 1998). To the extent that the sight of guns automatically activates aggressive thoughts, then, the weapons effect represents a hidden influence on behavior.

Guns are omnipresent in the movies and on TV

Media Effects on Aggression

According to some estimates, guns are present in over 40 percent of U.S. households. Even those people who don't own guns may have trouble avoiding them, however, given the prevalence of gun violence in the media. Nearly 100 percent of U.S. households own at least one television set, and 79 percent of children in the United States play video games on a regular basis.

Violence in various forms, gun violence included, has been a mainstay on television for some time. Researchers who conducted the National Television Violence Survey (Wilson et al., 1998) analyzed the amount and content of violence on TV for three consecutive years. They found that:

- 61 percent of TV programs contained some violence, and only 4 percent of programs with violent themes featured an "antiviolence" theme.
- 44 percent of the violent interactions on TV involved perpetrators who had some attractive qualities that were worthy of emulation.
- 43 percent of violent scenes involved humor, either directed at the violence itself or used by characters who were involved with the violence.

- Nearly 75 percent of violent scenes on TV featured no immediate punishment for or condemnation of the violence.
- 40 percent of programs featured "bad" characters who were never or rarely punished for their aggressive acts.

Remarkably, the depiction of violence on TV continues to rise. Consider the following numbers, compiled by the Parents Television Council, based on 400 hours of prime-time programming on six major TV networks during the November ratings sweeps of 1998, 2000, and 2002:

- On all the networks, violence increased in every time slot in the period between 1998 and 2002. The frequency of violence increased 41 percent during the first hour of prime time (8 P.M.–9 P.M.), 134 percent during the second hour of prime time (9 P.M.–10 P.M.), and 63 percent during the third hour (10 P.M.–11 P.M.).
- Fox and UPN were the worst offenders, showing 4.67 and 7.5 instances of violence per hour, respectively. ABC registered the largest increase in violence during the first prime-time hour, from .13 instances per hour to 2.0.

Two examples of videogames containing aggression

- In qualitative terms, violence committed with a gun or other weapons increased during all hours of prime time. At the same time, less lethal forms of violence such as fistfights and martial arts fights declined.
- Violent scenes featuring blood increased in a similar fashion, with a particularly noteworthy increase of 141 percent during the second hour of prime time.

These statistics may provide only a conservative estimate of the amount of violence on TV, because the study was limited to network television programming. If the programming on premium cable or satellite TV channels had been included, the numbers might have been even more dramatic.

In case you're wondering, foregoing the TV for an outing to the multiplex doesn't necessarily provide a safe haven from exposure to violence. Although the rating system devised by the Motion Picture Association of America allows individuals to regulate their exposure to violent content, an increase in gun violence depicted in PG-13 movies puts teenagers at an increasing risk of getting more violence than they bargained for. When the rating was first introduced in 1985, PG-13 movies had virtually no scenes depicting gun violence. However, since then, the number has been rising, and by 2012, movies rated PG-13 depicted more gun violence than R-rated movies (Bushman, Jamieson, Weitz, & Romer, 2013).

What appears to be true of TV and the movies seems to hold for video games as well. Ever since 1972, when Nolan Bushnell started selling a simple ping-pong game that could be played on a console hooked up to a black-and-white TV, the video game industry has been increasingly dominated by games with high levels of graphic violence. Numerous Internet-based games offer levels of violence and gore that make commercially available video games like *Resident Evil* and *Kill Zone* look tame by comparison.

Evidence for Media Effects on Aggression

How does prolonged and repeated exposure to violent media affect viewers? Consider the following example: A little over six years before Adam Lanza created the bloodbath at Sandy Hook Elementary School in Newtown, Connecticut, 25-year-old Kimveer Gill parked his car, retrieved a gun from the trunk, and entered the campus of Dawson College in Montreal, where he opened fire on the students, first on the lawn and later in the cafeteria. His rampage lasted only three minutes, but by the time Gill put the gun to his own head and ended his life, 19 students had been injured. One of them, 18- year-old Anastasia De Sousa, later succumbed to her injuries.

What makes Gill's case unique is the seeming absence of a motive for the shootings. When Marc Lepine killed 14 female students at the Ecole Polytechnique in Montreal 17 years earlier, he apparently did so to get even with the feminists he blamed for his failure to get into the school. When Dylan Klebold and Eric Harris shot teachers and classmates at Columbine High School in April 1999, they did so to get even with those who had teased, ostracized, and bullied them. Gill had no such motive. In fact, he had no association with Dawson College. He was a young man who, according to one of his Internet postings, hated everything and everyone, but nothing and no one in particular. Gill did, however, have one thing in common with Klebold and Davis. In one of his Internet postings, he indicated that he was fond of *Super Columbine Massacre*, an Internet-based game that allows users to reenact the shootings at Columbine.

Concerns over the harmful effects of media violence predate the Dawson College shootings by more than five decades. As early as 1952, the U.S. House of Representatives held hearings to explore the impact of television violence on viewers. In 1972, the Surgeon General of the United States, after reviewing existing studies, concluded in his Report on Television and Social Behavior that television violence did indeed contribute to increases in violent crimes and antisocial behavior. The 2001 Surgeon General's Report on Youth Violence, ordered by President Clinton in the wake of the Columbine High School shooting, echoed that theme.

Evidence for the link between aggression and exposure to media violence does not rest entirely on anecdotes. The results of over 1,000 studies conducted over four decades suggest that concern about the effects of media violence rests on solid empirical ground. Research on the link falls into three broad categories. *Experimental studies* generally expose participants to a brief presentation of violent behavior on TV and then measure its immediate effects on their aggressive behavior (for example, Meyer, 1972) and aggressive thoughts or emotions (for example, Huesmann & Guerra, 1997). *Cross-sectional surveys* focus on establishing a link between the current level of aggressiveness of participants (typically children) and the amount of violence they watch regularly (see the review by Bushman & Huesmann, 2000). Finally, *longitudinal studies* (for example, Lefkowitz et al., 1977) trace participants over the long term, looking for a link between exposure to media violence in their early childhood and physical and verbal aggression (through peer assessments) later in their lives.

Paik and Comstock (1994) conducted a meta-analysis of the effects reported by laboratory studies and cross-sectional studies conducted between 1957 and 1990. As defined by Glass (2006), a **meta-analysis** is an "analysis of analyses" of individual studies, for the purpose of integrating the results. Using this method, researchers typically identify relevant studies, describe their characteristics, and then calculate the average size or magnitude of the reported effects across all studies. One way to look at the effect size is as a correlation coefficient, which can range from -1 (indicating a perfect inverse relationship) to 0 (indicating no relationship) to +1 (indicating a perfect positive relationship). Paik and Comstock's (1994) analysis reveals a moderate-to-large effect of media violence in experimental studies, with correlation coefficients of .37 for the relationship between exposure to media violence and all forms of aggression and .32 for the relationship between exposure to media violence and physical aggression alone. In cross-sectional studies, the same effects were small to moderate, but still significant (correlations of .19 and .20, respectively). The difference in the size of the effects seen in experimental and cross-sectional studies is hardly surprising, given that the latter lack the controls typical of experimental research. A more recent meta-analysis (Anderson & Bushman, 2001) shows a similar pattern of results.

The results of longitudinal studies complete the picture. Lefkowitz et al. (1977) showed a significant correlation between the amount of exposure to media violence at age eight and aggressive behavior a decade later for boys, but not for girls. This curious relationship is not confined to the United States. Huesmann and Eron (1986) looked at exposure to media violence and aggression in five countries over a three-year period and found similar results. In contrast to Lefkowitz et al. (1977), however, they reported a significant correlation for both boys *and* girls—but only in the United States.

Recent research designed to study the effects of playing violent video games adds to the picture in disturbing ways. Simply interacting with an aggressive virtual character for a short time decreases trust and cooperation in a subsequent game with a real other (Rothmund, Gollwitzer, & Klimmt, 2011). These effects are relatively benign, considering a longitudinal study of 295 German adolescents (Möller & Krahé, 2008). The study showed that playing violent games influenced levels of physical aggression 30 months later by way of an increased endorsement of aggressive norms and a higher prevalence of the hostile attribution bias. Barlett, Harris, & Bruey (2007) demonstrated that games with high levels of bloodshed increased the levels of hostility and arousal in those who played them. Finally, a recent meta-analysis of 136 studies from around the globe (Anderson et al., 2010) concluded that exposure to violent video games is a causal risk factor for increased aggressive behavior, aggressive thought, and aggressive affect and for decreased empathy and prosocial behavior. Moreover, the analysis uncovered little in the way of cultural or gender differences for the deleterious effects of violent video games!

The precise mechanisms by which playing video games high in violence content increases aggressive behavior are presently not well understood. Although a decrease in empathy would seem like a plausible candidate, the results across studies show a mixed bag of evidence, at best (Vachon, Lynam, & Johnson, 2013). However, recent research (Greitemeyer, 2014) suggests that causing injury and death to a fellow player makes everyday aggressive behavior such as shouting at or shoving others seem innocuous by comparison.

Arguments against Media Effects on Aggression

Although most social psychologists would agree that there is solid—perhaps overwhelming—evidence that exposure to media violence is related to increased aggression and violence, much of the public is skeptical. In light of the increases in violence shown on television between 1998 and 2002, those who are responsible for TV programming seem to concur. This skepticism is based on three different arguments.

One frequently heard argument is that watching violent TV may be cathartic for viewers. This argument follows from Freud's (1920) speculations about the *Thanatos*, the drive that compels humans toward self-destruction (discussed earlier in this chapter). Recall that according to Freud, aggressing against others is essentially a defense mechanism that allows people to avoid aggressing against the self. Of course, most cultures prohibit aggressing against others, which poses a problem for the *Thanatos*. Freud thought that through **catharsis**, people can substitute vicarious aggression for actual aggression. In other words, they can meet their aggressive drives without harming the self or others, simply by watching the clash of gladiators, a Shakespearean tragedy, a violent TV show, or playing a game of *Mortal Kombat*. As with many of Freud's ideas, there is virtually no empirical evidence to suggest that catharsis really works. Of all the studies conducted over the past 40 years, fewer than 10 percent show a *decrease* in aggression as a result of watching violent media (Anderson & Bushman, 2001; Paik & Comstock, 1994).

A second set of arguments concerns the methodology commonly used in social psychological research on aggression and media violence: specifically, the artificiality of the social psychological laboratory. By their very nature, experiments allow causal inferences about the effects of an independent variable on a dependent variable. But does an experiment in which participants watch a short, violent video or play a violent video game and then complete a measure of their level of aggression really tell us about the results of exposure to media violence in the real world? Similarly, cross-sectional research, although much less artificial than experimental research, is often—and rightly—criticized as showing correlations, rather than causality. However, the mantra "Correlation does not imply causation" rings a bit hollow when the findings of correlational studies converge with those from experimental research. The point is, though one can criticize both methodologies, their relative weaknesses tend to cancel each other out. What matters is the extent to which their findings converge.

A third set of arguments has to do with the sizes of the effects in the studies analyzed by Paik and Comstock (1994) and Anderson and Bushman (2001). A correlation of .37 may seem puny compared to the theoretical high of 1.0. If we compare the size of the effects obtained in studies of media violence and aggression with those obtained in other types of research, however, the results seem much more impressive. According to Bushman and Huesmann (2001), the average size of the effect in studies of the relationship between media violence and aggression is only slightly smaller than the size of the effect in research on the relationship between smoking and lung cancer. It is considerably *higher* than the size of the effects in research on the relationships between:

—calcium intake and bone mass
—passive smoking in the workplace and lung cancer
—exposure to asbestos and cancer of the larynx
—homework and academic achievement

Oddly enough, few people would doubt that taking calcium strengthens bones, and smoking is now prohibited in many public places because of the health risks posed by passive smoking. On the face of it, then, curbing violence in the media would seem to be a sound public health policy.

How to do so is another matter, though. Censorship is hardly a viable solution, because it would deprive those who broadcast violent images of their First Amendment rights. It would also deprive consumers of their right to watch what they want to watch. What about ratings based on content and age, as well as warning labels indicating violent or restricted programming? They are a double-edged sword, because they can also elevate a program, video, or game to the status of forbidden fruit, becoming an enticement rather than a deterrent (Bushman & Cantor, 2003). Perhaps the best solution would be a combination of self-imposed restrictions by the media, technology that allows viewers to control what they see, and public health campaigns that raise awareness of the potentially harmful effects of media violence.

The call for such measures seems further warranted because of some other hidden influences of media violence that go beyond increased aggression and violence. There is evidence to suggest that extensive exposure to TV violence may produce a "mean world syndrome" (Gerbner et al., 1994), which leads viewers to overestimate their own risk of victimization. Because the media construct a version of social reality in which violence is commonplace and frequently rewarded, they cultivate a view of the world as far more dangerous than it is. Viewers can come to see the world as a place to be feared and distrusted. As a result, they may become more likely to arm themselves and respond to perceived threats in an aggressive fashion (Nabi & Sullivan, 2001). Of course, in doing so, they contribute to the culture of violence.

Desensitization to the effects of real violence is another important hidden influence of prolonged exposure to media violence (Smith & Donnerstein, 1998). Just like real violence, media violence at first produces fear and disgust in viewers (Cantor, 1998), but repeated exposure produces emotional states that are compatible with

SOCIAL PSYCHOLOGY AND HEALTH: PLAYING VIOLENT VIDEO GAMES MAY ALTER YOUR BRAIN

Although media violence may disgust us at first, repeated exposure to it reduces its psychological impact and diminishes the intensity of our emotional reactions (Geen, 1981). In essence, we become desensitized to it.

To examine the brain activity behind this type of desensitization, Bartholow, Bushman, and Sestir (2006) asked male participants to list their five favorite video games and indicate how often they played each, and how violent it was. Relatively high scores on this measure indicated that an individual was a *violent game player*, who spent a lot of time playing violent games. Relatively low scores indicated that an individual was a *nonviolent game player*, who either played violent games infrequently or played primarily nonviolent games.

All participants then completed a reaction time task, which they believed was a game in which they were competing against another player. They were told that on any given trial, the faster player could aggress against the slower player by delivering a blast of noise of varying intensity and duration through the headphones the player wore. In reality, participants did not compete against a partner. Instead, a computer controlled their wins and losses so that they always lost on the first trial, as well as about half the remaining trials, in random fashion. The computer also varied the intensity and duration of the noise blasts delivered by the "partners" in randomized fashion.

Not surprisingly, given earlier research on media violence and aggression, participants identified as violent video game players attempted to deliver more aggressive noise blasts than nonviolent video game players. To find out if their increased aggression was related to desensitization, researchers later showed the participants several images that varied in the degree and type of violence shown. *Neutral images* included pictures of a man on a bicycle, a towel on a table, and a mushroom. *Violent images* included pictures of a man holding a gun to another man's head and a man holding a knife to a woman's throat. Negative nonviolent images included pictures of a baby with a large tumor on her face and a skinhead standing in front of a Nazi flag. Participants viewed the images while wearing a cap wired with electrodes that recorded their electroencephalographic activity (EEG).

The researchers were particularly interested in the P300 component of the participants' event-related brain potential, because it is generally implicated in the processing of emotionally relevant stimuli (e.g., Cacioppo et al., 1993). The amplitude of the P300 component provides an indication of how much processing an emotion-eliciting stimulus receives. Large P300 amplitudes indicate a high level of processing, and thus a strong emotional response; small P300 amplitudes indicate relatively little processing, and thus a more muted emotional response.

To the extent that violent video game players have become desensitized to violence, their P300 amplitudes in response to viewing *violent images* should be smaller than those of nonviolent video game players viewing the same images. That is exactly what researchers found. As one would expect, the observed differences between the two types of video game players were limited to violent images; there were no differences in response to neutral and negative nonviolent images. Moreover, the P300 amplitudes elicited by the violent images were inversely related to aggression in the competitive reaction time task. Small amplitudes indicative of desensitization were associated with high levels of aggression; large amplitudes indicative of a more normal reaction to violence were associated with lower levels of aggression.

In sum, this study linked exposure to violent video games to a reduction in the brain activity related to the processing of emotional stimuli. Furthermore, it linked that reduced brain activity to increased aggression. Playing violent video games, in other words, may have profound and disturbing long-term consequences for a person's behavior.

aggression (Linz, Donnerstein, & Adams, 1989). At the same time, prolonged exposure reduces normal inhibitions against aggression, making individuals less responsive to the pain and suffering endured by real victims of violence (Funk et al., 2004). There is reason to believe that desensitization can change the brain function of heavy users of violent video games. The Social Psychology and Health box on **pages 624-625** examine the relationship between the two.

Pornography and Aggression

In Francis Ford Coppola's movie, *Apocalypse Now*, set during the Vietnam War, the renegade Colonel Kurtz laments that although the military allows pilots to drop bombs that can kill hundreds of civilians at a time, it doesn't allow them to write "Fuck" on the airplane's fuselage. His remarks are a poignant commentary on the way our culture views violence and sex. Flip through the TV channels any time after 8 p.m., and within minutes you will be inundated with images of violence. You will not see nudity or explicit sex, however. The imbalance in content arises from an uneven application of the Television Code, a voluntary code of conduct in which broadcasters pledge to show the "highest standards of respect for the American home."

Whether the results are intentional or not, the way the Television Code has been applied reflects how our culture conceives of the potentially detrimental effects of violence and pornography. Judging by what is on television and what is not, Americans seem to think that the consequences of viewing pornography are far more serious than the consequences of viewing violence. Are they?

The answer depends to some extent on how we define pornography. Defined broadly, pornography includes everything from nudity to violent and coercive sex. As such, the scientific evidence on the effects of pornography is mixed. Some studies have shown increases in aggression against both men and women after participants

SOCIAL PSYCHOLOGY ENCOUNTERS THE DARK SIDE: THE BEHAVIORAL AND ATTITUDINAL EFFECTS OF VIOLENT PORNOGRAPHY

Many studies of the effects of violent pornography on aggression examine those effects in terms of male aggression against another male or female in response to an insult or a provocation. One early study suggests that a provocation followed by a viewing of violent pornography leads to aggression primarily when it comes from another man (Donnerstein & Barrett, 1978). However, evidence from later studies indicates that violent pornography figures prominently in male-to-female aggression as well (Linz, Donnerstein, & Penrod, 1987).

In one such experiment (Donnerstein & Berkowitz, 1981), male participants were insulted by either a male or female confederate before watching one of four videos: (1) a documentary; (2) erotica involving consensual sex; (3) a movie showing nonsexual violence; or (4) a movie showing a woman being raped at gunpoint. All participants then had the opportunity to retaliate against the person who had insulted them by delivering electric shocks of varying intensity. As expected, the only experimental condition in which male subjects shocked the female confederate more than the male confederate was the one in which participants had watched the rape movie. Watching a violent movie that did not show sex led to increases in aggression against both male and female confederates. Interestingly, participants who had watched the erotic movie shocked the female confederate less than the male confederate.

Although in this study, the viewing of pornography promoted aggression, or retaliation, in response to an *insult*, one study (Donnerstein, 1980) showed that men aggressed against a woman more intensely after watching violent pornography than after watching erotica, even in the absence of an insult or attack.

Violent pornography that perpetuates the **rape myth** (Burt, 1980) may be particularly dangerous, because in addition to increasing aggression, it may affect men's attitudes toward women. The rape myth is the erroneous belief that women may at first resist being raped, but eventually become sexually aroused and begin to enjoy the forced sex. It is in stark contrast with the fact that rape is, in reality, a traumatic experience for women and that coercive sex of any kind is an assault that is treated as such by police. Watching a rape myth movie increases aggression against women more than all other types of violent pornography (Donnerstein & Berkowitz, 1981). Moreover, men who watched several rape myth movies were more likely to endorse the belief that women who get raped deserve it, as well as to endorse leniency in the penalties rapists receive (Linz, Donnerstein, & Penrod, 1984). Even a single exposure to a movie based on the rape myth (Sam Peckinpah's *The Getaway*) led male participants to adopt more callous attitudes toward men hurting women (Malamuth & Check, 1981). These studies suggest that men who view violent pornography may come to accept violence against women as legitimate.

view pornography (for example, Zillmann et al., 1981). Other studies (for example, Baron 1978) have shown a decrease in aggression.

To make sense of these conflicting findings, it is helpful to distinguish between *erotica* and *violent pornography*. **Erotica** includes depictions of nudity and of consenting adults engaging in enjoyable sex. **Violent pornography** encompasses depictions of coercive sex, which generally requires women to engage in humiliating and degrading

SOCIAL PSYCHOLOGY ENCOUNTERS THE BRIGHT SIDE: THE POTENTIAL AND REAL BENEFITS OF EROTICA

When actress Brooke Shields proclaimed –at the tender age of 15- that nothing would get between her and her Calvins, most people who saw the commercial thought of her as an attractive woman who wasn't wearing panties. Of course, that image dissipated quickly once Shields made it clear that she was talking about a new line of underwear from the maker of her jeans. Cynics were quick to point out that Shields's Calvin Klein commercial was just more proof that sex sells. And it does. Sex sells whenever the positive feelings it produces become associated with a product.

To the extent that sexual images can produce positive feelings, they create an emotional state that is incompatible with aggression. As a result, some erotica may actually reduce aggression. Evidence for this effect comes from a series of studies by Baron (1974, 1978, 1983). In an early demonstration of the aggression-reducing potential of erotica, male participants were angered by a male confederate. They then viewed either nonerotic photographs of scenery or furniture or erotic photographs of nude and seminude women in sexually suggestive poses. All participants then had a chance to retaliate against the confederate by delivering electric shocks. As expected, the men who had viewed the erotic photographs shocked the confederate less often than the men who had seen the relatively neutral pictures, presumably because the erotic images had produced feelings that were incompatible with aggression. Asking male participants to view sexually explicit cartoons had a similar effect (Baron, 1978).

In an ingenious field study, researchers looked to the real world for emotional responses that are in-compatible with aggression (Baron, 1983). A male motorist who was a confederate of the experimenters blocked other motorists at a traffic light by failing to drive away when the light turned green. Just before that, while the light was still red, a female confederate crossed the street. Depending on the condition of the experiment, the female confederate (1) wore a business suit; (2) hobbled across the street on crutches; (3) wore a clown suit; or (4) wore next to nothing. In a control condition, the confederate did not cross the street before the light turned green.

As one might expect, a full 90 percent of motorists honked their horns in the control condition, as well as when the woman crossed the street wearing a business suit. However, honking was drastically reduced when she crossed the street on crutches, wearing a clown suit, or wearing very little. In all likelihood, the feelings elicited by seeing someone on crutches, wearing a clown suit, or wearing next to nothing are quite different. They do have one thing in common, however: all are positive feelings that are incompatible with aggression.

Of course, partial nudity is a far cry from watching people enjoy consensual sex. Nevertheless, erotic scenes may also reduce aggression because they may distract men from being insulted and because they may remind men of caring and tender lovemaking, an activity that is incompatible with aggression (Baron, 1983).

sex acts. These two types of pornography have very different effects on aggression. The Social Psychology Encounters the Dark Side box on **page 626-627** explores the detrimental effects of violent pornography.

Our encounter with the dark side of pornography suggests that by itself, viewing erotic images does not increase aggression against women. Of course, this is perhaps best understood as a relative benefit. In fact, the experiment described in the Dark Side of Social Psychology (Donnerstein, 1981) shows that men aggressed less against a woman than against another man after watching erotica. Could viewing erotic images have beneficial effects? The Social Psychology Encounters the Bright Side box on **pages 627-628** explore that issue.

The legendary head butt that led to Zinedine Zidane's ejection from the 2006 Soccer World Cup final, preserved in bronze

Cultures of Honor and Aggression

French soccer star Zinedine Zidane came out of retirement for the 2006 World Cup. His inspired play helped the French National Team to reach the championship game against Italy. In the closing minutes, with the score tied at zero-zero and the game in overtime, Zidane head-butted Italian defender Marco Materazzi in the chest. For this inexplicably violent action, Zidane was ejected from the game, putting an ugly end to his storied career. France lost the game in a penalty kick shootout.

What compelled Zidane to undermine his reputation, his legacy, and his team's chances of winning the World Cup? He and Materazzi had tangled through much of the overtime period, exchanging words more than once. Materazzi said he offered only the usual kind of insult players toss around during competitive soccer games. However, Zidane, the son of Algerian immigrants, thought Materazzi had insulted his mother and sister, forcing him to defend their honor. Later that summer, Materazzi admitted to making a sexual innuendo concerning Zidane's sister. Whatever his exact words, they were less important than Zidane's perception that a member of his family had been dishonored. Because Zidane had been raised in a **culture of honor** in Algeria known as *nif*, defending the honor of a family member mattered more to him than the chance that his team might lose the World Cup.

Cultures of honor exist around the world. Researchers (Rodriguez Mosquera, Manstead, & Fisher, 2000) have tied the concept of honor, which appears to be related to *machismo*, to violence among the Spanish. Machismo is a code of honor that stresses pride in a man's virility. It is important not just in Spain, but in the

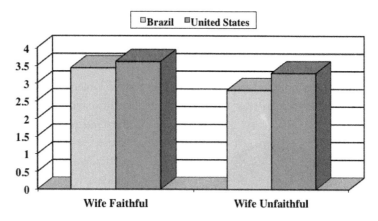

Figure 13.5: Ratings of husband's masculinity as a result of wife's fidelity

Source: Vandello, J. A., & Cohen, D. (2003). Male honor and female fidelity: Implicit cultural scripts that perpetuate domestic violence. *Journal of Personality and Social Psychology, 84,* 997–1010.

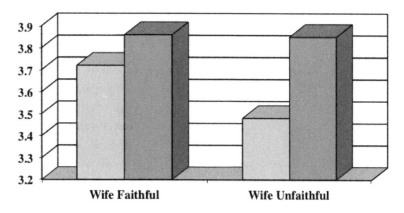

Figure 13.6: Ratings of husband's character as a result of wife's fidelity

Source: Vandello, J. A., & Cohen, D. (2003). Male honor and female fidelity: Implicit cultural scripts that perpetuate domestic violence. *Journal of Personality and Social Psychology, 84,* 997–1010.

Hispanic cultures of Latin America, which are characterized by traditional gender roles, strong family ties, and patriarchy (Delgado et al., 1997). Latin Americans place a heavy emphasis on virility and respect for the family.

How do members of such cultures respond to dishonor? To find out, Vandello and Cohen (2003) presented students from Brazil and the United States with scenarios in which a man's wife had been either faithful or unfaithful to him. They then asked the students to rate how the woman's fidelity or infidelity reflected on the *husband's* masculinity and good character. **Figures 13.5** and **13.6** show the results of these measures.

Participants from Brazil and the United States differed markedly in their ratings of the husband. Although both groups thought the woman's affair reflected negatively on the husband's manliness, Brazilian participants felt so to a greater extent than U.S. participants (**Figure 13.5**). Though U.S. participants did not think that the woman's affair had implications for the husband's character, Brazilian participants rated him significantly lower on that dimension (**Figure 13.6**).

Are such perceptual differences reflected in people's attitudes toward violence? To answer this question, the researchers presented participants with another scenario in which the husband either yelled at his wife to stop

A strong cultural emphasis on honor increases the likelihood that an insult will be met with aggression

the affair or yelled at her, slapped her hard across the face, and pushed her around. All participants felt that the husband who used violence was less justified than the husband who merely yelled. U.S. participants saw yelling as more justified than the Brazilians, whereas the Brazilians saw violence as more justified than the U.S. participants.

As it happens, we do not need to go to a foreign country to find cultures of honor. Nisbett (1993) has argued that in the United States, the South, and to some extent the West, are characterized by a culture of honor. He bases his argument on the observation that in the South, the murder rate among white males is significantly higher than it is in the North, especially in rural areas. In general, Southerners do not endorse violence any more than Northerners, but they are more accepting of violence that is committed in response to insults and provocation. Perhaps as a result, homicide rates in the rural South are triple those of the rural North (Nisbett & Cohen, 1996).

Nisbett and colleagues (Nisbett, 1993; Nisbett & Cohen, 1996; Cohen & Nisbett, 1997) trace the roots of the Southern culture of honor to a unique form of agricultural production. Whereas the Northern Great Plains were conducive to planting crops, the hilly South lent itself to raising cattle. Unlike corn and wheat, cows and sheep could be rustled away with relative ease, dealing a devastating blow to a man's wealth. In such a culture, in which citizens could depend only on themselves for protection, harsh retaliation to insults and challenges became imperative, especially for those with relatively low socioeconomic status (Henry, 2009). As it exists today, the Southern culture of honor is a legacy left over from the time when people had to raise cattle for a living in an often lawless environment.

Several other studies suggest that the Southern culture of honor is alive and well. At the University of Michigan, Cohen et al. (1996) compared how students from the North and South reacted to an obvious provocation. As male participants were walking down a narrow hallway on their way to an experiment, a male confederate of the experimenters bumped into them and called them an asshole to their faces. As expected, Northerners and Southerners responded much differently. Although the experimenters did not measure the participants' aggression directly, for obvious ethical reasons, they used several proxies to measure the participants' readiness for aggression. Compared to Northerners, Southerners were more likely to think that the incident had threatened their masculinity. They also had higher testosterone levels, suggesting that they were physiologically primed for aggression. Southerners were more upset, and more likely to reassert their dominance, when a second confederate challenged them.

The Southern culture of honor may also be reflected in a higher tolerance for violence in a man's past. Cohen and Nisbett (1997) sent job inquiries to 921 businesses in the North, South, and West. All the businesses belonged to national chains, and all the letters came from a purportedly qualified, hard-working applicant who had once broken the law. The letters were identical, except for an explanation of the conviction at the end. In

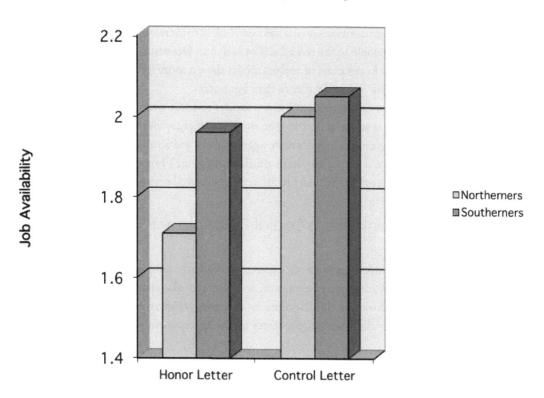

Figure 13.4: Willingness to Respond to a Job Inquiry from Applicants Convicted of Manslaughter (Honor Letter) or Car Theft (Control Letter)

Source: Cohen, D., & Nisbett, R. E. (1997). Field experiments examining the culture of honor: The role of institutions in perpetuating norms about violence. *Personality and Social Psychology Bulletin, 23*, 1188–1199.

the *honor letter*, the applicant explained that he had been convicted of manslaughter after killing a romantic rival, who had laughed at him and challenged him to a fight. In the *control letter*, the applicant explained that he had been convicted of motor vehicle theft after stealing cars to support his family. The researchers tracked the number of employers who sent an application packet or suggested the name of a person to contact. They also rated employers' responses in terms of how sympathetic they were to the applicant.

As shown in **Figure 13.4**, Northern and Southern employers did not differ in the extent to which they responded to the inquiry from the convicted car thief. The tone of their responses was equally sympathetic or unsympathetic. Compared to Northern employers, however, Southern employers were more willing to respond to the convicted killer in the first place, and their responses showed a higher degree of sympathy and forgiveness. Although most people think of killing someone as a more severe offense than stealing a car, the fact that the applicant had killed in defense of his honor appears to have rendered him more attractive than the car thief, at least to Southerners.

Aggression—The Culture: A Summary

Our culture promotes violence in numerous ways. Unrestricted access to guns makes it more likely that they will be used, and their mere presence can serve as a cue to aggression. Violence also permeates the media, including television and video games. Exposure to violent media has been linked to increases in aggression, in part because these games and films desensitize people to the real effects of violence. Desensitization manifests itself through lasting changes in the brain, so that heavy users of violent media show a more muted neural response—indicative of a negative emotional response—to real violence than light users.

Violent pornography has effects on aggression that are similar to those produced by other violent media. Moreover, violent pornography that is based on the rape myth encourages viewers to adopt more callous attitudes toward women. Conversely, erotica can decrease aggression by inducing feelings that are incompatible with aggression. Cultures that place a strong emphasis on defending one's honor promote argument- related aggression, in large part because they alter the interpretation of a perceived provocation.

Think Like a Social Psychologist

Making connections
—Much of the research that links aggression to exposure to violent media has been conducted with children. Does that imply that adults may be immune to the effects of violent media? Could an adult who never saw a violent TV show as a child become more aggressive as a result of repeated exposure to violent media? If so, what social-cognitive processes might be responsible?

Confronting social issues
—What role could the federal government play in making television programming less violent? To the extent that censorship is not an option, could the government influence broadcasters in the same way that it influences automobile makers to improve gas mileage and reduce emissions?

Designing research
—Social psychologists generally frown on the use of scenarios in experiments, primarily because they often elicit what participants think they should do rather than what they might actually do in

response to a real situation. What about the scenario in Vandello and Cohen's (2003) study rendered it a useful tool for their research?

Thinking critically

—The account of the origins of the Southern culture of honor, which revolves around a history of cattle raising, does not explain the culture of honor that exists among urban gangs, in which "dissing" is considered an attack on their honor. What variables may underlie the cultures of honor that are found in such settings? Can you think of a set of variables that could explain the cultures of honor in both the rural South and urban settings?

THE SOCIAL COGNITION OF AGGRESSION

Time to Act

As the evening wore on, the walls of Brian's apartment seemed to be closing in on him. Watching *The Texas Chainsaw Massacre* and playing *Grand Theft Auto 2* distracted him for a while, but he didn't enjoy them as much as he had in the past. To make matters worse, it was only 10 p.m.—too early to go to bed hoping that he would wake up to find that the day's events had been nothing more than a nightmare. Brian checked his pockets for his car keys, grabbed the last cold beer from the refrigerator, and got into his car. He wasn't sure where he was going, but he needed to keep moving. He soon found himself passing places that reminded him of his lost relationship with Suzie—the multiplex near the mall, the now dark and strangely quiet coffee shop, even the university campus, where students were still playing Frisbee under the lights. Seeing it all instilled a profound loneliness in him.

Hoping that he might be able to fix things if he could just talk to Suzie, Brian turned in the direction of her apartment. Pulling into a parking spot across the street, he noticed that the lights in her apartment were still on. Maybe she would agree to see him if he called and told her he was outside, he thought. As he reached for his cell phone, Brian saw something he had almost expected to see, but for which he was ill prepared: He had pulled in right behind Eric's pickup. Eric must be upstairs with Suzie, and the very thought of it made his blood boil. He was going to teach Eric a lesson!

To this point, we have been examining the role of the person and the situation in aggression. Heat, alcohol consumption, testosterone and serotonin levels, the sight of a gun, media violence, codes of honor—all are *related* to aggression. Yet, by themselves, none of these variables *cause* aggression. The extent to which they and other variables produce aggression depends in large part on a complex interplay between cognition and emotion. We will conclude this chapter with a brief review of four theories of how people's conscious and unconscious thoughts and feelings interact to produce aggression.

The Frustration-Aggression Hypothesis

One of the earliest social psychological theories of aggression downplayed the importance of emotion. According to the **frustration-aggression hypothesis** (Dollard et al., 1939), all aggression results from frustration. That is, whenever our path toward achieving a goal is blocked, we feel frustrated and are likely to react with aggression. This simple hypothesis helps to explain Brian's urge to aggress against Eric, whose arrival on the scene

Frustration arising from difficult life conditions, including poverty and injustice, can lead to scapegoating of an ethnic group (such as these Bosnian refugees in 1999) that is then targeted for extermination

had thwarted Brian's attempt to live happily ever after with Suzie. It also explains why a caller who has spent a considerable amount of time on hold is particularly likely to yell at a customer service representative.

The frustration-aggression hypothesis has garnered a fair amount of support over the years. In a classic study (Barker, Dembo, & Lewin, 1941), children who had to wait for a long time to play with toys that were placed in full view played with them more roughly than children who got to play with them right away. On a collective level, Staub (1992, 2002) has linksed genocide and mass killings to the frustration that arises from difficult life conditions. Such conditions promote *scapegoating*, a tendency to blame a particular ethnic group for existing conditions. We will discuss scapegoating in detail in Chapter 14.

A field experiment (Harris, 1974), in which a confederate cut in line while people were waiting to buy movie tickets, pay for groceries, or get a table at a restaurant, further suggests that aggression increases with frustration. The unwitting participants were more verbally aggressive when the intruder cut in as they stood second in line than when they stood 12th in line. Evidently, frustration was stronger when the participants were closer to achieving their goal, leading them to show more aggression. Again, similar observations have been made on a collective level. In studying the specific locations of the race riots of the 1960s, Spilerman (1970) found that they did not occur in places where conditions for African Americans were the worst. Rather, they happened in places where African Americans had made some progress toward improving their living conditions. Their relative closeness to their goal may have left them particularly frustrated by setbacks such as the assassination of the Reverend Martin Luther King Jr.

Despite its promise and the empirical support it received, the frustration- aggression hypothesis has been challenged. One important criticism is a logical one. In its original formulation, frustration is considered both necessary and sufficient to cause aggression. In other words, all frustration leads to aggression, and all aggression results from frustration. This proposition turned out to be false, however (Miller, 1941). Frustration does not always and necessarily lead to aggression, and aggression can arise from several different sources, frustration being one of them.

Whether or not frustration leads to aggression may depend on the presence or absence of additional conditions that facilitate or inhibit aggression. For example, attributions may matter (Baron & Richardson, 1994). If we are thwarted in achieving our goal by another's action, dispositional attributions will probably make us feel more frustrated (and consequently more prone to aggression) than situational attributions. For example, you will probably feel more frustrated if you conclude that your professor's refusal to change your low grade is due to her mean disposition than if you conclude that she is prevented from doing so because of a university policy.

Frustration may also lead to aggression because of the negative feelings it produces. From this perspective, frustration acts very much like insults and uncomfortable temperatures. That is, it is merely one of many experiences that can produce negative feelings, starting a causal chain whose endpoint may or may not be aggression (Berkowitz, 1989). The next theory we will look at stresses the cognitive processes that operate as the causal chain unwinds.

Being unable to engage in controlled processing increases the likelihood that we will respond to an insult with aggression

Cognitive Neoassociation Theory

Cognitive neoassociation theory (Berkowitz, 1990, 1993) provides a comprehensive framework through which to understand how aversive events may ultimately produce aggression. According to this theory, the unpleasant feelings induced by aversive events like frustration, excessive heat, and insults are fairly rudimentary. They may lead to anger or fear, and can also trigger thoughts, memories, and physiological responses associated with the fight-or-flight impulse. Whether we respond aggressively to an aversive situation depends on the outcomes of both automatic and controlled cognitive processes.

Aggressive thoughts, emotions, and behavioral tendencies are linked together in memory. The links between concepts that have similar meanings (for example, hurt and harm) are particularly strong, as they are between concepts that are frequently activated together (say, gun and shooting). Exposure to a weapon or to violent media automatically primes aggressive thoughts by activating these existing memory links, thus serving as a hidden influence on our behavior (Anderson, Benjamin, & Bartholow, 1998; Bushman, 1998). Such hidden influences can be offset when we are motivated to engage in more controlled, higher-order processing. Deliberately thinking about how we feel, making causal attributions for why we feel the way we do, and considering the consequences of acting on our feelings ultimately leads to more complex and differentiated feelings of anger or fear.

Negative feelings that have become more differentiated as a result of appraisals and attributions do not necessarily reduce the tendency toward aggression, however. Differentiated anger or fear can both attenuate and exacerbate aggression. For example, Brian may be less prone to aggress against Eric after learning that he was once a linebacker on the college football team. On the other hand, he may be more likely to aggress against Eric if a careful inspection of his feelings suggests that his anger is indeed justified. Moreover, his resulting tendency toward aggression may be further exacerbated by the ease with which he can retrieve relevant scripts to guide his behavior.

A. BACALL

"We'll start with a menu and a glass of water."

Because scripts form unitary concepts in memory, they allow us to infer the sequence of events that unfolds for activities like eating in a restaurant

Script Theory

Script theory expands on social learning theory (Bandura, 1977; Mischel, 1973) by specifying what people learn from watching violent media. Scripts are cognitive representations that define situations and guide behavior by supplying highly associated concepts in memory, including causal links, goals, and action plans (Schank & Abelson, 1977). Because the items in a script are strongly linked to one another, scripts become unitary concepts in memory. That's why most people who learn that a person entered a restaurant and paid for the check infer automatically that he also ate a meal there. Although the story is incomplete, the "restaurant script" fills in the details of what happened between two events.

The example of the restaurant script suggests that scripts are easily learned because of their sequential nature.

Additional rehearsal only strengthens the links between the items in a script and may create additional links to other concepts in memory. If nothing else, those additional links increase the number of paths through which a script can be activated, further strengthening the memory links. Huesmann (1986, 1998) suggested that children in particular learn aggressive scripts from the media.

Watching thousands of television shows in which guns are used to settle a dispute likely results in the acquisition of a highly accessible script that generalizes across many different situations, especially among children. By the time children reach adulthood, the script may have become chronically accessible, providing a mental blueprint of how to respond to situations marked by provocation, frustration, and the like. This observation helps to explain the relative stability of aggression over the life cycle, mentioned earlier in this chapter.

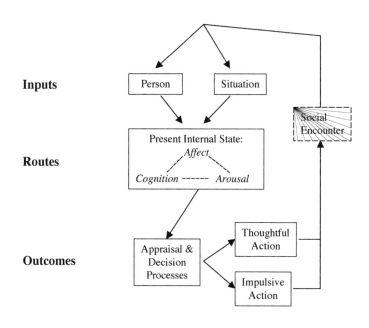

Figure 13.7: The General Aggression Model

Source: Anderson, C. A., & Bushman, B. J. (2002). Human aggression. *Annual Review of Psychology*, 53, 27–51.

The General Aggression Model (GAM)

Although it was first proposed to account primarily for the effects of heat on aggression (Anderson, 1989), the **general aggression model (GAM)** has since been expanded to integrate theories of aggression that consider other variables (Anderson & Bushman, 2002). This model focuses on a single event or episode related to a person who is engaged in an ongoing social interaction. To explain whether the episode will be marked by aggression, we must consider (1) *inputs* from the person and the situation; (2) the affective and cognitive *routes* through which those inputs have their effects; and (3) the *outcomes* of an appraisal and decision process that can lead to both thoughtful and impulsive actions. **Figure 13.7** shows a diagram of the general aggression model.

Inputs refer to the antecedents of aggression, which pertain to the characteristics of the person and the situation. Personal variables include gender, personality traits, attitudes, beliefs, and values. Situation variables include heat and alcohol, along with frustration and aggressive cues. According to the GAM, none of these variables influences aggression directly. Whether or not they lead to aggression depends on the extent to which they produce affect, cognitions, and levels of physiological arousal that are compatible with aggression.

Feelings and thoughts are highly connected with arousal in memory. Together, these three routes characterize an individual's present internal state. Some specific inputs such as exposure to media violence can increase the accessibility of hostile thoughts and aggression scripts (Huesmann, 1998). They can also lead to negative affect like anger and fear (Berkowitz, 1993). Arousal can influence aggression by strengthening an existing action tendency (Bushman & Anderson, 2002) or by excitation transfer identified by Zillmann (1983, 1988).

Internal states and the input variables that created them are subject to specific appraisals and decisions. Immediate appraisals are generally affected by whatever is accessible in memory. Thus, they are automatic and represent hidden influences that lead to relatively "thoughtless" behavior. For example, a person who is bumped by another person may be particularly likely to interpret the behavior as an act of aggression after watching a violent television program. To the extent that time and energy permit, however, he or she may reappraise the incident in a more deliberate and controlled fashion. Reappraisals often involve a search for alternative interpretations of the situation. If the search turns up a suitable alternative, it may replace the "thoughtless," aggressive course of action with a nonaggressive one. However, if it confirms the immediate appraisal, it will likely result in "thoughtful" rather than "thoughtless" aggression.

The general aggression model may seem highly complex, but despite that apparent complexity (or perhaps because of it), it can explain most forms of aggression with relative ease. The GAM provides a singular framework with which to understand how the seemingly disparate inputs we have considered in this chapter can lead to aggression in its many forms, including intimate partner violence, intergroup violence, and even suicide (DeWall, Anderson, & Bushman, 2011).

The Social Cognition of Aggression: A Summary

Historically, theories of aggression have increased in both their complexity and sophistication over time. Whereas the frustration-aggression hypothesis focuses on frustration as the main cause of aggression, subsequent theories emphasize the role of both conscious and unconscious processes in producing emotions that are compatible with aggression. Cognitive neoassociation theory stresses the importance of conscious processes that help to transform the rudimentary emotions elicited by a provocation or attack into complex emotions that may or may not lead to aggression. Script theory emphasizes the role of well-rehearsed aggression scripts, which can lead to aggressive behavior in the absence of conscious thought. The general aggression model focuses on the impact of various inputs from the person and the situation on the person's internal state, including affect, cognition, and arousal. It stresses the importance of both conscious and unconscious appraisals in determining the end result. Despite their differences, all these theories acknowledge the importance of hidden influences on aggression.

EPILOGUE: COPING COMES TO A CRASHING HALT

Brian sat in his car, contemplating what to do next. Briefly, he entertained the idea of abandoning his mission, but decided that since he had come this far, he should follow through with his intentions. Exactly what to do was an altogether different matter. He had fantasized about confronting Eric the minute he left the building, although he was not sure whether he should merely give him a piece of his mind or physically confront him.

Brian's deliberations came to an abrupt end when the lights in Suzie's apartment went dark. Eric wasn't coming out through that front door—he was going to spend the night with Suzie! The sight of the darkened window left Brian frustrated, further boosting his anger. Deprived of a chance take it out on Eric directly, he decided that taking it out on Eric's truck would be the next best thing to do. Brian's car key, if properly applied, would do a real job on the paint.

Brian flung his car door open and immediately felt a swoosh, followed quickly by a loud bang and a groan. The swoosh, it turned out, had been caused by a cyclist who was forced to swerve when Brian opened his car door. The bang happened when the bicycle crashed into Eric's truck, and the groan came from the young woman who had been riding the bicycle. The impact of the crash had left a big, ugly dent in the driver's side door of Eric's truck. Fortunately, the woman seemed unhurt and was concerned primarily with brushing the dirt off her fashionable cycling shorts and halter top. As Brian walked toward her, he saw no trace of anger on her face. If anything, he detected a faint smile as she removed her helmet and straightened out her long, dark hair. Brian was no longer thinking about Eric—or Suzie.

HIDDEN INFLUENCES ON AGGRESSION: A SUMMARY

Instinctual aggression: aggression stemming from basic human instincts that operate outside of conscious awareness and are directed toward self-preservation

Excitation transfer: the process through which physiological arousal from a prior setting spills over to the next, where it may be falsely attributed as the result of a provocation

The weapons effect: the extent to which the sight of a weapon automatically activates aggressive thoughts

The mean world syndrome: the belief that the world is a more dangerous place than it actually is; results from exposure to media violence, causing individuals to overestimate their own risk of victimization

Desensitization: the process by which exposure to media violence reduces initial fear and disgust and instead produces emotional states compatible with aggression; manifests itself in reduced inhibitions against aggression and lowered responsiveness to the victims of real violence

Automatic priming of aggressive thoughts: an unconscious process through which aggressive thoughts automatically activate existing memory links between aggression- related concepts

Immediate appraisals: automatic appraisals of internal states that are affected primarily by whatever is accessible in memory

KEY TERMS AND DEFINITIONS

Instrumental aggression: aggression undertaken to achieve goals (p. 601)

Hostile aggression: reactive aggression that is motivated by anger and intended specifically to harm another (p. 601)

Parental investment: the contributions males and females make to create and raise their offspring (p. 605)

Testosterone: the hormone that contributes to heightened aggression, particularly among males (p. 605)

Serotonin: a neurotransmitter that plays a role in the expression and regulation of aggression by providing the biological basis for impulse control (p. 605)

Hostile attribution bias: a chronic pattern of attributing ambiguous behavior to hostile intentions (p. 607)

Alcohol myopia: a general impairment of all cognitive processes that results from intoxication (p. 610)

Excitation transfer: the spillover of physiological arousal from one context to another (p. 612)

Weapons effect: heightened aggression resulting from exposure to a weapon (p. 614)

Meta-analysis: the quantitative analysis of the results of a large number of studies (p. 620)

Catharsis: vicarious aggression that substitutes for actual aggression, reducing the motivation to aggress (p. 621)

Erotica: pornographic material that shows nudity and sex among consenting adults (p. 625)

Rape myth: the erroneous belief that women become sexually aroused by being raped, and eventually come to enjoy the experience (p. 624)

Violent pornography: pornographic material that shows coercive sex, which generally requires women to engage in humiliating and degrading sex acts (p. 625)

Culture of honor: a culture that permits aggression in defense of one's honor (p. 627)

Frustration-aggression hypothesis: the theory that frustration is both necessary and sufficient for aggression to occur (p. 631)

Cognitive neoassociation theory: a theory of aggression that explains how cognitive processes transform rudimentary emotions into more complex, differentiated emotions (p. 634)

Script theory: a theory that explains aggression in terms of the acquisition and application of aggression scripts, starting in childhood (p. 634)

General aggression model (GAM): a complex theory that explains aggression as the product of specific inputs and internal states, subject to both conscious and unconscious appraisal (p. 635)

REFERENCES

Anderson, C. A. (1989). Temperature and aggression: Ubiquitous effects of heat on occurrence of human violence. *Psychological Bulletin, 106,* 74–96.

Anderson, C. A., & Anderson, K. B. (1996). Violent crime rate studies in philosophical context: A destructive testing approach to heat and southern culture of violence effects. *Journal of Personality and Social Psychology, 70,* 740–756.

Anderson, C. A., & Bushman, B. J. (1997). External validity of "trivial" experiments: The case of laboratory aggression. *Review of General Psychology, 1,* 19–41.

Anderson, C. A., & Bushman, B. J. (2001). Effects of violent video games on aggressive behavior, aggressive cognition, aggressive affect, physiological arousal, and prosocial behavior: A meta-analytic review of the scientific literature. *Psychological Science, 12,* 353–359.

Anderson, C. A., & Bushman, B. J. (2002). Human aggression. *Annual Review of Psychology, 53,* 27–51.

Anderson, C. A., Anderson, K. B., Dorr, N., DeNeve, K. M., & Flanagan, M. (2000). Temperature and aggression. In M. Zana (Ed.), *Advances in experimental social psychology* (Vol. 33, pp. 63–133). New York: Academic Press.

Anderson, C. A., Benjamin, A. J. Jr., & Bartholow, B. D. (1998). Does the gun pull the trigger? Automatic priming effects of weapon pictures and weapon names. *Psychological Science, 9,* 308–314.

Anderson, C. A., Bushman, B. J., & Groom, R. W. (1997). Hot years and serious and deadly assault: Empirical tests of the heat hypothesis. *Journal of Personality and Social Psychology, 73,* 1213–1223.

Anderson, C. A., et al. (2010). Violent video game effects on aggression, empathy, and prosocial behavior in Eastern and Western countries: A meta-analytic review. *Psychological Bulletin, 136,* 151–173.

Archer, J. (2004). Sex differences in aggression in real-world settings: A meta-analytic review. *Review of General Psychology, 8,* 291–322.

Archer, J., & Coyne, S. M. (2005). An integrated review of indirect, relational, and social aggression. *Personality and Social Psychology Review, 9,* 212–230.

Bandura, A. (1977). *Social learning theory.* Englewood Cliffs, NJ: Prentice Hall. Barker, R., Dembo, T., & Lewin, K. (1941). *Frustration and regression: An experiment with young children.* University of Iowa Press.

Barker, R., Dembo, T., & Lewin, K. (1941). Frustration and aggression: An experiment with young children. *University of Iowa Studies in Child Welfare, 18,* 1–314.

Barlett, C. P., Harris, R. J., & Bruey, C. (2007). The effect of the amount of blood in a violent videogame on aggression, hostility, and arousal. *Journal of Experimental Social Psychology, 44,* 539–546.

Baron, R. A. (1972). Aggression as a function of ambient temperature and prior anger arousal. *Journal of Personality and Social Psychology, 21,* 183–189.

Baron, R. A. (1974). The aggression-inhibiting influence of heightened sexual arousal. *Journal of Personality and Social Psychology, 30,* 318–322.

Baron, R. A. (1978). Aggression-inhibiting influence of sexual humor. *Journal of Personality and Social Psychology, 36,* 189–197.

Baron, R. A. (1983). The control of human aggression: An optimistic perspective. *Journal of Social & Clinical Psychology, 1,* 97–119.

Baron, R. A., & Ransberger, V. M. (1978). Ambient temperature and the occurrence of collective violence: The "long, hot summer" revisited. *Journal of Personality and Social Psychology, 36,* 351–360.

Baron, R. A., & Richardson, D.R. (1994). *Human aggression.* New York: Plenum.

Bartholow, B. D., Bushman, B. J., & Sestir, M. A. (2006). Chronic violent video game exposure and desensitization to violence: Behavioral and event-related brain potential data. *Journal of Experimental Social Psychology, 42,* 532–539.

Bègue, L., Bushman, B. J., Giancola, P. R., Subra, B., & Rosset, E. (2010). "There is no such thing as an accident," especially when people are drunk. *Personality and Social Psychology Bulletin, 36,* 1301–1304.

Berkowitz, L. (1989). Frustration-aggression hypothesis: Examination and reformulation. *Psychological Bulletin, 106,* 59–73.

Berkowitz, L. (1990). On the formation and regulation of anger and aggression: A cognitive-neoassociationistic analysis. *American Psychologist, 45,* 494–503.

Berkowitz, L. (1993). Towards a general theory of anger and emotional aggression: Implications of the cognitive-neoassociationistic perspective for the analysis of anger and other emotions. In R. S. Wyer Jr., & T. K. Srull, (Eds.), *Perspectives on anger and emotion* (pp. 1–46). Hillsdale, NJ: Erlbaum.

Berkowitz, L. (1994). On the escalation of aggression. In M. Potegal & J. F. Knutson (Eds.), *The dynamics of aggression: Biological and social processes in dyads and groups* (pp. 33–41). Hillsdale, NJ: Erlbaum.

Berkowitz, L., & LePage, A. (1967). Weapons as aggression-eliciting stimuli. *Journal of Personality and Social Psychology, 7,* 202–207.

Bonta, J. (1997). *Offender Rehabilitation: From Research to Practise 1997–01.* Canada: Ministry of the Solicitor General.

Burt, M. R. (1980). Cultural myths and supports for rape. *Journal of Personality and Social Psychology, 38,* 217–230.

Bushman, B. J. (1998). Priming effects of media violence on the accessibility of aggressive constructs in memory. *Personality and Social Psychology Bulletin, 24,* 537–545.

Bushman, B. J., & Anderson, C. A. (2002). Violent video games and hostile expectations: A test of the General Aggression Model. *Personality and Social Psychology Bulletin, 28,* 1679–1689.

Bushman, B. J., & Baumeister, R. F. (1998). Threatened egotism, narcissism, self- esteem, and direct and displaced aggression: Does self-love or self-hate lead to violence? *Journal of Personality and Social Psychology, 75,* 219–229.

Bushman, B. J., Bonacci, A. M., Pederson, W. C., Vasquez, E. A., & Miller, N. (2005). Chewing on it can chew you up: Effects of rumination on triggered displaced aggression. *Journal of Personality and Social Psychology, 88,* 969–983.

Bushman, B. J., & Cantor, J. (2003). Media ratings for violence and sex: Implications for policymakers and parents. *American Psychologist, 58,* 130–141.

Bushman, B. J., & Cooper, H. M. (1990). Alcohol and human aggression: An integrative research review. *Psychological Bulletin, 107,* 341–354.

Bushman, B. J., & Huesmann, L. R. (2000). Effects of televised violence on aggression. In D. G. Singer & J. L. Singer (Eds.), *Handbook of children and the media* (pp. 223–254). Thousand Oaks, CA: Sage.

Bushman, B. J., & Huesmann, L. R. (2010). Aggression. In S. T. Fiske, D. T. Gilbert, & G. Lindzey (Eds.), *Handbook of social psychology* (5th ed., pp. 833–863). New York: Wiley & Sons.

Bushman, B. J., Jamieson, P. E., Weitz, I., & Romer, D. (2013). Gun violence trends in movies. *Pediatrics, 132,* 1014–1018.

Bushman, B. J., Wang, M. C., & Anderson, C. A. (2005). Is the curve relating temperature to aggression linear or curvilinear? Assaults and temperature in Minneapolis reexamined. *Journal of Personality and Social Psychology, 89,* 62– 66.

Buss, A. H. (1961). *The psychology of aggression.* New York: Wiley.

Cacioppo, J. T., Crites, S. L., Berntson, G. G., & Coles, M. G. (1993). If attitudes affect how stimuli are processed, should they not affect the event-related brain potential? *Psychological Science, 4*(2), 108–112.

Campbell, A. (2002). *A mind of her own: The evolutionary psychology of women.* New York: Oxford University Press.

Cantor, J. (1998). *"Mommy, I'm scared": How TV and movies frighten children and what we can do to protect them.* New York: Mariner Books.

Carlsmith, J. M., & Anderson, C. A. (1979). Ambient temperature and the occurrence of collective violence: A new analysis. *Journal of Personality and Social Psychology, 37,* 337–344.

Chance, S. E., Brown, R. T., Dabbs, J. M. Jr., & Casey, R. (2000). Testosterone, intelligence and behavior disorders in young boys. *Personality and Individual Differences, 28,* 437–445.

Cohen, D., & Nisbett, R. E. (1997). Field experiments examining the culture of honor: The role of institutions in perpetuating norms about violence. *Personality and Social Psychology Bulletin, 23,* 1188–1199.

Cohen, D., Nisbett, R. E., Bowdle, B., & Schwarz, N. (1996). Insult, aggression, and the southern culture of honor: An "experimental ethnography." *Journal of Personality and Social Psychology, 70,* 945–960.

Cohn, E. G., & Rotton, J. (1997). Assault as a function of time and temperature: A moderator-variable time-series analysis. *Journal of Personality and Social Psychology, 72*, 1322–1334.

Cohn, E. G., & Rotton, J. (2005). The curve is still out there: A reply to Bushman, Wang, and Anderson's "Is the curve relating temperature to aggression linear or curvilinear?" *Journal of Personality and Social Psychology, 89*, 67–70.

Coie, J. D., Cillessen, A. H. N., Dodge, K. A., Hubbard, J. A., Schwartz, D., Lemerise, E. A., et al. (1999). It takes two to fight: A test of relational factors and a method for assessing aggressive dyads. *Developmental Psychology, 35*, 1179–1188.

Crick, N. R., & Dodge, K. (1994). A review and reformulation of social information- processing mechanisms in children's social adjustment. *Psychological Bulletin, 115*, 74–101.

Crick, N. R, & Rose, A. J. (2000). Toward a gender-balanced approach to the study of social-emotional development: A look at relational aggression. In P. H. Miller & E. K. Scholnick (Eds.), *Feminist approaches to developmental psychology* (pp. 153–168). New York: Routledge.

Dabbs, J. M. Jr., Carr, T. S., Frady, R. L., & Riad, J. (1995). Testosterone, crime, and misbehavior among 692 male prison inmates. *Personality and Individual Differences 18*, 627–633.

Dabbs, J. M. Jr., Hargrove, M. F., & Heusel, C. (1996). Testosterone differences among college fraternities: Well-behaved vs. rambunctious. *Personality and Individual Differences 20*, 157–161.

Dabbs, J. M. Jr., Hopper, C. H., & Jurkovic, G. J. (1990). Testosterone and personality among college students and military veterans. *Personality and Individual Differences, 11*, 1263–1269.

Dabbs, J. M. Jr., & Morris, R. (1990). Testosterone, social class, and antisocial behavior in a sample of 4,462 men. *Psychological Science, 1*, 209–211.

Daly, M., & Wilson, M. (1988). Evolutionary social psychology and family homicide. *Science, 242*, 519–524.

Deaux, K., & LaFrance, M. (1998). Gender. In D. Gilbert, S. T. Fiske, & G. Lindzey (Eds.), *The handbook of social psychology* (4th ed., Vol. 1, pp. 788–827). New York: McGraw-Hill.

Delgado, A. R., Prieto, G., & Bond, R. A. (1997). The cultural factor in lay perception of jealousy as a motive for wife battery. *Journal of Applied Social Psychology, 27*, 1824–1841.

Denson, T. F., Pederson, W. C., Friese, M., Hahm, A., & Roberts, L. (2011). Understanding impulsive aggression: Angry rumination and reduced self-control capacity are mechanisms underlying the provocation-aggression relationship. *Personality and Social Psychology Bulletin, 37*, 850–862.

Denson, T. F., White, A. J., & Warburton, W. A. (2009). Trait-displaced aggression and psychopathy differentially moderate the effects of acute alcohol intoxication and rumination on triggered displaced aggression. *Journal of Research in Personality, 43*, 673–681.

DeWall, C. N., Anderson, C. A., & Bushman, B. J. (2011). The general aggression model: Theoretical extensions to violence. *Psychology of Violence, 1*, 245–258.

DiPietro, J. A. (1981). Rough and tumble play: A function of gender. *Developmental Psychology, 17*, 50–58.

Dodge, K., & Tomlin, A. (1987). Utilization of self-schemas as a mechanism of interpretational bias in aggressive children. *Social Cognition, 5*, 280–300.

Dollard, J., Miller, N. E., Doob, L. W., Mowrer, O. H., & Sears, R. R. (1939). *Frustration and aggression.* New Haven, CT: Yale University Press.

Donnerstein, E. (1980). Aggressive erotica and violence against women. *Journal of Personality and Social Psychology, 39*, 269–277.

Donnerstein, E., & Barrett, G. (1978). Effects of erotic stimuli on male aggression toward females. *Journal of Personality and Social Psychology, 36*, 180–188.

Donnerstein, E., & Berkowitz, L. (1981). Victim reactions in aggressive erotic films as a factor in violence against women. *Journal of Personality and Social Psychology, 41,* 710–724.

Dutton, D. G., & Aron, A. P. (1974). Some evidence for heightened sexual attraction under conditions of high anxiety. *Journal of Personality and Social Psychology, 30,* 510–517.

Freud, S. (1920). *A general introduction to psychoanalysis.* New York: Horace Liveright.

Funk, J. B., Baldacci, H. B., Pasold, T., & Baumgardner, J. (2004). Violence exposure in real-life, video games, television, movies, and the internet: Is there desensitization? *Journal of Adolescence, 27,* 23–39.

Geen, R. G. (1981). Behavioral and physiological reactions to observed violence: Effects of prior exposure to aggressive stimuli. *Journal of Personality and Social Psychology, 40,* 868–875.

Geen, R. G., & Donnerstein, E. (1998*). Human aggression: Theories, research, and implications for social policy.* San Diego, CA: Academic Press.

Gerbner, G., Gross, L., Morgan, M., & Signorielli, N. (1994). Growing up with television: The cultivation perspective. In J. Bryant, & D. Zillmann (Eds.), *Media effects: Advances in theory and research* (pp. 17–41). Hillsdale, NJ: Erlbaum.

Giancola, P. R., & Corman, M. D. (2007). Alcohol and aggression: A test of the attention-allocation model. *Psychological Science, 18,* 649–655.

Glass, G. V. (2006). Meta-Analysis: The quantitative synthesis of research findings. In J. L. Green, G. Camilli, & P. B. Elmore, (Eds.), *Handbook of complementary methods in education research* (pp. 427–438). Mahwah, NJ: Erlbaum.

Greitemeyer, T. (2014). Intense acts of violence during video game play make daily aggression appear innocuous: A new mechanism why violent videogames increase aggression. *Journal of Experimental Social Psychology, 50,* 52–56.

Harris, M. B. (1974). Mediators between frustration and aggression in a field experiment. *Journal of Experimental Social Psychology, 10,* 561–571.

Henry, P. J. (2009). Low-status compensation: A theory for understanding the role of status in cultures of honor. *Journal of Personality and Social Psychology, 97,* 451–466.

Higley, J. D., Mehlman, P. T., Poland, R. E., & Taub, D. M. (1996). CSF testosterone and 5-HIAA correlate with different types of aggressive behaviors. *Biological Psychiatry, 40,* 1067–1082.

Huesmann, L. R. (1986). Psychological processes promoting the relation between exposure to media violence and aggressive behavior by the viewer. *Journal of Social Issues, 42,* 125–139.

Huesmann, L. R. (1998). The role of social information processing and cognitive schemas in the acquisition and maintenance of habitual aggressive behavior. In R. G. Geen & E. Donnerstein (Eds.), *Human aggression: Theories, research, and implications for policy* (pp. 73–109). New York: Academic Press.

Huesmann, L. R., & Eron, L. D. (1986). *Television and the aggressive child: A cross- national comparison.* Hillsdale, NJ: Erlbaum.

Huesmann, L. R., & Guerra, N. G. (1997). Children's normative beliefs about aggression and aggressive behavior. *Journal of Personality and Social Psychology, 72,* 408– 419.

Hull, J. G., & Bond, C. F. (1986). Social and behavioral consequences of alcohol consumption and expectancy: A meta-analysis. *Psychological Bulletin, 99,* 347–360.

Ito, T. A., Miller, N., & Pollock, V. E. (1996). Alcohol and aggression: A meta-analysis on the moderating effects of inhibitory cues, triggering events, and self-focused attention. *Psychological Bulletin, 120,* 60–82.

Kenrick, D. T., & MacFarlane, S. W. (1986). Ambient temperature and horn-honking: A field study of the heat/aggression relationship. *Environment and Behavior, 18,* 74– 96.

Kernis, M. H., Brockner, J., & Frankel, B. S. (1989). Self-esteem and reactions to failure: The mediating role of overgeneralization. *Journal of Personality and Social Psychology, 57,* 707–714.

Kring, A. M. (2000). Gender and anger. In Fischer, A. H. (Ed.), *Gender and emotion: Social psychological perspectives* (pp. 211–231). New York: Cambridge University Press.

Lefkowitz, M. M., Eron, L. D., Walder, L. O., & Huesmann, L. R. (1977). *Growing up to be violent: A longitudinal study of the development of aggression.* Oxford, England: Pergamon.

Linnoila, V. M., & Virkkunen, M. (1992). Aggression, suicidality, and serotonin. *Journal of Clinical Psychiatry, 53,* Suppl: 46–51.

Linz, D., Donnerstein, E., & Adams, S. M. (1989). Physiological desensitization and judgments about female victims of violence. *Human Communication Research, 15,* 509–522.

Linz, D., Donnerstein, E., & Penrod, S. (1984). The effects of long-term exposure to filmed violence against women. *Journal of Communication, 34,* 130–147.

Linz, D., Donnerstein, E., & Penrod, S. (1987). Effects of long-term exposure to violent and sexually degrading depictions of women. *Journal of Personality and Social Psychology, 55,* 758–768.

Lorenz, K. (1966). *On Aggression* (M. K. Wilson, Trans.). New York: Harcourt, Brace & World.

Malamuth, N. M., & Check, J. V. (1981). The effects of mass media exposure on acceptance of violence against women: A field experiment. *Journal of Research in Personality, 15,* 436–446.

Marcus-Newhall, A., Pedersen, W. C., Carlson, M., & Miller, N. (2000). Displaced aggression is alive and well: A meta-analytic review. *Journal of Personality and Social Psychology, 78,* 670–689.

Mazur, A. (1983). Hormones, aggression, and dominance in humans. In B. B. Svare (Ed.), *Hormones and aggressive behavior* (pp. 563–576). New York: Plenum Press.

Mazur, A., Booth, A., & Dabbs, J. M. Jr. (1992). Testosterone and chess competition. *Social Psychology Quarterly, 55,* 70–77.

Meyer, T. P. (1972). Effects of viewing justified and unjustified real film violence on aggressive behavior. *Journal of Personality and Social Psychology, 23,* 21–29.

Miller, N. E. (1941). The frustration-aggression hypothesis. *Psychological Review, 48,* 337–342.

Miller, N., Pederson, W. C., Earlywine, M., & Pollock, V. (2003). A theoretical model of displaced aggression. *Personality and Social Psychology Review, 7,* 75–97.

Mischel, W. (1973). Toward a cognitive social learning reconceptualization of personality. *Psychological Review, 80,* 252–283.

Möller, I., & Krahé, B. (2008). Exposure to violent videogames and aggression in German adolescents: A longitudinal analysis. *Aggressive Behavior, 35,* 75–89.

Mueller, C. W., & Donnerstein, E. (1983). Film-induced arousal and aggressive behavior. *Journal of Social Psychology, 119,* 61–67.

Mueller, C. W., Donnerstein, E., & Hallam, J. (1983). Violent films and prosocial behavior. *Personality and Social Psychology Bulletin, 9,* 83–89.

Nabi, R. L., & Sullivan, J. L. (2001). Does television viewing relate to engagement in protective action against crime? A cultivation analysis from a theory of reasoned action perspective. *Communication Research, 28,* 802–825.

Nagin, D. S., & Tremblay R. E. (1999). Trajectories of boys' physical aggression, opposition, and hyperactivity on the path to physically violent and nonviolent juvenile delinquency. *Child Development 70,* 1181–1196.

Nasby, W., Hayden, B., & DePaulo, B. M. (1979). Attributional bias among aggressive boys to interpret unambiguous social stimuli as displays of hostility. *Journal of Abnormal Psychology, 89,* 459–468.

Nisbett, R. E. (1993). Violence and U.S. regional culture. *American Psychologist, 48,* 441–449.

Nisbett, R. E., & Cohen, D. (1996). *Culture of honour: The psychology of violence in the South.* Boulder, CO: Westview.

Österman, K., Bjorkqvist, K., Lagerspetz, K. M. J., Charpentier, S., Caprara, G. V., & Pastorelli, C. (1999). Locus of control and three types of aggression. *Aggressive Behavior, 25*, 61–65.

Paik, H., & Comstock, G. A. (1994). The effects of television violence on antisocial behavior: A meta-analysis. *Communication Research, 21*, 516–546.

Ramirez, J., Bryant, J., & Zillmann, D. (1982). Effects of erotica on retaliatory behavior as a function of level of prior provocation. *Journal of Personality and Social Psychology, 43*, 971–978.

Reifman, A. S., Larrick, R. P., & Fein, S. (1991). Temper and temperature on the diamond: The heat-aggression relationship in major league baseball. *Personality and Social Psychology Bulletin, 17*, 580–585.

Reijntjes, A., Thomas, S., Kamphuis, J. H., Bushman, B. J., deCastro, B. O., & Telch, M. J. (2011). Explaining the paradoxical rejection-aggression link: The mediating effects of hostile intent attributions, anger, and decrease in state self-esteem on peer rejection-induced aggression in youth. *Personality and Social Psychology Bulletin, 37*, 955–963.

Rodriguez Mosquera, P. M., Manstead, A. S. R., & Fischer, A. H. (2000). The role of honour-related values in the elicitation, experience and communication of pride, shame and anger: Spain and the Netherlands compared. *Personality and Social Psychology Bulletin, 26*, 833–844.

Rothmund, T., Gollwitzer, M., & Klimmt, C. (2011). Of virtual victims and victimized virtues: Differential effects of experienced aggression in video games on social cooperation. *Personality and Social Psychology Bulletin, 37*, 102–119.

Rotton, J., & Cohn, E. G. (2000). Violence is a curvilinear function of temperature in Dallas: A replication. *Journal of Personality and Social Psychology, 78*, 1074–1081.

Schank, R., & Abelson, R. (1977). *Scripts, plans, goals, and understanding.* Mahwah, NJ: Erlbaum.

Singer, D. G. (1994). Play as healing. In J. H. Goldstein (Ed.), *Toys, play, and child development* (pp. 147–165). New York: Cambridge University Press.

Singer, J. L. (1994). Imaginative play and adaptive development. In J. H. Goldstein (Ed.), *Toys, play, and child development* (pp. 6–26). New York: Cambridge University Press.

Singer, J. L. (1994). The scientific foundations of play therapy. In J. Hellendoorn, R. van der Kooij, & B. Sutton-Smith (Eds.), *Play and intervention* (pp. 27–38). Albany: State University of New York Press.

Sloan, J. H., Kellermann, A. L., Reay, D. T., & Ferris, J. A. (1988). Handgun regulations, crime, assaults, and homicide: A tale of two cities. *New England Journal of Medicine, 319*, 1256–1262.

Smith, S. L., & Donnerstein, E. (1988). Harmful effects of exposure to media violence: Learning of aggression, emotional desensitization, and fear. In R. G. Geen & E. Donnerstein (Eds.), *Human aggression: Theories, research, and implications for social policy* (pp. 167–202). San Diego, CA: Academic Press.

Spilerman, S. (1970). The causes of racial disturbances: A comparison of alternative explanations. *American Sociological Review, 35*, 627–649.

Staub, E. (1992). The origins of aggression and the creation of positive relations among groups. In S. Staub & P. Green (Eds.), *Psychology and social responsibility: Facing global challenges* (pp. 89–120). New York: New York University Press.

Staub, E. (2002). Emergency helping, genocidal violence, and the evolution of responsibility and altruism in children. In R. J. Davidson & A. Harrington (Eds.), *Visions of compassion: Western scientists and Tibetan Buddhists examine human nature* (pp. 165–181). New York: Oxford University Press.

Steele, C. M., & Josephs, R. A. (1990). Alcohol myopia: Its prized and dangerous effects. *American Psychologist, 45*, 921–933.

Steele, C. M., & Southwick, L. (1985). Alcohol and social behavior I: The psychology of drunken excess. *Journal of Personality and Social Psychology, 48*, 18–34.

Taylor, S. E., Klein, L. C., Lewis, B. P., Gruenewald, T. L., Gurung, R. A. R., & Updegraff, J. A. (2000). Biobehavioral responses to stress in females: Tend-and- befriend, not fight-or-flight. *Psychological Review, 107*, 411–429.

Tremblay, R. E., Nagin, D. S., Séguin, J. R., Zoccolillo, M., Zelazo, P., Boivin, M., et al. (2005). Physical Aggression During Early Childhood: Trajectories and Predictors. *Canadian Child and Adolescent Psychiatry Review, 14, Feb. 2005*, 3–9.

Vachon, D. D., Lynam, D. R., & Johnson, J. A. (2013). The (non)relation between empathy and aggression: Surprising results from a meta-analysis. *Psychological Bulletin, 140*, 751-773.

Vandello, J. A., & Cohen, D. (2003). Male honor and female fidelity: Implicit cultural scripts that perpetuate domestic violence. *Journal of Personality and Social Psychology, 84*, 997–1010.

Westergaard, G. C., Suomi, S. J., Chavanne, T. J., Houser, L., Hurley, A., Cleveland, A., Snoy, P. J., & Higley, J. D. (2003). Physiological correlates of aggression on impulsivity in free-ranging female primates. *Neuropsychopharmacology, 28*(6), 1045–1055.

Wilson, B. J., Kunkel, D., Linz, D., Potter, J., Donnerstein, E., Smith, S. L., et al. (1998). Violence in television programming overall: University of California, Santa Barbara study. In M. Seawall (Ed.), *National television violence study* (Vol. 2, pp. 3–204). Thousand Oaks, CA: Sage Publications.

Zillmann, D. (1983). Arousal and aggression. In R. Geen & E. Donnerstein (Eds.), *Aggression: Theoretical and empirical reviews* (Vol. 1, pp. 75–102). New York: Academic Press.

Zillmann, D. (1988). Cognition-excitation interdependencies in aggressive behavior. *Aggressive Behavior, 14* (Special issue: Current theoretical perspectives on aggressive and antisocial behavior), 51–64.

Zillmann, D., Bryant, J. & Carveth, R. A. (1981). The effects of erotica featuring sadomasochism and bestiality on motivated internal aggression. Personality and Social Psychology Bulletin 7, 153–59.

CHAPTER 14

THE SOCIAL PSYCHOLOGY OF GENOCIDE, TERRORISM—AND HEROISM

n Chapter 1 of this book, we defined social psychology as "the study of how people think, behave, and feel in a social context." Because the term *social context* is broad, we have seen that research by social psychologists sheds light on people's behavior in a wide variety of social settings. Every chapter, for example, includes sections describing how the field's findings apply to health care and the legal system. In addition, we have discussed how research in social psychology applies to (among others) the classroom, the marketplace and business world, and intimate relationships.

In this chapter, we focus on yet another aspect of social behavior—one that is quite clearly an aspect of what we have called the "Dark Side" of human behavior. Our goal is to show how the theories and research discussed in the preceding chapters can help to explain the thoughts, behaviors, and feelings of people involved in the intentional, systematic, and wholesale murder of other human beings (see also Newman & Erber, 2002b; Staub, 1989; Waller, 2002). In other words, this chapter focuses on the social psychology of genocide, mass killing, and terrorism.

Like all the chapters in this book, this one is organized as a story. In this case, the story does not focus on a particular person or group, but on how genocidal killings and terrorist campaigns unfold over time. Specifically, it focuses on (1) the first rumblings of trouble in a society; (2) the selection of scapegoats for the society's troubles; (3) the persecution of the scapegoated group, and how people come to accept and cooperate with it; (4) the attempt to eliminate the group; and (5) the aftermath of genocide, during which people must come to terms with the crime.

THE DARKEST OF DARK SIDES: GENOCIDE, MASS KILLING, AND TERRORISM

For most readers, the term **genocide** (Powers, 2002) requires no introduction. Moshman (2005, p. 186) defines it as "the extermination, entirely or in part, of an abstractly defined group of people" based on "racial, ethnic, national, religious, cultural, linguistic, political, economic, sexual," or other characteristics. Not all cases of mass killing fit this definition unambiguously. In many examples of indiscriminate, organized mass killing (such as civilian massacres during the Vietnam War in the 1960s), the goal was not necessarily the systematic extermination of a group of people. Nevertheless, the processes reviewed in this chapter are relevant to those episodes, too. Therefore, although most of our discussion will focus on well-known cases of genocide, we will also use the more general term "mass killing" (Staub, 2002), without worrying about distinguishing between the two.

Perhaps the best-known and intensively studied episode of genocide is the attempt to exterminate Jews—starting with those in Europe—during the Second World War (1939–1945). This extended killing campaign, initiated by the German dictator Adolf Hitler and his National Socialist (Nazi) Party, was carried out with the assistance of people across Europe. The Holocaust, as it has come to be known, resulted in the wholesale murder of about six million Jews.

Scholars have approached the Holocaust from many different perspectives—historical, political, philosophical, and so forth. From the standpoint of social psychologists, the key questions are:

1. How could one group of people become convinced that another group was worthy of death?
2. How could people bring themselves to carry out the systematic killing of men, women, and children, and how could others stand by passively and watch?
3. How did the killers come to terms with what they had done?

Table 14.1: Representative cases of genocide and mass killing

THE HOLOCAUST

Under Adolf Hitler, when the Nazi Party gained power in Germany in 1933, the government began to discriminate against Jews. Their persecution intensified over the years. After the start of the Second World War in 1939, mass murders of Jews took place in German-occupied countries. In early 1942, the Nazis adopted the "Final Solution," a plan to exterminate all the Jews in Europe by gassing and other means. By the time the war ended in 1945, approximately six million Jews had been killed. Millions of other people were persecuted and killed by the Nazis, although only Jews and Gypsies/Roma were targeted for total annihilation.

THE ARMENIAN GENOCIDE

The Armenian genocide began in the late 19th century, with several massacres of Christian Armenians living in the Muslim Ottoman Empire. Then, shortly after the start of the First World War, the Ottoman military suffered humiliating defeats at the hands of Russia. The Armenians were accused of sabotage and were targeted for annihilation. Not even the end of the war put a stop to the violence. Approximately one million Armenians were killed or starved to death.

THE RWANDAN GENOCIDE

In 1994, the president of the African nation of Rwanda died in a plane crash. Members of the president's ethnic group, the Hutus, accused members of another ethnic group, the Tutsis, of being responsible (falsely, most people now agree). In a short period, approximately 800,000 Tutsis were murdered, along with suspected Hutu "collaborators," in a centrally organized killing spree.

THE RAPE OF NANKING

Japanese soldiers murdered, raped, and otherwise brutalized approximately 350,000 Chinese soldiers and civilians after the Chinese city of Nanking fell in battle in late 1937.

These are the questions we will address in this chapter. In addition to the Holocaust, several other historical events will figure heavily in our discussion (see **Table 14.1**). One is the genocidal killing of as many as a million Armenians in the Ottoman Turkish Empire. This killing occurred in stages between the 1890s and 1920s, climaxing shortly after the outbreak of the First World War in 1914. Another is the killing frenzy that took place in the African nation of Rwanda in 1994, in which one ethnic group, the Hutus, slaughtered hundreds of thousands of members of another ethnic group, the Tutsis, in a matter of weeks. Finally, we will consider the mass killings of Chinese soldiers and civilians by Japanese soldiers following the defeat of the city of Nanking in 1937–1938. The number of Chinese killed in the Rape of Nanking is commonly estimated at around 350,000.

Armenian refugees forced to flee their homes in Turkey shortly after the outbreak of the first World War. Many others, however, perished in massacres.

A memorial to some of the Tutsi victims of genocide in Butare, Rwanda

Although we will focus on four specific tragedies, other examples will also figure briefly in our discussion. Indeed, the message of this chapter is definitely *not* that genocide arises from some pathology specific to Germany, Turkey, Rwanda, and Japan. As we noted in Chapter 11, no nation, group, or culture is immune to prejudice and discrimination. Similarly, no people should feel confident that mass killings could never take place on their soil. The sequence of events we will review here could emerge anywhere, for although the events are themselves extraordinary, they result from quite ordinary social psychological processes.

In this chapter, we will also briefly consider terrorism, another organized human activity aimed at indiscriminate killing (Davis & Cragin, 2009; Kressel, 2002; Moghaddam & Marsella, 2004; Reich, 1998; Stout, 2002; Victoroff & Kruglanski, 2009). **Terrorism** can be hard to define (Hallett, 2004); in fact, Schmid and Jongman (1988) list over 100 possible definitions. We will use the term to refer to "(a) the use of force or violence (b) by individuals or groups (c) that is directed toward civilian populations (d) and intended to instill fear (e) as a means of coercing individuals or groups to change their political or social positions" (Marsella, 2004). Like genocide, terrorism is a concept that does not require an elaborate introduction. A prototypical example is the destruction of New York City's World Trade Center and the deaths of thousands of people inside the Twin Towers on September 11, 2001. To find other examples, we need only pick up a daily newspaper. **Figure 14.1** shows the frequency of international terrorist attacks over the last two decades of the 20th century.

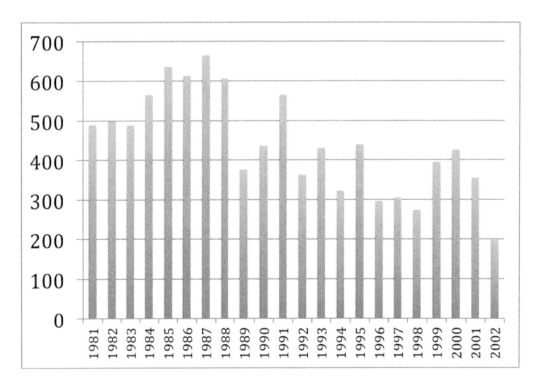

Figure 14.1: Number of international terrorist attacks per year, 1981–2002.

Source: From the United States Department of State report, "Patterns of Global Terrorism 2002," **http://www.state.gov/j/ct/rls/crt/2002/html/19997.htm**

Most readers of this book, if they try, can probably imagine circumstances under which the groups they belong to might be treated with such extreme injustice that formerly unacceptable forms of violence would seem justifiable. We are not interested in resolving debates over whether any specific act of violence should be labeled as terrorism or something else (such as "freedom fighting"). Doing so would involve moral, theological, political, and historical issues well beyond the scope of this book. We will simply note that terrorism exists, and that "to cold-bloodedly slaughter innocent women and children in buses, department stores, and airports" (Bandura, 2004, p. 124) does not come naturally to people. We will also assume that there are cases in which such behavior is not justified, largely because it is based on an exaggerated perception of wrongdoing and/or threat.

Terrorists in the United States: A member of the Symbionese Liberation Army The Symbionese Liberation Army, a radical revolutionary group in the early 1970s. Its activities included robbing banks, kidnapping, and other acts of violence—including murder.

Finally, just as people are capable of behavior that is shockingly brutal, they are also capable of behavior that is amazingly selfless and altruistic. This chapter will, therefore, conclude with a discussion of heroism. Indeed, most accounts of genocide and mass killing include stories of individuals who risked their lives to save others. We will discuss some of the factors that encourage and maintain such heroic behavior.

A NIGHTMARE UNFOLDS, PART I: CRISES AND THE SEARCH FOR SIMPLE SOLUTIONS

As we saw in Chapter 11, people who perceive themselves as members of a group find it difficult not to feel competitive toward other groups. In fact, research conducted using the minimal group technique (Tajfel, 1982; Tajfel & Billig, 1974) reveals that intergroup tensions can develop, even when people are grouped for trivial reasons. The tendency to be suspicious of or prejudiced toward members of an out-group may be rooted in our own—and other social animals'—evolutionary history (Diamond, 1992; Waller, 2002). Thus, it should not be surprising that hostilities often break out between rival groups. We might argue that inevitably, some of those confrontations will escalate into murderous conflicts.

On the other hand, groups can co-exist peacefully for long periods. Even when they do clash, the result is not always well-organized, systematic violence. Thus, understanding the causes of genocide and terrorism requires more than a general analysis of the reasons for friction between different groups, and more than an appreciation of the fact that social animals sometimes aggress against one another (Zajonc, 2002).

Genocide and Mass Killing

Typically, the chain of events that leads to genocide starts with some sort of economic or political crisis (Newman & Erber, 2002a; Staub, 1989, 2002). For example, the slaughter of the Armenians in 1914 erupted after the Ottoman Empire had suffered several serious military setbacks. In addition, the Turkish people were experiencing a general sense of political instability as their centuries-old system of government was challenged by reformers known as the Young Turks. Similarly, in the 1920s and 1930s, the German people were dissatis-

Difficult life conditions in Germany between the World Wars. Because of hyperinflation, by late 1923, the German government was issuing two-trillion Mark banknotes and postage stamps with a face value of fifty billion Marks. Here, a woman burns currency that had become essentially worthless for heat.

fied, not only because of their country's loss of territory and prestige following the First World War, but because of a major economic depression. That was the context in which the Nazis' anti-Semitic political program developed. In general, crises lead to widespread frustration, and frustration, as we know, is a major instigator of aggressive behavior (see the discussion of frustration-aggression theory in Chapter 13).

However, no necessary and sufficient criteria can be used to predict how bad circumstances must be before a nation experiences a crisis, let alone one sufficient to produce genocide. As we saw in Chapter 11, research on relative deprivation shows that dissatisfaction and distress result less from objective circumstances than from the feeling that your group is faring more poorly than others. (In Germany's case, the comparison may not have been just to other European nations, but to Germany's own past glories.) Therefore, what a group of people experiences as a major crisis will vary across time and place.

Some theorists maintain that the *feelings* triggered by a crisis are the key to whether a group will turn to extreme and violent solutions. The first of these feelings is loss of control. Frey and Rez (2002) argue that negative economic, political, and social conditions, no matter how severe, are not enough to convince people that all their problems can be solved by wiping out another group. After all, a better way to solve such problems would be to address them directly. Instead, a key precondition to extreme and violent actions is the feeling of a loss of control—the conclusion that nothing can be done to change a group's negative circumstances.

Germany, for example, experienced a great deal of economic, political, and social chaos in the early 1920s. After a brief period of relative stability, the worldwide economic depression that began in 1929 triggered a second period of distress and confusion. The recurrence of the crisis—along with the feeling that old approaches and solutions were no longer effective—led to a loss of public confidence and a belief that the situation was out of control. Frey and Rez note that the need for control is a basic human need; when it is blocked or frustrated, we can expect extreme reactions.

Evidence suggests that another psychological state, humiliation or threatened egotism, may also play a role in causing groups to lash out violently against others. As we saw in Chapter 4, people with very high self-regard often react to a blow to their egos with aggressive thoughts, feelings, and behavior toward others, especially those they see as the source of the ego threat (Baumeister & Butz, 2005; Baumeister & Campbell, 2002; Baumeister, Smart, & Boden, 1996; Bushman & Baumeister, 1998). Simply put, people lash out at others who threaten their inflated opinions of themselves. Baumeister (2002) suggests that the same principle that is used to explain the behavior of individuals could be used to explain the behavior of groups—even whole nations.

Indeed, circumstances that preceded several acts of genocide seem to support that hypothesis. For example, Turkey's genocidal actions against the Armenians followed events that were perceived as national humiliations, such as military defeat in the Russo-Turkish War of 1876–1877, the Balkan Wars of 1912–1913, and the First World War (Balakian, 2003). Similarly, the chaos that occurred in Germany between the two world wars was difficult for Germans to reconcile with their belief that their country was the most sophisticated, culturally refined, and dynamic nation in Europe. The feeling of national humiliation was widespread. Finally, it probably is not a coincidence that the murder of the Tutsis in Rwanda followed the intensification of a political movement known as "Hutu power." Challenges to that kind of intense pride and sense of collective greatness can be extremely threatening. (It also seems true, however, that Hutu Power was promoted to justify the violence *after* it was planned—see Staub, 1999.)

The causes of widespread crises are almost always extremely complex. Unfortunately, if the people who are experiencing a crisis are feeling humiliated, or if they believe they have lost their ability to control their destiny, they will not be inclined to engage in a careful, lengthy analysis of the causes. They will want a simple way of understanding their predicament and a straightforward, unambiguous course of action to follow (Kruglanski, Pierro, Manetti, & De Grada, 2006). All too often, that means finding and punishing a group of scapegoats.

Terrorism

Many of the same considerations involved in understanding why groups might turn to genocide apply to understanding what motivates people to become terrorists. Terrorists do not necessarily emerge from the most oppressed, disadvantaged sectors of society (Moghaddam, 2005; Taylor & Louis, 2004). In fact, they typically emerge from "an elite group that is headed by well-educated middle-class or upper-middle-class young people" (Sprinzak, 1998, p. 78). For example, many of the men who carried out the plot to destroy the World Trade Center in 2001 came from relatively privileged families and were better educated than most of their peers. Again, what seems most crucial in determining who is inspired to commit violence is not the nature of a person's objective circumstances, but the extent to which the person's life does not fulfill expectations. In other words, relative deprivation is more important than actual deprivation.

Threatened egotism, too, seems to be just as strong a motivator of terrorism as it is of genocide. In justifying their actions, terrorists typically speak of the need to avenge some national humiliation at the hands of another, more debased culture. Once terrorists have become isolated in small groups, they are especially likely to develop inflated (but unstable) self-concepts (Moghaddam, 2004). Challenges to their self-declared identities as the saviors of their people are likely to prove especially threatening.

Difficult Conditions, Crises, and Murderous Solutions: A Summary

Saying that those societies that are most likely to explode are the ones that are experiencing a crisis (as opposed to the ones experiencing peace and prosperity) is not particularly enlightening. Fortunately, we can say more than that. Frustration is likely to become widespread when people feel that their lives are falling far short of their expectations (that is, when they are experiencing a sense of relative deprivation). Moreover, when people feel that the undesirable situation they are experiencing is a function of forces beyond their control, they will be especially receptive to extreme solutions to their problems. Ego threat may be an even more explosive element; if a crisis triggers feelings of collective humiliation, aggression against the perceived causes of the humiliation is even more likely to occur.

Think Like a Social Psychologist

Making connections

—Based on what you have learned about evolutionary social psychology, can you speculate about what kinds of evolved psychological mechanisms may play a role in leading one group of people to attempt to exterminate another? What mechanisms may have evolved to *inhibit* that kind of aggression?

THE NIGHTMARE, PART II: SELECTING SCAPEGOATS

In times of crisis, which groups are likely to be selected as scapegoats? And when does that scapegoating lead to murder? In order to answer those questions, we need to take into account the relationship between the victim and the perpetrator groups, the nature of interpersonal interactions within the perpetrator group, and the crucial role played by a group's leaders.

Genocide and Mass Killing

The simplest prediction we could make about scapegoating would be that the out-group that is most hated by the majority will be the one targeted for victimization. Extreme prejudice leads to (and may be synonymous with) hatred (Dovidio, Gaertner, & Pearson, 2005). Hence, a minority group's chances of being selected as a scapegoat may be directly related to the sheer negativity with which the majority group views it.

Increasingly, however, social psychologists are discovering that just knowing how generally disliked a minority group is will not help much in predicting how that group will be treated (Bilewicz, & Vollhardt, 2012; Cottrell & Neuberg, 2005). Instead, it is important to know about the specific relationships between groups to better understand how members of those groups perceive and treat each other.

Envious prejudice. According to Fiske, Cuddy, Glick, and Xu's (2002) theory of stereotype content (see Chapter 11), reactions to another group depend to a great extent on two broad factors. The first is the out-group's competence or status; the second is the extent to which it is seen as having a cooperative or competitive relationship with the in-group. For example, some groups are perceived to be low in intelligence and power, but are not perceived as a threat because they are seen as obedient to (or cooperative with) their "superiors." Attitudes toward such groups are characterized by *benevolent prejudice.* Although they may be on the receiving end of extreme prejudice—others may view them with intense pity and disgust—they typically are not the ones targeted for extermination.

According to Glick (2002), groups that are subject to *envious prejudice* (high in competence, low in cooperation) are often most at risk of being scapegoated. These groups not only are thought to compete with the majority; they are feared and grudgingly admired because of their abilities and achievements. Besides being disliked, they are considered a plausible cause for a country's problems. In other words, people can easily imagine that successful minorities have the power to work behind the scenes to undermine a society's political and economic institutions for their own gain (see **Table 14.2**). Certainly not all Jews in Germany in the early 20th century were wealthy, but as a group, Jews had done quite well for themselves and had attained many prominent positions in business, politics, and the arts. Similarly, Armenians in the Ottoman Empire were relatively prosperous and were admired (and envied) for their financial acumen. And in Rwanda, members of the Tutsi minority—because of the privileged position they had occupied in the colonial system before the country gained its independence (Smith, 1998)—were perceived by the Hutu majority as an arrogant elite. In all these cases, the majority developed a belief that the out-group was organized into a conspiracy to control the country from behind the scenes.

Table 14.2 Some targets of envious prejudice that were also targets of genocidal killing

Armenians in the Ottoman Empire, late 19th and early 20th centuries
Kulaks (independent farmers) in the Soviet Union, 1930s
Jews in Germany, 1930s and 1940s
Arabs and Indians in Zanzibar, 1960s
Chinese in Indonesia, 1960s
Igbo people in Nigeria, 1960s
Educated classes in Cambodia, 1970s
Tutsis in Rwanda, 1990s

Not all cases of genocide involve groups that are subject to envious prejudice. Groups who are subject to what Fiske et al. (2002) call contemptuous prejudice may also find themselves in a precarious situation. Such groups are seen as both hostile *and* low in competence; in extreme cases, they are seen essentially as dangerous animals. In the past, indigenous peoples have sometimes been viewed in this way by colonizers. Both the native peoples of North America and Tasmania (to give just two examples) were targets of contemptuous prejudice. Both became victims of brutal extermination campaigns.

Group processes that intensify prejudice

Some groups, then, have more potential than others to become scapegoats. For that potential to become a reality, members of perpetrator groups must collectively agree that the out-group poses a threat that must be

Ankole-Watusi cattle, a much admired breed associated with the Tutsis, and a symbol of the alleged wealth and power that led them to be the targets of envious prejudice in Rwanda.

retaliated against. Several of the group processes discussed in Chapter 8 (see also Tindale, Munier, Wasserman, & Smith, 2002) take place when people communicate with each other about a crisis. Together, they can cement an out-group's status as a dangerous enemy.

For example, when members of a group discuss any issue, widely shared attitudes, beliefs, and knowledge are more likely to be brought up than the idiosyncratic, unshared information that is available to relatively few individuals (Larson, Foster-Fishman, & Keys, 1994; Stasser & Titus, 1985), as we learned in Chapter 8. Stereotypes and prejudices tend to be widely shared; even people who are not convinced of their validity are familiar with such shared "social representations" (Moscovici, 1984). Thus, stereotypes are likely to come up when groups deliberate (Stawiski, Dykema-Engblade, & Tindale, 2012). As a result, many—if not most—group members will be ready to suspect that the supposedly unsavory, suspicious people in their midst could be responsible for societal crises. Consequently, groups of people seeking the source of an unfortunate state of affairs they are experiencing may be drawn inexorably to explanations that involve scapegoating.

In addition, research on group polarization (Isenberg, 1986) reveals that if people share attitudes or preferences, discussions of those attitudes and preferences can intensify them. If people already have negative attitudes toward an out-group, communicating with other people who share those attitudes can lead the group to cling to those prejudices even more strongly and confidently. Myers and Bishop (1970) found that when prejudiced white participants discussed their attitudes toward black people with each other, their attitudes became even more negative. Some research suggests that even the mere presence of other group members can activate any prejudices a person harbors, through a process of social facilitation (see Chapter 8). In other words, if the dominant, most immediate response to members of a group is negative, the arousal caused by the presence of others can enhance that response (Lambert et al., 2003).

Needless to say, crises can be attributed to many causes other than the actions of an out-group. Economic downturns, political instability, and social chaos could be explained in terms of environmental disaster, foreign aggression, or even an act of God. Unfortunately, if even a small faction of people in a society are motivated to pin the blame on some racial, religious, or ethnic group, they can, in some cases, convert others to their view. Research on the phenomenon of minority influence (Levine & Russo, 1987; Moscovici, Lage, & Naffrechoux, 1969; Nemeth, 1986; see Chapter 7) shows that a small, energetic, and committed subgroup can change others' perspectives on important issues or problems. Furthermore, minorities within a group are most influential not when they try to radically change the majority's basic assumptions, but when they argue that their minority view is consistent with values and beliefs almost everyone shares—such as stereotypes and prejudices (Smith, Dykema-Engblade, Walker, Niven, & McGrough, 2000; Tindale, Smith, Thomas, Filkins, & Sheffey, 1996). For many years, the Nazi Party, formed shortly after the First World War, captured only a small percentage of the popular vote. In part by exploiting widespread anti-Semitism, however, it eventually won the support of a sizable proportion of the electorate (Tindale et al., 2002).

The role of leaders

Mass murder is a collective project that is based on a group's shared experiences. That is, genocides take place when many people in a society develop the beliefs and feelings that motivate them to target other groups for extreme violence. Nonetheless, mass killings rarely break out spontaneously; they must be instigated by people with social power (Mandel, 2002), usually political or military leaders. As we noted in Chapter 6, powerful people can be very persuasive. All the preconditions for genocide could be in place, but without an opportunistic leader who is willing to "increase the propensity for violence" and "accelerate its pace once it has started," genocide is not inevitable (Mandel, 2002, p. 262).

Leaders and the institutions they oversee do not just instigate genocide; they also administer it. Genocide typically is not perpetrated by out-of-control mobs caught up in frenzied killing sprees. Rather, ambitious extermination projects are well planned, organized, and coordinated (Balakian, 2003; Hilberg, 1961; Prunier, 1995; Zajonc, 2002). In Rwanda, broadcasters on government-controlled radio stations exhorted Hutus to slaughter Tutsis, even directing them to the locations of potential victims (Gourevitch, 1998). Although ordinary people can become perpetrators (and blaming their conduct on "bad leaders" who led them astray cannot absolve them of responsibility), we should not forget that some kind of elite leadership group is almost always necessary to initiate and sustain mass killing.

Terrorism

The role of leaders could be even more crucial in the case of terrorist activity. As Staub (2004, p. 160) notes, "many terrorist groups are extremely hierarchical and are often headed by a single figure who assumes paramount importance for group members." For that reason, many terrorist groups do not outlive their charismatic leaders' death or capture.

In addition, many of the group processes that spark fear, hatred, and violence are arguably even more directly linked to terrorism than to genocide. A great deal of the research on those processes (which documents the power of shared information, group polarization, and so on) has been conducted with small groups. Significantly, terrorists are often organized into small groups of like-minded individuals, who intentionally isolate themselves from other people (Sageman, 2004). As one researcher has noted, "belonging to a group and remaining isolated from society at large reinforces the terrorists' ideology and strengthens their motivations" (Ferracuti, 1998). Thus, many of the psychological pressures associated with small group processes will be especially potent influences on terrorists' beliefs and intentions.

It would be a mistake, though, to conclude that decisions to engage in terrorism always result from subtle psychological processes whose effects build over time, influencing people without their awareness. In Chapter 5, we reviewed the theory of reasoned action (Ajzen & Fishbein, 1980), a model of how people decide on courses of action in a thoughtful way. According to that theory, people's behaviors are based on their intentions, and their intentions are based on their assessment of the likely outcomes of different courses of action. Those actions that are highly likely to yield the outcomes a particular person favors are the ones most likely to drive that person's intentions. Disturbing as it may seem, the theory of reasoned action can shed light on what causes people to engage in terrorism. Crenshaw (1998) and Kruglanski and Fishman (2006) note that groups often launch terror campaigns because they have come to the conclusion that terrorism is the most effective and efficient way to reach their goals—political independence, the withdrawal of an occupation force, and so on. Consistent with that idea, terrorist groups on many occasions have disbanded (or ceased engaging in terrorism) when alternatives to terrorism have become available as a result of political reforms or other major changes in a society (Davis & Cragin, 2009).

Thus, terrorism can be less the result of insidious group processes and other hidden influences than of cold, remorseless logic.

Selecting Scapegoats and Targeting Victims: A Summary

It is not surprising to hear that the victims of genocide and terrorism belong to groups that are perceived negatively by the perpetrators. What is less obvious is that certain kinds of negative perceptions are more strongly associated with mass killing than others. Groups that are the target of envious prejudice (that is, groups that are seen as competent but hostile) are victimized because the perpetrators see them as being responsible for major crises and disasters. Groups that are the target of contemptuous prejudice (groups that are seen as both incompetent and hostile) are victimized because they are considered to be subhuman people who must be brushed aside so that the perpetrators can achieve their goals.

Though such prejudices may be shared at first by only a small group of people, influential minorities can persuade others to share their views. Once those prejudices begin to take hold in a society, they can be embraced more widely and intensely through a variety of group processes such as the tendency to preferentially discuss shared knowledge and the way in which such discussions often polarize people's attitudes. These processes play themselves out over time without people's awareness. In other words, they are hidden influences on people's attitudes and beliefs. However, murderous attitudes are more likely to lead to murderous behavior when a group's leaders instigate the killing.

Think Like a Social Psychologist

Making connections

—Genocide clearly is not closely associated with any particular culture. However, can you identify aspects of (1) individualism; and (2) collectivism that would both facilitate and inhibit people's willingness to participate in genocide?

THE NIGHTMARE, PART III: PERSECUTION, BYSTANDER ACQUIESCENCE—AND MURDER

It is one thing to blame your misfortunes on the actions of some group of people and perhaps experience intense hatred of those people. It is another thing to acquiesce to violent persecution of that group and even participate in the violence. However, history shows that securing people's cooperation with genocidal policies and operations is less difficult than we might imagine. If the perpetrators of genocide engage in behavior that violates most people's moral standards, why do so many people fail to intervene or even speak up? And why do so many ultimately join in?

Claiming Coercion

Leaders always justify the decision to embark on a campaign of mass killing by referring to extraordinary circumstances. Supposedly, the threat posed by the out-group is so immense that its existence can no longer be tolerated (Bandura, 1999). It would not be difficult to imagine, then, that any attempts to prevent the slaughter also would not be tolerated. Perhaps people who do not see the need to exterminate the out-group go along with it because they are afraid to resist.

Certainly, in all the episodes of genocide described in this chapter, some people believed (often with justification) that not cooperating with the killing would lead to negative consequences. In one of the areas where massacres of Armenians took place, for example, residents were told that "If any Moslem protect a Christian, first, his house shall be burned, then the Christian killed before his eyes, and then his [the Moslem's] family and himself" (Balakian, 2003, p. 204). Elsewhere, orders posted on the streets stated that "any Muslim who protected or hid an Armenian would be punished by hanging" (Balakian, 2003, p. 266). In Rwanda, too, many Hutus described being told that they themselves would be killed if they did not participate in murdering Tutsis (Gourevitch, 1998).

On the other hand, the vast majority of people who play some passive or active role in genocide do so in the absence of explicit threats—without even the belief that they will be punished for failing to comply. Speaking about the aftermath of the Holocaust, for example, Browning (1992, p. 170) notes that "no defense attorney or defendant in any of the hundreds of postwar trials has been able to document a single case in which refusal to obey an order to kill unarmed civilians resulted in the allegedly inevitable dire punishment." Even in Rwanda, many perpetrators freely admitted that they never saw or heard of a person being punished for refusing to take part in the killings (Hatzfeld, 2003). Why, then, do people cooperate?

Recognizing Evil

As we saw in Chapter 12, if a person is going to intervene in some emergency—whether that means helping someone who has fallen down in a subway car or trying to prevent someone from being killed because of her ethnicity—that person must first clearly recognize what is happening (Latane & Darley, 1970). Of course, it is easier to imagine not noticing someone who has stumbled in a crowded train than to imagine being unaware that your neighbors have been targeted for extermination. As we learned in Chapter 6, however, when circumstances permit, people will often ignore information or stimuli that are threatening to them (Baumeister & Newman, 1994; Sweeney & Gruber, 1984)—and the mass suffering of others is likely to be especially hard to come to terms with (Cameron & Payne, 2011). For instance, when Mayer (1955) interviewed a German man after the Second World War about the deportation and murder of Jews, the man said that "… I didn't want to see it, because I would then have had to think about the consequences of seeing it, what followed from seeing it, what I must do to be decent" (p. 201). Mayer concluded that many of the people he talked with "didn't know because they didn't want to know" (p. 126).

People who claim that they did not notice anything are not always being truthful—a point to which we will return. Still, a passage from the memoirs of Albert Speer, who in the early 1930s was Hitler's personal architect and frequent companion, is revealing. He wrote that

> Only today have I recalled that on our tours of the country, when we were met with so much cheering, we again and again drove under streamers repeating the antisemitic slogans of the very man with whom I had sat at an idyllic picnic … Sometimes I ask myself: Didn't I even notice those slogans, "Jews undesirable here," or "Jews enter this locality at their own risk"? (Speer, 1976, p. 24)

Needless to say, it is not always possible to avoid noticing that people are being evicted from their homes, stripped of their property, publicly humiliated, or worse. Observers who are not convinced that these actions are justified will experience guilt, shame, sadness, and other forms of distress. In short, we can expect that they will feel bad about themselves for playing even an indirect role in the persecution. The most direct route available for dealing with such bad feelings would be to repudiate the violence or even attempt to prevent it. As we saw in Chapter 4, however, people who are experiencing a specific threat to their self-concepts (for example, a

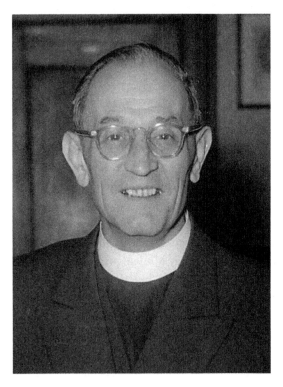

The costs of being a passive bystander From a poem attributed to Martin Niemöller (1892–1984), a German Pastor: "In Germany, they came first for the Communists, And I didn't speak up because I wasn't a Communist; And then they came for the trade unionists, And I didn't speak up because I wasn't a trade unionist; And then they came for the Jews, And I didn't speak up because I wasn't a Jew; And then... they came for me... And by that time there was no one left to speak up."

challenge to their sense of themselves as decent, moral people) do not always need to address that threat directly to feel better about themselves. Through the process of self-affirmation (Steele, 1988), a boost to their self-esteem in some other area might ease their discomfort. As a result, people who are uncomfortable standing by while their fellow citizens are subjected to intense discrimination might need only to read their children an extra bedtime story or give some money to a needy person on the street to live easily with themselves.

Finally, as we saw in Chapter 12, research on bystander intervention reveals that recognition of someone else's distress is not enough to ensure that we will help that person. If many other people witness the emergency—as is almost always the case in large-scale mass killings—the resulting diffusion of responsibility will reduce the likelihood of any one person taking any action (Latane & Darley, 1970). No individual person will feel he or she is the one who should do something, especially when the best course of action is unclear.

Regardless of why people remain passive or apathetic in the face of injustice and mass killing (see also Vincent, Emich, & Goncalo, 2013), inaction can create conditions in which violence is even more likely to occur, for several reasons. First, doing nothing can embolden the perpetrators. Second, a community's apathy about an out-group's fate can cause members of the group to feel hopeless, and thus to do less to resist victimization. In contrast, community support can embolden a group to act to save itself (Staub, 1989).

As we will see next, in the process of rationalizing their own passivity, people can develop attitudes that justify and support further cooperation with genocide (Staub, 2002).

Justifying Evil

To feel any degree of responsibility for helping others in these situations, it is necessary to label an event as an emergency (Latane & Darley, 1970). In some cases, people may not interpret an event as one that calls for intervention because its meaning is ambiguous (Has that woman fainted, or is she just taking a nap?). In other cases, though, people may be motivated to perceive an event in a particular way. Specifically, they may be motivated *not* to see the targets of violence as victims deserving of compassion (Imhoff & Banse, 2009).

As we saw in Chapters 4 and 6, when people engage in behavior that makes them feel uncomfortable—especially behavior they could control and that could lead to negative consequences—they experience an uncomfortable mental state called cognitive dissonance (Cooper, 2007; Cooper & Fazio, 1984; Festinger, 1957). People are motivated to get rid of dissonance, and one way to do so is to change their attitudes. As a result, one way to deal with the dissonance caused by failing to help others avoid a

The first step down the continuum of passivity? A woman complying with the Nazis' boycott of Jewish businesses, Germany, 1933. Will her inaction make it easier for her to later ignore even more serious acts of persecution?

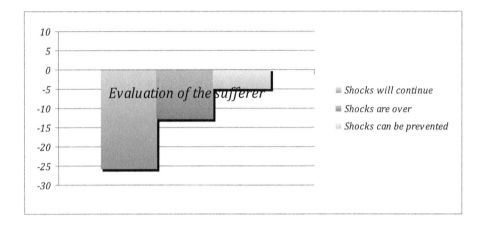

Figure 14.2: The just-world phenomenon: Impressions of a woman subjected to painful electric shocks as a function of whether the suffering will continue or can be controlled.

More negative ratings mean that the woman was evaluated more harshly (seen as less likable, attractive, mature, etc.).

Source: Lerner & Simmons (1966).

cruel and unjustified death is for people to change their attitude toward the victims. Unfortunately, concluding that the victims deserved their fate prepares a person to accept even harsher behavior toward them. In essence, deciding to remain a bystander can be the first step down what could be called the **continuum of passivity**. In other words, it can initiate a process that leads people to become more and more comfortable with acquiescing to genocide as they try to resolve their mounting dissonance.

The tendency for people to believe that those who experience misfortune deserve their fate is known as the **just-world phenomenon** (Hafer & Bègue, 2005; Lerner, 1980; Lerner & Simmons, 1966). Derogating others in this way is especially likely when people feel they have no control over the fate of the sufferers. For example, participants in Lerner and Simmons's (1966) study who observed a woman receiving painful electric shocks while participating in a memory experiment formed a negative impression of her—even though the woman received the shocks for making just a few understandable memory errors. Participants' reactions were especially negative when they were told that the experiment would have a second part, during which the poor woman would presumably receive more shocks. Because they expected to see more suffering, they were especially motivated to justify it. When participants believed they would be able to reassign the woman to a kinder, gentler "positive reinforcement" condition for the second part of the experiment—that is, when they felt they had the power to end her suffering—their impressions of her were more neutral (only slightly negative: see **Figure 14.2**).

To convince themselves that others deserve to suffer, people have at their disposal all the motivated reasoning strategies discussed in Chapters 3, 4, and 6. For example, members of perpetrator groups commonly convince themselves that they are actually the "victims" of the very people they are persecuting. What the group targeted for killing is experiencing is seen as mild compared to the wrongdoings they engaged in, which caused them to deserve their fate (Bandura, 1999, 2004). Many Germans convinced themselves that Jews were to blame for the treatment they were receiving because they had allegedly stabbed Germany in the back, causing the country's defeat in the First World War. Similarly, many of the Turks who took part in killing Armenians told themselves they were doing so because the Armenians had collaborated with the Russians, who had defeated them early in the same war.

Participating in Evil

Clearly, if a program of extermination is going to be carried out, the instigators of the killing need more than just passive acceptance and tacit approval. Someone has to do the actual killing. Typically, the front-line killers operate as organized groups and include soldiers, police, members of paramilitary groups, death camp personnel, or members of specially organized death squads. Although in some cases people are almost randomly assigned to such groups (Browning, 1992), often some sort of self-selection takes place. In other words, people who are already motivated to punish the victim group are more likely than others to join (Staub, 2002). However, it is one thing to hate a group, and another to be "perfectly comfortable with engaging in activities such as shooting people through the head, burying them alive, and even killing infants" (Newman, 2002, p. 52). What leads people to begin participating in such horrors?

Obedience

Most genocidal killings certainly are not the work of reluctant killers, who feel they have no choice but to obey orders (Berkowitz, 1989; Fenigstein, 1998; Mandel, 1998). However, obedience could play a role in encouraging people to begin participating in mass killings (Blass, 2002; Newman & Erber, 2002a; Sabini & Silver, 1980). As we saw in Chapter 7, when people believe that authorities can legitimately demand their compliance, they often do as they are told. Milgram's (1974) experiments showed that even when people do not have any past experience cooperating with an authority or any reason to believe their actions will produce a desirable outcome, they will follow orders to hurt others. If people will engage in potentially lethal behavior in response to a request from an "experimenter" for the sake of a "learning experiment," they are probably even more likely to engage in brutal behavior when the orders come from established leaders of what they believe is a historic national struggle.

Browning (1992) describes a case in which members of the German Reserve Police Battalion 101, none of whom had ever participated in the systematic murder of civilians, were assigned to round up and shoot all the Jews in a small Polish village. The vast majority of the men complied. As Browning (1992, pp. 173–174) noted, this event could be thought of as "a kind of radical Milgram experiment that took place in a Polish forest with real killers and victims rather than in a social psychology laboratory with naïve subjects." Many similar incidents could be described. However, Muñoz-Rojas and Frésard (2004) argue that it is less common for leaders to explicitly direct people to carry out atrocities than to implicitly or indirectly authorize brutality, by indicating that some goal must be accomplished and failing to rule out any means of achieving that goal.

Conformity

Perpetrators of genocide are responsive not only to pressure from above, but to perceived pressure from their peers. In other words, conformity (Asch, 1956) also leads people to become perpetrators. Disagreement with members of one's group can be psychologically uncomfortable (Matz & Wood, 2005). In addition, when people resist going along with what their peers are doing or saying for moral reasons, they can face resentment and rejection (Monin, Sawyer, & Marquez, 2008; see **Figure 14.3**). Conformity can help people to escape both these predicaments.

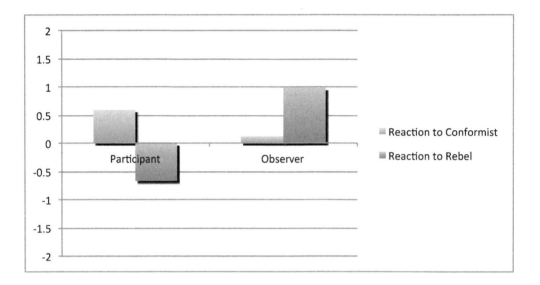

Figure 14.3: How do people react to those who fail to conform—rebels—versus those who do? Participants in one experiment (none of them African American) made a group decision to identify an African American as the probable perpetrator of a crime. Later (left), they reacted more positively to a person who conformed to their decision (blue) than to a rebel who did not (red). Interestingly, a separate group of people, who did not play a role in the decision (observers, right), reacted more positively to the rebel than to the conformist.

Note: Impressions could range from +5 (positive impression) to −5 (negative impression). Source: Monin, Sawyer, & Marquez (2008, Study 2).

Studies have shown that during wartime, soldiers report being motivated less by hatred of the enemy than by a desire not to let their fellow soldiers down (Muñoz-Rojas & Frésard, 2004; Stouffer et al., 1949). Indeed, the men of Reserve Police Battalion 101, after receiving their assignment to shoot all the Jews in the village, were told by their commanding officer that anyone who was uncomfortable with participating could be excused. Very few took advantage of the opportunity to escape the assignment. Many of those who participated in the killing later reported that they did not want to stand out or "lose face" (Browning, 1992, p. 72). More generally, as Bourke (1999, p. 81) suggests, "Taunts about virility and competence could be irresistible to young, immature men trapped in hostile environments far from home."

The concept of conformity sheds light on the behavior not just of people engaged in face-to-face killing. In Rwanda, for example, Gourevitch (1998) encountered prominent Hutus who had close friendships with Tutsis, and had taken a public stand against the virulent hatred directed at them. One Hutu, who had served as minister of justice not long before the genocide, had even tried to arrest a politician who encouraged the killing of Tutsis in a radio broadcast. But he soon "saw which way the wind was blowing" (p. 97) and brought his attitudes into alignment with the Hutus' ideology. Ultimately, he played an active role in encouraging and administering the killing.

Mandler (2002) documented another case of conformity: the behavior of the German Society for Psychology, whose members played a shameful role in the Nazi persecution of the Jews. Before Hitler's rise to power early in 1933, many Jews held prominent leadership roles in the society. Within months of the Nazis' takeover of the government, however, the society had allied itself with the new regime. Jews were dismissed from the editorial boards of journals and from the society's executive board. The biannual meeting of the group that year featured lectures on racial purity and speeches extolling the "great psychologist Adolf Hitler" (p. 192). As Mandler notes, none of these actions was required by law. In fact, they were taken at a time when "one did not need to be a hero or to risk one's life and liberty to express opposition or distance from the regime" (p. 193).

Pluralistic ignorance

Some see no sense in explaining participation in genocide and mass killings in terms of conformity (see Goldhagen, 1996). After all, people generally conform to majority viewpoints. In other words, if a person is being pressured to participate in atrocities, then most members of the group must already favor participating in such activities. Therefore, the massacres and other brutal actions would take place anyway, with or without pressure to conform.

Such arguments miss a crucial point. People conform to what they *believe* is the group's attitude, not necessarily to the *actual* attitude. In addition, people's judgments about what their peers are thinking and feeling are often mistaken. This phenomenon, discussed in Chapter 12, is known as pluralistic ignorance (Miller & Prentice, 1994). Pluralistic ignorance is especially likely to occur in situations in which people are afraid or embarrassed to express their opinions publicly. Miller and Prentice (1994) present a clear and relevant example in discussing Matza's (1964) research on juvenile delinquents:

> Matza argued that the individual members of juvenile gangs actually lacked a firm commitment to their antisocial behavior, at least initially. In fact, each of the youths in the gang was privately very uncomfortable with his own behavior. But because the youths were unwilling to express their reservations publicly, they each appeared to the others as fully committed to, and comfortable with, the

Pluralistic Ignorance in Nazi Germany Shortly after the Nazis came to power in Germany, "Heil Hitler" (with an upraised arm) became the standard greeting. Although many made the gesture enthusiastically, others felt pressured or coerced to do so. But because they went along with the practice anyway, "it looked as though everyone was turning into a Nazi, a view that stepped up pressure to conform" (Fritzsche, 2008, p. 23).

group's delinquency. The facade of toughness thus created "a system of shared misunderstandings," which, in turn, led to a level of antisocial behavior that no individual member fully embraced. (p. 543)

Similarly, people who sympathize with a group that has been labeled as their "enemy" or are revolted by what they are being asked to do to that group might be reluctant to speak up; they might fear being seen as traitors or cowards. Such could be the case, even if the people who feel that way are in the majority. Strange as it may seem, then, perpetrators could end up conforming to an attitude that might not be held by any other individual in the group.

Roles and deindividuation

In some cases, people are led to violate their usual norms neither by pressure from above nor by direct pressure from peers. Instead, they are encouraged to engage in aggressive, violent behavior, simply by virtue of the roles they play in social situations. The most well-known demonstration of this phenomenon is the Stanford prison experiment (Haney, Banks, & Zimbardo, 1973; Zimbardo, Maslach, & Haney, 2000), discussed in Chapter 7. In that study, a group of young men, none of whom had any history of mental illness or criminal behavior, was randomly divided into "guards" and "prisoners." Within a short time, the guards spontaneously began to humiliate and abuse the prisoners.

In many or most cases outside the psychology laboratory, people take on roles because they have sought them out or volunteered for them (Staub, 2002). Thus, a sadistic concentration camp guard might hold that job in part because he or she finds the work attractive, exciting, or at the least, tolerable. However, the Stanford prison experiment suggests that roles themselves can shape people's behavior. People will adjust their behavior and make decisions based on what they perceive to be their role requirements, rather than on their usual moral standards.

Wearing a mask can lead to deindividuation—and the loosening of one's usual standards for behavior.

Some roles are especially likely to cause people to disengage from their usual ways of thinking, feeling, and behaving. In other words, it is easier to lose oneself in some roles than in others. When people wear uniforms or masks, and/or when they are identified and addressed in terms of their job title, rank, or even number, they can become deindividuated—a state in which people feel less recognizable as individuals and less accountable for their behavior (Zimbardo, 1970; see Chapter 8). Jobs in military, paramilitary, and police organizations—groups that often play a central role in genocidal operations—tend to fit those characteristics, and thus to foster deindividuation.

However, any situational variable that leads people to relax their usual standards of behavior can promote violence. Mullen (1986; Leader, Mullen, & Abrams, D., 2007) studied lynchings of black people by white mobs that took place in the United States between 1899 and 1946. He suggested that the more numerous lynchers were relative to their victims, the more deindividuated they would be. As a result, he hypothesized, the more savage their atrocities would be (for example, the more their assaults would involve prolonged torture or dismemberment). His findings supported that hypothesis. A lynch mob of 100 will engage in more horrifying behavior toward two victims than toward four victims and will behave more brutally than a group of 20 toward two victims.

Initiating and Tolerating Killing: A Summary

How and why do people become participants in and accomplices to genocide? Undeniably, some people become parties to genocide because they are afraid to do otherwise. However, people will become passive bystanders or active perpetrators, even when they are not being directly coerced and would not be punished for behaving with decency and compassion.

Still, taking an active stance against brutality is more difficult than simply going about one's business as if nothing were happening. As a result, people may do what they can to avoid noticing or being aware of the injustices another group is experiencing. If they cannot avoid coming face to face with the group's persecution, they may instead convince themselves that the victims deserve their fate. Alternatively, diffusion of responsibility may allow them to conclude that even if they themselves take no action, others will surely help the victimized group. Unfortunately, the more often a person does nothing to prevent violence against a group, the easier it becomes to continue doing nothing. Without reflecting on the process—and without much or even any awareness—people can easily slide down the continuum of passivity.

Some people, of course, do more than acquiesce in a group's persecution; they actively carry it out. To be sure, many people who play major roles in mass killings seek out those roles because their attitudes and beliefs make doing so relatively easy. However, even "ordinary men" (Browning, 1992) can become perpetrators of genocide in response to pressure to be obedient and conform. People can even conform to group attitudes that do not exist—that is, pluralistic ignorance can prevent them from discovering that their peers have the same qualms they do. When people blend into a group or are perceived by others in terms of their formal roles rather than their uniqueness as individuals, they can become deindividuated. Deindividuation loosens the normal constraints on their behavior, making it easier for them to violate their usual moral standards.

Think Like a Social Psychologist

Making connections
—Many members of groups that attempt to exterminate others later claim that they did not know what was going on. Imagine a person whose neighbors—members of a victimized group—are all disappearing. What mental maneuvers might he or she engage in to keep from becoming aware of what is going on?

THE NIGHTMARE, PART IV: INCREASING COMMITMENT, INCREASING BRUTALITY

Facing the fact that human beings will passively accept the extermination of a group of people is troubling. Knowing that they may cooperate with the work of the perpetrators is even more disturbing, and learning that some may take an active role, even without coercion, can be profoundly depressing. Reviewing the details of an actual genocide, however, can be an experience of almost unimaginable horror and disgust. In Nanking, some soldiers competed to see who could behead the most victims in the shortest time. Women—even pregnant women—were disemboweled after being raped. Some victims were buried or burned alive. There were even reports of people being buried up to their waists and then ripped apart by dogs. Unfortunately, that is only an abbreviated list of the cruelties inflicted on the Chinese people during the Rape of Nanking (Chang, 1997).

Unquestionably, some people are more likely than others to initiate and participate in such unspeakable behavior. As we saw in Chapter 13, males are more physically aggressive than females (Archer, 2004), and that holds true in the context of genocide and mass killings. There are exceptions to this generalization, of course. Among the more notorious tormenters of concentration camp inmates during the Second World War were Ilse Koch—"the Witch of Buchenwald"—and Hermine Braunsteiner, "the Stomping Mare" of Ravensbrück and Majdanek. And in Rwanda, Pauline Nyiramasuhuko, the minister of family and women's affairs, played a major role in the roundup and execution of the Tutsis; she even orchestrated mass rapes (Landesman, 2002). Nonetheless, the vast majority of active perpetrators (that is, those who actually do the killing) are male.

What about personality characteristics? It would be a mistake to assume that perpetrators are simply sick, evil human beings who operate under a different set of rules from "normal" people. Specifying in advance how involved any given person will become in a mass killing campaign or how brutal his or her actions will be is difficult or impossible. Violent perpetrators simply are not characterized by any consistent sets of personality traits (Browning, 1992; Suedfeld & Schaller, 2002; Zillmer, Harrower, Ritzler, & Archer, 1995). Similarly, as one researcher puts it, "Terrorism is not the product of mentally deranged persons" (Sprinzak, 1998, p. 78; see also Kruglanski & Fishman, 2006). The behavior of perpetrators may seem abnormal, but the psychological processes that lead to it can be normal and predictable.

Genocide and Mass Killing

The continuum of destructiveness

People are not naturally comfortable with lopping off their neighbors' heads, murdering babies, or herding people over a cliff (a common fate of victims of the Armenian genocide). Indeed, even trained soldiers do not find it easy to aim their guns at other human beings and shoot them, especially during their first few battles (Bourke, 1999). Humans must be transformed into the kind of person who can do such things. How does that transformation take place?

As we have learned throughout this book (see Chapters 4 and 6, for example), several social psychological theories (especially cognitive dissonance and self-perception theory) make the point that just as attitudes affect behavior (see Chapter 5), behavior affects a person's attitudes. When people are subtly coerced to tell a lie, they tend to start believing that lie. When they find themselves publicly advocating a policy with which they disagree, their attitude toward the policy becomes more positive. If people are made to think of themselves as extraverted, they begin to see themselves as being extraverted and even to behave in a more extraverted way. Finally—and most relevant to this discussion—if a situation leads people to harm others (or at least to believe they are harming others), their feelings about their victims become more negative (Goldstein, Davis, & Herman, 1975). That is, they see them as more deserving of punishment. In sum, persecution and killing makes yet more persecution and killing easier (Martens, Kosloff, Greenberg, Landau, & Schmader, 2007).

Whatever leads people to participate in discrimination and persecution, continued involvement in such activity will create pressure to justify it (Valdesolo & DeSteno, 2007). One way to justify it is to decide that victims deserve what they get. That, in turn, can encourage people to intensify their brutality. Overall, the situational influences that first lead people to participate in persecution can launch them down what Staub (1989, 2002) calls the **continuum of destructiveness**, or what Bandura (1999) refers to as **gradualistic moral disengagement**. This process, which unfolds over time, can transform normal people into perpetrators who feel profound hatred and disgust toward their victims (Bilewicz & Vollhardt, 2012). Once people reach the point of believing that their attitudes and behaviors are not only reasonable, but morally necessary, anything becomes permissible (Skitka & Mullen, 2002).

What follows is a summary of some of the ways in which perpetrators convince themselves that their behavior is just, and their victims deserve to be exterminated.

Rationalization and justification

It might seem reasonable to assume that people are capable of participating in horrific activities because they have somehow removed themselves from the situation psychologically—that is, they have "gone numb." But a study of soldiers who killed during war led to the conclusion that "one of the most disturbing features in the private letters and diaries of combatants is the extent to which they were not 'numbed.'" That is, the soldiers felt they had to make sense of what they were doing, to rationalize it somehow (Bourke, 1999, p. 7).

The same is true of the perpetrators of genocide (Bandura, 1999). As we have seen, bystanders to persecution and murder are often driven to justify their behavior. Needless to say, active participants feel even more pressure to do so. Invariably, they insist that their victims are responsible for their own fate because of their aggression toward the perpetrator group. The Nazis justified the attempted extermination of the Jews by pointing to an alleged Jewish conspiracy to weaken and destroy Germany. The Turks accused the Armenians of a similar subterfuge; many of the perpetrators reported believing that they were only doing what their victims would have done to them, had they had the chance (Balakian, 2003).

A Rwandan rubbing a machete on a whetstone during the genocide in 1994 might be less likely to think of what he was doing as "preparing to kill my neighbors" as he would to think of it as "sharpening a tool" (more concrete) or "helping set my people free" (more abstract).

Reinterpretation

As we saw in Chapter 4, people can sometimes avoid facing the implications of their behavior by changing the way they think about it. According to action identification theory (Vallacher & Wegner, 1987), any given action can be labeled in many different ways. In the midst of criminal activity, for example, burglars may not think about what they are doing as "breaking the law," "stealing," or "causing pain and distress to other people." Instead, they may focus on technical details, such as "figuring out which tool is needed to unlock this door" or "plotting the best escape route" (Baumeister, 1990). Similarly, fighter pilots and snipers who are engaged in armed conflicts often report thinking of their activities as practicing a skill rather than killing people (Bourke, 1999). Bandura (1999) refers to this strategy for disguising the meaning of one's behavior as the use of euphemistic language.

Euphemistic language abounds during times of persecution. One historian has observed that in Nazi Germany,

> the rationales behind mass murder were linked to the resolution of various dangers or threats that could be warded off by "liquidating" the Jews: the "cleansing of the hinterland" on the eastern front or the "roundup of partisan nests," the elimination of the black market or of diseases, the punishment of sabotage and of assassination of German soldiers, or just the extermination of Bolshevism. (Herbert, 1998, p. 114)

An extreme example of this approach to justifying genocide is to think of exterminating a group of people as a way of creating a more perfect and peaceful world (Koons, 2003; Norfolk & Ignatieff, 1998). In the 1989 documentary film, *The Architecture of Doom*, Nazi leaders (many of whom had backgrounds in the arts)

Table 14.3: My group is more human than your group—or at least, we're more linked to human-related words

HUMAN WORDS	ANIMAL WORDS
Wife	Pet
Maiden	Mongrel
Woman	Pedigree
Person	Breed
Husband	Wildlife
Humanity	Critter
People	Cub
Civilian	Creature
Man	Feral
Citizen	Wild

Research participants found it easier to associate human words with their own country and its people and easier to associate animal words with people of another nationality (as assessed with an Implicit Association Test).

Source: Viki et al. (2006).

are shown to have idealized the Holocaust, seeing it as a project to create a more beautiful, aesthetically pleasing Europe.

Dehumanization played a central role in the persecution and killing of Native Americans

Dehumanization of Victims

Perpetrators do not just relabel their own behavior; they relabel their victims. Specifically, they **dehumanize** them (Bandura, 1999; Haslam, 2006; Hodson & Costello, 2007), a process made easier by the fact that in general, people tend to implicitly see members of out-groups as less human than members of their in-groups (Boccato, Capozza, Falvo, & Durante, 2008; Viki et al., 2006; see **Table 14.3**). Not surprisingly, perpetrators find it much easier to aggress against people who have been labeled subhuman (Bandura, Underwood, & Fromson, 1975). During the genocide in Rwanda, Tutsis were commonly referred to as "cockroaches" (Gourevitch, 1998). In the Ottoman Empire, Armenians were labeled "dangerous microbes" that had to be destroyed to safeguard the nation's health (Balakian, 2003, p. 164). During the Second World War, a member of a Japanese military unit that conducted unethical medical experiments insisted on calling the subjects of the experiments "logs," rather than "people" (Blumenthal & Miller, 1999, p. A10). And a Holocaust survivor who had been forced to dig up the graves of murdered Jews recalled that his German supervisors insisted the bodies they unearthed be referred to as "rags" (Lanzmann, 1995).

An attributional bias that encourages dehumanization: Perceiver-induced constraint

People who have been targeted for extermination are eventually reduced to a pitiful state. The fact that they are starving, emaciated, dirty, ragged, and in a state of constant terror helps perpetrators to see them as less than human, if they are motivated to see them in that way. Of course, the only reason the victimized group is in that state is because of the perpetrators' actions. Surely, the perpetrators could not ignore that fact. Some accounts of genocide, however, suggest that they do.

Rudolf Höss, the Nazi commandant of the notorious Auschwitz concentration camp, reportedly remarked to a visitor that the camp's inmates "are not like you and me. You saw them yourself; they are different. They look different. They do not behave like human beings." The visitor later remarked that

> It had never occurred to Hoss that he had created the conditions that reduced the prisoners to the level of rats scraping and fighting for every crumb of bread. Beset by malnutrition and disease, how could they have looked like average human beings when the camp was devised to reduce the human being to his bare animal state? (Paskuly, in *Hoss*, 1992, p. 198)

Similarly, Goldhagen (1996) describes how in one Nazi work camp, female prisoners were not provided with latrines in their barracks, but were instead forced to use buckets. Not enough buckets were provided, so of course they would overflow.

> As if the permanent stench was not itself a sufficient form of punishment, the camp's guards beat the Jewish women daily, including the seriously ill, ostensibly for the soiling of their barracks. Yet they would not provide the Jews with the additional buckets that would have altered the conditions producing these "punishments." (p. 341)

In other words, the Germans "'punished' the Jews for things which the Germans themselves guaranteed that the Jews could not avoid doing" (p. 342).

How can we understand the perpetrators' apparent failure to take into account the impact of their own behavior on their victims' appearance and behavior? One possibility is that they actually do, but pretend not to out of maliciousness (Goldhagen, 1996). In other words, perpetrators may well be aware that they are being unreasonable and unfair, and may simply be looking for new and creative ways to torment their victims.

Though ruling out that possibility is difficult in any given case, there is a more subtle interpretation. In Chapter 3, we reviewed research on perceiver-induced constraint (Gilbert & Jones, 1986; Gilbert, Jones, & Pelham, 1987). In those studies, participants actively directed and controlled other people's behavior, yet they still committed the fundamental attribution error. That is, they took people's behavior at face value, without taking the situational constraints into account. For example, participants who signaled others to express politically conservative opinions concluded that those participants actually were more conservative than participants who were instructed to express liberal opinions.

Research on perceiver-induced constraint reveals that people are capable of ignoring the obvious effects of their own actions on others, even when they have no vested interest in reaching a biased conclusion. After all, participants in the study just described had no reason to want to find evidence for one political orientation or the other. What happens, then, if people are motivated to ignore their own influence on others? What if doing so would help them to justify the brutal way in which others have been treated? In such cases, we could reasonably expect even more of an illogical and unjust disregard for their own influence on others. In sum, perpetrators may well be able to justify their behavior by reasoning that their victims are less than human, even when they themselves created the conditions that reduced their victims to a state of desperation.

Terrorism

Like the perpetrators of genocide, terrorists are molded gradually, in a step-by-step process of increasing radicalization (McCauley & Segal, 1989; Moghaddam, 2005; Sprinzak, E., 1998; Staub, 2004; see **Figure 14.4**).

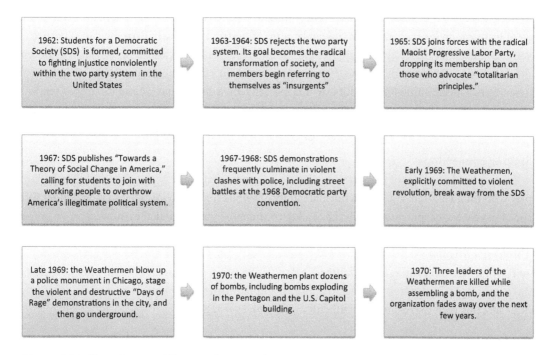

Figure 14.4: Terrorism and the continuum of destructiveness: The case of the Weathermen.

Source: Based on Sprinzak, 1998.

Some terrorist organizations arise out of groups engaged in normal political activity such as running for election or trying to influence the legislative process. Frustration at the ineffectiveness of those efforts or the slow pace of change can push them toward increasingly confrontational and violent behavior. As each extreme action is justified, it lays the groundwork for another even more extreme one. Once people have totally committed themselves to terrorism, repenting or turning back becomes difficult or impossible (Ferracuti, 1998).

Furthermore, many of the psychological maneuvers people use to rationalize mass killing can be observed in members of terrorist groups (Kressel, 2002). Acts of violence may be justified as "God's will." Potential victims (including anyone associated in any way with the institution or system seen by terrorists as the oppressor) may be labeled as "infidels"—a way of dehumanizing them and excluding them from normal moral considerations (Rapoport, 1998).

The Emergence and Maintenance of Brutal Behavior: A Summary

It is difficult for many people to understand how anyone could become actively involved in an extermination campaign. Understanding the almost unbelievable brutality of many perpetrators' behavior is even harder. The vast majority of those who participate in genocide do not see mass killing as a normal or appropriate thing to do. When their behavior causes them to feel dissonance and discomfort, they try to justify their actions to reduce their distress. They may rationalize the killing as a response to a provocation or convince themselves that their victims were not really human beings. They may even relabel their behavior so they can think of themselves as (for example) "making the world safe for my family" instead of "executing everyone in the village." The more the perpetrators justify their behavior, the easier it becomes for them to engage in even more brutal acts. That is, the process of justification leads them down the continuum of destructiveness. In extreme cases, perpetrators will not even recognize that they caused their victims' "subhuman" behavior (for example, stealing food or eating leaves) by their own actions (for instance, by starving them). In effect, the perpetrators' need to justify their cruelty serves as a hidden influence on the way they perceive their own behavior and its consequences.

Think Like a Social Psychologist

Making connections

—Biographical accounts of perpetrators of genocide show that many of them were able to go home, play with their children, and have a normal family life while they were involved in mass killing. What social-psychological processes might have allowed them to live such a dual existence?

Thinking critically

—To what extent do you agree with the idea that perpetrators of genocide often are not conscious of the psychological processes they use to adjust to and rationalize their own behavior? To what extent does agreeing with that claim raise difficult moral and legal issues?

DOES SOCIAL PSYCHOLOGY CONDONE PERPETRATORS?

We have reviewed a wide range of social psychological research to answer the basic question addressed by this chapter: How and why do people participate in genocidal killing and acts of terrorism? Some readers, though, may wonder if studying this material has been worth the effort. After all, they already have an answer to this question: People who do terrible things are terrible people. Terrorists and perpetrators of genocide are simply brutal, sadistic people, and such people commit brutal, sadistic crimes. More to the point, many readers—probably most—surely believe that mass killers are highly unusual people, who do not have much in common with them or the people they know and love.

As we saw in Chapter 3, people—especially those in individualistic cultures—have a tendency to explain others' behavior in terms of stable dispositions (Ross & Nisbett, 1991). The bias to label others with traits that describe their behavior is even more pronounced when people are motivated to infer specific traits (Spencer, Fein, Zanna, & Olson, 2003). The assumption that people would be motivated to conclude that those who engage in horrible behavior have horrible traits seems reasonable, then. After all, the alternative might be to conclude that such people were affected by situational factors, to which we all might be exposed someday. Diamond (1992, p. 277) summarizes this idea by noting that "we'd like to believe that nice people don't commit genocide, only Nazis do." As should be clear by now, however, perpetrators of genocide (and of terrorism) are often quite ordinary people (see Browning, 1992, 1998; Darley, 1992; Gross, 2001; Staub, 1989).

Not only do people embrace simple trait explanations for evil behavior; they can be actively dismissive of—perhaps even hostile toward—accounts that involve social and other contextual factors (Miller, Buddie, & Kretschmar, 2002; Rosenbaum, 1998). Miller, Gordon, and Buddie (1999) presented student research participants with a description of a hypothetical study of a particular form of wrongdoing, cheating. They told participants that the experimenters expected people to cheat less on a test if they were made to feel highly self-aware (see Chapter 4). Specifically, people were expected to cheat less than others if they worked in front of a mirror, because mirrors increase self-awareness. This hypothesis was tested and supported two decades earlier by Diener and Wallbom (1976).

Miller et al., however, presented each participant with one of two different summaries of the study's alleged results. They told half the participants (those in the situational explanation condition) of a powerful situational effect: only 5 percent of the participants in the mirror condition cheated, compared to 90 percent in the no-mirror condition. They told the other participants (those in the dispositional explanation condition) that there was no mirror effect at all. Moreover, participants in the hypothetical study had completed an individual-difference measure of honesty, and the researchers found a powerful dispositional effect. Specifically, only 5 percent of those who scored high on honesty cheated, compared to 90 percent of those who scored low on honesty.

Finally, Miller et al. asked participants to report the degree to which they thought the cheaters in these studies were personally responsible for what they did; the extent to which they thought the cheaters' behavior was intentional; and the degree to which they thought the cheaters should be blamed for what they did. They also asked participants to guess how the *researchers who had conducted the study* would answer the same questions.

Not surprisingly, participants in the dispositional explanation condition attributed high levels of responsibility, intentionality, and blameworthiness to the cheaters. They predicted that the researchers would feel the same way. The responses of participants in the situational explanation condition, however, were noteworthy in two respects. First, they too attributed high levels of responsibility, intentionality, and blameworthiness to the cheaters—in fact, they perceived them no differently than participants in the dispositional explanation condition. Thus, these participants seemed to resist taking situational influences into account in judging people who engage in antisocial behavior. Second, despite their own feelings, these participants predicted that the researchers would *not* see the cheaters' behavior as intentional, and would not hold the cheaters responsible or blame them for what they did (see **Table 14.4**).

Table 14.4: Judgments of evildoers (cheaters) as a function of the apparent cause of the behavior (situation or trait) and the participant's perspective (the participant's own perspective or beliefs about the researchers' perspective)

JUDGMENT	OWN PERSPECTIVE		RESEARCHERS' ASSUMED PERSPECTIVE	
	SITUATION	TRAIT	SITUATION	TRAIT
Responsible	8.12	8.77	5.00	7.65
Intentional	6.97	7.23	4.82	7.16
Blameworthy	6.88	7.13	3.82	5.65

Judgments were made on 11-point scales ranging from 0 (not at all) to 10 (extremely). Participants thought that psychologists emphasizing situational influences on wrongdoing were exonerating the wrongdoers (that is, absolving them of responsibility).

Source: Based on the results of Miller, Gordon, & Buddie (1999).

Participants were perfectly able to understand the results of the study described to them. They were also aware that other observers might be more hesitant to demonize wrongdoers after learning about situational influences on people's decisions to engage in antisocial behavior. Yet, they seemed to actively resist acknowledging the implications of the situational manipulation (the presence or absence of the mirror) on people's behavior. These findings were replicated in another study conducted by Miller et al. (1999; see also Newman & Bakina,

2009), in which participants were told that people's tendency to engage in aggressive behavior was strongly predicted either by their disposition to aggress or by a situational variable, hot weather (see Chapter 13 and Anderson, Anderson, & Deuser, 1996).

We have already discussed why people might be motivated to infer that evil behavior is the work of evil people, regardless of the context in which that behavior takes place. Why, however, would participants believe that the researchers who conducted the study would be more forgiving than they were toward cheaters or aggressors? They may have fallen prey to the **naturalistic fallacy**—the tendency to think that studies that show *what* people do imply what people *ought* to do (Friedrich, 2005; Friedrich, Kierniesky, & Cardon, 1989). Unfortunately, when participants make this error and assume that researchers endorse a behavior that the study is only describing, they may become angry or hostile toward the researchers (Friedrich, 2005; Lilienfeld, 2002). Perhaps that is why some people resist social-psychological attempts to understand the roots of evil behavior that go beyond simply condemning the evildoers.

But social-psychological thinking about the causes of genocide, mass killing, and terrorism is not aimed at providing excuses for the perpetrators. Instead, the goal is to educate people about the ways in which social situations may lead them to violate their usual standards of behavior. People are *not* helpless in the face of social and contextual factors—a point that has been made repeatedly in this book. True, they are not always aware of those factors. As we have seen, however, most—if not all—hidden influences on behavior lose much of their power when people become aware of their influence and are motivated to overcome them. In sum, it is true that the social psychologist's role is to encourage people to become less complacent about their resistance to evil and to counteract their tendency to believe that only terrible people do terrible things. Nonetheless, acknowledging the power of social and other situational factors does not excuse criminal behavior. People do resist the pressure or temptation to engage in wrongdoing, and it is everyone's responsibility to do so.

Finally, as we saw in Chapter 1, although social psychologists focus on how situations influence people's behavior and on the normal psychological processes that all people share, they do not ignore the existence of individual differences among people. Social psychologists recognize the importance of personality variables, and even more so, the importance of the interaction between personality and situational variables (Caprara & Cervone, 2000; Magnusson, 1990). As we have stated before (see Chapter 1), just as some situations are more likely than others to elicit aggression, some people are more likely than others to act aggressively. Not only that; situations do not always have the same effects on everyone. Certain situations will trigger hostile feelings in some people, but not in others. Thus, some people are more likely than others to participate in terrorism or genocide. However, no reader of this book should believe that he or she is immune from the possibility of doing so

Think Like a Social Psychologist

Thinking critically

—We have just seen that an interactionist perspective is helpful in understanding the role of personality in influencing people to participate in genocide. Imagine a set of circumstances that might make lazy, unmotivated people more likely than others to participate in mass killing. Now, imagine a different set of circumstances that might make energetic, ambitious people more likely than others to participate. Do the same for the traits anxious/high-strung versus calm/collected.

—When perpetrators of genocide are brought to trial, they commonly claim that they were not responsible for their actions because circumstances compelled them to do what they did. How valid do you think that defense is, and why?

THE PAST IS TRANSFORMED

Eventually, genocidal killings come to an end. In some cases (for example, Rwanda and Nazi Germany), the governments that sponsor them are defeated. In others, the killings continue until the target group has been reduced to a remnant (Native Americans in the United States, for instance). In at least one case—the systematic murder of Tasmanian natives by Australian colonists (see Diamond, 1992)—the genocide was complete, and an entire group of people was wiped off the face of the earth.

As we have seen, while mass killings take place, the perpetrators often believe that their actions are necessary, even just. After the fact, however, perpetrators rarely acknowledge what they have done or describe the details, let alone boast about it, either because other groups (often, conquering countries) refuse to accept their justifications, or because over time, those justifications no longer seem convincing, even to the killers. As a result, the perpetrators of genocide must eventually come to terms with their behavior, and they have a number of ways of doing so.

Lies and Distortions

In many cases, individual participants in genocide resort to a simple strategy for dealing with their past behavior: they lie about it. Perpetrators often deny their crimes, even when their deep involvement in genocide has been clearly documented. (See Blum [1977] for examples of Holocaust perpetrators hiding in the United States, who clearly lied about their pasts.) Although it might seem more difficult for entire countries to deny responsibility for genocidal campaigns, even that has been known to occur (Balakian, 2003; Chang, 1997).

Refusing to admit participating in genocide is bad enough because of the violence it does to the truth, but there are other unfortunate consequences. First, people who distort or even fabricate their memories and beliefs (especially those who do so repeatedly) can actually come to believe their lies (Erber, 2002; Schlenker & Trudeau, 1990). The self-perception processes discussed in Chapters 4 and 6 can perhaps explain this kind of self-deception. Second, if other people and other nations accept such false denials, those who are contemplating similar acts of violence can be emboldened. On the eve of the Second World War, Hitler is said to have asked his military leaders, "Who today, after all, speaks of the annihilation of the Armenians?" (Balakian, 2003, p. 377).

Probably more common than flat denials of participation in genocide are the kinds of self-serving attributions and biased inference processes discussed in Chapters 3 and 4. In other words, perpetrators often downplay the magnitude of their involvement and/or the extent to which they were responsible for their own or others' behavior (Opton, 1973; Stanton, 2005). Sometimes they downplay the seriousness of their actions by telling themselves that their victims were a little less than human to begin with. That is, they deny that the people they killed were capable of experiencing the full range of human feelings and emotions (Castano & Giner-Sorolla, 2006).

The fact that mass killings (and often, terrorist plots) are complicated operations that involve many people on different hierarchical levels is particularly useful to perpetrators who seek to escape responsibility (Darley,

1992). Those at the top of a hierarchy can claim to have been far removed from any actual killing and profess ignorance about what exactly was happening. They can even claim that their intentions and orders were misconstrued by subordinates. Those on the lower levels of the hierarchy can claim that they did not initiate the killings and even personally disapproved of them. They can maintain that they were simply participants in a legitimate political or military system, following orders from above"orders they were compelled to obey. Using obedience in this way as an alibi for one's behavior is an extremely common strategy (Muñoz-Rojas & Frésard, 2004), even when history shows that refusing to carry out immoral and illegal orders was, in fact, possible (Browning, 1992; Kelman & Hamilton, 1989).

When whole groups of people engage in this kind of self-serving reconstruction of the past, collectively sharing their distorted recollections with each other, self-deception can be even more effective. As we saw in Chapter 8, groups can have memories just as individuals do. Autobiographical memories are significantly affected by the way in which they are communicated to other people (Skowronski & Walker, 2004). In other words, an effective way for people to transform their perceptions of the past is to share biased recollections with each other.

Even people who did not directly participate in the killing, but could possibly have done more to prevent it, can feel the need to transform the past. Citizens of nations that were passive bystanders, for example, may suspect that their governments and armed services could have intervened to prevent the carnage. One way in

Self-serving reconstructions of the past European-Americans long preferred to recall their conflict with Native Americans as a series of glorious battles between well-matched opponents—not as a series of expulsions and massacres.

which people from other countries have been known to downplay the importance of their inaction is by arguing that the *victims* were too passive and did not do enough to help themselves. Even many Jews in Israel struggled with the disgust they felt because of the way Holocaust victims seemed to have gone like "sheep to the slaughter," putting up little resistance (Segev, 1993). Such reactions are a clear example of the fundamental attribution error (see Chapter 3), or the tendency to ignore how people's behavior can be constrained by the situation. Much more often than not, the targets of genocide are truly helpless in the face of overwhelming aggression. When persecuted groups do have the means to confront perpetrators, they fight fiercely and heroically to avoid extermination (see Balakian, 2003; Cohen, 2000; Kurzman, 1993).

Collective Guilt

Efforts to reconstruct and distort the past will be even more intense among people who strongly identify with a perpetrator group. Rensmann (2004, p. 172), referring to Germany after the Second World War, argued that "If a collective identity (i.e., belief in the 'fatherland') is highly valued, it may be an especially hard struggle to establish a self-critical political discourse on the country's guilt." Recall that according to social identity theory (Kuhl, 1997; Tajfel & Turner, 1979, 1986; see Chapter 11), people define themselves in terms of both their personal identities and their social identities. In other words, although people can think of themselves as individuals, they also think of themselves as members of groups. Just as they are motivated to see themselves as possessing favorable characteristics, they are also motivated to see the groups they identify with in positive terms. People want to feel good about their groups, especially the ones that are important to them. As a result, strong identification with a group that is associated with genocide or mass killing produces a desire to deny, justify, and/or minimize the group's actions (Branscombe & Doosje, 2004b; Doosje & Branscombe, 2003). This tendency is especially pronounced among people who glorify their groups, seeing them as superior to others (Roccas, Klar, & Liviatan, 2006).

Sometimes the evidence for a group's wrongdoing is so overwhelming that attempts to downplay it are doomed to failure. In such cases, people may deal with the distress caused by the objectionable behavior simply by dissociating themselves from the group (Glasford, Pratto, & Dovidio, 2008). That cannot always be done, however, both for practical reasons (for example, people cannot change their ethnicity) and for psychological reasons (people's identification with a group may be so complete that disentangling the group from their self-concepts may be impossible). In such cases, a person will experience **collective guilt** (Branscombe & Doosje, 2004a; Imhoff, Wohl, & Erb, 2013; Wohl, Branscombe, & Klar, 2006), an emotion that members of the perpetrator group feel individually on behalf of the group as a whole. Although collective guilt is unpleasant, it can lead to positive consequences, including efforts to repair the damage done to other groups (Lickel, Schmader, & Barquissau, 2004). Such efforts can include formal apologies or even concrete reparations—for example, financial compensation. Thus, collective guilt can be crucial to defusing tension between perpetrators and victims and paving the way to reconciliation.

A different group-based emotion, collective *shame*, seems to have less beneficial effects (Brown, González, Zagefka, Manzi, & Cehajic, 2008; Lickel et al., 2004). Focusing less on the nature of the offense committed by the group and more on the possibility that a group's actions could affect how the group is perceived—that is, that those actions could cause the group to be labeled as bloodthirsty and/or amoral—can trigger collective shame. In brief, "people feel guilty for what they have done, but feel ashamed for who they are" (Lickel et al., 2004, p. 41). Unfortunately, shame does not seem to promote the desire to atone for the group's behavior or

An expression of collective guilt feelings: The German Holocaust memorial in Berlin

offer the victims compensation. Instead, people seem to deal with shame by attempting to avoid the victimized group (Lickel et al., 2004). Collective guilt and collective shame are not mutually exclusive. But guilt is likely to predominate when members of a perpetrator group focus less on how they could be criticized or even stigmatized by others than on how they might control the negative repercussions of the group's behavior. Guilt is an even more likely reaction if a person feels he or she could personally have done something to prevent the wrongdoing.

Up to this point, we have been discussing collective guilt as if it is generated entirely from within. However, collective guilt can be encouraged or imposed by others—especially by victims of a group's wrongdoing (Cherfas, Rozin, Cohen, Davidson, & McCauley, 2006). For example, in 2005, tensions erupted between Japan and China after the Chinese charged that newly issued Japanese history textbooks showed insufficient remorse for the Nanking massacre (although these books were denounced by the Japanese Teachers' Union and were used in very few schools). According to Wohl and Branscombe (2004), the extent to which victims will assign collective guilt to a perpetrator group depends in part on how they categorize the people who perpetrated the violence. In a study conducted with Jewish participants (Wohl & Branscombe, 2005), the experimenters referred to the Holocaust in different terms with different participants. With some participants, they referred to it as a historical event in which "Germans behaved aggressively toward Jews"; with others, as an example of how "humans behaved aggressively toward other humans." Participants in the latter group were less likely than participants in the former group to assign collective guilt to contemporary Germans and more likely to feel forgiving toward them. Hence, seeing perpetrators as flawed human beings rather than as an out-group could reduce mistrust and hostility between the groups.

Of course, people vary in terms of how willing or able they are to experience collective guilt. The Collective Guilt Scale (Branscombe, Slugoski, & Kappen, 2004), which measures this individual difference (see **Table 14.5**),

Table 14.5 The collective guilt scale

COLLECTIVE GUILT ACCEPTANCE SUBSCALE

I feel regret for my group's harmful past actions towards other groups.

I feel guilty about the negative things my ancestors did to other groups.

I feel regret for some of the things my group did to other groups in the past.

I believe that I should repair the damage caused to others by my group.

I can easily feel guilty for the bad outcomes brought about by members of my group.

COLLECTIVE GUILT ASSIGNMENT SUBSCALE

Other groups have benefited at the expense of my group for generations.

It makes me upset that my group has been used to benefit other groups throughout history.

I feel entitled to concessions for past wrongs that other groups have done to my group.

Other groups that have benefited at the expense of my group owe us now.

It distresses me that my group suffers today because of the wrongs of former generations of another group.

WHOLE GROUP ACCOUNTABILITY SUBSCALE

If a group harms members of another group, then the whole group should feel guilty.

A group ought to be held responsible for the actions of its members.

I can see holding people responsible for the harmful things their group has done.

Whole groups, like individuals, ought to be held accountable for their actions.

I think that the members of a group are accountable for what others in their group do.

Each item is paired with a scale ranging from 1 to 8; higher numbers indicate greater agreement.

Source: Branscombe, Slugoski, & Kappen (2004).

consists of three subscales. The first, Collective Guilt Acceptance, assesses the tendency to experience collective guilt personally. The second, Collective Guilt Assignment, measures the extent to which a person feels that *other* groups should accept and experience collective guilt. Both acceptance and assignment depend on the more general belief that a group as a whole—as opposed to individuals in that group—can be held accountable for anything. The third subscale, Whole Group Accountability, gets at that belief; as might be expected, it correlates significantly with the other two subscales. Although the scale is presented here in its general form, it can also be tailored to relationships between specific groups (for example, Israelis and Palestinians, white and indigenous Australians, or Tutsis and Hutus).

Revisiting and Transforming the Past: A Summary

Many victims of attempted extermination have written memoirs recounting their experiences in great detail, but few, if any, books have been written by perpetrators who are proud of their genocidal activities. For reasons both external (fear of censure or punishment) and internal (belated realization that they may actually have committed a crime), perpetrators are usually motivated to deny their participation in mass killing, both to other people and to themselves.

Sometimes perpetrators simply lie about their pasts. Even simple lies have far from simple consequences: if people tell these lies often enough, they can come to believe them. Probably more common than lying is distortion of the past. Perpetrators downplay their own responsibility or the consequences of their behavior and may even come to believe that their victims were complicit in their own destruction.

People who strongly identify with perpetrator groups will be especially tormented by the past, and will make vigorous efforts to minimize their distress. When their psychological maneuvers prove ineffective, they may succumb to collective guilt, a feeling that results from the belief that the group as a whole is responsible for past wrongdoing. Collective guilt (as opposed to a related emotion, collective shame) can motivate people to try to compensate or atone for the harm done by their group. Not everyone is equally prone to feelings of collective guilt, however.

HEROISM—THE "BRIGHT SIDE"

Clearly, during times of crisis, many forces converge to cause groups to select scapegoats and individuals to participate in persecuting those scapegoats. As Rochat and Modigliani (2000, p. 107) note, however, "Knowing how nearly everyone behaved in a given situation … cannot tell us about the realm of the possible—about what might have happened." Among the other courses of action possible in such crises are a refusal to participate in victimizing scapegoats and active resistance to genocide. Indeed, in every episode of genocide, heroes have emerged, both men and women (Becker & Eagly, 2004), some of whom became famous for their actions.

Consider Oskar Schindler (Brecher, 1994; Crowe, 2004; see also the film *Schindler's List*). A member of the Nazi Party, Schindler took over a factory in Poland after the Germans occupied that country and staffed it with Jewish slave laborers. He even built his own concentration camp to house the workers. You may be surprised to hear that a man like that is celebrated as a great humanitarian, but he is. For Schindler's primary agenda was not financial success, but the protection of the Jews under his control. By the end of the war, his "factory," a front for his rescue operation, was producing nothing at all. It had, however, saved the lives of approximately 1,200 people.

Schindler, of course, was not alone in his remarkable altruism. The Swedish diplomat Raoul Wallenberg saved even more lives during the Holocaust by giving people false passports (Marton, 1982). Because of Wallenberg's efforts, tens of thousands of Hungarian Jews who would otherwise have been exterminated were spared. And from 1938 to 1939, Captain Paul Grüninger, a Swiss police chief in charge of a border crossing with Austria, ignored government orders to refuse entry to Jews trying to escape Nazi persecution. Grüninger did more than just open the border to Jews; he took active steps to save people, such as crossing the border to pick up refugees in his car, and arranging for relatives who were left behind to receive entry visas. In the end, Grüninger facilitated the entry into Switzerland of about 3,000 Jews, who would almost certainly have perished without his assistance (Rochat & Modigliani, 2000). As a result, he was fired from his job, which caused him severe financial hardship.

Similarly, many people who might have been raped, maimed, or killed during the brutal subjugation of Nanking by the Japanese army in 1937–1938 were saved by a small group of Europeans and Americans, who created a "safety zone" in the city (Chang, 1997). The leader of this group was a German businessman named John Rabe, who did more than organize and administer the safety zone. Rabe actually ventured out into the city to forcibly prevent atrocities, at times literally pulling rapists off their victims. Likewise, in 1914–1915, in the midst of the bloodshed in the Ottoman Empire, a sizable contingent of American missionaries and diplomats worked around the clock, putting their lives on the line to rescue, feed, and shelter Armenians (Balakian, 2003). And in Rwanda in 1994, among the many people who helped Tutsis escape a horrible death, hotel manager Paul Rusesabagina was especially effective (Gourevitch, 1998). The film *Hotel Rwanda* vividly portrays his heroism.

There is no "bright side" to genocide and mass killing. But the behavior of some people during these spasms of violence at least allows us to once again appreciate the bright sides of human nature and social interaction.

What Makes a Hero?

As we have seen, it is tempting to account for genocide and mass killing by branding the perpetrators as abnormal brutes. Heroism, too, seems to lend itself to straightforward dispositional explanations. What led the people we have just described to behave so altruistically (see Chapter 12)? Perhaps they were extremely brave and saintly people who expressed those traits consistently throughout their lives, in all situations?

That approach to understanding heroic behavior, however, is probably another example of the fundamental attribution error (Ross, 1977; Jones, 1990; see Chapter 3). A review of Paul Grüninger's life suggests that he "was not a heroic type, not a fighter, not someone working for a cause, not a rebel confronting the government in a defiant manner" (Rochat & Modigliani, 2000, p. 99). As for those who saved Chinese lives in Nanking, Chang (1997, pp. 138–139) notes:

Another unlikely hero: Giorgio Perlasca Perlasca was an Italian Fascist who posed as the Spanish consul-general to Hungary in 1944. In that role, he was able to save thousands of Jews from Nazi Germany and the Holocaust.

> Bookish and genteel, most of the zone leaders had little experience in handling a horde of rapists, murderers, and street brawlers. Yet they acted as bodyguards for even the Chinese police in the city, and somehow, like warriors, found the physical energy and raw courage to throw themselves in the line of fire—wresting Chinese men away from execution sites, knocking Japanese soldiers off of women, even jumping in front of cannons and machine guns …

As for John Rabe, the hero of Nanking, our description of him omitted one fascinating detail: He was an admirer of Adolf Hitler, an enthusiastic and dedicated Nazi. In fact, Rabe was the leader of the Nazi Party in Nanking.

It would be incorrect to claim that no personality traits are correlated with heroism. Research on people who acted heroically during the Holocaust reveals that most were empathic people, with clear moral principles they were strongly motivated to uphold (London, 1970; Oliner & Oliner, 1988). Staub (2002) argues that these people were also notable for their confidence in their ability to take effective action in the situations in which they found themselves—that is, they had high levels of self-efficacy (Bandura, 1997; see Chapter 4). Nonetheless, countless people with those same characteristics did *not* distinguish themselves by behaving altruistically, let alone heroically, during the Holocaust.

Other traits that may predispose people to play an active role in rescuing the targets of genocide are far from obvious. In Chapter 11, we described the trait of authoritarianism (Adorno, Frenkel-Brunswik, Levinson, & Sanford, 1950; Altemeyer, 1994). Authoritarians adhere strictly to conventional thinking and behavior and are not very tolerant of people whose values and perspectives differ from their own. They have also been found to be ethnocentric and to mistrust members of out-groups. For that reason, much research on authoritarianism has examined its close connection to stereotyping and prejudice. Of course, another characteristic of authoritarians is their tendency to obey authority figures. What if those authority figures were to direct their followers to avoid participating in mass killing, even to do what they could to help potential victims? Suedfeld and Schaller (2002) note that in eastern Europe, quite a few community and church leaders did, in fact, urge resistance to the Nazis' murderous campaign. In such cases, authoritarianism may actually have increased the chances that people would play a role in rescuing Jews. As Staub (2002, p. 33) observes, many rescuers of Jews "followed the guidance of leaders who set a policy of rescue."

In sum, trying to explain why some people become heroic helpers in times of crisis using either simple trait explanations or simple situational explanations is almost certainly fruitless. An interactionist approach is necessary. That is, in certain contexts, certain people who are exposed to certain kinds of situational influences (including many of those discussed in Chapter 12) will become heroes, although it is difficult to predict who those people will be.

A Social Identity Perspective

As we noted earlier in this chapter, when people identify strongly with a group—that is, when their membership in the group is an important aspect of their self-concepts—they find it difficult to distance themselves from the group's collective behavior. Consistent with social identity theory, such people will have difficulty acknowledging their group's unjust policy of persecution and will not be likely to resist it. They are, of course, unlikely to become heroic helpers.

In light of that observation, it is interesting to note that in many cases, Holocaust rescuers "were marginal to their community: they had a different religious background, were new to the community, or had a parent of foreign birth." Furthermore, "Many were 'inclusive' and regarded people in groups other than their own as human beings to whom human considerations apply" (Staub, 2002, p. 32). We have already noted that when victims perceive their persecutors as fellow human beings, rather than as members of an out-group, they are more open to forgiveness. Similarly, seeing others as sharing a common human identity makes a person more likely to come to their aid when they are in need or peril (Buchan et al., 2011; Gaertner & Dovidio, 2012; McFarland, Brown, & Webb, 2013; Monroe, Barton, & Klingemann, 1990). This observation is consistent with social identity theory.

As anecdotal evidence for that claim, consider how Clara Barton (the first president of the American Red Cross) convinced the Ottoman Empire's minister of foreign affairs to extend humanitarian relief to Armenians after the massacres of 1896. It is notable that in communicating with the minister, Barton purposely never used the word "Armenian." Instead, she referred to the suffering "people" who needed assistance (Balakian, 2003).

The Heroism of Groups

Heroic helpers rarely function in isolation. More typically, they are part of a network of like-minded and mutually supportive individuals (Isenberg, 2001; Roseman, 2011). Such groups vary in size. In some cases, coming to the aid of potential victims can become a national project. Perhaps the most celebrated example is the mass rescue effort in Denmark in 1943 to rescue that country's Jews from deportation to death camps. Ordinary citizens all over the country helped transport thousands of Jews across the sea to neutral Sweden.

Less well known is the resistance in Bulgaria (Todorov, 2001). Unlike Denmark, Bulgaria was not occupied by Germany—it was allied with it. Under pressure from Hitler's government, it enacted anti-Semitic legislation in 1941, and also permitted Jews from foreign territory it was occupying to be deported (and killed). However, proposals in 1943 to round up Jews in prewar Bulgarian territory ("Old Bulgaria") were met with widespread protest—including public demonstrations and marches involving thousands of people. As a result, Bulgaria's king Boris refused Nazi requests to deport the country's Jews. When the war ended, there were actually more Jews living in Bulgaria than there had been before the war started.

A tribute in Israel to the successful Bulgarian protest against the deportation of the country's Jewish population to the death camps.

What motivated Bulgarian resistance to genocide? Reicher, Cassidy, Wolpert, Hopkins, and Levine (2006) carefully analyzed a series of public statements made at the time by groups opposing the deportations (such as the Bulgarian Writers Union, the Bulgarian Lawyers Union, and the Bulgarian Orthodox Church). A variety of themes ran through the statements, but one of the most prominent was what they called "category inclusion." Arguments and appeals of this kind emphasized that Jews were Bulgarians, and more than that, human beings. In other words, they encouraged Bulgarians to view Jews as sharing with them a common in-group identity. Once again, this is exactly the kind of approach to encouraging assistance that social identity theory would predict would be effective.

The Continuum of Benevolence

We have seen that when people participate in victimizing members of an out-group, each unkind or violent act makes it easier to commit the next one. Indeed, each act of aggression prepares one to commit even more

Table 14.6: Three continua

THE CONTINUUM OF PASSIVITY

What it involves: becoming more and more apathetic about the evil behavior being directed at others

Some key processes: the just-world phenomenon, diffusion of responsibility, pluralistic ignorance, conformity, and obedience

Concrete example: People remain silent when others make disparaging remarks about members of another group, or when they are exposed to propaganda that demonizes the group. No one else is speaking up, after all. After being immersed in all that hate, it seems unremarkable to them when members of the stigmatized group are fired from their jobs or restricted from living in certain areas. By the time the scapegoats are evicted from their homes, publicly assaulted, or deported, there isn't much that can be done, anyway—and surely, members of the group must have done *something* to be treated in this way.

THE CONTINUUM OF DESTRUCTIVENESS

What it involves: becoming more and more brutal toward members of another group

Some key processes: dissonance reduction, biased reasoning, dehumanization, and motivated action identification

Concrete example: A soldier is asked to round up members of a group for "relocation." Doing so effectively, it turns out, requires being rough with some of them. The next time he receives a similar assignment, he behaves brutally from the start. The dirty, desperate people he is gathering and herding along remind him of animals anyway, so why should he treat them like human beings? In fact, they deserve inhuman treatment. Over time, the soldier comes up with new and creative ways to punish and humiliate his victims.

THE CONTINUUM OF BENEVOLENCE

What it involves: becoming more and more helpful and altruistic toward members of a victimized group

Some key processes: self-efficacy, strong attitudes, and attitude change via self-perception

Concrete example: A woman refuses to stop treating her neighbors courteously, even though propaganda is encouraging her to think of the ethnic group to which they belong as the enemy. When she sees they are going hungry because very little food is being rationed to them, she surreptitiously sends over some meat and vegetables for the children. During a period of mob violence, she allows her neighbors to hide in her cellar. Finally, when she suspects they are going to be taken away to be exterminated, she hides them in her home. They remain hidden for years.

violent acts. Similarly, tolerating or ignoring brutal behavior sets in motion psychological processes that allow a person to tolerate increasingly horrifying acts of persecution. These phenomena have come to be known as the continuum of destructiveness and the continuum of passivity.

Research into the behavior of heroic helpers reveals a related but heartening phenomenon: the **continuum of benevolence** (Staub, 2002; see **Table 14.6**). That is, like engaging in behavior that is unusually cruel, engaging in behavior that is unusually altruistic can cause a person to reexamine his attitudes and beliefs. As a result, each act of kindness a person engages in can lead to subtle changes in the person's self-concept, making the person even more likely to engage in altruistic behavior in the future. In fact, the heroic behavior seen during outbreaks of genocide is often the culmination of a series of deeds that began with more modest prosocial behavior (Suedfeld, 2000).

Becoming a Heroic Helper: A Summary

Although this chapter focuses on the dark side of social psychology, there is also a bright side. When difficult life conditions trigger extreme violence between groups, not everyone becomes a perpetrator of genocide or a terrorist. In fact, some people are notable for the efforts they make to spare others from harm. Empathic people with high moral standards and an awareness of others' humanity may be especially likely to become heroes. Still, in any given situation, it is very difficult to predict who the heroes will be. One thing is clear, though: Doing good can become a habit, so that small acts of kindness set people on a path leading to extraordinary acts of heroism.

Think Like a Social Psychologist

Thinking critically
—What role could collective guilt play in becoming (or not becoming) a heroic helper?

Confronting social issues
—If you were to learn about an episode of genocide taking place somewhere in the world, what could you do to avoid being a totally passive bystander?

CONCLUSION: THE POWER OF AWARENESS

Stories of heroic helpers can be inspiring. It is good to know that the social psychological processes discussed in this chapter do not inevitably lead all people to participate in mass killings. Needless to say, it would be even more heartening to live in a world where there is no need for heroes—in other words, a world where we would never encounter the circumstances that call for such heroism.

We cannot, alas, outline a plan to rid the world of genocide, mass killing, and terrorism. Instead, we close with a modest suggestion that follows from the material covered in the first 13 chapters of this book. Over and over again, we have seen that hidden influences on our behavior lose much of their power when we become aware of those influences and how they work. Primed concepts, for example, cease to have a direct effect on our judgment when we become aware of their biasing influence (Chapter 3). The same can be said for many of the effects of stereotypes (Chapter 11). When people become aware of the factors that can inhibit helping behavior, they are less likely to remain passive bystanders in an emergency (Chapter 12). When they become aware of the hidden influences of arousal, they can prevent themselves from misattributing it to the behavior of others (Chapter 9). Attitude reports are less contaminated by mood when a person's attention is called to the mood, and the mere exposure effect—the tendency to prefer things simply because we have encountered them many times—is undermined when people become conscious of the exposures (Chapter 5).

These are just a few examples of a general principle; we could add many more to the list. Instead, we will conclude with just one more. In the aftermath of the genocidal violence in Rwanda, the social psychologist Irvin Staub and his colleagues traveled to that country to help stabilize it and to try to prevent another outbreak. The team conducted an experiment in which they organized community members into groups to discuss people's experiences (Staub, 2004; Staub & Pearlman, 2005; Staub, Pearlman, Gubin, & Hagengimana, 2005). In the key experimental condition, the meetings were led by Rwandans who had participated in a seminar on the origins of genocide. In other words, these group leaders, or facilitators, had received training based on a review of material much like that covered in this chapter. Two months later, people in this experimental condition had come to feel more positively about members of the other ethnic group than those in groups led by facilitators who had been trained differently or had not been trained at all. In other words, an understanding of the social-psychological processes involved in mass killing seemed to diminish the hatred and suspicion that can fuel such tragedies.

Clearly, genocide, mass killing, and terrorism are complicated phenomena that can be fully understood only through a combination of philosophical, historical, political, geographical, anthropological, and psychological perspectives. However, if people are unaware of the psychological factors that prepare them for the indiscriminate killing of other human beings and if (as we assume) most people are uncomfortable assuming the identity of a brutal perpetrator, then the results of Staub and his colleagues' study should be encouraging. It is reasonable to assume that raising people's awareness of the relevant hidden influences can be an effective intervention. Thus, familiarity with social-psychological research is useful, not only to individuals facing everyday challenges, but to groups facing extraordinary and deadly ones.

KEY TERMS AND DEFINITIONS

Genocide: the extermination, entirely or in part, of an ethnic, national, religious, or other group

Terrorism: the use of violence against civilians to create fear and bring about political or other social changes

Continuum of passivity: the process of becoming more and more apathetic toward evil behavior as a result of justifying our passivity and changing our attitudes toward victims of evil behavior

Just-world phenomenon: the tendency to believe that people who experience misfortune deserve their fate

Continuum of destructiveness: the process of becoming more and more brutal as a result of justifying our brutality and changing our attitudes toward victims of that brutality

Gradualistic moral disengagement: another term for the continuum of destructiveness

Dehumanization: perceiving other people to be less than human

Naturalistic fallacy: the tendency to think that research showing what people do implies what they should or ought to do

Collective guilt: the feeling that can result from concluding that a group to which we belong is responsible for the suffering of another group

Continuum of benevolence: the process of becoming more and more altruistic as a result of justifying our helpfulness and changing our attitudes toward ourselves and the people we help

REFERENCES

Adorno, T. W., Frenkel-Brunswik, E., Levinson, D. J., & Sanford, R. (1950). *The authoritarian personality*. New York: Harper.

Ajzen, I., & Fishbein, M. (1980). *Understanding attitudes and predicting social behavior*. Englewood Cliffs, NJ: Prentice Hall.

Altemeyer, B. (1994). Reducing prejudice in right-wing authoritarians. In M. P. Zanna & J. M. Olson (Eds.), *The psychology of prejudice: The Ontario symposium* (Vol. 7, pp. 131–148). Hillsdale, NJ: Lawrence Erlbaum.

Anderson, C. A., Anderson, K. B., & Deuser, W. E. (1996). A general framework for the study of affective aggression: Effects of weapons and extreme temperature on accessibility of aggressive thoughts, affect, and attitude. *Personality and Social Psychology Bulletin, 22*, 366–376.

Archer, J. (2004). Sex differences in aggression in real-world settings: A meta-analytic review. *Review of General Psychology, 8*, 291–322.

Asch, S. E. (1956). Studies of independence and conformity: I. A minority of one against a unanimous majority. *Psychological Monographs, 70*(9, Whole No. 416).

Balakian, P. (2003). *The burning Tigris: The Armenian genocide and America's response.* New York: Harper Collins.

Bandura, A. (1997). *Self-efficacy: The exercise of control.* New York: W. H. Freeman.

Bandura, A. (1999). Moral disengagement in the perpetration of inhumanities. *Personality and Social Psychology Review, 3*, 193–209.

Bandura, A. (2004). The role of selective moral disengagement in terrorism and counterterrorism. In F. M. Moghaddam & A. J. Marsella (Eds.), *Understanding terrorism: Psychosocial roots, consequence, and interventions* (pp. 121–150). Washington, DC: American Psychological Association.

Bandura, A., Underwood, B., & Fromson, M. E. (1975). Disinhibition of aggression through diffusion of responsibility and dehumanization of victims. *Journal of Research in Personality, 9*, 253–269.

Baumeister, R. F. (1990). Anxiety and deconstruction: On escaping the self. In J. M. Olson & M. P. Zanna (Eds.), *Self-inference processes: The Ontario symposium* (Vol. 6, pp. 259–261). Hillsdale, NJ: Erlbaum.

Baumeister, R. F., & Butz, D. A. (2005). In R. J. Sternberg (Ed.), *The psychology of hate* (pp. 87–102). Washington, DC: American Psychological Association.

Baumeister, R. F., & Campbell, W. K. (2002). The intrinsic appeal of evil: Sadism, sensational thrills, and threatened egotism. *Personality and Social Psychology Review, 3*, 210–221.

Baumeister, R. F., & Newman, L. S. (1994). Self-regulation of cognitive inference and decision processes. *Personality and Social Psychology Bulletin, 20*, 3–19.

Baumeister, R. F., Smart, L., & Boden, J. M. (1996). Relationship of threatened egotism to violence and aggression. *Psychological Review, 103*, 5–33.

Becker, S. W., & Eagly, A. H. (2004). The heroism of women and men. *American Psychologist, 59*, 163–178.

Berkowitz, L. (1999). Evil is more than banal: Situationism and the concept of evil. *Personality and Social Psychology Review, 3*, 246–253.

Bilewicz, M., & Vollhardt, J. R. (2012). Evil transformations: Psychological processes underlying genocide and mass killing. In A. Golec de Zavala & A. Cichocka (Eds.), *Social psychology of social problems: The intergroup context* (pp. 280–307). New York: Palgrave Macmillan.

Blass, T. (2002). Perpetrator behavior as destructive obedience: An evaluation of Stanley Milgram's perspective, the most influential social-psychological approach to the Holocaust. In L. S. Newman & R. Erber (Eds.), *Understanding genocide: The social psychology of the Holocaust* (pp. 11–42). New York: Oxford University Press.

Blum, H. (1977). *Wanted! The search for Nazis in America.* Greenwich, CT: Fawcett Books.

Blumenthal, R., & Miller, J. (1999, March 4). Japanese germ-war atrocities: A half-century of stonewalling the world. *New York Times*, p. A10.

Boccato, G., Capozza, D., Falvo, R., & Durante, F. (2008). The missing link: Ingroup, outgroup and the human species. *Social Cognition, 26*, 224–234.

Bourke, J. (1999). *An intimate history of killing: Face-to-face killing in twentieth-century warfare.* London, UK: Granta Books.

Branscombe, N. R., & Doosje, B. (Eds.) (2004a). *Collective guilt: International perspectives.* New York: Cambridge University Press.

Branscombe, N. R., & Doosje, B. (2004b). International perspectives on the experience of collective guilt. In N. R. Branscombe & B. Doosje (Eds.), *Collective guilt: International perspectives* (pp. 3–15). New York: Cambridge University Press.

Branscombe, N. R., Slugoski, B., & Kappen, D. M. (2004). The measurement of collective guilt: What it is and what it is not. In N. R. Branscombe & B. Doosje (Eds.), *Collective guilt: International perspectives* (pp. 16–34). New York: Cambridge University Press.

Brecher, E. J. (1994). *Schindler's Legacy: True Stories of the List Survivors.* New York: Penguin Books.

Brown, R., González, R., Zagefka, H., Manzi, J., & Cehajic, S. (2008). Nuestra culpa: Collective guilt and shame as predictors of reparation for historical wrongdoing. *Journal of Personality and Social Psychology, 94,* 75–90.

Browning, C. R. (1992). *Ordinary men: Reserve police battalion 101 and the final solution in Poland.* New York: Harper Collins.

Browning, C. R. (1998). Ordinary men or ordinary Germans. In R. R. Shandley (Ed.), *Unwilling Germans? The Goldhagen debate* (pp. 55–73). Minneapolis: University of Minnesota Press.

Buchan, N. R., Brewer, M. B., Grimalda, G., Wilson, R. K., Fatas, E., & Foddy, M. (2011). Global social identity and global cooperation. *Psychological Science, 22,* 821–828.

Bushman, B. J., & Baumeister, R. F. (1998). Threatened egotism, narcissism, self-esteem, and direct and displaced aggression: Does self-love or self-hate lead to violence? *Journal of Personality and Social Psychology, 75,* 219–229.

Cameron, C. D., & Payne, B. K. (2011). Escaping affect: How motivated emotion regulation creates insensitivity to mass suffering. *Journal of Personality and Social Psychology, 100,* 1–15.

Castano, E., & Giner-Sorolla, R. (2006). Not quite human: Infrahumanization in response to collective responsibility for intergroup killing. *Journal of Personality and Social Psychology, 90,* 804–818.

Chang, I. (1997). *The rape of Nanking: The forgotten holocaust of World War II.* New York: Basic Books.

Cherfas, L., Rozin, P., Cohen, A. B., Davidson, A., & McCauley, C. (2006). The framing of atrocities: Documenting and exploring wide variation in aversion to Germans and German-related activities among Holocaust survivors. *Peace and Conflict: Journal of Peace Psychology, 12,* 65–80.

Cohen, R. (2000). *The avengers: A Jewish war story.* New York: Vintage Books.

Cooper, J. (2007). *Cognitive dissonance: 50 years of a classic theory.* London, UK: Sage Publications.

Cooper, J., & Fazio, R. H. (1984). A new look at dissonance theory. In L. Berkowitz (Ed.), *Advances in experimental social psychology* (Vol. 17, pp. 229–266). New York: Academic Press.

Cottrell, C. A., & Neuberg, S. L. (2005). Different emotional reactions to different groups: A sociofunctional threat-based approach to "prejudice." *Journal of Personality and Social Psychology, 88,* 770–789.

Crenshaw, M. (1998). The logic of terrorism: Terrorist behavior as a product of strategic choice. In W. Reich (Ed.), *Origins of terrorism: Psychologies, ideologies, theologies, states of mind* (pp. 7–24). Washington, DC: Woodrow Wilson Center Press.

Crowe, D. (2004). *Oskar Schindler: The untold account of his life, wartime activities, and the true story behind the list.* Boulder, CO: Westview Press.

Darley, J. M. (1992). Social organization for the production of evil. *Psychological Inquiry, 3,* 199–218.

Davis, P. K., & Cragin, K. C. (Eds.) (2009). *Social science for counterterrorism: Putting the pieces together.* Santa Monica, CA: RAND Corporation.

Deaglio, E. (1998). *The banality of goodness: The story of Georgio Perlasca*. Notre Dame, IN: University of Notre Dame Press.

Diamond, J. (1992). *The third chimpanzee*. New York: Harper Perennial.

Diener, E., & Wallbom, M. (1976). Effects of self-awareness on antinormative behavior. *Journal of Research in Personality, 10*, 107–111.

Doosje, B., & Branscombe, N. R. (2003). Attributions for the negative historical actions of a group. *European Journal of Social Psychology, 33*, 235–248.

Dovidio, J. F., Gaertner, S. L., & Pearson, A. R. (2005). On the nature of prejudice: The psychological foundations of hate. In R. J. Sternberg (Ed.), *The psychology of hate* (pp. 211–234). Washington, DC: American Psychological Association.

Erber, R. (2002). Perpetrators with a clear conscience: Lying self-deception and belief change. In L. S. Newman & R. Erber (Eds.), *Understanding genocide: The social psychology of the Holocaust* (pp. 285–300). New York: Oxford University Press.

Fenigstein, A. (1998). Were obedience pressures a factor in the Holocaust? *Analyse & Kritik, 20*, 54–73.

Ferracuti, F. (1998). Ideology and repentance: Terrorism in Italy. In W. Reich (Ed.), *Origins of terrorism: Psychologies, ideologies, theologies, states of mind* (pp. 59–64). Washington, DC: Woodrow Wilson Center Press.

Festinger, L. (1957). *A theory of cognitive dissonance*. Stanford, CA: Stanford University Press.

Frey, D., & Rez, H. (2002). Population and predators: Preconditions for the Holocaust from a control-theoretical perspective. In L. S. Newman & R. Erber (Eds.), *Understanding genocide: The social psychology of the Holocaust* (pp. 188–221). New York: Oxford University Press.

Friedrich, J. (2005). Naturalistic fallacy errors in lay interpretations of psychological science: Data and reflections on the Rind, Tromovitch, and Bauserman (1998) controversy. *Basic and Applied Social Psychology, 27*, 59–70.

Friedrich, J., Kierniesky, N., & Cardon, L. (1989). Drawing moral inferences from descriptive science: The impact of attitudes on naturalistic fallacy errors. *Personality and Social Psychology Bulletin, 15*, 414–425.

Fritzsche, P. (2008). *Life and death in the Third Reich*. Cambridge, MA: Belknap Press.

Gaertner, S. L., & Dovidio, J. F. (2012). The common ingroup identity model. In P. M. Van Lange, A. W. Kruglanski, E. Higgins (Eds.), *Handbook of theories of social psychology* (Vol. 2, pp. 439–457). Thousand Oaks, CA: Sage Publications Ltd.

Gilbert, D. T., & Jones, E. E. (1986). Perceiver-induced constraint: Interpretations of self-generated reality. *Journal of Personality and Social Psychology, 50*, 269–280.

Gilbert, D. T., Jones, E. E., & Pelham, B. W. (1987). Influence and inference: What the active perceiver overlooks. *Journal of Personality and Social Psychology, 52*, 861–870.

Glasford, D. E., Pratto, F., & Dovidio, J. F. (2008). Intragroup dissonance: Responses to ingroup violation of personal values. *Journal of Experimental Social Psychology, 44*, 1057–1064.

Glick, P. (2002). Sacrificial lambs dressed in wolves' clothing: Envious prejudice, ideology, and the scapegoating of Jews. In L. S. Newman & R. Erber (Eds.), *Understanding genocide: The social psychology of the Holocaust* (pp. 113–142). New York: Oxford University Press.

Goldhagen, D. J. (1996). *Hitler's willing executioners: Ordinary Germans and the Holocaust*. New York: Alfred A. Knopf.

Goldstein, J. H., Davis, R. W., & Herman, D. (1975). Escalation of aggression: Experimental studies. *Journal of Personality and Social Psychology, 31*, 162–170.

Gourevitch, P. (1998). *We wish to inform you that tomorrow we will be killed with our families*. New York: Farrar, Straus, & Giroux.

Gross, J. T. (2001). *Neighbors: The destruction of the Jewish community in Jedwabne, Poland*. New York: Penguin Books.

Hafer, C. L., & Bègue, L. (2005). Experimental research on just-world theory: Problems, developments, and future challenges. *Psychological Bulletin, 131*, 128–167.

Hallett, B. (2004). Dishonest crimes, dishonest language: An argument about terrorism. In F. M. Moghaddam & A. J. Marsella (Eds.), *Understanding terrorism: Psychosocial roots, consequence, and interventions* (pp. 49–67). Washington, DC: American Psychological Association.

Haney, C., Banks, C., & Zimbardo, P. (1973). Interpersonal dynamics in a simulated prison. *International Journal of Criminology and Penology, 1,* 69–97.

Haslam, N. (2006). Dehumanization: An integrative review. *Personality and Social Psychology Review, 10,* 252–264.

Hatzfeld, J. (2003). *Machete season.* New York: Picador.

Herbert, U. (1998). The right question. In R. R. Shandley (Ed.), *Unwilling Germans? The Goldhagen debate* (pp. 109–116). Minneapolis: University of Minnesota Press.

Hilberg, R. (1961). *The destruction of the European Jews.* New York: Harper & Row.

Hodson, G., & Costello, K. (2007). Interpersonal disgust, ideological orientations, and dehumanization as predictors of intergroup attitudes. *Psychological Science, 18,* 691–698.

Hoss, R. (1992). *Death dealer: The memoirs of the SS Kommandant of Auschwitz.* (Edited by S. Paskuly). Buffalo, NY: Prometheus.

Hu, H. L. (2000). *American goddess at the Rape of Nanking: The courage of Minnie Vautrin.* Carbondale: Southern Illinois University Press.

Imhoff, R., & Banse, R. (2009). Ongoing victim suffering increases prejudice: The case of secondary anti-Semitism. *Psychological Science, 20,* 1443–1447.

Imhoff, R., Wohl, M. A., & Erb, H. (2013). When the past is far from dead: How ongoing consequences of genocides committed by the ingroup impact collective guilt. *Journal of Social Issues, 69,* 74–91.

Isenberg, D. J. (1986). Group polarization: A critical review and meta-analysis. *Journal of Personality and Social Psychology, 50,* 1141–1151.

Isenberg, S. (2001). *A hero of our own: The story of Varian Fry.* New York: Random House.

Jones, E. E. (1990). *Interpersonal perception.* New York: Macmillan.

Kelman, V. L., & Hamilton, D. (1989). *Crimes of obedience: Toward a social psychology of authority and responsibility.* New Haven, CT: Yale University Press.

Keneally, T. (1982). *Schindler's list.* New York: Penguin.

Koons, C. (2003). *The Nazi conscience.* Cambridge, MA: Belknap Press.

Kressel, N. J. (2002). *Mass hate: The global rise of genocide and terror* (updated edition). Cambridge, MA: Westview Press.

Kruglanski, A. W., & Fishman, S. (2006). Terrorism between "Syndrome" and "tool." *Current Directions in Psychological Science, 15,* 45–48.

Kruglanski, A. W., Pierro, A., Manetti, L., & De Grada, E. (2006). Groups as epistemic providers: Need for closure and the unfolding of group-centrism. *Psychological Review, 113,* 84–100.

Kurzman, D. (1993). *The bravest battle: The 28 days of the Warsaw Ghetto uprising.* Cambridge, MA: Da Capo Press.

Lambert, A. J., Payne, B. K., Jacoby, L. L., Shaffer, L. M., Chasteen, A. L, & Khan, S. R. (2003). Stereotypes as dominant responses: On the "social facilitation" of prejudice in anticipated public contexts. *Journal of Personality and Social Psychology, 84,* 277–295.

Landesman, P. (2002, September 15). A woman's work. *New York Times Magazine,* pp. 82–89, 116, 125, 130–132.

Lanzmann, C. (1995). *Shoah: The complete text of the acclaimed Holocaust film.* New York: DaCapo Press.

Larson, J. R. Jr., Foster-Fishman, P. G., & Keys, C. B. (1994). Discussion of shared and unshared information in decision-making groups. *Journal of Personality and Social Psychology, 67*, 446–461.

Latane, B., & Darley, J. M. (1970). *The unresponsive bystander: Why doesn't he help?* Englewood Cliffs, NJ: Prentice-Hall.

Leader, T., Mullen, B., & Abrams, D. (2007). Without mercy: The immediate impact of group size on lynch mob atrocity. *Personality and Social Psychology Bulletin, 33*, 1340–1352.

Lerner, M. (1980). *The belief in a just world: A fundamental delusion.* New York: Plenum Press.

Lerner, M., & Simmons, C. H. (1966). Observer's reaction to the "innocent victim": Compassion or rejection? *Journal of Personality and Social Psychology, 4*, 203–210.

Levine, J. M., & Russo, E. M. (1987). Majority and minority influence. In C. Hendrick (Ed.), *Group processes: Review of personality and social psychology* (Vol. 8, pp. 13–54). Newbury Park, CA: Sage.

Lickel, B., Schmader, T., & Barquissau, M. (2004). The evocation of moral emotions in intergroup contexts: The distinction between collective guilt and collective shame. In N. R. Branscombe & B. Doosje (Eds.), *Collective guilt: International perspectives* (pp. 35–55). New York: Cambridge University Press.

Lilienfeld, S. O. (2002). When worlds collide: Social science, politics, and the Rind et al. (1998) child sexual abuse meta-analysis. *American Psychologist, 57*, 176–188.

London, P. (1970). The rescuers: Motivational hypotheses about Christians who saved Jews from Nazis. In J. Macauley & L. Berkowitz (Eds.), *Altruism and helping behavior.* New York: Academic Press.

Mandel, D. R. (1998). The obedience alibi: Milgram's account of the Holocaust reconsidered. *Analyse & Kritik, 20*, 74–94.

Mandel, D. R. (2002). Instigators of genocide: Examining Hitler from a social-psychological perspective. In L. S. Newman & R. Erber (Eds.), *Understanding genocide: The social psychology of the Holocaust* (pp. 259–284). New York: Oxford University Press.

Mandler, G. (2002). Psychologists and the National Socialist access to power. *History of Psychology, 5*, 190–200.

Marsella, A. J. (2004). Reflections on international terrorism: Issues, concepts, and directions. In F. M. Moghaddam & A. J. Marsella (Eds.), *Understanding terrorism: Psychosocial roots, consequence, and interventions* (pp. 11–47). Washington, DC: American Psychological Association.

Martens, A., Kosloff, S., Greenberg, J., Landau, M. J., & Schmader, T. (2007). Killing begets killing: Evidence from a bug-killing paradigm that initial killing fuels subsequent killing. *Personality and Social Psychology Bulletin, 33*, 1251–1264.

Marton, K. (1982). *Wallenberg.* New York: Ballantine.

Matz, D. C., & Wood, W. (2005). Cognitive dissonance in groups: The consequences of disagreement. *Journal of Personality and Social Psychology, 88*, 22–37.

Matza, D. (1964). *Delinquency and drift.* New York: Wiley.

Mayer, M. (1955). *They thought they were free: The Germans, 1933–1945.* Chicago: University of Chicago Press.

McCauley, C. R., & Segal, M. D. (1989). Terrorist individuals and terrorist groups: The normal psychology of extreme behavior. In J. Groebel & J. F. Goldstein (Eds.), *Terrorism* (pp. 39–64). Seville, Spain: Publicaciones de la Universidad de Sevilla.

McFarland, S., Brown, D., & Webb, M. (2013). Identification with all humanity as a moral concept and psychological construct. *Current Directions in Psychological Science, 22*, 194–198.

Milgram, S. (1974). *Obedience to authority.* New York: Harper & Row.

Miller, A. G., Buddie, A. M., & Kretschmar, J. (2002). Explaining the Holocaust: Does social psychology exonerate the perpetrators? In L. S. Newman & R. Erber (Eds.), *Understanding genocide: The social psychology of the Holocaust* (pp. 310–324). New York: Oxford University Press.

Miller, A. G., Gordon, A. K., & Buddie, A. M. (1999). Accounting for evil and cruelty: Is to explain to condone? *Personality and Social Psychology Review, 3*, 254–268.

Miller, D. T., & Prentice, D. A. (1994). Collective errors and errors about the collective. *Personality and Social Psychology Bulletin, 20*, 541–550.

Moghaddam, F. M. (2004). Cultural preconditions for potential terrorist groups: Terrorism and societal change. In F. M. Moghaddam & A. J. Marsella (Eds.), *Understanding terrorism: Psychosocial roots, consequence, and interventions* (pp. 103–117). Washington, DC: American Psychological Association.

Moghaddam, F. M. (2005). A staircase to terrorism: A psychological exploration. *American Psychologist, 60*, 161–169.

Moghaddam, F. M. & Marsella, A. J. (Eds.). (2004). *Understanding terrorism: Psychosocial roots, consequence, and interventions*. Washington, DC: American Psychological Association.

Monin, B., Sawyer, P. J., & Marquez, M. J. (2008). The rejection of moral rebels: Resenting those who do the right thing. *Journal of Personality and Social Psychology, 95*, 76–93.

Monroe, K. R., Barton, M. C., & Klingemann, U. (1990). Altruism and the theory of rational action: Rescuers of Jews in Nazi Europe. *Ethics, 101*, 103–122.

Moscovici, S. (1984). The phenomenon of social representations. In R. M. Farr & S. Moscovici (Eds.), *Social representations* (pp. 3–69). Cambridge, UK: Cambridge University Press.

Moscovici, S., Lage, S., & Naffrechoux, M. (1969). Influence of a consistent minority on the responses of a majority in a color perception task. *Sociometry, 32*, 365–380.

Moshman, D. (2005). Genocidal hatred: Now you see it, now you don't. In R. J. Sternberg (Ed.), *The psychology of hate* (pp. 185–209). Washington, DC: American Psychological Association.

Mullen, B. (1986). Atrocity as a function of lynch mob composition: A self-attention perspective. *Personality and Social Psychology Bulletin, 12*, 187–197.

Muñoz-Rojas, D., & Frésard, J. J. (2004). The roots of behaviour in war: Understanding and preventing IHL violations. *Reports and Documents, International Committee of the Red Cross*, www.icrc.org

Myers, D. G., & Bishop, G. D. (1970). Discussion effects on racial attitudes. *Science, 169*, 778–789.

Nemeth, C. J. (1986). Differential contributions of majority and minority influence. *Psychological Review, 93*, 23–32.

Newman, L. S. (2002). What is a "social-psychological" account of perpetrator behavior? The person versus the situation in Goldhagen's *Hitler's Willing Executioners*. In L. S. Newman & R. Erber (Eds.), *Understanding genocide: The social psychology of the Holocaust* (pp. 43–67). New York: Oxford University Press.

Newman, L. S., & Bakina, D. A. (2009). Do people resist social-psychological perspectives on wrongdoing? Reactions to dispositional, situational, and interactionist explanations. *Social Influence, 4*, 256–273.

Newman, L. S., & Erber, R. (2002a). Epilogue: Social psychologists confront the Holocaust. In L. S. Newman & R. Erber (Eds.), *Understanding genocide: The social psychology of the Holocaust* (pp. 325–345). New York: Oxford University Press.

Newman, L. S., & Erber, R. (Eds.) (2002b). *Understanding genocide: The social psychology of the Holocaust*. New York: Oxford University Press.

Norfolk, S., & Ignatieff, M. (autumn, 1998). The scene of the crime. *Granta, 63*, 121–150.

Oliner, S. B., & Oliner, P. (1988). *The altruistic personality: Rescuers of Jews in Nazi Europe*. New York: Free Press.

Opton, E. M. (1973). It never happened and besides they deserved it. In N. Sanford & C. Comstock (Eds.), *Sanctions for evil* (pp. 49–70). San Francisco: Jossey-Bass.

Powers, S. T. (2002). *"A problem from hell": America and the age of genocide*. New York: Basic Books.

Prunier, G. (1995). *The Rwanda crisis: History of genocide*. New York: Columbia University Press.

Rapoport, D. C. (1998). Sacred terror: A contemporary example from Islam. In W. Reich (Ed.), *Origins of terrorism: Psychologies, ideologies, theologies, states of mind* (pp. 103–130). Washington, DC: Woodrow Wilson Center Press.

Reich, W. (Ed.). (1998). *Origins of terrorism: Psychologies, ideologies, theologies, states of mind*. Washington, DC: Woodrow Wilson Center Press.

Reicher, S., Cassidy, C., Wolpert, I., Hopkins, N., & Levine, M. (2006). Saving Bulgaria's Jews: An analysis of social identity and the mobilisation of social solidarity. *European Journal of Social Psychology, 36*, 49–72.

Rensmann, L. (2004). Collective guilt, national identity, and political processes in contemporary Germany. In N. R. Branscombe & B. Doosje (Eds.), *Collective guilt: International perspectives* (pp. 169–190). New York: Cambridge University Press.

Roccas, S., Klar, Y., & Liviatan, I. (2006). The paradox of group-based guilt: Modes of national identification, conflict vehemence, and reactions to the in-group's moral violations. *Journal of Personality and Social Psychology, 91*, 698–711.

Rochat, F., & Modigliani, A. (2000). Captain Paul Grueninger: The chief of police who saved Jewish refugees by refusing to do his duty. In T. Blass (Ed.), *Obedience to authority: Current perspectives on the Milgram paradigm* (pp. 91–110). Mahwah, NJ: Erlbaum.

Roseman, M. (2011). The pleasures of opposition: Leisure, solidarity and resistance of a life-reform group. In P. E. Swett, C. Ross, & F. d'Almeida (Eds.), *Pleasure and power in Nazi Germany* (pp. 256–277). NY: Palgrave Macmillan.

Rosenbaum, R. (1998). *Explaining Hitler: The search for the origins of his evil*. New York: Random House.

Ross, L. (1977). The intuitive psychologist and his shortcomings. In L. Berkowitz (Ed.), *Advances in experimental social psychology* (Vol. 10, pp. 173–220). San Diego, CA: Academic Press.

Ross, L., & Nisbett, R. E. (1991). *The person and the situation: Perspectives of social psychology*. New York: McGraw-Hill.

Sabini, J. P., & Silver, M. (1980). Destroying the innocent with a clear conscience: A sociopsychology of the Holocaust. In J. E. Dimsdale (Ed.), *Survivors, victims, and perpetrators: Essays on the Nazi Holocaust* (pp. 329–358). New York: Hemisphere.

Sageman, M. (2004). *Understanding terror networks*. Pennsylvania: University of Pennsylvania Press.

Schlenker, B. R., & Trudeau, J. V. (1990). Impact of self-presentations on private self-beliefs: Effects of prior self-beliefs and misattribution. *Journal of Personality and Social Psychology, 58*, 22–32.

Schmid, A. P., & Jongman, A. J. (1988). *Political terrorism*. Amsterdam: North Holland Publishing Company.

Segev, T. (1993). *The seventh million: The Israelis and the Holocaust*. New York: Hill and Wang.

Skitka, L. J., & Mullen, E. (2002). The dark side of moral conviction. *Analyses of Social Issues and Public Policy*, pp. 35–41.

Skowronski, J. J., & Walker, W. R. (2004). How describing autobiographical events can affect autobiographical memories. *Social Cognition, 22*, 555–590.

Smith, C. M., Dykema-Engblade, A., Walker, A., Niven, T. S., & McGrough, T. (2000). Asymmetrical social influence in freely interacting groups discussing the death penalty: A shared representation interpretation. *Group Processes and Intergroup Relations, 3*, 387–402.

Smith, D. N. (1998). The psychocultural roots of genocide: Legitimacy and crisis in Rwanda. *American Psychologist, 7*, 743–753.

Speer, A. (1976). *Spandau: The secret diaries*. New York: Macmillan Publishing Company.

Spencer, S. J., Fein, S., Zanna, M. P., & Olson, J. M. (Eds.). (1993). *Motivated social perception: The Ontario symposium* (Vol. 9). Mahwah, NJ: Erlbaum.

Sprinzak, E. (1998). The psychopolitical formation of extreme left terrorism in a democracy: The case of the Weathermen. In W. Reich (Ed.), *Origins of terrorism: Psychologies, ideologies, theologies, states of mind* (pp. 65–85). Washington, DC: Woodrow Wilson Center Press.

Stanton, G. H. (2005). Twelve ways to deny a genocide. In J. Apsel (Ed.), *Darfur: Genocide before our eyes* (pp. 43–47). New York: Institute for the Study of Genocide.

Stasser, G., & Titus, W. (1985). Pooling of unshared information in group decision-making: Biased information sampling during discussion. *Journal of Personality and Social Psychology, 53*, 81–93.

Staub, E. (1989). *The roots of evil: The origins of genocide and other group violence.* New York: Cambridge University Press.

Staub, E. (1999). The origins and prevention of genocide, mass killing, and other collective violence. *Peace and Conflict, 5,* 303–336.

Staub, E. (2002). The psychology of bystanders, perpetrators, and heroic helpers. In L. S. Newman & R. Erber (Eds.), *Understanding genocide: The social psychology of the Holocaust* (pp. 91–112). New York: Oxford University Press.

Staub, E. (2004). Understanding and responding to group violence: Genocide, mass killing, and terrorism. In F. M. Moghaddam & A. J. Marsella (Eds.), *Understanding terrorism: Psychosocial roots, consequence, and interventions* (pp. 151–168). Washington, DC: American Psychological Association.

Staub, E., & Pearlman, L. A. (2005). Psychological recovery and reconciliation after the genocide in Rwanda and in other post-conflict settings. In L. Barbanel & R. Sternberg (Eds.), *Psychological interventions in times of crisis* (pp. 213–244). New York: Springer-Verlag.

Staub, E., Pearlman, L. A., Gubin, A., & Hagengimana, A. (2005). Healing, reconciliation, forgiveness and the prevention of violence after genocide or mass killing: An intervention and its experimental evaluation in Rwanda. *Journal of Social and Clinical Psychology, 24,* 297–334.

Stawiski, S., Dykema-Engblade, A., & Tindale, R. S. (2012). The Roles of Shared Stereotypes and Shared Processing Goals on Mock Jury Decision Making. *Basic and Applied Social Psychology, 34,* 88–97.

Steele, C. M. (1988). The psychology of self-affirmation: Sustaining the integrity of the self. In L. Berkowitz (Ed.), *Advances in experimental social psychology* (Vol. 21, pp. 261–302). New York: Academic Press.

Stouffer, S. A., Lumsdaine, A. A., Lumsdaine, M. H., Williams, R. M. Jr., Smith, M. B., Janis, I. L., Star, S. A., & Cottrell, L. S. Jr. (1949). *The American soldier: Combat and its aftermath. Volume II.* Princeton University Press.

Stout, C. E. (Ed.). (2002). *The psychology of terrorism.* Westport, CT: Greenwood Publishing.

Suedfeld, P. (2000). Reverberations of the Holocaust fifty years later: Psychology's contributions to understanding persecution and genocide. *Canadian Psychology, 41,* 1–9.

Suedfeld, P., & Schaller, M. (2002). Authoritarianism and the Holocaust: Some cognitive and affective implications. In L. S. Newman & R. Erber (Eds.), *Understanding genocide: The social psychology of the Holocaust* (pp. 68–90). New York: Oxford University Press.

Sweeney, P. D., & Gruber, K. L. (1984). Selective exposure: Voter information preferences and the Watergate affair. *Journal of Personality and Social Psychology, 46,* 1208–1221.

Tajfel, H. (1982). *Social identity and intergroup relations.* Cambridge, UK: Cambridge University Press.

Tajfel, H., & Billig, M. G. (1974). Familiarity and categorization in intergroup behavior. *Journal of Experimental Social Psychology, 10,* 159–170.

Taylor, D. M., & Louis, W. (2004). Terrorism and the quest for identity. In F. M. Moghaddam & A. J. Marsella (Eds.), *Understanding terrorism: Psychosocial roots, consequence, and interventions* (pp. 169–185). Washington, DC: American Psychological Association.

Tindale, R. S., Munier, C., Wasserman, M., & Smith, C. M. (2002). Group processes and the Holocaust. In L. S. Newman & R. Erber (Eds.), *Understanding genocide: The social psychology of the Holocaust* (pp. 143–161). New York: Oxford University Press.

Tindale R. S., Smith, C. M., Thomas, L. S., Filkins, J., & Sheffey, S. (1996). Shared representations and asymmetric social influence processes in small groups. In E. Witte & J. H. Davis (Eds.), *Understanding group behavior: Consensual action by small groups* (Vol. 1, pp. 81–103). Mahwah, NJ: Erlbaum.

Todorov, T. (2001). *The Fragility of Goodness: Why Bulgaria's Jews Survived the Holocaust*. Princeton University Press

Valdesolo, P., & DeSteno, D. (2007). Moral hypocrisy: Social groups and the flexibility of virtue. *Psychological Science, 18*, 689–690.

Vallacher, R. R., & Wegner, D. M. (1987). What do people think they're doing? Action identification and human behavior. *Psychological Review, 94*, 3–15.

Victoroff, J., & Kruglanski, A. W. (Eds.). (2009). *Psychology of terrorism: Classic and contemporary insights (key readings in social psychology)*. New York: Psychology Press.

Viki, G. T., Winchester, L., Titshall, L., Chisango, T., Pina, A., & Russell. R. (2006). Beyond secondary emotions: The infrahumanization of outgroups using human-related and animal-related words. *Social Cognition, 24*, 753–775.

Vincent, L. C., Emich, K. J., & Goncalo, J. A. (2013). Stretching the moral gray zone: Positive affect, moral disengagement, and dishonesty. *Psychological Science, 24*, 595–599.

Waller, J. (2002). *Becoming evil: How ordinary people commit genocide and mass killing*. New York: Oxford University Press.

Wohl, M. J. A., & Branscombe, N. R. (2004). Importance of categorization for forgiveness and collective guilt assignment for the Holocaust. In N. R. Branscombe & B. Doosje (Eds.), *Collective guilt: International perspectives* (pp. 284–305). New York: Cambridge University Press.

Wohl, M. J. A., & Branscombe, N. R. (2005). Forgiveness and collective guilt assignment to historical perpetrator groups depend on level of social category inclusiveness. *Journal of Personality and Social Psychology, 88*, 288–303.

Wohl, M. J. A., Branscombe, N. R., & Klar, Y. (2006). Collective guilt: Emotional reactions when one's group has done wrong or been wronged. *European Review of Social Psychology, 17*, 1–37.

Zajonc, R. (2002). The zoomorphism of human collective violence. In L. S. Newman & R. Erber (Eds.), *Understanding genocide: The social psychology of the Holocaust* (pp. 222–238). New York: Oxford University Press.

Zillmer, E. A., Harrower, M., Ritzler, B. A., & Archer, R. P. (1995). *The quest for the Nazi personality: A psychological investigation of Nazi war criminals*. Hillsdale, NJ: Lawrence Erlbaum.

Zimbardo, P. G. (1970). The human choice: Individuation, reason, and order versus deindividuation, impulse, and chaos. In W. J. Arnold & D. Levine (Eds.), *1969 Nebraska symposium on motivation* (Vol. 27, pp. 237–307). Lincoln: University of Nebraska Press.

Zimbardo, P. G., Maslach, C., & Haney, C. (2000). Reflections on the Stanford Prison Experiment: Genesis, transformations, consequences. In T. Blass (Ed.), *Obedience to authority: Current perspectives on the Milgram paradigm* (pp. 193–237). Mahwah, NJ: Erlbaum.

IMAGE CREDITS

CHAPTER 1

1. Copyright © 2007 by Ernie / Flickr / CC BY 2.0.
2. Copyright © 2011 by Depositphotos / lunamarina.
3. Copyright © 2014 by Depositphotos / creatista.
4. Copyright © 2013 by Miguel Discart / CC BY-SA 2.0.
5. Copyright © 2011 by Depositphotos / alptraum.
6. Copyright © 2012 by Chris Hope / CC BY 2.0.
7. Copyright © 2010 by Shima Ovaysikia, Khalid A. Tahir, Jason L. Chan, and Joseph F. X. DeSouza / CC BY 2.5.
8. Dominique M. Lasco / Public Domain.
9. Copyright © 2007 by User:Solmeber / Wikimedia Commons / CC BY 2.5.
10. Copyright © 2006 by User:Ludahai / Wikimedia Commons / CC BY-SA 2.5.
11. François Dubois / Public Domain.
12. Copyright © 2013 by Cartoonstock.com / Christ Wildt.
13. Copyright © 2005 by Mark Knobil / CC BY 2.0.

CHAPTER 2

1. Copyright © 2012 by Depositphotos / ronleishman.
2. Chad J. McNeeley / U.S. Army / CC BY 2.0.
3. Copyright © 2006 by Johannes Jansson / norden.org / CC BY 2.5 DK.
4. Frank C. Müller / Public Domain.

5. Copyright © 2013 by Adam Glanzman / CC BY 2.0.
6. Copyright © 2013 by Depositphotos / acceleratorhams.
7. Copyright © 2012 by Depositphotos / izmask.
8. Copyright © 2011 by Depositphotos / SergeyNivens.
9. Copyright © 2012 by Depositphotos / andrewgenn.

CHAPTER 3

1. Copyright © 2004 by Ante Perkovic / CC BY-SA 3.0.
2. Copyright © 2010 by User:bpsusf / Flickr / CC BY 2.0.
3. Copyright © 2013 by Depositphotos / Dejan.Ristovski.
4. Copyright © 2013 by Depositphotos / sararoom.
5. Copyright © 2003 by User:J.J. / Wikimedia Commons / CC BY-SA 3.0.
6. Copyright © 2008 by Cartoonstock.com / Wilbur Dawbarn.
7. NBC Television / Public Domain.
8. Copyright © 2008 by Evgeny Pavlov / CC BY-SA 2.0.
9. Copyright © 2012 by Eva Rinaldi / CC BY-SA 2.0.
10. Copyright © 2009 by User:Schlauwiestrumpf / Wikimedia Commons / CC BY 3.0.
11. Copyright © 2012 by Depositphotos / photography33.
12. Copyright © 2005 by Cartoonstock.com / Kes.
13. Copyright © 2006 by theopie / Flickr / CC BY 2.0.
14. Copyright © 2011 by Depositphotos / lisafx.
15. Copyright © 2012 by Depositphotos / photography33.

3. Copyright © 2013 by Depositphotos / andrewgenn.
4. Copyright © 2007 by User:JP.Neri / Wikimedia Commons / CC BY-SA 3.0.
5. Copyright © 2009 by Depositphotos / poznyakov.
6. Oliver F. Atkins / Public Domain.
7. Copyright © 2007 by User:Expiring frog / Wikimedia Commons / CC BY-SA 3.0.
8. Ronald L. Haeberle / U.S. Army / Public Domain.

CHAPTER 8

1. U.S. Army / Public Domain.
2. Harless Todd / FWS / Public Domain.
3. Copyright © 2012 by Benoit Rochon / CC BY 3.0.
4. Copyright © 2012 by Depositphotos / andresr.
5. Copyright © 2013 by Depositphotos / Deborah Kolb.
6. Copyright © 2013 by Depositphotos / Vadymvdrobot.
7. Copyright © 2012 by Depositphotos / photography33.
8. Copyright © 2008 by Thomas Bresson / CC BY 2.0.
9. Copyright © 2008 by South Africa The Good News / CC BY 2.0.
10. Chris Gardner / U.S. Army Corps of Engineers / Public Domain.
11. Copyright © 2006 by Mike Ingalls / www.thesabre.com.
12. Copyright © 2012 by Depositphotos / photography33.
13. User:Aurbina / Wikimedia Commons / Public Domain.
14. User:RoyHalzenski / Wikimedia Commons / Public Domain.
15. Copyright © 2009 by Mark Parisi. Reprinted with permission.

CHAPTER 9

1. Copyright © 2012 by Depositphotos / BestPhotoStudio.
2. Copyright © 2013 by Depositphotos / Kryzhov.
3. Copyright © 2013 by Depositphotos / halfpoint.
4. Copyright © 2013 by Depositphotos / william87.
5. Copyright © 2012 by Depositphotos / PicterArt.
6. Copyright © 2012 by Depositphotos / photography33.
7. Copyright © 2011 by Depositphotos / monkeybusiness.
8. Copyright © 2012 by Depositphotos / Subbotina.

9. Copyright © 2013 by Depositphotos / rudall30.
10. Copyright © 2012 by Depositphotos / benchyb.
11. Copyright © 2013 by Depositphotos / pohodenko.maria.
12. Copyright © 2012 by Depositphotos / zetwe.

CHAPTER 10

1. Brooks Atkinson Theatre / Public Domain.
2. Metro-Goldwyn-Mayer / Public Domain.
3. Copyright © 2014 by Depositphotos / imtmphoto.
4. Copyright © 2008 by Cartoonstock.com / Stan Eales.
5. Copyright © 2013 by Depositphotos / luislouro.
6. Copyright © 2012 by Depositphotos / pressmaster.
7. Copyright © 2013 by Depositphotos / Jim_Filim.
8. Copyright © 2013 by Depositphotos / peus.
9. Copyright © 2012 by Depositphotos / pressmaster.
10. Copyright © 2008 by Cartoonstock.com / Patrick Hardin.
11. Copyright © 2007 by Cartoonstock.com / Rosie Brooks.
12. Copyright © 2005 by Cartoonstock.com / Elmer Parolini.

CHAPTER 11

1. Copyright © 2006 by User:dusdin / Wikimedia Commons / CC BY 2.0.
2. Copyright © 2003 by Mark Pett. Reprinted with permission.
3. Architect of the Capitol / Public Domain.
4. Thomas J. O'Halloran / Public Domain.
5. Warren K. Leffler / Public Domain.
6. Copyright © 2012 by Depositphotos / thefinalmiracle.
7. Copyright © 2009 by User:Angiejgray / Wikimedia Commons / CC BY-SA 3.0.
8. Copyright © 2011 by Depositphotos / Mirage3.
9. Copyright © 2013 by Depositphotos / achaphoto.
10. Copyright © 2013 by Depositphotos / genious2000de.
11. Copyright © 2011 by Depositphotos / monkeybusiness.
12. Copyright © 2010 by Vitaly Ragulin / CC BY-SA 3.0.
13. Copyright © 2005 by Mark Knobil / CC BY 2.0.

CHAPTER 12

CHAPTER 13

CHAPTER 14

INDEX

CPSIA information can be obtained at www.ICGtesting.com
Printed in the USA
LVOW02s2007180915

454814LV00001B/1/P